THE OXFORD HANDBOOK OF

THE USE OF FORCE IN INTERNATIONAL LAW

AF767353

THE OXFORD HANDBOOK OF

THE USE OF FORCE IN INTERNATIONAL LAW

Edited by

MARC WELLER

Assistant Editors

ALEXIA SOLOMOU

JAKE WILLIAM RYLATT

OXFORD
UNIVERSITY PRESS

OXFORD
UNIVERSITY PRESS

Great Clarendon Street, Oxford, OX2 6DP,
United Kingdom

Oxford University Press is a department of the University of Oxford.
It furthers the University's objective of excellence in research, scholarship,
and education by publishing worldwide. Oxford is a registered trade mark of
Oxford University Press in the UK and in certain other countries

© The several contributors 2015

The moral rights of the authors have been asserted

First published 2015
First published in paperback 2017

All rights reserved. No part of this publication may be reproduced, stored in
a retrieval system, or transmitted, in any form or by any means, without the
prior permission in writing of Oxford University Press, or as expressly permitted
by law, by licence or under terms agreed with the appropriate reprographics
rights organization. Enquiries concerning reproduction outside the scope of the
above should be sent to the Rights Department, Oxford University Press, at the
address above

You must not circulate this work in any other form
and you must impose this same condition on any acquirer

Published in the United States of America by Oxford University Press
198 Madison Avenue, New York, NY 10016, United States of America

British Library Cataloguing in Publication Data
Data available

Library of Congress Cataloging in Publication Data
Data available

ISBN 978–0–19–967304–9 (Hbk.)
ISBN 978–0–19–880621–9 (Pbk.)

Printed and bound by
CPI Group (UK) Ltd, Croydon, CR0 4YY

Links to third party websites are provided by Oxford in good faith and
for information only. Oxford disclaims any responsibility for the materials
contained in any third party website referenced in this work.

The manufacturer's authorised representative in the EU for product safety is Oxford
University Press España S.A. of El Parque Empresarial San Fernando de Henares, Avenida de
Castilla, 2 – 28830 Madrid (www.oup.es/en or product.safety@oup.com). OUP España S.A.
also acts as importer into Spain of products made by the manufacturer.

Preface and Acknowledgement

It is every child's dream: to enter a sweetshop and be allowed the freedom to pick the best and most tasty treats on offer. Putting together this *Handbook* has been a somewhat similar experience. Over the years, many issues of the law on the use of force were neglected throughout. Others have remained contested, leaving the status of the law on key issues unresolved. And, of course, since the end of the Cold War, the old certainties underpinning this field of study have been shaken to the core. This book offered the opportunity to address these issues, and to address them through a cast of the most highly qualified and sought-after contributors. Indeed, in most cases, our first choice of author responded favourably to the invitation to contribute on the topic proposed to them. I am most grateful for their cheerful collaboration over a period that turned out to be somewhat longer than expected.

The list of actual or imagined recent challenges to the established law on the use of force is long. First, there is the changing role of non-state entities as agents of conflict, including the ability of terrorist movements to mount armed attacks on a scale previously reserved for regular armed forces maintained by states. Then, there is the availability of new weapons technologies and their effects on warfare, exemplified by the debate about targeted killings, drones and autonomous weapons systems. The concept of 'cyber war' has gained some currency in the debate. The increased availability of weapons of mass destruction to a broader range of states, and even to non-state actors, was a prominent factor in the controversies surrounding the use of force against Iraq in 2003.

There were also claims that 'rogue states' and others have placed themselves outside of the legal framework on the use of force, or that a 'global war on terror' might be waged without specific reference to the well-established criteria relating to self-defence in each individual instance of the use of force. Moreover, significant pressure for forcible humanitarian action emerged in relation to circumstances of overwhelming humanitarian emergency, in part driven by the shock caused by the international failings in responding to the horrors of the situations in Bosnia and Herzegovina and Rwanda.

These developments had an impact on the discussion of legal doctrines relating to the use of force. The idea of negative exceptionalism concerning so-called rogue states was matched by a concept of positive exceptionalism. This would hold that certain states have to shoulder a disproportionate load of military operations to maintain international peace and security. Hence their actions should be considered according to differing standards, chiefly informed by the supposedly beneficial aims of such operations for the international community as a whole, rather than judged according to the established legal criteria. Both types of exceptionalist explanations, negative and positive, threaten the universality of the very rules of the international system that have hitherto been regarded as indispensably universal.

The debate about forcible humanitarian action added a further conceptual challenge. The majority of commentators found, in the wake of the Kosovo operation of 1999, that forcible humanitarian action may not be strictly legal, but it is nevertheless legitimate. At least at first sight, this approach appeared to strain the view that one of the key conditions for political legitimacy must be compliance with law, or in this instance, with the legal rules on the use of force.

In addition, the content of some well-established rules on the use of force was challenged. This included, for instance, the criteria for self-defence. Over the decades since the advent of Article 51 of the UN Charter, a consensus had stabilized in practice and scholarly evaluation concerning the doctrine of anticipatory self-defence. This consensus was threatened by the argument that new threats require new measures and associated legal doctrines to counter them. In the ensuing debate the old controversy about preventative or pre-emptive uses of force was reopened. The debate carried over from the political/strategic level onto the tactical plane. The conditions for the use of self-defence shifted in the tactical rule of operation of some countries in certain instances of conflict from the protection of soldiers, airplanes or other assets from immediate, deadly threats to more abstract challenges that might manifest a latent threat.

Another aspect that appeared reminiscent of pre-UN Charter practice concerned, more generally, the apparently resurgence of the use of force as a means of national, or perhaps at least, international policy. 19th century concepts such as ultimata, threatening the use of force unless a state or other actor engages in certain conduct, resurfaced. In part, such ultimata were administered by the UN Security Council, for instance when it gave Iraq a certain number of days before the authorization to evict its forces from Kuwait would become operational. However, ultimata were also used in cases that were only loosely covered by a UN mandate, as was the case in relation to forcible operations concerning Bosnia and Herzegovina. In relation to Kosovo, a Contact Group composed of a small number of states, and NATO, threatened the use of force without formal cover from the Council.

There was also a return to arguments that force might be a means to enforce international obligations—an assertion of forcible self-help that had been thought to have been long overcome. The most famous case of this assertion was of course the US argument that it would be empowered to enforce militarily the obligations agreed to by Iraq when it accepted the cease-fire with coalition forces at the conclusion of the Kuwait conflict in 1991.

Other developments somewhat blurred important distinctions among legal categories determining what is and what is not lawful. Hence, it is clear that forcible reprisals or retaliation are no longer permitted in international law. Instead, unilateral forcible action requires the application of self-defence in relation to an actual or imminent armed attack. However, on several occasions force was used in response to past events, rather than current or imminent armed actions, sometimes with considerable delay. While justified as self-defence, the actions seemed more akin to forcible retaliation. An example is the 1993 US bombing of the Iraqi Intelligence Service headquarters that seemed like payback for an alleged plot to assassinate former US President George H.W. Bush.

Even where the right of self-defence could be applied, important additional issues arose. For instance, what is a proportionate response to an outrage like the attack on the World Trade Centre on 9/11? How far, and for how long, does the right of self-defence extend? How do we judge when a future attack mounted by a non-territorial terrorist group, operating underground, is imminent, and how can such a claim be internationally validated? And to what extent can self-defence be applied in relation to terrorist groups based in foreign states? Does that state have to be implicated in terrorist attacks at the very high level of attribution established by the International Court of Justice in the *Nicaragua* case before force can be used against terrorist actors based on its territory?

According to that test, self-defence could only be invoked against a state that is exercising overall control over an armed movement. In other words, the group must be virtually an agent of that state. Or does a state expose itself to the use of force by another by merely failing to remove such a group from its territory, or supressing its activities. Or is there after all a kind of middle ground test, taking account the level of support granted to such a group falling short of the exercise of overall control?

To some, these kinds of questions seemed too difficult to answer within the known and accepted legal standards. A whole series of new exceptional doctrines were proposed, which, if accepted, would have significantly weakened the prohibition of the use of force. However, both in practice and in scholarship, cooler heads prevailed. At the 2005 United Nations World Summit, the organized international community committed itself to the existing legal framework on the use of force established in the UN Charter. It determined that this framework does provide the necessary flexibility to accommodate new challenges, while retaining the strong presumption against the use of force in international relations.

The challenge therefore is how the existing legal rules can be construed to reflect this balance in relation to specific situations. This book hopes to offer a range of perspectives addressing most of the well known, but unresolved areas of controversy in this area of international law, alongside those that have emerged in more recent practice.

As the dimensions of this work indicate, this has been a significant effort which has taken several years from inception to completion. In view of the high quality of contributors, and their various other commitments, it is not surprising that there was a considerable gap between the first submissions of chapters, and the very last ones.

Some authors who submitted according to the original deadline have taken the opportunity to update their chapters in the final editorial round, which brought us up to September 2014. Others were unable to do so, leaving their contributions current as to the point of initial submission and the first round of editing, as may be evident from the footnotes.

I am most grateful to the two Assistant Editors who have borne a large element of the work involved with great efficiency and engagement. Ms Alexia Solomou supported the initial editorial rounds. She was replaced by Mr Jake Rylatt, who helped to steer the project through its final rounds of editing and proofing. Ms Rumiana Yotova contributed as well, most ably bridging the period between the tenure of the two. At the Lauterpacht Centre, the project also benefitted from the wonderful support provided, as ever, by Ms Anita Rutherford and Ms Karen Fachechi.

We are also very grateful for the steady support for this venture on the part of Oxford University Press. This includes in particular Mr John Louth, Ms Merel Alstein and Mr Anthony Hinton, who commissioned the work and kept faith with it, Ms Emma Endean who offered additional support, the production editor, Ms Catherine Cragg, and Ms Kumudhavalli Narasimhan and Ms Deepikaa Mercileen.

Marc Weller
Cambridge, November 2014

Contents

PART II COLLECTIVE SECURITY AND THE NON-USE OF FORCE

PART III THE PROHIBITION OF THE USE OF FORCE, SELF-DEFENCE, AND OTHER CONCEPTS

PART IV ACTION ON BEHALF OF PEOPLES AND POPULATIONS

PART V REVIVAL OF CLASSICAL CONCEPTS?

PART VI EMERGING AREAS?

PART VII GENERAL PROBLEMS

Table of Cases

European Court of Human Rights

International Court of Justice

Permanent Court of International Justice

International Arbitrations

International Tribunal on the Law of the Sea

International Criminal Tribunals

International Criminal Tribunal for the former Yugoslavia

Nuremberg

National Courts

Belgium

Canada

France

Italy

The Netherlands

Republic of Ireland

United Kingdom

United States

Table of Legislation

International Treaties, Conventions and United Nations Resolutions

National Legislation

Canada

Italy

United Kingdom

Statutes

Subordinate Legislation

United States

List of Abbreviations

AC	Appeal Cases
ADF	Allied Democratic Forces
AFISMA	African-led International Support Mission to Mali
AFL	Armed Forces of Liberia
AFRC	Armed Forces Revolutionary Council
All ER	All England Reports
AMC	American Maritime Cases
AMIB	African Mission in Burundi
AMIS	AU Mission in Sudan
AMISON	AU Mission in Somalia
ANZUS	Australia, New Zealand, United States Security
ARIO	Articles on Responsibility of International Organizations
ARISWA	Articles on the Responsibility of States for Internationally Wrongful Acts
AU	African Union
Bevans	Bevans' Treaties and Other International Agreements of the United States of America
CAR	Canadian Airborne Regiment
CERTS	Computer Emergency Response Teams
CIA	Central Intelligence Agency
CIS	Commonwealth of Independent States
CIWS	Close-In Weapons System
Cox CC	Cox's Criminal Cases
CTS	Consolidated Treaty Series
DFS	Department of Field Support
DLR	Dominion Law Reports
DPAA	direct participant in armed attacks
DPH	direct participant in hostilities
DPKO	Department of Peacekeeping Operations
DPRK	Democratic People's Republic of Korea
DRC	Democratic Republic of the Congo
DUF	directives on the use of force
EASBRIG	East African brigade
EC	European Community
ECCAS	Central Africa brigade
ECHR	European Convention on Human Rights
ECOBRIG	West Africa brigade
ECOMOG	Economic Community of West African States Monitoring Group
ECOWAS	Economic Community of West African States
ECtHR	European Court of Human Rights

EECC	Eritrea–Ethiopia Claims Commission
EEZ	exclusive economic zone
EFTA	European Free Trade Association
EITI	Extractive Industry Transparency Initiative
EU	European Union
EUFOR	European Union Force
EWCA Civ	England and Wales Court of Appeal, Civil Division
F3d	Federal Reporter, Third Series
FARC	Revolutionary Armed Forces of Colombia
FOMUC	Force Multinationale en Centrafrique (Multinational Force in the Central African Republic)
FRY	Federal Republic of Yugoslavia
FSA	Fish Stocks Agreement
FSupp	Federal Supplement
GAOR	General Assembly Official Records
HCPR	Humanitarian Policy and Conflict Research
HJRes	House [of Representatives] Joint Resolution
HL	House of Lords
HRC	Human Rights Council
HSC	Convention on the High Seas
IAC	international armed conflict
IAEA	International Atomic Energy Agency
ICC	International Criminal Court
ICISS	International Commission on Intervention and State Sovereignty
ICJ	International Court of Justice
ICoC	International Code of Conduct
ICRC	International Committee of the Red Cross
ICTR	International Criminal Tribunal for Rwanda
ICTY	International Criminal Tribunal for the former Yugoslavia
IEMF	Interim Emergency Multinational Force
IFOR	Implementation Force
IGAD	Intergovernmental Authority on Development
IGASOM	IGAD Peace Support Mission in Somalia
IHL	international humanitarian law
ILA	International Law Association
ILC	International Law Commission
ILM	International Legal Materials
ILR	International Law Reports
IMO	International Maritime Organization
IMT	International Military Tribunal
INTERFET	International Force for East Timor
ISAF	International Security Assistance Force
ITLOS	International Tribunal for the Law of the Sea
JCC	Joint Control Commission
KFOR	Kosovo Force
KLA	Kosovo Liberation Army
LAS	League of Arab States

Lloyd's Rep	Lloyd's Law Reports
LN	law of nations
LNOJ	League of Nations Official Journal
LNTS	League of Nations Treaty Series
LOAC	law of armed conflict
MAES	AU Electoral and Security Assistance Mission
MEZ	maritime exclusion zone
MILS	mainstream international legal scholarship
MINUCI	United Nations Mission in Côte d'Ivoire
MINURCAT	United Nations Mission in the Central African Republic and Chad
MINUSCA	United Nations Multidimensional Integrated Stabilization Mission in the Central African Republic
MINUSMA	United Nations Multidimensional Integrated Stabilization Mission in Mali
MINUSTAH	UN Stabilization Mission in Haiti
MIO	maritime interception operations/maritime interdiction operations
MNF	Multinational Force
MONUC	Mission de l'Organisation de Nations Unies en République Démocratique du Congo (United Nations Observer Mission in the Democratic Republic of the Congo)
MONUSCO	Mission de l'Organisation des Nations Unies pour la Stabilisation en République Démocratique du Congo (United Nations Stabilization Mission in the Democratic Republic of the Congo)
NAM	Non-Aligned Movement
NASBRIG	North Africa brigade
NATO	North Atlantic Treaty Organization
NFZ	no-fly zone
NGO	non-governmental organization
NIAC	non-international armed conflict
NSA	non-state actor
OAS	Organization of American States
OAU	Organisation of African Unity
OCHA	Office for the Coordination of Humanitarian Affairs
OECS	Organisation of Eastern Caribbean States
OFOF	orders for opening fire
OIC	Organisation of Islamic Cooperation
ONUB	Opération des Nations Unies au Burundi (United Nations Operation in Burundi)
ONUC	Opération des Nations Unies au Congo (United Nations Operation in the Congo)
OPANAL	Agency for the Prohibition of Nuclear Weapons in Latin America and the Caribbean
OSCE	Organization for Security and Co-operation in Europe
P5	five permanent members of the UN Security Council
PCASP	Privately Contracted Armed Security Personnel
PCIJ	Permanent Court of International Justice
PMC	private military company

PMSC	Private Military and Security Company
POC	protection of civilians
PPP	perpetual peace projects
PSC	private security company
PSI	Proliferation Security Initiative
PSNR	Permanent Sovereignty over Natural Resources
QB	Queen's Bench Reports
R2P	Responsibility to Protect
RAMSI	Regional Assistance Mission to Solomon Islands
RIAA	Reports of International Arbitral Awards
ROE	rules of engagement
RPA	remotely piloted aircraft
RUF	Revolutionary United Front
SADC	Southern African Development Community
SADCBRIG	South African brigade
SAS	Special Air Service
SCOR	Security Council Official Records
SCR	Supreme Court Reports
SEATO	South East Asia Treaty Organization
SFOR	Stabilization Force
SI	Statutory Instrument
SOLAS	Safety of Life at Sea
SOMA/SOFA	Status of Mission/Status of Forces Agreement
Stat	Statutes at Large
SUA	Suppression of Unlawful Acts
TCC	troop contributing countries
TEZ	total exclusion zone
TFG	Transitional Federal Government
TS	Treaty Series
TWAIL	Third World Approaches to International Law
UNCLOS	United Nations Convention on the Law of the Sea
UKHL	UK House of Lords Reports
UKTS	UK Treaty Series
UN	United Nations
UNAFIL	United Nations Interim Force in Lebanon
UNAMID	African Union/United Nations Hybrid Operation in Darfur
UNAMIR	United Nations Assistance Mission for Rwanda
UNAMSIL	United Nations Mission in Sierra Leone
UNCIO	United Nations Conference on International Organization
UNDOF	United Nations Disengagement Observer Force
UNEF	United Nations Emergency Force
UNFICYP	United Nations Peacekeeping Force in Cyprus
UNGA	United Nations General Assembly
UNIFIL	United Nations Interim Force in Lebanon
UNISFA	United Nations Interim Security Force for Abyei
UNITA	National Union for the Total Independence of Angola
UNITAF	Unified Task Force

UNMIBH	United Nations Mission in Bosnia and Herzegovina
UNMIK	United Nations Mission in Kosovo
UNMIL	United Nations Mission in Liberia
UNMIS	United Nations Mission in Sudan
UNMISET	United Nations Mission of Support in East Timor
UNMISS	United Nations Mission in South Sudan
UNMOGIP	United Nations Military Observer Group in India and Pakistan
UNMOVIC	United Nations Monitoring, Verification and Inspection Commission
UNOC	United Nations Operation in the Congo
UNOCI	United Nations Operation in Côte d'Ivoire
UNOMIL	United Nations Observer Mission in Liberia
UNOSOM	United Nations Operation in Somalia
UNPREDEP	United Nations Preventive Deployment Force
UNPROFOR	United Nations Protection Force
UNRRA	United Nations Relief and Rehabilitation Administration
UNSMIL	United Nations Support Mission in Libya
UNSMIS	United Nations Supervision Mission in Syria
UNTAC	United Nations Transitional Authority in Cambodia
UNTAET	United Nations Transitional Administration in East Timor
UNTS	United Nations Treaty Series
UNTSO	United Nations Truce Supervision Organization
US	US Supreme Court Reports
UST	United States Treaties
VCLT	Vienna Convention on the Law of Treaties
VPD	Vessel Protection Detachment
WEU	Western European Union
Wheat	Wheaton's US Supreme Court Reports
WHO	World Health Organization
WLR	Weekly Law Reports
WMD	weapons of mass destruction
WTO	World Trade Organization

Notes on the Contributors

Daniele Archibugi is a Research Director at the Italian National Research Council, affiliated at the Institute on Population and Social Policy (IRPPS), and Professor of Innovation, Governance and Public Policy at the University of London, Birkbeck College.

Jean Michel Arrighi is Professor of Public International Law (University of Uruguay), Secretary for Legal Affairs at the Organization of American States, and Member of the Institut de droit international. Jean Michel Arrighi was born in Montevideo, Uruguay in 1953. He is Doctor of Law and Social Sciences at the Universidad de la República Oriental del Uruguay and Professor of Public International Law at the Universidad de la República, Uruguay. He has lectured at numerous universities and at The Hague Academy of International Law. Arrighi is a Member of the Institut de droit international and Vice-President of the Latin-American Society of International Law. He is the author of books and articles on international law, consumer law, and inter-American law, and has published in journals in the Americas and Europe as well as having collaborated in the treaty on Public International Law under the direction of Eduardo Jiménez de Aréchaga. Arrighi is also a contributor to the *Max Planck Encyclopedia of Public International Law* (Oxford University Press).

Jean d'Aspremont is Professor of Public International Law at the University of Manchester and Professor of International Legal Theory at the University of Amsterdam. He is the director of the Manchester International Law Centre (MILC). He used to be Editor-in-Chief of the *Leiden Journal of International Law*. He acted as counsel in proceedings before the International Court of Justice. He is a member of the Scientific Advisory Board of the European Journal of International Law.

Vasco Becker-Weinberg, Dr iur (Hamburg), Masters of Laws (Lisbon), is currently deputy and legal adviser to the Portuguese Secretary of State of the Sea. Before joining the Government of Portugal, he practised law for several years and was a full-time scholar at the International Max Planck Research School for Maritime Affairs at the University of Hamburg. He has a law degree from the Portuguese Catholic University, a Masters from the University of Lisbon and a PhD from the University of Hamburg. He has published several works in public international law and the law of the sea. His research has also focused on maritime disputes and the use and development of marine natural resources in disputed maritime areas. He has recently written *Joint Development of Offshore Hydrocarbon Deposits in the Law of the Sea* (Springer, 2014). He has further written on international dispute resolution, maritime law, international environmental law, maritime security, and the use of force at sea.

Niels Blokker is Professor of International Institutional Law, Grotius Centre for International Legal Studies, Leiden Law School, Leiden University, The Netherlands. He was appointed as Professor of International Institutional Law to the 'Schermers Chair' in 2003. He graduated from Leiden University (1984), where he also defended his dissertation (1989). From 1984 he was a lecturer, subsequently a senior lecturer in the law of international organizations at Leiden University. In 2000, he was appointed senior legal counsel at the Netherlands Ministry of Foreign Affairs. In 2007, he became Deputy Legal Adviser at that ministry. In August 2013, he left the Foreign Ministry and started working full-time at Leiden University. His publications include *International Regulation of World Trade in Textiles* (dissertation, 1989), *International Institutional Law* (5th edn, Brill, 2011, co-authored with the late Henry G. Schermers), *Proliferation of International Organizations* (2000, Martinus Nijhoff, co-authored with the late Henry G. Schermers), *The Security Council and the Use of Force* (2005, Martinus Nijhoff, co-edited with Nico Schrijver). He is co-founder and co-editor-in-chief of the journal *International Organizations Law Review*.

Dr Elizabeth Chadwick has been a Reader by research at Nottingham Law School, Nottingham Trent University since 2007. Her main research interests lie in the related fields of international humanitarian law, the self-determination of 'peoples', and international terrorism. Among her various publications, Elizabeth is the author of *Self-Determination in the Post-9/11 Era* (Routledge Research in International Law, 2011), and more recently of 'Terrorism and Self-Determination' in Ben Saul (ed), *Research Handbook on Terrorism and International Law* (Edward Elgar, 2014). She also has a long-standing interest in the laws of armed neutrality, and recently contributed the chapter on 'Neutrality' in Tony Carty (ed), *Oxford Bibliographies in International Law* (Oxford University Press, 2014).

Kalliopi Chainoglou is a Lecturer in International and European Institutions at the University of Macedonia, Greece, a Visiting Fellow at the Centre on Human Rights in Conflict at the University of East London, UK, and a Lecturer in Law at the University of Bolton, UK.

Theodora Christodoulidou, LLB (Athens), LLM (Bristol), PhD (London), Counsel (Human Rights Sector) for the Republic of Cyprus.

Olivier Corten, Professor at Université Libre de Bruxelles, Director of the Centre de droit international et de sociologie appliquée au droit international, Director of the *Revue belge de droit international*, and deputy director of the LLM in international law.

James Crawford, AC SC FBA, is Whewell Professor of International Law, University of Cambridge. He was the first Australian Member of the United Nations International Law Commission and in that capacity was responsible for the ILC's work on the International Criminal Court (1994) and for the second reading of the ILC Articles on State Responsibility (2001). In addition to scholarly work on statehood, collective rights, investment law, and international responsibility, he has appeared in more than 100 cases before the International Court of Justice and other international tribunals, and is engaged as expert, counsel, and arbitrator in international arbitration. In 2012, he was awarded the Hudson Medal by the American Society of International Law. Recent work includes *The Cambridge Companion to International Law* (Cambridge University Press, 2012, co-edited with Martti Koskenniemi), *Brownlie's Principles of Public International Law* (8th edn, Oxford University Press, 2012), *State Responsibility: The General Part* (Cambridge University Press, 2013), and the 2013 Hague Academy General Course, entitled *Chance, Order, Change: The Course of International Law* (Brill, 2014). He was elected to the International Court in November 2014.

Mariano Croce (MA, PhD). Mariano Croce is FWO Pegasus Marie Curie Fellow at the Centre for Law and Cosmopolitan Values of the University of Antwerp. He held the position of Adjunct Professor of Philosophy of Law at Sapienza—University of Rome from 2007 to 2012. He has published *Self-Sufficiency of Law: A Critical-Institutional Theory of Social Order* (Springer, 2012) and *The Legal Theory of Carl Schmitt* (Routledge, 2013, with Andrea Salvatore). His articles have been published by journals such as the *Canadian Journal of Law and Jurisprudence*, *Cultural Critique*, the *European Journal of Social Theory*, the *Journal of Legal Pluralism*, *Law & Critique*, *Ratio Juris*, and others. His research interests lie in the areas of political philosophy, jurisprudence, legal pluralism, and law and sexuality.

Dr Shane Darcy is a lecturer at the Irish Centre for Human Rights at the National University of Ireland Galway. He teaches and researches in the fields of international humanitarian law, international criminal law, business and human rights, and transitional justice. He is the author of several books and articles in these fields, including most recently *Judges, Law and War: The Judicial Development of International Humanitarian Law* (Cambridge University Press, 2014). In 2007, he was awarded the Eda Sagarra Medal for Excellence in the Humanities and Social Sciences by the Irish Research Council for the Humanities and Social Sciences, and in 2010 the Journal of International Criminal Justice Prize.

Ashley S. Deeks is Associate Professor, University of Virginia Law School, and a former Academic Fellow at Columbia Law School. Her primary research and teaching interests are in the areas of international law, national security, and the laws of war. Before joining Columbia in 2010, she served as the assistant legal adviser for political-military affairs in the US Department of State's Office of the Legal Adviser, where she worked on issues related to the law of armed conflict, the use of force, conventional weapons, and intelligence. In previous positions at the State Department, Deeks advised on international law enforcement, extradition, and diplomatic property questions. In 2005, she served as the embassy legal adviser at the US Embassy in Baghdad, during Iraq's constitutional negotiations. Deeks was a 2007–8 Council on Foreign Relations International Affairs Fellow. Deeks received her JD with honours from the University of Chicago Law School, where she was elected to the Order of the Coif and served as comment editor on the *Law Review*. After graduation, she clerked for Judge Edward R. Becker of the US Court of Appeals for the Third Circuit. She serves on the State Department's Advisory Committee on International Law and is a senior contributor to the Lawfare blog.

François Dubuisson is Professor at Université Libre de Bruxelles (ULB), member of the Centre de droit international et de sociologie appliquée au droit international (ULB), director of the LLM in International Law (ULB), and President of the Réseau francophone de droit international (RFDI).

Professor Mathias Forteau is Professor of Law at the University of Paris Ouest, Nanterre La Défense (France); Member of the International Law Commission; Former Secretary-General of the French Society for International Law. Author of many books and articles in various fields of international law (Law of Responsibility, UN Law, Statehood, International Organizations Law, Settlement of Disputes, Investment Law, etc). Co-author (with P. Daillier and A. Pellet) of the last edition of the Treatise of 'Droit international public (Nguyen Quoc Dinh†)' (2009, 1709 p.) and co-editor (with J.-P. Cot and A. Pellet) of the French Commentary, article by article, of the UN Charter (2005, XX + 2363 p.). Advocate-counsel for states before international courts and tribunals (ICJ, ITLOS, International Arbitration).

Gregory H. Fox is Professor of Law and Director of the Program for International Legal Studies at Wayne State University Law School. Professor Fox has been a visiting professor or researcher at the Universidad Iberoamericana in Mexico City, the Lauterpacht Research Centre for International Law at Cambridge University, the Max Planck Institute for Comparative Public Law and Public International Law in Heidelberg, Germany, and at the Schell Center for Human Rights at Yale Law School. He is the author of *Humanitarian Occupation* (Cambridge University Press, 2008) and the editor of *Democratic Governance and International Law* (Cambridge University Press, 2000, with Brad Roth), as well as the author of numerous articles and book chapters on topics such as democratic governance, the law of belligerent occupation, and the nature of statehood in the international legal system. Professor Fox was co-counsel to the State of Eritrea in the Zuqar-Hanish Islands Arbitration with the Republic of Yemen, as well as counsel in several international human rights cases in US courts.

Professor Dr Terry D. Gill (1952): BA 1982, LLM 1985, PhD (cum laude) 1989, is Professor of Military Law at the University of Amsterdam and the Netherlands Defence Academy and was first Assistant and later Associate Professor of Public International Law at Utrecht University from July 1985 until February 2013. He is Director of the Research Program on the Law of Armed Conflict and Peace Operations at the Amsterdam Centre for International Law and of the Netherlands Research Forum on the Law of Armed Conflict and Peace Operations (LACPO). He is Editor-in-Chief of the *Yearbook of International Humanitarian Law* and is on the editorial board of the *Journal of Conflict and Security Law* and the *Journal of International Peacekeeping*. He was Fulbright Visiting Scholar at Columbia University and Visiting Fellow at Cambridge University, The International Institute of Humanitarian Law (San Remo), University of Coimbra, and University of Granada. He is co-editor/author of *The Handbook of the International Law of Military Operations* (Oxford University Press, 2010) and of numerous publications in the areas of the use of force, international humanitarian law, and related topics.

William C. Gilmore is Emeritus Professor of International Criminal Law in the School of Law of the University of Edinburgh, Scotland. He was Dean and Head of School from 2004 to 2007. He has written extensively in the field of transnational criminal law. Other areas of scholarly interest are the law of the sea and the law relating to armed conflict and the use of force. He has been the Legal Scientific Expert to the MONEYVAL Committee of the Council of Europe since its creation in 1997.

Michael J. Glennon is Professor of International Law at the Fletcher School of Law and Diplomacy, Tufts University. He has been Legal Counsel to the Senate Foreign Relations Committee (1977–80); Fulbright Distinguished Professor of International and Constitutional Law, Vytautus Magnus University School of Law, Kaunas, Lithuania (1998); a Fellow at the Woodrow Wilson International Center for Scholars in Washington, DC (2001–2); Thomas Hawkins Johnson Visiting Scholar at the United States Military Academy, West Point (2005); Director of Studies at the Hague Academy of International Law (2006); and professeur invité at the University of Paris II (Panthéon-Assas). Professor Glennon has served as a consultant to various congressional committees, the US State Department, and the International Atomic Energy Agency. He is a Member of the American Law Institute, the Council on Foreign Relations, and the Board of Editors of the *American Journal of International Law*. Professor Glennon is the author of numerous articles on constitutional and international law as well as several books. A frequent commentator on public affairs, he has spoken widely within the United States and abroad and appeared on *Nightline*, the *Today Show*, NPR's *All Things Considered*, and other national news programmes. His op-ed pieces have appeared in the *New York Times*, *Washington Post*, *Los Angeles*

Times, *International Herald-Tribune*, *Financial Times*, and *Frankfurt Allgemeine Zeitung*. His latest book, *National Security and Double Government*, will be published in October 2014, by Oxford University Press.

Douglas Guilfoyle is a Reader in Law at the Faculty of Laws, University College London where he teaches the international law of the sea and international criminal law. He is the author of *Shipping Interdiction and the Law of the Sea* (Cambridge University Press, 2009) and numerous articles on Somali piracy and maritime security and law enforcement. He has acted as a consultant on piracy and maritime security issues to the Contact Group on Piracy off the Coast of Somalia (Working Group 2), the Foreign Affairs Committee of the House of Commons, and the UN Office on Drugs and Crime. He holds a PhD and LLM from the University of Cambridge, where he was a Gates Scholar, and undergraduate degrees in law and history from the Australian National University.

Gina Heathcote is a senior lecturer at the School of Law and the Centre for Gender Studies at SOAS, University of London where she teaches courses on international law, armed conflict, and gender and feminist legal theory and writes on issues in relation to collective security, peacekeeping, and feminism. She is the author of *The Law on the Use of Force: A Feminist Analysis* (Routledge, 2012). She is the co-editor, with Professor Dianne Otto, of *Rethinking Peacekeeping, Gender Equality and Collective Security* (Palgrave, 2014), a member of the *Feminist Review* editorial collective, and the author of numerous journal articles.

Professor Dr Wolff Heintschel von Heinegg holds the Chair of Public Law, especially Public International Law, European Law and Foreign Constitutional Law at the Europa-Universität Viadrina in Frankfurt (Oder), Germany. In the academic year 2003/4 he was the Charles H. Stockton Professor of International Law at the US Naval War College and he held that position for the academic year 2012/13. From October 2004 until October 2008, he was the Dean of the Law Faculty of the Europa-Universität. From October 2008 until November 2012, he was the Vice-President of that university. Previously, he served as Professor of Public International Law at the University of Augsburg. He had been a Visiting Professor at the Universities of Kaliningrad (Russia), Almaty (Kazakhstan), Santiago de Cuba (Cuba), and Nice (France). He was the Rapporteur of the International Law Association Committee on Maritime Neutrality and was the Vice-President of the German Society of Military Law and the Law of War. Since 2007, he has been a Member of the Council of the International Institute of Humanitarian Law in San Remo, Italy. Since May 2012 he has been the Vice-President of the International Society for Military Law and the Law of War.

Dr André de Hoogh is a senior lecturer in International Law at the University of Groningen. In 1996, he defended his PhD dissertation at the (Radboud) University of Nijmegen, which dealt with the topics of obligations *erga omnes* and international crimes of state. Having worked for a while at Utrecht University, he transferred to Groningen in 1998. In the following year he served as an international observer, accredited by the UN, to the popular consultation in East Timor to determine the political future of the former Portuguese colony. His publications have focused on the powers of the Security Council, the Tadić case and attribution of conduct in the law of state responsibility, legislative powers of UN peacekeeping operations, the war against Iraq (2003), the Bush doctrine of pre-emptive self-defence, non-proliferation of nuclear weapons, jurisdiction of states, and the rules of treaty interpretation.

Ian Johnstone is Academic Dean and Professor of International Law at the Fletcher School of Law and Diplomacy, Tufts University. Prior to joining Fletcher in 2000, he served as a political and legal officer in the United Nations, including for five years in the Executive Office of the Secretary-General. He continues to work as a consultant to the UN Department of Peacekeeping Operations and Department of Political Affairs on an ad hoc basis. Past positions include Adjunct Professor of International Law at New York University Law School, Senior Fellow in International Law at the Center on International Cooperation, Warren Weaver Fellow at the Rockefeller Foundation, and Judicial Clerk at the Ontario Court of Appeal. His most recent book is *The Power of Deliberation: International Law, Politics, and Organizations* (Oxford University Press, 2011). From 2005 to 2007, Johnstone was the lead author and founding editor of the *Annual Review of Global Peace Operations*. He is currently co-writing the second edition of *Law and Practice of the United Nations* and co-editing *The Oxford Handbook on International Organizations*. Both will be published in 2015. A citizen of Canada, he holds an LLM degree from Columbia University and JD and BA degrees from the University of Toronto.

Daniel H. Joyner, JD, MA, PhD is Professor of Law, University of Alabama School of Law. He received his BA from Brigham Young University, his JD from Duke University School of Law, his MA from the University of Georgia, and his PhD from the University of Warwick. His books include *International Law and the Proliferation of Weapons of Mass Destruction* (Oxford University Press, 2009) and *Interpreting the Nuclear Non-Proliferation Treaty* (Oxford University Press, 2011). He is the founder of the online blog Arms Control Law.

Jörg Kammerhofer, (Mag. iur., Dr. iur., Vienna; LL.M., Cantab) is a Senior Research Fellow and Senior Lecturer at the Faculty of Law, University of Freiburg, Germany. He is currently working on international law with a focus on its general, procedural and theoretical aspects, as well as on the jurisprudence of the Vienna School. As a member of the Hans Kelsen Research Group he is also involved in publishing the collected works edition of Hans Kelsen's writings. Since 2006 he has been a member of the Co-ordinating Committee of the ESIL Interest Group on International Legal Theory. He is a co-organiser of the Annual ASIL-ESIL-MPIL Workshop Series on International Legal Theory. For a number of years he has been a reviewer for publishers, journals and research institutes (e.g. CUP, OUP, EJIL, LJIL, Wissenschaftskolleg zu Berlin). Together with Jean d'Aspremont he recently directed the project "International Legal Positivism in a Post-Modern World", funded by the German Research Fund (DFG).

Jan Klabbers is Academy Professor (Martti Ahtisaari Chair), University of Helsinki. He studied international law and political science at the University of Amsterdam, where he also obtained his doctorate (with distinction). Having taught at the same university, he moved to Helsinki in 1996. He has held visiting positions at, amongst others, New York University, the Graduate Institute of International and Development Studies (Geneva), and the University of Paris II (Pantheon-Assas). In 2013, he was appointed as the first incumbent of the Martti Ahtisaari Chair. Main publications include *International Law* (Cambridge University Press, 2013), *Treaty Conflict and the European Union* (Cambridge University Press, 2008), *The Concept of Treaty in International Law* (Brill, 1996) and *An Introduction to International Institutional Law* (2nd edn, Cambridge University Press, 2009; 3rd edn in preparation).

Vaios Koutroulis is Lecturer at the Centre de droit international, Université Libre de Bruxelles. Vaios Koutroulis studied law at the University of Athens and the Université Libre de Bruxelles (ULB). He received his PhD in 2011 for a thesis on the relations between *jus contra bellum* and *jus in bello*, under publication by Bruylant editions (Brussels). Vaios has taught public international law, international humanitarian law, international criminal law, and the law of international responsibility at the ULB and the Royal Military School of Belgium. He has also given lectures at various training courses for members of the armed forces. Since 2012, Vaios has also taught as a visiting lecturer at the Faculté Libre de Droit de Lille and the Université Catholique de Lille. His publications focus on jus contra bellum and jus in bello and include a monograph on belligerent occupation published by Pedone editions (Paris).

Claus Kreß is Professor for Criminal Law and Public International Law. He is Director of the Institute of International Peace and Security Law as well as Chair for German and International Criminal Law at the University of Cologne.

Charlotte Ku is Professor of Law and Assistant Dean of Graduate and International Legal Studies at the University of Illinois College of Law. She is director of the College's Graduate and International Studies Program, including the LLM and JSD programmes and has spearheaded College-wide efforts to increase awareness of law as a global profession through the Global Fellows Initiative. She is also co-director of the Center on Law and Globalization at the College of Law. Recent publications include *International Law, International Relations and Global Governance* published as part of the Routledge Global Institutions Series.

Anne Lagerwall is a Professor at the Université libre de Bruxelles, affiliated to the Centre de droit international et de sociologie appliquée au droit international at the Université libre de Bruxelles in Belgium. As a researcher, she is mainly concerned with the rules relating to *jus contra bellum* and the interactions between different legal orders. Amongst others, she teaches the courses of International Legal Theory and International Litigation in the LLM in International Law. She is the co-Editor-in-Chief with Olivier Corten of the *Belgian Review of International Law*.

Randall Lesaffer is Professor of Legal History, Tilburg University, Professor of International and European Legal History, University of Leuven. He is a historian of international law, and studied law and history at Ghent and Leuven. In 1998, he obtained a PhD in Law at the University of Leuven on a study of peace and alliance treaties of the Early Modern Age and the Cold War. Since 1999, he has been Professor of Legal History at Tilburg Law School. He also holds a part-time position as Professor of International and European Legal History at the University of Leuven. From 2008 to 2012, he served as Dean of Tilburg Law School. He is founding co-president of the Law Schools Global League. He is the author of *European Legal History: A Political and Cultural Perspective* (Cambridge University Press, 2009) and the editor of *Peace Treaties and International Law in European History: From the End of the Middle Ages to World War I* (Cambridge University Press, 2004).

Noam Lubell is a Professor in the School of Law at the University of Essex, and was appointed Head of the School in January 2014. He holds a PhD in Law and an LLM, as well as a BA in Philosophy. In previous years, he has taught courses on international humanitarian law and human rights law in a number of academic institutions in Ireland, Israel, the UK, and the United States. In addition to his academic work, during the last 15 years he has worked for human rights NGOs, as international law adviser, and director of a prisoners and detainees project. He has also provided consultancies and training in human rights law and the laws of armed conflict, for international bodies such as Amnesty International, government bodies, and the BBC. He is the Rapporteur of the International Law Association's Committee on the Use of Force, and holds the 2013–15 Swiss Chair of International Humanitarian Law at the Geneva Academy. He has published on a variety of topics in the field of international law, including on new technologies such as drones and cyber operations, and is the author of *Extraterritorial Use of Force Against Non-State Actors* (Oxford University Press, 2010).

Ralph Mamiya served on the Protection of Civilians Team for the UN Department Peacekeeping Operations/Department of Field Support and has spent most of his career working on conflict issues in Africa, including tours with the UN peacekeeping missions in Sudan and South Sudan. He has also taught as an Adjunct Professor with the Human Rights Program at Hunter College in New York. Mr Mamiya holds a Juris Doctor from Cornell Law School.

Marina Mancini, JD, PhD is Senior Lecturer in International Law, Mediterranean University of Reggio Calabria and Adjunct Professor of International Criminal Law at LUISS University in Rome. She holds a PhD in International Law from Sapienza

University of Rome (2003) and is the author of *Stato di guerra e conflitto armato nel diritto internazionale* (Giappichelli, 2009), a book that explores the concept of 'state of war' and investigates the consequences of the outbreak of international armed conflicts in contemporary international law. She is a member of the editorial committee of the *Italian Yearbook of International Law*.

Jean-Christophe Martin is Professor of International and European Law, University of Nice Sophia Antipolis (France); Centre d'Etudes sur le Droit des organisations européennes (EA 2139). He has been Professor of Public Law (international and european law) since 2008 at the University of Nice Sophia Antipolis, France. He has also been the Vice-President in charge of International Relations at the university since May 2012. In 2006, he published his thesis on 'Les règles internationales relatives à la lutte contre le terrorisme' (defended in 2005 at the University Aix-Marseille), and has published many articles mainly related to international security issues, the law of the sea, and environmental law.

Rob McLaughlin, Associate Professor, Australian National University College of Law. He is Director of the Centre for Military and Security Law in the College of Law at the Australian National University. He served in the Royal Australian Navy as a seaman officer and a legal officer, including as the Director of the Naval Legal Service, and Director of Operations and International Law in the Department of Defence.

Lindsay Moir is Professor of International Law and Deputy Director of the McCoubrey Centre for International Law at the University of Hull Law School, UK and has held a Visiting Fellowship at the International Human Rights Law Institute, DePaul University College of Law, Chicago. He has written extensively on the use of force and international humanitarian law, with publications including *Reappraising the Resort to Force: International Law, Jus ad Bellum and the War on Terror* (Hart Publishing, 2010) and *The Law of Internal Armed Conflict* (Cambridge University Press, 2002).

Sean D. Murphy is the Patricia Roberts Harris Research Professor of Law at the George Washington University Law School in Washington, DC, where he teaches international law and US foreign relations law. Since 2012, he is also a Member of the UN International Law Commission. Professor Murphy received his JD from Columbia University, LLM from Cambridge University, and SJD from the University of Virginia. From 1987 to 1995, Professor Murphy served in the Office of the Legal Adviser at the US Department of State, specializing in international dispute resolution, international environmental law, and the law of war. From July 1995 to July 1998, Professor Murphy served as the Legal Counselor of the US Embassy in The Hague, representing the US Government before the International Court of Justice and the International Criminal Tribunal for the former Yugoslavia, and as the US Agent to the Iran-US Claims Tribunal. Professor Murphy has represented several countries in international courts and tribunals, including Ethiopia, Kosovo, Macedonia, Suriname, and the United States. He has published articles in a variety of national and international law journals and his books include *International Law: Cases and Materials* (6th edn, 2014, with Damrosch); *Litigating War: Mass Civil Injury and the Eritrea-Ethiopia Claims Commission* (2013), with Kidane and Snider); *Public International Law in a Nutshell* (5th edn, 2013), with Buergenthal); *Principles of International Law* (2nd edn, 2012); *Foreign Relations and National Security Law* (4th edn, 2012), with Franck, Glennon, and Swaine); and *Humanitarian Intervention: The United Nations in an Evolving World Order* (1996). Professor Murphy is a Member of the American Law Institute and a Counselor to the American Society of International Law, and served for a decade on the Board of Editors of the *American Journal of International Law*.

Penelope Nevill, LLB (Hons)/BA (Auck); LLM (Cantab), is a Barrister at 20 Essex Street. Penelope specializes in public international law and related areas of EU and commercial law. In addition to her professional work, Penelope lectures on the Law of Armed Conflict LLM course at the University of Cambridge, where she is an affiliated lecturer. She also teaches at King's College, London, on undergraduate and postgraduate courses in international law, and is a visiting lecturer at the University of Auckland, where she teaches the LLM course on International Dispute Resolution. Before going to the bar in 2010, Penelope was a Fellow and College Lecturer in Law at Downing College, Cambridge, where she taught international law and EU law, and a Fellow of the Lauterpacht Centre of International Law. She is also a qualified barrister and solicitor in New Zealand, where she practised in the litigation team at Chapman Tripp for four and a half years.

Rowan Nicholson is the Senior Associate to Professor James Crawford, Lauterpacht Centre for International Law, Cambridge. He is a PhD candidate in international law, University of Cambridge, and has an LLM in international law, also from Cambridge.

André Nollkaemper is Professor of Public International Law at the Faculty of Law of the University of Amsterdam. He is also a Member of the Permanent Court of Arbitration, External legal adviser to the Minister of Foreign Affairs of the Netherlands, President of the European Society of International Law, and a member of the Royal Academy of Sciences of the Netherlands.

Keiichiro Okimoto is a Member of the Office of the Legal Counsel, Office of Legal Affairs, Secretariat of the United Nations. Visiting Professor (2012, 2013, 2014), Department of International Law and Human Rights, University for Peace. Formerly a member of the Treaty Section, Office of Legal Affairs, Secretariat of the United Nations; a legal adviser and a delegate of the International Committee of the Red Cross in Iraq, Israel and the Occupied Territories, the Philippines, and Rwanda. PhD, University of Cambridge; LLM, London School of Economics and Political Science.

Alexander Orakhelashvili, LLM Leiden, PhD Cantab, is a lecturer in law at Birmingham University, UK. Previously he was Shaw Foundation Junior Research Fellow at Jesus College, Oxford (2005–8), and has taught international law at the universities of London, Oxford, and Cambridge. He has authored *Peremptory Norms in International Law* (Oxford University Press, 2006), *Interpretation of Acts and Rules in International Law* (Oxford University Press, 2008), *Collective Security* (Oxford University Press, 2011), as well as over 65 articles and chapters in leading journals and edited collections.

Paolo Palchetti, PhD (University of Milan), is Professor of International Law at the Department of Law of the University of Macerata (Italy). He is the director of the PhD programme in Legal Studies of the University of Macerata and was visiting professor in several universities (including Université Panthéon-Assas/Paris 2, Université de Nice/Sophie Antipolis, and Universidade Federal de Santa Catarina). He is co-editor of *QIL—Questions of International Law*, member of the Board of Directors of *Diritti Umani e Diritto Internazionale*, member of the editorial committee of the *Rivista di diritto internazionale*. He has sometimes acted as adviser to the Italian Ministry for Foreign Affairs and was counsel of several states in international disputes before the International Court of Justice.

Jordan J. Paust is the Mike and Teresa Baker Law Center Professor of International Law at the Law Center of the University of Houston. He received an AB and JD from UCLA, an LLM from the University of Virginia, and is a JSD Candidate, Yale University (in residence, Ford Foundation Fellowship, 1973–5). Professor Paust has also been a Visiting Edward Ball Eminent Scholar University Chair in International Law at Florida State University (Spring, 1997), a Fulbright Professor at the University of Salzburg, Austria (1978–9), and a member of the faculty of the US Army Judge Advocate General's School, International Law Division (1969–73, mob. des. 1973–5). He has served on several committees on international law, human rights, laws of war, terrorism, and the use of force in the American Society of International Law, the American Branch of the International Law Association, and the American Bar Association, and was the Co-Chair of the American Society's International Criminal Law Interest Group (1992–2008). He was also the Chair of the Section on International Law of the Association of American Law Schools and was on the Executive Council and the President's Committee of the American Society of International Law. He is one of the most widely cited law professors in the United States and is ranked among the top 2 per cent in Leiter's studies for 2000–7 and 2005–9. Professor Paust has published over 190 articles, book chapters, papers, and essays in law journals in Belgium, Canada, China, England, Germany, Greece, Israel, Japan, the Netherlands, Serbia, and the United States.

Marco Pertile, PhD, is Senior Lecturer in International Law, Faculty of Law, School of International Studies, University of Trento, where he teaches public international law and the international law of armed conflict. Until 2012, he was Marie Curie Fellow at the Graduate Institute for International and Development Studies, in Geneva, where he worked on a project on the linkage between natural resources and armed conflicts. He is now Visiting Professor in the interdisciplinary programmes of the Graduate Institute, where he teaches a course on Natural Resources and Armed Conflicts under International Law. Previously, he was Visiting Fellow at the Max Planck Institute for Comparative Public Law and International Law in Heidelberg and Visiting Professional at the International Criminal Court.

Ian M. Ralby is Executive Director of I.R. Consilium, Ltd. As Executive Director, Dr Ralby provides high-level advice and assistance to governments and organizations, employing a multi-disciplinary approach to complex problem solving. He has extensive experience in legal and policy advisory work, as well as political negotiation, having worked with governments on five continents. His background includes practice in maritime, military, criminal, international and national security law. He is a leading expert on the regulation, governance, and oversight of private security companies—both land and maritime—and has played a major role for five years in various national and international efforts to develop codes, standards, and governance mechanisms for that industry. Dr Ralby lectures widely on matters of private military and security companies, maritime security, and international law. He earned a BA in Modern Languages and Linguistics and an MA in Intercultural Communication at the University of Maryland, Baltimore County; a JD at the College of William and Mary; and an MPhil in International Relations and a PhD in Politics and International Studies at St John's College of the University of Cambridge.

Professor Sir Nigel Rodley KBE, PhD, LLD (hon) is Professor of Law and Chair of the Human Rights Centre at the University of Essex, where he has taught since 1990. He is the UK-nominated Member of the UN Human Rights Committee (since 2001), of which he is currently the Chair. Starting as an Assistant Professor of Law at Dalhousie University, Canada (1965–8), he worked as an Associate Economic Affairs Officer at UN Headquarters in New York (1968–9) and then as a Visiting Lecturer in Political Science at the Graduate Faculty of the New School for Social Research (1969–72) and Research Fellow at the NYU Center for International Studies (1970–2). He was appointed the first legal adviser at the International Secretariat of Amnesty International (1973–90). He served as the Special Rapporteur on Torture of the UN Commission on Human Rights (1993–2001). Since 2012, he has been the President of the International Commission of Jurists. His extensive publications include *The Treatment of Prisoners under International Law* (3rd edn, Oxford University Press, 2009, with M. Pollard).

Andrea Salvatore is Post-Doctoral Research Fellow of Political Philosophy at Sapienza—University of Rome and Adjunct Professor of Business Ethics at the Università Cattolica del Sacro Cuore (Rome). His research interests include contemporary political philosophy, legal theory and applied ethics, with a focus on political violence (Schmitt, Girard, Walzer), and the philosophy of war and peace (pacifism, just war theory, anarchism). His publications include *Undoing Ties: Political Philosophy at the Waning of the State* (Bloomsbury, 2015, with Mariano Croce), *The Legal Theory of Carl Schmitt* (Routledge, 2013, with Mariano Croce), *Giustizia in contesto. La filosofia politica di Michael Walzer* (Liguori, 2010), *Il pacifismo* (Carocci, 2010).

Michael N. Schmitt, Charles H. Stockton Professor of International Law and Director, Stockton Center for the Study of International Law, United States Naval War College; Professor of Public International Law, Exeter University; Senior Fellow, NATO Cooperative Cyber Defence Centre of Excellence. He was previously Dean of the George C. Marshall Center in Germany. Professor Schmitt directed the International Group of Experts who produced the *Tallinn Manual on the International Law of Cyberwarfare*. He also participated as an international expert in the Harvard's Air and Missile Warfare and the ICRC's Direct Participation in Hostilities projects. He is a member of the Council on Foreign Relations and sits on many editorial and advisory boards in the field of international law and conflict.

Nico Schrijver is Professor of International Law and Academic Director of the Grotius Centre for International Legal Studies, Leiden University and a member of the Dutch Upperhouse. He is also a member of the Royal Netherlands Academy of Arts and Sciences and the chairperson of its Legal Section. From 2010 to 2012 he served as the President of the worldwide International Law Association. Furthermore, he is a member of the UN Committee on Economic, Social and Cultural Rights, a member of the Permanent Court of Arbitration, and a member of the Institut de droit international. From 2009 to 2010 he was the international law member on the Dutch Inquiry Commission on the War in Iraq. Among many other publications Nico Schrijver is the author of *Sovereignty over Natural Resources. Balancing Rights and Duties* (Cambridge University Press, 1997), *The Evolution of Sustainable Development in International Law* (Brill, 2008), and *Development without Destruction: The UN and Global Resource Management* (Indiana University Press/UN Intellectual History Project, 2010). With Niels Blokker, he co-edited *The Security Council and the Use of Force. Theory and Reality—A Need for Change* (Leiden, 2005).

Scott Sheeran is Senior Lecturer and Director of the LLMs and MAs in Human Rights, at the School of Law and Human Rights Centre, University of Essex. He is also Director of the Human Rights in Iran Unit, providing support to the UN Special Rapporteur for Iran. He worked previously as a New Zealand diplomat and legal adviser, including in New York and Geneva and as Vice-Chair of the Legal Committee of the UN General Assembly, and is on the advisory council of several human rights NGOs. He has published on international human rights law, public international law, and law of the United Nations.

Ramesh Thakur is Director of the Centre for Nuclear Non-Proliferation and Disarmament, Crawford School of Public Policy, Australian National University. He was Senior Vice Rector of the UN University (and UN Assistant Secretary-General), Commissioner and a principal author of *The Responsibility to Protect*, and the principal writer of Secretary-General Kofi Annan's second reform report (2002). The author/editor of 50 books and 400 articles/book chapters and the Editor-in-Chief of *Global Governance*, he serves on the international advisory boards of institutes in Africa, Asia, Europe, and North America. His books include *The United Nations, Peace and Security: From Collective Security to the Responsibility to Protect* (Cambridge University Press, 2006); *Global Governance and the UN: An Unfinished Journey* (Indiana University Press, 2010); *The Responsibility to Protect: Norms, Laws and the Use of Force in International Politics* (Routledge, 2011); *The Group of Twenty (G20)* (Routledge, 2013); and *The Oxford Handbook of Modern Diplomacy* (Oxford University Press, 2013). He is also Co-Editor of *Nuclear Politics*.

Kimberley N. Trapp is a Senior Lecturer in Public International Law at the Faculty of Laws, UCL. Prior to joining UCL in 2012, she was a Lecturer at Newnham College and an Affiliated Lecturer at the Faculty of Law, University of Cambridge. Kimberley obtained a BA (philosophy), BCL and LLB (all with great distinction) from McGill University, and an LLM and PhD from the University of Cambridge. During her doctoral studies, Kimberley clerked for Vice-President Al-Kasawneh and Judge Simma at the International Court of Justice. Her doctoral thesis was awarded the Cambridge Yorke Prize for a dissertation of distinction, and is the basis of her OUP monograph *State Responsibility for International Terrorism* (2011). Kimberley collaborates as an academic advisor on issues of international humanitarian law with various NGOs and Government departments, has published widely on issues relating to the use of force, state responsibility, the interaction between international humanitarian law and terrorism suppression and the settlement of international disputes, and has presented related scholarship at various forums, including the Annual Meetings of the Canadian Council on International Law and American Society of International Law.

Nicholas Tsagourias, Professor of International Law, University of Sheffield. Nicholas Tsagourias also sits on the editorial board of the *Journal of Conflict and Security Law* and is a member of the cyber terrorism study group of the International Law Association. He has published widely on issues relating to the use of force, cyberwar, collective security, peacekeeping, and international responsibility. He is co-author with Nigel D. White of *Collective Security: Theory, Law and Practice* (Cambridge University Press, 2013).

Guglielmo Verdirame is Professor of International Law, King's College London and Barrister, 20 Essex Street, London.

Martin Wählisch serves as Political Affairs Officer in the Office of the Special Coordinator for Lebanon (UNSCOL). Among others, he is an Affiliated Scholar of the Issam Fares Institute for Public Policy and International Affairs (American University of Beirut). He is a Lecturer at the Center for Peace Mediation and the Institute for Conflict Management at the European University Viadrina and La Sagesse University in Beirut (Master's Program in Diplomacy and Strategic Negotiations). Among others, he has been a visiting scholar at the Harriman Institute (Columbia University), Institute for Global Law, Justice & Policy (New York Law School), Durham University (Faculty of Law), and the Lauterpacht Centre for International Law (University of Cambridge).

A. Mark Weisburd is Reef C. Ivey, II Distinguished Professor of Law, School of Law, University of North Carolina at Chapel Hill. A native Arkansan he received his AB from Princeton University in 1970 and his JD from the University of Michigan in 1976. He joined the United States Foreign Service after earning his undergraduate degree, serving in East Pakistan/Bangladesh from 1971 to 1973. From 1976 to 1981, he was an associate with the Washington, DC, law firm of Wilmer, Cutler & Pickering. He joined the faculty at the School of Law of the University of North Carolina at Chapel Hill in 1981. His writing addresses questions related to public international law and to the relationship between that body of law and federal law in the United States.

Marc Weller, MA, MALD, Dr jur, Dr phil, PhD, FCIArb, Barrister (Middle Temple) is Professor of International Law and International Constitutional Studies at the University of Cambridge, and Director of the Lauterpacht Centre for International Law. He served as Senior Mediation Expert in the UN Secretariat and as Senior Legal Advisor in a significant number of international peace negotiations. He is the author, editor or co-editor of some 25 books, including specialist works on conflict and the use of force in international law.

Erika de Wet is Professor of International Law in the Faculty of Law of the University of Pretoria and Co-Director of the Institute for International and Comparative Law in Africa. Since 2011 Erika de Wet has been Co-Director of the Institute for International and Comparative Law in Africa and Professor of International Law in the Faculty of Law of the University of Pretoria. Between 2004 and 2010 she was tenured Professor of International Constitutional Law at the Amsterdam Center for International Law, University of Amsterdam, a position which she thereafter held part-time until December 2013. She further lectures in international law at the University of Zurich (Switzerland) and the University of Bonn (Germany) on a regular basis. Between 2006 and 2014 Erika de Wet was co-Editor-in-Chief of the *Oxford Reports on International Law in Domestic Courts* (ILDC); and between 2011 and 2014 she was one of the General Editors of *Oxford Constitutions Online*. She currently serves on the Scientific Advisory Board for Development Policy of the Max Planck Foundation for International Peace and the Rules of Law, as well as the General Council of the International Society of Public Law (ICON*S).

Nigel D. White is Professor of Public International Law, Faculty of Social Sciences, University of Nottingham. Professor White re-joined the School of Law at Nottingham in 2009 as Chair in Public International Law. Prior to that he held the Chair of International Law at the University of Sheffield from 2005 to 2009, and the Chair in International Organisations at the University of Nottingham from 2000 to 2005. He has held an academic post in law since 1987, and gained his doctorate from Nottingham in 1988. He gained a First Class BA (Hons) in Jurisprudence from Oxford in 1982. He has served as Head of the School of Law at Nottingham and Dean of the Faculty of Law at Sheffield. He is currently Head of School at the University of Nottingham and Co-Director of Research. He is also Co-Director of the Nottingham International Law and Security Centre with Professor Mary Footer.

Haidi Willmot serves in the Office of the Chief of Staff of the United Nations Department of Peacekeeping Operations/Department of Field Support. She has held a number of positions in the United Nations Secretariat, including in the United Nations Operations and Crisis Centre and the Office of Military Affairs. Prior to joining the Secretariat, Ms Willmot was the Peacekeeping Policy Officer at the Australian Mission to the United Nations, and worked as an analyst with the New Zealand Government. She previously worked in Vanuatu with the Australian Agency for International Development (AusAid) and in legal practice in Australia and throughout the island nations of the Pacific. Ms Willmot holds an BA/LLB (Hons) from the Australian National University and a MPhil in International Relations from the University of Cambridge.

Professor David Wippman is Dean of the University of Minnesota Law School and William S. Pattee Professor of Law. He writes and teaches on international law, human rights, and law of war issues. Previously, he was a professor and Associate Dean at Cornell Law School and served as Vice Provost for International Relations at Cornell University. In 1998–9, he served as a director in the US National Security Council's Office of Multilateral and Humanitarian Affairs, where he worked on war crimes issues, the International Criminal Court, economic sanctions, and UN political issues. Before joining Cornell, Professor Wippman practised law for nine years in Washington DC, with a focus on international arbitration, political consulting on public and private international law issues, and representation of developing countries in litigation.

Sir Michael Wood, KCMG, MA, LLB, member of the English Bar, is a member of the International Law Commission and a Senior Fellow of the Lauterpacht Centre for International Law, University of Cambridge. He is a barrister at 20 Essex Street, London, where he practises in the field of public international law, including before international courts and tribunals. He was Legal Adviser to the UK's Foreign and Commonwealth Office between 1999 and 2006, having joined as an Assistant Legal Adviser in 1970.

PART I

INTRODUCTION

INTRODUCTION: INTERNATIONAL LAW AND THE PROBLEM OF WAR

MARC WELLER

I. Preliminary Remarks

Homo homini lupus—man is mankind's wolf. This claim, put forward by Maccius Plautus in his comedy *Asinaria* of 195 BC, has struck a chord throughout the millennia. For it reflects what many regard as a universal and eternal truth: the greatest danger faced by humankind lies in our own predatory instincts. Life would be stable and secure for all, if only we could tame that inner wolf bent on aggression against its own kind. Hence, throughout history, humankind has decried the suffering brought about by war, and called for eternal peace, while plaintively accepting armed conflict as a necessary element of the human condition. International law has played, and continues to play a key role in this regard. Indeed, the question of whether international law can effectively prevent war and armed conflict is often seen as synonymous with the question of whether international law is law.[1] The persistence of war and international violence is taken as evidence for the proposition that the international legal system does not transcend the realm of disposable morality. In international life, law becomes irrelevant where it should matter most—in relation to the prevention of war and the immense suffering it imposes upon humankind.

[1] See Chapter 3.

Of course, we live in a world of our making. Law as an abstract conception cannot be said to be responsible for the state of the world. Instead, law is made for social ends. It reflects the state of the society it serves. Hence, the law that operates within the international system is one of the tools that can be used to shape the world. The shape of the international system depends on the corporate will of the constituencies represented in it, as does the role law can play within that system.

It may be an anarchical system in which law merely plays a tactical role among competing states. Or, in a more integrated international society law serves the purpose of managing interactions and conflicts between states. Finally, in an international community, it can be the instrument of an international constitutional system, where the law reflects, transmits, and operationalizes global community values. One such key value would be the absence of organized violence, of war.

II. Approaches to Peace and War

These three basic types of international system correspond in some measure to three schools of thought about war and law in the international system. These are the realist approach, the managerial approach, and the utopian visionary approach.

A. 'Realists' and Anarchy

The realist approach assumes that human beings are inherently prone to organized violence; they carry the seeds of war within their genetic code. True, social anthropologists point to evidence of peaceful societies throughout history. The first organized human communities lived in settlements without walls, it is argued, confirming that human beings can exist in a peaceable environment. And yet, from stone-age cave paintings, to the triumphalist reliefs carved in granite showing the battles of Mesopotamia, exhibiting the unhappy fate of the losers in battle, decapitated or led away into slavery, to the eternal litany of conquests and defeats over some 5,000 years of recorded history, the history of violence seems to be the history of humankind.

Those who believe that humankind is inherently violent tend to advance the so-called realist techniques of restraining the drive towards war. *Si vis pacem para bellum—if you want peace, prepare for war*, is another ancient Latin maxim. Hence, societies need to make defensive preparations, build walls and warships, and maintain and train armies. They need to conclude alliances in order to maintain a balance of power, or strike an enemy first, before it has developed its full military potential.

Or, they need to dominate others, in order to pacify the region or the known world through empire.

Of course, some argue that preparing for war tends to lead to war, whether intended or not. The preparations of the one side, even if motivated by considerations of defence, may appear as preparation for aggression to the other side. Castles and walls can serve as defences, but they were in fact often used by invading forces to consolidate their conquest. What is billed as a defensive alliance may seem to be a coalition of predators to those outside it. Preparations for defence have been made for as many hundreds and thousands of years as wars have occurred. Evidently, they do not end the risk of armed conflict.

Is there room for law in such an inherently unstable system which seeks to avoid war through the threat of war? The answer is clearly yes. The earliest defensive alliances aiming to establish a balance of power among states were concluded as sacred, as legal texts. Maintaining a balance of the power system through alliances required means of communication, with friends and foes alike. This led to the development of the doctrine of the sanctity of ambassadors and other envoys. In addition, rules and customs of warfare developed over time. In Europe, the code of chivalry was replaced by the codes of conduct among increasingly professional armies, which later ripened into the early emanations of the law of armed conflict. Moreover, attempts were made to achieve strategic stability between the states or alliances through arms control. The first significant attempt in this direction were the treaties seeking to constrain the currency of empire at the beginning of the 20th century—battleships. During the second half of that century, arms control extended significantly further, seeking to outlaw the possession or use of certain types of weapons, such as chemical or biological weapons, to limit conventional weapons, and to limit the spread of nuclear weapons while supporting the doctrine of nuclear deterrence through mutual assured destruction by way of strategic arms limitation treaties among the superpowers.

Throughout, though, in view of the so-called realists, law remained a tactical undertaking. It avoided war where all involved were interested in avoiding it. It limited the effects of war, or the 'temperament' of war, where this lay in the mutual interest of all. It required good reasons (or a just cause) for going to war.[2] But, at the same time, war remained very much a means of policy when it seemed advantageous to the one or other side.

B. Society and the Managerial Approach

The second approach is based on the view that human beings may not necessarily be warlike by their very nature. However, it is the organization into states that turns mankind into its own wolf. Organized societies will develop the technology

[2] See Chapters 1 and 3.

and capacity to wage war. More crucially, organized societies will inevitably compete for scarce resources. Throughout most of human history the crucial resource was land, along with the labour needed to exploit it. One city-state will want to conquer the fertile lands of its neighbour, one kingdom will want to absorb another, or form an empire to dominate everything within its reach. Modern analysts of geopolitics focus on other resources, be it the control over strategic resources such as oil or uranium, or water, or over avenues of global transport and communication.

If the drive towards war is not inherent in the human condition, but in human organization, the obvious answer is a managerial one. War is not the most rational way of satisfying claims to territory or resources. Instead, the trend towards violent competition over resources is counterbalanced by mechanisms to find other means of resolving such conflicts. In a more integrated international society it is assumed that the constituents of the international system, the people constituting states, would not rationally choose war, and will therefore opt for alternative means of settling disputes.

That vision takes concrete shape through increasing the interaction and interdependence among states. Increasingly sophisticated mechanisms of 'peaceful change' have been developed to resolve conflicts without resort to arms so as to manage the increasingly complex interests of, and relations among, states.

Initially, the Concert of Europe came into existence. Wars and conflicts continued, but were banished to the periphery of the system, avoiding, by and large, a cataclysmic clash of the great powers. These powers shared an interest in maintaining relative stability amongst themselves, to facilitate their uninterrupted overseas expansion, trade, and industry, while still competing with one another for resources and areas of influence and control. This competition and potential conflict among the powers was managed through ad hoc conference diplomacy. The legal approach of offering dispute settlement was added to the conference system. The example of the Jay Treaty (1794)[3] and the ensuing arbitrations was replicated. The Hague Conventions for the Pacific Settlement of International Disputes of 1899[4] and 1907[5] established the Permanent Court of Arbitration. The Dogger Bank incident (1904) and other cases proved that accidental wars can be avoided by means such as inquiry and conciliation.

The carnage of the first global conflagration of 1914 strengthened the view that in the age of mechanized warfare and new weapons technology such as chemical weapons, no state would resort to something as irrational as war when offered a peaceful alternative to address its claimed rights or interests. The managerial approach to conflict and dispute settlement was therefore strongly evident in the design of the League of Nations system at the conclusion of the war to end all wars.

[3] Treaty of Amity, Commerce and Navigation between Great Britain and the United States, 52 CTS 243.
[4] 32 Stat 1779, TS No 392. [5] 36 Stat 2199, TS No 536.

The League offered several layers of dispute settlement or crisis management mechanisms, and added adjudication in the form of the Permanent Court of Justice to the arsenal of instruments for peaceful change. War remained legal under the Treaty of Versailles that instituted the League.[6] However, in order to be able to make war lawfully, a state had to go through the mechanisms for peaceful change offered in the League Covenant. If states complied with this involving process, war would be practically impossible.

Of course, such a system based on the peaceful settlement of disputes will only function where the protagonists are actually interested in settling their disputes and avoiding war. Where a state is determined to vindicate its claimed rights through force, no system of war avoidance through peaceful change can operate. Hence, when the League of Nations was confronted by major powers wishing to upset the status quo or even to overturn the system, as was the intention of the Axis powers, Nazi Germany, fascist Italy, and Japan, the system collapsed.

c. Utopia and Collective Security

A third approach is the more radical, or utopian one.[7] If war is a culturally learnt behaviour by societies coming into contact with one another, rather than an inherent trait of life in an international environment, perhaps it can be unlearnt. War would no longer be seen as the normal condition, but as an aberration. War is no longer a heroic pursuit allowing a nation to develop its identity and destiny fully, as has been the dominant view through the millennia, up to and including the ultra-nationalist 19th century. Instead of an agent of national advancement and a measure of cultural achievement, war is painted as the ultimate cultural failure. It is no *ultima ratio* of international politics, it is simply irrational.

Once this realization has been made, the answer to the problem of war is simple. All that is required is a global cultural act, transforming mankind's plea for a warless world into a reality through a collective act of will to abolish war as an acceptable form of human interaction.

Over the centuries, the ideal of a world without war appeared to be consigned to a phantasy. True, pacifist ideals and movements have existed for a long time. This tendency gained momentum at the turn of the 19th to the 20th century, as mechanized warfare brought home the horrors and inhumanity of war, and again during the second half of the 20th century, in response to the fear of nuclear annihilation. But the peace movement was unable to overcome the key objection put by the so-called realists—that pacifism is passive. Pacifists declare that they will never contemplate force. But short of self-denial and a willingness to be subjugated by others, the doctrine can only operate if it is universally shared. As long as war remains possible

[6] BTS 4(1919), Cmd 153. [7] See Chapter 2.

to the minds of some, the others, however much they might wish to embrace the ideal of pacifism, will tend to feel the need to be prepared for defence unless they can accept the prospect of being forcibly incorporated into more warlike societies or empires.

The idea of collective security developed in answer to this dilemma. It offered a practicable utopia, although not necessarily a warless world. Instead of renouncing war as such, war is replaced by the doctrine of war in the common interest—in the interest of maintaining peace. The various peace plans emanating from distinguished pens such as those of the Abbé de Saint-Pierre, Rousseau, and Kant, combined three elements.[8] There would be renunciation of war as a means of state policy, a mechanism to settle disputes peacefully through conciliation or arbitration, and a pledge of all members of the system to take common action against any state failing to comply with prohibition of the use of force.

Incredible though it may seem, the League of Nations essentially attempted to put this utopian design into practice. This was innovative and quite radical, and can only be explained by the extent of suffering imposed, at the time mainly on the combatants, the soldiers who died in the fields of Flanders and elsewhere by the millions. The Preamble to the League Covenant exhorted member states to promote international cooperation and to achieve international peace and security 'by the acceptance of obligations not to resort to war'. This fell short of an outright prohibition of the use of force by states, but it was still a tangible beginning in the cultural revolution branding war as an international wrong, rather than a heroic act.

The second important element concerns the relative position of individual states vis-à-vis the international system represented by the League structure. While classical international law was focused on the advancement of the national or vital interests of states and their self-preservation as the ultimate aim of the system, the League was focused on the preservation of the system for peace that it established as the key goal. Action in support of a victim of a use of force was not characterized, in the first instance, as a kind of collective self-defence of the state under attack. Instead, military action might be taken collectively to 'protect the covenants of the League', as Article 16 of the Covenant put it. In other words, the object of protection of the collective security mechanism was the integrity and credibility of that mechanism itself, which was aimed at achieving international peace and security for all. This does represent a very fundamental shift in approach, although it was somewhat undermined by those states which continued to emphasize self-defence and self-preservation.

The third innovation of revolutionary magnitude in the Covenant was that it could apply universally. It regarded the aim of achieving international peace and security as an aim of mankind. Hence, the institutions and mechanisms addressing

[8] See Chapter 2.

international peace and security could be invoked and applied against members and non-members of the League alike. The Covenant declared in Article 11(1):

> Any war or threat of war, whether immediately affecting any of the Members of the League or not, is hereby declared a matter of concern to the whole League, and the League shall take any action that may be deemed wise and effectual to safeguard the peace of nations.

In this way, the Covenant breached the classical precepts of the international system, according to which states can only be bound by international arrangements to which they have consented. Here, there was a recognition of a superior public good, the peace of nations, the preservation of which was deemed to displace this classic requirement of consent.

Of course, somewhat ironically, one of the problems of the League was its failure to attract universal membership. Its founder, the US, never became a party. Japan withdrew in the wake of the Manchuko episode and Germany, which regarded the Versailles treaties of which the Covenant was a part as a punitive settlement of the First World War, opposed the system and left it, before overturning it through aggressive war, as did Italy. Stalin's Russia was expelled in view of its aggressive attitude.

There were also important structural deficiencies. First, as already noted, there was no definite prohibition of the use of force. Instead of being outlawed more formally, war was subjected to an involving procedure that would have to be exhausted before it could be lawfully made. An unlawful war was one launched in violation of these requirements of seeking to achieve peaceful change.

Secondly, there were many layers of mechanisms for peaceful change. However, there was no mechanism for comprehensive, compulsory jurisdiction. That is to say, states were not obliged to submit their disputes to one particular binding and final settlement mechanism if they had failed to come to a settlement by other means. The newly established World Court was not a court of final instance that would take on that role. Instead, it operated on the basis of quite strict consent by the states party to a dispute in relation to the exercise of its jurisdiction.

Thirdly, the enforcement mechanism was not automatic, at least where forcible measures were concerned. Article 16(1) of the Covenant declared that, should any member of the League resort to war in disregard of its commitments under the Covenant, it would be deemed to have committed an act of war against all other members of the League. In principle, there would follow an automatic imposition of trade and financial sanctions. In practice, even this was not achieved when Council members found themselves confronted with a use of force by a potential ally, such as Italy in the case of Abyssinia. In Article 16(2), the Covenant also imposed a duty to protect the common interest of all in the suppression of the procedurally unlawful use of force. However, critically, that duty was imposed upon the Council of the League, rather than its members.

Somewhat oddly, the Council would discharge its duty to act in the face of unlawful war by merely recommending to the governments concerned what military, naval, or air force might be used for the preservation of peace. Hence, in deference to the sovereignty of its member states, the Council would not make binding determinations. It was left to states to assess individually whether and how they would act in response to an unlawful war and to the recommendation of the Council.

Collective security was therefore only as credible as the willingness of states to act in defence of the system, rather than in pursuit of their own specific interests or alliances that persisted during the League era. This issue of credibility arose in two ways. In the first instance, it concerned the willingness and ability of Council members to agree on a recommendation. Secondly, it related to their willingness to enforce their own recommendation militarily if necessary. To function, this system would have required a tremendous degree of homogeneity and coherence among its member states—which was exactly what was lacking in the turbulent and revanchist 1930s.

Of course, the deficiencies of the actual design of the League were apparent to most from its very inception. A race was on to 'plug the gaps' in the Covenant. In 1924, the Geneva Protocol was proposed. It would have prohibited the threat of aggressive war, instituted compulsory dispute settlement through arbitration or the PCIJ, and even imposed disarmament obligations upon states to maintain the military balance. However, the Act, which was meant to be implemented through amendments to the League Covenant, failed to gain acceptance.

In 1928, this result was overturned through two important legal instruments—the Kellogg–Briand Pact and the Geneva General Act for the Pacific Settlement of Disputes. In the Preamble to the Kellogg–Briand Pact, the parties declared themselves 'deeply sensible of their solemn duty to promote the welfare of mankind' and 'persuaded that the time has come when a frank renunciation of war as a national policy should be made to the end that the peaceful and friendly relations now existing between their peoples may be perpetuated.'[9] In Article 1, the parties:

> Solemnly declare in the names of their respective peoples that they condemn recourse to war for the solution of international controversies, and renounce it as an instrument of national policy in their relations with one another.

This solemn declaration must surely rank as a crowning achievement of human civilization. The determination of the 15 major signatory governments, soon followed by another 43 accessions, to formally outlaw war as a means of national policy marks a key turning point in the attempt to turn war from a glorious and legitimate pursuit of states to an unlawful activity. Of course, the onset of mankind's most destructive war soon afterwards rather undermines this sentiment. As this volume amply demonstrates, the struggle to give meaning and reality to the prohibition of the use of force continues to this day. Yet, the importance of this cultural shift against the normality of war in international law is immense. The terms of the debate about war have definitely shifted as a consequence of the simple determination that war is, in principle, illegal.

9 94 LNOJ (1929) 57, No 2137.

The parties also agreed, in Article 2 of the Pact, that the settlement or solution of all disputes or conflicts of whatever nature or of whatever origin, which may arise among them, shall never be sought except by pacific means. Hence, the Pact reflected the two necessary sides of the one coin—if no dispute can be settled through the use of force, all disputes must be settled by peaceful means. However, the Pact did not fully succeed in plugging the gaps in the Covenant. The obligation of peaceful settlement was not matched by compulsory, comprehensive jurisdiction. That is to say, there was no specific means or method that would ultimately need to be employed in order to ensure that all disputes would be settled.

This issue was addressed in the Geneva General Act for the Pacific Settlement of Disputes concluded that same year.[10] It provided for 'disputes of every kind' between the participating states to be subjected to conciliation and ultimately arbitration.[11] All disputes relating to the respective rights of the parties (ie 'legal disputes') would be submitted for decision by the Permanent Court of International Justice or to arbitration. In principle, the General Act added the capstone to the architecture for peace of the League of Nations era, adding the element of comprehensive, compulsory dispute settlement. On paper, the dream of a warless world had been realized. However, the time for these radical innovations in international law and in international organization was of course anything but auspicious. The General Act only attracted 22 states parties. Only three years after the Kellogg–Briand Pact and the General Act had been concluded, Japan's invasion of Chinese Manchuria, soon followed by Italy's forcible acquisition of Abyssinia (Ethiopia) and then Germany's conquests of neighbouring territories, sounded the death knell for this initial experiment with collective security.

III. The United Nations System

It would be wrong to claim that the League of Nations period represents a failure for the attempts to restrain war that remained without consequence. The 'legal approach' of peaceful change that had characterized the League was discredited in the eyes of many, in particular those who emerged as 'realists' from the experience of the inter-war period and of the war. But the United Nations system combines a number of features drawn from the innovative League of Nations experience.

[10] 93 LNTS 343. [11] 93 LNOJ (1929) 343, No 2123.

A. Enforcement

The successor of the League, the United Nations Organization, purported to represent a decisive departure from what was now termed the naive or utopian vision of Wilson's League. And yet, reflecting the utopian vision, the UN too was meant to 'save succeeding generations from the scourge of war', as the Preamble to the Charter proclaims.[12] In order to achieve this aim the drafters of the UN Charter hoped to add the one element that had been missing from the League of Nations—a commitment to definite enforcement of the collective security commitment contained in the Charter. The UN Charter therefore emphasizes as its principal purpose, in the opening of its first substantive article, the maintenance of international peace and security through effective collective measures for the prevention and removal of threats to the peace, and for the suppression of acts of aggression or other breaches of the peace. Of course, the UN system conceived in this way could never fulfil its promise. From its inception, the one key element on which the system was based—a commitment of the great victorious powers to enforce peace through common action—was lacking, given the outbreak of the Cold War.

The two structural deficiencies of the League of Nations in relation to the enforcement of its decisions were meant to be addressed in the Charter. First, the powers of recommendation of the League Council or Assembly are replaced with the mandatory enforcement powers of the Security Council—a small executive body intended to keep the key victors of the Second World War united around the goal of making future wars impossible. The Council exercises the primary responsibility for international peace and security (Art 24 of the UN Charter). It can take preventative action, anticipating and preventing war, if necessary through forcible means, and it can respond to acts of aggression or breaches of the peace through powerful enforcement action, including military measures (Chapter VII). All member states are obliged to accept and carry out the decision of the Council (Art 25). Towards that end, they are obliged to make available to the Council armed forces, assistance, and facilities necessary for the purpose of maintaining peace and security (Art 43).

The primary authority over the use of force in international life, over war and peace, is assigned to a supranational executive body, the UN Security Council. Its powers extend to UN members. They also extended to the enemy states of the Second World War, not originally intended to qualify as 'peace-loving' states eligible for membership according to Article 4 of the Charter. They would be prevented by the war-time alliance made permanent in the shape of the Security Council from ever launching aggressive wars again. But, more generally, in Article 2(6) of the Charter, the club of states represented at the founding of the UN also gave themselves the power 'to ensure that States which are not Members of the United Nations act in accordance with these Principles so far as may be necessary for the maintenance of

[12] 1 UNTS 16.

international peace and security.' Hence, the UN claims objective legal personality, claiming full universality, at least where matters of peace or war are concerned. Its founding was conceived as a global constitutional moment, establishing the basis for a peaceful, post-war order.

In other aspects, the UN system represented an extension of the template of the League of Nations Covenant, supplemented by the Kellogg–Briand Pact and the Geneva General Act. The obligation to settle all disputes, without exception, peacefully, was clearly stated, as was the prohibition of the use of force, in Article 2(3) and (4) of the Charter. Due to the objective character of the UN Charter, these two matching obligations were now fully universalized. Moreover, the more modern concept of the 'use of force' had replaced the renunciation of war as a means of national policy. In addition, it was made clear that the threat of the use of force was just as unlawful as the actual use of force.

B. Disputes

Still, the Charter retained a number of very conservative elements. However vast the enforcement powers of the Security Council under Chapter VII relating to threats to the peace, breaches of the peace, and acts of aggression, the authority of the UN in relation to other disputes remains rather limited. International disputes are subjected to the very weak system of Chapter VI. Article 33 of the Charter confirms that states must settle their disputes peacefully, listing the principal tools available towards that end. But crucially, there is still no comprehensive, compulsory dispute settlement mechanism. That is to say, states remain free to determine how they will seek to address disputes. Even where disputes or situations are likely to endanger international peace and security, the Security Council can merely recommend the terms of a possible settlement, acting in the manner of a conciliator, or recommend means of a settlement. This reflects a highly traditional, sovereignty-conscious approach, asserting that strict consent of the respective states is required in relation to third party settlement of disputes. In practice, the Council has mainly abstained from even recommending the terms of a particular settlement, and it has only once referred a dispute to the International Court of Justice (ICJ). In the *Corfu Channel* case, the Court did not, however, rely on that referral as a source of its jurisdiction, preferring to invoke the doctrine of *forum prorogatum* instead. The dominant view remains that the Security Council lacks the authority to create jurisdiction for the Court where disputes have not been settled through other means and are likely to endanger international peace and security. It can only recommend judicial settlement.

This defect has left a considerable gap in the UN Charter system. States have in fact been willing to refer a number of important territorial disputes bearing the risk of armed conflict to the Court. One example is the dispute between Libya and Chad over the Anzou strip. In a number of other instances, the actual use of force has been referred to the Court, for instance in the *Nicaragua* case. However, the point remains that such settlement is possible, but it is not required as a matter of law. The gap caused by the lack of comprehensive compulsory jurisdiction is being healed to some extent by the proliferation of individual compulsory dispute settlement clauses and mechanisms. In particular since the end of the Cold War, the number of acceptances of the compulsory jurisdiction of the ICJ without special agreement has increased considerably, to a total of 70 states. Some 300 international treaties nominate the ICJ as the body entrusted to settle disputes relating to their interpretation and application. Moreover, a whole set of specialist international courts and tribunals has been established, including the Law of the Sea Tribunal and the WTO/GATT dispute settlement mechanism. This is supplemented by regional courts and tribunals, such as the Court of Justice of the European Union, and the European, Inter-American, and African human rights courts. Following upon the examples of the Yugoslav and Rwanda tribunals, the International Criminal Court has been established—a court that will in the future have the authority to address individual responsibility for the crime of aggression. In Europe, a system of arbitration, fact-finding, and directed conciliation has also been established within the framework of the Organization for Security and Co-operation in Europe (OSCE).

c. The Rule of Law and Enforcement

The purported clean break between the legal approach of the League of Nations era and the emphasis on effective enforcement of the UN system has had one consequence that is difficult to grasp for some. The Security Council is not an executive body dedicated to the enforcement of international law, or even just to the enforcement of the prohibition of the use of force. Instead, it is a mechanism to maintain or restore peace. This is clearly a political function, and one which is only partially circumscribed by law.

At a late point in its drafting, a reference to principles of justice and international law was added to Article 1(1) of the Charter, addressing the maintenance of peace and dispute settlement as part of the purposes and principles of the organization. However, the reference occurs in the second half of the sentence constituting that paragraph, relating to the adjustment or settlement of international disputes or situations that may lead to a breach of the peace. No such qualification attaches to the first half of the sentence, addressing effective collective measures for the prevention and removal of threats to the peace and the suppression of acts of aggression. Article 24 conferring the primary responsibility for international peace and security on the Council emphasizes again prompt and effective action. However, such action is to be undertaken in accordance only with the provisions of the Charter itself, rather than international law more broadly conceived. Essentially, the great victorious powers were keen to preserve their freedom of action in relation to action taken under Chapter VII.

This means that the Council has broad discretion to interpret its authority when acting under Chapter VII.[13] As Chapter VII applies in relation to threats to the peace, the substantive scope of its activities is determined principally through the political judgement of its members, rather than by legal criteria. The Council can act in circumstances that go beyond a violation of Article 2(4) prohibiting the use of force by states.

During the 1950s, the Council engaged in a heated debate about whether it could address colonial conflicts—conflicts which France and other states argued were internal to their own area of exclusive jurisdiction. By 1960 this issue was resolved in favour of expanding the authority of the Council in relation to such conflicts, along with the related issues of apartheid in South Africa and South Africa's continued presence in the former mandated territory of Namibia. In the early 1990s, the Council started to consider essentially internal situations of civil conflict and humanitarian suffering. Initially, it argued that it was the external ramifications of internal situations that allowed it to act, such as instability caused by the outpouring of refugees into neighbouring territories, or the risk of armed border incidents flowing from internal conflict. However, when addressing the desperate humanitarian situation in Somalia through Resolution 794 (1992), the Council accepted that the 'magnitude of humanitarian suffering' of the population concerned in itself constituted a threat to international peace and security, allowing the Council to proceed according to Chapter VII.

With the end of the Cold War, it appeared that the Security Council might involve itself more closely in the resolution of disputes. In the rather controversial instance concerning the purported Libyan Lockerbie bombers, the Council appeared to attempt to bypass the ICJ which was hearing the case.[14] This dispute was essentially a legal dispute, concerning the obligation of Libya to try or extradite the two suspects according to the Montreal Convention on the Suppression of Unlawful Acts against the Safety of Civil Aviation.[15] However, instead of acting under the weak, recommendatory powers of Chapter VI of the Charter addressing international disputes, the Council acted under Chapter VII. In Resolution 748 (1992) it ordered Libya to surrender the two suspects for trial to the UK and imposed sanctions against Libya to enforce this demand.

While this instance of semantically converting a legal dispute into a 'threat to international peace and security' that could be addressed under Chapter VII has remained highly controversial, it is clear that the past decades have witnessed an increasing breadth and depth of activity by the UN Security Council. This has included authorization for the use of force for the liberation of Kuwait and the imposition of ceasefire terms on Iraq upon the conclusion of the conflict, the

[13] See Chapters 8, 9, and 10. [14] See Chapter 15. [15] 974 UNTS 177.

granting of authority for the use of force on behalf of populations under threat of destruction or in response to counter-constitutional coups, the adoption of targeted sanctions against individuals involved in conflict, or in support of acts of international terrorism, and the establishment of the ad hoc criminal tribunals for Yugoslavia and Rwanda.

There has been some considerable debate about the exercise by the Council of a quasi-legislative function, threatening the application of the traditional precepts of state sovereignty and the principle that states can only be legally bound through their own consent. This debate has also extended to the question of the rights of individuals touched upon by Security Council action. Targeted sanctions address individuals by freezing their assets, inhibiting financial transactions, and imposing travel bans. They impose significant restrictions on their lives and livelihoods, akin to a criminal sanction. The question of whether such sanctions can be subject to judicial review, at least within the domestic legal orders in which such sanctions are being enforced, has caused a perceived clash between human rights, on the one hand, and the need for effective preventative action on the part of the Council, on the other.

This controversy also extends to the international administrative function exercised under the authority of the Security Council. There have been a number of instances of 'complex' peacekeeping operations, assigning to forces or authorities operating under a Security Council mandate functions and powers akin to those of a domestic government. However, for some time there existed no checks and balances or legal remedies that might be invoked by individuals in relation to such acts.[16] This problem became even more pronounced when the UN started to engage in international governance operations, taking over public authority in a given territory for a certain period, as it did in Cambodia, certain areas of Bosnia and Herzegovina, Eastern Slavonia, East Timor, and, for an extensive period, Kosovo. This practice led to an increased emphasis on human rights compliance by UN-mandated bodies, and on their legal accountability.

The question of whether the Council is bound by law also arose in relation to the possible clashes between *jus cogens* rules and Chapter VII resolutions. Bosnia and Herzegovina, for instance, asserted that the arms embargo imposed upon it under Resolution 713 (1991) deprived it of the ability to protect its population from a campaign of genocide perpetrated by armed elements operating on its territory. In addition to the possibility of the Council acting against *jus cogens* rules, there also exists the reverse effect. In its practice, the Council has often exercised an important international constitutional function in manifesting the effects of grave violations of *jus cogens*. For instance, it declared null and void and without legal consequence certain violations, such as the purported annexation of Kuwait by Iraq.

[16] See Chapters 15 and 19.

It is now becoming accepted that the Council is indeed a key element of the emerging international constitutional order—a legal order which also establishes boundaries for actions by the Council. Hence, the Council could not conceivably remove itself, or those acting under its mandates, from fundamental rules of international law enjoying the status of *jus cogens*. If *jus cogens* rules are rules no state can ever contract out of, the states represented on the Security Council cannot exempt themselves from the application of such rules when exercising their functions in the Council. Moreover, the Council, itself based on a treaty subject to the concept of *jus cogens*, and as a high institution of the organized international community, is itself subjected to the high order international rules of international constitutional standing. This would include the application of the essential principles of humanitarian law and the very core of human rights to UN action or to action performed under a UN mandate.

If it is accepted that international law does in some way circumscribe the action of the Security Council, then the question arises whether the legality of its actions can be tested before the ICJ, the principal judicial organ of the UN.[17] It is clear from the practice of the Council and the Court that both can act in parallel, reinforcing one another. That is to say, the fact that the Council is acting, even under Chapter VII, does not in itself render a case inadmissible in the Court. The Court has also interpreted the pronouncements of the Security Council in a significant number of cases. In the *Namibia Opinion*, it also ruled on the procedural validity of the Council action. However, the question of whether the Court would be willing to question the substance of a decision of the Council taken under Chapter VII has not as yet been fully addressed by the Court.

D. Prohibition of the Use of Force

The UN Charter is based on the abolition of war as a means of national politics. Article 2(4) obliges members 'to refrain in their international relations from the threat or use of force against the territorial integrity or political independence of any State, or in any other manner inconsistent with the purposes of the United Nations.'

It is by now principally uncontested that the prohibition of the use of force enjoys the status of a *jus cogens* rule.[18] This means that no state can contract out of the obligation. Moreover, a violation of this essential rule of the emerging international constitutional order triggers consequences for the organized international community. States must not recognize results brought about through the use of force, and they must not assist the offending state in keeping it in place. In addition, states should cooperate with a view to reversing the violation and its consequences, most likely through collective action within the framework of the UN.

[17] See Chapter 15. [18] See Chapters 7 and 54.

The concept of the prohibition of the threat or use of force is related to, but not the same as, a number of other legal terms.[19] Intervention denotes the action of one state in relation to the domestic jurisdiction of another without the consent of the latter. Armed intervention adds the element of the use of force. Once a use of force attains a certain intensity, it may amount to an armed attack, triggering the application of the right to individual and collective self-defence. The concept of aggression has been added, principally for two purposes. In the annex to Resolution 3314 (XXV), the UN General Assembly defined acts of aggression, seeking to assist the UN Security Council in using its powers of enforcement as foreseen in Chapter VII of the Charter. More recently, the concept of aggression has been revived in the context of criminal responsibility, in the Kampala accord which will, in a number of years, enable the International Criminal Court, to consider the responsibility of individuals for aggression.[20]

The language used in Article 2(4) is comprehensive, imposing a blanket prohibition on the threat or use of force.[21] The article covers any use of force. This is borne out by consistent practice. For instance, the Security Council will routinely condemn armed raids, or aerial attacks, even if these do not permanently infringe upon the territorial integrity or political independence of a state. Victim states of such attacks will invoke Article 2(4), and the states conducting such operations inevitably feel constrained to refer to self-defence as a justification for what is, even to their eyes, a prima facie violation of the prohibition of the use of force.

Similarly, the argument that certain unilateral uses of force are not precluded because they are not 'inconsistent with the purposes of the United Nations', has not been accepted. Like the reference to territorial integrity and political independence of states, this sub-clause was inserted into the article to ensure its comprehensive coverage, rather than to undermine it.

The comprehensive nature of the prohibition of the use of force excludes a number of other traditional doctrines or considerations that would classically justify armed action. In a major shift to the position in classical international law, the doctrine of self-help can no longer be invoked in defence of the use of force. In other words, force is not a lawful means for the vindication of claims or rights advanced by states, whatever their nature, including the invocation of 'vital interests' by a state. More specifically, the doctrine of armed reprisal can no longer be invoked to justify armed action to constrain a state to resume compliance with its international obligations. Similarly, the doctrine of necessity, which allows a state to injure the rights of another state to safeguard essential interests against grave and imminent peril, recognized as a circumstance precluding wrongfulness in the law of state responsibility, cannot be invoked in the context of the use of force. Moreover, the punitive use of force is no longer accepted. That is to say, a state can no longer respond to an infraction of its rights, or even to a use of force directed against it, by way of armed retaliation.

[19] See Chapter 22. [20] See Chapter 24. [21] See Chapter 21.

The ICJ has confirmed in the *Nuclear Weapons Advisory Opinion* that the threat of the use of force is just as unlawful as the actual use of force.[22] However, the concept of a threat of force is not open-ended. There must be a specific demand made by one state or a group of states against another, backed by a specific threat of the use of force. Hence, the practice of ultimata involving the threat of the use of force should have been removed from the diplomatic lexicon. Yet, in recent practice, formal threats of the use of force have recurred, although in connection with collective security; that is, the purported threat of force in the common interest. In Resolution 678 (1990), the UN Security Council authorized the use of force against Iraq, unless Iraq withdrew from Kuwait by a specified date. NATO (the North Atlantic Treaty Organization) threatened the use of force in implementation of Resolution 836 (1993), when demanding the withdrawal of heavy weapons around the UN-proclaimed safe areas in Bosnia and Herzegovina. An international contact group threatened force in 1999, unless the protagonists in the Kosovo conflict came to a rapid political settlement of that crisis in accordance with Security Council resolutions. NATO subsequently used force. In a few instances connected with counterterrorism, threats of force have also been made unilaterally.

It has of course been questioned what types of act are prohibited by Article 2(4). During the 1970s, developing states argued that economic sanctions could have an effect similar to the use of force in terms of their effect on civilian populations. These claims have not been widely accepted. Instead, it is clear that the term 'force' concerns physical force, administered through military-type agencies using military means. More recently, this issue has been reopened in connection with so-called cyberwars.[23] The argument is that an electronic 'attack' by one state on another can have effects that are just as severe as those caused by a more conventional military operation.

Another important point relates to the scope of application of Article 2(4). The conventional view remains that it only applies in an interstate context. Since 1945, the prevailing types of armed conflict, causing the largest number of deaths, have been the internal ones. Casualties in this kind of conflict tend to be mainly civilians. Despite these facts, no serious attempt has been made as yet to extend the prohibition of the use of force to the domestic context. The regulation of internal armed conflicts remains a matter for the domestic law of the state concerned, and of humanitarian law and human rights.

This deficiency is balanced somewhat by the determination of the Security Council that internal conflicts can threaten international peace and security. They can therefore be subject to Chapter VII action. In the larger number of such conflicts, the Council has at least imposed arms embargoes upon the sides. Some other internal conflicts have triggered Council mandates for robust peacekeeping including, increasingly, measures for the protection of civilians or for armed intervention

[22] See Chapter 42. [23] See Chapter 52.

by coalitions of states or regional organizations. The contested Security Council mandate granted in Resolution 1973 (2011) in relation to the conflict in Libya, and the dispute about its implementation by Western states, has however made such mandates more difficult to achieve. The inability of the UN Security Council to act decisively in the face of the carnage in Syria from 2012–14 was in part an outcome of this controversy.

A final issue concerns the question of whether the acts of non-state actors can constitute a use of force in the sense of Article 2(4). Traditionally, this question would have been answered in the negative. However, the UN Security Council determined that the events of 11 September 2001 amounted to an armed attack—a use of force so sustained that it triggered a right of self-defence on the part of the US.

The removal of armed self-help and associated concepts through the comprehensive prohibition of the use of force has meant that states have had to justify forcible action with reference to self-defence, the only remaining classical legal justification for the use of force.

E. Self-Defence

In contrast to the Kellogg–Briand Pact, the UN Charter contains a full article on the right to self-defence. The formulation of Article 51 on self-defence has given rise to a number of issues of interpretation.

The first issue concerns the very nature of the right. Article 51 refers to the 'inherent' right of individual and collective self-defence. If the right is inherent, does Article 51 merely reflect the traditional customary law standard on self-defence? According to the well-established *Caroline* formula, self-defence applies classically in response to an instant and overwhelming necessity, leaving no choice of means and no moment of deliberation.[24] Any act of self-defence must, moreover, be proportionate to the attack that triggered the right. However, if Article 51 merely refers to pre-existing custom, what would have been the point of defining the right in novel terms in the Charter?

This question is best answered by interpreting the terms of Article 51 in the light of the natural meaning attaching to the terms used, and with reference to the classical standard. This is possible as the formulation in Article 51 is not in fact fundamentally incompatible with the *Caroline* test.

The first issue that arises concerns the objects of protection of the right to self-defence. In addition to territory, this includes ships and aircraft registered to the relevant state. Where an armed attack is specifically targeted at a group of nationals of a particular state in another state's territory, self-defence also applies. For instance, Israel could invoke the right to self-defence when mounting an operation

[24] 2 *Moore's Digest* (1837), 409.

to rescue the mainly Israeli hostages held by terrorists and Ugandan armed forces in Entebbe after an aircraft hijacking in 1976. This is somewhat different to the doctrine of rescue of nationals abroad—a doctrine which is often deployed to justify the extraction of foreign nationals from areas of crisis. Those instances will be ordinarily characterized by an absence of public order, rather than an armed attack against a defined group of foreign nationals.

The ICJ has clarified in the *Nicaragua* case that not all use of force amounts to an armed attack. Instead, the armed action has to be sufficiently sustained, using military means at a certain level of intensity. This would rule out border incidents or minor skirmishes. The attack must be specifically aimed at the victim state. Firing a missile at undefined targets would not meet that criterion.[25]

Self-defence applies automatically, without the need of authorization from the Security Council or any other body. The defending state can invite others to join it in exercising the right to collective self-defence. However, third states can only invoke the right to collective self-defence if they have been so invited.

It is not necessary to be able to point to prior defence treaties between the victim and the supporting states, nor do the states rendering assistance have to have their own economic or strategic interests at stake. In a significant change to the previous understanding of the right, the co-defending states are not only rendering assistance to the victim of an armed attack. They are, at the same time, defending one of the cardinal principles of the international legal order—the prohibition of the use of force, which has an *erga omnes* character. That is to say, all states have a legal interest in compliance by all other states with this rule.

Article 51 is placed within Chapter VII of the Charter. This implies that it is seen as an element of the collective security architecture, rather than as its antithesis. Self-defence is seen as ancillary to collective security. It is meant to preserve the rights and integrity of a state under attack until the issue can be addressed through the collective security mechanism. Hence, states are required to notify the Council when acting in self-defence. This offers the Council the opportunity to review the claim to self-defence and, potentially, to overrule it. Moreover, according to Article 51, self-defence is only available until the Council has taken measures necessary to maintain international peace and security.

It is sometimes argued that self-defence is therefore suspended as soon as the Council takes action.[26] Surely the action of the Council must be what it considers the 'measures necessary' to maintain international peace and security, it is sometimes asserted. At the other extreme, it is argued that the doctrine of self-preservation means that self-defence persists until the victim state itself finds that the necessary measures have been adopted. Neither view is persuasive. Clearly, the Council may

[25] *Military and Paramilitary Activities in and against Nicaragua (Nicaragua v. US)*, Merits, Judgment, ICJ Rep 1986, 14, 103.

[26] See Chapters 28 and 33.

not be in a position to take all the measures necessary to restore peace and security in any given instance. Hence, it is clear that self-defence is not suspended by any resolution or decision taken by the Council. On the other hand, the post-1945 international legal order does privilege community interest over the interests of individual states. The Security Council could deprive a state of the right to self-defence even if that state does not regard the actions taken by the Council as sufficient to safeguard its security or integrity. The right view is therefore one that balances the interest of states and of the international community as a whole. Self-defence would be suspended in two cases: either when the Council specifically determines when acting under Chapter VII that self-defence is suspended, or when it makes demands under Chapter VII which, if implemented, would reverse the consequences of the armed attack, and which are backed by formal enforcement action under Article 41 and/or Article 42. In practice, it has been found prudent to reserve the continuing application of the right to self-defence in Chapter VII resolutions imposing sanctions, as was the case in Resolution 661 (1990) concerning Kuwait.

In other circumstances, self-defence remains bounded by international law. The right ceases when the armed attack has been reversed. It may be permissible to pursue an attacking force that is eventually retreating across its state boundary, and to continue military operations. However, such a right only extends to the extent necessary to ensure that the armed attack has definitely been defeated. It would not be permissible to continue the conflict in order to diminish and degrade the military capacity of the attacking state, for instance in order to alter the military balance in a way that would make a further, future attack less likely.

Self-defence is, moreover, bounded by the doctrine of proportionality. The response to the armed attack must remain in proportion to the original attack.

Article 51 allows for self-defence 'if an armed attack occurs'. In harmony with the previous *Caroline* doctrine, this means that an armed attack has to have taken place, or, according to the doctrine of anticipatory self-defence, it must be imminent.[27] Imminence contains an objective and a subjective element. Objectively, all the actions necessary for the launch of the attack must have taken place—the missiles are fuelled, armed, and stand erect on their launch-pads, as it were. This must be matched by the subjective element. There must be clear evidence of intent to launch the attack. Anticipatory self-defence can therefore take place at the last possible moment enabling the defending state to prevent an attack that would otherwise be inevitably undertaken against it.

There was some evidence of an erosion of the standard of imminence during the 1990s. An example is furnished by the activities of the American, British, and to a lesser extent, French air forces conducting operations over certain areas of northern and southern Iraq. These areas had been declared no-fly zones, in support of action to preserve the respective Kurdish and Shia populations from aggressive actions

[27] See Chapter 31.

by their own government. Initially, rules of operation allowed overflying coalition aircraft to engage Iraqi anti-air installations, such as anti-air missiles and radar, and Iraqi aircraft, when they illuminated and locked on to coalition targets. At that point, it was clear that an attack was imminent, and it would have been unreasonable to await the actual launch of the attack before responding.

Subsequently, however, the requirements were relaxed. In a second stage, merely switching on ground-based radar was seen as sufficient evidence of imminent attack to engage these installations. Later, the mere presence of anti-aircraft facilities exposed them to attack, in view of the more abstract risk they posed to coalition jets. Finally, even targets lying outside the aerial exclusion zone were targeted, if perceived to be linked to potential anti-aircraft operations against the coalition.

In reality, of course, by that time a campaign to diminish and degrade Iraqi military assets had commenced—essentially a preventative aim. However, this campaign had to be presented as consistent with self-defence. Hence, the requirements of imminence according to self-defence were becoming more elastic as time progressed.

These restrictive requirements as understood up to that point rule out preventative attacks, or preventative war.[28] Prevention means that one state strikes another at a time when it can do so effectively, in order to forestall an attack that may occur in the future. A state uses its temporary advantage to destroy, hinder, or delay the ability of another state to develop the ability to mount an attack at some other point. The requirement of imminence is not fulfilled. The threat that is engaged is in some aspects still remote and hypothetical. Hence, Israel's attack against the Iraqi Osirak nuclear facility in 1983 was condemned by the UN Security Council in Resolution 487 (1991). The Council invoked Article 2(4) and condemned what it termed a 'military attack' as a violation of the UN Charter and of norms of international conduct.

A related concept is pre-emptive war. Pre-emption applies when there is a high likelihood of conflict. While an attack may not be immediately imminent, armed conflict seems unavoidable. The side launching a pre-emptive attack seeks to gain the advantage through a surprise first strike that would diminish the military potential of the other side. Most would argue that such action is impermissible too, unless pre-emption is the only way of mounting an effective defence. Israel asserted a right of pre-emption in 1967, arguing that its geographical and military posture would not have allowed it to mount a defence if it had awaited the launch of the armed attack expected from its neighbouring states.

The issue of prevention or pre-emption was raised when the US published a national security strategy in 2002, indicating that the 'United States cannot remain idle while dangers gather'.[29] Against the backdrop of the events of 9/11, the doctrine

[28] See Chapter 29.

[29] National Security Strategy of the United States of America, Sept 2002, reproduced in John Ehrenberg et al (eds), *The Iraq Papers* (Oxford: Oxford University Press, 2010), 81, 84.

pointed to the great risks posed by terrorist attacks, including potentially those using weapons of mass destruction.

IV. New Threats

Up to 9/11 it was assumed that only states could mount an armed attack. However, the Security Council confirmed in Resolutions 1368 (2001) and 1373 (2001) that self-defence is also available in response to armed attacks undertaken by non-state actors, such as terrorist movements, provided the attack has the character and intensity that would ordinarily be achieved by military means. The collapse of the World Trade Center towers, causing the death of some 3,000 individuals, clearly crossed that threshold.

While military preparations of states can generally be observed, this is not the case where preparations for acts of terrorism are concerned. Hence, it will be impossible to determine with any accuracy when a terrorist attack is 'imminent'. Accordingly, it has been suggested that the classical criteria restricting the application of self-defence, including the criterion of imminence, cannot find application in this context. However, the right answer may be less one of a dilution of the criterion of imminence. Rather, it appears to be an issue of evidence. A state claiming that action has to be taken to forestall an imminent terrorist attack would need to make available evidence supporting its claim. This may take the form of evidence demonstrating that the terrorist organization is engaged in a continuous campaign which, unless disrupted, will inevitably result in further terrorist attacks.

Several other challenges have been put forward against the application of the law on self-defence as traditionally understood. It is now accepted that a non-state actor can mount an armed attack. But even if it is a non-state actor, it will necessarily be based somewhere, most likely on foreign soil. If self-defence is to be exercised, this would mean that force would be used not only against emanations of the terrorist movement, but also against the state on whose territory it is based.[30]

The answer to this issue comes in three forms. First, there is the law enforcement approach. If a terrorist movement is active on the territory of a foreign state, that state is under a legal obligation to establish jurisdiction over the relevant individuals and to prevent the commissioning of acts harmful to other states. Under international terrorism conventions, most of which have attracted very widespread participation, there would also be an obligation either to try the individuals or to extradite them for trial.

[30] See Chapters 32 and 34.

The second approach concerns situations where the host state is in fact colluding with the terrorists and knowingly offers them shelter and possibly other means of support. This situation is legally complex, as it involves two different legal regimes that are sometimes confused. The first is the law on attribution, based on state responsibility. The territorial state may well share legal responsibility for the terrorist act, depending on the extent of its support for, or even sponsorship of it. The victim state would be entitled to deploy all means available under international law to vindicate its rights, including against the state supporting the terrorist group. This would include the right to adopt countermeasures, although only peaceable ones.

The use of force in self-defence, on the other hand, does not become available once attribution has been demonstrated. The dominant view in international law would only make self-defence available if: (1) the act of terrorism amounted to an armed attack; there is (2) an imminent further attack; and (3) this act is not only supported and sponsored by another state, but it is virtually an act of that state. In addition to supporting the terrorist movement, the state concerned would need to control and direct the operations of the relevant group.

Hence, the US was entitled to use force in self-defence when engaging Al Qaeda in Afghanistan in the aftermath of 9/11. Al Qaeda was mainly based in the territory of Afghanistan, including its head, Osama bin Laden. Afghanistan had failed to comply with Chapter VII resolutions of the Security Council demanding that it cease its support for terrorism and establish jurisdiction over bin Laden. Indeed, Al Qaeda and the Taliban regime were so closely intertwined that it was possible to argue that the one was an instrumentality of the other.

In other cases, the situation may be less clear, and the emphasis must lie on seeking to deploy the Security Council in support of addressing it. This also applies in the third category of cases where the hosting state is unable to fulfil its obligation to restrain terrorism emanating from its territory. It may have lost control over certain sections of its territory, or the government may have collapsed in its entirety. Loss of governmental control does not affect the continuing legal personality of a state, including its right to be free from the use of force. However, if the state is persistently unable to discharge obligations essential for the maintenance of international peace and security, this is likely to affect the question of whether self-defence may be available. After all, in such a situation it would not be possible to determine whether the state concerned, or a portion of it, is coextensive with a terrorist organization by controlling or directing its activities. Hence, it would not be possible to insist on the application of this involving test for self-defence. Instead, the lawfulness of the action would depend increasingly on the ability to demonstrate that further terrorist acts akin to an armed attack will definitely be launched from the territory in question, and that such attacks are imminent, and can only be averted through force.

The failure on occasion to demonstrate that force was used in order to forestall an imminent armed attack emanating from a terrorist movement also undermined the proposition that no punitive action is permissible. For instance, in June 1993, the US launched 21 cruise missiles against the Iraqi intelligence headquarters in Baghdad. It argued that it had been convincingly proven that Iraqi intelligence had been implicated in a terrorist plot to assassinate former US President George Bush Sr some months earlier. No evidence of any threat of further action of that kind was put forward, nor any evidence of an imminent threat. Instead, the operation seemed to serve as retaliation and, as then President Clinton explained, deterrence of future acts.[31]

Given the legal difficulties in grappling with the mainly US campaign concerning international terrorism, a further development took place challenging the traditional legal categories. This concerned drone attacks against terrorist suspects.[32] It appears that these attacks were conducted in three types of circumstances. First, they were undertaken with the full consent and cooperation of the local government. This was the case in Yemen. Secondly, there were operations in territories where there was no effective structure of government (Somalia). Thirdly, they were undertaken in conditions where the host government appeared to oppose the operations publicly, although it was rumoured that there may have been tacit or secret agreement (Pakistan). While the appreciation of these instances at a state-to-state level may differ according to the extent of consent of the local state, it is clear that important human rights considerations concerning the victims of the attack, whether intended or 'collateral', remain.

An additional issue relates to the concept of proportionality. It may be possible to judge what is proportionate and necessary in order to reverse a particular armed attack conducted by the armed forces of a state. But how can one judge what is proportionate in relation to an attack of the magnitude of 9/11? Was it proportionate to dislodge the entire structure of governance in Afghanistan in order to forestall further attacks of that kind? The answer may well be yes, given the particularities of that situation. But the US, and at the time some others, went further, advancing the thesis of the 'war on terror'.

That thesis seemed to hold that 9/11 had been the opening shot in a global war, entitling the US to use force against associated terrorist movements wherever they might operate. It would not be necessary to justify individual acts according to the criteria of self-defence enumerated earlier. Instead, force would now be available without reference to international law as it was previously known.

In fact, the thesis of the war on terror was soon disowned by some of states that had originally advanced it, while others abandoned it more silently. Instead, a concerted effort was made to return to a commitment to the prohibition of the use of force as contained in Article 2(4) and the application of self-defence as defined in Article 51 of the Charter.

[31] David Von Drehle and R. Jeffrey Smith, 'US Strikes Iraq for Plot to Kill Bush', *Washington Post*, 27 June 1993, p A01, available at <http://www.washingtonpost.com/wp-srv/inatl/longterm/iraq/timeline/062793.htm>.

[32] See Chapter 51.

A UN High-Level Panel on Threats, Challenges and Change was established, inter alia to consider the status of international law in this area. It confirmed the continued application of the concept of imminence as traditionally understood.[33] In relation to other less tangible or immediate threats, the Panel ruled that the Security Council offered the best avenue for addressing them. In his document 'In Larger Freedom', the UN Secretary-General added:[34]

> Imminent threats are fully covered by Article 51, which safeguards the inherent right of sovereign states to defend themselves against armed attack. Lawyers have long recognized that this covers an imminent attack as well as one that has already happened.

At the 2005 UN World Summit, a universal consensus reaffirmed 'that the relevant provisions of the Charter are sufficient to address the full range of threats to international peace and security.'[35] Even if it was possible to restore to some extent a consensus on the interpretation of the prohibition of the use of force and the right to self-defence, a number of further challenges emerged.

V. New Challenges

The law on the use of force has not remained unaffected by other changes in the understanding of the international system. It had been expected that the prohibition of the use of force and the collective security mechanisms of the UN would come to operate as originally intended, once the Cold War dissolved around 1990. At that time, and under the impression of international cooperation under a UN mandate to liberate Kuwait, George Bush Sr proclaimed the existence of a New World Order. However, the end of the ideological confrontation of East and West brought with it new potential for armed conflict.

A. Territorial Change and the Use of Force

In Eastern and Central Europe, the unfreezing of the Cold War also meant the unfreezing of ethnic and boundary issues that had been forgotten since the League of Nations period. As the Soviet Union dissolved, the territorial integrity of Georgia was threatened by secessionist movements in South Ossetia and Abkhazia. Both territories managed to displace Georgian authorities. In 2008, in consequence of the use of

[33] A/59/565 (2 Dec 2004).

[34] Report of the Secretary-General, S/59/205 (21 Mar 2005), para 124.

[35] A/60/1 (24 Oct 2005).

force by the newly confident Russian Federation, they were forcibly separated from Georgia, declaring nominal independence. In Moldova, Transnistria established virtual independence, again under the protection of a significant Russian garrison stationed there. Moreover, Armenia captured the mainly ethnic Armenian populated territory of Nagorno Karabakh from Azerbaijan and has occupied it ever since. Most recently, the Russian Federation forcibly removed Crimea from Ukraine, purporting to annex the territory a few days after it had nominally declared independence.

Given the involvement or interest of the Russian Federation in all of these instances, the collective security mechanism could not function. For instance, a draft resolution condemning the referendum in Crimea that led to its incorporation in the Russian Federation and declaring it without effect failed by 13 votes in favour, due to the negative vote of the Russian Federation, with China abstaining.[36]

In addition to these instances of forcible 'realignment' of Russia's borders, a number of other conflicts straining the international system occurred. Chechnya pursued an armed campaign for independence from the Russian Federation. Although the European Union (EU) and some states continued to endorse the territorial unity of Russia, Chechnya managed in 1996 to obtain agreements from General Lebed and then President Yeltsin, promising self-determination and possible independence after an interim period. However, Russia unilaterally abrogated these commitments and instead forcibly reincorporated Chechnya in 1999. This controversial action remained generally unopposed by other states.

The European Community (EC) and its members states confirmed, on the other hand, that Slovenia and Croatia were entitled to the protection of the prohibition of the use of force, only a few weeks after both entities had declared independence from the Socialist Federal Republic of Yugoslavia, and several months before they achieved international recognition. This development gave credence to the view that pre-state entities, or emergent states, can be the objects of protection of international law even before they gain full effectiveness.

Previously, this view had only been held in relation to colonial territories. According to UN standards, such territories were protected from repression by their metropolitan state while struggling for self-determination.[37] Controversially, it was added that there existed a positive right to struggle against colonialism. This right was to be exercised by the recognized national liberation movement of the territory in question. This right could be explained in one of three ways. According to one view, colonial territories were already subjects of international law. Their right to struggle for liberation was a type of self-defence against alien oppression or occupation. Secondly, it was asserted that the right to struggle for national liberation was a new exception to the prohibition of the use of force, recognizing the unique justice of the cause of anti-colonialism. Thirdly, and most simply, it could be argued that there was no need to invoke a right to use force on the part of national liberation

[36] SC/11319 (15 Mar 2014). [37] See Chapter 38.

movements, inasmuch as the prohibition of the use of force only applies in interstate relations. As there was no international prohibition to use force internally, no international legal justification was required.

Of course, by the end of the Cold War, the principal anti-colonial struggles had been all but concluded. Even East Timor, which had been invaded at the point of its independence from Portugal, eventually gained statehood. This left only Western Sahara, which had been similarly occupied by its neighbour Morocco at the point of independence from Spain, and the case of Palestine on the international agenda of liberation from colonialism (disregarding a number of less noted non-self-governing territories). Given the peace processes that have been active in relation to both in stops and starts, offering a peaceful alternative towards a settlement, it has been argued that the doctrine of national liberation in the colonial sense is now virtually desuetude.

The dissolution of Yugoslavia also gave rise to a number of additional issues concerning the use of force. Bosnia and Herzegovina was subjected to armed occupation of most of its territory by armed forces of, or sponsored by, Croatia and Serbia respectively. Under the Dayton Accords of 1995, it was narrowly possible to claim that the legal personality of Bosnia and Herzegovina had been retained in rejection of ethno-territorial claims pursued forcibly by its neighbours.

Kosovo, which had declared independence from the former Yugoslavia, or later Serbia, at the outset of the Yugoslav crisis, eventually obtained independence in 2008. After some five years of peaceful resistance to what its mainly ethnic Albanian population perceived as repression by the government in Belgrade, an armed conflict erupted in 1995. NATO intervened in 1999, leading to the withdrawal of Yugoslav authorities and forces from the territory. Under Security Council Resolution 1244 (1999) Kosovo was placed under UN administration. Attempts to mediate a settlement of its final status with Belgrade failed. Eventually, the UN mediator Martti Ahtisaari recommended independence for Kosovo as the only realistic option, also in view of the severe repression that had previously been experienced by the mainly ethnic Albanian population. This result led to the revival of the arguments in favour of the doctrine of remedial secession—a doctrine which suggests that an entity gains an entitlement to self-determination in consequence of armed repression, grave human rights violations, or political disenfranchisement administered by the central state.

In its subsequent advisory opinion, the ICJ addressed the doctrine of territorial unity and integrity of states. It confirmed that the obligation to respect the territorial integrity of existing states only applies between states—it is akin to an obligation to refrain from intervention in secessionist disputes on behalf of the secessionist side. However, groups within the state concerned are not restrained by international law in seeking secession.

Although this issue was not addressed by the ICJ, the Kosovo case also raised the question of the impact of the use of force on the claimed status. In that instance, it could be argued that Kosovo would not have been able to obtain independence, had NATO not forcibly displaced the Serbian authorities from the territory. On the other hand, it was argued that the situation changed, given that NATO did not occupy the territory, but instead handed it over to UN administration. The UN exhausted attempts to obtain a negotiated settlement with Serbia. And while Kosovo's independence was not endorsed by the Security Council, Kosovo transformed the entire draft settlement generated by the UN mediator Ahtisaari into its own constitution. Hence, it was not a case of unilateral independence, but instead one of independence achieved under UN guidance.

Another argument in this context is somewhat more fundamental. It would assert that NATO's use of force in Kosovo was lawful, according to the doctrine of humanitarian intervention. If the use of force was lawful, then Kosovo's independence, even if ultimately the outcome of that use of force, would not have been tainted by a transgression against the *jus cogens* prohibition of the use of force.

B. Humanitarian Intervention

Humanitarian intervention was widely regarded as unlawful, at least until the end of the Cold War. Since then, the doctrine has inspired vigorous debate.[38] It is clear that the UN Security Council can act under Chapter VII to authorize the use of force on behalf of populations threatened by extermination, starvation, or forcible expulsion at the hands of their own government, or other groups exercising effective control over them. While the Council has had to emphasize the unique nature of virtually every situation it has addressed in this way, a pattern of practice has emerged which puts the authority of the Council to address essentially internal matters of this kind beyond question.

In the initial period following the end of the Cold War, there appeared to be a number of instances of forcible action undertaken by states outside a formal UN mandate which were not internationally resisted. These included actions on behalf of the mainly Kurdish population in the north of Iraq and the Shia so-called Marsh Arabs of the south. These operations were not internationally resisted. The operations of the Economic Community of West African States (ECOWAS), a sub-regional integration organization, in relation to Liberia and Sierra Leone were retroactively endorsed by the Security Council. However, NATO's operation on behalf of the mainly ethnic Albanian population of Kosovo caused significant controversy, leading some to doubt that the doctrine of humanitarian intervention is consolidating as a new justification for the use of force in international custom. As this would imply a deviation from an existing *jus cogens* rule, the prohibition of the use of force, the legal requirements for effecting such a change would be particularly

[38] See Chapter 35.

stringent.[39] This would require uniform practice and a special legislative intent on the part of the organized international community as a whole directed at modifying an existing rule of *jus cogens*, or creating a new one.

A more successful avenue of argument lies in the re-evaluation of the concept of state sovereignty. Action undertaken on behalf of a population to save it from manifest abuses of its rights, or a threat of extinction or displacement, would, according to this view, not amount to intervention. After all, such action would be undertaken to vindicate the rights, or presumed will, of the population under threat. That population, of course, is the true sovereign of the state, rather than the government or effective authority.

The doctrine of responsibility to protect has since been developed with a view to unifying the positions of states in this area. The doctrine was formally accepted at the 2005 World Summit, to which reference was made earlier. However, this acceptance does not fully resolve the issue, as the doctrine expressed in that document appears to relate mainly to the expectation that the UN Security Council will fulfil its responsibility to protect populations under threat, rather than individual states acting unilaterally. It has, however, been asserted that other international organs can exercise this responsibility if the Council is unable to act, due to the application of a veto. This would include the UN General Assembly and possibly regional organizations.

A further development relating to the use of force concerns pro-democratic action.[40] The Security Council itself has authorized armed action to restore a government that was removed through a counter-constitutional coup, in Resolution 940 (1994) concerning Haiti. It has repeatedly condemned counter-constitutional coups and the failure to implement election results. The Organisation of African Unity, now the African Union, and sub-regional organizations have on several occasions used force towards these ends. The Organization of American States has similarly established a system to provide for action in defence of democratic governance.

More controversially, in cases of internal armed conflict, significant numbers of states have either recognized opposition governments before they fully displaced the existing authority, or confirmed at least that an opposition leadership has the authority to represent a population during a period of prolonged uprising and conflict. The former occurred in relation to the Libyan Transitional National Council, the latter in the case of the umbrella organization of the Syrian groups fighting the government of Bashar Assad in Syria.

C. Claims to Enforcement of Global Community Values

Many instances of humanitarian or pro-democratic intervention, even if not formally mandated by a Security Council resolution, have at least made reference to demands

[39] See Chapters 7 and 54. [40] See Chapter 36.

made by the Council. In such cases, the Council would have confirmed that the situation at hand threatens international peace and security. Hence, it can no longer be considered a matter of entirely domestic concern. The Council would also have identified the nature of an overwhelming humanitarian emergency, and the means necessary to avert it. States mounting an intervention operation would then be able to argue that they are in fact enforcing the demands made by the Council.

Such references avoid the allegation that a state is intervening in pursuit of its own national interests, provided the intervening state or states limit themselves strictly to achieving the aims established by the Council. However, references to aims established by the Council do not in themselves furnish legal authority to act, if the Council has not granted a forcible mandate. The authority to act only exists to the extent that humanitarian intervention is accepted as a legal justification for the use of force.

No such underlying justification exists in relation to other claims put forward by states to enforce the will of the Security Council. This issue was borne out most sharply in relation to the Iraq conflict of 2003. The US argued that it had the authority to enforce disarmament obligations imposed upon Iraq in the ceasefire terms imposed by the Council through Resolution 687 (1991). This claim was generally rejected. The use of force by the US and some others was accordingly widely condemned as unlawful. This episode resulted in something of a crisis for the credibility of the prohibition of the use of force.

Other claims to enforce global community values have been made outside the context of Security Council resolutions. For instance, the US has claimed certain rights in relation to nuclear non-proliferation.[41] Its Proliferation Security Initiative, providing in particular for the possibility of enforced stop and search of ships, has given rise to controversy. However, the US has attempted to gain consent for this initiative, and has mainly only taken action against suspect ships with the consent of the flag state.

VI. Conclusions

The attempts to deploy international law in the pursuit of peace have utilized all three of the approaches identified at the outset of this Introduction. International law still supports the 'realist' doctrine of nuclear deterrence through arms control

[41] See Chapters 47 and 48.

agreements. It accepts that wars may occur by providing for rules of warfare and humanitarian law.

In addition, the international legal system offers an ever denser network of mechanisms for conflict management, as is foreseen in the society-based approach. Peaceful change is the norm. International armed conflict remains a spectacular, but generally rare, exception.

Finally, the international system has progressed to a perhaps surprising extent along the utopian route. It has outlawed war. Indeed, it has elevated the prohibition of the use of force to the status of the highest order norms of the emerging international constitutional system. Although the rule is not always complied with, states remain strongly attached to this significant cultural achievement.

Perhaps surprisingly, the world emerged from the difficult period of the Cold War with a fairly clear understanding and universal consensus relating to the meaning of the prohibition of the use of force and its principal exception, self-defence. Developments since then have challenged traditional views, but the rules concerned have proven quite resilient.[42] While some violations could have put their survival in question, the opposite seems to have been the case, at least thus far. The use of force against Iraq was met by an impressive stand by many populations around the globe in favour of peace. The war resulted in a re-commitment to the rules on the use of force by many states.

For now, the unipolar moment of the US, which seems to have placed particular stresses on the system, appears to have passed. The doctrine of positive exceptionalism, which would have held that the rules concerning the use of force may not apply to the US in the same measures as they apply to other states, given the large responsibility of the US for world peace, has been overcome. Similarly, negative exceptionalism, which would argue that certain rogue states lie outside the international legal order and can therefore not benefit from its protective rules, is no longer expounded with any vigour.

It remains to be seen whether the Russian Federation and China, which were previously strong defenders of the restrictive rules on the use of force, will challenge the system now that their geopolitical position is shifting away from being status quo powers. In addition to the conflicts on Russia's Western borders, disputes relating to the Antarctic, the South China Sea, and a whole host of other issues are emerging.

The weakness of the system remains the enforcement of the prohibition of the use of force. In attempting to provide for effective enforcement through cooperation of the great powers that emerged in 1945, the drafters of the UN Charter have in fact ensured that any one of them can inhibit collective action in the pursuit of peace. The present situation concerning Syria and Ukraine offers a stark reminder of this fact.

42 See Chapter 27.

The international system relating to war and peace often finds itself accused of double standards. Why was it possible to act in relation to the crisis in Haiti, but not in Rwanda, where some 800,000 civilians died through genocide observed by the UN and its members? Why has the issue of Palestine not been resolved? And why could the unlawful war against Iraq of 2003 not have been prevented? All of these questions are troublesome, but they are also misguided.

It is the function of the legal system to channel conduct into socially desirable paths and to offer avenues for action where these paths are not taken. The mechanisms that are so provided cannot in themselves assure that corrective action is taken in every instance that warrants it. This function falls to those who operate the system, to states, and to their constituents. The civilizational task of delegitimizing the use of force through law continues.

CHAPTER 1

TOO MUCH HISTORY: FROM WAR AS SANCTION TO THE SANCTIONING OF WAR

RANDALL LESAFFER*

I. Introduction

The enshrinement of the prohibition for states to use force in Article 2(4) of the Charter of the United Nations of 26 June 1945 is mankind's most ambitious attempt, to date, to ban war. The UN Charter stands at the end of an evolution by which the right of states to use force was progressively limited. This evolution started at the turn of the 20th century with the two Hague Peace Conferences (1899/1907). Historians of international law and international lawyers alike have written about the rise of the *jus contra bellum* as one of the key changes that revolutionized international law and divided the 'classical international law' of the 19th century from

* Many thanks to Shavana Musa (Tilburg Law School) for her help in editing this chapter.

the 'modern international law' of the 20th century.[1] They have caught this revolution in terms of a stark contradiction between the licence of the 19th century for states to resort to force and the almost complete, albeit far from effective, prohibition of force in the Charter era. Under this historical narrative, the *jus ad bellum*—the laws about the conditions under which war is legal—of the 19th century was reduced to the mere acceptance that the decision to resort to war fell within the preserve of state sovereignty and was a matter of policy rather than law. The *jus ad bellum* shrunk from a 'law to war' to a 'right to war'. Some scholars have added that the revolution of use of force law after the First World War reached back beyond the 19th century towards the tradition of the just war of the late Middle Ages.[2]

This narrative has historical merit. It is sustained by the writings of some late 19th- and early 20th-century international lawyers.[3] But, we should be careful not to turn a blind eye to the elements of continuity in the history of use of force law. Two important nuances need to be made. First, although ultimately the sovereign states of the 19th century had a right to resort to force, the *jus ad bellum* had not been emptied of all meaning. State practice of the 19th century showed that states still justified or condemned forcible actions under a widely accepted, albeit evolving, framework of reference that partook in the tradition of just war. Doctrinal writers may indeed have relayed these justifications to the domain of morals and politics, but facts show that a customary use of force law that had not shed the influences of the just war doctrine persisted. This sheds new light on the so-called return of the just war of the 20th century. Secondly, the gradual rise of the *jus contra bellum* did not occur in a context where there was hardly any material use of force law. This rise occurred in constant dialogue with the existing customary use of force law. In that sense, the *jus contra bellum* of the Charter did not mark a clear and utter break with the old *jus ad bellum*.

[1] Ian Brownlie, *International Law and the Use of Force by States* (Oxford: Clarendon Press, 1963), 19–111; Yoram Dinstein, *War, Aggression and Self-Defence* (3rd edn, Cambridge: Cambridge University Press, 2001), 71–85; Wilhelm Georg Grewe, *The Epochs of International Law* (Berlin/New York: De Gruyter, 2000), 575–8; Malcom Shaw, *International Law* (6th edn, Cambridge: Cambridge University Press, 2008), 1119–22.

[2] eg Cornelius van Vollenhoven, *The Three Stages in the Evolution of the Law of Nations* (Leiden: Martinus Nijhoff, 1919). The works of James Brown Scott and Arthur Vanderpol were instrumental in reviving the interest of international lawyers in scholastic just war doctrine. Christopher Rossi, *Broken Chain of Being: James Brown Scott and the Origins of Modern International Law* (The Hague: Kluwer, 1998); Arthur Vanderpol, *Le droit de la guerre d'après les théologiens et les canonistes du moyen-âge* (Paris/Brussels: Tralin/Goemaere, 1911).

[3] Amos Hershey, *The International Law and Diplomacy of the Russo-Japanese War* (New York: Macmillan, 1906), 67.

II. The Just War in the Middle Ages (12th–15th Centuries)

Throughout the narrative of the intellectual history of war in the West runs the scarlet thread of the just war tradition. Throughout the ages, ideas about the justification of war have been changed, twisted, and turned around a stable nucleus of ideas. The central core of that tradition is that war is a reaction to an injustice committed by the enemy. The just war tradition has its roots back in the Roman *jus fetiale*, the stoic concept of natural law as evidenced in the work of the Roman orator Marcus Tullius Cicero (106–43 BC)[4] and early Christian theology, in particular the writings of Saint Augustine (354–430).[5] Augustine's thought found its way into the *Decretum Gratiani* (c 1140), the basic authoritative text of late-medieval canon law. The just war doctrine came to its full articulation in the writings of the theologians and canon lawyers of the 12th to 14th centuries. The Dominican theologian Saint Thomas Aquinas (1225–74) moulded it into its classical form.

Aquinas distinguished three conditions for a war to be just: *auctoritas*, *causa justa*, and *recta intentio*. *Auctoritas* meant that a war could only be waged by or under the authority of a sovereign. Most late-medieval writers did not list possible just causes, but confined themselves to a broad definition. In general, it boiled down to the view that a just war was a reaction against a prior or threatening injury by the enemy—'ulcisci iniuriam' in the words of Augustine.[6] It was a form of law enforcement (*executio juris*), of forcible self-help in the absence of a superior authority to which to turn.

In his *De jure belli ac pacis* (1625), the Dutch humanist Hugo Grotius (1583–1645) discerned three just causes: defence, the re-vindication of property or rights, and the infliction of punishment.[7] The final condition, *recta intentio*, implied that the war needed to be waged with the intention of doing justice, and ultimately, to attain a just peace.[8]

In relation to the classical just war doctrine, three important remarks must be made. First, war was discriminatory. Except for the rare case when both sides had to be considered unjust, a just war was a war between a just and an unjust side. In

[4] Cicero, *De officiis* 1.11.33–1.13.41; idem, *De re publica* 3.33.

[5] Robert A. Markus, 'Saint Augustine's Views of the "Just War"' in W. J. Sheils (ed), *The Church and War* (Oxford: Blackwell, 1983), 1–13; Stephen C. Neff, *War and the Law of Nations. A General History* (Cambridge: Cambridge University Press, 2005), 29–38 and 45–7; Alan Watson, *International Law in Archaic Rome. War and Religion* (Baltimore, MD: John Hopkins University Press, 1993).

[6] Augustine, *Quaestionum in Heptateuchum liber sextus (in Iesum Nave)*, X, *PL*, 354, coll 780–1.

[7] Hugo Grotius, *De jure belli ac pacis libri tres* (1625) in James Brown Scott (ed), *Classics of International Law* (Oxford: Clarendon Press, 1925), 2.1.2.

[8] Thomas Aquinas, *Summa Theologiae* IIaIIae 40.1.

a consequential application of the doctrine, the *jus ad bellum* spilled into both the *jus in bello*—the laws of war properly speaking, that is, the laws regulating warfare itself—as well as the *jus post bellum*—the laws about the ending of war. Only one side had a right to be in the war and could thus benefit from the so-called *jura belli*, the rights of war such as the right to use violence, to take loot, to hold enemy persons to ransom, or make conquests. The soldiers on the unjust side only retained their natural right of self-defence in the case of personal attack. A just peace stood at the end of a just war. This implied that the claim over which the war had been fought had to be attributed to the just belligerent and that he would receive compensation for all the damages suffered because of the war. The just side had a right to punish the enemy as a guarantee against new wrongs. In the words of the neo-scholastic theologian Francisco de Vitoria (c 1480–1546), the victor of a war had to 'think of himself as a judge, sitting in judgment between two commonwealths, one the injured party and the other the offender.'[9] This, however, did not mean that the writers of the just war doctrine equated victory to justice. Just war was not an ordeal; nothing guaranteed the victory of the just side. It could only be deplored that its defeat would lead to injustice.

Secondly, the scope of the just war doctrine was theological because it was chiefly the product of theologians and canon lawyers. The just war doctrine was the answer to the question of what partaking in war did to one's eternal soul. Nevertheless, the just war doctrine was also picked up by late-medieval Roman lawyers and those writers who discussed the actual practices of war under the code of chivalry.[10] To these authors, the matter at hand was the actual effects of the justice of war in the here and now. At this level, some of the foremost civilians struggled with the discriminatory application of the *jura belli*, which was not sustainable in practice. In this context, they made reference to the concept of *postliminium* from classical Roman law. According to the Digest, *postliminium*—the right of a prisoner of war to be restored to all his prior rights and property after his liberation—applied between *hostes*—enemies in a properly authorized war between independent peoples.[11] On this basis, Bartolus of Sassoferrato (1314–57) acknowledged the indiscriminate application of the *jura belli* to both sides in a war between sovereigns. The later commentator Raphael Fulgosius (1367–1427) and the humanist jurist Andrea Alciato (1492–1550) would take this a step further by accepting that a war could be just on both sides, so that all belligerents enjoyed equal rights during the war. This

[9] Francisco de Vitoria, *Relectio de Jure Belli, in fine* in Anthony Pagden (ed), *Francisco de Vitoria, Political Writings* (Cambridge: Cambridge University Press, 1991).

[10] eg Honoré de Bonet, *L'arbre des batailles* (c 1386) in *The Tree of Battles of Honoré de Bonet* (transl G. W. Coopland, Liverpool: Liverpool University Press, 1949), whose work was largely based on that of the commentator Johannes da Legnano (d 1383), *De bello, de represaliis et de duello* in James Brown Scott (ed), *Classics of International Law* (Oxford: Carnegie Institution, 1917). See Maurice Hugh Keen, *The Laws of War in the Middle Ages* (London: Routledge/Kegan Paul, 1965).

[11] D 49.15.5.1, in combination with D 49.15.24.

concession, however, only pertained to its effects on earth; it left the effects of the justice of war at the Last Judgement untouched.[12]

Thirdly, the religious scope of the theory, combined with its law enforcement character, accounted for the fact that war was conceived of as a limited forcible action between a lessor and a lessee and their respective adherents to enforce a claim, rather than an all-out war. War was not thought of as a state of war in which all normal, peaceful relations between the belligerents and their people were broken, but as a set of concrete hostile actions.[13]

III. Just and Legal War in the Early Modern Age (16th–18th Centuries)

Although the just war doctrine could not mould the practices of war and peace-making to its farthest consequences, it did have a real impact in late-medieval Europe. Wars were often justified in terms which were derived from the just war doctrine. The 'universal' authority of canon law and ecclesiastical courts, and in particular the papal court, provided a mechanism for discriminating between just and unjust belligerents and sanctioning the latter.

During the first half of the 16th century, the context in which the old *jus ad bellum* operated radically changed. The Reformation caused the collapse of the religious unity of the Latin West and struck a mortal blow to the main pillars of authority—canon law and ecclesiastical jurisdiction—upon which the bridge between the doctrine and reality of just war rested. The discoveries and conquests in the New World necessitated a frame of reference for the laws of war other than those of Christian theology, canon and Roman law. The rise of great dynastic power complexes such as Habsburg Spain, Valois France, and Tudor England, out of which the modern sovereign states grew as well as the Military Revolution and the massification of armies, navies, and warfare it brought, denied the notion of war as a limited law enforcement action. All this brought important changes in the *jus ad bellum*, without however signalling the utter demise of the just war doctrine.

[12] Bartolus, *Digestum novum in tertium tomum Pandectarum commentaria Secunda super Digesto novo* (Basel, 1592), ad D 49.15.24; Raphael Fulgosius, *In Pandectas* (Lyon, 1554), ad D 1.1.5; Andrea Alciato, *Commentarii in Pandectas* (Lyon, 1550), ad D 1.1.5 and idem, *Paradoxorum juris civilis* 2.21, in *Opera Omnia*, 4 vols (Basel, 1549), vol 3.

[13] On the just war in the Middle Ages: Peter Haggenmacher, *Grotius et la doctrine de la guerre juste* (Paris: PUF, 1983), 51–444; Neff, *War and the Law of Nations*, 45–82; Frederick H. Russell, *The Just War in the Middle Ages* (Cambridge: Cambridge University Press, 1975).

The vast majority of jurists and theologians of the 16th to 18th centuries who applied themselves to the laws of war and peace sustained the general outline of the just war doctrine, time and again repeating the three conditions of Aquinas in one form or another. But building on the work of their medieval predecessors, they made some all-important amendments that changed the *jus ad bellum* at its core.

First, early-modern writers did away with the discriminatory character of war in relation to actual warfare (*jus in bello*) and peace-making (*just post bellum*). Vitoria, while sustaining the objective impossibility of a war to be just on both sides, acknowledged that each side could be excused, on the basis of an invincible error, from believing in good faith that he was waging a just war. Thus, he introduced the concept of *bellum justum ex utraque parte* (war just on both sides) at the subjective level. For Vitoria, the implication of this was that the unjust party would not condemn his eternal soul. But through this, he also opened the door to a non-discriminatory conception of war in which both sides had the right to wage war and enjoy the benefits of the laws of war in the here and now.[14]

The civil lawyers Baltasar de Ayala (1548–84) and Alberico Gentili (1552–1608) took a more radical step. Building on the tradition of Roman law, they focused on the effects of war in the earthly life rather than those in the eternal life. They articulated the concept of legal war, or war in due form as it was later known.[15] As long as war was waged by a sovereign and was formally declared, it was legal. This did not signify a rejection of the just war doctrine, but neutralized its effect on the *jus in bello* and the *just post bellum*. Gentili held that because human fallibility made it impossible in most cases to establish who was in the right, it had to be accepted that both sides had a right to wage war. As such, the laws of war were to be applied indiscriminately to both sides. Gentili brought this new conception of war to its full complement in his *just post bellum*. Since one could not be certain about the justice of war and since victory did not indicate justice, the outcome of war itself—or in the absence of clear victory, of the peace negotiations—determined the attribution of the claims over which the war was waged. This radically changed the conception of war from a law enforcement action (*executio juris*) into a substitute for a legal trial: a form of dispute settlement.[16] Whereas under the just war doctrine, the attribution of property and all kinds of claim had to be vested in the justice of a cause preceding

[14] Vitoria, *De jure belli* 2.4-5.

[15] Hugo Grotius used the term '*bellum solemne*' (formal war) in his *De jure belli ac pacis libri tres* 1.3.3.4–5. Emer de Vattel preferred the terms '*guerre légitime*' (legitimate war) and '*guerre dans les formes*' (war in due form); Emer de Vattel, *Le Droit des gens, ou Principes de la loi naturelle appliqués à la conduit et aux affaires des Nations et des Souverains* (1758) in James Brown Scott (ed), *Classics of International Law* (Washington DC: Carnegie Institution, 1916), 3.4.66.

[16] Gentili likened a war to a duel as well as to a civil trial. Alberico Gentili, *De jure belli libri tres* (1598) in James Brown Scott (ed), *Classics of International Law* (Oxford: Clarendon Press, 1933), 1.2.18 and 1.6.47–52.

the war, under the doctrine of legal war it was vested in the outcome of war itself. The *jus post bellum* became a *jus victoriae*.[17]

Grotius synthesized the theological-canonist tradition of just war with the civilian tradition of legal war. In *De jure belli ac pacis*, Grotius sustained both conceptions of war, just war and legal war (*bellum solemne*). He relayed the question of the justice of war to the domain of natural law, which applied in conscience (*in foro interno*), while the question of the legality of war fell within the domain of the positive, human law of nations, which was externally enforceable (*in foro externo*).[18] After Grotius, this inherently dualistic scheme became part and parcel of mainstream thought on the laws of war and peace. Emer de Vattel (1714–67) still adhered to it.[19] Modern minds have often described the Grotian move in terms of sidelining the just war doctrine. This was not the case for the deeply religious men and women of the Early Modern Age. In fact, the Grotian move hardly changed anything in the material terms of the law. It only put the long-existing difference between theologians and canon lawyers on one side and civilians on the other side into a single system of thought. The question of justice of war remained as ever a matter of eternal salvation or damnation. Natural law may not have been enforceable in the courts of man, but it was enforceable in the court of God. It was only when religion started to recede into the background—which happened at the earliest from the mid-18th century onwards—that the just war doctrine lost its primary position.

Secondly, the concept of war as a state, rather than a string of separate belligerent actions, was introduced. Whereas under the medieval just war doctrine, war had been conceived of as a limited law enforcement action by a prince and his adherents against the perpetrator of the injury which had caused the war, in Early Modern Europe, war became clashes between sovereign states in their entirety. By the late 16th century, it had become customary for belligerents, at the inception of war, to take a series of measures in relation to trade, enemy property, and personnel, which fundamentally disrupted normal peacetime relations. Thus, war became an encompassing state of affairs, which differed from the state of peace.[20] Whereas Gentili and others had already operated this notion, Grotius was the first expressly to define war as a state of affairs.[21] The concept of 'state of war' had two implications. First, it related to the legal effects of war. The concept served to distinguish two spheres of

[17] Balthasar de Ayala, *De Jure et Officiis Bellicis et Disciplina Militaris* (1584) in James Brown Scott (ed), *Classics of International Law* (Oxford: Clarendon Press, 1944), 1.2.34; Gentili, *De jure belli* 1.2 and 1.6; Randall Lesaffer, 'Alberico Gentili's *ius post bellum* and Early Modern Peace Treaties' in Benedict Kingsbury and Benjamin Straumann (eds), *The Roman Foundations of the Law of Nations. Alberico Gentili and the Justice of Empire* (Oxford: Oxford University Press, 2010), 210–40. See on the conception of war as a form of dispute settlement, James Q. Whitman, *The Verdict of Battle. The Law of Victory and the Making of Modern War* (Cambridge, MA: Harvard University Press, 2012).

[18] Grotius, *De jure belli ac pacis* 1.3.4.1, 3.3.4–5 and 3.3.12–13; Haggenmacher, *Grotius et la doctrine de la guerre juste*, 457–62.

[19] Vattel, *Le Droit des gens* 3.3.24–28 and 3.3.40.

[20] Lesaffer, 'Alberico Gentili's *ius post bellum*' in Kingsbury and Straumann, *The Roman Foundations of the Law of Nations*, 210–14.

[21] Grotius, *De jure belli ac pacis* 1.2.1.1.

applicable laws. To the state of peace, the normal laws of peace (*jus in pace*) applied; to the state of war the laws of war (*jus in bello*) applied for belligerents, while for third parties the laws of neutrality applied.[22] Secondly, the doctrine of state of war allowed taking away all brakes on the expansion of war. Under the just war doctrine, hostile action had to be limited to the perpetrator and those who personally supported his injustices, including his unjustified resistance. Under the new doctrine, war constituted an all-out struggle between two sovereigns and their subjects. Whereas under the old doctrine, violence was only allowed against the guilty and the taking of property was limited to the object of contention and compensation for damages, now all enemy subjects and property became liable to attack or seizure in the service of victory.[23]

More than just a feature of doctrine, the dualism of just and legal war reflected the realities of early-modern state practice. On the one hand, state practice operated the conception of legal war in relation to its effects on the waging of war itself (*jus in bello*) as well as the making of peace (*jus post bellum*). The very rare cases in which the indiscriminate application of the laws of war was challenged all related to rebellion, whereby one party refused to recognize that the other had *auctoritas*. This was, however, a consequential application of the doctrine of legal war. The concept of legal war also dominated the way wars were ended. In Early Modern Europe, almost all wars were ended by peace treaties. With a single exception, no peace treaty of the 15th to 18th centuries among European sovereigns included an attribution of justice or guilt for the war.[24] Concessions were not based on the justice of the causes of war, but on its outcome (*jus victoriae*), or, in the vast majority of cases where there was no clear victor, on the outcome of the peace negotiations. Nothing illustrated the rejection of the just war doctrine in peace treaties better than the so-called amnesty clauses. From the late 15th to late 18th centuries, almost all peace treaties included such a clause. Under this provision, the former belligerents denounced all rights for themselves and their subjects or adherents to bring forward any kind of claim for the harm or damage that had been inflicted upon them by the enemy because of the war, thus wiping away all questions of the justice of the war and of the legality of wartime actions. After 1800, these clauses disappeared from most peace treaties, but by then it was generally accepted in the doctrine that they were silently implied.[25]

[22] Stephen C. Neff, *The Rights and Duties of Neutrals. A General History* (Manchester: Manchester University Press, 2000).

[23] Neff, *War and the Law of Nations*, 100–2.

[24] The Preamble to the Peace Treaty of Madrid of 14 Jan 1526 between the Emperor Charles V and Francis I of France, who was held in captivity by Charles, stated that Francis had been taken captive in a just war. P. Mariño (ed), *Tratados internationales de España. Periode de la preponderencia española* (Madrid: Consejo Superior de Investigaciones Cientificas, 1986), vol 3.3, 128. For a list and the text of early-modern peace treaties, see the 'Publikationsportal Europäische Friedensverträge' of the Institut für Europäische Geschichte in Mainz at <http://www.ieg-mainz.de/likecms/likecms.php?site=site%2Ehtm&nav=209iteid=312>.

[25] Randall Lesaffer, 'Peace Treaties and the Formation of International Law' in Bardo Fassbender and Anne Peters (eds), *The Oxford Handbook of the History of International Law* (Oxford: Oxford

On the other hand, the just war doctrine was still very much alive with regard to the practice of the justification of war (*jus ad bellum*). In most cases, the princes and republics of Early Modern Europe went to a lot of trouble to justify their decision to resort to war. Formal declarations of war were often substantial texts in which the reasons for the war were explained in detail; these, as well as the less formal manifestos of war, were widely distributed. In these declarations and manifestos, the discourse of just war was utilized.[26]

One could say that when the sovereigns of Early Modern Europe went to war, they went to a just war; but when they waged or ended war, they waged or ended a legal war. To the modern mind, this might all seem to be a grand exercise in propaganda and duplicity, but, at least until deep into the 18th century, there was more to the resilience of the just war doctrine. There was no inherent contradiction between just and legal war. The two concepts played out on a different field. Sovereigns might have been legally safe from sanction for an unjust war by their peers or any human power, but they were not safe from divine sanction. To the vast majority of the princes of Early Modern Europe, this counted for much. It was widespread practice for princes to consult a council of specialists, on which theologians regularly took a seat, before the decision to go to war was taken. It was only late into the 18th century that the religious dimension began to recede and the justifications for war became commonly criticized for being mere propaganda or pretext. A now secularized natural law lost its teeth and its commands became truly unenforceable natural obligations, to be re-coined as natural or political morality. But this did not cause princes and other rulers to stop rendering justifications in terms of the demands of natural justice.[27]

Two important remarks must be added with regard to early-modern state practice. First, the conception of war as a state led to a distinction between full wars and hostile actions not amounting to full war—in the language of early-modern doctrine, perfect and imperfect wars. From this distinction, in the 19th century, the category of 'measures short of war' emerged. The justifications for imperfect war drew heavily

University Press, 2012), 71–94. For a good example of an amnesty clause: Peace of Utrecht of 13 July 1713 between France and Great Britain, Art 3 in Clive Parry (ed), *The Consolidated Treaty Series* (Dobbs Ferry, NY: Oceana, 1969), vol 27, 475–501.

[26] eg justification by Gustav Adolph of Sweden (1611–32) for his invasion of the Holy Roman Empire in 1630; the justifications put forward in the French declaration and manifesto of war of 1635 and the Spanish counter-declarations, see Randall Lesaffer, 'Defensive Warfare, Prevention and Hegemony. The Justifications for the Franco-Spanish War of 1635' (2006) 8 *Journal of the History of International Law* 91–123 and 141–79; Partel Piirimäe, 'Just War in Theory and Practice. The Legitimation of Swedish Intervention in the Thirty Years War' (2002) 45 *Historical Journal* 499–523. See for more examples from the 17th and 18th centuries, Bernd Klesmann, *Bellum solemne. Formen und Funktionen europäischer Kriegserklärungen des 17. Jahrhunderts* (Mainz: Zabern, 2007); Stephen Whatley (ed), *A General Collection of Treatys, Declarations of War, Manifestos, and other Publick Papers, Relating to Peace and War, Among the Potentates of Europe, from 1648 to the Present Time*, 4 vols (London: Knapton, 1710–32).

[27] Vattel, *Le Droit des gens*, 3.3.32; Whitman, *Verdict of Battle*, ch 3.

on the just war tradition. During the Early Modern Age, the most common instances of 'imperfect wars' were actions in reprisal or as an auxiliary. Reprisal was rooted in old late-medieval institution whereby a sovereign authorized a subject forcefully to seize property from the subjects of another prince in compensation for an injury committed by a subject of that prince. Out of this original form of 'particular' reprisal, grew the practice of 'general' reprisal, which formed the legal foundation for privateering. Thereby a private person was granted the authorization to seize all ships belonging to the subjects of a foreign prince. Auxiliaries were non-belligerents who actively supported an ally during a war without declaring war on the enemy. The actions of auxiliaries could stretch to the intervention of their troops or fleet.[28]

Secondly, there is the question of defence. Already in medieval doctrine, a distinction was made between self-defence and defensive war. Self-defence was the natural right of an individual to defend himself or his property against armed attack. Under early-modern doctrine, it was also attributed to states. Self-defence was not a major justification of force in medieval Europe, as it did not sit well with Christian theology. The fundamental justification for the use of force, which Augustine had forwarded to overcome original Christian pacifism, was that of an instrument to correct the unjust and to restore justice for all. As such, it was an altruistic action.[29] Self-defence, in contrast, was an egoistic action. Nevertheless, as theology faded into the background in the discourse of the *jus ad bellum* between the 17th and 19th centuries, self-defence came to be seen in a more positive light. Under the impact of humanism and the writers from the Modern School of Natural Law, self-defence gained traction as the most natural of human instincts and rights. However, in early-modern state practice, self-defence was rarely invoked on behalf of the state. Most often it was used to justify the actions of individual soldiers or units, for example a border garrison repelling a raid.

A defensive war was a perfect war for which the just cause was defence against an unjust armed attack by the enemy. There were some major differences between the two categories. First, self-defence was more limited in terms of duration, both with regard to its beginning and its end. Whereas self-defence was only justified in the case of actual or imminent attack, defensive war was also put forward in the case of threat of a future attack. A person or state had to desist from hostile action once the attack had stopped. At most, he could continue his action to get back what was taken, but only immediately contingent upon the end of the enemy's attack. A defensive war could be pursued until total victory. Secondly, self-defence had to be proportional and directed towards the actual attackers, whereas defensive war did not. In a defensive war, the defender could use all violence, including against enemy subjects innocent in the war, necessary to secure victory.

[28] Neff, *War and the Law of Nations*, 121–6.

[29] Augustine, *Letter* 238, see Henry Paolucci (ed), *Augustine of Hippo, The Political Writings of St Augustine* (Cambridge: Cambridge University Press, 1962).

Whereas self-defence was only rarely invoked in early-modern state practice, the argument of defence was used with much and increasing frequency to justify 'perfect' war. One of the main drives behind the increasing popularity of the notion of defence was the all-important role alliance treaties played as instruments of diplomacy and warfare from the 17th century onwards. Most of these alliance treaties were defensive, meaning that they were only triggered in the case of prior attack by the enemy. For this reason, belligerents went to great lengths to argue that they were fighting a defensive war. The term 'defensive war' was thus relaxed and expanded. Under the just war doctrine, all just wars were defensive *sensu lato* to the extent that they constituted a reaction against prior injury by the enemy—armed or otherwise. But they were only defensive *sensu stricto* if they were fought in reaction to a prior or threatening armed attack by the enemy, however big or small it might have been. Other wars were offensive. In their endeavours to justify wars as defensive, the rulers and diplomats of the 17th and 18th centuries blurred the lines. Declarations and manifestos of war of the 17th and 18th centuries show a standardized line of argument for the justification of war, which was meant to trigger the *casus belli* of defensive alliance treaties. In most cases, a belligerent when declaring war argued that the enemy had committed a long and incessant series of wrongs against the legitimate claims of the state. Ideally, but not always, one could point to a few instances of the use of force, such as reprisals or border incidents, or attacking an ally. As all other measures had failed, war was said to be necessary as the last resort to stop this and secure the most fundamental legitimate claims of the state. As the 18th century progressed, the language changed to the extent that the protection of the security and interests of the state came to supplement, and with time, supplant the invocation of rights.[30]

IV. Just War in the Shadows (19th Century)

Since the days of Grotius, the law of nations had been thought of as an inherently dualist system existing of two interconnected bodies of law: natural law and positive law. The legal positivism of the 19th century brought this dualism to an end, as natural law was cast out of the world of law and reduced to a code of morality. Thus, modern international law shrunk to what had been the secondary, voluntary or

[30] Klesmann, *Bellum solemne*; Randall Lesaffer, 'Paix et guerre dans les grands traités du XVIIIe siècle' (2005) 7 *Journal of the History of International Law* 25–41; idem, 'Defensive Warfare'; Neff, *War and the Law of Nations*, 126–30.

positive law of nations. The just war doctrine was therefore ousted from the field of international law. Under the pens of some of the leading international lawyers of the late 19th and early 20th centuries, the *jus ad bellum* withered to the mere recognition that sovereign states had a right to resort to force or war to pursue their claims or protect their security and interests. Some even brought this to its ultimate consequence: the decision to go to war was not a matter of law, but one of expediency.

Mainstream international legal doctrine does not wholly reflect 19th-century state practice. The just war tradition proved somewhat more resilient. First, over the course of the 19th century, states continued to offer express justifications to their subjects and allies when they resorted to war or force. Certainly, states more often than before neglected to make a formal declaration of war to the enemy, the forms in which justifications were made became more diverse, and explanations became less extensive.[31] The language shifted further away from war as a means of legal self-help to that of war as a means of self-help altogether—or war as 'a pursuit of policy by other means' to use the famous phrase of Carl von Clausewitz (1780–1831)[32]—as wars became justified in terms of the safeguarding of security, territorial integrity, 'vital interests', or honour of states rather than legitimate rights. But wars were by and large justified as reactions to prior unwarranted action, preferably armed action, by the enemy. They were justified for being defensive.[33] By the late 19th and the early 20th centuries, this focus on defensive war found its correlation in an increasingly general rejection of aggression by the international community. Although doctrine preached the free arbiter of states in relation to war and force, in practice a weak and vague international customary law that condemned aggression and extolled defence unfolded. But states expanded the term 'defensive' to its widest possible extent, completely blurring the lines between defence against an armed attack and reaction against a prior injury of rights or interests. One might say that defence became an empty vessel. The important thing, however, is that defence moved to the centre of modern international law's *jus ad bellum*.[34]

Secondly, the 19th century also saw the rise of 'measures short of war' in doctrine and practice. The different types of measures short of war were all rooted in the tradition of just war. The major categories were humanitarian and political intervention, self-defence, defence of nationals, and reprisal. Humanitarian and

[31] While formal declarations delivered to the enemy were still often used, the preferred form of the 19th century was the ultimatum delivered to the enemy or a general public declaration of war. Neff, *War and the Law of Nations*, 184–5 and examples therein.

[32] Carl von Clausewitz, *Vom Kriege* (1832) in Michael Howard (ed), *On War* (Princeton, NJ: Princeton University Press, 1976), 69.

[33] eg the Russian declaration of war against the Ottoman Empire of 26 Apr 1828, in *British Foreign and State Papers* (London: HMSO, 1842), vol 15, 656–62; the declaration of the British Queen Victoria announcing the war against Russia on 27 Mar 1854, 44 *British Foreign and State Papers* 110; and the diplomatic discussions just before the outbreak of war in 1914 as well as the declarations of war themselves, *Collected Diplomatic Documents Relating to the Outbreak of the European War* (London: Foreign Office, 1915).

[34] Brownlie, *Use of Force*, 19–50; Neff, *War and the Law of Nations*, 161–214.

political interventions were justified as actions to safeguard or restore other people's fundamental rights or actions for the sake of international order and stability. Self-defence of a state and defence by a state of its own nationals on foreign territory drew on the doctrine of the natural right of self-defence. The stress was now on the immediate necessity of the action under the imminence of the threat of greater harm in the absence of a non-violent alternative. These were also the elements in the famous definition of self-defence rendered by the US Secretary of State Daniel Webster (1782–1852) on the occasion of the *Caroline Incident* (1837).[35] Reprisal had evolved from its traditional meaning of the authorization for private individuals to use force into the modern meaning of an armed action by a state against another state in retribution for an injury and enforcement of the right that had been injured. This category remained the closest to the original meaning of just war, both with regard to its cause and its extension. Through the practice and doctrine of measures short of war, some concepts and rules from the old natural law of nations were transplanted into modern positive international law.[36]

The reasons why Western rulers, in spite of international legal doctrine, continued to offer their justifications of war has partly to be sought in the emerging role of public opinion in the formation of international policy and the rise of a clamour against war amongst the public. In the wake of the Napoleonic War, in different countries of the West, peace associations emerged from civil society. By the midst of the 19th century, international peace conferences were convened by these peace societies. For all of the 19th century, the organized peace movement remained a rather elitist affair. It had, however, some foothold in politics and from time to time attracted attention at the highest level.

The peace movement drew on two great European historical traditions. First, there was Christian pacifism. Early Christianity had been radically pacifist but by the 3rd and 4th centuries, when Christian faith won acceptance in the Roman Empire, pacifism had to cede to a more pragmatic attitude that found its expression in the just war doctrine. Pacifism remained in the margins until it gained a constituency in some protestant denominations from the 17th century onwards, particularly in Britain and its North American colonies. Anglo-American Protestants would play an important role in the 19th-century peace movement.[37] Secondly, from the

[35] '. . . a necessity of self-defence, instant, overwhelming, leaving no choice of means, and no moment for deliberation', letter from Daniel Webster of 24 Apr 1841, 29 *British Foreign and State Papers* 1137–8.

[36] Stanimir A. Alexandrov, *Self-Defense Against the Use of Force in International Law* (The Hague: Kluwer, 1996), 11–27; Neff, *War and the Law of Nations*, 215–49; Brendan Simms and D. J. B. Trim (eds), *Humanitarian Intervention. A History* (Cambridge: Cambridge University Press, 2011); Gerry Simpson, *Great Powers and Outlaw States. Unequal Sovereigns in the International Legal Order* (Cambridge: Cambridge University Press, 2004), 227–53; Ellery Cory Stowell, *Intervention in International Law* (Washington DC: Byrne, 1921).

[37] Roland Bainton, *Christian Attitudes towards War and Peace: A Historical Survey and Critical Re-examination* (New York: Abingdon Press, 1960).

Late Middle Ages, a tradition of peace plans in European literature emerged. Writers from Jean Dubois (c 1305) to the Duke of Sully (Maximilien de Béthune, 1559–1641), Emeric de Crucé (c 1590–1648), Godfried Wilhelm Leibniz (1646–1716), William Penn (1644–1718), and Saint-Pierre (Charles-Irénée Castel, 1658–1743) and through to Immanuel Kant (1724–1804) and Jeremy Bentham (1748–1832) laid out schemes to stabilize peace and ban war.[38] Many of these plans proposed a combination of the peaceful settlement of disputes through arbitration with a form of collective security whereby all powers committed themselves to combine against a power which did not respect the outcome of such a settlement or unjustly attacked a third power.[39]

From early on, a division existed between radical pacifists and moderate reformists. The latter sought gradually to limit the frequency and the devastation of war. After the crisis of the peace movement in the 1850s and 1860s wreaked by the Crimean War (1853–6) and the American Civil War (1861–5), the moderate peace movement gained traction and influence. It gained strength through its alliance with international lawyers, who from around 1870 started to organize their field into an autonomous, international academic discipline and pressure group.[40] A programme to limit warfare through international law was articulated and set on the agenda of international civil society and public diplomacy. This programme rested on four pillars: disarmament through binding international agreements, furthering the peaceful settlement of disputes through arbitration, codification of the laws of war, and collective security.[41]

[38] Pierre Dubois, *De recuperatione Terrae Sanctae* (1306) in *The Recovery of the Holy Land* (transl Walther Brandt, New York: Columbia University Press, 1956); Maximilien de Béthune de Sully, *Oecomomies royales* (1640) in David Buisseret and Bernard Barbiche (eds), *Les oeconomies royales de Sully* (Paris: Klincksieck, 1970–88); Emeric de Crucé, *Le nouveau Cynée ou Discours d'Etat représentant les occasions et moyens d'établir une paix générale et liberté de commerce par tout le monde* (1626) (ed Alain Fénet and Astrid Guillaume, Rennes: Presses Universitaires de Rennes, 2004); Gottfried Wilhelm Leibniz, *Codex juris gentium diplomaticus* (Hannover, S. Ammonus, 1693); idem (anon), *Caesarini Fuerstenerii, Tractatus de Jure suprematus ac Legationis principum Germaniae* (sl 1678); William Penn, *An Essay towards the Present and Future Peace of Europe by the Establishment of an European Dyet, Parliament or Estates* (London, 1693–4; repr Olms Hildesheim, 1983); Charles-Irénée Castel de Saint-Pierre, *Mémoires pour rendre la Paix perpétuelle en Europe* (Cologne, 1712; 2nd edn, Utrecht, 1713–17; repr Paris: Fayard, 1986) in Hugh Hale Bellot (transl), *Selections from the second edition of the Abrégé du Project de Paix Perpétuelle by C. I. Castel de Saint-Pierre* (London: Sweet & Maxwell, 1927); Imanuel Kant, *Zum Ewigen Frieden. Ein philosophischen Entwurf* (Konigsberg: Friedrich Nicolovius, 1795) in Mary Campbell Smith (transl), *Perpetual Peace. A Philosophical Essay* (London: Allen & Unwin, 1917); Jeremy Bentham, *Plan for a Universal and Perpetual Peace* (1786–9) (ed C. John Colombos, London: Sweet & Maxwell, 1927).

[39] F. H. Hinsley, *Power and the Pursuit of Peace. Theory and Practice in the Relations between States* (Cambridge: Cambridge University Press, 1963), 13–91; Jacob ter Meulen, *Der Gedanke der internationaler Organisation in seiner Entwicklung*, 2 vols (Leiden: Martinus Nijhoff, 1917–40); Kurt von Raumer, *Ewiger Friede. Friedensrufe und Friedenspläne seit der Renaissance* (Freiburg: Alber, 1953).

[40] Martti Koskenniemi, *The Gentle Civilizer of Nations. The Rise and Fall of International Law 1870–1960* (Cambridge: Cambridge University Press, 2001).

[41] On the 19th- and early 20th-century peace movement: David Cortright, *Peace. A History of Movements and Ideas* (Cambridge: Cambridge University Press, 2008), 25–62; Cecelia Lynch, 'Peace

V. The Limitation of the Right to War (1899–1945)

The invitation by the Russian Tsar Nicholas II (1894–1917) to an international peace conference in The Hague in 1899 moved this programme to the centre of international diplomacy. The 1899 and 1907 Conferences, however, achieved little aside from the partial codification of the laws of war.[42] The proposal to introduce obligatory arbitration as a means to settle disputes between states was rejected. The Hague Convention I on the Pacific Settlement of International Disputes (29 July 1899) did not go beyond a promise by the contracting parties 'to use their best efforts to ensure the pacific settlement of international disputes.'[43] The Convention provided for the establishment of a Permanent Court of Arbitration.[44] The Hague Conferences also codified the age-old obligation of states to formally declare war before starting hostilities, which had somewhat lapsed in practice over the 19th century (Hague Convention III Relative to the Opening of Hostilities, 18 Oct 1907).[45] The failure of the Peace Conferences did nothing to stop the attempts to promote international arbitration as the ultimate way to prevent war. During the first four decades of the 20th century, an impressive number of bilateral arbitration treaties were signed, if not always ratified. But many of these treaties mitigated the obligation to subject disputes to arbitration or to other forms of peaceful settlement by the exclusion of disputes which touched on the security and vital interests of the state, thus effectively excluding those disputes that most endangered peace. As such, these treaties made a distinction between disputes that were deemed to be of a legal nature and those that were deemed to be of a political nature, limiting the scope of application of international law to the former.[46] The series of 'Treaties for the Advancement of Peace', also known as the Bryan Treaties (1913–14) after the US Secretary of State William Jennings Bryan (1860–1925), provided for the submission of all disputes, without restriction, to an international commission for investigation. They also stipulated that the parties to the dispute could not resort to war for a period of 12 months.[47]

Movements, Civil Society, and the Development of Law' in Fassbender and Peters, *The Oxford Handbook of the History of International Law*, 198–221.

[42] Arthur Eyffinger, *The 1899 Hague Peace Conference. 'The Parliament of Man, the Federation of the World'* (The Hague: Kluwer, 1999); idem, *The 1907 Peace Conference. The Conscience of the Civilized World* (Oisterwijk: Wolf Legal Publishers, 2011).

[43] Art 1, 187 *The Consolidated Treaty Series* 410–28.

[44] Art 20.

[45] (1908) 2 AJIL Supp 85–90.

[46] eg the Arbitration Treaties between the US and respectively Britain and France of 3 Aug 1911, Art 1 in Ruhl Bartlett (ed), *The Record of American Diplomacy. Documents and readings in the history of American Foreign Relations* (New York: Prager, 1964), 338.

[47] eg Treaty between the United States and Austria–Hungary of 6 May 1914, 220 *The Consolidated Treaty Series* 6–7. On arbitration in the era of the League of Nations, Francis Paul Walters, *A History of the League of Nations* (Toronto: Oxford University Press, 1952), vol 1, 377–87.

The entry of the US under President Woodrow Wilson (1856–1924) in the Great War in 1917 pushed collective security to the centre of the international agenda. Wilson refused to adhere to a traditional strategy for peace and pushed his allies at the Paris Peace Conference (1919–20) towards a new world order. At the heart of this stood collective security, a combination of an obligation to settle disputes peacefully by international law, the limitation of the right to wage war, and collective action against aggression by an organized international community, the League of Nations. The Peace Treaty of Versailles of 28 June 1919 between the Allied and Associate Powers and Germany was an amalgam of Wilson's radical ideas and tradition, but altogether caused a revolution in the *jus ad bellum*.

The Versailles Peace Treaty was the first peace treaty among sovereigns in centuries that broke with the tradition of silence over the justice of war. Article 231 attributed responsibility for the war to Germany and its allies. Germany was designated as the aggressor. In Articles 231 and 232, Germany was held liable for all the loss and damages the Allied and Associated Powers, their governments, and nationals had suffered because of the war—with the exception of most of the costs of warfare itself. The German Emperor Wilhelm II (1888–1918) would be indicted before an international tribunal 'for a supreme offense against international morality and the sanctity of treaties.'[48] Articles 228 and 229 provided for the prosecution before military tribunals of Germans who had violated the laws and customs of war or committed crimes against the nationals of the Allied and Associate Powers.

These clauses constituted a return to the just war tradition. This revival was only partial and it was not followed up in general peace treaty practice after 1920. Nevertheless, it was far-reaching. The Versailles Peace Treaty restored the discriminatory concept of war from the old just war tradition. Only one side of the belligerents had a right to wage war; the other side had not and was therefore liable for all the costs of damages due to the war. The Treaty went beyond early-modern practices and doctrine, which had restricted the enforceability of just war to the court of God, by providing for criminal prosecution for infringements against both the *jus ad bellum* and the *jus in bello* by the unjust side. The basis for the attribution of responsibility to Germany and its allies were aggression and disregard for treaty obligations, most of all in relation to Belgian neutrality.[49] Some elements of the just war tradition were thus drawn into the sphere of positive international law.

The Paris Peace Conference also agreed upon the Covenant of the League of Nations, which was inscribed in all the peace treaties.[50] Articles 10–17 regarded collective security and the *jus ad bellum*. The founders of the League refrained from inscribing a general prohibition of war, but focused on preventing war by imposing upon states the duty first to resort to peaceful ways of dispute settlement.

[48] Art 227 of the Peace Treaty of Versailles, 28 June 1919, *The Treaties of Peace 1919–1923* (New York: Carnegie, 1924), vol 1, 3–264; 225 *The Consolidated Treaty Series: 1648–1918*, 188 (1981).

[49] 'Report of the Commission on the Responsibility of the Authors of the War and the Enforcement of Penalties', 29 Mar 1919 (1920) 14 AJIL 95–154.

[50] eg Arts 1–24 of the Versailles Treaty.

Articles 12, 13, and 15 imposed upon the members of the League the obligation to refer any dispute that was likely to lead to war either to arbitration or to the Council of the League. Article 12 stipulated a cooling-off period of three months after the award of the arbitrators or the report of the Council in which the parties could not resort to war. If the Council voted unanimously on a report regarding the dispute, no state could wage war on a member which abided by the report. If no such unanimity was reached, the members had a right to take all actions that they deemed 'necessary for the maintenance of right and justice'. Article 14 provided for the establishment of a Permanent Court of International Justice to rule over disputes between states, but its jurisdiction was not mandatory. Articles 10, 11, and 16 enshrined the compromise the allies had reached on collective security. Article 16 provided for automatic economic sanctions against a member which resorted to war in contravention of Articles 12, 13, and 15. It stated that in such a case states had to indicate which armed forces they would contribute to protect the members of the League. In 1921, the League Assembly stipulated that economic sanctions could stretch to naval blockades.[51] Article 10 was at one time the most encompassing but also the vaguest of the Covenant's *jus ad bellum* clauses. It imposed upon the members the commitment 'to respect and preserve as against external aggression the territorial integrity and existing political independence of all Members of the League' and made any threat or danger of aggression a matter for the League's Council. Article 11 provided that any war or threat of war should be referred to the Council.

These clauses from the League's Covenant did not lay down a new, coherent, and all-encompassing *jus ad bellum*. They neither emerged in a juridical vacuum nor did they sweep away existing practices and customary law. During the first decade of the League's existence, several attempts were made to interpret and supplement the Covenant to clarify and fill in the gaps in the system which were perceived to exist. One of these attempts concerned the so-called General Act of Geneva on the Pacific Settlement of Disputes of 26 September 1928, which provided that all disputes should ultimately be settled by peaceful means.[52]

Apart from the difficulties of interpretation and the unsystematic character of the Covenant clauses, there were more fundamental reasons to leave the peace movement far from satisfied with the outcome of the Paris Peace Conference. The refusal of the US to join the League and the initial exclusion of communist Russia and the former Central Powers weakened and reduced it to a club of the European victors of the Great War and their allies, minus the main one. The League system neither provided for an effective mechanism of collective security nor for a general prohibition to use force. Its major lacunae in this respect were that it only condemned

[51] 'League of Nations Assembly Resolution on the Economic Weapon', 4 Oct 1921, LNOJ, Special Supp 6, 24, see also 'Legal Position Arising from the Enforcement in Time of Peace of the Measures of Economic Pressure Indicated in Article 16 of the Covenant, Particularly by a Maritime Blockade', 15 June 1927 (1927) 8 LNOJ 834–45.

[52] (1931) 25 AJIL Supp 204–24.

aggression, but it did not exclude war if peaceful dispute settlement procedures failed after a period of cooling down had been respected—it even seemed to confirm the right to war in Article 15—and it did not restrict use of force other than war and aggression.[53]

In the 1920s, part of the US peace movement, in concordance with some major political figures, retook the battle and redirected the agenda. As League membership was, after rejection by the US Senate, deemed impossible or even undesirable because of its commitment to the security of other states, the focus was now on the peaceful settlement of disputes—through the accession by the US to the Permanent Court of International Justice—and through what became known as 'the outlawry of war'. Aided by the desire of the French to obtain at least some security agreement with the US, in 1928 the peace movement saw a major success through the General Treaty for the Renunciation of War of 27 August 1928, better known as the Pact of Paris or the Kellogg–Briand Pact. The Pact was initially signed by 15 states, among which were the major powers of the West. Some 48 other states joined later. The Pact condemned 'recourse to war for the resolution of international controversies' and renounced it 'as an instrument of national policy in their relations with one another.' [54] Article 2 provided for the pursuit of settlement of disputes by pacific means.[55]

The international community of states had thus abolished the concept of legal war. The Kellogg–Briand Pact did not provide for any sanctions, but this did not mean that violation remained without legal consequences. Neff indicated the major consequences attached to the resort to war in breach of the Pact of Paris. First, resort to war in contravention of the Pact made the state liable for all the costs and damages ensuing from the war. Secondly, a violation of the Pact gave all parties to the Pact the right to intervene against the perpetrator. Whereas there was hardly any state practice of armed intervention pursuant to violations of the Pact, during the 1930s a practice of relaxing the duties of neutrality by third parties—as with the US in the case of the German aggression against Western Europe in 1939–40—arose. Also, the 1930s saw the emergence of a form of non-belligerency, whereby a third power one-sidedly supported one belligerent with supplies, arms, subsidies, and the like without resorting to force or declaring war. Thirdly, over the 1930s, there arose a rule in state practice that a war in contravention of the Pact could not give rise to any conquest or acquisition of rights of any kind, under the old maxim *ex injuria non oritur jus*. This was enshrined in the so-called Stimson Doctrine, laid out by US

[53] Brownlie, *Use of Force*, 59–65. [54] Art 1, 94 LNTS 57.

[55] Charles Chatfield, *For Peace and Justice: Pacifism in America, 1914–1941* (Knoxville, TN: University of Tennessee Press, 1981); Cortright, *Peace*, 62–6; Robert H. Ferrell, *Peace in their Time. The Origins of the Kellogg–Briand Pact* (New Haven, CT: Yale University Press, 1952); idem, *Beyond Appeasement: Interpreting Interwar Peace Movements in World Politics* (Ithaca, NY: Cornell University Press, 1999); Bernhard Roscher, *Der Briand-Kellogg-Pakt von 1928. Der 'Verzicht auf den Krieg als Mittel Nationaler Politik' im völkerrechtlichen Denken des Zwischenkriegszeit* (Baden-Baden: Nomos, 2004); Hatsue Shinohara, *US International Lawyers in the Interwar Years. A Forgotten Crusade* (Cambridge: Cambridge University Press, 2012).

Secretary of State Henry Stimson (1867–1950) in 1932.[56] To these three consequences put forward by Neff should be added that resort to war in violation of the Paris Pact was equated to aggression, triggering the obligations of third states under Article 10 of the Covenant.[57]

Similarly to the Covenant, the Paris Pact referred to 'resort to war' rather than 'force'. Whether 'war' in the Pact was used in its technical meaning and all other uses of force were excluded was and remains a matter of contention among international lawyers.[58] What is certain is that actions in self-defence were excluded from it.[59] Self-defence gained a lot of traction in state practice during the 1920s and it would gain even more after the Paris Pact. The negotiators at the Paris Peace Conference of 1919–20 put the spotlight on aggression by making it the touchstone of Germany's responsibility for the war and by making it the concern of all League members. In putting aggression at the heart of the new *jus contra bellum*, the drafters of the Covenant and the peace treaties inevitably lifted its correlate, self-defence, to the heart of the newly emerging *jus ad bellum*. After 1920, states began more than ever before to invoke self-defence. They did so either as a justification for their actions against a so-called aggressor or to trigger collective defence by the international community under Article 10 of the Covenant. In the state practice of the interwar period, these actions were not considered to amount to full war. Thus, the old natural right of self-defence was given a central place within positive international law, without however shedding the cloak of necessity that hung together with its origins. States followed this strategy for two main practical reasons. First, by invoking self-defence they attempted to avoid the restrictions on war from the Covenant and the Paris Pact and the consequences of its violations. Secondly, by not considering a conflict as war, third states could relax the strict duties of neutrality and act with partiality towards the two sides in the conflict. This would prove a crucial element in the strategy of US President Franklin Delano Roosevelt (1882–1945) to overcome the strict laws of 'New Neutrality' in the face of German aggression.

The major treaties and state practice in relation to war and self-defence in the interwar period allowed for the claim that by the end of the 1930s an international customary rule against aggression had been formed.[60] This conclusion gives too rosy a picture of how far the prohibition to use force had progressed before its inscription in the UN Charter. The Covenant of the League and the Paris Pact ended the legality of war, but only in a discriminatory way. State practice from the Second World War

[56] Neff, *War and the Law of Nations*, 294–6. The Stimson doctrine in relation to territorial acquisition was also inscribed in the so-called Saavedra-Lamas Treaty of 16 Dec 1933 between most American and European powers, banning wars of aggression, 163 LNTS 393.

[57] 'Draft Treaty on the Rights and Duties of States in Case of Aggression', Introductory Comment (1939) 33 AJIL Supp 819–909, 823.

[58] Brownlie, *Use of Force*, 84–92.

[59] Note by Kellogg to the French ambassador, 1 Mar 1928 in David Hunter Miller, *The Peace Pact of Paris* (London: Putnam, 1928), 43.

[60] Brownlie, *Use of Force*, 105–11.

indicates that states still considered themselves to have a right to resort to war and formally declare war in the case of prior aggression by an enemy. Moreover, the Covenant and the Paris Pact had left the door wide open for an alternative strategy to resort to force rather than war, primarily in the guise of self-defence. Whereas states claimed to operate the limited, by origin natural, right of self-defence in the face of aggression, they did in fact draw from the rich tradition of defensive war to justify their own actions. State practice agreed with the notion of defence *sensu stricto* as a reaction against a prior attack, but states would use the smallest instance of use of force by the enemy to justify a disproportionate and all-out reaction. To that end, they beefed up their arguments by referring to injuries against their rights and interests, thus persisting with much of the language of early-modern and 19th-century justifications for war. Also, states pushed their defensive actions beyond the limits that the traditional notion of natural self-defence imposed, so that at times there was little or nothing to distinguish self-defence from full-blown war. In the end, the Covenant and the Paris Pact did very little to stop the tradition of defensive war or restrict the lax interpretation of the term 'defensive'. On the contrary, the transfer of the natural right of self-defence to the domain of positive international law allowed for an even stronger association with the lax justifications of defensive war and opened Pandora's box.[61]

VI. Conclusion

The founders of the UN attempted but failed to close that box. The drafters of the UN Charter at the conferences of Dumbarton Oaks (1944) and San Francisco (1945) consciously tried to stop some of the gaps the earlier treaties had left. In rephrasing the term 'resort to war' to 'use or threat of force' they attempted to settle the discussion on the extent of the prohibition of 'war' under the Paris Pact.[62] The choice to inscribe the right to self-defence in the Charter was not a major step in itself, as the principle had already become well established in positive international law. The merit of the Charter lay in the qualification of the right. By using the word 'inherent' the drafters of the Charter referred to the origins of the right as a natural right,

[61] D. W. Bowett, *Self-Defense in International Law* (New York: Praeger, 1958), 120–31; Neff, *War and the Law of Nations*, 303–13.

[62] Robert Hildebrand, *Dumbarton Oaks. The Origins of the United Nations and the Search for Postwar Security* (Chapel Hill, NC: University of North Carolina Press, 1990). See also the contribution by Nico Schrijver, 'The Ban on the Use of Force in the UN Charter', Chapter 21 in this volume, Section III.

with all its restrictions and limitations. Furthermore, the right was clearly defined in terms of a reaction against an *occurring armed* attack and the duty was imposed upon states to refer to the UN Security Council. Through this, the founders of the UN did everything possible to restrict the sole exception to the prohibition of inter-state use of force, short of banning it. But, as state practice since 1945 proves, in this the UN has met with only very partial success.[63]

[63] Thomas M. Franck, *Recourse to Force. State Action Against Threats and Armed Force* (Cambridge: Cambridge University Press, 2002), 45–134; Christine Gray, *International Law and the Use of Force* (3rd edn, Oxford: Oxford University Press, 2008); Neff, *War and the Law of Nations*, 326–34.

CHAPTER 2

LAW OF NATIONS OR PERPETUAL PEACE? TWO EARLY INTERNATIONAL THEORIES ON THE USE OF FORCE

DANIELE ARCHIBUGI
MARIANO CROCE
ANDREA SALVATORE

I. Introduction

THIS chapter deals with what is considered to be the legitimate use of force in two intellectual traditions that are at the origins of modern international thought: the law of nations (LN) and the perpetual peace projects (PPP). These two traditions emerged in the late 16th century and lasted until the Congress of Vienna, when their late developments gave rise to modern international law, on the one hand, and to international organizations and peace movements, on the other hand. Both the LN and the PPP influenced and were influenced by the emergence and growth of the modern states in Europe (and, progressively, outside the Old Continent) and tackled the question of how these new institutional entities should regulate their mutual relations. As a consequence, the main issue addressed by these two traditions was the question of war and, therefore, the achievement of peace. In considering the development of the LN and the PPP, we need to bear in mind that both these traditions arose and developed in transitional historical contexts, and often advocated changes that would take place in the following centuries.

In order to account for the different assessment of the recourse to armed force advanced by the LN and PPP, it is important to place the discussion in its proper historical context. This is why in Section II we focus on the emergence of the state as the main player of internal and international politics, progressively becoming the only legitimate authority in declaring war. As war became the primary activity of the state, this was also the primary issue discussed in both the LN and the PPP. We argue in Section III that this also led to a change in the meaning of the term 'war', which was no longer used to describe types of social conflict, but was limited to the political domain. Conversely, peace was no longer regarded as an internal and spiritual value (a sort of overall harmony), but as a stable political condition. Although LN and PPP shared the new way of conceiving war and peace, the two traditions pursued different aims. While the LN tradition aimed at regulating and restraining war (Section III.A), the PPP tradition aimed at banning and abolishing any armed conflict (Section III.B). After a basic insight—in Section IV—into the significant developments of the two traditions that took place at the end of 17th century, in Section V we focus on the use of armed force concerning four main occurrences, fiercely debated within both traditions. The cases we examine are the following: war among states (V.A), resistance against an oppressive regime (V.B), humanitarian intervention (V.C), and the use of force towards stateless indigenous populations (V.D).

II. The Historical Context: The Rise of the State and of the States System

The constitution of the state as the main player in national and international politics necessitated a fundamental revision of the concepts and practices of both coercive power and war which had dominated since the Middle Ages. The pre-modern era was fundamentally characterized by indirect rule,[1] where governments relied on a

[1] 'Indirect rule' means a particular type of administration of territories adopted by state governments and relying on the traditional authorities and local powers of those territories. On the one hand,

plethora of sub-state actors that were entitled both to impose taxes, to wage war, and thus to recruit private armies. The subsequent transition from indirect to direct rule occurred over centuries and through violent struggles. Rulers who controlled substantial coercive means tried to draw the boundaries of a secure area within their territories and, to achieve this, they had to demote or wipe out many of the protagonists of indirect rule; those who were successful evolved as state rulers. Within this framework, three activities were particularly interrelated:

(1) state-making (eradication of internal rivals);
(2) war-making (attack on external rivals);
(3) protection (defence of internal populations).

Indeed, between the 16th and the 18th centuries, the new central governments expended great efforts in trying to disarm or co-opt those who could claim to exercise rival political and legal power. The best way to further this aim was to outlaw the use of private armies by all those who were not formally authorized by the state. Disarmament of non-state agents occurred in many different ways, such as collection of weapons, prohibition of duels, and control over the production of weapons. These strategies made it increasingly difficult for rivals and rebels to organize forms of counter-power and, in turn, the state progressively became the sole controller of legitimate force. All this led to a radical transformation of war, which was doomed to become a conflict between sovereign states—that is, states became the only agents permitted to use force to achieve their political goals. Therefore, the act of making of war turned into a means by which to reinforce the sovereignty of the state; thus, war became one means among many to strengthen the link between the supremacy of the state and the monocratic administration of legitimate force.[2] War became the primary activity of the state.

In an epoch in which armies were mainly comprised of mercenaries and national mass conscription was still unthinkable, warfare prompted states to obtain financial and material resources by subjugating the population and forcing them to provide the revenue (taxes) necessary to pay for a private armed force. The disarmament of civilians brought about the need for state protection, and the former were asked to provide financial support for the warfare of the latter. In this way, states became the only actors able to protect the population from attack by external enemies or internal irregular forces. The possibility of waging war entailed the state, at one

this type of rule requires less investment in terms of material and financial resources by state governments, as traditional authorities were called upon to employ their own resources; on the other hand, precisely because of this, it granted remarkable power and autonomy to the latter. This reconstruction, as well as the historical framework we set out in this chapter, was originally advanced by Charles Tilly, *Coercion, Capital, and European States, AD 990–1992* (Oxford: Blackwell, 1992).

[2] We prefer to rephrase the standard Weberian definition of 'monopoly on the legitimate use of violence' since literally monopoly refers to the existence of a single vendor, whereas violence is not sold but administered.

and the same time, to eliminate internal rivals, to subjugate the population, and to obtain financial support.

The role of war turned out to be pivotal well beyond the 18th century, when the connection between war-making and state-making began to collapse and new players (basically, the states) started to emerge. In fact, the costs and risks of using mercenaries—and especially foreign mercenaries—induced states to substitute them with civilians. The emergence of popular armies was inspired by the French Revolution, which (even more than enlightened absolutism) favoured the transition from indirect to direct rule. French revolutionaries provided a model of centralized government that was followed by many other states. In fact, the *levée en masse* of 1793 transformed war into a national enterprise, instrumental in the construction and reinforcement of the nation-state. This allowed both a greater orientation towards war outside the state territory and an increase in the already extensive apparatus of extraction and control. With this new connection between nation-making and war-making, the territory, the population, and the state government could be said to be three faces of the same entity.[3]

In brief, the formation of powerful states increasingly narrowed the limits within which struggles for power occurred. The elimination of the players entitled to use force and wage war led to the formation of a restricted number of states, organized in a system founded not only on the effective control of force and territories, but also on reciprocal recognition. The need to gather recognition from other states also led each political unit to reflect a similar basic structure. Standard models for armies and organized bureaucracies favoured a twofold process of a collective guarantee of internal peace and an international system of sovereigns states based on rules that, over the 17th and the 18th centuries, shaped into the rhythm of major wars.

III. The Origin of International Thought

Arising from the historical context sketched in the previous section, both the LN and the PPP conceived of states as the main or even the only actors in international politics. In particular, the internationalist thought developed by these two theories

[3] In addition to Tilly's *Coercion, Capital, and European States*, a very instructive book on the transition we have discussed so far is Wolfgang Reinhard, *Power Elites and State Building* (Oxford: Oxford University Press, 1996). Reinhard explains the roles of elites in shaping the state as a political form and the connection between central and peripheral authorities. A further groundbreaking work in the study of the way the state managed to become *the* political form of modernity, and irreversibly to shape both modern and current politics, is Peter B. Evans, Dietrich Rueschemeyer, and Theda Skocpol (eds), *Bringing the State Back In* (Cambridge: Cambridge University Press, 1985).

aimed to regulate or even abolish the use of armed force. Although both traditions obviously also dealt with other types of interstate relationship—such as international trade, diplomatic relations, cross-cultural contacts, dynastic controversies—opposition between war and peace undoubtedly represented the central issue.

The LN and the PPP broke with the earlier traditions that also conceived of peace as a familiar, religious or social problem, and thus failed adequately to distinguish between peace as a private and spiritual value and peace as a public and political condition. These latter traditions were perfectly summarized by two of the most influential tracts of Renaissance political thought; that is, the *Querela pacis* by Erasmus of Rotterdam (1519) and the *De pacificatione* by Juan Luis Vives (1529). According to the Renaissance perspective developed by Erasmus and Vives, the conceptual opposite of peace was, in compliance with the ancient and medieval traditions, discord. In contrast, the LN and the PPP conceived of war and peace exclusively in a strictly political sense. War became the only opposite of peace which, in turn, no longer referred to a polyphonic harmony but merely to the absence of armed conflict among organized and sovereign groups. Beside these similarities, the LN and the PPP also show marked differences, which are highlighted and summarized in Table 2.1.

Table 2.1 A comparative overview between the law of nations and the perpetual peace projects

	Law of nations	Perpetual peace projects
Method of inquiry	Rational and realistic	Pleading and utopian
Attitude to war	Regulated/restrained (just/legitimate on both sides, on the basis of multilaterally recognized procedural criteria)	Banned/abolished (unjust/illegitimate on both sides, on the basis of generally shared substantial criteria)
Concept of peace	Contextual, transitory, and negative (peace as a mere truce between two wars)	Universal, perpetual, and positive (peace as the enforcement of a lasting well-ordered society)
Sovereign institution (legitimate authority for the *jus belli*)	State sovereignty (lack of a third party); strong distinction between domestic and foreign politics	Supra-state sovereignty (effectiveness of a third party); weak distinction between domestic and foreign politics
Members of international community	States represented by their sovereign or diplomatic representative	States usually represented by their sovereign; in some projects, delegates exercising an independent mandate

	Law of nations	Perpetual peace projects
Interstate relationships	Bilateral	Multilateral
Forms of regulation of interstate relationships	Treatises, voluntary respected by member states, with no coercive powers	Permanent and indissoluble international organizations, sometimes with coercive powers
Method for addressing controversy	Diplomatic negotiations or armed conflict	Refereed by international organizations (either courts or intergovernmental institutions)
Changes to the interstate system	Allowed as a consequence of war, but limited and regulated by the LN	Strictly forbidden unless achieved by consensus
Relationship with political reality	Rational, aiming at the regulation of existing relationships	Utopian, aiming at the creation of new relationships
Authors	Mostly legal theorists, often working with courts as legal advisers and lawyers, authors of systematic and comprehensive treaties (predominantly written in Latin), with strong academic content	Mostly philosophers, authors of advocacy papers (written in modern languages), designed to support a cause rather than to define content and boundaries of a discipline

A. The Law of Nations

The LN was one of the most important attempts at justifying and regulating the rise and consolidation of independent states at the international level.[4] We call this tradition the 'law of nations' since that was the term already being used in English-speaking nations at the start of the 17th century. But the original Latin term *jus gentium* had a different meaning since 'gentes' were not necessarily nations: in

[4] For a more comprehensive account of the crucial turn from the medieval just war tradition to the modern law of nations, see William Ballis, *The Legal Position of War: Changes in Its Practice and Theory from Plato to Vattel* (London: Garland, 1973); John Gitting, *The Glorious Art of Peace: From the Iliad to Iraq* (Oxford: Oxford University Press, 2012); James Turner Johnson, *Ideology, Reason, and the Limitation of War: Religious and Secular Concepts, 1200–1740* (Princeton, NJ: Princeton University Press, 1975); Stephen C. Neff, *War and the Law of Nations: A General History* (Cambridge: Cambridge University Press, 2005); Frederick H. Russell, *The Just War in the Middle Ages* (Cambridge: Cambridge University Press, 1975); Richard Tuck, *The Rights of War and Peace: Political Thought and the International Order From Grotius to Kant* (Oxford: Oxford University Press, 1999); Alfred Vanderpol, *La doctrine scolastique du droit de guerre* (Paris: Pedone, 1919).

Roman law, the *jus gentium* was the body of norms used by the Roman Empire to deal with stateless communities or conquered dependencies. When the term re-emerged in Europe via the Spanish theorists of the 16th century, such as Vitoria and Suarez, it was intended to deal with a problem which had already been encountered by the Romans. The main concern was to deal with the stateless communities of the New World, for which norms had to be created from scratch rather than left to the brutal methods of the Conquistadores.

A few decades later, these insights began to be formulated in a more systematic manner. Both Alberico Gentili (1588–9) and Grotius (1625) drew up comprehensive treaties devoted to the problems of war and peace and with their main focus on the European system of states rather than stateless communities. This line of thought further developed with a plethora of treaties, including Pufendorf (1672), Wolff (1748), and Vattel (1758). The last of the *jus gentium* treaties, and the first of modern international law, Martens (1789), was published in the same year as the French Revolution.[5]

Francisco de Vitoria's writings were crucial in going beyond the prior theological presuppositions of the just war tradition as the only, necessary, and ultimate foundations of the law of war. Vitoria made the first serious attempt at developing a natural law theory able to be applied across religious and territorial boundaries. His conceptualization of an international society of independent and sovereign communities (with a composite law of nations replacing the canonical concept of universal sovereignty) stood at the beginning of the fundamental shift from the study of interstate relations as a subtle case-based reasoning to international law as a consistent scientific domain. The first epochal consequence of this new approach was the substantial rejection of both religious differences (and, more generally, of matters of faith) and claims of universal jurisdiction as just causes of war.

Some decades later, Gentili (1588–9) definitely distanced his treatise on the laws of war from the classical doctrine of just war. His famous warning—'Let theologians keep silence about matters outside their province'[6]—has been rightly considered as the inaugural address of the modern theory of international law. Finally, Grotius, as

[5] In other languages, including French and German, the historic term (respectively *droit des gens* and *Völkerrecht*) is still used as an equivalent in international law. In this regard, Kant was the first to note the semantic difference between '*ius gentium*' and 'law of nations': 'What we are now about to consider under the name of international right or the right of nations is the right of *states* in relation to one another (although it is not strictly correct to speak, as we usually do, of the *right of nations* [*Völkerrecht*]; it should rather be called the *right of states, jus publicum civitatum*)' (Immanuel Kant, 'The Metaphysics of Morals' in Hans S. Reiss (ed), *Kant: Political Writings* (Cambridge: Cambridge University Press, 1991), 165). The texts of the LN tradition under discussion are: Alberico Gentili, *De Iure Belli Libri Tres* (Oxford: Clarendon Press, 1933); Hugo Grotius, *On the Law of War and Peace* (Whitefish, MT: Kessinger Publishing, 2010); Samuel von Pufendorf, *De Jure Naturae et Gentium Libri Octo* (Buffalo, NY: Hein, 1995); Christian Wolff, *The Law of Nations Treated According to a Scientific Method* (Oxford: Clarendon Press, 1934); Emerich de Vattel, *The Law of Nations* (Indianapolis, IN: Liberty Fund, 2008); Georg Friedrich von Martens, *The Law of Nations* (London: Cobbett, 1829).

[6] Gentili, *De Iure Belli*, 57 (translation partially revised).

a theorist of interstate relations, paved the way—most probably beyond his actual intention—for the complete secularization of the LN. However, the revolutionary potentialities of his famous speculative hypothesis—'even if we concede that there is no God . . . or that human affairs are of no concern to him'[7]—would be gradually pushed to the extreme by his successors. Grotius based his whole theory on two explicit distinctions: the first between natural law and volitional law; the second, strictly (but not completely) connected to the former, between just war and legal war. Drawing on this crucial distinction, Grotius stated that while only one side in a war acts justly, it may be the case that both sides act legally. Despite some degree of ambiguity and uncertainty, these two distinctions represented the great and definitive divide between the early-modern theory of interstate relations and modern international law.

This new paradigm disposes of the theological universalism embedded in the just war tradition (based on the concept of an all-embracing *Res publica Christiana*) and replaced the canonical concept of universal sovereignty with a composite law of states as a self-sufficient legal regulation apt to be applied across religious and territorial boundaries. According to this new paradigm, sovereign states—conceived as self-constituent, independent, and equal subjects—became the primary institutional agents in an interstate system of relations that aimed to stabilize and preserve the balance of political power and territorial subdivision in continental Europe. From this perspective, the normative rationale of the LN can essentially be reduced to a multilateral and shared insurance against any attempt, either internal or external to the state, to alter *substantially*—that is, beyond a minor or limited change in the border between two or more countries—established power relations.

The basic aim of keeping competing nation-states in check and preventing one from overriding another, was pursued by means of a binding regulation of the use of force, with regard to both the legitimate justifications for waging war (*jus ad bellum*) and the limits of legitimate conduct in war (*jus in bello*). As long as it was confined to the field of interstate relations, war was no longer conceived of as an irrational exception that must be justified (let alone, barbarism that must be abolished), but instead as a foreseeable and rational outcome. This did not necessarily mean that war should be seen as a normal condition of international relations and peace and, consequently, viewed as simply a truce between two wars. Rather, war had to be regarded as a possible and practicable political solution. Accordingly, peace no longer appeared as a condition of harmony among human beings or as a moral ideal or spiritual value, but simply as the valuable condition of a stable political assessment that was able to minimize the risk of unrestrained armed conflict.

The canon law developed by theologians, according to whom a just war primarily concerned the moral sphere and was to be viewed mainly as retributive punishment

[7] Grotius, *On the Law of War and Peace*, 'Prolegomena', § 11 (translation partially revised).

for an offence, gradually gave way to secular conceptions of natural law. These latter conceptions were based on the reason of the state, according to which a justified war pertained exclusively to the political domain and needed to be considered essentially as the restoration of a violated right. From this institutional perspective, far from needing to be banned or taken to the extreme, war was to be effectively bracketed and restrained in order to settle armed disputes among states without destroying the institutional system. The LN therefore aimed to make of war a type of duel between states, in which each should accept and respect a set of shared rules. Provided the participants agreed to those rules, there was no moral judgement on their behaviour.

The basic conviction shared by states may also be translated in a precept of strategic rationality. According to this interpretation, the maximum gain that a state could make—say, by waging an unrestrained war in order to take over the leadership of the European continent—was less relevant than the maximum loss that a state could suffer if the structural framework of interdependent relationships and multilateral balance—that represented the institutional core of the LN as a whole—collapsed. This 'strategic' interpretation of the modern LN was clearly developed in Martens' systematization in terms of general positive law, and in whose opinion the legal foundation of the law of nations lay solely in 'the mutual *will* of the nations concerned'[8] and the *jus ad bellum* could be reduced to the state's self-interest. War was consequently enshrined in an institutionalized legal framework that, by formalizing the rules of warfare, sought to limit and restrain the use of arms and the intensity of the violence used. Thus, in order to preserve an overall political balance among leading powers, the *theoretical* growth in the liberty of states to wage war went hand in hand with the *practical* self-limitation of their own freedom of action.

This new institutional model rested on three main pillars:

(1) formal equality of states—in compliance with the principle of sovereignty—regardless of any material difference (military force, economic power, territorial extension) between them;
(2) respect of neutrality and non-interference in another state's affairs;
(3) dynastic legitimacy as a practical foundation of absolutism—consequently, there was no third party which had the power and the right to settle a dispute between two (or more) states.

Within the perspective developed by the LN, any conceivable type of supranational court of last resort would jeopardize the existing political balance as a whole and, indirectly, the very existence of the sovereign states that supported it. Indeed, if a sovereign state set itself up to judge the political actions carried out by another sovereign state, the former would infringe the legal equality of the latter. Consequently,

[8] Martens, *The Law of Nations*, 48. As Neff rightly points out, 'the period might be known more aptly as the Age of Calculation than the Age of Reason' (Neff, *War and the Law of Nations*, 90).

if the legal equality of a state was violated, and the political balance thereby broken, any contractual resolution among states that aimed to restrain violence would turn out to be impossible.

From these pillars we can deduce one of the considerations of the LN approach that has often baffled commentators: according to this paradigm, both the opponents could fight a 'just war'. Once it is granted that any war declared by a sovereign is a legitimate war and that there is no legitimate third party to determine who is right, it follows that both opponents have justice on their side (with the sole exception of the view propounded by Wolff[9]). This was the revolutionary conclusion reached by all theorists of the modern LN: war was claimed to be just on both sides, without distinction. Insofar as the *jus ad bellum* prescriptions declined, the restrictions imposed by the *jus in bello* requirements rose in prominence. Indeed, if both sides had the same degree of justice on their side, the overall justice of each could be determined, if at all, only by their relative adherence to the proper conduct of hostilities:

> Thus the rights founded on the state of war, the lawfulness of its effects, the validity of the acquisitions made by arms, do not, externally and between mankind, depend on the justice of the cause, but on the legality of the means in themselves—that is, on everything requisite to constitute a *regular war* [*guerre en forme*].[10]

Discrimination between belligerents and civilians—according to which violence was to be limited to regular soldiers and, more specifically, to those soldiers who actively took part in hostilities—was formalized by means of the creation of a national army, that is, military units raised, selected, sustained, and controlled directly by the state. The enemy, usually depicted as a criminal, turned to be a *justus hostis*, that is, a legitimate opponent who complied with a substantially shared set of rules of engagement and conduct. There was no room, then, at least theoretically, for an absolute conflict against an enemy regarded as an existential and anthropological other than oneself, who needed to be annihilated because of his distinctive way of life. As Spinoza pointed out, 'it is not hatred but the state's right that makes a man an enemy'.[11] Accordingly, a political opponent could be described as someone other than oneself only with regard to her or his political aims, which were by definition fluid and conditional (as proved by the quickly shifting alliances that characterized the Cabinet Wars). Conflict was limited to a single and determined *casus belli*: meant to counter and force back a state army, not to ravage and destroy a whole nation.

B. The Perpetual Peace Projects

While the LN aimed to restrain war, the goal pursued by the PPP was much more ambitious—that is, the abolition of all wars. This is the reason why in PPP peace was

[9] Wolff, *The Law of Nations*, 513–15 (§§ 1010–16). [10] Vattel, The Law of Nations, 591.

[11] Baruch Spinoza, *Theological-Political Treatise* (Indianapolis, IN: Hackett Publishing, 2001), 180.

qualified as 'perpetual' (Kant's well-known *Toward Perpetual Peace* (1795) borrowed, as did many others, the term introduced more than 80 years earlier by Abbot Saint-Pierre). The first projects, those of Crucé (1623) and Saint-Pierre (1713–17), boldly promoted the idea of an International Union composed of all sovereigns. Others, such as Penn (1693) and Saint-Simon (1814), suggested the creation of a European parliament. Others, such as Bentham (1786–9) and Kant (1795), were less keen to present clear institutional proposals, but indicated practical and ethical norms that, if implemented, would have led to the abolition of war.[12]

By advancing both moral and utilitarian arguments, advocates of the PPP stressed the point that, for achieving a lasting peace, a radical transformation of the rules of the interstate system was required. Accordingly, within the PPP's perspective, the chief cause of war could be seen in the anarchy which was typical of interstate relations, and which did not recognize any authority above the state. The PPP shared with the LN the notion of equality of all states as members of the international community but they still attempted to envisage the institutionalization of a third party, endowed with effective power, that is, able to persuade or compel states to accept its ultimate decision on any given issue. This third party could be an International Union composed of ambassadors representing all states (as suggested by Crucé (1623) and Saint-Pierre (1713–17)), or an elected parliament (as suggested by Penn (1693) and Saint-Simon (1814)), or independent courts. From this perspective, once the establishment of a third party was agreed, states would accept the status quo and all territorial, political, and dynastic claims would be abandoned. Any change to the interstate system would be achieved through consensus and shared procedures.

The means for settling interstate disputes was no longer war (however limited it may have been), but international arbitration, to which the parties referred and by whose decision they agreed to be bound (by consent or even by force as a last resort, depending on the type of project considered). If not formally authorized by the

[12] The texts of the PPP tradition under discussion are: Émeric Crucé, *The New Cineas* (New York: Garland, 1972); Abbé de Saint-Pierre, *An Abridged Version of the Project for Perpetual Peace* (Valletta: Midsea, 2009); William Penn, *An Essay Towards the Present and Future Peace of Europe, by the Establishment of an European Diet, Parliament, or Estates* (London: Peace Committee of the Society of Friends, 1936); Henri de Saint-Simon (with Augustin Thierry), 'On the Reorganisation of European Society' in Keith Taylor (ed), *Henri Saint Simon (1760–1825): Selected Writings on Science, Industry and Social Organisation* (New York: Holmes & Meier, 1975); Jeremy Bentham, 'Of War, Considered in Respect of its Causes and Consequences' and 'A Plan for an Universal and Perpetual Peace' in John Bowring (ed), *The Works of Jeremy Bentham*, vol II (Edinburgh: Tait, 1838–43); Immanuel Kant, 'To Perpetual Peace: A Philosophical Project' in Hans S. Reiss (ed), *Kant: Political Writings* (Cambridge: Cambridge University Press, 1991). For a comprehensive account of the history of the PPP, see Daniele Archibugi, 'Models of International Organization in Perpetual Peace Projects' (1992) 18 *Review of International Studies* 295–317; Murray Forsyth, *Unions of States. The Theory and Practice of Confederation* (Leicester: Leicester University Press, 1981); Sylvester J. Hemleben, *Plans for World Peace through Six Centuries* (Chicago, IL: Chicago University Press, 1943); Christian L. Lange and August Schou, *Histoire de l'internationalisme* (Oslo: Aschehoug, 1963); Jacob ter Meulen, *Der Gedanke der Internationalen Organisation in seiner Entwicklung* (The Hague: Martinus Nijhoff, 1968).

supranational authority, any use of military force was absolutely forbidden, except in cases of self-defence. In the strong variant of the PPP, developed by Crucé and Saint-Pierre, the newly formed International Union should even have the power to administer sanctions against states that did not comply with its decisions.

The PPP model rested on the same three main pillars mentioned previously in regard to the LN model. Yet they were differently conceived and deeply revised in order to account for a very different institutional setting.

(1) Formal equality of states was strongly radicalized. Indeed, the legal statute of the supranational assembly, by enforcing the rule 'one state, one vote' (at least in the strong variant proposed by Crucé and Saint-Pierre), turned the formal equality of states into substantial parity, ensured by institutional practice. Then, each state had to count for one and no state for more than one, regardless of any material difference (military force, economic power, territorial extension). The UN General Assembly and many other international organizations have endorsed this principle. The early PPP (Crucé and Saint-Pierre, but also Penn) also dared to identify the core players of this international system: with the purpose of indicating the states that should become members of the International Union, for the first time in international theory they provided a list of the then existing European states.[13]
(2) Respect of neutrality and non-interference in another state's affairs.
(3) Dynastic legitimacy as a practical foundation of absolutism inasmuch as it was necessary to strengthen the pacification of Europe. But on this point the PPP model was even more radical than the LN one. While the latter saw the reconfiguration of state borders as an expected and natural outcome of international conflict (and, more generally, of interstate relationships), the former intended to maintain the status quo at all costs. Any secession, annexation, or fusion among states—as well as any change in borders—was explicitly forbidden, unless agreed by *every* member of the international community.

However, apart from the different conception of the unavoidability of armed conflict, the LN and the PPP agreed on the fact that the right to wage war in no way pertained to non-state actors. In both traditions, any non-state subject willing to resort to armed force faced condemnation as an outlaw actor and was declared an enemy of the public peace and social order. Non-state subjects could be internal or external to the state. Among the violent conflicts carried out by intrastate subjects, the most relevant for our purposes were private conflicts and civil rebellions fought by duellists,

[13] Noted that no LN text provides a list of states. This is because within the tradition it is accepted that states could merge, could be conquered, or could be created *ex novo*. In the LN it is force that provides the legitimacy to become a member of the international community. However, in the PPP tradition, the system of states is somehow 'frozen' and change can be achieved only by consent. For this reason, advocates of the tradition do not dare to list the political players that deserve to be part of the interstate system and, therefore, of the international organization.

knights, nobles, or cities. Among the violent conflicts carried out by extra-state subjects, the most important were pirate wars and colonial wars. Any armed conflicts waged by these non-state actors (as with any armed repression against them conducted by a state or by a supranational union) were no longer defined as war. War was only *interstate*. In the first book of *The Social Contract*, Rousseau summed up perfectly the state-centred nature of war that we are discussing:

> War then is a relation, not between man and man, but between State and State, and individuals are enemies only accidentally, not as men, nor even as citizens, but as soldiers; not as members of their country, but as its defenders. Finally, each State can have for enemies only other States, and not men; for between things disparate in nature there can be no real relation.[14]

Eventually, the PPP made a suggestion addressed to the rulers that it was rather simple: it was in their interest to establish an International Union since this would reinforce their internal sovereignty. Once the International Union was established, the rulers of other states would refrain from instigating or supporting internal opponents, up to the point that, in the strong version of Crucé and Saint-Pierre, the joint forces of the members of the Union would potentially be used to repress rebels and rebellions. However, the price to be paid was to give up the key aspect of external sovereignty; namely, the legitimacy to wage war without any further authorization. But this was precisely the legitimacy that the LN wished to guarantee to state rulers and which ultimately marked the core difference between the two traditions.

IV. Evolutionary Lines of the Law of Nations and the Perpetual Peace Projects

What were the evolutionary lines of these two traditions? They emerged at the end of the 16th century and evolved in relation to the expansion of states in the 17th and the 18th centuries. Though parallel, they cannot be said to be perfectly coeval: if the LN reached its high point in the 17th century, the most significant advocates of the PPP belonged to the 18th century. In reality, this temporal gap tells us much about the way the European system of states evolved: while still in its infancy in the 17th century, in the 18th century it developed more fully.

In the 17th century, in the wake of the development of the modern LN, the first requirement was to grant states as much autonomy as possible and then the possibility

[14] Jean-Jacques Rousseau, *The Social Contract* (New York: Cosimo, 2007), 19–20.

of deciding when to resort to violence. In the 18th century, many European states had already developed and the principle of legitimate violence eventually triumphed, to such an extent that it became conceivable to envisage at least a limitation on external sovereignty through a prohibition of the unilateral use of force, as suggested by the PPP.

The influence of the LN that characterized the *Jus Publicum Europaeum* declined at the end of the 18th century. After the French Revolution—which in 1793 introduced mass conscription (*levée en masse*, literally 'mass uprising')—and the Napoleonic wars, revolutionary ideals and subsequent nationalistic ideology marked the end of the *guerre en forme* as the exclusive paradigm of modern warfare. Collective goals other than state security (mainly the demand for liberty from domination and the quest for political equality) were gradually considered not only as legitimate reasons for waging war, but often as the only justifiable ground for resorting to violence. This shift heralded the end of both the absolutist right of states to self-determination and the corresponding duty of non-interference in another state's affairs. As Clausewitz (1832) pointed out, by reviewing his own previous idea on the nature of modern armed conflict, the absolute war—that is, a war with no restraints—was not merely a 'a pure concept' (Book I) but also a 'real possibility' (Book VIII):

> Since Bonaparte, then, war, first among the French and subsequently among their enemies, again became the concern of the people as a whole, took on an entirely different character, or rather closely approached its true character, its absolute perfection. There seemed no end to the resources mobilised; all limits disappeared in the vigor and enthusiasm shown by governments and their subjects. Various factors powerfully increased that vigor: the vastness of available resources, the ample field of opportunity, and the depth of feeling generally aroused. The sole aim of war was to overthrow the opponent. Not until he was prostrate was it considered possible to pause and try to reconcile the opposing interests.[15]

It is precisely at the end of the 18th century and during the Napoleonic wars that the PPP flourished and often transformed themselves from the rigid and somewhat conservative approach they inherited from the early authors such as Crucé and Saint-Pierre to an attempt to generate a new legal framework for Europe based on peace and human rights. In France and Germany—the countries most involved in conflict—many thinkers debated the possibility of a peace which could be different from merely a truce. In the eyes of diverse revolutionaries such as James Madison (1792) and Johann Fichte (1796), the PPP appeared to be a mutual warranty by which sovereigns could retain their arbitrary power.[16] In the

[15] Carl von Clausewitz, *On War* (Cambridge: Cambridge University Press, 2007), 239.

[16] See James Madison, 'Universal Peace' in Marvin Meyers (ed), *The Mind of the Founder: Sources of the Political Thought of James Madison* (Hanover, NH: Brandeis University Press, 1981); Johann Gottlieb Fichte, 'Zum ewigen Frieden. Ein philosophischer Entwurf von Immanuel Kant' in Id., *Gesamtausgabe*, vol III (Stuttgart: Bayerischen Akademie der Wissenschaften, 1962). Hegel is also of the same opinion and asserts that 'Kant proposed a league of sovereigns to settle disputes between states, and the Holy Alliance was meant to be an institution more or less of this kind' (Georg Wilhelm Friedrich Hegel, *Elements of the Philosophy of Right* (Cambridge: Cambridge University Press, 1991), 362).

new historical context, these authors grasped the critical analysis of the early PPP already developed by Leibniz (1715), Voltaire (1761), and, above all, Rousseau (1758–9).[17] Based on the old tradition, during that period the link between the adjective 'perpetual' and the noun 'peace' was deemed to be the way to ward off war, and also to devise an organization of European society based on respect of individual rights and the autonomy of peoples—in sum, on the values of justice and freedom which had been proclaimed by the French and American revolutions. This required rethinking some of the basic presuppositions of the PPP of the pre-revolutionary era.[18]

That said, at the end of the Napoleonic wars the situation was drastically reversed and the idea of a perpetual peace, brokered by permanent institutions, was firmly set aside. The Congress of Vienna, however, recovered the conservative aspects of the projects elaborated by Crucé and Saint-Pierre: no formal International Union was needed to allow the powers of old Europe mutually to assist each other against any further revolutionary movement. The pleas of Bentham and Kant for transparency in international affairs were also put aside, as well as the idea that elected governments were a precondition for interstate peace. But even such a loose agreement required a recognition of the need to foster diplomatic relations; the law of nations gradually developed into international law thus providing interstate relations with a much needed juridical framework. But that leads to another story—the story of the 19th and 20th centuries.

V. The Use of Violence

With regard to the use of violence, there were salient inner differences within each tradition. In particular, the following points should be noted.

- What are the reasons authorizing a state to declare war on another state (V.A)?
- Do state subgroups have the right to resist state authority (V.B)?

[17] See Gottfried Wilhelm von Leibniz, 'Observations on the Abbé de St Pierre's *Project for Perpetual Peace*' in Patrick Riley (ed), *The Political Writings of Leibniz* (Cambridge: Cambridge University Press, 1972). On the controversy between Voltaire and Saint-Pierre, see Merle L. Perkins, 'Voltaire and the Abbé de Saint-Pierre on World Peace' (1961) 17 *Studies on Voltaire and the Eighteenth Century* 9–34. Finally, see Jean-Jacques Rousseau, 'Abstract on Monsieur l'Abbé de Saint-Pierre's Plan for Perpetual Peace' and 'Judgement on Perpetual Peace' in Stanley Hoffmann and David P. Fidler (eds), *Rousseau on International Relations* (Oxford: Oxford University Press, 1991).

[18] Some of the key texts of this period are collected in Anita Dietze and Walter Dietze (eds), *Ewiger Friede? Dokumente einer deutschen Diskussion um 1800* (Leipzig: Kiepenheuer, 1989).

- Can a third state have the facility to encourage and support the resistance of subgroups in another state (V.C)?
- When and how can a state use violence against indigenous populations who are deemed to be stateless (V.D)?

A. The Legitimacy of Waging War Between States

According to the PPP, once an International Union had been established, the legitimacy of a state waging war against another state vanished. Every dispute had to be brought before the International Union. In the strong variant, that of Crucé and Saint-Pierre, the Union also had the coercive power granted by the armies of its member states. If a state continued to ignore its precepts, the International Union, when attempts at mediation had been ruled out, had to take it upon itself to restore legality by way of joint military intervention. In effect, this variant is not far from that prescribed by the Charter of the United Nations, since the Military Staff Committee should have had precisely that function. As a matter of fact, there are few circumstances in which Security Council resolutions have led to joint military interventions against a state which continues not to comply with them: the most important case being the intervention in Iraq in 1991–2 to restore Kuwait's sovereignty. In the weak variant, advocated by authors such as Penn (1693), Kant (1795), and Saint-Simon (1814), the International Union lacked coercive powers and was conceived of as an arbitral tribunal to which parties could bring their dispute. In both cases, the PPP required states to relinquish an important component of their own sovereignty, the external one.

In the LN approach, any war waged by a state was, by that very fact and at least prima facie, legitimate. Since armed conflict was considered the ultimate but still necessary means for organizing interstate relations, war could no longer be regarded as an outlaw solution. From the 16th century onwards, the paradigm of just war was thus eventually replaced by the theory of legitimate war. Because of this shift, the criterion of just cause was removed, or better, was included within (and effectively reduced to) the key criterion of legitimate authority: there were no longer just and unjust wars, only legitimate and illegitimate wars—wars waged (or not) only by the proper authority, that is, the state. Accordingly, even though the three classical just causes of war—self-defence, claim of goods or rights taken or infringed in an illegal way, and (less generally accepted) the punishment of the aggressor—were reaffirmed, the substantive principles of the *jus ad bellum* (just cause, comparative justice, and right intention) became secondary, while its procedural criteria (last resort, legitimate authority, and proper declaration) attained more prominence. In order to be considered lawful, at least from a legal point of view (lawful conflict), a war had only to fulfil a set of procedural steps, regardless of any substantive criterion concerning its justice—in some treatises considered indeterminable, in others irrelevant—other than the preservation of the overall balance of power among (leading) states. Put another way, the only—but absolutely pivotal—actual limit set on resort to war was a functional (or structural) constraint and not a normative requirement.

B. The Right to Resist

According to the PPP—above all, in the strong variant of Crucé and Saint-Pierre—subjects had no right to resist. Indeed, if they were intent on combating the sovereign, the International Union would have the task of intervening militarily in order to restore the status quo ante. This was the argument that Crucé and Saint-Pierre usually advanced in order to persuade sovereigns to create such an institution: this would actually corroborate the internal power of sovereigns, since it would not only prevent possible wars of aggression, but also internal rebellion. The armies of the Union would be called upon not only to intervene against states that violated international norms, but also to punish the rebellions of their subjects.

Obviously, this position was doomed to be criticized by those who, even though in favour of peace, believed it to be a necessity to confer legitimacy on the reasoning of a sovereign's subjects. As we saw earlier, Voltaire, Rousseau, and Madison fiercely criticized Saint-Pierre's argument, while Leibniz and Saint-Simon (1814) remained sceptical. Kant's (1795) position was emblematic: although in his project there was no reference to the coercive force of the Union, and although he aimed at a reduction in force (as can be evinced, for instance, by his request for progressive abolition of permanent armies), it is precisely in this writing that he, departing from his disciples, took a stand against the right of a people to fight a revolution.

Nonetheless, it is worth considering that, unlike for example the situation in the LN, in the PPP there was no clear-cut distinction between the violence exercised between states and that exercised in civil wars. In principle, the rejection of violence entails both domestic and international politics.

Throughout the history of the LN, the question of the right to revolution can be roughly summarized by the following trend: the more that states extended their control over society and strengthened their mutual relations within the interstate system, the more the legal theorists of the LN were prepared to endorse the right to revolution. At the outset of the LN tradition, there was fierce opposition to the right to revolution: Balthasar de Ayala (1582), for example, reaffirmed the medieval relationship between the crime of rebellion and the crime of heresy. Yet, the classical condemnation of both groups by the medieval and early-modern canonists was in some way reversed: the infidels acquired the legal status of opponents, whilst the rebels and any other non-state subject were not only declared as outlaws but also considered immoral (echoed a few years later by Gentili, who affirmed that the main incentive for cruelty in war was rebellion[19]). By discussing the status of rebels, Ayala asserted:

Now rebels ought not to be classed as enemies, the two being quite distinct, and so it is more correct to term the armed contention with rebel subjects execution or legal process, or prosecution, and not war.... For the same reason, the laws of war and of captivity and of postliminy, which apply to enemies, do not apply to rebels, any more than they apply to pirates and robbers (these not being included in the term of 'enemy').... [I]t follows that a war waged by a prince with rebels is a most just and that all measures allowed in war are available against them...[20]

Grotius also continued to deny a right to take up arms against the sovereign, even if the latter was patently unjust. According to the Dutch jurist, if a sovereign, by provoking her or his people to despair, 'loses the rights of independent sovereigns and can no longer claim the privilege of the law of nations', the people had no right to take up arms:

Admitting that it would be fraught with the greatest dangers if subjects were allowed to redress grievances by force of arms, it does not necessarily follow that other powers are prohibited from giving them assistance when labouring under grievous oppressions.... The impediment, which prohibits a *subject* from making resistance, does not depend upon the nature of the *occasion*, which would operate equally upon the feelings of men, whether they were subjects or not, but upon the character of the persons, who cannot transfer their natural allegiance from their own sovereign to another.[21]

Yet, as stated previously, Grotius's misgivings about the right of resistance were an exception which could not be sustained for any length of time. Indeed, in 1690 John Locke, who is still the theorist of the 'federative power' as a separate political power, advocated the right of resistance against any oppressive and illiberal government. Finally, at the other end of the continuum we have sketched, a few decades before the French Revolution, Vattel (1758) spoke of the right to resist as an 'indisputable right':

But this high attribute of sovereignty [a right belonging to the prince] is no reason why the nation should not curb an insupportable tyrant, pronounce sentence on him (still respecting in his person the majesty of his rank), and withdraw itself from his obedience.[22]

What is the reason behind this unexpected shift from the total denial of a right to revolution—when states were still in their infancy—to its explicit recognition—when states were almost at the peak of their development? In our opinion, the reason is to be found in the degree of systemic development reached by the interstate system in the 18th century. On the one hand, the internal stability of every member of the

[19] See Gentili, *De Iure Belli*, III, 7.

[20] Balthasar de Ayala, *Three Books On the Law of War And on the Duties Connected with War And on Military Discipline* (Washington, DC: Carnegie Institution of Washington, 1912), 11–12. For the comparison between rebels and infidels, see § 23, significantly titled 'Rebellion a most heinous offense'.

[21] Grotius, *On the Law of War and Peace*, 227.

[22] Vattel, *The Law of Nations*, 104.

system turned out to be more important, for the overall balance of the international domain, than the specific form of government and the dynastic continuity of any given state. On the other hand, the foreign policy of a state appeared to be increasingly independent of its form of government (which, therefore, whatever form it may take, did not represent a systemic threat).

c. Humanitarian Intervention

Directly tied to the right to resistance is humanitarian intervention. In the strong variant of the PPP the same possibility of humanitarian intervention was certainly not taken into account: the fact that a sovereign may have been cruel to her or his subjects and that those subjects may have had good reasons to resist, went well beyond the perspective of Crucé and Saint-Pierre. This issue was seldom tackled in the other perpetual peace projects: Rousseau, Bentham, and Kant were aware that sovereigns could be brutal to their own subjects, but not one of them thought that the solution relied on external intervention. In brief, the PPP, in their strong version, were against humanitarian intervention and, indeed, supported intervention aimed at suppressing revolt; in the weak version, they simply disregarded the problem.

There was no generally shared opinion about humanitarian intervention among the theorists of the LN. Grotius was undoubtedly the staunchest advocate of the legal right—not the moral duty—of an intervention on behalf of the oppressed. In his argument, the question of justice shifted from the discussion about *what was right* to the problem of *having a right*. As noted, Grotius's firm endorsement of this right seemed to be at odds with his conviction that subjects could not take up arms against an unjust sovereign even in the toughest situations: basically, he granted external players—that is, third states endowed with sovereign power—the right that he denied to the internal players (ie the subjects), who did not have sovereign power. However, it seems contradictory that external players should risk their lives when the internal players, those who suffer most from the actions of an unjust sovereign, cannot do the same.

On this matter, Vattel's position was highly significant because he successfully managed to provide a justification for humanitarian intervention that was compatible with respect of state sovereignty: only when oppressed subjects had begun an open rebellion that effectively brought into question the authority and the power of the incumbent sovereign, could a third state interfere. And it was up to the third state to decide whether to intervene in favour of the incumbent authority or the challenging authority. In the chapter titled 'Of the right to security, and the effects of the sovereignty and independence of nations', Vattel wrote:

It is an evident consequence of the liberty and independence of nations, that all have a right to be governed as they think proper, and that no state has the smallest right to interfere in the government of another.... It does not then belong to any foreign power to take cognisance of the administration of that sovereign, to set himself up for a judge of his conduct, and to oblige him to alter it.... But if the prince, by violating the fundamental laws, gives his subjects a legal right to resist him—if tyranny becoming insupportable obliges the nation to rise in their own defence—every foreign power has a right to succour an oppressed people who implore their assistance.... [W]hen a people from good reasons take up arms against an oppressor, it is but an act of justice and generosity to assist brave men in the defence of their liberties. Whenever therefore matters are carried so far as to produce a civil war, foreign powers may assist that party which appears to them to have justice on its side.[23]

For our purposes, perhaps the most interesting arguments are those advanced by Martens (1789). In the section titled 'Of the Rights of each State relative to its own Constitution', he wrote:

The internal constitution of a state rests, in general, on these two points: viz. on the principles adopted with respect to him or them in whose hands the sovereign power is lodged, not only at present, but for the future also; and on those adopted with respect to the manner in which this sovereign power is to be exercised. Both these depend on the will of the state, foreign nations having not the least right to interfere in arrangements which are purely domestic. However, there are some exceptions to this rule. In case a dispute should arise concerning either of the points above-mentioned, a foreign power may: 1. offer its good offices, and interpose them, if accepted; 2. if called in to the aid of that of the two parties which has justice on its side, it may act coercively; 3. it may have a right, from positive title, to intermeddle; and 4. if its own preservation requires it to take a part in the quarrel, that consideration overbalances its obligations to either of the parties.[24]

Indeed, Martens seemed to run into great difficulties in finding a viable solution to the question of humanitarian intervention. On the one hand, he was suspicious of a right that allowed one state to enforce the rights of subjects in another state, because of the risks that a horizontally organized state system may meet in recognizing it. On the other hand, Martens did not seem entirely indifferent to the questions of when, if ever, a foreign state could legitimately intervene on behalf of the faction that it considered to be the morally legitimate opponent.

D. The Use of Force Towards Stateless Indigenous Populations

It was at the very beginning of the LN that the question of non-state communities (generally identified with the American aborigines) was more comprehensively discussed. In 1539 Vitoria had already set the agenda of an emerging problem that, unsurprisingly, had not been addressed since the end of the Roman Empire, in his two essays *Relectio de indis* (On the American Indians) and *Relectio de iure belli* (On the Law of

[23] Vattel, *The Law of Nations*, 289–291. [24] Martens, *The Law of Nations*, 69–70.

War).[25] Even though Vitoria judged the Spanish dominion in America as ultimately legitimate, he stated that the legitimation at issue could not be claimed by referring to just causes of war other than those concerning war among Christian states. Vitoria affirmed that aborigines should be considered as much human as any other peoples and therefore should keep a basic right to their land, sovereignty, and resources. Yet this 'humanization' of the American natives goes hand in hand with a new discrimination. Indeed, the reasons that, according to Vitoria, represented a legitimate title to the occupation of the American land by the Spanish were not the same as those that, in his view, might justify a war waged by a European state against another European state (above all, the freedoms of trade and religion across boundaries).

The flawed and hypocritical sophistry systematized by Vitoria was followed, with very few differences, by Gentili, Suarez, and even Grotius and Pufendorf, when they referred to (what they considered to be) the *contra naturam* (eg human sacrifices, zoophilia, sodomy) customs and practices adopted by the aborigines (often again compared to animals) as just causes for war. Clearly, none of these European thinkers ever dared, for example, to discuss the custom in Europe of burning witches or other practices of the Christian Inquisition as being just causes for war.

Far from being merely the first (and more cautious) author of an enlightened series of 'legal critics', Vitoria was actually the sole theorist who attributed some of the state's characteristics to the American land and its native people. The further we delve into the history and consolidation of a more stable system of interstate relations in Europe (at least until the second half of the 20th century), the more fiercely the would-be statehood of any native or intrastate community was denied (and consequently the would-be injustice of any past or possible war against them). It is certainly highly significant that at the peak of colonial expansion, the LN—the main and most recognized approach of international norms—substantially ignored the relationship of European states with stateless non-European communities.

Neither are Indigenous peoples particularly addressed in the PPP tradition which was mainly a European project designed for Europeans. There are, however, significant exceptions, one of which is the first PPP by Crucé. In this work, he envisaged a truly world assembly of states from which no nation should be excluded. But he did not enter into the detail of who should represent the peoples who did not have a state to represent them.

When subsequent projects, and most notably those of Penn and Saint-Pierre, began to identify the members of the international community by naming them, they ignored those outside Europe. The most significant example is Penn himself: the founder of Pennsylvania, the man who made a brave and avant-garde attempt to establish peaceful relations with the American aborigines, did not suggest involving

[25] Anthony Pagden and Jeremy Lawrance (eds), *Vitoria: Political Writings* (Cambridge: Cambridge University Press, 1991).

either non-European peoples or even the inhabitants of the American colonies in his own European parliament.

A significant exception was represented by Kant: following Vitoria, he forcefully condemned the fact that European states and their companies subjugated and conquered other continents, and the fact that those territories were considered devoid of any rights. By contrast, Kant assumed that the Europeans should grant these populations the same rights that they granted to each other.

VI. Conclusion

In this chapter, we sketched the main similarities and differences between two important traditions that have contributed to the foundation of modern international theory, the LN and the PPP. Both traditions reflected the rise of the new states but they also anticipated in their theorizing an international system that only became dominant several decades later. In fact, they contributed substantially to providing legitimacy for the modern system of states.

In spite of the important variations encountered within the LN and the PPP, we also emphasized the core distinctive factor between the two traditions as summarized in Table 2.1. However, one distinctive core element would be sufficient to distinguish between them: the legitimacy of war in interstate relations. While the LN never attempted to abolish war, simply to regulate it, the PPP had a much more utopian approach and aimed to abolish interstate war all together.

We also noted that, although the two traditions developed almost in parallel from the 17th to the 18th centuries, there was a significant difference: the LN splendour occurs in the 17th century, reflecting the need of the fresh new states to be guaranteed total autonomy. As soon as this aim was achieved, another issue arose on the international relations agenda; namely, the possibility of having an institutionalized system of states based on shared procedures and cooperation.

There is, however, one baffling factor: the PPP and the LN basically ignored each other. Faced with the same historical events and the same subject, the PPP and the LN were unable to confront each other, either to stress their points of agreement or to emphasize their disagreements. Seldom do the authors of one tradition cite the authors of another, confirming that it is often easier to ignore opposite views than to deal with them. Can we assume that the authors of the PPP did not know the views of the LN and vice versa? Not quite: Kant, for example, knew very well most texts of the LN, but he called three of their main representatives—Grotius, Pufendorf, and Vattel—'sorry comforters', one of the most derogative terms he ever used. Not even

Rousseau (1756–8), who was a most careful reader of Grotius, found it necessary to discuss his views on peace and war when he summarized and criticized Saint-Pierre's project. Conversely, within each tradition careful attention was paid to the legacy left by its ancestors.

Both the LN and the PPP were very influential in the subsequent development of international theory and practice. The LN is generally considered the precursor of international law and almost all texts on the discipline were introduced by a chapter devoted to the forefathers. We argue that the PPP were also equally influential in inspiring the creation of international organizations, although they are often neglected. They also inspired a distinctive stream of peace movements, namely institutional pacifism.

Finally, we examined what each tradition authorized in the use of force and identified four categories: (1) interstate wars; (2) the right to resist state authority; (3) what in modern terminology has been called humanitarian intervention; and (4) the use of force against stateless populations. A clear distinction between the LN and the PPP emerged in the first category: the main aim of the LN is to regulate interstate wars, while the main aim of the PPP is to abolish them. This distinction suffices to classify the international theorists of the 16th, 17th, and 18th centuries into one of the two traditions.

There is a much less clear-cut distinction across the LN and the PPP in the other three categories considered since authors belonging to the same tradition may have held very different positions. In particular, LN theorists had different views on the right to resist, with Grotius leading those who believed that subjects should never resist their sovereign and Vattel leading those who extended to international theory Locke's lesson in defence of the right to resist.

In most cases, the PPP denied the right and even more the duty of a state to practise humanitarian intervention; where this was not explicitly made clear, there was a lack of consideration of the issue. Each LN author, on the other hand, provided a somewhat different list of legitimate reasons to resort to humanitarian intervention.

With regard to the use of force against stateless communities, this was a problem ignored by both the LN and the PPP. Only the early theorists of both traditions, such as Vitoria for the former and Crucé for the latter, acknowledged the existence of non-European peoples. Kant provided forceful criticism of colonial practices by European states and companies, but he was an exception among the international theorists. The others tended to ignore the problem: at the peak of colonial expansion in the 17th and 18th centuries, international theorists were primarily concerned with the European system of states rather than on how those same European states were acting outside Europe.

CHAPTER 3

THE LIMITATIONS OF TRADITIONAL RULES AND INSTITUTIONS RELATING TO THE USE OF FORCE

MICHAEL J. GLENNON

> In politics as in mechanics, the power which is to keep the engine going must be sought for outside the machinery; and if it is not forthcoming, or is insufficient to surmount the obstacles which may reasonably be expected, the confidence will fail.
>
> (John Stuart Mill[1])

I. Introduction

What is outside the formal machinery of legal rules and institutions keeps the engine of law going. It is, alas, what is *not* outside the formal machinery of those rules and institutions relating to the use of force that has created obstacles and caused confidence in them to fail.

[1] John Stuart Mill, *Considerations on Representative Government* (1862), 21.

Law is a form of cooperation. When cooperative mechanisms such as law function properly, certain exogenous conditions normally prevail. Social scientists have identified a number of these conditions.[2] For example, the community in which cooperative mechanisms arise is relatively homogeneous.[3] A high degree of consensus obtains. Actors are more equal and trusting. Reinforcing social norms are stronger. The cost of non-cooperation to defectors is higher. Free-riders are more easily identified and penalized. Individual and collective interests are more aligned. Future dealings are expected. This sub-legal scaffolding accounts for the comparative success of legal systems of the sort that prevail in advanced constitutional democracies.

In contrast, in the more heterogeneous international legal community, relatively little agreement exists concerning the use of force. Actors are unequal. A low degree of trust prevails. Social norms are weak. The costs of exclusion to non-cooperators are low. Free-riding is easy. Individual and collective interests often clash. Expectations concerning future dealings are limited. Centrifugal geopolitical forces such as these represent, in George Kennan's profound words, 'the deeper sources of international instability'.[4]

The strength or weakness of such conditions varies geographically and topically; not all international law is alike. In some sub-regimes, international rules and institutions are more robust than in others. The supportive sub-legal scaffolding is stronger in the realm of 'low politics' that comprises trade, communication, transit, and economic concerns. In the realm of 'high politics', on the other hand, where the issues are core questions of state security and survival, underlying economic and geopolitical features of the system, which produce power disparities and value conflicts, limit the impact of legal rules on state behaviour. Thus, if the legal rules happen to coincide with the underlying dynamic, states will appear to be acting in accordance with the rules. 'If, however, the legal rules conflict with other policy goals,' Anthony Arend concludes, 'states will almost certainly act contrary to legal rules.'[5]

The *jus ad bellum* comprises quintessential 'high politics'. In it, the requisite background conditions have not been present to the degree necessary to generate consistent international cooperation in managing the use of force. That conclusion

[2] Simon Maxwell, 'Why Cooperate?', paper distributed at symposium, 'Reforming the United Nations Once and for All', World Economic Forum, Davos, Switzerland, 23 Jan 2004. Seminal works include Robert O. Keohane, *After Hegemony* (Princeton, NJ: Princeton University Press, 1984); Robert Axelrod, *The Evolution of Cooperation* (New York: Basic Books, 1984); Kenneth A. Oye (ed), *Cooperation Under Anarchy* (Princeton, NJ: Princeton University Press, 1986).

[3] John Jay referred to the US as 'one connected country, to one united people, a people descended from the same ancestors, speaking the same language, professing the same religion, attached to the same principles of government, [and] very similar in their manners and customs. …' The Federalist No 2 (Jay).

[4] George F. Kennan, 'Diplomacy in the Modern World' in Robert J. Beck et al (eds), *International Rules: Approaches from International Law and International Relations* (New York: Oxford University Press, 1996), 99, 104.

[5] Anthony Arend, 'Do Legal Rules Matter? International Law and International Politics' (1997–8) 38 *Virginia Journal of International Law* 107, 123.

is particularly striking with respect to the most important condition, the need for a common understanding concerning whether and when the use of force is justified. This was one of the issues addressed in a lengthy study published in November 2009 by the Council on Foreign Relations that compiled recent international polls comparing the views of different nations' populations.[6] The attitudinal differences concerning use of force, terrorism, and the proliferation of weapons of mass destruction are striking.

- When asked whether the UN Security Council should or should not have the right to authorize the use of military force to restore by force a democratic government that has been overthrown, 57 per cent of Americans said yes—but only 35 per cent of Russians and 37 per cent of Chinese.
- People were asked to imagine that North Korea has acquired weapons of mass destruction, and that the US government has decided to attack North Korea to force that country to give up those weapons. They were then asked whether they would support a decision by their government to take part in this military action. In the US, 58 per cent said yes and 31 per cent no—but in Germany, only 20 per cent said yes and 76 per cent said no; in Italy, 24 per cent said yes and 70 per cent said no. In the European Union as a whole, 31 per cent said yes and 63 per cent said no. If such action against North Korea were undertaken by the North Atlantic Treaty Organization (NATO), Americans continued to approve, 68–24, but military action was still disapproved by Germans (34–64), Italians (32–63), and Europeans (41–54). Even authorization by the UN Security Council had little effect. Americans continued to approve the action (72–24) but it was opposed by Germans (33–66), Italians (37–59), and Europeans (43–53).
- The results differed little with respect to Iran. People were asked to imagine that Iran has acquired weapons of mass destruction, and that the US government has decided to attack Iran to force that country to give up those weapons. They were then asked whether they would support a decision by their government to take part in this military action. In the US, 67 per cent said yes and 23 per cent said no—but in Germany, only 32 per cent said yes and 66 per cent said no; in Italy, 26 per cent said yes and 68 per cent said no. In the European Union (EU) as a whole, 38 per cent said yes and 56 per cent said no. If such action against Iran were undertaken by NATO, Americans continued to approve (78–17), but military action was still disapproved by Germans (29–67), Italians (34–62), and Europeans (48–48). Even authorization by the UN Security Council again had little effect. Americans continued to approve the action (75–16) but it was opposed by Germans (46–51), Italians (44–52)—but now supported by Europeans (50–44).

[6] Council on Foreign Relations, Public Opinion on Global Issues: A Web-based Digest of Polling from Around the World (2009), available at <http://www.cfr.org/public_opinion>.

- In 2009, 66 per cent of Americans believed that the NATO mission in Afghanistan should be continued, but only 14 per cent of Russians, 14 per cent of Chinese, and 13 per cent of Pakistanis.
- Asked in 2006 whether the possibility of an unfriendly country becoming a nuclear power represented an important threat, 3 per cent of Americans said it was not important, compared with 17 per cent of Chinese and 12 per cent of Indians who considered it an unimportant threat.

The lesson of these and many similar polls[7] is clear: the consensus needed for the formulation and enforcement of effective international rules governing the use of force does not exist.

II. Weaknesses in Secondary Rules

The weakness of the sub-legal infrastructure underpinning international rules and institutions relating to the use of force tends to amplify pre-existing ambiguities in international law's secondary rules[8] that pertain to the use of force, concerning three questions in particular: consent, obligation, and causation.

The prevailing theory of validity in international law is, at its core, the classic positivist idea that states are obliged to follow only those rules to which they consent. They consent explicitly through words, or treaties, and implicitly through deeds, or custom. If a state has not consented to a given rule, it is free to disregard the rule. Moreover, in the face of uncertainty whether a state has consented to the rule or not, a state is presumed not to have consented and remains free to disregard the rule.[9] Neo-naturalists

[7] See eg *The German Marshall Fund of the United States, Transatlantic Trends* (2003). In 2003, eg, 53 per cent of Americans believed that war is sometimes necessary to obtain justice—compared with only 18 per cent of Europeans.

[8] H. L. A. Hart regarded international law as a primitive legal system because it lacked secondary rules altogether. See H. L. A Hart, *The Concept of Law* (Oxford: Clarendon Press, 1994), 214.

[9] 'The rules of law binding upon states ... emanate from their own free will as expressed in conventions. ... [R]estrictions upon the independence of states therefore cannot be presumed.' *The SS Lotus (France v. Turkey)*, 1927 PCIJ, Ser A, No 10, 18. See also Hans Kelsen, *Principles of International Law* (Clark, NJ: Lawbook Exchange, 1952), 305; Louis Henkin, 'International Law: Politics, Values and Functions' (1989) 216 *Recueil des cours de l'Académie de droit international* 27 ('a State is not subject to any external authority unless it has voluntarily consented to such authority'); Daphne Richemond, 'Normativity in International Law: The Case of Unilateral Humanitarian Intervention' (2003) 6 *Yale Human Rights and Development Law Journal* 45; Ian Brownlie, *Principles of Public International Law* (Oxford: Oxford University Press, 1973), 2 (international rules are law because 'the general consent of states creates rules of general application'). For a discussion of difficulties in consent-based theories generally, see Jack Goldsmith and Daryl Levinson, 'Law for States: International Law, Constitutional

dislike this so-called 'freedom principle' and would prefer that judges be permitted to find rules in some 'brooding omnipresence in the sky'—that is, to make up rules when none can be found to which states have consented. That the freedom principle of *The Lotus*[10] continues to be the *Grundnorm* of international law, however, cannot be disputed. The International Court of Justice (ICJ), in the *Nuclear Weapons* advisory opinion, was invited by the UN General Assembly to reconsider the rule—and it declined and, 15 years later, in its advisory opinion on Kosovo, it declined again.[11]

It would have been untenable for the Court to do otherwise. International law long ago took a positivist turn, embracing the familiar empiricist idea that international rules are created by states, not discovered, and that states are therefore bound to obey only treaties and customary rules fashioned with their consent. One of the rules that states have posited is the rule that states will comply with their obligations (*pacta sunt servanda*). Yet this approach is also, in one major conception, naturalist in that it presupposes an a priori obligation to obey the rule requiring compliance. An infinite regress is created if the rationale for compliance consists only of another positive rule requiring compliance with the antecedent rule—the foundation of this positive framework would be little more than turtles all the way down. Again, as Brierly observes, 'A consistently consensual theory … would have to admit that if consent is withdrawn, the obligation created by it comes to an end.'[12] H. L. A. Hart

Law, Public Law' (2009) 122 *Harvard Law Review* 1791. I suggest later in the chapter that 'consent' cannot be taken to imply unfettered free movement of the mind on the part of a state's policymakers, but this qualification does not affect the previous analysis, which relates to the default rule applied by international law when clear signals of state intent are absent.

[10] The words of the Permanent Court of International Justice in *The Lotus* case, 19, para 44, are worth recalling:

> International law governs relations between independent States. The rules of law binding upon States therefore emanate from their own free will as expressed in conventions or by usages generally accepted as expressing principles of law and established in order to regulate the relations between these co-existing independent communities or with a view to the achievement of common aims. Restrictions upon the independence of States cannot therefore be presumed.

[11] In framing the question before it ('Is the unilateral declaration of independence by the Provisional Institutions of Self-Government of Kosovo in accordance with international law?'), the ICJ noted that:

> The task which the Court is called upon to perform is to determine whether or not the declaration of independence was adopted in violation of international law. The Court is not required by the question it has been asked to take a position on whether international law conferred a positive entitlement on Kosovo unilaterally to declare its independence or, *a fortiori*, on whether international law generally confers an entitlement on entities situated within a State unilaterally to break away from it. Indeed, it is entirely possible for a particular act–such as a unilateral declaration of independence–not to be in violation of international law without necessarily constituting the exercise of a right conferred by it. The Court has been asked for an opinion on the first point, not the second.

Accordance with International Law of the Unilateral Declaration of Independence in respect of Kosovo, Advisory Opinion of 22 July 2010, ICJ Rep 2010, para 56. The Court concluded that no such prohibition existed. See para 122.

[12] James Leslie Brierly, *The Law of Nations: An Introduction to the International Law of Peace* (ed Sir Humphrey Waldock, Oxford: Clarendon Press, 1963), 53.

wrote that international law is binding simply because it is treated as binding, but he did not go much beyond that.[13] Had he done so, he might have examined the social and cultural infrastructure upon which international law rests and concluded that it is that infrastructure, rather than something endogenous to the rules, that makes *some* rules of international law binding on *some* states *some* of the time. The bindingness of an international rule, in other words, is not at its heart a *legal* question; 'compliance pull', so-called, is a function of the political, historical, and cultural infrastructure—'what is outside the formal machinery'—on which the functioning of law depends.

Causation poses a third difficulty. The issue arises in connection with customary international law but treaty law as well, to the extent that de facto textual modifications are attributed to *ex post* custom. The doctrine of *opinio juris* suggests that customary norms emerge only when a general and consistent practice of states is 'followed by them from a sense of legal obligation'.[14] From this premise, some international law scholars have embraced the notion that state conduct that is consistent with international law must necessarily have been caused by international law; the whole point of the doctrine, of course, is that the norm in question must motivate pertinent state behaviour. The state must act as it does out of a sense of juridical obligation. If it does not, the doctrine warns, a juridical norm cannot be distinguished from a norm motivated by considerations of courtesy, comity, convenience, or some other non-legal cause. Last year, Canada did not attack Mongolia; Guatemala did not attack New Zealand; Syria did not attack Luxembourg. States generally act consistently with the rule; is not that evidence that they accept the rule as binding law?

Of course, it is not. In the *North Sea Continental Shelf* cases, the ICJ proclaimed that pertinent states must 'feel that they are conforming to what amounts to a legal obligation'.[15] The states in question must have 'acted because they felt legally compelled to [act] in this way by reason of a rule of customary law obliging them to do so—especially considering that they might have been motivated by other obvious factors'.[16] Applying this test, the ICJ in 1996 declined to find a rule prohibiting the use of nuclear weapons. The argument had been made that the reason that nuclear weapons had not been used since 1945 was not that a legal rule prohibited their use, but that other factors, such as deterrence, were responsible for states' restraint. The Court, therefore, did 'not consider itself able to find' *opinio juris* with respect to the supposed customary rule.[17] Correlation is not causation, in international law or anywhere else.

[13] See H. L. A. Hart, *The Concept of Law* (2nd edn, Oxford: Clarendon Press, 1994), 216–20.

[14] Restatement (Third) of Foreign Relations Law, § 102 (1987). For a thoughtful comparison of custom in domestic and international contexts, see Eugene Kontorovich, 'Inefficient Customs In International Law' (2006) 48 *William and Mary Law Review* 859.

[15] *North Sea Continental Shelf (Federal Republic of Germany v. Denmark) (Federal Republic of Germany v. Netherlands)*, 20 Feb 1969, ICJ Rep 3, 44, para 77.

[16] *North Sea Continental Shelf*, 44–5, para 78.

[17] *Legality of the Threat or Use of Nuclear Weapons*, Advisory Opinion of 8 July 1996, ICJ Rep 1996, 226, 254, para 67.

III. Weaknesses in the Charter Rules

The shaky support provided by what is outside the formal machinery of international legal rules governing use of force has thus been exacerbated by the weakness of international law's secondary rules concerning consent, obligation, and causation. These difficulties are compounded by deficiencies in the wording of the rules themselves. Article 2(4) of the Charter, resurrected from the burnt timbers of the League of Nations Covenant, would hardly be drafted as it is had that provision been intended—as now widely interpreted—flatly and simply to prohibit any use of force by states. The reference to 'territorial integrity and political independence' plainly qualifies the prohibition; any use or threat of force that is not against the territorial integrity or political independence of a state is not prohibited. What the text excludes is anyone's guess. Perhaps use of force that is not intended to result in territorial acquisition is excluded from the prohibition, as some have suggested; however, this would have exempted, among other things, the Japanese attack on Pearl Harbor (had the Charter been in effect at the time), something probably not intended. Article 2(4) prohibits, in addition, other uses of force that are inconsistent with the Charter. Again, what actually is forbidden is baffling. The Charter espouses many inconsistent values—antinomies such as state sovereignty and human rights, peace and justice foremost among them—leaving one to conclude that use of force is forbidden, permitted, or perhaps even encouraged for opposite purposes.

Article 51 poses the first of two exceptions to the ban on force set out in Article 2(4). The article professes that neither Article 51 itself, nor anything else in the UN Charter, 'shall impair' the inherent right of a state to act in self-defence in response to an armed attack.[18] The implication is not only that an inherent right to self-defence existed prior to ratification of the UN Charter, but also that an inherent right continues to exist—unimpaired—after ratification. But Article 51 then proceeds to do precisely what it says it will not and cannot do. It begins by adding an explicit 'if': if an armed attack has not yet occurred, a state's inherent right to pre-empt that attack is removed.[19] Then, Article 51 adds another, implicit 'if': if the Security Council takes 'measures necessary to maintain international peace and security' following an armed attack, Article 51 not only impairs the inherent right of self-defence but in fact extinguishes it because the right exists only 'until' the Security Council takes such measures.[20] Lest any doubt exist that the right to self-defence is impaired, Article 51 asserts that it is the Security Council, not the state acting in its own self-defence,

[18] UN Charter, Art 51.

[19] 'Nothing in the present Charter shall impair the inherent right of individual or collective self defense if an armed attack occurs', UN Charter, Art 51.

[20] UN Charter, Art 51. The inherent right of self-defence may be impaired even if the Security Council takes no measures. The Council may conclude that peace and security are best maintained by

that prevails in the event of a conflict between the two. Article 51 further provides that the defending state's report to the Security Council 'shall not in any way affect the authority of the Security Council … to take at any time such action as it deems necessary…'[21] Thus, the right to self-defence, supposedly protected from impairment by the Charter, is permitted under the actual text of Article 51 to be impaired to the extent the Security Council chooses to impair it (but the right, of course, remains inherent).[22]

What, then, does the self-defence exception actually permit? Though the ICJ has never blessed the interpretation, Article 51 is now widely taken to permit the use of at least some pre-emptive force, when an attack is imminent. The text of the Charter and *travaux préparatoires* however, offer little support for this view. The text of Article 51 explicitly requires an 'armed attack' as a pre-condition for the use of defensive force. Its terms contrast, in their asymmetry, with the terms of Article 2(4). Article 2(4) prohibits not only the use of force but also the 'threat of' force. Article 51, however, makes no reference to the 'threat' of force; under the article, no threat of force (or of an armed attack, which presumably is different) by one state justifies the use of defensive force by another. The intent of the Charter's framers was to make acceptable uses of force readily distinguishable from unacceptable uses of force. Drawing the line at the precise point of an armed attack, an event the occurrence of which could be objectively established, served the purpose of eliminating uncertainty.[23]

Arguments that the Charter permits pre-emptive self-defence are unpersuasive. It has been suggested, for example, that the phrase 'if an armed attack occurs' does

doing nothing, in which case its purposeful inaction could have the effect of precluding a state from using force to defend itself.

[21] UN Charter, Art 51. A member state is required to 'accept and carry out' decisions of the Security Council: UN Charter, Art 25.

[22] Some of this is cursorily considered by the ICJ in a quick sweep over the language of Art 51. See *Military and Paramilitary Activities (Nicaragua v. US)*, 27 June 1986, ICJ Rep 14, 102–3, 105. But one is left to ask why it goes to the trouble: if a customary right is still available to states, as the *Nicaragua* Court assures us it is, what is the point of parsing the precise wording of Art 51? See Ian Brownie, *International Law and the Use of Force by States* (Oxford: Oxford University Press, 1963), 279.

[23] During the first three decades after the Charter's ratification, the US appears not to have challenged the proposition that Art 51 permits the use of force only in response to an actual armed attack. See eg 'The President's Proposal on the Middle East: Hearings Before the Senate Comm. on Foreign Relations and the Senate Comm. on Armed Services', 85th Cong 6–7, 27–8 (1957) (statement of US Secretary of State John Foster Dulles). During the Cuban Missile Crisis, US officials declined to rely upon Art 51, claiming instead that the quarantine of Cuba was justified under Art 52. See Abram Chayes, 'The Legal Case for U.S. Action on Cuba', *State Department Bulletin*, 19 Nov 1962, 763–5. In supporting the UN Security Council resolution that condemned Israel's 1981 raid on an Iraqi nuclear reactor, however, the US representative did not address the scope of self-defence under Art 51 or the claim of Israel that it acted in self-defence. See UN SCOR, 36th Sess, 2288th mtg at 3–5, S/PV.2288 (1981). In recent years, however, the US has come implicitly to question that proposition, and in the so-called 'Bush doctrine' the US explicitly rejected the notion that defensive force can be used only in response to an armed attack.

not mean 'only if an armed attack occurs'.[24] The suggestion is that an armed attack is but one of several factual bases that might permit defensive use of force. But the possibility of multiple, unspecified bases for the use of force other than armed attack would swallow up the 'armed attack' limit and render pointless the singularity of its enumeration. The argument that an attack actually begins before its physical manifestations occur must also be wrong. The contention is that the planning, organization, and logistical preparation are, properly conceived, part of the actual armed attack.[25] This argument would render chimerical the armed attack requirement as well, because an attack would then begin not with bullets and bombs but with pencils and paper, possibly deployed months or even years before actual hostilities. Nothing in the *travaux préparatoires* suggests that the plain language of Article 51 does not convey precisely the meaning that was intended.[26] 'The fair reading of Article 51 is persuasive,' Louis Henkin has written, 'that the Charter intended to permit unilateral use of force only in a very narrow and clear circumstance, in self-defense if an armed attack occurs.'[27]

The second exception to Article 2(4) is set out in Chapter VII: use of force is permitted when authorized by the Security Council. A fair reading of the text of the Charter discloses, however, that as drafted the Charter was intended to limit the authority of the Council to do so. The relevant provision is Article 39, which permits the Council to engage in enforcement actions only in specified circumstances, that is, upon the occasion of a threat to the peace, breach of the peace, or act of aggression. None of those terms is defined in the Charter. Article 39 authorizes the Council 'to maintain or restore international peace and security' upon finding one of those three factual predicates, suggesting that the Council does not have carte blanche to approve the use of force by one state against another for purely domestic threats that pose no risk to *international* peace and security. Council practice in recent years has increasingly transgressed those limits, however, leading some to insist that, as a 'living' document, it must be construed to keep pace with the times. Others—including representatives of China and Russia during the Council's consideration of the Syrian question—dispute that the Charter has been altered by practice, leaving the breadth of the Security Council exception, like that of the self-defence exception, very much up in the air.

[24] See Julius Stone, *Aggression and World Order: A Critique of United Nations Theories of Aggression* (Clark, NY: Lawbook Exchange, 1958), 44; Derek W. Bowett, *Self-Defense in International Law* (New York: Praeger, 1958), 187–92.

[25] See eg Sir Humphrey Waldock, 'The Regulation of the Use of Force by Individual States in International Law' (1952) 81 *Recueil des cours de l'Académie de droit international* 451, 498.

[26] See Ian Brownlie, *International Law and the Use of Force by States* (Oxford: Oxford University Press, 1963), 278.

[27] Louis Henkin, *How Nations Behave: Law and Foreign Policy* (2nd edn, Columbia, NY: Columbia University Press, 1979), 295. See also Brownlie, *International Law and the Use of Force by States*, 278 ('The view that Article 51 does not permit anticipatory self-defense is correct and ... arguments to the contrary are either unconvincing or based on inconclusive pieces of evidence'); 2 Lasa Oppenheim,

IV. Weakness in Compliance by Sovereign Equals

A final limitation on the effectiveness of these rules and institutions lies in the fatal deficiencies of the regime's enforcement entity, the Security Council, which became evident once again in its consideration of the crises in Libya and Syria. The Council proved, as it had in the earlier crisis concerning Iraq, that it is incapable of stopping a war—even when the matter is squarely before it. It was claimed that the Council's approval of Resolution 1973 finally breathed life into the 'responsibility to protect'. The intervention, it was said, fulfilled the promise of the Security Council as humanity's ultimate guarantor of human decency and reversed the unhappy precedent of Kosovo, where NATO, faced with likely Russian or Chinese vetoes, was forced to act without the Security Council's approval.

The facts, unfortunately, suggest otherwise. The Council approved use of force against Libya on 17 March 2011.[28] China, Russia, Brazil, India, and Germany abstained. The resolution authorized use of force for two and only two purposes: 'to protect civilians ... under threat of attack' and to enforce a no-fly zone.[29] On 28 March 2011

International Law: A Treatise (ed Hersh Lauterpacht, 7th edn, London: Longmans, 1952), 156 ('The Charter confines the right of armed self-defence to the case of an armed attack as distinguished from anticipated attack or from various forms of unfriendly conduct falling short of armed attack'). Philip Jessup stated: 'Article 51 of the Charter suggests a further limitation on the right of self-defense: it may be exercised only "if an armed attack occurs." ... This restriction in Article 51 very definitely narrows the freedom of action which states had under traditional law. A case could be made out for self-defense under the traditional law where the injury was threatened but no attack had yet taken place. Under the Charter, alarming military preparations by a neighboring state would justify a resort to the Security Council, but would not justify resort to anticipatory force by the state which believed itself threatened.' Phillip C. Jessup, *A Modern Law of Nations* (London: Read Books, 1948), 166.

[28] SC Res 1973, S/RES/1973 (17 Mar 2011).

[29] The Council did so in paras 4, 6, and 8 of Resolution 1973. Paragraph 4 provides as follows:

> Authorizes Member States that have notified the Secretary-General, acting nationally or through regional organizations or arrangements, and acting in cooperation with the Secretary-General, to take all necessary measures, notwithstanding paragraph 9 of resolution 1970 (2011), to protect civilians and civilian populated areas under threat of attack in the Libyan Arab Jamahiriya, including Benghazi, while excluding a foreign occupation force of any form on any part of Libyan territory, and requests the Member States concerned to inform the Secretary-General immediately of the measures they take pursuant to the authorization conferred by this paragraph which shall be immediately reported to the Security Council ...

Paragraph 6 provides as follows:

> Decides to establish a ban on all flights in the airspace of the Libyan Arab Jamahiriya in order to help protect civilians. ...

Paragraph 8 proves as follows:

> Authorizes Member States that have notified the Secretary-General and the Secretary-General of the League of Arab States, acting nationally or through regional organizations or arrangements, to

President Obama underscored the narrow limits on force permitted by the resolution.[30] The UN mandate, he said, was only 'to protect the Libyan people from immediate danger, and to establish a no-fly zone. ...'[31] 'If we tried to overthrow Qaddafi by force,' he said, 'our coalition would splinter.'[32] So it would be a mistake, he said, to try to 'bring down Qaddafi and usher in a new government.'[33]

Nonetheless, NATO military action came to be directed at precisely the objective that the president said the Security Council did not approve—regime change. Messrs Obama, Cameron, and Sarkozy publicly acknowledged as much. According to an op-ed piece co-authored by the three leaders on 14 April 2011, NATO's real objective was to ensure that 'the Libyan people can choose their own future.'[34] 'Qaddafi must go and go for good,' they wrote.[35] What NATO did in Libya was legally the equivalent of what NATO did in Kosovo—it acted without Security Council approval. Libya was not a repudiation of the Kosovo precedent—Libya was an affirmation of the Kosovo precedent. It was no answer to insist that getting rid of Gaddafi was necessary to protect civilians. Rightly or wrongly, the Security Council rejected that logic by refusing to authorize regime change, which again would have split the coalition. Rather, in waging a war for regime change in the face of Security Council opposition, the interveners transformed Libya into Kosovo. Both are now precedents involving the use of force without Security Council approval, in violation of the Charter.

One reason for the Council's dysfunctionality lies in the UN's professed reliance upon the principle of sovereign equality. As George Kennan pointed out, the notion of sovereign equality is a myth; disparities among states 'make a mockery' of the concept.[36] Applied to states, the proposition that all are equal is belied by evidence everywhere that they are not—neither in their power, nor in their wealth, nor in their respect for international order or for human rights. Yet the principle of sovereign equality animates the entire structure of the UN—and disables it from effectively addressing emerging crises, such as murderous human rights violations, that derive precisely from the presupposition of sovereign equality. Treating states as equals prevents treating individuals as equals. If Yugoslavia, Libya, and Syria truly

take all necessary measures to enforce compliance with the ban on flights imposed by paragraph 6 above, as necessary, and requests the States concerned in cooperation with the League of Arab States to coordinate closely with the Secretary General on the measures they are taking to implement this ban, including by establishing an appropriate mechanism for implementing the provisions of paragraphs 6 and 7 above.

[30] 'Obama's Remarks on Libya,' *New York Times*, 28 Mar 2011, available at <http://www.nytimes.com/2011/03/29/us/politics/29prexy-text.html?pagewanted=all>.

[31] 'Obama's Remarks on Libya.' [32] 'Obama's Remarks on Libya.'

[33] 'Obama's Remarks on Libya.'

[34] Barack Obama, David Cameron, and Nicholas Sarkozy, 'Libya's Pathway to Peace,' *New York Times*, 14 Apr 2011.

[35] 'Libya's Pathway to Peace.'

[36] George Kennan, *Around the Cragged Hill: A Personal and Political Philosophy* (London: W.W. Norton, 1993), 89.

enjoyed a right to non-intervention equal to that of every other state, then their citizens would have been denied human rights equal to those of individuals in other states, because their human rights could be vindicated only by intervention. The irrationality of treating states as equals was brought home as never before when it emerged that the will of the Security Council concerning the Libya intervention would be determined by the votes of Bosnia and Herzegovina, Colombia, and Gabon—nations whose representatives sat side by side and exercised an equal voice and vote with those of Brazil, Germany, and India. The equality principle permitted two of those rotating council members to cast a de facto veto (by denying a majority the critical ninth vote necessary for potential victory). Granting a de jure veto to the permanent five was the Charter's intended antidote to unbridled egalitarianism. But it did not work. The de jure veto simultaneously under-corrected and over-corrected for the problem, lowering the US and China to the level of France and raising France above India (which did not even hold a rotating seat on the Council during the Iraq debate). Yet the de jure veto did nothing to dilute the rotating members' de facto veto. The upshot has been a Security Council that reflects the real world's power structure with the accuracy of a fun-house mirror.

V. The Collapse of the Charter's Use of Force Regime

A shaky sub-legal infrastructure; undeveloped secondary rules concerning consent; obligation, and causation; confused and contradictory textual rules; and process grounded upon misconceived principles of sovereign equality—these elements reinforce one another and, together, help to explain why rules and institutions that regulate the use of force have failed to meet the hopes of their framers, in several respects.

First, and most notably, the rules and institutions were intended 'to save succeeding generations from the scourge of war'.[37] This is the UN's first and most prominent objective, set out as its first goal in the Charter's preamble. But the Charter's use-of-force rules have become, in Michael Walzer's blunt assessment, 'paper' rules, not working rules.[38] The record, alas, is indisputable. As the Secretary-General's High-Level Panel on Threats, Challenges and Change put it, 'for the first 44 years of the United Nations,

[37] Preamble, UN Charter.

[38] Michael Walzer, *Just and Unjust Wars: A Moral Argument with Historical Illustrations* (4th edn, New York: Basic Books, 2006), xxi.

Member States often violated [the Charter] rules and used military force literally hundreds of times, with a paralysed Security Council passing very few Chapter VII resolutions and Article 51 rarely providing credible cover.'[39] By one count, the Panel said, from 1945 to 1989 'force was employed 200 times, and by another count, 680 times'.[40] Other studies have reported similar results.[41]

How, then, are these attitudinal divisions and the breakdown of use-of-force rules reflected in the international legal system? How ought paper rules to be described in the language of international law? Let me emphasize the word *described*. The task is to describe, not prescribe. The question is not what the rules *should* be, not whether international law is really law, not whether the Charter's desiccated use-of-force rules are in some moral sense good or bad, not whether there is, or was at some point, a moral obligation to obey those rules, and not what has become of other sub-regimes, such as the *jus in bello*. The issue is one of analytic clarity and relates, ultimately, to international law's rule of recognition: in the light of the prevailing international legal standard by which legal rules are recognized, is it accurate to continue to describe these rules of the *jus ad bellum* as law?

I think not. The international legal system is consent-based.[42] Given the established view that states are bound only to rules to which they consent by 'their own free will', the status of a putative rule is an empirical question. In the light of all the evidence, states' words, as well as their deeds, is it reasonable to conclude that they have consented to the supposed rule? No. When a rule has been violated many times by many states over many years, it is sensible to suppose that they do not consent to it, and that it is not international law. This does not mean that some policymakers in some states are not influenced by the rule, or that the rule is not honoured in some regions. But it does mean that a tipping point has been reached, that the quantum of violation has become too great, and that the international community as a whole no longer views the rule as a binding rule of international law. That is what happened to the first treaty banning war, the Kellogg–Briand Pact.[43] This, sadly, is what also

[39] Secretary-General's High-Level Panel on Threats, Challenges and Change, 'A More Secure World: Our Shared Responsibility', Report of the Secretary General's High-Level Panel on Threats, Challenges and Change, A/59/565 (2 Dec 2004), para 186.

[40] 'A More Secure World', 140.

[41] eg Arthur M. Weisburd, *Use of Force: The Practice of States Since World War II* (University Park, PA: Penn State University Press, 1997) (Weisburd counted 100 interstate wars between 1945 and 1997); see also Kalevi J. Holsti, *The State, War, and the State of War* (Cambridge: Cambridge University Press, 1996), 24 (Holsti counted 38 between 1945 and 1995); Meredith Reid Sarkees, 'The Correlates of War Data on War: An Update to 1997' (2000) 18 *Conflict Management and Peace Science* 123, 135 (the Correlates of War Project counted 23 between 1945 and 1997); Herbert K. Tillema, 'Risks of Battle and the Deadliness of War: International Armed Conflicts: 1945–1991', unpublished manuscript, 16 Apr 1996 (quoted in Peter Wallensteen, 'New Actors, New Issues, New Actions' in Peter Wallensteen (ed), *International Intervention: New Norms in the Post-Cold War Era?* (1997), 5, 6 (Tillema counted 690 overt foreign military interventions between 1945 and 1996); Carter Centre, *Conflict Resolution Update: Update on World Conflicts* (Uppsala: Uppsala University Press, 1998) (identifies 30 'major ongoing wars' today).

[42] See nn 9–11 and accompanying text.

[43] General Treaty Providing for the Renunciation of War (Kellogg–Briand Pact), Art 1, 27 Aug 1928 (2 Bevans 732) ((1929) UKTS 29, Cmd 3410).

happened to the use-of-force rules of the UN Charter. Walzer sums it up well: the legalist paradigm 'is more restrictive than the judgments we actually make'.[44]

I have addressed elsewhere various objections that have been raised to this view.[45] Three in particular are worth revisiting.

The first is that a rule of international law is not diminished but rather is confirmed and strengthened when violation of the rule is coupled with a claim of compliance. The ICJ made this argument in justifying its conclusion in the 1984 *Nicaragua* case.[46] 'If a State acts in a way prima facie incompatible with a recognized rule,' the court said, 'but defends its conduct by appealing to exceptions or justifications contained within the rule itself, then *whether or not the State's conduct is in fact justifiable on that basis*, the significance of that attitude is to confirm rather than to weaken the rule.'[47]

It is true that what a state says is entitled to some weight. Because the question is whether the state consents (or continues to consent) to the rule in question, all probative evidence of its intent must be considered. But it makes no sense to accord a state's words *dispositive* effect in all circumstances, ignoring all evidence to the contrary. A state's conduct counts, too, and when a state's words and deeds conflict, what the state does would seem to be more persuasive evidence of what it believes than what it says. States' words—even assuming that they represent an 'appeal' to the rule, which they frequently do not[48]—need to be taken with a grain

[44] Walzer, *Just and Unjust Wars*, 72.

[45] See generally Michael J. Glennon, *The Fog of Law: Pragmatism, Security and International Law* (Stanford, CA: Stanford University Press, 2010). See also Michael J. Glennon, 'How International Rules Die' (2005) 93 *Georgetown Law Journal* 939; Michael J. Glennon, 'Sometimes A Great Notion' (2003) 27 *Woodrow Wilson Quarterly* 45; Michael J. Glennon, 'Why the Security Council Failed' (2003) *Foreign Affairs* May/June, all of which I draw upon for this chapter.

[46] *Military and Paramilitary Activities in and against Nicaragua (Nicaragua v. US)*, 27 June 1986, ICJ Rep 1986, 14.

[47] *Nicaragua*, para 186 (emphasis added).

[48] See generally John Mearsheimer, *Why Leaders Lie: The Truth About Lying in International Politics* (Oxford: Oxford University Press, 2012). It is often claimed that US policymakers justify non-compliance with the Charter's use of force rules by appeal to the Charter itself. In fact, numerous statements of US officials over the last decade, in Thomas Franck's words, 'boldly proclaim a new policy that openly repudiates the Article 2(4) obligation.' See Thomas M. Franck, 'Future Implications of the Iraq Conflict: What Happens Now? The United Nations After Iraq' (2003) 97 *American Journal of International Law* 607, 608. Eg the national security strategy statement issued by the executive branch in Sept 2002, was said by John Ikenberry to 'render international norms of self-defense—enshrined by Article 51 of the UN Charter—almost meaningless.' See G. John Ikenberry, 'America's Imperial Ambition' (2002) 81 *Foreign Affairs* 44, 51. On 10 Nov 2002, Secretary of State Colin Powell said that the US would not consider itself bound by the Security Council's decision concerning Iraq, even though it expected Iraq to comply with the Council's decisions. Nothing in the Charter exempts the US from the obligation to comply but imposes an obligation upon other countries to do so. Powell said on 26 Jan 2003: 'We continue to reserve our sovereign right to take military action against Iraq alone or in a coalition of the willing.' Michael R. Gordon, 'Threats and Responses: Strategy; Serving Notice of a New U.S., Poised to Hit First and Alone', *New York Times*, 27 Jan 2003, p A1. Of course, states' 'sovereign right' to take military action is limited by Art 2(4) of the Charter; if it is reserved, the limitation of the Charter does not apply. In his 2003 State of the Union Address, President Bush said, 'The course of this nation does not depend on the decisions of others.' Michael R. Gordon, 'State of the Union: The Iraq

of salt; it would often, indeed, be naive to accept states' own explanations of their motives and beliefs as the final word. Words prove only so much. In the *North Sea Continental Shelf* cases, the ICJ opined that a rule can be 'carried out in such a way' as to indicate whether a state actually believes that the rule is obligatory.[49] Many international law scholars have been among the first to question states' self-serving justifications in other contexts. Elsewhere in its *Nicaragua* judgment the Court was more realistic. 'The mere fact that States declare their recognition of certain rules,' it said, 'is not sufficient for the Court to consider these as being part of customary international law, and as applicable as such to those States.'[50] If a state flouts a rule, it is more sensible to conclude that its policymakers disagree with the rule than to assume that their 'cheap talk' authoritatively reveals their deeper motives. As the WikiLeaks cables confirm on issue after issue, what policymakers say publicly is not always consistent with what they in fact believe or do.[51]

The second objection is that the notion of desuetude gives unjustified, asymmetric weight to instances of non-compliance. An accurate evaluation of a rule's effect, it is argued, must examine not only evidence of non-compliance but also evidence of compliance. One cannot judge the 'vitality of a law by looking only at its failures.... A better test is whether state decision-makers continue to accept it as a general standard of accepted conduct powerful enough to constrain state behavior.'[52]

The concerns underpinning this objection are valid but misdirected. Desuetude, as I refer to it, *does* reflect both sides of the ledger. All pertinent evidence of what 'state decision-makers continue to accept' *is* considered, for whatever that evidence might be worth. Sometimes the evidence in question will be decision-makers' approving words. When words and deeds conflict, however, it is necessary to decide which evidence is more probative. For the reasons indicated previously, deeds often seem more persuasive than contradictory speech. Sometimes that evidence will be deeds—behaviour that leads their state to act in a manner consistent with a given rule. Obviously that evidence, too, must be evaluated. But in the light of the number

Issue; Bush Enlarges Case for War by Linking Iraq With Terrorists', *New York Times*, 29 Jan 2003, p A1. But the Charter has it that the authority of a state to use armed force depends, absent an armed attack, on the decision of the Security Council; the course of the nation does in that sense depend upon the decision of the Security Council. President Bush, in his 2004 State of the Union Address, said: 'America will never seek a permission slip to defend the security of our country.' David E. Sanger, 'State of the Union: Diplomacy; Emphasis on Iraq Remains, but From a Different Angle', *New York Times*, 21 Jan 2004 available at <http://www.nytimes.com/2004/01/21/us/state-of-the-union-diplomacy-emphasis-on-iraq-remains-but-from-a-different-angle.html>. But again, only when an armed attack occurs does the Charter permit a state to act without permission.

49 *North Sea Continental Shelf*, 20 Feb 1969, ICJ Rep 1969, 3, para 77.

50 See *Military and Paramilitary Activities*, para 184.

51 Scott Shane and Andrew W. Lehren, 'Leaked Cables Offer a Raw Look Inside U.S. Diplomacy: Dispatches Chronicle Threats and Tensions', *New York Times*, 29 Nov 2010, p 1.

52 David Wippman, 'War on Terror Symposium: The Nine Lives of 2(4)' (2007) 16 *Minnesota Journal of International Law* 387.

of officials involved in decisions to comply or not to comply and in the light of the multifariousness of causes that invariably animate such decisions—and which can create an illusion of compliance—it must be acknowledged that evidence of behaviour consistent with a rule is seldom as probative as evidence of clear-cut violation. Behaviour that is consistent with a rule creates only a possibility that a rule worked. Violation establishes to a certainty that it did not. Put another way, two propositions on each side of the ledger are at issue: first, there are numerous instances of non-compliance; and, secondly, there might be instances of compliance. The first proposition is falsifiable. The second is not.

A third objection is related but slightly different. Even if there exist more instances of non-compliance than of compliance, it is suggested, that negative balance ought not necessarily be taken as evidence of desuetude. A given legal rule might have some effect upon behaviour without necessarily carrying the day. That a rule has been violated, even frequently violated, does not mean that the rule has no effect and has fallen into desuetude. Although its effects might not rise to the level of compliance, the salutary effects of such a rule might not be non-existent. Too broad a view of desuetude could be destructive of rules that are suboptimal but still beneficial.

This third objection raises, in effect, a category question. Is it sensible to categorize as non-law a rule the effects of which do not meet a certain minimal level? It is true that labelling such a rule as 'no longer law' could induce further deviant behaviour. The objection seems to suggest, however, that no amount of non-compliance should ever trigger a not-law categorization if any possibility exists that the decaying rule continues to exert even a scintilla of compliance pull. It is possible, for example, even after the massive flouting of the Kellogg–Briand Pact during the Second World War that the Pact continued to generate some salutary effect. But the question is whether it ought still to have been considered binding law. To suggest as much would seemingly disregard overwhelming evidence, in the form of states' deeds, that they no longer considered the Pact to be obligatory. It is worth recalling that the traditional methodology of customary international law does not counsel that evidence of non-compliance eroding customary rule be disregarded so as to preserve potential vestigial effects. What is at issue in the context of desuetude is something virtually identical—the replacement of an existing rule not with another substantive rule but with, in effect, a null-set rule that triggers application of the freedom principle. The reasons that support recognition of a tipping point that gives way to a new substantive rule also support recognition of a tipping point that gives way to no rule.

It therefore makes no sense to engage in what Michael Walzer has called 'utopian quibbling' over the breadth of the self-defence exception to a prophylactic ban on use of force that does not exist.[53] Whether Article 51 requires an actual 'armed attack' or merely an imminent threat of attack, whether it permits preventive or

[53] Michael Walzer, *Just and Unjust Wars: A Moral Argument with Historical Illustrations* (4th edn, New York: Basic Books, 2006), xx–xxi.

pre-emptive force, whether it permits humanitarian intervention or cyberwarfare, whether the acquisition of nuclear weapons provides *casus bellum*—these are utopian quibbles for Walzer, as they are for me, and compel those interested in realistic answers to look elsewhere.

VI. Conclusion

'Elsewhere', unfortunately, has too often meant misguided neo-naturalist efforts to find other ways to impose effective restraints, including a circular concept of peremptory norms, retreat to alternate, tautological systems of validation (eg morality and legitimacy), and resort to a vacuous 'responsibility to protect'. As with other pre-empirical naturalist schools, however, these suffer from an indeterminacy, subjectivity, and parochialism that undermine the possibility of shoring up those rules or institutions with a universalist justification of the sort to which supporters claim adherence. A realistic effort to replace paper rules with working rules would begin with an examination of the background conditions needed to make rules work and with a slow, patient, national, and international effort to create conditions that now are lacking. To leapfrog that stage yet again by formulating new rules and institutions not anchored on solid geopolitical ground will be, yet again, to build legalist castles in the air—objects for useful moralization but for little else. Moralists will, as always, regard such realism as illiberal; George Kennan, as usual, got it right. 'Whatever is realistic in concept,' he said, 'and founded in an endeavor to see both ourselves and others as we really are, cannot be illiberal.'[54] The beginning of progress in forging international rules and institutions that manage the use of force effectively is to see ourselves not as we wish we were but as we really are.

[54] George Kennan, *American Diplomacy* (Chicago, IL: University of Chicago Press, 1984), 107.

CHAPTER 4

THE CONTINUED RELEVANCE OF ESTABLISHED RULES AND INSTITUTIONS RELATING TO THE USE OF FORCE

JAMES CRAWFORD
ROWAN NICHOLSON

I. Introduction

In 1864, William Tecumseh Sherman—early exponent of 'hard' or total war, major-general, and commander of the amassed armies of the Union—ordered the people of Atlanta to leave the city and burned its government buildings to the ground. Before doing so, he rebuffed a plea by its mayor. His words echo the Melian Dialogue of two thousand years earlier and ring on today in the ears of international lawyers: 'War is cruelty and you cannot refine it ... You might as well appeal against the thunder-storm as against these terrible hardships of war. They are inevitable'.[1] A necessary implication is that war is beyond the reach of effective legal rules.

Yet neither all wars nor all their hardships are inevitable. It may be that war can never be entirely eliminated. But we do have some means of 'refining' or even averting it, and one of them is the international law on the use of force (*jus ad bellum*) as it has developed since 1945. That was the year of the United Nations Charter, which provides that 'Member States shall refrain in their international relations from the threat or use of force against the territorial integrity or political independence of any State, or in any other manner inconsistent with the Purposes of the United Nations' (Art 2(4)), subject to the right of self-defence (Art 51) and the system of collective security authorized by the Security Council (Chapter VII).[2] In this chapter, we will argue that this body of law and the institutions connected with it remain relevant despite two lines of critique, articulated in especially strong terms in a series of publications by Michael Glennon. The first is the realist argument that the rules on the use of force are ineffective. Distinct from this is an argument from within international law: that the prohibition on the use of force has been breached so often that it no longer amounts to international law at all. We will argue that there is no basis for that conclusion and that, though the rules may not always be optimally effective, there is reason to believe that they have contributed to a sustained decline in interstate armed conflict since 1945.

II. The Realist Critique

Glennon is among those who argue that in 'the realm of "high politics," where the issues are core questions of state security and survival, structural forces, which produce power disparities and value conflict ..., limit the impact of legal rules on state behavior'.[3] States may sometimes *seem* to comply with the rules on the use of

[1] Letter from Major-General W. T. Sherman to Mayor J. M. Calhoun, 12 Sept 1864, collected in *The War of the Rebellion: A Compilation of the Official Records of the Union and Confederate Armies*, series I vol XXXIX part 2, available at <http://ebooks.library.cornell.edu/m/moawar/waro_fulltext.html>. The Melian Dialogue of 416 BCE is recorded in Thucydides, *The History of the Peloponnesian War* (trans R. Crawley and rev R. C. Feetham, Avon, CT: Cardavon Press, 1974), book 5, 293–9. Athens insisted that the Melians not remain neutral in the Second Peloponnesian War and responded to their pleas by ruling out in advance any talk of right or justice: 'you know as well as we do that right, as the world goes, is only in question between equals in power, while the strong do what they can and the weak suffer what they must'. This similarly implies that war, at least between unequals, is beyond the reach of effective legal rules.

[2] Charter of the United Nations, 26 June 1945, 892 UNTS 119.

[3] Michael J. Glennon, 'How International Rules Die' (2005) 93 *Georgetown Law Journal* 939, 987.

force, but perhaps that is only because the rules happen to coincide for the time being with the underlying geopolitical interests that *really* shape their behaviour.[4] Andreas Paulus sums up this 'realist' approach to international law:

> when the basic interests of states are at stake, in 'high politics,' international law is considered marginal to international politics. In this optic, international law is merely a superstructure, a Marxian *Überbau* that masks the real forces of international law—above all, power and military capabilities. This 'search for the actual laws' in political reality, not legal norms, characterizes realism. At the heart of international relations, it is power relationships that count: at the personal level, at the state level, at the interstate level.[5]

Realism has a certain intellectual elegance and has contributed useful insights to international relations and even to international law.[6] As Paulus comments, 'We need legalists who do not build utopias that are either irrelevant or turn into nightmares, but who look at the chances of legal prescriptions in the real world'.[7] In the context of the *jus ad bellum*, realism is especially alluring. Hans Morgenthau, founding father of modern realist thought in international relations, accepted that 'to deny that international law exists at all as a system of binding legal rules flies in the face of all evidence' in that it routinely governs such matters of low politics as 'the limits of territorial jurisdiction, the rights of vessels in foreign waters, and the status of diplomatic representatives'.[8] But in matters directly concerning political and especially military power, Morgenthau thought international law was ineffective.

The realist critique has two intertwined strands: a jurisprudential argument about the nature of international law and a practical one about whether it is effective. The jurisprudential argument draws on the debate about whether international law (or some subset of it, such as the law on the use of force) constitutes 'law' in the strict sense of H. L. A. Hart or Joseph Raz. Hart argued that 'the absence of an international legislature, courts with compulsory jurisdiction, and centrally organized sanctions' in international law 'means that the rules for states resemble that simple form of social structure, consisting only of primary rules of obligation, which ... we

[4] This section draws on the discussion of the realist critique of international law more generally in James Crawford, 'Chance, Order, Change: The Course of International Law' (2013) 365 *Recueil des Cours de l'Académie de Droit International*, ch 1.

[5] Andreas Paulus, 'Realism and International Law: Two Optics in Need of Each Other' (2002) 96 *American Society of International Law Proceedings* 269, 269. See further other contributions in the same volume.

[6] eg Eyal Benvenisti and George Downs, 'The Empire's New Clothes: Political Economy and the Fragmentation of International Law' (2007) 60 *Stanford Law Review* 595; Jack Goldsmith and Eric Posner, *The Limits of International Law* (New York: Oxford University Press, 2005); Lloyd Gruber, *Ruling the World: Power Politics and the Rise of Supranational Institutions* (Princeton, NJ: Princeton University Press, 2000); Stephen Krasner, *Sovereignty: Organized Hypocrisy* (Princeton, NJ: Princeton University Press, 1999); Stephen Krasner et al, 'Symposium on International Regimes' (1982) 36 *International Organization* 185.

[7] Paulus, 'Realism and International Law', 272.

[8] Hans J. Morgenthau, *Politics among Nations: The Struggle for Power and Peace* (2nd edn, New York: Alfred A. Knopf, 1954), 251. See also Hans J. Morgenthau, 'Positivism, Functionalism and International Law' (1944) 34 *American Journal of International Law* 271.

are accustomed to contrast with a developed legal system'.[9] In other words: international law suffers from inherent weaknesses as compared with domestic law that might lead us to question whether it truly constitutes law at all. This line of thinking has been largely accepted by some international lawyers, including Hersch Lauterpacht, who saw the international law of his time as a contingent and unsatisfactory stage in a transition to something more like domestic law.[10]

It also informs much of Glennon's critique. He adopts a 'definition of international law grounded upon nonviolation as a test of obligation': a norm is obligatory not 'because states have somehow consented to be obliged' but only if 'the costs of violation outweigh the benefits for nearly all of the states nearly all of the time, so violations are rare'.[11] This is a step beyond Otto von Bismarck, who only thought treaties ceased to be binding when they came 'in conflict with the struggle for existence'.[12] It is as confused and unreal as it sounds. The 'costs of violation' have nothing whatsoever to do with whether particular rules, such as those on the use of force and, notably, treaties, are obligatory as a matter of law. As a matter of practice, the rules on the use of force form part of and underpin a larger system of law—on international investment, trade, transportation, and so on—that states and other international actors treat as binding. They are reaffirmed routinely by the Security Council[13] and have been described by the International Court of Justice as 'a cornerstone of the United Nations Charter'.[14] Yet Glennon's approach seems to deny even the possibility of analysing international law as a system with secondary rules of obligation, instead dealing with each situation ad hoc. He endorses the view that 'if you want to know what the law is, ... look at it from the perspective of the person contemplating violation', which 'will vary from one person (or state) to another, from one norm to another, and from one context to another'.[15] It is hard

[9] H. L. A. Hart, *The Concept of Law* (2nd edn, Oxford: Oxford University Press, 1994), 214. Cf Joseph Raz, *Practical Reason and Norms* (London: Hutchinson, 1975), 35–48.

[10] See eg Hersch Lauterpacht, 'Westlake and Present Day International Law' (1925) in Elihu Lauterpacht (ed), *International Law, being the Collected Papers of Hersch Lauterpacht*, vol 2 (Cambridge: Cambridge University Press, 1975), 401; Hersch Lauterpacht, '*A Modern Law of Nations: An Introduction* by P. C. Jessup' (review) (1947) 24 *British Yearbook of International Law* 502; Hersch Lauterpacht, *The Function of Law in the International Community* (Oxford: Oxford University Press, 1933; repr 2011), 440. Cf Martti Koskenniemi, 'Introduction' in ibid, xlii–xliii; Martti Koskenniemi, *The Gentle Civiliser of Nations: The Rise and Fall of International Law 1870–1960* (Cambridge: Cambridge University Press, 2002), ch 5.

[11] Glennon, 'How International Rules Die', 952–3.

[12] 'All treaties between great states cease to be binding when they come in conflict with the struggle for existence': attributed to Bismarck (1815–98), George Seldes, *The Great Thoughts* (rev edn, New York: Ballentine Books, 1996).

[13] eg even without accounting for indirect references and references to previous resolutions, in the 12 months from Apr 2012 to Mar 2013 the Security Council expressly reaffirmed the rules on the use of force in SC Res 2046, 2 May 2012 (on Sudan); SC Res 2047, 17 May 2012 (on Sudan); SC Res 2074, 14 Nov 2012 (on Bosnia and Herzegovina); SC Res 2075, 16 Nov 2012 (on Sudan); SC Res 2086, 21 Jan 2013 (on peacekeeping operations); and SC Res 2098, 28 Mar 2013 (on the Democratic Republic of the Congo).

[14] *Armed Activities on the Territory of the Congo (DRC v. Uganda)* ICJ Rep 2005, 168, 223.

[15] Glennon, 'How International Rules Die', 952.

to imagine a state taking this position before an international court, or even in a diplomatic note.

More generally, jurisprudential debates about the nature of international law can tell us only so much about the reality of how states behave. The classification as 'law' of any system, including international law, does not predetermine its effectiveness or the effectiveness of specific rules: that should be clear from the many ineffective domestic systems that are still treated as 'law'. Let us turn, then, to the practical question of whether the rules on the use of force really *are* ineffective. We will then look at two factors said to constrain their effectiveness.

A. Whether the Charter Rules are Effective in Practice

Throughout the 19th century, the prevailing view in international law was that resort to war was an attribute of statehood and that sovereignty could be acquired by conquest.[16] This began to change in the first half of the 20th century: the League of Nations Covenant of 1919 imposed procedural constraints on resort to war (while retaining the older view that resort to it was permissible), and the parties to the Kellogg–Briand Pact of 1928 purported to renounce it entirely.[17] Realists such as Morgenthau were influenced by the failure of these agreements to prevent the Second World War.[18]

Their successors argue that the Charter rules, which redoubled the efforts of the Kellogg–Briand Pact, have similarly failed to have effect. They might point to a report by a UN panel in 2004: 'for the first 44 years of the United Nations, Member States often violated [the Charter] rules and used military force literally hundreds of times, with a paralysed Security Council passing very few Chapter VII resolutions and Article 51 only rarely providing credible cover'.[19]

[16] Sovereignty was acquired either under a subsequent peace treaty effectively imposed on the defeated state or by reason of the complete disappearance (*debellatio*) of a defeated state, such as the South African Republic at the end of the Boer War. See further: Ian Brownlie, *International Law and the Use of Force by States* (Oxford: Clarendon Press, 1963), 3–50; Christine Gray, *International Law and the Use of Force* (3rd edn, Oxford: Oxford University Press, 2008); James Crawford, *Brownlie's Principles of Public International Law* (8th edn, Oxford: Oxford University Press, 2013), 744–74.

[17] Covenant of the League of Nations, 28 June 1919, 225 CTS 195; General Treaty for the Renunciation of War as an Instrument of National Policy (Kellogg–Briand Pact), 27 Aug 1928, 94 LNTS 57.

[18] Though the Kellogg–Briand Pact was not totally ignored: the US invoked it in relation to hostilities between China and the Soviet Union in 1929, the conflict between China and Japan in the 1930s, and the Leticia dispute between Peru and Ecuador in 1933; and the League of Nations Assembly cited it as late as 1939 in condemning the Soviet invasion of Finland: see Crawford, *Brownlie's Principles*, 744–5 and sources cited therein.

[19] Secretary-General's High-Level Panel on Threats, Challenges and Change, 'A More Secure World: Our Shared Responsibility', A/59/565 (2 Dec 2004), para 286. The report tempers this by adding that 'Since the end of the cold war, however, the yearning for an international system governed by the rule of law has grown'.

But it is—to put it mildly—far from clear that the Charter system has gone the way of the League. There has been a sustained decline in both the incidence and severity of state-based armed conflict. Steven Pinker has collated evidence from numerous sources. There have been no wars between 'great powers' since 1945 except perhaps the Korean War, in which both China and the US participated but where the latter was authorized by the Security Council.[20] Nor has any widely recognized state ceased to exist through 'conquest', compared with the 22 that were occupied or absorbed in the first half of the 20th century.[21] Indeed, between 1946 and 1975, only 12 'interstate territorial aggressions' resulted in *any* major change to state borders, including cases where entirely new states were established (eg Bangladesh). Russia's purported annexation of Crimea in 2014 may be the first case since 1975.[22] Genuinely interstate wars, with a few notable exceptions such as the 1991 and 2003 wars against Iraq and the 1998–2000 war between Ethiopia and Eritrea, have almost vanished since the end of the Cold War. It might be objected that the number of notionally civil wars—some of them 'internationalized' by foreign intervention—has increased since 1945. But even if we include them (and not all civil wars involve breaches of the Charter), all wars together have become less severe: battle deaths in state-based armed conflict have dwindled by more than 90 per cent, from about 500,000 per year in the late 1940s to about 30,000 per year in the early 2000s.[23]

Of course, this does not demonstrate any causal relationship with the Charter rules. Since states are not unitary entities and we often lack evidence of their internal processes, it can be difficult to determine what ultimately influences their behaviour.[24]

[20] Steven Pinker, *The Better Angels of Our Nature* (London: Penguin, 2011), 302. Whether China was a 'great power' at this time is debatable.

[21] With the arguable exception of the 'conquest' of South Vietnam by the North: Pinker, *The Better Angels*, 303.

[22] This chapter was drafted before the events in Crimea and eastern Ukraine. Mark Zacher identifies the following 12 'major changes' resulting from 'interstate territorial aggressions' since 1946: Pakistan in part of Kashmir (1947–8); the creation of Israel (1948); India in Goa (1961); Indonesia in West New Guinea (1961–2); China in Aksai Chin (1962); Israel in the West Bank, the Gaza Strip, and the Golan Heights (1967); the creation of Bangladesh (1971); Iran in islands in the Strait of Hormuz (1971); China in the Paracel Islands (1974); Turkey in northern Cyprus (1974); Morocco in Western Sahara (1975); and the reunification of Vietnam (1975): Mark Zacher, 'The Territorial Integrity Norm: International Boundaries and the Use of Force' (2001) 55 *International Organization* 215; see also Pinker, *The Better Angels*, 303 fn 145, 312–13. This is an ill-assorted list from the perspective of international law; at least half of the cases involving territorial acquisition do not begin to qualify as 'conquest', eg West New Guinea, as to which see James Crawford, *The Creation of States in International Law* (2nd edn, Oxford: Clarendon Press, 2006), 555–6. Other cases, such as Iraq's short-lived 'conquest' of Kuwait and Indonesia's purported annexation of East Timor (discussed in more detail later), have since been reversed.

[23] Pinker, *The Better Angels*, 363. Pinker's figures are based on the armed conflict dataset from the Uppsala Conflict Data Project and Peace Research Institute of Oslo: see Human Security Report Project, *Human Security Brief 2007* (Vancouver: 2007), based on data from B. Lacina and N. P. Gleditsch, 'Monitoring Trends in Global Combat: A New Dataset in Battle Deaths' (2005) 21 *European Journal of Population* 145, updated in 2010 by T. Cooper.

[24] Gray, *International Law and the Use of Force*, 26.

A number of factors have been cited to explain the decline of war since 1945, including the nuclear deterrent, democracy, trade, membership of international organizations (including the UN), the vastly greater expense of modern means of warfare, and underlying attitudinal shifts.[25] The decline could be due to some or all of these factors. But it has been sustained over time and is plainly not a mere statistical aberration. In the circumstances it is plausible to suggest that it could be at least partly due to a progressively embedded norm of state behaviour, reflected in rules of international law, against the use of force other than for self-defence or collective security. As Christine Gray remarks, this explanation for the general reluctance of states to use force is consistent with what they actually say:

> Given that in fact they choose to use this language to explain their behaviour and to respond to that of others, anyone involved in any way in advising states or in assessing their actions will have to be able to engage in this discourse. Simple assertions that this use of language is mere cynical manipulation of the rules, and no more than *ex post facto* rationalization for actions reached on other grounds, are not justified in the absence of empirical evidence that this is in fact the case, and such assertions are no more plausible than the opposite version that states are in fact influenced by the law. Of course, it is common for states to offer other justifications as well; it is rare for a state to use the language of international law exclusively…but with only a tiny number of exceptions they take care to offer a legal argument for their use of force.[26]

In any event, one thing is clear from the evidence since 1945: there is no empirical basis for the view that the Charter system has failed to arrest the unlawful use of force. On the contrary, the most remarkable feature of international relations under the Charter system is the comparative rarity of interstate armed conflict when compared with previous periods.

It is certainly possible to identify specific breaches of the rules on the use of force, but in itself that proves little. The global homicide rate (8.8 per 100,000 persons per year) is far higher than the global rate of battle deaths in state-based armed conflicts (about 0.5 per 100,000 persons per year, not necessarily resulting from uses of force that are unlawful under the Charter).[27] But the fact that some individuals commit murder does not prove that domestic laws against it are ineffective. Equally, the fact that some states may unlawfully use force cannot in itself demonstrate the ineffectiveness of the Charter rules.

[25] See further the discussion in Pinker, *The Better Angels*, 322–54.

[26] The 'tiny number of exceptions' might include the action by the US, the UK, and France to protect the Kurds in 1991 and Turkey's incursions into Iraq in the 1990s and 2007: Gray, *International Law and the Use of Force*, 28–9. See also Christine Gray and Simon Olleson, 'The Limits of the Law on the Use of Force: Turkey, Iraq and the Kurds' (2001) 12 *Finnish Yearbook of International Law* 355.

[27] Pinker, *The Better Angels*, 363, citing homicide statistics from Etienne G. Krug et al (eds), *World Report on Violence and Health* (Geneva: World Health Organization, 2002), 10; the average rate of battle deaths for 2000–5 from the previously mentioned Uppsala Conflict Data Project and Peace Research Institute of Oslo dataset; and population figures from the US Census Bureau, *International Data Base: Total Midyear Population of the World: 1950–2020* (2010).

In addition to the empirical evidence, there is also a more fundamental problem with the realist critique. To focus solely on 'effectiveness', defined as general compliance with a rule, obscures the complexity of the reasons we have law. Gray remarks that the rules on the use of force 'clearly also serve a declaratory function; they set out a goal to be aimed at, the ideal that states adhere to'.[28] Although the law on the use of force may be constrained by power relationships in some cases, it can still exercise a significant normative pull. This might be called a 'processual' response to the realist critique: the test of the relevance of international law rules should not be whether powerful states sometimes flout the rules, nor whether such states must submit to sanctions or binding dispute settlement; it should be a broader test of how the international norms and institutions influence the process of resolving a dispute.

An example of where the Charter rules on the use of force have influenced the resolution of a dispute against the geopolitical interests of the powerful is East Timor. On one side was a regional power, Indonesia, tacitly supported by the US. On the other were the 700,000 people of a small, poor, and divided non-self-governing territory, which Portugal, itself the weakest colonial power, had effectively abandoned after its 1974 revolution.[29] To a realist, the geopolitical situation was obvious. US Secretary of State Henry Kissinger—a realist by any measure—told his staff, 'the Indonesians are going to take the island sooner or later'.[30] And indeed they did. Indonesia's invasion in 1975, ostensibly to restore order, and its annexation of East Timor as a province in 1976 indisputably constituted an unlawful use of force in violation of the Charter and other international law rules. It was roundly criticized as such by the General Assembly and Security Council.[31] A realist conclusion that the law on the use of force had been proved ineffective might have been strengthened by Australia's ensuing realpolitik. In 1989, it expressly recognized Indonesian sovereignty over East Timor as the price for negotiating a zone of cooperation for exploiting oil and gas in the Timor Sea, off its northern coast.[32]

In 1991, Portugal brought an action against Australia in the International Court. It claimed that by recognizing Indonesian sovereignty Australia had breached Portugal's rights and various UN resolutions.[33] The case was held inadmissible (on the *Monetary*

[28] Gray, *International Law and the Use of Force*, 27.

[29] East Timor had been a Portuguese colony since 1702 and was declared a non-self-governing territory under Chapter XI of the Charter in 1960: GA Res 1542 (XV), 15 Dec 1960.

[30] Henry Kissinger at Secretary's Principal's and Regional Staff Meeting, US Department of State, 12 Aug 1975, available at <http://www.gwu.edu/~nsarchiv/NSAEBB/NSAEBB62/doc2.pdf>.

[31] SC Res 384, 22 Dec 1975; SC Res 389, 22 Apr 1976; GA Res 3485 (XXX), 12 Dec 1975; GA Res 31/53, 1 Dec 1976; GA Res 32/34, 28 Nov 1977; GA Res 33/39, 13 Dec 1978; GA Res 34/40, 21 Nov 1979; GA Res 35/27, 11 Nov 1980; GA Res 36/50, 24 Nov 1981; GA Res 37/30, 23 Nov 1982. The General Assembly resolutions ceased in 1982 when majority support was no longer guaranteed.

[32] Treaty on a Zone of Cooperation in an Area between the Indonesian Province of East Timor and Northern Australia, Timor Sea, 11 Dec 1989, 1654 UNTS 105.

[33] *East Timor (Portugal v. Australia)*, ICJ Rep 1995, 90.

Gold principle: Portugal did not have a claim that could be severed from a dispute with Indonesia, a non-party[34]). But the Court acknowledged a significant practical consequence of East Timor's status: 'For the two Parties, the Territory of East Timor remains a non-self-governing territory and its people has the right to self-determination', a right that 'as it evolved from the Charter and from United Nations practice, has an *erga omnes* character'.[35] Even Australia, in defending itself, accepted this principle and affirmed that its treaty with Indonesia would not be opposable to an independent East Timor.[36] No other state was willing to recognize expressly that Indonesia's unlawful use of force and subsequent actual control could have entitled it to sovereignty. Although realists may have thought the case closed, it was still open as a matter of international law and international relations. In fact, after Indonesia came under a new government in 1998, the consequences of its unlawful use of force were reversed. It agreed with Portugal on an act of 'popular consultation' under UN auspices, in which the East Timorese voted for independence.[37] When they ultimately achieved it, in the face of violence, displacement, and chaos, it was with the assistance of an Australian-led force with a mandate under Chapter VII.[38]

Not every unlawful use of force is reversed. Nor can a reversal undo the suffering experienced by peoples such as the East Timorese in the meantime.[39] But East Timor illustrates that even where the rules on the use of force have been 'ineffective' in that states have flouted them—and recall that states have flouted them less and less since 1945—they may still be of considerable practical relevance in shaping the responses of other states and international institutions, in keeping disputes alive, and potentially in influencing their eventual resolution. True, the situation in East Timor from 1975 to 2000 was not effectively governed by rules of international law. But contrary to the realist critique, their relevance was also not a priori excluded: the principle that sovereignty cannot be acquired by the unlawful use of force continued to have salience, and ultimately it was with UN involvement that the situation was resolved.

[34] *Monetary Gold Removed from Rome in 1943 (Italy v. France, UK and US)*, ICJ Rep 1954 19; *East Timor*, 102.

[35] *East Timor*, 102–3.

[36] This decision was made by Australia at Cabinet level: CR 95/14, 16 Feb 1995, 12, 14 (G. Griffith QC, agent of Australia); *East Timor*, 99, 105–6. Much else passed between the parties that is not reflected in the judgment, though there is more in some of the separate and dissenting opinions: see especially *East Timor*, 108 (Judge Oda on the limited extent of the judgment); 133 (Judge Ranjeva on how 'realism' requires appropriateness, not expediency); 136–8 (Judge Vereschetin on the need to consult the people of East Timor and the possibilities of doing so); 204 (Judge Weeramantry on Australia's duty of non-recognition); 262, 265 (Judge Skubiszewski on how 'realities' are neither stable nor permanent and thus there is no basis for disregarding respect for international law). Generally see Crawford, *The Creation of States*, 168–72.

[37] Special Committee on the Situation with Regard to the Implementation of the Declaration on the Granting of Independence to Colonial Countries and Peoples, 'East Timor: Working paper prepared by the Secretariat', A/AC.109/2000/12 (22 June 2000), paras 4, 12.

[38] SC Res 1264, 15 Sept 1999; Special Committee, 'East Timor', para 17.

[39] From 1975 to 2000 it is estimated that some 200,000 East Timorese died, almost one-third of the population before the conflict: see Crawford, *The Creation of States*, 560–2 and sources cited therein.

The realist assumption that the Charter rules are ineffective in practice thus fails on two counts: first, the evidence since 1945 does not support it and, if anything, contradicts it; and, secondly, the critique is misconceived in that it ignores how, even in the realm of high politics, international law can have both symbolic and practical relevance to state behaviour beyond its strictly defined effectiveness.

B. Whether the Charter Rules are Too Indeterminate

The fact that the Charter rules are substantially more effective than realists would credit does not mean they are optimal. They probably are not. There also remain problems of interpretation, including the meaning of the word 'threat' in Article 2(4)[40] and the legality of anticipatory or pre-emptive self-defence under Article 51, which protects the 'inherent right' of self-defence 'if an armed attack occurs' (though the more expansive notion of 'preventive' self-defence propounded by the US in the 2000s clearly has no legal basis).[41] Gray notes that insofar as the General Assembly has adopted resolutions that might be seen as authoritative interpretations of the Charter, 'Typically the price of consensus has been ambiguity on the crucial issues that divide states'.[42]

Nonetheless, claims that textual deficiencies render the rules ineffective have been much exaggerated. Glennon calls them 'malleable' and 'incoherent' and implies that there may not even exist 'a single determinate "Charter system" governing the use of force on which all reasonable observers must agree'.[43] But this seems to disregard the ongoing elaboration of the law on the use of force by institutions such as the International Court. A well-known example is *Corfu Channel*. The UK argued that the phrase 'threat or use of force against the territorial and political independence of any State' in Article 2(4) excluded a minesweeping operation in Albanian waters to collect evidence in support of an international claim. But the Court held that it could 'only regard the alleged right of intervention as the manifestation of a policy of force, such as has, in the past, given rise to the most serious abuses' and that 'Intervention is perhaps still less admissible in the particular form it would take

[40] Compare *Corfu Channel (UK v. Albania)*, ICJ Rep 1949, 4, *Military and Paramilitary Activities in and against Nicaragua (Nicaragua v. US)*, ICJ Rep 1986, 14, and *Legality of the Threat or Use of Nuclear Weapons*, ICJ Rep 1996, 226 with the more eccentric interpretation of the term in *Guyana v. Suriname* (2007) 139 ILR 566, 690–7. See also: Nikolas Stürchler, *The Threat of Force in International Law* (Cambridge: Cambridge University Press, 2007).

[41] See Brownlie, *International Law and the Use of Force by States*, 251–80; Gray, *International Law and the Use of Force*, 128–66; Stephen C. Neff, *War and the Law of Nations: A General History* (Cambridge: Cambridge University Press, 2005), 329–30; Thomas M. Franck, *Recourse to Force: State Action against Threats and Armed Attacks* (Cambridge: Cambridge University Press, 2002), 45–108; and relevant contributions in this volume.

[42] Gray, *International Law and the Use of Force*, 9.

[43] Glennon, 'How International Rules Die', 962–3.

here', since 'it would be reserved for the most powerful States, and might easily lead to perverting the administration of international justice itself'.[44] In *Nicaragua*, the Court confirmed that this was a blanket rejection of a narrow interpretation of the provision: 'A prohibited intervention must ... be one bearing on matters in which each State is permitted, by the principle of State sovereignty, to decide freely'.[45]

Gray remarks that in *Nicaragua* the Court 'apparently regarded the Charter provisions as dynamic rather than fixed, and thus capable of change over time through state practice'.[46] Such 'open texture' is inherent in any general legal rule. As Hart wrote:

> When we are bold enough to frame some general rule of conduct (e.g. a rule that no vehicle may be taken into the park) the language used in this context fixes necessary conditions which anything must satisfy if it is to be within its scope, and certain clear examples of what is certainly within its scope may be present in our minds. ... We have initially settled the question that peace and quiet in the park is to be maintained at the cost, at any rate, of the exclusion of these things. ... When the unenvisaged case does arise, we confront the issues at stake and can then settle the question by choosing between the competing interests in a way which best satisfies us. In doing so we shall have rendered more determinate our initial aim and shall incidentally have settled a question as to the meaning, for the purposes of this rule, of a general word.[47]

For 'peace in the park' read 'peace in the world'. The fact that the outer bounds of concepts such as 'threat or use of force' may remain indeterminate is not problematic in itself; the question is whether the rules are *so* indeterminate as to abrogate their effectiveness. The answer is no.

c. Whether the Charter Rules are Too Strict

A further line of argument is not that the Charter is ineffective in general or too indeterminate but that in some sense it is *too strict*—in particular, that in order to intervene in humanitarian crises states are compelled to use force unlawfully, as the North Atlantic Treaty Organization (NATO) arguably did when it bombed

[44] *Corfu Channel*, 35. Gray comments that the UK's argument was a 'relatively isolated example' of a state relying on a narrow view of Art 2(4). Others may include Israel's interpretation during the Entebbe incident in 1976, when hijackers diverted an aircraft from Tel Aviv and Israeli forces mounted a successful rescue operation in Uganda; and the US invasion of Grenada in 1983, when it suggested that the Charter justified the use of force in pursuit of values such as freedom, democracy, and peace. But both Israel and the US also relied on more traditional arguments to justify their actions within the terms of the Charter, principally self-defence: Gray, *International Law and the Use of Force*, 31–3. Brownlie observes that the *travaux préparatoires* make it clear that the words 'territorial integrity and political independence' were introduced precisely to provide guarantees to small states: Brownlie, *International Law and the Use of Force by States*, 265–8. See also Franck, *Recourse to Force*, 12.

[45] *Nicaragua*, 106–8. Similarly in *Armed Activities*, 227, Uganda violated the prohibition even if its objective was not to overthrow the Congolese president.

[46] *Armed Activities*, 227, citing *Nicaragua*, 94.

[47] Hart, *The Concept of Law*, 128–9.

Yugoslavia in 1999. Some postulate that the law on the use of force *does* permit humanitarian intervention.[48] The UK claimed that renewed repression by Yugoslavia in Kosovo 'would cause further loss of civilian life and would lead to the displacement of the civilian population' and that 'as an exceptional measure on grounds of overwhelming humanitarian necessity, military intervention is legally justifiable'.[49] But there is little basis for such an approach in state practice and no place for it within the Charter framework; it is not *lex lata*.[50] So the question here is whether the effectiveness of the Charter is limited by the fact that interventions on humanitarian or other grounds are only permissible under Chapter VII.

Glennon blames 'the principle of sovereign equality' for disabling the UN—especially the Security Council—'from addressing emerging crises, such as access to [weapons of mass destruction], that derive precisely from the presupposition of sovereign equality'.[51] He argues that states such as Yugoslavia under Slobodan Milošević, despite acts of repression, enjoy 'a right to nonintervention equal to that of every other state', which serves in practice to deny equal human rights to their citizens.[52]

It is undeniable that the collective security system has often been incapacitated and that its incapacitation can limit the effectiveness of the Charter. But attributing the problem to 'sovereign equality' is a misdiagnosis. The Security Council is not hostage to sovereign equality: Article 2(7) of the Charter protects states against intervention 'in matters which are essentially within the domestic jurisdiction of any State', but it expressly adds that 'this principle shall not prejudice the application of enforcement measures under Chapter VII'. The immediate cause of Security Council inaction is usually the *inequality* institutionalized in its structure. In Yugoslavia in 1999 and in other recent cases, the reason the Security Council's role was limited was

[48] See the discussion and sources cited in Gray, *International Law and the Use of Force*, 33–9; Crawford, *Brownlie's Principles*, 752–4; Franck, *Recourse to Force*, 135–73; and relevant contributions in this volume.

[49] S/PV.3988 (24 Mar 1999), 12. Whether the NATO intervention actually did breach the Charter is a matter of debate. A preliminary difficulty is that from Oct 1998 the threat of force against Yugoslavia by NATO members was conditioned on various 'demands' concerning the status of Kosovo. There was also little authority or state practice at the time to support a right of humanitarian intervention, as the UK itself recognized when it informed a parliamentary committee that it aimed to establish 'new principles governing humanitarian intervention': House of Commons Foreign Affairs Committee, Fourth Report—Kosovo (HC 28-I), 7 June 2000, para 144. Further: Gray, *International Law and the Use of Force*, 39–51. In the cases brought by Yugoslavia (Serbia and Montenegro) against 10 NATO members, the International Court held that it did not have jurisdiction over the question: *Legality of the Use of Force (Serbia and Montenegro v. Belgium)*, ICJ Rep 2004, 279.

[50] Other putative instances of state practice often cited—also somewhat problematically—are the air exclusion zones created over northern Iraq in 1991 and over southern Iraq in 1992 and the operations of the Economic Community of West African States in Liberia in 1990: see Crawford, *Brownlie's Principles*, 754.

[51] Michael J. Glennon, 'Why the Security Council Failed' (2003) 82 *Foreign Affairs* 16, 33.

[52] Glennon, 'Why the Security Council Failed', 33.

that one or more of its permanent members exercised or certainly would have exercised a veto. Indeed, during the Cold War the likelihood of a veto by the US or the Soviet Union rendered the collective security system effectively prostrate—much more so than now. The only use of force it authorized in that period in response to a breach of the peace by a state was in Korea in 1950 (and in that case the Soviet Union was absent from the Security Council, a mistake it did not repeat).[53]

This institutionalized inequality is a manifestation of the familiar spectre of *actual* inequality. As Glennon observes, the Security Council does not accurately reflect 'the real world's power structure':[54] all five permanent members (the P5) are elevated to the same plane despite their inequality relative to each other; and such powers as Brazil and India are excluded.[55] But insofar as the Charter does acknowledge actual inequality (or was meant to do so in 1945) it is an attempt to remedy the defects of the League. Stephen Neff argues that whereas it contrasts with the more starry-eyed League, the Charter is reminiscent of the Concert of Europe established in 1815: 'more political than legal in nature' and addressed 'chiefly to dangerous and destabilising political situations' (though it is also 'somewhat more democratic' than the Concert in that the Security Council includes elected rotating members as well as the P5).[56]

If the institutionalized inequality of the collective security system does generate a problem of effectiveness, it is that its effectiveness is asymmetric. Although the Charter rules may have reduced the incidence of the use of force by states in general, and although their direct and indirect influence may extend to regional powers such as Indonesia, they may be less consistently effective where the interests of great powers are engaged. Russia's actions in Ukraine in 2014 are a case in point. Gerry Simpson explains this asymmetry by distinguishing two groups of states:

> an elite group of states, commonly referred to as the 'Great Powers', and a large mass of middle and smaller powers who defer to these larger powers in the operation and constitution of international legal order. These Great Powers occupy a position of authority within each of the legal regimes that has arisen since 1815. Sometimes these regimes are constructed around loose affiliations of interested Great Powers (the Vienna Congress), at other times the role of the Great Powers is laid out in the detailed provisions of an originating document (The United Nations Charter). In each instance, these powers have policed the international order from a position of assumed cultural, material and legal superiority. A key prerogative of this position has been a right to intervene in the affairs of other states in order to promote some proclaimed community goal.[57]

[53] Gray, *International Law and the Use of Force*, 255–9. See also the discussion of UN practice in Franck, *Recourse to Force*, 21–44.

[54] Glennon, 'Why the Security Council Failed', 33.

[55] For a survey of proposals for Security Council reform, see Wolfram Karl, Bernd Mützelburg, and Georg Witschel, 'Article 108' in Bruno Simma et al (eds), *The Charter of the United Nations: A Commentary*, vol 2 (2nd edn, Oxford: Oxford University Press, 2002), 1341, 1361–3.

[56] Neff, *War and the Law of Nations*, 323–4.

[57] Gerry Simpson, *Great Powers and Outlaw States: Unequal Sovereigns in the International Legal Order* (Cambridge: Cambridge University Press, 2004), 5. See also Crawford, 'Practice and Process of the Law of Nations', ch 11.

III. A Critique From Within International Law

The realist critique is an extralegal one. The debate about whether international law constitutes 'law' in a Hartian or some other sense is distinct from whether a particular proposition constitutes 'the law' within the boundaries of the system of international law. Whether the law on the use of force is effective in practice is also separate from what the law actually is. But in addition to making this extralegal critique, Glennon has argued that the Charter rules are no longer international law at all. Since he does not clearly distinguish between arguments internal and external to international law, it may not be possible to sever this from his solipsistic theory of international law: he begins with the presupposition that 'The term "law" in an international law sense does not, to me, include norms that are violated often by many states'.[58] But his conclusion still takes the form of a statement from *within* international law: a categorical claim that Article 2(4) 'has fallen into desuetude and is no longer obligatory'.[59] It can therefore be answered on the basis of international law as ordinarily understood.

The claim relies on an assertion about the frequency of violations that, as discussed earlier, contradicts the fact that the use of interstate force has sharply declined during the Charter period. But even if we leave that aside, it is a hopeless argument.

To start with, Glennon seeks support for it in the wrong places. He asks whether 'state practice that is inconsistent with a norm is simply too thick to justify the conclusion that states really accept the norm as obligatory' and identifies examples of such inconsistent state practice.[60] He deflects the 'important objection' that we should weigh this against instances of apparent compliance ('Canada did not attack Mongolia; Guatemala did not attack New Zealand'), by observing that 'state behaviour consistent with a rule, without more' is not 'practice corroborating state consent to the rule'.[61] That is not exactly an iconoclastic view; it is the whole point of *opinio juris*. Nor is there much traction in his argument that '"cheap talk" … does not mean that states in fact embrace the rule of law to which they avert':[62] *opinio juris* is not undermined merely because officials' words may not reflect their motives. But more importantly, these discussions are largely beside the point. State practice and *opinio juris* are requirements for the identification of *customary* international law. There is indeed a parallel customary prohibition on the use of force,[63] but the more

[58] Glennon, 'How International Rules Die', 952.
[59] Glennon, 'How International Rules Die', 960.
[60] Glennon, 'How International Rules Die', 960.
[61] Glennon, 'How International Rules Die', 974.
[62] Glennon, 'How International Rules Die', 977.
[63] See *Nicaragua*, 99–101: the Court noted that 'both Parties take the view that the principles as to the use of force incorporated in the United Nations Charter correspond, in essentials, to those found

pressing task for a critic is to show that the rules *in the Charter* are not international law—and they are first and foremost *treaty* rules, subject to the law of treaties.

As recognized in the Vienna Convention on the Law of Treaties (VCLT), 'Every treaty in force is binding upon the parties to it'.[64] The VCLT also provides that 'The validity of a treaty or of the consent of a State to be bound by a treaty may be impeached only through the application of the [VCLT]'; and it may cease to be in force 'only as a result of the application of the provisions of the treaty or of the [VCLT]'.[65] A treaty may be amended 'by agreement between the parties'.[66] The Charter also imposes specific requirements on formal amendments: a vote by two-thirds of the General Assembly and ratification by two-thirds of UN members, including the P5 (Art 108). It is thus not enough for a critic to assert that states do not 'feel obliged to comply'[67] with the law on the use of force in some vague, extralegal sense. The rules are contained in a treaty that is prima facie in force and binding on its parties, which include all widely recognized states.[68] Their consent to the Charter can be impeached only through the principles reflected in the VCLT.

There are only two potential bases for a claim that the prohibition on the use of force is no longer the law. The first is to show that the rules have been amended or terminated. Glennon is correct that there is a concept of 'desuetude' in international law. For example, in the *Affaire Yuille, Shortridge et Compagnie* arbitration, the arbitrator acknowledged the possibility that the 1654 Anglo-Portuguese Treaty of Peace, Commerce and Alliance might have fallen into desuetude, though he held that it had not.[69] But state practice is scarce, and the circumstances surrounding the

in customary international law', though the treaty and customary rules may not necessarily be the same. For a survey of the customary rules on the use of force, see Enzo Cannizzaro and Paolo Palchetti (eds), *Customary International Law on the Use of Force: A Methodological Approach* (Leiden: Martinus Nijhoff, 2005). *Opinio juris* may, of course, be relevant to the customary rules on the use of force: see the discussion in Gray, *International Law and the Use of Force*, 25. The existence of a customary rule, far from lowering the threshold for a critic, in fact raises it: it would have to be shown that *both* the Charter and customary rules are no longer international law.

[64] Vienna Convention on the Law of Treaties, 22 May 1969, 1155 UNTS 331, Art 26. This is generally accepted as reflecting customary international law. Eg in *Gabčíkovo-Nagymaros (Hungary/Slovakia)*, ICJ Rep 1997, 7, 36–8, 62, the International Court applied certain of the VCLT provisions on termination as generally reflecting custom, even though the treaty in question predated the entry into force of the VCLT for the parties. Since, under Art 4, the VCLT itself strictly applies only to treaties concluded after its entry into force (and not all UN members are parties to the VCLT anyway) it is customary international law that governs the Charter.

[65] VCLT, Art 42.

[66] VCLT, Art 39. The rules in VCLT Arts 40–1 'apply to such an agreement except in so far as the treaty may otherwise provide'. As discussed later, Art 108 of the Charter does make specific provision for amendments.

[67] Glennon, 'How International Rules Die', 960.

[68] The UN has 193 members. The Holy See and Palestine are 'non-member permanent observer states'. The Cook Islands and Niue, both associated states of New Zealand, are members of some UN specialized agencies such as the World Health Organization and are also treated as non-member states. There are no other widely recognized states. So the Charter rules are virtually universal even without accounting for the parallel customary rules.

[69] Treaty of Peace, Commerce and Alliance, 10 July 1654, 3 CTS 281; *Affaire Yuille, Shortridge et Cie (Grande Bretagne/Portugal)*, 21 Oct 1861, Albert Geouffre de la Pradelle and Nicolas Politis,

Charter rules on the use of force do not remotely qualify. In fact, desuetude is not even a distinct legal rule; rather, it is a consequence of a tacit agreement between the parties to amend or terminate a treaty in whole or in part. It was on this basis that the International Law Commission omitted a reference to desuetude from the VCLT:

> the Rapporteur does not believe that there is any objective principle of law terminative of treaties on the mere ground of age, obsolescence, or desuetude as such. Indeed it would be possible to point to a number of treaties centuries old, framed in archaic language, and seldom invoked in terms or referred to by the parties, which the latter nevertheless regard as being still in force and effective. On the other hand, where the parties themselves, without denouncing or purporting actually to terminate the treaty, have, over a long period, conducted themselves in relation to it more or less as though it did not exist, by failing to apply or invoke it, or by other conduct evincing lack of interest in or reliance on it, it may be said that there exists what amounts to a tacit agreement of the parties, by conduct, to disregard the treaty and to consider it as being at an end. In such event, however, the basis of the termination would be the presumption of a tacit agreement of the parties—or, alternatively, of an assent to or acceptance by each party of the non-application of the treaty by the other—and not age or desuetude as such, although the latter would be relevant factors in estimating the real attitude and intentions of the parties.[70]

In principle, desuetude might apply to the Charter, but it is much more likely that the provisions of the Charter—a living instrument—will be interpreted with sufficient flexibility to reflect any new consensus and to respond to emerging needs. For instance, Article 27(3) states that Security Council decisions 'shall be made by an affirmative vote of nine members including the concurring votes of the permanent members', but the International Court held in the *Namibia* advisory opinion that there was 'abundant evidence' that voluntary abstentions by P5 states were 'consistently and uniformly interpreted ... as not constituting a bar to the adoption of resolutions' and that this had been generally accepted by UN members 'and evidences a general practice' of the UN.[71] Note that this was a tacit agreement on interpretation, not an amendment.[72] Karl, Mützelburg, and Witschel remark that 'What happens ...

Recueil des Arbitrages Internationaux, vol 2, *1856–1872* (Paris: Éditions Internationales Paris, 1932), 101. Further: Marcelo G. Kohen and Sarah Heathcote, '1969 Vienna Convention: Article 42' in Olivier Corten and Pierre Klein (eds), *The Vienna Convention on the Law of Treaties: A Commentary*, vol 2 (Oxford: Oxford University Press, 2011), 1015, 1023–4.

70 Gerald G. Fitzmaurice, Second Report of the Special Rapporteur on the Law of Treaties, *Yearbook of the International Law Commission*, 1957, vol II, 48. See also ibid, 28 and more generally on desuetude, Athanassios Vamvoukos, *Termination of Treaties in International Law: The Doctrine of Rebus Sic Stantibus and Desuetude* (Oxford: Clarendon Press, 1985); Jan Wouters and Sten Verhoeven, 'Desuetudo' (2008) in Rüdiger Wolfrum (ed), *Max Planck Encyclopedia of Public International Law* (Oxford: Oxford University Press, 2013), available at <http://www.mpepil.com>.

71 *Legal Consequences of the Continued Presence of South Africa in Namibia (South West Africa)*, ICJ Rep 1971, 16, 22. This has been called 'The most famous instance of desuetudo': Wouters and Verhoeven, 'Desuetudo' in Wolfrum, *Max Planck Encyclopedia of Public International Law*.

72 Parties may enter into a subsequent agreement 'regarding the interpretation of the treaty or the application of its provisions', and 'subsequent practice in the application of the treaty' may establish

under the guise of interpretation is in fact often a modification of the treaty', and tacit amendment outside the formal procedure in Article 108 may also be possible.[73] But in that case it would be necessary that all or virtually all member states had either participated in the practice or had, at least, acquiesced in it.[74]

There is patently no tacit amendment here. There is no evidence that even a single state considers the prohibition on the use of force not to be binding, let alone the evidence actually required: that virtually *every UN member* has at least accepted an amendment to it by conduct. Glennon attempts to adduce 'verbal evidence that the United States does not consider itself bound by Article 2(4)' (he has less to say on the views of other states).[75] But even when, for instance, the Reagan administration suggested that the US might not need to comply with the rules in response to an enemy that did not itself comply, the US continued to offer legal arguments in the Security Council.[76]

The only other avenue a critic might have is to argue that the Charter provisions, though still in force, have been modified in their operation by a supervening customary rule. This may be possible under some circumstances. For instance, in the *Fisheries Jurisdiction* cases the International Court held that even though the 1958 High Seas Convention provided for freedom of fishing on the high seas, a customary rule had since emerged entitling states to 12 nautical mile fishing zones and the states involved had accepted the rule.[77] But what would have to be shown is essentially similar to evidence of a tacit amendment to the Charter: put baldly, that states had consented to a new rule of customary international law allowing other states to use force against them.

Even that might not be enough. Even if it could somehow be shown that the Charter rules had been modified by a new customary rule or tacitly amended, it

such an agreement. The subsequent agreement is taken into account in the interpretation of the treaty: VCLT, Art 31(3)(a)–(b).

[73] Karl, Mützelburg, and Witschel, 'Article 108' in Simma et al, *The Charter of the United Nations: A Commentary*, 1246.

[74] Karl, Mützelburg, and Witschel, 'Article 108' in Simma et al, *The Charter of the United Nations: A Commentary*, 1246. There may be some limits on such tacit amendments. Jochen Frowein has argued that a majority amendment provision such as Art 108 cannot change completely the object, purpose or basic structure of an international organization: Jochen Frowein, 'Are There Limits to the Amendment Procedures in Treaties Constituting International Organisations?' in Gerhard Hafner et al (eds), *Liber Amicorum Professor Ignaz Seidl-Hohenveldern* (The Hague: Kluwer Law International, 1998), 201–18. If this is correct, it might not apply *ipso facto* to a tacit amendment (which would be not by majority but by consensus), but it might seem equally incongruous for a tacit agreement to modify a basic tenet of the Charter.

[75] Glennon, 'How International Rules Die', 960, 979.

[76] Gray, *International Law and the Use of Force*, 29, citing a statement by the US representative to the UN during the Reagan administration that 'unilateral compliance with the Charter's principles of non-intervention and non-use of force may make sense in some instance but it is hardly in itself a sound basis for either US policy or for international peace and security' in Jeane Kirkpatrick, 'Law and Reciprocity' (1986) *American Society of International Law Proceedings* 59.

[77] *Fisheries Jurisdiction (UK v. Iceland)*, ICJ Rep 1974, 3, 22–4; *Fisheries Jurisdiction (Germany v. Iceland)*, ICJ Rep 1974, 175, 191–2; Convention on the High Seas, 29 Apr 1958, 450 UNTS 11.

would then *also* have to be shown that the parallel customary prohibition on the use of force no longer operated. Since this is probably a peremptory (*jus cogens*) norm, and such a norm can be modified only by a subsequent norm having the same character,[78] any new rule permitting force would presumably also have to be peremptory. There is not the slightest evidence of this.

IV. Conclusion

We have considered the relevance of the Charter rules on the use of force from a number of perspectives. The argument that they may not be binding 'law' in some stipulated sense, whatever its merits, says nothing about their relevance in practice. And there is no empirical basis for a more practical realist critique of their effectiveness: on the contrary, a distinctive feature of the Charter period is the *decline* of interstate armed conflict. This is not to say that there are no limits on the effectiveness of the rules; there are many, including limits on the effectiveness of the asymmetric collective security system. But as Gray points out, 'it tends to be non-lawyers rather than lawyers whose expectations are unreasonably elevated and who attack international law as having no significant role when there is anything less than perfect compliance'.[79] As we have also seen, there is no doubt whatsoever that the prohibition on the use of force remains a binding rule of international law. It has given the lie to Sherman's assertion that the hardships of war are 'inevitable'. That is not mere aspiration; it is what the facts suggest.

[78] The International Court has noted that the rule codified in Art 2(4) is frequently referred to as peremptory: *Nicaragua*, 100. VCLT, Art 53 states: 'a peremptory norm of general international law is a norm accepted and recognized by the international community of States as a whole as a norm from which no derogation is permitted and which can be modified only by a subsequent norm of general international law having the same character'.

[79] Gray, *International Law and the Use of Force*, 25.

CHAPTER 5

FEMINIST PERSPECTIVES ON THE LAW ON THE USE OF FORCE

GINA HEATHCOTE

> We don't know what 'being human' is, we are still in the process of becoming
>
> (Shelly Wright[1])

I. Introduction

This chapter articulates the idea that, rather than discussing when force is justified or how force is authorized, it is time to re-imagine and expand the parameters of the prohibition on the use of force contained in Article 2(4) of the UN Charter. In returning to the prohibition, I use structural bias feminist approaches to consider how the law on the use of force has fared in the first two decades after the advent of feminist approaches addressing international law.[2] Structural bias

[1] Shelly Wright, *International Human Rights, Decolonisation and Globalisation: Becoming Human* (New York: Routledge Research in International Law, 2001).

[2] Hilary Charlesworth, Christine Chinkin, and Shelly Wright, 'Feminist Approaches to International Law' (1991) 85 *American Journal of International Law* 379.

feminism focuses on both organizational and normative structures to demonstrate the gendering of international legal categories and how this contributes to the harm and discrimination women experience globally.[3] I focus on women's low participation in decision-making structures, the need for an expanded institutional take-up of feminist approaches, and the neglect of feminist peace studies in international legal scholarship, to draw conclusions about the law on the use of force, in particular the prohibition on the use of force. I reflect on when force has been authorized, using the Security Council action in Libya in 2011 as an example of the normative and organizational exclusion of women, and when force has been justified, in particular contemporary US justifications for targeted strikes against terrorist actors on the territory of another state, to challenge the Council's contemporary understanding of the relationship between women, peace, and security. I note the Security Council's women, peace, and security resolutions[4] to highlight how the women, peace, and security framework supports and legitimates the use of force. This is an outcome of which I am critical and I recommend a focus on strengthening the prohibition on the use of force instead.

In Section II, I focus on women as participants in decision-making structures, reflecting on the access some women have to the Security Council and the impact the Security Council's resolutions on women, peace, and security have had on country-specific resolutions. Using the authorization of force in Libya in 2011, I demonstrate how decisions with respect to the use of force remain untouched by the women, peace, and security framework. This raises questions about the organizational and normative capacity for women's participation as an embedded international norm.

In Section III, I consider the intersection of race and gender privilege in international law and, drawing on the work of Orford,[5] call for the Council's ongoing work on women, peace, and security to respond to the diversity of feminist approaches. Recognition of diversity complicates our legal projects and mitigates against a single sentence—even if a long one—such as the prohibition on the use of force, in Article 2(4) of the UN Charter, as the only law prohibiting the deployment of military force by states. This section recalls Charlesworth, Chinkin, and Wright's claim in 1991 that 'no single approach can deal with the complexity of international organisations, processes or rules or the diversity of women's experiences'.[6] Acknowledging the diversity of feminist approaches, and of women's experiences, challenges the

[3] Charlesworth, Chinkin, and Wright, 'Feminist Approaches to International Law', 621.

[4] The Council has issued seven resolutions on women, peace, and security, see: SC Res 1325: UN SCOR 4213th mtg, S/RES/1325 (31 Oct 2000); SC Res 1820: UN SCOR 5916th mtg, S/RES/1820 (19 June 2008); SC Res 1888: UN SCOR 6195th mtg, S/RES/1888 (30 Sept 2009); SC Res 1889: UN SCOR, 6196th mtg, S/RES/1889 (5 Oct 2009); SC Res 1960: UN SCOR, 6453 mtg, S/RES/1960 (16 Dec 2010); SC Res 2106 UN SCOR 7044th mtg (24th June 2013); SC Res 2122 UN SCOR, 6984th mtg (18th October 2013).

[5] Anne Orford, *Reading Humanitarian Intervention: Human Rights and the Use of Force in International Law* (Cambridge, Cambridge University Press, 2003).

[6] Charlesworth, Chinkin, and Wright, 'Feminist Approaches to International Law', 634.

Security Council's framework on women, peace, and security which I describe as legitimating the Council rather than representing a feminist understanding of security.[7] I use targeted strikes on the territory of other states as an example of the type of force that is insufficiently attended to by the Council yet in violation of Article 2(4). As the justification for targeted strikes in part rests on the failure of states to implement the Council's targeted sanctions regime,[8] attention to the risks of the targeted sanctions being implicated in targeted strikes requires further attention. Rather than the instigation of new forms of targeted sanctions, such as those developed under the 1325 framework against suspected perpetrators of widespread and systematic sexual violence in armed conflict, recalling the prohibition on the use of force requires condemnation of targeted strikes. As such, Section III demonstrates how the complicity of (some) feminist approaches in legitimating the Security Council's action (and inaction) directly undermines the prohibition on the use of force while equally undermining the perceived legitimacy of feminist analysis in non-Western states.

In Section IV, I turn to feminist peace activism. Feminist peace activism is a persistent yet hidden component of the law on the use of force, recognized as an element of the international structure since at least 1915.[9] Acknowledging the role of women and feminists as organizing for peace and disarmament, forces us to recognize that to speak of war (or force) and not to speak of peace is to begin from a premise that ultimately favours rather than restrains military action. This results in the prohibition functioning as a trigger to arguments for justified or authorized force rather than as a restraint on the use of force. For feminist approaches, the references to the potential use of 'necessary means' in response to widespread and systematic sexual violence in situations before the Council—found in Security Council Resolutions 1820 (2008), 1888 (2009), and 1960 (2009)—further challenges the Council's women, peace, and security agenda as counterintuitive to the history and the diversity of feminist approaches.

In articulating feminist perspectives on the prohibition on the use of force, I demonstrate persistent themes that engage gender, the law on the use of force, and the prohibition contained in Article 2(4) of the UN Charter. The isolation of traditional (or mainstream)[10] approaches to the law on the use of force from gender

[7] See also: Dianne Otto, 'The Security Council's Gender Legitimacy: The Symbolic Capital of Resolution 1325' in Hilary Charlesworth and Jean Marc Coicard (eds), *Faultlines of International Legitimacy* (Cambridge: Cambridge University Press, 2010).

[8] Harold Koh, 'Keynote Address: The Obama Administration and International Law' (2010) 104 *Proceedings of the American Society of International Law* 207, 219.

[9] See: Felicity Ruby, 'Security Council Resolution 1325: A Tool for Conflict Prevention?' in Gina Heathcote and Dianne Otto (eds), *Rethinking Peacekeeping, Gender Perspectives and Collective Security* (London: Pluto Press, 2013).

[10] For a definition and analysis of what constitutes the 'mainstream' of international law, see: B. S. Chimni, 'A Prolegomena to a Class Approach to International Law' (2010) 21 *European Journal of International Law* 57; also see B. S. Chimni, 'An Outline of a Marxist Course on Public International

analysis requires acknowledgement.[11] In addition, appreciation of non-Western feminist understandings of governance, of gender, and of insecurity are vital to challenging the limited perspectives and answers prevalent in mainstream international legal scholarship (MILS).[12] I reflect on the feminist project within international law, its strengths and weaknesses, as well as an emergent division between contemporary Western feminist approaches that have increasingly gained leverage at the UN and the spectrum of feminist thinking on the use of force.[13] I conclude with a return to Shelly Wright's article, 'The Horizon of Becoming',[14] emphasizing the role that humanity plays as a persistent motif in feminist approaches, so that the prohibition on the use of force is articulated as a useful beginning for imagining the potential of humanity rather than, as international actors often assume, a starting point for justifying further force, further violence, or further destruction.

II. Women's Participation: Organizational and Normative Approaches

In 1992 Chinkin noted the 'invisibility of women in nationalist movements and their invisibility in determining the legality or otherwise of any international use of force'.[15] In 2011, as protest in the Middle East garnered global attention, the role of women

Law' (2004) 17 *Leiden Journal of International Law* 1 defining MILS as 'an ensemble of methods, practices and understandings in relation to the identification, interpretation, and enforcement of enforcement of international law' (at 2). Of the four features of MILS that Chimini identifies, pertinent to the analysis in this chapter, is that 'practitioners of MILS do not recognise that there are structural constraints in the international system that greatly limit the pursuit of common good through law' (ibid).

[11] eg the four central pieces of Western scholarship on the use of force, despite being published after the first Security Council resolution on women, peace, and security, have no index reference to women or gender: Yoram Dinstein, *War, Aggression and Self-Defense* (5th edn, Cambridge: Cambridge University Press, 2011); Christine Gray, *International Law and the Use of Force* (3rd edn, Cambridge: Cambridge University Press, 2008); Thomas Franck, *Recourse to Force* (Cambridge: Cambridge University Press, 2002); Mary Ellen O'Connell, *International Law and the Use of Force: Cases and Materials* (New York: Federation Press, 2005).

[12] See n 10.

[13] See: Doris Buss, 'The New Man of International Law' in Amy Bartholomew (ed), *Empire's Law: The American Imperial Project and the 'War to Remake the World'* (London: Pluto Press, 2006).

[14] Wright, *The Horizon of Becoming*, 1.

[15] Christine Chinkin, 'A Gendered Perspective to the International Use of Force' (1992) 12 *Australian Yearbook of International Law* 279, 280.

in popular revolutions was given both media[16] and academic attention.[17] The topic of 'Women and the Arab Spring' has attracted continuing global attention yet elections in Tunisia and Egypt demonstrate the difficulties of transforming women's role in the articulation of dissatisfaction with the state into concrete political reform that is attentive to gender equality. At the same time, women's movements have struggled to challenge local perceptions that women's rights are concepts that have been exported from the West and that should be rejected post-revolution.[18] When force has been authorized, women's rights have been deployed as rhetoric[19] or in post-conflict resolutions but not as a component of the decision-making process with respect to the use of force. This is illustrated below in analysis of the 2011 Libyan intervention.

Security Council Resolution 1973 (2011) authorized the use of force to protect the Libyan people from state-led violence.[20] Despite the authorization coming over a decade after the first Security Council resolution on women, peace, and security (Resolution 1325) and four subsequent resolutions also emphasizing the need to consider women's security and to incorporate women's participation into all stages of the decision-making process, Resolution 1973 was silent on the normative and organizational requirements of Resolution 1325, in particular the need for women's participation in the decision to authorize force. While the structure of the Security Council in 2011 included some high-profile women, notably Susan Rice representing the US, Maria Luiza Riberio Viotti representing Brazil, and Joy Ogwu representing Nigeria, these women were not charged with representing women's interests. The presence of three women sitting on the Council when the decision was made to authorize force in Libya highlights the limitations of strategies centred on adding women to existing institutions: as this does little to challenge the organization's structure or the normative outputs of the institution.

It is not until after the Gaddafi regime had been deposed from power and the UN action in Libya shifted from the authorized use of force to post-conflict strategies for peacebuilding that women were recognized within the Council's debates as participants and stakeholders within the security discourse. Security Council Resolution 2009 (2011), issued seven months after Resolution 1973, established the United Nations Support Mission in Libya (UNSMIL)[21] and included a condemnation

[16] See eg <http://www.bbc.co.uk/news/world-middle-east-20726942>, <http://www.opendemocracy.net/5050/deniz-kandiyoti/fear-and-fury-women-and-post-revolutionary-violence>, and <http://www.washingtonpost.com/blogs/worldviews/wp/2012/10/25/what-the-arab-spring-has-done-for-womens-equality-in-one-chart/>.

[17] See eg Nadje Al-Ali, 'Gendering the Arab Spring' (2012) 5 *Middle East Journal of Culture and Communication* 26.

[18] Al-Ali, 'Gendering the Arab Spring'.

[19] Starting just before the invasion of Iraq in 2003, Iraqi women were heralded by the US administration as promoters of freedom and democracy, see <http://www.gwi-boell.de/web/un-resolutions-embedded-feminism-nadje-al-ali-2811.html> and contrast with <http://2001-2009.state.gov/g/rls/rm/2003/18477.htm>.

[20] SC Res 1973: UN SCOR 6598th mtg, S/RES/1973 (17 Mar 2011).

[21] SC Res 2009 (16 Sept 2011).

of sexual violence in its Preamble, and a call for accountability for human rights violations, including sexual violence, as well as protection for vulnerable groups.[22] The subsequent Security Council resolution on the situation in Libya, Resolution 2016 (2011), identified the participation of women (and minority groups) as a concern in its Preamble. Resolutions 2017 (2011) and 2022 (2011) on Libya made no mention of women or of the risk of gender-based violence during armed conflict.[23] So it is in Resolution 2040 (2012), issued by the Security Council a year after the authorization of the use of force,[24] where these strands are drawn together and the Council condemned sexual violence (of men, women, and children) in the Preamble, addressed issues of protection from and accountability for acts of sexual violence in operative paragraph 3,[25] and encouraged UNSMIL to promote 'the empowerment and the political participation of women',[26] as well as the need for the protection of women and children's human rights.[27] In March 2013, with the renewal of UNSMIL's mandate by the Council, a similar set of concerns were articulated.[28] The separation of the authorization of force from attention to women's security is thus visible across this sequence of resolutions.

Consequently, the Security Council's resolutions on Libya demonstrate the extent to which the evolving agenda on women, peace, and security is developed away from decisions on the use of force. There was no attention to the women, peace, and security agenda in the decision to authorize force: this was not attended to by the Council until well into the post-conflict peacebuilding process (and after the creation of UNSMIL in Resolution 2009) and without consistency across the post-conflict initiatives. The approach to women, peace, and security in the Libya resolutions was developed without any requirement that the Council itself be attentive to the participation of women in its own committees and decision-making structures. For example, in Resolution 1973 the Council also established a Panel of Experts, to monitor the situation in Libya, yet again ignored its own decree for women's participation in decision-making structures at all levels.[29] This indicates that the women, peace, and security agenda of the Council would be better understood as a women and peace agenda that perpetuates an understanding that the 'hard work' of security, or the decision to authorize the use of force, is inimical to the Council's development of gender perspectives.

Furthermore, even when the Security Council addresses women's participation in post-conflict communities, the focus is grounded within a liberal feminist model that is narrow in its focus on strategies to obtain women's formal equality in

[22] SC Res 2009, operative para 7.

[23] SC Res 2016: UN SCOR 6640th mtg, S/RES/2016 (27 Oct 2011); SC Res 2017: UN SCOR 6644th mtg, S/RES/2017 (31 Oct 2011); SC Res 2022: UN SCOR 6673rd mtg, S/RES/2022 (2 Dec 2011).

[24] SC Res 2040: UN SCOR 6733rd mtg, S/RES/2040 (12 Mar 2012).

[25] SC Res 2040, operative para 3.

[26] SC Res 2040, operative para 6(a).

[27] SC Res 2040, operative para 6(b).

[28] SC Res 2095: UN SCOR 6934th mtg, S/RES/2095 (14 Mar 2013).

[29] SC Res 2095, operative para 24.

access to decision-making structures; often within a constricted set of substantive concerns that are identified as of relevance to gender.[30] As such, any call for the increased participation of women in the Council's own decision-making structures, such as was hinted at earlier, should not be a quota-type strategy. The empirical aspect of the participation claim lies in the recognition of the relative absence of women in international and national decision-making structures, yet to address this absence the incorporation of women's narratives from outside the mainstream of international law to explain, analyse, and challenge the international law on the use of force is necessary.

A structural bias strategy centred on women's participation replaces demands for gender equality, in terms of women's proportionate or numerical representation, with a sophisticated and long-term commitment to enhancing women's capacity for participation in international and state structures, via attention to education, health, maternal support, and addressing restrictive social narratives on women's roles within communities. This would involve seeking out women's understanding of their own and society's needs, as well as understanding the role of women on the 'peripheries' in challenging social, cultural, and legal norms.[31]

Strategies that encourage women to value themselves, their opinions, and their capabilities, through education, through empowerment strategies, and through the challenging of gendered violence that is tolerated because it is directed against them as women, are the types of strategies that are relevant to enlarging women's participation in institutional and state structures. This also involves thinking through the existing gender imbalances within powerful structures, including the Council, to ask how education of existing participants might assist recognition of how privilege perpetuates gendered harms. None of these structural bias reforms are currently apparent in the resolutions of the Council and without this level of gender reform the Council will continue to contribute to the lack of women's participation in high-level decision-making structures.

For decision-making structures on the use of force, the disproportionately low representation of women (ie in the Security Council) is simple to acknowledge yet this does not mean that either proportionate representation would be the optimal outcome (although it might be a start) or that women do not already work in a multitude of positions that support the work of the Council and remain unrecognized in terms of the formal participants and decision-makers in the Council. The democratic deficit in the make-up of Security Council is easy to identify, more difficult to reform. While the Council is a political body with legal powers that might not be expected to reflect global diversity, the shifts since the early 1990s to expand the range of resolutions the Council issues, including thematic resolutions

[30] Gina Heathcote, *The Law on the Use of Force: A Feminist Analysis* (London: Routledge, 2012), ch 6.

[31] Ratna Kapur, *Erotic Justice: Law and the New Politics of Postcolonialism* (New York: Routledge, 2005), ch 4.

such as those on women, peace, and security, has considerably altered the nature of the Security Council output. The creation of normative frameworks considerably expands the Council's powers and demonstrates a need for a representative Council. In addition, greater regional representation is now an established norm of the Council demonstrating that transformation is possible.

To propose women's full participation in legal processes is, therefore, to embark on a (slow) reworking of legal structures and normative categories, including the Security Council itself. The organization of Council is linked to the normative outputs of the Council, with a beginning point being attention to the maintenance of gender imbalances in the Council's own structure. Consequently, when authorizations of force are made, such as in response to the crisis in Libya in 2011, without attention to the impact of force on women or to the gender structures military force functions within, the Council remains complicit in the undermining of women's security. When justifications for the use of force, or authorizations from the Security Council, are articulated and maintained/extended through a narrowly selected group of elite men, with occasional representations from elite women, women's participation—and specifically feminist concerns regarding the deployment of force—remain outside our understandings of the prohibition.

III. The Misrepresentation of Western Feminism as a Universal Feminism

Orford's seminal text, *Reading Humanitarian Intervention: Human Rights and the Use of Force in International Law* draws on critical legal theory, Third World Approaches to International Law (TWAIL),[32] feminist and postcolonial theory to demonstrate a core feature of feminist approaches to international law that has resonance for the law on the use of force: feminist thinking is immersed in debates and dialogues with a range of other contemporary theoretical approaches that both inform and springboard from feminist thinking. As such, recognition and understanding of the intersection between race and gender needs to be adequately integrated to the feminist reappraisal of women's participation within decision-making structures, so that this can be acknowledged and developed within approaches to the prohibition on the use of force. The intersection of race and gender are extensively theorized in feminist and critical approaches, yet overlooked at the institutional level, in particular

[32] For an introduction see: Antony Anghie, B. S. Chimni, Karin Mickelson, and Obiora Okafor (eds), *The Third World and the International Order* (Leiden: Martinus Nijhoff, 2003).

Security Council work on women, peace, and security. For Wright (writing in the context of international human rights law) this requires open engagement with the legacy and reach of decolonization, such that she proclaims:

> I would suggest that decolonisation is an immensely more complex process than international law has hitherto acknowledged. It involves seriously questioning the meaning of universality and its association with European humanism.[33]

To take Wright's project seriously is, therefore, to openly question and acknowledge the racial and gendered power imbalances that are at once invisible and visible in international relations. These imbalances are often unconsciously propagated in mainstream understandings of the prohibition on the use of force that prioritize justified and authorized violence.[34] This also requires reflection on Wright's quest for expanding our understanding of what it means to be human, acknowledging the limited frameworks that dominant political, moral, and philosophical models were born from, in particular the gender and racial exclusions that created the conditions for Enlightenment thinking that continues to influence the structures of international law today.

Recognition of the embedded dialogues of feminist approaches allows for greater recognition of the transnational and anti-imperialist dimensions of feminist methods. This also demonstrates the narrow focus of specific institutional, and some Western, feminist dialogues (particularly those that have been developed within the Security Council's women, peace, and security framework) that often fail to reflect, develop, or integrate the established links between feminist and other critical approaches. Orford, writing in 2003, was able to fuse the strengths of TWAIL, postcolonial, and critical legal scholarship with a feminist appraisal of the narratives produced to underpin and justify humanitarian interventions at the onset of the new millennium, compelling readers to work against 'forgetting law's imperial history'[35] and thus allowing the text to explore the limits of gender as a mechanism for analysis when used in isolation from other critical models.[36] This permits Orford to recognize the role that the prohibition on the use of force plays in reasserting the status quo of international law while permitting powerful states to intervene in extreme circumstances.

The post-millennium use of force through targeted strikes starkly demonstrates this need for a diversity of feminist and critical thinking to be developed within approaches to the prohibition on the use of force. Within the women, peace, and security framework, akin to the work of the Security Council more generally, targeted strikes are not broached. Justifications for the use of targeted strikes on the territory of another state, by the US, relies upon consent of the state where the

[33] Wright, *International Human Rights, Decolonisation and Globalisation*, 10.

[34] Heathcote, *The Law on the Use of Force*.

[35] Orford, *Reading Humanitarian Intervention*, 39.

[36] Orford, *Reading Humanitarian Intervention*, 39.

force occurs or the failure of the territorial state to implement Security Council targeted sanctions to establish the legality of the strikes.[37] Regardless of whether these justifications are representative of international law, the parallel development of a targeted sanctions regime within the women, peace, and security framework seemingly provides a feminist endorsement of both the Council's targeted sanctions regime and the Council's silence on the legality of targeted strikes. Yet a feminist analysis of the targeted strikes conducted by the US on the territory of other states would focus precisely on the intersectional harm these attacks produce, including the creation of two tiers of rules on the use of force, the lack of protection for civilians from targeted strikes, and the disproportionate risks to foreign communities as opposed to drone operators in the US.

In addition, the use of targeted strikes by the US has occurred in parallel with the US and the UK's shift on the women, peace, and security framework from the general Security Council Resolution 1325 (2000) to the production, under the US presidency of the Council, of four resolutions on women, peace, and security that centre primarily on sexual violence during armed conflict. An intersectional feminist analysis raises questions of how both race and gender are constructed in these two moves by the US in relation to security in the post-millennium period. That is, the period where the US developed the technology to use force on the territory of another state without deploying troops to the location of force, has coincided with the period where vast discussion of the dangers of sexual violence during armed conflict has emerged and been led by the US in the Security Council. This allows a form of 'civilized' force to be conducted by the US through targeted strikes, not only with low risks to US actors but with low risks of sexual violence to foreign women (at least from US service personnel). As such, the atrocities of militaries in relation to the perpetration of sexual violence are documented and recorded to demonstrate the non-civilized nature of other forms of warfare and distinguished from the manner in which the US conducts conflicts. A narrative of technologically advanced, precise, and 'safe' warfare conducted by the US is juxtaposed with the brutal stories of conflict documented in the global south. The complicity of Western militaries in the production of negative sexual cultures and sexual crimes is thus rendered less visible while new forms of forceful intervention are proposed as less damaging forms of warfare, justified through the exceptionalism of the global war on terror.

While feminist scholarship directly addressing the prohibition on the use of force may be less in comparison to the mainstream material available on the use of force, the complexity of a feminist approach to the prohibition on the use of force—if embedded in larger critical dialogues on race and global privilege—speaks to contemporary conditions in global relations and demands a remembrance of being human, as articulated by Wright. Becoming human requires we re-imagine and redevelop the boundaries of our thinking, recalling the essence of the prohibition

[37] Koh, 'Keynote Address'.

as a restraint on force rather than a space to argue for further force, justified, authorized, or legitimized.

In relation to targeted strikes, this raises new questions about the perpetuation of imperial structures as civilized and uncivilized that, not surprisingly, co-opt ideas about women's protection, particularly the protection of foreign (non-Western) women from non-Western men, which ignore the global prevalence of gendered violence and the manner in which women's rights are deployed to construct standards that reinforce a model of the West as technologically advanced and civilized. Targeted strikes kill men and women producing local narratives that are harmful to the protection of women's rights due to the anti-US sentiment that emerges in the locations of targeted strikes. This often becomes a suspicion of other forms of 'Western' interventions of which feminist action is included. As such, the combination of the Council's own women, peace, and security agenda and the failure of the Council to address or regulate the practice of targeted strikes, as well as the implicit endorsement of targeted strikes via the targeted sanctions regime, including targeted sanctions against perpetrators of sexual violence in armed conflict, re-appropriates feminist thinking as a Western theory, when it is not. This contributes not only to global inequalities, but also to the articulation of important local feminist concerns and women's rights generally, in spaces where anti-US sentiments arise in response to the risk of targeted strikes, as dangerous.

Consequently there is a need for both targeted strikes and targeted sanctions, including those against actors suspected of being responsible for widespread and systematic sexual violence, to be understood from diverse feminist perspectives and from larger critical writing on international law to expose the power relations that embed rather than dismantle gender, race, and economic privilege.

IV. The Enduring Relevance of Feminist Peace Studies

The failure to engage effectively with feminist peace studies within the Security Council's women, peace, and security framework has been matched with a failure to engage the prohibition on the use of force as a gendered component of international relations.[38] As such, in recalling feminist peace activism, for example the work of the

[38] eg see Fionnula Ni Aoláin, Dina Francesca Haynes, and Naomi Cahn, *On the Frontlines: Gender, War and the Post Conflict Process* (Oxford: Oxford University Press, 2011) which focuses on post-conflict processes.

Women's International League for Peace and Freedom in the creation of the League and the UN,[39] the simplicity of Article 2(4) is challenged and a quest for the development of the prohibition in response to contemporary understandings of the nexus between global inequalities, gendered understandings of violence, and the diversity of feminist approaches needs to be developed.

I have argued elsewhere that a failure to develop the legal finesse of Article 2(4) as a prohibition on the use of force is linked with histories of international institutions, such as the UN and the League of Nations, that do not recognise the role of feminist peace activism.[40] In turn, this leads to the preoccupation of states and scholars with the articulation of justifications, rather than the prohibition on the use of force. This constructs a status quo that contributes to, rather than diminishes, the level of conflict globally.

The placement of Article 2(4) as the epitome of state agreement on the nature of prohibited force was a significant legal development in 1945: the failure of states to continue to develop the legal reach of the prohibition does not mean this must always be the case. From a feminist perspective, Article 2(4) must be regarded as the beginning of the outlawing of state violence, so that the elaboration and development of what it means to have a prohibition on the use of force, its limits, its regulation, and its co-option into a gendered understanding of law and violence is connected to global feminist peace activism. Unfortunately, feminist peace activism remains a footnote, a sign, or completely invisible rather than a site of analytical and practical inquiry within MILS.

Within the Security Council's women, peace, and security resolutions, the possibility of force as a mechanism to halt widespread and systematic sexual violence is proposed in operative paragraph 1 of Resolutions 1820, 1888, and 1960.[41] This is markedly different from a feminist politics of peace, which emphasizes the need to work to prevent conflict through attention to social and economic inequalities both within and across states. Nor does the policy of taking 'necessary measures', via the Security Council as operative paragraph 1 of these resolutions proposes, work to challenge existing insecurities, the role of social and cultural constructions of gender, the persistence of gender-based violence within communities, or the need for disarmament rather than deployment of weapons into conflict zones. Like all of the resolutions on women, peace, and security, the provisions imagining the use of force to stop systematic and

[39] Lela B. Costin, 'Feminism, Pacificism, Internationalism and the 1915 International Congress of Women' (1982) 5 *Women's Studies International Forum* 301; Anne Wiltsher, *Most Dangerous Women: Feminist Peace Campaigners of the Great War* (London: Pandora, 1985); Leila Rupp, *Worlds of Women: The Making of an International Women's Movement* (Princeton, NJ: Princeton University Press, 1997).

[40] Heathcote, *The Law on the Use of Force*.

[41] See further: Gina Heathcote, 'Feminist Politics and the Use of Force: Theorising Feminist Action and Security Council Resolution 1325' (2011) 7 *Socio-Legal Review* 23–43; Letita Anderson, 'Politics by Other Means: When Does Sexual Violence Threaten International Peace and Security?' (2010) 17 *International Peacekeeping* 244.

widespread sexual violence in armed conflict construct responses to violence rather than working to stop it occurring in the first place.

The 2009 General Assembly debates on the Responsibility to Protect[42] demonstrate how, outside powerful Western states, support for increased interventions, authorized or otherwise, is low. In contrast, states in conflict zones recognize the strength of the first pillar of the Responsibility to Protect doctrine: the Responsibility to Prevent. This further indicates the complexity of harnessing the plural perspectives on the use of force that exist globally. That this is difficult, complex, and undoubtedly time-consuming is no reason to avoid commencing such a project.

Feminist perspectives that acknowledge peace activism as a vital voice within global feminism challenge our communities to continue to return to the prohibition, allowing those who have experienced the impact of force to contribute to the future refinement and application of the prohibition. It is, however, important to note that feminist peace activism is not a movement that is premised on women as peacemakers: such an approach would get us no further than the attempts to add women in political structures, discussed earlier, as this relies on stereotypes of femininity that feminist projects work towards disrupting. Feminist peace activism is, instead, a method and a means for speaking about peace through disarmament, through attention to the continuum of violence from the intimate to the international, and through identifying the persistence of gender-based violence in communities defined as peaceful and in those enduring conflict.

The endorsement of the Definition of Aggression[43] within the Crime of Aggression by the State Parties to the Rome Statute for the International Criminal Court in 2010 illustrates the difficulties of any attempt to build state consensus on force and aggression. At the same time, the agreement by the state parties to the Rome Statute in Kampala in 2010, and the slow shift towards establishing individual criminal responsibility for the crime of aggression, do demonstrate the possibilities that law offers.[44] Yet, international criminal law is reactive; in this sense, it cannot stop the use of force although it may, in the future, punish those who instigate force. As such, it is also time to initiate refinement and development of the prohibition on the use of force. Return to the prohibition requires acknowledgement of those who were excluded during international law's formation and from the expression of global values in the early years of the UN. As it is no longer possible to proclaim the inherent universality of a system that overtly excluded on the grounds of gender and ethnicity, strategies for inclusive and pluralist future outcomes need to be incorporated

[42] Transcript of the 63rd session of the UN General Assembly, 97th–101st Plenary Meeting, 21–28 July 2009, available at <http://www.responsibilitytoprotect.org/index.php/component/content/article/35-r2pcs-topics/2493-general-assembly-debate-on-the-responsibility-to-protect-and-informal-interactive-dialogue-#debate>.

[43] GA Res 3314 (XXIX) UN GAOR, 29th Sess, Supp No 31 (14 Dec 1974).

[44] For International Criminal Court developments with respect to the Crime of Aggression, see <http://www.iccnow.org/?mod=aggression>.

from this stage forward: as a global community we are well past discussing whether this is necessary.

Incorporating the participation of women and non-Western actors, with cross-class and cross-cultural perspectives to develop and extend the prohibition on the use of force is not a short-term project; however, few of the projects international law has embarked upon have been short term. If, as MILS tells us, international law began in 1648 with the Peace of Westphalia and the writings of the father of international law, Hugo Grotius, then tri-millennium recognition of the very limited perspective this model affords our understandings of international law are long overdue. The transfer of this recognition into challenging our accepted ways of acting is the next stage. Addressing the diversity of perspectives that feminist approaches bring to future debates needs to commence with attention to existing gender imbalances, which were discussed earlier. This is a project that equally requires attention as to who is permitted to speak on women's issues within international law and who is empowered within our communities to speak to power.

My recommendation, to develop the parameters of Article 2(4), is in contrast to the increasing emphasis placed on justifications and is voiced in the context of the previous recommendations regarding women's participation and agency. To develop Article 2(4) would require recognition of the inadequacy of the prohibition because it has been consistently read as accommodating justifications for violence rather than as a reason for state restraint. Development of the prohibition requires strategies that seek to disassociate constructions of the nation-state under international law from understandings of the Western-sexed legal subject.[45] Consequently, what begins as a strategy 'within' the contemporary contours of international law also requires a larger feminist project of re-imagining the basic norms and values that shape international law. Underlying this claim is an expectation that a renewed focus on the prohibition encourages peacebuilding initiatives and preventative strategies.

V. Conclusion

In her article on the 11 September 2011 attacks on the US, Wright argues, 'international law might be positively transformed if it were to take the critical approaches of feminist and other scholars seriously.'[46] This recalls Chinkin's approach in 1992 when a structural bias feminism, that recognized the harm and inequalities that

[45] See further: Heathcote, *The Law on the Use of Force*, 9–10.
[46] Wright, *The Horizon of Becoming*, 216.

women live with, globally, and the foundational bias of international law, was perceived as the path for the development of feminist perspectives. The Security Council has elaborated an agenda on women, peace, and security that downplays, and at times renders invisible, the diversity of these feminist approaches to law. The consequence is a failure of international institutions to see the prohibition on the use of force as a starting point for a transformative approach to the foundations of international law: indeed, military force is embedded within the women, peace, and security resolutions as a potential mechanism for halting widespread and systematic sexual violence despite the history of feminist scholarship highlighting the need for preventative strategies, the social and cultural causes of violence against women, and the role military force plays in perpetuating negative gender relations that create risks to women within communities.

Additionally, the failure to develop the spectrum of feminist perspectives within security documents and debates can be linked to the failure to regard the imperial history of international law, and the persistent inequalities both across and within communities, as contributing to the normative contours of debates on the use of force. A strategy of understanding the prohibition as a component of 'becoming human', rather than an endpoint in our debates on force, requires attention to the range of structural biases within international structures: gender, race, economic. Seeing the prohibition on the use of force as a foundational law that lacks sufficient interrogation and development is a first step in moving away from debates on when force should be deployed towards understanding that force is prohibited.

The prohibition on the use of force is the lynchpin of the international relationship between law and violence. Feminist scholarship demonstrates the co-option of gendered assumptions into the law and violence relationship[47] that emerges in the legal enforcement of public and private violence,[48] state and individual violence.[49] To reconsider the prohibition, to develop its reach and purpose, to talk seriously about what it means to prohibit the use of force, is a relevant starting point for the next generations of feminist scholars writing on international law. The approach I have outlined in this chapter begins with attention to the persistent gender imbalances in institutional structures at all levels, reconsiders the contemporary approach to combating sexual violence in armed conflict to remove the nexus with force, and returns to the diversity of feminist approaches that demonstrate the intersectionality of discriminations and that recall the history and concerns of feminist peace activism. This is also a timely project for international lawyers who seek to better incorporate global understandings of the law on the use of force that are sensitive to the persistence of gender inequalities.

[47] Lucinda Joy Peach in Jennifer Rycenga and Marguerite Waller (eds), *Frontline Feminisms: Women, War and Resistance* (London: Routledge, 2001).

[48] Cynthia Cockburn and Dubravka Zarkov (eds), *The Postwar Moment: Militaries, Masculinities and International Peacekeeping* (London: Lawrence and Wishart, 2002).

[49] Caroline Moser and Fiona Clark, *Victims, Perpetrators or Actors? Gender, Armed Conflict and Political Violence* (London: Zed Books, 2001).

CHAPTER 6

THE COLLECTIVE SECURITY SYSTEM AND THE ENFORCEMENT OF INTERNATIONAL LAW

JEAN D'ASPREMONT*

I. Introduction

HERE is a famous fable about international law: international law is riven by an enforcement disability, for it lacks a general mechanism to ensure that any behaviour unwanted by its primary rules is systematically and automatically sanctioned. Although commonly heard among circles of neophytes and non-specialists, this perennial tale has never been totally ridiculed by international lawyers as, like most fables, it touches on a sensitive chord. Though international lawyers have developed powerful argumentative tools to diminish the ontologically devastating consequences of this fable, they do not like to be reminded that international law somehow suffers from an enforcement disability. Indeed, the fable points to a recurrent complex afflicting them. Certainly, it is an emotional discomfort that international lawyers have learnt to live with and which they have successfully repressed over time. Yet,

* The author wishes to thank Madeleine Gorman for her assistance.

like any complex, it is never completely reined in and it resurfaces from time to time,[1] especially when they venture beyond their closed peer circles. When they step out of the epistemic community of international law, international lawyers, confronted with the enforcement disability of international law, feel compelled to rehabilitate international law as law. The enforcement complex of international lawyers is particularly rekindled each time blatant violations of international law dominate the headlines of mainstream news media worldwide. This is why international lawyers constantly feel the need to reaffirm how such disability does not strip international law of its legal pedigree.

In this context, it seems hard to deny that the two-step process that led to the creation of a collective security system in the 20th century bore a sweeping therapeutic effect on the previously mentioned complex of international lawyers. Whilst the failure of the League of Nations procedural framework for the resort to coercive powers exacerbated the enforcement complex of the discipline, the subsequent design of the 'Chapter VII' mechanism of the UN Charter, envisaged in the suburbs of Washington DC and finalized in San Francisco, created the hope that an enforcement procedure, endowed with real credentials, had finally been delivered. Despite being mainly oriented towards the settlement of disputes, the UN Charter was enthusiastically received by the international legal community for improving enforcement capabilities of international law. Although those hopes were quickly dashed by the Cold War stalemate, the collective security system put in place by the UN Charter fundamentally vindicated the ambitions of the epistemic community of international law and assuaged their complex.

These introductory epistemological considerations explain why, since 1945, it has become impossible to reflect upon the enforcement of international law in isolation from developments affecting the collective security system. It is against this backdrop that a parallel is drawn between the incremental sophistication of the enforcement of international law through the gradual consolidation of the collective security system and the evolving perceptions about the international legal system itself. More precisely, this chapter argues that the extent to which the collective security system contributes to the enforcement of international law informs how international lawyers understand international law as a whole. It is important to emphasize, however, that, although grappling with the contribution made by the collective security system to international law as a whole, this chapter maintains its distance from the perennial endeavours traditionally made by international lawyers to rehabilitate international law as law.[2]

[1] Despite the unanimity in rejecting the Austinian imperatival handicap, this charge 'still left traces in the international discourse'. See Alain Pellet, 'Sanctions' in Rüdiger Wolfrum (ed), *Max Planck Encyclopedia of Public International Law* (Oxford: Oxford University Press), available at <http://www.mpepil.com/home>, para 3.

[2] International lawyers making these efforts are usually those who feel existentially engaged in, and responsible for, international law and are especially troubled by its enforcement inability.

This chapter will briefly recall the theoretical debates about the role of enforcement in our understanding of international law (Section II). A few observations will then be formulated as to how the creation of a collective security system regulating the use of force, irrespective of its actual enforcement function, came to upend the way in which enforcement of international law is understood by international lawyers (Section III). Taking into account recent developments pertaining to non-state actors, as well as targeted and smart sanctions, it will re-evaluate the coercive role that can be performed by the collective security system (Section IV). Finally, this chapter will explain how the various steps in the development of the collective security system and our understanding thereof directly impinge on how international law as a whole is perceived. The concluding remarks will invite some critical reflections on the need of a catharsis that will purge international lawyers' enforcement complex vis-à-vis their reading of the collective security system (Section V).

II. Neutralizing the Austinian Imperatival Handicap of International Law

The enforcement disability of international law is often addressed in reference to John Austin who derided international law as morality for this same shortcoming. From such a perspective, international law cannot be properly considered law in a strict sense, that is, a set of commands, for it can only be enforced by moral sanctions.[3] Austin's demotion of international law to morality was informed by his view that law ought necessarily to be backed by sanctions. This conception was shared with Jeremy Bentham, although the latter contended that some commands would still be law even if supported only by moral and religious sanctions or if accompanied by an offer of reward.[4] The Austinian handicap of international law is well known and widely discussed in the literature.[5] It constitutes a common charge made by critics

[3] See John Austin, *The Province of Jurisprudence Determined and the Uses of the Study of Jurisprudence* (Indianapolis, IN: Hackett Publishing, 1832, repr 1998), para 201.

[4] J. Bentham, *A Fragment on Government* (Cambridge: Cambridge University Press 1988), 51.

[5] On the Austinian handicap of international law, see generally Anthony D'Amato, 'Is International Law Really "Law"' (1985) 79 *Northwestern University Law Review* 1293. See also Jean d'Aspremont, 'Herbert Hart and the Enforcement of International Law: Substituting Social Disability to the Austinian Imperatival Handicap of the International Legal System' (29 Jan 2012), available at SSRN: <http://ssrn.com/abstract=1995041>.

who are often called the 'deniers'.[6] These thinkers position themselves against the legal pedigree of international law and, hence, against the international legal scholarship as a whole, which they ridicule for deifying its object of study.

It will come as no surprise that international legal scholars promptly rebuffed such a charge. Threatened by what they perceived as a compelling attack against the nobility of their object of study and thus their own identity, international lawyers have unanimously rejected the Austinian charge against international law.[7] The rejection of the Austinian handicap of international law by international lawyers manifests itself in the adoption of some powerful counter-arguments. Two different argumentative tools against the Austinian imperatival handicap of international law have been devised by international legal scholars. Although there may be others, these tools represent the chief avenues through which one may circumvent the Austinian objection.

Two classical counter-objections against the Austinian imperatival handicap must thus be briefly recalled here. One the one hand, scholars like Kelsen, while embracing a coercive conception of international law, strive to demonstrate that international law is indeed a set of commands 'armed with sanctions' (Section II.A). On the other hand, other scholars challenge the definitional premise on which the Austinian imperatival charge is based and claim that the legal pedigree of international law is not dependent on it being a coercive order (Section II.B).

A. International Law as a Coercive Normative Order

The first argumentative construction to rebut the Austinian imperatival handicap turns Austin's argument on its head. Kelsen embodies such a rejection as he did not deny the necessity to ground law in coercion, but affirmed that international law was a coercive order where sanctions are mainly decentralized.[8] He relied on decentralized coercion to affirm the coercive character of international law, an approach that was not entirely unprecedented but is personified by his work.[9]

For Kelsen, a legal order is different from other kinds of positive normative orders, particularly morality, because they are coercive orders 'in the sense that

[6] For an illustration, see John R. Bolton, 'War and the United States Military: Is there Really "Law" in International Affairs?' (2000) 10 *Transnational Law and Contemporary Problems* 1.

[7] Prosper Weil, 'Le droit international en quête de son identité. Cours général de droit international public' (1992-IV) 237 *Recueil des cours de l'Académie de droit international* 54.

[8] See generally Hans Kelsen, 'Théorie du droit international public' (1953) 84 *Recueil des cours de l'Académie de droit international* 1, esp 13–17. For a discussion of that aspect of Kelsen's theory, see Jörg Kammerhofer, 'Kelsen—Which Kelsen? A Reapplication of the Pure Theory to International Law' (2009) 22 *Leiden Journal of International Law* 235, 227–8; see also Jochen von Bernstorff, *The Public International Law Theory of Hans Kelsen* (Cambridge: Cambridge University Press, 2010), 84–92.

[9] See Kaltenborn as studied by Bernstorff, *The Public International Law Theory of Hans Kelsen*, 15–20.

they react to antisocial "facts"...if necessary using physical force...inflicted as a coercive measure'.[10] Indeed, for Kelsen, coercion is what distinguishes a legal order from an 'ought-order' such as morality and religion.[11] While, in this respect, there is certainly kinship with the Austinian imperatival conception of law, Kelsen stops short of saying that membership to the legal order hinges on this norm being accompanied by a sanction. Non-coercive norms are not invalid. Coercion is a constitutive element of the legal order as a whole but not a validity criterion of each of the norms composing that legal order.[12]

For Kelsen, the extent to which the exercise of coercion against the unwanted behaviour is organized and institutionalized will usually serve as an indication of the development of the legal order. If the use of physical coercion becomes a delict while, at the same time, a sanction is authorized by the legal order that is claiming a monopoly on the use of physical coercion, then the legal order concerned is no longer a primitive legal order. In his view, primitive legal orders fall short of empowering an organ with the task of applying (physical) coercion. They allow self-help and leave this function to subjects injured by the delict.[13] In Kelsen's view, international law was undoubtedly such an underdeveloped order because coercion was mainly decentralized. Yet, he never went as far as Austin to deny that international law was actual law and even explained why it was undeniably so.[14] His demonstration that international law is endowed with enforcement powers was informed by his agenda to help international law to survive its inability to prevent the Second World War and buoy the emergence of an international order of peace.[15]

Kelsen's concept of law, when applied to international law, leads to the conclusion that international law is 'true law' for it contains institutions performing coercion. In particular, Kelsen found that reprisals and war, the 'legally stipulated consequence(s) of breach of law', perform such a function.[16] International law, in Kelsen's eyes, regulates the resort to both reprisals and wars and found some

[10] Hans Kelsen, *The Law of the United Nations: A Critical Analysis of Its Fundamental Problems* (London: Stevens and Sons, 1950), 34.

[11] Bernstorff, *The Public International Law Theory of Hans Kelsen*, 86.

[12] Kammerhofer, 'Kelsen—Which Kelsen?', 228.

[13] Hans Kelsen, *Principles of International Law* (New York: Rinehart, 1952), 14–15. See the remarks of Kammerhofer, 'Kelsen—Which Kelsen?', 228; see also Bernstorff, *The Public International Law Theory of Hans Kelsen*, 90–1.

[14] Kelsen, *Principles of International Law*, 18–64.

[15] The implicit agenda behind some aspects of Kelsen's Pure Theory has been the object of much discussion. See eg Bernstorff, *The Public International Law Theory of Hans Kelsen*, 84; Bruno Simma, according to whom Kelsen was intent on countering Hegel which had been translated into legal theory by Jellinek and thus aimed at strengthening the idea of an international rule of law: Bruno Simma, 'The Contribution of Alfred Verdross to the Theory of International Law' (1995) 6 *European Journal of International Law* 33, 41. Some similar arguments are made by Francois Rigaux, who argues that Kelsen opposed not only Hegel but also Triepel's dualism: Francois Rigaux, 'Hans Kelsen on International Law' (1998) 9 *European Journal of International Law* 325, 326.

[16] Bernstorff, *The Public International Law Theory of Hans Kelsen*, 88.

institutional forms of decentralized coercion in wars and reprisals.[17] Discussing the Chapter VII mechanism of the UN Charter, he affirmed that enforcement actions under Articles 39, 41, and 42 could *potentially* be interpreted as sanctions because such measures react to violations of the UN Charter.[18] He insisted that the sanctions adopted under Article 41 do not formally presuppose a violation of international law but only necessitate a finding that there has been a breach of the peace and security.[19]

Some famous international lawyers expressly endorsed Kelsen's neutralization of the Austinian imperatival handicap of international law.[20] Many others, while not expressly espousing Kelsen's approach, similarly contested Austin's contention that there were no enforcement mechanisms, even at his own time.[21] This view also finds support in the case law of the International Court of Justice (ICJ).[22] Others pushed the Kelsenian counterargument further by arguing that international law was a coercive order not only because of the existence of decentralized forms of sanctions but also by virtue of a wide range of soft enforcement mechanisms.[23] Although sanctions in international law are sometimes perceived as 'weak' or 'ineffective',[24] especially in some strands of the American international legal scholarship, the finding that international law is endowed with sanctions mechanisms has enjoyed wide support, even among American legal scholars.[25]

[17] To that end, he relied on the theory of *bellum justum* by virtue of which some wars could be deemed legal and others not. This is an aspect of Kelsen's theory which is most controversial for it is not certain that wars were unlawful before the Kellogg–Briand Pact.

[18] Bernstorff, *The Public International Law Theory of Hans Kelsen*, 735–6 (for Kelsen, Art 41 plays the role of 'reprisals' and Art 42 plays the role of war).

[19] Kelsen, *The Law of the United Nations*, 734.

[20] Paul Guggenheim, *Traité de droit international public*, Book 1 (Geneva: Librairie de l'Université, Georg & Cie, 1953). See also *Oppenheim's International Law* (8th edn, Oxford: Oxford University Press, 1908), 8, para 8. For a similar view, but in a milder form, see Ch. Leben, it is the 'possibility to have resort to a judge, although this remains very minimalistic in fact' (Ch. Lebel, 'La jurisdiction internationale' (1989) *Droits* 143 ff); see also Anthony D'Amato, 'The Coerciveness of International Law' (2009) 52 *German Yearbook of International Law* 437–60.

[21] Dino Kritsiotis, 'International Law and the Relative of Enforcement' in James Crawford and Martti Koskenniemi (eds), *The Cambridge Companion to International Law* (Cambridge: Cambridge University Press, 2012), 266.

[22] See the rather confident and upbeat reading of international law by the ICJ in 1966: 'In the international field, the existence of obligations that cannot in the last resort be enforced by any legal process, has always been the rule rather than the exception...' (*South West Africa*, Second Phase *(Ethiopia v. South Africa; Liberia v. South Africa)*, 18 July 1966, ICJ Rep 1966, para 86).

[23] For an interesting attempt to refute the Austinian handicap of international law by virtue of a conception of enforcement based on 'outcasting', see Oona Hathaway and Scott J. Shapiro, 'Outcasting: Enforcement in Domestic and International Law' (2011) 212 *Yale Law Journal* 252.

[24] See Jack L. Goldsmith and Eric A. Posner, *The Limits of International Law* (New York: Oxford University Press, 2005). This echoes the earlier position advocated by Hans Morgenthau, *Politics Among Nations* (New York: Alfred A. Knopf, 1948), 211, esp 229. For a challenge of this position, see Mary Ellen O'Connell, *The Power and Purpose of International Law: Insights from the Theory and Practice of Enforcement* (Oxford: Oxford University Press, 2011), esp 99–149.

[25] For a different view among American international legal scholars, see D'Amato, 'Is International Law Really "Law"'.

B. International Law as a Source-Based Order

Another avenue overcoming the Austinian imperatival handicap is to strip the concept of international law of any coercive feature and demote sanctions to, at the most, a condition of the effectiveness of international law, as opposed to a condition of its existence. It is not unreasonable to say that this is the route commonly taken by most international lawyers nowadays, albeit sometimes unconsciously or unreflectively. International law is thought of in isolation from its sanctions, the latter being at best construed as an effectiveness-enhancement mechanism.

It is not certain that the paternity for such an approach should be ascribed to Hart. Yet, it is usually under the banner of a Hartian approach to international law, which is quite dominant in the international legal scholarship, though not always for good reasons,[26] that the Austinian imperatival handicap was rejected.[27] Hart expressly broke with the sanction-based conception of law popular in the, until then, dominant utilitarian tradition of Hobbes, Bentham, and Austin. Even if Hart agreed that law is an expression of will, coercive mechanisms no longer constitute a central feature of any legal system, for it is entirely conceivable that a legal system does not need coercive mechanisms.[28] He recognized that enforcement mechanisms are common, but that they are not necessary for such systems to be legal systems.[29]

This is the extent to which Hart helps to accommodate the enforcement deficiencies of international law when it comes to enforcement. First, although for different reasons, Hart demoted international law to 'law improperly so called'.[30] More fundamentally, enforcement, while having been wiped out from the surface of Hart's theory, re-enters through the back door. While not being a constitutive feature of Hart's concept of law, enforcement is an implied prerequisite of a Hartian legal system. Hart's Concept of Law, preserves the role of enforcement on its surface, but then restores its prominent role by way of repercussion. Indeed, Hart's concept of law presupposes the existence of law-applying authority, thereby making an enforcement mechanism absolutely essential. In my view, although secondary at first glance, enforcement in Hart's theory resurfaces in the form of law-application.[31] Without law-applying authorities, there cannot be meaningful rules of recognition—no law-applying authority means no production of meaning for the rule of recognition, and thus no meaningful theory of

[26] See generally Jean d'Aspremont, 'Herbert Hart in Post-Modern International Legal Scholarship' in Jean d'Aspremont and Jörg Kammerhofer, *International Legal Positivism in a Post-Modern World* (Cambridge: Cambridge University Press, 2014).

[27] Pellet makes a similar finding, Pellet, 'Sanctions'.

[28] H. L. A. Hart, *The Concept of Law* (2nd edn, Oxford: Clarendon Press, 1994), 216–20. See also Joseph Raz, *Practical Reason and Norms* (Princeton, NJ: Princeton University Press, 1990), 154–62.

[29] Hart, *The Concept of Law*, 179–80.

[30] Hart, *The Concept of Law*, 232–7.

[31] I have defended this elsewhere. See d'Aspremont, 'Herbert Hart'.

sources. Law-application, and the practice of law-identification (ascertainment) that comes with it, is thus an indispensable condition for the existence of a legal system.

By elevating the practice of ascertainment by law-applying authorities to a linchpin of the rule of recognition, Hart substituted one handicap for another. In this sense, Hart only provides a temporary respite from the Austinian handicap, which he subsequently reintroduces in another form.[32] A social requirement, which is not necessarily fulfilled by international law, follows the imperatival Austinian requirement. It is uncertain that international law can always accumulate a sufficient amount of social practice for meaningful rules of recognition to emerge. It is not that we lack law-applying authority. Nor is it that courts and tribunals fail to sufficiently apply and identify international rules. It is simply that there is little awareness by law-applying authorities that they share a linguistic community. In practice, international judges do not cultivate a strong sense of membership to the same linguistic community. Each court, in isolation from others' activities, carries out the practice of law-ascertainment.[33]

Here is certainly not the place to dwell on such theoretical questions. For the sake of these brief observations, it suffices to highlight that a Hartian take on international law plays down the Austinian imperatival handicap of international law but unearths another form of disability: the deficient social conscience of courts and tribunals in relation to the social practice relating to the rule of recognition, and the great inability of the system to produce a consistent social practice of law-identification, without which there cannot be sound and meaningful rules of recognition. In Hart's understanding of law, the Austinian disability of the international legal system is superseded by another equally serious ailment.

Whatever the actual value of Hart's rebuttal of the Austinian imperatival handicap, it is important to highlight that such an approach has been followed by many international lawyers who construe sanction at best as a condition of the effectiveness of international law and not as a condition of its existence.[34] According to these lawyers, the organization and institutionalization of the sanction are only indications of the degree of institutionalization of a legal order,[35] which in that sense must

[32] d'Aspremont, 'Herbert Hart'.

[33] For a discussion on the social deficiency of international law and the absence of social conscience of international courts and tribunal, see Jean d'Aspremont, *Formalism and the Sources of International Law* (Oxford: Oxford University Press, 2011), 213 ff.

[34] Gerald G. Fitzmaurice, 'The Foundations of the Authority of International Law and the Problem of Enforcement' (1956) 19 *Modern Law Review* 1 ff. On a similar move on this question in 19th century-German scholarship, see Bernstorff, *The Public International Law Theory of Hans Kelsen*, 85; the so-called 'Manhattan School' of international law has even contended that sanction is not necessary for the effectiveness of international law. See the famous contention by Thomas Franck that 'powerless' rules are obeyed, even by powerful states. See Thomas M. Franck, *The Power of Legitimacy Among Nations* (Oxford: Oxford University Press, 1990), 3.

[35] Weil, 'Le droit international en quête de son identité', 55.

be seen as lagging behind domestic or regional legal orders. This view received some support from the ICJ in the *Barcelona Traction* case.[36]

It is interesting to note that in American legal scholarship, the Hartian rejection of the constitutive role of sanctions was energetically vindicated by a number of scholars who, following Louis Henkin,[37] endeavoured to reject realist scepticism towards international law.[38] Yet, it was interpreted slightly differently by these scholars, for, drawing on Hart,[39] they claimed that, at the heart of international law, lies a belief.[40] Such a belief, in their view, manifests itself in the dominant compliant behaviour of states. This behaviourist and necessarily empirical turn is important to mention, even though it is not strictly in line with a Hartian understanding of law that favours compliance by law-applying authorities over acts of primary actors. Indeed, this turn opened the way for a new strand of scholarship in American literature focused on compliance by primary actors and the driving forces behind the pull for compliance of international law.[41]

III. Centralization and Individualization of Enforcement of International Law

Enforcement in international law has witnessed two key moves over the last two centuries. There is a lot of controversy regarding the extent to which the collective security system can itself be considered a centralized enforcement mechanism

[36] *Barcelona Traction*, Second Phase, 5 Feb 1970, ICJ Rep 1970, para 82: 'The lack of a jurisdictional link cannot be regarded either in this or in other fields of international law as entailing the non-existence of a right'.

[37] Louis Henkin, *How Nations Behave* (2nd edn, New York: Columbia University Press, 1979), 329–32.

[38] For a follower of Henkin's use of Hart, see eg Mary Ellen O'Connell, *The Power and Purpose of International Law: Insights from the Theory and Practice of Enforcement* (Oxford: Oxford University Press, 2011). See also Abram Chayes and Antonia Handler Chayes, *The New Sovereignty* (Cambridge, MA: Harvard University Press, 1995) according to which resources allocated to coercive sanctions are misplaced and would be better allocated by attempting to change states' behaviour through managerial strategies.

[39] See Louis Henkin, *How Nations Behave*, 58.

[40] Mary Ellen O'Connell, *The Power and Purpose of International Law*, esp 99–149, 78.

[41] For a famous embodiment of this approach, see Thomas Frank, *The Power of Legitimacy among Nations*. See also Anne-Marie Slaughter's embrace of the democratic peace theory and her contention that the march towards democracy necessarily brings about greater compliance with rules on the prohibition to use force. See Anne-Marie Slaughter, 'International Law in a World of Liberal States' (1995) 6 *EJIL* 503. For criticism, see Jose Alvarez, 'Do Liberal States Behave Better? A Critique of Slaughter's Liberal Theory' (2001) 12 *European Journal of International Law* 183–2.

of international law. Irrespective of whether the collective security system can be elevated into an enforcement mechanism per se, its creation has fundamentally impinged the understanding of sanctions by the international legal system of unwanted behaviours at the international level. Whatever the ultimate function performed by the collective security system, its creation has led to a decommissioning of self-help as the primary enforcement tool of international law. For this reason, the first major evolution affecting enforcement is the gradual move to a collective security system and the partial decommissioning of self-help as an enforcement tool (Section III.A). Over the years, however, the sanction mechanism of the collective security system has itself undergone significant changes, and accordingly sanctions of unwanted behaviours have been customized to an unprecedented degree (Section III.B). These two moves, however, should not obfuscate the persistence of other more disparate mechanisms endowed with some enforcement function (Section III.C).

A. Decommissioning Self-Help: The Move to the Collective Security System

Until the 20th century, international law adopted a very permissive posture towards self-help, which was largely unregulated. As a result, self-help, which includes forcible measures, was elevated into the primary enforcement mechanism of the international legal order.[42] Although performing other functions, such as punitive and retributive,[43] the enforcement function of self-help was both backward-looking and forward-looking. Self-help constituted a means for a state to coerce another state to cease the breach of an obligation owed to it and possibly to repair the harm resulting therefrom.

The central position of self-help as a tool for the enforcement of international law was gradually dismantled in the first half of the 20th century.[44] Indeed, although it did not disappear completely from the range of reactions available under international law, self-help was decommissioned as the central tool of enforcement of international law as a result of a move that, curiously, is considered in retrospect by the epistemic community of international law to be a very positive development

[42] James Leslie Brierly, *The Law of Nations: An Introduction to the International Law of Peace* (6th edn, Oxford: Clarendon Press, 1963), 398; Derek W. Bowett, *Self-Defence in International Law* (Manchester: Manchester University Press, 1958), 11; Fitzmaurice, 'The Foundations of the Authority of International Law and the Problem of Enforcement', 8.

[43] Elisabeth Zoller, *Peacetime Unilateral Remedies: An Analysis of Countermeasures* (Ardsley, NY: Transnational, 1984), 55. See also Section IV.D.

[44] See generally Math Noortmann, *Enforcing International Law: From Self-Help to Self-Contained Regimes* (Farnham: Ashgate, 2005).

and a factor of progress.[45] This shift brought an end to what was perceived as the dark age of international law.[46]

The various steps of this move towards a centralized collective security system are well known.[47] After the adoption of the 1907 Hague Convention Respecting the Limitation of the Employment of Force for the Recovery of Contract Debts[48] and the partial proceduralization and institutionalization of war under the League of Nations,[49] the adoption of the Kellogg–Briand Pact[50] was the death knell of self-help as the central enforcement tool of international law. Such a decommissioning of self-help was confirmed and generalized by the UN Charter in 1945, which prohibited both the threat and the use of force.[51] Although not excluding decentralized forms of authorized non-forcible coercion, it empowered one central body with coercive powers. In contrast with the Pact of the League of Nations, the UN Charter placed the power to make a finding that could trigger the sanction mechanism in one centralized body, rather than leaving the determination to member states.[52] Also in contrast with the Pact, the determination of non-forcible coercive measures was left to the discretion of the Council and not formally designed *ex ante*.[53] The centralization inherent in the Chapter VII architecture coexisted with a high degree of politicization. The resulting politicization of the policing function of the Security Council was informed both by the need to place more emphasis on dispute settlement rather than the restoration of legality,[54] and by a

[45] See also the critical remarks of David Kennedy, 'The Move to Institutions' (1987) 8 *Cardozo Law Review* 841. See also Thomas Skouteris, *The Notion of Progress in International Law Discourse* (The Hague: T.M.C. Asser Press, 2010).

[46] Hector A. Munro, 'The Case of the Corfu Minefield' (1947) 10 *Modern Law Review* 363–76; interestingly, that period of time is sometimes—oddly—portrayed as being very positivistic—see Joachim von Elbe, 'The Evolution of the Concept of Just War in International Law' (1939) 33 *American Journal of International Law* 684–5.

[47] See Ramesh Thakur, 'Reconfiguring the UN System of Collective Security', Chapter 8 in this volume.

[48] See generally James Brown Scott, *The Hague convention (II) of 1907 respecting the limitation of the employment of force for the recovery of contract debts* (Washington DC: Carnegie, 1915).

[49] See generally David Kennedy, 'The Move to Institutions' (1987) 8 *Cardozo Law Review* 841.

[50] See generally Georges Rambert, *Le Droit de la Guerre et le Pacte Briand–Kellogg* (Lausanne: Payot & cie, 1931); David H. Miller, *The Peace Pact of Paris: A Study of the Briand–Kellogg Treaty* (New York: Putnam, 1928).

[51] On the prohibition of the treaty of force, see generally Nikolaos Tsagourias, 'The Prohibition of Threats of Force' in Nigel White and Christian Henderson (eds), *Research Handbook on International Conflict and Security Law* (Cheltenham: Edward Elgar, 2012), available at SSRN: <http://ssrn.com/abstract=2074015>; see also François Dubuisson and Anne Lagerwall, 'Que signifie encore l'interdiction de recourir a la menace de la force?' in Karine Bannelier, Theodore Christakis, Olivier Corten, and Barbara Delcourt (eds), *L'intervention en Irak et le Droit International* (Paris: Pedone, 2004), 83.

[52] Art 16 of the Pact of the League of Nations.

[53] Art 16 of the Pact of the League of Nations. For an unsuccessful application, see Albert E. Highley, 'The Actions of the States Members of the League of Nations in Application of Sanctions against Italy', thesis Université de Genève, 1938.

[54] On this equilibrium in the UN Charter, see Oscar Schachter, 'United Nations Law' (1994) 88 *American Journal of International Law* 14.

sense of realism after the fate of Article 16 of the Pact of the League of Nations. Accordingly, political discretion was expressly provided for in the Charter and the automaticity found in the Pact of the League, which is often construed as one of the causes of the failure of the League system, was abandoned. The Pact of the League of Nations and the UN Charter did not dovetail either as regards the implementation of forcible and non-forcible measures. There is little doubt that the centralization of the exercise of coercive powers by and through the Security Council is the hallmark of the move to a collective security regime in the first half of the 20th century.

This does not mean that the move towards the collective security system is uncontroversial. Much debate persists both as to whether Chapter VII itself puts in place an enforcement mechanism *stricto sensu* and whether the prohibition to use force by the Kellogg–Briand Pact and subsequently by the UN Charter still left some room for decentralized enforcement performed through forcible self-help. It is slightly uncertain whether the *forcible* coercive powers centralized in the Security Council necessarily exclude the decentralized *forcible* coercive powers of states. This largely depends on how one construes self-defence. It seems that the dominant position among experts is that, whether in the form of self-defence[55] or the state of necessity,[56] the UN Charter has eliminated any measure of *forcible* self-help. The rejection of military countermeasures by the International Law Commission buttresses that position.[57]

The ICJ expressly acknowledged this principled decommissioning of self-help as an enforcement measure in its first contentious case:

> The Court can only regard the alleged right of intervention as the manifestation of a policy of force, such as has, in the past, given rise to most serious abuses and such as cannot, whatever be the present defects in international organization, find a place in international law. Intervention is perhaps still less admissible in the particular form it would take here; for,

[55] Olivier Corten, *The Law Against War* (Oxford: Hart, 2010), 348–400; Christine Gray, *International Law and the Use of Force* (3rd edn, Oxford: Oxford University Press, 2008), 348–69. In the same vein, Kammerhofer, 'Kelsen—Which Kelsen?', 244–5; on the rejection of collective self-defence as an enforcement mechanism, see Dissenting Opinion of Judge Jennings, *Military and Paramilitary Activities in and against Nicaragua (Nicaragua v. US)*, 27 June 1986, ICJ Rep 1986, 545.

[56] Sarah Heathcote, 'Est-ce que l'état de nécessité est un principe de droit international coutumier?' (2007) 40 *Revue Belge de Droit International* 53; see also Jean d'Aspremont, 'Mapping the Concepts Behind the Contemporary Liberalization of the Use of Force in International Law' (2010) 31 *University of Pennsylvania Journal of International Law* 1133–5.

[57] See Art 50 of the Articles on the Responsibility of States, Report of the International Law Commission (ILC) on the work of its 53rd session, UN GAOR, 56th Sess, Supp No 10, A/56/10, ch IV.E.1 There is, however, some ambiguity in the earlier work of the ILC. See ILC, Report 1979, *Yearbook of the International Law Commission*, 1979, vol II (2), 131, note 593 (where self-defence is seen as the only case of military reactive measures).

from the nature of things, it would be reserved for the most powerful States, and might easily lead to perverting the administration of international justice itself.[58]

A similar position was echoed in the *Nicaragua* case:

In any event, while the United States might form its own appraisal of the situation as to respect for human rights in Nicaragua, the use of force could not be the appropriate method to monitor or ensure such respect.[59]

Equally important for the sake of this chapter is to recall that the Security Council was empowered not only with a monopoly on forcible coercive measures, but also with express competences to take *non-forcible* coercive measures.[60] The other fundamental feature of the Charter's collective security system that impacted the debate about the enforcement of international law is the power to adopt non-forcible measures, which can potentially trump any conflicting rule of international law. Whilst the possibility for a central body to resort to non-forcible coercive measures was already present in the Pact of the League of Nations,[61] the UN Charter reinforced, centralized, and systematized such a mechanism.

These provisions were first used during the crisis in Rhodesia in 1965,[62] which was quickly followed by many other instances.[63] It is known to all observers that the use of these non-forcible coercive measures came to surpass the maintenance of international peace and security *stricto senso*. It is sometimes argued that some of the Security Council's main achievements lie in the non-military measures that it has ordered,[64] as is illustrated today by the Security Council's use of its Chapter VII powers for mostly non-military purposes.[65] Moreover, the measures that the Security Council typically orders are not conceived as measures preceding a possible authorization to use force; they are construed as the final end of the Council's action.

[58] *Corfu Channel (UK v. Albania)*, Judgment of 9 Apr 1949, ICJ Rep 1949, 35; see the critical remarks on that aspect of the case by Theodore Christakis, 'Intervention and Self-Help' in Karine Bannelier, Theodore Christakis, and Sarah Heathcote (eds), *The ICJ and the Evolution of International Law: The Enduring Impact of the 'Corfu Channel' Case* (London: Routledge, 2012), 211–25; see also Christine Gray, 'A Policy of Force' in Bannelier, Christakis, and Heathcote, *The ICJ and the Evolution of International Law*, 226–41.

[59] *Military and Paramilitary Activities in and against Nicaragua (Nicaragua v. US)*, 27 June 1986, ICJ Rep 1986, 134, para 268.

[60] See in particular UN Charter, Arts 25 and 41.

[61] See Pact of the League of Nations, Art 16.

[62] Res 216 (1965) and Res 217 (1965) on Southern Rhodesia.

[63] Among others see, South Africa, Res 418 (1977); Iraq, Res 661 and 662 (1990); Libya, Res 748 (1992); Yugoslavia, Res 713 (1991); Sudan, Res 1054 (1996); Angola, Res 1173 (1998) and 1295 (2000); Sierra Leone, Res 1306 (2000); Liberia, Res 1343 (2001).

[64] This is one of the ideas behind Vera Gowlland-Debbas (ed), *United Nations Sanctions and International Law* (Dordrecht: Kluwer Law International, 2001).

[65] For an analysis of that practice, see Lori Damrosch, 'Enforcing International Law through Non-Forcible Measures' (1997) 269 *Recueil des cours de l'Académie de droit international* 9–250, esp 102–54. More recently, see Andrea Charron, *UN Sanctions and Conflict: Responding to Peace and Security Threats* (London: Routledge, 2011).

The exercise of the Council's powers to take non-forcible measures has been the theatre of another fundamental move affecting the question of enforcement: individualization. This second move must now be discussed, for it brought about a great and unprecedented sophistication of the non-forcible coercive powers of the Security Council, which in turn has had consequences on the perceived enforcement functions bestowed upon the Council.

B. Customizing International Security: The Move to Individualization of Sanctions

The conferral of non-forcible coercive powers to the Security Council is as important a change as the monopoly on measures involving the use of force with which it was endowed. By virtue of non-forcible measures under Article 41 of the UN Charter, the Security Council has been implementing a broad range of policies, such as reconstructing states[66] or fighting impunity through the creation of judicial bodies.[67] Additional tasks alien to the maintenance of peace and security have been conferred upon the Council through non-UN mechanisms. For example, the Security Council can refer country-specific situations to the International Criminal Court, which then has the power to launch investigations even in countries that are not signatories to the Rome Statute.[68] All in all, the Council has increasingly vacated its role of guardian of the *order* and has focused on problems of *justice*. In doing so, the 'Police' has, in Martti Koskenniemi's famous words, ventured into the 'Temple',[69] a development that is at odds with the idea that the promotion of justice is reserved for the General Assembly.[70]

It is unnecessary to discuss the legality of these radical alterations to the Charter, which were brought about by 'subsequent practice'.[71] The substance *ratione*

[66] See SC Res 1244 (1999) on Kosovo.

[67] See SC Res 827, S/RES/827 (25 May 1993) (on the establishment of the International Criminal Tribunal for the former Yugoslavia, ICTY); SC Res 955, S/RES/955 (8 Nov 1994) (on the establishment of the International Criminal Tribunal for Rwanda, ICTR). See more generally, SC Res 1757, S/RES/1757 (30 May 2007) (on the creation of the Special Tribunal for Lebanon).

[68] See Rome Statute of the International Criminal Court, 17 July 1998, 2187 UNTS 90, Art 13.

[69] Martti Koskenniemi, 'The Police in the Temple: Order, Justice and the UN: A Dialectical View' (1995) 6 *European Journal of International Law* 325, 328–9.

[70] See Declaration on the Establishment of a New International Economic Order, GA Res 3201 (S-VII), A/RES/3201 (S-VII) (1 May 1974); see also Declaration on the granting of independence to colonial countries and peoples, GA Res 1514 (XV), A/RES/1514 (XV) (14 Dec 1960); Request for an advisory opinion from the International Court of Justice on the legality of the threat or use of nuclear weapons, GA Res 49/75, A/RES/49/75 (15 Dec 1994).

[71] On the notion of subsequent practice, see ILC, Study on Treaties and Times: Effect on Treaties of Subsequent Agreement and Practice, see preliminary study by Georg Nolte, A/63/10, Annex A. On the motives that can potentially inform the choice for the use of subsequent practice in treaty interpretations, see Julian Arato, 'Subsequent Practice and Evolutive Interpretation: Techniques of Treaty Interpretation over Time and Their Diverse Consequences' (2010) 9 *Law and Practice of International Courts and Tribunals* 443–94.

personae of the measures adopted in the exercise of the Security Council's non-forcible coercive powers have evolved dramatically. Originally thought of as sanctions against states, the sanctions practice by the Security Council has increasingly been aimed at more specific and carefully delineated subjects, including the targeting of non-state entities.[72] The ICJ subsequently recognized the legality of this practice.[73] Simultaneously, resulting from concern over the humanitarian fallout of broad sanctions regimes, the Council turned to the use of 'smart sanctions' and in particular to individual-oriented sanctions resting on a listing system by sanctions committees.[74] As early as the crisis in Haiti in the early 1990s, the Security Council had initiated a new model of sanctions based on listings nominally designating individuals.[75] The targeting of the leaders of the National Union for the Total Independence of Angola (UNITA)[76] and individuals in Sierra Leone followed this trend.[77]

It is important to realize that such practices still continued to be of a collective nature as targeted individuals were being identified by virtue of their *formal* participation in a government or an organized insurgent group. This is why the final step towards full individualization and de-territorialization[78] only came later with the anti-terrorist policies which member states decided to carry out through the collective security system, rather than through fully decentralized channels.[79] The smart and targeted sanctions which they designed on that occasion—and which further institutionalized the Council's exercise of its coercive powers[80]—reached an unprecedented level of sophistication meant to avoid the fallout witnessed in the case of general and broad sanctions regimes. This practice of smart and targeted sanctions continued to consolidate itself; which did not prove unproblematic, especially in terms of the protection owed to the rights of individuals.[81] Controversies were spurred by the challenge of the European Court of Justice[82] and the creation of an ombudsperson.[83] Interestingly, these

[72] See Res 942 (1994), Bosnian Serbs; or UNITA in Angola Res 864 (1993).

[73] *Accordance with international law of the unilateral declaration of independence in respect of Kosovo (Request for Advisory Opinion)*, 22 July 2010, ICJ Rep 2010, paras 116–17.

[74] Pellet, 'Sanctions', paras 33–8. [75] Res 917 (1994). [76] Res 1127 (1997).

[77] Res 1171 (1998). [78] Pellet, 'Sanctions', para 36.

[79] Res 1390 (2002); 1452 (2002); 1455 (2003); 1526 (2004); 1617 (2005); 1735 (2006); 1904 (2009); 1989 (2011).

[80] On the Terrorism Committee, see generally Eric Rosand, 'Security Council Resolution 1373, the Counter-Terrorism Committee, and the Fight Against Terrorism' (2003) 97 *American Journal of International Law* 333–41.

[81] See generally Larissa van den Herik, 'The Security Council's Targeted Sanctions Regimes: In Need of Better Protection of the Individual' (2007) 20 *Leiden Journal of International Law* 797–807.

[82] Jean d'Aspremont and Frédéric Dopagne, '*Kadi*: The ECJ's Reminder of the Elementary Divide Between Legal Orders' (2008) 5 *International Organizations Law Review* 371–9.

[83] Laurence Boisson de Chazournes and Pieter-Jan Kuyper, 'Mr. Kadi and Mrs. Prost: Is the UN Ombudsperson Going to Find Herself Between a Rock and a Hard Place?' in Eva Rieter and Henri de Waele (eds), *Evolving Principles of International Law: Studies in Honour of Karel C. Wellens* (Leiden: Martinus Nijhoff, 2012), 71–90; Kimberly Prost, 'Fair Process and the Security Council: A Case

recent developments have required the use of coercion by the Security Council to undergo a further process of customization and sophistication.[84] Such practice shows that the coercion 'authorized' by the international legal system has grown more precise and specific. The customization and sophistication of the exercise of non-forcible coercive power by the Council have reinforced the conviction of international lawyers that the collective security system can effectively perform enforcement functions.

c. Coexistence with Other Coercive Reactive Mechanisms

The creation of a collective security system, and its growing individualization, customization, and overall sophistication, have not occurred in a vacuum. The main change brought about by the collective security system is that coercive powers outside the UN framework can only be non-forcible. Forcible self-help was decommissioned and the power to resort to forcible coercive measures was bestowed exclusively upon the Council. Conversely, the non-forcible coercive powers of the Council were never meant to be exclusive of other coercive measures, either centralized or decentralized. Many of these measures even came with a much more explicit reactive character and were expressly geared towards enforcement.

Three types of such measures can be identified. They can be centralized and internal as in some institutional regimes like the World Trade Organization (WTO) or the European Union (EU).[85] They can be completely decentralized, being the object of some coordination by virtue of an international organization, such as the obligation not to recognize.[86] Or, they can be completely decentralized like countermeasures, though coordination is not excluded. These measures perform

for the Office of the Ombudsperson' in Ana María Salinas de Frías, Katja L.H. Samuel, and Nigel D. White (eds), *Counter-Terrorism: International Law and Practice* (Oxford: Oxford University Press, 2012), 409–23; Grant L. Willis, 'Security Council Targeted Sanctions, Due Process and the 1267 Ombudsperson' (2011) 42 *Georgetown Journal of International Law* 673–745.

[84] On the mechanisms put in place after the European contestation, see Francesco Francioni, 'The Right of Access to Justice to Challenge the Security Council's Targeted Sanctions: After-thoughts on "Kadi"' in Ulrich Fastenrath et al (ed), *From Bilateralism to Community Interest: Essays in Honour of Judge Bruno Simma* (Oxford: Oxford University Press, 2011), 908–22. See also Grant L. Willis, 'Security Council Targeted Sanctions, Due Process and the 1267 Ombudsperson' (2011) 42 *Georgetown Journal of International Law* 673–745.

[85] On these regimes, see the remarks of Bruno Simma, 'Self-Contained Regimes' (1985) 16 *Netherlands Yearbook of International Law* 111.

[86] See Art 41 of the Articles on States Responsibility (2001).

enforcement functions. Among them, countermeasures probably constitute the enforcement measure 'par excellence'.[87] Such decentralized modes of enforcement of international law can, among other things, even constitute a very powerful tool for the enforcement of international law in the general interest.[88] They can also perform other functions, such as measures possessing a coercive character but not aimed at enforcement. Instances of this latter type of measure include the termination of a treaty by virtue of the *exceptio non adimpleti contractus*[89] or the invalidity of a treaty by virtue of unauthorized coercion.[90]

Furthermore, there is a range of informal mechanisms which have not been formally organized by international law and which nonetheless can be coercive and geared towards enforcement. This is the case for all measures that constitute retorsion and which do not need to be 'authorized' by the international legal system.[91] Finally, there are all those measures the coercive effect of which is purely 'reputational'[92] or 'spontaneous',[93] whereby the interference boils down to damaging reputation.

A collective security system thus emerged in the 20th century. The development of targeted and smart sanctions did not necessarily generate a simplification of the range of coercive measures available in international law. It is beyond the scope of this chapter to discuss how the sophisticated collective security system is to be articulated with regard to other coercive reactive mechanisms. The internal and external complexity of the exercise of coercive powers on the international law plane has been demonstrated; it will now be shown how the design of a collective security system and its great sophistication over the last two decades reinforced the conviction that the collective security system could be endowed with enforcement functions.

[87] See the critical remarks by Pierre-Marie Dupuy, 'Observations sur la pratique récente des 'sanctions' de l'illicite' (1983) 87 *Revue générale de droit international public* 505, esp 526 ff.

[88] Christian Tams, 'Individual States as Guardians of Community Interests' in Fastenrath et al, *From Bilateralism to Community Interest*, 379–405; Christian Tams even argues that decentralization of enforcement is no longer a second-best (at 405).

[89] Art 60 of the 1969 and 1986 Vienna Conventions on the Law of Treaties.

[90] Arts 52 and 53 of the 1969 and 1986 Vienna Conventions on the Law of Treaties.

[91] On retorsion as enforcement measures, see generally Lori Fisler Damrosch, 'Enforcing International Law through Non-Forcible Measures' (1998) 269 *Recueil des cours de l'Académie de droit international* 9–250.

[92] Andrew Guzman, *How International Law Works—A Rational Choice Theory* (Oxford: Oxford University Press, 2008), 33.

[93] De Visscher distinguished between techniques institutionnelles, techniques d'autoprotection, and techniques spontanées (technically institutional, technically self-protective, and technically spontaneous) (Paul De Visscher, 'Cours general de droit international public' (1972) 136 *Recueil des cours de l'Académie de droit international* 138–53).

IV. Enforcement of International Law Through the Collective Security System

While there seems to be unanimity among experts and observers that forcible self-help was banned by virtue of the collective security system and the prohibition to use force,[94] there is much disagreement as to the impact of these instruments on the enforcement of international law through non-forcible measures. The decommissioning of self-help[95] and the aforementioned sophistication of the Security Council's exercise of non-forcible coercive power,[96] led to the growing expectation that the collective security system could perform enforcement functions, in one way or another. In spite of this general inclination to assign these enforcement responsibilities, there has not been much agreement as to the type of enforcement role that could be bestowed upon the UN system. In particular, there have been four diverging views on the enforcement role that such mechanisms could play and which ought to be briefly outlined here. Mention is made of the enforcement of international law as a whole (Section IV.A), the enforcement of the UN Charter prescriptions (Section IV.B), the enforcement of peace (Section IV.C), as well the enforcement of justice though retribution (Section IV.D) that the collective security system is said to be capable of performing.

A. The Collective Security System as an Enforcement Mechanism of International Law

According to that view, the use of the sanctions regime of Chapter VII can be considered an enforcement mechanism of international law when the threat to the peace is grounded in violations of international law. A number of authors accordingly argue for the coincidence of the maintenance of peace and security and the enforcement of international law.[97] Some of those embracing this view have gone so far as to claim that, at least in explicit cases, the finding or determination of a violation recognized by the Council should be held to bear definitive legal effect.[98]

[94] See n 56. [95] See Section III.A. [96] See Section III.B.

[97] Pellet, 'Sanctions', para 17. Daniel Joyner, *International Law and the Proliferation of Weapons of Mass Destruction* (Oxford: Oxford University Press, 2009), 178; Jean Combacau, *Le pouvoir de sanction de l'ONU. Étude théorique de la coercition non militaire* (Paris: Pedone, 1974), 9–16; Louis Cavaré, 'Les sanctions dans le cadre de l'ONU' (1951-I) *Recueil des cours de l'Académie de droit international* 191–291, 221; Michel Virally, *L'Organisation Mondiale* (Paris: Armand Colin, 1972), 453; Marco Roscini, 'The United Nations Security Council and the Enforcement of International Humanitarian Law' (2010) 43 *Israel Law Review* 334.

[98] Vera Gowlland-Debbas, 'Security Council Enforcement Action and Issues of State Responsibility' (1994) 43 *International and Comparative Law Quarterly* 74–90; see also Lori Damrosch, 'The Permanent

This view is contested. Traditionally, the most compelling objection raised against this view pertains to the absence of any formal prerequisite for the Council to make a finding of wrongdoing by the subjects of the coercive measures.[99] It is true that in practice, as discussed later,[100] many situations qualified as a 'breach of the peace' as well as many of the situations qualified as a 'threat to the peace' involved violations of the UN Charter and the corresponding customary rules.[101] Likewise, systematic violations of human rights or humanitarian law have sometimes underpinned findings of a threat to the peace.[102] However, there cannot be any automaticity between the two types of violation, because, as a matter of principle, the process of qualification remains entirely discretionary. Moreover, practice shows a plethora of examples where situations short of indicating any clear violation of international law were qualified as threats to the peace. It nonetheless happens that the Security Council raises the promotion of legality as one of the rationales for taking action under Chapter VII.[103] Even if these express references were to be considered as anything more than diplomatic discourse, such a rationale remains purely occasional and thus no systemic conclusion can be drawn as to the enforcement role of the Security Council.[104] It could also be argued that Chapter VII actions remain primarily aimed at the maintenance or establishment of a factual situation, rather than a legal one,[105] and accordingly cannot be seen from the standpoint of international law, as constituting enforcement action per se. It is true, however, that

Five as Enforcers of Controls on Weapons of Mass Destruction: Building on the Iraq "Precedent"?' (2002) 13 *European Journal of International Law* 305–21. See the criticism of this position by Gaetano Arangio Ruiz, 'On the Security Council's "Law-Making"' (2000) 83 *Rivista di diritto internazionale* 609, 633–4. See also the criticism by Pierre d'Argent, Jean d'Aspremont, Frédéric Dopagne, and Raphael van Steenberghe, 'Article 39' in Cot, Pellet, and Forteau, *La Charte des Nations Unies*, 1139. On this question, see generally Mathias Forteau, *Droit de la sécurité collective et droit de la responsabilité internationale de l'Etat* (Paris: Pedone, 2006).

[99] Kelsen, *The Law of the United Nations*, 294; P.-M. Dupuy, 'Securité collective et organisation de la paix' (1993) 97 *Revue générale de droit international public* 625; Derek Bowett, 'The Impact of Security Council Decisions on Dispute Settlement Procedures' (1994) 5 *European Journal of International Law* 84–101; Rosalyn Higgins, 'The Legal Limits to the Use of Force by Sovereign States: United Nations Practice' (1961) 37 *British Yearbook of International Law* 269, 275; Kammerhofer, 'Kelsen—Which Kelsen?', 245; Arangio Ruiz, 'On the Security Council's "Law-Making"', 633; Giorgio Gaja, 'Réflexions sur le role du Conseil de sécurité dans le nouvel ordre mondial' (1993) *Revue générale de droit international public* 306.

[100] See Section IV.B. [101] cf Section IV.B.

[102] For examples of resolutions pertaining to the situation in Kosovo, see SC Res 1160, S/RES/1160 (1998); SC Res 1199, S/RES/1199 (1998); SC Res 1203, S/RES/1203 (24 Oct 1998); SC Res 1239, S/RES/1239 (14 May 1999); SC Res 1244, S/RES/1244 (10 June 1999); for the situation in Darfur, see SC Res 1593, S/RES/1593 (31 Mar 2005); For the situation in Rwanda, see SC Res 929, S/RES/929 (22 June 1994), or for the situation in Somalia, see SC Res 794, S/RES/794 (3 Dec 1992); SC Res 733, S/RES/733 (23 Jan 1992); SC Res 751, S/RES/751 (24 Apr 1992).

[103] See the preamble to the resolutions creating the ICTY and ICTR: promotion of legality is not the main goal but only in the interests of peace and security. See also S/PV.3175 (22 Feb 1993) and S/PV.3217 (25 May 1993).

[104] Mathias Forteau, *Droit de la sécurité collective et droit de la responsabilité internationale de l'Etat* (Paris: Pedone, 2006), 250

[105] Forteau, *Droit de la sécurité collective et droit de la responsabilité internationale de l'Etat*, 251.

there are a number of regimes bestowing some enforcement responsibilities upon the Security Council or other UN organs.[106] It must, however, be observed that these responsibilities conferred upon the Council are mostly intended as incentives for compliance and do not give the Council enforcement responsibilities per se.[107]

These reservations explain why the view that the collective security system, especially the Chapter VII mechanism, has more commonly been conceived of either as a regime geared towards the enforcement of the rules of the Charter (Section IV.B), as a peace-enforcement regime (Section IV.C), or, albeit more rarely, as a punitive regime (Section IV.D).

B. The Collective Security System as a Self-Enforcing Regime

The argument that any sanction adopted by virtue of Chapter VII can be seen as an enforcement measure of the Charter itself is likely to be less controversial than the understanding previously mentioned. According to this view, Chapter VII is not a mechanism geared towards law enforcement in general but solely against types of conduct unwanted by the Charter.[108] Such a position is commonly premised on the idea that any threat to the peace, breach of the peace, or act of aggression necessarily constitutes a violation of the Charter and especially of Article 2(4). The Charter itself could also be said to provide a limited underpinning for such a reading, particularly regarding non-forcible measures taken under Article 41, which envisages such measures as the enforcement of previous decisions taken by the Council itself.

Generally, the actual occurrence of an act of aggression or a breach of the peace will automatically constitute a violation of Article 2(4), as well as other international obligations.[109] From an empirical perspective, this seems to have been the case when the Security Council sought to sanction what it qualified as an 'aggressive act' or

[106] See eg ICC Statute, Art 13(b); Art V of the Convention the Prohibition of Military or any other Hostile Use of Environmental Modification Techniques, 1108 UNTS 151; Art XII(4) of the 1993 Chemical Weapons Convention, 1974 UNTS 45; Art 89 of 1977 Additional Protocol I to the Geneva Conventions, 1125 UNTS 3.

[107] This necessity to distinguish between compliance control and enforcement does not, however, bar the charge of effectiveness and compliance. According to some scholars, whether or not such measures constitute enforcement measures, they are barely compliance-incentives and do little to enhance compliance with international law. The argument could thus be made that, from the standpoint of compliance, it is in vain to seek to elevate the exercise of coercive powers by the Security Council in enforcement responsibility. See criticisms and proposals for reform: Laurie Rosensweig, 'United Nations Sanctions: Creating a More Effective Tool for the Enforcement of International Law' (1995) 48 *Austrian Journal of Public and International Law* 161–95.

[108] Gerald Fitzmaurice, 'The Foundations of the Authority of International Law and the Problem of Enforcement' (1956) 19 *Modern Law Review* 5.

[109] Forteau, *Droit de la sécurité collective et droit de la responsabilité internationale de l'Etat*, 328–9.

an 'act of aggression',[110] or when the Council resorted to the qualification of 'breach of the peace'.[111] Nevertheless, this finding cannot be generalized because situations qualified as a 'threat to peace' constitute the overwhelming majority of situations in which the Council resorts to the use of its Chapter VII powers. In some cases, the Council acknowledges that its own injunctions have not been respected and it subsequently adopts sanctions to address those infringements or it formulates injunctions directly accompanied by a set of sanctions to be imposed if the injunction is not complied with by the set deadline.[112] Sanctions of this nature taken by the Council can certainly be seen as enforcement measures of the Council's own decisions, but these are rather limited situations of self-enforcement and cannot be extrapolated either. Moreover, even in cases of self-enforcement, the Council continues to make use of its wide discretion in picking and choosing which of its injunctions it wishes to see enforced.[113] More fundamentally, there are two objections against the idea that the Chapter VII mechanism necessarily operates as a Charter-enforcing tool. First, textually, one could argue that it is not accidental that Article 2(4) speaks of a threat or use of force and Article 39 of any threat to the peace, breach of the peace, or act of aggression.[114] A second objection can be derived from this practice, especially when it involves a threat to the peace; the Council has qualified a whole range of different situations as threats to the peace, despite the fact that they did not come close to a violation of Article 2(4).[115]

Mention must nonetheless be made of situations where the Security Council enforced decisions of the ICJ. Such situations can be analysed as cases of self-enforcement given the organic link between the Court and the UN Charter. Such

[110] See SC Res 326, S/RES/326 (2 Feb 1973); SC Res 387, S/RES/387 (31 Mar 1976); SC Res 405, S/RES/405 (14 Apr 1977); SC Res 573, S/RES/573 (4 Oct 1985); SC Res 611, S/RES/611 (25 Apr 1988); SC Res 667, S/RES/667 (16 Sept 1990).

[111] Res 82, 83, and 84 (1950) on the Situation in Korea; Res 598 (1987) on the situation in Iraq and Iran; Res 660 (1990) on the situation in Kuwait; Res 502 (1982) on the situation of the Falklands. For some critical remarks, see d'Argent, d'Aspremont, Dopagne, and van Steenberghe, 'Article 39', 1151–3.

[112] See SC Res 748, S/RES/748 (31 Mar 1992) (imposing sanctions on Libya for failing to comply with SC Res 731 (1992) despite the fact that the latter had not been adopted under Chapter VII). See generally SC Res 1737, S/RES/1737 (2006) (adopting sanctions against Iran for, inter alia, failing to comply with SC Res 1696 (2006)).

[113] Gaja, 'Réflexions sur le role du Conseil de sécurité dans le nouvel ordre mondial', 317; Schachter, 'United Nations Law', 12; for some criticism of the selective and opportunistic decisions by the Security Council in terms of enforcement, see Michael Bothe, 'Les limites du pouvoir du Conseil de Sécurité' in René-Jean Dupuy (ed), *The Development of the Role of the Security Council* (Dordrecht: Martinus Nijhoff, 1992), 227; Roscini, 'The United Nations Security Council and the Enforcement of International Humanitarian Law', 353–5; Andrea Bianchi, 'Ad-Hocism and the Rule of Law' (2002) 13 *European Journal of International Law* 262.

[114] d'Argent, d'Aspremont, Dopagne, and van Steenberghe, 'Article 39', 1146–64.

[115] On this finding, see generally d'Argent, d'Aspremont, Dopagne, and van Steenberghe, 'Article 39', 1133–45; for a recent example, see Declaration by the Security Council that Global warming may constitute threat to the peace. See S/PV.6587; see also Press Release of 20 July 2011, SC/10332, 6587th Meeting, available at <http://www.un.org/News/Press/docs/2011/sc10332.doc.htm>.

situations of self-enforcement are the object of Article 94 of the UN Charter, which sets up a partial and non-exclusive enforcement regime.[116] In that case, the Security Council's action, for instance in the form of a recommendation, is said not to be dependent on a finding under Article 39 of the Charter.[117]

c. The Collective Security System as a Peace-Enforcement Regime

The aforementioned objections to an understanding of the collective security system as a Charter-enforcement mechanism explain why the most common view is that, outside any finding of a violation of international law or of the Charter itself, the collective security system is only a peace enforcement regime. This view is premised on the idea that coercive measures under Chapter VII cannot be construed as sanctions because they are not necessarily a response to a wrong.[118] Simply speaking, such measures are either forcible or non-forcible police measures that are geared towards the maintenance of peace and security. Such conclusions also hold true for complex peacekeeping missions, irrespective of whether they are created by the General Assembly or the Security Council.[119]

While mainstream, this understanding of the UN Charter is certainly not without paradox, especially if the legal pedigree of a normative order is similarly conditioned on the existence of sanction mechanisms.[120] Indeed, if the Chapter VII mechanism cannot be considered an enforcement mechanism and if it did eliminate all forms of self-help as many authors argue,[121] the adoption of the UN Charter could be seen as depriving international law as a whole of its natural enforcement tool.[122] If one

[116] See generally Alain Pillepich, 'Article 94' in Cot, Pellet, and Forteau, *La Charte des Nations Unies*, 1987–8.

[117] See Constanze Schulte, *Compliance with Decisions of the International Court of Justice* (New York: Oxford University Press, 2004), esp 40–52 (who argues that Art 94, para 2 of the UN Charter only refers to non-forcible measures and sets an autonomous regime not dependent on Chapter VII).

[118] Kelsen, *The Law of the United Nations*, 294; P.-M. Dupuy, 'Securité collective et organisation de la paix' (1993) 97 *Revue générale de droit international public* 625; Derek Bowett, 'The Impact of Security Council Decisions on Dispute Settlement Procedures' (1994) 5 *European Journal of International Law* 84–101; Higgins, 'The Legal Limits to the Use of Force by Sovereign States', 269, 275; Kammerhofer, 'Kelsen—Which Kelsen?', 245; Alexandros Kolliopoulos, *La Commission d'indemnisation des Nations Unies et le droit de la responsabilité international* (Paris: LGDJ, 2001), 61; Arangio Ruiz, 'On the Security Council's "Law-Making"', 633; Gaja, 'Réflexions sur le role du Conseil de sécurité dans le nouvel ordre mondial', 306; this is also how legal theorists have read the UN Charter. Hart, *The Concept of Law*, 217.

[119] Schachter, 'United Nations Law', 11. For recent and compelling criticism of the use of peacekeeping missions as peace-enforcement mechanisms, see James Sloan, *The Militarisation of Peacekeeping in the Twenty-First Century* (Oxford: Hart, 2011).

[120] cf Section IV.A. [121] See n 56.

[122] Fitzmaurice, 'The Foundations of the Authority of International Law and the Problem of Enforcement', 4–5.

embraces a sanction-based conception of international law in the manner of Kelsen, Oppenheim, or Guggenheim, the creation of the collective security system could be understood as enfeebling international law as law properly so called.

This paradox should not be overblown. The previously mentioned reading of the UN Charter, and the practice thereunder, does not exclude the possibility that the collective security system plays an indirect enforcement role for either Charter obligations or international law as a whole. Violations of both international law and Charter obligations can be construed as being constitutive of a threat to or breach of the peace or an act of aggression. It is the breach itself that is constitutive of a threat to the peace in such a textbook case. Practice provides examples of situations where a violation of humanitarian law, human rights law, or the right to self-determination directly informed the finding of a threat to the peace.[123] It is, however, difficult to draw any firm conclusions. Even when the Council expressly refers to a violation of international law in its qualification of a situation as a threat to the peace, it is never clear whether it is the violation itself that generates the threat to the peace or only the consequences thereof.[124] Affirming that such references to violations of international law were, in themselves, threatening international peace and security remains speculative. It must be acknowledged that the wording of the sanctions grounded in situations of violations of the right to self-determination could seem to indicate that the violations themselves, more than their actual and factual consequences, lead to a more automatic qualification as threats to the peace.[125] This is not entirely surprising given the high place that such a principle and the policy carried out in its name features in the agenda of the international community and that of the UN. Nonetheless, this remains highly speculative. The practice of deriving the finding of a threat to the peace from a violation of a positive rule of international law or the UN Charter could at best elevate the collective security system to an *indirect* enforcement mechanism of either the former or the latter.

D. The Collective Security System as Punitive System

Although such a view is more isolated, it has been argued that measures adopted under Chapter VII ultimately have a retributive function. Such a function can complement any of the other enforcement functions mentioned earlier. Authors amenable to this idea of retribution argue that the collective security system is not devoid of punitive dimensions in its Charter-enforcement or peace-enforcement role.[126] In this sense, forcible and non-forcible measures under Chapter VII can be construed

[123] See n 106. [124] See Res 794 (1992) or Res 808 (1993).

[125] Res 216 (1965) and Res 217 (1965) on the situation in Rhodesia.

[126] Wolfgang Friedman, *The Changing Structure of International Law* (London: Stevens and Sons, 1964), 84; Combacau, *Le pouvoir de sanction de l'ONU*, 133; Michel Virally, *L'Organisation Mondiale* (Paris: Armand Colin, 1972), 451; P.-M. Dupuy, 'Observations sur le crime international de l'Etat' (1980)

as retributive, at least in part. This finding may be true as a matter of fact and as a matter of diplomatic discourse.[127] It is probably less a matter of the formal architecture of the UN Charter.[128] Support for a retributive function of the Chapter VII mechanisms shows that another enforcement function can nonetheless be assigned to the collective security system; namely, the enforcement of a vague idea of justice embedded in the Charter.[129]

The previous paragraphs have laid out the varying enforcement functions which international lawyers, buoyed by the decommissioning of self-help and the unprecedented sophistication of the collective security system, have assigned to the latter. Although there are diverging opinions as to the nature and extent of the enforcement role that has been bestowed upon the collective security system, most international lawyers ascribe a specific enforcement dimension to the Charter and the collective security system that it establishes. The final section of this chapter will formulate some epistemological observations on the place of enforcement in the ethos of the epistemic community of international law.

V. Enforcement of International Law Through the Collective Security System: The Need of a Catharsis

The epistemic context in which the debate regarding the functions of the collective security system unfolds will now be examined. Attention is paid to the therapeutic effect continuously sought by international lawyers to be drawn from the collective

Revue générale de droit international public 477; Otto Kimminich, 'Article 6' in Bruno Simma (ed), *The Charter of the United Nations—A Commentary* (Munich: Beck, 1994), 189; Alain Pellet, 'Vive le crime!: Remarques sur les Degrés de l'Illicite en Droit International', *International Law on the Eve of the Twenty-First Century: Views from the International Law Commission* (New York: United Nations, 1997), 304; Rosalyn Higgins, 'International Law and the Avoidance, Containment and Resolution of Disputes—General Course on Public International Law' (1991-V) *Recueil des cours de l'Académie de droit international* 230, 220; Schachter, 'United Nations Law', 13; see generally Anthony F. Lang, 'Punitive Intervention: Enforcing Justice or Generating Conflict?' in Mark Evans (ed), *Just War Theory: A Reappraisal* (New York: Palgrave MacMillan, 2005), 50–70.

[127] This sometimes pervades the political discourse of members of the Council (see debate about Iraq in 1990, S/PV.2943 (25 Sept 1990), 58; S/PV.2951 (29 Oct 1990); or debate about Libya, S/PV.3063 (31 Mar 1992), 66).

[128] Critique by Forteau, *Droit de la sécurité collective et droit de la responsabilité internationale de l'Etat*, 260–5.

[129] On the UN Charter and the idea of justice, see Koskenniemi, 'The Police in the Temple', 325–48.

security system. As alluded to in the introduction to this chapter, there is no doubt that the collective security system and the institution of coercive mechanisms aimed at the maintenance or re-establishment of peace have sustained the self-confidence of a profession long racked with distress caused by the enforcement disability of the international legal order. Put differently, confronted with the Austinian imperatival handicap of international law, international lawyers have been able to find solace in a collective security system that, despite being focused on dispute resolution, appeared to provide the teeth that international law was long lacking.

The therapeutic effect of the collective security system has not been limited solely to the rehabilitation of (the project of) international law as law. It has taken on the rehabilitation of a profession as a whole. In turn, the confidence of international lawyers in the credentials of 'their law' has been conducive to the self-esteem of the entire profession. Indeed, the confidence in the ability of international law to enforce and maintain order, an aptitude they attribute to the UN Charter, has generated self-assuredness about the usefulness of their own efforts to streamline, understand, and, for some of them, develop a system of rules that is not derided as toothless and inoffensive.

This confidence in international law as a whole is derived from the inception of the collective security system, and hence, the profession's self-esteem resulting therefrom has remained hugely dependent on the stability of the system of collective security. When the collective security system enters a zone of dangerous turbulence, the confidence in international law as a whole and in its guardians can usually be seen to dwindle. These fluctuations have continued to hinge significantly on varying perceptions of the authority and effectiveness of the prohibition on the use of force, which the collective security system as a whole is both predicated on and designed to protect. For this reason, I argue that the perceived solidity of the collective security system is a direct consequence of the state of the ethos of the profession.

It is hardly controversial to say that the belief of international lawyers in the solidity of the collective security system has fluctuated over time. The prohibition on the use of force, as well as the ability of the UN collective system to preserve its authority and effectiveness, have been regularly put under strain. Each controversial use of force by a state has sparked dire predictions from international legal scholars who came to envisage the demise of this prohibition.[130] On occasion, claims have been made

[130] For an earlier controversy, see the famous debate between Thomas M. Franck and Louis Henkin. See Thomas M. Franck, 'Who killed Article 2(4) or: Changing Norms Governing the Use of Force by States' (1970) 64 *American Journal of International Law* 809 (arguing that the prohibition against the use of force has been eroded beyond recognition). But see Louis Henkin, 'The Reports of the Death of Article 2(4) Are Greatly Exaggerated' (1971) 65 *American Journal of International Law* 544, 544 (arguing that while Art 2(4) is under assault, it is not dead). Franck has grown even more pessimistic in recent years, see Thomas M. Franck, 'What Happens Now? The United Nations After Iraq' (2003) 97 *American Journal of International Law* 607.

that Article 2(4) of the Charter is clinically dead,[131] even by those who usually advocate a rather favourable and progressive reading of the international legal system.[132]

We have now entered an era of greater liberalization of the use of force.[133] In my view, such liberalization has not manifested itself in either the dislocation of the prohibition on the use of force or the invocation of new 'limitations'[134] to the prohibition. This conclusion is illustrated by the almost unanimous rejection of the doctrine of humanitarian intervention[135] and the absence of any alteration of *jus ad bellum* by the surprisingly successful doctrine of the Responsibility to Protect. Instead, the liberalization of the use of force in international law has materialized in a loosening of the framework for collective security and in the particular dilution of the existing limitations. The latter phenomenon can be seen in particular in the broadening of both the limits of Security Council's authorizations[136] and the concept of

[131] See generally Anthony C. Arend, *Legal Rules and International Society* (Oxford: Oxford University Press, 1999), 75; Michael J. Glennon, 'The Collapse of Consent: Is a Legalist Use-of-Force Regime Possible?' in Beth A. Simmons (ed), *International Law* (London: Sage, 2008), 220; Jack L. Goldsmith and Eric A. Posner, *The Limits of International Law* (Oxford: Oxford University Press, 2005), 143, 198; Michael J. Glennon, 'Rise and Fall of the U.N. Charter's Use of Force Rules' (2003–4) 27 *Hastings International and Comparative Law Review* 497, 508.

[132] Henkin, 'The Reports of the Death of Article 2(4) Are Greatly Exaggerated', 544 (arguing that while Art 2(4) is under assault, it is not dead).

[133] d'Aspremont, 'Mapping the Concepts', 101–59.

[134] A note on terminology is necessary here: situations where force can legally be used under current international law are better seen as 'limitations'. Indeed, the term 'limitation' seems better suited than the term 'exception' or 'qualification' in the sense that situations where the use of force is allowed do not, strictly speaking, derogate from the prohibition. They simply *limit* its ambit. Likewise, situations where force can lawfully be used, although being enshrined in provisions scattered throughout the entire UN Charter, can be seen as constitutive parts of a single rule. Envisaging the prohibition on the use of force as one single legal rule embracing the multilateral use of force authorized by the Security Council as well as the concept of self-defence enshrined in both Art 51 and customary international law also underpins the use of the term limitation instead of exception. Such terminology is also reflected in the case law of the ICJ which in its decision in the *Oil Platforms* case ceased to consider self-defence an exception to the prohibition to use force and qualified it a 'limitation'. See *Oil Platforms (Iran v. US)*, ICJ Rep 2003, 161, 183 (addressing the requirements for measures to qualify as necessary self-defence). It is interesting to note that prior to that judgment, the Court considered self-defence an 'exception' to the prohibition on the use of force. See Pierre d'Argent, 'Du Commerce à l'Emploi de la Force: L'Affaire des Plates-Formes Pétrolières (Arrêt sur le Fond)' (2003) 49 *Annuaire Français de droit International* 266.

[135] Christine Gray, *International Law and the Use of Force* (3rd edn, Oxford: Oxford University Press, 2008), 51; Olivier Corten, *Le droit contre la guerre* (Paris: Pedone, 2008), 792. See also Jean d'Aspremont and Jérôme de Hemptinne, *Droit international humanitaire* (Paris: Pedone, 2013), ch 12.

[136] d'Aspremont, 'Mapping the Concepts', 125. In particular, the multiple attempts—especially by the US and the UK between 1991 and 2003 to 'revive' the authorization to use force contained in Res 678 (1991) of the Security Council have convinced other states that future authorizations should be more carefully doled out. It cannot be excluded that this also stems from the overly generous and unlimited authorizations issued by an overactive Security Council in the immediate aftermath of the Cold War. See Lord Goldsmith, 'Attorney General Clarifies Legal Basis for Use of Force Against Iraq', 18 Mar 2003, cited in Franck, 'What Happens Now?', 611 (citing Press Release, UK Foreign and Commonwealth Office, 'Attorney General Clarifies Legal Basis for Use of Force Against Iraq', 18 Mar 2003, available at <http://www.fco.gov.uk/resources/en/news/2003/03/fco_not_180303_legaladvice>); see also UK Materials on International Law (1993) 64 *British Yearbook of International Law* 736–40. See also Sean D. Murphy, 'Contemporary Practice of the United States' (2003) 97 *American Journal of International Law* 419, 427.

self-defence,[137] especially in cases of armed attack by and against non-state actors.[138] Notwithstanding such a liberalization, we have witnessed a continued vindication of the prohibition on the use of force and the existing system[139] which has been further underpinned by the strong tendency of states using force in ambiguous circumstances still to strive to justify their deeds by referring to the rules of international law pertaining to the use of force.[140]

An overwhelming majority of international lawyers, myself included, believe that the prohibition enshrined in Article 2(4) of the Charter, as well as the corresponding rule of customary international law, remains a central rule of international law. This conviction is held despite faltering authority and effectiveness in practice. I submit that international lawyers are inextricably inclined to vindicate Article 2(4) of the Charter as a result of their awareness of its critical importance to the enforceability of international law, and hence to the profession's self-esteem as a whole. The community realizes that the prohibition on the use of force is the cornerstone of their system of thoughts, and their ethos. It is this realization that leads international lawyers to deride those who venture to claim that contemporary practice has been lethal for the prohibition at the heart of the collective security system. The epistemic community of international law is dominated by bigotry towards the collective security system and its basic foundational norm. This prejudice in favour of Article 2(4) and the customary corresponding rule is probably what informs, for instance, the common resort to the argumentative construction of an enduring *opinio juris*[141]

[137] d'Aspremont, 'Mapping the Concepts', 127–31.

[138] Nicholas Tsagourias, 'Non-State Actors and the Use of Force' in Jean d'Aspremont (ed), *Participants in the International Legal System: Multiple Perspectives on Non-State Actors in International Law* (Oxford: Routledge, 2011), 326–41; see also d'Aspremont, 'Mapping the Concepts', 131–40; Christian Tams, 'Light Treatment of a Complex Problem: The Law of Self-Defence in the Wall Case' (2005) 16 *European Journal of International Law* 963; Lindsay Moir, *Reappraising the Resort to Force: International Law, Jus ad Bellum and the War on Terror* (Oxford: Hart, 2010). The extension of self-defence to situations of indirect attack—namely, cases of harbouring terrorists or supporting them—has received implied agreement in the 2005 African Union Non-Aggression and Common Defence Pact, Art 1(c)(xi) of which states:

> The following shall constitute acts of aggression, regardless of a declaration of war by a State, group of States, organization of States, or non-State actor(s) or by any foreign entity: ... the encouragement, support, harbouring or provision of any assistance for the commission of terrorist acts and other violent trans-national organized crimes against a Member State.

African Union, Non-Aggression and Common Defence Pact, Art 1(c)(xi), 31 Jan 2005, available at <http://www.africa-union.org/root/AU/Documents/Treaties/text/Non%20Aggression%20Common%20Defence%20Pact.pdf>. On the relationship between the African Union Defence Pact and the UN Charter, see Raphaël van Steenberghe, 'Le Pacte de non-agression et de défense commune de l'Union africaine: entre unilatéralisme et responsabilité collective' (2009) 113 *Revue générale de droit international public* 125. On the specificities of the African Union Non-Aggression and Common Defense Pact, see Marco Roscini, 'Neighbourhood Watch? The African Great Lakes Pact and ius ad bellum' (2009) 69 *Zeitschrift für ausländisches öffentliches Recht und Völkerrecht* 931.

[139] For an illustration, see Moir, *Reappraising the Resort to Force*, 3.

[140] *Military and Paramilitary Activities (Nicaragua v. US)*, 27 June 1986, ICJ Rep 1986, 14, 95, para 186.

[141] *Military and Paramilitary Activities (Nicaragua v. US)*, 27 June 1986, ICJ Rep 1986, 14, 99–100; see also Tom J. Farer, 'The Prospect for International Law and Order in the Wake of Iraq' (2003) 97 *American Journal of International Law* 621, 622.

to try to salvage the customary rule corresponding to Article 2(4) in the face of extremely contradictory practice.[142]

This prejudice in favour of Article 2(4) and the corresponding customary rule is what brings me back to the question of enforcement. It is uncontested that international lawyers' understanding of the collective security system remains deeply affected by the respective conception of each scholar of the rules regulating the use of force and the aspirations that each has vested in the collective security system.[143] The particular necessity felt by an entire epistemic community to uphold Article 2(4) and its corresponding customary rule constitutes the manifestation of its aspirations in terms of enforcement of international law. The prejudice in favour of an everlasting prohibition on the use of force is the direct consequence of the assignment of enforcement tasks to the collective security system. In other words, it is because international lawyers endow some enforcement function to the collective security system based on Article 2(4) that they avoid confronting anything that would demote Article 2(4) to a norm close to desuetude. Accordingly, I suspect that, whether consciously or not, international lawyers have been balking at considering the death of the prohibition on the use of force out of fear that this would wreak havoc on a collective security system that is crucial to their confidence in international law as a whole.

In the light of the foregoing, I believe that stripping our understandings of the collective security system entirely of its enforcement dimensions would certainly help to assuage our fears of losing confidence in the system and of enfeebling our self-esteem. Such a move would allow us to look without complex at Article 2(4) and the collective security system. In this sense, it is not until we overcome the projection of our desire for enforcement into the collective security system that we will be capable of liberating ourselves from a constraining complex. Disempowering the collective security system of any enforcement function would allow us to bolster the profession towards self-empowerment and enable us to regain our ability to look more transparently at the collective security system. What the profession needs is not another round of studies on the enforcement function performed by the collective security mechanism. What it needs is a catharsis to purge the mindset of the epistemic community of international law from its multifaceted obsession for construing the coercive powers authorized by the UN Charter as being geared towards the performance of enforcement functions.

[142] Jane E. Stromseth, 'Law and Force After Iraq: A Transitional Moment' (2008) 97 *American Journal of International Law* 628, 631–3 (reflecting the belief that the core of Art 2(4)—that wars of territorial expansion and conquest are unlawful—is still alive).

[143] On this question, see generally Andrea Bianchi, 'The International Regulation of the Use of Force: The Politics of Interpretive Method' (2009) 22 *Leiden Journal of International Law* 651.

CHAPTER 7

CHANGING *JUS COGENS* THROUGH STATE PRACTICE? THE CASE OF THE PROHIBITION OF THE USE OF FORCE AND ITS EXCEPTIONS

ALEXANDER ORAKHELASHVILI

I. Introduction

AFTER the adoption in 1945 of the UN Charter and its comprehensive prohibition of the use of force under Article 2(4), multiple attempts took place in state practice to fragment or alter its content. In the Cold War period, there were repeated state claims as to the various exceptions from this prohibition, such as in relation to protecting nationals abroad, regarding humanitarian intervention, and regarding various extended versions of self-defence, whether termed anticipatory or interceptive. The post-Cold War period witnessed further activation of the humanitarian intervention argument, mainly with the example of the use of force against the Federal Republic of Yugoslavia (FRY) in 1999, and its modified version termed 'Responsibility to Protect' and attempts to further extend anticipatory self-defence to encompass broader uses of force that would at times have pre-emptive character (Iraq 2003) and at times essentially constitute an armed reprisal (Afghanistan 2001).

All these claims effectively asserted something that the terms of Articles 2(4) and 51 of the UN Charter do not admit at face value. In terms of international lawmaking, these 'emerging exceptions' are essentially attempts to consolidate the positions that are either derogatory from or amendatory of the legal position under the Charter and corresponding customary international law.

The reasoning thus runs into two separate, though conceptually similar, normative processes. For, the claims in practice purported the creation of a new customary rule that also aims to reinterpret or effectively amend the terms of the Charter. It seems to be generally agreed that the amendment of a treaty through custom should satisfy the requirements of subsequent practice under Article 31(1)(b) of the 1969 Vienna Convention on the Law of Treaties (VCLT).[1] The threshold requirements are then very high. The practice in question must positively command the agreement of all state parties to the effect of clarification of the content, or modification, of treaty obligations.[2] In relation to customary law proper, the requirement of a regular, or even arguably special, *opinio juris* is crucial. More so, as in the area of *jus cogens* any normative change should command, if the requirements under Article 53 of the same Convention are considered, the acceptance of the international community as a whole.

Conceptually, the ways in which state practice interacts with the rules of *jus cogens* can involve either a wholesale abolition or replacement of the relevant peremptory norm; a consolidation of a new exception to an existing peremptory norm; or validation of the concrete situation produced through the breach of that peremptory norm. Article 53 VCLT outlaws derogations from *jus cogens*, but allows for its modification through a newer peremptory rule. When state practice prima facie conflicting with *jus cogens* is developed, the question is whether it goes to derogation from, or modification of, *jus cogens* norms.

The complexity of this process requires a similarly complex analysis. We should first understand what state practice is about and what difference it makes. Then we should focus on the nature of *jus cogens*, including its state practice elements. Lastly, it has to be examined how state practice on the actual or claimed exceptions to and derogations from the peremptory prohibition of the use of force is received in international law.

[1] Yoram Dinstein, 'The Interaction between Customary International Law and Treaties' (2006) 322 *Recueil des cours de l'Académie de droit international* 259, chs IX, X, and XI, and esp 414–15.

[2] cf Alexander Orakhelashvili, *The Interpretation of Acts and Rules in Public International Law* (Oxford: Oxford University Press, 2008), ch 10.

II. The Nature and Relevance of State Practice

State practice is frequently resorted to by writers and government officials, as is often tempting and opportune, to justify multiple lines of state conduct and policy by events from the past. Officials will obviously refer to any state practice they consider to be useful, which raises the question how far their elbow room can be maintained without compromising the predictable and reliable framework of international lawmaking. For the sake of methodological clarity, it should be emphasized that particular activities do not amount to state practice merely because they are performed by states. Multiple state actions and omissions—whether for reasons of ceremony, comity, courtesy, or discretion—are unrelated to international legal rights and obligations. For what is left, no action performed or position uttered by a state takes place in a legal vacuum. All of it instead relates to the complex framework of the sources of international law, and purports to impact the existing allocation of rights and obligations, with the intention to preserve or alter it.

Consequently, 'state practice' is not self-fulfilling or self-explanatory. Its relevance derives from a source backed by a constitutional authority of lawmaking, which then determines what kind of state practice matters and on what conditions. We should consequently be interested only in such state practice that fulfils the requirements under Article 38(1)(b) of the International Court's Statute—general practice of states accepted as law through their concordance of wills (accompanied by *opinio juris*). In the consensual framework of international law, state practice has to consist in an act, offer, claim, protest, or other expression of attitude displayed internationally. Manifestation of a view is required, for no communication is possible without exchanging views. Statements and claims are just as indicative of state practice as are actual material facts and actions.[3]

The whole reason why state practice is relevant is to give a material substratum to the process of the identification of customary rules. Those rules must relate to something materially tangible that states see, experience, perform, or react to. They cannot sensibly be derived from policy aspirations and perceptions, or ideological preferences that officials may unilaterally entertain, but have instead to be grounded in the process of mutual communication of states that ultimately leads to an unwritten agreement. To illustrate, the International Court in the *Anglo-Norwegian Fisheries* case and in the *Minquiers and Echrehos* case had to examine the validity of claims as to the ownership of territorial and maritime spaces, respectively between the UK and Norway and the

[3] The 'lawmaking power of facts' will not be critiqued here; see instead Orakhelashvili, *The Interpretation of Acts and Rules in Public International Law*, ch 5.

UK and France.[4] In both cases the Court extensively examined the practice of litigating states in relation to disputed areas and identified critical dates—well before the commencement of litigation—after which their claims and acts would no longer be taken into consideration. The reason is that states should not raise and pursue self-serving opportunistic claims, but only those relating to facts and positions with the potential to lead to an agreement through practice—those displayed within the material time period. Such approach objectivizes the whole issue, preventing it from degenerating into the chaotic process where any statement by one litigant state could be set off against any statement by another litigant state, leaving no objectively ascertainable criteria as to which claim is better founded in law. Seen this way, state practice constrains the freedom of auto-interpretation by states of their legal rights and obligations, reduces the relevance and validity of claims to a narrower, historically ascertainable set of events, and filters out the claims that do not correspond to its requirements.

As for the particular elements of state practice as part of customary law, it has to be general, settled, consistent, and durable. As the International Court observed in the *Nicaragua* case, addressing the customary law status of the rules on the use of force, the application and observance of the rules in practice does not have to be perfect. Instead, 'the conduct of States should, in general, be consistent with such rules, and that instances of State conduct inconsistent with a given rule should generally have been treated as breaches of that rule, not as indications of the recognition of a new rule.'[5] This emphasizes the standing of the state that uses force, and that of other states that express positions as to the legality of such use of force. The consensual positivist element of custom-generation is thereby reinforced, to the effect that state practice that does not point to the formation of an agreement or consensus as to the newer rule has to be disregarded.

General customary law is produced the way that it applies to all states, some of which consolidate it by active practice and contribution, and others by acquiescence motivated by interest or indifference. Even if not all states' affirmative consent is, strictly speaking, a requirement, the practice in question should nevertheless be displayed in the way that brings it to the attention of the entire international society. Not just that every state must be aware that certain things happen in practice but also that those things are done by the relevant states with the intention of impacting the existing legal rights and obligations. From here, other states can figure out their own position, either agreeing to, or preventing the emergence of, a new customary rule.

As an initial step, the position of the state that wishes to attain normative change through customary law has to be coherent and consistent so that other states can

[4] *Anglo-Norwegian Fisheries (UK v. Norway)*, ICJ Rep 1951, 116; *The Minquiers and Echrehos Case (France v. UK)*, ICJ Rep 1953, 47.

[5] *Military and Paramilitary Activities in and against Nicaragua (Nicaragua v. US)*, Merits, Judgment of 27 June 1986, ICJ Rep 1986, 14, para 186.

identify the parameters of the offer made. As the International Court observed in *Nicaragua*:

> If a State acts in a way prima facie incompatible with a recognized rule, but defends its conduct by appealing to exceptions or justifications contained within the rule itself, then whether or not the State's conduct is in fact justifiable on that basis, the significance of that attitude is to confirm rather than to weaken the rule.[6]

A sufficient number of states must therefore be involved. The International Criminal Tribunal for the former Yugoslavia (ICTY) confronted in the *Brđanin* case the argument that the US government's position regarding the threshold of pain as an element of the definition of torture impacted the customary law definition of torture. However, 'no matter how powerful or influential a country is, its practice [did] not automatically become customary international law.'[7] Even if multiple states back the potential customary rule, the chances of its emergence will be slim if the international society is divided on the issue. As the International Court pointed out in the *Nuclear Weapons* advisory opinion, even if 'the desire of a very large section of the international community' was there, 'the emergence, as *lex lata*, of a customary rule specifically prohibiting the use of nuclear weapons as such is hampered by the continuing tensions between the nascent *opinio juris* on the one hand, and the still strong adherence to the practice of deterrence on the other.'[8]

When state practice is identified to support an entitlement or claim, it should relate precisely to the subject matter of that claim or entitlement; as opposed to conceptually endorsing the relevant type of action. Furthermore, all relevant state practice relating to the issues at hand should be addressed. Without such complete focus, state practice can be hijacked by the natural law agenda. Some amount of state practice identified in the relevant case, but falling short of the reach and intensity to satisfy the requirements of generality and durability, could be used to project customary law on the relevant subject matter to give expression to whatever the relevant decision-maker considers right, just, reasonable, sensible, or useful. This is a problematic attitude, replicating Pufendorf's naturalist approach that state practice is there to reflect overarching principles derived from natural law and matters only to the extent it can be used to serve that task.[9]

Two cases where the Court positively identified the existence of customary law on the basis of state practice are the *Arrest Warrant* case and the *Germany v. Italy* case, dealing with the immunity of states and their officials before foreign courts. In

[6] ICJ Rep 1986, 98.

[7] *Brđanin*, ICTY Appeal Chamber, IT-99-36-A, 3 Apr 2007, para 247.

[8] *Legality of the Threat or Use of Nuclear Weapons*, Advisory Opinion of 8 July 1996, ICJ Rep 1996, 226, 255.

[9] cf Samuel von Pufendorf, 'The Law of Nature and Nations' in James Brown Scott (ed), *Classics of International Law* (Oxford: Clarendon Press, 1934), 228; see further Alexander Orakhelashvili, 'The Origins of Consensual Positivism—Pufendorf, Wolff, and Vattel' in Orakhelashvili (ed), *Research Handbook on Theory and History of International Law* (Cheltenham: Edward Elgar, 2011), 93.

both cases the Court posited an essentially natural law premise as to the necessity, usefulness, or reasonableness of a particular type of immunity. It then identified a rather limited set of state practice through which it projected the customary law on immunities that meets the requirements of those natural law premises.

In the *Arrest Warrant* case, the Court first linked the issue of the immunity of incumbent foreign ministers to the general need of states to be duly represented in foreign relations. Proceeding from this essentially naturalist premise, the Court identified the 'firmly established' rule on immunity from two national court decisions. The first was the *Pinochet* decision of the UK House of Lords, which related to the former head of state not an incumbent foreign minister.[10] The second case was the *Gaddafi* decision of the French Cour de Cassation,[11] which related to the immunity of a serving head of state, whose immunity was actually held to be subjected to some exceptions even if those were not dealt with then and there.[12]

In *Germany v. Italy*,[13] the Court initially linked state immunity to the principle of sovereign equality of states under Article 2(1) of the UN Charter, even though there is no indispensable connection between the two.[14] Based on this natural law premise, the Court referred to the limited body of evidence and prioritized such state practice, mainly national court decisions, as support for its conclusions, over other elements of state practice that contradicted its approach.[15] When confronted with the reality that most of the relevant national statutes deny immunity for territorial torts, either generally or in conjunction with the acts of armed forces, the Court simply pled unawareness that those statutory provisions had been applied by national courts to that effect; and then recast the issue of tort immunity into that of armed forces immunity.[16]

[10] *Pinochet* [1999] 2 All ER 97 (HL).

[11] *Gaddafi*, 125 ILR 508 (Cour de Cassation).

[12] *Arrest Warrant of 11 April 2000*, Merits, General List No 121, ICJ Rep 2002, 14 Feb 2002, paras 51–4.

[13] *Jurisdictional Immunities of the State (Germany v. Italy)*, ICJ, Judgment of 3 Feb 2012, General List No 143.

[14] In *Libya/Malta*, the Court denied that the principle of sovereign equality required equidistance in delimiting the continental shelf area between the two states. *Libya/Malta*, ICJ Rep 1985, 43. Also, 'there is no obvious impairment of the rights of equality, or independence, or dignity of a State if it is subjected to ordinary judicial processes within the territory of a foreign State,' Robert Jennings and Arthur Watts, *Oppenheim's International Law* (9th edn, London: Longman, 1992), 342.

[15] For state practice that denies that immunities are part of customary international law, see *I Congreso* [1983] 1 AC 260–1 (HL); *Trendtex Trading v. Bank of Nigeria* [1977] 1 QB 552–3; *McElhinney*, 104 ILR 701 (Irish Supreme Court, 15 Dec 1995); *US v. Noriega*, 99 ILR 162–3; *Lafontant v. Aristide*, 103 ILR 586, stating that 'the grant of immunity is a privilege which the United States may withhold from any claimant.' For a doctrinal opinion to the same effect, see DP O'Connell, *International Law* (London: Stevens & Sons, 1970), 846; Hersch Lauterpacht (ed), *Oppenheim's International Law* (London: Longman, 1955), 274; Rosalyn Higgins, *Problems and Process* (Oxford: Oxford University Press, 1994), 81; Arthur Watts, 'The Legal Position in International Law of Heads of States, Heads of Governments and Foreign Ministers' (1994) 247 *Recueil des cours de l'Académie de droit international* 36, 53.

[16] *Germany v. Italy*, paras 70–7.

In both of the aforementioned cases the majority of the Court seems to have engaged in political opportunism, and the existence of customary rule was imagined where in fact there was none. The legal position was, and remains, that there is no positive customary law on state immunity, because it lacks a sufficient and consistent substratum in state practice.[17]

Natural law reasoning creates a problem that is exacerbated by the fact that one's understanding of state practice on occasion depends on one's political orientation. For instance, the New Haven policy-oriented school operates with the notion of the process of authoritative policy decisions to further the overarching policy goal of 'human dignity', thus validating particular decisions, irrespective whether they comply with legal rules.[18] What follows from this is that the official or the legal adviser serving a particular government that aspires to be the guardian of 'human dignity' can advance a justification for any action that suits its political goals. The 'policy decision process' certainly refers to past decisions, and therefore it is to some extent reflective of state practice. But, it purports to recast that process, the way that state practice is made relevant, not in terms of whether it corresponds to the requirements of Article 38 of the Statute of the International Court, but in terms of whether it serves the political goals of those who claim to be guardians of 'human dignity'.

The New Haven approach is more widespread than meets the eye among writers, officials, and advisers. One can be an undeclared McDougalite and try to 'translate', to the benefit of the audience, one's preferred policy decision process into state practice language. Practice fitting within a particular political agenda or ideological perception would then appear to matter more than practice falling outside it.

The next requirement is that state practice must bear on the subject matter that is actually regulated by international law, or is purported to be brought within its realm. State practice, as part of domestic law, would not matter as such. For example, national legislation on state immunity excludes the consideration of international law from the task of national courts and thus diminishes their potential to contribute to state practice internationally.[19] The Special Tribunal for Lebanon interlocutory decision on the applicable law specifies, pursuant to Anzilotti's reasoning, that the mere existence of concordant laws does not prove the existence of a customary rule, 'for it may simply result from an identical view that States freely take and can change at any moment'. To illustrate:

> the fact that all States of the world punish murder through their legislation does not entail that murder has become an international crime. To turn into an international crime, a

[17] See for detail Alexander Orakhelashvili, *Peremptory Norms in International Law* (Oxford: Oxford University Press, 2006), ch 10.

[18] Myres McDougal, 'The Hydrogen Bomb Tests and the International Law of the Sea' (1955) 49 *American Journal of International Law* 356.

[19] F. A. Mann, 'The State Immunity Act 1978' (1980) 51 *British Yearbook of International Law* 43; James Crawford, 'A Foreign State Immunities Act for Australia?' (1983) *Australian Yearbook of International Law* 71, 105–6.

domestic offence needs to be regarded by the world community as an attack on universal values (such as peace or human rights) or on values held to be of paramount importance in that community; in addition, it is necessary that States and intergovernmental organisations, through their acts and pronouncements, sanction this attitude by clearly expressing the view that the world community considers the offence at issue as amounting to an international crime.[20]

The ICTY addressed in *Furundžija* the domestic legislation of a number of states on rape and similarly concluded that it did not matter in identifying the customary law of rape. What mattered is practice that can evidence the correlation of views and positions of states internationally.[21]

A further requirement is that the process of normative change in the area of custom-generation should not contradict the sources and frameworks of law that are by definition beyond the reach of that process of custom-generation. State practice contrary to multilateral treaty obligations is unlikely to create customary law, because it will be unopposable in a large number of states. In theory, it could create a limited custom as between non-signatory states. Nevertheless, chances of consolidation are slim. Practice falling short of the Article 38 generality requirement might then require, pursuant to the International Court's approach in the *Asylum* case, a greater degree of consensus, in the sense that it must be positively established that the customary rule in question has become binding specifically in relation to the relevant state, through constant and uniform usage.[22] For example, Article 51 of the 1977 Additional Protocol I to the 1949 Geneva Conventions unconditionally prohibits reprisals against civilians. While outside the scope of the Protocol, customary law could still theoretically allow resorting to reprisals against civilians in some circumstances. However, the burden is too heavy on those who attempt to prove this position. All parties to Additional Protocol I being excluded (even in their relations with non-parties),[23] it is almost impossible to find evidence that general, or special, customary law could exist in relation to non-parties in the way that allows reprisals in defiance of Additional Protocol I.

On balance, some state practice matters and some does not. The complex factors examined previously testify that state practice as part of customary international law may not always be there when a particular legal argument projects or desires it.

[20] Interlocutory Decision on the Applicable Law, STL-II-01/I, 16 Feb 2011, para 91 (referring to Dionisio Anzilotti, *Corso di diritto internazionale*, vol I (4th edn, Padua: CEDAM, 1955), 100).

[21] *Furundžija*, 10 Dec 1998, IT-95-17/I-T, paras 182–3.

[22] *Asylum (Colombia v. Peru)*, Merits, ICJ Rep 1950, 266, 276.

[23] Humanitarian law treaties codify rules and obligations that do not fit within the patterns of bilateralism, see for detail Orakhelashvili, *Peremptory Norms in International Law*, ch 4.

III. The *Jus Cogens* Status of the Prohibition of the Use of Force

Even though there may be some divergences of detail, UN Charter law and customary law regarding the use of force are identical in outlawing all uses of force against states apart from a response to an armed attack under Article 51 of the Charter. It is this legal position, reflecting Articles 2(4) and 51 of the Charter, that commands the status of *jus cogens*. The International Court affirmed the peremptory status of the prohibition of the use of force in *Nicaragua*, mainly by relying on UN General Assembly resolutions.[24] Although there are repeated doctrinal attempts to deny this,[25] a careful reading of *Nicaragua* shows that the Court pointed to the qualification by the International Law Commission (ILC) of the relevant norm as peremptory, and inferred from this its customary status. There is no authority to contest this position. There are remarks by writers that in practice states do not frequently reaffirm that the prohibition of the use of force is part of *jus cogens*.[26] Looking at individual states could produce the impression that only a minority of states have expressly accepted this position. This approach further projects a double burden of proof in relation to the acceptance of the prohibition of the use of force as a customary rule and then as a peremptory norm. It seems, however, that the super-imposition of such double requirement goes substantially beyond what the legal framework requires.

Article 53 VCLT is the consensual positivist recognition of the relevance of *jus cogens*. Article 53 does not subsume *jus cogens* within, nor exclude it from the ambit of, any particular source of law listed in Article 38 of the Statute of the International Court of Justice. The key requirement under Article 53 is that of acceptance and recognition by the international community as a whole. What we need to search for is the ways in which the community as a whole speaks. This leads to the evidentiary relevance of multilateral treaties and UN General Assembly resolutions. Although none of these can independently generate—as opposed to reflect—a peremptory norm, they serve as evidence of the international community's attitude as to the relevant norm's content and status. If need be, international courts can repeatedly

[24] *Nicaragua*, ICJ Rep 1986, 100–1, 103 (referring to GA Res 2625 (1970) on Principles of International Law (also known as the Friendly Relations Declaration; and Res 3314 (1974), on the Definition of Aggression)). The House of Lords has affirmed the peremptory status of the prohibition of the use of force following *Nicaragua*, see *R v. Jones* [2006] UKHL 16, para 18.

[25] Dinah Shelton, 'Normative Hierarchy in International Law' (2006) 100 *American Journal of International Law* 291, 304; Bruno Simma, 'Universality of International Law from the Perspective of a Practitioner' (2009) 20 *European Journal of International Law* 265, 272.

[26] James A. Green, 'Questioning the Peremptory Status of the Prohibition of the Use of Force' (2010–11) 32 *Michigan Journal of International Law* 215, 243.

apply the requirements of custom-generation, namely state practice and *opinio juris*, the way that explains the emergence of *jus cogens* rules. Whether this leads to the emergence of a special *opinio juris* is a theoretical question, for international courts and tribunals have placed this whole process within the context of requirements of Article 38, much as it is obvious that the elements of state practice they use differ from context to context.[27] Article 38(1)(b) of the Court's Statute does not limit the acceptable headings of practice. Treaty practice and collective multilateral practice can be just as good as practice performed by states individually. The overall positivist balance is thus observed: the more widespread the support expressed for the rule through the channels of the community will, the more obvious the evidence of *opinio juris*.

Against this background, viewing the peremptory status of the prohibition of the use of force—or indeed of any *jus cogens* norm—as dependent on occasional affirmation by individual states constitutes a methodological error. It matters what the community of states pronounces through the community channels, not how often individual states additionally utter similar pronouncements or refrain from such.

IV. State Practice and Exceptions to the Peremptory Prohibition of the Use of Force

The task now is to identify whether the prohibition of the use of force can be changed against the background of the requirements of Article 53 VCLT. Such change will inevitably require general consistent practice aimed at such legal change specifically, and it is subject to a heavy burden of proof for those who wish to prove it. The impact of *jus cogens* on derogatory state practice was most recently witnessed in the International Court's advisory opinion in relation to the Unilateral Declaration of Independence in Kosovo, where it was reaffirmed that the involvement of a breach of *jus cogens* can invalidate subsequent acts and actions whether performed by states or non-state actors, notably unilateral declarations of independence.[28] If,

[27] For a detailed analysis of the practice consisting of decisions of ICJ, ICTY, and national courts to this effect, see Orakhelashvili, *Peremptory Norms in International Law*, ch 5.

[28] *Accordance with international law of the unilateral declaration of independence in respect of Kosovo*, Advisory Opinion of 22 July 2010, ICJ Rep 2010, 402, 437–8 (para 81). For previous practice, see Orakhelashvili, *Peremptory Norms in International Law*, chs 7 and 11. For the relevance of these principles in the law of state responsibility, see James Crawford, Fourth Report, *Yearbook of the*

therefore, a specific concrete action or situation can be tainted with invalidity, it is an even more pressing outcome that normative attempts to secure a change in the applicable law that, should they succeed, they will operate on a continuous basis will even more obviously command such consequence. In the end, both conceptually and normatively, and if the overall impact of the overarching concept of derogation under Article 53 VCLT is considered, the issue of the validity of individual breaches of *jus cogens* will inevitably run into that of an attempted normative change, and vice versa.

State consent to foreign military presence and operations is one area that tests the resilience of the peremptory *jus ad bellum* to derogation attempts. Intervention by consent is lawful, provided that it rests on a clearly expressed request, authored by the government of the territorial state, to be interpreted strictly in terms of duration, space, and type of pertinent military activities.[29] If exceeding such strictly construed grant, the use of force will qualify as aggression. In practice, the claims that consent of the government of the target state has been obtained have not always been found to be authentic.[30]

Unlike ad hoc consent, a prospective consent to authorize the use of force by one state against another, irrespective or against its will at the moment when force is being used, constitutes a derogation from the prohibition of the use of force. Such consent embodied in a treaty or in a unilateral act would be void for its conflict with *jus cogens* on the basis of Article 53 VCLT and general international law.[31] The use of force in question will still be governed by, and be unlawful under, the general international law of the use of force.

One pattern of forcible intervention that raises the issue of the validity and authenticity of consent to a foreign intervention relates to interventions to restore democratic government and constitutional order within the target state. In relation to pro-democratic intervention, the argument in doctrine and practice addresses the significance of the consent to intervention and who is more eligible to give it—a de facto illegitimate government, a lawful government in exile, or an insurgent entity aspiring to capture the entire territory of the state.[32] Once it is ascertained

International Law Commission, 2001, vol II (1), 12 ff, and 2001 Articles on State Responsibility, *Yearbook of the International Law Commission*, 2001, vol II (2), Arts 41–2 and Commentary.

[29] *Case Concerning the Armed Activities on the Territory of the Congo (Democratic Republic of the Congo v. Uganda)*, 19 Dec 2005, ICJ, General List No 116, paras 43–7.

[30] As can be seen from the reaction of the UN General Assembly to the US invasions in Grenada 1983, Panama 1989, and to that by USSR in Afghanistan 1979. See Simon Chesterman, *Just War or Just Peace?: Humanitarian Intervention and International Law* (Oxford: Oxford University Press, 2001), 99–106.

[31] See also ILC Draft Articles on Unilateral Acts and Commentary; see more generally Brad Roth, 'The Illegality of "Pro-Democratic" Invasion Pacts' in Gregory Fox and Brad Roth (eds), *Democratic Governance and International Law* (Cambridge: Cambridge University Press, 2000), 328; and Orakhelashvili, *Peremptory Norms in International Law*, ch 6, focusing on the 1960 Cyprus Guarantee Treaty and other similar instances.

[32] Most practice in this respect, such as the cases of Grenada in the 1980s, Haiti, Liberia, and Sierra Leone in the 1990s, has actually centred on the mandate given to intervening forces by the UN or

in casu that consent was given by the entity entitled to give it, which according to prevailing practice must be the constitutionally legitimate government, *and* in relation to that one specific case, it is certain that the use of force in question is not one directed against the sovereign state. The issue of *jus cogens* illegality will not arise, and correspondingly there will be no attempt of derogation. Otherwise, as was the case in Grenada in 1983 or Panama in 1989, the issue of *jus cogens* invalidity would arise if the relevant state practice will witness an inclination to validate the fruits of that use of force, or use it as a test case intended to consolidate a normative change in that direction. In this latter respect, the underlying claims will at some stage—and implausibly—run into attempts to reinterpret Article 2(4) of the UN Charter in the way that allows uses of force short of encroaching upon the territorial integrity and political independence of the state,[33] and into the invalidating process pursuant to the doctrine of *jus cogens*.

As for claims to use force on the basis of generally applicable law, as opposed to the will and consent of the target state, it is always important to understand in the context of which legal framework the pertinent state practice gets displayed. Pre-1945 state practice was displayed with different constitutional settings in mind. Before 1945, there could be no feasible argument regarding the exceptions from the prohibition of the use of force, because there was no such prohibition in the first place. To justify the use of force, the 1841 statement by US Secretary of State Webster regarding the *Caroline* incident relied on the appreciation of events as instant, overwhelming, leaving no time for choice and no moment for deliberation. *Caroline* is essentially an instance of practice displayed against the background of the natural law-based right to self-preservation, even though it refers to the notion of self-defence which 'crept into the correspondence'.[34] Modern law of the use of force would not admit such claims, because the only state practice that matters is the one that its authors were in a position to apply their minds to, which is the positive law under the UN Charter and corresponding customary rules. This positive law as dealt with in *Nicaragua* constitutes the starting point against which any entitlement to use force must be described, characterized, and qualified, if the claim behind it is ever to become valid.

Any state using force is aware of the prohibitions and exceptions under the Charter. If the state acts with a belief that those arrangements do not apply to its

regional organizations such as the Economic Community of West African States (ECOWAS), in conjunction with consent from the entities that were, at the time of intervention, deemed to be legitimate governments of those states, for a more detailed discussion, see Alexander Orakhelashvili, *Collective Security* (Oxford: Oxford University Press, 2001), chs 5 and 7.

[33] cf Oscar Schachter, 'The Legality of Pro-Democratic Invasion' (1984) 78 *American Journal of International Law* 645.

[34] R. Y. Jennings, 'The *Caroline* and *McLeod* Cases' (1938) 32 *American Journal of International Law* 82, 91–2. Lord Ashburton maintained in the note of 28 July 1841 that 'self-defence is the first law of our nature'.

use of force, then this belief can taint the validity of its action as a first step in the process of state practice. If, however, a state uses force claiming that its action is in accordance with the UN Charter provisions even if not prima facie covered thereby, that state has the burden of proof to demonstrate how exactly that is the case. Other states witnessing such action and reacting to it must also be deemed to be aware that their response and reaction of whatever description will not take place in a legal vacuum, but against the background of the existing sources of law.

In the first place, state practice claiming an extra-Charter exception from the prohibition of the use of force has to involve a coherent manifestation of a pertinent view; otherwise it cannot produce legal positions under which state actions are lawful or unlawful. The context of the day, especially material factors on the ground (also which audience one is speaking to and whether there is international organ with jurisdiction that could ultimately hear the case), will often influence policymakers and legal advisers in choosing the plausible justification: it will tempt advancing some justifications and deterring others; it will influence the alteration of stated motives and claims while force is being used. There have been several such instances, as was the case with the US in Dominican Republic in 1965 (referring first to protection of nationals and then to the spreading of communist threat) and Grenada in 1983 (referring first to the invitation from the government and then to the approval by the Organisation of Eastern Caribbean States (OECS) and the need to combat the regional threat consisting in the spread of armaments). The changing allusion to multiple justifications casts doubt on the validity of all related claims, because it undermines the continuity of practice.

What is the real motivation of a state claiming exception also matters: to genuinely transform a legal position by making, through practice, a respective offer to other states, or just to make a claim that appears plausible to the relevant audience[35] and then hope to get away with it because other states may find it politically unwise to object or be indifferent to doing so, or because the case would not be covered by the regular jurisdiction of international tribunals to adjudge the merit of the relevant claims? In this latter case the official or adviser will also understand that the claim or action in question will not be plausibly contributing to the process of creation or alteration of legal rules. Whichever of these two premises one acts upon in particular situations, a sound official or adviser will not fail to apply their mind to the possibilities or consequences arising from either of them.

As for the specific claims relating to extra-Charter exceptions, claims to protect nationals pertinently illustrate the essence of this process. As Bowett explained, before 1945 states used to assume the right to forcibly protect nationals abroad, but after the introduction of a comprehensive prohibition in 1945, these claims can only

[35] cf Arthur Watts, 'The Importance of International Law' in Michael Byers (ed), *The Role of Law in International Politics* (Oxford: Oxford University Press, 2000), 5, 8.

be validated if covered by the right to self-defence as the only exception from that prohibition.[36] What authors of such claims have to substantiate is how the state that forcibly protects its nationals abroad can be seen as a victim of an armed attack under Article 51 of the Charter. This is not without relevance to the fact that most if not all claims in relation to incidents of forcible rescuing of nationals against the will of the territorial state have been subjected to condemnation as unlawful.[37]

In relation to self-defence particularly, states have claimed anticipatory self-defence that a state can resort to before it becomes the victim of an armed attack. The incident in point is Israel's attack on the Osirak nuclear reactor in Iraq in 1981 that the Security Council condemned in Resolution 487 (1981). The Council's position at that point essentially signified the opposition of the community of states to acts such as those, with the effect that state practice leading to the relevant change in the Charter-based legal framework would be difficult to consolidate.[38]

The war against Iraq in 2003 witnessed a further articulation of a claim in state practice that the use of force was permitted in a pre-emptive manner.[39] The initial claim was derived from the 2002 US National Security Strategy. In the wake of adopting Resolution 1441 (2002), the US claimed the right to use force pre-emptively against threats caused by Iraq, even without the authorization of the Security Council, indeed conceding at that point that there was no such authorization.[40] Later on, however, the US ceased claiming the entitlement to defend itself pre-emptively and instead advanced the claim that Resolution 1441 authorized the use of force, contrary to its previous position.[41]

In relation to the US-led use of force in Afghanistan in 2001, no plausible evidence has been presented to demonstrate that it was undertaken in response to an armed attack under Article 51 of the UN Charter.[42] This use of force resembled more

[36] Derek W. Bowett, 'The Use of Force for the Protection of Nationals Abroad' in Antonio Cassese (ed), *The Current Legal Regulation of the Use of Force* (Dordrecht: Martinus Nijhoff, 1986), 39, 40.

[37] In relation to the Stanleyville operation in 1964, see Bowett, 'The Use of Force for the Protection of Nationals Abroad' in Cassese, *The Current Legal Regulation of the Use of Force*, 45; GA Res 38 (1983), 44/240 (1989), respectively on operations against Grenada and Panama.

[38] That anticipatory self-defence is not permitted, see Yoram Dinstein, *War, Aggression and Self-Defence* (5th edn, Cambridge: Cambridge University Press, 2011), 199; and a comprehensive study by Abdul Ghafur Hamid, 'The Legality of Anticipatory Self-Defence in the 21st Century World Order: A Reappraisal' (2007) 54 *Netherlands International Law Review* 441–90.

[39] As Dinstein usefully illustrates, the difference between anticipatory and pre-emptive use of force is essentially that of semantics, Dinstein, *War, Aggression and Self-Defence*, 199.

[40] Security Council 4644th Meeting, SC Press Release SC/7564; S/2003/351; for detail and analysis, see Orakhelashvili, *Collective Security*, ch 5.

[41] Ghafur Hamid, 'The Legality of Anticipatory Self-Defence in the 21st Century World Order', 479; Sean Murphy, 'Assessing the Legality of Invading Iraq' (2004) 92 *Georgetown Law Journal* 173; see for detailed analysis of the pre-emption argument, Marc Weller, *Iraq and the Use of Force in International Law* (Oxford: Oxford University Press, 2010), 134 ff.

[42] Eric Myjer and Nigel White, 'The Twin Tower Attack: An Unlimited Right to Self-Defence?' (2002) 7 *Journal of Conflict and Security Law* 5, 7.

a reprisal than self-defence.[43] Armed reprisals are prohibited.[44] It is in the nature of reprisals to be retaliatory and punitive, which is inimical to the nature of self-defence under Article 51. Although there are doctrinal attempts to subsume armed reprisals within self-defence, it is acknowledged that reprisals are essentially aimed at retaliating and forestalling recurrence, mostly well after the initial attack has taken place, as opposed to responding to an ongoing armed attack.[45] The aims of the two kinds of responses are thus qualitatively different, which means that Article 51 cannot encompass reprisals. If Article 51 allowed retaliatory response, no need for the separate reprisal talking would ever arise. It is much easier for states to point to obvious justifications under the Charter than look for dubious grounds outside it that will place them under an increasing burden of proof in terms of reclassification and justification of the relevant forcible acts.

There are claims that the silence of many states could have validated the use of force in Afghanistan. As Quigley explains, the failure of states to demand compliance with applicable rules does not change the substance of these rules.[46] As the Permanent Court of International Justice clarified in the *Danube* case, toleration of practice is not the same as acceptance of its legality.[47] Toleration occurs because nothing can be physically done about the particular situation, but this is short of acceptance, which represents the confirmation of its legality. Such legal acceptance must be—and was not—shown with the relevant evidence.

Relatively recent claims relate to the expansion, through state practice, of the entitlement to use force in self-defence when the initial attack comes from a non-state actor as opposed to a state. As a background, Article 51 mandates the use of force in self-defence only where it responds to an armed attack that has been perpetrated by one state against another. The International Court has repeatedly pronounced accordingly.[48] The doctrinal reaction to the Court's clear and consistent position has been to overlook the content of the Court's pronouncements and suggest that the Court was vague, or to describe the Court's findings as inadequate by not justifying

[43] Javaid Rehman and Saptarshi Ghosh, 'International Law, US Foreign Policy and Post-9/11 Islamic Fundamentalism: The Legal Status of the "War on Terror"' (2008) 77 *Nordic Journal of International Law* 87, 94.

[44] Art 50, ILC's Articles on State Responsibility, ILC Report 2001, UN GAOR, 56th Sess, Supp No 10, A/56/10.

[45] Dinstein, *War, Aggression and Self-Defence*, 245, 249–55.

[46] John Quigley, 'The Afghanistan War and Self-Defense' (2002–3) 37 *Valparaiso University Law Review* 541, 554; see also Ghafur Hamid, 'The Legality of Anticipatory Self-Defence in the 21st Century World Order', 477.

[47] *Jurisdiction of the European Commission of the Danube*, Advisory Opinion, Ser B, No 14, 8 Dec 1927, 36–7.

[48] *Legal Consequences of the Construction of the Wall in the Occupied Palestinian Territory*, 9 July 2004, ICJ, Advisory Opinion, General List No 131, para 138; *DRC v. Uganda*, 19 Dec 2005, General List No 116, para 146. For analysis see Alexander Orakhelashvili, 'Legal Stability and Claims of Change: The International Court's Treatment of *Jus ad Bellum* and *Jus in Bello*' (2006) 75 *Nordic Journal of International Law* 371.

action that states might take against terrorist networks around the globe.[49] But both categories of criticism fail, because the Court was straightforwardly and consistently clear on the principles it upheld, and there is no international authority postulating the law of self-defence in a different manner.

Dinstein points to two examples from practice in favour of self-defence encompassing attacks by non-state actors. The first example relates to Security Council Resolutions 405 and 419 (1977) regarding aggression against Benin without mentioning the role of any state. The second example relates to the 2005 African Union Non-Aggression Pact referring to acts of aggression by non-state actors.[50] As for the first example regarding Benin, the Security Council deliberations demonstrated that the mercenaries involved in the attack launched through an unauthorized landing at Cotonou airport had significant connections to France and were in fact led by a French colonel. Benin submitted 'that high-level French officials in Cotonou were aware of the aggression long before its execution and that two French agents in Cotonou had participated in its actual preparation and execution.' France publicly distanced itself from those mercenaries and joined their condemnation.[51] For obvious reasons, these two resolutions would never have been adopted had they referred to the French role expressly. As for the second example, the 2005 Abuja Pact contrasts starkly with the 1974 Definition of Aggression under General Assembly Resolution 3314, which states that 'aggression is the use of armed force by a State against the sovereignty, territorial integrity or political independence of another State.' The International Court has confirmed that this resolution embodies customary law.[52] The position under the Abuja Pact is plainly insufficient to modify the general law of the use of force and could at most constitute an African *lex specialis* (should the provisions of the Pact, especially Art 1(c), be interpreted to authorize uses of force against the state without its consent). Such outcome cannot be sustained, however, given that the general *jus ad bellum* is peremptory. There can, quite simply, be no two diverging streams of *jus ad bellum*. Nor was such admitted by the International Court in the *DRC/Uganda* decision that relates precisely to the African context.

This position came under increasing challenge after the terrorist attacks against the US on 11 September 2001, especially with the adoption of Security Council

[49] Elizabeth Wilmshurst et al, 'The Chatham House Principles of International Law on the Use of Force in Self-Defence' (2006) 55 *International and Comparative Law Quarterly* 963; Michael Wood, 'The Law on the Use of Force: Current Challenges' (2007) 11 *Singapore Yearbook of International Law* 1; Daniel Bethlehem, 'Self-Defense against an Imminent or Actual Armed Attack by Nonstate Actors' (2012) 106 *American Journal of International Law* 769.

[50] Dinstein, *War, Aggression and Self-Defence*, 227. Art 1(c) of the Abuja Pact specifies, in its relevant part, that aggression means 'the use, intentionally and knowingly, of armed force or any other hostile act by a State, a group of States, an organization of States or non-State actor(s) or by any foreign or external entity, against the sovereignty, political independence, territorial integrity and human security of the population of a State Party to this Pact . . .'

[51] *Yearbook of the United Nations*, 1977, 210–14.

[52] ICJ Rep 1986, 103.

Resolutions 1368 (2001) and 1373 (2001) which focus on counterterrorist measures and mention the right to self-defence.[53] However, nothing in these resolutions reveals that non-state actors can on their own be the source of an 'armed attack'. On closer inspection, the two resolutions have recognized the inherent right to self-defence under the Charter and reaffirmed the responsibility of states and non-state actors for terrorist acts. This has been emphasized, however, by two separate principles, and the fact that they were mentioned together does not establish a conceptual or normative link between them.

In the *Wall* case, Judge Kooijmans offered a rather light treatment of this question, arguing that the Security Council resolutions 'recognize the inherent right of individual or collective self-defence without making any reference to an armed attack by a State', which therefore amounted to a 'completely new element' in the legal picture. Judge Kooijmans went as far as arguing that 'This new element is not excluded by the terms of Article 51 since this conditions the exercise of the inherent right of self-defence on a previous armed attack without saying that this armed attack must come from another State *even if this has been the generally accepted interpretation for more than 50 years*',[54] and thus construed these resolutions as effecting an instant or momentous alteration of the well-established legal position, even as those resolutions do not by their text and wording reveal a result as far-reaching as that. There was no clear indication how the desired legal position had turned into an actual one through the sources of international law. Kooijmans' argument of instantaneous change could be conceivable under naturalist reasoning of various descriptions but that has, quite simply, no place in the legal system that depends on the consent and agreement of states to be clearly demonstrated in relation to each and every claimed rule.

Lastly, claims as to humanitarian intervention should be addressed. Despite the moral and political attractiveness of this idea in various governmental and academic circles, no legal entitlement to humanitarian intervention has ever emerged in state practice. In 1986, the British Foreign Policy statement emphasized that state practice behind this 'right' was uncertain and the motives behind interventions were not always laudable. It was added, in policy terms, that the case against allowing humanitarian intervention was: 'that its doubtful benefits would be heavily outweighed by its costs in terms of respect for international law.'[55]

[53] Dinstein, *War, Aggression and Self-Defence*, 227, regards this as the 'defining moment' to clarify that attacks by non-state actors are included. Wolff Heintschel von Heinegg, 'Legality of Maritime Interdiction Operations in Operation Enduring Freedom' in Michael Bothe, Mary Ellen O'Connell, and Natalino Ronzitti (eds), *Redefining Sovereignty: the Use of Force after the End of Cold War* (The Hague: Brill, 2005), 364, 385, suggests that Resolution 1373 'has made sufficiently clear' that self-defence is not restricted to armed attacks attributable to a state.

[54] ICJ Rep 2004, 230 (emphasis added).

[55] Foreign and Commonwealth Office, Policy Document, 'UK Materials on International Law' (1986) *British Yearbook of International Law* 618–19.

When in 1999 North Atlantic Treaty Organization (NATO) states used force against the FRY to protect Kosovo Albanians from governmental oppression, the response of the community of states was plainly negative. This use of force was instantly condemned by India, China, and a group of Latin American states as unlawful.[56] Later in the same year, the statement of the Non-Allied Movement, backed by 132 states, 'reject[ed] the so-called "right" of humanitarian intervention, which has no legal basis in the UN Charter or in the general principles of international law.'[57] Nor has the failure of the Security Council to condemn this use of force altered the legal landscape, for as the International Court has specified, the failure by an international organ to adopt a particular proposal does not equate to its support for the opposite proposal.[58]

The notion of the 'Responsibility to Protect' relates to protecting vulnerable populations from governments that expose them to war crimes, genocide, or crimes against humanity, or governments that refrain from protecting them from such atrocities. This concept has not been framed to purport to validate forcible interventions outside the context of Chapter VII of the UN Charter.[59] In any case, the unilateral uses of force pursuant to the 'Responsibility to Protect' doctrine would not be different from the previously examined humanitarian intervention claims in any conceptual, generic, or normative respect, and their merit would fall to be assessed accordingly.

A unifying feature of nearly all claims to the use of force on extra-Charter grounds is that they rely on the naturalist articulation of values and their common-sense understanding, in the sense that it is necessary and useful to act to protect oppressed people or to prevent terrorists or rogue regimes from using force first. This naturalist thinking inevitably claims that one's own political morality is universal and that which is necessary must be law too. This way, it has little in common with the positivist reasoning regarding the sources of law.

Claims in favour of the extra-Charter exceptions have always been incoherent to constitute valid state practice for the purposes of custom-generation, and fallen far short of commanding the support of states to produce an amending peremptory norm under Article 53 VCLT. All this practice has either been fragmented and not general; or inconsistent in relation to the same state, same incident, or as between

[56] Statement by the Rio Group, 26 Mar 1999, A/53/884, S/1999/347, 2; see also S/PV.3988 (23 Mar 1999), for the positions of India and China.

[57] Statement by the Non-Aligned States (132 states), 24 Sept 1999, in Ian Brownlie, *Principles of Public International Law* (Oxford: Oxford University Press, 2008), 744; and the statement made in Havana, 10–14 Apr 2000, para 54.

[58] *Legal Consequences of the Continuing Presence of South Africa in Namibia,* ICJ Rep 1971, 36, para 69.

[59] World Summit Outcome Document, A/RES/60/1 (2005), para 138, refers to 'collective action, in a timely and decisive manner, through the Security Council, in accordance with the Charter, including Chapter VII.'

multiple states; or it has consolidated within a group of states but been rebuffed by the rest of the community of states. The whole practice in relation to anticipatory self-defence, pre-emption, humanitarian intervention, or self-defence against non-state actors has attempted to gain higher ground by professing to follow the UN Charter framework of *jus ad bellum*, and is therefore subsumable within the previous dictum from *Nicaragua* that unilateral claims reinterpreting the established legal framework are generally counterproductive.

V. Conclusion

The previous analysis has demonstrated that whenever the state practice argument is raised, it is a point at which to start inquiry, not to draw conclusions. The framework of *jus ad bellum* both under customary law and the UN Charter has proved to be rigorous and robust enough to withstand the pressures for momentous and situational change.

At the end of the day the argument against the *jus cogens* status of the prohibition of the use of force is unlikely to produce effect. The censuring power that accrues under general international law to the *jus cogens* prohibition of the use of force does not stand alone. Its content is shadowed by the cluster of parallel rules under the UN Charter. The *jus cogens* prohibition, however, retains its independent relevance to prevent the consolidation of *lex specialis* that could develop through state practice as between the limited number of states or in relation to individual states or incidents, exempting them from the general requirements of *jus ad bellum* on the basis of general acquiescence when states are deterred from voicing opposition. Under this scenario, the overall standards of *jus ad bellum* under the UN Charter and the relevant customary law would continue intact, but they would be fragmented by the diverging sets of *lex specialis*. The strict requirement of uniformity inherent in *jus cogens* and its non-derogability is practically the only tool at the disposal of the legal system to prevent such position from materializing.

PART II

COLLECTIVE SECURITY AND THE NON-USE OF FORCE

CHAPTER 8

RECONFIGURING THE UN SYSTEM OF COLLECTIVE SECURITY

RAMESH THAKUR

I. Introduction

THE incidence of war in human society is as pervasive as the wish for peace is universal. The 20th century captured the paradox only too well. On the one hand, increasing normative, legislative, and operational fetters were placed on the right of states to go to war. Yet the last century turned out to be the most murderous in history, with more dead than in all previous wars of the past two thousand years.

This chapter situates the changing role of the United Nations regarding peace and security within the larger context of its evolution from consensual pacific settlement and coercive collective security, including economic sanctions, to consent-based peacekeeping, robust peace operations, the coercive responsibility to protect (R2P), and nuclear security. The use of force—when and how it may justly be used—is a central element in this story. According to Secretary-General Kofi Annan's High-Level Panel on Threats, Challenges and Change, 'the maintenance of world peace and security depends importantly on there being a common global understanding, and acceptance, of when the application of force is both legal and legitimate'.[1]

[1] High-Level Panel on Threats, Challenges and Change (HLP), 'A More Secure World: Our Shared Responsibility', A/59/565 (Dec 2004), para 184.

Established to provide predictability and order in a world in constant flux, the UN—a bridge between power and principles, between state-based realism and international idealism—is at once the symbol of humanity's collective aspirations for a better life in a safer world for all, a forum for negotiating the terms of converting the collective aspirations into a common programme of action, and the principal international instrument for the realization of the aspirations and the implementation of the plans. On balance, albeit with some major qualifications, the world has been a better and safer place because of the existence of the UN, because of what it does, and because of how it works.

The chapter begins with an account of pacific settlement and collective security as the main UN instruments for promoting and underwriting international security. Their shortcomings and failures were the backdrop for the emergence of peacekeeping as a new form of international activity. This too metamorphosed over the decades under the impact of changing circumstances and requirements. In the new millennium, the understanding and scope of security threats have broadened considerably, necessitating newer approaches to UN-centred collective security. This is illustrated through the principle-cum-norm of R2P and nuclear security. The chapter concludes with a comment on the shift from collective security to global governance.

II. Pacific Settlement and Collective Security

The problem of peace and order is not new. Napoleon Bonaparte imposed temporary order and unity on Europe through conquest. Other European powers set up an alternative concert system in reaction and transformed the original impulse, of a military alliance for the single purpose of defeating Napoleon, into the longer term political goal of preventing a similar domination of Europe by any one power in the future. The Concert of Europe was the most comprehensive attempt until then to construct new machinery for keeping the peace among and by the great powers.

The Hague Conferences of 1899 and 1907 broadened international relations in participation and agenda. The two major international organizations of the 20th century were the League of Nations after the First World War and the UN after the Second World War—the first attempts in history to create a universal collective security system.[2] In both instances, people horrified by the destructiveness of modern wars decided to create institutions for avoiding a repetition of such catastrophes.

[2] For the origins of international organization, see Inis L. Claude, *Swords into Plowshares: The Problems and Progress of International Organization* (3rd edn, New York: Random House, 1964).

The League was prepared to condemn Japanese aggression in Manchuria in 1931 despite no prospect of any collective action being undertaken. The Italian invasion of Ethiopia in 1935 presented the League with its moment of greatest triumph: for the first time, the international community, acting through institutionalized channels, condemned aggression, identified the aggressor, and imposed sanctions. Their eventual failure does not negate the advancement of the *ideal* that the world community can take joint coercive measures against international outlaws. But Ethiopia also stands as the symbol of failure to realize the high hopes held of the League at its creation, for the aggressor secured his ends through forcible conquest.

The League was destroyed with the outbreak of the Second World War; its collective security legacy lives on in the UN. The UN incorporated the League proscription on the use of force for national objectives, but inserted the additional prescription to use force in support of international, that is UN, authority. The UN Security Council was envisaged as the equivalent of a supreme war-making organization of the international community. It was given the power to decide whether international peace was threatened, whether sanctions were to be imposed, and, if so, the nature of the sanctions, including military force as the instrument of last resort. Moreover, such decisions by the Security Council would be binding upon all member states, even on those which voted against the measures.

Narrowing the scope and circumstances of the permissible use of force by states has been matched by the historical movement to broaden the range of international instruments available to states to settle their disputes peacefully. The techniques of peaceful settlement, set out in Chapter VI of the UN Charter, range from bilateral negotiations between the disputants to formal adjudication by third parties. The normative primacy of peaceful over forceful means is firmly entrenched, as is the proposition that the international community has a stake in war-avoidance justifying its involvement in bilateral disputes between member states. The UN has helped states to bring down levels of armed conflict as a proportion of interstate interactions, form habits of cooperation, and develop shared norms and perceptions.[3]

After the First World War, collective security was a conscious substitute for systems of alliances and balance of power policies that were 'forever discredited'. Predicated on the proposition that war can be prevented by the deterrent effect of overwhelming power being brought to bear against any state contemplating the use of force, collective security entails the imposition of diplomatic, economic, and military sanctions against international outlaws. Unlike pacific settlement, collective security is not concerned with the causes and conditions of war.[4] Only one assumption is necessary,

[3] See esp Harold K. Jacobsen, *Networks of Interdependence* (New York: Knopf, 1979).

[4] For elaboration of the differences between pacific settlement and collective security, see Claude, *Swords into Plowshares*, ch 11, 'Peaceful Settlement of Disputes' and ch 12, 'Collective Security as an Approach to Peace'.

that wars are probable; only one normative premise is required, that wars must be prevented or stopped. Enforcement measures are outlined in Chapter VII of the Charter. Articles 42 and 43 in particular authorize the Security Council to 'take such action by air, sea or land forces as may be necessary to maintain or restore international peace and security', and require member states to make available to the UN such 'armed forces, assistance, and facilities' as may be necessary for this purpose.

There turned out to be many a slip between the theory of collective security as written in the Charter and its practice in the real world of international politics. Efforts to devise an operational collective security system have been thwarted by a conceptual conundrum. War between lesser states may be deplorable and unhealthy for their nationals, but cannot of itself endanger *world* peace. Only the prospect of war between powerful states directly, or their involvement on rival sides in a quarrel between minor powers, can threaten international order. Collective security understood as the maintenance of international peace and security is therefore superfluous in respect of small states. Equally, however, collective security is impossible to enforce against major powers. For any attempt to launch military measures against a great power would bring about the very calamity that the system is designed to avoid, namely a world war. Both these propositions hold true from the very definitions of 'major' and 'minor' powers.

The UN sought to avoid the latter eventuality by conferring permanent membership of the Security Council upon the great powers with the accompanying right of veto. The practical effect of the veto is that 'the extensive decision-making competence' of the Security Council, necessary for the successful operation of a collective security system, is severely curtailed by the equally 'extensive decision-blocking competence' of the five permanent members (P5).[5] The mistrust among the Cold War great powers also put paid to the idea of a Military Staff Committee which was to have functioned as the Security Council's strategic adviser (Art 47 of the UN Charter).

The closest that the UN has come to engaging in collective enforcement action was in Korea in 1950: the US intervened against communist North Korean invasion, the UN followed the US intervention. The initiative was American, taken in the context of the Cold War and invoking the moral support of the UN for a resort to force that would have occurred anyway. That is, the UN action in Korea was made possible by a temporary marriage of convenience between collective security and collective defence,[6] and by a fortuitous combination of other circumstances. The Soviet Union, absent from the Security Council in protest at an unrelated

[5] Claude, *Swords into Plowshares*, 242.

[6] See Arnold Wolfers, *Discord and Collaboration: Essays on International Politics* (Baltimore, MD: Johns Hopkins University Press, 1962), chs 11, 'Collective Security and the War in Korea', and 12, 'Collective Defense versus Collective Security'.

issue, was not able to veto the action. The UN had its own commission on the ground which was able to confirm immediately that aggression had occurred and by whom. The ready availability of US troops in nearby Japan allowed the UN to overcome the problems posed by the non-implementation of Article 43. In this early test of the UN, member states and foundation Secretary-General Trygve Lie were more readily inclined to adopt robust measures against a clear case of unprovoked aggression.

The next large-scale military action under UN mandate came four decades later in the Persian Gulf (1990–1) in response to Iraq's invasion and annexation of Kuwait.[7] Its most important long-term significance lay in the crossing of the conceptual Rubicon by authorizing enforcement of sanctions and military eviction of the aggressor by troops not even nominally under UN command. As in Korea in the 1950s, the advantage of the procedure was that it allowed the UN to approximate the achievement of collective security within a clear chain of command necessary for large-scale military operations. The cost was that the Gulf War, like the Korean War, became identified with US policy over which the organization exercised little real control.

III. From Peacekeeping to Peace Operations

The word 'peacekeeping' famously does not appear in the UN Charter, and yet it has been one of the most visible symbols of the UN's role in international peace and security: hundreds of thousands of military personnel and tens of thousands of police officers and civilian officials from around 120 countries—over 60 per cent of the UN membership—have taken part in UN peacekeeping.[8] With the attainment of a reliable system of collective security being deferred to a distant date, states moved to guarantee national security by means of collective defence and the international community groped towards damage-limitation techniques

[7] The Security Council dealt with the Iraqi invasion of Kuwait in a number of resolutions: S/RES/660 (2 Aug 1990) condemned the invasion of Kuwait by Iraq; S/RES/661 (6 Aug 1990) imposed economic sanctions on Iraq; S/RES/665 (25 Aug 1990) authorized a naval blockade to enforce the sanctions; S/RES 678 (29 Nov 1990) set a deadline of 15 Jan 1991 for Iraq to withdraw from Kuwait and authorized member states 'to use all necessary means' if Iraq failed to comply; and S/RES/686 (2 Mar 1991) provided the formal framework for a ceasefire after the coalition victory over Saddam Hussein.

[8] Statistics on all the operations are available on the UN website at <http://www.un.org/en/peacekeeping/>.

to avoid and contain conflicts. Peacekeeping evolved in the grey zone between pacific settlement and military enforcement. It grew side by side with preventive diplomacy which Secretary-General Dag Hammarskjöld used to forestall the competitive intrusion of the rival power blocs into conflict situations that were either the result or potential cause of a power vacuum in the Cold War. It was given concrete expression by inserting the thin blue wedge of blue beret UN soldiers between enemy combatants.

Terms like 'peacekeeping', 'peace support operations', and 'peace operations' are used generically to refer to missions and operations that fall short of military combat between clearly recognizable enemies. While specific UN activities have been varied, the theme common to all is to promote international stability and support peaceful change outside the axis of great power rivalry. Peacekeeping operations have been diverse in function and size, ranging from a few observers on the India–Pakistan border,[9] to a 20,000-man force in the Congo.[10] Traditional peacekeeping forces could never *keep* world peace, for they lacked both mandated authority and operational capability to do so. But they did succeed in stabilizing several potentially dangerous situations.

One of the originators of classical UN peacekeeping, the Canadian foreign minister, Lester Pearson, aptly characterized it as 'an intermediate technique between merely passing resolutions and actually fighting'.[11] The constraining effect of many of the core principles of classical UN peacekeeping—non-use of force because of military neutrality between the belligerents, non-intervention in domestic quarrels because of political neutrality with respect to the conflict, non-participation by great powers because of their mutual suspicions—produced controversy and frustration in the organization. The UN refused to abandon them, however, because they represented a middle way between abdication of responsibility for management of the international order and turmoil if the organization attempted to shake off the Charter shackles on collective military action. Brian Urquhart argued that 'It is precisely because the [Security] Council cannot agree on enforcement operations that the peacekeeping technique has been devised, and it is precisely because an operation is a peacekeeping operation that governments are prepared to make troops available to serve on it'.[12] There is another important implication which follows from this. Since peacekeeping evolved as a second-best substitute for a

[9] United Nations Military Observer Group in India and Pakistan (UNMOGIP, 24 Jan 1949–present), established by S/RES/39 (20 Jan 1948) and S/RES/47 (21 Apr 1948).

[10] United Nations Operations in the Congo (ONUC, 15 July 1960–30 June 1964), established by S/RES/143 (14 July 1960). S/RES/161 (21 Feb 1961) and S/RES/169 (24 Nov 1961) are also important for having mandated 'all appropriate measures' and 'vigorous action' respectively.

[11] Lester B. Pearson, 'Force for U.N.' (1957) 35 *Foreign Affairs* 401.

[12] Brian E. Urquhart, 'Peacekeeping: A View from the Operational Center' in Henry Wiseman (ed), *Peacekeeping: Appraisals and Proposals* (New York: Pergamon, 1983), 165.

non-obtainable collective security system, it cannot rightly be assessed on the criterion of collective enforcement.

A. Peace Operations

The number of UN operations increased dramatically after the end of the Cold War as the UN was placed centre stage in efforts to resolve outstanding conflicts. In the first 40 years, from May 1948 to April 1988, a total of 13 missions were established. In the next ten years, from May 1988 to April 1998, another 35 were established; from May 1988 to April 2012, a total of 44 peacekeeping missions were set up.[13] However, the multiplication of missions was not always accompanied by coherent policy or integrated military and political responses.[14] Traditional peacekeeping was under UN auspices, command, and control. There was a reaction against UN peacekeeping because of widespread, if often inaccurate, perceptions that UN operations led to diplomatic ennui and could not be freed of the Cold War rivalry and other highly politicized antagonisms that had infected large parts of the UN system. The second generation of peacekeeping operations were mounted either unilaterally or multilaterally, but in any case outside the UN system, in Zimbabwe, the Sinai, Beirut, and Sri Lanka. The precursors to this sort of extra-UN peacekeeping operations were the international control commissions in Indochina set up by the Geneva Agreements of 1954. On the one hand, the non-UN operations adopted from traditional UN peacekeeping most of the principles of third party military interposition and buffer. On the other hand, they expanded the range of tasks and functions that were required to beyond just military interposition.

Traditional peacekeeping aimed to contain and stabilize volatile regions and interstate conflicts until such time as negotiations produced lasting peace agreements. By contrast, the third generation of peacekeeping saw UN missions being mounted as part of package deals of peace agreements, for example in Namibia and Cambodia. The peacekeeping mission was an integral component of the peace agreement and aimed to complete the peace settlement by providing third party international military reinforcement for the peace process. Reflecting the changing nature of modern armed conflict, UN operations expanded not just in numbers but also in the nature and scope of their missions. The newer 'complex emergencies' produced multiple crises all at once:[15] collapsed state structures; humanitarian

[13] United Nations, Department of Peacekeeping Operations, 'List of Peacekeeping Operations, 1948–2012', available at <http://www.un.org/en/peacekeeping/documents/operationslist.pdf>.

[14] See Ramesh Thakur and Albrecht Schnabel (eds), *United Nations Peacekeeping Operations: Ad Hoc Missions, Permanent Engagement* (Tokyo: United Nations University Press, 2001).

[15] The Congo crisis of the 1960s and the UN operation there (1960–4) were precursors to the complex emergencies and third generation missions.

tragedies caused by starvation, disease, or genocide; large-scale fighting and slaughter between rival ethnic or bandit groups; horrific human rights atrocities; and the intermingling of criminal elements and child soldiers with irregular forces. Reflecting this, third generation operations had to undertake additional types of tasks like military disengagement, demobilization and cantonment, policing, human rights monitoring and enforcement, observation, organization and conduct of elections, and rehabilitation and repatriation.

In Somalia and elsewhere the UN attempted the fourth generation of 'peace-enforcement' operations, with results that were anything but encouraging, hence General Sir Michael Rose's metaphor of 'the Mogadishu Line' that peacekeeping forces dare cross only at their peril.[16] A peacekeeping operation in a theatre where there was no peace to keep, the UN Protection Force (UNPROFOR) in former Yugoslavia failed to prevent the horrors of Srebrenica in 1995.[17] The incident remains a stain on world conscience for passivity in the face of the calculated return of 'evil' to Europe and a tragedy that, in the words of the official UN report, 'will haunt our history forever'.[18]

Partly in consequence of the disastrous venture into peace-enforcement, in Bosnia and Haiti UN peacekeeping underwent a further metamorphosis into the fifth generation of enforcement operations being *authorized* by the Security Council, but *undertaken* by a single power or ad hoc multilateral coalition. There was not a single such operation during the Cold War (1945–89); there were 15 such operations set up between November 1990 and September 2003.[19] The UN itself took back responsibility for a traditional-type consensual peacekeeping, once the situation had stabilized, for a temporary period, but with the tasks of third generation expanded peacekeeping. Modifying the Gulf War precedent somewhat, this was the pattern that emerged of UN-authorized military action by the US in Haiti, France in Rwanda, Russia in Georgia, and the North Atlantic Treaty Organization (NATO) in Bosnia.[20]

East Timor represents the evolution into the sixth generation of peacekeeping. A UN-authorized multinational force was prepared for combat action if necessary and was given the mandate, troops, equipment, and robust rules of engagement that are required for such a mission.[21] However, the military operation was but the prelude

[16] Michael Rose, 'The Bosnia Experience' in Ramesh Thakur (ed), *Past Imperfect, Future UNcertain: The United Nations at Fifty* (London/New York: Macmillan/St Martin's Press, 1998), 139.

[17] UNPROFOR (Feb 1992–Mar 1995) was established by S/RES/743 (21 Feb 1992), and Res 749 (7 Apr 1992) authorized its full deployment.

[18] Report of the Secretary-General Pursuant to General Assembly Resolution 53/35 (1998), A/54/549, UN Secretariat (Nov 1999), para 503.

[19] For a complete listing of the 15 cases, see David M. Malone (ed), *The UN Security Council: From the Cold War to the 21st Century* (Boulder, CO: Lynne Rienner, 2004), App 2, 665–8.

[20] The last one, eg, was the NATO-run Kosovo Force (KFOR) authorized by S/RES/1244 (10 June 1999).

[21] The International Force for East Timor (INTERFET, Sept 1999–Feb 2000), established by S/RES/1264 (15 Sept 1999). This was supported by the UN Transitional Administration in East Timor (UNTAET, Oct 1999–May 2002), set up by S/RES/1272 (25 Oct 1999); and followed by the UN Mission of Support in East Timor (UNMISET, May 2002–May 2005), set up by S/RES/1410 (17 May 2002).

to a de facto UN administration, which engaged in state-making for a transitional period.[22] That is, a 'nation' was granted independence as a result of UN-organized elections. But the nation concerned had no structures of 'state' to speak of. It was not even, like Somalia, a case of a failed state; in East Timor a state had to be created from scratch. In the latter, the UN finally confronted and addressed the dilemma that haunted it in the Congo in the 1960s and Somalia in the 1990s, namely that peace-restoration is not possible without the establishment of law and order. In a country where the writ of government has either collapsed or is non-existent, the law that is made and enforced so as to provide order can only be that of the UN or of another foreign power (or coalition).

B. Brahimi Report

A significant cost of the cascade of generations of peacekeeping within a highly compressed time frame was that most of the newer operations had little real precedent to go by; each had to make and learn from its own mistakes. UN Secretary-General Kofi Annan appointed a high-level international panel, chaired by veteran Algerian diplomat Lakhdar Brahimi, to make recommendations for changes in UN peacekeeping. Its report was unusual in the candour of its analysis and recommendations.[23] Most of the recommendations were accepted and several have been implemented.

The Brahimi Report concluded that 'when the United Nations does send its forces to uphold the peace, they must be prepared to confront the lingering forces of war and violence with the ability and determination to defeat them'. For in the final analysis, 'no amount of good intentions can substitute for the fundamental ability to project credible force if complex peacekeeping, in particular, is to succeed'.[24] Mandates, and the resources to match them, have to be guided by pragmatic, realistic analysis and thinking. The UN Secretariat 'must not apply best-case planning assumptions to situations where the local actors have historically exhibited worst-case behaviour'.[25] The UN needs to develop the professional civil service culture of providing advice that is sound, based on a thorough assessment of options, independent of what might be politically popular or fit the preconceptions of the decision-makers, and free of fear of consequences for politically neutral officials. The Secretariat was urged to tell the Security Council what it needs to hear, not what it wants to hear. Where clearly

[22] For a critical evaluation of the UN's record of transitional administration, see Simon Chesterman, *You, the People: The United Nations, Transitional Administration, and State-Building* (Oxford: Oxford University Press, 2004).

[23] Report of the Panel on United Nations Peace Operations, A/55/305-S/2000/809 (21 Aug 2000). See also David M. Malone and Ramesh Thakur, 'UN Peacekeeping: Lessons Learned?' (2001) 7 *Global Governance* 11–17.

[24] Report of the Panel on United Nations Peace Operations, viii.

[25] Report of the Panel on United Nations Peace Operations, para 51.

unimplementable missions have been approved because of confused, unclear, or severely under-resourced mandates, the UN has to learn to say 'No'.

Nor should the need for impartial peacekeeping translate automatically into moral equivalence among the conflict parties on the ground: in some cases local parties consist not of moral equals but obvious aggressors and victims.[26] The panel concluded that political neutrality has too often degenerated into military timidity, the abdication of the duty to protect civilians, and an operational failure to confront openly those who challenge peacekeeping missions in the field. Impartiality should not translate into complicity with evil. The Charter sets out the principles that the UN must defend and the values that it must uphold. The reluctance to distinguish victim from aggressor implies a degree of moral equivalency between the two and damages the institution of UN peacekeeping.

IV. Sanctions

Coercive economic sanctions developed as a conceptual and policy bridge between diplomacy and force for ensuring compliance with UN demands. Their use as a tool of foreign and international policy increased dramatically in the 20th century, yet their track record in ensuring compliance is modest.[27] Sanctions all too often are a poor alibi for, not a sound supplement to, good policy. They are ineffective, counterproductive, harmful to the economic interests of those imposing sanctions, damaging to relations with allies, morally questionable, yet difficult to lift once imposed. They inflict pain on ordinary citizens while imposing questionable costs on leaders who are often enriched and strengthened on the back of their impoverished and oppressed people. Annan acknowledged that 'humanitarian and human rights policy goals cannot easily be reconciled with those of a sanctions regime'.[28]

[26] Report of the Panel on United Nations Peace Operations, para 50.

[27] See Gary Clyde Hufbauer, Jeffrey J. Schott, Kimberley Ann Elliot, and Barbara Oegg, *Economic Sanctions Reconsidered* (3rd edn, Washington DC: Petersen Institute for International Economics, 2009); Daniel W. Drezner, *The Sanctions Paradox: Economic Statecraft and International Relations* (Cambridge: Cambridge University Press, 1999); Jeremy Farrall, *United Nations Sanctions and the Rule of Law* (Cambridge: Cambridge University Press, 2009); Robert A. Pape, 'Why Economic Sanctions Do Not Work' (1997) 22 *International Security* 90–136; and David Cortright, George A. Lopez, and Linda Gerber-Stellingwerf, 'Sanctions' in Thomas G. Weiss and Sam Daws (eds), *The Oxford Handbook on the United Nations* (Oxford: Oxford University Press, 2007), 349–69.

[28] Kofi A. Annan, 'Partnerships for Global Community: Annual Report on the Work of the Organization 1998' (1998), para 64.

The target country can choose from a range of sellers in the international marketplace. It is virtually impossible to secure universal participation in embargoes and difficult to police their application in participating countries. The incentive to make large profits by circumventing sanctions is more powerful than the motive for enforcing them, and a variety of means and routes exist to camouflage sanctions-busting contacts. Seyed Hossein Mousavian, described as the highest ranking member of Iran's political elite living in the US, notes that since the Security Council-imposed sanctions on Iran in 2006, 'the number of centrifuges increased eight times. Instead of one enrichment facility in 2006, Iran now possesses two facilities. Additionally, the fact the unilateral US sanctions are not readily reversible exacerbates Iran's skepticism about Washington's real intentions behind sanctions and removes any incentives for cooperation with the West'.[29]

Sanctions are counterproductive through two effects: political and economic. Politically, their goal is to reduce the support for sanctioned leaders among their own people. But sanctions offer an easy scapegoat for ruinous economic policies: economic pain is simply blamed on hostile and ill-intentioned foreigners. Bearing pain in order to cope with sanctions is portrayed as patriotic duty. Dissent is stifled and political opposition muted, silenced, or liquidated.

Economically, sanctions create shortages and raise prices in conditions of scarcity. The poor suffer; the middle class, essential to building the foundations of democracy, shrinks; the ruling class extracts fatter rents from monopoly controls over the illicit trade in banned goods. Scarcity increases the dependence of the population on the distribution of necessities by the regime, so sanctions give leaders yet another tool with which to exercise control and leverage over their people. Family cliques surrounding dictators under international sanctions can monopolize the black market spawned by the imposition of sanctions and the resulting scarcities and shortages of goods on the open market.

Violent conflicts are increasingly internal and involve rapacious and criminal behaviour in a regional environment of failed or criminalized states and warring and profiteering factions exploiting a shadow economy. On whom are the sanctions to be imposed, how are they be to enforced, and where is the financial incentive for the armed factions to comply with international demands instead of simply absorbing the extra costs? Where are the border-control mechanisms and state institutions for regulating and controlling the flow of goods that are subject to sanctions? The people at large, already victims of war, dispossession, and dislocation, are further victimized by warlords, black marketeers, and armed gangs. The most marked effect of sanctions in such circumstances may be to disrupt relief efforts and activities. All this explains why all UN sanctions

[29] Quoted in Ali Vaez, 'Seyed Hossein Mousavian: The West is pushing Iran in the Wrong Direction', *Bulletin of the Atomic Scientists*, 18 Nov 2011, available at <http://www.thebulletin.org/web-edition/features/seyed-hossein-mousavian-the-west-pushing-iran-the-wrong-direction>.

'should be effectively implemented and enforced by strengthening State capacity to implement sanctions, establishing well resourced monitoring mechanisms and mitigating humanitarian consequences'.[30]

The motives for the imposition and continuation of sanctions are often rooted in domestic politics. Rivals for office seek to reap electoral advantage by depicting opponents as 'soft' on the enemy. US sanctions on Cuba remain in place, not because they serve any purpose, not because they are achieving their original goals, but because of the power of a domestic electoral lobby which gives them a crucial swing-vote role in determining the outcome of Florida's electoral votes.

Sanctions inflict pain on innocent countries in the neighbourhood. The long history of sanctions on Cuba has many times brought US policy into conflict with those of its allies. They can damage producer groups in the countries imposing them, for example farmers. In addition, because of the frequency with which a country resorts to sanctions, the long-term reliability of its supplier status becomes suspect, with the result that foreign purchasers may not switch back to its products even after sanctions are lifted.

Public support for sanctions rests in their image as a humane alternative, and perhaps a necessary prelude, to war, which is increasingly regarded as a tool of the very last resort. Yet they can cause large-scale death and destruction through 'structural violence'—starvation, malnutrition, and the spread of deadly diseases—that exceeds the 'cleaner' alternative of open warfare. John Mueller and Karl Mueller concluded that sanctions caused more deaths in the 20th century than all weapons of mass destruction throughout history.[31] Their deadly impact on civilians in Saddam Hussein's Iraq was especially pernicious and instrumental in draining international public support from sanctions as a tool of statecraft.[32]

Against a formidable list of non-sanctions because some countries are too big to punish (who will bell the P5?) and others who are their allies, dubious sanctions, and the failure of sanctions, the list of successful outcomes of sanctions policies is thin and patchy. Sanctions advocacy relies on an ideological faith in the instrument quite disconnected from the mass of evidence since before the Second World War (eg Italy in Abyssinia),[33] that point to their futility. When national drug approval regulators scrutinize new (or already on the market) medicines, any drug that

[30] Kofi A. Annan, Report of the Secretary-General, 'In Larger Freedom: Towards Development, Security and Human Rights for All', A/59/2005 (21 Mar 2005), paras 109–10.

[31] John Mueller and Karl Mueller, 'Sanctions of Mass Destruction' (1999) 78 *Foreign Affairs* 43–53.

[32] See *Child Mortality: Iraq* (New York: UNICEF, 1999), doc GJ-99.8; Alberto Ascherio et al, 'Effect of the Gulf War on Infant and Child Mortality in Iraq' (1992) 327 *New England Journal of Medicine* 931–6; Richard Garfield, 'Morbidity and Mortality among Iraqi Children from 1990 to 1998: Assessing the Impact of Economic Sanctions', Occasional Paper Series 16:OP:3, Joan B. Kroc Institute for International Peace Studies of the University of Notre Dame and the Fourth Freedom Forum, Mar 1999; and Mohamed M. Ali and Iqbal H. Shah, 'Sanctions and Childhood Mortality in Iraq' (2000) 355 *Lancet* 1837–57.

[33] See George W. Baer, 'Sanctions and Security: The League of Nations and the Italian–Ethiopian War, 1935–1936' (1973) 27 *International Organization* 165–79.

betrays, say, a 10 per cent gravely damaging health side effect will be banned. Yet with sanctions, the international community seems prepared to tolerate a 20–30 per cent success rate alongside a 70–80 per cent failure rate,[34] some of it with very grave consequences indeed.[35]

[34] These figures are meant to be illustrative, not authoritative. The literature on the success and effectiveness of sanctions is in something of a mess, for a number of reasons. First, the literature in the English language is dominated almost exclusively by authors from sanctions-imposing countries in the West, who approach the subject from the point of view of the rights, interests, and objectives of those applying sanctions, not the experience of those living under sanctions. Secondly, there is no agreement on how to define and measure success, failure, and effectiveness, and therefore the indicators employed vary from one study to another. Thirdly, some indicators are remarkably lax, implying that the capacity to demonstrate *some* effects of the imposition of sanctions should be enough to refute criticisms that sanctions are a failure of policy. Thus, sanctions imposed by rival Cold War countries on Olympic Games held in countries of the rival bloc were affected to some degree; but who gets to decide whether the Moscow (1980) and Los Angeles Olympics (1984) were overall successes or failures? On the one hand, some countries did boycott the two and it is safe to assume that winners, medal tallies, and even some records would have been different had they all taken part. On the other hand, the Games were held and the official records on individual medal winners, country total medals, and performance measurements will forever stand. Fourthly, there is little to no effort to weight the variables with respect to the major cases and minor examples. Fifthly, on any rigorous assessment, failures of sanctions are easier to demonstrate than it is to argue conclusively for their effectiveness. Eg the South African apartheid regime collapsed. But it did so after living under sanctions for decades. It is impossible to prove that the collapse was caused by the sanctions, as opposed to, say, worsening economic straits caused by a deteriorating investment climate which saw foreign and domestic investors resort to capital flight. Similarly, it seems more plausible to posit that the change in policies in Myanmar has come about due to internal regime change rather than external sanctions. By contrast, if economic sanctions are followed by war against the target regime, or if the regime stays in power for years and decades under international sanctions, then clearly the sanctions have failed. With these comments in mind, it is instructive to consider just some of the major examples since the First World War. In the interwar period (1919–39), the two big cases were sanctions imposed on Italy and Japan for their invasions of Abyssinia and Manchuria; both were total failures. Since 1945, one of the few clear cases of sanctions success is against Mu'ammer Gaddafi of Libya who buckled to international demands in 2003. By contrast, sanctions on Saddam Hussein in Iraq failed, as proven by the very fact of war against him in 2003; those on Southern Rhodesia failed, for black liberation was achieved primarily as a result of an armed liberation struggle, while sanctions on Zimbabwe's Robert Mugabe have failed to dislodge him from power; sanctions imposed by the former Soviet Union on Josef Tito's Yugoslavia failed; sanctions maintained on Cuba have arguably helped to keep Fidel Castro in power instead of removing him; sanctions on Vietnam for its invasion of Cambodia did not achieve much; in the South Pacific, sanctions imposed on Fiji for the overthrow of its civilian government have been eased without any discernible concessions to outsiders; sanctions imposed on India and Pakistan for their nuclear weapons tests in 1998 have long since been abandoned and instead the non-proliferation regime has itself been 'reinterpreted' to accommodate India as a de facto nuclear weapon power with the signing of the India–US civil nuclear cooperation agreement; Iran's nuclear weapon capability has broadened and deepened while it has been under US, UN, and European Union sanctions with the number of centrifuges increasing eightfold since 2006, as noted earlier; and North Korea remains as defiant as ever.... For my review of the sanctions theory, practice, and literature, see Ramesh Thakur, *The United Nations, Peace and Security: From Collective Security to the Responsibility to Protect* (Cambridge: Cambridge University Press, 2006), ch 6, 'International Sanctions', 134–55.

[35] See esp Joy Gordon, *Invisible War: The United States and the Iraq Sanctions* (Cambridge, MA: Harvard University Press, 2012).

A. Smart Sanctions

Several of the problems associated with sanctions can be minimized through the imposition of 'smart' sanctions that target members of the ruling elite and are limited in their application to restrictions on overseas travel and financial transactions, a freeze on foreign assets, and arms embargoes.[36] Smart sanctions, the norm for this century, help the UN to mitigate the subversion of humanitarian goals and efforts. Their costs to third party countries are negligible. They reduce perverse incentives and consequences and deny regimes the use of aid as a tool for establishing control over people by controlling its delivery. They avoid long-term damage to the social, educational, health, and physical infrastructure. Above all, they make clear to the people that the international community does discriminate between the sins of the leaders and the distress of the people.

Humanitarian impact assessments, involving the use of such indicators as public health and population displacement, are now standard practice in sanctions policy. However, the difficulties associated with the imposition, monitoring, and enforcement of smart sanctions will become known only with experience. With respect to arms embargoes, for example, the well-intentioned effort runs into the problem of a buyer's market. In sum, 'while smart sanctions may seem logically compelling and conceptually attractive…[t]he operational problems—due to persistent technical inadequacies, legal loopholes, institutional weaknesses, budgetary and staff scarcities, and political constraints—are daunting'.[37] There remains a pressing need for serious studies of the compliance and transaction costs of targeted, well-thought-out sanctions regimes with built-in monitoring and enforcement mechanisms. Only then will the international community learn how to impose secondary sanctions on sanctions-busting countries while supporting states adversely affected by sanctions, the criteria and ground rules for exceptions and exemptions, and time limits and sunset clauses. The studies might also help to clarify the criteria for smart sanctions and whether they should be established on the basis of efficacy or, alternatively, if they are not proving efficacious, whether they should be lifted, expanded to comprehensive sanctions, or lead to military enforcement.

Thus, even when much improved from a moral, political, and technical point of view, smart sanctions remain unproven in actual practice. And the bigger question remains: within the larger framework of collective security, are sanctions a substitute for, complement to, or precursor to war?

[36] See David Cortright and George A. Lopez (eds), *Smart Sanctions: Targeting Economic Statecraft* (Lanham, MD: Rowman & Littlefield, 2002); Peter Wallensteen, Carina Staibano, and Mikail Erikson (eds), *Making Targeted Sanctions Effective: Guidelines for the Implementation of UN Policy Options* (Uppsala: Uppsala University, Department of Peace and Conflict Research, 2003).

[37] Michael Brzoska, 'From Dumb to Smart? Recent Reforms of UN Sanctions' (2003) 9 *Global Governance* 530–1.

V. The High-Level Panel and After

In order to forge a new consensus on the norms and laws governing the use of force in world affairs, Annan brought together a group of distinguished experts to probe the nature and gravity of today's threats and to recommend collective solutions to them through a reformed UN. The panel's report provided a useful analysis of the contemporary challenges confronting the UN and a set of broad and specific proposals to improve its performance and relevance.[38] The overarching themes were shared vulnerability, and the primacy of the rule of law embedded in universal institutions and procedures that are efficient, effective, and equitable. Its central thesis was that no country can afford to deal with contemporary threats alone, and no threat can be dealt with effectively unless other threats are addressed at the same time.

The report identified the major threats as war and violence among and within states, the use and proliferation of weapons of mass destruction, terrorism, transnational organized crime, and poverty, infectious disease, and environmental degradation. The threats can come from state and non-state actors and endanger human as well as national security. Collective security is necessary because today's threats cannot be contained within national boundaries, are interconnected and have to be addressed simultaneously at all levels. But the report did not address the challenge of how to institute and operationalize a workable collective security *system*.

For reasons of space, not all the categories of contemporary threats requiring a UN-centred collective security response can be discussed here. But two of the newer developments are worth examining: the responsibility to protect and nuclear security.

A. The Responsibility to Protect (R2P)

R2P is the normative instrument of choice for converting a shocked international conscience into decisive collective action—for channelling selective moral indignation into collective policy remedies—to prevent and stop atrocities. The origins of the UN lie in the anti-Nazi wartime military alliance between Britain, the US, and the Soviet Union. Its primary purpose is the maintenance of international peace and security. But in the decades after 1945, the nature of armed conflict was transformed as interstate warfare between uniformed armies gave way to irregular conflict between rival armed groups.[39] The nature of the state too changed from its idealized European version. Many communist and some newly decolonized countries were internal security states whose regimes ruled through terror. Increasingly, the

[38] HLP, 'A More Secure World'.

[39] See Andrew Mack et al, *Human Security Report 2005* (Oxford: Oxford University Press, 2005).

principal victims of both types of violence were civilians. Advances in telecommunications brought the full horror of their plight into the world's living rooms. In the meantime, the goals of promoting human rights and democratic governance, protecting civilian victims of humanitarian atrocities, and punishing governmental perpetrators of mass crimes became more important.

Created from the ashes of the Second World War with the Allies determined to prevent a repeat of Adolf Hitler's horrors, the UN for most of its existence focused more on external aggression than internal mass killings. Yet Nazi Germany was guilty of both. Unlike aggression against other countries, the systematic and large-scale extermination of Jews was a new horror. The 21st century began with the UN elevating the doctrine of preventing mass atrocities against people to the same level of collective responsibility as preventing and repelling armed aggression against states.

For 350 years after the Treaty of Westphalia (1648), sovereignty shielded tyrants from external accountability for acts of domestic brutality. International interventions in Kosovo and East Timor in 1999 broke that mould and were the backdrop to Annan's search for a new norm. With Canada's help, an independent international commission formulated the principle of R2P.[40] This principle spoke eloquently to the need to change the UN's normative framework in line with the changed reality of threats and victims.[41]

The 2001 report of the International Commission on Intervention and State Sovereignty (ICISS) argued that the essential nature of sovereignty had changed from state privileges and immunities to the responsibility to protect people from atrocity crimes.[42] Where the state defaulted on its solemn responsibility owing to lack of will or capacity, or because it was itself complicit in the commission of the atrocities, the responsibility to protect tripped upwards to the international community acting through the UN. The unanimous endorsement of R2P by world leaders in 2005 added clarity, rigour, and specificity, whilst limiting the triggering events to war crimes, genocide, ethnic cleansing, and crimes against humanity and so realigning the emerging global political norm to existing categories of international legal crimes.[43]

UN Secretary-General Ban Ki-moon's reports on R2P have sustained and consolidated the new international consensus on this inherently controversial and

[40] See Gareth Evans, *The Responsibility to Protect: Ending Mass Atrocity Crimes Once and for All* (Washington DC: Brookings Institution, 2008); Ramesh Thakur, *The Responsibility to Protect: Norms, Laws and the Use of Force in International Politics* (London: Routledge, 2011) and *People vs. the State: Reflections on UN Authority, US Power and the Responsibility to Protect* (Tokyo: United Nations University Press, 2011); Thomas G. Weiss, *Humanitarian Intervention* (London: Polity, 2007); and Alex J. Bellamy, *Responsibility to Protect: The Global Effort to End Mass Atrocities* (Cambridge: Polity, 2009).

[41] For an account of the UN's transformation since 1945, see Thakur, *The United Nations, Peace and Security*.

[42] International Commission on Intervention and State Sovereignty, *The Responsibility to Protect* (Ottawa: International Development Research Centre for ICISS, 2001).

[43] World Summit Outcome Document, adopted by GA Res A/RES/60/1 (24 Oct 2005), paras 138–40.

contentious subject.[44] Civil society organizations have promoted a vigorous process of R2P norm socialization and crystallization. The annual debates by the UN General Assembly on Ban's special reports have helped to forge a shared understanding of R2P to distinguish it from humanitarian intervention and align it with building capacity to help states to exercise their sovereignty more effectively. The debates show that the consensus on R2P is broadening, its legitimacy is strengthening, and most states are more concerned to move on to questions of implementation.[45] In the vacuum of responsibility for the safety of the marginalized, stigmatized, and dehumanized out-group subject to mass atrocities, R2P provides an entry point for the international community to step in and take up the moral and military slack. Pared down to its essence, R2P is the acceptance of a duty of care by all those who live in zones of safety towards those trapped in zones of danger. It strikes a balance between unilateral interference rooted in the arrogance of power and institutionalized indifference that dislocates the 'Other' from the Self.

In a speech on 18 January 2012 to a conference to honour ICISS on the tenth anniversary of the R2P report,[46] Ban Ki-moon noted that historically, the international community's 'chief failing' has not been too much intervention, but rather 'the reluctance to act in the face of serious threats'. In his view, Libya in 2011 'demonstrated that human protection is a defining purpose of the United Nations'. But 'the execution of our collective responsibilities was not always perfect' in Libya and some innocent lives were lost in the name of R2P.[47]

R2P was the discourse of choice in debating how best to respond to the Libya crisis. In Security Council Resolutions 1970 and 1973 (2011), the UN for the first time invoked R2P under the coercive Chapter VII of the UN Charter.[48] By year's end, Mu'ammer Gaddafi had been ousted, captured, and killed. The outcome was a triumph for R2P: it *is* possible for the international community, working through the authenticated, UN-centred structures and procedures of organized multilateralism, to deploy international force to neutralize the military might of a dictator and intervene between

44 Implementing the Responsibility to Protect, A/63/677 (12 Jan 2009); Early Warning, Assessment, and the Responsibility to Protect, A/64/864 (14 July 2010); The Role of Regional and Subregional Arrangements in Implementing the Responsibility to Protect, A/65/877–S/2011/393 (28 June 2011); and Timely and Decisive Response, A/66/874–S/2012/578 (25 July 2012).

45 Mónica Serrano, 'The Responsibility to Protect and Its Critics: Explaining the Consensus' (2011) 3 *Global Responsibility to Protect (GR2P)* 425–37.

46 Disclosure: I was an ICISS Commissioner and one of the three principal authors of its report.

47 Ban Ki-moon, 'Address to Stanley Foundation Conference on the Responsibility to Protect', New York, 18 July 2012 (UN News Centre, 18 Jan 2012), available at <http://www.un.org/apps/news/infocus/sgspeeches/statments_full.asp?statID=1433>.

48 For a range of diverse opinions and perspectives on R2P and Libya, see the collection of essays in e-International Relations, 'The Responsibility to Protect: Challenges and Opportunities in Light of the Libyan Intervention', 21 Nov 2011, available at <http://www.e-ir.info/2011/11/21/the-responsibility-to-protect-challenges-opportunities-in-light-of-the-libyan-intervention/comment-page-1/#comment-37850>.

him and his victims. Albeit qualified and incomplete, Libya marks a milestone in taming atrocities on their own people by tyrants.

By 2012 there was no substantial opposition to R2P as a principle or norm—an international standard of conduct. During the day-long discussions at the event where Ban Ki-moon spoke, there was a striking depth of consensus in support of R2P principles among state representatives, UN officials, and other policy and civil society actors. Yet there was also deep disquiet among many participants, verging on outright distrust in some key sections, about how UN authorization for the Libyan operation had been overstretched.

Consequently, the jury is still out on whether NATO military action in Libya will consolidate or soften the R2P norm. Inevitably, the first UN-authorized military intervention showed flaws and imperfections in the machinery of implementation that will need to be addressed. Carefully crafted both to authorize and delimit the scope of intervention, Resolution 1973 specified the purpose of military action as humanitarian protection and limited the means to that goal. NATO ignored its restrictions, spurned hints of a negotiated ceasefire, and broke the arms embargo of the UN by supplying weaponry to the rebels. Denials to the contrary rest on 'legal sophistries'.[49]

Brazil offered a paper on 'Responsibility while Protecting' with the potential to bring in some agreed parameters on the conditions that will govern the use of UN-authorized R2P operations.[50] Its two key elements were to formulate an agreed set of criteria or guidelines to help the Security Council in the debate before an R2P military intervention is authorized, and a monitoring or review mechanism to ensure that the Council has an oversight role and exercises supervisory control over the operation after authorization and during implementation. Specifically, 'the authorization for the use of force must be limited in its legal, operational and temporal elements'; and 'Enhanced Security Council procedures are needed to monitor and assess the manner in which resolutions are interpreted and implemented to ensure responsibility while protecting'.[51]

Had R2P merely repackaged the Western humanitarian warriors' wishes and brushed aside the sensitivities of the rest, it never would have gained rapid uptake and traction culminating in unanimous endorsement in 2005. The R2P consensus underpinning Resolution 1973 in 2011 was damaged by gaps in expectation, communication, and accountability between those who mandated the operation and those who executed it. One important result of the gaps was a split in the international response to the worsening crisis in Syria. The Arab and Western countries introduced draft

[49] Jonathan Eyal, 'The Responsibility to Protect: A Chance Missed' in Adrian Johnson and Saqeb Mueen (eds), *Short War, Long Shadows: The Political and Military Legacies of the 2011 Libyan Campaign* (London: Royal United Services Institute, Whitehall Report 1-12, 2012), 59.

[50] 'Responsibility while Protecting: Elements for the Development and Promotion of a Concept', United Nations, General Assembly, and Security Council, A/66/551–S/2011/701 (11 Nov 2011).

[51] 'Responsibility while Protecting', paras 11(d) and 11(h).

Security Council resolutions in October 2011, February 2012, and July 2012 that were vetoed by China and Russia still smarting from the over-interpretation of Resolution 1973 in Libya and the abuse of their goodwill in abstaining on a resolution they disliked. Both were defiantly opposed to any resolution that could set in train a sequence of events leading to a Resolution 1973-type authorization for outside military operations in Syria.[52]

The R2P operation in Libya in 2011 was thus successful, but also controversial and contested. Above all, the Libyan example shows that success in an R2P intervention is no more self-guaranteeing than in any other type of external intervention. Good intention is not a magical formula by which to shape good outcomes in foreign lands. On the contrary, there is no humanitarian crisis so grave that an outside military intervention cannot make it worse. Although no intervention will mean grave harm in some cases, fewer interventions may do less good but also will do less harm. The guiding R2P motto therefore should be: first do less harm.

B. Nuclear Security

After the terrorist attacks on the US on 11 September 2001, fears of a nuclear war intersected with fears of an act of nuclear terrorism. A major nuclear security vulnerability or crisis anywhere would pose an unacceptable risk and threat everywhere: a classic collective security dilemma. All countries need to work individually and collaboratively in all aspects of the storage, use, transportation, and disposal of nuclear and radiological materials. In his famous speech in Prague on 5 April 2009 outlining his dream of a world free of nuclear weapons, President Barack Obama described the risk of nuclear terrorism as the most immediate and most extreme threat to global security.[53] He announced the start of a new international effort to secure the world's vulnerable nuclear material within four years.

Thousands of tons of nuclear materials, enough for another 100,000 bombs compared to the present stockpiles of around 18,000, are stored in hundreds of sites in 32 countries.[54] While some of the sites are well secured, many are not. Hence, there is risk of sabotage and theft by, or illicit sales to, terrorists and others. The risks are multiplied in conditions of fragile and failing states, of fragmented authority structures, of a pervasive culture of corruption among public officials, or when widespread unemployment, underemployment, and poverty can weaken resistance

[52] See Ramesh Thakur, 'Syrians are paying the price of NATO excesses in Libya', e-International Relations, 2 Mar 2012, available at <http://www.e-ir.info/2012/03/02/syrians-are-paying-the-price-of-nato-excesses-in-libya>.

[53] 'Remarks by President Barack Obama, Hradcany Square, Prague, 5 April 2009', White House, Office of the Press Secretary, 2009, available at <http://www.whitehouse.gov/video/The-President-in-Prague#transcript>.

[54] See Ramesh Thakur and Gareth Evans (eds), *Nuclear Weapons: The State of Play* (Canberra: Centre for Nuclear Non-proliferation and Disarmament, 2013).

to inducements offered by various shady groups. According to the International Atomic Energy Agency (IAEA), between January 1993 and December 2011, there were 2,164 cases of illegal trafficking, theft, or loss of nuclear and radiological materials around the world, of which only 40 per cent has been recovered.[55] These incidents show the urgent need to raise international nuclear security standards.

Terrorists need only to identify and exploit the weakest link in the chain of international nuclear security to acquire enough fissile material to make and detonate a bomb in a major city. Measures for the physical protection of all nuclear materials, facilities, and activities are an essential and critical component of nuclear collective security. As well as guards, gates, and fences at nuclear plants and facilities, this requires thorough background checks on personnel employed there and rigorous training after recruitment in order to inculcate a culture of nuclear security. Weapon-grade fissile material even for peaceful purposes should be subject to security controls no less stringent than those prescribed for nuclear weapons, or what the US National Academy of Sciences describes as 'the stored-weapon standard'.[56]

The global norms and international instruments for addressing nuclear security include the IAEA's Informational Circular (INFCIRC) 225 as revised in 2011, the cornerstone of the international physical protection regime for nuclear materials and facilities; the IAEA Code of Conduct on the Safety and Security of Radioactive Sources (2003); the Convention on the Physical Protection of Nuclear Materials (1980, with an important amendment in 2005); and Security Council Resolution 1540 (2004) which obligates all states to enact and enforce laws to prohibit non-state actors to develop, acquire, transfer, or use weapons of mass destruction; to take and enforce effective domestic control, physical protection, accounting, and border-control measures to prevent proliferation, and prohibit assisting or financing such proliferation; to control the provision of funds and services that contribute to proliferation; and to set up a committee of the whole to oversee implementation of the resolution.

Following Obama's initiative, three nuclear security summits were held in Washington (April 2010), Seoul (March 2012), and The Hague (2014). They were convened to strengthen, consolidate, elevate, and energize the many existing national, multilateral, and cooperative institutions and structures to ensure nuclear security and prevent nuclear smuggling. The summits recognized that global nuclear security is only as strong as the weakest national link in the chain of state-operated nuclear programmes.[57] If terrorists manage to get their hands on weapon-usable nuclear

[55] Of these, 399 involved unauthorized possession or use of, or trade in, nuclear material or radioactive sources; 588 incidents involved the theft or loss of such material; and 1,124 cases involved such other activities as the unauthorized disposal of radioactive materials; see <http://www-ns.iaea.org/security/itdb.asp>.

[56] Quoted in Weapons of Mass Destruction Commission, *Weapons of Terror: Freeing the World of Nuclear, Biological and Chemical Arms* (Stockholm: Weapons of Mass Destruction Secretariat, 2006), 84.

[57] 'Highlights of the National Commitments made at the Nuclear Security Summit', Office of the Press Secretary, White House, 13 Apr 2010, available at <http://www.whitehouse.gov/the-press-office/highlights-national-commitments-made-nss>.

material from any one particular facility in any one country, they could threaten to use them anywhere else in the world against the people and interests of any country. This makes nuclear security a shared global interest and enterprise. Every state maintaining nuclear facilities and operating nuclear programmes has an international as well as a national responsibility to secure them. All states are responsible for ensuring the security of nuclear materials and facilities under their control, to seek assistance from others if necessary, and to provide assistance to others if asked.

But the force of the communiqués was weakened by the fact that they were vague, non-binding, and full of escape clauses like 'as appropriate', 'where technically and economically feasible', 'taking into account the need for assured supplies of medical isotopes', and 'consistent with national security considerations and development objectives'.[58] Given the gravity of the threat, a credible and effective nuclear security regime must be mandatory, legally binding, and create globally uniform standards and monitoring-cum-verification systems.

VI. From UN Collective Security to UN-Centred Global Governance

This survey of the changing requirements and manifestations of the UN-centred system of collective security shows that, within the parameters of the 1945 Charter, the UN has demonstrated remarkable policy innovation, institutional adaptation, and organizational learning. On policy innovation, the best example is peacekeeping itself, a word missing from the Charter, as well as R2P and international criminal justice as a legal sanction. On institutional adaptation, the Department of Peacekeeping Operations, the Peacebuilding Commission, the Joint Office on Genocide Prevention and R2P, and the International Criminal Court are entities that did not exist in 1945. On organizational learning, the Brahimi Report on peace operations and the Secretary-General's special reports on R2P are good examples.

The core of the collective security system is the Security Council which has proven impossible to reform since the last restructuring in the mid-1960s.[59] The many efforts made to do so recall the fate of Sisyphus, condemned to watch his boulder roll

[58] See <http://www.whitehouse.gov/the-press-office/communiqu-washington-nuclear-security-summit> and <http://www.thenuclearsecuritysummit.org/userfiles/Seoul%20Communique_FINAL.pdf>.

[59] See Thakur, *United Nations, Peace and Security*, ch 13.

down every time he pushed it to the top of the hill. It violates many fundamental precepts of contemporary good governance, including representivity, accountability, and transparency.[60] The irreducible minimum for any credible system of collective security is that the key actors making and enforcing the coercive decisions in the name and on behalf of the collectivity are the major powers of the day. This is the logic justifying permanent membership with veto rights of the Security Council. This is the criterion on which, more than any other single factor, the Council fails the test comprehensively. Consequently, the Council in particular and the UN in general are experiencing accumulating legitimacy deficits, with challenges both to the legality and the legitimacy of their edicts on a broad range of fronts.[61] Thus, in the press release accompanying the publication of its annual report in May 2012 on the state of the world's human rights, Amnesty International drew attention to 'a failure of leadership that makes the UN Security Council seem tired, out of step and increasingly unfit for purpose'.[62]

In the light of the suboptimal effectiveness of UN operations, NATO is replacing UN-commanded operations as the enforcement arm of the international organization when (albeit not only when) duly authorized by the Security Council. But this is far from a risk-free partnership for the UN. The use of force depends on: (1) the mandate as written in the authorizing Security Council resolution; (2) the rules of engagement (ROE); and (3) the decision of military commanders on the ground. For UN operations, the use of force is restricted to self-defence, protecting UN personnel and property against attacks, protecting civilians targeted by spoilers, and protecting the mandate. With UN-authorized but non-UN-led operations, as in Kosovo and Afghanistan, the ROE are approved by the coalition or by NATO. The restrictions are much less stringent and the resources are far more robust. The Security Council gives them international legitimacy but has no say over the ROE nor does it exercise any effective authority over these forces. NATO countries, which provide the troops, equipment, and logistics, have the military capability and the political clout to act independently of the UN; they have leverage over the UN, not the other way round. The Security Council is not the oversight body to which NATO forces in Afghanistan report.

In addition to NATO as the outsourced enforcement arm of the UN, the gathering crisis of confidence-cum-authority has produced a shift away from UN-centred collective security to a more diffuse set of multilateral arrangements signifying

[60] See Thomas G. Weiss, *What's Wrong with the United Nations and How to Fix It* (Oxford: Polity, 2008).

[61] See Ramesh Thakur, 'Law, Legitimacy, and the United Nations' in Richard Falk, Mark Juergensmeyer, and Vesselin Popovski (eds), *Legality and Legitimacy in Global Affairs* (Oxford: Oxford University Press, 2012), 45–71.

[62] Press release, Amnesty International, available at <http://www.amnesty.org/en/annual-report/2012/press-release>.

global governance with a range of governmental, intergovernmental, and civil society actors.[63] The global governance architecture is made up of:

- formal global organizations like the UN system, the World Bank, the International Monetary Fund, the World Health Organization, and the World Trade Organization;
- formal regional and sub-regional organizations like the African Union, the Economic Community of West African States, the Commonwealth of Nations, the Organization of American States, and the Association of Southeast Asian Nations;
- collective defence pacts like NATO;
- informal general-purpose institutions like the G8 and the G20; and
- informal but functionally specific and single-problem-oriented institutions like the Proliferation Security Initiative and the nuclear security summits.

In this framework of multiple and complementary actors of global governance, the potential of the G20, for example, lies in augmenting the formal fora of organized multilateralism with an informal institutional setting for the key players to engage each other directly and personally in pre-negotiations to break some particularly obdurate global deadlocks.[64] But they will still require ratification by the UN system as the world's premier and, for this purpose, indispensable and irreplaceable mandated multilateral organization.

[63] See Thomas G. Weiss and Ramesh Thakur, *Global Governance and the UN: An Unfinished Journey* (Bloomington, IN: Indiana University Press, 2010).

[64] See Andrew F. Cooper and Ramesh Thakur, *The Group of Twenty (G20)* (London: Routledge, 2013).

CHAPTER 9

OUTSOURCING THE USE OF FORCE: TOWARDS MORE SECURITY COUNCIL CONTROL OF AUTHORIZED OPERATIONS?

NIELS BLOKKER*

I. Introduction

The analysis of authorizations by the Security Council to use force must be seen in the context of the basic rules governing the use of force in international relations: the obligation for states to refrain from the threat or use of force in international relations[1] and the two exceptions to this prohibition, the right of

* This chapter was written in a personal capacity; the views expressed are those of the author. I thank Sir Michael Wood and Dr Marten Zwanenburg for their comments on a previous version, and Kim Lelieveld for her research assistance.

[1] UN Charter, Art 2(4).

self-defence against armed attacks[2] and the use of force by or authorized by the Security Council. The obligation to refrain from the threat or use of force is a key provision in the UN Charter. The Charter is replete with provisions supporting this key provision, from the preambular aim 'to save succeeding generations from the scourge of war' and the requirement that new members are 'peace-loving'[3] to the powers attributed to the Security Council. But the weight of the two exceptions to this key provision is considerable, as these exceptions often relate to situations in which the security of a state and/or the survival of a regime is, or is perceived to be, at stake.

There is a delicate balance between the prohibition in Article 2(4) and the two exceptions to this prohibition. With regard to self-defence, while Article 51 recognizes that this is an 'inherent right', it also stipulates that this right may be exercised only 'until the Security Council has taken the measures necessary to maintain international peace and security'. In addition, self-defence actions must be immediately reported to the Council and 'shall not in any way affect the authority and responsibility of the Security Council under the present Charter to take at any time such action as it deems necessary in order to maintain or restore international peace and security'. With respect to the other exception, authorizations to use force by the Security Council, the Charter does not offer much guidance. When the Charter was negotiated, it was agreed that the Security Council would have the power to use force through armed forces put at its disposal on the basis of agreements concluded with member states.[4] However, such agreements have not been concluded and practice had to find acceptable alternatives that would—albeit second best—fill some of the resulting 'collective security gap'. These alternatives are UN peacekeeping operations and operations carried out by one or more states or by international organizations on the basis of a Security Council authorization ('authorized operations'). One of the fundamental differences between these two types of operations is that the former are implemented and financed by the UN; they are UN organs, for whose conduct the UN may be held responsible. The latter are authorized by the Security Council, but are implemented largely outside its control, and therefore also, in principle, outside UN responsibility. The link between peacekeeping operations and the UN is generally much closer than that of authorized operations and the UN.

Both in the case of UN peacekeeping operations and in the case of authorized operations, it is for the Security Council to prescribe when force may be used. In the case of peacekeeping operations, the scope for the use of force was originally restricted to self-defence. Over the years this scope has been much broadened. In some cases, particularly since the 1990s, the Security Council has given extensive authorizations to use force to UN peacekeeping forces. At the same time, such

[2] UN Charter, Art 51. [3] UN Charter, Art 4(1). [4] UN Charter, Art 43.

authorizations have always remained under the control of the Security Council. This is different for authorized operations. They are placed outside the institutional structure of the UN and are carried out and financed by others who are 'able and willing' (states or international organizations such as the North Atlantic Treaty Organization (NATO), the European Union (EU), or the African Union (AU)).

The name 'authorized operation' is not a generally used term of art. Various names have been used for these operations, such as 'operations by coalitions of the able and willing'. However, this term does not cover authorizations to a single state, such as the authorization to use force to the French forces in the case of Côte d'Ivoire (discussed in the next section). Other terms, such as the 'franchise model' or the 'privatization' of Security Council enforcement action have other shortcomings.[5] The term 'authorized operation' has the advantage of staying close to Security Council terminology and to the precise function of the Council in relation to these operations. The resolutions on the basis of which these operations are carried out usually state: 'The Security Council... authorises the establishment [or: the deployment] of a multinational force [or: specific name, such as SFOR (Bosnia) or ISAF (Afghanistan)]'. In contrast, if the Security Council decides not to use this technique but prefers a UN peacekeeping force, the relevant resolutions usually state: 'The Security Council decides to establish the United Nations Mission in ...'[6] In the case of authorized operations, the actual *establishment* of the operation is done by the relevant state(s) or organization; the Security Council's role is to *authorize* the establishment of the operation. This is a more limited role, although it is essential. The authorization is a *conditio sine qua non* for these operations, which are therefore named authorized operations.

While the technique of authorized operations offers the relevant state(s) or international organization considerable leeway, it has at times been subject to legal and political criticism. The Security Council has at times been criticized for 'outsourcing' or 'delegating away' its authority and its primary responsibility for the maintenance of international peace and security. In addition, implementing states or international organizations have been accused of acting outside the scope of their authorization. For example, in 2011 certain member states were authorized 'to take all necessary measures... to protect civilians and civilian populated areas under threat of attack in the Libyan Arab Jamahiriya, including Benghazi' (NATO operation 'Unified Protector').[7] However, a number of states and commentators suggested that NATO had in fact carried out regime change.[8] NATO

[5] On this terminology, see Niels Blokker, 'Is the Authorisation Authorised? Powers and Practice of the UN Security Council to Authorise the Use of Force by "Coalitions of the Able and Willing"' (2000) 11 *European Journal of International Law* 541, 543 fn 3.

[6] See eg Res 1509 (UNMIL, Liberia), Res 1542 (MINUSTAH, Haiti), Res 1996 (UNMISS, South Sudan).

[7] SC Res (1973), para 4.

[8] eg Russian Foreign Minister Lavrov stated on 4 July 2011 that weapons supplies and deployment of military advisers to help the rebels violated Res 1973 (see <http://www.reuters.com/assets/print?aid=USTRE76326J20110704>). See also the statements by Russia and China in the Security Council on 4 May 2011 (S/PV.6528, 8–10).

has rejected this.[9] In December 2011—after NATO had ended the operation—UN Secretary-General Ban Ki-moon stated that NATO had acted within its mandate.[10]

Criticism of the NATO operation in Libya also influenced decision-making in the Security Council in relation to the situation in Syria, for example when on 4 October 2011 a draft resolution submitted by France, Germany, Portugal, and the UK was vetoed by China and Russia.[11]

This criticism of the 2011 NATO operation in Libya is far from new. It follows criticism expressed in the 1990s, particularly in relation to Security Council Resolution 678 (1990), authorizing the use of 'all necessary means' against Iraq following Iraq's invasion of Kuwait. On the one hand, the adoption of Resolution 678 was widely welcomed, as it marked the end of an era in which the Security Council had generally been unable to play the role foreseen in the UN Charter. On the other hand, however, the Security Council not only carried out its responsibility under the Charter by adopting this resolution, at the same time it left the implementation of the military operation almost exclusively to the coalition led by the US, hardly keeping any control over it.

The criticism of the carte blanche nature of Resolution 678 consists of three elements. First of all, there is no time limit for the authorization. The authorization to use all necessary means would therefore remain in force until another resolution had been adopted to terminate it, and the US and others could use their veto to prevent such a termination. Secondly, the mandate given in the authorization is extremely broad. The use of force is authorized 'to uphold and implement resolution 660 (1990) and all subsequent relevant resolutions and to restore international peace and security in the area'. Thirdly, Resolution 678 requested the coalition forces 'to keep the Security Council regularly informed'. It was not specified how often this would need

[9] eg during a press conference (15 Apr 2011) NATO Secretary-General Rasmussen stated: 'in the conduct of that operation we do not go beyond the text or the spirit of UN Security Council resolution 1973. On the contrary, we are implementing the Security Council resolution in strict conformity with both the letter and the spirit of that resolution' (<http://www.nato.int/cps/en/natolive/opinions_72785.htm>). During a meeting of the NATO–Russia Council, 4 July 2011, the NATO Secretary-General made similar remarks (<http://www.bbc.co.uk/news/world-europe-14010305>).

[10] During a press conference on 14 Dec 2011: 'I believe that these changes of regime were done by the people, not by the intervention of any foreign forces, including the United Nations. Security Council resolution 1973, I believe, was strictly enforced within that limit, within the mandate. This military operation done by the NATO forces was strictly within [Resolution] 1973' (<http://www.un.org/apps/sg/sgstats.asp?nid=5762>). In turn, this statement was criticized by the Russian Ambassador to the UN: '[we] expect the [UN] Secretariat to be more careful when it passes its judgment on very important issues which the Security Council is dealing with' (<http://www.reuters.com/assets/print?aid=USTRE7BI29920111219>).

[11] See S/PV.6627. During this meeting Russia stated, inter alia: 'The situation in Syria cannot be considered in the Council separate from the Libyan experience. The international community is alarmed by statements that compliance with Security Council resolutions on Libya in the NATO interpretation is a model for the future actions of NATO in implementing the responsibility to protect' (at 4). South Africa abstained and stated, inter alia: 'We are concerned that this draft resolution not be part of a hidden agenda aimed at once again instituting regime change...' (at 11).

to be, or what information would have to be provided. In practice, several member states submitted very brief reports (one or a few pages) to the Council, without much detail and essentially indicating that the operation was going smoothly and was under (their) control.[12] Thus, the Security Council was unable to play any effective supervisory role in relation to this operation. Moreover, because of its very general and elastic nature, Resolution 678 has also been used much later, as part of the legal underpinning for the use of force against Iraq in 2003.

The carte blanche nature of Resolution 678 has been criticized, both by states and by academic commentators. For example, Weston argued in 1991 that the Security Council 'eschewed direct UN responsibility *and* accountability for the military force that ultimately was deployed, favoring, instead, a delegated, essentially unilateralist determination and orchestration of world policy, coordinated and controlled almost exclusively by the United States.'[13] Within the Security Council, similar criticism was expressed.[14]

In an earlier publication, I have analysed Security Council practice in relation to authorization resolutions post-Resolution 678.[15] The main finding of that analysis was that the Security Council exercised more control over these authorized operations than it did over the operation against Iraq in 1991. Its authorization resolutions adopted during the period from 1990 to 2000 are different from Resolution 678, with respect to the three elements previously mentioned. In a number of cases—but not always—the authorization is limited in time. The mandate of the operation, that is, the purpose for which the authorization is given, has never again been as broad and general as in Resolution 678. Furthermore, there are stricter requirements for reporting to the Security Council.

This chapter will analyse developments relating to operations authorized by the Security Council since 2000. Has the trend towards more Security Council control persisted, taking into account the three elements mentioned earlier? And if this is the case, what are the implications? The relevant authorization resolutions will be analysed, as well as the reports of the meetings of the Security Council, in which

[12] eg S/22341 (Letter dated 5 March 1991 from the permanent representative of the United States of America to the United Nations addressed to the President of the Security Council; 8 Mar 1991).

[13] Burns Weston, 'Security Council Resolution 678 and Persian Gulf Decision Making: Precarious Legitimacy' (1991) 85 *American Journal of International Law* 516, 517. For similar criticism, see John Quigley, 'The Privatization of Security Council Enforcement Action: A Threat to Multilateralism' (1996) 17 *Michigan Journal of International Law* 249. See also Giorgio Gaja, 'Use of Force made or authorised by the United Nations' in Christian Tomuschat (ed), *The United Nations at Age Fifty—A Legal Perspective* (The Hague: Kluwer, 1995), 39 (at 46: 'the preservation of some essential elements of the Charter system appears to require that the Council refrain from giving "blank" authorisations, but keep a strict control over the objectives of the operation, the rules of engagement, and the organization of the force'); Frank Berman, 'The Authorization Model: Resolution 678 and Its Effects' in David M. Malone (ed), *The UN Security Council—From the Cold War to the 21st Century* (Boulder, CO: Lynne Rienner, 2004), 153. For more references to authorization literature of the 1990s, see Blokker, 'Is the Authorisation Authorised?'.

[14] See S/PV.2963, eg at 58 (Cuba) and 76 (Malaysia).

[15] Blokker, 'Is the Authorisation Authorised?'.

these resolutions were adopted, and the practice under these resolutions. Following a brief general overview in Section II, various relevant elements of the authorization resolutions adopted by the Security Council in the period from 2000 to 2012 will be analysed (Sections III to VIII). Subsequently, Section VIII will discuss the relevance of this analysis for questions regarding the potential responsibility of the UN. Section IX will offer a few conclusions and recommendations.

II. General Overview

Between 1 January 2000 and 1 January 2012, the Security Council adopted 80 resolutions in which it authorized states and international organizations to establish or to continue an operation that would have the right to use armed force ('authorization resolutions'). Of these 80 resolutions, 75 were adopted unanimously. There were no negative votes, only abstentions when the five other resolutions were adopted. These abstentions did not relate to the technique of authorizations, but to other issues.[16]

As indicated in the following list, these 80 authorization resolutions relate to 13 cases or situations and involve ten host states; most of these resolutions are extensions of authorizations given earlier for a limited period (eg six months or one year).

(1) Bosnia and Herzegovina: Resolution 1305 (2000),[17] 15 extensions; originally the authorization was given to 'the Member States acting through or in cooperation with the organization referred to in Annex 1-A of the Peace Agreement' (NATO), since Resolution 1575 (2004) it was also given to 'the Member States acting through or in cooperation with the EU'.

(2) Afghanistan: Resolution 1386 (2001), 11 extensions; authorization given to 'the Member States participating in the International Security Assistance Force' (led by NATO).

(3) Côte d'Ivoire: Resolution 1464 (2003), 21 extensions;[18] authorization originally given to 'Member States participating in the ECOWAS [Economic Community of West African States] forces in accordance with Chapter VIII together with

[16] These five resolutions are 1305 (Russia abstained), 1776 (Russia abstained), 1483 (Syria did not participate in the vote; later it indicated that it would have voted in favour, see S/PV.4761, 2 fn), 1497 (France, Germany, and Mexico abstained), 1973 (Brazil, China, Germany, India, and Russia abstained).

[17] The original authorization is given in Res 1031 (1995).

[18] One extension was given almost one month after the existing authorization expired: Res 1962 extended the existing Security Council authorization until 30 June 2011, but the next extension was only adopted on 27 July 2011 (Res 2000). As a result, there was no legal basis for the operation of the French forces in Côte d'Ivoire in the period 30 June–27 July 2011.

the French forces supporting them', since Resolution 1594 (2005) only to 'the French forces'.

(4) Iraq: Resolution 1483 (2003), five extensions;[19] originally not specified to whom the authorization was given; since Resolution 1511 this was to 'a multinational force under unified command'.

(5) Democratic Republic of the Congo: Resolution 1484 (2003), one extension; authorization given to 'the Member States participating in the Interim Emergency Multinational Force in Bunia'.

(6) Liberia: Resolution 1497 (2003); authorization given to 'the Member States participating in the Multinational Force in Liberia'.

(7) Haiti: Resolution 1529 (2004), one extension; authorization given to 'the Member States participating in the Multinational Interim Force in Haiti'.

(8) Democratic Republic of the Congo: Resolution 1671 (2006); authorization given to the EU force 'Eufor R.D. Congo'.

(9) Somalia: resolution 1725 (2006); authorization given to 'IGAD [Intergovernmental Authority on Development] and Member States of the African Union'.

(10) Somalia: Resolution 1744 (2007), eight extensions; authorization given to 'member States of the African Union'.

(11) Chad, the Central African Republic, and the sub-region: Resolution 1778 (2007); authorization given to 'the European Union'.

(12) Somalia—piracy: Resolution 1816 (2008), five extensions; authorization given to 'States cooperating with the TFG [Transitional Federal Government]'.

[19] It may be questioned whether Res 1483 is an authorization resolution, since it does not contain the standard language 'all necessary means' or 'all necessary measures'. However, Res 1483 'Appeals to Member States and concerned organizations to assist the people of Iraq in their efforts to reform their institutions and rebuild their country and to contribute to conditions of stability and security in Iraq in accordance with this resolution'. In the preamble, the Council welcomed 'the willingness of Member States to contribute to stability and security in Iraq by contributing personnel, equipment, and other resources under the Authority'. The report of the meeting of the Council during which Res 1483 was adopted (S/PV.4761) demonstrates the relief of the members that the Council was united again and was able to agree upon the assistance that the international community should give to Iraq. Finally, the conclusion that Res 1483 can be qualified as an authorization resolution was confirmed in practice: a number of states considered Res 1483 as a sufficient basis to send troops to Iraq (see eg the Netherlands, parliamentary doc. TK 2002–2003, 23432, nos 115, 116, 121). Overall, this resolution should be seen against the background of the preceding negotiations on the adoption of a 'second resolution' authorizing the use of force against Iraq. Such a resolution was not adopted, but the US and the UK nevertheless attacked Iraq and removed Saddam Hussein from power. Res 1483 represented the end of the impasse in the Security Council. It did not legitimize *ex post facto* the US/UK attack, but it provided the general legal basis and the legal framework for assistance to Iraq post-Saddam Hussein. For these reasons, against this exceptional background, Res 1483 is considered as an authorization resolution, even though only a few months later the 'successor' resolution, Res 1511, authorized the taking of 'all necessary measures'.

(13) Libya: Resolution 1973 (2011); authorizations given to 'Member States that have notified the Secretary-General, acting nationally or through regional organizations or arrangements, and acting in cooperation with the Secretary-General' (OP 4—protection of civilians); 'Member States that have notified the Secretary-General and the Secretary-General of the League of Arab States, acting nationally or through regional organizations or arrangements' (OP 8—enforcement of the no-fly zone); 'all Member States, in particular States of the region, acting nationally or through regional organizations or arrangements' (OP 13—enforcement of the arms embargo).

The size and nature of the operations carried out on the basis of these authorizations vary widely. Some operations, notably those in Afghanistan, Iraq, and Libya, have extensive mandates, cover most or a great part of the territory of the country concerned, and need thousands or tens of thousands of soldiers. Others are more limited and specific. But they have in common that they are all based on Security Council resolutions and may all use force to the extent authorized by the Council.

As the previous list shows, Security Council authorizations are in most cases given to states, and in a few cases to international organizations (EU, IGAD). Authorizations given to states often indicate that these states 'act through or in cooperation with', or 'participate in' an organization or ad hoc multinational force.

III. Legal Basis

Almost all 80 authorization resolutions explicitly determine that the situation concerned constitutes 'a threat to international peace and security' and refer to Chapter VII of the UN Charter. Only Resolutions 1498 (2003, Côte d'Ivoire) and 1542 (2004, Haiti) lack an explicit reference to Chapter VII and merely extend the original authorization.[20] The reference to Chapter VII is usually located at the end of the preamble to these resolutions, and reads as follows: '*Acting* under Chapter VII of the Charter of the United Nations'. In a few cases, this reference is not in the preamble, but in the operative paragraph of the resolution, in which the authorization is given.[21] This does not affect the authorization as such, but it implies that only

[20] Res 1542 only refers to Chapter VII in relation to the UN force MINUSTAH, not in relation to the authorized operation ('the Multinational Interim Force'). The original authorizations (Res 1464 (2003) in the case of Côte d'Ivoire and Res 1529 (2004) in the case of Haiti) explicitly refer to Chapter VII. Res 1542 is the only extension of the authorization in Res 1529, for a maximum period of 30 days. In the case of Côte d'Ivoire, all 20 further extensions adopted after Res 1498 explicitly refer to Chapter VII.

[21] Res 1464 (2003), 1542 (2004), and 1778 (2007).

the authorization to use force is based on Chapter VII, not the entire resolution. However, in these cases the preamble explicitly determines that the relevant situation constitutes 'a threat to international peace and security', which can only be done by the Security Council under Chapter VII.[22]

In most cases, the Security Council merely states in the preamble, without further explanation, that the situation concerned constitutes a threat to international peace and security. In a few cases the Security Council also explains why this is the case. For example, the Somalia resolutions relating to piracy (Resolution 1816, extended in five resolutions) indicate the following: '*[d]etermining* that the incidents of piracy and armed robbery against vessels in the territorial waters of Somalia and the high seas off the coast of Somalia exacerbate the situation in Somalia which continues to constitute a threat to international peace and security in the region'.

A reference to Chapter VII in Security Council resolutions *in itself* is not sufficient to authorize the use of force. The reference to Chapter VII indicates that the Security Council characterizes a particular situation as a threat to the peace, breach of the peace, or act of aggression. Under Chapter VII, the Security Council may make recommendations and take a wide variety of measures, and Chapter VII explicitly distinguishes between measures that do and do not involve the use of armed force.[23] If the Security Council decides to authorize the use of force, more specific language is required (usually the 'all necessary measures' or the 'all necessary means' phrase), as discussed in the next section. Sometimes the Security Council has explicitly excluded that 'Chapter VII resolutions' authorize the use of force, for example when imposing economic sanctions on Iran, by explicitly mentioning Article 41 as the legal basis of the resolution.[24]

Enforcement measures taken under Chapter VII of the Charter will normally lack the consent of the 'target state'. However, a few authorization resolutions explicitly indicate some degree of agreement of this state. For example, some of the resolutions adopted to authorize the use of force in Iraq explicitly state that 'the presence of the MNF [multinational force] is at the request of the Government of Iraq'.[25] Legally, this is not required. However, it is clear that this may facilitate not only the adoption of the resolution, but also its implementation: it may make it less difficult to find states able and willing to contribute to the operation, and the UN may rely on this request when the operation is later criticized by the host state.

[22] UN Charter, Art 39. [23] See Arts 41 and 42 of the Charter.

[24] Res 1737 (2006), 1747 (2007), 1803 (2008), and 1929 (2010). See also the draft resolution relating to the situation in Syria, vetoed by China and the Russian Federation on 4 Feb 2012: 'nothing in this resolution authorises measures under Article 42 of the Charter' (S/2012/77, preamble, penultimate para).

[25] Res 1637 (2005), 1723 (2006), and 1790 (2007). See also Res 1546 (2004). In the case of Iraq, the requirement of the consent of the Iraqi government should be seen against the background of the 2003 military operation by the US and the UK against Iraq, and the subsequent aim 'to restore Iraq's sovereignty'. The US stated in the Security Council that by 30 June 2004 the government of Iraq 'will have the final say on the presence of the multinational force' (S/PV.4987 (8 June 2004), 2); the UK stated that 'The sovereign Government will be able to require a review of that multinational force or its termination' (at 3).

IV. Terminology: 'Means', 'Measures', and the Need for Clarity and Certainty

The Security Council has only exceptionally *explicitly* referred to the use of armed force in authorization resolutions. An early example is Resolution 221 (1966), in which the Security Council called upon the UK 'to prevent, by the use of force if necessary' the arrival at Beira of oil vessels destined for Southern Rhodesia.[26] In 1990, during the negotiations on what was to become Resolution 678, the US proposed to refer explicitly to the authorization of the use of military force against Iraq,[27] but the Soviet Union objected, and the Security Council decided to use the words 'all necessary means'.[28] Ever since, this wording, or the phrase 'all necessary measures', is used by the Security Council to authorize the use of military force. It has never been questioned that a Security Council authorization to take 'all necessary means/ measures' includes an authorization to use armed force.[29]

In two of the 80 authorization resolutions the phrase 'all necessary means' or 'all necessary measures' is lacking: Resolutions 1483 (2003, Iraq) and 1725 (2006, Somalia). Nevertheless, on the basis of the text of these resolutions, the context, and the reports of the meetings of the Security Council during which these resolutions were adopted, it must be concluded that these are authorizations to use force.[30] It is not clear why the usual phrase was not used in these two cases. In the case of Resolution 1483, this may perhaps to some extent be explained by the fact that it was adopted after weeks

[26] A more recent example is Res 836 (1993), in which the Council authorized member states 'to take all necessary measures, through the use of air power' (to support the UN peacekeeping operation UNPROFOR in and around the safe areas in Bosnia and Herzegovina).

[27] Bob Woodward, *The Commanders* (New York: Simon & Schuster, 1991), 333: 'Bush administration lawyers had said it would be best for the resolution language to be a model of clarity, spelling out directly the authority for use of force'.

[28] Woodward, *The Commanders*, 333–4: 'The Soviet Union could not go to the United Nations and be seen voting for war. At home, war still meant Afghanistan.'

[29] See eg with regard to Res 678, the statement by Minister for Foreign Affairs Qian Qichen of China in the Security Council: 'the wording "use all necessary means", in essence, permits the use of military action' (S/PV.2963, 62; China abstained from voting). Likewise, US Secretary of State Baker stated in the same meeting: 'Today's resolution is very clear. The words authorise the use of force' (at 103). Of course, an authorization to use force does not mean that force *will* be used in practice, although this is usually the case.

[30] For the reports of these meeting see S/PV.4761 (Res 1483) and S/PV.5579 (Res 1725). For the interpretation of decisions of the Security Council factors other than in the case of interpretation of treaties may have to be taken into account. Eg statements of representatives of the members of the Security Council may play an important role in interpreting Security Council decisions. See Michael C. Wood, 'The Interpretation of Security Council Resolutions' (1998) 2 *Max Planck Yearbook of United Nations Law* 73–95; see also the International Court of Justice (ICJ), *Accordance with international law of the unilateral declaration of independence in respect of Kosovo*, Advisory Opinion of 22 July 2010, para 94.

of difficult negotiations following the 2003 US/UK military operation against Iraq, in which a renewed basis for UN presence in Iraq had to be found, without any legitimization afterwards of the US/UK operation. In the case of Resolution 1725, it is unclear why there is no reference to the phrase 'all necessary measures', while the mandate leaves little doubt that an authorization to use force is given.

Such unclear authorizations are exceptional. An earlier example, not relating to an authorized operation but to a UN operation, is Resolution 1509 (establishing the UN Mission in Liberia). The Security Council intended to give this mission permission to use force in carrying out its mandate, but did not include the 'all necessary means/measures' phrase in the resolution. The Office of Legal Affairs of the UN Secretariat advised in this case that:

> it does not follow from the fact that no such express wording appears in the resolution that the Security Council has not exercised that power and granted such authorisation. Whether it has done so depends upon the interpretation of the resolution, specifically, on the ordinary and natural meaning which is to be given to its terms when they are read in the context of the resolution as a whole and in the light of its object and purpose, and against the background of the discussions leading to, and the circumstances of, its adoption, in particular the report that the Secretary-General submitted pursuant to resolution 1497 (2003).[31]

Nevertheless, if it is the intention of the Security Council to authorize the use of force, with respect to UN operations and in the case of authorized operations, the Council should say so explicitly,[32] since the prohibition to use force is a fundamental Charter rule and since certainty is required in the volatile situations in which both UN operations and authorized operations have to perform their functions. It is true that the political dynamics of Security Council decision-making may make it difficult to adopt a resolution that is sufficiently 'black or white', providing a clear answer to the question whether or not armed force may be used, and may make it more feasible to adopt a 'grey' compromise text. However, while this may be more feasible in a particular situation in the short term, it may also lead to deep international confrontation in relation to that situation (when armed force is actually used by some, but the authorization to do so is disputed by others). Moreover, it may in the long run undermine the legitimacy and the authority of the Security Council. While the ambiguity of a resolution concealing disagreement amongst the members of the Security Council on the authorization to use force may be helpful from a short-term perspective, it is harmful from a long-term perspective. As Secretary-General Kofi Annan stated in the Security Council: 'the unity of the Council is the indispensable foundation for effective action to maintain international peace and security and international law'.[33]

[31] *United Nations Juridical Yearbook*, 2003, 538–9.

[32] See on this requirement, Jules Lobel and Michael Ratner, 'Bypassing the Security Council: Ambiguous Authorisations to Use Force, Cease-Fires and the Iraqi Inspection Regime' (1999) 93 *American Journal of International Law* 124.

[33] On the occasion of the adoption of Res 1483, the legal basis for the authorization operation in Iraq (S/PV.4761, 12).

When authorizing the use of force by authorized operations, most of the 80 resolutions adopted from 2000 to 2012 use the phrase 'all necessary measures'.[34] This was different during the 1990s, when the Security Council generally used the phrase 'all necessary means'.[35] It is not clear why 'measures' is nowadays usually preferred over 'means'. In recent years, the phrase 'all necessary means' is generally used to authorize the use of force in UN peacekeeping operations.[36]

When comparing the word 'measures' in Resolution 1529 (2004, Haiti) to 'means' in Resolution 678, Kirgis has observed that this difference in terminology 'presumably reflects a difference in purpose.... An authorisation in resolution 1529 to use "all necessary means" might be interpreted simply as an authorisation to use force.... "all necessary measures" apparently would include not only an authorisation to use force if it is necessary to achieve the Council's goals in Haiti, including restoring and maintaining public order, but also to take other measures that would be appropriate to achieve the Council's humanitarian goals'.[37] However, Security Council practice does not seem to support this explanation. As indicated previously, the Security Council has used both the phrase 'all necessary measures' (particularly since 2000) and the phrase 'all necessary means' (particularly in the 1990s) in the case of authorized operations. There is no indication in Security Council practice that the use of the words 'means' or 'measures' would have implications for the scope or the nature of the means/measures concerned and of the authorization to use force. Rather, the choice between these words seems to depend on the coincidental outcome of the negotiations preceding the adoption of the relevant resolution. The Security Council is a political body and, moreover, international law does not require the Council to choose a particular phraseology for use of force authorizations.

Another phrase to authorize the use of force can be found in so-called Article 41½ resolutions: these are resolutions authorizing the use of force to enforce compliance with economic sanctions. Often in these resolutions, the Security Council authorizes states 'to use the measures commensurate to the specific circumstances ... '[38] Only in this context, on one occasion, did a member state claim that the phrase concerned did not cover the use of armed force.[39]

[34] Exceptionally, the Security Council has used the word 'means' in authorizations for authorized operations: SC Res 1739, para 8 (2007, Côte d' Ivoire), SC Res 1846, para 10 (2008, Somalia), and the extensions of these authorizations.

[35] The most important examples are Res 678 (Iraq), 794 (Somalia), 929 (Rwanda), 940 (Haiti), and 1080 (Great Lakes region).

[36] Although, exceptionally, Security Council resolutions relating to UN peacekeeping operations use the phrase 'all necessary measures'. See eg Res 1861, para 7 (UN Mission in the Central African Republic and Chad). See for an early example Res 787 (para 9), in which the Council authorized the UN peacekeeping operation UNPROFOR 'to take the necessary measures, including the use of force'.

[37] Frederic L. Kirgis, 'Security Council Resolution on Multinational Interim Force in Haiti', 8(4) *American Society of International Law Insights*, 17 Mar 2004, para 6.

[38] eg Res 1973, para 13 (2011, Libya). For earlier examples, see Res 665, para 1 (1990, Iraq); Res 787, para 12 (1992, former Yugoslavia); Res 875, para 1 (1993, Haiti).

[39] China, in relation to Res 665 (see S/PV.2938, 54–5: 'We think that the reference in the draft resolution to using "such measures commensurate to the specific circumstances as may be necessary" does

V. Mandate

The mandate, indicated in the authorization resolution, describes the task that has to be performed by the authorized operation. If the description of the mandate is general and broad, as was the case in Resolution 678 (1990) mentioned in the previous section, there is considerable implementing freedom for the states or organizations that carry out the mandate, and there cannot be much Security Council control over the operation. As mentioned previously, during the 1990s mandates have generally become more specific. This tendency has continued since 2000, although there are a great variety of mandates in the 80 authorization resolutions adopted from 2000 until 2012. Some are still of a rather general nature, others are clearly more limited.

For the mandate of the operation, some authorization resolutions refer to a pre-existing agreement concluded between the relevant states and other parties. This is the case for the resolutions relating to Bosnia and Herzegovina, Afghanistan, and Liberia.[40] These mandates are broad. The task of the forces concerned is to assist in ensuring compliance with the pre-existing agreement (eg that obliges the parties to cease hostilities). A similarly broad task was given to the multinational force authorized to operate in Iraq since mid-2003; this force had 'to contribute to the maintenance of security and stability in Iraq.'[41] The mandate of the other authorization resolutions is more specific. Often it mentions the protection of civilians.[42] The mandate mentioned in the Somalia anti-piracy resolutions is 'to repress acts of piracy and armed robbery'.[43]

Even though most of these mandates are more or less specific, the Libya authorization has demonstrated the elasticity of the language of the mandate. In that case, the mandate was 'to protect civilians and civilian populated areas under threat of attack in the Libyan Arab Jamahiriya, including Benghazi, while excluding

not contain the concept of using force'). However, in subsequent cases where this language was used China did not repeat this interpretation (see eg S/PV.3137, 119–21 (Res 787); S/PV.3293, 17–18 (Res 875); S/PV.6498, 10 (Res 1973)).

[40] Res 1305 and subsequent resolutions relating to Bosnia and Herzegovina refer to Annex 1A of the 1995 General Framework Agreement for Peace in Bosnia and Herzegovina; Res 1386 and subsequent resolutions relating to Afghanistan refer to Annex 1 to the 2001 Bonn Agreement; Res 1497 refers to the 17 June 2003 ceasefire agreement relating to Liberia.

[41] Res 1483, operative para 1; Res 1511, operative para 13; Res 1546, operative para 10.

[42] Res 1464 (Côte d'Ivoire): 'the protection of civilians immediately threatened with physical violence within their zones of operation'. Res 1484 (DRC): 'to contribute to the safety of the civilian population'. Res 1671 (DRC): 'to contribute to the protection of civilians under imminent threat of physical violence in the areas of its deployment, and without prejudice to the responsibility of the Government of the Democratic Republic of the Congo'. Res 1778 (Chad, the Central African Republic, and the subregion): 'to contribute to protecting civilians in danger, particularly refugees and displaced persons'. Res 1973 (Libya): 'to protect civilians and civilian populated areas under threat of attack in the Libyan Arab Jamahiriya, including Benghazi'.

[43] Res 1816 and subsequent resolutions.

a foreign occupation force of any form on any part of Libyan territory'. In practice, a few months of fighting resulted in regime change. It is, of course, not certain whether this outcome would have been the same without the NATO operation, but regime change was certainly not what some members of the Security Council, in particular the Russian Federation, had in mind when the Security Council adopted Resolution 1973. At least Russia now had some ground for its criticism, even though the majority view appears to be that the way in which this authorization was carried out, with regime change as a result, still fell within the scope of protection of civilians and civilian-populated areas and could be justified on the basis of the mandate.[44] The mandate was certainly less elastic as far as it explicitly excluded a foreign occupation force. There is no doubt that a new resolution would have been required if NATO had wanted to have troops on Libyan territory, to occupy (part of) the territory.

The mandates, included in some other authorizations, also contain elements that do not offer room for extensive interpretations: these elements relate to the geographical limitation of the authorized mission. The original Afghanistan authorization was limited to 'Kabul and its surrounding areas',[45] and clearly could not be interpreted to also cover operations in other parts of Afghanistan. Therefore, when it was agreed to extend NATO operations to such other parts, the authorization had to be changed. The mandate was expanded to also cover 'areas of Afghanistan outside of Kabul and its environs'.[46] Likewise, the geographical scope of the original Somalia counter-piracy authorizations was limited to the territorial waters of Somalia.[47] Resolution 1851 extended this to 'all necessary measures that are appropriate in Somalia', thereby also authorizing the use of force on Somali territory, against those who plan, facilitate, or undertake acts of piracy from the territory of Somalia.[48] Some other authorization resolutions also have (parts of) mandates of limited geographical scope, for example Resolution 1484 (DRC, limited to Bunia) and Resolution 1671 (DRC, 'to contribute to airport protection in Kinshasa').

While the limited number of authorized operations and the wide variety of their mandates hardly justify a typology, some operations clearly perform similar functions. For example, mandates in a number of authorization resolutions include the protection of UN missions and humanitarian organizations.[49] Another function is to prepare the ground for a future UN peacekeeping operation: some authorized

[44] This view was taken by many states; in addition not only by NATO Secretary-General Rasmussen but also by UN Secretary-General Ban Ki-moon (see n 10). For discussion of the question whether Res 1973 covered the regime change, see Mehrdad Payandeh, 'The United Nations, Military Intervention, and Regime Change in Libya' (2012) 52 *Virginia Journal of International Law* 355, esp 387–91.

[45] Res 1386, operative para 1. [46] Res 1510, operative para 1. [47] Res 1816 and Res 1846.

[48] SC/9541; explanation of vote by UK Foreign Minister Miliband in the Security Council (S/PV.6046, 4).

[49] Res 1511 (Iraq); Res 1484 (DRC); Res 1671 (DRC); Res 1778 (Chad, the Central African Republic, and the sub-region).

operations were established for a brief interim period (eg a few months), before a UN force would be established to take over all or most of the mandate. This was the case when Resolution 1497 (Liberia) authorized member states to establish a multinational force in order to, inter alia, 'prepare for the introduction of a longer-term United Nations stabilization force to relieve the Multinational Force'. Similarly, when the Security Council in 2004 established the multinational force for Haiti for a period of three months, it also declared 'its readiness to establish a follow-on United Nations stabilization force';[50] this force (the UN Stabilization Mission in Haiti, MINUSTAH) was created a few months later.[51] The same idea prevailed with regard to the Somalia authorization to members of the AU (Resolution 1744 and the extensions of this authorization). However, in that case the preconditions for the creation of a UN peacekeeping force were not considered fulfilled.[52]

It can be concluded that the authorization resolutions adopted between 2000 and 2012 contain a wide variety of mandates. In some cases (eg Afghanistan, Bosnia and Herzegovina) the Security Council decided to leave considerable room for interpretation in their implementation and therefore kept only limited control over the operation on the ground. In other cases (Liberia, DRC, Somalia—piracy) the mandate was much more specific. The previous overview also demonstrates that there are hard and soft elements in the mandate. A hard element is the definition of the geographical scope of the mandate. Even the most elastic interpretation of the mandate would not allow forces on the ground to operate outside this area without a new authorization extending the geographical scope. Another example of a hard element is the explicit exclusion, in Resolution 1973 (Libya), of 'a foreign occupation force of any form on any part of Libyan territory', which prevented NATO from having 'boots on the ground' occupying (part of) Libya. However, the mandate in this authorization also contained an important soft element: 'to protect civilians and civilian populated areas'. In practice, this was also used to support the opposition in its successful fight for regime change. Soft elements such as this have the advantage of offering the flexibility that subsequent developments on the ground may require. However, they also carry the risk of broad interpretation by those who implement the authorization, as a result of which the general support for the authorization at the moment of the adoption of the resolution may dwindle or even disappear. In the long run, this may make it more difficult to muster the necessary support when future authorizations are proposed.[53]

[50] Res 1529. [51] Res 1542.

[52] The AU repeatedly urged the Security Council to establish a UN peacekeeping operation (eg S/2007/34). However, according to the UN Secretary-General, time was not yet ripe: 'A United Nations operation will only succeed if it is deployed in support of a political process, not as a substitution for one' (S/2007/381, 21, para 100). This observation was based on earlier UN peacekeeping experience. A first general lesson from the fall of Srebrenica was: 'when peacekeeping operations are used as a substitute for such political consensus [on a particular response to active military conflicts] they are likely to fail' (Report by the UN Secretary-General, A/54/549 (1999), 110, para 498).

[53] As was illustrated by the Security Council discussions on the situation in Syria in 2011–12, which took place against the background of the 2011 authorization to use force against Libya (Res 1973).

VI. Duration

The Security Council may decide to give authorizations without any time limit or for a specified period of time. If there is no time limit, the Security Council renounces considerable control over the operation, since the adoption of a new resolution is required to terminate the authorization. This will only happen if one or more permanent members that support the authorization do not block the adoption of such a new resolution.

The authorization to use force against Iraq (Resolution 678 (1990)) did not have any time limit which has been part of the criticism raised against this open-ended authorization. It is also part of the reason why this resolution could still be invoked by the US and the UK as the basis of their legal underpinning of the 2003 military operation against Iraq, even though this operation had no connection with Iraq's 1990 invasion of Kuwait (the reason for the adoption of Resolution 678). Almost all other authorizations adopted by the Security Council during the 1990s have time limits, covering periods of not more than one year. The same is true for the authorization resolutions adopted in the period from 2000 to 2012: of these 80 resolutions, only Resolution 1973 (2011) on Libya did not have a time limit for its three authorizations (protection of civilians; no-fly zone; enforcement of the arms embargo).[54] The Security Council decided to terminate both the authorizations to use force to protect civilians and civilian-populated areas and the authorization to enforce the no-fly zone seven-and-a-half months later (Resolution 2016). It terminated the authorization to use force to enforce the arms embargo almost one year later (Resolution 2040). All other 79 authorization resolutions adopted in this 12-year period have time limits, varying from a few days to one year.

See in this context the report of Security Council meeting of 4 Oct 2011 (S/PV.6627), in which a draft resolution on the situation in Syria (referring to 'the Syrian Government's primary responsibility to protect its population') was vetoed by China and Russia (Brazil, India, Lebanon, and South Africa abstaining). Russia stated that 'The situation in Syria cannot be considered in the Council separately from the Libyan experience. The international community is alarmed by statements that compliance with Security Council resolutions on Libya in the NATO interpretation is a model for the future actions of NATO in implementing the responsibility to protect' (at 4). South Africa stated: 'We are concerned that this draft resolution not be part of a hidden agenda aimed at once again instituting regime change, which has been an objective clearly stated by some' (at 11). See also the report of the Security Council meeting of 4 Feb 2012, in which China and Russia again used their vetoes to prevent the adoption of a resolution on the situation in Syria.

[54] It is not known whether Security Council members that abstained from voting on Res 1973 (Brazil, China, Germany, India, and Russia) proposed to include a time limit for the Libya authorization during the negotiations on the resolution. Their statements in the Security Council meeting during which the resolution was adopted do not mention such a proposal (see S/PV.6498).

VII. Reporting

The third and final aspect of authorization resolutions that is important for the Security Council to exercise control over the authorized operation is the reporting by those who carry out the operation. Strictly speaking, this reporting requirement is not as such an instrument for control, but rather a precondition for effective supervision. As mentioned earlier, there was hardly any reporting when in 1991 Operation Desert Storm carried out the authorization to use force against Iraq. This situation improved considerably during the 1990s, when the Security Council requested regular reporting and in some cases also required that reports fulfilled certain conditions.[55]

The 80 authorization resolutions adopted in the period from 2000 to 2012 contain divergent reporting arrangements. First of all there are resolutions that require reporting at specified intervals. This is the case for the Bosnia and Herzegovina authorizations (reporting originally 'at least at monthly intervals', as of Resolution 1575 (2004) 'at least at three-monthly intervals'), for almost all Afghanistan authorizations,[56] for the last few Iraq authorizations,[57] and for Resolution 1778 (Chad, the Central African Republic, and the sub-region—six months). Secondly, a number of other authorization resolutions require those who are authorized to report 'periodically' or 'regularly' (without specifying how often reports must be submitted).[58] Thirdly, the Libya authorization (Resolution 1973) requires member states to report 'immediately' the measures they take,[59] without specifying whether this should be done through periodic reporting.[60] Fourthly, in the case of Liberia there was no reporting obligation for the member states participating in the multinational

[55] Blokker, 'Is the Authorisation Authorised?', 564.

[56] Only the first Afghanistan authorization (Res 1386) requires 'periodic reports'. The second resolution (Res 1413) requests monthly reports. The third (Res 1444) and subsequent authorizations request quarterly reports.

[57] The reporting requirements in the Iraq authorizations have become stricter over time. While Res 1483 only '*encourages* the United Kingdom of Great Britain and Northern Ireland and the United States of America to inform the Council at regular intervals of their efforts under this resolution', Res 1511 '*[r]equests* that the United States, on behalf of the multinational force..., report to the Security Council on the efforts and progress of this force as appropriate and not less than every six months'. The subsequent Iraq authorizations (Res 1546, 1637, 1723, and 1790) request reports every three months ('on a quarterly basis').

[58] eg Res 1386 ('periodic reports'), 1464, 1484, 1497, 1529, and 1671.

[59] Both with respect to the authorization to use force to protect civilians (Res 1973, para 4) and with respect to the enforcement of the no-fly zone (Res 1973, para 11). The latter reporting arrangement is exceptional, since reports had to be sent not only to the UN Secretary-General, but also to the Secretary-General of the League of Arab States.

[60] In practice, the NATO Secretary-General sent four monthly reports to the UN Secretary-General, as well as some weekly reports and four 'technical update reports'. These reports have not been published. They were circulated to the members of the Security Council and mentioned in briefings by the UN Secretariat (Under-Secretary-General for Political Affairs Lynn Pascoe), see S/PV.6541, S/PV.6566, and S/PV.6595.

force, only for the UN Secretary-General;[61] the same is true for some of the Somalia authorizations (the AU Mission in Somalia, AMISOM), which only contains a reporting obligation for the UN Secretary-General, in the more recent authorizations.[62]

It may be concluded that, overall, although reporting is a standard element of Security Council authorizations, the requirements for reporting as laid down in these resolutions could have been more rigorous, for example by using as standard practice the requirement that reporting would be at least at monthly or three-monthly intervals. In the period from 2000 to 2012 reporting at such intervals was far from standard.

Reporting in this context is much more than a mere procedural requirement. It should provide the Security Council with information on how its authorization is put into practice. Those who carry out the authorized operation must be accountable to the Security Council. An analogy may be drawn with the reporting requirements for self-defence. According to Article 51 of the UN Charter, 'Measures taken by Members in the exercise of this right of self-defence shall be immediately reported to the Security Council and shall not in any way affect the authority and responsibility of the Security Council under the present Charter to take at any time such action as it seems necessary in order to maintain or restore international peace and security'.[63] Likewise, in authorized operations there is a delicate balance between the role and powers of the Security Council and UN members (or international organizations) that act on the basis of the Security Council authorization. Reporting by these UN members (or by international organizations) should take place at specified, brief intervals to enable the Security Council to perform its functions and, more specifically, to supervise the implementation of the authorization.

VIII. Responsibility Implications

The previous analysis demonstrates that the tendency towards more Security Council control of authorized operations has continued during the years from 2000 to 2012. This raises the question whether the Security Council should also

[61] Res 1497, operative para 15 (requesting the Secretary-General 'through his Special Representative to report to the Council periodically on the situation in Liberia in relation to the implementation of this resolution, including information on implementation by the Multinational Force of its mandate').

[62] Res 1744, 1772, 1863, 1872, 1910, 1964, and 2010. The UN Secretary-General is requested to report 'every four months, on all aspects of this resolution'.

[63] In its case law, the ICJ has taken into account the absence of reporting under Art 51 when coming to the conclusion that there had not been an armed attack (*Military and Paramilitary Activities in and against Nicaragua (Nicaragua v. US)*, Merits, ICJ Rep 1986, 121–2, para 235; *Case concerning armed activities on the territory of the Congo (DRC v. Uganda)*, ICJ Rep 2005, 222–3, paras 145–7). See in general on the reporting requirement of Art 51: Tom Ruys, *'Armed Attack' and Article 51 of the UN Charter* (Cambridge: Cambridge University Press, 2010), 68.

be responsible if an internationally wrongful act is committed by an authorized operation. This question has been the subject of considerable debate, in particular in relation to the work of the International Law Commission (ILC) on the topic of responsibility of international organizations and in relation to decisions of the European Court of Human Rights (ECtHR).

In 2011, the ILC adopted the Articles on Responsibility of International Organizations (ARIO).[64] According to Article 3 of the ARIO, 'Every internationally wrongful act of an international organization entails the international responsibility of that organization'. According to Article 4, there is an internationally wrongful act of an international organization 'when conduct consisting of an action or omission: (a) is attributable to that organization under international law; and (b) constitutes a breach of an international obligation of that organization'. With regard to the issues discussed in the present chapter, a key question is whether the UN is responsible for wrongful acts by states or international organizations implementing Security Council authorizations. For example, if NATO had committed wrongful acts in Libya in 2011, would the UN be responsible (or co-responsible with NATO or its participating member states), since the Security Council adopted Resolution 1973 and thereby authorized the military operation in the context of which wrongful acts were committed? The key ingredient for the answer to this question is laid down in Article 7 of the ARIO: 'The conduct of an organ of a State or an organ or agent of an international organization that is placed at the disposal of another international organization shall be considered under international law an act of the latter organization if the organization exercises effective control over that conduct'. Therefore, using the example of NATO in Libya, the question must be whether the UN exercised effective control over the relevant conduct of NATO in Libya. More generally, the question is if the UN, through the Security Council use of force authorizations for authorized operations, has effective control over the conduct of states and/or international organizations that implement those authorizations.

The UN Secretariat has denied this. It has always taken the view that a distinction must be made between UN peacekeeping forces, on the one hand, and authorized operations, on the other. The former are UN organs for whose acts the UN is responsible, the latter are outsourced operations over which the Security Council exercises only limited control and for whose acts the UN is not responsible. As stated in a 1996 report by the UN Secretariat:[65]

> The international responsibility of the United Nations for combat-related activities of United Nations forces is premised on the assumption that the operation in question is under the exclusive command and control of the United Nations. Where a Chapter VII-authorised operation is conducted under national command and control, international responsibility

[64] For the text of these articles and the commentary by the ILC, see Report of the International Law Commission, 63rd Sess, A/66/10, 52 ff.

[65] A/51/389, paras 17–18. See also A/CN.4/545, II.G, and *Yearbook of the International Law Commission*, 2011, vol II (2), Commentary to Art 7.

for the activities of the force is vested in the State or States conducting the operation.... In joint operations, international responsibility for the conduct of the troops lies where operational command and control is vested according to the arrangements establishing the modalities of cooperation between the State or States providing the troops and the United Nations. In the absence of formal arrangements between the United Nations and the State or States providing troops, responsibility would be determined in each and every case according to the degree of effective control exercised by either party in the conduct of the operation.

The ILC has followed this approach in the ARIO. Since effective control is usually with the states and/or international organizations that implement a Security Council authorization, it is those states and/or international organizations that are, as a rule, responsible for wrongful acts committed within the context of the authorized operation. In principle, there is no responsibility for the UN, as the Security Council authorization does not prescribe effective control by the UN over the operation.

However, while the distinction between UN peacekeeping forces and authorized operations is essential for answering responsibility questions and while, as a rule, the UN could be held responsible for acts of the former, not of the latter, in concrete cases the facts of each specific situation are decisive for the answer to where the responsibility lies. The practice of both UN peacekeeping operations and of authorized operations is full of nuances. It cannot be excluded that, under certain specific circumstances, member states, not the UN, may be held responsible for acts of UN peacekeeping operations.[66] Also, with respect to authorized operations, it cannot be excluded that, under certain specific circumstances, the UN, not the member states, is held responsible for certain wrongful acts committed within the context of the authorized operation.[67]

There is another ARIO provision that is of particular relevance for possible UN responsibility for its authorizations for authorized operations. According to Article 17, paragraph 2, 'An international organization incurs international responsibility if it circumvents one of its international obligations by authorising member States or international organizations to commit an act that would be internationally wrongful if committed by the former organization and the act in question is committed because of that authorisation'. This provision was adopted to prevent an international organization from 'delegating away' its responsibility for breaches of one of its own obligations.[68] In its Commentary to Article 17, the ILC explained:[69]

When a member State or organization is authorised to commit an act, it is apparently free not to avail itself of the authorisation received. However, this may be only in theory, because

[66] eg see the 5 July 2011 judgments by the Court of Appeal of The Hague in two of the Srebrenica cases (LJN: BR0132 and BR0133), available at <http://www.rechtspraak.nl/ljn.asp?ljn=BR0132> and <http://www.rechtspraak.nl/ljn.asp?ljn=BR0133>. For more examples, see the ILC Commentary to Art 7 of the ARIO (A/66/10, 89–90 (No 8)).

[67] eg see the *Behrami* and *Saramati* cases decided by the ECtHR, discussed later in this section.

[68] The authorizing organizations 'would clearly not be responsible for any other breach that the member state or international organization to which the authorisation is addressed might commit' (Commentary No 13 to Art 17, Report of the International Law Commission, 63rd Sess, at 110).

[69] Report of the International Law Commission, 63rd Sess, at 109 (No 8).

an authorisation often implies the conferral by an organization of certain functions to the member or members concerned so that they would exercise these functions instead of the organization. Moreover, by authorising an act, the organization generally expects the authorisation to be acted upon.

Therefore, this provision would prevent the UN from escaping its responsibility by authorizing action by authorized operations, if it would be responsible were such action carried out by the UN itself.

The ECtHR has in several cases been confronted with questions relating to responsibility for unlawful acts committed in the context of both UN peacekeeping operations and authorized operations. The *Behrami* and *Saramati* cases concerned the operation of the UN and NATO in Kosovo following the 1999 NATO military action against Serbia and the adoption of Security Council Resolution 1244.[70] The key question was whether states—France and Norway in these cases—could be held responsible for their conduct within the framework of KFOR (Kosovo Force, the NATO security presence in Kosovo) and UNMIK (the UN Mission in Kosovo). France and Norway argued that the acts concerned (supervision of demining; detention) could not be attributed to them, as the UN exercised overall effective control of the territory. However, the UN claimed before the ECtHR that these acts could not be attributed to the UN.

The Court found that 'issuing detention orders fell within the security mandate of KFOR and that the supervision of demining fell within UNMIK's mandate'. What KFOR and UNMIK had done or had failed to do 'was, in principle, "attributable" to the UN', because the UN Security Council retained 'ultimate authority and control'. Since the UN is not a party to the European Convention on Human Rights and is not subject to the Court's jurisdiction, the Court concluded that the complaints by Behrami and Saramati were incompatible *ratione personae* with the provisions of the Convention. Therefore it declared the complaints inadmissible.[71]

This decision was strongly criticized by commentators, both from a human rights perspective and in view of the 'ultimate authority and control' test that departs from

[70] *Behrami v. France* (App no 71412/01) and *Saramati v. France, Germany and Norway* (App no 78166/01), Decision of 2 May 2007 (Grand Chamber). This summary of *Behrami* and *Saramati*, as well as the comments later, are taken from Henry G. Schermers and Niels Blokker, *International Institutional Law* (5th edn, Leiden: Martinus Nijhoff, 2011), 1014–16. The ECtHR has used the same approach in subsequent decisions: see Decision of 5 July 2007 on the admissibility of App no 6974/05, Decision of 28 Aug 2007 on the admissibility of App no 31446/02, Decision of 16 Oct 2007 on the admissibility of App nos 36357/04, 36360/04, 38346/04, 41705/04, 45190/04, 45578/04, 45579/04, 45580/04, 91/05, 97/05, 100/05, 1121/05, 1123/05, 1125/05, 1129/05, 1132/05, 1133/05, 1169/05, 1172/05, 1175/05, 1177/05, 1180/05, 1185/05, 20793/05, and 25496/05. See also the *Al-Jedda* case (related to the authorization laid down in Security Council Res 1546 (2004)), in which the ECtHR considered that 'the United Nations Security Council had neither effective control nor ultimate authority and control over the acts and omissions of foreign troops within the Multi-National Force and that the applicant's detention was not, therefore, attributable to the United Nations' (Judgment of 7 July 2011 (Grand Chamber), para 84).

[71] *Behrami v. France* (App no 71412/01) and *Saramati v. France, Germany and Norway* (App no 78166/01).

the effective control test suggested by the ILC in the (then) draft ARIO.[72] The UN Secretary-General did not accept the Court's conclusion, when he stated that it is 'understood that the international responsibility of the United Nations will be limited to the extent of its effective operational control'.[73] More generally, the Court's decision demonstrated how much disagreement there may be over the answer to the question who is responsible in scenarios such as this: the organization or its members. The judicial review implications of this answer are far-reaching, as the ECtHR has jurisdiction over states, not over international organizations.[74] While individual states are within the jurisdictional reach of the Court, their conduct within the framework of international organizations is not, unless—in the opinion of the Court—the latter lack 'ultimate authority and control'. This controversial 'ultimate authority and control' test will not easily result in piercing the organizational veil and holding its members responsible. This may have been the precise reason that this test was used by the Court. Towards the end of its decision, it considers the following:[75]

> Since operations established by UNSC resolutions under Chapter VII of the UN Charter are fundamental to the mission of the UN to secure international peace and security and since they rely for their effectiveness on support from member states, the Convention cannot be interpreted in a manner which would subject the acts and omissions of Contracting Parties which are covered by UNSC resolutions and occur prior to or in the course of such missions, to the scrutiny of the Court. To do so would be to interfere with the fulfillment of the UN's key mission in this field including, as argued by certain parties, with the effective conduct of its operations. It would also be tantamount to imposing conditions on the implementation of a UNSC resolution which were not provided for in the text of the resolution itself.

The question remains, however, whether it was necessary for the Court to have recourse to the 'ultimate authority and control' test in order to achieve the result it had in mind. It does not seem impossible that the effective control test could have yielded the same result. The UN was clearly responsible for UNMIK. KFOR

[72] See eg Pierre Klein, 'Responsabilité pour les faits commis dans le cadre d'opérations de paix et étendue du pouvoir de contrôle de la Cour européenne des droits de l'homme: quelques considérations critiques sur l'arrêt *Behrami et Saramati*' (2007) 53 *Annuaire français de droit international* 43; Rick Lawson, 'Mission Impossible—Het EVRM is niet van toepassing op VN-vredesmissies' (2008) 33 *Nederlands juristen Comité voor de Mensenrechten Bull* 39; P. Bodeau-Livinec, G. P. Buzzini, and S. Villalpando, 'Note' (2008) 102 *American Journal of International Law* 323; Kjetil M. Larsen, 'Attribution of Conduct in Peace Operations: The "Ultimate Authority and Control" Test' (2008) 19 *European Journal of International Law* 509; Marco Milanovic and Tatjana Papic, 'As Bad As It Gets: The European Court of Human Rights' *"Behrami and Saramati"* Decision and General International Law' (2009) 58 *International and Comparative Law Quarterly* 267. See also the implied criticism expressed *sotto voce* by ILC Special Rapporteur Gaja in his Seventh Report, A/CN.4/610, 9–10, para 26. In its decision the Court extensively refers to the work of the ILC and to the effective control test (paras 28–34), but it does not explicitly indicate why it uses a different test.

[73] S/2008/354, 4, para 16 (12 June 2008, report on UNMIK).

[74] This will change with respect to the EU when it accedes to the European Convention on Human Rights (see Art 6(2) of the Treaty on European Union).

[75] *Behrami v. France* (App no 71412/01) and *Saramati v. France, Germany and Norway* (App no 78166/01), Decision of 2 May 2007 (Grand Chamber), para 149 of the decision of the Court.

or NATO could have been held responsible for KFOR's conduct (not the UN, even though the role of the UN was certainly not limited to authorizing KFOR operations in a carte blanche way,[76] without exercising any further control over their implementation).

It may be concluded that the tendency towards more Security Council control of authorized operations, as analysed in Sections II to VII, may have responsibility implications. Normally there will not be effective control by the Security Council of authorized operations. It is an inherent characteristic of the technique of authorizations for such operations that operational decision-making is not carried out by the UN, but is outsourced to implementing states or international organizations. However, it cannot be excluded that in specific cases, depending on the facts of those cases, Security Council control may reach the level of effective control, so that the UN may be held responsible for wrongful acts committed by the authorized operation.

IX. Conclusions and Recommendations

A first conclusion is that the technique of authorized operations is generally accepted. During the period from 2000 to 2012 fundamental objections against this technique were never expressed during the Security Council meetings in which the 80 authorization resolutions were adopted. This technique has been regularly used, particularly in cases in which the establishment of a UN peacekeeping mission was not, or not yet, considered feasible, and in which it was considered necessary to have the possibility of using force more intensively than is common in UN peacekeeping operations.

Secondly, it can be concluded that the need for Security Council control of authorized operations, prescribed by the Charter, is well reflected in the tendency of the move away from blank cheque authorizations such as Resolution 678. This tendency—already prevalent in the authorization resolutions adopted during the 1990s—has continued in the period from 2000 to 2012. Most of the mandates have become more specific, almost all authorizations have time limits (Resolution 1973 (Libya) being the only exception), and reporting requirements enable the Security Council to perform its supervisory functions.

At the same time, the earlier analysis of the 80 authorization resolutions adopted in the period from 2000 to 2012 also leads to three recommendations. First, as indicated in Section IV, two of the 80 authorization resolutions do not explicitly use

[76] eg there was monthly reporting to the UN on the operations of KFOR (eg S/2001/333). The arrest of Saramati was even mentioned in a meeting of the Security Council (see S/PV.4350, 6).

the terms 'all necessary measures' or 'all necessary means'. While there is no legal preference for use of either of these phrases, at least one of them should be used, or other explicit language that leaves no doubt that the Security Council authorizes the use of force. If it is the intention of the Security Council to authorize the use of force, the Council should say so explicitly, since the prohibition to use force is a fundamental rule in the Charter and since certainty is required in the volatile situations in which both UN operations and authorized operations have to perform their functions.

Secondly, against the background of the Charter and given the need for Security Council control of authorized operations, there is a strong preference for having a time limit in all authorization resolutions. While it is true that a precise description of the mandate also responds to the need for Security Council control, the Libya example has demonstrated that even a precise description may be given a broad interpretation by those who implement the authorization, that is not shared by all or most members of the Security Council. This is inherent in the concept of authorized operations, which are carried out not by the UN itself but by 'coalitions of the able and willing', or by an individual UN member state (eg France in the case of the Côte d'Ivoire authorizations). For this reason, it is necessary that there is another way for the Council to keep control of authorized operations, and this is by limiting the time period of the authorization, to ensure that operations for which support within the Security Council is diminishing or has even disappeared, will not automatically continue *sine die*.

This strong preference for time limits is, strictly speaking, not a *conditio sine qua non* for the lawfulness of authorization resolutions. It remains for the Security Council to decide on such limits. It cannot be excluded that in a specific future case there may be particular policy reasons not to include time limits and to leave more flexibility to the parties carrying out the operation. However, at the same time, there may also be long-term policy reasons for including time limits: it may be seen as a guarantee that a possible disagreement within the Security Council about the way in which the authorization is implemented cannot last indefinitely. Time limits serve as a check on the true or perceived abuse of authorizations. This strong preference for time limits is, as analysed previously, fully supported by practice: all but one of the 80 authorization resolutions adopted from 2000 to 2012 have time limits.

The third recommendation following from the analysis is that the reporting requirements included in authorization resolutions should be improved, for example by specifying that those who implement the authorization must at least every month or every two or three months report on how the operation is proceeding. At present, a wide variety of reporting provisions is used in authorization resolutions, and some of these provisions do not specify how often reports must be sent, merely requiring that reporting must be done periodically or regularly. As a result of the tendency towards more Security Council control of authorized operations, these operations now more closely resemble UN peacekeeping operations.[77] This is also because UN peacekeeping operations have developed from operations of more limited scope during the Cold War era to much more complex operations since 1990, often Chapter VII operations with substantive use of force mandates.[78] Nevertheless, there will remain a fundamental difference between authorized operations and UN peacekeeping operations. Only the latter are UN organs; command and control is exercised by the UN and these operations are financed by the UN. Of course, authorized operations are linked to the UN as well, but this link is much weaker. The Security Council authorization is essential, but only defines the broad contours of the operation, leaving the implementation, the command and control, and the financing of the operation to states or international organizations, without micromanagement by the UN. It seems realistic to assume that in the foreseeable future—in the continued absence of Article 43 agreements—practice will require both UN peacekeeping operations and authorized operations.

A final conclusion is that, in principle, the 'responsibility implications' of more Security Council control of authorized operations are limited. As indicated in Section VIII, it is an inherent characteristic of the technique of authorizations that operational decision-making is not carried out by the UN, but is outsourced to implementing states or international organizations. However, it cannot be excluded that in specific cases, depending on the facts of the cases, Security Council control may reach the level of effective control, so that the UN may be held responsible for wrongful acts committed by an authorized operation.

[77] As is also demonstrated in the *Behrami* and *Saramati* cases, discussed in Section VIII. The ECtHR concluded that the UN had 'ultimate control' over the relevant acts of both UNMIK (a UN mission) and KFOR (an authorized operation).

[78] See in more detail, Niels Blokker, 'The Security Council and the Use of Force: On Recent Practice' in Niels Blokker and Nico Schrijver (eds), *The Security Council and the Use of Force—Theory and Reality, A Need for Change?* (Leiden: Martinus Nijhoff, 2005), 1, esp 15–21, 28.

CHAPTER 10

WHEN THE SECURITY COUNCIL IS DIVIDED: IMPRECISE AUTHORIZATIONS, IMPLIED MANDATES, AND THE 'UNREASONABLE VETO'

IAN JOHNSTONE*

I. Introduction

MANY of the issues covered in this chapter are rooted in the failure of the collective security scheme embodied in the United Nations Charter to function as intended. Article 43 'special agreements' were never reached, Articles 44 and 45 became moot,

* I would like to thank Jessica Dedic and Mumtaz Baloch for their research assistance. I would also like to thank Tom Weiss for his comments on this draft, and Marc Weller and Alexia Solomou for their perceptive edits.

and the Military Staff Committee has played a minor role. As a result, the Security Council has either been paralysed when it came to situations requiring the use of force, as it was during much of the Cold War and at critical post-Cold War moments, or it has innovated. The principal innovation during the Cold War was peacekeeping, but those missions rarely had occasion to use force. It was not until the post-Cold War era that the Security Council became active in authorizing forcible action. Two developments in particular have given rise to interesting questions about the scope and limits of the Security Council's competence: the delegation of enforcement action to regional organizations or coalitions of the willing; and the establishment or authorization of robust peacekeeping missions with some enforcement powers.

The UN Charter explicitly empowers the Security Council to delegate enforcement action to regional organizations, but the Council is often imprecise about the scope of powers it has delegated in particular cases. The Charter does not provide for delegation of enforcement to individual states or coalitions, but this has become common practice and is generally regarded as falling within the Council's competence. Both regional organizations and coalitions have sometimes acted on the basis of implicit authorizations to use force, or have claimed retroactive approval for their actions. Adding a layer of complexity, ambiguity in how the Council acts (or does not act) is often intentional, as a way of papering over or managing political differences. Most controversially, states have on occasion claimed a unilateral right to use force when—in the view of those states—the Council should have acted, but did not due to the veto.

This chapter proceeds as follows. Section II provides an overview of the Charter provisions on delegated enforcement action and the legal issues that have arisen in practice. The remaining three sections address three types of cases that tend to arise when the Security Council is divided: imprecise authorization; implied mandates; and the failure to act. The first covers cases when the Security Council expressly authorizes the use of force, but the objectives and scope of the authorization are unclear. Recent examples are the authorization in Resolution 1973 (2011) for the North Atlantic Treaty Organization (NATO)-led coalition to use force to protect Libyan civilians, and the reaffirmation in Resolution 1975 (2011) for the United Nations Operation in Côte d'Ivoire (UNOCI) and Operation Licorne to protect civilians there. The second set of cases, implied authorizations, are when the Security Council adopts a resolution that may or may not authorize the use of force at all, like Resolution 688 (1991) on a safe haven and no-fly zones in Iraq, Resolution 1441 (2002) on Iraq's weapons of mass destruction, and Resolution 2085 (2012) on Mali. The final section covers cases when, in not acting, the Security Council is accused of failing to discharge its responsibilities for the maintenance of international peace and security. Two theories have been invoked in these cases: unilateral enforcement of the collective will; and 'unreasonable' exercise of the veto. Both came up in Kosovo in 1999 and echoes were heard in Iraq 2003 and Syria 2011–12.

A thread that runs through these cases is the need to avoid Security Council paralysis while preserving its status as the principal international body responsible for international peace and security. On the one hand, there are good reasons for looking at ways to finesse the political divisions that often plague the Council, which after all is dominated by five countries that do not have a monopoly on wisdom or legitimacy when it comes to the use of force in international affairs. On the other hand, playing fast and loose with the Council's authority could lead to complete breakdown of the fragile system we have for regulating the use of force. While cases of uncertain authority are troubling, in the rough and tumble of Council politics, it is too much to expect perfect consistency. Indeed, what the cases considered in this chapter highlight is the discursive function of the Council, a place for contestation and deliberation when the international community is divided on how to address threats to the peace. This contestation has not led to a complete collapse of Charter-based law and institutions. If anything, it has reinforced the function of the Council as the centre of a discursive process that helps to manage tensions about the use of force that inevitably arise in a pluralistic world.

II. The UN Charter on Delegation of Enforcement Powers

A. Delegation to Regional Organizations

Chapter VIII, Article 53 of the UN Charter provides for the delegation of enforcement action to regional organizations as follows:

> The Security Council shall, where appropriate, utilize such regional arrangements or agencies for enforcement action under its authority. But no enforcement action shall be taken under regional arrangements or by regional agencies without the authorization of the Security Council …

Much ink has been spilled over what constitutes a 'regional arrangement or agency' within the meaning of Chapter VIII, whether 'enforcement action' includes economic sanctions, the relative primacy of regional organizations versus the UN in peace operations, and the degree of control the Security Council must maintain over military action by regional organizations.[1] These issues are addressed elsewhere

[1] Dan Sarooshi, *The United Nations and the Development of Collective Security: The Delegation by the UN Security Council of its Chapter VII Powers* (Oxford: Oxford University Press, 1999); Ademola Abass, *Regional Organisations and the Development of Collective Security: Beyond Chapter VIII of the*

in this volume. For the purposes of this chapter, it is enough for me to join with scholars who assert that what matters is not the nature of the organization that is taking the action, but the nature of the action itself.[2] When NATO uses force, the important question is not whether NATO is a Chapter VIII regional organization (it insists it is not), but whether it is acting in collective self-defence in response to an armed attack. If so, then according to Article 51, it does not require Security Council authorization; if not, it does. Declaring that NATO was established on the basis of Article 51 rather than Chapter VIII does not exempt it from the rest of the Charter rules on the use of force.[3]

The most difficult legal questions arise not when a regional organization engages in a warlike military intervention, but rather in the context of robust peace operations. As originally conceived, peacekeeping was a consent-based, Chapter VI enterprise, in which force was used only in self-defence. The early missions were typically managed by the UN and had Security Council authorization, although strictly speaking that was not necessary as long as they had the reliable consent and cooperation of the main parties to the conflict.[4] However, in the post-Cold War era especially, peacekeeping missions became more robust: consent of the parties was not reliable, strict impartiality (defined as neutrality) was hard to maintain, and the use of force beyond self-defence was required. Many of the UN missions were deployed either wholly or partially under Chapter VII.

UN Charter (Portland, OR: Hart, 2004); Suyash Paliwal, 'The Primacy of Regional Organizations in International Peacekeeping: The African Example' (2010) 51 *Virginia Journal of International Law* 185; Monica Hakimi, 'To Condone or Condemn? Regional Enforcement Actions in the Absence of Security Council Authorization' (2007) 40 *Vanderbilt Journal of Transnational Law* 643; Niels Blokker, 'Is the Authorization Authorized? Powers and Practice of the UN Security Council to Authorize the Use of Force by "Coalitions of the Able and Willing"' (2000) 11 *European Journal of International Law* 541; Marten Zwanenburg, 'Regional Organizations and the Maintenance of International Peace and Security: Three Recent Regional African Peace Operations' (2006) 11 *Journal of Conflict and Security Law* 490; Bryan D. Kreykes, 'A Case for Delegation: The UN Security Council. Regional Conflicts, and Regional Organizations' (2008) 11 *Touro International Law Review* 1; Ugo Villani, 'The Security Council's Authorization of Enforcement Action by Regional Organizations' (2002) *Max Planck Yearbook of United Nations Law* 535; Zsuzsanna Deen-Racsmany, 'A Redistribution of Authority between the UN and Regional Organizations in the Field of the Maintenance of Peace and Security' (2000) 13 *Leiden Journal of International Law* 297.

[2] Christine Gray, *International Law and the Use of Force* (Oxford: Oxford University Press, 2008); Hakimi, 'To Condone or Condemn?', 9–10; Michael Akehurst, 'Enforcement Action by Regional Agencies, with Special Reference to the Organization of American States' (1967) 42 *British Yearbook of International Law* 175, 184.

[3] As Bruno Simma asserts: 'Article 53 is not formally applicable to NATO but Chapter VII is'. Bruno Simma, 'NATO, the UN and the Use of Force: Legal Aspects' (1999) 10 *European Journal of International Law* 1, 10.

[4] This logic led the International Court of Justice (ICJ) to conclude in the *Certain Expenses* case that the UN General Assembly had the competence to establish peacekeeping missions, despite Art 11(2) of the Charter, since it was tantamount to a recommendation to all concerned to deploy and accept the deployment of troops for that purpose. *Certain Expenses of the United Nations*, Advisory Opinion, ICJ Rep 1962, 151.

For regional organizations, a question that has arisen is whether peacekeeping constitutes 'enforcement action' within the meaning of Article 53. Some scholars argue that peace operations *within the organization's membership* never require Council authorization, while so-called out-of-area operations always do.[5] An alternative perspective is that the circumstances and purpose for which the peacekeepers use force is more important than where it is used. If it is to deliver humanitarian relief and the major parties have not consented to it, for example, then Security Council authorization is required.[6] This standard can be difficult to apply—for example, when the host government consents to the presence of the peacekeepers but not to each forcible act[7]—but a blanket rule one way or the other is not required by the UN Charter nor does it accord with practice. There are many examples of peacekeeping missions being deployed by regional organizations without Security Council authorization, to which no legal objection was raised.[8] Conversely, there are many cases of regional organizations seeking authorization for robust peace operations even when deployed in a member state of the organization.[9]

A final question about Article 53 is whether after-the-fact Security Council approval meets the requirement. The cases cited most often for this proposition are Liberia and Sierra Leone, where ECOWAS used force without Security Council authorization but the Council later welcomed both interventions.[10] Other cases some scholars point to are Kosovo (1999), the Central African Republic (2002), Côte d'Ivoire (2002), and Darfur (2004).[11] Thomas Franck argues that this cumulated

[5] Abass, *Regional Organisations and the Development of Collective Security*, 45, 157; Sean D. Murphy, *Humanitarian Intervention: The United Nations in an Evolving World Order* (Philadelphia, PA: University of Pennsylvania Press, 1996), 342–43; Alexander Orakhelashvili, 'The Legal Basis of the United Nations Peace-Keeping Operations' (2002–3) 43 *Virginia Journal of International Law* 514; Alexander Orakhelashvili, *The Interpretation of Act and Rules in Public International Law* (Oxford: Oxford University Press, 2008).

[6] Paliwal, 'The Primacy of Regional Organizations in International Peacekeeping', 219; Zwanenburg, 'Regional Organizations and the Maintenance of International Peace and Security', 490; Gray, *International Law and the Use of Force*.

[7] The UN's Capstone Doctrine seeks to address this issue by distinguishing strategic from tactical consent: 'UN Peacekeeping Operations: "Principles and Guidelines"' (2008).

[8] eg the Multinational Force in the Central African Republic (Force Multinationale en Centrafrique, FOMUC); the Organization for Security and Co-operation in Europe (OSCE) and now the EU in Georgia; the Organization of American States (OAS) in Colombia; and the Regional Assistance Mission to Solomon Islands (RAMSI). For a survey of current missions, see *Annual Review of Global Peace Operations 2013* (New York: Center on International Cooperation, New York University, 2013).

[9] The AU in Burundi, Darfur, and Somalia; the OSCE in the Balkans; and the Economic Community of West African States (ECOWAS) in Côte d'Ivoire and Sierra Leone. See id and earlier *Annual Reviews of Global Peace Operations*.

[10] SC Res 788 (19 Nov 1992) on Liberia; SC Res 1162 (17 Apr 1998) on Sierra Leone.

[11] Thomas M. Franck, *Recourse to Force: State Action Against Threats and Armed Attacks* (Cambridge: Cambridge University Press, 2002); Paliwal, 'The Primacy of Regional Organizations in International Peacekeeping'; Zwanenburg, 'Regional Organizations and the Maintenance of International Peace and Security'.

practice amounts to a reinterpretation of Article 53.[12] Others claim that the relevant practice is too slim: even in Liberia and Sierra Leone the language used by the Security Council was equivocal; the main parties in Darfur, the Central African Republic and Côte d'Ivoire all consented to the initial deployment of the missions and, by the time they took robust action, the Security Council had granted Chapter VII authority.[13] There is nothing in the resolution that established the United Nations Mission in Kosovo (UNMIK) and the Kosovo Force (KFOR) in July 1999 to suggest *ex post* authorization of NATO's intervention in March.[14] Similarly, the first resolution adopted after the military action in Iraq in 2003 was carefully drafted to preclude any claim that it provided *ex post* authorization for the war.[15]

Either way, debate over when regional organizations require Security Council authorization for peace operations is likely to continue. At what point is a consent-based peacekeeping operation 'robust' enough that it requires Security Council authorization under Article 53? Whose consent matters? Consider Mali in June 2012, where ECOWAS was prepared to send an intervention force of some 4,000 troops provided by Nigeria, Niger, and Senegal, yet the Security Council was not ready to back it.[16] To deal with these situations, Bryan Kreykes proposes that the Security Council delegate Chapter VII enforcement powers to regional organizations *in advance*, as a way of getting around 'capricious use of the veto'.[17] While a creative proposal, it is unrealistic to expect the Security Council to write a blank cheque or to be able to agree on appropriate safeguards as he suggests.

B. Delegation to Individual States or Coalitions

The UN Charter is silent on delegated enforcement action by coalitions of the willing or member states. The first true case is military action by the US-led coalition to drive Iraq out of Kuwait in 1991. Smaller scale missions include the Unified Task Force (UNITAF) in Somalia (Resolution 794 (1992), para 10), the multinational

[12] Franck, *Recourse to Force*, 162; See also Abass, *Regional Organisations and the Development of Collective Security*, 53–4; Paliwal, 'The Primacy of Regional Organizations in International Peacekeeping', 220; Simma, 'NATO, the UN and the Use of Force', 4; Deen-Racsmany, 'A Redistribution of Authority between the UN and Regional Organizations'; Ruth Wedgewood, 'NATO's Campaign in Yugoslavia' (1999) 93 *American Journal of International Law* 828, 832.

[13] Zwanenburg, 'Regional Organizations and the Maintenance of International Peace and Security', 502–7; Villani, 'The Security Council's Authorization of Enforcement Action', 553.

[14] SC Res 1244 (10 June 1999) on Kosovo.

[15] SC Res 1483 (22 May 2003) on Iraq; Michael Byers, 'Agreeing to Disagree: The Security Council Resolution 1441 and Intentional Ambiguity' (2004) 10 *Global Governance* 165, 181.

[16] Ange Aba, 'ECOWAS has Mali Force Troop Pledge, Still Lacks Backing', *Reuters*, 17 June 2012, available at <http://www.reuters.com/article/2012/06/17/us-mali-crisis-idUSBRE85G0HE20120617>.

[17] Kreykes, 'A Case for Delegation'.

force in Haiti (Resolution 940 (1994), para 4), the Australian-led coalition in East Timor (Resolution 1264 (1999), para 3), and the NATO-led coalition in Libya (Resolution 1973 (2011), paras 4 and 8). The Security Council has also authorized individual states to use force, like France's Operation Licorne in Côte d'Ivoire (Resolution 1528 (2004), para 16), Operation Serval in Mali (Resolution 2100 (2013), para 18), and Operation Sangaris in Central African Republic (Resolution 2127 (2013), para 50). The legality of the 1991 Iraq war was challenged by Cuba, Malaysia and by some scholars, but the weight of scholarly and official opinion is now that the Council can subcontract in this way.[18] Dan Sarooshi makes a strong legal case that it is an implied power of the Security Council, subject to limitations.[19] As these cases demonstrate, this quasi-constitutional reading of the UN Charter as a 'living tree' is confirmed by extensive Council practice and acquiescence to that practice by the vast majority of UN member states which have never objected to these 'subcontracted' operations.

While this interpretation of the Council's power is widely accepted, there is less evidence of state practice to support the limitations identified by Sarooshi, which he claims are rooted in general international law. He insists that the delegating resolution must be clear and specific, that the Security Council must retain supervisory power over the delegated action, and that the delegate must report to the Council often and extensively.[20] Other scholars have presented variations on this list, always with the emphasis on accountability—the notion that a principal (the Security Council) cannot delegate more power than it has, and must retain substantial control over the agent (states or coalitions).[21] Though questions about the degree of supervision and control are important, this chapter focuses on Sarooshi's first condition—that vague mandates are unacceptable and that the Security Council must spell out the scope and objectives of its delegation precisely. I now turn to cases where the Security Council has *not* satisfied that condition.

[18] Oscar Schachter, 'United Nations Law in the Gulf Crisis' (1991) 85 *American Journal of International Law* 452; Blokker, 'Is the Authorization Authorized?'; Helmut Freudenschuss, 'Between Unilateralism and Collective Security: Authorizations of the Use of Force by the UN Security Council' (1994) 5 *European Journal of International Law* 492; Gray, *Use of Force*, 328; Sarooshi, *The United Nations and the Development of Collective Security*. For a contrary view see, Burns H. Weston, 'Security Council Resolution 678 and Persian Gulf Decision Making: Precarious Legitimacy' (1991) 85 *American Journal of International Law* 516.

[19] Sarooshi, *The United Nations and the Development of Collective Security*.

[20] Sarooshi, *The United Nations and the Development of Collective Security*, 32–46, 156–63.

[21] Blokker, 'Is the Authorization Authorized?', 561–8; Gray, *Use of Force*, 333–4; Marc Weller, *Iraq and the Use of Force in International Law* (New York: Oxford University Press, 2010), 56–7; Jules Lobel and Michael Ratner, 'Bypassing the Security Council: Ambiguous Authorizations to Use of Force, Cease-Fires and the Iraqi Inspection Regime' (1999) 93 *American Journal of International Law* 124; Villani, 'The Security Council's Authorization of Enforcement Action'.

III. Imprecise Authorization

In 1950, the Security Council authorized 'members of the United Nations to furnish such assistance to the Republic of Korea as may be necessary to repel the armed attack [from the North] and to restore peace and security in the area.'[22] Setting aside questions about the absence of the Soviet Union at the table (in protest against the absence of the People's Republic of China) and the later adoption of the Uniting for Peace resolution by the General Assembly,[23] what does 'the restoration of international peace and security in the area' mean? Could the US pursue the North Koreans across the 38th parallel in order to eliminate their ability to launch future attacks?[24] The US believed it could, although it ultimately submitted the issue to the General Assembly. In any case, this is an early example of the Security Council authorizing military action for an ill-defined objective, using the very words that became the subject of controversy in Iraq.

Resolution 678 authorized member states cooperating with Kuwait to 'use all necessary means to uphold and implement resolution 660 (1990) and all subsequent relevant resolutions and to restore international peace and security in the area.'[25] The meaning of 'uphold and implement resolution 660' was well understood (drive Iraq out of Kuwait), but the implications of 'all subsequent resolutions' and 'restore international peace and security in the area' were less clear. Both became issues in the aftermath of the Gulf War, but even during the war itself there were debates over whether the resolution granted the US-led coalition the authority to use force in response to Iraqi war crimes, or to march on Baghdad and overthrow the government. Marc Weller finds good legal reasons for doubting these broad interpretations and notes that most states, including the US and the UK at the time, did not read the resolution as providing a 'blank cheque' for the use of force to achieve objectives beyond the liberation of Kuwait.[26]

A striking recent case of the Security Council authorizing the use of force in terms that led to conflicting interpretations is Resolution 1973 (2011) on Libya, which imposed a no-fly zone and authorized 'all necessary means' to protect the civilian population. The vote on the resolution was ten in favour, with five abstentions from Russia, China, Germany, India, and Brazil. There were many motives for the intervention in Libya, not all humanitarian, but a strong argument can be made that the intervention would not have happened if the notion of a 'responsibility to protect' (R2P) had not been central to the discourse. It made it easier for reluctant interveners

[22] SC Res 83 (27 June 1950) on Korea. [23] GA Res 377 (V) (3 Nov 1950).

[24] Lobel and Ratner, 'Bypassing the Security Council', 138–9.

[25] SC Res 678 (29 Nov 1990) on Iraq, para 2.

[26] See Weller, *Iraq and the Use of Force*, 43–4; Lobel and Ratner, 'Bypassing the Security Council', 140. Both cite the statements of various Security Council government officials.

to approve the intervention and harder for the sceptics to say no. In other words, Libya's failure to protect its civilian population was the hook that made it possible to squeeze that resolution through the Security Council, regardless of motives—which are very difficult to define anyway. And without that resolution, there would have been no intervention.[27]

A separate question is whether in implementing the resolution the NATO-led coalition exceeded its terms. Russia and others were sharply critical of how the intervention was carried out. Many of the criticisms were expressed in legal terms—namely, that the actions of the NATO coalition went beyond the authority granted in Resolution 1973 (2011). For example, the resolution prohibits deployment of a 'foreign occupation force' (para 4): did that cover the special forces France and the UK had on the ground? Did the embargo imposed in Resolution 1970 preclude arming the rebels? Most consequentially, did the authorization to protect civilians (para 4) and impose a no-fly zone (para 8) permit regime change? The US, the UK, and France all claimed that targeting Gaddafi strongholds was necessary to protect civilians. Others, including Russia, China, and India, insisted that NATO's actions exceeded the mandate.

A more common type of imprecise authorization occurs in the context of robust peace operations. This can be traced back to the UN's expansion of the concept of self-defence employed in UN peacekeeping, to include defence of the mandate. Thus guidelines issued for the second United Nations Emergency Force (UNEF II) in 1973 state that 'self-defence would include resistance to attempts by forceful means to prevent the force from discharging duties under the mandate of the Security Council.'[28] While this expanded concept of self-defence was rarely invoked by commanders in the field during the Cold War (for fear of escalation), Ralph Zacklin—long-time Deputy Legal Counsel in the UN—states that it 'represents a major development in the use of force in peacekeeping'.[29] The implication is that even for Chapter VI missions, UN doctrine holds that use of force in defence of a mandate is permissible. The Security Council normally invokes Chapter VII nowadays when the use of force beyond the peacekeeper's defence of his person and property is contemplated. But there are exceptions, like Resolution 1701 (2006) on

[27] For a good series of articles assessing the impact of R2P on the Libya intervention, see *Ethics in International Affairs*, Sept 2011: Alex J. Bellamy, 'Libya and the Responsibility to Protect: The Exception and the Norm' (2011) 25 *Ethics & International Affairs* 263–9; Simon Chesterman, '"Leading from Behind": The Responsibility to Protect, the Obama Doctrine, and Humanitarian Intervention after Libya' (2011) 25 *Ethics & International Affairs* 279; Thomas G. Weiss, 'RtoP Alive and Well after Libya' (2011) 25 *Ethics & International Affairs* 287; Jennifer Welsh, 'Civilian Protection in Libya: Putting Coercion and Controversy Back into RtoP', (2011) 25 *Ethics & International Affairs* 255.

[28] Report of the Secretary-General on the Implementation of Security Council Resolution 340 (1973), S/11052/Rev.1 (1973), 27 Oct 1973, para 4(d).

[29] Ralph Zacklin, 'The Use of Force in Peacekeeping Operations' in Niels Blokker and Nico Schrijver (eds), *The Security Council and the Use of Force: Theory and Reality—A Need for Change?* (Leiden: Martinus Nijhoff, 2005), 91, 94.

Lebanon, which—under Chapter VI—authorizes the United Nations Interim Force in Lebanon (UNIFIL) to 'take all necessary action' to protect civilians and to ensure its area of operations is not used for hostile activity.

Many peace operations have mixed Chapter VI and VII mandates. The most common is when a consent-based, multidimensional mission is given coercive power to protect civilians. The first UN mission to be given the mandate explicitly was the UN Assistance Mission in Sierra Leone in 2000, as a compromise between those who wanted the entire mission to be under Chapter VII given the insecure environment and those who feared the degree of commitment this would require and were reluctant to convert UN peacekeepers into fighting forces.[30] The Democratic Republic of the Congo (DRC) has been the most complex setting for robust peacekeeping. The UN operation there (Mission de l'Organisation de Nations Unies en République Démocratique du Congo, MONUC) went from being a small liaison mission of 90 observers, to a robust force of 20,000 with a mandate that got ever more complicated. In addition to all the civilian functions MONUC was tasked with performing, Resolution 1493, adopted in the aftermath of a crisis in eastern DRC in July 2003, delineated a set of purposes for which force could be used: in self-defence; to protect UN personnel and facilities; to ensure the security and freedom of movement of its personnel; to protect civilians under imminent threat of physical violence; and to contribute to the improvement of the security conditions in which humanitarian assistance is provided. These specific mandated tasks were followed by the more generic authorization for MONUC to use 'all necessary means to fulfill its mandate in the Ituri district and, as it deems within its capabilities, in North and South Kivu'.[31] Thus, in 2003 MONUC had Chapter VII authority for its entire mandate, full enforcement power in Ituri, and limited enforcement power 'within its capabilities' for the protection of civilians and in the Kivus. An army of lawyers would have trouble understanding, let alone implementing, that mandate.

This rather complicated formulation was simplified in subsequent resolutions that prioritized the protection of civilians. The robustness of the mandate was taken a significant step further in March 2013 when an 'Intervention Brigade' was attached to MONUSCO (Mission de l'Organisation des Nations Unies pour la Stabilisation en République Démocratique du Congo) with a mandate to carry out 'targeted offensive operations' to neutralize and disarm armed groups (Resolution 2098 (2013), para 12(b)). While the language is straightforward, its application is complicated by a provision earlier in the resolution that the Intervention Brigade is to operate 'without prejudice to the agreed principles of peacekeeping' (para 9). It is not easy to

[30] Ian Johnstone, 'Dilemmas of Robust Peace Operations' (2006) *Annual Review of Global Peace Operations 2006* 7; SC Res 1289 (7 Feb 2000) on Sierra Leone, para 10.

[31] SC Res 1493 (28 July 2003) on the Democratic Republic of the Congo, para 26.

reconcile those principles with offensive operations, which are based on a peace enforcement or even war-fighting mandate, not peacekeeping.

The peacekeeping protection of civilians mandate was put to the test in Côte d'Ivoire, around the same time as the Libya intervention. UNOCI and Operation Licorne were first deployed in 2004 with a Chapter VII mandate to protect civilians while facilitating a transitional peace process that would culminate in presidential elections. After repeated delays, those elections were finally held in late 2010. Alasane Ouatarra was declared the winner by an independent electoral commission, the UN, the African Union (AU), and ECOWAS, but the incumbent Laurent Gbagbo refused to accept the results. In late 2010 and early 2011, ECOWAS called for the removal of Gbagbo by force, but the Security Council instead strengthened the mandates of UNOCI and Licorne to protect civilians. The Security Council vote on Resolution 1975 was unanimous, but in the explanation of votes, there were important differences of emphasis, displaying tension over the line between protection of civilians and regime change.[32] ECOWAS members (Nigeria and Gabon) wanted military action to install Ouatarra, but others like India, South Africa, Brazil, and China were not prepared to go that far. The Western powers and Russia were all quite cautious in their statements. Thus we have an example of 15 members of the Security Council unanimously agreeing to something quite far-reaching, namely the transfer of power away from an incumbent, while engaging with each other on how best to make that happen. After a protracted period of escalating violence, the UN and France interpreted Resolution 1975 as giving them the authority to prevent the use of heavy weapons against the civilian population.[33] A sustained period of bombardment, including with UN attack helicopters, cleared the way for Ouatarra supporters to enter Gbagbo's compound and arrest him on 11 April 2011.

To summarize, the previous cases signify not a failure to act on the part of the Security Council, but a failure to specify the scope of action. This can be troublesome for those executing the mandate, but it is an inevitable consequence of the Security Council being a political body that cannot be expected to anticipate every contingency, let alone agree on what to do about those contingencies. While perfect clarity would be helpful in implementing a mandate, that is asking too much of the Council and may be a recipe for paralysis. The same issue arises even more acutely when the Security Council adopts a resolution that does not expressly authorize the use of force, but is interpreted that way by some UN member states.

[32] Record of the Meeting of the Security Council on the Situation in Côte d'Ivoire held on 30 March 2011 in New York, S/PV.6508 (30 Mar 2011).

[33] Cross-Cutting Report No 2 on Protection of Civilians in Armed Conflict, Security Council Report, 20 July 2011.

IV. Implied Mandates

This section considers cases of so-called implied authorizations to use force. The next section reviews some of the same cases under the heading of 'failure to act'. The difference is in the type of argument used to justify military action. The first employs a purposive approach to interpreting Security Council resolutions, claiming that the Council has acted, albeit ambiguously; the latter claims that the Security Council has failed to act in circumstances when it should have, thereby opening the door to unilateral action.

The first post-Cold War case to give rise to a dispute over whether the Security Council had authorized the use of force concerned the sanctions imposed on Iraq in 1990. The US and the UK claimed they had the authority to interdict ships that were in breach of Resolution 661, as well as on the basis of self-defence.[34] Canada and others insisted that only the Security Council could authorize the enforcement of sanctions by military force.[35] The matter was largely though not fully resolved with the adoption of Resolution 665, which 'call[ed] upon Member States cooperating with Kuwait…to use such measures commensurate to the specific circumstances as may be necessary under the authority of the Security Council to halt all inward and outward maritime shipping.'[36] Because it was not explicitly adopted under Chapter VII, the Soviet Union and China expressed some doubt over whether the resolution authorized the use of force, but those views did not prevail.[37]

A more lasting division arose over interpretation of Resolution 688, adopted shortly after the so-called 'ceasefire' resolution that brought the Gulf War to an end in April 1991.[38] In a tightly worded eight paragraphs, the Council 'condemned' Iraq's repression of its Kurdish and Shia populations and declared the consequences to be a threat to international peace and security (para 1); it 'demanded' an end to the repression (para 2); it 'insisted' that Iraq provide immediate access to those in need of assistance (para 3); and it 'appealed' to member states to contribute to the humanitarian relief effort (para 6). The resolution was not explicitly adopted under Chapter VII, but was interpreted by the US, the UK, and France as authorizing a safe haven in northern Iraq and no-fly zones in the north and south. The reaction in 1991 was relatively muted, but as time passed, the objections grew, prompting France to drop out of the triumvirate and the UK to shift away from an argument of implied authorization to one of humanitarian intervention in support of collective purposes (which I will return to in Section V below).[39]

[34] Weller, *Iraq and the Use of Force*, 24–5. [35] Weller, *Iraq and the Use of Force*, 25.

[36] SC Res 665 (25 Aug 1990) on the situation between Iraq and Kuwait, para 1.

[37] Freudenschuss, 'Unilateralism and Collective Security', 496; Weller, *Iraq and the Use of Force*, 27.

[38] SC Res 688 (5 Apr 1991) on Iraq, paras 1–3.

[39] Weller, *Iraq and the Use of Force*, 74–80; Gray, *Use of Force*, 349–50; Lobel and Ratner, 'Bypassing the Security Council', 133.

Whether Resolutions 678 and 687 authorized coercive enforcement of the Iraq weapons inspection regimes was a major source of controversy long before the 2003 intervention. It came up first in 1993 when the US, the UK, and France launched missile and air attacks against suspect sites in response to Iraq's non-cooperation with the inspectors. In an extraordinary move, Secretary-General Boutros-Ghali declared that those carrying out the strikes 'had a mandate from the Security Council, according to resolution 678 (1990), and the cause of the raid was the violation by Iraq of resolution 687 (1991) concerning the cease-fire'.[40] The issue arose again in 1998 in the context of Operation Desert Fox, with the added twist that Resolutions 1154 (1998), 1155 (1998), and 1205 (1998) had been adopted, warning of serious consequences for non-cooperation, condemning Iraq for violations of the resolutions, and demanding compliance. The resolutions did not use the term 'material breach' that was so important later in 2003, but the US and the UK insisted that Iraq's non-compliance revived the authorization to use force contained in Resolution 678 (1990). The merits of this argument—including the reactions of other states—have been debated extensively in the scholarly literature and will not be repeated here.[41] Suffice to say that the argumentation revolved around differing interpretations of Resolutions 678 (1990), 687 (1991), and the later resolutions. There was no doubt that the actions of Iraq constituted a threat to international peace and security that *could* justify the use of force. The question was whether the resolutions *did* authorize the use of force, or whether a new Security Council decision was needed.

A similar question arose again several months later, when NATO launched a 14-week bombing campaign in response to Belgrade's violence against the civilian population in Kosovo. Much of the debate on Kosovo has been about the legality of humanitarian intervention *without* Security Council authorization, but the argument put forward by most participants in the intervention was that they had the authority to act based on Resolutions 1160 (1998), 1199 (1998), and 1203 (1998).[42] The resolutions, all adopted under Chapter VII, condemned the use of force by Serbs and made demands on Belgrade. According to the logic of the argument, failure of the Serbs to

[40] Press Release, United Nations Department of Public Information, 'Transcript of Press Conference by Secretary-General Boutros Boutros-Ghali, Following Diplomatic Press Club Luncheon in Paris on 14 January 1993', SG/SM/4902/Rev.1, 15 Jan 1993.

[41] Ian Johnstone, *The Power of Deliberation: International Law, Politics, and Organizations* (New York: Oxford University Press, 2011), 125–6; Gray, *Use of Force*, 350–1; Sarooshi, *The United Nations and the Development of Collective Security*, 177–83; Weller, 'Iraq and the Use of Force', 115–30; Lori Fisler Damrosch and Bernard Oxman, 'Agora: Future Implication of the Iraq Conflict' (2003) 97 *American Journal of International Law* 553; Lori Fisler Damrosch and Bernard Oxman, 'Agora (continued): Future Implication of the Iraq Conflict' (2003) 97 *American Journal of International Law* 803.

[42] The US, the UK, France, Germany, Italy, Belgium, Greece, the Netherlands, and Slovenia all claimed the resolutions provided legal authority for the action, though many invoked other legal justifications as well. Gray, *Use of Force*, 353–4; Michael W. Reisman, 'Acting Before Victims Become Victims: Preventing and Arresting Mass Murder' (2007) 40 *Case Western Reserve Journal of International Law* 57, 79–80; Nico Krisch, 'Unilateral Enforcement of the Collective Will: Kosovo, Iraq, and the Security Council' (1999) *Max Planck Yearbook of United Nations Law* 59, 81–3.

meet those demands triggered the right of NATO to use force. Germany presented the most nuanced position along these lines, claiming the action was in conformity with the 'sense and logic' of the resolutions, if not their precise terms.[43] The argument is a stretch, not only because the resolutions lack even an ambiguous reference to the use of force, but also because China, Russia, and others made it clear in debates before and at the time the resolutions were adopted that they did not read them that way.[44]

Resolution 1441 (2002) on Iraq sparked the greatest controversy. The US, the UK, and others attacked based on a combined reading of Resolution 678 (1990), 687 (1991), and 1441 (2002).[45] Some of the language in Resolution 1441 (2002) made the case for war stronger than it had been in 1993 and 1998: it recalled Resolution 678 (1990) and repeated the phrase 'all necessary means' in the preamble; it declared Iraq to be in material breach of its obligations under Resolution 687 (1991) and decided that non-cooperation with Resolution 1441 (2002) would be a 'further material breach'; it warned of 'serious consequences' for violations; and while it agreed to reconvene to 'assess' the situation and to 'consider' what to do in the event of non-cooperation, the resolution did not explicitly stipulate that the Security Council must 'decide' what to do. Thus the best argument that can be made for the US/UK position is that the authorization to use force in Resolution 678 was suspended by Resolution 687 (1991) only insofar as Iraq remained in compliance with the terms of the ceasefire. In Resolution 1441 (2002), the Council as a whole found that Iraq's non-compliance was not trivial but a 'material breach', reviving the right to use force without a new authorization.[46] Clever lawyers embellished the argument by claiming that while the Security Council does not authorize the use of force lightly, nor does it terminate that authorization lightly.[47] Further support comes from looking at the purpose of Resolution 687 (1991), which was disarmament. The only way of keeping pressure on Iraq to comply with its disarmament obligations was through the credible threat of force; the threat would not

[43] Simma, 'NATO, the UN and the Use of Force', 12. [44] Gray, *Use of Force*, 352–3.

[45] Letter dated 20 March 2003 from the Permanent Representative of the United Kingdom of Great Britain and Northern Ireland to the United Nations addressed to the President of the Security Council, S/2003/350 (21 Mar 2003); Letter dated 20 March 2003 from the Permanent Representative of the United States to the United Nations addressed to the President of the Security Council, S/2003/351 (21 Mar 2003); William H. Taft and Todd F. Buckwald, 'Preemption, Iraq, and International Law' (2003) 93 *American Journal of International Law* 557; the US also sought to make the case for war on the basis of self-defence as an extension of the war on terrorism, but by March 2003 it had ceased making that claim to international audiences. Ian Johnstone, 'US–UN Relations After Iraq: The End of the World (Order) As We Know It?' (2004) 15 *European Journal of International Law* 813.

[46] The US and the UK made much of the term 'material breach' because it signified the Council's judgement that a fundamental term of the ceasefire had been broken, pre-empting a counterargument that individual member states should not have the unilateral right to determine whether a particular violation of the resolution justified military action. As Sarooshi argues, the Security Council has been delegated the authority to determine whether a threat to the peace exists and cannot sub-delegate that. Sarooshi, *The United Nations and the Development of Collective Security*, 33, 179.

[47] John Yoo, 'International Law and the War in Iraq' (2003) 97 *American Journal of International Law* 563, 567.

be credible if the Security Council had to decide collectively whether to act each time Iraq was being obstructive. Saddam Hussein would simply bide his time, cooperating only enough to drive a wedge between Council members. Thus, according to this line of argument, in order to achieve the object and purpose of Resolution 687 (1991), the resolutions should be read broadly to permit the use of force until such time as the Security Council explicitly decides peace and security has been restored.

The counterarguments are at least as powerful. Resolution 687 (1991) did not merely suspend Resolution 678 (1990), but superseded it. When the conditions for a ceasefire were formally established and a framework for implementing those conditions was set out in Resolution 687 (1991), the authorization to use force expired. Resolution 1441 (2002) added nothing to the legal case for military action. It was a compromise, by which Council members agreed to put pressure on Iraq and, in the event of non-compliance, to reconvene. The Security Council may have declared Iraq to be in material breach, but it never declared it to be in 'further material breach' nor did it decide what to do about it.[48] As France, Russia, and China put it in a joint statement, the resolution contained 'no automaticity'. This line of reasoning is supported by the argument that an open-ended delegation of authority to individual member states would fly in the face of the Security Council's primary responsibility for the maintenance of international peace and security. A resolution that delegates something as fundamental as the use of force should be construed narrowly and in favour of the prerogatives of the Security Council as a collective decision-making body. In other words, if the Council wants to authorize military action, it should do so unambiguously.

The debate raged in policy and academic circles for many years, with repercussions that extend to today.[49] What is more important than who is right or wrong is that the Security Council 'knowingly adopted a resolution the language of which would permit both sides to claim victory'.[50] Both sides knew how the other would interpret the resolution if and/or when push came to shove. The unanimous adoption of the resolution (in the absence of Syria) was meant to send a strong message to Saddam Hussein, hoping either that he would comply without the need to force him to do so or that, when it became clear he would not comply, the passage of time would make it possible to agree on what to do about that non-compliance (ie agree on how to interpret the resolutions).

This take on events is reinforced by French Ambassador Jean-David Levitte's admission that, weeks before the US had planned to table the famous second resolution that would have explicitly authorized the use of force, he 'went to the State Department and to the White House to say, don't do it. First, because you'll split the

[48] Weller, *Iraq and the Use of Force*; Gray, *Use of Force*, 363.

[49] For a range of opinions on both sides, see the symposium 'Agora: Future Implications of the Iraq Conflict' (2003) 97 *American Journal of International Law*, issues 3 and 4.

[50] Stephen D. Mathias, 'The United States and the Security Council' in Blokker and Schrijver, *The Security Council and the Use of Force*, 176, 176. Mathias was Assistant Legal Adviser for UN Affairs in the US Department of State at the time. He is currently Deputy Legal Counsel at the UN.

Council and second, because you don't need it. Let's agree to disagree between gentlemen...'[51] Levitte was not signalling France's acceptance of the US interpretation of the resolution, but rather was trying to preserve the credibility of the Council. If the second resolution had been put to a vote and vetoed by France and Russia, the US and the UK going to war would have destroyed the Council as an institution. By allowing the US and the UK to claim legal authority based on existing resolutions and France and Russia to deny it—in other words by agreeing to disagree—then it was possible to return to the Council to help to clean up the diplomatic mess in the aftermath of the war.

What does this episode tell us about implied authorizations? As a matter of law, it is not hard to make the case for clarity over ambiguity.[52] And as a matter of policy, one can see the danger in finding the authority to use force too readily in ambiguous language, not only because international peace and security is better served by a presumption against the use of force, but also because the ability of the Security Council to send strong signals would be compromised. Indeed, there is evidence that the Council learned that lesson. Resolutions imposing sanctions on North Korea and Iran unusually included explicit references to Article 41 of the Charter, to pre-empt any argument that they could be read as implicitly authorizing the use of force under Article 42.[53] Conversely, the Council was unable to send a strong message to Syria in 2011. In vetoing a condemnatory resolution, Russia stated in reference to the Libya precedent, 'it is very important to know how [Resolution 1973] was implemented and how a Security Council resolution was turned into its opposite.'[54]

Mali is another case of implied authorization. As the situation in the north of the country deteriorated through the latter half of 2012, the UN, ECOWAS, and the AU were all busy trying to devise a plan for intervention. The result was Resolution 2085 (2012), which authorized an African-led International Support Mission to Mali (AFISMA) to deploy once certain preconditions were met. Paragraph 14 of the resolution 'urges Member States, regional organizations and international organizations to provide... any necessary assistance in efforts to reduce the threat posed by terrorist organizations.' Did that authorize military action by France? The question was put to the test in early January 2013, when Al Qaeda in the Islamic Maghreb and its allies seized the town of Konna, long before AFISMA had deployed. French forces intervened, engaging in major combat operations over a period of months. France presented three legal justifications: the invitation by Malian authorities to intervene;

[51] Quoted in Jane E. Stromseth, 'Law and Force After Iraq: A Transitional Moment' (2003) 97 *American Journal of International Law* 628, 631; Weller, *Iraq and the Use of Force*, 169. See also Byers, 'Agreeing to Disagree', 73; Johnstone, 'US–UN Relations After Iraq'.

[52] Sarooshi, *The United Nations and the Development of Collective Security*.

[53] SC Res 1874 (12 June 2009) on North Korea; SC Res 1929 (9 June 2010) on Iran.

[54] Record of the Meeting of the Security Council, S/PV.6627 (4 Oct 2011), 4.

self-defence based on Article 51 of the UN Charter; and authority based on Security Council Resolution 2085.[55] None of the claims were put forward in great detail, and they tended to be intermingled. Significantly, the Security Council tacitly endorsed the French position as follows:

> The members of the Security Council recall resolutions 2056 (2012), 2071 (2012) and 2085 (2012) adopted under Chapter VII of the Charter of the United Nations, as well as the urgent need to counter the increasing terrorist threat in Mali. The members of the SC reiterate their call to Member States to assist the settlement of the crisis in Mali and, in particular to provide assistance to the Malian Defence and Security Forces in order to reduce the threat proposed by terrorist organizations and associated groups.[56]

The implication seems to be that the French interpretation of Resolution 2085 (2012), as implicitly authorizing the use of force, was accepted.

A categorical position against implied authorizations seems overly formalistic as it assumes that the line between implicit and explicit authorization is self-evident. All words are in need of interpretation; 'plain' or 'ordinary' meanings are only plain or ordinary in the light of their context. Important terms in Security Council resolutions are and should be read in context, requiring an inquiry into object, purpose, subsequent practice, negotiating history, and all the other techniques of treaty interpretation.[57] When one delves into that kind of inquiry, the distinction between implicit and explicit authorization is question-begging. Moreover, sometimes the ambiguity is intentional. In the case of Iraq, Resolution 1441 (2002) was meant to kick the problem down the road, in the (perhaps vain) hope that it would not come to a head. Would the alternative—no resolution at all—have been better? That would have resulted in either continued paralysis with no weapons inspectors in Iraq, or US unilateral action without even the fig leaf of authority. As Michael Byers argues, deliberate ambiguity can protect international law from permanent harm by cushioning it from the effects of deep political differences.[58] This may be less than ideal, but it is better than demanding an unrealistic level of lawmaking precision from the Security Council, thereby rendering it irrelevant.

[55] 'Mali—Press conference given by M. Laurent Fabius, Minister of Foreign Affairs—excerpts', French Ministry of Foreign and European Affairs, Official Speeches and Statement of 14 Jan 2013, available at <http://basedoc.diplomatie.gouv.fr/exl-doc/FranceDiplomatie/PDF/baen2013-01-14.pdf>.

[56] Security Council Press statement SC/10878, AFR/2502, 10 Jan 2013. See also SC Res 2100 (2013), preambular para 5, and ECOWAS Press Release No 006/2013, 12 Jan 2013.

[57] This approach to interpretation borrows from Arts 31–2 of the Vienna Convention on the Law of Treaties (1969).

[58] Byers, 'Agreeing to Disagree', 181; see also Mathias, 'The United States and the Security Council' in Blokker and Schrijver, *The Security Council and the Use of Force*, 177, who says the arguments over the interpretation of Res 678 (29 Nov 1990), 687 (3 Apr 1991), and 1441 (8 Nov 2002) on Iraq 'support rather than undermine the existing legal regime' because they are premised on the authority of the Security Council to authorize force.

V. Failure to Act

The most controversial cases are when regional organizations or coalitions claim a right to use force with no Security Council authorization at all (and no plausible self-defence claim). The contestation occurs not when a state asserts a right to act unilaterally whenever its security interests are at stake—few officials or scholars make that broad claim—but when the Security Council is said to have failed in its responsibility to maintain peace and security.[59] The issue arises most frequently in the context of humanitarian intervention. It is captured by Thomas Franck who, in paraphrasing a Supreme Court Justice's comment on the US Constitution, quipped 'surely the UN Charter is not a genocide pact'.[60] Two related but distinct theories have been put forward to justify 'unauthorized' intervention: unilateral enforcement of the collective will expressed in Security Council resolutions; and the 'unreasonable' or 'capricious' veto.

The 'enforcement of the collective will' theory is close to but differs from implied authorization. The latter finds authority to use force implicit in a resolution; the former acknowledges that the Security Council did not authorize military action, but nevertheless expressed its will on objectives to be achieved. States relying on this theory claim the right to take military action in order to achieve the Council's purposes.[61] The argument was made with respect to the no-fly zones in Iraq, Operation Desert Fox in 1998, Kosovo in 1999, and Iraq again in 2003. On the no-fly zones, the US and the UK argued that they were 'consistent with' and 'in support' of UN Security Council Resolution 688, even if not authorized by it.[62] When force was used in response to Iraq's obstruction of UN weapons inspectors in 1998, British

[59] By responsibility, I mean a Charter-based political responsibility not a legal obligation. The World Summit Outcome Document was carefully drafted to preclude an interpretation that R2P imposed a legal obligation on the Security Council to end or prevent mass atrocities (UN General Assembly, World Summit Outcome Document: resolution/adopted by the General Assembly, A/RES/60/1 (24 Oct 2005)). See paras 138–9. For an analysis of the negotiation history of those paragraphs, see Johnstone, *The Power of Deliberation*, 71–2. On the other hand, Louise Arbour has argued that the Genocide Convention, as interpreted by the ICJ in the *Bosnia* case (ICJ (1993), 325) imposes an obligation on the P5 not to exercise their veto to end genocide. Louse Arbour, 'The Responsibility to Protect as a Duty of Care in International Law and Practice' (2008) 34 *Review of International Studies* 445.

[60] Franck, *Recourse to Force*, 182; Michael W. Reisman, 'Kosovo Antinomies' (1999) 93 *American Journal of International Law* 860, 860; Mathias, 'The United States and the Security Council', 182.

[61] Krisch, 'Unilateral Enforcement of the Collective Will'; Carsten Stahn, 'Enforcement of the Collective Will After Iraq' (2003) 97 *American Journal of International Law* 804, 809, 816–19; Weller, *Iraq and the Use of Force*, 81–8; Simma, 'NATO, the UN and the Use of Force', 9–13; Christian Henderson, *The Persistent Advocate and the Use of Force: The Impact of the United States upon the Jus ad Bellum in the Post-Cold War Era* (Farnham: Ashgate, 2010), 100.

[62] For statements from various US and UK officials, see Henderson, *The Impact of the United States upon the Jus ad Bellum*, 99, 110–14; Weller, *Iraq and the Use of Force*, 75; Krisch, *Unilateral Enforcement of the Collective Will*, 75.

Prime Minister Tony Blair claimed that it 'was to enforce the Security Council's will'. The German position that NATO's intervention in Kosovo followed the 'sense and logic' of Security Council resolutions is a variant of the claim. So are UK statements that the resolutions were 'an important part of the legal framework within which NATO acted' and US views about the 'synergy' between NATO and the UN 'on behalf of an urgent common cause'.[63] Regarding Iraq 2003, the claim that a material breach of Resolution 687 triggers the right to use force is in effect an argument that enforcement authority devolves upon individual states in the event of Security Council paralysis.[64]

The majority of states did not accept the 'enforcement of the collective will' line of thinking in all of the previous cases. The sentiment is well captured by the Russian Permanent Representative to the UN in 1998: 'no [one] is entitled to act independently on behalf of the UN and even less to assume the functions of world policeman'.[65] Among scholars, Marc Weller observes 'that a general right of states to appoint themselves the executors of the "will" of the Security Council would lead to very significant instability'.[66] Nico Krisch concludes that unilateral enforcement is more likely to threaten than enhance community interests.[67] Those who see merit in this approach believe adequate safeguards can be put in place, for example by insisting on a prior determination of the gravity of the humanitarian situation by the Security Council.[68] Carsten Stahn argues for a principled approach to 'unauthorized enforcement action', which would look at whether common interests enshrined in resolutions are being enforced, who the interveners are, and whether a participatory process of legal discourse involving all relevant actors was pursued.[69]

The 'unreasonable veto' theory has a long history. In San Francisco, France and other states proposed that UN member states should have the right to act 'in the interest of peace, right and justice' if the Security Council was paralysed by the veto.[70] This was not accepted then, but it became the basis for the General Assembly's Uniting for Peace resolution of 1950 (discussed in Chapter 13 of this volume). It resonated during the Cold War when the Security Council found it difficult to act on

[63] Simma, 'NATO, the UN and the Use of Force', 11–12; Krisch, *Unilateral Enforcement of the Collective Will*, 81–5; Henderson, *The Impact of the United States upon the Jus ad Bellum*, 105, 114–19; Christopher Greenwood, 'International Law and the NATO Intervention in Kosovo' (2000) 49 *International and Comparative Law Quarterly* 926, 927–9.

[64] Weller, *Iraq and the Use of Force*, 160–72. See also Gray, *Use of Force*, 369.

[65] For that statement and the position of other states, see Krisch, *Unilateral Enforcement of the Collective Will*, 67, 77–9, 82–5.

[66] Marc Weller, 'The US, Iraq and the Use of Force in a Unipolar World' (1999) 41 *Survival* 81, 89.

[67] Krisch, *Unilateral Enforcement of the Collective Will*, 92–4.

[68] Vaughan Lowe, 'International Legal Issues Arising in the Kosovo Crisis' (2000) 49 *International and Comparative Law Quarterly* 934, 939.

[69] Stahn, 'Enforcement of the Collective Will After Iraq', 815.

[70] eg France and Australia. Ruth B. Russell, *A History of the United Nations Charter* (Washington DC: Brookings Institution, 1958); Stahn, 'Enforcement of the Collective Will After Iraq', 810.

any threat to the peace because of the superpower rivalry. It also served a rhetorical purpose in the post-Cold War after the Security Council was criticized for doing too little in Bosnia and Rwanda. A version was invoked by the Dutch Permanent Representative to the UN at the start of the Kosovo crisis:

> [If] due to one or two permanent members' rigid interpretation of the concept of domestic jurisdiction, such a resolution is not attainable, we cannot sit back and simply let the humanitarian catastrophe occur. In such a situation we will act on the legal basis we have available, and what we have available in this case is more than adequate.[71]

The North Atlantic Parliamentary Assembly hinted at the doctrine with its resolution calling for NATO to 'stand ready to act should the UN Security Council be prevented from discharging its purpose of maintaining international peace and security'.[72]

The most full-bodied scholarly articulation of the concept is provided by Christopher Greenwood (now ICJ judge) in his testimony before the UK House of Commons Foreign Affairs Committee in June 2000:

> Under international law it is the Security Council which has the primary responsibility for maintaining international peace and security. That does not mean, however, that if the Security Council is unable to take action in a particular case—for example because of a veto, or the threat of a veto, by a permanent member of the Council—no action is possible. As demonstrated above, States have intervened on humanitarian grounds without the authorisation of the Security Council in extreme cases. Furthermore, an interpretation of international law which would forbid intervention to prevent something as terrible as the Holocaust, unless a permanent member could be persuaded to lift its veto, would be contrary to the principles on which modern international law is based as well as flying in the face of the developments of the last 50 years.[73]

The idea is that the threatened or actual use of an 'unreasonable' veto triggers a unilateral right to act. One can see the logic (if not necessarily the merit) of the argument when the motive for using the veto is unrelated to the issue at hand, for example when China vetoed the extension of the United Nations Preventive Deployment Force (UNPREDEP) because of Macedonia's relations with Taiwan, or when the US threatened to veto the UN police mission in Bosnia (United Nations Mission in Bosnia and Herzegovina, UNMIBH) unless the Security Council approved a blanket exemption for the US and other non-parties of the International Criminal Court (ICC) from investigation and prosecution by the ICC.[74]

The problem is that there are no criteria for determining when a veto is 'unreasonable'. The theory can be traced to Council inaction in the face of extreme humanitarian and human rights crises, like the Rwanda genocide. If a state or group of states had been

[71] Record of the Meeting of the Security Council on the Situation in Kosovo held on 24 March 1999 in New York, S/PV.3988 (24 Mar 1999), 8. Also quoted in Weller, *Iraq and the Use of Force*, 85.

[72] Quoted in Simma, 'NATO, the UN and the Use of Force', 16.

[73] Greenwood, 'NATO Intervention in Kosovo', 930.

[74] The resolution on the ICC is SC Res 1422 (12 July 2002).

prepared to act then and the Security Council was prepared to authorize it, but for the objection of one permanent member, would that veto not be 'unreasonable'? This is what stimulated the R2P phenomenon, including the six criteria set out by the International Commission on Intervention and State Sovereignty on when intervention would (and would not) be appropriate, ideally with Security Council authorization but if necessary without it.[75] In the context of discussions on Security Council reform, it inspired appeals for a gentlemen's agreement among the five permanent members of the Council (P5) not to use the veto to block humanitarian intervention.

The 'unreasonable veto' theory is also connected to the notion of humanitarian necessity as an excuse for violations of the law. Based on the 'defence of necessity' in common and civil law jurisdictions, as well as the International Law Commission Articles on State Responsibility,[76] the idea is that humanitarian intervention is not another exception to the prohibition against the use of force, but rather will be excused in extreme cases of humanitarian need. In other words, the world will turn a blind eye to the violation and in effect pardon those responsible.[77] It is a difficult argument that assumes an amorphous 'interpretive community' is capable of making a subtle distinction between interventions that are legal, those that are illegal but excusable, and those that are both illegal and inexcusable. Arguably it did this in the Kosovo case: NATO's intervention was never condoned by the Security Council, General Assembly, or in the legal discourse surrounding them; but nor was it condemned in a manner that cost NATO a great price.[78] That still begs the question, is it possible for the international community to treat an act as illegal but excusable without fatally undermining the prohibition against the use of force? Elsewhere I have argued that it can, but there is certainly room for debate.[79]

In any case, the theory still has resonance even if it has not gained much traction among lawyers. Echoes of it were heard in Iraq 2003 and more recently in Syria. After the Houla massacre in May 2012, US Permanent Representative to the UN Susan Rice was quoted as saying states may have little choice but to pursue military options outside of the UN Security Council:

I think we may be beginning to see the wheels coming off this bus ... [The worst case scenario is that] the Council's unity is exploded, the Annan plan is dead, and this becomes a proxy

[75] 'Responsibility to Protect', Report of the International Commission on Intervention and State Sovereignty (2001).

[76] Art 25 of Responsibility of States for Internationally Wrongful Acts, Annex to GA Res 56/83 (12 Dec 2001), corrected by A/56/49 (vol 1).

[77] Oscar Schachter, *International Law in Theory and Practice* (Leiden: Martinus Nijhoff, 1991), 268. See also Franck, *Recourse to Force*, 285; Ian Johnstone, 'The Plea of "Necessity" in International Legal Discourse: Humanitarian Intervention and Counter-Terrorism' (2005) 43 *Columbia Journal of Transnational Law* 337, 357–66.

[78] Ian Johnstone, 'Security Council Deliberations: The Power of the Better Argument' (2003) 14 *European Journal of International Law* 437.

[79] Johnstone, 'The Plea of Necessity', 379; But see Anthea Roberts, 'Legality vs. Legitimacy: Can Uses of Force be Illegal but Justified?' in Philip Alston and Euan Macdonald (eds), *Human Rights, Intervention, and the Use of Force* (Oxford: Oxford University Press, 2008).

conflict with arms flowing in from all sides. And members of this council and members of the international community are left with the option only of having to consider whether they're prepared to take action outside the Annan plan and the authority of this council.[80]

Russia and others would strongly disagree with the notion that their use of the veto was unreasonable in the circumstances, let alone that others would be justified in acting outside the Council because of the veto. But to suggest that there is no objective way of deciding between these two positions misses the point. The fact of the matter is that between early 2011 and mid-2012 there had been extended public contestation among the P5; emerging powers like India, Brazil, South Africa, and Turkey; those with a stake in the region like Qatar, Egypt, and Jordan; representatives of the Arab League, AU, the Organisation of Islamic Cooperation (OIC), the EU, and NATO; as well as a large constellation of non-governmental actors on what the 'responsibility to protect' requires and appropriate role of the Security Council in giving effect to the doctrine. There is no objective answer to the question when a veto is unreasonable, but reasoned deliberation about that question is possible. It is a fundamental principle of justice that like cases ought to be treated alike. Yet in the real world of international politics, perfect consistency is not possible: power matters and inequalities in power will inevitably result in inconsistency. That does not mean we must resign ourselves to hypocrisy and double standards. One of the functions of international law and norms is to generate more consistency, to serve as advocacy tools to pressure decision-makers to treat like cases alike. Consider R2P: a cynical view is that it is simply an excuse the powerful states use to intervene for ulterior motives; a less cynical view is that while the risk of abuse is real, norms like R2P can be a tool to minimize abuse, to make Security Council-authorized intervention a little more likely when appropriate and a little less likely when not.

VI. Conclusion

For reasons of both law and policy, it is tempting to denigrate strained interpretations of Security Council action and inaction as providing justification for the use of force. There are ample reasons for wanting the Security Council to say what it means and to mean what it says when it comes to something as fundamental as the use of force. Acting on the basis of imprecise authorizations, implied authorizations, and authorizations that *should* have happened deprives international law of

[80] Colum Lynch, 'Rice warns that Annan peace plan may be on last legs', blog Foreign Policy, 30 May, 2012, available at <http://turtlebay.foreignpolicy.com/posts/2012/05/30/rice_warns_that_annan_peace_plan_may_be_on_its_last_legs>.

determinacy.[81] Vague delegation of power may run afoul of basic principles of international institutional law,[82] as well as the UN Charter itself.[83] It abdicates responsibility for control over military operations[84] and raises legal questions about accountability for wrongful acts committed in the execution of those operations.[85] Expansive interpretations of Security Council (in)action may deter members from ever agreeing to strongly worded resolutions or even discussing contentious issues for fear of being accused of threatening an 'unreasonable' veto. This not only limits the range of instruments in the Security Council's toolbox, but undermines the stability that the rule of law is meant to bring to the international system.

All true, but as noted earlier, to expect perfect clarity from the Security Council is expecting too much. Undoubtedly clear, precise resolutions are better than vague, implied, or after-the fact authorizations to use force. But when Resolution 1441 was adopted, the choice was not between a vague and a more tightly worded resolution, but rather between that and no resolution at all. The likely impact of no resolution would have been no weapons inspectors back in Iraq and unilateral US action with the support of a few allies. There would have been much less legal and justificatory discourse between November 2002 and March 2003. The Council itself would have been spared the rancour that characterized that period, but it would also have looked irrelevant. As it turns out, the Council was damaged by the Iraq episode, but not destroyed by it.[86] Even 'misuses' of concepts like R2P, such as Russia's claim that it justified intervention in Georgia in 2008 or France's claim that it justified intervention in Myanmar in the aftermath of Cyclone Nargis, can reinforce it if rejected in the discursive process; making clear what a norm is not gives it greater precision and can shore up support for what it is.[87]

Formalistic legal analyses of what the Council has and has not authorized tend to overlook the useful discursive function it plays. The Council is not just a decision-making body, but also a place where claims about appropriate international behaviour and the requirements of international law are proffered, challenged, defended, and criticized. In the discursive process, the rules of international life are interpreted, reinterpreted, and on occasion rewritten. Findings of (il)legality are not derived objectively, but inter-subjectively, through the push and pull of international politics

[81] Orakhelashvili, *Act and Rules in Public International Law*, 9–23; Thomas M. Franck, *The Power of Legitimacy* (New York: Oxford University Press, 1990); Lon L. Fuller, *The Morality of Law* (rvsd edn, New Haven, CT: Yale University Press, 1969), 221.

[82] Sarooshi, *The United Nations and the Development of Collective Security*, 8.

[83] Lobel and Ratner, 'Bypassing the Security Council', 128–9.

[84] Sarooshi, *The United Nations and the Development of Collective Security*, 159–60; Freudenschuss, 'Unilateralism and Collective Security', 524–7; Gray, *Use of Force*, 333–4.

[85] Blokker, 'Is the Authorization Authorized?', 546; Weller, *Iraq and the Use of Force*; International Law Commission, 'Draft Articles on the Responsibility of International Organizations', *Yearbook of the International Law Commission*, 2011, vol II (2).

[86] Johnstone, 'US–UN Relations After Iraq'.

[87] Christina G. Badescu and Thomas G. Weiss, 'Misrepresenting R2p and Advancing Norms: An Alternative Spiral?' (2010) 11 *International Studies Perspectives* 354.

framed by accepted understandings of the techniques of interpretation and the conventions of legal discourse.[88] This discourse includes not only Security Council members, but also other countries affected by what the Security Council and the broad constellation of intergovernmental and non-governmental actors who participate in or find a way of impacting what the Security Council does. The process, as I have argued elsewhere, is more inclusive than meets the eye.[89]

Viewing the Security Council in this way does not lead to any particular conclusion about the merits of narrow versus broad readings of Council acts and failures to act. A broad, purposive approach to Charter interpretation can cut both ways. It may remove any vestige of predictable behaviour that rules on the use of force are meant to provide. Or it may cushion the impact of deep political divisions over when the use of force is justified. The former perspective sees rigid adherence to explicit rules as the only way of protecting the law from subjective interpretation, hypocrisy, and irrelevance. The latter sees legal discourse as a vehicle for problem-solving—a way of managing the tensions and competing normative claims that characterize any pluralistic society. From either perspective, discourse in and around the Security Council about when the use of force is legal and appropriate reinforces the value of the institution rather than undermines it.

[88] See generally Johnstone, *The Power of Deliberation*; Henderson, *The Impact of the United States upon the Jus ad Bellum*; Stahn, 'Enforcement of the Collective Will After Iraq', 806, 808, 822; Stromseth, 'Law and Force After Iraq', 632–3.

[89] Johnstone, *The Power of Deliberation*. See also Reisman, 'Kosovo Antinomies', 862.

CHAPTER 11

UNITED NATIONS SECURITY COUNCIL PRACTICE IN RELATION TO USE OF FORCE IN NO-FLY ZONES AND MARITIME EXCLUSION ZONES

ROB MCLAUGHLIN

I. Introduction

In terms of authorizations and justifications for use of force, the United Nations Security Council (UNSC) has been, on the whole, fairly reticent to either approve or condemn no-fly zones (NFZs) and maritime exclusion zones (MEZs) asserted by states.[1] They have

[1] eg the Cuban Quarantine of Oct 1962; see US Department of State, *Foreign Relations of the United States, 1961–1963, Vol XI: Cuban Missile Crisis and Aftermath*, available at <http://www.state.gov/www/

been less reticent, however, to employ these operational air and ocean space control mechanisms under the cover of Chapter VII mandates. This is not to say that the UNSC utilizes NFZs and MEZs routinely—it does not. But there is a sufficient body of practice in relation to these two mechanisms to allow some assessment of the use of force contours of their utilization by the UNSC, and some analysis of the uncertainties that remain.

NFZs and MEZs, on their face, are sibling concepts in that both are targeted at regulating access to ocean and/or airspace in order to achieve a particular operational objective. These objectives range from the relatively benign (surface or airspace picture simplification), through defensive (force protection), to offensive (effectively, delineating 'engagement zones').[2] Understanding the UNSC's relationship with both NFZs and MEZs is at core a function of three interlinked questions:

(1) Is the law governing the zone law of armed conflict (LOAC) or non-LOAC-based?
(2) Is the law on use of force inside the zone fundamentally the same as the law on use of force applying outside the zone?
(3) Has the UNSC's act of declaring or acquiescing in the zone altered the law normally applicable in the ocean or airspace enclosed by the zone?

There is, however, one ongoing debate which is fundamental to the issue of UNSC use of force with respect to NFZs and MEZs, the relevance of which I will note at certain points. This is the broader issue of whether the UNSC can authorize use of *lethal* force for a mandate-enforcement purpose, even where there is no LOAC authorization available, and the situation is not one of immediate individual or unit self-defence (or defence of others), as understood by most national legal systems. This debate is complicated by uncertainty with respect to two fundamental and

about_state/history/frusXI/index.html>; 'Presidential Proclamation Announcing Quarantine of Cuba, 23 October 1962' (in Richard Jaques (ed), *Maritime Operational Zones* (Newport, RI: US Naval War College, 2006), C-2–C-3). The Kennedy administration considered declaring a limited blockade, recognizing that this would constitute 'an act of war' (eg Doc 27, 'Memorandum by Director of Central Intelligence McCone', 17 Oct 1962) but ultimately settled on the 'quarantine' concept—partially so as to avoid any legal implication of blockade, and thus a state of armed conflict; Doc 38, 'Minutes of 506th Meeting of the National Security Council', 21 Oct 1962. See generally, Errol Henriques, 'Zones in Crisis Conditions—Control of Sea and Airspace During Times of National Emergency and Enforcing Collective Security' in Jaques, *Maritime Operational Zones*, 3-5–3-12. In relation to the TEZ (total exclusion zone) declared during the Falklands conflict by the UK on 28 Apr 1982 (to come into effect on 30 Apr 1982, thereby upgrading the 7 Apr 1982 'MEZ'), see generally: 'Declaration of United Kingdom Total Exclusion Zone (TEZ) 28 April 1982', in Jaques, *Maritime Operational Zones*, C-11; Lawrence Freedman, 'The War of the Falklands Islands, 1982' (1982) 61 *Foreign Affairs* 196; Anthony Parsons, 'The Falklands crisis in the United Nations, 31 March–14 June 1982' (1983) 59 *International Affairs* 169; Nicholas J. Watkins, 'Disputed Sovereignty in the Falklands Islands: The Argentina–Great Britain Conflict of 1982' (1984) 11 *Florida State University Law Review* 649.

[2] During the Falklands crisis, for example, neither SC Res 502 (3 Apr 1982) nor SC Res 505 (26 May 1982) mentioned the British or Argentinian declared exclusion zones. A range of factors could have influenced this outcome: the UNSCs recognition of the legitimacy of declaring exclusion zones during armed conflict at sea; the UK veto; and the fact that both parties had declared similar zones.

closely linked concerns. The first is the existence (or otherwise) of a 'third paradigm' for use of lethal force (individual and unit self-defence and defence of others; in accordance with LOAC; and as a third paradigm, to implement a Chapter VII 'all necessary means' authorized mandate). It is assumed in this chapter that such a third paradigm for use of lethal force does not exist.[3] The second concern is the broad scope of the concept of 'self-defence' to which the UNSC (and, indeed, the UN generally) subscribes. There is a good deal of UNSC practice supporting an approach to 'self-defence' for UN-authorized or sanctioned forces which includes the capacity to use force—including lethal force—to 'defend' the mandate and/or achieve mandate purposes.[4] This debate will simply be outlined, but my view is that this broad UN conception of use of *lethal* force in 'self-defence' is at the least intensely problematic, and most likely (for many states) unlawful. It is important to recognize the legal distinction between mandate enforcement (for which lethal force—outside LOAC-governed situations—is not available), and self-defence/defence of others (which generally permits lethal force only in situations where there is a degree of imminent threat to life or of serious injury).

II. Outline

In order to examine UNSC practice in relation to NFZs and MEZs, it is useful to adopt differentiated approaches to each. With respect to UNSC-mandated NFZs, because practice is concisely centred upon three examples, it is instructive to examine each in turn and to then draw general conclusions. MEZs, on the other hand, are a more regular feature of UNSC action, but in a broader array of guises. As a consequence, greater clarity in relation to UNSC MEZ practice is arguably achieved through a more thematic or 'typological' approach. This chapter reflects this analytical premise.

[3] Rob McLaughlin, 'The Legal Regime Applicable to Use of Lethal Force When Operating under a United Nations Security Council Chapter VII Mandate Authorising "All Necessary Means"' (2008) 12 *Journal of Conflict and Security Law* 389.

[4] eg Report of the Secretary-General on the Implementation of Security Council Resolution 425, S/12611 (1978) (on the establishment of the United Nations Interim Force in Lebanon (UNIFIL))—the force 'shall not use force except in self-defence. Self-defence would include resistance to attempts by forceful means to prevent it from discharging its duties under the mandate of the Security Council...' (para 4d); January 2000 Rules of Engagement for the United Nations Transitional Administration in East Timor (UNTAET), rule 1.9: 'Use of force, up to and including deadly force, against any individual or party who limits or intends to limit the freedom of movement of UNTAET personnel, is authorized' (in Australian Defence Force Military Law Centre/Asia Pacific Centre for Military Law, *Law and Military Operations in East Timor (UNTAET) Feb 2000–May 2002*; Annex Y); see generally Trevor Findlay, *The Use of Force in UN Peace Operations* (Oxford: SIPRI/Oxford University Press, 2002).

III. UNSC-Endorsed or Mandated No-Fly Zones

A. General Description

Descriptions of air exclusion zones, or NFZs, are relatively consistent. Timothy McIlmail describes the purpose of NFZs as 'prohibit[ing] the entry of unauthorised aircraft into airspace over specified territory'.[5] Michael Schmitt defines NFZs as 'a *de facto* aerial occupation of sovereign airspace in which, absent consent of the entity authorising the occupation, only aircraft of the enforcement forces may fly'.[6] The essence of a NFZ in UNSC practice, consequently, is that it is declared over sovereign airspace (ie the airspace above all or part of the landmass and territorial sea of the state of concern), purports to exclude certain classes of aircraft from that airspace, and is enforceable by UNSC-authorized or sanctioned forces from both within and outside that airspace.

To date, UNSC practice in relation to NFZs is essentially limited to three sets of NFZs: in Iraqi airspace (PROVIDE COMFORT/NORTHERN WATCH and SOUTHERN WATCH); in the airspace of Bosnia and Herzegovina (DENY FLIGHT); and in Libyan airspace (UNIFIED PROTECTOR, once it evolved into a single North Atlantic Treaty Organization (NATO) operation). The UNSC-mandated International Security Assistance Force (ISAF) operation in Afghanistan also exerts some regulatory and exclusory control over Afghan airspace, but this measure is not generally referred to in terms of a UNSC-mandated NFZ—it is conceptualized almost exclusively in terms of airspace controls routinely permissible under LOAC and also as consented to by the government of Afghanistan. As such, it does not presage any requirement for a specific UNSC head of authorization in relation to a NFZ.

B. Iraq NFZs

The NFZ declared in northern Iraq was, as Schmitt observes, 'a product of the way the Gulf War [of 1991] ended'.[7] As a component of the ceasefire, Iraqi military

[5] Timothy P. McIlmail, 'No-Fly Zones: The Imposition and Enforcement of Air Exclusion Regimes over Bosnia and Iraq' (1995) 17 *Loyola LA International and Comparative Law Journal* 35, 36.

[6] Schmitt notes that use of the term 'occupation' in this sense does not necessarily presage 'occupation' in terms of LOAC: Michael N. Schmitt, 'Clipped Wings: Effective and Legal No-Fly Zone Rules of Engagement' (1998) 20 *Loyola LA International and Comparative Law Journal* 727, 729. This is similar to the UN Charter Art 41 reference to the UNSC's power to 'blockade'—another term of art in LOAC which needs to be distinguished from the UN Charter's usage of the term in a more general sense.

[7] Schmitt, 'Clipped Wings', 733.

aircraft—with the exception of helicopters in certain areas—were prohibited from flying in Iraqi airspace.[8] As Kurdish and Shia populations rebelled in northern and southern Iraq respectively, the Iraqi regime used helicopters to suppress the rebels and target associated populations. In UNSC Resolution 688, the UNSC expressed its grave concern at this repression and called upon Iraq to facilitate humanitarian relief.[9] By 10 April 1991 a NFZ was established (excluding all Iraqi aircraft, including helicopters, unless they had received prior authorization), relief flights had commenced, and a force comprising elements from 13 states entered northern Iraq. The NFZ was enforced with Turkish, UK, US, and (initially) French aircraft. By August 1991, the situation in the north was further complicated by conflict between two Kurdish factions, one of which was supported by the Iraqi regime. Although singling out the Kurdish areas in northern Iraq for specific humanitarian assistance, the general tenor of Resolution 688 was equally applicable to the Shia in southern Iraq. However, it was not until August 1992 that the UK, the US, and France implemented and enforced a NFZ over southern Iraq.[10]

For those who consider the northern Iraq NFZ lawful, its UNSC authority was derived implicitly, as opposed to expressly, from the interaction between Resolution 688 (demanding an end to repression and mandating humanitarian assistance, but not explicitly authorizing a NFZ), interpretations of the post-conflict UNSC resolutions permitting further coalition force actions where ceasefire conditions were not observed, and lingering Chapter VII authorizations attendant upon the general Iraq–Kuwait UNSC resolutions and the ceasefire UNSC resolutions (most specifically Resolutions 678 and 687).[11] This provenance is not without controversy. On one view, these zones were effectively enforced, but illegally imposed.[12] On another, the northern Iraq NFZ was appropriately authorized, but the southern NFZ's authority was perhaps more tenuous. Further, given the absence of an explicit Resolution 688 linkage, its extension in September 1996 (from latitude 32N to 33N) was even more problematic than its establishment.[13] The UN itself did not condemn the NFZs, but its public statements upon their legality are equivocal at best—for example (as Boileau notes), a formal UN reference to a group of states enforcing the NFZs as acting

[8] See generally SC Res 686 on Iraq–Kuwait (2 Mar 1991), operative para 3: 'Also demands that Iraq (a) cease hostile or provocative actions by its forces against all Member States, including missile attacks and flights of combat aircraft…'

[9] SC Res 688 on Iraq (5 Apr 1991), operative paras 1 and 4 (noting the general repression of, and requirement for humanitarian assistance for, the population in general, but with specific reference to the Kurdish population).

[10] See generally Schmitt, 'Clipped Wings'; McIlmail, 'No-Fly Zones'; Alain Boileau, 'To the Suburbs of Baghdad: Clinton's Extension of the Southern Iraqi No-Fly Zone' (1997) 3 *ILSA Journal of International and Comparative Law* 875; Alan D. Surchin, 'Terror and the Law: The Unilateral Use of Force and the June 1993 Bombing of Baghdad' (1995) 5 *Duke Journal or Comparative and International Law* 457.

[11] The debate focusing on almost identical legal issues and interpretations in the lead-up to renewed action in 2003 was not, it will be evident, fundamentally unique.

[12] See generally: McIlmail, 'No-Fly Zones'; Surchin, 'Terror and the Law'.

[13] See generally: Schmitt, 'Clipped Wings'; Boileau, 'To the Suburbs of Baghdad'.

'in what they stated was an effort to enforce and monitor compliance with resolution 688'.[14] Perhaps the best that might be said is that there remains significant debate as to the existence of a clear UNSC authority for both Iraq NFZs.

There is also debate as to the precise nature of the legal regime actually governing enforcement of the Iraq NFZs. Schmitt—who was a legal adviser to the Iraq NFZ operations—characterizes the applicable law generally in terms of self-defence and mandate enforcement.[15] McIlmail, on the other hand, refers extensively to the aerial components of LOAC in his assessment of *jus in bello* conduct in support of NFZ enforcement.[16] Given the uncertainty surrounding the parent UNSC authority for these NFZs, this debate is very difficult to settle—claims to non-LOAC or LOAC-based use of force rights in enforcement will always be at the mercy of overarching uncertainty as to the preliminary authority and mandate of the NFZs. Thus, although a seminal instance of UNSC NFZ enforcement in terms of actual operational practice, the Iraq NFZs—whilst significantly more effective in implementation than the next instance (Bosnia)—are of problematic provenance in terms of drawing lessons for 'UNSC-authorised' NFZ practice with respect to use of force.

c. Bosnia and Herzegovina NFZ

Whilst debate as to the provenance of the Iraq NFZs complicates their status as a UNSC precedent, there is no debate as to the clear UNSC-mandated status of the Bosnia and Herzegovina NFZ. In the face of routine flouting of an earlier flight ban, Resolution 781 formalized this flight ban, but limited enforcement measures to tracking and monitoring (as opposed to use of force). In March 1993, Resolution 816 implemented a NFZ under Chapter VII and granted the UN force the 'all necessary measures' authority it required to use force in implementing the NFZ.[17] Authority and responsibility for enforcing the NFZ then paralleled the evolution of UN operations in the Federal Republic of Yugoslavia (FRY), passing through the United Nations Protection Force (UNPROFOR), NATO, the Implementation Force (IFOR), and the Stabilization Force (SFOR).

In terms of scope, the Bosnia NFZ was in practice directed at military flights in Bosnian airspace. It remains an elusive precedent, however, for whilst the *jus ad bellum* authority permitting use of force was ironclad, the *jus in bello* authorizations detailing how, when, and at what level of lethality that force could be used remain problematic. First, questions as to precisely which sorts of military flights can be targeted—only combat capable aircraft? intelligence and surveillance flights? logistics support flights?—will always need to be resolved on an operation-by-operation/

[14] Boileau, 'To the Suburbs of Baghdad', 881, quoting from UN and the Iraq–Kuwait Conflict 1990–1996, S/23295.

[15] Schmitt, 'Clipped Wings', 753–66. [16] McIlmail, 'No-Fly Zones', 71–80.

[17] SC Res 816 on Bosnia and Herzegovina (31 Mar 1993), operative para 4.

case-by-case basis. Additionally, any implementation of a NFZ must necessarily take account of suppression of ground-based anti-aircraft capabilities which can threaten the NFZ-enforcing force's own aircraft and freedom of manoeuvre within the NFZ. Such assessments will always need to consider the nature of the threats the NFZ is designed to neutralize, the mandated tasks the NFZ is anticipated to support, and the legal context of the NFZ-enforcer's engagement—primarily in terms of whether the force is a UNSC-sanctioned belligerent with access to LOAC authorizations such as attack, or as a UNSC-mandated stabilization agent which is not a belligerent in the armed conflict, and thus has no de jure access to LOAC authorizations.

In this sense, the Bosnia NFZ is a lacklustre use of force precedent, precisely because of such confusions. At first glance, it appears generally safe to assert that successive Bosnia NFZ enforcement agents understood their general role to be that of stabilization and mitigation, not as a belligerent party to the armed conflict. This is a threshold issue because it removes from the outset any de jure access to LOAC authorizations in enforcing the NFZ. Thus, use of force in enforcing the Bosnia NFZ has to be assessed against, and understood in terms of, non-LOAC authorizations and law. At this point, however, we return to uncertainty, for there are several types of 'use of force' which must be considered. The first is use of force in self-defence. There is little argument that the UNSC authorized or sanctioned force could use force against delinquent military aircraft, in self-defence of force aircraft enforcing the NFZ, force units on the ground, and civilians. This is well encapsulated in Schmitt's analysis of self-defence in NFZ enforcement in terms of a NFZ-enforcing aircraft being illuminated by a missile guidance radar from a ground installation: Under 'self-defence' (as generally understood), the aircraft has an immediate option to neutralize that threat with force, or to exit the radar's envelope or its associated missiles' range. But at that point the hostile act/hostile intent is ended. There is no:

> 'self-defence' option for the aircraft to exit the area, plan an attack, and then return some time later to destroy the ground threat (unless it again lights the aircraft up, thus creating a new hostile intent/hostile act and, consequently, an immediate self-defence situation).[18]

That the UN conceived of this form of 'use of force' as a distinct sub-category in the Bosnia and Herzegovina operation appears clear from the operational distinction the UN drew between 'close air support' for situations of self-defence, and 'air strikes' for other situations.[19] Use of force in self-defence in this sense is not geographically

[18] Schmitt, 'Clipped Wings', 761–2.

[19] See Report of the Secretary-General pursuant to General Assembly Resolution 53/35: The fall of Srebrenica, A/54/549 (15 Nov 1999), paras 185–9, 277–96, 480–3; see eg the confusion inherent in the UNSC's mixing of self-defence and mandate enforcement in operative paras 5, 9, and 10 of SC Res 836 on Bosnia and Herzegovina (4 June 1993), and the attempt to differentiate 'air strikes' (for enforcement) and 'close air support' (for self-defence) in Letter from the Secretary-General to the President of the UNSC, S/1994/94 (28 Jan 1994).

constrained by the NFZ—if an enforcing force aircraft were to encounter (for example) a Serb military aircraft outside the NFZ, and that aircraft engaged in a hostile act or demonstrated hostile intent against the UNSC-authorized aircraft, there is absolutely no doubt that the latter could engage the former in self-defence regardless of the fact that the event was taking place outside the NFZ. The two issues are not legally linked—self-defence as a legal right exists and operates to the same extent both inside and outside the NFZ. Where the NFZ may serve a self-defence purpose it is only in the form of an additional self-defence trigger, in that crossing into a lawful, notified, and well-publicized NFZ is an additional hostile-intent indicator which is not readily available in other airspace.

However, the Bosnia NFZ also raises a further legal conundrum with respect to use of force in NFZ enforcement outside LOAC—namely, the degree to which lethal force can be used to enforce a NFZ where there is no imminent threat such as to create a 'self-defence' situation. In short, the question is: what level of force can be employed to achieve the mandate aims (eg ensuring access for humanitarian assistance or reducing potential air threats to 'safe areas') which the NFZ was established to support? Put another way, what level of force is permissible to enforce the NFZ? This legal conundrum is particularly acute in relation to NFZ enforcement against delinquent aircraft, in that once standard signalling and escalation of force procedures (proximity, waggling of wings, radio interrogations, and so on) are exhausted, the options tend to narrow to two—continue to monitor, or shoot it down and almost certainly kill the occupant(s) and potentially others on the ground. This conundrum is not generally as sharp in escalation of force procedures against vessels and vehicles where targeted disabling fire can be a less than lethal option. I submit that a Chapter VII 'all necessary means' authorization does *not* provide a general authority to use lethal force solely to 'implement' or 'enforce' the mandate, unless the UNSC-sanctioned or authorized force is acting in immediate individual or unit self-defence or defence of others, or is a belligerent party in the conflict and is thus able to access LOAC authorizations. This is a highly contentious issue with respect to NFZs precisely because—in relation to delinquent aircraft—there is no readily available middle ground in terms of use of force options between warnings and lethal force. The consequence is that NFZ enforcement is faced with a particularly acute, but not insurmountable, credibility problem in that where a delinquent military aircraft continues its transit through a NFZ, but in a non-threatening manner, the only legal option is to continue to escort it through until it exits the NFZ. This is not as parlous a problem as it appears, for the option of lethal force in self-defence is always available in the background. Should a delinquent aircraft—which has been subject to the full range of non-lethal warning and escalation of force measures—deviate from its non-threatening transit such that it commits a hostile act or demonstrates hostile intent against forces or others on the ground, or against the monitoring aircraft, then lethal force may be justified in self-defence.

D. Libya NFZ

The 2011 'unprecedentedly robust'[20] Libya NFZ was expressly established by the UNSC through a Chapter VII 'all necessary means' authorization, and in this sense shares an unimpeachable *jus ad bellum* authority with the Bosnia NFZ.[21] Beyond this point, however, the Libya NFZ does not necessarily clarify any of the problems associated with understanding use of force options arising out of the Bosnia NFZ. This is because the Libya NFZ in many respects returns us to the broader confusion evident in the Iraq NFZs (leaving aside their underpinning legality) as regards the *jus in bello* of use of force within the NFZ being based in LOAC authorizations, or in non-LOAC-based mandate-enforcement and self-defence.

The Libya NFZ, established in Resolution 1973, was clearly focused on protection of civilians, and (via its caveats) was targeted at (essentially) Libyan military aircraft.[22] At this level, it is uncontroversial—protecting civilians in situations such as the Libya conflict is clearly within UNSC competence, and establishing a NFZ in relation to military aircraft which threaten those civilians is clearly a legitimate UNSC response enjoying at least one clear precedent. The problem, however, is the confusion or obfuscation which surrounds the precise legal characterization of individual NFZ-enforcement tasks, and protection of civilian tasks. The first issue is whether the UNSC-sanctioned NATO force implementing the NFZ was a party to the armed conflict between Libyan government forces and rebel groups. NATO statements were equivocal, and vacillate between explaining that Libyan government installations and forces were prosecuted from the air as 'legitimate military targets', or 'in self-defence'.[23] Clearly, self-defence

[20] Michael Schmitt, 'Wings over Libya: The No-Fly Zone in Legal Perspective' (2011) 36 *Yale Journal of International Law Online* 45, 46, available at <http://the-beacon.info/blog/wp-content/uploads/2011/05/wings-over-libya.pdf>.

[21] SC Res 1973 on Libya (17 Mar 2011), operative paras 4, 6–9; as adjusted by SC Res 2009 on Libya (16 Sept 2011), operative paras 20–1.

[22] The SC Res 1973 NFZ is stated to apply to 'all flights' in the airspace of Libya, but then grants a standing approval for 'humanitarian' flights (broadly defined to include extracting third party nationals from the conflict), other flights 'deemed necessary by States acting under the authorisation conferred in paragraph 8 to be for the benefit of the Libyan people' (operative para 7), flights that are targeted at the protection of civilians (operative para 4), and flights otherwise approved under the approval mechanisms established in operative paras 8–9.

[23] eg 'By maintaining a high operational tempo and carrying out precision strikes against *legitimate military targets*, we have seriously degraded the ability of the Qadhafi regime to *attack civilians* and relieved the pressure on civilian populated areas such as Misratah' (NATO, 'Statement on Libya Following the Working Lunch of NATO Ministers of Defence with non-NATO Contributors to Operation Unified Protector', 8 June 2011, available at <http://www.nato.int/cps/en/natolive/news_75177.htm>); compared with (25 Mar 2011) '[NATO Spokesman]: ... What I am saying is if you are threatened by say a surface to air missile system that's stopping you enforcing the NFZ, *you have the right of self defence ... The NFZ does not give you the right to just go if you like, as you put it, bomb targets on the ground ...*', (<http://www.nato.int/cps/en/natolive/opinions_71781.htm>); (26 July 2011) 'We are ... acting where it is required to prevent attacks on civilians or to prevent a build-up of military capabilities that could stop humanitarian aid, for example. *So we are not a party in that conflict, and we have no intent to be*', (<http://www.nato.int/cps/en/natolive/opinions_76680.htm>)—emphasis added.

remains a legal option for forces engaged in armed conflict, but when those forces are engaging 'the adversary' the proper criterion against which to assess use of force is LOAC, not the law of self-defence. As Additional Protocol I makes clear, even when a combatant force takes defensive action against an attack by the adversary, its conduct is still governed by LOAC 'attack' rules.[24] If NATO were engaged as a belligerent, and its attacks on Libyan targets were thus governed by LOAC, then the existence of a specific authority to enforce the NFZ is relatively inconsequential in terms of providing authority for the actions of NATO aircraft against both legitimate military targets on the ground and in the air. Schmitt, discussing the Libyan NFZ, finds it clear that the fact '[t]hat a no-fly zone may be established pursuant to a Security Council mandate has no effect on the applicability of the law of armed conflict'[25]—the two issues are subject to different legal thresholds.

This issue is closely linked to the second complication in distilling clear use of force guidance from the Libya NFZ—the argument that the NFZ was exploited for other purposes.[26] The essence of this argument is that the UNSC-mandated NFZ was narrowly concerned with aerial threats to civilians in Libya, but that it was used to justify much more wide-scale operations against Libyan government forces on the ground. If UNSC-sanctioned NATO forces operating to enforce the mandate were in fact belligerents in the armed conflict (which is my view) then in many respects the NFZ authorization is irrelevant to the question, for once approved to intervene, it was LOAC authorizations which were utilized.[27] In these terms, conducting attacks against Libyan government forces and other legitimate military targets was clearly lawful *jus in bello*; the broader question is whether this was what the UNSC was actually authorizing the NATO force to do.

E. Conclusions as to UNSC Use of Force Practice

1. *Is the law governing the zone LOAC- or non-LOAC-based?*

Practice on use of force in relation to UNSC-authorized NFZs is mixed, and coherence between the two or three sets of precedents (depending upon one's view of the Iraq NFZs) is elusive. Whilst the context of the Bosnia NFZ clearly evidenced that the UNSC-sanctioned enforcing force was not a belligerent in the armed conflict attending the establishment of the NFZ, it is less clear that this

[24] Additional Protocol I of 1977 to the Geneva Conventions of 1949, Art 49(1).

[25] Schmitt, 'Wings over Libya', 50.

[26] See eg Letter dated 9 November from the Permanent Representative of Brazil to the United Nations addressed to the Secretary-General, A/66/551–S/2011/701, para 11, which (although relating to the issue of 'responsibility while protecting') has been broadly understood as a critique of NATO's use of force in implementing the 2011 Libya mandate.

[27] The corollary at sea is the furore over the 1982 sinking of the Argentinian warship *General Belgrano* outside the Falkland Islands TEZ—an entirely legitimate act under LOAC regardless of the existence of that TEZ.

was the case with respect to the Libya NFZ. What can be said is that UNSC NFZs (including the contested Iraq NFZs) have in practice focused upon military aircraft and ground-based military anti-aircraft capabilities inside or proximate to the NFZ. In that sense, UNSC NFZ practice is consistently limited to concern with military capabilities—making it quite distinct from UNSC MEZ practice, which focuses much more broadly upon delinquency in non-military (primarily merchant) vessels.

2. *For UNSC non-LOAC-based NFZs, is the law on use of force inside the zone fundamentally the same as the law on use of force applying outside the zone?*

As UNSC NFZ practice appears to be concerned with military capabilities, there is no indication—nor any reason—to assume that civil air traffic which breached a UNSC NFZ should or would be treated by the NFZ-enforcement force other than in accordance with Article 3bis of the Chicago Convention. This rule—civilian aircraft should only ever be shot down as a last resort in grave self-defence situations—is widely considered to be customary international law, including by the UNSC.[28] Consequently, one's position on the trumping power of Article 103 of the UN Charter, and its effect (if any) in relation to customary international law, is central to interpreting the *legality* of such an action. However, shooting down a delinquent civilian aircraft which enters a UNSC NFZ on the basis of 'mandate enforcement' would be a radical act, and would indeed represent a distinct challenge to the coherence of the law on use of force within and without the NFZ. I suspect that should such an incident ever occur it would only ever arise in a hostile act or hostile intent scenario, and would thus be understood in terms of the legally safer justification of self-defence, rather than a use of lethal force for mandate enforcement. It is important to note, however, that this is a highly contentious question upon which there is little practice. Views will inevitably differ: Schmitt, for example, argues that:

> However, enforcement of a Security Council-authorized no-fly zone applying to all aircraft, such as that over Libya, necessarily alters the equation. A civilian aircraft violating a no-fly zone forfeits its civilian status and becomes a 'military objective,' because it is making an 'effective contribution to military action' and its 'destruction, capture or neutralization, in the circumstances ruling at the time, offers a definite military advantage' to the states enforcing the no-fly zone. Were this not the case, the establishment of a no-fly zone prohibiting all flights would be meaningless.[29]

[28] See eg SC Res 1067 on the shooting down of two civil aircraft on 24 February 1996 (26 July 1996)—concerning the shooting down of two US civil aircraft by the Cuban Air Force, resulting in four deaths—operative para 6: 'Condemns the use of weapons against civil aircraft in flight *as being incompatible with elementary considerations of humanity, the rules of customary international law as codified in article 3 bis of the Chicago Convention*, and the standards and recommended practices set out in the annexes of the Convention . . .' (emphasis added).

[29] Schmitt, 'Wings over Libya', 51.

3. *Has the UNSC actually altered the law normally applicable in the airspace enclosed by the zone?*

When imposing a NFZ in sovereign airspace (or, indeed, in international airspace) as a Chapter VII 'all necessary means' measure, the UNSC clearly alters the law normally applicable in the airspace enclosed by the NFZ. As McIlmail notes, NFZs effectively 'deprive [a] state … of a large measure of its territorial sovereignty'.[30] Although there is no practice on point, it follows that the UNSC's imposition of a NFZ in international airspace could also lawfully alter the routine airspace rights normally applicable in the enclosed area.

IV. UNSC-Endorsed or Mandated Maritime Exclusion Zones

A. General Description

There is no settled general legal definition of a 'MEZ'. The start point is to note a general definition of 'maritime operational zone' and to refine the concept by reference to this parent context. The US Naval War College's 2006 publication *Maritime Operational Zones* asserts that such zones comprise 'designated ocean areas and superjacent airspace in which a nation [or the UNSC] purports to restrict the freedom of navigation and/or overflight of other users or otherwise impact the exercise of those freedoms'.[31] Another related description is that for 'exclusion zone' in the International Institute of Humanitarian Law's *Rules of Engagement Handbook*: 'A zone established by a sanctioning body to prohibit specific activities in a specific geographic area'.[32] Historically, terms such as cordon sanitaire, quarantine, warning zone,[33]

[30] McIlmail, 'No-Fly Zones', 36.

[31] Dennis Mandsager, 'Foreword' in Jaques, *Maritime Operational Zones*, xiii.

[32] Alan Cole et al, *Rules of Engagement Handbook* (San Remo: International Institute of Humanitarian Law, 2009), 82.

[33] See generally, Henriques, 'Zones in Crisis Conditions' in Jaques, *Maritime Operational Zones*; Henriques has described a non-LOAC-based 'warning zone' as 'an identified area of the ocean in which a State is conducting or intends to conduct lawful activities which might pose a hazard to or interfere with other use of the oceans' (at 2-1). Whilst there is considerable debate about the lawfulness or otherwise of such zones, advocates do not in general assert that the mere declaration of a warning zone actually generates or enlivens a different law applicable within the zone. At most, the legal effect of a warning zone is to offer a defined tripwire for assessing hostile intent: if a vessel ignores warnings and continues to close the unit, the order to engage is still only valid if it is an exercise of self-defence, informed by the hostile intent indicator of crossing the line and continuing to close in a heightened threat environment. There is no 'zone of death' argument available—the infringing vessel could not be engaged simply because it crossed the line.

security zone,[34] safety zone,[35] blockade zone,[36] and exclusion zone have been used with little distinction in terms of linking particular terms with differentiated powers. For the purposes of this analysis, a UNSC-authorized or sanctioned MEZ is conceived of as follows: a maritime area or zone in which the UNSC, or an agent acting under its authority or with its sanction, asserts a legal right to prohibit entry, or to regulate the conditions of entry, and to enforce that prohibition or those conditions by force as necessary.

There are, arguably, only two types of MEZ—LOAC MEZs and non-LOAC MEZs. The distinction between them is important on two levels. First, LOAC-based MEZs are centred upon the potential for use of offensive force (targeting; attack) in that certain conduct breaching the regulatory scope of a blockade zone, or a visit and search zone, creates a rebuttable LOAC-based right to attack the delinquent vessel.[37] Breaching a non-LOAC-based MEZ does not automatically enliven a right to use

[34] Some forms of 'security zone' are anticipated in UNCLOS—eg the right of the coastal state to temporarily suspend innocent passage through a part of its Territorial Sea, for security purposes, as long as it is not discriminatory amongst foreign vessels in either form or fact: Art 25. Some states also claim 'security zones' in areas analogous to the contiguous zone (where additional fiscal, immigration, sanitary, and customs powers coexist with the EEZ rights already available in the 12–24 nautical mile zone). Such claims are contentious, to say the least. See also Frederick C. Leiner, 'Maritime Security Zones: Prohibited Yet Perpetuated' (1984) 24 *Virginia Journal of International Law* 967—this analysis focuses more narrowly upon security zones that are contiguous to the territorial seas of the states asserting them. On use of maritime warning and exclusion zones during the Iran/Iraq 'Tanker War' and the 1990–1 Gulf War, see (inter alia) John H. McNeill, 'Neutral Rights and Maritime Sanctions: The Effects of Two Gulf Wars' (1991) 31 *Virginia Journal of International Law* 631; Ross Leckow, 'The Iran–Iraq Conflict in the Gulf: The Law of War Zones' (1988) 37 *International and Comparative Law Quarterly* 629; Lois E. Fielding, 'Maritime Interception: Centrepiece of Economic Sanctions in the New World Order' (1993) 53 *Louisiana Law Review* 1191; Maxwell Jenkins, 'Air Attacks on Neutral Shipping in the Persian Gulf: The Legality of the Iraqi Exclusion Zone and Iranian Reprisals' (1985) 8 *Boston College International and Comparative Law Review* 517; George K. Walker, 'The Tanker War 1980–1988: Law and Policy' (2000) *International Law Studies* 74.

[35] eg the 500-yard safety zone coastal states may assert around an installation in their EEZ or over their continental shelf: See UNCLOS, Art 60(5) via Art 80.

[36] Most recently by Israel in relation to the Gaza Strip, as was at issue in relation to the *Mavi Marmara* incident. See: 'Report of the Secretary-General's Panel of Inquiry on the 31 May 2010 Flotilla Incident' (Palmer Report), July 2011; 'The Public Commission to Examine the Maritime Incident of 31 May 2010: Report Part I' (Turkel Report), released 23 Jan 2011, available at <http://www.turkel-committee.gov.il/files/wordocs//8707200211english.pdf>; 'Report on the Israeli attack on the humanitarian aid convoy to Gaza on 31 May 2010' (Turkish National Commission of Inquiry), Feb 2011.

[37] Louise Doswald-Beck (ed), *San Remo Manual on International Law Applicable to Armed Conflicts at Sea* (Cambridge: International Institute of Humanitarian Law/Cambridge University Press, 1995), rule 98 (blockade), rule 60(e) (activities which may render enemy merchant vessels military objectives, and thus liable to attack), and rule 67(a) (neutral merchant vessels may not be attacked unless believed on reasonable grounds to be, inter alia, carrying contraband, and, after prior warning, intentionally and clearly refuse to stop or resist visit, search, or capture). Note, however, that a third LOAC-based authority—the power to control (including in some cases to exclude) neutral vessels and aircraft 'in the immediate vicinity of naval operations' (rule 108) does not necessarily carry with it a rebuttable presumption for attack. In fact, however, the actual operational effect can be the same, for a neutral vessel which ignores repeated warnings to depart the immediate area of operations may then be reassessed in terms of belligerent conduct (under LOAC) or hostile intent (as a trigger for unit self-defence).

offensive force, however—if there is no armed conflict then LOAC does not apply, and the attack rules are not available. This does not mean that no force can be used in such zones—clearly force in individual and unit self-defence is always available where the preconditions that enliven this right are manifest. Similarly, non-lethal force in a 'constabulary' or 'law enforcement' context is also routinely available to support stopping, boarding, searching, detaining, and diverting vessels which transgress the regulatory purpose of a lawful MEZ.

B. Sanctions Enforcement Generally

Within this broader LOAC/non-LOAC bivalency, there are three forms of MEZ which the UNSC has utilized in practice. The first is the zone associated with Chapter VII compulsory sanctions-enforcement operations, and is an 'exclusion' zone insofar as it supports discriminatory regulation—the exclusion of only a particular class of vessels (ie vessels carrying sanctioned cargoes) as opposed to all vessels generally. By this, I mean those sanctions regimes where the UNSC has used the necessary form of words to temporarily displace or alter the general international law regime applicable to boarding, searching, detaining, and diverting vessels on the high seas, and indeed in territorial seas. It is important to note, however, that not all Chapter VII sanctions regimes are of this nature. Some regimes—such as that established in response to the Democratic People's Republic of Korea (DPRK) nuclear test—avoid using the necessary phrases. The enforcement consequence is that use of force remains or becomes available only in each state's own ports and sovereign waters, on its own flagged vessels, and with flag state consent for all other shipping.[38]

In practice, consequently, it is only when the UNSC employs the form of words first utilized in Resolution 665 in relation to the Iraq–Kuwait sanctions regime, that it consciously and explicitly empowers mandated forces to conduct such operations without the need to gain flag state consent, even though the purpose of the operation is unrelated to Article 110 of the 1982 United Nations Convention on the Law of the Sea (UNCLOS) five routine exceptions to the requirement to seek flag state consent (the 'right of visit'),[39] or to any other (non-UN Charter) treaty-based waiver of the requirement to seek or confirm positive flag state consent.[40] The form of words used in Resolution 665 was:

Calls upon those member states cooperating with the government of Kuwait…to use such measures commensurate to the specific circumstances as may be necessary under the

[38] SC Res 1718 on Non-proliferation / Democratic People's Republic of Korea (14 Oct 2006), operative para 8(f).

[39] In relation to vessels suspected of being engaged in piracy, slave trading, unauthorized broadcasting, being without nationality, or despite the visible flag (or even no flag) the vessel is suspected of being of the same nationality as the warship engaging the right of visit.

[40] eg Agreement Between the Government of the United States of America and the Government of the Republic of the Marshall Islands Concerning Cooperation to Suppress the Proliferation of Weapons

authority of the Security Council to halt all inward and outward maritime shipping in order to inspect and verify their cargoes and destinations and to ensure strict implementation of the provisions related to such shipping laid down in resolution 661 (1990)...[41]

This phraseology has been repeated in subsequent UNSC maritime sanctions regimes—for example, in relation to the former Yugoslavia (see the following section), Haiti, and Sierra Leone.[42] Such sanctions regimes are buttressed by an actual—if not always specifically declared—MEZ to which entry is regulated by the terms of the UNSC mandate. In general, this regulation is narrow, specific, and discriminatory in that vessels not carrying or suspected of carrying sanctioned cargoes will generally be permitted to transit through the MEZ (often on the basis of a standing authority for vessels of certain classes to proceed). However, this power to regulate entry and grant standing approvals is always read in the context of the overarching power to enforce the sanctions regime, and thus it may be a precondition of entry that even non-suspect vessels undergo basic prior vetting—generally through radio interrogation and, if necessary, board and search where radio interrogation, or the vessel's conduct, generate suspicion as to its true cargo and/or intentions.

c. UNSC Non-LOAC-Based MEZs

Practice related to UNSC-approved MEZs that go beyond routine sanctions enforcement is very limited. In effect, there is only a single clear instance where the UNSC has gone one step beyond a sanctions enforcement regime—whereby shipping is permitted to pass through the designated zone as long as it has been checked, or it is not liable to the sanctions regime—to actually prohibiting entry into and transit through the relevant MEZ. This was the MEZ which the UNSC imposed in relation to the Territorial Sea of Serbia and Montenegro during the conflict in the former Yugoslavia.

Following the descent into widespread conflict as the FRY broke apart from September 1991, the UNSC implemented a general embargo on military equipment entering the FRY,[43] followed by a broader sanctions regime over FRY exports which states were called upon to implement within their territory and in relation to their

of Mass Destruction, Their Delivery Systems, and Related Materials by Sea 2004 (entered into force 24 Nov 2004); Art 4(3)(d) 'If there is no response from the Competent Authority of the requested Party within four hours of its acknowledgment of receipt of the request, the requesting Party will be deemed to have been authorized to board the suspect vessel for the purpose of inspecting the vessel's documents, questioning the persons on board, and searching the vessel to determine if it is engaged in proliferation by sea'—available at <http://www.state.gov/t/isn/trty/35237.htm>.

[41] SC Res 665 on Iraq–Kuwait (25 Aug 1990), operative para 1.

[42] See eg SC Res 875 on Haiti (16 Oct 1993), operative para 1; SC Res 1132 on Sierra Leone (8 Oct 1997), operative paras 6 and 8.

[43] SC Res 713 on the Socialist Federal Republic of Yugoslavia (25 Sept 1991), operative para 6; SC Res 724 on the Socialist Federal Republic of Yugoslavia (15 Dec 1991), operative para 5.

flagged vessels.[44] On 16 November 1992, the UNSC further expanded the sanctions regime by reference to specified prohibited imports into the FRY and transformed its enforcement by reference to the form of words underpinning the Resolution 665 Iraq–Kuwait authorization.[45] In April 1993, Resolution 820 further expanded the sanctions regime to cover 'all commodities and products' being imported into or exported from the FRY, with the exception of specified humanitarian supplies.[46]

What sets the UNSC's FRY sanctions MEZ—and, indeed, Resolution 820—apart from the general course of UNSC non-LOAC-based MEZs in support of sanctions enforcement is that Resolution 820 transformed a *regulated* entry MEZ into a *prohibited* entry MEZ in a portion of the maritime area of operations—the Serbia and Montenegro Territorial Sea. Prior to Resolution 820, commercial traffic which indicated it was merely transiting through this Territorial Sea was permitted to proceed, whilst traffic reporting (or suspected to have as its actual aim) an intention to enter a Serbia and Montenegro port was subject to board and search in line with the sanctions regime. The effect of Resolution 820, however, was to prohibit even non-Serbia and Montenegro destined commercial traffic from transiting this area, unless it had received prior sanctions committee permission, or was facing a situation or *force majeure*.[47] This prohibitive (as opposed to more permissively regulatory) form of UNSC non-LOAC-based MEZ is evidence that declaring and enforcing such a MEZ is certainly within the UNSC's Chapter VII powers.

D. UNSC LOAC-Based MEZs

It is not routine for UNSC-authorized forces to descend into the arena as belligerents in an armed conflict. In general, UNSC-authorized forces stand apart from the belligerents and attempt to act as a stabilization force in the midst of the armed conflict, whilst not being a party to that armed conflict. UNPROFOR is one example: the parties to the armed conflict were Serb, Croat, and Bosniac states/entities; the UN force was not a party to the armed conflict and thus did not have access, de jure, to LOAC authorizations.[48] On occasion, however, the UNSC effectively authorizes a force to engage as a party in the armed conflict (eg ISAF in Afghanistan[49]) or the UN force ends up as a party through circumstance (eg the United Nations Operation in the Congo (ONUC)[50] and perhaps—very temporarily—the United Nations Operation

[44] SC Res 757 on Bosnia and Herzegovina (30 May 1992), operative para 4.

[45] SC Res 787 on Bosnia and Herzegovina (16 Nov 1992), operative paras 9 (expanded sanctions regime) and 12 (crossing the 'Iraq–Kuwait line' in terms of enforcement authority).

[46] SC Res 820 on Bosnia and Herzegovina (17 Apr 1993), section B.

[47] SC Res 820 on Bosnia and Herzegovina (17 Apr 1993), operative paras 28–9.

[48] Hence the previously noted tortuous 'mandate enforcement' and 'self-defence' language used in, inter alia, SC Res 836 on Bosnia and Herzegovina (4 June 1993).

[49] eg SC Res 1510 on Afghanistan (13 Oct 2003), operative paras 1–2.

[50] See generally, Findlay, *Use of Force in UN Peace Operations*, ch 3.

in Côte d'Ivoire (UNOCI) in 2011[51] or the Intervention Brigade in the Democratic Republic of the Congo under SC Res 2098 (2013)). In terms of the former, given that the Afghanistan conflict is not accompanied by any related armed conflict at sea, there has been no potential for a coexisting UNSC LOAC-based MEZ authorization. In terms of the latter, such instances have centred upon unanticipated and transient operations ashore and there has been little time, need, or opportunity to implement a relevant LOAC-based MEZ.

This leaves us with a single clear, but highly contentious, instance of an alleged use of a LOAC-based MEZ under the authority of a Chapter VII mandate (Iraq 2003), and a more recent incident of potential use which is obscured by continuing uncertainty as to the status of UNSC-authorized forces involved in the conflict (Libya 2011). I shall examine the Iraq context first. Leaving aside the *jus ad bellum* debate as to a claimed rejuvenation of the mandate attendant upon the initial ceasefire in 1991, there is no legal reason why a UNSC-mandated or authorized force cannot access LOAC-based MEZ powers in the same way and for the same reasons as UNSC-mandated or authorized forces ashore can access LOAC powers when they are a party to the armed conflict. In this sense, it is thus useful to briefly explore how this occurred in Iraq in 2003.

In essence, at the time of the invasion, there were two MEZ regimes in operation in the north Arabian Gulf. The first was the continuing sanctions-enforcement regime which had been underway since Resolution 665 in 1990.[52] The second was the belligerent right of visit and search claimed by coalition naval forces as an adjunct to the armed conflict against Iraq.[53] Each regime is governed by separate 'rules' in relation to use of force, and governs different 'scopes' in relation to infringing conduct. Thus, whilst the visit and search regime was available to deal with contraband (as defined in LOAC) and the option of attack was available in relation to certain vessels which breached the visit and search regime, this regime could not be readily applied to 'neutral' merchant shipping exiting Iraq. The coexisting UNSC sanctions regime, however, could be applied to shipping exiting Iraq (specifically in relation to the regulated cargoes), but the available options for use of force in enforcement did not extend to LOAC-based attack. The lesson, it is clear, is that whilst the UNSC may authorize a force to engage in LOAC-based operations whilst at the same time continuing to implement a pre-existing sanctions regime, it is vital—both legally and operationally—to be

[51] See eg 'Pro-Gbagbo forces attack on Ouatara's HQ', 10 Apr 2011, available at <http://www.thisdaylive.com/articles/pro-gbagbo-forces-attack-on-ouattaras-hq/89357/>; 'Côte d'Ivoire's UN Peacekeepers', *The Economist*, 10 June 2012, available at <http://www.economist.com/blogs/baobab/2012/06/c%C3%B4te-divoires-un-peacekeepers>.

[52] This sanctions regime continued in force—albeit with some amendments, from 1990–2003, and in more limited form after mid-2003—eg SC Res 1546 on Iraq (8 June 2004), operative para 21.

[53] See eg 'Special Warning 121 Persian Gulf' (20 Mar 2003) available in Jaques, *Maritime Operational Zones*, C59.

clear which regime is being utilized in any given situation, as the legal boundary between the regimes is not necessarily permeable. It would be a grave error—and unlawful—to assume that the coexistence of the regimes also authorized the transferral of powers between them. It would be legally questionable to assume that the UNSC had tacitly authorized use of LOAC attack rules in sanctions enforcement, or conversely that the visit and search regime could be used on exiting shipping in the same way that the sanctions regime could be so applied.

The second context is Libya in 2011. Although the tortuous mechanism of replacing an operative paragraph in Resolution 1970 (implementing a sanctions regime with limited enforcement mechanisms)[54] with a different operative paragraph from Resolution 1973 (implementing a fully enforceable sanctions regime)[55] is notable, the fundamental effect of Resolution 1973 was to institute a compulsory 'Iraq–Kuwait' style MEZ sanctions regime. The question raised by the Libyan maritime sanctions regime, however, is whether it was underpinned only by a non-LOAC-based UNSC-approved MEZ—in the same way as the FRY regime was—or whether it provides a second (more defensible) example of a UNSC-approved LOAC-based MEZ. It is clear that NATO maritime forces were engaged in a 'standard' UNSC sanctions-enforcement operation, and that the MEZ reflected this authority: 'NATO maritime assets stopped and searched any vessel they suspected of carrying arms, related materials or mercenaries to or from Libya'; 'By the end of the operation, NATO had conducted over 3,000 hailings at sea and almost 300 boardings for inspection, with 11 vessels denied transit to their next port of call'.[56] This is the public language of traditional Chapter VII 'all necessary means' sanctions enforcement with no LOAC overlay. Similarly, there was no LOAC-based Notice to Mariners or Special Warning of a nature similar to that promulgated in relation to operations against Iraq in 2003.[57] These tentative indications (at least until further details of the maritime operation emerge) tend towards the conclusion that NATO maritime forces involved in UNSC Libyan sanctions enforcement did not in fact rely upon LOAC-based MEZ authorizations (eg blockade or visit and search). At this stage, consequently, the Libyan MEZ operation is perhaps better viewed as yet another example of the Iraq 1990 and FRY non-LOAC-based

[54] SC Res 1970 on Peace and Security in Africa (26 Feb 2011), operative para 11.

[55] SC Res 1973 on Libya (17 Mar 2011), operative para 13. The sanctions regime was further adjusted by SC Res 2009 on Libya (16 Sep 2011), operative para 13. See generally, Martin D. Fink, 'UN-Mandated Maritime Arms Embargo Operations in Operation Unified Protector' (2011) 50 *Military Law and the Law of War Review* 237.

[56] 'NATO and Libya', available at <http://www.nato.int/cps/en/natolive/topics_71652.htm>.

[57] See eg NAVAREA III NAVWARN 395/11—'NATO is coordinating a maritime embargo operation in vicinity of LIBYA in accordance with UNITED NATIONS SECURITY COUNCIL RESOLUTIONS (UNSCR) 1970, 1973 and 2009', available at <http://www.shipping.nato.int/operations/UP/Pages/NavWarn.aspx>. NAVAREA III 445/2011 cancelled the NAVWARN on the Libyan maritime sanctions-enforcement operation in the Mediterranean Sea on 31 Oct 2011—available at <http://www.armada.mde.es/ArmadaPortal/page/Portal/ArmadaEspannola/ciencia_ihm_1/02_Productos Servicios--02_NAVAREAS>.

MEZ approach than as a more legitimate example of the Iraq 2003 joint LOAC and non-LOAC-based MEZ approach.

E. Conclusions as to UNSC Use of Force Practice

1. *Is the law governing the zone LOAC or non-LOAC-based?*

This threshold paradigmatic question is vital for understanding the law applicable in enforcing the MEZ once the UNSC has authorized its creation, or a UNSC-sanctioned force has created such a zone as a component of its operational plan to implement the mandate the UNSC has conferred upon it. UNSC practice with LOAC-based MEZs is very limited and is indirect in that it is not the UNSC itself which declares a LOAC-based blockade or visit and search regime—rather, these are operational options which the UNSC-sanctioned or mandated force may employ amongst its suite of use of force options where it is actually participating as a belligerent in the armed conflict. In most cases, the UNSC's clear preference is to employ MEZs of varying scope via the mechanism of non-LOAC-based sanctions-enforcement regimes. These MEZs are generally of limited regulatory discrimination (targeted at specific vessels and cargoes, leaving all other maritime traffic free to transit the MEZ), but there is at least one instance of UNSC practice supporting a more general exclusionary power.

2. *For UNSC non-LOAC-based MEZs, is the law on use of force inside the zone fundamentally the same as the law on use of force applying outside the zone?*

This question must always be assessed at two levels—use of non-lethal force, and use of lethal force. In terms of use of non-lethal force, the law applicable inside a Chapter VII 'all necessary means' MEZ does change in that the UNSC has created an authority to use maritime law enforcement powers in situations where they generally are only available on the basis of flag or coastal state consent. In a second sense, however, the applicable law does not change in that the permission for authorized forces to employ routine law enforcement levels of force to implement the sanctions—that is, use of force to halt, board, search, detain, seize, and divert—is linked to a mandate purpose, not necessarily a closely defined geographic zone. Unless expressly limited to a particular geographic zone by the UNSC, this authority is general in that it is not expressly tied to a specific area of ocean space. In practice, the forces mandated to implement the sanctions regime will generally do so only within a defined area—the MEZ—but this is a self-imposed operational limitation as opposed to a legal one. If the sanctions regime is not expressly geographically confined, then there is no legal reason that a UNSC-mandated force could not undertake a sanctions-related boarding and seizure in ocean space outside the declared operational zone. In this sense, the law inside the MEZ and outside the MEZ is the same.

The same is so in terms of lethal force. In general, lethal force is available to UNSC-mandated or sanctioned forces, which are not engaged as belligerents in an armed conflict, only in circumstances focusing upon individual, unit, and force self-defence or defence of others. In terms of use of lethal force, declaring a 'line in the water' does not create a new legal regime inside the zone where lethal force is available merely by virtue of the fact that a vessel has crossed that line. As with the MEZs declared around the Iraqi oil platforms in the aftermath of the 2003 conflict, the line in the water did not create a new authority to engage vessels that crossed that line with lethal force merely *because they crossed the line*. What these lines in the water actually did was to create a tripwire which could then act as a significant indicator of hostile intent, which could in turn support (in conjunction with other available information) a decision to employ lethal force in self-defence.

3. *For non-LOAC-based MEZs, has the UNSC actually altered the law normally applicable in the ocean space enclosed by the zone?*

The declaration of a UNSC-authorized and compulsory MEZ does indeed create a legal option for the UNSC to alter the law normally applicable in the ocean space enclosed by the zone. The establishment of such an exclusory MEZ in international waters clearly anticipates that the routinely applicable law is temporarily displaced to the extent of any inconsistency with the UNSC-mandated regime. Thus, the default setting on freedom of navigation encapsulated in customary international law and in Article 87 of UNCLOS (the 'High Seas freedoms') can be legally curtailed in the MEZ to the extent necessary for such an exclusory regime to be effectively implemented. Similarly, in the territorial sea, the routine right of innocent passage can also be displaced where this is implicit in the UNSC mandate. This was the case with the MEZ created in the Territorial Sea of Serbia and Montenegro by Resolution 820—an MEZ for which the default setting was a prohibition on entry unless authorized. The general sanctions regime MEZ default, however, is for 'entry as usual' except for certain classes of vessels, which are generally defined by their declared cargo and destination or suspicions as to actual cargo and intentions.

V. Conclusion

UNSC practice with respect to use of force in relation to NFZs and MEZs is mixed, and only partially coherent. In a *jus ad bellum* sense, it is clear that in utilizing its Chapter VII powers the UNSC can and does impose NFZs and MEZs in a variety of forms, albeit with practice on MEZs being both more regular and of broader scope. It is equally clear that in authorizing or acquiescing in the creation of NFZs and MEZs, the UNSC can and often does alter the legal regime within the zone in terms of both restricting or regulating entry and transit through the zone, and granting a general permission to authorized or mandated forces to use force in enforcing the purposes for which the zone is established. Beyond this point, however, as the NFZ or MEZ mandate is 'operationalized', there is significantly less coherence in practice. This is most evident in the variable interplay between legal contexts which governs each situation. One such context question is whether the zone is a LOAC or non-LOAC-based zone. In this regard, UNSC practice appears to endorse remaining silently acquiescent on the use of LOAC-based zones and their attendant authorizations, and this is nowhere more evident than in its practice in relation to NFZs. This is not inherently problematic, however, as LOAC authorizations draw their authority from a body of law that is not dependent upon the UNSC for its power, and such authorizations can and do coexist with related UNSC authorizations. However, the UNSC is much less reticent to give directions on the implementation and enforcement of non-LOAC-based exclusion zones—a logical and necessary requirement given that such zones may not rest upon any other authority than that of the UNSC. Another fundamental context question that is central to any analysis of UNSC NFZ and MEZ use of force practice—but which also contributes to the confusion still evident in this practice—is the issue of 'expanded' legal authorizations for use of lethal force for a mandate enforcement purpose that is linked neither to immediate individual self-defence or defence of others, nor to LOAC authorizations. Definitively describing or defining UNSC practice on use of *lethal* force in enforcing NFZs and MEZs will, however, remain an elusive task. Whilst debates as to the precise nature and legal authority of the UN's conception of 'self-defence', and the ambit of Chapter VII powers in relation to use of lethal force remain unresolved, tracing coherence within this disparate body of practice will continue to prove difficult.

CHAPTER 12

MILITARY SANCTIONS ENFORCEMENT IN THE ABSENCE OF EXPRESS AUTHORIZATION?

PENELOPE NEVILL*

I. Introduction

'Around 80 per cent of global trade by volume and over 70 per cent by value is carried by sea and is handled by ports worldwide; these shares are even higher in the case of most developing countries'.[1] Thus, whether we are talking about arms embargoes or measures aimed at countering proliferation of weapons of mass destruction (WMD) or trade and economic sanctions, enforcing sanctions to prevent the transport and delivery of such goods, by the use of force if necessary, primarily concerns action by navies or coastguards. Action at sea by state authorities to enforce

* Many thanks to my research assistant Majida Rasul, without whom this chapter would not have come together, and to Lieutenant Commander James Farrant of Her Majesty's Royal Navy for his helpful advice.

[1] United Nations Conference on Trade and Development (UNCTAD), Review of Maritime Transport 2012, UNCTAD/RMT/2012, available at <http://unctad.org/en/pages/PublicationWebflyer.aspx?publicationid=380>.

sanctions raises two key considerations. Is a 'use of force' in this context a 'use of force' in the Article 2(4) sense or in the police or law enforcement sense, or are these the same thing? And what are the legal bases for the use of force to enforce sanctions at sea?

The absence of express UN Security Council authorization might arise in various ways: a Council resolution imposing sanctions does not contain provisions for enforcement; a unilateral, non-UN sanctions regime is imposed by a state or regional organization; or a use of force falls outside the scope of the Council's authorization. The absence of Council authorization will not automatically render the use of force to enforce sanctions unlawful. An assessment of unlawfulness turns on the facts of the case: by whom is the force used or threatened; against whom; where; what is the level and kind of force used or threatened; and what is the legal basis of the enforcement action?

This chapter is structured as follows: Section II sets out the history and background to enforcement of sanctions at sea; Section III addresses the question of what constitutes a use of force in this context; and Section IV considers the legal bases for enforcement action.

II. History and Background to Forcible Measures at Sea

The sanctions regimes with which we are familiar today typically impose one or more of a range of measures, including embargoes on weapons and related technology, or trade in specified goods that are either used by the target state or non-state actor to fund armed conflicts or which, if cut off, might bring enough economic pressure to bear on the target to cause them to comply with their international obligations.[2] As such, sanctions are the descendants of various categories of state action recognized by the law of nations as it crystallized over the 19th century: the rights of belligerents against enemies and neutrals under the law of war to impose blockades and contraband of war measures[3] and, during relations of peace, the self-help

[2] eg the UN embargoes on the import of charcoal from Somalia, a significant revenue source for Al Shabaab and exacerbating the humanitarian crisis, imposed by Res 2036 (2012) (Preamble, p 3 and paras 22–3), the export of luxury goods to North Korea imposed by Res 1718 (2006) (para 8(a)(iii)), and the import of round logs and timber products and rough diamonds from Liberia (Res 1521 (2003), paras 6 and 10); the EU sanctions on the import and shipment of Iranian and Syrian oil and related contracts now contained in Council Regulation (EU) No 267/2012 (Iran) and Council Regulation (EU) No 36/2012 (Syria), in addition to an arms embargo and sanctions on other goods, including gold, precious metal, and diamonds.

[3] Kern Alexander, *Economic Sanctions: Law and Public Policy* (Basingstoke: Palgrave Macmillan, 2009), 9.

measures of retorsion, reprisal, intervention, and self-defence.[4] An understanding of the historical background to sanctions and their enforcement is key to an understanding of the evolution of Council and state practice concerning sanctions after 1945, the attendant legal debates, and the current position regarding the legal bases for military enforcement of sanctions and similar measures without Council authorization.

Under 19th-century international law, no legal basis was required for going to war. Rather, the law focused on regulating armed conflict, viewed as inevitable, through the law of war. The application of the law of war and (importantly for an understanding of this topic) the law of neutrality followed automatically upon the commencement of war.[5] The law of war entitled belligerent states to impose a blockade (the sealing off of an enemy state's ports preventing all shipping in and out[6]), and contraband measures falling short of a full blockade against cargoes of arms and goods carried by neutral shipping[7] which might be used in the enemy's war effort.[8] Blockade and contraband were enforced by naval action against enemy and neutral merchant vessels in accordance with the rules of war governing naval warfare (the *jus in bello*),[9] including: stopping, boarding and searching, or capture of merchant vessels on the high seas and in the waters of the enemy state;[10] the condemnation or destruction of cargos or vessels; or the forced rerouting to another port of

[4] J. L. Brierly, *The Law of Nations: An Introduction to the Law of Peace* (6th edn, New York: Oxford University Press, 1963), revised by Sir Humphrey Waldock, 397–408. See also, William Edward Hall, *Treatise on International Law* (3rd edn, Oxford: Clarendon Press, 1890), 265–93 and 364–73. It should be noted that the legal category of self-defence under this conception was a strictly limited right and much narrower than we understand it to be today: see Stephen C. Neff, *War and the Law of Nations: A General History* (Cambridge: Cambridge University Press, 2005) and Brierly, *The Law of Nations*, 405–7.

[5] With the development of the *jus ad bellum* in the 20th century, it was doubted whether that meant one could speak of a 'right' to resort to war: see eg Richard Baxter, 'So-Called "Unprivileged Belligerency": Spies, Guerrillas, and Saboteurs' (1951) 28 *British Yearbook of International Law* 323, 323–4; Christopher Greenwood, *Essays on War in International Law* (London: Cameron May, 2008), 58.

[6] See the Declaration Respecting Maritime Law (Declaration of Paris) 1856 in Adam Roberts and Richard Guelff, *Documents on the Laws of War* (3rd edn, Oxford: Oxford University Press, 2000), 47, incidentally the first major example of states legislating by way of treaty (Stephen C. Neff, 'A Short History of International Law', in Malcolm D. Evans (ed), *International Law* (3rd edn, Oxford: Oxford University Press, 2010), 3, 20).

[7] Enemy vessels and cargo being subject to capture.

[8] The 'absolute case' of 'contraband of war' was arms and ammunition. For an attempt to codify a list of absolute contraband, see the London Declaration Concerning the Laws of Naval War 1909 (Art 22). Additional articles had to be notified under a contraband list (Art 23). 'Dual use' or 'conditional contraband' items, ie those susceptible of use in peace as well as war, including food, foodstuffs for animals, gold and silver, and money, were subject to capture without notice (Art 24); again, the list of 'conditional contraband' could be extended by a published 'contraband list' (Art 25). The London Declaration sought to set out a comprehensive code covering blockade and contraband measures with a view to establishing an International Prize Court to hear appeals from domestic courts, but it was never ratified by any of its signatories.

[9] See the 1856 Paris Declaration Respecting Maritime Law in Roberts and Guelff, *Documents on the Laws of War*, 47.

[10] Measures on the high seas against vessels flagged to their own state fell within their jurisdiction as a matter of international law. Under English law, eg, trading with the enemy was prohibited.

destination. Belligerent rights of blockade and contraband thus allowed the exercise of extraterritorial jurisdiction over foreign-flagged vessels in the high seas and waters of the enemy state. The law of neutrality prohibited neutral states from, inter alia, moving troops or munitions or supplies across their territory or otherwise supporting any of the belligerents.[11] Neutral states were not, however, obliged to prevent their nationals from engaging in the export or transport of arms or other supplies that might be of use to an army or fleet on behalf of the belligerents, but if restrictions were introduced they had to be applied without discrimination as between belligerents.[12] The law of neutrality and rights of belligerents against neutral shipping also applied to a 'true' civil war, beyond rebellion or insurgency, where a state of belligerency was recognized.[13] The recognition of insurgency produced less wide-ranging legal effects and was, for that reason, more common in practice: neutral trading with the insurgents was not precluded and de jure governments could only close ports in areas under insurgent control by imposing an effective blockade.[14]

Outside a 'state of war', states might take 'measures falling short of war' which could entail the use of force:[15] retorsions, reprisals, intervention, and self-defence.[16] Reprisals were resorted to when a specific wrong had been committed, including the seizure and condemnation[17] of property belonging to the offending state or its subjects as compensation or to compel the state to grant redress (usually in respect of damage to the property or person of subjects of the state carrying out the reprisal), or the suspension of treaties (such as those concerning freedom of navigation and commerce).[18]

[11] Codified in Hague Convention (V) 1907, Respecting the Rights and Duties of Neutral Powers and Persons in Case of War on Land: Roberts and Guelff, *Documents on the Laws of War*, 87, Art 5; Convention (XIII) 1907, Concerning the Rights and Duties of Neutral Powers in Naval War, Roberts and Guelff, *Documents on the Laws of War*, 127, Arts 7–9.

[12] Arts 7, 9.

[13] Neff, *War and the Law of Nations*, 258–64. In state practice developed in the first half of the 19th century, recognition of belligerency marked a 'true' civil war from the lesser condition of insurgency, and entitled the belligerents to exercise rights against neutral shipping and required third states to observe the rules on neutrality.

[14] Neff, *War and the Law of Nations*, 268–72. Insurgency did not preclude the provision of assistance to the government of the state fighting the insurgency and recognition of insurgency did not entitle either side to visit and search foreign flagged vessels on the high seas and confiscate contraband (at 269). See also Robert Jennings and Arthur Watts (eds), *Oppenheim's International Law*, Vol I, Peace (9th edn, London: Longman, 1992), 161–9.

[15] Hall, *Treatise on International Law*, 364–73; Brierly, *The Law of Nations*, 399–402.

[16] As noted earlier (n 4), much more narrowly conceived than the doctrine of self-defence with which we are familiar today.

[17] Meaning confiscation and, subject to a holding of a (domestic) prize court, the transfer of property in the vessel or cargo.

[18] Hall explained in his 1890 edition that such acts were '*prima facie* acts of war; and that they can be done consistently with the maintenance of peace must be accounted for…by exceptional reasons…They are supposed to be used when an injury has been done, in the commission of which a state cannot get redress by purely amicable means and which is of scarcely sufficient magnitude to be a motive of immediate war…It of course remains true that reprisals are acts of war in fact, though not in intention, and that…the state affected determines for itself whether the relation of war is set up by them or not' (Hall, *Treatise on International Law*, 365).

The form of reprisal most commonly employed was the seizing of vessels of the target state lying in the ports of the state employing the reprisal or on the high seas, and the seizing of any public or private property belonging to the target state within the state making the reprisal 'not entrusted to the public faith'.[19] So-called 'pacific blockades', limited (for the most part) to property of the target state and its subjects,[20] were also deployed as reprisal measures short of war,[21] although some commentators doubted their legality at least as applied against vessels not belonging or flagged to the target state.[22] Even then, a pacific blockade might be treated as an act of war by the target state[23] or an arbitral tribunal.[24]

Merchant vessels might also be subject to similar forms of enforcement action (ie stop and search, condemnation, etc) in an entirely different context: the enforcement of domestic laws (for example customs or sanitary laws) within a state's internal waters, territorial sea, or on the high seas subject to the limits of international law (that is, against that state's own flagged vessels or consequent on a hot pursuit from the state's waters).[25] Extraterritorial jurisdiction might also be exercised against pirates and their vessels.[26]

The development over the 20th century of rules limiting states' freedom to go to war and use force (the *jus ad bellum*) and an institutional system of collective security raised fundamental questions about the rights of belligerents against neutral shipping and the rights and obligations of neutral states. The first attempt at collective sanction measures was Article 16(1) of the Covenant of the League of Nations, the so-called 'automatic sanctions' provision. Members of the League which resorted to war in breach of the Covenant committed an act of war against all the other members, which undertook to immediately sever all trade and financial relations and prohibit their nationals from trading with the covenant-breaking state or its nationals, and prevent trade between the covenant-breaking state and the nationals of any other state. The Council of the League could recommend 'what effective military, naval or air force the Members of the League shall severally contribute to the armed forces to be used to protect the covenants of the League'.[27] A 1921 supplementary

[19] Hall, *Treatise on International Law*, 366.

[20] See the Insitut de droit international, Déclaration concernant le blocus en dehors de l'état de guerre 1887.

[21] See the examples given by Hall, *Treatise on International Law*, 369–70. A pacific blockade might differ from a blockade under the law of war because only the ships and property of the target state and its subjects would be sequestered and ownership in the property would not be pass (ie it would not be 'condemned') unless and until a state of war was declared.

[22] Hall, *Treatise on International Law*, 371; Neff, *War and the Law of Nations*, 230–9.

[23] States subsequently agreed in the Second Hague Peace Conference of 1907 to forgo the use of armed force to enforce debts owed by another state to their nationals, unless the alleged debtor state refused to submit to arbitration (Hague Convention Respecting the Limitation of the Employment of Force for the Recovery of Contract Debts 1907, Art 1).

[24] Neff, *War and the Law of Nations*, 236.

[25] See further William C. Gilmore, 'Hot Pursuit', Chapter 41 in this volume.

[26] See further Douglas Guilfoyle, 'The Use of Force Against Pirates', Chapter 49 in this volume.

[27] Art 16(2). Art 17 applied for the application of equivalent economic sanctions and enforcement measures against non-member states which resorted to war against a member.

resolution of the League Assembly made it clear that economic sanctions might require the establishment of a naval blockade of the covenant-breaking state in 'special circumstances', and that the execution of the blockade operations might be entrusted to some members of the League. A naval blockade in support of economic sanctions under the Covenant was characterized, not as an act of 'war', but a pacific blockade;[28] that is, a collective forcible reprisal.[29]

As has been well documented, the flaw of the League system was that by focusing on the legal state of 'war', the Covenant left open various measures short of war,[30] which the UN Charter sought to remove by prohibiting all measures falling short of war as well as war.[31] Forcible reprisals, such as pacific blockades, were prohibited, as subsequently expressly affirmed in the Declaration on Friendly Relations 1970. The 1974 Definition of Aggression spelt out that blockades qualified as an act of aggression.[32] The Council was empowered to impose collective sanctions under Article 41. Where these were inadequate, the UN might take armed enforcement action under Article 42, including by 'blockade' and 'operations by air, sea or land forces'. That is, traditional belligerent rights were recast as UN sanctions-enforcement measures.

The difficult question that then arose was whether, if 'war' as a legal concept or institution no longer existed because it had been replaced by the Charter system (the predominant view), the laws of war—the *jus in bello* and laws on neutrality—had disappeared with it.[33] So, for example, it was doubted whether states continued to have any belligerent 'rights' of blockade or contraband against merchant shipping. These uncertainties can be illustrated by two examples from US practice. The US rejected the description 'blockade' for the naval action taken in the 1962 Cuban Missile Crisis to prevent the delivery of Soviet ballistic missiles and warheads to Cuba because it might have implied a state of war or belligerency, prohibited by the Charter.[34] It refused to characterize its closure of Haiphong

[28] Neff, *War and the Law of Nations*, 292.

[29] In the event, automatic sanctions operated only once, against Italy on its invasion of Ethiopia in 1935. A naval blockade was never imposed by the League.

[30] See eg Brierly, *The Law of Nations*, 411–12; Neff, *War and the Law of Nations*, 285–6.

[31] See, eg, Neff, *War and the Law of Nations*, 318.

[32] See the Resolution on the Definition of Aggression (1974), UN Res 3314 (XXIX), Art 3(c).

[33] Neff, *War and the Law of Nations*, describes the Charter and the initial steps towards it taken in the Covenant of the League of Nations and the Kellogg–Briand Pact 1928 as a recasting of the 'just war' approach, replacing the 'dualing nations' conception of war, from which the rights of belligerents and the rights and obligations of neutral states could be deduced. The view was even taken during this period that the *jus in bello* was rendered superfluous because war had been prohibited: see the proceedings of the 1949 International Law Commission, cited by Greenwood, *Essays on War in International Law*, 13; see also 50–4.

[34] Leonard C. Meeker, 'Defensive Quarantine and the Law' (1963) 57 *American Journal of International Law* 515. Some authors suggest that the US relied on anticipatory self-defence in 1962 when it imposed a naval quarantine on Cuba to compel the removal of soviet missiles said to pose an immediate threat to US security (Thomas M. Franck, 'When, If Ever, may States Deploy Military Force Without Prior Security Council Authorization?' (2001) 5 *Washington University Journal of Law and Policy* 51, 59. President John F. Kennedy, Proclamation 3504: Interdiction of the Delivery of

Harbour in 1971–2 during the Vietnam war as a blockade. Instead, the US based its actions on self-defence and, in order to avoid any interference with third states shipping on the high seas, carried out more restricted naval operations than would have been allowed in a blockade under the traditional *jus in bello*.[35]

Commentators also doubted whether the rules of neutrality had survived, for example the obligation of impartiality of treatment between belligerents in the provision of arms and other supplies and the freedom of nationals to trade in these goods with belligerents.[36] Article 2(5) of the Charter required member states 'to give the United Nations every assistance' in cases of enforcement action, which in effect did away with neutrality as regards collective action under the Charter. Moreover, neutral states were freed from the obligation of impartiality—at least as regards those states clearly identified as an aggressor by the UN—and could support the victim state by imposing an arms embargo as a non-forcible reprisal or countermeasure against the aggressor.[37]

Despite the early doubts, the rules governing blockade, contraband and related aspects of the law of neutrality in the *jus in bello* appear to have survived the development of the *jus ad bellum*. There are still questions as to their scope and application in contemporary situations, which tend to be worked through as they arise. The rules are included in the 1994 San Remo Manual on International Law Applicable to Armed Conflicts at Sea which, while not binding, is considered a persuasive restatement and progressive development of the law,[38] and states' military manuals.[39] The 'rights and obligations' of parties to an armed conflict under the *jus in bello* undertaking a blockade were affirmed by the recent reports of the UN Human Rights Council and Secretary-General's Panel of Inquiry on the Israeli blockade of Gaza and the flotilla incident of 31 May 2010 involving the *Mavi Marmara*.[40] The *jus in bello* does not, however, provide a legal basis

Offensive Weapons to Cuba (1963) 57 *American Journal of International Law* 512. See also Anthony C. Arend and Robert J. Beck, *International Law and the Use of Force: Beyond the UN Charter Paradigm* (Abingdon: Routledge, 1993), 11–13). Others suggest it relied instead on a resolution passed by the Organization of American States because of the absence of an armed attack and qualms (since quelled) about whether the Charter allowed anticipatory self-defence (Neff, *War and the Law of Nations*, 328).

35 Neff, *War and the Law of Nations*, 353.

36 Daniel Patrick O'Connell, 'International Law and Contemporary Naval Operations' (1970) 44 *British Yearbook of International Law* 19 and the *Law of the Sea* (1984), vol II, 1094 ff. Prior to the Charter there had been some steps towards the development of a new form of limited neutrality by the US, which entailed an even-handed arms embargo going beyond traditional requirements by prohibiting nationals from selling arms and munitions to either party. The 1930 Harvard draft Convention on the Rights and Duties of States in Case of Aggression was based on the premise that an aggressor state might have all the duties but none of the rights of belligerency (ie as regards blockade and contraband) and that states supporting the victim state might be entitled to depart from the traditional rules of neutrality without incurring legal liability: Neff, *War and the Law of Nations*, 310–13.

37 Neff, *War and the Law of Nations*, 320.

38 Roberts and Guelff, *Documents on the Laws of War*, 574, Arts 93–104.

39 eg UK Ministry of Defence, *The Manual of the Law of Armed Conflict* (2004), ch 13.

40 Report of the international fact-finding mission to investigate violations of international law, including international humanitarian and human rights law, resulting from the Israeli attacks on the flotilla of ships carrying humanitarian assistance, A/HRC/15/21 (27 Sept 2010), paras 48–61; Report of

for imposing blockades and contraband measures and the deployment of force to secure their implementation. This is explored in Section IV of this chapter. Before doing so it is first useful to ask whether the forcible actions typically employed by states against vessels to enforce blockades, contraband measures, and sanctions fall within the meaning of a 'use of force' in the sense in which that term is used in Article 2(4) of the Charter and customary international law.

III. What Amounts to a 'Use Of Force' in this Context?

It might appear to follow from the historical background outlined previously that the imposition of blockades and contraband measures and the naval force used to enforce them, as acts of war or forcible reprisals under pre-Charter law, would be considered as a use or threat of use of (armed) force within the meaning of Article 2(4) of the Charter. However, it has been questioned whether sanctions enforcement is 'law enforcement' or 'police action' which therefore falls outside the prohibition.

A typical operation at sea against a merchant, fishing, or other private vessel, such as visit and search, starts with giving an auditory or visual signal to stop using internationally recognized signals.[41] Where the master and crew are compliant with a request this might not involve any use of force. It is, however, implicit that forcible measures might be used if the orders are not complied with: a warning shot might be fired over the bow to force the vessel to stop, to disable it, or force it to change course. Force might also be used to board the vessel and confiscate the vessel or its cargo and detain its master and crew.[42] Thus, maritime enforcement actions necessarily entail the threat to use forcible measures. It has, however, been doubted whether such 'law enforcement' can constitute a use of, or threat to use, armed or

the Secretary-General's Panel of Inquiry on the 31 May 2010 Flotilla Incident (Sept 2011), paras 157–60. See also Wolff Heintschel von Heinegg, 'Blockades and Interdictions', Chapter 43 in this volume.

[41] *M/V 'Saiga' (No 2) (Saint Vincent and the Grenadines v. Guinea)*, Judgment, 1 July 1999, ITLOS Reports 1999, para 156.

[42] As reflected in Iran's arguments in *Oil Platforms*: it asserted a right to attack merchant vessels in the Persian Gulf which refused a proper request for stop and search (para 23). In November 2010 the Indian navy fired warning shots over the bow of a Bahamas-flagged merchant vessel, the *Dynamic Stryker*, forcing it to stop and return to the port of Mumbai after an extended sea chase resulting from its departure from the port in breach of orders by port officials: Deeptiman Tiwary, 'Rogue ship stopped after dramatic 14-hour chase', available at <http://epaper.timesofindia.com/Default/Layout/Includes/MIRRORNEW/ArtWin.asp?From=Archive&Source=Page&Skin=MIRRORNEW&BaseHref=MMIR%2F2010%2F11%2F24&GZ=T&ViewMode=HTML&EntityId=Ar00200&AppName=1>.

military force caught by Article 2(4) and requiring Council authorization under Article 42.[43] The jurisprudence suggests that the answer to this question turns on a contextual analysis of the circumstances, rather than the nature or quality of the force actually used or threatened.

The International Court of Justice has considered the use of naval force on three occasions. In the *Corfu Channel* case the Court referred to the gunfire by Albanian authorities from a land base in the direction of the British naval cruisers *Orion* and *Superb*, and shots fired at a United Nations Relief and Rehabilitation Administration (UNRRA) tug and barges, as involving the use of force.[44] In the *Oil Platforms* case the Court appeared to accept that the hit on the *Sea Isle City*, a US-flagged oil tanker, allegedly by an anti-ship missile, during the Iran–Iraq War (in which Iran and Iraq asserted belligerent rights over neutral merchant shipping[45]) would have been a use of force by Iran against the US[46] had it been established that the hit was attributable to Iran and that the missile was aimed at the *Sea Isle City*.[47] However, in *Fisheries Jurisdiction (Spain v. Canada)*,[48] where a Canadian fisheries patrol vessel fired four warning bursts from a .50 calibre machine gun across the bow of a Spanish fishing vessel, the *Estai*, in the high seas before it was boarded and seized by armed officers from the Canadian Department of Fisheries and Oceans and the Royal Canadian Mounted Police,[49] the Court implicitly rejected Spain's claim that Canada had used

[43] See eg Martin D. Fink, 'Maritime Embargo Operations: Naval Implementation of UN Sanctions at Sea Under Articles 41 and 42 of the UN Charter' (2013) LX *Netherlands International Law Review* 73; Wolff Heintschel von Heinegg, 'Maritime Interception/Interdiction Operations' in Terry D. Gill and Dieter Fleck (eds), *The Handbook of the International Law of Military Operations* (Oxford: Oxford University Press, 2011), 375.

[44] *Corfu Channel*, Merits, ICJ Rep 1949, 4, 19. The order to fire was given by the Coastal Commander, in execution of a General Order (at 19). The firing started when the ships had passed an Albanian battery, consisted of between 12–120 rounds and a number of 'shorts' and 'overs', and lasted for 12 minutes, although the ships were not hit (at 27).

[45] Both belligerents declared prohibited war zones around their coasts and Iraq targeted tankers carrying Iranian oil (para 42).

[46] If not an armed attack for the purposes of Art 51: see paras 64 and 77. It is not entirely clear from the Court's reasoning whether the hit on the *Sea Isle City* would have amounted to an armed attack under Art 51 if both attribution to Iran and an intention to hit the *Sea Isle City* had been established. Cf para 72, where the Court did 'not exclude the possibility that the mining of a single military vessel might be sufficient to bring into play the 'inherent right of self-defence'. See more generally the discussion at para 35 of the commentary on Art 2(4) by Albrecht Randelzhofer and Oliver Dörr in Bruno Simma et al (eds), *The Charter of the United Nations: A Commentary* (3rd edn, Oxford: Oxford University Press, 2012), vol 1, 200.

[47] Alleged by the US to have been a 'Silkworm', an HY-2 cruise missile of Chinese manufacture designed for use as an anti-ship weapon. The Court concluded on the evidence presented that a Silkworm missile fired from more than 100 km away, as alleged, could not have been aimed at the specific vessel, but could only have been programmed to hit some target in Kuwaiti waters (para 64).

[48] ICJ Rep 1998, 432.

[49] A. Lopez, 'Case Study 1.92: Special Meeting to Discuss the "Turbot War": Canada's Preservation of the Turbot and Code Fish Stocks vs Portugal and Spain's Right to Fish in International Waters', The Institute of Public Administration of Canada, 4. The authorities only fired on the *Estai* after receiving high-level authorization from Ottawa.

force in breach of Article 2(4).[50] The Court held that Section 8.1 of the Coastal Fisheries Protection Act 1994, on which the Canadian authorities had based their actions and which authorized the 'use of force', was a provision of a character and type to be found in legislation of various states dealing with fisheries conservation and management and Article 22(1)(f) of the UN Agreement on Straddling Stocks 1995.[51] As such, the Canadian actions fell within what was commonly understood as enforcement of conservation and management measures and therefore within the terms of the Canadian reservation in its Article 36 Declaration, notwithstanding that the reservation did not refer to the use of force.[52]

Similarly in the *MV Saiga (No 2)* case[53] the International Tribunal for the Law of the Sea treated actions by a Guinean patrol boat under its Customs Code against the *MV Saiga*, an oil tanker, and its crew—alleged to include firing at the ship with live ammunition and using solid shot from large-calibre automatic guns[54]—as law enforcement.[55] It found (under the heading 'Use of force') that Guinea had used excessive force in its law enforcement in breach of the United Nations Convention on the Law of the Sea (UNCLOS) by firing at the ship from a fast-moving patrol boat without issuing any of the signals and warnings required by international law and practice, firing indiscriminately while on deck, and using gunfire to stop the engine of the ship.[56]

An UNCLOS Annex VII arbitral tribunal reached a somewhat different conclusion in *Guyana v. Suriname*[57] where Suriname also defended naval action against an oil platform and its support vessels as law enforcement. Guyana claimed, in the context of a maritime delimitation dispute under Articles 74 and 83 of the United Nations Convention on the Law of the Sea (UNCLOS), that Suriname had breached

[50] The question for the Court at the jurisdictional stage was whether Spain's claim fell within the Canadian reservation to its Optional Protocol Art 36 declaration for 'disputes arising out of or concerning conservation and management measures taken by Canada with respect to vessels fishing in the NAFO Regulatory area…and the enforcement of such measures.' Spain argued that its claim fell outside the scope of the reservation because its object was not a dispute over conservation and management of fisheries, but whether Canada was entitled to exercise its jurisdiction on the high seas against Spanish-flagged ships and their crews by armed force: para 24; see also para 53. Spain also asserted that the use of force against the *Estai* amounted to a violation of Art 2(4): paras 78–80. The Court avoided directly answering the question as to whether there had been a breach of Art 2(4), responding that there was no requirement to interpret a reservation as covering only acts compatible with international law, and so it did not need to consider this aspect of Spain's argument.

[51] Para 81; see also para 82. Section 8.1 of the Coastal Fisheries Protection Act 1994 provided that fisheries protection officers 'may, in the manner and to the extent prescribed in the regulations, use force that is intended or is likely to disable a foreign fishing vessel' and fisheries protection officers were included amongst the law enforcement officers covered by section 25 of the Canadian Criminal Code relating to the use of force in law enforcement.

[52] Para 84. [53] *M/V 'Saiga' (No 2)* (n 41). [54] Para 153. [55] Para 154.

[56] Paras 157–8. There was no evidence of any use or threat of use of force by the crew of the *CE hornton*.

[57] *Guyana v. Suriname*, Award of the Arbitral Tribunal, 17 Sept 2007. The Tribunal's assumption of jurisdiction over Guyana's use of force claim has been controversial.

its obligations under UNCLOS and Article 2(3) of the UN Charter and customary law to settle disputes by peaceful means by using armed force against the CGX exploratory rig and the drill ship *CE Thornton*. The facts were that shortly after midnight on 3 June 2000, gunboats from the Suriname Airforce and Navy established contact with the *CE Thornton* and its service vessels (which were working in the disputed maritime area under concessions granted by Guyana), ordered them to leave within 12 hours because they were in Suriname waters, and warned that there would be 'consequences' if they did not.[58] Suriname maintained that its actions were reasonable and proportionate law enforcement measures to prevent unauthorized drilling in a disputed area of continental shelf[59] and that law enforcement measures could not be a violation of the prohibition on the use of force in international law.[60] While the Tribunal accepted 'the argument that in international law force may be used in law enforcement activities if it is unavoidable, reasonable and necessary', in the circumstances of the case 'the action mounted by Suriname on 3 June 2000 seemed more akin to a threat of military action rather than a mere law enforcement activity'.[61] The Tribunal found as a matter of fact that there was an explicit threat to use force if the order to leave was not complied with. This constituted a threat of the use of force in contravention of UNCLOS, the UN Charter, and general international law.[62] The Tribunal accordingly rejected Suriname's argument that the action was a lawful countermeasure.[63]

The conclusion that can be drawn from these decisions is that any typical forcible measures used or threatened by state authorities against vessels or oil rigs and platforms are 'uses of force'. Whether a particular use of force, for example firing across the bow, is treated as law enforcement or a use of force under the Charter turns on an objective assessment of the state's intention and the surrounding circumstances, not the gun or ammunition used, the number of shots fired, or the identity of the state authority (warships or military aircraft or the coastguard and fisheries protection officers), although these may be relevant to that assessment. That is, there is no difference in the meaning of the term 'use of force' in Article 2(4) of the Charter or Article 22 of the Straddling Fish Stocks Agreement.[64]

As in other aspects of this area of law, a contextual analysis of the circumstances is required.[65] This has implications for identifying the legal basis—or lack thereof—of

[58] Paras 432–8. [59] Para 441. [60] Para 442. [61] Para 445.

[62] Para 445. Guyana had characterized its use of force claim as a breach of the obligation in Art 2(3) of the Charter to settle international disputes 'in such a manner that international peace and security, and justice, are not endangered', the point being that, as the area was disputed, a use of force would not be against the territorial integrity or independence of a state. However, the Tribunal's finding does not specifically invoke Art 2(3).

[63] Para 446.

[64] cf Vera Gowlland-Debbas, 'The Limits of Unilateral Enforcement of Community Objectives in the Framework of UN Peace Maintenance' (2000) 11 *European Journal of International Law* 361, 366.

[65] A contextual approach has a long history in this area of law. Eg Hall records that the intention of a state imposing a blockade distinguishes a reprisal from an act of war (at 367). The Commission of Jurists held that whether measures short of war were undertaken in breach of the obligation to resolve

a use of force by a state to enforce arms embargoes and restrictions on trade and the grounds of any related responsibility for a wrongful act.[66] It is also relevant to an analysis of whether Council authorization to enforce sanctions by force must be express and whether it is engaging its powers under Article 42 as well as Article 41. The answer to these questions does not turn on the meaning of the term 'use of force' or any argument that law enforcement action might be distinguished from other uses of military force by a difference in the kind or degree of force used.[67]

IV. Legal Bases for the Use of Force to Enforce Sanctions

One reason that debate has arisen over whether sanctions enforcement, including enforcement of UN sanctions, is law enforcement rather than a use of armed force is because sanctions, whether imposed by the UN or unilaterally by the European Union (EU) or some other regional entity[68] or an individual state, are typically implemented

disputes peacefully was to be determined by the League Council in each case 'having due regard to all the circumstances of the case and the nature of the measures adopted' (Council Meeting 13 Mar 1924, LNOJ 1924, 524, discussed by Neff, *War and the Law of Nations*, 299–300). The International Court also takes a contextual approach to a threat to use force in *Legality of the Threat or Use of Nuclear Weapons*, Advisory Opinion, ICJ Rep 1996, 226, 246: 'Whether a signalled intention to use force if certain events occur is or is not a "threat" within Article 2, paragraph 4, of the Charter depends on various factors... Thus it would be illegal for a State to threaten force *to secure* territory from another State, or *to cause* it to follow or not to follow certain political or economic paths' (para 47, emphasis added). See also *Corfu Channel (UK v. Albania)*, Merits, ICJ Rep 1949, 4, 35; Dino Kritsiotis, 'Close Encounters of a Sovereign Kind' (2009) 20 *European Journal of International Law* 299, 322–9. For a similar analysis of the Court's approach to Art 51, see Thomas M. Franck, 'When, If Ever, may States Deploy Military Force Without Prior Security Council Authorization?' (2001) 5 *Washington University Journal of Law and Policy* 51, 63 and consent, see Randelzhofer and Dörr, 'Article 2(4)' in Simma et al, *The Charter of the United Nations*, 213.

[66] eg an excessive exercise of jurisdiction or going beyond what is an acceptable level of force in law enforcement, as in *Medvedyev and Others v. France*, App no 3394/03, Judgment of the European Court of Human Rights (Grand Chamber), 29 Mar 2010, 51 EHRR 39.

[67] As suggested by some commentators (see the reference in Christine Gray, *International Law and the Use of Force* (3rd edn, Oxford: Oxford University Press, 2008), 30). Perhaps the answer does not matter, if in most instances the act could not be characterized as an 'armed attack' (ie it may no longer be treated as an 'act of war' providing justification for declaring war) and state responsibility will in any event be engaged on some additional ground, eg a breach of the prohibition on intervention in domestic affairs or the rules governing the use of force in maritime law enforcement.

[68] The EU has competence under its treaties to implement UN sanctions and impose its own in pursuit of common foreign and security policy. Whether the sanctions originate with the UN or the EU itself, they are implemented by EU regulation (following a Council Decision) which is directly

through domestic legislation which provides the legal basis as a matter of domestic law for the use of coercive force by state authorities against an individual's person and property.[69] Provided the prescription of a sanction is lawful, no breach of international law will be entailed by a naval asset's use of force, within the limits of that state's enforcement jurisdiction, to enforce domestic law imposing sanctions.[70] States do not require Council authorization to use force to enforce sanctions within their enforcement jurisdiction, that is, within their territory,[71] against their own flagged vessels or, in

applicable in the legal systems of member states. Those within the jurisdiction of EU member states are bound by the sanctions from the date of publication of the regulation in the Official Journal. EU sanctions regulations require additional implementing legislation by EU member states to prescribe criminal sanctions and, like UN sanctions, depend for their enforcement on the legal systems and authorities of the member states.

[69] Vera Gowlland-Debbas, *National Implementation of United Nations Sanctions: A Comparative Study* (Leiden: Martinus Nijhoff, 2004). Eg the UK implements UN resolutions by statutory instruments (Orders in Council, Regulations) passed under the United Nations Act 1946 or the Export Control Act 2002. EU sanctions regulations, which implement UN sanctions as well as non-UN EU sanctions (eg those against Syria in May 2011), imposing embargoes on goods and transport and related contracts are implemented by Orders in Council under the Export Control Act 2002. Financial sanctions are implemented by regulations under the European Communities Act 1972. The use of force in law enforcement is governed by the law on self-defence and section 3(1) of the Criminal Law Act 1967 ('A person may use such force as is reasonable in the circumstances in the prevention of crime, or in effecting or assisting in the lawful arrest of offenders or suspected offenders or of persons unlawfully at large').

[70] Prescription of such sanctions and any action to enforce them will usually engage the state's responsibility under one or more rules of international law, eg law of the sea (the right of innocent passage), international human rights (the right to property, freedom from arbitrary arrest and detention—see eg *Medvedyev and Others v. France* (n 66)), or breach of a trade treaty. Regional or unilateral sanctions may entail an excessive exercise of prescriptive jurisdiction, ie because the state concerned is purporting to regulate the persons and property outside its territorial jurisdiction in a way which unlawfully interferes in the domestic affairs of third states. See eg Vaughan Lowe, 'US Extraterritorial Jurisdiction: The Helms–Burton and D'Amato Acts' (1997) 46 *International and Comparative Law Quarterly* 378 and Andrea Bianchi, 'Extraterritoriality and Export Controls: Some Remarks on the Alleged Antimony Between the US and the European Approach' (1992) 35 *German Yearbook of International Law* 366. There must, therefore, be an accepted legal basis for prescription of a sanction, eg a retorsion, countermeasure implementation of a Security Council resolution, or self-defence. According to the International Law Commission, the lawfulness of collective countermeasures (outside the case of UN sanctions) taken in the general or collective interest by non-injured states is uncertain: see Art 54 and commentary of the Articles on the Responsibility of States for Internationally Wrongful Acts 2001, International Law Commission, *Yearbook of the International Law Commission*, 2001, vol II (2), 31, 137–9. See also P.-E. Dupont, 'Countermeasures and Collective Security: The Case of the EU Sanctions Against Iran' (2012) 17 *Journal of Conflict and Security Law* 301.

[71] As this chapter is concerned with the use of force, it focuses on the enforcement actions by states that involve the use of force against persons and property, rather than the equally and perhaps more important use of national regulation and criminal law to prohibit the contracts and commercial relationships at one or more stages removed from the target state or non-state actor, eg the activities of traders, bankers and financiers, insurers, vessel owners, and charterers within their jurisdiction. An example of the effectiveness of targeting the secondary players is the case of *The Alaed* in June 2012. *The Alaed*, at the time flagged to Curacao, was returning reconditioned Soviet warship helicopters from Russia to Syria when its UK insurers Standard Chartered, in response to the EU's Syria sanctions regime, terminated the vessel's insurance on 19 June 2012, causing the vessel to turn around. Council

accordance with the provisions now laid down in UNCLOS 1982,[72] against foreign-flagged vessels in internal waters and the territorial sea and, if in hot pursuit, the contiguous zone, exclusion economic zone (EEZ), and high seas. A state may also use force to enforce sanctions extraterritorially without Council authorization within the territory, territorial waters, or against vessels flagged to a third state with that state's consent.[73] In that case, the lawfulness of a particular use of military force will also turn on the scope of the third state's consent. Any enforcement must also comply with human rights.[74]

A state might also enforce arms embargoes and restrictions on trade extraterritorially, without Council authorization, where it is a party to an international armed conflict or a non-international armed conflict within Additional Protocol II of 1977 (APII) or a non-APII non-international armed conflict where the non-state party is otherwise in control of territory.[75] As explained previously, the rules governing the rights and obligations of parties to an armed conflict to impose blockade and contraband measures have survived the prohibition on 'war' and are found in the *jus in bello* or international humanitarian law (IHL). According to military manuals, in the context of an international armed conflict, '[b]elligerent warships and military aircraft have a right to visit and search merchant vessels and civil aircraft where there are reasonable grounds for suspicion that they are subject to capture'.[76]

As IHL rules will apply to all parties to an armed conflict irrespective of the legality of a resort to force, it could be said that IHL provides a *legal basis* for the enforcement of blockades and contraband measures against vessels and aircraft by the use or threat of use of military force without Council authorization. However, it has been

Regulation (EU) No 36/2012 was subsequently amended by Regulation (EU) No 545/2012 on 26 June 2012 to prohibit insurance contracts related to such transport in addition to the transport of sanctioned weapons and goods.

[72] A useful summary of the position under the law of the sea can be found in Douglas Guilfoyle, 'Maritime Interdiction of Weapons of Mass Destruction' (2007) 12 *Journal of Conflict and Security Law* 1.

[73] eg the Convention for the Suppression of Unlawful Acts Against the Safety of Maritime Navigation, 1988 facilitates enforcement by making it easier to secure flag-state consent.

[74] In the law enforcement context, see eg *Medvedyev and Others v. France* (n 66), which involved the arrest and detention of the *Winner* and its crew in international waters on suspicions of drug trafficking. In the context of armed conflict, it is now well established that human rights obligations will continue to apply alongside the *jus in bello*/IHL as the *lex specialis*.

[75] This may be because the non-state actor does not meet the requirements of Additional Protocol II, but would have qualified for recognition under the traditional rules of belligerency and to which IHL would apply for the reasons given by the International Criminal Tribunal for the former Yugoslavia in *Prosecutor v. Tadić*, Case No IT-94-1-A, 15 July 1999, 38 ILM 1518.

[76] Wolff Heintschel von Heinegg, 'Economic Warfare at Sea' in Gill and Fleck, *The Handbook of the International Law of Military Operations*, paras 19.7 and 19.21, reflecting paras 118 and 125 of the *San Remo Manual on International Law Applicable to Armed Conflicts at Sea* (Cambridge: International Institute of Humanitarian Law/Cambridge University Press, 1994). Neutral vessels are subject to capture if they are, inter alia, carrying contraband or breaching or attempting to breach a blockade (which meets the requirements of effectiveness) (rule 19.23). 'Contraband' is defined to mean goods which are ultimately destined for territory under the control of an enemy belligerent and which are susceptible for use in an armed conflict (at 372). Under the law of armed conflict, enemy merchant vessels are subject to capture simply because they possess enemy nationality (para 20.13).

questioned whether the affirmation of the principle of equality of application of IHL[77] extends positive 'rights', such as those against neutral shipping, to states in breach of the *jus ad bellum* and whether the duties of neutrality continue to apply where no aggressor has been authoritatively identified.[78] It has also been questioned whether the requirements of necessity and proportionality of self-defence are consistent with the application of extensive rights against merchant shipping under IHL.[79] These questions have been addressed to some extent in the responses to Israel's blockade of Gaza from 2007 and, in particular, its actions against a flotilla of passenger and other vessels flagged to third states in May 2010.[80] Israel justified its actions on the basis of self-defence, claiming that the blockade was necessary to prevent the supply of arms and other goods used in the rocket attacks against Israel from Gaza. The UN Human Rights Council and the UN Secretary-General's inquiry into the flotilla incidents, while they reached different conclusions on the facts, both accepted that in principle states could justify the imposition of a blockade on the basis of self-defence, could exercise traditional rights against neutral shipping under IHL and were obliged to adhere to the rights of neutral states.[81] In any event, IHL does not preclude the wrongfulness of a state's resort to force. Where the resort to armed force is itself unlawful, losses incurred by reason of a blockade or contraband measures which are otherwise compliant with IHL provide the basis for reparations claims.

A related question is whether states coming to the assistance of another in response to an unlawful armed attack, accepted as such by the Council, can rely on a right of collective self-defence or require Council authorization before using military force to enforce UN sanctions against merchant vessels. The answer is not entirely clear. In the first Gulf War (1990–1) the UK and the US imposed a blockade to enforce the trade embargo imposed by the Council in Resolution 661 (1990), relying on the right of collective self-defence and a request for assistance from Kuwait. Nevertheless, they subsequently sought Council authorization, given in Resolution 665 (1990), for forcible maritime interdiction against foreign-flagged vessels.

If a state is not a belligerent or co-belligerent because it is acting in a peacekeeping capacity (eg Rhodesia in 1966 or Yugoslavia in 1992) or because the sanctions regime is directed at countering proliferation of WMD rather than being imposed in the context of an ongoing armed conflict (eg North Korea, Iran), then the contingent basis for the automatic application of the rules of naval warfare does not exist (although it has been accepted that IHL applies in the context of UN action[82]).

[77] As to which, see Greenwood, *Essays on War in International Law*, paras 3.10–3.15.

[78] Neff, *War and the Law of Nations*, 346; 353 ff.

[79] Neff, *War and the Law of Nations*, 346, 349–51; 353–4, 376; see also Lois E. Fielding, *Maritime Interception and UN Sanctions* (San Francisco, CA: Austin & Winfield, 2007), 6–8.

[80] See eg Andrew Sanger, 'The Contemporary Law of Blockade and the Gaza Freedom Flotilla' (2010) 13 *Yearbook of Humanitarian Law* 397 and James Farrant, 'The Gaza Flotilla Incident and the Modern Law of Blockade' (2013) 66 *Naval College Law Review* 81.

[81] See n 40.

[82] Neff, *War and the Law of Nations*, 344–5.

Authors typically refer to the stopping, boarding, or redirecting of merchant vessels or destruction or confiscation of cargoes or vessels in these circumstances as maritime interception or interdiction operations (MIO), distinguishing them from the exercise of the rights of a belligerent against foreign-flagged merchant vessels and aircraft in an armed conflict.[83] The possible legal bases for the use or threat of use of force against a foreign-flagged vessel in these circumstances will be that it is within the limits of extraterritorial jurisdiction allowed by international law, or with the consent of the flag state, or under a Council resolution.

The Security Council has authorized maritime operations by states to enforce arms and economic sanctions against Southern Rhodesia (1966),[84] Iraq (1990),[85] the former Yugoslavia (1992),[86] Haiti (1993),[87] and Sierra Leone (1997).[88] However, because of the parallels between law enforcement and the Council's Chapter VII powers and member states' enforcement operations at sea, there was some doubt over whether an express authorization to enforce sanctions was required or was entailed in the sanction itself, and whether any express authorization was an exercise of the Council's powers under Article 41 or 42. These questions were first voiced when British naval forces commenced enforcement of the oil embargo imposed by the Security Council on Rhodesia in Resolution 217 (1965) in Operation London, prior to the Council's Resolution 221 (1966) which expressly authorized the UK 'to prevent by the use of force if necessary, the arrival at Beira of vessels reasonably believed to be carrying oil destined for Southern Rhodesia'.[89] At the time, some commentators assumed that

[83] Heintschel von Heinegg, 'Maritime Interception/Interdiction Operations' in Gill and Fleck, *The Handbook of the International Law of Military Operations*, 375. As Heintschel von Heinegg observes, 'the legal basis for maritime interception/interdiction operations will differ in accordance with the aims pursued' and they will only be lawful if public international law provides a—treaty or customary—rule explicitly authorizing interference with foreign vessels or aircraft (at 375; see also para 20.13). Military Interception Operations are naval operations which are not governed by the law of armed conflict, and are used in times of peace or of crisis only: 'This of course does not rule out the possibility that MIO are conducted simultaneously with an ongoing armed conflict. For example, there may exist an international armed conflict between States A and B. On the one hand the Security Council, acting under Chapter VII of the Charter, may have determined a threat to the peace and may have authorized UN Member States to prevent the flow of arms into the region. While those States acting under the authorization will conduct MIO, the States parties to the conflict may continue to take measures against foreign vessels and aircraft under the law of international armed conflict' (at 376). See also Richard Zeigler, 'Ubi Sumus? Quo Vadimus?: Charting the Course of Maritime Interception Operations' (1996) 46 *Naval Law Review* 1.

[84] SC Res 2221 (1966) authorizing measures to implement Res 217 (1966). See also Res 232 (1966) and 460 (1979).

[85] SC Res 665 (1990) authorizing measures to implement Res 661 (1990).

[86] SC Res 757 (1992) authorizing measures to implement Res 713 (1991).

[87] SC Res 875 (1993).

[88] SC Res 1132 (1997). The Security Council authorized ECOWAS under Chapter VIII to enforce the embargo: see further Karsten Nowrot and Emily W. Schbacker, 'The Use of Force to Restore Democracy: International Legal Implications of the ECOWAS Intervention in Sierra Leone' (1998) 14 *American University International Law Review* 321, 357.

[89] Martin D. Fink, 'Maritime Embargo Operations'; Heintschel von Heinegg, 'Maritime Interception/ Interdiction Operations' in Gill and Fleck, *The Handbook of the International Law of Military*

the Council was acting under Article 41, although Resolution 221 never expressly said so.[90] This was influenced by the view that Article 42 was intended for traditional large-scale military enforcement and blockades, which suggested that maritime embargo operations in terms of their scope and the low level of force employed did not fall within it.[91] The debate received renewed attention in the first Gulf War following Resolution 665 (1990), in which the Council called on:

> those Member States co-operating with the Government of Kuwait which are deploying maritime forces to use such measures commensurate to the specific circumstances as may be necessary... to halt all inward and outward maritime shipping, in order to inspect and verify their cargoes and destinations and to ensure strict implementation of the provisions related to such shipping laid down in resolution 661 (1990).[92]

As in the example of Rhodesia some 25 years earlier, states (the UK and the US) had commenced maritime operations to enforce the embargo before the Council had passed Resolution 665.

The debate was subsequently influenced by the discussion on the legal basis for the Council's authorization of peacekeeping action and the limits on peacekeepers' rights to use lethal force. It was suggested that the use of minimal force to enforce sanctions could be authorized by the Council under Article 41 in the same way as a minimal use of force by land-based peacekeeping missions under the 'active self-defence' doctrine might be authorized by reference to Article 40.[93]

Operations, para 20.03 and commentary. Cf Dan Sarooshi, *The United Nations & the Development of Collective Security: The Delegation by the United Nations Security Council of it Chapter VII Powers* (Oxford: Clarendon Press, 1999), 194–210.

[90] See eg Rob McLaughlin, 'United Nations Mandated Naval Interdiction Operations in the Territorial Sea?' (2002) 51 *International and Comparative Law Quarterly* 249, 258, citing earlier commentaries.

[91] The debate is summarized by Martin D. Fink, 'Maritime Embargo Operations', 83–5.

[92] Para 1. States concerned in the maritime action were requested to coordinate their actions using the mechanisms of the Military Staff Committee and to submit reports to the Security Council and Security Council Committee established in Res 661 to facilitate the monitoring and implementation of Res 665 (para 4). See further McLaughlin, 'United Nations Mandated Naval Interdiction Operations in the Territorial Sea?'.

[93] Roslyn Higgins, cited in McLaughlin, 'United Nations Mandated Naval Interdiction Operations in the Territorial Sea?', 256. However, she also says that it is hard not to characterize the US and UK actions in the Beira Patrol as a blockade under Art 42. For a discussion of the distinction between the 'law enforcement' and 'armed conflict' paradigms and the concept of 'active self-defence' under the former in UN peacekeeping operations (which presupposes a legal basis for actions on the territory of another state—ie the Council 'overrides' the territorial state's jurisdiction), see Rob McLaughlin, 'The Legal Regime Applicable to Use of Lethal Force When Operating under a United Nations Security Council Chapter VII Mandate Authorising "All Necessary Means"' (2008) 12 *Journal of Conflict and Security Law* 389 and Chapter 11. The question that arises from this analysis is its application to resolutions authorizing maritime interdiction: is the use of (potentially) lethal force restricted to self-defence of self and unit? Does 'self-defence of others', eg civilians, require an additional legal basis as a matter of international law? See also Scott Sheeran, 'The Use of Force in United Nations Peacekeeping Operations', Chapter 16 in this volume.

Looking back from the vantage point of some 20 years of Council practice on sanctions, we can see the development of some consistent approaches which resolve the debate.[94] The Council expressly authorizes the enforcement of sanctions by states outside their jurisdiction,[95] which suggests that imposition of sanctions measures alone does not provide a basis for the use or threat of force in maritime operations to enforce those sanctions,[96] whether or not such action is considered law enforcement. Furthermore, the authorization for sanctions-enforcement operations is contained in a separate paragraph or resolution from those authorizing use of 'all necessary means' to restore international peace and security, which suggests that an authorization to 'use all necessary means' does not encompass forcible enforcement of sanctions at sea.[97]

Recent arms embargoes and economic sanctions have not authorized enforcement by states outside their jurisdiction, but instead emphasized states' obligations to take necessary measures within their jurisdiction (Côte d'Ivoire (Resolution 1572 (2004)), Lebanon (Resolution 1701 (2006)),[98] and Eritrea (Resolution 1907 (2009)). In each of these resolutions (other than Resolution 1701[99]) the Council stated that it was acting under Chapter VII, but did not otherwise refer to specific Charter provisions. The wording used in the resolutions imposing sanctions on North Korea[100] and Iran[101] specifically stated that the Council was acting under Article 41 as well as Chapter VII, which was intended to make it clear that the Council was not authorizing the use of force.[102] Instead, the most recent resolution containing measures concerning Iran (Resolution 1929 (2010)) calls on flag states to cooperate by consenting to requests by other states to stop and search vessels.[103] This new approach is not

[94] Nevertheless, it continues to receive attention. See Martin D. Fink, 'Maritime Embargo Operations', 91. Martin Fink's concern is the 'legal parameters under which naval assets can perform their task', which he considers have not completely crystallized.

[95] As distinct from their obligation to implement and enforce sanctions within their jurisdiction. This point is often lost in discussions of sanctions enforcement.

[96] See eg Natalie Klein, *Maritime Security and the Law of the Sea* (Oxford: Oxford University Press, 2011), 278; Martin D. Fink, 'Maritime Embargo Operations', 89–90; McLaughlin, 'United Nations Mandated Naval Interdiction Operations in the Territorial Sea?', citing Politakis and Soons and placing express provision for maritime interdiction measures under Art 41, rather than Art 42.

[97] Martin D. Fink, 'Maritime Embargo Operations', 86–7. He cites Marc Weller's observation with regard to Res 665 that Art 42 was specifically not included in the resolution to preclude an expansive interpretation of the authority that was granted: 'The United Nations and the *Ius Ad Bellum*' in Peter Rowe (ed), *The Gulf War 1990–1991 in International and English Law* (Abingdon: Routledge, 1993), 29, 36.

[98] Para 15.

[99] But the Council does determine that the situation is a threat to international peace and security.

[100] Res 1718 (2006) and 1874 (2009).

[101] Res 1737 (2006), 1747 (2007), 1803 (2008), and 1929 (2010).

[102] Nico Krisch, 'Article 41' in Simma et al, *The Charter of the United Nations*, paras 13 and 44; Gray, *International Law and the Use of Force*, 266.

[103] Para 15. See further Vasco Becker-Weinberg and Guglielmo Verdirame, 'Proliferation of Weapons of Mass Destruction and Shipping Interdiction', Chapter 47 and Rob McLaughlin, 'United Nations Security Council Practice in Relation to Use of Force in No-Fly Zones and Maritime Exclusion Zones', Chapter 11 both in this volume.

limited to sanctions targeting proliferation of WMD. Resolution 1970 (2011) imposing an arms embargo on Libya in response to its actions against civilians in the 'Arab Spring' also expressly stated that the Council was taking measures under Article 41. Subsequently, Resolution 1973 (2011) of 17 March 2011, dropping any reference to Article 41, authorized Member States 'to use all measures commensurate to the specific circumstances to carry out… inspections' of inward vessels and aircraft to implement the arms embargo.[104]

Various examples are given by commentators of the use or threat of naval force to enforce sanctions without Council authorization—the launch by the UK of Operation London to enforce the UN embargo on Rhodesia before Resolution 221 (1966) was passed, the maritime enforcement actions of the UK and the US in the Gulf before Resolution 665 (1990),[105] and the launch by the North Atlantic Treaty Organization (NATO) and the Western European Union (WEU) of Operations Maritime Monitor and Sharp Vigilance in support of Resolutions 713 (1991) and 757 (1992) four months before the passage of Resolution 757 (1992). However, they do not provide clear support for an argument that express authorization is not required.[106] In Operation London the UK sought the consent of the third party flag state before stopping and boarding suspect merchant vessels before Resolution 221 was passed.[107] In the early stages of the Gulf War the UK and the US relied on a request for assistance they had sought from Kuwait so that stopping and searching merchant vessels in the Gulf could be justified as an act of collective self-defence under Article 51[108] and, despite that legal justification, sought Council authorization for the military blockade they had established. It was later observed that 'international support seemed to be stronger when collective authorization was obtained'.[109] As for the Yugoslav example, the NATO and the WEU Operations Maritime Monitor and Sharp Vigilance were limited to 'surveillance, identification and reporting of maritime traffic in areas

[104] Para 13. The resolution is much more detailed than its earlier counterparts. The authority to enforce the arms embargos was terminated 12 months later by Res 2040 (2012) (para 8).

[105] The Iraqi-flagged tankers *Al Fao*, *Al Byaa*, and *Al Abid* were stopped and searched on 17 Aug 1990. On 18 Aug warning shots were fired across the bows of Iraqi tankers by two US warships. French warships were authorized to fire shots across the bow with presidential authorization. Eight days later on 25 Aug the Council expressly authorized maritime interdictions in Res 665: see Jane Gilliland Dalton, 'The Influence of Law on Seapower in Desert Shield/Desert Storm' (1993) 41 *Naval Law Review* 27.

[106] cf Martin Fink, who suggests that the unilateral maritime measures by the UK and NATO and the WEU respectively prior to Res 221 and 787 to implement earlier Council resolutions amount to 'implied maritime embargo operations' based on Art 41.

[107] Martin D. Fink, 'Maritime Embargo Operations', 77 and fn 18.

[108] Jon E. Fink, 'From Peacekeeping to Peace Enforcement: The Blurring of the Mandate for the Use of Force in Maintaining International Peace and Security' (1995) 19 *Maryland Journal of International Law* 1.

[109] Nico Krisch, 'Unilateral Enforcement of the Collective Will: Kosovo, Iraq, and the Security Council' (1993) 3 *Max Planck Yearbook of United Nations Law* 59, 96–7 fn 162.

to be defined in international waters in the Adriatic Sea': stop and search operations were not carried out until after Resolution 787 was passed.[110] This practice would tend to suggest that the states involved were not of the view that they had any clear 'implied consent' from the Security Council to take forcible actions to enforce sanctions, nor that the exercise of a collective right of self-defence conferred belligerent rights against neutral shipping. Furthermore, the debates at the time over the naval interdictions called for in the case of Rhodesia, Iraq, Yugoslavia, and Haiti made it clear that only a specific Security Council authorization would 'absolve States undertaking such action from responsibility for breaching their obligations under international law'.[111]

V. Conclusion

Despite earlier uncertainties about whether blockade, contraband and the law of neutrality survived the Charter and the questions surrounding the legal basis for the military enforcement of sanctions imposed by the Council, the law in this area appears to have settled to a reasonable extent. The Council's recent sanctions practice suggests that extraterritorial enforcement of UN sanctions at sea, whether called law enforcement or military action, may not be undertaken other than with its express authorization or with flag state consent,[112] and that such authorization is an exercise of its powers to authorize member states to use armed force under Article 42 rather than Article 41. If the Council has not given express authorization or the sanctions measure in question is not a UN sanction but a unilateral measure imposed by a state or regional entity such as the EU, states are limited to taking enforcement measures within the limits of their enforcement jurisdiction under international law. An exception lies where the state is exercising the right of

[110] Operations Maritime Monitor and Sharp Vigilance were replaced by Operation Maritime Guard on 22 Nov, in response to the passage of Res 787. All ships bound to or from the territorial waters of Yugoslavia (Serbia and Montenegro) were halted to inspect and verify their cargoes and destinations, as well as all ships proceeding to all other ports of the former Yugoslavia (<http://www.manp.nato.int/NAVSOUTH/OperationMaritimeGuard.htm>). The earlier NATO and WEU operation merely reported on vessels' movements, presumably relying on the pressure this would place on the flag state or any port State so comply with their obligations to enforce UN sanctions within their jurisdiction.

[111] See Gowlland-Debbas, 'The Limits of Unilateral Enforcement of Community Objectives in the Framework of UN Peace Maintenance', 371.

[112] Martin D. Fink, 'Maritime Embargo Operations', 75.

self-defence against a state or non-state actor, and may extend to the case of collective self-defence, provided action is taken in accordance with the provisions of IHL concerning blockade and contraband. From recent practice, it does not appear that the *vires* of any claim to self-defence affects the 'rights' of the state party to the armed conflict to take action against neutral vessels.

CHAPTER 13

THE RELATIONSHIP BETWEEN THE UN SECURITY COUNCIL AND GENERAL ASSEMBLY IN MATTERS OF INTERNATIONAL PEACE AND SECURITY

NIGEL D. WHITE

1. Introduction

Although the Security Council has the 'primary responsibility for the maintenance of peace and security',[1] and is granted an impressive array of powers under Chapters VI and VII of the UN Charter, the General Assembly has competence

[1] UN Charter, Art 24(1).

to make recommendations to the Security Council and to the member states on 'any questions or any matter within the scope of the present Charter',[2] thereby having a secondary competence in matters of peace and security. As clearly stated by the International Court of Justice in the *Expenses* opinion delivered in 1962, the 'responsibility conferred' on the Security Council is 'primary' not 'exclusive', and the Charter 'makes it abundantly clear' that the General Assembly is 'also to be concerned with international peace and security'.[3]

The purpose of this chapter will be to understand and explore this division of competence as it has evolved since the inception of the UN Charter in 1945. It also aims to explore this division within the context of the prohibition on the use of force. While it is clear that the Security Council can authorize the use of force by states, as an express Charter exception to the prohibition there is disagreement as to whether the General Assembly can recommend that states take military action, for instance when the Council is deadlocked and the UN is faced with an imminent and catastrophic use of force or act of violence. To examine this conundrum, the debate over the legality of the (in)famous Uniting for Peace resolution of 1950, will be revisited within the context of the emergence of a Responsibility to Protect (R2P).

II. Purposes and Powers of the UN

The primary or, more accurately, the first-listed purpose of the UN is:

> To maintain international peace and security, and to that end: to take effective collective measures for the prevention and removal of threats to the peace, and for the suppression of acts of aggression or other breaches of the peace, and to bring about by peaceful means, and in conformity with the principles of justice and international law, adjustment or settlement of international disputes or situations which might lead to a breach of the peace.[4]

If any organization is to fulfil its purposes it must have the legal personality, competence, and powers to achieve these goals, or certain aspects of them. This could be the power to recommend that member states behave in a certain way, or it could be the legal power to bind member states to so behave, with the power to impose sanctions (expulsion, suspension, denial of certain rights and privileges, boycotts, economic measures, and military measures) on those members that do not comply. Furthermore, those powers might be delegated to differing organs within the organization.

[2] UN Charter, Art 10.

[3] *Certain Expenses of the United Nations (Article 17, paragraph 2, of the Charter)*, Advisory Opinion, ICJ Rep 1962, 151, 163.

[4] UN Charter, Art 1(1).

The recently re-emerged 'orthodoxy' that organizations should be limited to those powers, expressly delegated to them by the founding states and those that are strictly necessary to read into the text to give effect to the express powers,[5] represents an attempt to restrict the constitutional growth of organizations. Such a view is very much in the tradition of viewing organizations as the servants of their creators (the founding states). According to this vision, states have created organizations by an act of free will and they cannot thereafter be restricted in the subsequent exercise of their free will by their creations, unless they have clearly agreed to such limitations, in the express grant of competences or by necessary implication.[6] However, one is reminded at this point of Jean-Jacques Rousseau's memorable reflection on the human condition: 'l'homme est né libre, et partout il est dans les fers' ('man is born free but everywhere is in chains').[7] If a condition of pure freedom between states ever existed on the international plane (and there is little evidence that this was the case), then it was restricted upon the agreement of the first treaty, more so by the emergence of customary rules of international law, and significantly further by the creation of international organizations not based on unanimity. Furthermore, while a narrow approach to powers may be applicable to specialized agencies such as the World Health Organization (WHO), it has not been applied to the UN itself. Thus, a contrast can be made between those liberal interpretations of the UN's powers in matters of peace and security found in judgments of the International Court of Justice, such as in the *Reparations* and *Expenses* cases,[8] with the narrow view of the powers of the specialized agencies found in the Court's response to a request for an advisory opinion by the WHO on the *Legality of the Use by a State of Nuclear Weapons in Armed Conflict*.[9]

An organization with a broad constitutional base, such as the UN, means that though states may control the creation of the organization, once created it can develop a significant separate will. Although state representatives sit in the organs, the fact of majority rule, and the interpretation of the mandates of organs by entities and individuals working within the organization, signify that it is no longer in the control of each state. The establishment of a constitutional order signifies the importance of the purposes and principles of the Charter—found in the Preamble and Articles 1 and 2. These express the object and purpose of the Charter, and delineate the maximum extent of constitutional growth. Thus, the practice of the various organs as a means of developing and protecting these purposes and principles becomes important, as

[5] *Legality of the Use by a State of Nuclear Weapons in Armed Conflict*, Advisory Opinion, ICJ Rep 1996, 66, 78–9.

[6] Jan Klabbers, *An Introduction to International Institutional Law* (Cambridge: Cambridge University Press, 2009), 73.

[7] Jean-Jacques Rousseau, *Du Contrat Social* (Paris: Garnier Flammarion, 1966), 41.

[8] *Reparations for Injuries Suffered in the Service of the United Nations*, Advisory Opinion, ICJ Rep 1949, 174, 182–3; *Certain Expenses*, Advisory Opinion, 168.

[9] *Legality of the Use by a State of Nuclear Weapons in Armed Conflict*, Advisory Opinion, 78–9.

does the implication of powers, though not expressly granted, to achieve the aims of the organization.[10] The text becomes less important, but there are still clear legal limits as set by the constitution. For instance, Article 2(7) states that nothing in the Charter permits the UN to intervene within the domestic affairs of states and thus represents a restriction on the competence of the UN, though its scope has been narrowed over the years.[11] Both the Security Council and the General Assembly have increasingly intervened in the internal affairs of states, tackling issues such as the denial of human rights and self-determination on the basis that abuse can constitute a danger or threat to the peace, when asserting competence over matters of peace and security, or on the basis that the promotion and development of human rights and self-determination is, in itself, within the purposes and competence of the UN.[12] Thus, the Charter is a living instrument—it evolves and develops—thereby enabling it to keep pace with developments in the international order.

Constitutional documents such as the UN Charter go through different stages of evolution as the surrounding politics and the underlying balance of power change. The expansion of the competence of the General Assembly during the Cold War, evidenced early on in the enactment of the Uniting for Peace resolution in 1950,[13] is paralleled by the expansion in competence of the Security Council after the end of the Cold War. The latter does not somehow cancel out the former, but it does mean that advances in competence made by the General Assembly during the Cold War years are unlikely to be utilized in the post-Cold War era, when the Security Council is so dominant politically.

III. The Prohibition on the Use of Force, the UN, and Peace and Security

The prohibition on the threat or use of force is the most important principle in the UN Charter. The absence of widespread use of force by members, as well as the presence of a centralized and legitimate monopoly on the use of violence, are the basic elements for the survival of any society. Since Article 2(4) purports to control the threat or use of force by stating a norm of international law to which states must

[10] José E. Alvarez, 'Constitutional Interpretation in International Organizations' in Jean-Marc Coicaud and Veijo Heiskanen (eds), *The Legitimacy of International Organizations* (Tokyo: United Nations University Press, 2001), 104, 136–7.

[11] Georg Nolte, 'Article 2(7)' in Bruno Simma et al (eds), *The Charter of the United Nations* (Oxford: Oxford University Press, 2002), 171.

[12] UN Charter, Arts 1(2), 1(3), 55, and 56.

[13] Uniting for Peace, GA Res 377 (1950).

conform, and the Security Council is concerned with maintaining international peace by, inter alia, taking action against states using force in contravention of Article 2(4), it is plausible to examine the possibility of a correlation between Article 2(4) and the competence of the Security Council. One possible (narrow) approach is to restrict the Security Council's coercive competence under Chapter VII to threats or uses of force prohibited by Article 2(4). Following from this, Chapter VI empowers the Council to deal with potential breaches, whereas Chapter VII allows it to deal with actual breaches of Article 2(4). Indeed, further to this argument there is a direct relationship between the concept of 'threat of force' under Article 2(4) and the concept of 'threat to the peace' under Article 39, and that of 'use of force' under Article 2(4) and those of 'breach of the peace' or 'act of aggression' under Article 39. Such a thesis envisages that the Charter established a 'closed' rather than an 'open' system. The Security Council's competence would be defined, at its limits, by Article 2(4); and to determine that a situation was a 'threat to the peace' when it was not a 'threat of force' would be *ultra vires*.[14]

Nevertheless, the Charter was neither constructed with such precision in mind, nor has it been interpreted in that manner. The trigger for Chapter VI, that the situation or dispute endangers international peace found in Article 34, is not confined to potential breaches of Article 2(4). Furthermore, the triggers for Chapter VII are not to be equated with breaches of Article 2(4) since the concern of the Security Council is with world peace and security, much broader notions than the threat of armed force or the actual use of armed force. This concern for peace and security spreads to issues such as the proliferation in armaments, the spread of terrorism, the disintegration of failed and failing states, massive flows of refugees, egregious violations of human rights—all issues that might threaten international peace and security, but all matters that fall outside Article 2(4).[15]

IV. Breaches of International Law, the UN, and Peace and Security

Very few authors have argued that the Charter is 'closed' to the extent that the Security Council's ultimate competence is defined by Article 2(4).[16] Others have

[14] Nigel D. White, *Keeping the Peace: The United Nations and the Maintenance of International Peace and Security* (Manchester: Manchester University Press, 1997), 33–6.

[15] Rüdiger Wolfrum, 'Article 1' in Simma et al, *The Charter of the United Nations*, 41–2.

[16] But see Joachim Arntz, *Der Begriff der Friendensbedrohung in Satzung und Praxis der Vereinten Nationen* (Berlin: Duncker & Humblot, 1975), 63–4, 102–6.

argued that the Security Council's competence is or should be triggered by breaches of international law, so that measures taken under Chapter VII are seen as sanctions for breaches of international law.[17] While it is true that the Security Council has over recent decades responded to major breaches of humanitarian law for instance, and responded in ways that have led to the punishment of criminal behaviour, such as by the creation of criminal tribunals, its core concern remains peace and security.[18] Thus, a state possessing weapons of mass destruction may or may not be in breach of non-proliferation treaties and it may or may not represent a threat to international peace and security. The Security Council is concerned with the latter issue so, for instance, it may decide that there is no threat even though an arms control treaty has been breached, or alternatively it may decide that there is a threat and that is evidenced in part by the breach of the treaty; or it might decide that there is a threat even though the treaty has not been breached.[19]

Kelsen is of the opinion that it is 'completely within the discretion of the Security Council as to what constitutes a threat to the peace'.[20] Both Kelsen and Higgins state that because the Council is not fettered in its powers of determination under Article 39, such a determination can create new law as to what constitutes a threat to or breach of the peace.[21] It can be seen from this that the Council has a lawmaking role, but it does not necessarily follow that the Council is unfettered by international and Charter law. After all, the idea that key actors in international law are both lawmakers and subjects of the law is not new. While states accept obligations on a consensual basis in a bilateral or multilateral exchange with other states, at least in the pure Westphalian model of international law, the Security Council seems to be able to impose obligations without any reciprocal obligations being imposed on it. However, this seems to disregard the fact that, according to Article 24, the Security Council acts on behalf of member states, suggesting at least some form of reciprocal relationship, and that in so doing it is required to act in accordance with the purposes and principles of the Charter, agreed to by all member states. Article 1 includes as a purpose of the UN the maintenance of peace and security by means of collective measures if necessary, but also the promotion and encouragement of respect for human rights. Thus, even within the UN Charter, hard security concerns run alongside human rights, so that when fulfilling its primary purpose, the Council must have regard to human rights. As will be seen, the Assembly too has a

[17] Jost Delbrück, 'The Impact of the Allocation of International Law Enforcement Authority on the International Legal Order' in Jost Delbrück (ed), *The Allocation of Law Enforcement Authority in the International System* (Berlin: Duncker and Humblot, 1995), 135, 158; Vera Gowlland-Debbas, 'Introduction' in Vera Gowlland-Debbas (ed), *United Nations Sanctions and International Law* (The Hague: Kluwer, 2001), 7–9.

[18] *Tadić*, Case No IT-94-1-T (1995), para 19 (ICTY Appeals Chamber).

[19] See eg SC Res 1718 (2006) on North Korea; SC Res 1737 (2006) on Iran.

[20] Hans Kelsen, *Law of the United Nations* (London: Stevens, 1951), 727.

[21] Rosalyn Higgins, *The Development of International Law through the Political Organs of the United Nations* (Oxford: Oxford University Press, 1963), 266.

concern for both peace and security, and for human rights and self-determination, and though it does not have mandatory powers in these fields, it is governed in the exercise of its powers by the purposes and principles of the Charter, as well as any express limitations.

The UN, in both the Security Council and the General Assembly has, in practice, manifested a preference for an open system. In particular, it has applied the concept of a 'threat to the peace' in Article 39 to essentially internal situations.[22] Arntz argues that internal situations are not within the ambit of Article 39 because they do not constitute a 'threat of force' against another state within the meaning of Article 2(4). He argues that the text of the Charter, particularly the Preamble and Article 1, indicate that peace is the antithesis of war, and so the Charter only deals with threats to or breaches of interstate or international peace, and not to intrastate or internal peace.[23] However, the evidence is that if an internal situation or conflict such as found relatively early in the life of the UN, in the Congo and Southern Rhodesia in the 1960s,[24] is serious enough to threaten international peace and security then the Security Council will become involved. Hence, although there may be an overlap between the competences of UN organs and the rules on the use of force, the concern of the former is so much broader—the maintenance of international peace and security.

V. The UN and the Responsibility to Protect

In the broader context of international law, a strong argument can be made that the Security Council ought to act to prevent genocide, crimes against humanity, and other egregious violations of human rights, either because there is a duty on states and therefore on other actors possessing rights and duties to act within their legal competences to prevent such violations of international law,[25] or simply because such actions inherently undermine peace and security—they are antithetical to global order as well as being international crimes. However, given the Council's primary responsibility for peace, there may be problems in placing a further

[22] See eg SC Res 418 (1977) on South Africa. The General Assembly had determined that the situation in South Africa constituted a threat to the peace in 1965—GA Res 2054 (1965).

[23] Arntz, *Der Begriff der Friendensbedrohung in Satzung und Praxis der Vereinten Nationen*, 63–4.

[24] SC Res 161 (1961) re the Congo; SC Res 232 (1966) re Southern Rhodesia.

[25] See Art I of the Convention on the Prevention and Punishment of the Crime of Genocide 1948 which obligates states parties to 'prevent and punish' the crime of genocide.

responsibility upon it, especially if, in a particular instance, a military action to prevent a crime against humanity actually worsens the security situation and endangers world peace.

Nonetheless, in 2011 the Council took action to tackle crimes against humanity in the context of increasing violence within Libya. During the meeting at which Resolution 1973 (2011) on Libya was adopted,[26] the unanimity behind Resolution 1970 (in which the Security Council imposed non-forcible measures on Libya and Libyan leaders and referred the situation to the International Criminal Court (ICC)) was broken, but not to the extent of disabling the adoption of Resolution 1973 (2011) by 10 votes to 0 with 5 abstentions (Brazil, China, Germany, India, Russia). Those abstaining were not only the usual advocates of non-intervention (China and Russia) but important states, each with a strong case for permanent membership themselves.

The political change within the Council from the situation in Kosovo in 1999 when it could not agree on military action to protect the Kosovars,[27] to Libya in 2011 was marginal, but sufficient to give the initial action by the North Atlantic Treaty Organization (NATO) in Libya a sound legal basis. That marginal push may have been helped by the emergence in the early 21st century of the idea that there is a responsibility to protect (R2P) on the part of the international community, when a state has failed to protect its population from crimes against humanity or other similar egregious acts.[28] The UN World Summit Outcome Document of 2005 placed this responsibility on the government of the state, but then on the Security Council if the government failed to protect its population from genocide, crimes against humanity, or war crimes.[29] Both Council Resolutions 1970 (2011) and 1973 (2011) on Libya stated in the Preamble that the Libyan authorities bore responsibility to protect the population of Libya, which could be seen as a reference to R2P, though tellingly neither resolution went on to state that since the Libyan government had failed to protect its population, the Security Council had a responsibility to do so. Instead, the Council seemed to be exercising its primary responsibility for the maintenance of international peace and security, its traditional concern, making no reference to any other form of responsibility it might have. While there is no doubt that the Libyan crisis will be lauded as a precedent for R2P, the resolutions themselves do not support such an interpretation. At most, in the face of an imminent and brutal attack on the city of Benghazi, R2P arguments may have helped to persuade wavering permanent members not to veto the resolution authorizing necessary measures to protect civilians and civilian-populated areas.

[26] UNSC 6498th mtg (2011).

[27] See SC Res 1199 (1998); SC Res 1203 (1998) on the situation in Kosovo. Neither resolution expressly authorized 'necessary measures' to protect the people of Kosovo.

[28] See International Commission on Intervention and State Sovereignty, *The Responsibility To Protect* (Ottowa: International Development Research Centre, 2001); Report of the High-Level Panel, *A More Secure World* (2004), recommendation 55; Report of the Secretary-General, 'In Larger Freedom: Towards Security, Development and Freedom for All' (2005), para 135.

[29] World Summit Outcome Document, GA Res 60/1 (2005), para 139.

The obvious weakness in placing a responsibility to respond to specific acts of violence on a body in which a veto can block any effective action, leads to the question of whether there are legitimate and lawful configurations of states that can fulfil the responsibility to protect on behalf of the international community. In other words, when the Security Council is deadlocked in the face of imminent and catastrophic violence can other security institutions, principally the General Assembly and regional organizations, authorize necessary measures to prevent such violence? The potential R2P role of the Assembly will be returned to after considering its competence for matters of peace and security under the Charter in the next section, which not only relates those powers but discusses the sometimes fraught relationship between the Assembly and the Council in matters of peace and security.

VI. Division of Competence under the Charter

Normally the constitutive treaty of an international organization provides for a division of competence between organs. Occasionally it is argued that this is or should be along the lines of the separation of powers, with one organ being given executive powers, and another judicial, another legislative.[30] However, this pure form of separation is rarely found at the international level. Rather, the constitutive treaties divide and arguably balance powers between organs. The division of competence between the 'primary' organ for international peace and security, the Security Council, and the General Assembly has been a constant source of contention since the Korean War in 1950.

The powers of the Security Council are relatively clearly delineated in Chapters VI and VII of the UN Charter, with the former containing a range of recommendatory powers in relation to the peaceful settlement of disputes or situations that might endanger the peace, including fact-finding and recommending methods of adjustment or terms of settlement.[31] The powers contained in Chapter VII, to demand provisional measures such as ceasefires, to take a range of non-forcible measures including economic sanctions, and to take military action,[32] are contingent upon the Security Council finding a 'threat to the peace', 'breach of the peace', or 'act of aggression'.[33]

The Security Council has been creative in developing a range of non-forcible measures beyond general and targeted sanctions to include the creation of international

[30] Matthew Happold, 'Security Council Resolution 1373 and the Constitution of the United Nations' (2003) 16 *Leiden Journal of International Law* 593.

[31] UN Charter, Arts 34, 36, 37, and 38.

[32] UN Charter, Arts 40, 41, and 42.

[33] UN Charter, Art 39.

criminal tribunals and international territorial administrations.[34] In taking military measures against aggressor states and in tackling threats to the peace, the Security Council has relied on a system of 'coalitions of the willing' acting under a broad mandate, in lieu of the express Charter scheme of special agreements by states under the control of the Military Staff Committee and ultimately the Security Council.[35] Thus, the Security Council has significantly developed its competence in the field of peace and security, but the majority of these developments occurred after the end of the Cold War and with it the extended pernicious use of the veto. The first coalition of the willing was put in place by the Security Council in 1950 in response to North Korea's attack on South Korea.[36] It was dismissed as a historical aberration at the time and it remained so until the Cold War ended, Iraq invaded Kuwait in 1990, and Operation Desert Storm was authorized to take necessary measures to restore peace.[37] The coalition model has been used on many occasions since to tackle threats to the peace as well as the acts of aggression of North Korea and Iraq.

During the Cold War, with the Security Council deadlocked most of the time, emphasis was switched to the General Assembly and its secondary responsibility for peace and security. Inevitably, there is a division of views on whether the General Assembly has wide or narrow competence. A wide view of the competence of the UN General Assembly would point to Articles 10 and 14 of the Charter. Article 10 empowers the Assembly to 'discuss any questions or any matters within the scope of the present Charter or relating to the powers or functions of any organs provided for in the present Charter, and, except as provided in Article 12, [and] make recommendations to the Members of the United Nations or to the Security Council or to both on any such questions or matters.' As a result, Article 10 establishes a general competence for the Assembly to discuss any matter within the remit of the UN as determined by the Charter.[38] This power indeed makes the Assembly the 'town meeting place of the world', and 'the open conscience of humanity', as intended at San Francisco.[39] It follows that its power to adopt recommendations on any such matter must also cover the same area as the more concrete recommendatory powers of the Security Council under Chapters VI and VII.[40]

If Article 10 is insufficient to grant the Assembly the full range of recommendatory powers, Article 14 re-emphasizes its potentially wide jurisdiction with specific reference to international security by providing that 'subject to the provisions of Article 12, the General Assembly may recommend measures for the peaceful adjustment of any situation, regardless of origin, which it deems likely to impair the general welfare or friendly relations among nations, including situations resulting from a violation of the present Charter setting forth the Purposes and Principles of the

[34] eg SC Res 827 (1993) re ICTY; and SC Res 1244 (1999) re Kosovo.

[35] UN Charter, Arts 43–7. [36] SC Res 83 (1950) re Korea. [37] SC Res 678 (1990) re Iraq.

[38] Hans Kelsen, *The Law of the United Nations* (London: Stevens, 1951), 198.

[39] *Yearbook of the United Nations*, 1946–7, 51.

[40] Kay Hailbronner and Eckart Klein, 'Article 10' in Simma et al, *The Charter of the United Nations*, 264.

United Nations'. Article 14 with its jurisdictional threshold of a situation deemed 'likely to impair the general welfare or friendly relations among nations' appears to give the Assembly access to a much wider range of situations in the field of international peace and security than the Security Council. The Assembly can, under Articles 10 and 14, discuss situations covered by Articles 34 and 39, but to prevent any clash between the work of the Security Council, which is primarily concerned with such situations, and the General Assembly, Article 14, as well as Article 10, are subject to the limitation contained in Article 12. Article 12(1) provides that the 'General Assembly shall not make any recommendations with regard to that dispute or situation' while the Council is 'exercising in respect of any dispute or situation the functions assigned to it in the present Charter'. In practice, the Assembly often adopts resolutions on a matter at the same time at which the Security Council is considering the question.[41]

It seems to have been accepted practice at least in the early life of the UN that when an item was placed on the Security Council's agenda it was deemed to be exercising its functions in accordance with Article 12(1). The theory behind the list of matters which the Secretary General submits to the General Assembly is that it tells the Assembly which issues it is not allowed to discuss because they are receiving attention in the Security Council. In effect, this approach amounted to defining 'functions' in Article 12(1) with reference to Article 12(2).

The procedure in which the list of matters seized by the Security Council was also deemed to contain those matters in relation to which it is exercising the functions assigned to it may have been accepted at a very formal level, but in practice it has been disregarded. Western states could use their early dominance of both organs in the first decade to remove, by procedural vote, items from the agenda of the Security Council, where the Soviet veto might have been preventing action being taken, to put the issue before the Assembly.[42]

Whereas the Western states could use this method of transferring issues from the Council to the Assembly during the early Cold War period, the Non-Aligned Movement (NAM), once it became an established force in the 1960s, was not assured of winning a procedural vote in the Council and so in practice it tended to ignore procedural technicalities. In view of the importance of the UN to the NAM, it was not surprising that they took the attitude that their disregard of a technical procedure adopted during a period of Western domination was no more reprehensible than the manipulation by the West of the same procedure during the earlier period. Indeed, the Assembly's approach breaks what in many ways was an artificial link between Article 12(2) and (1). The approach developed during the Cold War was that the Assembly would decide for itself whether the Council was functioning within the meaning of Article 12(1), thereby instituting a crude form

[41] Hailbronner and Klein, 'Article 12' in Simma et al, *The Charter of the United Nations*, 290.
[42] See the Greek Question (1947–8) discussed in White, *Keeping the Peace*, 153–4.

of political accountability in the organization. This attitude to Article 12 has been maintained despite the ending of the Cold War, and seems to have received the qualified endorsement of the International Court in 2004 in its advisory opinion on the *Legal Consequences of the Construction of a Wall in the Occupied Palestinian Territory*.[43] Nevertheless, with the Security Council now 'functioning' more or less continuously and dealing positively with many issues brought before it, the Assembly has considerably fewer opportunities to assert its authority.

Articles 10 and 14 empower the General Assembly to discuss and make recommendations on matters which may be a danger to international peace within the meaning of Article 34, Chapter VI, or which constitute a threat to or breach of the peace within the meaning of Article 39, Chapter VII. Since these are the jurisdictional thresholds to the Security Council's competence in the field of international peace and security, there is a large area of overlap between the two organs. It is clear from Article 24(1) that the Security Council has 'primary responsibility' for peace and security, a position that Articles 11 and 12 of the UN Charter attempt to elaborate upon. Article 11(3) deals specifically with a situation which comes within Chapter VI, as defined by Article 34, by stating that the 'General Assembly may call the attention of the Security Council to situations which are likely to endanger international peace'. Article 11(3) seems to envisage the possibility of concurrent jurisdiction between the two organs in that it does not place an obligation on the Assembly to refer any such situation to the Council.

Article 11(2) addresses the issue of whether the Assembly can purport to exercise any powers similar to those possessed by the Council under Chapter VII by providing that the Assembly 'may discuss any questions relating to the maintenance of international peace and security brought before it' and 'may make recommendations with regard to any such questions to the state or states concerned or to the Security Council or to both'. However, Article 11(2) then crucially provides that 'any such question on which action is necessary shall be referred to the Security Council by the General Assembly either before or after discussion'.

Article 11(2) accords the General Assembly a general competence in peace and security and thereby empowers it to find a 'threat to the peace', a 'breach of the peace', or an 'act of aggression' and to make recommendations thereon to restore international peace, a power concurrent with that of the Security Council under Article 39, and one utilized by the Assembly in practice (reviewed in Section VIII). Though objected to by a minority of members,[44] such a power is reconcilable with the Charter. It is a recommendatory power only, any coercive measures under Chapter VII requiring a mandatory decision can only be adopted by the Security Council.[45]

[43] *Legal Consequences of the Construction of a Wall in the Occupied Palestinian Territory*, Advisory Opinion, ICJ Rep 2004, 136, 150.

[44] UNGA 1395th plen mtg, 1965 (Norway); UNGA 1671st plen mtg, 1968 (Netherlands).

[45] Jean-Pierre Cot and Alain Pellet, *La Charte des Nations Unies* (2nd edn, Paris: Economica, 1991), 283–5.

Support for this interpretation of Article 11(2) can be found in the *Expenses* opinion of 1962, though the Court considered the measures under review (namely peacekeeping forces in the Middle East and in the Congo) were based on the consent of the states in question and therefore did not constitute coercive measures against states. However, in its more abstract discussion of powers, the Court stated that 'only the Security Council…can *require* enforcement by coercive action', and further that 'it is the Security Council which, exclusively, may *order* coercive action'.[46] It follows from this that the Assembly can go as far as to recommend action by the Security Council, or to suggest voluntary sanctions, or further to recommend military measures.[47] There is a limited amount of General Assembly practice to support this contention (reviewed in Section VIII), although the power to recommend military measures has not been utilized in the full sense, and in the current post-Cold War climate, has become more a theoretical rather than a practical issue. The fact remains, however, that the General Assembly does appear, on balance, to have this power and it is not impossible to envisage a situation in which its future use may be considered.

Nevertheless, the power of the Assembly to recommend economic or military action is controversial in that in the original Charter scheme the only way in which the UN could undertake economic or military action was by a *mandatory* decision of the *Security Council* under Article 41 or 42. It is argued that since the UN has the power to order military action, then it must have the lesser power to *recommend* military action, and once this recommendatory power is recognized there is nothing in the Charter which prohibits the Assembly as well as the Council from exercising it. This contention, however, disguises the fact that recommendatory military action allows for the potential of greater abuse by member states, but it is the model that has in effect been adopted by the UN. Though it is practice for the Security Council to 'authorize' military action, the difference between this power and that belonging to the General Assembly to 'recommend' military action may be more than semantic,[48] but does not mean that the Security Council has 'required' or 'ordered' coercive military action. The reality is that under both the 'authorization' and 'recommendation' versions of the decentralized military option developed by the Security Council, states volunteer their forces to the UN for military action, and volunteering states decide on the extent of their commitment to the cause within

[46] *Certain Expenses*, Advisory Opinion, 163, emphasis added.

[47] Robert Y. Jennings, 'International Court of Justice Advisory Opinion of July 20, 1962' (1962) 11 *International and Comparative Law Quarterly* 1169, 1173; Juraj Andrassy, 'Uniting for Peace' (1956) 50 *American Journal of International Law* 563, 567–8, 571–2.

[48] Danesh Sarooshi, *The United Nations and the Development of Collective Security* (Oxford: Oxford University Press, 1999), 13; Jochen A. Frowein and Nico Krisch, 'Article 42' in Simma et al, *The Charter of the United Nations*, 759; Niels Blokker, 'Is the Authorization Authorized: Powers and Practice of the UN Security Council to Authorize the Use of Force by Coalitions of the Willing and Able' (2000) 11 *European Journal of International Law* 541, 562–3; Benedetto Conforti, *The Law and Practice of the United Nations* (The Hague: Kluwer, 2000), 204.

the terms of the mandate and subject to a duty to report to the mandating organ on measures taken.

VII. Division of Competence in Practice

The reference in Article 14 to the purposes and principles of the UN explains the development of one of the major roles of the General Assembly—the shaping of the right to self-determination referenced in Article 1(2). While the Security Council is established to further the first-listed purpose of the UN in Article 1(1), namely the maintenance of international peace and security, the Assembly's functions extend to cover the development and promotion of self-determination in Article 1(2) and human rights in Article 1(3),[49] in addition to its secondary competence in peace and security as evidenced in Articles 10 and 11. The division between peace and security on the one hand, and human rights and self-determination on the other, does not exclude the Security Council, as primary organ for peace and security, from dealing with violations of human rights and self-determination whenever the peace is threatened, nor does it prevent the General Assembly as the main UN organ for human rights and self-determination from addressing matters of peace and security, particularly where violations of human rights are occurring.

Another way of understanding the issue is to consider the purposes in Article 1 as defining the framework within which subsequent practice of the UN develops. Further limitations will be found in express prohibitions or limitations—for example, in Article 2(7). The International Court of Justice recognized that the main limitation on the practice of the UN was the purposes of the organization when it stated in the *Expenses* case that 'When the Organization takes action which warrants the assertion that it was appropriate for the fulfilment of one of the stated purposes of the United Nations, the presumption is that such an action is not *ultra vires*',[50] but it also discussed potential limitations on the powers of the organization in the Charter, especially Article 11(2) as regards the General Assembly.

Issues of peace and security often involve questions of self-determination and human rights and thus frequently both the Security Council and General Assembly are involved. Arguably, if the Council is functioning in relation to the issue, then the Assembly should only become involved if it concentrates on the issues of self-determination and human rights, and it does not transgress any express

[49] See further UN Charter, Arts 13(1)(b) and 55.

[50] *Certain Expenses*, Advisory Opinion, 168.

limitations such as found in Article 11(2) with its limitation of 'action' to the Security Council. Confining the General Assembly in this way did not prove to be possible during the Cold War as the majority of members (excluding Western states) viewed the denial of self-determination in the colonial context as a threat to peace.[51]

The example of Southern Rhodesia is dealt with at this stage, though a similar story emerges from the Assembly's practice during the Cold War in relation to the Portuguese Territories, apartheid South Africa, and the question of Palestine.[52] In the Southern Rhodesia situation, the Assembly was initially concerned with the failure to implement the 1960 Declaration on the Granting of Independence to Colonial Countries and Peoples,[53] and not with problems of international peace and security.[54] However, the Assembly moved beyond the issue of denial of self-determination in 1963 when it determined that the failure to extend basic political rights to the 'vast majority of the African population', and the 'entrenchment of the minority regime in power' created an 'explosive situation' which constituted a 'threat to international peace and security'.[55] It is arguable that after the Council had made a similar determination of a threat to the peace,[56] and started taking measures against Southern Rhodesia following the Unilateral Declaration of Independence in 1965, the Assembly should have left the situation to be dealt with by the Council. Nonetheless, the Assembly kept up its pressure on the Council as well as the white minority regime until settlement of the situation in 1980.[57]

Furthermore, the International Court of Justice confirmed the legality of Assembly practice as a means of interpreting its competence in 2004,[58] which was given in response to a General Assembly request for a Court opinion concerning the legal consequences arising from the construction of a security wall in the occupied Palestinian territory in the light of the rules and principles of international law. The resolution was adopted during the Assembly's reconvened 10th Emergency Special Session, and expressed its awareness of the inadmissibility of the acquisition of territory by the use of force and the denial of the principle of self-determination.[59] Thus, the Assembly combined its competence in matters of peace and security with its concern with issues of human rights and self-determination. The Court accepted the Assembly's competence to do so under Articles 10 and 11, thereby endorsing its competence to determine a threat to international peace and security.[60] The Court stated that Assembly practice had moved towards consistently acting in 'parallel' with the same matter concerning international peace and security.[61] Furthermore, the Court also stated that it was 'often the case that, while the Security Council has

[51] White, *Keeping the Peace*, 169. [52] White, *Keeping the Peace*, 170–2. See n 67.
[53] GA Res 1514 (1960). [54] GA Res 1747 (1962). [55] GA Res 1889 (1963).
[56] SC Res 221 (1966). [57] See eg GA Res 2562 (1970); GA Res 3116 (1973).
[58] *Wall*, Advisory Opinion, 136. [59] GA Res ES-10/14 (2003).
[60] *Wall*, Advisory Opinion, 145.
[61] *Wall*, Advisory Opinion, 149. See White, *Keeping the Peace*, 161–3, where the present author introduces the concept of the Assembly acting in a parallel fashion to the Security Council.

tended to focus on aspects of such matters related to international peace and security, the General Assembly has taken a broader view, considering also their humanitarian, social and economic aspects'.[62] The Court considered that this 'accepted practice' was consistent with the UN Charter specifically Article 12,[63] and in so doing dismissed Israel's argument that such practice was *ultra vires* as it argued that the Security Council was the body entrusted with matters of peace and security.[64]

The question remains whether the General Assembly can step into the shoes of the Security Council not only to determine a threat to the peace, but to tackle issues that are primarily if not exclusively issues of peace and security by recommending measures, either non-forcible or forcible. The issue of military measures was raised during the Korean War (1950–3), which will be discussed in the next section. Korea also involved one of the first instances of the Assembly recommending voluntary non-forcible sanctions. These were instigated by the pro-Western majority and directed not only against the North Korea aggressors, but also against the People's Republic of China, which had entered the war when the US-led forces approached the Chinese border in their bid to unify the country, and involved an embargo on military supplies and equipment.[65] Unsurprisingly, the Soviet Union declared that it viewed these sanctions as invalid since, it argued, they constituted 'action' within the competence of the Security Council according to Article 11(2).[66]

Assembly practice during the Cold War consolidated this competence, though the instigators in this period were the NAM and Socialist majority. Voluntary sanctions were called for by the General Assembly in the cases of South Africa, the Portuguese Territories, and Southern Rhodesia.[67] The Assembly's power to recommend voluntary measures was confined to colonial or racist regimes, and the sanctions mentioned previously were terminated with the end of colonial or racist domination. However, by tying zionism to racism in 1975,[68] the Assembly was able to subsequently justify recommending voluntary measures against Israel.[69] A US-led campaign led to the 'repeal' of the resolution that equated zionism to racism in 1991.[70]

VIII. Uniting for Peace

Controversy over the extent of the General Assembly's competence, as well as the extent of its encroachment on the functions and powers of the Security Council, is

[62] *Wall*, Advisory Opinion, 150. See White, *Keeping the Peace*, 169–72, where the present author analyses the practice to establish the Assembly wider competence.

[63] *Wall*, Advisory Opinion, 150. [64] *Wall*, Advisory Opinion, 148. [65] GA Res 500 (1951).

[66] UNGA 330th mtg (1951). [67] GA Res 1663 (1961); GA Res 2107 (1965); GA Res 2151 (1966).

[68] GA Res 3379 (1975). [69] See eg GA Res 39/146 (1984). [70] GA Res 46/86 (1991).

often centred on the Uniting for Peace resolution of 3 November 1950.[71] The immediate reason for the adoption of the resolution was the return, in August 1950, of the Soviet Union to the Security Council, leading to the discontinuation of the Council as the body able to address the Korean War. Previously, in the absence of the Soviet Union from the Council Chamber (in protest over the continued occupation of the Chinese permanent seat by the Nationalists instead of the Communists), the Council had recommended that the US-led coalition take necessary measures to repel the attack of North Korea and to restore international peace and security to the area.[72] In fact, the Assembly adopted an 'enforcement' resolution on Korea after the Soviets had returned to the Security Council but before the Uniting for Peace resolution was adopted.[73]

In reality, the reasons for Uniting for Peace went beyond Korea, in that the Western-influenced majority in the General Assembly at the time was also of the view that the frequent use of the Soviet veto during the period 1946–50 was an abuse of that right, and that the ideal of great power unanimity at San Francisco was no longer attainable. Western states wanted an alternative form of collective security, based not on permanent member agreement in the Security Council, but on the basis of the will of the majority in the Assembly. Such a concept of collective security, whilst opening up the potential for economic and military actions against transgressors, also had the potential, in theory, to allow the General Assembly to recommend military action against one of the permanent members. A more likely scenario would be for the Assembly to recommend military action that would affect the interests of a permanent member. It may be because this system of collective security was so potentially dangerous in upsetting the underlying balance of power that existed in the Cold War that the Uniting for Peace resolution restricted the Assembly's power to recommend military measures to the most flagrant violations of international peace, namely breaches of the peace or acts of aggression, and did not expressly permit the Assembly to take such measures as a response to threats to the peace.

The Soviet Union objected strongly to the resolution, in particular it argued that it violated the Charter requirement that coercive power was granted solely to the Security Council.[74] In the *Expenses* case the Court stated that 'action', which is the preserve of the Security Council,[75] refers to coercive action but it failed to state whether this excluded the Assembly from recommending coercive measures. At some points the Court suggested that 'action' was restricted to mandatory, coercive action 'ordered' by the Security Council. Thus, the Assembly did not appear to be barred from recommending enforcement action as part of its significant responsibility for the maintenance of peace as recognized by the Court.[76] There was no provision that clearly prohibited the Assembly from adopting this resolution.

[71] GA Res 377 (1950). [72] SC Res 83 (1950). [73] GA Res 376 (1950).
[74] UNGA 301st plen mtg, 1950, pointing to Art 42. [75] UN Charter, Art 11(2).
[76] *Certain Expenses*, Advisory Opinion, 162–5.

Furthermore, despite the wording of the Uniting for Peace resolution, there appears to be no cogent argument against allowing the Assembly to recommend military measures to combat a threat to the peace.[77]

There can be no doubt that Uniting for Peace was designed to enable the UN to achieve one of its primary purposes: the maintenance or restoration of international peace and security. In addition to fulfilling the UN's purposes, such a power must also be consistent with the principles of the UN contained in Article 2. Although Article 2(7), prohibiting UN intervention in domestic affairs, only expressly exempts Chapter VII measures by the Security Council, there can be little doubt that threats to or breaches of the peace are not domestic matters to which the provision applies. More problematic for Uniting for Peace is the rule prohibiting the threat or use of force in international relations contained in Article 2(4), since if the Assembly is empowered to recommend states to use force, this appears to be a prima facie breach. The exceptions to Article 2(4) are explicitly stated in the UN Charter to be self-defence by states under Article 51 of the UN Charter, and military action taken (in practice authorized) by the Security Council under Article 42 or 53. To state that the General Assembly can recommend military action arguably creates a third exception, which would appear to be contrary to Article 2(4), unless the General Assembly's power is restricted to the endorsement of the right of individual or collective self-defence under Article 51. Such endorsement is not a legal requirement but may be sought to increase the legitimacy of any proposed military operation. Clearly the debates preceding the adoption of Uniting for Peace showed that the envisaged power was not restricted to a legitimating function, whereby self-defence would be endorsed by the Assembly.[78]

Furthermore, the argument that the Security Council was simply endorsing the right of self-defence in the Korean and Kuwait operations of 1950 and 1990 respectively is misconceived, shown by the fact that contributing, neutral, and target states, as well as crucial actors such as the UN Secretary-General, viewed both operations as UN military operations, not actions in self-defence.[79] Though there is clearly an overlap between the right of self-defence under Article 51 and the power to take military action to restore peace and security under Article 42 when an armed attack/armed aggression has taken place, the legal basis of any military operation has to be judged by a combination of objective analysis of whether the necessary conditions for the exercise of the legal power are present, as well as the claims and reactions of states in relation to such military action.

[77] Sydney D. Bailey and Sam Daws, *The Procedure of the UN Security Council* (3rd edn, Oxford: Oxford University Press, 1998), 296; Hailbronner and Klein, 'Article 10' in Simma et al, *The Charter of the United Nations*, 266.

[78] UNGA 299th mtg (1950), France and the US; UNGA 300th mtg (1950), UK.

[79] Nigel D. White, 'From Korea to Kuwait: The Legal Basis of United Nations' Military Action' (1998) 20 *International History Review* 507, 612–16.

The Security Council in exercising its power under Chapter VII to authorize military action acts on behalf of the membership of the UN,[80] and so arguably the exceptions to the ban on force are those undertaken in legitimate self-defence and those authorized by organs representing the membership of the UN in matters of peace and security. The question of which organ within the UN authorizes them is an internal issue and does not affect the legitimacy of UN action vis-à-vis a transgressing state.[81] This internal issue can be resolved in favour of both organs having the ability to authorize (in the case of the Security Council) or recommend (in the case of the General Assembly) military action. It is submitted that the Assembly possessed a power to recommend military action in 1945, but its conversion from power *in abstracto*, to power in reality, has been achieved through the practice of the Assembly, including the Uniting for Peace resolution.

The Uniting for Peace resolution, whereby the Assembly can be activated in the face of a deadlocked Security Council by means of a procedural vote in the Council that is not subject to the veto, has been used to gain UN authority for innovative military actions. In the face of a military intervention by two permanent members (France and the UK) in the Suez crisis of 1956, and in the face of a threat to the peace in the Congo in 1960, which was in a state of collapse, the Security Council, unable to take substantive action itself due to the veto, transferred the matter to the Assembly,[82] which duly became the mandating organ in the case of the United Nations Emergency Force (UNEF), a traditional peacekeeping force, and temporarily in the case of the United Nations Operation in the Congo (ONUC), which acted in a more muscular fashion. Although it may be argued that these two operations were more 'peacekeeping' than 'enforcement', and thus are not direct precedents for seeking an enforcement mandate, the reality was that the Congo operation constituted enforcement action against non-state actors (secessionist fighters and mercenaries).[83]

In addition, the General Assembly had, even before the adoption of the Uniting for Peace resolution, become involved in the direction of the Korean military enforcement operation. In fact, the Assembly made a substantial contribution to the UN-mandated action in Korea by passing a resolution on 7 October 1950 which allowed the UN force to continue its military operations in order to establish 'a unified, independent and democratic government of Korea', after the Security Council had been deadlocked by the return of the Soviet representative.[84] This resolution was seen as permitting the US-led force's crossing of the 38th parallel and so can be classified as recommending enforcement action. The British Foreign Secretary,

[80] UN Charter, Art 24(1). [81] *Certain Expenses*, Advisory Opinion, 168.

[82] SC Res 119, 31 Oct 1956 (UK and France voted against); SC Res 157 (17 Sept 1960) (USSR voted against).

[83] White, *Keeping the Peace*, 254–61. But see *Certain Expenses of the United Nations*, 177.

[84] GA Res 376 (1950).

Ernest Bevin, who was instrumental in drafting the resolution, saw it as essential to have the mandate from the UN for the non-defensive intervention in North Korea.[85]

Though actual practice by the General Assembly in recommending that states take military action is extremely limited, the previous analysis has established that the Assembly has the power to make such recommendations, to combat threats to the peace as well as breaches and acts of aggression. The Assembly reluctance to exercise its powers is a reflection of the dominance of the Security Council in matters of peace and security, and increasingly in matters of international criminal law. However, when there is strong evidence of a threat to the peace and of egregious violations of human rights, there are compelling reasons to recognize that the Assembly needs to revive its apparently long-lost competence to recommend military action. In the face of genocide or crimes against humanity, both egregious violations of human rights that sit squarely in the remit of the General Assembly, and in the face of a deadlocked Security Council, the Assembly should come under increasing pressure to fulfil the UN's responsibility to protect.

It is somewhat ironic that a procedure advocated by Western states in 1950 was conveniently 'forgotten' in the case of the Kosovo crisis of 1999, when Western states (in the form of NATO) threatened and then used force to end the crimes against humanity being committed by Serb forces. The threat of Chinese and Russian vetoes seemed to have blocked further Council action beyond non-forcible measures. The cumbersome nature of convening an emergency special session of the Assembly, which can be done by the Assembly itself, was not a legitimate excuse for failing to activate Uniting for Peace, given that NATO first threatened to use force without express authority in October 1998 when the Assembly was meeting in its 53rd annual session. Canada briefly considered taking such an initiative,[86] as apparently did the UK. The reasons for not doing so were not primarily legal but political—a fear of losing the vote and a fear of resurrecting a precedent that might be used against Western states in the future, although the UK later stated that it doubted the legality of such a move.[87] Uniting for Peace provokes controversy, not only out of legal concerns, but because it embodies a very different approach to collective security than that envisaged by the Security Council.

Finally, it is interesting to note that the legality of the Uniting for Peace resolution was not really questioned when the Assembly utilized its reconvened tenth emergency special session in 2003 to request an advisory opinion of the International Court of Justice on the legal consequences of the construction of a security wall in

85 See Anthony Farrar-Hockley, *The British Part in the Korean War: Volume 1: A Distant Obligation* (London: HMSO, 1990), 209.

86 Paul Heinbecker, 'Kosovo' in David Malone (ed), *The UN Security Council: From the Cold War to the 21st Century* (Boulder, CO: Lynne Rienner, 2004), 543.

87 House of Commons Select Committee on Foreign Affairs, 18 Nov 1999, 63–4 (Emyr Jones Parry). But see 4th Report of the Select Committee on Foreign Affairs, 23 May 2000, para 128; Ian Brownlie and Christine J. Appleby, 'Kosovo Crisis Inquiry: Memorandum on International Law Aspects' (2000) 49 *International and Comparative Law Quarterly* 904.

the occupied Palestinian territory, in which the Court determined that the construction of the security wall by Israel was illegal.[88] In determining it had jurisdiction the Court was concerned, inter alia, with whether the conditions of the resolution were satisfied rather than with the legality of Uniting for Peace itself.[89] However, in determining that those conditions were—first that the Council had failed to exercise its primary responsibility as a result of one or more vetoes and, secondly, that the situation is one where there appeared to be a threat to the peace, breach of the peace, or act of aggression[90]—the Court was effectively endorsing the Assembly's competence in matters of peace and security as contained in the resolution.

IX. Conclusion

The Assembly is a slumbering giant, in thrall to the smaller but sporadically powerful Council. While the Council is equipped with an impressive array of powers, their use is not guaranteed even though the Council has become much more active in the post-Cold War period. Its failure to act in Kosovo in 1999 and in Syria in 2012, either side of its humanitarian military action in Libya in 2011, puts in perspective the true nature of its 'responsibility' to prevent and react to genocide and crimes against humanity. Such crimes were being committed in all three cases, and moreover all three were threats to the peace. In such situations, if a plan were to come from (a group of) member states and the Secretary-General involving peacekeeping, peace enforcement, or humanitarian action, and that plan were to be endorsed by the General Assembly,[91] this would neither be a breach of the Charter nor would it be confusing police action with issues of justice.[92] Rather, it would be a powerful form of collective security based on the principles of the Charter and on upholding the purposes of the UN.[93]

[88] *Wall*, Advisory Opinion, 197.
[89] *Wall*, Advisory Opinion, 136.
[90] *Wall*, Advisory Opinion, 151–2.
[91] Lester Pearson of Canada and Dag Hammarskjöld combined effectively in 1956 to put in place the first peacekeeping force under a General Assembly mandate—see William Roger Louis, 'The Suez Crisis and the British Dilemma at the United Nations' in Vaughan Lowe et al (eds), *The United Nations Security Council and War* (Oxford: Oxford University Press, 2008), 280, 297.
[92] But see Martti Koskenniemi, 'The Police in the Temple Order, Justice and the UN: A Dialectical View' (1996) 6 *European Journal of International Law* 325, 337–8.
[93] International Commission on Intervention and State Sovereignty, *The Responsibility to Protect* (Ottawa: International Development Research Centre, 2001), xii. But see Dominik Zaum, 'The Security Council, the General Assembly and War: The Uniting for Peace Resolution' in Lowe et al, *The United Nations Security Council*, 154, 156, 173–4.

CHAPTER 14

REGIONAL ORGANIZATIONS AND ARRANGEMENTS: AUTHORIZATION, RATIFICATION, OR INDEPENDENT ACTION

ERIKA DE WET

I. Introduction

This chapter examines the evolution of military operations by the African Union (AU) since the turn of the century. In doing so, it places particular emphasis on the development of the legal framework pertaining to regional security of the AU, as well as its relationship with the United Nations Charter. The latter emphasis is motivated by the fact that the AU has become increasingly involved in peace operations since the late 1990s. In addition, its constitutive documents underwent significant amendment in order to accommodate their new regional security role. In the analysis, reference is also made to the North Atlantic Treaty Organization (NATO), due to its impact on the evolution of the concept of 'regional organizations' and its military involvement in Africa during the Libya conflict in 2011.

After examining the meaning of the term 'regional organizations', the chapter reflects on whether and to what extent the UN Charter (still) requires prior authorization by the United Nations Security Council (UNSC) of a military intervention by a regional organization. This question has become particularly pertinent since the adoption of the Constitutive Act of the AU in 2000, which seems to allow for military intervention independent of any UNSC authorization under certain circumstances. Thereafter the chapter illuminates core aspects of the legal framework pertaining to regional security of the AU. It further gives an overview of the respective military operations in which the AU has been involved up to the time of writing (April 2014), including an assessment of the legal basis of these operations and their relationship with the UNSC.

II. Defining Regional Organizations

Article 53(1) of the UN Charter determines that:

> The Security Council shall, where appropriate, utilize such regional arrangements or agencies for enforcement action under its authority. But no enforcement action shall be taken under regional arrangements or by regional agencies without the authorisation of the Security Council.

The first pertinent question raised by Article 53(1) concerns the definition of 'regional arrangements or agencies' (which in this chapter are used interchangeably with the concept 'regional organizations'). The only article in the UN Charter that sheds light on this question is the first sentence of Article 52(1), according to which:

> Nothing in the present Charter precludes the existence of regional arrangements or agencies for dealing with such matters relating to the maintenance of international peace and security as are appropriate for regional action...[1]

From this article one can deduce that a regional organisation should have the task of taking care of the peaceful settlement of disputes within its own region.[2] The term 'regional' implies a distinctive feature about the members of the organization,

[1] The Charter of the United Nations of 26 June 1945, available at <http://www.un.org/en/documents/charter/>; see also Christian Walter, *Vereinte Nationen und Regionalorganisationen* (Berlin: Springer, 1996), 276.

[2] Ige Dekker and Eric Myjer, 'Air Strikes on Bosnian Positions: Is NATO Also Legally the Proper Instrument of the UN?' (1996) 9 *Leiden Journal of International Law* 413; Walter, *Vereinte Nationen*, 276.

which is generally understood to be of a geographic nature.[3] It can either relate to the geographic region from which all the member states come, or to the geographic area in which the organization will operate, or a combination of these factors.[4] Whatever the combination, the activities of the regional organization are limited to its own region and amongst its own members.[5]

The AU fulfils this requirement. However, there is still some debate as to whether NATO, which has thus far been the only organization to engage in full-scale enforcement action, qualifies as a regional organization in the sense of Article 53(1) of the UN Charter.[6] The reason is that NATO was originally adopted for the purpose of collective self-defence and would therefore be a regional *defence* organization which (initially) had as its sole purpose the offering of protection against external aggression.[7]

NATO was thus established as a collective defence organization in the sense of Article 51 of the UN Charter and not as a regional organization under Chapter VIII.[8] Its purpose was to deter a Soviet military attack in Western Europe, and to defend Europe from an attack should deterrence fail.[9] However, from NATO's activity in the former Yugoslavia onwards, one can conclude that the organization's constitution has been amended through the practice of its member states. Even though the alliance remains committed to self-defence, it now serves a broad concept of collective security that includes crisis management.[10] This change in the character of NATO's mandate has been endorsed implicitly within the membership of the UN by authorizing its involvement in Kosovo, Afghanistan, and most recently Libya.[11]

In spite of its expanded mandate, it is nonetheless still questionable whether NATO has evolved into a regional organization in terms of Article 53(1) of the UN Charter. Whereas a regional organization's activities are limited to its own

[3] Walter, *Vereinte Nationen*, 40.

[4] Walter, *Vereinte Nationen*, 40–1. The distinctive geographic factor can also be accompanied by cultural and historical ties such as those between the members of the Commonwealth.

[5] Walter, *Vereinte Nationen*, 276–7; Dekker and Myjer, 'Air Strikes on Bosnian Positions', 416; Mary Ellen O'Connell, 'The UN, NATO, and International Law After Kosovo' (2000) 22 *Human Rights Quarterly* 66.

[6] Heike Gading, *Der Schutz grundlegender Menschenrechte durch militärische Massnahmen des Sicherheitsrates—das Ende staatlicher Souveränität?* (Berlin: Dunker & Humblot, 1996), 32.

[7] Dekker and Myjer, 'Air Strikes on Bosnian Positions', 413.

[8] Dekker and Myjer, 'Air Strikes on Bosnian Positions', 414; Walter, *Vereinte Nationen*, 51.

[9] Celeste Wallander, 'Institutional Assets and Adaptability: NATO After the Cold War' (2000) 54 *International Organisation* 712.

[10] See the Declaration on Peace and Co-operation issued by the Heads of State and Government participating in the meeting of the North Atlantic Council (including decisions leading to the creation of the North Atlantic Co-operation Council (NACC)) of 8 November 1991, at <http://www.nato.int>. See also Wallander, 'Institutional Assets', 718.

[11] See eg S/RES/1244 (1999) that authorized the NATO presence in Kosovo; S/RES/1386 (2001) which was the first resolution that authorized a NATO presence in Afghanistan; and S/RES/1973 (2011) that authorized the NATO intervention in Libya.

members, NATO's expanded notion of its security role has exclusively crystallized in activities beyond the borders of its members.[12] Moreover, even if one were to regard NATO as a regional organization in terms of Chapter VIII of the UN Charter, the UNSC would most likely not be able to rely on Article 53(1) when deploying NATO troops 'out of area'. In keeping with the purpose of regional organizations (ie to maintain peace and security within their own area) the UNSC would only be able to rely on Article 53(1) of the UN Charter where it authorizes the regional organization to engage in military action within its own region *and* against (a) member State(s).[13]

When authorizing NATO to engage in 'out of area' enforcement action, the UNSC would have to rely on Articles 42 and 48(2) of the UN Charter. Whereas Article 42 allows the UNSC to designate the member states which will participate in the military action, Article 48(2) allows for such decisions to be carried out by the members of the UN directly and through their action in the appropriate international agencies of which they are members. Although this article first and foremost relates to the UN specialized agencies, its wide formulation makes it applicable to all types of international organizations (including NATO) whose members are also members of the UN.[14] This would inter alia imply that the NATO action in Libya in 2011 was based on Articles 42 and 48(2) of the UN Charter. Such a conclusion is further supported by the fact that the UNSC based the authorization to use force by states acting through 'regional organizations or arrangements'[15] under Chapter VII of the UN Charter and with no reference to Chapter VIII.[16]

The extent to which the AU relied on Article 53(1) of the UN Charter when participating in peace operations will be analysed in Section IV. Before doing so, however, it is necessary to discuss the extent to which this article requires an (explicit) authorization to the regional organization for engaging in enforcement action. This issue has been a bone of contention notably in relation to Article 4(h) of the Constitutive Act of the AU, which allows for intervention by the AU in member states in instances where certain grave circumstances are present.

[12] cf Niels Blokker and Sam Muller, 'NATO as the UN Security Council's Instrument: Question Marks from the Perspective of International Law?' (1996) 9 *Leiden Journal of International Law* 419, 420, who regarded NATO's evolution as sufficient for it to qualify as a regional organization.

[13] Walter, *Vereinte Nationen*, 278.

[14] Walter, *Vereinte Nationen*, 277; see also Michael Bothe, 'Die NATO nach dem Kosovo-Konflikt und das Völkerrecht' (2000) 10 *Schweizerische Zeitschrift für internationales und europäisches Recht* 183.

[15] S/RES/1973 (2011), para 4.

[16] See also as further examples the wording of S/RES/1244 (1999) which authorized the NATO military presence in Kosovo, as well as S/RES/1386 (2001) authorizing the International Security Assistance Force (ISAF) in Afghanistan.

III. Does Regional Enforcement Action Require (Prior) Authorization by the UNSC?

The second sentence of Article 53(1) of the UN Charter explicitly determines that no enforcement action shall be taken under regional arrangements or by regional agencies without the authorization of the UNSC.[17] Already in 1962 the International Court of Justice (ICJ) had defined 'enforcement action' as coercive military action in terms of Chapter VII of the Charter.[18] This in turn implies that Article 53(1) will only come into play in situations where the UNSC has made a prior determination that a threat to the peace, breach of the peace, or act of aggression exists. This fact combined with the clear wording of Article 53(1) indicates that the legality of a mandate for enforcement action by a regional organization is dependent on an explicit prior UNSC authorization to this effect.

Where no such authorization exists, the regional intervention would be illegal, unless it amounts to individual or collective self-defence in accordance with Article 51 of the UN Charter, or to military measures which do not amount to coercive measures and therefore fall beyond the scope of Article 2(4) of the UN Charter. These include peacekeeping ('Chapter VI½') operations performed with the consent of the affected state(s), in a neutral manner during which force is used only in self-defence.[19] It also includes military action by one or more states in another upon the request of the latter's lawful government (intervention by invitation).[20] One concretization of intervention by invitation is Article 4(j) of the AU Constitutive Act of 2000,[21] according to which member states can request intervention from the AU in order to restore peace and security.

Some authors have persistently argued that regional organizations have a residual power to adopt enforcement measures when the UNSC remains inactive in situations of gross and systematic human rights violations.[22] This argument is

[17] See generally Suyash Paliwal, 'The Primacy of Regional Organisations in International Peacekeeping: the African Example' (2011) 51 *Virginia Journal of International Law* 185 ff.

[18] *Certain Expenses of the United Nations*, Advisory Opinion, ICJ Rep 1962, 178. See Sir Robert Jennings, 'Advisory Opinion of July 20, 1962' (1962) 11 *International and Comparative Law Quarterly* 1173; see also Erika de Wet, *The Chapter VII Powers of the United Nations Security Council* (Oxford: Hart, 2004), 32–3.

[19] *Certain Expenses*, Advisory Opinion.

[20] For an analysis, see Georg Nolte, 'Restoring Peace by Regional Action' (1993) 53 *Zeitschrift für ausländisches öffentliches Recht und Völkerrecht* 635.

[21] The Constitutive Act of the African Union of 11 July 2000, available at <http://au.int/en/about/constitutive_act>.

[22] Nolte, 'Restoring Peace by Regional Action'. See also Matthias Herdegen, 'Der Wegfall effektiver Staatsgewalt: "The Failed State"' (1995) 34 *Berichte der Deutschen Gesellschaft für Völkerrecht* 76 ff, who supported humanitarian intervention by regional organizations without prior UNSC authorization in the case of a failed state.

underpinned by the rationale that the chances for abuse of the military mandate by a regional organization are less likely, due to the institutional and collective control provided within the regional body, as well as by the higher degree of disinterest and objectivity within an organization composed of mutually independent states.[23]

From a UN Charter perspective, this line of thinking would violate the second sentence of Article 53(1), which explicitly states that no enforcement action shall be taken by regional organizations without authorization by the UNSC.[24] Moreover, it also negates the fact that the UNSC may be deliberately refraining from action, because the major powers are not convinced that enforcement action is called for. Another problem with this argument is that it seems to assume that the UNSC could prevent the respective regional organization from intervening by adopting a Chapter VII resolution to that affect.[25] However, any such decision could be frustrated in practice by a veto of a permanent member which is silently condoning the illegal military operation. This is a real risk where the interests of a permanent member of the UNSC coincide with those of a regional (defence) organization. It is also aggravated where the institutional structures and controls exerted by regional organizations are rudimentary in practice, enabling the enforcement action to be dominated by the interests of the more powerful nations within the regional organization.[26]

The central role of the UNSC in authorizing any enforcement action, including those aimed at protecting the civilian population against gross human rights violations, was affirmed by the World Summit Outcome of 2006. This document, which was adopted by the United Nations General Assembly (UNGA), acknowledged that where a state failed to protect its population against suffering or serious harm resulting from internal armed conflict, the international community had a residual responsibility to do so. In such circumstances, the principle of non-intervention yielded to the 'international responsibility to protect' which can also include military action.[27] However, the document simultaneously underscored that any military intervention in the interest of the protection of the civilian population had to be authorized by the UNSC.[28] This would imply that there is no scope for states or regional (defence) organizations to engage in military action for protective purposes in the absence of a UNSC authorization.[29]

[23] Walter, *Vereinte Nationen*, 262, 264; see Nolte, 'Restoring Peace by Regional Action', 635; Nigel White and Özlem Ülgen, 'The Security Council and the Decentralized Military Option: Constitutionality and Function' (1997) 44 *Netherlands International Law Review* 388, 406.

[24] Dan Sarooshi, *The United Nations and the Development of Collective Security* (Oxford: Oxford University Press, 1999), 33–4.

[25] As suggested by Walter, *Vereinte Nationen*, 261.

[26] White and Ülgen, 'The Security Council and the Decentralized Military Option', 262, 264.

[27] World Summit Outcome, A/RES/60/1 (2005), para 79; see also 'In Larger Freedom', A/59/2005, para 135. See generally also Carsten Stahn, 'Responsibility to Protect: Political Rhetoric or Emerging Legal Norm?' (2007) 101 *American Journal of International Law* 99 ff.

[28] World Summit Outcome, para 79; 'In Larger Freedom', para 135.

[29] S/RES/1973 (2011), para 4 is an example of where such authorization was indeed obtained by NATO, for the protection of the civilian population under threat of attack in Libya.

Despite these objections, the AU seems to have formally claimed for itself the residual right to authorize enforcement action in instances of grave humanitarian concern. In accordance with Article 4(h) of the Constitutive Act of the AU, the organization may intervene in a member state pursuant to a decision of the Assembly of Heads of State and Government in respect of grave circumstances including war crimes, genocide and crimes against humanity.[30] The inclusion of this clause was motivated by the persistent inaction of the UNSC in the face of widespread and systematic human rights atrocities committed on the continent, including the genocide in Rwanda.

In accordance with Article 7(1) of the Constitutive Act, the Assembly takes such a decision on the basis of a two-thirds majority. No reference is made to any involvement of the UNSC. This suggests that prior authorization by the UNSC is not anticipated in instances where the AU relies on Article 4(h) of its Constitutive Act.[31] Subsequent legal and policy documents are more ambivalent, as illustrated by the Protocol Relating to the Establishment of the Peace and Security Council of the AU of 9 July 2002 (the Peace and Security Protocol). On the one hand, Article 17 acknowledges the primacy of the UNSC in the maintenance of international peace and security and pledges close cooperation with the UNSC in promoting and maintaining peace, security, and stability in Africa and in keeping with Chapter VIII of the UN Charter.[32] On the other hand, Article 16 of the Peace and Security Protocol determines that, insofar as the AU's relationship with sub-regional organizations is concerned, the AU would have the primary role in relation to the maintenance of peace and security on the continent. Some see this statement as running counter to the primacy conferred upon the UNSC, unless it were to mean that the AU decisions take primacy over those of sub-regional organizations such as the Economic Community of West African States (ECOWAS) and the Southern African Development Community (SADC).[33]

[30] Ademola Abass and Mashood Baderin, 'Towards Effective Collective Security and Human Rights Protection in Africa: An Assessment of the Constitutive Act of the New African Union' (2002) 49 *Netherlands International Law Review* 15.

[31] Anel Ferreira-Snyman, 'Intervention with Specific Reference to the Relationship Between the United Nations Security Council and the African Union' (2010) 63 *Comparative and International Law Journal of Southern Africa* 160.

[32] Protocol Relating to the Establishment of the Peace and Security Council of the African Union of 2 July 2002 (hereinafter AUPSC Protocol), Art 17(1) and (2), available at <http://www.au.int/en/content/protocol-relating-establishment-peace-and-security-council-african-union>; Alexander Orakhelashvili, 'The Legal Framework of Peace Operations by Regional Organisations' (2007) 11 *International Peacekeeping* 136.

[33] See 'The common African position on the proposed reform of the UN: The Ezulwini Consensus' (7th extraordinary session of the AU Executive Council, Addis Ababa, Ethiopia, 7–8 Mar 2005). In S/RES/1233 (2012) the UNSC for its part stressed the importance of cooperation with regional and sub-regional organizations in matters relating to the maintenance of peace and security, consistent with Chapter VIII of the UN Charter. See also Jeremy Sarkin, 'The Role of the United Nations, the African Union and Africa's Sub-Regional Organisations in Dealing with Africa's Human Rights

However, at this point in time, the debate about the (perceived) absence of a link between Article 4(h) of the AU Constitutive Act and Article 53(1) of the UN Charter remains academic. As will be illustrated in the following section, it has yet to be relied on for any intervention by the AU. So far the only full-scale military intervention in the interest of the protection of a civilian population in Africa concerned the military intervention in Libya in 2011 in accordance with UNSC Resolution 1973 (2011).[34] This operation was executed by NATO forces and took place under the overall control of the UNSC under Chapter VII of the UN Charter.

It is further unlikely that any large-scale military operation exercised by the AU will occur without UNSC approval as neither the AU nor its member states are currently in a position to finance or administer extended military operations on its own. The subsequent analysis will reveal that most operations thus far undertaken by the AU have been heavily dependent on Western logistical and financial support.[35]

IV. Military Intervention by the AU

The AU came into being as successor to the Organisation of African Unity (OAU) with the adoption of its Constitutive Act on 11 July 2000 and at the time of writing consisted of 54 African states. The involvement of the OAU in peace operations remained limited and the organization was unable to prevent any of the major civil conflicts of the late 20th century, including the genocide in Rwanda and conflicts

Problems: Connecting Humanitarian Intervention and the Responsibility to Protect' (2009) 53 *Journal of African Law* 77; Paliwal, 'The Primacy of Regional Organisations in International Peacekeeping', 197; Orakhelashvili, 'The Legal Framework of Peace Operations', 135.

[34] Art 4(h) of the AU Constitutive Act has since been amended by the Assembly of Heads of State and Government to read: 'the right of the Union to intervene in a Member State pursuant to a decision of the Assembly in respect of grave circumstances, namely war crimes, genocide and crimes against humanity *as well as a serious threat to legitimate order to restore peace and stability to the Member State of the Union upon the recommendation of the Peace and Security Council*' (emphasis added). However, this amendment is not yet in force. It requires ratification by two-thirds of the AU member states, which has not yet occurred. See First Extraordinary Session of the AU Assembly in Addis Ababa, Ethiopia (3 Feb 2003) and Second Ordinary Session of the AU in Maputo, Mozambique (11 July 2003). The precise meaning of what constitutes a serious threat to the legitimate order and how it relates to the other grounds of intervention in Art 4(h), which are all international crimes, is not clear. Neither is it clear what criteria the AU will apply in order to determine the legitimacy of a regime in an African state. See Sarkin, 'The Role of the United Nations', 18; Ferreira-Snyman, 'Intervention with Specific Reference to the Relationship Between the United Nations Security Council and the African Union', 157.

[35] This includes the EU-funded African Peace Facility. See Solomon Dersso, 'The Role and Place of the African Standby Force within the African Peace and Security Architecture', Institute for Security Studies (ISS) Paper 209 (2010), 7, 9.

in Burundi, the Democratic Republic of Congo (DRC), Liberia, and Sierra Leone.[36] The metamorphosis of the OAU into the AU was driven in part by the realization that Africa needed to become more self-efficient in preventing and resolving situations of widespread and systematic human rights abuses resulting from military conflict on the continent.[37]

The preceding section already drew attention to the fact that the AU's Constitutive Act endorses the promotion of peace, security, and stability on the continent as well as authorizing the intervention by the AU in a member state in respect of grave circumstances including war crimes, genocide, and crimes against humanity.[38] That section also illuminated the fact that the right of intervention foreseen in Article 4(h) of the Constitutive Act can be interpreted as a defiance of the central role foreseen for the UNSC in Article 53(1) of the UN Charter in relation to coercive military action by regional organizations.

The legal framework pertaining to military interventions as articulated in the AU Constitutive Act is complemented by the Peace and Security Protocol.[39] This Protocol established the AU Peace and Security Council as well as paving the way for the African Standby Force, which is to be deployed during military interventions pursuant to Articles 4(h) and 4(j) of the AU Constitutive Act.[40] The mandate of the 15-member strong AU Peace and Security Council is broad: ranging from the implementation of a common AU defence policy to the harmonization of regional and continental efforts to combat international terrorism; the promotion of arms control and disarmament; and the maintenance of peace, security, and stability in Africa.[41]

It is envisaged that the African Standby Force, when fully operational, should be capable of rapid deployment within 14 to 90 days depending on the nature of the operation.[42] It will consist of five regional standby brigades to which the member states of the respective regions will contribute. The composition of these brigades will include military, police, and civilian components. The African Standby Force will operate under the authority of the chairperson of the African Commission,[43] who

[36] The largest OAU peacekeeping mission was deployed in Chad and included some 3,500 personnel. See Orakhelashvili, 'The Legal Framework of Peace Operations', 137; Sarkin, 'The Role of the United Nations', 17; Paul Williams, 'The African Union's Peace Operations: A Comparative Analysis' in Fredrik Söderbaum and Rodrigo Tavares (eds), *Regional Organisations in African Security* (London: Routledge, 2011), 29.

[37] Sarkin, 'The Role of the United Nations', 17.

[38] AU Constitutive Act, Art 4(h); Paliwal, 'The Primacy of Regional Organisations in International Peacekeeping', 195–6.

[39] AUPSC Protocol, Art 17(1)–(2); Orakhelashvili 'The Legal Framework of Peace Operations', 135.

[40] AUPSC Protocol, Art 16(1).

[41] AUPSC Protocol, Art 2, Art 7(h)–(k). It comprises 15 members of equitable geographic distribution of whom ten are elected to serve for two years and five for a period of three years. See Sarkin, 'The Role of the United Nations', 21.

[42] AUPSC Protocol, Art 13(1); Dersso, 'The Role and Place of the African Standby Force', 7.

[43] Established by the AU Constitutive Act, Art 20.

will appoint a special representative and a force commander for every operation.[44] The expectation that the African Standby Force would be fully operational by the end of 2010 proved overambitious. At the time only the development of the East African brigade (EASBRIG) was well advanced,[45] while the remaining brigades for West Africa (ECOBRIG), Southern Africa (SADCBRIG), Central Africa (ECCAS), and North Africa (NASBRIG) were advancing much more slowly.[46] Therefore, the AU cannot yet rely on the Standby Force to the extent envisaged, and support from notably Western countries within the UN system remains essential during peace operations.

The following overview of AU peace operations will reflect that the right of states to request intervention in order to restore peace and security would be the most common basis for military intervention. Since the year 2000, this right is also concretized in Article 4(j) of the AU Constitutive Act. In addition, these interventions were undertaken in consultation with the UN which in three of the four operations subsequently took control of the operation.

A. Burundi

The African Mission in Burundi (AMIB) in 2003 was the AU's first peace operation and consisted of 3,500 troops from Ethiopia, Mozambique, and South Africa. It constituted part of Africa's attempt to broker a settlement to Burundi's long-running civil war, sparked by a coup in 1993.[47] AMIB came into being subsequent to a peace agreement in December 2002 between the transitional government and the rebel Forces for the Defense of Democracy.[48] The mission's mandate included monitoring the ceasefire agreements; securing identified assembly and disengagement areas; ensuring safe passage for the parties during planned movements to designated assembly areas; facilitating and providing technical assistance to the disarmament and reintegration process; and facilitating the delivery of the humanitarian assistance and providing VIP protection for designated returning leaders.[49]

[44] Ulf Engel and João Gomes Porto, 'The African Union's New Peace and Security Architecture: Toward an Evolving Security Regime?' in Söderbaum and Tavares, *Regional Organisations in African Security*, 19.

[45] Dersso, 'The Role and Place of the African Standby Force', 8; Engel and Gomes Porto, 'The African Union's New Peace and Security Architecture' in Söderbaum and Tavares, *Regional Organisations in African Security*, 20.

[46] Engel and Gomes Porto, 'The African Union's New Peace and Security Architecture' in Söderbaum and Tavares, *Regional Organisations in African Security*, 20.

[47] This mission was preceded by a contingent of 750 South African troops, sent at the request of the Burundian government in order to protect Hutu politicians who had returned to the country, as well as to train a local protection force. Williams, 'The African Union's Peace Operations', 30–1.

[48] Williams, 'The African Union's Peace Operations', 31.

[49] Communiqué of the Ninety-First Ordinary Session of the Central Organ of the Mechanism for Conflict Prevention, Management and Resolution at Ambassadorial Level, Central Organ/MEC/AMB/

Already at the time of its initiation, the transition of the operation to a UN mission was anticipated, as the AU lacked the necessary military and financial capacity to implement the mandate in the long term.[50] Subsequently in Resolution 1545 of 21 May 2004, the transition of AMIB to the United Nations Operation in Burundi (ONUB) was authorized under Chapter VII of the UN Charter.[51] The mandate of ONUB contained more extensive responsibilities in relation to disarmament and the protection of civilians under imminent threat of physical violence.[52] The only aspect of the previous mission in Sudan that remained under the control of the AU (with the consent of the Burundian government) concerned the protection of political leaders, as this was not covered by the ONUB mandate.[53]

B. Sudan (Darfur)

During the civil war in Darfur the government of Sudan was initially unwilling to consent to the presence of UN personnel on the territory. It did, however, consent to the AU Mission in Sudan (AMIS). AMIS was formally created by a communiqué of the AU Peace and Security Council at its Seventeenth Meeting in October 2004.[54] With an initial strength of 2,341 military personnel which was ultimately expanded to 3,320, AMIS was charged with monitoring the ceasefire agreement in place between the government and opposition forces, protecting civilians, and returning internally displaced persons to their homes.[55] AMIS was based on the consent of the government of Sudan which notoriously also constituted a member of the AU Peace and Security Council at the time. It was additionally endorsed by the UN in Resolution 1574 of 19 November 2004, but without investing AMIS with any enforcement power under Chapter VII or VIII of the UN Charter.[56]

However, the AU did not possess the financial, military, or logistical capacity to sustain the mission on a long-term basis, which necessitated the eventual taking over of the mission by the UN.[57] In March 2005 the UNSC established the 10,000-man

Comm (XCI) (2 Apr 2003), para 5; Paliwal, 'The Primacy of Regional Organisations in International Peacekeeping', 201.

[50] Communiqué of the Ninety-First Ordinary Session, para 5; Orakhelashvili, 'The Legal Framework of Peace Operations', 138.

[51] S/RES/1545 (2005), paras 2, 3.

[52] Orakhelashvili, 'The Legal Framework of Peace Operations', 138; Paliwal, 'The Primacy of Regional Organisations in International Peacekeeping', 202.

[53] Communiqué of the Twentieth Meeting of the Peace and Security Council, PSC/PR/Comm (XX) (15 Nov 2004), paras B(1)–(7); Paliwal, 'The Primacy of Regional Organisations in International Peacekeeping', 202.

[54] Communiqué of the Seventeenth Meeting of the Peace and Security Council, para 4.

[55] Communiqué of the Seventeenth Meeting, para 7.

[56] S/RES/1574 (2004), para 13; Paliwal, 'The Primacy of Regional Organisations in International Peacekeeping', 199.

[57] Williams, 'The African Union's Peace Operations', 33; Orakhelashvili, 'The Legal Framework of Peace Operations', 138.

strong United Nations Mission in Sudan (UNMIS) in Resolution 1590 of 24 March 2005.[58] Although the mandate of UNMIS was similar to that of AMIS, UNMIS was authorized under Chapter VII of the UN Charter to take the necessary action to protect UN personnel and facilities and ensure the security and freedom of their movement and the movement of humanitarian workers, as well as protecting civilians under imminent threat of physical violence.[59] UNMIS initially coexisted alongside AMIS with which it was expected to coordinate and liaise closely.[60] Subsequently, with the adoption of Resolution 1679 of 16 May 2006 the UNSC initiated the transformation and integration of AMIS into a UN mission. This decision was taken under Chapter VII of the UN Charter and with the support of the AU Peace and Security Council.[61]

c. Somalia

Subsequent to his election as president of Somalia's Transitional Federal Government in 2004, Colonel Abulah Yusuf requested the AU to deploy a peacekeeping mission to assist him in stabilizing his government in Somalia.[62] Instead of giving effect to this request itself, the AU endorsed a decision of the Intergovernmental Authority on Development (IGAD)[63] in March 2005 to deploy a peacekeeping mission involving 10,000 troops. However, no state was willing to commit troops and the mission was never deployed.[64]

In late 2006, the creation of a peacekeeping operation gained new momentum with the adoption of UNSC Resolution 1725 of 6 December 2006. This resolution, which was adopted under Chapter VII of the Charter, authorized IGAD and member states of the AU to establish a protection and training mission in Somalia (the IGAD Peace Support Mission in Somalia, IGASOM). Its mandate inter alia included the monitoring of the dialogue between the Transitional Federal Institutions and the Union

[58] S/RES/1590 (2005), para 1. [59] S/RES/1590 (2005), paras 4, 16.

[60] S/RES/1590 (2005), para 2.

[61] S/RES/1679 (2006), para 3; Paliwal, 'The Primacy of Regional Organisations in International Peacekeeping', 200; Orakhelashvili, 'The Legal Framework of Peace Operations', 139.

[62] Williams, 'The African Union's Peace Operations', 33.

[63] IGAD constitutes the successor to the Authority on Drought and Development which was created in 1986 and comprised Djibouti, Eritrea, Kenya, Somalia, Sudan, and Uganda. This organization had a narrow mandate around the issue of drought and desertification. See Frederik Söderbaum and Björn Hettne, 'Regional Security in a Global Perspective' in Ulf Engel and João Gomes Porto (eds), *Africa's New Peace and Security Architecture* (Farnham: Ashgate, 2011), 25.

[64] Art 19 of the IGAD Charter determines that member states shall act collectively to preserve peace, security, and stability which are essential prerequisites for economic development and social progress. IGAD has thus far mainly focused on conflicts in Sudan and Somalia. It has created a standing Committee on Peace for each of these countries, which serves as a consultative forum for peace negotiations. See Sarkin, 'The Role of the United Nations', 27; Söderbaum and Hettne, 'Regional Security in a Global Perspective' in Engel and Gomes Porto, *Africa's New Peace and Security Architecture*, 26–7; Williams, 'The African Union's Peace Operations', 33, 40.

of Islamic Courts; ensuring free movement and safe passage of all those involved with the dialogue process; maintaining and monitoring security in Baidoa; providing protection for members of the Transitional Federal Institutions and government as well as their key infrastructure; and providing training for the Transitional Federal Institutions' security forces.[65]

Soon afterwards, in January 2007, the AU Peace and Security Council (led by Ethiopia) established the AU Mission in Somalia (AMISON) which replaced and subsumed IGASOM.[66] AMISON's mandate was very similar to that of IGASOM and was also approved by the UNSC. Resolution 1744 of 21 February 2007 authorized the mission under Chapter VII of the UN Charter to take all necessary measures as appropriate to carry out its mandate.[67]

AMISON faced many challenges after its inception. Its mandate to support the weak Transitional Federal Government met with disapproval from many Somalis who regarded it as illegitimate. In addition, there was widespread concern that Ethiopia was directly shaping the AU's position on the conflict in Somalia. These factors, combined with the fact that AMISON had to function in a situation of ongoing conflict, made many African states reluctant to contribute troops to the mission.[68]

D. The Comoros

Subsequent to the election of Abdallah Sambi as president of the Comoros in 2007, tensions rose as Mohammed Bacar (who had ruled the island of Anjouan since 2001) attempted to cling to power. Bacar organized an illegal election on the island after which he declared himself the winner and announced the independence of Anjouan from the Union of the Comoros.[69] This behaviour was criticized by the AU Electoral and Security Assistance Mission (MAES), which the AU had created in May 2007 to support and monitor the election process.[70]

The AU Peace and Security Council thereafter amended the mandate of MAES in March 2008 in order to authorize Operation Democracy. This involved a direct invasion of Anjouan, the installation of an interim leader for the island, and plans to resume or rerun the Anjouan presidential elections on the island.[71] Subsequently,

[65] S/RES/1725 (2006), para 3.

[66] Communiqué of the Sixty-Ninth Meeting of the Peace and Security Council, PSC/PR/Comm (LXIL) (19 Jan 2007); Paliwal, 'The Primacy of Regional Organisations in International Peacekeeping', 20.

[67] S/RES/1744 (2007), preamble, paras 4, 12; Paliwal, 'The Primacy of Regional Organisations in International Peacekeeping', 204.

[68] Williams, 'The African Union's Peace Operations', 41–2.

[69] Williams, 'The African Union's Peace Operations', 38.

[70] Williams, 'The African Union's Peace Operations', 38.

[71] Report of the Chairperson of the Commission on the Situation in the Comoros Since the 10th Ordinary Session of the Assembly of the African Union held in Addis Ababa from 31 January–2 February 2008, PSC/PR/2 (CXXIV) (30 Apr 2008), paras 13, 15–21.

the mandate of MAES was expanded to support the Comorian efforts to collect arms and ammunition in Anjouan and assist in organizing the election of a president for the island of Anjouan.[72]

The military intervention was undertaken with the consent and at the request of the legitimate government of the Comoros.[73] It would therefore seem that Article 4(j) of the AU Constitutive Act is the most likely basis for the intervention.[74] It was spearheaded by Tanzania and Sudan and with logistical support from Libya and France, but without any formal UN involvement. From a military perspective, the operation was an easy target, as the island was small and weak; politically, the operation was controversial, not least due to the involvement of Sudanese soldiers in an operation apparently directed at restoring democracy. In addition, it came across as selective as no military action was taken in other countries in the region which were also confronted with unconstitutional changes of government at the time, such as Mauritania and Togo.[75]

V. Conclusion

The previous analysis reflects a marked distinction between the AU's formal policy regarding regional security and the practical reality. The AU's legal framework and official policy initiatives reflect ambitious security goals and a proactive approach to peace operations which would have been difficult to imagine before the turn of the century. This new approach also reflects a willingness to operate independently from the UNSC. However, the current practice of peace operations within the AU reflects that the organization remains dependent on the (Western members of the) UN for logistical, financial, and military assistance. This reality makes any full-scale military intervention by the AU without a UNSC authorization unlikely.

All the military operations thus far carried out by the AU occurred on the invitation of the recognized government and sometimes also with the consent of rebel groups. This would imply that the principles of intervention by invitation or even classic peacekeeping would constitute the primary legal bases for these

[72] Communiqué of the 124th Meeting of the Peace and Security Council, PSC/PR/Comm (CXXIV) (30 Apr 2008), para 6; Williams, 'The African Union's Peace Operations', 38.

[73] Communiqué of the 124th Meeting, paras 3, 17.

[74] See also See Ferreira-Snyman, 'Intervention with Specific Reference to the Relationship Between the United Nations Security Council and the African Union', 157. She suggested that the rejection of unconstitutional changes of government in Art 4(p) of the AU Constitutive Act may have constituted the basis, although this is not formulated as a separate ground for intervention in the AU Constitutive Act.

[75] Williams, 'The African Union's Peace Operations', 39.

interventions. Both principles are well established in international law and do not amount to a violation of Article 2(4) of the UN Charter. This in turn would imply that a UNSC authorization would not have been necessary in these instances—if and to the extent that the scope and duration of the mandate remained in line with the consent of the recognized government. In practice, UNSC authorizations under Chapter VII of the UN Charter did complement the consensual basis of the mandates discussed earlier, either by endorsing AU intervention or in paving the way for its integration into a UN mission.

As a result, it seems premature to suggest that the practice of the AU amounts to the emergence of a new customary right to engage in 'first-instance enforcement action'.[76] Although several of the military interventions discussed previously reflected a division of labour in accordance with which the AU paved the way for a UN mission, this was based on practical considerations rather than due to any new legal basis for military intervention. Given the socio-economic realities on the African continent, sustainable free-standing AU peace enforcement that occurs politically, financially, and ultimately also legally independent from the UN is not likely to occur in the near future.

[76] As suggested by Paliwal, 'The Primacy of Regional Organisations in International Peacekeeping', 220, 221.

CHAPTER 15

USE OF FORCE: JUSTICIABILITY AND ADMISSIBILITY

A. MARK WEISBURD

I. Introduction

The International Court of Justice (ICJ) is the principal judicial organ of the United Nations.[1] When legal issues arise from the use of force, therefore, the ICJ may be asked to address the law governing the use of force. There are, however, limits on the ICJ's capacity to affect this body of law. This chapter addresses one set of such potential limitations: restrictions on the ICJ's capacity to act which arise from problems of admissibility or justiciability.

Considering admissibility first, it must initially be noted that the term is difficult to define clearly. The closest the Court has come to defining admissibility its observation that objections to admissibility normally take the form of an assertion that, even if the Court has jurisdiction and the facts stated by the applicant state are assumed to be correct, nonetheless there are reasons why the Court should not

1 UN Charter, Art 92.

proceed to an examination of the merits.[2] However, some of the Court's decisions add content to the concept.

While the Court has called several cases inadmissible, in which it found no concrete dispute between the parties,[3] and treated similarly a case involving a dispute affecting the rights of a non-party state,[4] the case with the most bearing on this discussion is the judgment of the Permanent Court of International Justice in *Free Zones of Upper Savoy and the District of Gex (Switzerland v. France)*.[5] In that case, the parties had asked the Court to, inter alia, devise rules for a customs regime affecting parts of their territories.[6] The Court refused to do so, characterizing such a task as unsuitable to the role of a court of justice.[7] It went on to observe that:

> the settlement of such matters is not a question of law, but is a matter depending on the interplay of economic interests on which no Government can afford to be controlled by an outside organ. Such questions are outside the sphere in which a Court of Justice, concerned with the application of rules of law, can help in the solution of disputes between two States.[8]

Two aspects of this language stand out. First, the Court considered the resolution of economic questions as not susceptible to control by legal rules, and therefore not a task for a judicial body. Secondly, the Court saw the matter as one so important that any government would necessarily have to reserve final decisions to itself; as to this second point, the Court's language implies that governments' maintaining control of such decisions was not only inevitable but, more fundamentally, proper.

Thus, we have three different bases for a determination that a case is not admissible: first, that the parties' dispute cannot be called a legal dispute; secondly, that the issue is not one resolvable by the application of legal rules; and, thirdly, that the issue is one that necessarily must be addressed by an institution other than the Court.

The Court has never addressed justiciability as such. However, that term too refers to the question whether there are reasons why a court ought not decide a particular case over which it has jurisdiction. The three categories of admissibility specified in the preceding paragraph also describe situations in which a case could be called non-justiciable. Indeed, the only difference between the two ideas in the practice of the Court would appear to be that, formally, admissibility issues are raised by respondents as preliminary objections, while the Court can find itself

[2] *Oil Platforms (Iran v. US)*, Merits, ICJ Rep 2003, 161, 177 (6 Nov).

[3] See eg *Northern Cameroons (Cameroon v. UK)*, Preliminary Objections, ICJ Rep 1963, 15; *Nuclear Tests (Australia v. France)*, Judgment, ICJ Rep 1974, 253; *Nuclear Tests (New Zealand v. France)*, Judgment, ICJ Rep 1974, 457.

[4] *Monetary Gold Removed from Rome in 1943 (Italy v. France, UK and US)*, ICJ Rep 1954 19. Compare *Certain Phosphate Lands in Nauru (Nauru v. Australia)*, ICJ Rep 1992, 240.

[5] PCIJ, Ser A/B, No 46. [6] At 160–1. [7] At 162. [8] At 161–2.

confronting justiciability issues at any stage of the proceedings. The discussion that follows therefore will treat the categories in the foregoing paragraph as applicable to both justiciability and admissibility.

This discussion will focus on the last two of those categories. That is, it will consider disputes involving the use of force that cannot be decided without the exercise of non-legal judgement. The chapter will also address cases that, though not outside the Court's jurisdiction, would be more properly resolved by a different body.

The problem presented when judges are asked to resolve an issue that turns on non-legal considerations is one with which lawyers should be generally familiar. However, as will be discussed in greater detail later, cases addressing the use of force can present unique difficulties.

The question of whether the Court or some other institution ought properly to deal with a given matter implicates the authority of the Security Council of the United Nations. Under the Charter, the Security Council has primary responsibility for the maintenance of international peace and security;[9] further, members of the UN are obliged to comply with its decisions,[10] and it is authorized to decide[11] among a virtually unlimited menu of tools[12] how best to respond to a situation it concludes is a threat to the peace, breach of the peace, or act of aggression.[13] Given the very broad scope of the Security Council's authority, it is important to understand how the Court deals with cases that arguably involve that authority.

The discussion which follows will examine these matters in greater detail.

II. The ICJ and Cases Requiring the Exercise of Non-Legal Judgement

A. Introduction

The Court may be called upon to decide cases requiring the exercise of non-legal judgement in at least two sets of circumstances. First, the nature of a particular dispute may make it difficult for someone without special training even to recount events. Secondly, there will be cases in which the problem is not so much

[9] UN Charter, Art 24. [10] Art 25. [11] Art 39. [12] Arts 40–9. [13] Art 39.

disagreement over historical facts as it is that of evaluating those facts by applying specialized knowledge of some subject other than law.

The first of these types of questions is not unique to use of force issues; it is not uncommon for triers of fact to face the task of assessing the testimony of witnesses. However, the unusual difficulties in obtaining facts regarding military operations can be exacerbated when the significance of the facts is not apparent to someone without military expertise. Such cases shade over into those involving the second sort of question as, for example, in a use of force case in which it is necessary to evaluate behaviour according to standards employed by persons with experience in the problems of making military decisions. If decisions in such cases are made by persons lacking the necessary specialized knowledge, the results may be doubtful. Indeed, even the Court in *Military and Paramilitary Activities in and against Nicaragua (Nicaragua v. US)* has acknowledged that its making determinations requiring the exercise of military judgement could be problematic.[14]

The discussion now turns to the cases arguably raising questions about the Court's capacity to determine and evaluate fact questions in the use of force context. It should be stressed that the Court discussed military considerations in resolving what it denominated as an admissibility issue only in *Military and Paramilitary Activities in and against Nicaragua (Nicaragua v. US)*.[15] However, it addressed issues analogous to admissibility in *Legality of Threat or Use of Nuclear Weapons*.[16] In the other three cases examined, as the following discussion will show, it was forced to deal with issues arguably requiring the evaluation of military considerations; these cases therefore provide further understanding of the Court's approach in such matters, albeit not in the context of admissibility.

1. *Corfu Channel (UK v. Albania)*

In this case,[17] the UK instituted proceedings against Albania alleging that Albania was responsible for the harm done to certain Royal Navy warships, which while traversing the Corfu Channel in October 1946, struck mines.[18] The case turned on

[14] Merits, ICJ Rep 1986, 14. In that case, the US sought to respond to allegations of US violations of international law by characterizing its actions as an exercise of the right of self-defence. As the Court noted, the US argued that its raising the issue of self-defence required determining whether the US faced the necessity of using force, and that such a determination involves a pronouncement on political and military matters, not a question of a kind that a court can usefully attempt to answer, para 34. The Court responded to this concern by stating that, in the light of the posture of the case, its resolution of the dispute would not necessarily involve it in any evaluation of military considerations, para 35. This response suggests that the Court agreed that it might face difficulties if it attempted to engage in such an evaluation.

[15] *Military and Paramilitary Activities in and against Nicaragua (Nicaragua v. US)*, Jurisdiction of the Court and Admissibility of the Application, ICJ Rep 1984, para 99.

[16] Advisory Opinion, ICJ Rep 1996, para 15.

[17] ICJ Rep 1949, 4.

[18] At 6, 12–13.

the questions of whether Albania, or Yugoslavia acting with Albania, had laid the mines and, if that question could not be answered, whether the mines could have been laid without the knowledge of the Albanian government.[19]

Resolving the case required the Court to decide a number of issues of fact. After hearing the parties' witnesses, it appointed, on its own initiative, a committee of neutral naval officers to investigate and report on certain disputed factual questions.[20] These questions related to crucial issues in the case, in particular, whether the mines could have been laid without Albania's knowledge.[21] In subsequently deciding that the Albanian government must have known of the minelaying, the Court relied heavily on the experts' reports.[22]

In this case, the Court actively sought to supplement the parties' evidence in order to address particular fact questions. It should also be noted, however, that the necessary evidence was apparently not difficult to obtain and the naval officers who assessed the evidence for the Court had only to answer relatively objective questions.[23] This case therefore differed from one where evidence was difficult to obtain, or where assessment of the evidence was less straightforward.

2. *Nicaragua v. US*

This case presented use of force issues different in kind from those in *Corfu Channel*. Nicaragua alleged that the US had violated international law by supporting the so-called contra rebels' efforts to overthrow Nicaragua's government and by mining Nicaraguan ports. The US raised numerous preliminary objections, among them the argument that the Court should treat the case as inadmissible 'in consideration of the inability of the judicial function to deal with situations involving ongoing conflict', referring to the difficulty in resolving factual issues in such cases.[24]

The Court rejected this argument, stating that a case was not inadmissible simply because one of the parties bore the burden of proof on an issue as to which evidence might well be unavailable:

> it is the litigant seeking to establish a fact who bears the burden of proving it; and in cases where evidence may not be forthcoming, a submission may in the judgment be rejected as unproved, but is not to be ruled out as inadmissible *in limine* on the basis of an anticipated lack of proof.[25]

[19] At 15–16. [20] At 7–9.

[21] *Corfu Channel (UK v. Albania)*, Order made on 17 Dec 1948, ICJ Rep 1948, 124, 124–6 (hereafter *Corfu Channel*, Order of 17 Dec).

[22] *Legality of Threat or Use of Nuclear Weapons*, Advisory Opinion, paras 20–2.

[23] eg the range of visibility from a given location at a specific time and day, *Corfu Channel*, Order of 17 Dec, 125, or whether whoever laid the mines in question could have acted without being observed by the Albanian authorities, *Corfu Channel*, Order of 17 Dec, 126.

[24] *Nicaragua*, Jurisdiction of the Court and Admissibility of the Application, para 99.

[25] *Nicaragua*, para 99.

The Court confronted another sort of question during the merits phase of this case.[26] The US did not appear in that phase, but its earlier pleadings made clear that it did not seriously contest the broad outlines of Nicaragua's factual allegations regarding US actions. Rather, it argued that those actions amounted to lawful self-defence or, more precisely, as collective self-defence in concert with El Salvador against Nicaragua's support for an insurgency in El Salvador.[27] In that connection, the US argued that considering that defence would require the Court to consider military matters beyond its expertise. The Court observed that it would not need to consider such issues if the legal prerequisites for the self-defence claim were absent.[28] In fact, it reached that conclusion.[29]

Nonetheless, the Court did not in fact refrain from an evaluation of military considerations. In its discussion of the facts of the case, the Court observed that, while the US had in 1981 raised with Nicaragua concerns regarding arms flows from Nicaragua to El Salvador, it had refused, citing security considerations, to provide Nicaragua with evidence of its claims.[30] For this reason, the Court stated, it could not assess the value of this evidence. It went on to observe:

> the Court would remark that, if [evidence of smuggling] really existed, the United States could be expected to have taken advantage of it in order to forestall or disrupt the traffic observed; it could presumably for example arrange for the deployment of a strong patrol force in El Salvador and Honduras, along the frontiers of these States with Nicaragua. It is difficult to accept that it should have continued to carry out military and paramilitary activities against Nicaragua if their only purpose was, as alleged, to serve as a riposte in the exercise of the right of collective self-defence.[31]

There were similarities between the Court's attitude on this issue and its treatment of Article XXI in the treaty between the US and Nicaragua,[32] which formed the basis of the Court's jurisdiction in the case. That article provided that 'the present Treaty shall not preclude the application of measures [by a party]...necessary to protect its essential security interests.'[33]

The Court held that it had the authority to determine whether particular actions by the parties to this treaty could be considered 'necessary to protect...essential security interests'. The Court justified this conclusion by noting, first, that it had jurisdiction to interpret Article XXI and, secondly, that the language in question, unlike that in some other treaties, did not expressly leave to the state concerned the determination whether a given action was 'necessary for the protection of its essential security interests.'[34] The Court then held:

> Taking into account the whole situation of the United States in relation to Central America, so far as the Court is informed of it (and even assuming that the justification of self-defence,

[26] Para 99. [27] Paras 15, 126. [28] See discussion at n 14.

[29] *Nicaragua*, paras 195, 211, 230. [30] Para 155. [31] Para 156.

[32] Treaty of Friendship, Commerce and Navigation Between the United States of America and the Republic of Nicaragua, Managua, 21 Jan 1956, 367 UNTS 3.

[33] Art XXI. [34] See *Nicaragua*, paras 222, 282.

which the Court has rejected on the legal level, had some validity on the political level), the Court considers that the mining of Nicaraguan ports, and the direct attacks on ports and oil installations, cannot possibly be justified as 'necessary' to protect the essential security interests of the United States.[35]

In this case, the Court's analysis in its preliminary objections judgment was incomplete. In contrast to the situation in the *Corfu Channel* case, obtaining the evidence necessary to the US self-defence argument was difficult. That argument centred on allegations regarding the behaviour of the applicant state. The best evidence on the issues raised by that defence was necessarily in the possession of Nicaragua, which would have no incentive to produce the evidence and every incentive to misrepresent it. While the US might have had available information obtained through espionage, it could not reveal that information without taking significant risks. Thus, these evidence-access problems meant that the US, had it proceeded with the case, would have had to either abandon its self-defence claim as not being able to be proved or compromise its intelligence-collection methods. The Court's reliance on burden of proof concepts in dealing with this situation was unsatisfactory. This was not a situation in which the party with the evidence problem had invoked the jurisdiction of the Court; rather, the US was an unwilling litigant. Nor was this case comparable to one in a domestic court in which a defendant could rely on subpoena power and discovery to obtain evidence necessary to a defence. Arguably, a case in which a respondent state would be unable to offer a defence, except at unreasonable cost, would seem to be one the Court should hesitate to hear, that is, treat as inadmissible, even assuming that it had jurisdiction and that the applicant's allegations were accurate.

Elements of the Court's merits judgment in this case were also questionable. Its assertion that if the US truly had evidence of arms being smuggled into El Salvador through Honduras, it would have arranged for the deployment of a strong patrol force assumes that such a deployment would have been possible. Whether that was true, however, depended on issues of military feasibility: whether such patrolling was possible in the light of the nature and the extent of the terrain to be patrolled and the availability of the necessary human and material resources. In assuming the possibility of such patrolling, the Court engaged in the evaluation of military considerations, an activity that it implied it would avoid.

The Court's purporting to determine the essential security interests of the US in its analysis of Article XXI of the Friendship Treaty between Nicaragua and the US was also problematic. The Court's discussion of its jurisdiction and its parsing of the treaty language were not relevant to the key point, that is, whether the Court, relying on legal analysis, could itself determine a state's essential security interests. To the extent that the Court was unable to do so, and in fact relied on its own

[35] Para 282.

political and military assessment, it, once again, was engaging in an activity requiring non-judicial expertise.

3. *Legality of the Threat or Use of Nuclear Weapons, Advisory Opinion*

This advisory opinion[36] responded to the following question from the General Assembly: 'Is the threat or use of nuclear weapons under any circumstances permitted under international law?' While the concept of admissibility as such does not seem applicable to the Court's advisory jurisdiction, the Court in this case was faced with the argument that it should decline to give the requested opinion, lest its conclusions amount to 'hypothetical or speculative declarations outside the scope of its judicial function'.[37] In rejecting this argument, the Court stated:

> The Court does not consider that…it would necessarily have to write 'scenarios', to study various types of nuclear weapons and to evaluate highly complex and controversial technological, strategic and scientific information. The Court will simply address the issues arising in all their aspects by applying the legal rules relevant to the situation.[38]

That is, the Court seemed to consider whether to render an advisory opinion as involving considerations analogous to those which, in its contentious jurisdiction, would be matters of admissibility.

On the substance of the case, the Court was quite cautious. Its focus was the behaviour of states. It noted that, regarding arms control, states had chosen to label certain weapons as prohibited rather than to label others as authorized. It found no prohibition of nuclear weapons either in existing treaties or deriving from Security Council actions.[39] It likewise found no such prohibition in customary international law in the light of states' deep differences of opinion and practice on the issue.[40] It further held that international humanitarian law, though applicable to the use of nuclear weapons, did not forbid their use in all circumstances.[41] The Court went on to observe that it could not 'lose sight of the fundamental right of every State to survival, and thus its right to resort to self-defence…when its survival is at stake'[42] and took note as well of the 'policy of deterrence' applied by 'an appreciable section of the international community'.[43] It concluded that it could not 'reach a definitive conclusion' on the question presented to it.[44] In the *dispositif*, the Court's answer to the General Assembly's question stated that the use of nuclear weapons was generally illegal, but added that the Court could not say that such weapons could not lawfully be used 'in an extreme circumstance of self-defence, in which the very survival of a State would be at stake'; this part of the *dispositif* was adopted only by the president's casting vote.[45]

[36] ICJ Rep 1996, 226. [37] Para 15. [38] Para 15. [39] Paras 52–63.
[40] Paras 64–73. [41] Paras 74–95. [42] Para 96. [43] Para 96. [44] Para 97.
[45] Para 105(2)E. Each of the 14 judges wrote separate opinions in this case; they were even more divided in their methods of analysis than they were in their voting. See ICJ Rep 1996, 268–593.

The Court's approach in this case was strikingly different from that it employed in the *Military and Paramilitary Activities* case. The *Nuclear Weapons* advisory opinion could be said to involve a pure question of law, while the earlier case turned on factual questions. Nonetheless, the Court made its own evaluations of military issues in the *Military and Paramilitary Activities* case while refraining from doing so in the advisory opinion. In particular, it did not attempt to determine the circumstances in which the use of nuclear weapons in self-defence could be said to be necessary. Given the importance of the issue, it is perhaps not surprising that the Court was unwilling to go further than it did in the absence of an international consensus.

4. *Oil Platforms (Iran v. US)*

In this case,[46] Iran sought reparations from the US because of US attacks on certain Iranian oil platforms in the Persian Gulf in October 1987 and April 1988. The attacks took place during the Iran–Iraq war, in the course of which the belligerents carried out numerous attacks in the Persian Gulf on ships flying the flags of neutral states.[47] The US argued that both of its sets of attacks were acts of lawful self-defence. The US characterized the 1987 attacks as a defensive response to attacks, attributed by the US to Iran, on US merchant vessels, in particular on the ship *Sea Isle City*.[48] It characterized the 1988 attacks as acts of self-defence after a US naval vessel struck a mine, allegedly laid by Iran in international waters.[49] It appears from the Court's decision that there was at least strong evidence that the laying of the mine struck by the warship was not an isolated incident, but an element of what the US argued was Iran's 'general practice of using mines to attack neutral shipping'.[50]

The Court rejected the US claims of self-defence. The Court had two grounds for its conclusion as to the 1987 attacks. First, the Court held that the evidence provided by the US to prove Iranian responsibility for the attack on the merchant vessel was insufficient.[51] Secondly, it stated that the *Sea Isle City* incident was not, in any event, an armed attack on the US, since the missile employed in that attack was so inaccurate that it could only have been directed at the general area in which the *Sea Isle City* happened to be, not specifically at that vessel.[52] Regarding the 1988 attacks, the Court held that mining of the naval vessel likewise did not support a claim of self-defence by the US, relying in part on its determination that the evidence of Iranian responsibility was 'highly suggestive, but not conclusive',[53] and also by observing:

> The Court does not exclude the possibility that the mining of a single military vessel might be sufficient to bring into play the 'inherent right of self-defence'; but in view of all the circumstances, including the inconclusiveness of the evidence of Iran's responsibility for the mining… the Court is unable to hold that the attacks on the…platforms have been shown

[46] Merits, ICJ Rep 2003, 161. [47] Paras 23–4. [48] Para 48. [49] Para 67.
[50] Paras 67–9. [51] Paras 50–61. [52] Para 64. [53] Para 71.

to have been justifiably made in response to an armed attack on the United States by Iran, in the form of the mining…[54]

The Court also considered the scale of the 1988 attacks, 'as a response to the mining, by an unidentified agency, of a single United States warship, which was severely damaged but not sunk, and without loss of life' violated the principle of proportionality.[55] The Court did not address the US allegation that Iran made a practice of mining shipping lanes in order to attack neutral shipping.

The Court's analysis of the attribution issue in connection with the 1987 attacks seems to assume that military commanders in the field should not attribute uses of force to particular states absent supporting evidence adequate for use in a court. As Judge Buergenthal observed in his separate opinion, the Court's approach did not consider the question to be whether, considering all the facts available to US decision-makers at the time, it was reasonable for the US to act as it did.[56] Expanding upon Judge Buergenthal's point, the Court could be said to have failed to take military considerations into account in a case in which they were at least arguably crucial.

Also, the Court reached a doubtful conclusion in holding that the incidents upon which the US relied could not be called armed attacks on the US because they could not be said to have been directed specifically at US vessels. By this logic, if a state directs attacks on other states in such a way that it cannot predict which other states will be harmed by those attacks, none of the victims can be said to have been a victim of an armed attack and therefore none could claim a right to self-defence. This amounts to treating attacks directed indiscriminately at a number of states as equivalent to a situation in which there are no attacks at all. Again, the issue would appear to involve military considerations, that is, how a commander could reasonably respond in the situation faced by the US. While it might be that the Court should be understood to have held that the rule it applied was binding whatever the dilemma confronting a commander attempting to defend ships in the position of the *Sea Isle City*, its opinion could also be read as failing to come to grips with this dilemma.

There are also problems with the Court's treatment of the US arguments regarding the 1988 attacks. First, the Court held that the mining of the US warship that triggered the response did not amount to an armed attack. However, it appears that the US presented at least some evidence that Iran was regularly mining international waters;[57] that is, while only one ship may have *struck* a mine, Iran had laid others. Perhaps laying one mine in international waters is not an armed attack on all vessels using those waters, but if a state lays enough mines, presumably at some point it has created so great a danger that the minelaying must be an armed attack on international shipping, regardless of the number of ships that actually strike mines.

[54] Para 72. [55] Para 77.

[56] *Oil Platforms (Iran v. US)*, Merits, Separate Opinion of Judge Buergenthal, ICJ Rep 2003, 270, para 40.

[57] See *Legality of the Threat or Use of Nuclear Weapons*, paras 67–9.

The characterization of the 1988 US attacks as a disproportionate response to the mining of a single vessel is a mistake at both the practical and legal levels. As a practical matter, a naval commander confronted with evidence of minelaying has to determine how to address the threat of *future* harm the mines present, however limited the damage that may have already been incurred. There is also strong legal authority that evaluating the proportionality element of the doctrine of self-defence requires comparing the defender's actions to the harm to be prevented from happening, not to that which has already occurred.[58]

As with its treatment of the 1987 attacks, the Court's approach here arguably suggests a failure to confront the military considerations involved in evaluating the 1988 attacks. The military problem the US faced was deciding how to respond, not only to past harms, but to the future dangers presented by Iran's apparent strategy of mining the Gulf. The Court's failure even to acknowledge the existence of this military problem raises doubts as to whether the judges truly understood the actual situation they were attempting to assess.

Taken together, the Court's mistakes in its analysis of this case demonstrate the rationale for treating the analysis of military considerations as generally beyond the competence of a court.

5. *Legal Consequences of the Construction of a Wall in the Occupied Palestinian Territory*

This advisory opinion[59] resulted from a General Assembly request for an assessment of the legality of Israel's construction of a barrier complex intended to forestall terrorist infiltration from the occupied Palestinian territories into Israel proper.[60] After an extensive discussion, the Court concluded that Israel's actions violated international law in a number of respects.[61] Once it had determined that Israel's actions violated international law, the Court considered arguments that could be seen as affirmative defences, that is, assertions of the form 'Even if Israel's actions would otherwise be in violation of international law, additional circumstances render those actions lawful.' In this connection, the Court first addressed the contention that the Israeli barrier complex should be seen as a lawful act of self-defence. It rejected that argument, asserting that a state could invoke the right of self-defence as set out in Article 51 of the UN Charter only in response to actions by another state; since the threats against which Israel sought to protect itself did not emanate from a state, Article 51 was irrelevant.[62] The Court also considered and rejected the argument that Israel could invoke the defence of necessity.[63] The Court observed that the necessity defence was only available if the action at issue was 'the only way for the State to

[58] See Noam Lubell, *Extraterritorial Use of Force Against Non-State Actors* (Oxford: Oxford University Press, 2010), 65 and authorities therein cited.

[59] Advisory Opinion, ICJ Rep 2004, 136. [60] Paras 66–82. [61] Paras 86–137.

[62] Paras 138–9. [63] Para 140.

safeguard an essential interest against a grave and imminent peril'.[64] Its only explanation for its rejection of that defence in this situation was its statement that it was 'not convinced that the construction of the wall along the route chosen was the only means to safeguard the interests of Israel against the peril which it has invoked as justification for that construction'.[65] The Court acknowledged the security problems on which Israel's reference to Article 51 was based, but did not address them in any detail.[66]

One might have expected the Court to support its conclusion that Israel had failed to demonstrate the necessity of the barrier complex by reference to alternative measures available to Israel, especially in the light of its acknowledgement of Israel's security problems. The Court did not do so. Judge Buergenthal took issue with the Court's approach in a vigorous separate opinion, arguing that the Court could not properly address the situation without an evidentiary record addressing the problems Israel faced and the options available to it and that it therefore should have declined to render the opinion.[67] With or without such evidence, analysis of such an argument would in any event require consideration of military factors. The Court's conclusory treatment of the issue explained neither how it performed that analysis nor why it saw itself as competent to do so.

III. Cases Involving Matters Arguably within the Province of the Security Council

A. Introduction

The preceding section addressed admissibility problems posed by cases presenting issues not readily justiciable. The discussion now turns to a second kind of admissibility issue: the Court's position in cases in which its actions might conflict with decisions of the Security Council.

There have been no instances in which both bodies addressed the same situation, but did so inconsistently. However, there have been developments that could be the seed of future conflicts. First, the Court's explanations for its decisions to proceed with a case despite some degree of Security Council involvement are formulated in

[64] Para 140, quoting Art 25 of the International Law Commission's Articles on Responsibility of States for Internationally Wrongful Acts, Annex, GA Res 56/83 (28 Jan 2002), A/RES/56/83.

[65] Para 140. [66] Para 141.

[67] *Legal Consequences of the Construction of a Wall in the Occupied Palestinian Territory*, Separate Opinion of Judge Buergenthal, ICJ Rep 2004, 240.

a way that leaves open the possibility of conflict. Also, the Court has taken a quite different view of the right of self-defence from that of the Security Council; in the light of the primary responsibility of the Security Council for the maintenance of international peace and security, one could argue that the Court should defer to the Council on such questions. A discussion of the cases will make these points clearer.

B. Cases

1. *Nicaragua v. US*

In its preliminary objections,[68] the US had argued that the case was inadmissible because the responsibility of dealing with alleged unlawful uses of force belonged exclusively to the political organs of the UN and that, in the light of the Security Council's refusal to act on Nicaragua's application, Nicaragua's taking the case to the Court amounted to asking the Court to review the Council's action.[69]

At the outset, it must be acknowledged that there was no prospect that the Security Council would address the situation in Nicaragua, given the fundamental disagreements among permanent members. However, the Court's rejection of the US arguments did not turn on that fact, focusing instead on other factors. It noted[70] that the Security Council had not objected to its order for provisional measures in *United States Diplomatic and Consular Staff in Tehran*.[71] It observed that, while the Charter expressly forbids the General Assembly to make recommendations when the Security Council is dealing with an issue, it imposes no such restrictions on the Court, which, the Court stated, reflects its crucial role in peaceful dispute settlement.[72] It also rejected the US characterization of the matter as involving an alleged unlawful use of force, noting that no notice of this conflict had been given to the Council and asserting that 'it is clear that the complaint of Nicaragua is not about an ongoing armed conflict between it and the United States . . .'[73] The Court also pointed out that the Charter vested in the Security Council primary but not exclusive responsibility for dealing with uses of force, stating that 'the Council has functions of a political nature assigned to it, whereas the Court exercises purely judicial functions. Both organs can therefore perform their separate, but complementary functions with respect to the same events'.[74] It stressed that the Court had never avoided a case because of its political elements or because it involved serious elements of the use of force.[75] It dismissed as irrelevant the distinction the US drew between cases involving uses of force in the past and those involving uses of force

[68] See n 15.

[69] *Nicaragua*, Jurisdiction of the Court and Admissibility of the Application, paras 89, 91.

[70] Para 93. [71] ICJ Rep 1980, 3.

[72] *Nicaragua*, Jurisdiction of the Court and Admissibility of the Application, para 93.

[73] Para 94. [74] Para 95. [75] Para 96.

contemporaneously, and argued that it could not be said to be hearing an appeal of the Security Council's actions, in that 'the Court is not asked to say that the Security Council was wrong in its decision, nor that there was anything inconsistent with law in the way in which the members of the Council employed their right to vote.'[76]

The Court's reasoning in this judgment is suspect. It relied on its decision in the *Diplomatic and Consular Staff in Tehran* case for the general proposition that the Court and the Council can consider a matter simultaneously. However, in the *Tehran* case, the Court was at pains to demonstrate that, as a matter of fact, its activities were not interfering with those of the Council.[77] The Court carried out no similar analysis in this case. The Court put weight on the US failure to report its actions to the Council; while that failure may raise issues about US compliance with Article 51 of the Charter, it seems irrelevant in this context, since the Council's authority does not depend on a report being made. Further, while it may have been clear that Nicaragua's complaint involved no 'ongoing armed conflict', it was hardly clear that the situation giving rise to the complaint was not an armed conflict, especially in the light of the US defence's focus on the internal armed conflict in El Salvador. The reference to the Court's history of not avoiding cases of this sort did not acknowledge that the Court had never before confronted a case of this type; in this connection, if the distinction between current and past uses of force was irrelevant, it would have been helpful for the Court to explain why this was so.

Aside from the foregoing, there are three especially serious weaknesses in the Court's analysis. The first is the Court's apparent conclusion that the Council's primary responsibility for the maintenance of international peace and security imposes no limitations on the Court's activity. Even though, as the Court noted, there is no language in the Charter regarding the Court analogous to the limits imposed on the General Assembly by Article 12,[78] the Charter's designating the Council as having *primary* responsibility for the maintenance of international peace and security must mean that all other organs of the UN must defer to the Council when it is exercising that responsibility. Otherwise, the designation of the Council as primary loses its meaning. The foregoing does not explain how the functions of the Court and Council are to be reconciled, but neither did the Court make any attempt to determine the consequences of the Council having 'primary responsibility'.

To be sure, the Court asserted that both it and the Council could perform their separate functions with regard to the same events, since the Council's functions were political while those of the Court were purely judicial.[79] That assertion was the second serious problem in this opinion. The Court neither considered the possibility that its judgment could, as a practical matter, impede a particular course of action the Council had chosen, nor addressed the implications of such a conflict. It simply

[76] Paras 97–8. [77] See n 71, paras 40–4. [78] See n 24, para 93. [79] Para 95.

relied on the formal political/legal distinction to justify its position. The Court's third mistake, similar to its second, was its rejection of the argument that it was, in effect, hearing an appeal from an action of the Security Council. The Court's disingenuous claim that it was not entertaining an appeal since it was not passing judgement on the legal validity of the Council's actions, once again, relied on a formal political/legal distinction and ignored the potential practical effects of its judgment.

2. *Questions of Interpretation and Application of the 1971 Montreal Convention Arising from the Aerial Incident at Lockerbie (Libyan Arab Jamahiriya v. US)*

This case[80] derived from the bombing of a US-registered aircraft while over the town of Lockerbie, Scotland, in 1988. Having become convinced that identified Libyan agents had planted the bomb, the UK and the US demanded that Libya, among other things, surrender those agents for trial.[81] In January 1992, the Security Council adopted a resolution urging Libya to comply with the demands;[82] after Libya had failed to comply, the Council adopted legally binding resolutions on 31 March 1992 and 11 November 1993, requiring Libya to surrender the suspects. The Council also imposed sanctions on Libya pending compliance.[83] Libya on 3 March 1992 had filed an application with the Court seeking a declaration that the so-called Montreal Convention[84] was applicable to the matter, that Libya had complied with its obligations under that treaty while the US and the UK had not, and that the two countries were obliged to refrain from threats of force and 'to respect Libya's right not to have the [Montreal] Convention set aside …'[85]

The Court denied Libya's requests for provisional measures in orders of 14 April 1992.[86] These orders relied on the broad authority of the Council; the Court expressly stated that Libya's obligation under Article 25 of the Charter, read in conjunction with

[80] ICJ Rep 1998, 115.

[81] Letter dated 20 December 1991 from the Permanent Representative of the United Kingdom of Great Britain and Northern Ireland to the United Nations addressed to the Secretary-General (31 Dec 1991), S/23307; Letter dated 20 December 1991 from the Permanent Representative of the United States of America to the United Nations addressed to the Secretary-General (31 Dec 1991), S/23308.

[82] SC Res 731 (21 Jan 1992), S/RES/731.

[83] SC Res 748 (31 Mar 1992), S/RES/748; SC Res 883 (21 Jan 1992), S/RES/731.

[84] Convention for the Suppression of Unlawful Acts Against the Safety of Civil Aviation, Montreal, 23 Sept 1971, 974 UNTS 177.

[85] *Questions of Interpretation and Application of the 1971 Montreal Convention Arising from the Aerial Incident at Lockerbie (Libyan Arab Jamahiriya v. UK)*, Preliminary Objections, ICJ Rep 1998, 9 [1]; *Questions of Interpretation and Application of the 1971 Montreal Convention Arising from the Aerial Incident at Lockerbie (Libyan Arab Jamahiriya v. US)*, Preliminary Objections, ICJ Rep 1998, 115 [1].

[86] *Questions of Interpretation and Application of the 1971 Montreal Convention Arising from the Aerial Incident at Lockerbie (Libyan Arab Jamahiriya v. UK)*, Provisional Measures, ICJ Rep 1992, 3; *Questions of Interpretation and Application of the 1971 Montreal Convention Arising from the Aerial Incident at Lockerbie (Libyan Arab Jamahiriya v. US)*, Provisional Measures, ICJ Rep 1992, 114.

Article 103, obliged it to comply with the Council's 31 March resolution and superseded any obligations under the Montreal Convention. It also stated that, whatever Convention rights Libya may have had prior to the adoption of that resolution, those rights were not appropriate for protection by provisional measures, given that resolution. The Court further noted that such measures would be likely to impair the respondents' rights under the resolution.[87]

The Court's approach to the Council's resolutions was quite different in its 1998 judgments rejecting the respondents' preliminary objections. Both respondents had argued that the case was without object in that, whatever the situation might be under the Montreal Convention, the Security Council's resolutions superseded that treaty and any rights Libya might have enjoyed under it.[88] The Court acknowledged that this argument could properly be labelled a preliminary objection, but observed that the parties disagreed as to whether the objection possessed an exclusively preliminary character.[89] The Court concluded that it did not, stressing that the very reasons offered by the respondents in support of their objections showed that Libya's rights on the merits would in fact be the subject of any judgment even though, in form, it would be a decision not to address the merits.[90]

This case reinforces the concerns raised by the Court's reasoning in *Military and Paramilitary Activities*. This becomes clear when one compares the reasoning in the 1992 orders denying Libya's request for provisional measures with that in the 1998 preliminary objections judgments. In the 1992 orders, the Court took it as established, prima facie, that Security Council resolutions clearly required Libya to extradite the two suspects and that they prevailed over the Montreal Convention.[91] It would seem, therefore, that the only questions left were whether this reading of the resolutions was correct and whether the Council was authorized to adopt the resolutions. If the resolutions in fact had the effect which the respondents contended and the Council had the requisite authority, the respondents were correct that Libya's claim was without object. The Court's 1998 judgment rightly observed that resolving these matters would have the same effect as a decision on the merits. However, if the Court was correct in asserting that this conclusion meant that the argument could not be raised as a preliminary objection, then the Court can never uphold any preliminary objection not directed at jurisdiction, since all such

[87] *Libya v. UK*, Provisional Measures, paras 39–41; *Libya v. US*, Provisional Measures, paras 42–4.

[88] *Libya v. UK*, Preliminary Objections, para 46; *Libya v. US*, Preliminary Objections, paras 39–40.

[89] *Libya v. UK*, Preliminary Objections, 47–8; *Libya v. US*, Preliminary Objections, paras 46–7.

[90] *Libya v. UK*, Preliminary Objections, para 50 (corresponding discussion in *Libya v. US* is substantially identical, *Libya v. US*, Preliminary Objections, para 49).

[91] *Libya v. UK*, Provisional Measures, ICJ Rep 1992, 3, paras 42–4; *Libya v. US*, Provisional Measures, ICJ Rep 1992, 114 paras 39–41.

objections necessarily go to what could be called the merits of the case.[92] Further, unless there was some doubt about the legal effect of the Council's resolutions, the claim was in fact without object. The Court's refusal to uphold the preliminary objections thus implied that the legal effect of the resolutions was not clear, which is puzzling in the light of its 1992 pronouncements regarding the Council's authority. The result is difficult to understand, and could even be read as a claim by the Court that it had the authority to treat Council resolutions as unlawful.

3. *Self-defence*

As noted previously,[93] the Court asserted in *Legal Consequences of the Construction of a Wall in the Occupied Palestinian Territory*[94] that a state could invoke the right of self-defence as justifying military operations on the territory of another state only if it was defending itself against that state; threats from non-state actors could not justify such operations.[95] The Court reiterated this position in *Armed Activities on the Territory of the Congo (DRC v. Uganda)*.[96] The case arose from military operations carried out by Uganda within the Congo.[97] Among other justifications for its conduct, Uganda asserted that it was acting in self-defence.[98] The Court's reasons for rejecting this defence included Uganda's failure to prove that the Congolese government was responsible for the attacks on Ugandan territory that had emanated from the territory of the Congo.[99]

The problem with the treatment of self-defence in these cases is that it is inconsistent with Security Council resolutions which recognized[100] and reaffirmed[101] the right of self-defence in the context of the attacks on the US on 11 September 2001. Since those attacks, of course, were not perpetrated by states, the position of the Court on this matter is flatly contrary to that taken by the Security Council.[102] Indeed, judges writing separately in those cases drew attention to just this point.[103] One would think that the Security Council's understanding of the concept of self-defence would have some bearing on the Court's analysis, but the Court neither followed the Council nor explained why it did not.

[92] Accord, Shabtai Rosenne, *The Law and Practice of the International Court* (4th edn, Leiden: Martinus Nijhoff, 2006), vol II, 891.

[93] See text at n 61. [94] ICJ Rep 2004, 136. [95] Paras 138–9.

[96] ICJ Rep 2005, 168. [97] Para 28. [98] Para 118. [99] Paras 146–7.

[100] SC Res 1368 (12 Sept 2001), S/RES/1368.

[101] SC Res 1373 (28 Sept 2001), S/RES/1373.

[102] See also Theresa Reinold, 'State Weakness, Irregular Warfare, and the Right to Self-Defence Post 9/11' (2011) 105 *American Journal of International Law* 244, 260–1.

[103] *Advisory Opinion on the Israeli Wall*, Separate Opinion of Judge Koojimans, ICJ Rep 2003, 219, para 35 and Declaration of Judge Buergenthal, paras 5–6; *Congo v. Uganda*, Separate Opinion of Judge Koojimans, ICJ Rep 2005, 306, paras 28–9 and Separate Opinion of Judge Simma, ICJ Rep 2005, 334, paras 10–13.

IV. Conclusion

In conclusion, the Court has faced few cases that it could not decide without engaging in what amounted to analyses requiring military, rather than legal, expertise. However, in those few cases, it has shown little willingness to apply the concept of inadmissibility or to deal in some other way with arguable justiciability issues. Aside from its action in the *Corfu Channel* case, it has not sought assistance to evaluate military considerations.[104] If the Court's attitude towards this subject stays constant, it is difficult to imagine a case that the Court will decline to hear solely because its resolution would require such an evaluation.

The Court has also characterized its authority vis-à-vis the Security Council in a way that arguably would permit it to question the Council's actions. If that is in fact the Court's position, it could have significant effects on the functioning of the UN.

The Court's treatment of these issues presents the risk that it will reach results in particular use of force cases that are suspect legally and ill-advised as a practical matter. More fundamentally, they force states to consider how much sense it makes to take seriously the Court's pronouncements on issues involving the use of force.

[104] The (closely divided) Court effectively deferred in its *Nuclear Weapons* advisory opinion to the strategic judgements of the nuclear weapons states. One might wonder whether the fact that an opposite result would have been ignored, thereby humiliating the Court, affected the deliberations.

CHAPTER 16

THE USE OF FORCE IN UNITED NATIONS PEACEKEEPING OPERATIONS

SCOTT SHEERAN

I. Introduction

The use of force by UN peacekeeping operations raises important and distinct issues for international law. The development of UN peacekeeping forces commanded by the Secretary-General on behalf of the organization was not envisaged or regulated in the Charter.[1] As one former Secretary-General stated, it 'can rightly be called the invention of the United Nations'.[2] From its modest beginnings, however, UN

[1] See Bruno Simma et al (eds), *The Charter of the United Nations: A Commentary* (2nd edn, Oxford: Oxford University Press, 2002), 590–2; Scott Sheeran, 'A Constitutional Moment?: United Nations Peacekeeping in the Democratic Republic of Congo' (2011) 8 *International Organizations Law Review* 55; Katherine Cox, 'Beyond Self-Defense: United Nations Peacekeeping Operations and the Use of Force' (1999) 27 *Denver Journal of International Law and Policy* 239; Benedetto Conforti, *The Law and Practice of the United Nations* (The Hague: Kluwer International Law, 1997), 200–1; Nigel D. White, 'The UN Charter and Peacekeeping Forces' in Michael Pugh (ed), *The UN, Peace and Force* (London: Frank Cass, 2001), 115.

[2] UN Secretary-General, 'An Agenda for Peace', A/47/277 (1992), para 46.

peacekeeping has become a central and indispensible activity of the organization and is now an accepted part of UN law and practice.[3]

The use of force by UN peacekeepers is an everyday reality and is integral to mission success and failure. It is relevant for strategic decisions at mission headquarters-level down to individual soldiers' decisions in the field based on their rules of engagement. Whether characterized by excess or timidity, the use of force has been central to all the major crises of UN peacekeeping. The two operations in which UN peacekeepers engaged in the use of force on a significant scale—Congo (1960–3) and Somalia (1993)—were traumatic experiences for the organization and civilians. The controversy of these operations was surpassed only in Rwanda (1994) and Srebrenica (1995) where lack of force used led to major atrocities.[4]

As the literature indicates, there are significant problems with understanding the legal authority of UN peacekeepers to use force.[5] The major scholarly work, Findlay's *The Use of Force in UN Peace Operations*, concludes that peacekeeping 'has been marked by political controversy, doctrinal vacuousness, conceptual confusion and failure in the field'.[6] As a major constitutional adaptation of the UN, from its beginnings to the present day there has not been a clear legal doctrine for application of force in UN peacekeeping operations. The concept of UN peacekeeping was 'invented long after praxis had begun; and improvisation has characterized its evolution ever since'.[7] This has led to 'truisms' in UN peacekeeping—such as the basic principles of *consent*, *impartiality*, and *non-use of force* except in self-defence—which are oft-repeated but seldom critically analysed. These problems are compounded as the law is also often conflated with or overshadowed by political or policy concerns.

This chapter seeks to provide greater clarity and a re-conceptualization of the legal authority of UN peacekeepers to use force. It accordingly explores and clarifies the nature, scope, and legitimacy for use of force under international law. First, it will review the historical and conceptual foundations and development of the use of force in UN peacekeeping. Secondly, it will explore the normative framework for use of force, including the categorization and legal bases for use of force under international law. Thirdly, it will consider the operational and practical challenges that arise due to the legal problems. Finally, the chapter will conclude with an overview and re-conceptualizing of the legal authority for UN peacekeepers to use force.

[3] Sheeran, 'A Constitutional Moment?', 106–7, for statistics see the current UN Department of Peacekeeping Operations/Department of Field Support (DPKO/DFS) Peacekeeping Fact Sheet, available at <https://www.un.org/en/peacekeeping/resources/statistics/factsheet.shtml>.

[4] Simon Chesterman, 'The Use of Force in UN Peace Operations', External Study, Best Practices Unit, UN Department of Peacekeeping Operations, 2004, 2; Alex Bellamy, Paul Williams, and Stuart Griffin, *Understanding Peacekeeping* (2nd edn, Cambridge: Polity, 2010), 119.

[5] Nigel D. White, *Keeping the Peace: The United Nations and the Maintenance of International Peace and Security* (Manchester: Manchester University Press, 1993), 204–6, 17; Cox, 'Beyond Self-Defense'; Frederick Fleitz, *Peacekeeping Fiascoes of the 1990s* (Westport, CT: Greenwood, 2002), 42–4.

[6] Trevor Findlay, *The Use of Force in UN Peace Operations* (Oxford: Oxford University Press, 2002), 351.

[7] Findlay, *The Use of Force in UN Peace Operations*, 4.

II. Historical and Conceptual Development

It is necessary first to delineate what is meant by UN peacekeeping operations for the purposes of this chapter. The term 'UN peacekeeping operations' is usually understood to mean Security Council-mandated missions in the field under UN command, which involve military or police as well as civilian personnel. Their purpose is commonly to facilitate implementation of a peace agreement or ceasefire.[8] They are distinct from those missions conducted under the authority of the UN Security Council, but commanded by regional bodies, such as the North Atlantic Treaty Organizaton (NATO), or by a coalition of single states.

A. The United Nations and Peacekeeping

The capacity, and historically the right, of states to use force was a part of Westphalian sovereignty and inherent in the nature of a decentralized and horizontal legal order. From the time of de Vattel through to the beginning of the 20th century, use of force was seen as one of the options for state action within the international order.[9] Grotius suggested that the 'right of self-defence... has its origin directly and chiefly in the fact that nature commits to each his own protection.'[10] This view was challenged when the idea of international collective security began to gain currency, including as expressed in Woodrow Wilson's Fourteen Points in 1918, a key influence in the internationalist and cosmopolitan ideas that led to the development of the League of Nations. While the League was involved in a number of limited peacekeeping-type activities, none of these featured collective security *stricto sensu* or use of force on behalf of the organization and its membership.[11]

As is often reiterated, the UN was founded to 'save succeeding generations from the scourge of war'.[12] The Charter built on the experience (and failures) of the Covenant

[8] There are multiple definitions, this draws from 'An Agenda for Peace', para 20. See also Derek H. Bowett, *United Nations Forces* (London: Stevens & Sons, 1964), 268–74. Vaughan Lowe, Adam Roberts, Jennifer Welsh, and Dominik Zaum, 'Introduction' in Vaughan Lowe et al (eds), *The United Nations Security Council and War* (Oxford: Oxford University Press, 2008), 1, 22.

[9] See generally Hugo Grotius, *The Law of War and Peace* (1625); Emmerich de Vattel, *The Law of Nations or the Principles of Natural Law* (1758).

[10] Grotius, *The Law of War and Peace*, Book 2, ch 1 (The Causes of War: First, Defence of Self and Property).

[11] The League was involved in the Administration of the German Saar territory (1920), Free City of Danzig (1920), a number of plebiscites such as Upper Silesia (now Poland and Czech Republic), and the Greek ceasefire observer mission (1925). See Alan James, 'The Peacekeeping Role of the League of Nations' (1999) 6 *International Peacekeeping* 154–160.

[12] Leland Goodrich and Edvard Hambro, *Charter of the United Nations* (Medford, MA: World Peace Foundation, 1946), 21, 59.

of the League of Nations, and was seen as a more advanced version of a collective security agreement.[13] Under the Charter, member states relinquished authority to use force but maintained the right of self-defence, and the UN itself was given the authority to authorize the use of force against its members for the purpose of maintaining international peace and security.[14] A central element of the Charter's collective security machinery, and an advance upon the Covenant, was provision in Article 43 for special agreements for UN standing forces under the Security Council's direction.[15]

The concept of UN peacekeeping developed as a response to failure of the collective security system envisaged in the Charter.[16] The Cold War struggle and veto had paralysed the Security Council and any hope of utilizing the Article 43 arrangements.[17] The first peacekeeping operation is most commonly understood as the United Nations Emergency Force (UNEF I) in the Sinai in 1956 established by the General Assembly.[18] The UK, France, and Israel had attacked Egypt in response to its nationalization of the Suez Canal, and the UK and France had vetoed attempts of the Security Council to deal with the matter. This mission of lightly armed UN peacekeepers was successfully deployed with the consent of all the states engaged to supervise the peace and withdrawal of foreign forces and act as a buffer. The idea of peacekeeping as Mats Berdal notes 'represented a functional adjustment by the organization to an international political system shaped by deep-seated rivalry and overshadowed by the threat of wider war.'[19]

B. Development of Use of Force in UN Peacekeeping

The use of force in UN peacekeeping was initially very limited and missions focused on self-defence. Such missions expanded over time driven by major events and operational demands. As mentioned earlier, the first UN peacekeeping operation

[13] Goodrich and Hambro, *Charter of the United Nations*, 3–4; Lowe et al, *The United Nations Security Council and War*, 11–17.

[14] See UN Charter, Arts 25, 39, 42, and 43.

[15] *Certain Expenses of the United Nations* (20 July 1962), Advisory Opinion, ICJ Rep 1962, 167; Goodrich and Hambro, *Charter of the United Nations*, 163–7, 170–2, 278–7; Lowe et al, *The United Nations Security Council and War*, 13. For description of the states' intent, see Christine Gray, *International Law and the Use of Force* (3rd edn, Oxford: Oxford University Press, 2008), 254.

[16] Edwin Smith, 'Collective Security, Peacekeeping, and *Ad Hoc* Multilateralism' in Charlotte Ku and Harold K. Jacobson (eds), *Democratic Accountability and the Use of Force in International Law* (Cambridge: Cambridge University Press, 2003), 83; Gray, *International Law and the Use of Force*, 261.

[17] Adam Roberts, 'Proposals for UN Standing Forces: A Critical History' in Lowe et al, *The United Nations Security Council and War*, 99, 100–5.

[18] White, *Keeping the Peace*, 200; Cox, 'Beyond Self-Defense', 239; Fleitz, *Peacekeeping Fiascoes of the 1990s*, 37. The United Nations Truce Supervision Organization (UNTSO) established in 1948 is sometimes referred to as the first UN peacekeeping operation. What differentiates UNEF I from UNTSO, and a number of League of Nations missions, however, is that the peacekeepers in UNEF I were armed and able to use force.

[19] Mats Berdal, 'The Security Council and Peacekeeping' in Lowe et al, *The United Nations Security Council and War*, 175, 180.

was UNEF I deployed to the Sinai to defuse the Suez Crisis in 1956.[20] The force was established by General Assembly Resolution 998 (ES-I) adopted under the Uniting for Peace resolution and with Egypt's consent.[21] The rationale for this novel development was not fully considered at the time. The 'basic principles' of peacekeeping—*consent*, *impartiality*, and the *non-use of force* except in self-defence—were set out *ex post facto* in Secretary-General Dag Hammarskjold's final report on UNEF I in 1958.[22] The report stated that:

> The rule is applied that men engaged in the operation may never take the initiative in the use of armed force, but are entitled to respond with force to an attack with arms, including attempts to use force to make them withdraw from positions which they occupy under orders from the Commander.... The basic element involved is clearly the prohibition against any initiative in the use of armed force.[23]

This recognized essentially the inherent right of a soldier as an individual, and the UN, to defend themselves against any attack, and was a practical precondition for deployment of military forces.[24] This use of force in simple self-defence was a natural corollary of a purely consent-based and impartial mission for the maintenance of international peace and security, in which the main tasks were monitoring and observation of peace agreements and ceasefires.

The next major UN peacekeeping operation was the United Nations Operation in the Congo (Opération des Nations Unies au Congo, ONUC) in the Congo from 1960–4. The operation was established by the Security Council at the request of the Congo, and initially supervised the withdrawal of Belgian colonial forces.[25] The ONUC operation commenced with a limited mandate similar to the successful UNEF I. However, after a series of setbacks and escalating conflict, in 1961 the Security Council authorized in a resolution 'all appropriate measures to prevent the occurrence of civil war in the Congo, including... the use of force, if necessary, in the last resort'.[26] The Council amended this mandate only seven days later to authorize ONUC, in theory still a UN peacekeeping operation, to:

> take vigorous action, including the use of the requisite measure of force, if necessary, for the immediate apprehension, detention pending legal action and/or deportation of all

[20] Gray, *International Law and the Use of Force*, 262–3; Berdal, 'The Security Council and Peacekeeping' in Lowe et al, *The United Nations Security Council and War*, 179.

[21] GA Res 998 (ES-1), 1000 (ES-1), and 1001 (ES-1) (4, 5, and 7 Nov 1956 respectively).

[22] UN Secretary-General, 'Summary Study of the Experience Derived from the Establishment and Operation of the Force', A/3943 (1958), para 127.

[23] 'Summary Study of the Experience Derived from the Establishment and Operation of the Force', para 179.

[24] 'Summary Study of the Experience Derived from the Establishment and Operation of the Force'; Trevor Findlay, 'The Use of Force in Self-Defence: Theory and Practice' in Alex Morrison, Douglas Fraser, and James Kiras, *Peacekeeping with Muscle: The Use of Force in International Conflict Resolution* (Ottawa: The Canadian Peacekeeping Press, 1997), 53.

[25] GA Res 143 (14 July 1960); Gray, *International Law and the Use of Force*, 263.

[26] GA Res 161 (21 Feb 1961); Findlay, *The Use of Force in UN Peace Operations*, 13.

foreign military and paramilitary personnel and political advisers not under United Nations Command, and mercenaries.[27]

While the UN maintained, throughout the operation and escalating conflict, that force was being used only in self-defence, or 'active' self-defence, ONUC's actions in practice became indistinguishable from a war-fighting role and standard military campaign.[28] The operation also included a relatively unique element at that time of protection of civilians, as the ONUC Operational Directive No 8 stated that:

> Where feasible, every protection will be afforded to unarmed groups who may be subjected by any armed party to acts of violence likely to lead to loss of life. In such cases, UN troops will interpose themselves, using armed force if necessary, to prevent such loss of life.[29]

The robust mandate of ONUC and how it was being implemented went well beyond the 'basic principles' of UN peacekeeping from UNEF I. This was naturally controversial and contributed to the Soviet, French, and others' refusal to fund the operation under the regular UN budget, resulting in the ICJ *Certain Expenses* advisory opinion on the legality of UN peacekeeping under the Charter, and subsequently a contraction in the UN membership's ambitions for peacekeeping.

In response to the Congo crisis, and significant limits on the use of force by UN peacekeepers, the UN undertook to redefine the use of force based upon a widened notion of self-defence.[30] The concept was extended to include use of force in self-defence *including in defence of the mandate*. This was first done in the United Nations Peacekeeping Force in Cyprus (UNFICYP) mission in 1964.[31] The Secretary-General stated that the UN peacekeepers in Cyprus could use force in self-defence where 'specific arrangements accepted by both communities [ie the parties] have been or ... are about to be violated, thus risking a recurrence of fighting or endangering law and order' or where there were 'attempts by force to prevent them from carrying out their responsibilities as ordered by their commanders.'[32] This expanded concept of self-defence was reaffirmed in 1973 and 1978 when the Security Council approved Secretary-General Kurt Waldheim's proposals for UNEF II and the United Nations Interim Force in Lebanon (UNIFIL) respectively, which stated that 'Self-defence would include resistance to attempts by forceful means to

[27] GA Res 169 (24 Nov 1961).

[28] Chesterman, 'The Use of Force in UN Peace Operations', 7; Katarina Mansson, 'Use of Force and Civilian Protection' (2005) 12 *International Peacekeeping* 503, 504; Bowett, *United Nations Forces*, 196; Simma et al, *The Charter of the United Nations*, 683.

[29] Operations Directive No 8 [untitled], Febr 1961, UN Archives DAG/13/1.6.5.0.0; Operations Directives Aug 1960–Jan 1964, Box 3, 2–3.

[30] Chesterman, 'The Use of Force in UN Peace Operations', 7.

[31] Hans Boddens Hosang, 'Force Protection, Unit Self-Defence and Extended Self-Defence' in Terry Gill and Dieter Fleck (eds), *The Handbook of the International Law of Military Operations* (Oxford: Oxford University Press, 2011), 415, 418.

[32] UN Secretary-General, Aide-Memoire of the Secretary-General Concerning Some Questions Relating to the Function and Operation of the United Nations Peacekeeping Force in Cyprus, S/5653 (10 Apr 1964), 17(c)–18(c).

prevent it from discharging its duties under the mandate of the Security Council'.[33] For the rest of the Cold War, the UN peacekeeping operations were traditional and did not significantly engage the requirement for use of force beyond simple self-defence.

After the end of the Cold War, the context within which force was used by UN peacekeepers changed radically. The use of UN peacekeeping rapidly expanded with more operations conducted in 1988–93 than there had been in the previous 40 years.[34] In this comparatively short period of time, UN peacekeepers were called on to use force in a wide range of situations beyond simple self-defence: to frustrate attempts to disarm them; to defend posts, vehicles and equipment, and UN civilian personnel from attack; and to protect humanitarian convoys, corridors, and 'safe havens'.[35] During the early and mid-1990s, particularly in Bosnia, Somalia, and Rwanda, the traditional principles of UN peacekeeping, including use of force only in self-defence, were 'strained to the breaking point'.[36]

The use of force and self-defence became central in the United Nations Protection Force (UNPROFOR) peacekeeping operation in the former Yugoslavia. As the situation and conflict began to escalate, UNPROFOR was authorized in September 1992 under a non-Chapter VII resolution to use force in self-defence, including where armed persons attempted by force to prevent them from carrying out their mandate.[37] In June 1993, the Security Council acting under Chapter VII authorized a wider mandate for UNPROFOR to use force.[38] UNPROFOR's mandate was based on an ambitious and strained interpretation of 'acting in self-defence' as the use of force was authorized in essentially three different situations: (1) to 'deter attacks against the safe areas'; (2) to 'ensure the freedom of movement of UNPROFOR' in and around these areas (and later everywhere); and (3) to 'protect humanitarian convoys'.[39] This was a broader application of the

[33] UN Secretary-General, Report of the Secretary-General on the Implementation of Security Council Resolution 340, S/11052/Rev.1 (27 Oct 1973), para 5; SC Res 426 (19 Mar 1978); Report of the Secretary-General on the implementation of Security Council Resolution 425, S/12611 (19 Mar 1978); Cox, 'Beyond Self-Defense', 254.

[34] Scott Sheeran, 'UN Peacekeeping and the Model Status of Forces Agreement', UN Peacekeeping Law Reform Project, University of Essex, 2010, paras 13–27, available at <http://www.essex.ac.uk/plrp/documents/default.aspx>.

[35] International Peace Academy, *Peacekeeper's Handbook* (Oxford: Pergamon Press, 1984), 57; Findlay, *The Use of Force in UN Peace Operations*, 15.

[36] Shashi Tharoor, 'The Changing Face of Peace-Keeping and Peace-Enforcement' (1995) 19 *Fordham International Law Journal* 408.

[37] In SC Res 776 (14 Sept 1992), which made no reference to Chapter VII of the Charter, the Security Council approved the Secretary-General's report which included this proposal. See also SC Res 819 (16 Apr 1993); SC Res 824 (6 May 1993); SC Res 836 (4 June 1993). For a discussion of UNPROFOR and use of force, see Nicholas Tsagourias, 'Self-Defence, Protection of Humanitarian Values, and the Doctrine of Impartiality and Neutrality in Enforcement Mandates', Chapter 18 in this volume, at 405.

[38] SC Res 836, para 5.

[39] SC Res 836, para 5.

self-defence (ie defence of the mandate) than for UNFICYP or UNEF II and was authorized by a Chapter VII resolution.

At around the same time in June 1993, the United Nations Operation in Somalia (UNOSOM II) became the first UN peacekeeping operation since ONUC to be granted a specific Chapter VII mandate to use force beyond 'self-defence'.[40] After an ambush resulted in the deaths of 24 Pakistani peacekeepers and left another 57 wounded, the Security Council authorized UNOSOM II to take 'all necessary measures against all those responsible', including 'their arrest and detention for prosecution, trial and punishment'.[41] The excessive force that followed led to a serious escalation in conflict and casualties, which gave rise to the notion espoused by Lieutenant-General Michael Rose, the Force Commander in UNPROFOR, of crossing the 'Mogadishu line' from peacekeeping to peace enforcement or war-fighting.[42] The other significant development in the 1990s was the UN beginning to deploy police on mass in the *sui generis* transitional administration operations, such as in Kosovo and Timor-Leste. In this mission, UN military and police were required in varied ways to use of force in 'Maintaining civil law and order' including in the context of detention for law enforcement.[43]

The next major development in use of force in UN peacekeeping operations was the use by the Security Council of 'protection of civilians' mandates acting under Chapter VII. In 1995, the Secretary-General's Supplement to the Agenda for Peace recognized that the trend from interstate to intrastate conflicts had led to conflicts in which 'Civilians are the main victims and often the main targets'.[44] It was not until the United Nations Mission in Sierra Leone (UNAMSIL) in 1999 and the United Nations Observer Mission in the Democratic Republic of the Congo (Mission de l'Organisation de Nations Unies en République Démocratique du Congo, MONUC) in 2000 that peacekeepers were provided mandates under Chapter VII to use 'all necessary means' to protect 'civilians under imminent threat of physical violence'.[45] This has become almost the standard authorization under Chapter

[40] Chesterman, 'The Use of Force in UN Peace Operations', 9.

[41] SC Res 837 (1993), paras 5, 33; Findlay, *The Use of Force in UN Peace Operations*, 196; Gray, *International Law and the Use of Force*, 286–9.

[42] Berdal, 'The Security Council and Peacekeeping' in Lowe et al, *The United Nations Security Council and War*, 70, 203–4.

[43] For discussion about use of force in the *sui generis* context of the UN transitional administrations in Kosovo and Timor-Leste, see Gray, *International Law and the Use of Force*, 298–9; Simma et al, *The Charter of the United Nations*, 295–7.

[44] UN Secretary-General, Supplement to an Agenda for Peace, A/50/60 (1995), para 12.

[45] UNAMSIL, SC Res 1270 (22 Oct 1999), para 14; MONUC, SC Res 1291 (24 Feb 2000), para 8. For an analysis of the 'protection of civilians' mandate, see Haidi Willmot and Scott Sheeran, 'The Protection of Civilians Mandate in Peacekeeping Operations: Reconciling Protection Concepts and Practices' (forthcoming 2014) *International Review of the Red Cross*, special edition on multinational operations; Victoria Holt and Glyn Taylor, 'Protecting Civilians in the Context of UN Peacekeeping Operations: Successes, Setbacks and Remaining Challenges', Independent study jointly commissioned by the Department of Peacekeeping Operations (DPKO) and the Office for the Coordination of Humanitarian Affairs (OCHA), United Nations, 2009, 8 and 160–72.

VII for UN peacekeepers to use force, with 12 operations in total having been given this mandate since 1999, and eight of the 14 current UN peacekeeping operations.[46] In 2009, the General Assembly endorsed the 'protection of civilians' concept in its annual peacekeeping resolution.[47] The practice of actual use of force for a protection of civilians mandates under Chapter VII has been patchy, however, and also almost never against the host state's forces but rather against non-state actors such as militia and armed groups.[48]

Finally, in April 2013 the Security Council authorized an 'Intervention Brigade' within the United Nations Stabilization Mission in the Democratic Republic of the Congo (Mission de l'Organisation des Nations Unies pour la Stabilisation en République Démocratique du Congo, MONUSCO) operation.[49] Despite the operation's efforts under its Chapter VII protection of civilians mandate, which some would say were too modest, the rebel groups in the Eastern Congo had continued to foment insecurity and to commit violations of human rights and humanitarian law. The Security Council decided 'on an exceptional basis and without creating a precedent or any prejudice to the agreed principles of peacekeeping' to authorize an '"Intervention Brigade"...with the responsibility of neutralising [these] armed groups'.[50] In particular, MONUSCO was authorized to use force and 'to take all necessary measures to perform the following tasks' which include to 'carry out targeted offensive operations through the Intervention Brigade...to prevent the expansion of all armed groups, neutralize these groups, and to disarm them.'[51] This was a significant decision and not without controversy,[52] which will be returned to further later in the chapter.

This brief review of the historical development of the concept of using force in UN peacekeeping demonstrates several points: it has been reactive to the demands put upon the UN peacekeeping instrument and crisis events; there has been a significant growth in the scope and nature of the concept of using force over time; and it has moved beyond a use of force based solely in self-defence to protecting the mandate of the mission and also civilians.

[46] For a review of practice, see Haidi Willmot and Ralph Mamiya, 'Mandated to Protect: Security Council Practice on the Protection of Civilians', Chapter 17 in this volume. The operations are UNAMSIL, MINURCAT, UNAMID, MONUSCO/MONUC, UNMIS, UNMISS, UNISFA, UNOCI, MINUSTAH, UNIFIL, UNMIL, ONUB.

[47] GA Res 63/280 (8 May 2009), para 2; Report of the Special Committee on Peacekeeping Operations and its Working Group, A/63/19 (2009), paras 125–8.

[48] Chesterman, 'The Use of Force in UN Peace Operations', 19.

[49] SC Res 2098 (28 Mar 2013); UN Press Release, '"Intervention Brigade" Authorised as Security Council Grants Mandate Renewal for United Nations Mission in Democratic Republic of Congo', SC/10964, 28 Mar 2013.

[50] SC Res 2098, para 9. [51] SC Res 2098, para 12(b).

[52] UN Press Release, '"Intervention Brigade" Authorised as Security Council Grants Mandate Renewal for United Nations Mission in Democratic Republic of Congo' (eg see comments by Guatemala and Argentina).

III. The Normative Framework

The development of the legal framework for UN peacekeeping has taken place in the context of the UN Charter's silence on the activity, and where there is arguably no complete theory of sources of international law for the organization.[53] To elaborate the legal framework therefore requires a review of foundation principles, the UN Charter, Security Council mandates, the status of forces agreement, other relevant instruments and resolutions, and UN practice. The legal framework is accordingly diffuse and opaque, and it is sometimes difficult to determine the precise legal authority for UN peacekeepers to use force vis-à-vis the host state's sovereignty guaranteed in the UN Charter in particular under Article 2(7). It is therefore essential to understand the *legal* position as distinct from policy, politics, or operational factors, which have been confused in cases such as Rwanda and Bosnia. It is also important to differentiate between the legal *authority* or *right* as compared to any legal *obligation* or *duty* of UN peacekeepers.

A. Relationship to the *Jus ad Bellum*

When starting with the conceptual framework in which to understand the law, it is important to note at the outset that the use of force in UN peacekeeping is effectively a sub-branch of the international law on use of force (the *jus ad bellum*). This is an issue often forgotten or not even realized, and one which permeates much of the legal analysis that follows. The use of force in UN peacekeeping has unique legal foundations and considerations, which translate to different understandings and interpretive approaches to the law.

The law, jurisprudence, and practice on use of force is often understood as the application of Articles 2(4) and 51 of the Charter and the associated customary international law.[54] Underlying this is the extent to which one state's intrusion on the sovereignty of another becomes contrary to the Article 2(4) prohibition and cannot be justified as self-defence under Article 51.[55] As the UN is accepted as a 'subject' of international law with a certain 'measure of international legal personality',[56] it too may impinge on and even violate the territorial sovereignty of a state. It is primarily the Security Council's authority and powers and Article 2(7) of the Charter which define the limits of authority to use force in a host state.[57] The extent

[53] Sheeran, 'A Constitutional Moment?', 118.

[54] See Gray, *International Law and the Use of Force*, 114–65; Simma et al, *The Charter of the United Nations*, 789–806.

[55] Findlay, *The Use of Force in UN Peace Operations*, 51.

[56] *Reparations for Injuries Suffered in the Service of the United Nations* (11 April 1949), Advisory Opinion, ICJ Rep 1949, 174, 179.

[57] Nicholas Tsagourias, 'Consent, Neutrality/Impartiality and the Use of Force in Peacekeeping' (2006) 11 *Journal of Conflict and Security Law*, 465; Simma et al, *The Charter of the United Nations*, 164–7.

of a UN peacekeeping operation's authority is, in this sense, the correlative of an imposition on the host state's sovereignty under the Charter. This represents the UN's multilateral mandate and legitimacy, and reflects that in using force the UN peacekeepers are acting 'on behalf of the international community at large'.[58] The UN's legal authority to use force is therefore fundamentally defined by the internal law and processes of the Charter, in particular Article 25, Chapters VI and VII, which may bind both the organization and UN member states.[59]

As this necessarily brief discussion suggests, while there are ostensible similarities in the nature and legal authority of the UN's use of force to that of states, including the nomenclature of 'self-defence', the legal foundations are substantially different.

B. Basic Principles of UN Peacekeeping and Use of Force

The 'basic principles' of UN peacekeeping, namely *consent* of the main parties to the conflict, *impartiality*, and *non use of force except in self-defence* all have an integral relationship with the use of force. In fact, the manner in which force is used helps to define and distinguish UN peacekeeping from non-UN-led operations mandated by the Security Council that are considered to be 'peace enforcement'.[60] The basic principles are affirmed in the annual General Assembly resolution on UN peacekeeping, the United Nations Peacekeeping Operations: Principles and Guidelines (Capstone Doctrine), and the Report on the Panel of United Nations Peace Operations (Brahimi Report),[61] but have not really guided the Security Council's work.[62] They provide a framework that purports to set policy boundaries for the use of force and, in the absence of a legal framework for peacekeeping under the Charter, they have been influential including at the normative level.[63]

[58] Daphna Shraga and Ralph Zacklin, 'The Applicability of International Humanitarian Law to United Nations Peacekeeping Operations: Conceptual, Legal and Practical Issues' in *Symposium on Humanitarian Action and Peacekeeping Operations* (Geneva: International Committee of the Red Cross, 1995), 39 and 43. Goodrich and Hambro, *Charter of the United Nations*, 64.

[59] UN Charter, Art 25 and 104, and Chapter VII.

[60] UN Department of Peacekeeping Operations and UN Department of Field Support, *United Nations Peacekeeping Operations: Principles and Guidelines* (Capstone Doctrine), 2008, 34, available at <http://www.peacekeepingbestpractices.unlb.org/Pbps/Library/Capstone_Doctrine_ENG.pdf>; Chesterman, 'The Use of Force in UN Peace Operations', 4, 3. The Intervention Brigade in MONUSCO may be an exception to this but MONUSCO is still considered by most, including the Organization, to be a UN peacekeeping operation.

[61] United Nations, Report on the Panel of United Nations Peace Operations (Brahimi Report), A/55/305 and S/2000/809 (2000), ix.

[62] eg the Security Council mandate for the MONUSCO intervention brigade.

[63] *Certain Expenses*, Advisory Opinion. For a discussion of the principles, see Nicholas Tsagourias, 'Self-Defence, Protection of Humanitarian Values, and the Doctrine of Impartiality and Neutrality in Enforcement Mandates', Chapter 18 in this volume, at 399–404.

The rationale for the *non-use of force* except in self-defence is closely connected to consent and impartiality and central to the UN peacekeeping concept. Shraga and Zacklin provided an orthodox view when they stated:

peacekeeping describes the inherently *peaceful action* of an internationally directed force of military, police and sometimes civilian personnel to assist with the implementation of agreements between governments or parties which have engaged in the conflict. It presumes cooperation, and the use of military force (other than self-defence) is *incompatible* with the concept.[64]

The challenge with use of force beyond self-defence is that, as Berdal comments, 'one cannot wage peace and make war in one location at the same time'.[65] This point was borne out in the Congo, Somalia, and Bosnia, where the UN peacekeeping operations became a de facto party to the conflict. The tension is not confined to theory and practice, as the UN Capstone Doctrine is internally contradictory on this issue. It endorses the basic principles but also that a 'robust' UN peacekeeping mandate may authorize the operation to 'use all necessary means' to deter forceful attempts to disrupt the political process, protect civilians under imminent threat of physical attack, and/or assist the national authorities in maintaining law and order.[66] This 'robust peacekeeping' is considered to be different to 'peace enforcement'.

As is clear from the basic principles, the use of force is central to the rationale and definition of UN peacekeeping. However, while the UNEF I mission was the defining precedent for UN peacekeeping, it differs significantly in nature to the complex, robust, multidimensional missions that have been mandated since, and the fit of contemporary operations with the principles is therefore strained.[67] Gray notes that in UN peacekeeping practice, and especially where the use of force is stretched beyond simple self-defence, it seems that the principles are rendered somewhat 'absurd'.[68] As was highlighted by some members of the Security Council, the MONUSCO 'intervention brigade' for example was directly contrary to the basic principles. This led to inclusion of language in the Security Council's resolution that the Intervention Brigade's mandate was provided 'on an exceptional basis and without creating a precedent or any prejudice to the agreed principles of peacekeeping'.[69] The strict adherence to the principles, regardless of the hostility of the mission's environment or need for civilian protection, can preclude more forceful options from being considered when they are appropriate.[70] In this regard, the basic principles of UN

[64] Shraga and Zacklin, 'The Applicability of International Humanitarian Law to United Nations Peacekeeping Operations' in *Symposium on Humanitarian Action and Peacekeeping Operations*, 44.

[65] Mats Berdal, 'The Use of Force in "Peace Operations" in the 1990s' (2000) 7 *International Peacekeeping* 55, 61.

[66] Capstone Doctrine, 34.

[67] Findlay, *The Use of Force in UN Peace Operations*, 412; Berdal, 'The Use of Force in "Peace Operations" in the 1990s', 58; Chesterman, 'The Use of Force in UN Peace Operations', 3.

[68] Gray, *International Law and the Use of Force*, 514.

[69] SC Res 2098, para 9.

[70] Berdal, 'The Security Council and Peacekeeping' in Lowe et al, *The United Nations Security Council and War*, 197.

peacekeeping do not act as either clear guidance in favour of, or a sensible constraint to, the use of force.

c. Legal Basis for Use of Force

The use of force in UN peacekeeping operations has one of two main legal bases: it is *implied* under the rubric of the right to self-defence, usually under a non-Chapter VII mandate; or it is *expressly* authorized under Chapter VII, such as a protection of civilians mandate. This has to be understood in the general context of the legal authority for UN peacekeeping under the Charter and the nature of a quasi-constitutional interpretation exercise. The competence and powers of a UN peacekeeping operation as a sub-organ of the organization are established by a mandate of the Security Council.[71] There are also specialist regimes of international law that are relevant to use of force in particular the law of armed conflict and human rights.

There are various approaches to the legal basis for UN peacekeeping operations under the Charter. One view is that peacekeeping is established under Articles 40, 41, and 42 depending on the type of mission.[72] Another is that there is no need for an express basis because the UN possesses an inherent or implied power[73] for peacekeeping, or that the legal foundation can be a customary rule of law.[74] At the time of UNEF I and ONUC, Dag Hammarskjöld the UN Secretary-General had located UN peacekeeping in the interstices between the peaceful and coercive measures available to the Security Council—'Chapter VI½' as he famously termed it—a blurring of the distinction between the two and the early origins of a doctrinal problem.[75] In the landmark legal ruling in the *Certain Expenses of the United*

[71] UN Charter, Arts 22 and 29; *Certain Expenses*, Advisory Opinion.

[72] Boris Kondoch, *International Peacekeeping: The Library of Essays of International Law* (Farnham: Ashgate, 2007), xvi; Alexander Orakhelashvili, 'The Legal Basis of the United-Nations Peacekeeping Operations' (2003) 43 *Virginia Journal of International Law* 485–524; Giorgio Gaja, 'Use of Force Made or Authorized by the United Nations' in Christian Tomuschat (ed), *The United Nations at Age Fifty: A Legal Perspective* (The Hague: Kluwer Law International, 1995), 39–58, 50–3; Michael Doyle, 'The UN Charter—A Global Constitution?' in Jeff Dunoff and Joel Trachtman (eds), *Ruling the World? Constitutionalism, International Law, and Global Governance* (Cambridge: Cambridge University Press, 2009), 122–3; Simma et al, *The Charter of the United Nations*, 648.

[73] On inherent powers, see Finn Seyersted, *United Nations Forces in the Law of Peace and War* (Leiden: Sijthoff, 1966), 133–4; Nigel D. White, 'The UN Charter and Peacekeeping Forces: Constitutional Issues' in Kondoch, *International Peacekeeping*, 90. In terms of implied powers, see the ICJ statement in *Reparations for Injuries Suffered in the Service of the United Nations*, Advisory Opinion, 82: 'under international law, the Organization must be deemed to have those powers which, though not expressly provided in the Charter, are conferred on it by necessary implication as being essential to the performance of its duties.'

[74] Kondoch, *International Peacekeeping*, xvi; White, 'The UN Charter and Peacekeeping Forces: Constitutional Issues' in Kondoch, *International Peacekeeping*, 77, 93.

[75] Chesterman, 'The Use of Force in UN Peace Operations', 5; White, 'The UN Charter and Peacekeeping Forces' in Pugh, *The UN, Peace and Force*, 60; Findlay, *The Use of Force in UN Peace Operations*, 351.

Nations advisory opinion of 1962, the International Court of Justice (ICJ) held that the Security Council and General Assembly have the general implied or inherent power to establish a UN peacekeeping operation.[76] As Alvarez indicates, therefore, the most accurate position is that today's UN peacekeeping operations are based on a loose interpretation of the 'general powers' of the Security Council acting under Chapter VII or under its general grant of authority in Articles 24 and 25.[77]

The UN legal order and its interpretation accordingly draw strong parallels to constitutional law. As explained by Franck: 'The law of, or about, international organizations is essentially constitutional law... [t]his is true not only because it is descriptive of the internal rules governing the operation of institutions and societies, but because it is treated by lawyers in a manner different to other law—treated as being capable of organic growth.'[78] This evidences a constitutional approach rather than full-fledged constitutionalism.[79] The law accordingly needs to be understood not so much in the light of usual interpretive methods for treaty law and customary international law, but in the light of methods associated with a constitutional approach, such as implied powers and the significant role of practice in the law's development.[80] It is important to understand the interpretive approach of inherent or implied powers of organs and sub-organs under the UN Charter, which is now widely accepted in Charter interpretation.[81] This includes the accepted role of each organ in determining its own jurisdiction, and the important role of practice, consent, and even acquiescence in validating legal interpretations.[82] As the Court has stated in the *Certain Expenses* case, 'each organ must, in the first place at least determine its own jurisdiction'.[83] This general background is central to understanding the extent of legal authority of UN peacekeepers to use force.

D. Implied Authority to Use Force: Basis of Self-Defence

The concept of use of force in self-defence in UN peacekeeping is fraught both because it is seldom spelt out, and its articulation is also inherently unclear in legal scope and foundation. The use of force in self-defence arises almost exclusively in the context of

[76] *Certain Expenses*, Advisory Opinion, 151, 167, 177.

[77] Alvarez, 'Constitutional Interpretation in International Organizations' in Coicaud and Heiskanen, *The Legitimacy of International Organizations*, 191.

[78] Thomas Franck, 'Book Review of Derek W. Bowett, The Law of International Institutions (Stevens, 1963)' (1964) 77 *Harvard Law Review* 1565.

[79] Jan Klabbers, 'Constitutionalism Lite' (2004) 1 *International Organizations Law Review* 31–58.

[80] *Certain Expenses*, Advisory Opinion; *Reparations*, Advisory Opinion; Sheeran, 'A Constitutional Moment?'.

[81] Alvarez, 'Constitutional Interpretation in International Organizations' in Coicaud and Heiskanen, *The Legitimacy of International Organizations*, 121; *Reparations*, Advisory Opinion, 174.

[82] *Reparations*, Advisory Opinion, 168 (that each organ must in the first place determine its own jurisdiction).

[83] *Certain Expenses*, Advisory Opinion, 168.

non-Chapter VII peacekeeping operations. This is because Chapter VII operations will usually have an express authority for use of force that goes beyond implied and simple self-defence. Where the legal authority to use force is implied, the consent of the host state has both political and legal significance. While the articulation that Article 25 of the Charter requires member states to 'accept and carry out' all Security Council decisions,[84] the practice tends to reflect that non-Chapter VII resolutions (or Chapter VI as most prefer to say) are seen as only recommendatory in nature.[85] The host state's legal consent is evident in acceptance or lack of objection to the Security Council's establishment of the UN peacekeeping operation, and eventually in the host state's conclusion of a status of forces agreement with the UN for the operation.

The use of force in self-defence is not usually spelt out in Security Council mandates, status of forces agreements,[86] or other instruments, nor positively expressed in any other way as a legal authorization. This is despite the UN Capstone Doctrine suggesting that Security Council express authorization is required even for self-defence.[87] The use of force in self-defence has been express in only a couple of Security Council resolutions, for example Resolution 467 in 1990 for the UNIFIL mission, and Resolution 918 in 1994 for the United Nations Assistance Mission for Rwanda (UNAMIR) adopted after the height of the genocide. However, both of these resolutions *reaffirm* rather than provide an independent basis, by respectively 'recalling' the guidelines of the Secretary-General's mission report and 'recognizing' self-defence. Historically, the Secretary-General had outlined the mandate and guidelines for a UN peacekeeping operation in his report, which would then be approved by the Security Council in its resolution, including through incorporation by reference.[88] This followed a pattern that began with the UNEF I operation, but is no longer the usual practice as operations have become more complex, multidimensional, and robust, and state sovereignty more salient. The Council now generally seeks to address use of force issues in its resolutions or not at all, rather than incorporate by reference from Secretary-General's reports. None of the current UN peacekeeping operations which are considered as non-Chapter VII have an express mandate to use force.

Without a positively expressed authority for UN peacekeepers to use force, the underlying legal basis must come more into focus, even if it is also unclear. Findlay uses a combination of two arguments based on the state and individual's right to

[84] Michael M. Bothe and Thomas Doerschel, 'The UN Peacekeeping Experience' in Dieter Fleck (ed), *The Handbook of the Law of Visiting Forces* (Oxford: Oxford University Press, 2001), 491; Lowe et al, *The United Nations Security Council and War*, 37.

[85] Findlay, *The Use of Force in UN Peace Operations*, 7.

[86] University of Essex, 'UN Peacekeeping and the Model Status of Forces Agreement', 13; Gray, *International Law and the Use of Force*, 300–4, 340.

[87] Capstone Doctrine, 34 ('it is widely understood that [UN peacekeeping operations] may use force at the tactical level, *with the authorization of the Security Council*, if acting in self-defense and defense of the mandate').

[88] UN Secretariat, *The Blue Helmets: A Review of United Nations Peacekeeping* (3rd edn, 1996), 60, 84; Gray, *International Law and the Use of Force*, 302.

self-defence for this underlying authority. He and others draw the analogy with the inherent right to self-defence of state armed forces as the main defenders of a state—essentially Article 51 of the Charter—and they argue that those forces continue to enjoy this right when acting on behalf of the UN.[89] This is obviously flawed to the extent that UN peacekeepers will not be defending their own state let alone any territory over which the UN is exercising sovereignty (unless exceptionally it is a transitional administration where the UN's authority is paramount). Another argument that Findlay makes is that self-defence in peacekeeping originates in individual self-defence that is escalated to the UN level.[90] This would be consistent with the way that many operational legal advisers of national armed forces apply self-defence in military law, as derived from national criminal law.[91] This approach is beset with many problems, however, including the relationships between the hierarchy of international and national law and consistency among different national laws of the contributing peacekeeping forces.

A better approach is to understand the legal basis for using force in self defence in the *specific context* of the UN organization and its peacekeeping operations, and given the hermeneutics and interpretation of the UN legal system. As the ICJ has stated, the rights and obligations of the UN are determined by 'its purposes and functions as specified or *implied* in its constituent documents and developed in practice'.[92] A UN peacekeeping operation's implied or inherent power to use force does not derive from an express mandate of the Security Council including under Chapter VII. It is also a general authority or right acknowledged and consented to by the UN membership, including through the 'basic principles' of UN peacekeeping, rather than established solely on a case-by-case basis with the host states for each peacekeeping operation. In other words, accepting a UN peacekeeping operation also means accepting that it may use force in self-defence including in defence of the mandate, and against parties to the conflict. This provides a stronger basis for the use of force against the host state in cases beyond simple self-defence.[93] This is also *necessary* for the fulfilment of the organization's purposes and functions through its peacekeeping operations, which is central to the implied powers test.[94] The parties, and especially the host state, do not consent to use of force per se, rather they consent to a UN peacekeeping operation as a whole package and on the basis that it may use force in self-defence, even if against the host state.

[89] Bowett, *United Nations Forces*, 284; Simma et al, *The Charter of the United Nations*, 683.

[90] Findlay, *The Use of Force in UN Peace Operations*, 14.

[91] Discussion of author with military legal adviser, eg see UK Ministry of Defence, *British Defence Doctrine*, Joint Doctrine Publication 0-01 (4th edn, 2011), 1B1.a.

[92] *Reparations*, Advisory Opinion, 179.

[93] Findlay, *The Use of Force in UN Peace Operations*, 8.

[94] *Reparations*, Advisory Opinion, 182–3. The ICJ's decision stated: 'Under international law, the Organization is deemed to have those powers which, though not necessarily expressly provided in the United Nations Charter, are conferred upon it by necessary implication as being essentially to the performance of its duties'.

It is possible for self-defence also to be understood as a right under customary international law for UN peacekeeping operations. It is well accepted that international organizations may be bound *mutatis mutandis* by customary international law,[95] and the ICJ has affirmed this for the organization.[96] A customary international law right for the UN relies on *opinio juris* and state practice and it will be similar in nature to establishing an implied power. As the law's content is still determined by the scope of the Charter and its practice, it is difficult to talk of any customary international law that is meaningfully independent of UN law and practice.[97]

E. Meaning of Self-Defence

The concept of use of force in self-defence by UN peacekeepers has undergone a quiet revolution, in particular with the expansion to include 'in defence of the mandate'. However, the current scope is both unclear and conceptually incoherent. There is no single articulated general definition in an authoritative UN document. A range of literature, statements, and practice therefore needs to be reviewed to construct the legal picture.

As demonstrated in the historical review, the UN's practice and statements on the scope of self-defence paint a picture of evolution and growth, but also inconsistency in the face of political pressure. This is well illustrated by two different missions' approaches to a similar question around the same time. In the United Nations Transitional Authority in Cambodia (UNTAC, 1992–3), Force Commander Lieutenant-General John Sanderson of Australia assumed that the rules of engagement permitted UNTAC to use force in self-defence of 'anyone going about their legitimate business under the Paris Agreement', including non-uniformed UN personnel and Cambodians.[98] The UNTAC military component was deployed ready

[95] Rosalyn Higgins, *The Development of International Law Through the Political Organs of the United Nations* (Oxford: Oxford University Press, 1963), 2; Andrew Clapham, *Human Rights Obligations of Non-State Actors* (Oxford: Oxford University Press, 2006), 19; Christian Tomuschat, 'International Law: Ensuring the Survival of Mankind on the Eve of a New Century: General Course on Public International Law' (2001) 281 *Recueil des cours de l'Académie de droit international* 34–5; Philippe Sands and Pierre Klein, *Bowett's Law of International Institutions* (6th edn, London: Sweet & Maxwell, 2009), 458–9.

[96] *Reparations*, Advisory Opinion, 179; Guglielmo Verdirame, *The UN and Human Rights: Who Guards the Guardians?* (Cambridge: Cambridge University Press, 2011), 56.

[97] eg see John Cerone, 'Reasonable Measures in Unreasonable Circumstances: A Legal Responsibility Framework for Human Rights Violations in Post-Conflict Territories under UN Administration' in Nigel D. White and Dirk Klaasen (eds), *The UN, Human Rights and Post Conflict Situations* (New York: Juris Publishing, 2005), 62.

[98] John Sanderson, 'A Review of Recent Peacekeeping Operations', paper presented at Pacific Armies Management Seminar, Dacca, Jan 1994, quoted in Findlay, *The Use of Force in UN Peace Operations*, 125–6; James Schear, 'Riding the Tiger: The UN and Cambodia' in William Durch (ed), *UN Peacekeeping, American Policy, and the Uncivil Wars of the 1990s* (Washington DC: Henry. L. Stimson Centre, 1996), 135, 143.

to use force to 'defend' the first national elections including the polling stations, which was in the end critical to the mission's success.[99]

By contrast, in Rwanda in 1994 the UNAMIR Force Commander Major-General Romeo Dallaire's cable to New York proposing the use of force to seize a weapons cache that was anticipated to be used in what became the genocide was refused by UN Headquarters as 'beyond the mandate entrusted to UNAMIR'.[100] As an exercise perhaps in retrospective interpretation or shifting the blame, after the genocide the Security Council stated in its Resolution 918 (1994) that it 'recognize[d] that UNAMIR may be required to take action in self-defence against persons or groups who threaten protected sites and populations, UN and other humanitarian personnel or the means of delivery and distribution of humanitarian relief'.[101]

Commentators and scholars have tended not to go beyond general descriptions of the scope of self-defence, including that it should be exercised as a matter of last resort and must conform to rules on self-defence under international law (which stipulate that it can only be exercised in a manner proportionate to the existing threat).[102] The more precise formulations of self-defence for UN peacekeepers have included the use of force for the following: (1) to defend themselves from an attack or imminent attack; (2) in response to attempts to disarm them; (3) to protect UN equipment against seizure or damage; (4) to support UN troops from other contingents; (5) to ensure freedom of movement; (6) to protect safe areas and protected sites; and (7) to protect humanitarian convoys and aid.[103]

There is no doubt that more than simple or traditional self-defence is required for the success of UN peacekeeping. In the light of the 'basic principles' and the Security Council's silence on use of force in most resolutions, it is not surprising that 'self-defence' became a conceptual vehicle for the expansion of use of force. The problem, however, is that the UN's broad concept of 'defence of the mandate' has few boundaries. As evident from the ONUC and UNPROFOR experiences, some commentators such as White observe: 'Allowing a force to

[99] For discussion see Chesterman, 'The Use of Force in UN Peace Operations', 14. In Haiti, the multinational force's interpretation of the rules of engagement was quickly changed in response to civilian deaths to permit troops to use force to prevent the loss of human life. See David Malone, *Decision-Making in the UN Security Council: The Case of Haiti, 1990–1997* (Oxford: Clarendon Press, 1998), 113; Findlay, *The Use of Force in UN Peace Operations*, 274.

[100] See Fred Grünfeld and Anke Huijboom, *Failure to Prevent Genocide in Rwanda* (Leiden: Brill, 2007), ch 8.2; Philip Gourevitch, *We Wish To Inform You That Tomorrow We Will Be Killed With Our Families* (New York: Farrar, Straus & Giroux, 1998), ch 8.

[101] SC Res 918 (1994).

[102] Findlay, *The Use of Force in UN Peace Operations*, 14; Ray Murphy, 'United Nations Peacekeeping in Lebanon and Somalia' (2003) 8 *Journal of Conflict and Security Law* 71; Bowett, *United Nations Forces*, 196; Simma et al, *The Charter of the United Nations*, 683. If the use of force is subject to international humanitarian law (IHL), then the general principles of IHL will apply, see Secretary-General's Bulletin etc.

[103] Boddens Hosang, 'Force Protection, Unit Self-Defence and Extended Self-Defence' in Gill and Fleck, *The Handbook of the International Law of Military Operations*, 417; Capstone Doctrine, section 2.2; Findlay, *The Use of Force in UN Peace Operations*, 15.

take positive action in defence of its purpose is no different from allowing them to enforce it'.[104]

The concept of self-defence is well established and reasonably clearly defined in international law. The extension of the concept to the protection of third parties such as civilians outside of the sovereign borders, obscures its content and makes it less clear and understandable. The problems associated with the sheer breadth of such active self-defence have been borne out in UN peacekeeping practice. In ONUC, self-defence was used 'as practically the sole justification for bringing down the [secessionist] Katangan regime'.[105] In UNPROFOR, self-defence became almost unidentifiable, as it justified using force for the protection of freedom of movement, safe areas, and humanitarian aid and convoys. As Findlay noted, the self-defence norm is 'stretched and ultimately broken'.[106] What the concept has evolved to mean today bears little resemblance to the common or legal understanding of self-defence, including in Article 51, or national criminal law. The difficulty is not only that it becomes unclear in substance, therefore losing its normative power (ie to authorize and to constrain), but also this obscures its true legal basis and the legitimacy of the use of force by UN peacekeepers and creates practical problems on the ground.

F. Express Authority to Use Force

The use of force by UN peacekeepers can also stem from the Security Council's express authorization in a Chapter VII resolution for a 'robust' UN peacekeeping operation.[107] A mandate under Chapter VII is obligatory, not merely recommendatory. As affirmed in the *Certain Expenses* advisory opinion, a Chapter VII resolution obviates the need for consent as the UN (or a force authorized but not led by the UN) is able to use force by Council authority under the Charter. This express authorization builds on the foundations of UN peacekeeping operations' inherent right to use force in self-defence. However, a mandate granted under Chapter VII for a UN peacekeeping operation does not always mean that express authority to use force is provided.[108] Such mandates are also employed for non-legal reasons to indicate the serious nature of the situation (ie an Article 39 threat to international peace and security) and also the Council's resolve.

[104] White, *Keeping the Peace*, 201. This is acknowledged also by the UN in the 1995 General Guidelines for Peacekeeping Operations which states that use of force in defence of the mandate 'might be interpreted as entitling United Nations personnel to open fire in a wide variety of situations'. UN Department of Peacekeeping Operations, General Guidelines for Peacekeeping Operations, UN/210/TC/GG95 (Oct 1995), available at <http://www.un.org/Depts/dpko/training>, 20.

[105] Findlay, *The Use of Force in UN Peace Operations*, 74, 356. Hammarskjöld even promoted anticipatory self-defence, an idea not generally accepted in the *jus ad bellum*. He stated 'the act of self-defence against attack could include the disarming and, if necessary, the detention of those *preparing* to attack UN troops'.

[106] Findlay, *The Use of Force in UN Peace Operations*, 356.

[107] Capstone Doctrine, section 3.1.

[108] eg UNMIL in Liberia, SC Res 1509 (2003); Gray, *International Law and the Use of Force*, 297.

A UN peacekeeping mandate under Chapter VII to use force is usually grounded in the wording 'all necessary means' or 'necessary actions' to achieve certain tasks set out in the mandate.[109] A range of different formulae are agreed by the Security Council, but as Gray notes 'there is no obvious reason for the diversity'.[110] The terminology is more proactive than self-defence, but it is also broad and imprecise if not appropriately qualified. Berdal points out that such mandates provided by UN political organs may be 'so vague as to provide little or no basis for translation into realizable military objectives'.[111] More recently, the Chapter VII resolutions for UN peacekeeping have consistently qualified the use of force with a 'protection of civilians' mandate. This is more limited and legitimate, in particular when compared to mandates for non-UN-led peace enforcement operations, which are also primarily based on the 'all necessary means' formula.[112]

It is beyond the scope of this chapter to fully review and categorize the use of force in Security Council mandates under Chapter VII, but key elements have included: (1) defence of personnel, facilities, installations, and equipment;[113] (2) in support of implementation of peace agreements;[114] (3) implementation of arms and other sanctions;[115] (4) resisting attempts by forceful means to prevent operations from discharging their duties under the mandate;[116] (5) ensuring freedom of movement of UN and humanitarian personnel and aid, observers, and others;[117] and (6) maintaining a safe and secure environment.[118]

Historically, mandates that have essentially called for the neutralization of a particular party of the conflict, such as in ONUC and the Unified Task Force (UNITAF) in Somalia, have been considered as too far reaching and led to escalation and peace enforcement rather than peacekeeping. This, however, is the mandate of the new MONUSCO 'Intervention Brigade'.[119] Not only is MONUSCO now 'taking sides', including when government forces are also responsible for violations of international

[109] Bothe and Doerschel, 'The UN Peacekeeping Experience' in Fleck, *The Handbook of the Law of Visiting Forces*, 500; Findlay, *The Use of Force in UN Peace Operations*, 8; Gray, *International Law and the Use of Force*, ch 8. Eg see SC Res 1493 (2003) ('all necessary means'); SC Res 1499 (2003) ('to take all necessary means'); SC Res 1565 (2004), or SC Res 1756 (2007) ('use all necessary means').

[110] Gray, *International Law and the Use of Force*, 304; Findlay, *The Use of Force in UN Peace Operations*, 7; Boddens Hosang, 'Force Protection, Unit Self-Defence and Extended Self-Defence' in Gill and Fleck, *The Handbook of the International Law of Military Operations*, 419.

[111] Berdal, 'The Use of Force in "Peace Operations" in the 1990s', 62; Gray, *International Law and the Use of Force*, 310.

[112] For more discussion of use of 'necessary means' in UN-authorized missions, see Gray, *International Law and the Use of Force*, 306.

[113] UNAMID in Darfur, SC Res 1769 (2007), para 15(a)(i).

[114] UNAMID in Darfur, SC Res 1769 (2007), para 15(a)(ii).

[115] MONUSCO, SC Res 1925 (2010), para 12(t).

[116] UNIFIL in Lebanon, SC Res 1701 (2006), para 12.

[117] UNISFA in Abyei, SC Res 1990 (2011), para 3.

[118] See an alternative list in Berdal, 'The Security Council and Peacekeeping' in Lowe et al, *The United Nations Security Council and War*, 191.

[119] See n 49; and Scott Sheeran and Stephanie Case, 'Legal Issues for the UN Intervention Brigade in the Democratic Republic of the Congo', International Institute for Peace (IPI), Issue Brief, 2014 forthcoming.

human rights and humanitarian law, but the Intervention Brigade's military operations are designed around eliminating particular parties to the conflict. This potentially goes beyond peace enforcement and into the realms of war-fighting, albeit within one component and aspect of the overall MONUSCO mission.

G. Protection of Civilians

While civilian protection may have been engaged in UN peacekeeping since the time of ONUC, the practice of protection of civilians mandates began only shortly after the Brahimi Report with the UNAMSIL operation in Sierra Leone in 1999. The protection of civilians has been mandated in numerous operations since. The usual wording has been an authorization to 'use all necessary means, within the limits of [the operation's] capacity and in the areas where its units are deployed' to '[e]nsure the protection of civilians, including humanitarian personnel, under imminent threat of physical violence, in particular violence emanating from *any of the parties* engaged in the conflict'.[120] The protection of civilians concept has been endorsed in general resolutions of both the Security Council and the General Assembly.[121] There is a trend driven by the humanitarian community to consider civilian protection in UN peacekeeping in a much broader sense,[122] which is partly evident in the most recent MONUSCO mandate. There are also significant and difficult questions about how broadly to interpret 'imminent threat' in this context. In MONUC, for example, it was read as demonstrated by an action 'preparatory to a hostile action' alongside 'available evidence which indicates an intention to attack'.[123]

A key manifestation of the UN's use of force for protection of civilians is the question of whether UN peacekeepers are permitted to protect civilians from harm regardless of their mandate. This obviously bears on their legal authority for use of force, and is well illustrated in the Brahimi Report which stated:

> peacekeepers—troops or police—who witness violence against civilians should be presumed to be authorized to stop it, within their means, in support of basic United Nations principles

[120] SC Res 1857 (2008), paras 5 and 3(a).

[121] GA Res 63/280 and Report of the Special Committee on Peacekeeping Operations and its Working Group, A/63/19 (2009).

[122] In 1999, the UN Inter-Agency Standing Committee (IASC) adopted the definition of protection as 'all efforts aimed at obtaining full respect for the rights of the individual and of the obligations of the authorities/arms bearers in accordance with the letter and the spirit of the relevant bodies of law'. See 'Protection of civilians in conflict—the ICRC perspective', Address by Angelo Gnaedinger, ICRC Director-General, Humanitarian and Resident Coordinators' Retreat, Geneva, 9 May 2007, available at <http://www.icrc.org/eng/resources/documents/statement/children-statement-140507.htm>. See discussion of protection of civilians in Willmot and Sheeran, 'The Protection of Civilians Mandate in Peacekeeping Operations: Reconciling Protection Concepts and Practices'; Holt and Taylor, *Protecting Civilians in the Context of UN Peacekeeping Operations*; Nicholas Tsagourias, 'Self-Defence, Protection of Humanitarian Values, and the Doctrine of Impartiality and Neutrality in Enforcement Mandates', Chapter 18 in this volume, at 407–14.

[123] Major General (Rtd) Patrick Cammaert, 'Learning to use force on the hoof in peacekeeping', Institute for Security Studies, Situation Report, 3 Apr 2007, 6.

and... consistent with 'the perception and the expectation of protection created by [an operation's] very presence'.[124]

After the Brahimi Report suggested this *presumed* authority to protect civilians, the UN Secretariat revised in 2002 what became known as the 'UN master list of numbered rules of engagement'.[125] One of the standard rules from that list, which applied to *all* UN peacekeeping operations regardless of the mandate, authorized the use of force 'up to, and including deadly force, to defend any civilian person who is in need of protection against a hostile act or hostile intent, when competent local authorities are not in a position to render immediate assistance'.[126] This reflects a position that protection of civilians is inherent in all UN peacekeeping and does not apply *only* in Chapter VII operations with an express mandate. That said, the potential scope of this task is shaped by military or other capability ('within their means'), which will be more limited in an operation without an express mandate to use force.

The use of force by UN peacekeepers for protection of civilians is a significant conceptual development. In terms of Security Council implementation, it has been more influential and utilized than the Responsibility to Protect.[127] Gray refers to it as a 'new legal and moral' dimension to the use of force,[128] in similar terms that were used by the Argentinian delegation during the adoption of the first protection of civilians mandate for UNAMSIL.[129] It is the crystallization of a trend that suggests that the most legitimate use of force on behalf of the international community is the protection of civilians.[130] This is consistent with impartiality, the purposes of the Charter, and the general level of agreement in support of the concept. It is a real movement from the state-centric focus on international peace and security and resolution of disputes of states, which was the central focus of Chapter VII at the time of

[124] Brahimi Report, para 62 (quoting the Rwanda lessons learnt report).

[125] Findlay, *The Use of Force in UN Peace Operations*, App 3; United Nations Master List of Numbered ROE, Guidelines for the Development of ROE for UNPKO, Provisional Sample ROE, Attachment 1 to FGS/0220.001, United Nations, Apr 2002.

[126] Rule 1.8. See discussion of UN Master List in Victoria Holt and Tobias Berkman, *Impossible Mandate? Military Preparedness, the Responsibility to Protect and Modern Peace Operations* (Washington DC: Henry L. Stimson Centre, 2006), 83–6; a UN template for ROE without model rules is provided in the UN Infantry Battalion Manual, 2012, Vol. II, Annex C model ROE, 254.

[127] This is in addition to the significant use in UN peacekeeping, eg the Security Council mandate for the Libya intervention had a reference in the preamble to 'the responsibility of the Libyan authorities to protect the Libyan population' but *decided* that coalition forces could 'take all necessary measures... to protect civilians and civilian populated areas under threat of attack'. SC Res 1973 (2011), para 4. See Nicholas Tsagourias, 'Self-Defence, Protection of Humanitarian Values, and the Doctrine of Impartiality and Neutrality in Enforcement Mandates', Chapter 18 in this volume, at 407–14.

[128] Gray, *International Law and the Use of Force*, 313.

[129] Security Council Meeting Record, S/PV.4054 (22 Oct 1999), 16 ('the protection of civilians under Chapter VII [of the Charter] is a pertinent development in the context of the mandate of a peace operation. This draft resolution is significant in that it introduces a new, fundamental political, legal and moral dimension').

[130] See Haidi Willmot and Ralph Mamiya, 'Mandated to Protect: Security Council Practice on the Protection of Civilians', Chapter 17 in this volume.

the Charter's drafting and adoption.[131] It can be also seen as a reaction to the failures of UNPROFOR and other operations in the 1990s, which had relied on mandates of extended self-defence and de facto peace enforcement. In this regard, it makes more sense to talk of the inherent right to use force in self-defence and for protection of civilians, than of self-defence including 'in defence of the mandate'. The UN by defending civilians in this context is not acting similar to an intervening state, but is acting as a supra-national organization defending the norms and values of the UN Charter.

The evolution of use of force in UN peacekeeping, as exemplified by protection of civilian issues and mandates discussed earlier, has become conceptually a manifestation of a human rights-focused approach.[132] As Berdal indicates, the growing international emphasis on good governance, human rights, and democracy has impacted on the development leading to humanitarian grounds increasingly becoming the justification for international use of force.[133] This is a shift in Charter interpretation and emphasis from Westphalian sovereignty and peace and security between states, to the inherent dignity and protection of the individual. The Security Council is required to respect the core content of fundamental human rights as set out in the Purposes under Article 1(3) of the Charter.[134] The Security Council's practice demonstrates that an essential foundation for the express mandate of protection of civilians is recognizing human rights abuses and violations of international humanitarian law.[135] This reflects also a parallel and earlier evolution in the meaning of Article 39—the trigger for the use of Chapter VII powers—from interstate to intrastate conflict in which civilians are the main victims and targets.[136]

H. Positive Duties and International Human Rights Law

Some commentators suggest not just an authority but a *duty* for UN peacekeepers to use force for protection of civilians. They consider that UN peacekeeping inaction in the face of violence against civilians could be a wrongful act under international law,[137] including in the light of the UN's stated policy expecting peacekeepers to recognize and respond correctly to violations of international human rights law.[138]

[131] Goodrich and Hambro, *Charter of the United Nations*, 35–6.

[132] Haidi Willmot and Ralph Mamiya, 'Mandated to Protect: Security Council Practice on the Protection of Civilians', Chapter 17 in this volume; Gray, *International Law and the Use of Force*, 313–14; Cox, 'Beyond Self-Defense', 258.

[133] Berdal, 'The Security Council and Peacekeeping', in Lowe et al, *The United Nations Security Council and War*, 189.

[134] Erika de Wet, *The Chapter VII Powers of the United Nations Security Council* (Oxford: Hart, 2004), 198; cf Martti Koskenniemi, 'The Police in the Temple. Order, Justice and the UN: A Dialectical View' (1995) 6 *European Journal of International Law* 327, 336–7.

[135] UNAMSIL, SC Res 1270 (1999), paras 17, 22; MONUC, SC Res 1291 (2000), preambular paras 18, 19, para 15.

[136] Simma et al, *The Charter of the United Nations*, 724–5.

[137] Mansson, 'Use of Force and Civilian Protection', 515; Kondoch, *International Peacekeeping*, 531.

[138] Capstone Doctrine, section 1.2.

As the authority to use force to protect civilians is either based on implied terms, or the express mandate from a Chapter VII resolution, it is quite difficult to articulate such a duty to act as a positive obligation within the *jus ad bellum*. There are also, no doubt, practical challenges to conceiving it as a positive obligation.

While it is beyond the scope of this chapter, the legal authority of UN peacekeepers to use force is connected to obligations under international human rights law. In particular, in Brahimi's scenario of civilian protection described earlier, it could be argued that the UN has an obligation to ensure respect of international human rights law (also known as the 'due diligence' obligation) by other actors—such as armed groups, private individuals, and even local authorities.[139] While there is real scope for this argument of *positive* obligation, it is complicated and requires untangling a range of legal issues outside the scope of this chapter, including: (1) the basis and scope of human rights obligations of the UN and its peacekeepers; (2) the extent to which derogation is possible (eg as for states of emergency) for any such applicable obligations; and (3) the UN's legal authority to use force in a peacekeeping operation without an express mandate from the Security Council to do so (which is usually the case for a non-Chapter VII operation).[140]

IV. Legal Issues at the Practical and Operational Level

While the overall command of the mission lies with the Secretary-General, the decision to use force is usually taken by those on the ground.[141] Such decisions are often taken by a force commander, officers in the field, or even individual soldiers faced with a situation which necessitates an immediate decision and action. In order to integrate the use of force into UN peacekeeping operations, the authority needs to be translated

139 UN Human Rights Committee, General Comment 31 (2004), CCPR/C/21/Rev.1/Add.13, paras 8 (due diligence), 10 (peacekeeping); Sheeran, 'A Constitutional Moment?', 80–4, 113–18.

140 Sheeran, 'A Constitutional Moment?', 113–18; Megret and F. Hoffman, DETAILS NEEDED; Verdirame, *The UN and Human Rights*; Erika de Wet, *The Chapter VII Powers of the United Nations Security Council* (Oxford: Hart, 2004), 201–2; Scott Sheeran and Catherine Bevilacqua, 'The UN Security Council and International Human Rights Obligations: Towards a Theory of Constraints and Derogation' in Scott Sheeran and Sir Nigel Rodley (eds), *The Routledge Handbook on International Human Rights Law* (London: Routledge, 2013); Michael Wood, 'The UN Security Council and International Law', Hersch Lauterpacht Memorial Lectures, Lauterpacht Centre for International Law, University of Cambridge, 8 Nov 2006, para 29, available at <http://www.lcil.cam.ac.uk/sites/default/files/LCIL/documents/lectures/2006_hersch_lecture_2.pdf>.

141 Cammaert, 'Learning to use force on the hoof in peacekeeping', 3–7.

into Standard Operating Procedures through rules of engagement (ROE), orders for opening fire (OFOF), and directives on the use of force (DUF).[142] While these documents specify the conditions and limits for initiating or responding by force, they are not legal documents per se, but they may represent orders and therefore can be the basis of disciplinary and even criminal sanction for individual soldiers and police.

A. Translation from Mandate to Rules of Engagement

There are real problems for the UN Secretariat in translating the broad principles on the use of force into succinct situation-specific guidance for use in missions.[143] The difficulties include that, while the use of force needs to be made operational through the ROE, OFOF, and DUF, it is still expected to embody peacekeeping principles such as restraint and impartiality,[144] and also reflect the mandate given to the operation.[145] These are high expectations as it is not easy to convey the delicate constraints and expectations for peacekeeping in concise orders to be followed by soldiers and others on the ground. This challenge is exacerbated by the lack of clarity in both the mandates provided by the Security Council and more generally in understanding the relevant law.[146] The UN's Model ROE referred to earlier may be helpful, but it is not clear on what authority those standards are based. As indicated later in this section, they also contain challenges. Furthermore, due to the mixture of law with strategy, policy, politics, and operational capability, for example, the ROE will usually be more restrictive than the mandate (ie 'read down'), which may hamper the fulfilment of the mission.[147]

B. UN and National Rules of Engagement

It is well documented that national contingents in a UN peacekeeping operation may have their own ROE which are different to the UN ROE.[148] This is partly as

[142] Bothe and Doerschel, 'The UN Peacekeeping Experience' in Fleck, *The Handbook of the Law of Visiting Forces*, 494.

[143] Jonathan Dworken, 'Rules of Engagement (ROE) for Humanitarian Intervention and Low-Intensity Conflict: Lessons From Restore Hope', Research Memorandum 93–120, Center for Naval Analyses, United States, 1, available at <http://www.fieldex.org/wp-content/uploads/2011/04/ROE-in-Humanitarian-Intervention.pdf>; Finlay, *The Use of Force in UN Peace Operations*, 356.

[144] Findlay, *The Use of Force in UN Peace Operations*, 14.

[145] Cox, 'Beyond Self-Defense', 270.

[146] eg see Australia's comments on Security Council resolutions and different interpretations and inconsistencies in the rules of engagement, UN Press Release (26 Feb 2007), GA/PK/192.

[147] Dale Stephens, 'The Lawful Use of Force by Peacekeeping Forces: The Tactical Imperative' (2007) 14 *International Peacekeeping* 157, 163.

[148] Stephens, 'The Lawful Use of Force by Peacekeeping Forces', 163–169; Chesterman, 'The Use of Force in UN Peace Operations', 3.

each nation may have its own ROE philosophy, different terminology, military culture, and training, as well as political imperatives for contributing states. As one military commander in Somalia commented, UNISOM II's various contingents came to the battlefield with many different rules of engagement, 'which makes life interesting when the shooting begins'.[149] One of the issues discussed for UNPROFOR in Bosnia was that many contingents were not legally able to use lethal force to protect property, which was authorized in the UN ROE (and also still is in the Model ROE).[150] The problem of differences with national ROE is also exacerbated further by the existence of 'national caveats', which are country-specific guidelines applying to individual troop contributing countries (TCC) that place restrictions and conditions on their contingents' activities and use of force.[151]

c. Decision-Making Based on Rules of Engagement

Another practical issue is that difficult decisions on using force have to be made on the basis of a few succinct and open-ended prescriptions in the operational guidance. There may be few decisions made under as much pressure, often without opportunity of consultation or reflection, as those by UN peacekeepers to use force. This is based on two main difficulties: a lack of clarity in the operational guidance; and the nature of military doctrine for peacekeeping compared to warfare. First, in terms of clarity, the ROE for UNOSOM II in Somalia for example authorized the use of 'deadly force' to 'resist attempts by forceful means to prevent the Force from discharging *its duties*'.[152] As the ROE provided no explanation of the mission 'duties', this is almost meaningless as practical and clear guidance for real-time decisions by soldiers.

Secondly, there is an important difference for military doctrine and ROE for peacekeeping as compared to warfare. The former focuses on use of force against 'hostile acts' or 'hostile intent' against the mission or mandate, while the latter focuses on the relatively clearer concept of 'hostile force' or belligerents. The UNOSOM II ROE, for example, authorized deadly force to 'defend themselves, other UN lives, or persons and areas under their protection against *hostile acts* or *hostile intent*'.[153] The ROE defined

[149] Anthony Zinni, 'It's Not Nice and Neat' (1995) 121 *Proceedings, US Naval Institute* 26, 30.

[150] eg British soldiers' actions in Bosnia were assessed in accordance with British criminal law legislation. See Peter Rowe, 'The United Nations Rules of Engagement and the British Soldier in Bosnia' (1994) 43 *International and Comparative Law Quarterly* 947, 954; Stephens, 'The Lawful Use of Force by Peacekeeping Forces', 165.

[151] Terry Gill, 'Characterization and Legal Basis for Peace Operations' in Gill and Fleck, *The Handbook of the International Law of Military Operations*.

[152] Findlay, *The Use of Force in UN Peace Operations*, App 2.5 (Rules of Engagement for UNOSOM II (May 1993), rule 1(b)).

[153] Findlay, *The Use of Force in UN Peace Operations*, App 2.5, rule 1(a).

a hostile act in essence as a 'use of force' against the operation, and hostile intent as the 'threat of imminent use of force' against the operation. As noted in a US military lessons learned report from Somalia, 'hostile intent' is difficult to determine at the best of times, and became even more difficult as guns were 'an ever-present aspect of Somali life and carrying them in the open became common'.[154]

The operational guidance on use of force, when combined with the difficult real-life context on the ground and lack of clarity in the law, makes for a broad range of possible interpretations based on individual judgement, training, predisposition, cultures, and values. As a consequence, relying on a force commander, officer, or soldier to make the right call in the difficult context explained previously may result in inaction, or indeed the wrong actions being taken, for use of force by UN peacekeepers.

V. Conclusion

The use of force in UN peacekeeping has been marked by political and doctrinal problems, conceptual incoherence, and failures on the ground. This is partly because the UN peacekeeping concept has developed in crises of international peace and security and in a reactive, ad hoc, and *ex post facto* manner. The legal principles have thus derived from operational needs and according to political and practical exigencies. Problems have been caused by UN peacekeeping lacking a foundational prescription in the Charter, and instead latching on to state-centric international law concepts such as Article 51, which do not fully reflect the *sui generis* nature of the UN and its authority. This has restricted the role of law as a clear guide and constraint, and more deeply impacted on the coherence and legitimacy of this crucial peacekeeping tool of the UN.

As the discussion demonstrates, there is a need for an update and reconceptualization of the theory of use of force by UN peacekeepers under international law. There are two key aspects to this re-conceptualization. The first is to discard the vague and unhelpful notion of defence of the mandate. The second is to recognize that protection of civilians is an *inherent* aspect of the UN's authority for use of force in *all* peacekeeping operations. This approach provides greater legitimacy, normativity, and clarity to the UN's use of force, and especially for non-Chapter VII peacekeeping operations. At the practical level, it means better guidance on when

[154] Dworken, 'Rules of Engagement (ROE) for Humanitarian Intervention and Low-Intensity Conflict', 4.

force can and should be used, and less of an excuse when it is not. The significant problems with the law explained in this chapter should not be left unresolved, only to be 'answered' by chance, or highlighted through political failures or future uses of force in the field. If further tragic failures and human suffering on a massive scale are to be avoided, such as in Somalia, Rwanda, and Srebrenica, the foundation and scope of the law explained in this chapter is one issue that needs to be openly discussed and resolved.

CHAPTER 17

MANDATED TO PROTECT: SECURITY COUNCIL PRACTICE ON THE PROTECTION OF CIVILIANS

HAIDI WILLMOT*

RALPH MAMIYA

I. Introduction

THE evolution of UN Security Council practice on the authorization of the use of force is intimately connected with the conception and growth of the protection of civilians mandate in UN peacekeeping operations. The use of force to protect civilians under threat of physical violence is now frequently mandated in such operations and broadly accepted by the international community, evidencing a new

* The authors serve with the United Nations Department of Peacekeeping Operations/Department of Field Support. They write in a personal capacity; the views expressed do not necessarily reflect those of the United Nations.

paradigm for the legitimate use of force. This chapter will trace the conception and evolution of the protection of civilians mandate through Security Council practice and examine the significance of the mandate in the broader evolution of the use of force under the UN Charter. While the Security Council deals with the protection of civilians both as a thematic issue and through its country-specific work, the former including a broad range of humanitarian and human rights issues,[1] it is the authorization of the direct physical protection of civilians by UN peacekeeping operations and other authorized military interventions that are the aspects of the protection agenda most relevant to the evolution of Security Council practice on the use of force.

The protection of civilians by UN peacekeepers is a subject that has garnered relatively little academic attention, despite the fact that it has become one of the most frequent and accepted uses of force by the international community, establishing a people-centred approach within what remains a state-centred system. The growth of the protection of civilians mandate represents an elemental shift in the nature of UN peacekeeping and its use as an instrument of international peace and security. While the international community struggled with the revolutionary strategic concepts of humanitarian intervention and the Responsibility to Protect, a quiet evolution was taking place through UN peacekeeping. The authorization of the use of force to protect civilians under threat of violence within the UN peacekeeping context has become a legitimate exercise of the Council's powers and created a new paradigm for the use of force under the UN Charter.

The apparent failures of peacekeepers to protect civilians have attracted far more attention than the mandate's positive implementation,[2] and peacekeeping missions have indeed faced numerous challenges. Many of the challenges have arisen from the traditional military configuration of most missions, comprising lightly armed infantry, with limited mobility or intelligence capabilities, designed for patrolling and static guard duty rather than actively using force.[3] Observers have noted that some troop contributors are reluctant to endorse military postures that would place their soldiers' lives at risk, and many of the world's best trained and equipped

[1] Issues considered as part of the thematic agenda include: compliance with and accountability for violations of international humanitarian and human rights law, safety of humanitarian personnel, and issues of humanitarian access.

[2] See eg International Crisis Group, 'Eastern Congo: Why Stabilisation Failed', Crisis Group Africa Briefing No 91, 4 Oct 2012, 12; David Smith, 'UN admits peacekeepers failed in Sudan clashes', *The Guardian*, 6 June 2011; Jessica Hatcher and Alex Perry, 'Defining Peacekeeping Downward: The UN Debacle in Eastern Congo', *Time*, 26 Nov 2012.

[3] See Alan Doss, 'Great Expectations: UN Peacekeeping, Civilian Protection, and the Use of Force', Geneva Centre for Security Policy, 2011; Refugees International, 'The Last Line of Defence: How Peacekeepers Can Better Protect Civilians', Feb 2010; International Forum on the Challenges of Peace Operations, 'Challenges of Protecting Civilians in Multidimensional Peace Operations', Challenges Forum Report 2010; Nicki Bennett, 'International peacekeeping missions and civilian protection mandates: Oxfam's experiences', *Humanitarian Exchange magazine*, issue 46, Mar 2010.

militaries provide no armed personnel to peacekeeping missions.[4] While such challenges are acknowledged, they should not detract from the fact that the use or threat of force exerted by UN peacekeepers to protect civilians is widespread, accepted, has led to significant decreases in civilian deaths,[5] and has had a significant normative impact.

II. Normative and Legal Framework

The use of force to protect civilians in UN peacekeeping operations is guided by a set of legal and operational instruments. The concept and practice derives from Security Council resolutions mandating peacekeeping operations in accordance with the UN Charter. The application of the use of force to protect civilians is shaped by other relevant bodies of international law, such as humanitarian and human rights law, the 'principles of UN peacekeeping',[6] and operational instruments, including the Status of Mission/Status of Forces Agreement (SOMA/SOFA), memoranda of understanding between the UN and troop contributing countries, and a mission's Concept of Operations and Rules of Engagement.[7] In practice, political and resource constraints have a critical impact.

There are several key legal aspects of the protection of civilians mandate that remain ambiguous. First, the obligatory nature of the mandate remains unclear. While it clearly provides a right for peacekeepers to use force to protect civilians, whether it implies an obligation to use force is uncertain.[8] In practice, there is little

[4] See Victoria Holt and Glyn Taylor, 'Protecting Civilians in the Context of UN Peacekeeping Operations: Successes, Setbacks and Remaining Challenges', independent study jointly commissioned by the Department of Peacekeeping Operations (DPKO) and the Office for the Coordination of Humanitarian Affairs (OCHA), United Nations, 2002, 142, 203, 219, 233, 251–2, and 257.

[5] See Lisa Hultman, 'Keeping Peace or Spurring Violence? Unintended Effects of Peace Operations on Violence against Civilians' (2010) 12 *Civil Wars* 29.

[6] UN Department of Peacekeeping Operations and UN Department of Field Support, *UN Peacekeeping Operations: Principles and Guidelines* (Capstone Doctrine), 2008, available at <http://pbpu.unlb.org/pbps/library/capstone_doctrine_eNg.pdf>, 31–5.

[7] See Scott Sheeran, 'The Use of Force in United Nations Peacekeeping Operations', Chapter 16 in this volume.

[8] A related question was at issue, but not settled, in *Mothers of Srebrenica et al v. State of the Netherlands and United Nations*, Case no 295247, published on <http://www.rechtspraak.nl>, LJN: BD6795 (LJN: BD6796 for the English translation). See also The Hague Justice Portal at <http://www.asser.nl/upload/documents/20120420T025954-Commentary%20Den%20Dekker%20District%20Court%20Decision%20(English).pdf> and the Asser Institute, Centre for International and European Law <http://www.asser.nl/default.aspx?site_id=36&level1=15248&level2=&level3=&textid=39956> for commentary. See also Scott Sheeran, 'The Use of Force in United Nations Peacekeeping Operations', Chapter 16 in this volume.

opportunity for recourse against troops that fail to effectively fulfil the mandate, including due to the absence of an explicit link between the mandate and substantive activities of a contingent in the memoranda of understanding between the UN and troop-contributing countries.[9] Secondly, the parameters of the right are also unclear. The extent to which force may be used proactively and pre-emptively has not been legally tested. Thirdly, whether UN peacekeeping operations have an inherent right or obligation to protect civilians *in the absence* of an explicit mandate remains a live legal question.[10]

A. UN Charter

The collective security agreement articulated in the UN Charter prohibits the use of force[11] except in self-defence[12] or as authorized by the Security Council in executing responsibilities for the maintenance of international peace and security.[13] In exercising the authorization of the use of force, the Council is obliged to discharge its powers in accordance with the purposes and principles of the UN.[14] In doing so, it is faced with balancing state sovereignty, and the principle of non-intervention,[15] with the protection and promotion of human rights.[16] In this way, the Charter provisions set general parameters as to the legitimate ends that may be pursued, and the means that may be applied; however, an ongoing challenge for the Council has been balancing the divergent imperatives of state sovereignty and the protection of human rights.[17]

It is fairly clear that the original objectives of the 1945 collective security agreement were focused on the use of force between states, and the Security Council was not intended to concern itself with purely internal situations.[18] However, Security Council practice quickly evolved in the direction of determining that threats to the peace can arise from internal conflicts and result from grave violations of human rights and humanitarian law, suggesting a move towards a more people-centred approach to the maintenance of international peace and security.[19] In the absence

[9] See Model Memorandum of Understanding between the UN and Troop Contributing Countries, A/C.5/66/8, ch 9.

[10] See Scott Sheeran, 'The Use of Force in United Nations Peacekeeping Operations', Chapter 16 in this volume.

[11] UN Charter, Art 2(4). [12] UN Charter, Art 51. [13] UN Charter, Arts 39 and 42.

[14] UN Charter, Art 24(2). [15] UN Charter, Art 2(7). [16] UN Charter, Art 1(3).

[17] For discussion, see Bruno Simma et al (eds), *The Charter of the United Nations: A Commentary* (Oxford: Oxford University Press, 1994), 39–47, 112–36, 148–71, 442–52, 648–729, 749–59, 788–806; Inger Österdahl, *Threat to the Peace: The interpretation by the Security Council of Article 39 of the UN Charter*, Swedish Institute of International Law, Studies in International Law, vol 13 (Uppsala: Iustus Förlag, 1998); and Erika de Wet, *The Chapter VII Powers of the United Nations Security Council*, vol. 3 (Portland, OR: Hart, 2004), 30–3, 133–216, 369–71, 375–85.

[18] See Simma et al, *The Charter of the United Nations*, 720; and Österdahl, *Threat to the Peace*, 11–12.

[19] See Simma et al, *The Charter of the United Nations*, 724–5; and Österdahl, *Threat to the Peace*, 33–5.

of the manifestation of a standing military capacity as envisaged by the Charter,[20] the primary measures of physical coercion used by the Council to respond to such threats have been UN peacekeeping operations and the authorization of military interventions by coalitions or single member states. The struggle between the divergent norms of non-intervention and the protection of human rights has, to some extent, played out through the development of the mandates of UN peacekeeping operations.

Early peacekeeping operations were unarmed observation missions with passive mandates, limited to observation, investigation, and reporting on troop movements.[21] Later missions were mandated to take a more coercive posture with armed personnel under UN command deployed primarily to monitor ceasefires and the withdrawal of forces.[22] The surge in UN peacekeeping at the end of the Cold War saw a transformation in the types of activities mandated, seeking to address the root causes through elections, development activity, and the promotion of human rights; some missions were also given sweeping civil administration functions.[23]

The inception of the protection of civilians mandate in 1999, described in greater detail later in the chapter, was a critical development in respect of the use of force. That year, the Security Council mandated the first UN peacekeeping mission, the United Nations Mission in Sierra Leone (UNAMSIL), to 'take the necessary action…to afford protection to civilians under imminent threat of physical violence'.[24] Almost every UN peacekeeping operation since that time has been mandated to protect civilians, and since 2007 it has been the priority mandate of many of the UN's largest missions.[25]

[20] See UN Charter, Art 43.

[21] Examples include the UN Truce Supervision Organization (UNTSO) and the UN Military Observer Group in India and Pakistan (UNMOGIP).

[22] Examples include the UN Emergency Force (UNEF I), United Nations Interim Force in Lebanon (UNIFIL), and the UN Peacekeeping Force in Cyprus (UNFICYP).

[23] In particular, the UN Interim Administration Mission in Kosovo (UNMIK) and the UN Transitional Administration in East Timor (UNTAET). For further discussion on the evolution of UN peacekeeping, see John Mackinlay and Jarat Chopra, 'Second Generation Multinational Operations' (1992) 15 *Washington Quarterly* 113–31; Marrack Goulding, 'The Evolution of United Nations Peacekeeping' (1993) 69 *International Affairs* 451; Mats Bedal, 'Whither UN Peacekeeping?', Adelphi Paper 281, International Institute of Strategic Studies, London, 1993; William J. Durch (ed), *The Evolution of UN Peacekeeping* (New York: St Martin's Press, 1993); William J. Durch (ed), *UN Peacekeeping, American Policy and the Uncivil Wars of the 1990s* (New York: St Martin's Press, 1996); William J. Durch (ed), *Twenty-First-Century Peace Operations* (Washington DC: United States Institute of Peace and the Henry L. Stimson Center, 2006); Paul F. Diehl, *Peace Operations* (Cambridge: Polity, 2008); and Alex Bellamy and Paul Williams, *Understanding Peacekeeping* (Cambridge: Polity, 2010).

[24] S/RES/1270 (1999), operative para 14.

[25] See Holt and Taylor, 'Protecting Civilians in the Context of UN Peacekeeping Operations'; and S/RES/1769 (2007); S/RES/1856 (2008); S/RES/1778 (2007); and S/RES/1996 (2011).

B. International Humanitarian and Human Rights Law

The legal foundation of the protection of civilians peacekeeping mandate lies firmly in the UN Charter. While both international humanitarian and human rights law have influenced the normative development and the implementation of the protection of civilians mandate, it goes well beyond the passive concept of protection articulated in international humanitarian law and the governance of the relationship between the state and individuals found in international human rights law.

The idea that civilians should not be subject to physical violence lies at the heart of international humanitarian and human rights law and, historically, both bodies of law have been instrumental in developing the associated norms. International humanitarian law prohibits attacks against civilians during hostilities,[26] while international human rights law enshrines the right to life and security of person, and prohibits torture and cruel, inhuman, or degrading treatment.[27] The interpretation of the UN Charter to authorize the use of force to protect civilians under imminent threat of physical violence, builds upon these fundamental norms adding a new dimension by introducing a recognition of the right of the international community, acting under the collective security agreement, to use force to pursue the fulfilment of such ideals.

Both international humanitarian and human rights law also influence the practical implementation of the protection of civilians mandate, including through restraining peacekeepers from committing war crimes and human rights abuses.[28] However, the direct application of the relevant instruments to UN peacekeepers and peacekeeping missions remains a complex and contested area.[29]

C. Principles of UN Peacekeeping

The development of UN peacekeeping—including the authorization of the use of force—has been significantly shaped by the well-established 'principles of UN peacekeeping'; namely, consent of the parties, impartiality, and non-use of force except in self-defence and in defence of the mandate.[30] Originally conceived in the context of

[26] Geneva Conventions, Common Art 3.

[27] International Covenant on Civil and Political Rights, Arts 6 and 7; and Universal Declaration of Human Rights, Art 3.

[28] See Secretary-General's Bulletin: Observance by United Nations forces of international humanitarian law, ST/SGB/1999/13; Human Rights Committee, General comment No 31, Nature of the General Legal Obligation on States Parties to the Covenant, CCPR/C/21/Rev.1/Add.13 (2004), para 10.

[29] See Scott Sheeran, 'The Use of Force in United Nations Peacekeeping Operations', Chapter 16 in this volume; Bruce Oswald, 'The Security Council and the Intervention Brigade: Some Legal Issues', American Society of International Law, 6 June 2013, available at <http://www.asil.org/insights130606.cfm>; Rule of Law and Armed Conflicts Project, 'Application of International Law: Haiti', available at <http://www.geneva-academy.ch/RULAC/applicable_international_law.php?id_state=84> (2012).

[30] See Capstone Doctrine, available at <http://pbpu.unlb.org/pbps/library/capstone_doctrine_eNg.pdf>; Trevor Findlay, *The Use of Force in UN Peace Operations* (Oxford: Oxford University Press, 2002),

the first United Nations Emergency Force (UNEF I) in 1956[31] and expanded in the United Nations Peacekeeping Force in Cyprus (UNFICYP) in 1964[32] and the second Emergency Force (UNEF II) in 1973,[33] the principles attempt to articulate the basis upon which UN peacekeeping operations should be deployed and executed to enable sustainable deployments founded upon political and practical realities. The principles have no formal legal standing, but have recently been referred to in the non-operative paragraphs of several Security Council resolutions.[34]

While the protection of civilians mandate in UN peacekeeping operations has fundamentally challenged each of the principles, the restraint imposed by the principles has allowed the mandate to achieve wide acceptance, where the Responsibility to Protect has remained contentious among many UN member states.[35] Most protection-mandated peacekeeping missions are explicitly authorized to use force under Chapter VII of the Charter, legally not requiring the consent of the host state, but in practice being deployed with host state consent (or at least acquiescence). Concerns have been raised about the impartiality of the mission being undermined by protection activity requiring UN peacekeepers to actively engage particular groups, thus potentially being viewed as a party to the conflict. The use, or threat, of force is a fundamental element of the mandate, but has been tempered by the precept of restraint and the imperatives of maintaining impartiality and strategic consent. This delicate balance has proved challenging for a number of protection-mandated missions.

D. Protection of Civilians and the Responsibility to Protect

While the protection of civilians mandate in UN peacekeeping operations and the Responsibility to Protect doctrine are borne of similar motivations, the protection

esp 3–5; and successive annual reports of the General Assembly Special Committee on Peacekeeping Operations, A/66/19 (2012), para 25; A/65/19 (2011), para 24; A/64/19 (2010), para 23; A/63/19 (2009), para 23.

[31] Second and final report of the Secretary-General on the plan for an emergency international United Nations force requested in the resolution adopted by the General Assembly on 4 November 1956 (A/3276), A/3302 (6 Nov 1956).

[32] Note by Secretary-General, Aide memoire concerning some questions relating to the function and operation of the United Nations Peace-keeping Force in Cyprus, S/5653 (1964).

[33] Report of the Secretary-General on the implementation of Security Council resolution 340 (1973), S/11052/Rev. 1 (1973).

[34] S/RES/2086 (2013), preambular para 6; S/RES/2098 (2013), preambular para 2; S/RES/2100 (2013), preambular para 3.

[35] See Benjamin de Carvalho and John Harald Sande Lie, 'Policy Brief: Challenges to Implementing the Protection of Civilians Agenda', Norwegian Institute of International Affairs (NUPI), 2009, 2; and Jeremy Sarkin, 'Is the Responsibility to Protect an Accepted Norm in the Post-Libya Era?' (2012) 1 *Groningen Journal of International Law* 21.

of civilians mandate preceded, and is distinct from, the Responsibility to Protect. Where the former is an operational mandate provided by the UN Security Council to peacekeeping operations deployed with the consent of the host state, the latter posits a set of principles for strategic action on the part of the international community where a state is unable or unwilling to protect its population.[36] Peacekeeping as a whole, and the protection of civilians mandate, could arguably fit within the 'second pillar' of the Responsibility to Protect framework, which aims at supporting host states in fulfilling their protection responsibilities.[37] However, the Responsibility to Protect is best known for its 'third pillar', providing for intervention.[38]

III. Security Council Practice 1960–99: Early UN Peacekeeping Operations Protection Activity—Stretching the Concept of Self-Defence

UN peacekeepers have been involved in the physical protection of civilians since 1961 when the Security Council mandated the United Nations Operation in the Congo (ONUC) to 'take immediately all appropriate measures to prevent the occurrence of civil war in the Congo, including arrangements for ceasefire, the halting of all military operations, the prevention of clashes, and the use of force, if necessary, in the last resort'.[39] However, when the mandate was promulgated there was no guidance on how it should be implemented, particularly regarding how force should be applied to achieve the objectives and whether it could legitimately be used to afford direct physical protection to civilians.[40]

[36] For further discussion, see Hugh Breakey et al, 'Enhancing Protection Capacity: Policy Guide to the Responsibility to Protect and the Protection of Civilians in Armed Conflicts', Institute for Ethics, Governance and Law, Griffith University, 2012; and Global Centre for the Responsibility to Protect, 'The Relationship Between the Responsibility to Protect and the Protection of Civilians in Armed Conflict', Policy Brief, 2009.

[37] Report of the Secretary-General: Implementing the Responsibility to Protect, A/63/67 (12 Jan 2009), paras 41–5.

[38] Report of the Secretary-General: Implementing the Responsibility to Protect, paras 49–65; Report of the Secretary General, Responsibility to Protect: Timely and Decisive Response, A/66/874–S/2012/578 (25 July 2012).

[39] S/RES/161 (1961), operative para 1.

[40] For a case study of the use of force in ONUC, see Findlay, *The Use of Force in UN Peace Operations*, 51–86.

Guidance on the use of force was developed in ONUC in the form of a series of operational directives, through which the mission took on an increasingly robust posture.[41] Early directives authorized the mission to 'take preventive and protective actions' in situations of ethnic conflict and banditry, but only to use force in self-defence.[42] Operational Directive No 8 asserted:

Where feasible, every protection will be afforded to unarmed groups who may be subjected by any armed party to acts of violence likely to lead to loss of life. In such cases, UN troops will interpose themselves, using armed force if necessary, to prevent such loss of life.[43]

Former Under-Secretary-General for Political Affairs, Brian Urquhart, indicated that the protection of civilians by ONUC peacekeepers was intended to be justified through a concept of self-defence expanded to include the defence of civilians in grave danger.[44] This treatment caused Oscar Schachter, a former director of the UN Legal Division, to note that 'because of the UN's reluctance to go beyond self-defence as the touchstone of peacekeeping, the concept of self-defence was stretched "to incredulity and beyond its usual legal meaning"'.[45]

Deployed in the midst of an active civil war, ONUC placed strains on the organization's political and financial resources.[46] While it was a precursor and precedent for the authorization of the robust use of force, including to protect civilians, it was also a chastening experience. As William Durch notes, 'many in the UN [viewed ONUC] as "the UN's Vietnam," as an experience never to be repeated. In mid-1992, when UN officials looked at Bosnia-Herzegovina, they saw the Congo.'[47]

The United Nations Protection Force deployed to the former Yugoslavia (UNPROFOR) was the UN's first real concerted attempt at civilian protection, although it was not mandated or resourced to provide direct physical protection to the civilian population.[48] UNPROFOR proceeded with an indirect civilian protection strategy based on protection *through* the delivery of humanitarian assistance and protection

[41] Findlay, *The Use of Force in UN Peace Operations*, 56.

[42] Operations Directive No 3, 'ONUC policy with regard to inter-tribal conflict', 17 Aug 1960, UN Archives DAG13/1.6.5.0.0, Ops Directives Aug 1960–Jan 1964, Box 3, s2(d), in Findlay, *The Use of Force in UN Peace Operations*, App 2.

[43] Operations Directive No 8 [untitled], Feb 1961, UN Archives DAG/13/1.6.5.0.0, Ops Directives Aug 1960–Jan 1964, Box 3, 2–3, in Findlay, *The Use of Force in UN Peace Operations*, App 2.

[44] Brian Urquhart, *Hammarskjöld* (New York: Alfred A. Knopf, 1972), 348, quoted in Findlay, *The Use of Force in UN Peace Operations*, 69.

[45] Findlay, *The Use of Force in UN Peace Operations*, 85, quoting Oscar Schachter, 'Authorised Uses of Force by the UN and Regional Organisations' in Lori Fisler Damrosch and David Scheffer (eds), *Law and Force in the New International Order* (Boulder, CO: Westview Press, 1992), 84.

[46] See Durch, *The Evolution of UN Peacekeeping*, 315–51, Bellamy and Williams, *Understanding Peacekeeping*, 86–7, and *Certain Expenses of the United Nations (Article 17, Paragraph 2 of the Charter)*, Advisory Opinion of 20 July 1962, ICJ Rep 1962, 151.

[47] Durch, *The Evolution of UN Peacekeeping*, 8.

[48] See William J. Durch and James A. Schear, 'Faultlines: UN Operations in the Former Yugoslavia' in Durch, *UN Peacekeeping, American Policy and the Uncivil Wars of the 1990s*, 197–202; and Findlay, *The Use of Force in UN Peace Operations*, 272–91.

through the demilitarization and defence of territory ('safe areas'), and was only authorized to use force in self-defence.[49] This concept of self-defence was expanded slightly to include the use of force to defend safe areas.[50] However, the UNPROFOR mandate was not interpreted to include the direct physical protection of civilians, and the use of force beyond self-defence was assumed to lie with the North Atlantic Treaty Organizaton (NATO).[51] Ambiguity regarding the responsibilities of UN troops and the authorized use of force, in addition to a strained and complex command chain and the insufficient allocation of resources, all contributed to the civilian protection failures experienced in UNPROFOR, particularly in the Srebrenica 'safe area'.[52]

The challenges faced in the former Yugoslavia, as well as the failures of the UN operations in Somalia (UNOSOM I and II) in the early 1990s,[53] played a key role in the UN's response to the Rwanda genocide. Established in the aftermath of the Somalia crisis and during UN operations in the former Yugoslavia, the United Nations Assistance Mission for Rwanda (UNAMIR) was mandated and structured along the lines of a traditional peacekeeping mission.[54] When Rwanda was plunged into extreme violence with the commencement of a campaign of genocidal massacres and the resumption of the civil war, the UN Force Commander, General Dallaire, sought to take a more active role to protect civilians, and the UN Secretary-General, Kofi Annan, called for reinforcement and a new mandate for UNAMIR.[55] The tragic series of events that followed are well covered in the literature.[56] UNAMIR eventually received a mandate to protect civilians, but was never provided with sufficient resources or support.[57]

During the crisis, General Dallaire argued that UNAMIR should be able to protect civilians based on the idea that the principle of 'self-defence' included the 'defence of the mandate'.[58] A similar justification was used by General Sanderson of the United Nations Transitional Authority in Cambodia (UNTAC) to justify deploying

[49] S/RES/743 (1992), S/RES/758 (1992), S/RES/776 (1992); and Findlay, *The Use of Force in UN Peace Operations*, 221–31.

[50] S/RES/836 (1993), operative para 9. [51] S/RES/836 (1993), operative para 10.

[52] See Report of the Secretary-General pursuant to General Assembly Resolution 53/35: The Fall of Srebrenica, A/54/549 (1999); Durch and Schea, 'Faultlines: UN Operations in the Former Yugoslavia' in Durch, *UN Peacekeeping, American Policy and the Uncivil Wars of the 1990s*, 197–202; and Findlay, *The Use of Force in UN Peace Operations*, 272–91.

[53] See Report of the Commission of Inquiry Established Pursuant to Security Council Resolution 885 (1993) to Investigate Armed Attacks on UMSOM II Personnel Which Led to Casualties Among Them, S/1994/653 (1994); Durch, *UN Peacekeeping, American Policy and the Uncivil Wars of the 1990s*, 311–65; Findlay, *The Use of Force in UN Peace Operations*, 278–9; and Bellamy and Williams, *Understanding Peacekeeping*, 223–6.

[54] S/RES/872 (1993). [55] S/1999/1257 (1999), 19.

[56] See Report of the Independent Inquiry into the actions of the United Nations during the 1994 genocide in Rwanda, S/1999/1257 (1999); Matthew J. Vaccaro, 'The Politics of Genocide: Peacekeeping and Disaster Relief in Rwanda' in Durch, *UN Peacekeeping, American Policy and the Uncivil Wars of the 1990s*, 382–3; and Findlay, *The Use of Force in UN Peace Operations*, 278–9.

[57] S/RES/918 (1994), operative para 3(a).

[58] Findlay, *The Use of Force in UN Peace Operations*, 358.

UN troops to provide security during that country's elections.[59] While using the guiding principles to push the boundaries of mandate interpretation failed to deliver General Dallaire the troops or political will required to take decisive action, the Security Council's hesitancy and inaction in Rwanda served as a poignant lesson to the international community, regarding the failure to use UN peacekeeping in the face of mass violence. The UN's experience in Rwanda no doubt contributed to the retreat from UN peacekeeping in the mid-1990s, but it also played a major role in the revitalized approach during its renaissance at the turn of the century.

IV. Security Council Practice 1999–2007: Inception and Development of the 'Protection of Civilians' Mandate—the Council Makes It Explicit

The year 1999 was particularly significant for the development of the protection of civilians as a key element in UN peacekeeping missions. The Council commenced a programme of thematic activity and mandated the first peacekeeping operation with the express authorization to use force 'to protect civilians under imminent threat of physical violence'.[60] However, while the Council asserted a commitment to protection ideals and evidenced a willingness to mandate the use of force for the protection of civilians in UN peacekeeping missions, the issue soon became overshadowed by the broader debate on the concept of the Responsibility to Protect.[61]

A. Thematic Activity

In 1999 comprehensive and candid UN-sponsored reviews of the causes of the peacekeeping failures in Bosnia[62] and Rwanda[63] were released. Both highlighted

[59] Findlay, *The Use of Force in UN Peace Operations*, 358.

[60] UN Mission in Sierra Leone (UNAMSIL), S/RES/1270 (1999).

[61] See World Summit Outcome Document, A/RES/60/1 (2005); Report of the Secretary-General on implementing the Responsibility to Protect, A/63/677 (2009); S/RES/1674 (2006); Alex J. Bellamy, 'Whither the Responsibility to Protect? Humanitarian Intervention and the 2005 World Summit' (2006) 20 *Ethics and International Affairs* 143; Alex J. Bellamy, 'The Responsibility to Protect and the Problem of Military Intervention' (2008) 48 *International Affairs* 615.

[62] A/54/549 (1999). [63] S/1999/1257 (1999).

a lack of political will, inappropriate Security Council mandates, and inadequate resources as key factors contributing to the failures. Following receipt of the reports, Secretary-General Annan established the Panel on UN Peace Operations to undertake a comprehensive review of peacekeeping. The resultant 'Brahimi Report' explicitly recognized that, 'United Nations peacekeepers—troops or police—who witness violence against civilians should be presumed to be authorized to stop it, within their means, in support of basic United Nations principles'.[64]

During the same year, the Security Council embarked upon an exercise to develop a more informed and systematic approach to the protection of civilians through its thematic activity. The Council held the first open debate on the protection of civilians,[65] beginning a cycle of thematic activity comprising biannual open debates and, between 1999 and 2007, the delivery of six Secretary-General's Reports,[66] five Security Council resolutions,[67] and six Presidential Statements[68] on the protection of civilians.

The Council's thematic activity addressed the protection of civilians holistically, covering humanitarian and legal issues, in addition to physical protection. Throughout its thematic work, the Council continually affirmed its commitment to the protection of civilians, including through ensuring 'where appropriate and feasible, that peacekeeping missions are given suitable mandates and adequate resources to protect civilians under imminent threat of physical danger'.[69] Through successive thematic resolutions, the physical protection element grew in prominence, and the Council devoted more attention to protection mandates in peacekeeping missions. In 2006, the Council adopted Resolution 1674 stating:

> [The Council] [*r*]*eaffirms* its practice of ensuring that the mandates of United Nations peacekeeping, political and peacebuilding missions include, where appropriate and on a case-by-case basis, provisions regarding (i) the protection of civilians, particularly those under imminent threat of physical danger within their zones of operation... and *expresses its intention* of ensuring that (i) such mandates include clear guidelines as to what missions can and should do to achieve those goals, (ii) the protection of civilians is given priority in decisions about the use of available capacity and resources, including information and intelligence resources, in the implementation of the mandates, and (iii) that protection mandates are implemented.[70]

B. The Council's Country-Specific Activity

In accordance with its thematic efforts, in 1999 the Security Council mandated the first UN peacekeeping mission, the United Nations Mission in Sierra Leone

[64] Report of the Panel on United Nations Peace Operations ('Brahimi Report'), A/55/305 and S/2000/809 (2000), 62 and x.

[65] S/PRST/1999/6 (1999).

[66] S/1999/957 (1999); S/2001/331 (2001); S/2002/1300 (2002); S/2004/431 (2004); S/2005/740 (2005); S/2007/643 (2007).

[67] S/RES/1265 (1999); S/RES/1296 (2000); S/RES/1502 (2003); S/RES/1674 (2006); S/RES/1738 (2006).

[68] S/PRST/1999/6 (1999); S/PRST/2002/6 (2002); S/PRST/2002/41 (2002); S/PRST/2003/27 (2003); S/PRST/2004/46 (2004); S/PRST/2005/25 (2005).

[69] S/RES/1296 (2000), operative para 13.

[70] S/RES/1674 (2006), operative para 16.

(UNAMSIL), to 'take the necessary action…within its capabilities and areas of deployment, to afford protection to civilians under imminent threat of physical violence, taking into account the responsibilities of the Government of Sierra Leone and ECOMOG [Economic Community of West African States Monitoring Group]'.[71] The language used in UNAMSIL set a precedent that has been employed in most subsequent UN peacekeeping missions:[72] MONUC (United Nations Observer Mission in the Democratic Republic of the Congo);[73] UNMIL (United Nations Mission in Liberia);[74] UNOCI (United Nations Operation in Côte d'Ivoire);[75] MINUSTAH (UN Stabilization Mission in Haiti);[76] ONUB (United Nations Operation in Burundi);[77] UNMIS (United Nations Mission in Sudan);[78] UNIFIL (United Nations Interim Force in Lebanon);[79] UNAMID (African Union/United Nations Hybrid Operation in Darfur);[80] MINURCAT (United Nations Mission in the Central African Republic and Chad);[81] MONUSCO (United Nations Stabilization Mission in the Democratic Republic of the Congo);[82] UNISFA (United Nations Interim Security Force for Abyei);[83] UNMISS (United Nations Mission in South Sudan);[84] MINUSMA (United Nations Multidimensional Integrated Stabilization Mission in Mali);[85] and MINUSCA (United Nations Multidimensional Integrated Stabilization Mission in the Central African Republic).[86, 87]

71 S/RES/1270 (1999), operative para 14.

72 The exceptions being the UN missions in East Timor (UNTAET, UNMISET, UNMIT), Ethiopia and Eritrea (UNMEE), and Syria (UNSMIS).

73 Protection of civilians language was added to the mandate on 24 Feb 2000, S/RES/1291 (2000), operative para 8.

74 Protection of civilians language was in the original mandate, S/RES/1509 (2003), operative para 3(j).

75 Protection of civilians language was in the original mandate, S/RES/1528 (2004), operative para 6(i).

76 Protection of civilians language was in the original mandate, S/RES/1542 (2004), operative para 7(I)(f).

77 Protection of civilians language was in the original mandate, S/RES/1545 (2004), operative para 5.

78 Protection of civilians language was in the original mandate, S/RES/1590 (2005), operative para 16(i).

79 Protection of civilians language was added to the mandate on 11 Aug 2006, S/RES/1701 (2006), operative para 12.

80 Protection of civilians language was in the original mandate, S/RES/1769 (2007), operative para 15(a)(2).

81 Protection of civilians language added to the mandate on 14 Jan 2009, S/RES/1861 (2009), operative para 7(a)(i).

82 Protection of civilians language was in the original mandate, S/RES/1925 (2010), operative paras 11 and 12(a).

83 S/RES/1990 (2011), operative para 3(d).

84 S/RES/1996 (2011), operative para 3(b).

85 S/RES/2039 (2012), operative para 16(c)(i).

86 S/RES/2149 (2014), operative para 30(a).

87 The Council has also authorized a number of non-UN peace operations with similar civilian protection functions: the Interim Emergency Multinational Force (IEMF), Operation Artemis, in Bunia, Democratic Republic of the Congo (S/RES/1484 (2003)); the French-led forces, Operation Licorne, in Côte d'Ivoire (S/RES/1464 (2003) and S/RES/1528 (2004)); ECOWAS in Côte d'Ivoire (ECOMICI) (S/RES/1464 (2003)); the AU in Darfur (AMIS) (S/RES/1574 (2004)); EUFOR RD Congo in the Democratic Republic of the Congo (S/RES/1671 (2006)); the EU operation in Chad (EUFOR) (S/RES/1778 (2007)); and the NATO Operation Unified Protector in Libya (S/RES/1973 (2011)); and most recently the African-led International Support Mission in Mali (AFISMA) (S/RES/2085 (2012)).

The protection of civilians language formulation has remained fairly consistent. Most mandates use the phrase 'protection of civilians under imminent threat of physical violence' including the caveats 'without prejudice to the responsibility of the host nation' and 'within capabilities and areas of deployment'. All of the mandates marry the protection of civilians with the authorization of the use of force, at times creating a special Chapter VII carve-out, to signal the differentiation of approach to protection tasks as opposed to an overall robust posture of the mission.[88] The protection of civilians mandate is often accompanied by, and delineated from, the tasks of protecting UN personnel and property and ensuring the freedom of movement of humanitarian personnel.[89]

When the Council began authorizing the use of force for the direct physical protection of civilians, it moved a step beyond earlier protection efforts. The distinction lay in the directness of the activity and the authorization of the use of force beyond passive defence. The protection mandate implied the use of pre-emptive and offensive force (when necessary) in order to actively protect civilians. Protection was no longer to occur only as the outcome of some other activity, such as the withdrawal of forces, or demilitarization of an area, the intervening elements disappeared and a direct link was created between the international community (through the Council) and the people to whom protection was to be afforded.

The debate which occurred in advance of the adoption of the UNAMSIL mandate[90] is revealing as to the intentions of the Security Council. The Argentinian delegation made the following insightful statement:

> We believe that the protection of civilians under Chapter VII is a pertinent development in the context of the mandate of a peace operation. This draft resolution is significant in that it introduces a new, fundamental political, legal and moral dimension. This bears on the credibility of the Security Council and shows that the Council has learned from its own experience and that it will not remain indifferent to indiscriminate attacks against the civilian population. At the same time, we are realistic. The objective to be fulfilled must be consonant with the means provided. For that reason, we agree with the limits that operative paragraph 14 of the draft resolution sets on UNAMSIL's actions.[91]

The comments delivered by Security Council delegations in advance of the adoption of the UNAMSIL mandate clearly demonstrated an express intention that UN peacekeepers would be mandated to use force to provide direct physical protection to civilians. There was a recognition that this was the introduction of a new dimension to UN peacekeeping operations and an awareness of the need to be realistic, hence the inclusion of the caveats. The clarity of purpose demonstrated in these early debates, however, seemed to dissipate as the language was regularly added to

[88] For further discussion see Holt and Taylor, 'Protecting Civilians in the Context of UN Peacekeeping Operations', 42–7.

[89] See eg S/RES/1996 (2011), operative para 3(b)(vi); S/RES/1925 (2010), operative para 12(a); S/RES/1769 (2007), and S/2007/307/Rev.1, operative para 55(b)(vii).

[90] S/PV.4054 (1999). [91] S/PV.4054 (1999), 16.

new mission mandates, and in the absence of operational guidance for implementing the mandate it became open to the widely varying interpretations of senior mission leadership on the ground.[92]

C. Hiatus in the Advancement of the Protection Mandate and the Responsibility to Protect

Between 2002 and 2006, the Security Council continued to hold thematic debates and mandate civilian protection in UN peacekeeping operations. However, Council engagement on the issue lost its dynamism, and focus on the issue waned. In part, this was due to the strained Security Council dynamics following the 2003 US-led invasion of Iraq.[93] However, there were other critical factors that contributed to the hiatus in the advancement of the mandate. In several of the operations in which the protection of civilians had been authorized, the mission was unable to implement the mandate in any meaningful way, and the use of force by UN peacekeepers to protect civilians became almost a moot point. In Sierra Leone, Côte d'Ivoire, and the Democratic Republic of the Congo, UN peacekeepers were outmatched by local insurgents and Council-mandated interventions by Western military forces—the British, French, and European Union (EU), respectively—were required to restore order. Additionally, the focus of the Security Council at the thematic level was turned towards the protection of specific at-risk groups such as women and children.[94]

Consideration of civilian protection issues also moved from the Security Council to the broader UN membership and focused on the overarching normative dilemmas. Following NATO's controversial 1999 'humanitarian intervention' in Kosovo, UN Secretary-General Annan, in his report in advance of the Millennium Summit, highlighted what he termed the 'intervention dilemma'.[95] In 2001, the International Commission on Intervention and State Sovereignty published a report introducing and advocating the concept of the Responsibility to Protect.[96] This became the focus of the debate on civilian protection over the next four years, leading up to (and to some extent following) the 2005 World Summit.[97] The dissonance among the

[92] Holt and Taylor, 'Protecting Civilians in the Context of UN Peacekeeping Operations', 8, 160–72.

[93] Security Council Report (2008), 8.

[94] S/RES/1325 (2000), and S/RES/1612 (2005). The concepts established in these resolutions would develop in later years. See S/RES/1889 (2009), S/RES/1882 (2009), S/RES/1820 (2008), and S/RES/1888 (2009).

[95] Report of the UN Secretary-General, 'We the Peoples: The Role of the United Nations in the 21st century', A/54/2000 (2000).

[96] International Commission on Intervention and State Sovereignty, *The Responsibility to Protect* (Ottawa: IDRC Books, 2001).

[97] See Alex J. Bellamy, 'Realizing the Responsibility to Protect' (2009) 10 *International Studies Perspectives* 111; Alex J. Bellamy, 'The Responsibility to Protect—Five Years On' (2010) 24 *Ethics and*

membership on the Responsibility to Protect impaired progressive engagement on the protection of civilians in UN peacekeeping until failures to protect once again threw a spotlight on the mandate language, its meaning, and utility.

V. Security Council Practice 2007–11: Prioritizing Protection—UNAMID, MONUC, UNOCI, and UNMISS

Following a number of grave failures to protect civilians on the part of UN peacekeeping operations, particularly in the Democratic Republic of the Congo,[98] in 2007, the Security Council once again became focused on the protection mandate. The Council's efforts shifted from thematic to country-specific activity and, in particular, the prioritization and implementation of protection mandates. The only thematic resolution adopted between 2007 and 2011 focused to a large extent upon the implementation of protection mandates in UN peacekeeping operations, stressing that protection activities should be given priority in resource allocation.[99]

Momentum on the issue was also gathering outside the Council. Although negotiations were sensitive and prolonged, in 2009 the UN General Assembly Special Committee on Peacekeeping Operations (C-34) included language on the protection of civilians in the report of its regular session, and has continued to do so in every subsequent annual report.[100] The UN Secretariat also undertook several major projects, including the development of an Operational Concept, training materials, and legal clarification of aspects of the mandate language. In the Operational Concept, the Secretariat interpreted the protection of civilians mandate as a holistic effort, encompassing physical protection activities alongside the mission's political and development work seeking to create a protective environment.[101]

The years since 2007 have witnessed a significant evolution in the Council's country-specific approach. Previously, the Council had included the protection of civilians as one of a spectrum of tasks in mission mandates, but from 2007 it began

International Affairs 143; Gareth Evans, 'The Responsibility to Protect: An Idea Whose Time Has Come…and Gone?' (2008) 22 *International Relations* 285; Thomas G. Weiss, 'R2P After 9/11 and the World Summit' (2006) 24 *Wisconsin International Law Journal* 741.

[98] eg in Kisangani (2002), Bunia (2003), Bukavu (2004). See Holt and Taylor, 'Protecting Civilians in the Context of UN Peacekeeping Operations', 246–59.

[99] S/RES/1894 (2009).

[100] A/63/19 (2009), A/64/19 (2010), A/65/19 (2011), and A/66/19 (2012).

[101] UN Department of Peacekeeping Operations—Department of Field Support, *Operational Concept on the Protection of Civilians in United Nations Peacekeeping Operations*, 2010.

prioritizing protection efforts. Significantly, when a number of missions were being criticized for civilian protection failures,[102] the Council's reaction was not to withdraw from the mandate, but to underscore its priority and provide guidance on implementation.

In 2007–8, civilian protection became the core of the mandates of the UN's two largest and most complex operations, in Darfur (UNAMID)[103] and the Democratic Republic of the Congo (MONUC).[104] In response to ongoing mass violence against civilians in the Democratic Republic of the Congo, in December 2008 the Council revised the mandate of MONUC to explicitly set the protection of civilians as the highest priority of the mission. The Council also prioritized the protection of civilians in the mandate of the missions deployed to Chad and the Central African Republic (MINURCAT),[105] South Sudan (UNMISS),[106] and Liberia (UNMIL).[107] In response to the violent fall-out of the contested presidential election in Côte d'Ivoire in late 2010, the Council not only prioritized the protection of civilians in UNOCI, but went further, providing the mission with specific authorization to use force to prevent the use of heavy weapons against the civilian population.[108] The language served not only to provide specific guidance on mandate implementation, but also to encourage implementation by demonstrating explicit political support for robust action.

VI. Security Council Practice from 2011 Onwards: Exploring the Boundaries of the Mandate

Since 2011, Security Council practice on the protection of civilians was characterized by an exploration of the boundaries of the mandate. This was in part a result of an expedient use of the broadly accepted mandate language and in part reflective of a broader debate on the scope and function of the UN peacekeeping instrument.

[102] See eg Human Rights Watch, *Killings in Kiwanja: The UN's Inability to Protect Civilians* (New York: Human Rights Watch, 2008); Human Rights Watch, *Abandoning Abyei: Destruction and Displacement* (New York: Human Rights Watch, May 2008); The Darfur Consortium, *Putting People First: The Protection Challenge Facing UNAMID in Darfur* (Kampala: The Darfur Consortium, July 2008).

[103] S/RES/2003 (2011), operative para 3(a); S/RES/1769 (2007), operative para 15(a)(ii).

[104] S/RES/1856 (2008), operative paras 3 and 6. See also S/PV.6055 (2008), 2–3.

[105] S/RES/1778 (2007). [106] S/RES/2057 (2012). [107] S/RES/2066 (2012).

[108] S/RES/1975 (2011), operative para 6.

The Security Council acted quickly and decisively in response to the violent conflict in Libya in early 2011. In March, the Council authorized member states 'to take all necessary measures . . . to protect civilians and civilian populated areas under threat of attack'.[109] However, this was not done in the context of a UN peacekeeping presence with the accompanying strategic consent, instead the Responsibility to Protect and protection of civilians concepts were conflated. The broadly accepted protection of civilians language, to which the membership had become accustomed in the context of UN peacekeeping, was used to describe what was essentially a Responsibility to Protect operation. While some in the international community hailed the Libya intervention as the Council finally taking up its responsibilities pursuant to the Responsibility to Protect doctrine, the NATO Operation Unified Protector quickly became the subject of much criticism (including on the part of some Council members), both in respect of a perceived failure to take necessary precautions to ensure that civilians were not harmed by its air strikes and for going beyond the purpose of the mandate and using it as a vehicle for regime change.[110]

Much has been made of the impact that the Libya intervention had on the Council's inability to effectively respond to the extreme levels of violence against civilians in Syria and, while it undoubtedly had an impact, the Council's deliberations were influenced by a range of political dynamics and strategic interests.[111] In April 2012, after months of disagreement, the Council finally adopted a resolution authorizing the establishment of the United Nations Supervision Mission in Syria (UNSMIS), however the mission was not mandated to protect civilians.[112] Like other UN missions without a protection mandate,[113] UNSMIS faced challenges associated with expectations of the local and international communities that wherever a UN mission is deployed it is both authorized and obligated to protect civilians.

The negative response to the Libya intervention did not have a fundamental impact on the ongoing development of the protection of civilians mandate in UN peacekeeping missions. In response to the conflict in Mali, in December 2012 the Council authorized the African-led International Support Mission to Mali (AFISMA) with a protection of civilians *support* function.[114] The mission operated in support of the Malian Amy and alongside French-led forces deployed as part of Operation Serval.[115] In April 2013, a UN peacekeeping mission in Mali was mandated (MINUSMA) and assumed authority

[109] S/RES/1973 (2011), operative para 4.

[110] Alex J. Bellamy, 'The Responsibility to Protect and the Problem of Regime Change', *e-International Relations* (Sept 2011); Alex J. Bellamy and Paul D. Williams, 'The New Politics of Protection? Côte d'Ivoire, Libya and the Responsibility to Protect' (2011) 87 *International Affairs* 838; John-Mark Lyi, 'The Duty of an Intervention Force to Protect Civilians: A Critical Analysis of NATO's Intervention in Libya' (2012) 2 *Conflict Trends* 41.

[111] Security Council Report, Cross-Cutting Report 2012 No 2: Protection of Civilians, 31 May 2012, 14–22.

[112] SC/RES/2043. [113] eg UNTSO. [114] SC/RES/2085, operative para 9(d).

[115] SC/RES/2100, preambular para 5, BBC News, 'France confirms Mali military intervention', 11 Jan 2013, available at <http://www.bbc.co.uk/news/world-africa-20991719>.

from AFISMA. The UN mission was mandated with a protection of civilians function using the standard language, although it was not explicitly prioritized.[116] The standard protection of civilian language was again used when the Security Council mandated the mission in the Central African Republic (MINUSCA) in April 2014.[117]

In the context of the Mali deployment, concern was raised about the UN operating in close cooperation with French forces undertaking counterterrorism activities and about the appropriateness of a UN peacekeeping operation potentially undertaking such activity itself.[118] Following the adoption of the MINUSMA mandate, the Under-Secretary-General for Peacekeeping, Hervé Ladsous, stated that '[MINUSMA] is not an enforcement mission, [it] is not an anti-terrorist operation, but it is clear at the same time that in an environment which will certainly see asymmetric attacks, the stabilization mission will have to defend itself and its mandate, depending on circumstances.'[119]

The debate that took place in respect of the potential counterterrorism activities of MINUSMA was in effect a debate on the scope of the protection of civilians mandate. Questions were raised about whether UN peacekeepers should be authorized or expected to undertake targeted, pre-emptive counterterrorism-type activity, when the threat to civilians emanates from a group employing terrorist tactics; about the impact that would have on the impartiality of the mission and the safety and security of UN personnel; and whether UN peacekeeping missions would even be capable of executing such a role. At the same time as the MINUSMA mandate was being negotiated, the Council was dealing with related issues in the Democratic Republic of the Congo.

Despite the UN peacekeeping mission in the Democratic Republic of the Congo (MONUSCO) having a prioritized protection of civilians mandate, and rules of engagement allowing the conduct of offensive operations, in March 2013 the Security Council mandated a supplementary 'Intervention Brigade' to undertake 'targeted offensive operations' to 'neutralize' rebel groups carrying out attacks against civilians.[120] The resolution stated that the Intervention Brigade was established 'on an exceptional basis and without creating a precedent or any prejudice to the agreed principles of peacekeeping.'[121] The mandate of the Intervention Brigade was viewed by many as unprecedented and a shift from 'peacekeeping' to 'peace enforcement'.[122]

[116] S/RES/2039 (2012), operative para 16(c)(i) [117] S/RES/2149 (2014), operative para 30(a).

[118] S/PV.6952, 2; Reuters, 'UN Security Council approves creation of Mali peacekeeping force', 25 Apr 2013, available at <http://uk.reuters.com/article/2013/04/25/us-mali-crisis-un-idUSBRE93O0R420130425>; Foreign Policy, 'UN authorizes controversial 12,000 man Mali peacekeeping mission', 25 Apr 2013, <http://turtlebay.foreignpolicy.com/posts/2013/04/25/un_authorizes_mali_peacekeeping_mission>.

[119] UN News and Media, 'Peacekeeping chief gives further details about new UN stabilization mission in Mali', available at <http://www.unmultimedia.org/radio/english/2013/04/peacekeeping-chief-gives-further-details-about-new-un-stabilization-mission-in-mali/>

[120] S/RES/2098 (2013), operative para 12(b). [121] S/RES/2098 (2013), operative para 9.

[122] See eg, 'UN sends force to look for a fight in Democratic Republic of the Congo', *The Guardian*, 5 May 2013, available at <http://www.theguardian.com/world/2013/may/05/un-force-democratic-republic-congo>;

Again, concerns were raised about maintaining the impartiality of UN peacekeeping, the potential impact upon the safety and security of UN personnel, and about unintended humanitarian fallout.[123] Others saw the mandating of the Intervention Brigade as unnecessary, and a reaction to the unwillingness of troop-contributing countries to robustly implement the existing mandate.[124] Major General Patrick Cammaert (Rtd), a former Force Divisional Commander for the UN in the Democratic Republic of the Congo stated: 'The issue is not that proactive operations are not already authorized, but that troop contributors are risk averse, and show time and again a lack of political will to employ a full reading of the mandate, leading to accusations that it lacks robustness… the mandate is only as strong as the will of the leadership and the [troop-contributing countries] to implement it.'[125]

It seems that by mandating the Intervention Brigade the Council did not intend to circumscribe the protection of civilians mandate, setting a boundary of offensive action beyond which specific authorization would be required. The pre-emptive and offensive use of force to protect civilians raises a spectrum of issues. These include strategic issues of the appropriateness of the UN peacekeeping instrument being used in such a way; legal issues related to UN peacekeepers potentially becoming combatants under international humanitarian law; and very practical issues associated with the need for resources such as attack helicopters and effective intelligence systems; how the UN can protect civilians if it becomes a target through active involvement in a conflict; the impact on the safety and security of other UN personnel; and not least, the willingness of troop-contributing countries to implement such mandates.

The use of protection of civilians language for the authorization of the NATO intervention in Libya, the deployment of the UN mission in Mali, and of the Intervention Brigade certainly demonstrated the Council exploring the boundaries of the protection of civilians mandate; an initiative that was reflected in policy work in the UN Secretariat and in practical initiatives undertaken in peacekeeping

'UN Approves New Force to Pursue Congo's Rebels', *New York Times*, 28 Mar 2013, <http://www.nytimes.com/2013/03/29/world/africa/un-approves-new-force-to-pursue-congos-rebels.html?_r=0>; Aljazeera, 'UN approves DR Congo "intervention brigade"', 29 Mar 2013, <http://www.aljazeera.com/news/africa/2013/03/2013328191551529953.html>.

[123] See eg S/PV.6943; BBC News Africa, 'DR Congo unrest: Fears over UN intervention', 25 July 2013, available at <http://www.bbc.co.uk/news/world-africa-23452735>; Stimson Centre, 'Spotlight: New UN Force May Increase Risks for Civilians', 11 July 2013, <http://www.stimson.org/spotlight/new-un-force-may-increase-risks-for-civilians/>; Refugees International, 'UN's New Solution for Congo Not Without Risk', 28 Mar 2013, <http://reliefweb.int/report/democratic-republic-congo/un%E2%80%99s-new-solution-congo-not-without-risk>.

[124] See Major General Patrick Cammaert (Rtd) and Fiona Blyth, 'Issue Brief: The UN Intervention Brigade in the Democratic Republic of the Congo, International Peace Academy', July 2013, available at <http://www.ipinst.org/media/pdf/publications/ipi_e_pub_un_intervention_brigade_rev.pdf>.

[125] See Fiona Blyth, 'Too Risk-Averse, UN Peacekeepers in the DRC Get New Mandate and More Challenges', International Peace Academy Global Observatory, 10 Apr 2013, available at <http://theglobalobservatory.org/component/myblog/too-risk-averse-un-peacekeepers-in-the-drc-get-new-mandate-and-more-challenges/blogger/Fiona%20Blyth/>.

missions. It also reignited a larger debate among Security Council members, major troop-contributing countries, and the Secretariat about the trajectory of the use of force in UN peacekeeping missions and the future of the UN peacekeeping instrument.[126]

VII. Conclusion

The use of force in UN peacekeeping operations to protect civilians was initially driven by initiatives from the field and approached as an extended concept of self-defence. Following the failures of UN peacekeeping in the 1990s and the release of the Brahimi Report, through a series of thematic resolutions, the Council indicated a willingness to ensure that peacekeeping missions were mandated and resourced to protect civilians under imminent threat of physical violence. It demonstrated a sustained commitment to the concept by mandating the use of force to protect civilians in almost all the peacekeeping operations deployed since 1999. Today, more than 90 per cent of UN peacekeeping personnel serve in missions mandated to protect.[127] Despite the challenges faced in the implementation of the protection of civilians mandate, the Council has prioritized protection efforts in the mandates of the largest UN missions and made efforts to provide specific guidance on implementation. Defining the substance and scope of the mandate is an ongoing process, taking place through an interaction of Security Council practice, legal interpretation, policy articulation, and importantly, the implementation of the mandate in the field impacted by the willingness of troop-contributing countries to use force and the resources effectively to do so.

The protection of civilians mandate has evolved under the aegis of the principles of UN peacekeeping, an evolution that has at times resulted in tension but ultimately led to an approach to the use of force that has won broad international acceptance. The influence of the principles, which emphasize maintaining the strategic consent of host states, restraint in the use of force, and impartial action, aim to provide interpretation of the mandate and a body of protection practice that is sustainable and achievable.

[126] See eg Security Council Report, The Secretary-General's 2013 Security Council Retreat, 22 Apr 2013, available at <http://www.whatsinblue.org/2013/04/the-secretary-generals-2013-security-council-retreat.php>; and Security Council Report, Peacekeeping Working Group Meeting on Safety and Security of Peacekeepers, 31 May 2013, <http://www.whatsinblue.org/2013/05/meeting-of-the-working-group-on-peacekeeping.php>.

[127] See UN Peacekeeping Fact Sheet, <http://www.un.org/en/peacekeeping/resources/statistics/factsheet.shtml>.

Although developed by the Council, the protection of civilians mandate has been endorsed by a much broader spectrum of the UN membership. The General Assembly Special Committee on Peacekeeping Operations, in which member states involved in peacekeeping are represented, has recognized the importance of the mandate by calling for actions to improve the implementation of protection mandates in successive annual reports. The General Assembly Administrative and Budgetary Committee (Fifth Committee), within which all UN member states are represented, has consistently agreed the financing of relevant missions.[128] Host states have accepted the concept with the provision of strategic consent for the deployment of missions with protection mandates. In agreeing to deploy national military and police personnel to implement protection mandates, troop- and police-contributing countries have also accepted the idea. Additionally, the UN Secretary-General and the Secretariat have contributed to legitimizing the concept both through reporting on protection mandate implementation in peacekeeping operations and through work being undertaken in respect of legal interpretation, policy development, and training delivery.

Questions have been raised about the depth of commitment to protection ideals across the membership.[129] The powerful liberal Western democracies which, propelled by domestic constituencies, are the main proponents of the protection agenda, are criticized for a seeming unwillingness to contribute troops and assets to implement protection mandates in UN peacekeeping missions. The commitment of some troop- and police-contributing countries is questioned on the basis that motivations for contributing may be more closely associated with financial incentives for deployment. That member states act in accordance with narrowly conceived national interests only serves to highlight the significance of the progress achieved to date. It does, however, indicate that the ongoing development of the concept may be challenged by changing power dynamics in the future.

As the foregoing illustrates, there has been an elemental shift from a purely state-centred approach to the maintenance of international peace and security to a more people-centred conception. The development and acceptance of the protection of civilians mandate in UN peacekeeping operations has both played a significant role in the shift, and is reflective of it. Through the protection of civilians mandate,

[128] The Fifth Committee is responsible for reviewing and approving peacekeeping mission budget proposals. Fifth Committee delegates, along with members of the Advisory Committee on Administrative and Budgetary Questions, engage in dialogue with the Secretariat during their deliberations and often alter budget proposals prior to approval. The Fifth Committee plays a critical role in shaping UN peacekeeping through the provision of resources to implement various aspects of a mission mandate, and has in the past been used to further or stymie political agendas. For further information on Fifth Committee working methods, see <http://www.un.org/en/ga/fifth/index.shtml> and UN Doc A/58/CRP.5.

[129] See eg William J. Durch and Madeline L. England, 'The Purposes of Peace Operations' in Centre on International Cooperation, *Robust Peacekeeping: The Politics of Force* (New York: New York University, 2009), 45–6.

a nuanced paradigm for the use of force has been developed which delicately balances the streams of sovereignty and non-intervention with the protection and promotion of human rights evident in the Charter. This careful balance born of pragmatism and politics, is a large part of the reason that the use of force for the protection of civilians in UN peacekeeping operations has achieved such wide acceptance. Security Council practice on the protection of civilians in UN peacekeeping missions has resulted in broad acceptance of the legitimacy of the application of the collective use of force by the international community for the defence of civilian lives, with the strategic consent of the host state. While this does not extend to a right or obligation of intervention when a state is unable or unwilling to protect its population, it is a significant development. The process has not been one of revolution, but the evolutionary development of a nuanced paradigm for the legitimate use of force, utilizing the tools at the Council's disposal to respond to modern conflicts and the acceptance of the importance of people within the framework of international peace and security.

CHAPTER 18

SELF-DEFENCE, PROTECTION OF HUMANITARIAN VALUES, AND THE DOCTRINE OF IMPARTIALITY AND NEUTRALITY IN ENFORCEMENT MANDATES

NICHOLAS TSAGOURIAS

I. Introduction

Since the inception of peacekeeping, it has been recognized that such operations should be based on the triptych of consent, neutrality/impartiality, and minimum use of force—only in self-defence. These principles were set out by the UN

Secretary-General Dag Hammarskjöld, as early as 1958, in connection with the United Nations Emergency Force (UNEF),[1] the first UN peacekeeping operation. Since then they have been constantly reaffirmed in UN peacekeeping doctrine and practice.[2] It can thus be plausibly argued that they form part of the constitutional structure of peacekeeping operations.[3] That having been said, these principles are subject to constant reinterpretation in view of the more complex and challenging environment within which peacekeeping operations operate as well as the changing nature of peacekeeping missions, which nowadays are tasked with the attainment of humanitarian objectives. More specifically, peacekeeping missions are now often deployed in situations characterized by systematic atrocities against people, violations of human rights and humanitarian law by state or non-state actors, and by fragile or disintegrating state authority. In these situations, peacekeeping missions are tasked with both the short-term and the long-term alleviation of human suffering, and are often endowed with an enforcement mandate for that reason.[4]

This chapter will consider the issue of how the protection of humanitarian values assigned to peacekeeping operations can be achieved through the use of force, and how such use of force interacts with the principles of neutrality and impartiality. In this regard, the implications of 'the responsibility to protect' and the 'protection of civilians' on the competence to use force will also be considered. Nevertheless, a caveat needs to be lodged: the protection of humanitarian values as part of the broader humanitarian agenda pursued by humanitarian actors, such as the International Committee of the Red Cross (ICRC), will not be dealt with.[5] Although such actors often operate alongside peacekeeping forces, are concerned with the alleviation of human suffering, and use the language of impartiality and neutrality,[6] their status and mandate as well as the meaning of the terms neutrality and impartiality as applied to their operations differ.

[1] UNEF: Summary Study of the Experience Derived from the Establishment and Operation of the Force: Report of the Secretary-General, UN GAOR, 13th Sess, Annex 1, Agenda Item 65, A/3943 (1958), paras 154–93.

[2] *The Blue Helmets: A Review of United Nations Peacekeeping Operations* (3rd edn, 1996), 7; An Agenda For Peace: Preventive Diplomacy, Peacemaking and Peace-Keeping, A/47/277–S/24111 (1992), paras 11–12; Supplement to An Agenda For Peace, A/50/60–S/1995/1 (1995), para 33; Report of the Panel on United Nations Peace Operations of 21 August 2000 (Brahimi Report), A/55/305, S/2000/809, para 48. *United Nations Peacekeeping Operations: Principles and Guidelines* (New York: Department of Peacekeeping Operations Best Practices Unit, 2008), ch 3 (Capstone Doctrine).

[3] Nicholas Tsagourias, 'Consent, Neutrality/Impartiality and the Use of Force in Peacekeeping: Their Constitutional Dimension' (2006) 11 *Journal of Conflict and Security Law* 465.

[4] Capstone Doctrine, 24

[5] See eg Sorcha O'Callaghan and Sara Pantullano, *Protective Action: Incorporating Civilian Protection into Humanitarian Response* (London: Humanitarian Policy Group, 2007); 'ICRC Protection Policy: Institutional Policy' (2008) 90 (871) *ICRC* 751; Office for the Coordination of Humanitarian Affairs (OCHA), Humanitarian Response Review (2005).

[6] See eg 'OCHA on Message: Humanitarian Principles', available at <http://ochanet.unocha.org/p/Documents/OOM_HumPrinciple_English.pdf>.

II. The Peacekeeping Principles of Neutrality and Impartiality and the Use of Force

The principles of neutrality, impartiality, and use of force in self-defence are interconnected and it is therefore necessary to explain the meaning of neutrality and impartiality before examining how their presence or absence affects the level of force that can be used by peacekeepers.

Neutrality holds that the peacekeeping operations should entertain no prejudice towards any of the participants in the conflict. As the former UN Secretary-General Dag Hammarskjöld stressed in one of his reports on UNEF, force should not 'be used to enforce any specific political solution of pending problems or to influence the political balance decisive to such a solution',[7] whereas with regard to the Opération des Nations Unies au Congo (ONUC), the Security Council mandated that the peacekeeping force should not be 'a party to or in any way intervene in or be used to influence the outcome of any internal conflict'.[8]

Some contend that the principle of neutrality derives from Article 40 of the UN Charter which, as the argument goes, is the legal basis of peacekeeping operations.[9] Article 40 gives the Security Council powers to take provisional measures 'to prevent an aggravation of the situation' and provides that such measures 'shall be without prejudice to the rights, claims, or position of the parties concerned'. Nevertheless, grounding neutrality on Article 40 is not convincing. It is one thing for the Security Council as a provisional measure to urge states to act in a certain manner, or to abstain from acting, which exhortation the parties may or may not heed; and a completely different thing for the Security Council, a third party to the dispute, to deploy a peacekeeping operation as a provisional measure.[10]

As a matter of fact, neutrality was not the product of legal considerations, but of political considerations. Indeed, it was instrumental in obtaining the consent of the

[7] UNEF: Summary Study, A/3943 (1958), para 167. Rosalyn Higgins, *United Nations Peacekeeping 1946–1967. Documents and Commentary* (Oxford: Oxford University Press, 1969), vol III, 132–3; Tsagourias, 'Consent, Neutrality/Impartiality and the Use of Force in Peacekeeping: Their Constitutional Dimension', 478.

[8] The Congo Question (9 Aug) SC Res 146 (1960), para 4.

[9] E. M. Miller (Oscar Schachter) 'Legal Aspects of the United Nations Action in the Congo' (1961) 55 *American Journal of International Law* 1, 4–6; Derek H. Bowett, *United Nations Forces: A Legal Study of United Nations Practice* (London: Stevens and Sons, 1964), 175–8 and 280–5; Higgins, *United Nations Peacekeeping 1946–1967*, vol III, 55–7; Nigel D. White, *Keeping the Peace* (Manchester: Manchester University Press, 1993), 197–202; Hitoshi Nasu, *Peacekeeping: A Study of Article 40 of the UN Charter* (Leiden: Martinus Nijhoff, 2009).

[10] Dan Ciobanu, 'The Powers of the Security Council to Organise Peace-Keeping Operations' in Antonio Cassese (ed), *United Nations Peace-Keeping: Legal Essays* (Alphen aan den Rijn: Sithoff and Noordhoff, 1978), 15, 20.

host state, because it provided political as well as psychological assurances that the sovereignty of the host state or the interests of the parties involved in the dispute would be respected. This will become immediately apparent if we recall the context within which peacekeeping came into being. Peacekeeping was the substitute for the original UN scheme of peace enforcement, which provided that enforcement action will be decided by the Security Council and will be carried out by a stand-by army under UN command.[11] This scheme did not materialize because states were determined to preserve important vestiges of their sovereignty and enforcement is too intrusive on state sovereignty. Thus, in its place, peacekeeping was invented as a neutral that is, non-intrusive or threatening force. Because of that, states would not only give their consent to have them deployed on their territory but would also contribute troops to peacekeeping missions knowing that the force will not be used to fight a war without their consent.

Impartiality implies equal treatment of all parties against certain standards which in a peacekeeping operation are the purposes of the UN, as the general and permanent standard, and the operation's mandate as the more specific standard. As the Brahimi Report put it 'impartiality...must mean adherence to the principles of the Charter and to the objectives of a mandate that is rooted in those Charter principles'.[12] Both standards reinforce each other and provide the framework within which impartiality is assessed.

It becomes apparent from the previous discussion that the principles of neutrality and impartiality are not synonymous, but distinguishable and separable—although they are often used interchangeably. Neutrality is the quality of being apolitical in regard to a situation or to parties, whereas impartiality is about treating all parties even-handedly in view of the mission's objectives. Put differently, whereas an impartial actor responds even-handedly to the actions of the parties irrespective of their identity, a neutral actor takes a non-judgemental position towards the parties or their actions. As the former Deputy Secretary-General Louise Fréchette put it 'impartiality is not the same as neutrality. Of course, United Nations forces must apply impartially the mandate given them by the Security Council. But that is not at all the same as being neutral between parties that obey that mandate and those that resist it, or between those who respect international humanitarian and human rights law, and those who grossly violate it.'[13]

A peacekeeping mission cannot be at the same time impartial and neutral. Neutrality translates into passivity and inaction. When the mission is challenged by any of the parties, it can only maintain its neutrality by scaling down its activities or

[11] UN Charter, Chapter VII.

[12] Brahimi Report, para 50; See further Capstone Doctrine, 33. Also Joint Publication 3-07.3, Peace Operations (17 Oct 2007), vii. Daniel H. Levine, 'Peacekeeper Impartiality: Standards, Processes and Operations' (2011) 15 *Journal of International Peacekeeping* 422.

[13] Louise Fréchette, 'United Nations Peacekeeping-A Changing Landscape', UN Press Release DSG/SM/96, 8 June 2000.

by retreating.[14] In contrast, impartiality, being value-oriented, translates into action, albeit in an even-handed manner.[15] As the Capstone Doctrine put it 'impartiality… should not be confused with neutrality or inactivity. United Nations peacekeepers should be impartial in their dealing with the parties to the conflict, but not neutral in the execution of their mandate'.[16]

The possibility of the coexistence of the principles of neutrality and impartiality has been further strained by the changing and more challenging environment within which peacekeeping missions are nowadays deployed, the diverse roles and tasks assigned to those operations, and, above all, by the broad humanitarian objectives attributed to peacekeeping missions. More specifically, peacekeeping operations are deployed in the midst of intrastate confrontation and their functions diversified to include observation, monitoring ceasefires, interposition, demobilization, electoral monitoring, protection of humanitarian assistance, preventive deployment, early warning, protection of safe areas, civilian protection, disarmament and demobilization, and reintegration of former combatants leading to state reconstruction.[17] Having broad and programmatic mandates, peacekeeping missions need to fulfil them effectively in order to justify their existence and garner legitimacy. As a result, neutrality has been abandoned and impartiality has become the guiding light in peacekeeping operations.[18]

The changing dynamics between neutrality and impartiality have inevitably affected the other ingredient of peacekeeping—the use force in self-defence—and, more specifically, its outer limits.[19] The original reading of self-defence included the personal defence of the peacekeeper, which is inherent to any person, including military personnel, the defence of other peacekeepers, or persons protected by peacekeepers, as well as the defence of peacekeeping equipment and posts occupied by peacekeepers.[20] This notion of self-defence reflects national criminal law

[14] Annual Report of the Secretary-General on the Work of the Organization, 16 June 1960–15 June 1961, A/4800 (1961), 17.

[15] Dominick Donald, 'Neutral is Not Impartial: The Confusing Legacy of Traditional Peacekeeping Operations Thinking' (2003) 29 *Armed Forces & Society* 415; Dominick Donald, 'Neutrality, Impartiality and UN Peacekeeping at the Beginning of the 21st Century' (2002) 9 *International Peacekeeping* 21, 22; Hikaru Yamashita, '"Impartial" Use of Force in United Nations Peacekeeping' (2008) 15 *International Peacekeeping* 615, 617; Marc Weller, 'The Relativity of Humanitarian Neutrality and Impartiality' (1997) 91 *Proceedings American Society of International Law* 441, 443.

[16] Capstone Doctrine, 33.

[17] eg see SC Res 1291 (2000) and SC Res 1565 (2004) with regard to MONUC (Congo); with regard to UNUCI (Côte d'Ivoire) see SC Res 1528 (2004), SC Res 1609 (2005), and SC Res 1739 (2007); with regard to UNAMID (Darfur) see SC Res 1769 (2007); with regard to UNISFA (Sudan) see SC Res 1990 (2011).

[18] eg the UN does not mention neutrality as one of its peacekeeping principles. See <http://www.un.org/en/peacekeeping/operations/principles.shtml>. In the same vein, Joint Publication 3-07.3 does not mention neutrality in the 15 fundamentals of peace operations although it still mentions consent and impartiality. Joint Publication 3-07.3 'Peace Operations', 17 Oct 2007.

[19] For further discussion, see Scott Sheeran, 'The Use of Force in United Nations Peacekeeping Operations', Chapter 16 in this volume.

[20] General Guidelines for Peace-Keeping Operations, UN/210/TC/CG95 (1995); UNEF: Summary Study, A/3943 (1958), para 179. With regard to UNFICYP, see S/5653 (11 Apr 1964), para 16: 'Troops of

stipulations of self-defence[21] and constitutes customary international law.[22] Such limited use of force also complemented the principle of neutrality. It reassured parties that armed force would not be used to influence the situation on the ground, whereas troop-contributing countries were reassured that their soldiers would be able to protect themselves and their positions. Although a certain margin of appreciation always existed, the defining line was that peacekeepers should never take the initiative in the use of armed force.[23]

When the mandates of peacekeeping operations expanded and neutrality was abandoned, the use of force in self-defence was broadened to include the defence of the mission. Perhaps the first time the defence of the mission was mentioned was with regard to UNEF II,[24] but previous missions, in particular ONUC, operated on a broader version of self-defence. For instance, the Security Council authorized ONUC to 'take vigorous action, including the requisite measure of force, if necessary, for the immediate apprehension, detention..., or deportation of all foreign military and paramilitary personnel...and mercenaries'[25] which, as the UN Secretary-General insisted,[26] and the International Court of Justice (ICJ) later confirmed,[27] fell within the remit of self-defence. The Brahimi Report explicitly states that force can be used to defend peacekeepers, the mission's components, and the mission's mandate.[28] It further states that 'rules of engagement should not limit contingents to stroke-for-stroke responses but should allow ripostes sufficient to silence a source of deadly fire that is directed at United Nations troops or at the people they are charged to protect, and, in particularly dangerous situations should not force United Nations contingents to cede the initiatives to the attackers'.[29] The Security Council consequently authorizes peacekeeping forces to take necessary action in this regard.[30] For all intents and purposes, this alludes to

UNFICYP shall not take the initiative in the use of armed force. The use of armed force is permissible only in self-defence. The expression "self-defence" includes:

(a) the defence of United Nations posts, premises and vehicles under armed attack;
(b) the support of other personnel of UNFICYP under armed attack.'

[21] eg see the UK Criminal Law Act 1967, section 3 and *Beckford* [1988] AC 130 (Privy Council).

[22] *Prosecutor v. Kordić et al*, IT-95-14/2, Trial Chamber Judgment of 28 Feb 2001, para 451.

[23] UNEF: Summary Study, A/3943 (1958), paras 178–9.

[24] Report of the Secretary-General on the Implementation of Security Council Resolution 340, S/11052/Rev.1 (27 Oct 1973), para 4(d): 'Self-defence would include resistance to attempts by forceful means to prevent it from discharging its duties...'

[25] SC Res 169 (1960).

[26] Report of the Secretary-General on Certain Steps Taken in Regard to the Implementation of the Security Council Resolution Adopted on 21 February 1961, S/4752 (1961), Annex 7; contra, see Trevor Findlay, *The Use of Force in UN Peace Operations* (Oxford: Oxford University Press, 2002), 86.

[27] *Certain Expenses of the United Nations (Article 17, paragraph 2, of the Charter)*, Advisory Opinion of 20 July 1962, Reports of Judgments, Advisory Opinions and Orders, ICJ Rep 1962, 150, 177.

[28] Brahimi Report, paras 48–51; Report of the Special Committee on Peace-Keeping Operations, Report A/57/767 (28 Mar 2003), para 46; Capstone Doctrine, ch 3.

[29] Brahimi Report, para 49.

[30] See eg SC Res 1291 (2000) and SC Res 1565 (2004) with regard to MONUC; also SC Res 1528 (2004) with regard to UNOCI (Côte d'Ivoire).

enforcement of the operation's mandate by means of force. It is therefore important to examine whether the use of force in the context of peacekeeping differs, if at all, from peace enforcement as envisaged in Chapter VII of the UN Charter, because both types of force are nowadays authorized by the Security Council but as the UN Secretary-General commented, 'peace-keeping and the use of force (other than self-defence) should be seen as alternative techniques and not as adjacent on a continuum, permitting easy transition from one to the other'.[31]

Peace enforcement is defined as an action involving the use of force which is directed against a state with the aim of overcoming its will.[32] In a peace enforcement operation, there is a culpable party, usually a state, which is treated as the enemy of international society and against whom enforcement action is taken. The aim of such enforcement action is to impose the will of the international society on that party through the use of force.[33] Peace enforcement is neither neutral nor impartial and the use of force is the essence and the principal instrument of the action. For example, the aim of the use of force against Iraq which the Security Council authorized in 1990 was to expel Iraq from Kuwait[34] because Iraq breached international peace by invading Kuwait. Moreover, the use of force was the main rationale of the action.

By way of contrast, in a peacekeeping operation with enforcement capabilities, the use of force does not impose a solution to the conflict, but it protects the peacekeeping operation's mandate and vies to create conditions conducive to resolving the dispute according to the mission's mandate. It is for this reason that all parties are treated impartially against the mission's mandate and force may be used against any party.[35] Furthermore, the use of force is not the primary aim or the *raison d'être* of the operation, but it is incidental thereto. Force is used when and if needed. Along similar lines, the Capstone Doctrine distinguishes between the use of force at the strategic level, which defines peace enforcement operations and the use of force at the tactical level, which characterizes peacekeeping operations.[36] The distinction between peace enforcement and peacekeeping with

[31] Report of the Secretary-General Pursuant to Security Council Resolution 982 (1995) and 987 (1995), S/1995/444 (30 May 1995), para 62.

[32] *Certain Expenses of the United Nations (Article 17, paragraph 2, of the Charter)*, Advisory Opinion, ICJ Rep 1962, 151, 166, 177; contra see Judge Koretsky, ibid, 276 and Judge Quintana, ibid, 246; Findlay, *The Use of Force in UN Peace Operations*, 374–378.

[33] See Allied Joint Publication (AJP) 3.4.1 Peace Support Operations, July 2001, available at <http://www.pronato.com/peacekeeping/AJP-3-4-1/index.htm>. Joint Publication 3-07.3, x and I-4.

[34] SC Res 660 (1990) and 678 (1990).

[35] Implementation of the Recommendations of the Special Committee on Peacekeeping Operations, Report of the Secretary-General, A/64/573 (22 Dec 2009), para 25; Report of the Special Committee on Peacekeeping Operations and its Working Group (C-34), 2009 Substantive Session, 23 Feb–20 Mar 2009, A/63/19, para 125; Report of the Special Committee on Peacekeeping Operations, 2010 substantive session, 22 Feb–19 Mar 2010, A/64/19, para 143; Joint Publication 3-07.3, viii–x.

[36] Capstone Doctrine, 34–5. Report by the Secretary-General's High-Level Panel on Threats, Challenges and Change, 'A More Secure World: Our Shared Responsibility' (2004), para 212, available at <http://www.un.org/secureworld>.

enforcement capabilities is also reflected in the way humanitarian law applies to such operations. Whereas in peace enforcement operations humanitarian law applies *in toto* and *ab initio*, in peacekeeping operations with enforcement capabilities it applies when the forces are engaged as combatants, and for the duration of their engagement.[37]

An example where the use of force was authorized both as part of a peacekeeping and an enforcement operation and in the same resolution was Security Council Resolution 836 (1993). It authorized the United Nations Protection Force deployed to the former Yugoslavia (UNPROFOR), 'acting in self-defence, to take the necessary measures, including the use of force, in reply to bombardments against the safe areas by any of the parties or to armed incursion into them or in the event of any deliberate obstruction in or around those areas to the freedom of movement of UNPROFOR or of protected humanitarian convoys'.[38] In the following paragraph it authorized 'member states, acting nationally or through regional organisations or arrangements, [to] take... all necessary measures, through the use of air power, in and around the safe areas... to support UNPROFOR in the performance of its mandate'.[39] It was the North Atlantic Treaty Organization (NATO) that enforced the latter prong of the mandate, and as Professor Marc Weller noted, NATO's actions were 'not an exercise of self-defence on behalf of UNPROFOR. Instead, the action represented a much wider reading of the resolution [836], which empowered NATO to take all necessary measures to ensure the implementation of the aims enunciated in paragraph 5 of that resolution.'[40] In contrast, the more limited mandate of UNPROFOR was justified by the UN Secretary-General on the basis of 'the nature of UNPROFOR as a lightly armed, impartial, international force'[41] and because, as he put it in one of his reports 'using force against only one party, whether directly or through regional arrangements, alters the party's perception of the neutrality of UNPROFOR'.[42]

What follows from the preceding discussion is that peacekeepers can use force without Security Council authorization in order to defend themselves and their positions, but when the Council authorizes the use of force, peacekeepers can use force to defend their mandate.[43] This expands the scope of force that can be used.

[37] Secretary-General's Bulletin, Observance by United Nations Forces of International Humanitarian Law, ST/SGB/1999/13 (1999).

[38] Bosnia and Herzegovina SC Res 836 (1993), para 9. [39] SC Res 836 (1993), para 10.

[40] Marc Weller, 'Peace-Keeping and Peace Enforcement in the Republic of Bosnia and Herzegovina' (1996) 70 *Zeitschrift for ausländisches öffentliches Recht und Völkerrecht* 163.

[41] Report of the Secretary-General Pursuant to Security Council Resolution 844, S/1994/555 (1994), para 20.

[42] Report of the Secretary-General Pursuant to Security Council Resolution 982 (1995) and 987 (1995), S/1995/444 (30 May 1995), para 58.

[43] Compare, eg, certain Security Council resolutions concerning UNPROFOR. Early resolutions such as SC Res 776 (1992) did not authorize the use of force, but the Secretary-General authorized force in self-defence. Report of the Secretary-General on the Situation in Bosnia and Herzegovina, S/24540 (1992), para 9. Later resolutions, eg SC Res 871 (1993), authorized the use of force in self-defence.

However, the use of self-defence language plays an important role in limiting such force to the objectives of the mission and thus prevents any mission-creep towards peace enforcement. Moreover, the language of self-defence reinforces the impartially of the peacekeeping operation, something that is lacking from peace enforcement operations.

The Independent International Fact-Finding Mission on the Conflict in Georgia has adopted a different approach to self-defence in the context of peacekeeping. In its report, it accepted that, in principle, attacks on Russian peacekeepers can trigger Russia's right of self-defence. Its contention was based on the fact that the Commonwealth of Independent States (CIS) peacekeeping operation, of which the Russian soldiers and bases were part, was not under UN command and control and also because the attack was aimed specifically at Russia.[44] For the Commission, the Russian peacekeeping forces were instruments of the state.

The report's conclusions are erroneous because they confuse peacekeeping and the right to use force by way of self-defence in the context of peacekeeping, with the right of self-defence, which is available to states pursuant to Article 51 of the UN Charter or customary international law. In the first place, peacekeepers can be organized and deployed by regional organizations without UN authority provided that the host state gives its consent. The CIS peacekeeping force which consisted of Russian, Georgian, and Ossetian troops was deployed with the agreement of the respective governments and authorities, which set out the mandate of the force. The peacekeeping force had the power to use force only in self-defence[45] and was placed under joint military command which in itself was under the authority of a Joint Control Commission (JCC).[46] Consequently, the real question the Commission should have answered was whether the use of force by the Russian peacekeepers exceeded their mandate or whether the use of force by Russia in Georgia can be justified under other headings, outside the peacekeeping framework.

[44] The Independent International Fact-Finding Mission on the Conflict in Georgia was established by the European Union Council with its decision 2008/901/CFSP of 2 Dec 2008, vol II, 264–9. The Report of the Fact-Finding Mission is available at <http://www.ceiig.ch>.

[45] See eg Protocol 2 of the Meeting of the Joint Control Commission (JCC) for the Georgian–Ossetian Conflict Settlement (12 July 1992) in Tamaz Diasamidze, *Regional Conflicts in Georgia—the Autonomous Oblast of South Ossetia, the Autonomous SSR of Abkhazia (1989–2006) The Collection of Political-Legal Acts* (Tbilisi: The Regionalism Research Centre, 2006), 105: 'the JPKF…shall use weapons for the purpose of self-defence…' Also Annex I of Joint Control Commission's decision of 6 Dec 1994 concerning the Basic Principles of Operation of the Military Contingents and of the Groups of Military Observers Designated for the Normalisation of the Situation in the Zone of the Georgian-Ossetian Conflict, in Diasamidze, 177.

[46] Arts 3(1) and 3(2) of the Agreement on Principles of Settlement of the Georgian–Ossetian Conflict in Diasamidze, *Regional Conflicts in Georgia*, 98. Also see Art 2 of Decision No 1 of the Session of Joint Control Commission (4 July 1992), in Diasamidze, 10; Art 2 of the Regulation Concerning the Basic Principles of Operation of the Military Contingents and of the Groups of Military Observers Designated for the Normalization of the Situation in the Zone of the Georgian–Ossetian Conflict (6 Dec 1994) in Diasamidze, 174.

III. Protection of Civilians, Responsibility to Protect, and the Use of Force in Peacekeeping

At this juncture it is important to consider the implications of the protection of civilians (POC) and the Responsibility to Protect (R2P) doctrines on the Security Council's readiness to authorize the use of force as well as on the readiness of peacekeepers to use force and on the level of force that they can use.

Both doctrines were developed by the UN following the acknowledged failure of its missions in Rwanda and Yugoslavia to protect people from mass atrocities.[47] The POC doctrine, which preceded R2P, is about the protection of civilians from violence in situations of armed conflict. Although in its basic form POC is founded in humanitarian law,[48] as a task or an objective assigned to a UN mission, it rests on UN values and principles, on local expectations as to the protection that should be afforded to people,[49] on considerations of legitimacy, and on the need to achieve durable peace, as the ultimate aim of modern integrated missions.[50] Thus, POC as a concept is broader and more far-reaching in the peacekeeping context.[51] Indeed, the UN has developed a comprehensive framework for the protection of civilians[52]—including the protection of certain vulnerable groups such as women[53] or children[54]—which goes beyond their physical protection or the securing of humanitarian access, and is about establishing conditions for their sustained protection.

For example, the Department of Peacekeeping Operations/Department of Field Support (DPKO/DFS) Operational Concept on the Protection of Civilians in UN Peacekeeping Operations organizes the work of UN peacekeeping missions in support of this mandated task into three tiers: first, protection through political process;

[47] See Report of the Secretary-General Pursuant to General Assembly Resolution 53/35: The Fall of Srebrenica, A/54/549 (1999), para 499; Report of the Independent Inquiry into the actions of the United Nations during the 1994 genocide in Rwanda, S/1999/1257, 16 Dec 1999, 50–2.

[48] Jean-Marie Henckaerts and Louise Doswald-Beck, *Customary International Humanitarian Law, Vol. I: Rules* (Geneva: International Committee of the Red Cross), rules 1–11; SC Res 1894 (2009).

[49] Brahimi Report, ix: 'No failure did more to damage the standing and credibility of United Nations peacekeeping in the 1990s than its failure to distinguish between victim and aggressor'.

[50] Victoria Holt and Glyn Taylor, *Protecting Civilians in the Context of UN Peacekeeping Operations: Successes, Setbacks and Remaining Challenges* (New York: United Nations, 2009), 22–4.

[51] See Siobhan Wills, *Protecting Civilians* (Oxford: Oxford University Press, 2009).

[52] See eg SC Res 1265 (1999), SC Res 1296 (2000), SC Res 1267 (2006), SC Res 1894 (2009) on the Protection of civilians in armed conflict; Presidential Statement S/PRST/1999/6 (1999), S/PRST/2002/6, and S/PRST/2009/1; Report of the Special Committee on Peacekeeping Operations and its Working Group (C-34), 2009 Substantive Session, 23 Feb–20 Mar 2009, A/63/19, 24; Reports by the Secretary-General on the protection of civilians in armed conflict (most recent 8th Report S/2010/579).

[53] SC Res 1325 (2000); SC Res 1820 (2008); SC Res 1889 (2009).

[54] SC Res 1612 (2005) and SC Res 1882 (2009).

secondly, providing protection from physical violence; and, thirdly, establishing a protective environment.[55] In the same vein, the African Union/United Nations Hybrid Operation in Darfur (UNAMID) Mission Directive on the Protection of Civilians in Darfur (Mission Directive No 1/2009) defines the POC doctrine very broadly, as 'all activities aimed at obtaining full respect for the rights of the individual in accordance with the letter and the spirit of the relevant bodies of law'.[56]

R2P as set out by the International Commission on Intervention and State Sovereignty in its 2001 Report concerns the protection of people from serious harm. Conceptually, R2P recalibrates the notion of sovereignty from its traditional Westphalian notion of control to a concept of 'sovereignty as responsibility'. States have the primary responsibility to protect their citizens whereas the international community, acting mainly through the UN, has a secondary responsibility, if a state is unable or unwilling to fulfil its own responsibility.[57] R2P in its original form was premised on three pillars: the responsibility to prevent, the responsibility to react, and the responsibility to rebuild.[58] In subsequent versions, R2P was gradually diluted. The 2005 UN World Summit Outcome Document limited the protective responsibility of states to four core crimes: 'genocide, war crimes, ethnic cleansing and crimes against humanity'.[59] It also relayed the responsibility of the international community on the UN 'to use appropriate diplomatic, humanitarian and other peaceful means, in accordance with Chapters VI and VII of the Charter' and to 'take collective action…through the Security Council…on a case by case basis and in cooperation with relevant regional organisations as appropriate.'[60] The way the doctrine has been reinterpreted since 2001 indicates a clear shift in perceptions from forcible to less forcible measures. This became evident in the Secretary-General's Report on 'Implementing the Responsibility to Protect' which identifies three pillars to R2P: first, the protection responsibilities of the state; secondly, international assistance and capacity-building; and, thirdly, timely and decisive response by the

[55] UN DPKO/DFS *Civil Affairs Handbook* (2012), 54–55 available at <http://www.un.org/en/peacekeeping/documents/civilhandbook/Chapter4.pdf>. See also UK Government Strategy on the Protection of Civilians in Armed Conflict (2010) which sets out four policy areas: (1) political engagement; (2) protection by peace support operations; (3) humanitarian action; and (4) state capacity. Available at <http://www.fco.gov.uk/en/publications-and-documents/publications1/protection-civilians-armed-conflict/>.

[56] Cited in Holt and Taylor, *Protecting Civilians in the Context of UN Peacekeeping Operations*, 181. See also Proposed Guidelines for the Protection of Civilians in African Union Peace Support Operations for consideration by the African Union, para 1 available at <http://www.operationspaix.net/DATA/…/8763.pdf>—Canada. Progress report of the Chairperson of the Commission on the Development of Guidelines for the Protection of Civilians in African Union Peace Support Operations, PSC/PR/2(CCLXXIX) (18 May 2011), available at <http://www.peaceau.org/…/progress-report-protection-of-civilians-eng-.pdf>.

[57] *The Responsibility to Protect, Report of the International Commission on Intervention and State Sovereignty* (2001), 13–18.

[58] *The Responsibility to Protect*, chs 3–5.

[59] World Summit Outcome Document, GA Res 60/1 (2005), para 138.

[60] World Summit Outcome Document (2005), para 139.

international community through the UN[61] with the first and second pillars receiving extensive attention.

Although POC and R2P have been introduced as separate concepts, they are interlinked and indeed constitute parts of the broader concept of protecting people.[62] First, both doctrines establish a normative framework for the protection of people, be they civilians caught in armed conflict or persons threatened with mass violence. Secondly, they both operationalize the protection concept and they reflect and operationalize the UN values of human dignity and peace. As the Representative of Brazil to the Security Council stated in 2011 'Protecting civilians is one of the most important ways in which the Organization gives expression to its ultimate objectives, as set out in the Charter.'[63] Thirdly, the protection of civilians under both doctrines is a primary responsibility of states[64] with the UN having secondary responsibility to provide protection when the state fails in this regard.[65] Fourthly, implementing measures often overlap. The POC concept is not just about the physical protection of endangered civilians but has become a normative concept that entails direct, as well as structural measures for prevention, reaction, and capacity-building in the same vein as the R2P does in its preventive and capacity-building aspects.[66] Fifthly, one can trace a conceptual shift as far as the protection of civilians is concerned in that often the relevant resolutions do not restrict such protection to armed conflict because threats to civilians can emanate from diverse sources not necessarily confined to situations of armed conflict.

It thus follows that the POC and the R2P as articulated in UN documents are streams of the same overarching concept, the protection of people, and peacekeeping has become the main tool for providing such protection. Although, and in contrast to POC, no explicit connection was made at the beginning between peacekeeping and the R2P, the UN Secretary-General in his Report on the Implementation of the Responsibility to Protect called for its mainstreaming through the work of the UN, including its peacekeeping.[67] This is explained by the fact that peacekeeping is one of the tools used by the UN to realize its aims, and, consequently, the links between

[61] Implementing the Responsibility to Protect: Report of the Secretary-General, 12 January 2009, A/63/677 and GA Res 63/308 (2009).

[62] For the interaction and merging of both concepts, see SC Res 1674 (2006) on Protection of civilians in armed conflict, para 4. See also SC Res 1706 (2006) with regard to Sudan which reaffirms SC Res 1674 and the responsibility to protect (para 2 of the preamble) and then goes on to authorize the use of force to protect civilians under threat of violence (para 12). Also SC Res 1894 (2009) on Protection of civilians in armed conflict, seventh preambular para.

[63] S/PV.6531 (10 May 2011), 11.

[64] As part of humanitarian law, it is a primary obligation of all belligerents, be they states or non-state actors.

[65] *The Responsibility to Protect*, 12–18. SC Res 1674 (2006), ninth preambular para; Res 1590 (2005), para 16 (UNMIS).

[66] Compare eg the Report of the Secretary-General to the Security Council on the Protection of Civilians in Armed Conflict, S/2010/579 (11 Nov 2010) with the Implementing the Responsibility to Protect: Report of the Secretary-General, A/63/677 (12 Jan 2009).

[67] Implementing the responsibility to protect, A/63/677, para 68.

the R2P and POC as UN concepts and peacekeeping are not only normative, but also institutional and operational. Indeed, protection is now the rule in peacekeeping missions either as the overall objective of the mission, or as one of its tasks or objectives.[68]

One of the implications of the adoption of the POC and R2P and, of course, the Brahimi Report is that it changed the rhetoric within the Security Council on whether to authorize the use of force. Since 2000, most peacekeeping operations are authorized to use all necessary means, including the use of force, to protect civilians.[69] However, questions still remain as to the level of force peacekeepers can use in this regard, particularly since the relevant Security Council resolutions do not explicitly mention self-defence.[70] It is submitted that any force that they may employ in order to protect civilians cannot exceed the self-defence threshold as interpreted by the Brahimi Report, or as was practised in previous peacekeeping operations because the use of force in this case is permitted only as 'a last resort when Government security services are unable to provide such security', its aim should be to protect civilians 'under imminent threat of physical violence' and peacekeepers should use force 'within their capabilities' and 'within their areas of deployment'.[71]

These are very important caveats that distinguish the use of force for the protection of civilians from the use of force as part of a peace enforcement operation in that enforcement requires a higher level of force to overcome the resistance of an identified actor and attain the overall aims of the operation. To these it should be added that the use of force in the context of POC proper, which is either authorized or 'presumed' as the Brahimi Report put it,[72] is incidental to the operation. It is not the rationale of the operation—as it is in peace enforcement—but it is conditional on civilians being threatened with imminent violence or conditional on the

[68] The first mission that referred to POC was UNAMSIL with regard to Liberia, see SC Res 1270 (1999), para 14: 'acting under Chapter VII ... UNAMSIL may take the necessary measures to ... to afford protection to civilians under imminent threat of physical violence, taking into account the responsibilities of the Government of Sierra Leone and ECOMOG'. See also MONUC, UNMIL, UNOCI, MINUSTAH, UNMIS, UNAMID, and MINURCAT among others.

[69] SC Res 1270 (1999), para 14 (UNAMSIL); SC Res 1291 (2000), para 8, SC Res 1417 (2002), para 7, SC Res 1493 (2003), paras 8, 12, 25, SC Res 1592 (2005), para 7, SC Res 1756 (2007), paras 2 and 3 (MONUC); SC Res 1925 (2010), para 12(a) (MONUSCO); SC Res 1509 (2003), para 3 (UNMIL); SC Res 1464 (2003), para 9 and SC Res 1528 (2004), para 6 (UNOCI); SC Res 1769 (2007), para 15 (UNAMID); SC Res 1990 (2011), para 3(d) (UNISFA); SC Res 1996 (2011), para 4 (UNMISS).

[70] For further discussion, see Scott Sheeran, 'The Use of Force in United Nations Peacekeeping Operations', Chapter 16 in this volume, 360–7.

[71] See among others, the resolutions included in n 69 as well as the Special Report of the Secretary-General on the Sudan, S/2011/314, 17 May 2011, paras 41 and 44–8; Report of the Secretary-General on South Sudan, S/2012/140, 7 Mar 2012, paras 48–55; Report of the Secretary-General on the United Nations Organization Stabilization Mission in the Democratic Republic of the Congo, S/2011/656, 24 Oct 2011, paras 31–2.

[72] Brahimi Report, para 62. Elsewhere it states that peacekeepers may not only be operationally justified in using force but also morally compelled so to do. Ibid, para 50.

mission's civilian protection objective being challenged by 'spoilers'. Force is used in this case to prevent or stop physical violence against civilians or to defend the mandate. The use of force in the context of POC is also impartial; it reacts equally to all challenges irrespective of source. For example, because of the threat governmental forces posed to civilians, the United Nations Observer Mission in the Democratic Republic of the Congo (Mission de l'Organisation de Nations Unies en République Démocratique du Congo, MONUC) needed to 'plan its deployments according to this risk, and identify possible coercive actions against FARDC [governmental forces] elements responsible for Human Rights violations, during and after operations'.[73] Finally, the fact that the resolutions authorizing the use of force for the protection of civilians at the same time recognize the primary responsibility of the incumbent government to afford protection means that the mission does not displace or replace the government which is the case with enforcement operations.[74]

These features also distinguish the use of force in the POC context from the use of force in the R2P context; in the latter case it is equivalent to enforcement. The Libya incident is instructive in this respect. Following the use of brutal violence by the Gaddafi regime to suppress a popular revolt, the Security Council in Resolution 1973 (2011) authorized states acting nationally or through regional organizations to take all necessary measures to protect civilians and civilian-populated areas in Libya.[75] On the basis of that authorization, NATO and other forces took military action against the Gaddafi regime which led to its overthrow. NATO's action in Libya was an enforcement action since it targeted a specific party (the Gaddafi regime) which was identified by the Security Council as the source of the threat to civilians, it used a high level of force, force was the rationale of the operation, and the operation terminated only when the threat was eclipsed. Granted, no formal reference to R2P was made in the relevant resolutions[76] but the language used is evocative of the R2P. In particular, the reference to the primary responsibility of the government to protect its people, the reference to gross and systematic attacks on civilian populations, and the referral of the case to the International Criminal Court invoke the R2P benchmarks.[77] Even if the use of force by NATO cannot be justified under the R2P doctrine, the situation in Libya still fell under the enforcement powers of the Security Council under Chapter VII of the UN Charter in that the

[73] Cited in Holt and Taylor, *Protecting Civilians in the Context of UN Peacekeeping Operations*, 188.

[74] Sudan, SC Res 1590 (2005), para 16(i) (UNMIS).

[75] SC Res 1973 (2011), preamble and para 4. See also SC Res 1970 (2011), preamble.

[76] The European Parliament referred to the concept of the 'Responsibility to Protect' in Resolution on the Southern Neighbourhood, and Libya in particular (P7_TA-PROV(2011)0095), para 10 (10 Mar 2011). Also see Press release by the UN Secretary-General Special Adviser on the Prevention of Genocide, Francis Deng, and Special Adviser on the Responsibility to Protect, Edward Luck, on the Situation in Libya (22 Feb 2011).

[77] SC Res 1973 (2011), preamble. Also SC Res 1970 (2011), preamble and paras 2, 4.

internal violations of human rights constituted a threat to the peace which justified enforcement action.[78]

Be that as it may and although the distinction between peace enforcement akin to R2P and peacekeeping with enforcement capabilities akin to POC is legally and politically helpful, there still remain problems in its operationalization on the ground. When, for example, authorizing resolutions affirm the primary responsibility of the government to provide protection or that the protection of civilians by the UN force should take place without prejudice to the responsibility of the government,[79] or that protection should be provided when the government fails in this regard,[80] questions immediately arise as to what constitutes failure by the government to provide protection, when should protection be provided, and how far should the force go in order to protect civilians. This is further complicated by the fact that sometimes the entire operation is authorized under Chapter VII,[81] whereas other times it is only the part concerning the protection of civilians.[82] Furthermore, certain missions such as UNAMID are authorized to protect civilians in general; other missions are authorized to protect civilians under imminent threat;[83] whereas other missions are authorized or encouraged to give the protection of civilians high priority,[84] which again raises questions about the timing and scope of the use of force. Related to this is the fact that in certain missions the protection of civilians is one of the mission's tasks, whereas in others it is an objective of the whole mission—which perhaps can justify more extensive use of force.

To this it should be added that there is always a grey area in the spectrum of force and in most cases it is there that most peacekeeping operations stumble. It could be argued that high and sustained levels of violence against people combined with local hostility will require a peace enforcement operation but when the peacekeeping force is already involved in the situation, yet the level of violence increases gradually, the boundaries can quickly shift. It is of course for the Security Council to change the mandate or to deploy a different operation but this may not be forthcoming for many reasons.

Also, peacekeeping operations often operate alongside enforcement operations. In the cases of Yugoslavia or Somalia, UN operations were supported by NATO or the US respectively. Mixing operations with different rationales can even inadvertently increase the level of force permitted by the peacekeeping operation and affect

[78] UN Charter, Arts 39 and 42. See also Bruno Simma (ed), *The Charter of the United Nations: A Commentary* (2nd edn, Oxford: Oxford University Press, 2002), Art 39, paras 7, 18–20. Also see with regard to the treatment of the Kurds by the Iraqi authorities, SC Res 688 (1991) and with regard to the humanitarian crisis in Somalia, SC Res 794 (1992). For Libya, see statement by Harold Hongju Koh at the American Society of International Law Annual Meeting (2011), available at <http://www.state.gov/s/l/releases/remarks/159201.htm>.

[79] SC Res 1590 (2005), para 16 (UNMISS).

[80] SC Res 1996 (2011), para 3(v) (UNMISS).

[81] eg UNMISS as per SC Res 1996 (2011), MONUSCO as per SC Res 1925 (2010).

[82] eg compare paras 1–2 and para 3 of SC Res 1990 (2011) (UNISFA).

[83] eg UNISFA as per SC Res 1990 (2011), para 3(d).

[84] SC Res 1856 (2008) (MONUC).

perceptions of impartiality. The Côte d'Ivoire case is indicative. The United Nations Mission in Côte d'Ivoire/United Nations Operation in Côte d'Ivoire (MINUCI/UNOCI) was deployed to facilitate and oversee the implementation of the 2003 Linas-Marcoussis Accords.[85] UNOCI was authorized to 'protect civilians under imminent threat of physical violence within its capabilities and areas of deployment' and to prevent the use of heavy weapons against the civilian population, whereas the French forces that operated alongside UNOCI were authorized to 'use all necessary means' to support UNOCI and intervene at the request of UNOCI and 'help protect civilians in the deployment areas of their units'.[86] When civil war erupted after a contested presidential election and the refusal of the incumbent President Laurent Gbagbo to step down,[87] the Security Council passed Resolution 1975 (2011) which authorized UNOCI forces, while 'impartially implementing its mandate, to use all necessary means to carry out its mandate to protect civilians under imminent threat of physical violence... including to prevent the use of heavy weapons against the civilian population'.[88] ONUCI was involved together with the French forces in attacking Gbagbo's stronghold, which took place against the warning of the Indian representative to the Security Council who said that UNOCI 'should not become party to the Ivorian political stalemate [and] should also not get involved in the civil war'; the force 'should not be made [an] instrument of regime change' but should 'carry out its mandate with impartiality and while ensuring the safety and security of peacekeepers and civilians'.[89] One may say that UNOCI's attacks were justified since heavy weapons were fired from Gbagbo's compound. Nevertheless, whether it impartially protected civilians may be questioned, since it failed to protect them against the forces of Alassane Ouattara, who was disputing the presidency with Gbagbo.[90] Yet the Secretary-General declared that ONUCI 'is not a party to the conflict. In line with its Security Council mandate, the mission has taken this action in self-defence and to protect civilians.'[91]

This leads to the next point, namely, that perceptions about the impartiality of peacekeeping missions can be damaged not only when they are perceived to favour one party but also when the operationalization of POC may require collaboration or joint operations with the government. As was said earlier, the government has the primary responsibility to protect civilians. It was also said that POC involves a wide spectrum of actions, including preventive and environment-building actions. For this reason, missions are often instructed to cooperate with and support the government

[85] SC Res 1479 (2003) and SC Res 1528 (2004).

[86] SC Res 1528 (2004), paras 6(i) and 16 and SC Res 1739 (2007), paras 2, 5, and 8; Res 1933 (2010), para 16; SC Res 1962 (2010), para 17.

[87] SC Res 1962 (2010). [88] SC Res 1975 (2011), para 6. [89] S/PV.6508 (30 Mar 2011).

[90] As the Russian representative to the Security Council said 'it is unacceptable for United Nations peacekeepers to be drawn into armed conflict and, in effect to take the side of one of the parties when implementing the mandate'. S/PV.6531 (10 May 2011), 9.

[91] SG/SM/13494, AFR/2157 (4 Apr 2011). See also SG/SM/13548 (6 May 2011).

in its civilian protection responsibilities.[92] It cannot be denied that even if the mission is determined to execute its mandate impartially and target the government if need be, maintaining the perception of impartiality is a difficult task if it also collaborates with the government. Yet, the cooperation of the government is critical for the success of the mission and action taken against the government may affect that relationship. The choice is often quite stark; either the mission turns a blind eye to governmental abuses or becomes an enforcement operation if the government withdraws its consent.

IV. Conclusion

The alleviation of human suffering is a fundamental UN principle. As a result UN peacekeeping missions have always been assigned humanitarian ends.[93] These humanitarian ends are nowadays channelled through the POC and R2P concepts and the use of force is often authorized to facilitate their attainment. However, a distinction should be made at the strategic, operational, and tactical level between securing humanitarian ends by enforcing the mandate against obstructionist parties, and securing them by defeating an enemy through the use of force. Whereas the former, performed by peacekeeping missions, requires controlled use of force, the latter requires force at the top end of the spectrum amounting to enforcement. This distinction applies to the two streams of protection available at the UN level; POC and R2P, with the latter requiring enforcement action as a response to extreme cases of state forfeiture of its responsibility to protect its own people. Keeping that distinction in mind is also important for purposes of resourcing the operation, for political and military planning and direction, for managing expectations, and, above all, for the legitimacy of the operation. Blurring the lines between peacekeeping and enforcement will affect the standing of peacekeeping as a separate tool for achieving humanitarian ends. The distinction is also important because it preserves a fundamental feature of peacekeeping operations, which is their impartiality.

[92] See SC Res 1767 (2007), para 18 with regard to UNMEE (Ethiopia and Eritrea). Also compare paras 5–14 and para 15 of SC Res 1769 (2007) (UNAMID). Implementation of the Recommendations of the Special Committee on Peacekeeping Operations, Report of the Secretary-General, A/64/573 (22 Dec 2009), para 19: 'Peacekeepers have a unique role to play in supporting national authorities in exercising their responsibility to protect civilians.' Report of the Special Committee on Peacekeeping Operations, 2010 substantive session (22 Feb–19 Mar 2010), A/64/19, para 151.

[93] As the French representative to the Security Council put it: 'The protection of civilians is at the heart of the mandate of United Nations peacekeeping operations. In that framework our Organization, on a daily basis, must fulfil that mission.' S/PV.6650 (9 Nov 2011), 19.

As the UN has acknowledged, for a peacekeeping operation to succeed, its 'strongest "weapon" is . . . impartiality'.[94]

Notwithstanding the considerable progress that has been made,[95] operationalizing the attainment of humanitarian ends through peacekeeping still faces challenges in resourcing, efficient decision-making, or planning, which are compounded by many other external challenges such as hostile environments and massive human rights abuses. Impartiality, as well as the authority and ability to employ force are not immune from such challenges. As far as the use of force is concerned, further clarification and guidance is needed as to when, how, against whom, and what level of force is required to achieve the mission's humanitarian ends; and as far as impartiality is concerned, clear designation of tasks, better management of expectations, and precise communication of information are called for.

[94] '1948–1998 50 Years of United Nations Peacekeeping Operations', available at <http://www.un.org/en/peacekeeping/sites/50years/2.htm>.

[95] Report of the Secretary-General on the implementation of the report of the Panel on United Nations Peace Operations, A/55/502 (20 Oct 2000); Implementation of the recommendations of the Special Committee on Peacekeeping Operations and the Panel on United Nations Peace Operations, Report of the Secretary-General, A/55/977 (1 June 2001); Implementation of the recommendations of the Special Committee on Peacekeeping Operations, Report of the Secretary-General, A/64/573 (22 Dec 2009); The New Horizon Initiative: Progress Report No 2 (DPKO/DFS, 2011).

CHAPTER 19

TRANSPARENCY, ACCOUNTABILITY, AND RESPONSIBILITY FOR INTERNATIONALLY MANDATED OPERATIONS

CHARLOTTE KU*

I. Introduction

INTERNATIONAL military operations at the direction of international organizations are a development of the 20th century. These operations have increased in number and in complexity and now involve a wide array of public and private actors and contributors. Yet, the transparency of decision-making that establishes the operations, the accountability of individual actors, and the responsibility of the institutions creating the mandates have not kept pace with operational developments. This underdeveloped state is further complicated by international bodies sharing functions in each

* I would like to acknowledge with gratitude the comments and suggestions received from Edwina Campbell, Paul Diehl, and colleagues from the May 2012 University of Illinois College of Law Faculty Retreat in the preparation of this chapter.

of these areas with one or more national entities and private actors including the latter's donors and governing boards.

Historically, the practice and posture of international institutions has largely been to leave accountability issues to national authorities. National institutions have adapted in order to discharge their obligations in a blended operational environment, but it is becoming clear that this is not enough and that international institutions need to develop their own concepts and systems of transparency, accountability, and responsibility to complement and to supplement existing national and private practices. This chapter will identify how selected milestones have developed with a view towards meeting ongoing and future needs of all actors involved in such operations.

II. Sources of International Mandates

Political thinkers and policymakers from around the world have engaged with issues, such as when and how to use military force and to what ends, for centuries. Historians have shown that the development of the modern state was tied to the search for an effective mode both to control and to regulate the use of force.[1] The 20th century contribution to this was to establish international institutions charged with authorizing and overseeing the use of force. January 1918 and US President Woodrow Wilson's Fourteen Points speech is a useful starting point. Point XIV provided that: 'A general association of nations must be formed under specific covenants for the purposes of affording mutual guarantees of political independence and territorial integrity to great and small states alike.'[2] The League of Nations Covenant in Articles 12, 13, and 15 obligated members to take preliminary steps through the League to settle disputes and conflicts before resorting to the use of military force. It was expected that by the time force was used, the case for doing so would be so self-evident to all League members that they would rally to punish the wrongdoer.[3] Members and prospective League members, such as the US, harboured deep reservations about binding themselves to such collective action. The US declined to join, and the League of Nations ultimately declined to act in the face of the invasions by Japan of Manchuria in 1931 and by Italy of Ethiopia in 1935.

Post-Second World War planners in the US undertook to fashion a new security institution that would overcome the perceived defects of the League of Nations

[1] See generally Hendrik Spruyt, *The Sovereign State and Its Competitors* (Princeton, NJ: Princeton University Press, 1994).

[2] Woodrow Wilson, Fourteen Points Speech (8 Jan 1918), available at <http://isinfo.state.gov/usa/infousa/democracy/51.htm>.

[3] Covenant of the League of Nations, Arts 10 and 11.

including the failure of the US to join. Under the terms of the United Nations Charter, primary responsibility for the maintenance of peace and security was entrusted to a Security Council made up of five permanent members (P5) representing the leading victors of 1945 and six, then ten, other elected members.[4] Decisions would be made by a majority vote with some decisions requiring the concurrence of all five permanent members. Only a negative vote is considered to be a 'veto' so that an abstention by one of the P5 will not block action if a majority of nine out of 15 votes is otherwise attained. Initially stymied by the Cold War and the veto threats of the Soviet Union, the US and the UK promoted the passage of the Uniting for Peace resolution in 1950 to enable the UN General Assembly to act if the Security Council were unable to respond to a threat to the peace.[5] British support for the resolution waned after it was used against the UK following the British–French takeover of the Suez Canal in 1956. By 1964, after decolonization changed the make-up of the UN General Assembly and the US could no longer expect an automatic majority, the US no longer regarded Uniting for Peace as a viable alternative to Security Council decision-making.

Despite the general focus on the UN in authorizing the use of military force, the UN has never been the sole source of such authorization. Chapter VIII of the UN Charter provided for regional arrangements 'for dealing with such matters relating to the maintenance of international peace and security as are appropriate for regional action…'[6] The 1948 Inter-American Treaty of Reciprocal Assistance providing for hemispheric defence in the Americas is an example of such an arrangement. Of a different character, but also an alternative to the UN security system, is the self-defence arrangement created by the 1949 North Atlantic Treaty whereby each member 'individually and in concert with the other Parties, [takes] such action as it deems necessary, including the use of armed force, to restore and maintain international peace and security of the North Atlantic area.'[7] Between 1945 and 2007, 34 regional arrangements emerged with security responsibilities.[8] While the UN Security Council remains the preferred international authority for the use of force, we have witnessed the increase in operations initiated by regional organizations—44 between 1999 and 2005 in comparison to 31 started by the UN in the same period.[9]

[4] UN Charter, Art 23 was amended in 1965 to expand the number of elected UN Security Council members.

[5] GA Res 377, UN GAOR, 5th Sess, Supp No 20, at 10, A/1775 (1950).

[6] UN Charter, Art 52.

[7] North Atlantic Treaty, Art 5 which goes on to say that NATO measures 'shall be terminated' once the UN Security Council acts.

[8] These include arrangements, such as the Warsaw Pact and the Southeast Asia Treaty Organisation, that no longer exist as well as arrangements that have undergone name and structural changes like the Organisation of African Unity that is now the African Union. See Alex J. Bellamy and Paul D. Williams, *Understanding Peacekeeping* (Cambridge: Polity, 2010), 302.

[9] Paul F. Diehl and Young-Im Cho, 'Passing the Buck in Conflict Management: The Role of Regional Organizations in the Post Cold War Era' (2006) 12 *Brown Journal of World Affairs* 195.

Although the UN is most closely identified with fielding international operations, particularly peace operations, it does not do so alone. The North Atlantic Treaty Organization (NATO)-led Kosovo Force (KFOR) in Kosovo, the Economic Community of West African States (ECOWAS) in Liberia, and the Southern African Development Community (SADC) in Lesotho are all examples of non-UN-led international operations.[10] Coalitions of the willing have also led UN-sanctioned international operations in Somalia (the US-led UNITAF—Unified Task Force) in 1992–3; the Australian-led International Force for East Timor (INTERFET) in 1994, and the NATO-led International Security Assistance Force (ISAF) in Afghanistan from 2002. There are also hybrid and coordinated operations where a mission may start under a regional organization, but then be turned over to the UN. Or, in the case of a hybrid operation, two organizations may run an operation together, as is the case with the UN-African Union Mission in Darfur (UNAMID).[11] Each of these types of international operation requires working out details of relationships among troop contributors and the relevant international institutions, including command structure and financing mechanisms. These operational conditions are further complicated if a mission starts under one institutional umbrella, but shifts to another, with multiple troop-contributing states which must comply with their own national standards and requirements, including what kinds of weapons their soldiers carry and for what purposes.

The first channels for transparency, responsibility, and accountability are at the international level, but quickly involve national authorities and processes once a mission is put into operation. This shared responsibility can result in blame shifting should problems arise, but is inevitable. Troops remain subject to national command authority, standards of conduct, and behaviour even while serving under international mandates. Practice over time has created a blended system, with the UN stepping into a more direct role of responsibility for the conduct of troops, particularly from countries with less developed command structures, rules of engagement, and standards of military conduct. While it has not replaced national command and control systems, it has created a more complicated situation where national systems are held accountable and must discharge their obligations under conditions not fully within their control.

Even at the exclusively international level, decision-making and accountability may not be straightforward. For example, practice has not yet provided a clear relationship between an international mandate as authorized by the UN Security Council and a regional mandate that may or may not have UN Security Council backing. The UN Charter provisions on self-defence in Article 51 and on regional

[10] Appendix: Peace Operations 1948–2006 in Paul F. Diehl, *Peace Operations* (Cambridge: Polity, 2008), 171–8.

[11] See Alexandru Balas, 'It Takes Two (or More) to Keep the Peace: Multiple Simultaneous Operations' (2011) 15 *Journal of International Peacekeeping* 384.

arrangements in Articles 53 and 54 require that the UN Security Council be 'kept fully informed' of actions taken or contemplated. Practice, however, has been inconsistent, with some operations following the Charter's requirements, but others ignoring them, and the Security Council doing little to address the issue. Critics of this practice worry that it might erode the authority of the Security Council, provide regional hegemons a cover of international authority and legitimacy that might not otherwise exist, and create conditions whereby some regions have better resource bases to respond to crises than others. Those who take a more positive view of active regional involvement argue that proximity, greater knowledge of the region, and potentially greater incentives to achieve success as reasons to support enhancing the capacity of regional organizations to respond.

Authorizing international operations is now further complicated in a post-Westphalian world where the treatment of individuals can warrant a protective response even if the UN and its member states fail to authorize such action. The emerging humanitarian practice is associated with the concept of a 'responsibility to protect'. The International Commission on Intervention and State Sovereignty explicitly provided as an alternative option to Security Council authorization 'action within the area of jurisdiction by regional or sub-regional organisations under Chapter VIII of the Charter, subject to seeking subsequent authorisation from the Security Council.'[12] With the UN's capacity limited, and an increased number of players—including private actors—the role of the UN in authorizing international operations may remain central, but is clearly not exclusive. The multiple sources of mandates for international operations complicate any effort to develop transparency, accountability, and responsibility at the international level since different organizations may have different procedures and requirements. This situation may create conditions whereby no one international authority is fully in control of, responsible for, and informed about an operation.

III. Carrying Out International Mandates: UN Operational and Legal Milestones

Although the founders of the UN had intended to provide the organization with the troops and resources to carry out its decisions, including a command structure through the Military Staff Committee, this system has never been operationalized.

[12] International Commission on Intervention and State Sovereignty, *The Responsibility to Protect* (Ottawa: International Development Research Centre, 2001), xiii.

Article 43 obligates members to make available by special agreement to the UN 'armed forces, assistance, and facilities, including rights of passage' for the purpose of maintaining peace and security. Article 43 agreements, however, were never concluded, and UN member states have decided on a case-by-case basis whether to contribute their military forces to various operations. Separate case-by-case decisions are further made as to the level of engagement states allow their armed forces. Nevertheless, from 1948 to 2011, the UN reports that it conducted 66 peacekeeping operations, 16 of which are presently being directed and supported by the UN's Department of Peacekeeping Operations.[13] Over 121,000 personnel are involved in these operations with the vast majority (nearly 99,000) in uniformed military forces, police (over 14,000), and military observers (just under 2,000).[14] The total cost of these UN-run operations from 1948 to 30 June 2010 is estimated at $69 billion.[15] These operations encompass a range of purposes including monitoring and observation, peacekeeping with host consent or traditional peacekeeping, peacekeeping plus state-building tasks, using force to ensure compliance with international mandates, and enforcement.[16]

The novelty of peacekeeping, a 'non-violent, international military operation', was recounted by British diplomat and long-time UN official Brian Urquhart, who worked closely in 1956 with UN Secretary-General Dag Hammarskjöld to set up the first peacekeeping operation, the United Nations Emergency Force (UNEF). 'Our efforts were almost exclusively an exercise in improvisation.'[17] The operation proved such a success that US Secretary of State John Foster Dulles, backed by a unanimous resolution of the US Congress, called for the creation of a standing UN peacekeeping force.[18] This did not come to pass, but a new form of military operation was born. Urquhart noted:

> The *modus operandi* of peacekeeping operations, now commonplace, was then a first experiment, a complete innovation. We were asking soldiers, against all tradition and training, to take part in non-violent operations in a critical situation—operations, moreover which were not under the control of their own governments. The new peacekeeping operations touched on the most delicate issues of military psychology, national sovereignty, international politics, and national and international law.[19]

Despite this early success, some years would pass before another peacekeeping mission was fielded. The United Nations Operation in the Congo (Opération des

[13] Information available at <http://www.un.org/en/peacekeeping/resources/statistics/factsheet.shtml>.

[14] See n 13.

[15] See UN Peacekeeping Fact Sheet, available at <http://www.un.org/en/peacekeeping/resources/statistics/factsheet.shtml>.

[16] See Charlotte Ku and Harold K. Jacobson (eds), *Democratic Accountability and the Use of Force in International Law* (Cambridge: Cambridge University Press, 2002), 19–25 for discussion of these categories.

[17] Brian Urquhart, *A Life in Peace and War* (New York: Harper & Row, 1987), 134.

[18] Urquhart, *A Life in Peace and War*, 137.

[19] Urquhart, *A Life in Peace and War*, 137.

Nations Unies au Congo, ONUC) marked another milestone in the development of peace operations.[20] Active from 1960 to 1964, ONUC involved nearly 20,000 troops with a substantial civilian component. Built initially on the model of UNEF I to secure law and order after the departure of Belgian colonial officials, ONUC ended up with the more robust and complicated task of maintaining the territorial integrity of the Congo and preventing the secession of Katanga province. This ramped-up mission drew the vociferous opposition of France and the Soviet Union which expressed their opposition by withholding their payments to the UN budget and subsequently triggering a financial crisis within the UN.

Two advisory opinions of the International Court of Justice (ICJ) address issues relating to UN peace operations in those early days. These opinions helped to define the transparency, accountability, and responsibility of internationally mandated operations that are still applicable today. The first, addressing the *Reparations for Injuries Suffered in the Service of the United Nations*, was prompted by the 1948 murder of UN Mediator Count Folke Bernadotte in Jerusalem. The UN General Assembly sought advice from the ICJ on whether the UN could pursue a claim on behalf of its agent, Count Bernadotte. It further asked for clarification as to how such a claim would affect the right to damages that Bernadotte's nationality state, Sweden, might have as a matter of general international law. The baseline question was whether the UN, as an international organization and not a state, possessed adequate international personality to claim damages on behalf of its agent. The ICJ acknowledged that the question was left open in the Charter, but concluded that 'the attribution of international legal personality [to the UN] is indispensable.'[21]

It reached this conclusion based on the understanding that the UN is not 'merely a centre for "harmonizing the actions of nations in the attainment of...common ends"', but that the Charter requires the organization to carry out special tasks through its Secretariat and particular organs:

> Practice—in particular the conclusion of Conventions to which the Organisation is a party—has confirmed this character of the Organisation which occupies a position in certain respects in detachment from its members, and which is under a duty to remind them, if need be, of certain obligations.[22]

The ICJ went on to say that:

> In the opinion of the Court, the Organisation was intended to exercise and enjoy, and is in fact exercising and enjoying, functions and rights which can only be explained on the basis of the possession of a large measure of international personality and the capacity to operate on the international plane.[23]

[20] ONUC was created by SC Res 163 (14 July 1960) and supplemented by SC Res 161 (21 Feb 1961) and SC Res 169 (24 Nov 1961) authorizing higher levels of the use of force by ONUC forces. Information available at <http://www.un.org/en/peacekeeping/missions/past/onucM.htm>.

[21] *Reparations for Injuries Suffered in the Service of the United Nations*, Advisory Opinion of 11 Apr 1949, ICJ Rep 1949, 178.

[22] *Reparations*, Advisory Opinion, 179.

[23] *Reparations*, Advisory Opinion, 179.

This means that the UN also incurs the duties and responsibilities that go with those rights. The UN has had to evolve its practice to discharge these duties and responsibilities because it was not equipped at the outset either with the capacity or the infrastructure to discharge them fully. The advent of increasingly complex UN-led military operations since 1990 has created the need to develop this capacity and infrastructure much more fully than from 1949 to 1989.

Further addressing the independence of the UN to undertake an operation without the full agreement of its members, the UN General Assembly sought an advisory opinion from the ICJ to determine whether 'certain expenditures authorised by the UN General Assembly constitute "expenses of the Organisation" within the meaning of Article 17, paragraph 2, of the Charter of the United Nations.'[24] The specific expenses in question were those relating to the UN operations in the Congo in 1960 and those of UNEF between 1956 and 1960. France and the Soviet Union, in particular, had opposed these operations and had refused to pay for their expenses. The ICJ concluded that these expenses were incurred in accordance with the purposes of the UN and therefore should be considered regular expenses to be borne by all members as stipulated in Article 17, paragraph 2. The ICJ acknowledged that no guidance was provided in the Charter as to types of expenses, and therefore it had to analyse whether the expenses in question were in accordance with the UN's functions. It further had to conclude whether the UN General Assembly could authorize action even though the UN Security Council was charged with the *primary* responsibility for issues of peace and security. The Court answered both questions in the affirmative. Indeed, the ICJ noted that the Charter contemplated 'a close collaboration between the two organs'.[25]

By concluding this and following the *Reparations for Injuries* advisory opinion, the ICJ opted to provide the UN with a voice and a role that was criticized as exceeding the bounds of international law. Leo Gross found that the Court's desire to provide the UN with 'institutional effectiveness' overshadowed the reality of the UN as a creature of its members, and that even if the UN was meant to have such an independent role, it could not force all its sovereign members to pay for it.[26] Whatever the strengths of the legal arguments, the political fallout of the opinion was such that it took the UN nearly three decades to recover both its credibility and its financial stability in the area of internationally mandated peacekeeping operations.

[24] *Certain Expenses of the United Nations (Article 17, paragraph 2, of the Charter)*, Advisory Opinion of 20 July 1962, ICJ Rep 1962, 152.

[25] *Certain Expenses*, Advisory Opinion, 163.

[26] Leo Gross, 'Expenses of the United Nations for Peace-Keeping Operations: The Advisory Opinion of the International Court of Justice' (1963) 17 *International Organization* 3.

IV. Agenda for Peace and the Advent of Complex Peace Operations

The controversy ignited by ONUC in the 1960s was such that UN peacekeeping largely fell out of favour as a means to address international crises through the 1970s and 1980s. This was to change dramatically with the end of the Cold War in 1989–91. More peace operations were fielded by the UN in the 1990s than in its entire previous history, with more countries taking part. The nature of UN operations also changed, with more complex demands and missions that were more intrusive into the affairs of host countries. Much of this was foreshadowed in 1992 by UN Secretary-General Boutros Boutros-Ghali's *An Agenda for Peace*, the first edition of which was prepared for the first ever meeting of the UN Security Council at the heads of state or government level on 31 January 1992. The Secretary-General set out to provide an 'analysis and recommendations on ways of strengthening and making more efficient within the framework and provisions of the Charter the capacity of the United Nations for preventive diplomacy, for peacemaking and for peace-keeping.'[27]

In the 1995 second edition of *An Agenda for Peace*, Boutros-Ghali noted the increased number of UN peace operations undertaken after the end of the Cold War and the qualitative difference in these missions—intervention in more intrastate than interstate conflicts. 'Of the five peace-keeping operations that existed in early 1988, four related to inter-state wars and only one (20 per cent of the total) to an intra-state conflict. Of the 21 operations established since then, only 8 have related to inter-state wars, whereas 13 (62 per cent) have related to intra-state conflicts. . . . Of the 11 operations established since January 1992, all but 2 (82 per cent) related to intra-state conflicts.'[28]

Intrastate conflicts present the kind of challenging operating environment first encountered by UN peacekeepers in the Congo. 'They are usually fought not only by regular armies but also by militias and armed civilians with little discipline and with ill-defined chains of command. They are often guerrilla wars without clear front lines. Civilians are the main victims and often the main targets. Humanitarian emergencies are commonplace and the combatant authorities, in so far as they can be called authorities, lack the capacity to cope with them.'[29] The major difference of operations in these less-defined environments requires UN forces to 'forfeit the consent of the parties, to behave in a way that was perceived to be partial and/or to use force other than in self-defense.'[30] In the wake of such increased complexity and particularly as soldiers come into closer contact with the local population, transparency, responsibility, and accountability issues were bound to arise.

[27] Boutros Boutros-Ghali, *An Agenda for Peace* (2nd edn, New York: UN Department of Public Information, 1995), 5.

[28] *Agenda for Peace*, 7–8.

[29] *Agenda for Peace*, 8–9.

[30] *Agenda for Peace*, 15.

V. Blended Accountability and Responsibility

The nature of internationally mandated operations, where organizations authorizing operations do not have troops of their own, is that they work in a blended system of accountability and responsibility. The starting point to understand transparency, accountability, and responsibility is to look at the command and control structures of UN operations. There are three general sources of direction: first, overall political direction, which belongs to the Security Council; secondly, executive direction and command, for which the Secretary-General is responsible; and, thirdly, command in the field, which is entrusted by the Secretary-General to the chief of mission (special representative or force commander/chief military observer).[31]

However, at no time do countries relinquish control of their troops as to discipline and code of conduct. Troop-contributing countries in fact were long considered to be the first and final lines of authority to deal with the conduct of their troops.[32] Troop-contributing countries have faced challenges when their forces are sent into missions that can change rapidly, for which they may not have prepared, and over which they have little control as to objectives and capabilities. This is made even more complicated because UN peacekeeping operations often rely on troops from countries other than the P5.[33]

Until 2000, many troop-contributing countries, once committed, were not part of any decision to deploy or redeploy their troops and were not even present at the operational briefings conducted for the UN Security Council. This creates further problems for countries with strong legislative bodies that also require information as to the nature, duration, and character of a military commitment. This operational reality has led international organizations, however, usually to provide broad authorization and approval, leaving specific direction to field commanders.

The type of mission raises different sets of transparency, accountability, and responsibility issues. In addition to thwarting cross-border aggression in Korea and Kuwait, the cases for which the doctrine of collective security was designed, UN missions now pursue objectives that were not envisaged when the League Covenant and UN Charter were signed. Among these objectives are: maintaining ceasefire agreements, preventing genocide and serious violations of human rights, and restoring a democratically elected government. As Boutros Boutros-Ghali wrote in 1995, many of

[31] *Agenda for Peace*, 16.

[32] See eg US Department of Defense Joint Publication 3–16, *Multinational Operations* (7 Mar 2007), x, that states: 'Forces participating in a multinational operation will always have at least two distinct chains of command: a national chain of command and a multinational chain of command.'

[33] Lists of troop-contributing countries are available at <http://www.un.org/en/peacekeeping/resources/statistics/contributors.shtml>.

the instances in which the UN deploys military forces involve intrastate rather than interstate conflicts. For missions supported and directed by the UN's Department of Peacekeeping Operations or its predecessor units, operations will be commanded by an individual appointed by and reporting to the UN Secretary-General. In the other cases, the UN might authorize states or coalitions of states to use military forces to achieve the goals specified in resolutions adopted by the Security Council. In these cases, the state or states conducting the operation will define their own command structures and are required to report to the Security Council on the conduct of the operations.[34] Such authorizations are typically renewed every six months to provide ongoing accountability to the international organization.

Accountability and responsibility will likely have to be established more than once at various stages of an operation, depending on its complexity and novelty. These stages can be seen as a series of questions. Is the international decision-making body the appropriate one to call for a particular action? How much latitude is allowed to states to define the conditions of their involvement? What standards of responsibility and accountability are needed to fulfil international and national requirements? Who is responsible for investigating and dealing with the misconduct of soldiers or harm to a population resulting from the presence of an international force?

Much of the practice for international operations is based on established domestic practices, including adherence to international humanitarian law on the conduct of war.

VI. Evolving National Accountability Mechanisms and the 2000 Report of the Panel on Peace Operations

Despite the novelty of pre-1990 peacekeeping operations, the consent of the conflicting parties and limited engagement with local populations meant that peacekeeping soldiers operated under less hostile conditions where their personal safety was concerned. Except for Korea and ONUC, traditional peacekeeping conducted with the consent of the host state contrasted sharply with the 1990s operations intended to enforce UN mandates and to protect safe zones and corridors for humanitarian relief. These placed UN forces in much less permissive environments. The higher the level of risk to the personnel, the higher the level of domestic scrutiny, particularly

[34] See eg US Department of Defense JP 3-16, *Multinational Operations*, ch II on multinational command structure.

in democratic countries, and demand for accountability in the country contributing the troops. Two prominent cases show how national systems have had to change in order to adapt to the requirements of these international operations.

A. Canada and UNITAF

In 1992, the Canadian Airborne Regiment (CAR) was deployed to Somalia as part of a coalition force, Unified Task Force (UNITAF), led by the US—a Chapter VII operation authorized by Security Council Resolution 794 to restore law and order in Somalia. Although Canadian troops had initially been assigned to support humanitarian relief operations in a more traditional peacekeeping role in another part of Somalia, Canada's view of itself as a country that supported UN operations led it to agree to their reassignment even though its troops were not trained for the level of violence and banditry they would face in the volatile area of Belet Huen. Up until the Somali operation, it was a badge of honour among Canadians that their armed forces had served in every UN mission from the inception of peacekeeping in 1956. There was a compelling desire to remain prominent in UN-mandated operations.

The misconduct of Canadian soldiers in Somalia became a problem not only for the UN mission, but also for Canada. The country subsequently undertook one of the most far-reaching reviews of its military training and force structures in its history. The specific event that triggered this prolonged period of public inquiry and recrimination was the revelation of the beating to death of a Somali youth by Canadian soldiers. These actions went against the good image Canadians had of their armed forces and created a political firestorm. A Commission of Inquiry conducted a sweeping investigation, but it was abruptly ended after two years by a government impatient to move on.[35] Despite this, the widespread public scrutiny of the Canadian military led by the Commission did result in major changes.

The CAR was disbanded and Canada took steps to break up traditional regiments and to de-emphasize regimental loyalty. It took note of the need for improved training both for its enlisted personnel and officers, particularly regarding the conditions and people they would encounter on the ground in international operations. The Inquiry found the lines of command and control blurred, troop discipline lacking, no assessment made of the suitability of deploying particular units into their assigned missions, and unclear rules of engagement.[36] It concluded that Canadian

[35] Commission on Inquiry into the Deployment of Canadian Forces to Somalia, 'Dishonored Legacy: The Lessons of the Somalia Affair', Minister of Public Works and Government Service, Ottawa, 1997; see also Donna Winslow and Christ Klep, 'The Public Inquiry into the Canadian Peace Mission in Somalia' in Hans Born and Heiner Hänggi (eds), *The 'Double Democratic Deficit': Parliamentary Accountability and the Use of Force Under International Auspices* (Farnham: Ashgate, 2004), 91–107.

[36] Commission of Inquiry at <http://www.dnd.ca/somalia/vol10/vos27e.htm>.

troops placed into the harsh operational conditions of Somalia were unable to respond appropriately.[37]

These findings, and substantial cuts in Canada's military budget since the 1990s, have made Ottawa more selective in deploying Canadian forces in international operations. Although formal parliamentary oversight over executive decisions to deploy forces may not have changed much in Canada since UNITAF, the problem remains an issue of public concern in an established democracy:

> Accountability is a principal mechanism for ensuring conformity to standards of action. In a free and democratic society, those exercising substantial power and discretionary authority must be answerable for all activities assigned or entrusted to them—in essence, for all activities for which they are responsible.[38]

Canada has remained active in developing specialized training in peacekeeping leadership and command and control.

B. The Netherlands and Srebrenica

The Bosnian town of Srebrenica was designated a safe area by Security Council Resolution 819 in April 1993, to be made safe from any armed attack or other hostile actions by forces in the ex-Yugoslavian conflict. United Nations Protection Force (UNPROFOR) troops were ordered to prevent attacks on the safe area. In 1995, the Dutch UNPROFOR battalion (Dutchbat) found itself under attack by an overwhelming Bosnian Serb force, but was ordered by the UN to assume blocking positions to prevent any further breakthrough into the safe area. NATO air support was expected, but did not materialize, in part because of concerns that the Bosnian Serb force would kill the Dutch battalion if air power were used. Srebrenica subsequently fell to Bosnian Serb forces and the Dutchbat commander was summoned to negotiate terms for the battalion's departure. According to the Dutch commander, it was expected that the Bosnian Muslim population that had sought shelter in the safe area would be allowed to evacuate 'voluntarily' and under UN military escort. As is now known, a massacre of nearly 8,000 Bosniaks occurred on the heels of the Dutch force's departure—6,000 or more as victims of mass executions.

As the scope of the killing was revealed, the consequences were severe not only for the UN, but also for the Netherlands. On the release of a Dutch government inquiry in 2002, the government of Prime Minister Wim Kok resigned. More than 15 years after Srebrenica, in 2011, a Dutch court of appeal decided that the Dutch government remains liable for the deaths of three Bosnian Muslim men, a decision that could lead to the eventual prosecution of the top commanders of the Dutch battalion. The court rejected the argument put forward by the Dutch government

[37] Commission of Inquiry at <http://www.dnd.ca/somalia/vol10/vos26e.htm>.

[38] Commission of Inquiry at <http://www.dnd.ca/somalia/vol10/vos26e.htm>.

that the state is not liable for acts committed by Dutchbat because they were acting under a UN mandate.[39]

A 2002 report published by the Netherlands Institute for War Documentation concluded that:

Dutch policy with regard to the former Yugoslavia was determined by two main factors. First, there was the desire to play a significant part in the international context. Second, there was the importance attached to human rights and humanitarian aid: moral politics. Apart from these two factors, there was no discernible direct national interest.[40]

Other factors that contributed to this tragedy were Dutchbat undertaking a mission with no clear mandate and no exit strategy, at a location described as a safe area without any understanding of what that meant. There was inadequate intelligence, including from the Canadian force that Dutchbat replaced, and a false belief that the UN leadership would use air power in the event of danger to Dutch forces and the local population.[41]

Prior to the Srebrenica tragedy, Dutch parliamentary involvement in sending troops to UN operations was minimal. Furthermore, as a middle power, the Netherlands was not included in the Contact Group[42] and other fora of the larger powers in determining policy with regard to the former Yugoslavia. Since Srebrenica, the Dutch have insisted on greater parliamentary involvement in decision-making on the deployment of troops and have amended their constitution accordingly.[43] Article 100 of the Dutch Constitution provides that 'the Government is to inform Parliament concerning the use or placing at the disposal [of an international organization] of armed forces for the maintenance or advancement of the international legal order. This includes the possible deployment of the military for humanitarian tasks in case of an armed conflict.'[44] This action follows the practice of the Scandinavian countries that enacted standing legislation to allow the participation of their troops in UN missions, but subject to further independent appraisal by each troop-contributing country on a case-by-case basis.[45]

[39] Srebrenica Appeal Decision, The Hague Court of Appeal (5 July 2011), LJN: BR0132, available at <http://www.rechtspraak.nl/ljn.asp?ljn=BR0132>.

[40] Netherlands Institute on War Documentation, Report on Srebrenica: A Safe Area available at <http://www.srebrenica.nl/en/menulinks.htm>, 5.

[41] Report on Srebrenica, 7.

[42] The Contact Group on Bosnia was organized in 1994 as an informal framework for negotiation after the failure of the combined efforts of the European Union, the Organization on Peace and Security in Europe, and the UN to get the warring parties to negotiate.

[43] It may be worth noting, however, that at the time there was widespread parliamentary support for the Dutch deployment to Srebrenica.

[44] Lori F. Damrosch, 'Trends in Executive and Legislative Powers' in Charlotte Ku and Harold K. Jacobson (eds), *Democratic Accountability and the Use of Force in International Law* (Cambridge: Cambridge University Press, 2002), 51.

[45] Damrosch, 'Trends in Executive and Legislative Powers' in Ku and Jacobson, *Democratic Accountability and the Use of Force in International Law*, 51.

c. Rwanda and the Failure of the International Community to Respond

In 1999, UN Secretary-General Kofi Annan appointed an independent inquiry into the actions of the UN during the 1994 genocide in Rwanda when approximately 800,000 people were killed between April and July. The Report of the Independent Inquiry into the Actions of the United Nations During the 1994 Genocide in Rwanda, issued in December 1999, pointed to the shortcomings of the UN itself as it struggled to adapt to the changing landscape of peace operations. It concluded that:

> The failure by the United Nations to prevent, and subsequently, to stop the genocide in Rwanda was a failure by the United Nations system as a whole. The fundamental failure was the lack of resources and political commitment devoted to developments in Rwanda and to the United Nations presence there. There was a persistent lack of political will by Member States to act, or to act with enough assertiveness. This lack of political will affected the response by the Secretariat and decision-making by the Security Council, but was also evident in the recurrent difficulties to get the necessary troops for the United Nations Assistance Mission for Rwanda (UNAMIR). Finally, although UNAMIR suffered from a chronic lack of resources and political priority, it must also be said that serious mistakes were made with those resources which were at the disposal of the United Nations.[46]

Rwanda was a turning point in UN peacekeeping. It came to symbolize a lack of will to commit to peacekeeping and, above all, to commit adequate resources and to take risks in the field. The Rwandan crisis occurred in the midst of the dramatically increased demand for peacekeeping troops after the end of the Cold War. As the UN report noted, 'by the second half of 1993, the enthusiasm for United Nations peacekeeping of previous years was on the wane among key member states, the capacity of the Secretariat, in particular the DPKO [Department of Peacekeeping Operations] to administer the approximately 70,000 peacekeepers wearing blue berets was overstretched, and several existing operations were facing severe difficulties.'[47] The UN was also facing financial constraints with over $1 billion in outstanding assessments in peacekeeping operations.

The problem, however, remained that the UN and its members felt an obligation to act in the face of genocide.[48] What all learned by 1999 was that operations based on such aspirations, but inadequately implemented, carried grave risks for both the populations in need of protection and those seeking to provide it.

[46] Report of the Independent Inquiry into the Actions of the United Nations during the 1994 Genocide in Rwanda, 15 Dec 1999 available at <http://www.un.org/News/ossg/rwanda_report.htm>, 1.

[47] UN report on Rwanda, 26.

[48] UN report on Rwanda, 34.

D. The Brahimi Report

The serious deficiencies revealed by these episodes in Somalia, Rwanda, and the Balkans indicated clearly that the improvisation and spirit of muddling through that had guided UN peace operations until 1990 were no longer adequate. There was a literally fatal weakness in complete reliance on national systems of accountability to ensure performance and oversight of troops put into situations for which they were ill-prepared and about which their governments were not fully informed or in control. Inattention to what was required had proven dangerous and deadly. This realization led to a review of UN peace and security operations convened in March 2000 by UN Secretary-General Kofi Annan, himself a former head of the UN's Department of Peacekeeping Operations, and led by Lakhdar Brahimi, the former foreign minister of Algeria.[49] The group was charged 'to present a clear set of specific, concrete and practical recommendations' to improve performance in this area.[50]

The Panel's recommendations were sweeping and direct with an initial observation that 'no amount of good intentions can substitute for the fundamental ability to project credible force if complex peacekeeping, in particular, is to succeed.'[51] The Panel concluded that:

> There are many tasks which the United Nations peacekeeping forces should not be asked to undertake, and many places they should not go. But when the United Nations does send its forces to uphold the peace, they must be prepared to confront the lingering forces of war and violence with the ability and determination to defeat them.[52]

The Panel further recommended that the UN regard headquarters support as a core activity of the organization to be funded through the UN's regular budget in place of the special funding that had to be made available each time an operation was authorized.[53] Finally, the Panel stressed the importance of 'clear, credible and adequately resourced Security Council mandates', and participation by troop-contributing states at briefings and discussions of the Security Council on issues related to the 'safety and security of mission personnel or to a change or reinterpretation of the mandate regarding the use of force.'[54]

On matters of responsibility and accountability, the Panel stressed 'the essential importance of the United Nations System adhering to and promoting international

[49] A/55/305–S/2000/809, Comprehensive review of the whole question of peacekeeping operations in all their aspects (21 Aug 2000) (the Brahimi Report). The report was prepared from more than 200 interviews with Permanent Missions of Member States, the Special Committee on Peacekeeping Operations, and personnel in peace and security-related departments at UN Headquarters in New York, the UN Office in Geneva, officials of the UN High Commissioner for Refugees, the World Bank, and peace operations.

[50] Transmittal Letter dated 21 Aug 2000 from the UN Secretary-General to the President of the UN Security Council and the President of the UN General Assembly. See A/55/305–S/2000/809.

[51] Brahimi Report, Executive Summary, viii.

[52] Brahimi Report, 1, para 1.

[53] Brahimi Report, Executive Summary, xiii.

[54] Brahimi Report, 1, para 6(b).

human rights instruments and international humanitarian law in all aspects of its peace and security activities.'[55] The Panel recommended the creation of a Lessons Learned Unit and the enhancement of support capacities of other UN programmes and institutions such as the UN High Commissioner for Human Rights. A final point to note from the Panel's report is the recognition that individuals at headquarters and in the field are to be held 'accountable for their performance, recognising that they need to be given commensurate responsibility, authority and resources to fulfill their assigned tasks.'[56] This included the need for a clear chain of command and unity of effort.

VII. Ramping up of International Responsibility

The Brahimi Report drew attention to the intricacies of what necessarily is a blended system of accountability and responsibility, given that decision-making at the strategic level to conduct an international operation has now generally shifted to an international or regional body. At the operational and tactical level, decision-making is often national or in the hands of an ad hoc coalition. However, this does not mean that the international organization mandating an operation does not bear its own share of responsibility both for the personnel serving in its missions and the people they aid and protect. Acknowledging the UN's own responsibility, UN Secretary-General Annan issued a Bulletin on Observance of International Humanitarian Law in 1999.[57] Taking a dramatic step away from the initial legal opinion provided by UN lawyers that the UN did not possess adequate capacity to undertake the obligations of international humanitarian law, the UN Secretary-General directed that UN forces act in compliance with any status of forces agreements and with full respect for the principles and rules of the general humanitarian law conventions applicable to the conduct of military personnel.[58] The UN also undertook to ensure that military personnel on UN-authorized missions were fully acquainted with the principles and rules of those international instruments and the obligation to comply with them regardless of whether or not a status of forces agreement exists.

[55] Brahimi Report, 1, para 6(e). [56] Brahimi Report, 1, para 6(k).

[57] ST/SGB/1999/13: Observance by United Nations Forces of International Humanitarian Law.

[58] Robert C. R. Siekmann, 'The Legal Responsibility of Military Personnel' in Ku and Jacobson, *Democratic Accountability and the Use of Force in International Law*, 109.

VIII. Personal Responsibility of UN Peacekeepers

Another area of development is that of the personal responsibility of UN peacekeepers. As 'experts on mission', UN peacekeepers are subject to the applicable laws of the host country. They are also protected by the 1994 Convention on the Safety of United Nations and Associated Personnel identifying them as non-combatants. The terms of this Convention necessarily exclude forces in Chapter VII enforcement actions when UN forces are engaged as combatants.[59] Despite the 1948 assassination of Bernadotte,[60] it was not until 1994 that the UN acknowledged that it could also become a target because of the positions it backed or the actions it took—even as a middleman. This was tragically underscored with the 2003 bombing of the UN headquarters in Baghdad that took the life of the UN's top envoy there, Sergio Vieira de Mello. The 1994 Convention imposes an obligation on the host country to protect UN personnel and property.[61] A 2005 Protocol amends the Convention also to cover operations (including non-governmental organization (NGO) operations) delivering humanitarian, political, or development assistance in peacebuilding, or delivering emergency humanitarian assistance.[62] None of these requirements replaces the troop-contributing countries' national responsibility for the conduct of their personnel. Nor do they replace host country obligations to do their utmost to provide for the safety of experts working on their territories.

The area of personal responsibility of troops has received particular attention since revelations of incidents of sexual exploitation and abuse by UN personnel including peacekeeping forces. The 2003 Bulletin on Special Measures for Protection from Sexual Exploitation and Sexual Abuse stipulates that any acts of sexual exploitation or sexual abuse committed by UN staff members or persons under contract to the UN 'constitute acts of serious misconduct and are therefore grounds for disciplinary measures, including summary dismissal.'[63] Since 2005, the UN has taken additional steps to address this problem by working with NGOs on creating complaint and response systems for complaints of sexual exploitation and abuse.[64] In 2007, the UN General Assembly adopted a new model Memorandum of

[59] Art 2, Convention on the Safety of United Nations and Associated Personnel 1994.

[60] See S/1005 (17 Sept 1948).

[61] Art 7 of the Convention on the Safety of UN and Associated Personnel.

[62] <http://untreaty.un.org/cod/avl/ha/csunap/csunap.html>.

[63] 2003 UN S-G Bulletin on Special Measures for Protection from Sexual Exploitation and Sexual Abuse (see <http://www.un.org.en/pseataskforce/achievements.shtml>).

[64] March 2005: Zeid Report: A comprehensive strategy to eliminate future sexual exploitation and abuse in United Nations Peacekeeping Operations, A/59/710.

Understanding between the UN and troop-contributing countries to cover sexual exploitation and abuse.[65]

The UN General Assembly further adopted a resolution on the individual criminal accountability of UN officials or experts on mission to address the extension of jurisdiction to cover criminal misconduct. The Assembly asked countries whose nationals are accused of wrongdoing to indicate what efforts have been undertaken 'to investigate and as appropriate, prosecute crimes of a serious nature, as well as the types of appropriate assistance states may wish to receive from the Secretariat for the purposes of such investigations and prosecutions.'[66] The UN has backed up this increased level of individual responsibility with materials setting out expectations as to standards of integrity and conduct and rules of personal conduct for UN peacekeepers.[67] These documents emphasize the professionalism of a soldier and the need to respect the population of a host country and its culture, traditions, customs, and practices.

IX. The Challenges of a Blended System of Transparency, Accountability, and Responsibility and the Ongoing Evolution of Peace Operations

In the wake of the attacks on the US on 11 September 2001 and the war in Iraq, the UN undertook a review of its security system to determine if the organization and the security framework created in 1945 remained relevant to the threats and concerns of the 21st century. UN Secretary-General Kofi Annan's Foreword to the report produced by the High-Level Panel on Threats, Challenges and Change summed up the key findings:

> I wholly endorse the report's core argument that what is needed is a comprehensive system of collective security: one that tackles both new and old threats, and addresses the security concerns of all states—rich and poor, weak and strong. Particularly important is the report's

[65] See <http://www.un.org/News/Press/docs/2007/gaspd368.doc.htm>.

[66] A/Res/62/63 (8 Jan 2008).

[67] See *We are United Nations Peacekeepers*, available at <http://www.un.org/en/peacekeeping/documents/un_inf.pdf> and *Ten Rules of Personal Conduct for Blue Helmets*, at <http://www.un.org/en/peacekeeping/documents/ten_in.pdf>.

insistence that today's threats to our security are all interconnected. We can no longer afford to see problems such as terrorism, or civil wars, or extreme poverty, in isolation. Our strategies must be comprehensive. Our institutions must overcome their narrow preoccupations and learn to work across the whole range of issues, in a concerted fashion.[68]

Addressing this new environment is a challenge for states, powerful and less powerful, as well as for institutions like the UN, for several reasons. The root causes of conflict can be complicated and may require costly and long involvement to correct. At the same time, the world is vulnerable as never before to the effects of conflict on an individual level because of the connections created by globalization. Individuals, as well as states, have ready access to weapons and technologies that can kill and destroy on a large scale. We have only to reflect on the challenges of piracy at sea, the desire to undertake mass killing by attacking subways and commercial aircraft, or the shelling of civilian populations to suppress uprisings to understand the nature of conflict today.

For all the new actors who may now be capable of igniting conflict and mass killing, the state remains the key actor to respond to security challenges. However, how the state responds has been steadily, but fundamentally, changed since the first modern efforts to regulate the use of force in the League of Nations Covenant. Collective security that was initially designed to constrain states has now become a necessity to address security threats because of the collective nature of those threats. The High-Level Panel on Threats, Challenges and Change noted that today's security challenges require 'Collective strategies, collective institutions and a sense of collective responsibility.'[69] Developments in internationally mandated operations since the creation of UNEF in 1956 show the progress that has been made not only in responding to new security challenges, but also in the adaptations that have taken place as the international community of international organizations, states, and NGOs works together. What we see is that all involved are changed by working together and that the sum of the parts is qualitatively different from the efforts of individual states or organizations.

It is now routine that an initial authorization or mandate be given by an international or regional body to undertake action. States respond and have adapted the organization of their armed forces to include service in international operations.[70] However, international institutions have only recently begun to develop accountability, transparency, and responsibility mechanisms. We have seen that necessity has compelled some level of compliance in the area of humanitarian law, but, as the Brahimi Report noted, such increased responsibility may work in the short run against transparency.[71] This does not imply that international institutions

[68] Report of the Secretary-General's High-Level Panel on Threats, Challenges and Change, 'A More Secure World: Our Shared Responsibility' (2004), vii.

[69] 'A More Secure World', 1.

[70] See eg US Department of Defense Joint Publication 3-16, *Multinational Operations*, ch II: Command and Coordination Relationships.

[71] Brahimi Report, paras 62 and 63.

and non-governmental actors do not have obligations to carry out their work in an accountable, transparent, and responsible manner. It only means that the three objectives may not always work consistently with each other and possibly even less so between international and national systems. This calls for a deeper understanding of the conceptual, operational, and legal relationship between international and national obligations, including host state obligations, in each of these areas. Given the unique nature of many international operations, no one answer will suffice, but given the number of operations and the level of experience now available, it might be possible to identify a range of such relationships.

So, although operationally we may have started to move beyond the 'muddling through' that characterized many early international operations, conceptually and legally, we are only beginning to understand the responsibility that is now shared by states and international and regional institutions as well as by NGOs. Transparency and accountability are not only important to the stakeholders of these institutions, but also vital for effective collective action and unity of effort. As the demand for and complexity of international operations increase, so will the need to develop greater conceptual, legal, and operational clarity as to how responsibility and accountability are shared and discharged by all parties concerned—the host country, the protected population, troop-contributing states, the international organization, and non-governmental humanitarian and other workers. The key problem is that international organizations can authorize action, but are much less equipped to direct action.

As we have learned, internationally mandated operations are not immune to attack by those opposed to any cessation of conflict or to personal misconduct by peacekeepers when working under dangerous and stressful conditions. More generally, we are only beginning to understand the implications of international operations in contributing to long-term peacemaking and the rebuilding of societies.[72] Effective collective action requires a common understanding of these shared duties that can then be adjusted as resource requirements or the nature of the mission changes. We have seen how inadequate attention to these requirements has led to poor and tragic outcomes. It should be no surprise that, as international operations have become more complex, the governing infrastructure needed to support these operations needs to change. Preliminary steps have been taken, but development of a coherent system of decision-making, shared responsibility, and accountability remains a work in progress.

[72] See eg Gugliermo Verdirame, *The UN and Human Rights: Who Guards the Guardians?* (Cambridge: Cambridge University Press, 2011).

CHAPTER 20

'FAILURES TO PROTECT' IN INTERNATIONAL LAW

ANDRÉ NOLLKAEMPER*

I. Introduction

Every new mass atrocity tends to provoke a critique of outside actors that failed to protect populations. Many observers are no longer content with condemning perpetrators and extend their moral outrage to bystanders who should have done more. Modern scholarship[1]

* The research leading to this chapter has received funding from the European Research Council under the European Union's Seventh Framework Programme (FP7/2007–2013)/ERC grant agreement no 249499, as part of the research project on Shared Responsibility in International Law (SHARES), carried out at the Amsterdam Center for International Law (ACIL) of the University of Amsterdam.

[1] eg Carla Bagnoli, 'Humanitarian Intervention as a Perfect Duty: A Kantian Argument' in Terry Nardin and Melissa S. Williams (eds), *Humanitarian Intervention. NOMOS XLVII* (New York: New York University Press, 2006); Susan C. Breau, 'The Impact of the Responsibility to Protect on Peacekeeping' (2006) 11 *Journal of Conflict & Security Law* 429; Luke Glanville, 'The Responsibility to Protect Beyond Borders' (2012) 12 *Human Rights Law Review* 1, 21 ('failure of the UN to prevent genocide'); Nick Grono, 'Briefing—Darfur: The International Community's Failure to Protect' (2006) 105 *African Affairs* 621; International Crisis Group, 'Darfur: The Failure to Protect', Africa Report No 89, 2005; Hitoshi Nasu, 'Operationalizing the "Responsibility to Protect" and Conflict Prevention: Dilemmas of Civilian Protection in Armed Conflict' (2009) 14 *Journal of Conflict & Security* 209, 235 ('failure to take action to protect civilians'); Hitoshi Nasu, 'The Responsibility to React? Lessons from the Security Council's Response to the Southern Lebanon Crisis of 2006' (2007) 14 *International Peacekeeping* 339 ('the Security Council's failure to react'); James Pattison, 'Legitimacy and Humanitarian Intervention: Who

and recent UN practice[2] are replete with such 'failures to protect critiques'.[3]

The shift of 'failures to protect-critiques' to include bystanders is a relatively recent phenomenon. Blame for the Armenian genocide, the Holocaust, the Cambodian crimes against humanity, and the mass killings in Uganda under Idi Amin was mainly attributed to perpetrators—even though outside actors could have made a difference by withdrawing support or by intervening.[4] In the wake of the Rwandan and Balkan atrocities in the 1990s, this has changed. While international law continues to place the primary responsibility to protect on the territorial state,[5] the blame for 'failures to protect' is now extended to outside actors. The emergence of the notion of 'responsibility to protect' has solidified this trend. Hardly any state is immune from a critique that it did not do enough in the face of a mass atrocity, if only because it did not allow the UN to respond effectively.

This discourse therefore construes mass atrocities as situations that result from a combination of acts by perpetrators and omissions by bystanders. Thus, the Rwandan genocide can only be understood if we consider not only the acts of individual perpetrators on the one hand, but also the role of Rwanda, the UN, its member states, and

Should Intervene?' (2008) 12 *International Journal of Human Rights* 395; Kok-Chor Tan, 'The Duty to Protect' in Nardin and Williams, *Humanitarian Intervention*, 84 ('failure to intervene to protect human rights'); Nsongurua J. Udombana, 'When Neutrality is a Sin: The Darfur Crisis and the Crisis of Humanitarian Intervention in Sudan' (2005) 27 *Human Rights Quarterly* 1149, 1172 ('the UNSC's "failure to perform the role assigned to it" '); Alex de Waal, 'Darfur and the Failure of the Responsibility to Protect' (2007) 83 *International Affairs* 1039; Jennifer M. Welsh and Maria Banda, 'International Law and the Responsibility to Protect: Clarifying or Expanding States' Responsibilities?' (2010) 2 *Global Responsibility to Protect* 213.

[2] See eg in relation to Srebrenica, UNGA 'Report of the Secretary-General pursuant to General Assembly Resolution 53/35: The Fall of Srebrenica' (15 Nov 1999), A/54/549, para 501; Rwanda: UNSC 'Letter dated 15 December 1999 from the Secretary-General addressed to the President of the Security Council' (16 Dec 1999) enclosing the 'Report of the Independent Inquiry into the Actions of the United Nations during the 1994 Genocide in Rwanda' (15 Dec 1999), S/1999/1257, 59; and Sri Lanka Report of the Secretary-General's Internal Review Panel on 'United Nations Action in Sri Lanka' (14 Nov 2012).

[3] The term 'protect' in the concept 'failure to protect' (indicating what should have been done) can stand for a wide variety of conduct, ranging from preventative acts (as in the prevention of genocide) to swift action when mass atrocities are carried out. In this respect, the term 'failure to protect' is the mirror image of 'responsibility to protect', and the wide variety of acts by which one can carry out that responsibility can each be translated as grounds for failure. What specifically had to be done to protect depends on the specifics and content of the obligation to protect that applies in a particular case.

[4] eg in the case of Uganda it could be argued that some of the atrocities could have been prevented if the main arms suppliers, which included Libya, the Soviet Union, and the German Democratic Republic, had withdrawn their support. See: on the support of the Idi Amin regime by Libya, Guy Arnold, *The A to Z of Civil Wars in Africa* (Plymouth: Scarecrow Press, 2008), 188; by the Soviet Union, Colin Legum, 'The Soviet Union, China and the West in Southern Africa' (1975) 54 *Foreign Affairs* 745, 749 and Dale C. Tatum, *Who Influenced Whom? Lessons from the Cold War* (Lanham, MD: University Press of America, 2002), 192; and by the German Democratic Republic, Gareth M. Winrow, *The Foreign Policy of the GDR in Africa* (Cambridge: Cambridge University Press, 1990), 141.

[5] World Summit Outcome Document, GA Res 60/1 (24 Oct 2005), A/RES/60/1, para 138.

especially France on the other.[6] Likewise, the genocide in Srebrenica is seen as a result of both the conduct of individual perpetrators and the Bosnian Serb Republic, and the acts and omissions of Serbia, the UN, its member states, in particular the Netherlands, and the North Atlantic Treaty Organization (NATO).[7] Similar analyses can be made for the atrocities committed in Sierra Leone and Liberia (1991–2002), Burundi (1972 and 1993), Darfur (from 2003 onwards), Sri Lanka (2009), and in Libya and Syria (2011–2012). Such situations would not have occurred were it not for the combination of acts and omissions of perpetrators and bystanders.

International law to a very limited extent, has followed the moral and political critiques of bystanders. In the past decades, international law has inched along in several respects and now has more to say to bystanders than, say, at the time of the Second World War. Indeed, international law now allows us to frame protection of populations as a shared responsibility of bystanders.[8]

However, from a legal perspective there is something disingenuous about applying a 'failure to protect-critique' in one stroke to both perpetrators and bystanders. While international law offers a firm basis for holding perpetrators (whether individuals or states) responsible, it treats bystanders radically differently. There may be good moral grounds for a judgement that a particular outside actor 'failed to protect',[9] but international law rarely offers a basis for an allocation of blame to individual bystanders.[10] This is unlikely to change in the near future. The failures to protect of bystanders are built in and to a large extent induced and legitimized by the international legal system. International law provides a framework for political debate on how this shared responsibility should be performed: who should protect, where, and when. But this framework allows individual bystanders to hide behind a failing political process and to escape individual responsibility for failures to protect.[11]

[6] See on the role of the UN, inter alia, Carlsson Commission, 'Report of the Independent Inquiry into the Actions of the United Nations During the 1994 Genocide in Rwanda' (15 Dec 1999), S/1999/1257, 3; Michael Barnett, *Eyewitness to a Genocide. The United Nations and Rwanda* (Ithaca, NY: Cornell University Press, 2002). See on the role of France, Andrew Wallis, *Silent Accomplice: The Untold Story of France's Role in the Rwandan Genocide* (London: I. B. Tauris, 2007).

[7] André Nollkaemper, 'Multi-Level Accountability: A Case Study of Accountability in the Aftermath of the Srebrenica Massacre' in Yuval Shany and Tomer Broude (eds), *The Shifting Allocation of Authority in International Law. Considering Sovereignty, Supremacy and Subsidiarity* (Portland, OR: Hart, 2008).

[8] See generally on the concept of 'shared responsibility', André Nollkaemper and Dov Jacobs, 'Shared Responsibility in International Law: A Conceptual Framework' (2013) 34 *Michigan Journal of International Law* 359.

[9] James Pattison, *Humanitarian Intervention and the Responsibility to Protect: Who Should Intervene?* (Oxford: Oxford University Press, 2010).

[10] With the exception of Serbia's fate in the Genocide case (*Application of the Convention on the Prevention and Punishment of the Crime of Genocide (Bosnia and Herzegovina v. Serbia and Montenegro)*, Judgment, ICJ Rep 2007, 43), we have not seen any successful claims against outside actors who failed to protect.

[11] In this respect the main argument of the chapter is comparable, and supported by, the argument by Scott Veitch, *Law and Irresponsibility: On the Legitimation of Human Suffering* (Abingdon: Routledge, 2007).

This chapter provides a critical review of the failure to protect-critique of bystanders.[12] It proceeds in four parts. Section II discusses the very limited degree to which international law provides a basis for holding individual bystander states responsible for a failure to protect, and explains that international law in fact discourages and, in essential respects, precludes individual action to respond to mass atrocities. Individual bystanders are to remain just that (even though they can, of course, protest and undertake other diplomatic action). Section III discusses the failure to protect-critique of international organizations, notably the UN. While one can argue that the shared responsibility to protect should be performed by the UN—and the distinct responsibilities of the UN in principle make it an easier target of failure to protect-critiques—the basis of the obligation is similarly weak; Section IV discusses how, as a result, international law allows states and international organizations to 'pass the buck' and hide behind other bystanders. The concluding Section V construes the failure to protect-critique as a critique of the political process within the parameters set by international law, rather than as a critique of the non-performance of individual obligations.

II. Bystander States

By and large, international law protects bystander states from a legal critique that they failed to protect a population in a foreign state. International law supports blaming both individual perpetrators and commanders, as well as the states to which their acts can be attributed. It is only in rather exceptional situations that a bystander state can become responsible for failing to act on the basis of a breach of an obligation to protect. Otherwise, omissions would be legally irrelevant. Critically, a mere omission to act cannot, as explained by the International Court of Justice (ICJ) in the *Genocide* case, result in responsibility based on complicity.[13]

[12] The chapter limits itself to failures to protect from mass atrocities, in particular those that can be qualified as genocide, crimes against humanity, and large-scale war crimes, rather than protection of all types of other human rights abuses. While there is nothing to prevent use of the term failure to protect in relation to incidental abuses or killings, it is in particular in relation to this more limited category of mass atrocities that the phrase 'failures to protect' has been used. In this respect, the concept of failures to protect is the mirror image of responsibility to protect. See General Assembly, 'Report of the Secretary-General', 'Early Warning, Assessment and the Responsibility to Protect' (2010), A/64/864; Jann K. Kleffner, 'The Scope of the Crimes Triggering the Responsibility to Protect' in Julia Hoffmann and André Nollkaemper, *Responsibility to Protect. From Principle to Practice* (Amsterdam: Amsterdam University Press, 2012), 85.

[13] *Application of the Convention on the Prevention and Punishment of the Crime of Genocide*, Judgment, para 432.

This section will explore these situations, distinguishing between states exercising jurisdiction in the state where mass atrocities take place (Section II.A), states that by virtue of their influence over perpetrators may have had to offer protection (Section II.B), and other bystander states (Section II.C). It then will explain that international law, rather than compelling action by individual bystander states, justifies and, to a large extent, requires inaction (Section II.D).

A. States Exercising Extraterritorial Jurisdiction

Bystander states that exercise jurisdiction in a territory where atrocities take place may, in particular situations, be responsible for failing to act. This covers situations such as Iraq or Afghanistan where third states, whether or not legitimized by the UN, exercised some form of authority during a period of continuing atrocities. Their presence may trigger obligations to protect under human rights and humanitarian law.[14] This category will also encompass states that occupy, whether or not based on a UN mandate, the territory of another state in which mass atrocities take place.[15] Such states may exercise (extraterritorial) jurisdiction over persons they have detained,[16] or over persons in respect of which they exercise 'public powers normally to be exercised by a sovereign government'.[17]

However, the scope of the obligation to protect of these states will be limited and will correspond to the extent of the exercise of jurisdiction. They will not generally provide a basis for claims that the state should have protected persons against mass atrocities, beyond the area where it exercises jurisdiction. For instance, while there were good grounds for arguing that the Netherlands failed to protect individuals that it had actively deported from its compound from Srebrenica,[18] it was

[14] Although both bodies of law are generally only in limited instances applicable in cases of extraterritorial jurisdiction. See for human rights law, eg Fons Coomans and Menno T. Kamminga (eds), *Extraterritorial Application of Human Rights Treaties* (Antwerp: Intersentia, 2004); Virginia Mantouvalou, 'Extending Judicial Control in International Law: Human Rights Treaties and Extraterritoriality' (2005) 9 *International Journal of Human Rights* 147; Alexander Orakhelashvili, 'Restrictive Interpretation of Human Rights Treaties in the Recent Jurisprudence of the European Court of Human Rights' (2003) 14 *European Journal of International Law* 529; Marko Milanovic, *Extraterritorial Application of Human Rights Treaties: Law, Principles and Policy* (Oxford: Oxford University Press, 2011).

[15] *Armed Activities on the Territory of the Congo (Democratic Republic of the Congo v. Uganda)*, Judgment, ICJ Rep 2005, 116, paras 172–80 (determining that Uganda had an obligation to protect in parts of the Congo that Uganda occupied). See also Dieter Fleck, *The Handbook of International Humanitarian Law* (2nd edn, Oxford: Oxford University Press, 2008), 280; Monica Hakimi, 'State Bystander Responsibility' (2010) 21 *European Journal of International Law* 341, 378.

[16] eg *Al-Skeini and Others v. UK* (App no 55721/07), ECtHR, 7 July 2011.

[17] *Al-Skeini and Others v. UK* (App no 55721/07), ECtHR 7 July 2011, para 149.

[18] Netherlands, The Hague Court of Appeal, *Nuhanović v. Netherlands* (5 July 2011), LJN: BR0133; ILDC 1742 (NL 2011); Bèrénice Boutin, 'Responsibility of the Netherlands for the Acts of Dutchbat in Nuhanović and Mustafić: The Continuous Quest for a Tangible Meaning for "Effective Control" in the Context of Peacekeeping' (2012) 25 *Leiden Journal of International Law* 521.

much harder to argue that the Netherlands did not accord protection to all 7,000 Bosnian men who were killed in Srebrenica—after all, these persons were not under the jurisdiction of the Netherlands.[19]

The situation of an occupying state is comparable: the scope of the obligation is in principle limited to the area where the occupying state exercises control. The ICJ suggested that occupying states are required to uphold, in the areas that they occupy, not only the human rights treaties to which they themselves are party to, but also the human rights treaties to which the occupied state is a party as well as customary human rights law.[20] In situations where one or more states occupy an entire territory (eg Iraq when it was occupied by the US and the UK), such obligations may indeed give rise to a failure to protect-critique. However, it is also true that the typical situations of mass atrocities that have given rise to failure to protect-critiques do not arise in situations of occupation.[21] That certainly holds true outside the areas where an occupying state exercises control.

B. Influential Bystander States

It is now commonly held that the fact that some bystander states have the capacity to exert influence over perpetrators may trigger obligations to protect. The legal basis for that proposition is provided by the ICJ which, in the *Genocide* case,[22] held that states which do not exercise jurisdiction, or otherwise have a presence, in a state in which mass atrocities occur, can nonetheless have an obligation to prevent genocide, and can be responsible for failing to perform that obligation. Surely a failure to perform an obligation to prevent is to 'fail to protect'.

[19] Netherlands, Supreme Court, *Stichting Mothers of Srebrenica v. Netherlands and United Nations* (13 Apr 2012), Final appeal judgment, LJN: BW1999; ILDC 1760 (NL 2012) (the Mothers of Srebrenica claimed that the Netherlands was partly responsible for the fall of the safe area in Srebrenica and the consequences thereof, namely the murder of their family members and their loss of property).

[20] *Legal Consequences of the Construction of a Wall in the Occupied Palestinian Territory*, Advisory Opinion, ICJ Rep 2004, 136, paras 102–14.

[21] It should be added that even within areas under their jurisdiction, the scope of obligations will be relatively limited. As noted by the UK House of Lords in *Al Skeini*, occupation does not necessarily give the occupying force sufficient control to secure the wide range of protections provided by the European Convention on Human Rights (ECHR); see *Al-Skeini and Others v. Secretary of State (Consolidated Appeals)* [2007] UKHL 26, paras 82–3.

[22] *Case Concerning the Application of the Convention on the Prevention and Punishment of the Crime of Genocide (Bosnia and Herzegovina v. Serbia and Montenegro)*, Judgment, ICJ Rep 2007, 43; Mark Gibney, 'Universal Duties: the Responsibility to Protect, the Duty to Prevent (Genocide) and Extraterritorial Human Rights Obligations' (2011) 3 *Global Responsibility to Protect* 123; Andrea Gattini, 'Breach of the Obligation to Prevent and Reparation Thereof in the ICJ's Genocide Judgment' (2007) 18 *European Journal of International Law* 695; Paola Gaeta, 'On What Elements Can a State Be Held Responsible for Genocide?' (2007) 18 *European Journal of International Law* 631; Marko Milanovic, 'State Responsibility for Genocide: A Follow-Up' (2007) 18 *European Journal of International Law* 669; William A. Schabas, 'Genocide and the International Court of Justice: Finally, a Duty to Prevent the Crime of Crimes' (2007) 4 *International Studies Journal* 17.

The Court was somewhat ambiguous as to which states would fall into this category. In one particular instance, it stated that: 'The obligation to prevent the commission of the crime of genocide is imposed by the Genocide Convention on any State party which, in a given situation, has it in its power to contribute to restraining in any degree the commission of genocide.'[23] It therefore suggested that not all states are under such an obligation, only those states that have the influence or otherwise the capacity to avert genocide.

Elsewhere, the Court suggested that capacity was not so much a trigger for an obligation to prevent, but rather a criterion for the assessment of the performance of that obligation. The Genocide Convention imposes an obligation upon *all states parties* 'to employ all means reasonably available to them, so as to prevent genocide so far as possible.'[24] Whether a state had discharged its obligation would then depend on its capacity to effectively influence the actions of persons likely to commit, or already committing, genocide.[25] That capacity would, in turn, depend on the geographical distance of the state concerned from the events, and on the strength of political links, as well as links of all other types, between the authorities of that state and the main actors in the events.[26] However, the apparent absence of any practice in terms of legal claims in cases of genocide, casts doubt on the support for this construction by states parties. It is doubtful whether we can say that *all* states are legally bound to prevent genocide wherever it occurs, and to employ to that end 'all means reasonably available to them so as to prevent genocide, as far as possible', and that failure to do so would entail for them a secondary international obligation to make reparation for breach of an international obligation.[27]

Also if we adopt the former, more limited, construction, the criterion of 'capacity to influence effectively the actions of persons likely to commit, or already committing, genocide' in principle allows for a much wider category of states subject to a failure to protect-critique than the category of states that exercise extraterritorial jurisdiction. The criterion employed by the Court makes it implausible that only one of a few states could be singled out for that purpose. The Court indeed recognized

[23] *Application of the Convention on the Prevention and Punishment of the Crime of Genocide*, Judgment, para 461.

[24] *Application of the Convention on the Prevention and Punishment of the Crime of Genocide*, Judgment, para 430.

[25] See on capacity as a foundation for an actor's role in protection (and thus also as a normative basis for condemnation for failures to protect): Anne Orford, *International Authority and the Responsibility to Protect* (Cambridge: Cambridge University Press, 2011), 16; James Pattison, 'Assigning Humanitarian Intervention and the Responsibility to Protect' in Hoffmann and Nollkaemper, *Responsibility to Protect*, 176; Jennifer M. Welsh and Maria Banda, 'International Law and the Responsibility to Protect: Clarifying or Expanding States' Responsibilities?' (2010) 2 *Global Responsibility to Protect* 213, 218–19; David Miller, 'The Responsibility to Protect Human Rights', Working Paper Series SJ006, Department of Politics and International Relations, University of Oxford, May 2007, 2–13.

[26] *Application of the Convention on the Prevention and Punishment of the Crime of Genocide*, Judgment, para 430.

[27] Daphna Shraga, 'The Security Council and Human Rights—from Discretion to Promote to Obligation to Protect' in Bardo Fassbender (ed), *Securing Human Rights: Achievements and Challenges of the UN Security Council* (Oxford: Oxford University Press, 2011), 11, 28.

the possibility that the combined efforts of several states, each complying with its obligation to prevent, might have achieved the result—averting the commission of genocide—which the efforts of only one state were insufficient to produce.[28] But it is not easy to determine which states could then be singled out for a failure to protect-critique. The criterion of geographical distance may be limiting, but that is not true for the criterion of 'strength of political links'. In many situations of mass atrocities, powerful actors like China, Russia, the US, or even the European Union could, depending on the case, not easily be excluded from this group. This possible extension casts serious doubt on the question whether capacity can be a workable criterion as a ground for obligations to protect.[29] A narrower criterion would be that a state 'may have to restrain external actors if it substantially enables them to violate rights'.[30] However, this is not what the Court said, and the Court's judgment opens the possibility for a wider group of potentially responsible actors.

It has been argued that the obligation to protect outside the relevant territory could extend to other 'responsibility to protect' crimes—such as war crimes, crimes against humanity, and ethnic cleansing[31]—which could potentially expand the network of actors covered by the category. However, the basis of this is not obvious. The concept of responsibility to protect in itself cannot fill the gap as it does not provide an independent legal basis. Furthermore, neither human rights law nor humanitarian law provide a comparable basis for targeting influential states.[32]

The net result is, if we accept the expansive interpretation of the Court, that it is only for the crime of genocide that bystander states can as a matter of law be the subject of a failure to protect-critique. However, the category of states to which this critique can be applied is rather ill-defined. The ambiguity of the criterion formulated by the Court makes it difficult to single out responsible states and invites a certain amount of buck-passing.[33]

c. Other bystander states

For situations not covered by the obligations discussed in the two preceding sections, it will be even more difficult to single out individual states which can be subject to a failure to protect-critique. International law is not entirely silent on such situations. In the *Wall* advisory opinion, the ICJ identified obligations that apply to all bystander states, and that are potentially relevant in situations of mass atrocities. The Court suggested that 'all States parties to the Fourth Geneva Convention

[28] Glanville, 'The Responsibility to Protect Beyond Borders', 17.

[29] Hakimi, 'State Bystander Responsibility', 356 (assigning the obligation primarily on the basis of capacity would be untenable).

[30] Hakimi, 'State Bystander Responsibility', 366–7.

[31] Glanville, 'The Responsibility to Protect Beyond Borders', 28.

[32] See Section IV.

[33] See further Section IV.

relative to the Protection of Civilian Persons in Time of War of 12 August 1949 have... the obligation... to ensure compliance by Israel with international humanitarian law as embodied in that Convention.'[34] It also stated that it is for all states 'to see to it that any impediment, resulting from the construction of the wall, to the exercise by the Palestinian people of its right to self-determination is brought to an end.'[35] Although made in the context of self-determination, the second statement seems to be a more general consequence of a breach of *erga omnes* obligations. The International Law Commission (ILC) indeed formulated a broader obligation to cooperate in relation to serious breaches of obligations under peremptory norms.[36]

Three comments are in order. First, in state practice there is little or no support for the proposition that states that do not act in the face of violations of the Geneva Conventions in and by a third state are responsible.[37] In this respect, the legal implications of the first statement of the Court appear to be very limited.

Secondly, in relation to a possible wider obligation to bring an end to violations of peremptory norms, there is no hint of state practice or *opinio juris* in relation to events in, for instance, Darfur or Syria, to suggest that any state that did not act to protect persons from mass atrocities would commit an internationally wrongful act. While responsibility to protect (R2P) presupposes some underlying obligations,[38] in itself it does not create obligations for all states, as a matter of law.[39] In this respect, Alvarez's observation that it would be 'absurdly premature'[40] for the UN to be liable in law for

[34] *Legal Consequences of the Construction of a Wall in the Occupied Palestinian Territory*, Advisory Opinion, para 159; see also Giorgio Gaja, 'Do States Have a Duty to Ensure Compliance with Obligations *Erga Omnes* by Other States?' in Maurizio Ragazzi (ed), *International Responsibility Today: Essays in Memory of Oscar Schachter* (Leiden: Martinus Nijhoff, 2005), 32–3.

[35] *Legal Consequences of the Construction of a Wall in the Occupied Palestinian Territory*, Advisory Opinion, para 159.

[36] Art 41 of the Articles on the Responsibility of States for Intentionally Wrongful Acts (ARISWA), in Report of the International Law Commission to the General Assembly on its Fifty-Third Session, 56 UN GAOR Supp No 10, at 1, 43, A/56/10 (2001), reprinted in *Yearbook of the International Law Commission*, 2001, vol II (2), 20. See generally, Nina H. B. Jørgensen, 'The Responsibility to Protect and the Obligations of States and Organisations under the Law of International Responsibility' in Hoffmann and Nollkaemper, *Responsibility to Protect*, 125.

[37] See eg Carlo Focarelli, 'Common Article 1 of the 1949 Geneva Conventions: A Soap Bubble?' (2010) 21 *European Journal of International Law* 125; Frits Kalshoven, 'The Undertaking to Respect and Ensure Respect in All Circumstances: From Tiny Seed to Ripening Fruit' (1999) 2 *Yearbook of International Humanitarian Law* 3, 60 (Art 1 'cannot be said to impose upon states a legal obligation to act against other states that fail in their respect of the Convention').

[38] Indeed, the change from the original International Commission on Intervention and State Sovereignty (ICCIS) Report, *The Responsibility to Protect* (Ottawa: International Development Research Centre, 2001) to the World Summit Outcome Document, GA Res 60/1 (24 Oct 2005), A/RES/60/1, with the limitation to the four 'core crimes', can be seen as a distinct legalization of the principle.

[39] See for discussion of moral philosophical foundations, James Pattison, 'Assigning Humanitarian Intervention and the Responsibility to Protect' in Hoffmann and Nollkaemper, *Responsibility to Protect*, 173; Jennifer M. Welsh, 'The Responsibility to Protect and Humanitarian Intervention' in Hoffmann and Nollkaemper, *Responsibility to Protect*, 185.

[40] José E. Alvarez, 'The Schizophrenias of R2P' in Philip Alston and Euan Macdonald (eds), *Human Rights, Intervention and the Use of Force* (New York: Oxford University Press, 2008), 282.

failing to act in the face of the Rwandan genocide, applies more generally to claims that all states could be responsible for failing to protect people from mass atrocities.

Thirdly, while the wording of the ICJ and the ILC does not exclude individual conduct, it seems to emphasize cooperation rather than unilateral action (if only because that would be more effective).[41] The basis for claims against individual bystander states faced with mass atrocities remains weak, if it exists at all, and such obligations would make it easy for states to point to each other so as to explain why nothing was done. Rather than providing for individual obligations, the obligation to cooperate supports a political process in order to respond to mass atrocities, in particular within the framework of the UN (see further Section V).

D. Justifying inaction

The mere fact that international law provides a basis for failure to protect-critiques of individual states, only in rare situations does not in itself mean that such states are not empowered to act. International law allows third states a variety of means to respond to mass atrocities, and many states (in particular the US and those in Western Europe) have made wide use of such powers. States that do not use the powers to act that international law allows them, may still be subject to a failure to protect-critique, even though such a critique would not then translate into a claim of international responsibility.

However, international law severely restricts the means to which bystander states can resort. While all states may (and many states do) protest against mass atrocities in other states, international law largely denies states the means to take effective action. Three such (related) limitations are particularly relevant.

First, international law limits the right to take countermeasures against states engaged in mass atrocities to 'lawful' measures'. As the Commentary to Article 54 ARISWA notes, at present 'there appears to be no clearly recognized entitlement of States referred to in article 48 to take countermeasures in the collective interest.'[42]

Secondly, the principle of non-intervention remains a formidable barrier for third states seeking to respond to mass atrocities in other states—such as when they seek to support an opposition against an oppressive state that is believed to be engaging in mass atrocities.[43] In the cases of Libya and Syria, several states seem to have explored and pushed the limits set by the principle of supporting the opposition,

[41] *Yearbook of the International Law Commission*, 2001, vol II (2), 114; James Crawford, *The International Law Commission's Articles on State Responsibility. Introduction, Text and Commentaries* (Cambridge: Cambridge University Press, 2002), 249; Gaja, 'Do States Have a Duty to Ensure Compliance with Obligations *Erga Omnes* by Other States?' in Ragazzi, *International Responsibility Today*, 34.

[42] Para 6 of the Commentary to Art 54 of the ARISWA.

[43] Generally Maziar Jamnejad and Michael Wood, 'The Principle of Non-Intervention' (2009) 22 *Leiden Journal of International Law* 345.

but the principle of non-intervention remains a powerful argument against the legality of such action, and in effect legitimizes inaction of bystanders.

Thirdly, international law precludes the use of force as a unilateral response to mass atrocities. This restriction is critical, as in most cases that we tend to characterize as failures to protect it would seem that only a threat or use of force could have resulted in actual protection.[44] By disallowing such use of force outside the context of the UN, international law justifies states to remain inactive. The debates in the UN concerning the responsibility to protect have made it clear that there is no emerging consensus among states to grant such a power to engage in forceful action in non-consenting states with a view to protecting the population in those states.[45] Though the idea that outsiders have a moral entitlement to intervene has a long pedigree, in particular in the form of the just war doctrine,[46] which sometimes takes the form of a (moral) *duty* to intervene,[47] and though some states do claim a right of humanitarian intervention[48] and some commentators find support in the R2P doctrine for such a right,[49] international law continues to ban (and for good reasons—notably to prevent the risk of abuse) [50] the use of force by individual states

[44] Daniel Jonah Goldhagen, *Worse than War: Genocide, Eliminationism, and the Ongoing Assault on Humanity* (New York: Public Affairs, 2009).

[45] The Outcome Document confines the right to use force to the Security Council (see para 139) and contains no trace of recognition of a right of individual states, or other international organizations, to use force for humanitarian purposes.

[46] Mark Evans (ed), *Just War Theory. A Reappraisal* (Edinburgh: Edinburgh University Press, 2005); Michael Walzer, *Just and Unjust Wars: A Moral Argument With Historical Illustrations* (4th edn, New York: Basic Books, 2006).

[47] Richard J. Regan, *Just War. Principles and Cases* (Washington DC: The Catholic University of America Press, 1996), 6, 17. See also Tan, 'The Duty to Protect' in Nardin and Williams, *Humanitarian Intervention*, 84; Carla Bagnoli, 'Humanitarian Intervention as a Perfect Duty: A Kantian Argument' in Nardin and Williams, *Humanitarian Intervention*, 118 ('there is a strict moral duty to intervene when fundamental rights are violated').

[48] See the coalition agreement of the Dutch cabinet 'Rutte II', which states that 'for a contribution to international crisis management operations, either a mandate in accordance with international law is required or there should be a humanitarian emergency situation. Requests in this regard will be considered in the light of our international responsibility and our national interests' (author's own translation). This agreement is available at <http://www.rijksoverheid.nl/regering/regeerakkoord/nederland-in-de-wereld>.

[49] Alicia L. Bannon, 'The Responsibility to Protect: the UN World Summit and the Question of Unilateralism' (2006) 115 *Yale Law Journal* 1157, 1164.

[50] Alex J. Bellamy and Nicholas J. Wheeler, 'Humanitarian Intervention in World Politics' in John Baylis, Steve Smith, and Patricia Owens (eds), *The Globalization of World Politics: An Introduction to International Relations* (5th edn, Oxford: Oxford University Press, 2008), 514; Burleigh Wilkins, 'Humanitarian Intervention: Some Doubts' in Aleksander Jokic (ed), *Humanitarian Intervention, Moral and Philosophical Issues* (Toronto: Broadview Press Ltd, 2003), 38; Clara Portela, 'Humanitarian Intervention, NATO and International Law. Can the Institution of Humanitarian Intervention Justify Unauthorized Action?', Research Report 00.4, Berlin Information Center for Transatlantic Security, Berlin, 2000, 16–17; Jonathan E. Davis, 'From Ideology to Pragmatism: China's Position on Humanitarian Intervention in the Post-Cold War Era' (2001) 44 *Vanderbilt Journal of Transnational Law* 217, 223.

or international organizations other than the UN.[51] It makes little sense to criticize states for not using powers that they do not have.[52]

It follows that international law not only provides no more than a thin basis for failure to protect-critiques of individual states, but fundamentally supports and legitimizes individual bystanders to remain bystanders.

III. The United Nations

Compared to individual states, the UN is a much more likely target for a failure to protect-critique in cases of mass atrocities. The Security Council's responsibility for the maintenance of peace and security, combined with the modern interpretation of seeing mass atrocities in terms of threats to peace and security,[53] automatically draws the Council into the network of actors that are expected to act in cases of mass atrocities and that will be subject to failure to protect-critiques when they do not do so.[54]

However, as in the case of individual states, failures to protect will rarely translate into a legal claim against the organization. The provision of the UN Charter, combined with the rules of human rights law, humanitarian law, and the Genocide Convention that may be applicable to the UN, primarily provide a framework for political debate over whether and when to intervene, rather than a basis for international responsibility in the case of inaction. I will explore this basis both with regard to the Security Council (Section III.A) and peacekeeping operations (Section III.B).

A. The Security Council

The record of the Council in relation to mass atrocities has not always been a good one. There have been ample examples where a moral or political 'failure to protect-critique'

[51] I will leave aside here the possible role of the General Assembly under the Uniting for Peace procedure. See generally, GA Res 377 A (V) 'Uniting for Peace' (3 Nov 195), A/RES/377(V) A; Christina Tomuschat, 'Uniting for Peace', UN Audiovisual Library of International Law, 2008, available at <http://untreaty.un.org/cod/avl/pdf/ha/ufp/ufp_e.pdf>; Dominik Zaum, 'The Security Council, the General Assembly, and War: The Uniting for Peace Resolution' in Vaughan Lowe et al (eds), *The United Nations Security Council and War The Evolution of Thought and Practice since 1945* (Oxford: Oxford University Press, 2008).

[52] But see the assumption of powers in the Constitutive Act of the African Union (adopted 11 July 2000, entered into force in 2001) 2158 UNTS 3, Art 4; Ademola Abass, 'The African Union and the Responsibility to Protect. Principles and Limitations' in Hoffmann and Nollkaemper, *Responsibility to Protect*, 213.

[53] Shraga, 'The Security Council and Human Rights' in Fassbender, *Securing Human Rights*, 11–14.

[54] UN Charter, Art 24.

is appropriate.[55] Its failures in respect of Srebrenica[56] and Rwanda are well documented.[57] As Shraga notes, while criminal responsibility for the genocides in Rwanda and Srebrenica, and for the crimes against humanity in Darfur, was that of the Hutus, the Bosnian-Serbs, and the Janjaweed militia supported by the government of Sudan, respectively, it was largely facilitated by the Security Council, which was unwilling to engage, or to engage with, decisive force.[58]

In such situations, there may also be grounds for a legal failure to protect-critique. The Charter gives the Council the responsibility for maintenance of international peace and security,[59] and the Council is bound by obligations resting on the UN.[60] The UN as an international organization with legal personality is bound by obligations under general international law pertaining to the protection of persons from mass atrocities.[61] To the extent that we accept the obligation to prevent genocide as an obligation under customary law, this would also bind the Council.[62] In the *Genocide* case, the ICJ did not express itself on the customary nature of the obligation to prevent genocide and it seems very doubtful that such an obligation could be construed on the basis of existing practice. However, if the obligation to prevent is read into the obligation not to commit, as the Court did,[63] and if that latter obligation is to be construed as an obligation under customary international law,[64] it would seem that the Council could indeed be

[55] See the overview in Victoria Holt, Glyn Taylor, and Max Kelly, 'Protecting Civilians in the Context of UN Peacekeeping Operations, Successes, Setbacks and Remaining Challenges', Independent study commissioned by the Department of Peacekeeping Operations and the Office for the Coordination of Humanitarian Affairs, 17 Nov 2009, 211.

[56] Shraga, 'The Security Council and Human Rights' in Fassbender, *Securing Human Rights*, 16.

[57] SC Res 912 (21 Apr 1994), S/RES/912, para 8; Shraga, 'The Security Council and Human Rights' in Fassbender, *Securing Human Rights*, 27.

[58] Shraga, 'The Security Council and Human Rights' in Fassbender, *Securing Human Rights*, 16.

[59] Leland M. Goodrich, Edvard Hambro and Ann P. Simons, *Charter of the United Nations: Commentary and Documents* (3rd edn, New York: Cambridge University Press, 1969), 203.

[60] Generally on UN Security Council obligations, see August Reinisch, 'Developing Human Rights and Humanitarian Law: Accountability of the Security Council for the Imposition of Economic Sanctions' (2001) 95 *American Journal of International Law* 851, 855–7. Footnotes in this excerpt are also copied from Reinisch. See also Finnur Magnússon, 'Targeted Sanctions and Accountability of the United Nations Security Council' (2008) 13 *Austrian Review of International and European Law* 35; Marcelo G. Kohen, 'There is No Need to Change the Composition of the Security Council: It Is Time for Stressing Accountability' in Laurence Boisson de Chazournes and Marcelo G. Kohen, *International Law and the Quest for its Implementation* (Leiden: Martinus Nijhoff, 2010), 85.

[61] Anne Peters, 'The Security Council's Responsibility to Protect' (2001) 8 *International Organizations Law Review* 15; Elias Davidsson, 'The Security Council's Obligations of Good Faith' (2003) 14 *Florida Journal of International Law* 541; Rudolf Dolzer, 'Lecture Commentary: Regime Change and the Changing Universe of Values in Contemporary International Law' (2004) 98 *American Society of International Law* 299; Gareth Evans and Mohammed Sahnoun, 'The Responsibility to Protect' (2002) 81 *Foreign Affairs* 99; August Reinisch, 'Developing Human Rights and Humanitarian Law: Accountability of the Security Council for the Imposition of Economic Sanctions' (2001) 95 *American Journal of International Law* 851, 857.

[62] Shraga, 'The Security Council and Human Rights' in Fassbender, *Securing Human Rights*, 25.

[63] *Application of the Convention on the Prevention and Punishment of the Crime of Genocide*, Judgment, para 382.

[64] The customary international law nature of the principles underlying the Genocide Convention was recognized by the ICJ in its 1951 advisory opinion on the *Reservations to the Genocide Convention*,

subject to an obligation to protect. This is particularly relevant since the UN, more than any other actor, would have both the capacity and the means (including those specified in Art 41 and 42 of the Charter) to protect.[65]

However, the combination of the Council's responsibility under the Charter with customary obligations resting on the UN will not easily allow a claim for wrongful omission in the case of inaction. The performance of international obligations has to be reconciled with, and remains subject to, the discretionary powers of the Council.[66] Any obligation of the organization as a whole has to accommodate the nature of the powers of the organs, and cannot in itself transform a power to authorize the use of force into a duty to do so. While it is perfectly possible to say that the Council, by failing to use its powers, contributed to a mass atrocity which it could have prevented or at least curtailed, inaction by the Council in the face of mass atrocities may not be easily qualified as a breach of an international obligation that would engage the international responsibility of the UN.

Owing to the difficulty of addressing a failure to protect-critique to the Council, it is not uncommon to address such a critique to the member states that did not allow the Council to act.[67] However, the bases for such a critique are of a moral or political, rather than a legal, nature. In current international law, there is no support for the proposition that member states of the Council are responsible for a failure of the Council to act[68] since, as a general proposition, member states are not responsible for a wrongful act of the organization.[69] More to the point, the participation of a state in the creation or adoption of an act of an organization does not in itself constitute a source of member state responsibility for the acts of the international organization.[70] This also holds true for the use of the veto by the permanent members of the Council.[71]

Reservations to the Convention on the Prevention and the Punishment of the Crime of Genocide, Advisory Opinion, ICJ Rep 1951, 15, 23; Shraga, 'The Security Council and Human Rights' in Fassbender, *Securing Human Rights*, 32.

[65] Shraga, 'The Security Council and Human Rights' in Fassbender, *Securing Human Rights*, 33.

[66] UN Charter, Art 42. See Shraga, 'The Security Council and Human Rights' in Fassbender, *Securing Human Rights*.

[67] eg Report of the Secretary-General's Internal Review Panel on 'United Nations Action in Sri Lanka' (14 Nov 2012), 29, para 81 (one of the elements of the systemic failure of the UN was 'inadequate political support from Member States as a whole').

[68] Davidsson, 'The Security Council's Obligations of Good Faith', 541, 543.

[69] Art 62, ILC Draft Articles on the Responsibility of International Organizations (DARIO) (2011), adopted at the 63rd Session, *Yearbook of the International Law Commission*, 2011, vol II, para 87.

[70] Anne Peters, 'The Responsibility to Protect: Spelling Out the Hard Legal Consequences for the UN Security Council and Its Members' in Ulrich Fastenrath et al (eds), *From Bilateralism to Community Interest: Essays in Honour of Bruno Simma* (Oxford: Oxford University Press, 2011), 320.

[71] Peters, 'The Responsibility to Protect' in Fastenrath et al, *From Bilateralism to Community Interest*, 320–1; Sienho Yee, '"Member Responsibility" and the ILC Articles on the Responsibility of International Organizations: Some Observations' in Maurizio Raggazi (ed), *Responsibility of International Organizations: Essays in Memory of Sir Ian Brownlie* (Leiden: Martinus Nijhoff, 2013), 325–36.

Of course, international legal responsibility can be incurred by member states for their own conduct, in breach of their own obligations which required them to act, under the Genocide Convention or under general international law.[72] There is no shortage of principles that lend themselves to creative interpretation in relation to member states that block effective action. However, in light of their reception and application in state practice, it would seem that neither the obligation to cooperate[73] nor the prohibition against aiding or assisting in the commission of a wrongful act by the organization[74] can provide a basis for a claim of wrongdoing against member states that did not allow the Council to act. The transfer of responsibility to the Council to act in situations of mass atrocities does not require individual members to act beyond that which they are required to do under their own obligations, and international law does not provide a basis for subjecting them to a failure to protect-critique.

B. Peacekeeping

Critique for failures to protect may not only be directed to the Security Council, but also to peacekeeping operations[75] mandated by the Council. For a long time, the absence of mandates to use force to protect civilians—traditionally a central element of UN peacekeeping practice[76]—made it pointless as a matter of law to blame peacekeepers for a failure to protect.[77] In regard to the atrocities in Rwanda[78] and Burundi,[79] where peacekeepers were in place but could not act, it is possible on moral or political grounds to blame the UN for not empowering the mission, but the blame can hardly be directed at the mission itself.

[72] ARISWA, Arts 40–1. [73] Section II.C.

[74] DARIO, Art 15; Peters, 'The Responsibility to Protect' in Fastenrath et al, *From Bilateralism to Community Interest*, 321–2.

[75] See Scott Sheeran, 'The Use of Force in United Nations Peacekeeping Operations', Chapter 16 in this volume and Nicholas Tsagourias, 'Self-Defence, Protections of Humanitarian Values, and the Doctrine of Impartiality and Neutrality in Enforcement Mandates', Chapter 18 in this volume.

[76] Ralph Zacklin, 'The Use of Force in Peacekeeping Operations' in Niels Blokker and Nico Schrijver (eds), *The Security Council and the Use of Force: Theory and Reality: A Need for Change?* (Leiden: Koninklijke Brill, 2005); Hitoshi Nasu, *International Law on Peacekeeping. A Study of Article 40 of the UN Charter* (Leiden: Koninklijke Brill, 2009), 25; Trevor Findlay, *The Use of Force in UN Peace Operations* (Oxford: Oxford University Press, 2002), 1, 20; Katherine E. Cox, 'Beyond Self-Defense: United Nations Peacekeeping Operations & the Use of Force' (1999) 27 *Denver Journal of International Law and Policy* 239.

[77] The question may be raised whether the absence of legal powers by peacekeeping troops to use force other than for self-defence is ever a legal justification for *not* using force. See Nasu, *International Law on Peacekeeping*, 25–6 (peacekeeping forces are 'urged to restrain the use of armed force, but are not prohibited from taking such a course of action').

[78] Ingvar Carlsson, 'The UN Inadequacies' (2003) 3 *Journal of International Criminal Justice* 837.

[79] Kristiana Powell, *The African Union's Emerging Peace and Security Regime: Opportunities and Challenges for Delivering on the Responsibility to Protect* (Institute for Security Studies, South Africa, 2005), 35.

For modern peacekeeping missions a failure to protect-critique has more bite. Mandates provide for the use of force for the protection of civilians,[80] and may in turn evolve into peace enforcement rather than peacekeeping.[81] Examples are the mandates of the African Union/United Nations Hybrid Operation in Darfur (UNAMID) to take 'the necessary action' to protect civilians,[82] Sierra Leone,[83] Liberia,[84] Côte d'Ivoire,[85] Haiti,[86] Chad and the Central African Republic,[87] the Democratic Republic of the Congo,[88] and Sudan.[89] Depending on the formulation of the mandate, they must protect, by force if necessary, civilian populations in imminent threat of physical violence.

Yet, failures by a peacekeeping force to perform its mandate cannot necessarily be qualified as a wrongful act. A mandate is not an obligation, certainly not one which correlates to a right of injured parties outside the UN. It could be argued that an empowerment creates a 'legitimate expectation' of injured parties that force will be used,[90] but it remains to be seen how far this would carry in a court of law.

Of course, general obligations under human rights law and humanitarian law, to the extent that they are binding on the UN, remain applicable. To the extent that such obligations apply, the question is how far they extend, and in particular whether they extend beyond the area where the peacekeeping force exercises control (eg its prisons and military camps), into the area where the territorial state, or armed groups, exercise control. The Brahimi Report noted that peacekeepers 'who witness violence against civilians should be presumed to be authorized to stop it, within their means, in support of basic United Nations principles.'[91] As indicated by the phrase 'within

[80] Nasu, *International Law on Peacekeeping*, 27; Shraga, 'The Security Council and Human Rights' in Fassbender, *Securing Human Rights*, 24; Breau, 'The Impact of the Responsibility to Protect on Peacekeeping', 429.

[81] Breau, 'The Impact of the Responsibility to Protect on Peacekeeping', 444–6.

[82] SC Res 1769 (31 July 2007), S/RES/1769, para 15; Shraga, 'The Security Council and Human Rights' in Fassbender, *Securing Human Rights*, 30.

[83] SC Res 1270 (22 Oct 1999), S/RES/1270, para 14.

[84] SC Res 1509 (19 Sept 2003), S/RES/1509, para 3j.

[85] SC Res 1528 (27 Feb 2004), S/RES/1528, paras 6i and 16 and SC Res 1933 (30 June 2010), S/RES/1933, para 16b.

[86] SC Res 1542 (30 Apr 2004), S/RES/1542, para 7If.

[87] SC Res 1778 (25 Sept 2007), S/RES/1778, para 6a; SC Res 1861 (14 Jan 2009), S/RES/1861, para 7ai; and SC Res 1923 (25 May 2010), S/RES/1923.

[88] SC Res 1291 (24 Feb 2000), S/RES/1291, para 8; SC Res 1484 (30 May 2003), S/RES/1484; SC Res 1493 (28 July 2003), S/RES/1493, para 25; SC Res 1565 (1 Oct 2004), S/RES/1565, para 4b; SC Res 1756 (15 May 2007), S/RES/1756, para 2a; SC Res 1794 (21 Dec 2007), S/RES/1794, paras 5 and 8; SC Res 1856 (22 Dec 2008), S/RES/1856, para 3a; SC Res 1906 (23 Dec 2009), S/RES/1906, paras 5a, 7, and 22–3; and SC Res 1925 (28 May 2010), S/RES/1925, para 12a–c.

[89] SC Res 1590 (24 Mar 2005), S/RES/1590, para 16; SC Res 1706 (31 Aug 2006), S/RES/1706, para 12a; SC Res 1769 (31 July 2007), S/RES/1769, para 15; SC Res 1919 (29 Apr 2010), S/RES/1919, para 4; and SC Res 1935 (30 July 2010), S/RES/1935, para 2.

[90] Generally on legitimate expectations, see Michael Byers, *Custom, Power, and the Power of Rules. International Relations and Customary International Law* (Cambridge: Cambridge University Press, 1999), ch 7.

[91] Report of the Panel on United Nations Peace Operations (Brahimi Report) (2000), A/55/305 and S/2000/809, para 62. See similarly Commentary of the International Committee of the Red Cross to

their means', the scope of a failure to protect-critique is limited to a combination of 'their areas of operation, capabilities, and available resources'.[92] If these conditions are satisfied, it may be possible to claim as a matter of law that a peacekeeping force (and thus the UN) failed to exercise its obligations to protect. However, it would seem that this has been the case in very few—if any—of the mass atrocities of the last decades. Given the notorious lack of actual capabilities granted to peacekeeping troops, it is only in rare cases that such a critique could translate into a viable legal claim. There are ample instances where the inability of troops to protect was not so much due to lack of legal powers, but to the lack of resources. These include the United Nations Assistance Mission for Rwanda (UNAMIR), which the Security Council had reduced to a minimal force,[93] the United Nations Protection Force in Bosnia and Herzegovina (UNPROFOR),[94] UNAMID in Burundi (2004), which 'lacked sufficient troop capacity, logistics, and funding',[95] and the African Union Mission in Sudan (AMIS), which 'was hampered by insecurity, lack of significant troops, logistical and operational challenges, the refusal of the government of Sudan to allow deployment of non-African troops, and the lack of contributions of means of transportation and critical aviation capabilities'.[96]

In such situations, a failure to protect-critique may well circumvent the peacekeeping mission as such, and direct itself to the member states that did not provide peacekeeping forces with the necessary means to perform their mandate (somewhat comparable to critiques of member states that did not allow the Security Council to act). The obligation to cooperate to bring to an end serious breaches of peremptory norms[97] may be relied on to support the proposition that member states should cooperate to enable peacekeeping missions to fulfill their mandates so as to protect civilians from mass atrocities. But the obligation lacks the power to remove the essentially voluntary nature of a decision to provide troops for peacekeeping missions, and does not provide a basis for singling out particular states for a legal failure-to-protect-critique.

Common Article 1 of the 1949 Geneva Conventions, Jean S. Pictet, *The Geneva Conventions of 12 August 1949: Commentary* (Geneva: International Committee of the Red Cross, 1952). See also Siobhân Wills, *Protecting Civilians: The Obligations of Peacekeepers* (Oxford: Oxford University Press, 2009), 267–8 (noting that 'where the force has a mandate to provide protection and the host-State is unable or unwilling to respond in sufficient time to protect the lives of the persons under imminent attack, it ought to be best practice to require peacekeepers to respond, if they have the capacity to do so. This would be in line with the principle of Article 1 and also with the expectations generated by deployment of a peacekeeping force').

[92] Shraga, 'The Security Council and Human Rights' in Fassbender, *Securing Human Rights*, 24.

[93] Ingvar Carlsson, 'The UN Inadequacies' (2005) 3 *Journal of International Criminal Justice* 837.

[94] General Assembly, 'Report of the Secretary General pursuant to General Assembly Resolution 53/35', 'The Fall of Srebrenica' (1999), A/54/549, para 56.

[95] Shraga, 'The Security Council and Human Rights' in Fassbender, *Securing Human Rights*, 16.

[96] Shraga, 'The Security Council and Human Rights' in Fassbender, *Securing Human Rights*, 16; Ademola Abass, 'The United Nations, The African Union and the Darfur Crisis. Of Apology and Utopia' (2007) 54 *Netherlands International Law Review* 415; Alex de Waal, 'Darfur and the Failure of the Responsibility to Protect' (2007) 83 *International Affairs* 1039; see also the Brahimi Report, para 63.

[97] ARISWA, Art 41.

IV. Diffused Responsibility

It follows from the previous two sections that it is possible to construe the responsibility to protect populations from mass atrocities as a shared responsibility.[98] International law empowers both states and the UN to act, even though it limits the means that may be employed by the former. In some cases, it also obliges bystanders to act. At a minimum, the obligation to cooperate applies to situations where mass atrocities are committed by a third state. In this respect, it may be said that all actors that refrain from acting are a cause, in the sense that they had to do something, and their omissions along with the acts of the perpetrators are empirically connected to the outcome.[99]

It also follows from this that international law does not generally translate this shared responsibility in particular obligations to specific obligations. The shared responsibility rests on all. In this respect, failures to protect can be said to arise out of 'problems of many hands'. This concept, originating in literature on public administration, is based on the proposition that when many persons contribute to harmful outcomes, 'it is difficult even in principle to identify who is morally responsible for political outcomes.'[100] Unless accompanied by a scheme for allocation of obligations and responsibilities to individual actors, the involvement of 'many hands' will lead to a diffusion of responsibility: 'As the responsibility for any given instance of conduct is scattered among more people, the discrete responsibility of every individual diminishes proportionately.'[101] With the exception of the perpetrators, it seems difficult if not impossible to say that the outcome would not have occurred but for the actor's act or omission. The actors are only a causal factor—one of 'a plurality of distinguishable causal conditions.'[102]

[98] See Nollkaemper and Jacobs, Shared Responsibility in International Law: A Conceptual Framework', see also Larry May, *Sharing Responsibility* (Chicago, IL: University of Chicago Press, 1992).

[99] Compare see Dennis Thompson, 'Designing Responsibility: The Problem of Many Hands in Complex Organizations' in Jeroen van den Hoven, Seumas Miller, and Thomas Pogge (eds), *The Design Turn in Applied Ethics* (Cambridge: Cambridge University Press, 2012), available at <http://scholar.harvard.edu/files/dft/files/designing_responsibility_1-28-11.pdf> ('to assert that an individual is a cause on this criterion only empirically connects his or her action with the outcome—along with the actions of many other hands and the influence of many other forces. It does not establish that the individual is the most important cause, even less that the individual is morally responsible for the entire outcome').

[100] Dennis F. Thompson, 'Moral Responsibility of Public Officials: the Problem of Many Hands' (1980) 74 *American Political Science Review* 905, 905. For further discussion on the subject, see Thompson, 'Designing Responsibility' in van den Hoven, Miller, and Pogge, *The Design Turn in Applied Ethics*.

[101] Mark Bovens, *The Quest for Responsibility: Accountability and Citizenship in Complex Organizations* (Cambridge: Cambridge University Press, 1998) 46. For a comparable point, see May, *Sharing Responsibility*, 37–8.

[102] See Thompson, 'Designing Responsibility' in van den Hoven, Miller, and Pogge, *The Design Turn in Applied Ethics*, citing Joel Feinberg, *Doing and Deserving* (Princeton, NJ: Princeton University Press,

This phenomenon thus magnifies the difficulty of singling out individual bystanders for their failure to protect in relation to mass atrocities. In addition to the weakness of the normative basis for claims against such states, the very multitude of actors who may be in a position to act diffuses the responsibility of any single actor.

It is true that, in the rare cases where multiple actors have international obligations to protect populations from mass atrocities, a multiplicity of actors in itself does not necessarily affect the obligations of each of the individual actors, nor does it otherwise affect their possible responsibility. International law in principle allows for the coexistence of multiple responsibilities in relation to failures to protect. This holds true for the coexistence of responsibility between perpetrators and bystanders, and within the category of bystanders itself.

As for the former, the obligation to protect of states exercising extraterritorial jurisdiction and of 'influential states' will generally coexist alongside those of the territorial state. The mere fact that a third state exercises jurisdiction does not relieve the territorial state of its obligations; just as the fact that the territorial state retains its obligation does not relieve the state that exercises extraterritorial jurisdiction of its obligations.[103] Also, the mandate of peacekeeping operations to protect civilians will be without prejudice to the government's responsibilities.[104] Likewise, while under the responsibility to protect doctrine, the territorial state's inability to protect triggers the responsibilities of third states and international organizations,[105] the transfer of responsibilities triggered by inability is not necessarily binary and exclusive. One illustration is that while Security Council Resolution 1973 allowed for military action (with a reference to R2P), it reiterated the primary responsibility of Libya.[106] Both the territorial state and outside actors may then be obliged to act—and in principle these responsibilities do not exclude or undermine one another.

As to the latter, the fact that an obligation to protect rests on a multitude of outside actors does not reduce the obligations of each individual actor. On this point, paragraph 430 of the *Genocide* case is relevant.[107] When considering whether the

1970), 201–2. See for a construction of shared responsibility in relation to situations where causation is not possible, May, *Sharing Responsibility*, 37–8.

[103] *Ilascu and Others v. Moldova and Russia* (App No. 48787/99) ECtHR, 8 July 2004, para 331; *Catan and Others v. Moldova and Russia* (App nos 43370/04, 18454/06, 8252/05) (Grand Chamber) ECtHR, 19 Oct 2012, paras 109–10. It should be added that while the fact that there are a multiplicity of actors obligated to take action to protect persons from mass atrocities, in principle this need not affect the responsibility of any single actor, it may affect the content of obligations or the scope of responsibility. Eg in case of civil strife, as in Sri Lanka or Colombia, because of the role and power of rebel movements, the ability of territorial states to take action to protect civilians from mass atrocities may be weak. While this will not relieve them of their obligations to protect civilians, it will influence what, as a legal matter, may be required and expected by them.

[104] Shraga, 'The Security Council and Human Rights' in Fassbender, *Securing Human Rights*, 24.

[105] World Summit Outcome Document (2005), para 139.

[106] SC Res 1973 (17 Mar 2011), S/RES/1973.

[107] *Application of the Convention on the Prevention and Punishment of the Crime of Genocide*, Judgment.

obligations of Serbia to prevent genocide would be affected by the action or inaction of other states, the ICJ held that:

> it is irrelevant whether the State whose responsibility is in issue claims, or even proves, that even if it had employed all means reasonably at its disposal, they would not have sufficed to prevent the commission of genocide. As well as being generally difficult to prove, this is irrelevant to the breach of the obligation of conduct in question, the more so since the possibility remains that the combined efforts of several States, each complying with its obligation to prevent, might have achieved the result—averting the commission of genocide—which the efforts of only one State were insufficient to produce.[108]

The Court thus held that the fact that multiple actors may act in the face of a mass atrocity, does not alter the fact that each state can be responsible for its failure to prevent genocide, even if it could not by itself have averted the genocide. The fact that a bystander state is one of many, does not as such affect its individual obligations.

However, despite the independence of individual obligations and responsibilities, the multitude of actors that potentially have a role in the protection of populations against mass atrocities may complicate the determination of the responsibility of any single actor. The fact that international law obliges, or empowers, multiple actors, without providing clear criteria for the allocation of obligations and powers between such actors, may allow actors that were (allegedly) responsible for (part of) the events to evade their responsibility and to 'pass the buck' to others.[109]

The phenomenon of buck-passing is well illustrated by the coexistence of obligations of individuals and states. The emergence of the possibility of attributing individual responsibility to perpetrators after 1945, and in particular in the late 1990s, has made it easier for states to deflect responsibility to individual authors of international crimes. It allowed them to escape state responsibility, and restrict responsibility to that of individual perpetrators.[110] It allowed third states (and 'the international community') to abstain from imposing formal responsibility on state perpetrators and to limit them to imposing responsibility on individual perpetrators.[111]

Buck-passing is also facilitated by the principles that apply to the relationship between territorial states and bystanders. Under the responsibility to protect doctrine, the territorial state's inability to protect triggers the responsibilities of third states and international organizations.[112] As noted previously, triggering the responsibility of outside actors does not necessarily terminate the responsibilities

[108] *Application of the Convention on the Prevention and Punishment of the Crime of Genocide*, Judgment, para 430.

[109] Nollkaemper, 'Multi-Level Accountability' in Shany and Broude, *The Shifting Allocation of Authority in International Law*.

[110] Yuval Shany and Tomer Broude (eds), *The Shifting Allocation of Authority in International Law* (Oxford: Hart, 2008).

[111] This also served the interests of stability: the international community had a prime interest to allow the state, eg Iraq or Serbia, to continue and re-establish itself quickly as a stable political entity—sacrificing individual state agents did not endanger that objective.

[112] World Summit Outcome Document (2005), para 139.

of the territorial state, and there exists a grey zone where both territorial states and outside actors can assume the responsibility to protect persons from mass atrocities, without any clarity as to who is to do what. The triggering device of 'inability' may induce a territorial state to deem itself to be relieved from its obligations once outside actors step in, and in that sense invites buck-passing. States may prefer this situation, since it does not carry the political costs of fighting a civil war.[113] At the same time, the primary responsibility of the territorial state, as well as the principle of non-intervention, will induce outside actors to continue to defer to the territorial state.

A similar ambiguity arises once external actors are present in the territory where the atrocities take place. For instance, while the obligations of peacekeeping operations to protect civilians are without prejudice to the government's responsibilities,[114] the relationship between the obligations and responsibilities of such operations on the one hand and the territorial state, on the other, is equivocal, and the law invites blame-shifting games.

In relation to 'influential states', a similar analysis can be made. Grounding the obligations and responsibilities of such states on the criteria of 'capacity' does not appear to provide a workable criterion to delineate obligations and responsibilities of multiple states.[115] The nature and contents of the criteria formulated by the Court are indeterminate and flexible and inevitably lead to blame-shifting.

It is only in rare cases that areas of responsibility may be of an exclusive nature. Arguably, though controversially, this applies to attribution of conduct between the UN and troop-contributing states. It is somewhat unclear whether the standard of effective control, used in the ARIO,[116] allows for multiple attribution.[117] In the *Nuhanović* case, the Court of Appeal of The Hague took the position that for determining who had effective control over an act, it needed to be established whether the UN or the state had the power to prevent the conduct.[118] If this is the relevant criterion, it would seem possible that both the UN and the troop-contributing state had the power to prevent the removal. The Dutch court expressly recognized the possibility of double attribution.[119] In the *Behrami and*

[113] Sarah M. H. Nouwen, 'Complementarity in Practice: Critical Lessons from the ICC for R2P' (Symposium: The International Criminal Court and the Responsibility to Protect) (2010) *Finnish Yearbook of International Law* 53; Sarah M. H. Nouwen and Wouter G. Werner, 'Doing Justice to the Political: The International Criminal Court in Uganda and Sudan' (2010) 21 *European Journal of International Law* 941, 949.

[114] Shraga, 'The Security Council and Human Rights' in Fassbender, *Securing Human Rights*, 24.

[115] Hakimi, 'State Bystander Responsibility', 356 (assigning the obligation primarily on the basis of capacity would be untenable).

[116] DARIO, para 87.

[117] James Crawford and Simon Olleson, 'The Nature and Forms of International Responsibility' in Malcolm D. Evans (ed), *International Law* (Oxford: Oxford University Press, 2010), 444.

[118] Netherlands, The Hague Court of Appeal, *Nuhanović v. Netherlands* (5 July 2011), LJN: BR0133; ILDC 1742 (NL 2011), para 5.9.

[119] *Nuhanović v. The Netherlands*, para 5.3. Also some scholars have taken the position that the conduct of contributing troops can always be attributed to both the sending state and the UN. See eg Aurel

Saramati cases,[120] the European Court of Human Rights (ECtHR) construed the applicable criterion for attribution in exclusive terms. The UN also supports an exclusive mode of attribution—albeit on a different ground—taking the position that peacekeeping troops are to be considered as subsidiary organs of the UN.[121]

Either way, the 'effective control debate' has proved unable to prevent blame-shifting arguments. For actors who construe the criterion in an exclusive manner, it seems to have induced and allowed actors to 'pass the buck' to others (in this case the UN, which may then profit from its immunity from litigation).[122] When the criterion is construed in a way that allows for double attribution, this does not necessarily solve the problem. The terms of the ARIO—where the question of attribution is governed by the standard of 'effective control'[123]—introduce inherent flexibility, allowing for arguments pointing to several actors. Also the argument that the entity *best* placed to prevent should take action[124] is inherently ambiguous, both allowing and inviting actors to point to others who would be more capable of preventing such abuses.

In those situations where multiple bystanders contribute through their omissions to a mass atrocity, this very multiplicity may thus complicate the possibility of holding each individual actor responsible. In such situations, the absence of third party institutions that can determine responsibility, of course, further supports the process of buck-passing.

A particular consequence of a multitude of bystanders is that while it may be possible to find individual actors responsible when specific obligations apply, it may be much more difficult to determine which actor(s) are to provide reparation. This problem may occur, in particular, when obligations are framed as obligations of conduct, and the rules on causation are construed in such a way that no sufficient connection can be found between individual wrongs and the harmful outcome. In such a case, states can be held responsible for their wrongs, but they will not be required to provide reparation in relation to the eventual harmful outcome that cannot fully be traced to their acts or omissions. There may thus be a mismatch

Sari, 'Jurisdiction and International Responsibility in Peace Support Operations: The *Behrami* and *Saramati* Cases' (2008) 8 *Human Rights Law Review* 151, 160–1; Luigi Condorelli, 'Le Statut des Forces de l'ONU et Le Droit International Humanitaire' (1995) 78 *Rivista di Diritto Internazionale* 881; Luigi Condorelli, 'Le Statut des Forces des Nations Unies et le Droit International Humanitaire' in Claude Emmanuelli (ed), *Les Casques Bleus: Policiers ou Combattants?* (Montreal: Wilson & Lafleur, 1997).

[120] *Behrami and Behrami v. France and Saramati v. France, Germany and Norway* (App nos 71412/01 and 78166/01), ECtHR, 2 May 2007.

[121] ILC, Report of the International Law Commission on the Work of its Sixty-First Session (4 May–5 June and 6 July–7 Aug 2009), A/64/10, 64.

[122] Netherlands, Supreme Court, *Stichting Mothers of Srebrenica v. Netherlands and United Nations* (13 Apr 2012), Final appeal judgment, LJN: BW1999; ILDC 1760 (NL 2012).

[123] DARIO, Art 7, para 87.

[124] Tom Dannenbaum, 'Translating the Standard of Effective Control into a System of Effective Accountability: How Liability Should be Apportioned for Violations of Human Rights by Member State Troop Contingents Serving as United Nations Peacekeepers' (2010) 51 *Harvard International Law Journal* 113, 158.

between individual responsibility of states for individual wrongful acts, and the harmful outcome that the collectivity produces.

This phenomenon of dilution of responsibility manifested itself with full force in respect of the obligation to provide reparation in the *Genocide case*. The ICJ found that it had not been shown that in the specific circumstances of the events, the use of the means of influence by Serbia and Montenegro 'would have sufficed to achieve the result which the Respondent should have sought'.[125] The Court declined to order Serbia and Montenegro to pay compensation because of the collective nature of the failures to prevent.

This example illustrates that international law structures its primary and secondary rules[126] relating to failures to protect in such a way that makes it possible for each of the multiple parties to contribute to a wrong, yet to remain below the threshold where their responsibility would be engaged or, in any event, where they would have to provide reparation for the consequences.

V. Failures to Protect-Critique as a Political Critique

Over time, the number of actors involved in the protection of persons against mass atrocities has expanded, with the recognition and development of positive obligations of the territorial state, the clarification of obligations of states exercising extraterritorial jurisdiction, the emergence of a general obligation to cooperate, with the ICJ's ruling in the *Genocide* case, and with the assumption of powers by the Security Council to act in cases of mass atrocities without physical transboundary effects.

However, it appears from the earlier discussion that this complex of obligations and powers only rarely allows for a failure to protect-critique of individual actors that is grounded in international law. The multiplicity of powers and obligations across various actors reflects the reality that effective power is not vested in any single institution—and, because of the discretionary nature of its powers, the Security Council also falls into that category. Perhaps the hope is that—to paraphrase the ICJ in the *Genocide* case—the combined efforts of several states, each complying

[125] *Application of the Convention on the Prevention and Punishment of the Crime of Genocide*, Judgment, para 463. See critical discussion by Gattini, 'Breach of the Obligation to Prevent and Reparation Thereof in the ICJ's Genocide Judgment', 707–12.

[126] See generally on the distinction, Ulf Linderfalk, 'State Responsibility and the Primary-Secondary Rules Terminology—The Role of Language for an Understanding of the International Legal System' (2009) 78 *Nordic Journal of International Law* 53, 72.

with its obligation to prevent or performing its power to prevent, might achieve the result (averting the commission of genocide) which the efforts of only one state would be insufficient to produce.[127] However, as illustrated in the preceding section, this reliance on multiple actors can easily transform from a strength of the system into a weakness, and allows states and international organizations to duck the question of responsibility.

It may be said that this failure to assign a special duty to act could be seen as a weakness of the normative system.[128] A clarification of obligations as well as secondary rules, that indicate more clearly who is responsible for what, may to some extent ameliorate this weakness. Such criteria can specify what individual actors should or should not do.[129] This can involve clarification of the task of peacekeeping missions[130] and of individual states.[131] In this respect at least, the ICJ's ruling on Serbia and Montenegro's responsibility for its failure to prevent was a welcome step forward.

Improvements may, to some extent, also be sought by strengthening the institutional and procedural avenues for holding various actors to account. Specific options may include broadening the *ex post facto* assessment, for instance by requiring the UN to make broader assessments of failures, not just internally but for all actors involved; and improving access to remedies against the UN.

However, it would seem that seeking clarification with regards to the allocation of obligations and responsibilities to individual actors will only, in rare cases, allow for the individualization of responsibilities, and may indeed start out from the wrong premise. Responding to mass atrocities is by its very nature a collective enterprise, which does not easily allow for individualization of responsibilities. 'Failure to protect' critiques thus do not put blame on an individual actor, but rather on the collectivity of states and international institutions (or 'the international community') that failed to use their powers to provide protection, without this triggering responsibility of individual actors.

The relevance of international law in relation to failures to protect is therefore not to provide a ground for responsibility of individual actors, but rather its ability to provide a framework for deliberation on whether and how to act.[132] This

[127] Glanville, 'The Responsibility to Protect Beyond Borders', 17.

[128] Jennifer M. Welsh and Maria Banda, 'International Law and the Responsibility to Protect: Clarifying or Expanding States' Responsibilities?' (2010) 2 *Global Responsibility to Protect* 213, 219; Miller, 'The Responsibility to Protect Human', 2, 3–4.

[129] See Thompson, 'Designing Responsibility' in van den Hoven, Miller, and Pogge, *The Design Turn in Applied Ethics*.

[130] eg Holt, Taylor, and Kelly, 'Protecting Civilians in the Context of UN Peacekeeping Operations, Successes, Setbacks and Remaining Challenges', 212–13.

[131] eg Alvarez, 'The Schizophrenias of R2P' in Alston and Macdonald, *Human Rights, Intervention and the Use of Force*, 279 ('Perhaps it is time, in light of the ICJ's Bosnia decision, for a protocol to the Genocide Convention indicating much more clearly what its signatories have a right to do in the face of on-going genocide in another signatory state').

[132] See also Martti Koskenniemi, 'Solidarity Measures: State Responsibility as a New International Order?' (2002) 72 *British Yearbook of International Law* 337.

framework is supported by the obligation to cooperate to bring to an end violations of peremptory norms, in combination with the responsibility and powers of the Security Council. The UN, and in particular the Council, thus provides the primary mechanism for performing the obligation of cooperation. The Genocide Convention, human rights law, and humanitarian law are relevant for such cooperation. These obligations may not easily provide a basis for claims for wrongfulness in cases of failures to protect, but they do circumscribe political processes and as such may underlie and support critiques of states and international organizations for the outcome of such processes.

PART III

THE PROHIBITION OF THE USE OF FORCE, SELF-DEFENCE, AND OTHER CONCEPTS

CHAPTER 21

THE BAN ON THE USE OF FORCE IN THE UN CHARTER

NICO SCHRIJVER*

> All members shall refrain in their international relations from the threat or use of force against the territorial integrity or political independence of any State, or in any other manner inconsistent with the Purposes of the United Nations.

I. Introduction

Few treaty provisions, if any, are as significant in international affairs as Article 2(4) of the UN Charter.[1] It establishes a (nearly) fully-fledged ban on the use of force in international relations. Its genesis is a long one, a topic which can only be briefly addressed in Section II of this chapter. Finally, its cradle stood in San Francisco, at the United Nations Conference on International Organization (UNCIO, April–June 1945). Section III reviews the making and delivery of what became Article 2(4) of

* The author records his appreciation for the assistance received from his student assistant Hilde Roskam in preparing this text.

This chapter builds upon the author's contribution on Art 2(4) in Jean-Pierre Cot, Alain Pellet, and Mathias Forteau (eds), *La Charte des Nations Unies, Commentaire article par article* (3rd edn, Paris: Economica, 2005), vol I, 437–64.

[1] Charter of the United Nations (1945), 892 UNTS 119, 26 June 1945.

the UN Charter. While without doubt being the principal provision on the use of force in the Charter, it is by no means the only one. Therefore, Section III also reviews the other articles of the UN Charter that touch upon the use of force.

Yet, when the prohibition on the use of force eventually became prominently embedded in the Charter of the UN, this did not by any means signal the end of the use of force in international relations. On the contrary, force has been used on numerous occasions throughout the existence of the UN, and nowadays frequently even with authorization by the UN Security Council. The exceptions to the Charter prohibition of the use of force are described in Section IV, while Section V examines the interpretation of Article 2(4) in the practice of three principal organs of the UN (General Assembly, Security Council, and International Court of Justice (ICJ)) as well as its incorporation in a number of multilateral treaties. The questions arise whether the post-1945 use of force is compatible with the object and purpose of Article 2(4) of the UN Charter and what the legal status of the prohibition to use force is in contemporary international law (Section VI). The final Section VII provides some concluding observations.

II. Pre-Charter Attempts to Restrict the Freedom of States to Resort to Warfare

Building on the work of theologians, most notably of Saint Augustine (354–430) and Saint Thomas Aquinas (1225–74), and the scholarly work of the founding fathers of international law such as Francisco Suarez and Hugo Grotius, it took a long time for a normative doctrine on a *bellum justum* to evolve. In fact, during the Westphalian order, only The Hague Peace Conferences of 1899 and 1907 introduced the first serious interstate diplomatic attempts to restrict the recourse to war. The Hague Convention (I) was aimed at the peaceful adjustment of international differences, 'before an appeal to arms'. Contracting parties were 'animated by a strong desire to concert for the maintenance of the general peace' and 'resolved to second by their best efforts the friendly settlement of international disputes'.[2] In Convention (III) relative to the Opening of Hostilities, contracting parties agree not to commence hostilities between them without previous and explicit warning, in

[2] Convention for the Pacific Settlement of International Disputes, The Hague Peace Conference, 1899, Preamble.

the form of either a declaration of war containing reasons for the commencement of hostilities, or an *ultimatum* with a conditional declaration of war.[3] Such mainly procedural limitations on the waging of war were followed by more substantive limitations. The so-called Drago-Porter Convention, adopted at the Second Hague Peace Conference, introduced an official ban on the use of force for the collection of debts.[4] Some further restrictions were introduced through a series of treaties concluded from 1913 by the US with as many as 19 other states 'to advance the general cause of peace' (Preamble); the so-called Bryan Treaties. Among other obligations, states parties committed themselves to submit all their disputes to a conciliation commission and 'not to declare war or begin hostilities' prior to the commission's report, which was to be submitted within one year.[5]

Despite these new treaties, the outbreak of the devastating Great War (1914–18) could not be prevented. The war resulted in renewed political commitment to restrict warfare and in the establishment of the League of Nations in order to 'promote international co-operation and to achieve international peace and security by the acceptance of obligations not to resort to war' (Preamble). Article 11 of the Covenant of the League of Nations stated that any war or threat of war was a matter of concern to the whole League, and that the League should take any action deemed to be wise and effectual for safeguarding the peace of nations. At first glance, Article 10 appears to include a prohibition of warfare as well as a collective security system: 'The Members of the League undertake to respect and preserve as against external aggression the territorial integrity and existing political independence of all Members of the League.' However, the following articles make clear that Article 10 can be explained merely as a duty to submit their disputes to consultation, arbitration, judicial settlement, or inquiry by the Council of the League of Nations. Article 12, for example, provides for a cooling-off period of three months after such procedures before countries may resort to war. In addition, Article 15(7) states that if the League's Council fails to reach a report which is unanimously agreed by its members, the members of the League reserve to themselves the right to take such action as they consider necessary for the maintenance of right and justice. It therefore follows that war is only prohibited against countries that comply with an arbitral award, within the cooling-off period, and in the case of a unanimous report of the Council of the League.[6]

[3] Convention relative to the Opening of Hostilities, 18 Oct 1907, Art 1.

[4] Hague Convention II respecting the Limitation of the Employment of Force for the Recovery of Contract Debts, 1907. See also: Henri-Alexis Moulin, 'La doctrine de Drago' (1907) 14 *Revue Générale de Droit International Public* 417–72; Wolfgang Benedeck, 'Drago-Porter Convention' in Rüdiger Wolfrum (ed), *Max Planck Encyclopedia of Pubic International Law*, vol III (Oxford: Oxford University Press, 2012), 234–6.

[5] See Hans-Jürgen Schlochauer, 'Bryan Treaties (1913–1914)' in Wolfrum, *Max Planck Encyclopedia of Pubic International Law*, vol. I, 1071–3.

[6] See Francis Paul Walters, *A History of the League of Nations* (Oxford: Oxford University Press, 1952).

During the period of the League of Nations, several further attempts were made to solidify and supplement the League's regime with respect to the use of force. The Geneva Protocol for the Pacific Settlement of International Disputes (1924) can be regarded as a first attempt to impose compulsory dispute settlement.[7] Any state in breach of that Protocol was to be identified as an 'aggressor'. In such case, all states were under an obligation to take collective enforcement measures, which could include the use of force.[8] However, the Geneva Protocol failed to generate widespread enthusiasm and never entered into force. After the first approval by all 47 members of the League of Nations on 2 October 1924, Great Britain did not ratify the Protocol because it was met with grave objections from the Dominions and India. Consequently, the Protocol failed to materialize.[9]

Another attempt to regulate the use of force was the Locarno Treaty of Mutual Guarantee of 16 October 1925. Germany and Belgium and Germany and France undertook that they would 'in no case attack or invade each other'.[10] A more significant attempt to regulate the use of force is the Kellogg–Briand Pact of 27 August 1928. This was a joint initiative by France and the US; interestingly, the latter was not a member of the League of Nations. The contracting parties were 'persuaded that the time has come when a frank renunciation of war as an instrument of national policy should be made to the end that the peaceful and friendly relations now existing between their peoples may be perpetuated'.[11] The parties condemned 'recourse to war for the solution of international controversies' and renounced it 'as an instrument of national policy in their relations with another'.[12] They agreed that the settlement or solution of conflicts that arose between them would never be sought, except by pacific means.[13] In contrast to the Geneva Protocol drafted under the auspices of the League and the Locarno Treaty with its limited geographical scope, the Pact was joined by many states. It entered into force on 24 June 1929 and is currently still valid. Consequently, the Kellogg–Briand Pact can be seen as the first widely accepted denunciation of war.

Nevertheless, the shortcomings of the Pact soon became apparent. First, there were no sanctions envisaged in the case of a breach of the Pact.[14] Secondly, the Pact specifically outlawed war and not the use of force in general. Soon states proved to be rather ingenious in avoiding labelling their actions 'war', and thereby prevented the application of the Pact. For example, Japan called its invasion in China's Manchuria an 'incident', and both the Chinese and Japanese governments insisted that no war

[7] Protocol for the Pacific Settlement of International Disputes (Geneva Protocol), 2 Oct 1924.

[8] Geneva Protocol, Art 10.

[9] The minutes of the meeting of the Cabinet of Great Britain are contained in the National Archive, available at <http://filestore.nationalarchives.gov.uk/pdfs/small/cab-23-49-cc-12-25-21.pdf>.

[10] Art 2, 54 LNTS 28.

[11] Kellogg–Briand Pact, 27 Aug 1928, Preamble.

[12] Kellogg–Briand Pact, Art 1.

[13] Kellogg–Briand Pact, Arts 1 and 2.

[14] See Randall Lesaffer, 'Too Much History: From War as Sanction to the Sanctioning of War', Chapter 1 in this volume, 52.

existed between them and continued their diplomatic relations. Another example is the statement by Mussolini that Italy's annexation of Abyssinia was an 'expedition'.[15] These shortcomings contributed to the erosion of the newly established norms on the use of force in international relations. The outbreak of the Second World War, starting with the forcible *Anschluss* of Austria to Hitler's Germany in 1938, rendered the new norm its final blow. Yet, at an early stage of the Second World War the Allied Powers recognized the necessity of reinstating the norm and establishing a collective security system. Thus, in the Atlantic Charter the US President and the British Prime Minister included among the common principles on which they based their hopes for 'a better future of the world'. Furthermore, 'they believe that all of the nations of the world, for realistic as well as spiritual reasons must come to the abandonment of the use of force.'[16]

III. Incorporating the Ban on the Use of Force in the UN Charter

This section discusses, first, the drafting history of the provision on the prohibition of the use of force which resulted in the text of Article 2(4) of the UN Charter. Secondly, it reviews other articles of the UN Charter which touch upon the use of force.

A. The Making of Article 2, Paragraph 4

The various violations of the Kellogg–Briand Pact and the devastations of the Second World War resulted in a determination by the Allied Powers to bolster the prohibition of warfare by adopting more stringent provisions. These included strengthening the duty to settle international disputes in a peaceful manner, specification of an absolute ban on the use of force, and institutionalization of a collective security system. These three key elements were already adopted in the US Tentative Proposals for a General International Organization.[17] In response to the shortcomings of the Kellogg–Briand Pact, the Proposals aimed at a prohibition of the use of

[15] See Bernardus V. A. Röling, 'On the Prohibition of the Use of Force' in D. Blackshield (ed), *Legal Change. Essays in Honour of Julius Stone* (Sydney: Butterworths, 1983), 274–98.

[16] Atlantic Charter, 14 Aug 1941. Text in *Documents on American Foreign Relations*, vol IV, 1941–2, 10.

[17] Text in *Department of State Bulletin*, vol XI, 368, 7 Oct 1944.

force in as absolute terms as possible, as well as the prohibition of the threat to use force. The Allied Powers were led by their desire to declare the independent use of armed force by any member of the organization as clearly unlawful, except in cases of self-defence against aggression.[18]

At the San Francisco Conference, several rounds of discussions took place on the text of the prohibition on the use of force, as now enshrined in Article 2(4) of the Charter.[19] Discussions included, first, proposals to expand the prohibition to types of force other than armed force. For example, Brazil proposed to prohibit economic force and Ecuador sought to repudiate moral or physical force.[20] In its turn, Iran demanded the inclusion of political force within the prohibition on the use of force: 'All the Member States of the Organization should refrain from intervening in their international relations, either directly or indirectly, in the internal affairs of the other States and from the threat or use of force in any manner inconsistent with the purposes of the Organization.'[21] None of these proposals were adopted.

A second main point of discussion was to include in Article 2(4) a reference to the prohibition of aggression. Brazil proposed to add the following provision: 'All threats or acts of violence committed by any state to the detriment of any other state shall be considered as acts of aggression committed against all the other members of the Organization.'[22] Similar proposals were submitted by Ecuador and Bolivia.[23] Another proposal was made by New Zealand, which advocated the inclusion of a collective undertaking against aggression in a separate paragraph: 'All members of the Organization undertake collectively to resist every act of aggression against any member.'[24] However, such proposals referring to the concept of aggression were opposed by China, the UK, and the US. In their view, these proposals would narrow, rather than broaden, the scope of Article 2(4). Aggression in all its potential forms would be better covered by the term 'threat to the peace'. The amendment of New Zealand received 26 votes in favour and 18 votes against, but was not adopted as it failed to receive the required two-thirds majority.[25]

[18] Leland M. Goodrich and Edvard Hambro, *Charter of the United Nations. Commentary and Documents* (3rd edn, Medford, MA: World Peace Foundation, 1969), 14.

[19] These proceedings are recorded, with the original proposals and the amendments submitted, in *Documents of the United Nations Conference on International Organization* (*UNCIO*), published by the United Nations Information Organizations in cooperation with the Library of Congress, 22 vols, 1945–55.

[20] *UNCIO*, vol 6, 559. Earlier Brazil submitted a more lengthy amendment covering a comprehensive prohibition of non-intervention (vol 3, 237); *UNCIO*, vol 6, 561 and vol 3, 399 and 423 (Ecuador).

[21] *UNCIO*, vol 6, 563 (Iran). [22] *UNCIO*, vol 6, 558.

[23] See *UNCIO*, vol 3, 422 (Ecuador) and vol 3, 582 (Bolivia).

[24] *UNCIO*, vol 6, 564 and vol 6, 342. The representative of New Zealand stated: 'that New Zealand was not asking for more than it would give, for battlefields all over the world were marked with the graves of New Zealanders who had given their lives for peace and for freedom'; see *UNCIO*, vol 6, 343.

[25] *UNCIO*, vol 6, 346. Similarly, a Panamanian amendment to add to the New Zealand amendment a phrase aimed at the protection of territorial integrity and independence of all member states against aggression received a simple majority only. *UNCIO*, vol 6, 346.

A third discussion focused on the final part of the draft provision 'or in any other manner inconsistent with the Purposes of the United Nations'.[26] Several delegations expressed concern that this provision could be interpreted in a way that states on their own could decide whether or not the use of force was prohibited. Therefore, Costa Rica proposed to delete this part of the provision in order to make clear that the prohibition on the use of force was absolute.[27] Norway supported the omission of the last part of Article 2(4) and proposed an alternative text aimed at the explicit prohibition of force or threat of force if not approved by the Security Council as a means to achieve the objectives of the organization.[28] Brazil also expressed the fear that the last phrase of Article 2(4) could well be interpreted as authorizing unilateral forcible actions by a state claiming that such action was in accordance with the objectives of the organization.[29] It proposed another sentence that only allowed for action 'being taken according to the procedures established by the Organization and in accordance with its decisions'.[30] All these amendments were opposed by the UK and the US. The British delegate stipulated that the wording had been carefully considered in order to preclude interference with the enforcement clauses of Chapter VII of the Charter. He was therefore convinced that the text of the draft represented the 'most intelligible, forceful and economical language'.[31] The US delegate confirmed that the intention of the authors of the original text was to state 'in the broadest terms an absolute all-inclusive prohibition'. He confirmed that the last part of the article (the phrase 'or in any other manner') was designed to ensure that there would be 'no loopholes'.[32] Finally, acting on the proposals of several small states, the Conference resolved to add the phrase 'against the territorial integrity or political independence of any State' to the text of Article 2(4). This addition was meant as an extra and specific guarantee for small states.[33] The final text of Article 2(4) was adopted on 5 June 1945, with only Norway abstaining.[34]

B. Other Charter Provisions Relating to the Use of Force

The UN Charter contains various other provisions directly relating to the use of force. First, the Preamble specifies that the UN is established to 'ensure, by the acceptance of principles and the institution of methods, that armed force shall not be used, save in the common interest'. Secondly, Article 1(1) states that one of the

[26] *UNCIO*, vol 6, 556–68.

[27] Proposals by Costa Rica, 5 Dec 1944 and 4 May 1945, *UNCIO*, vol 3, 274 and 278.

[28] *UNCIO*, vol 3, 366. [29] *UNCIO*, vol 6, 334. [30] *UNCIO*, vol 6, 334.

[31] *UNCIO*, vol 6, 335. [32] *UNCIO*, vol 6, 335.

[33] See *UNCIO*, vol 6, 304, 334–5, and 556–68. See also Ian Brownlie, *International Law and the Use of Force by States* (Oxford: Oxford University Press, 1963), 267.

[34] *UNCIO*, vol 6, 342.

purposes of the organization is 'to take effective collective measures for the prevention and removal of threats to the peace, and for the suppression of acts of aggression or other breaches of the peace'. Thirdly, Article 42 vests the Security Council with the power 'to take such action by air, sea, or land forces as may be necessary to maintain or restore international peace and security'. Fourthly, Article 44 specifies that 'when the Security Council has decided to use force' it shall invite concerned members to participate in the decision of the Security Council concerning the employment of contingents of that member's armed forces. Fifthly, Article 51 provides assurance that 'nothing in the present Charter shall impair the inherent right of individual or collective self-defense if an armed attack occurs against a Member of the United Nations, until the Security Council has taken measures necessary to maintain international peace and security'. Next, Article 53(1) uses a rather general term relating to the use of force in that it provides that 'the Security Council shall, where appropriate, utilize such regional arrangements or agencies for enforcement action under its authority'. Lastly, Articles 53 and 107 address the issue of action against former enemy states. Article 107 provides that 'nothing in the present Charter shall invalidate or preclude action, in relation to any State which during the Second World War has been an enemy of any signatory to the present Charter, taken or authorized as a result of that war by the Governments having responsibility for such action'. In sum, these Charter articles do not employ entirely consistent wording with respect to the use of force. Neither is the relationship between these articles entirely clear. Nevertheless, in the light of its central place and primordial significance, it is only logical to see Article 2(4) as the key provision, if not the mother of all provisions, on the prohibition on the use of force within the Charter.

IV. Exceptions to the Charter Prohibition on the Use of Force

This section discusses three categories of exceptions to the Charter prohibition of the threat or use of force: written Charter exceptions, implicit Charter exceptions, and alleged extra-Charter exceptions.[35]

[35] See also Albrecht Randelzhofer and Oliver Dörr, 'Article 2(4)' in Bruno Simma et al (eds), *The Charter of the United Nations: A Commentary* (3rd edn, Oxford: Oxford University Press, 2012), vol I, 200, 218–29.

A. Charter Exceptions

Part of the process restricting and regulating the use of force was the specification of exceptions under which use of force would be justified and unavoidable. Three exceptions are specifically laid down in the Charter. The first can be found in Articles 53(1), 77, and 107 and allows for measures against former enemy states from the Second World War without authorization by the Security Council. With the admission of Italy (1955), Japan (1956), and later Germany (1973) to the UN, this exception has become obsolete and lacks any current legal relevance.[36] There have even been attempts to remove these provisions from the Charter, most recently in the 2005 World Summit Outcome.[37]

The second exception emanates from the position of the Security Council as the principal organ of the UN with primary responsibility for the maintenance of international peace and security (Art 24). The Council is thus vested with the power to recommend or command military enforcement action when a threat to the peace, breach of the peace, or act of aggression takes place.[38] The wording of Article 39 (*recommendations*) and Article 42 (it *may* take such action) make clear that this is a discretionary power.

The third exception is laid down in Article 51, which provides that 'Nothing in the present Charter shall impair the inherent right of individual or collective self-defence if an armed attack occurs against a Member of the United Nations, until the Security Council has taken measures necessary to maintain international peace and security'. Self-defence is often considered to belong to the realm of customary international law.[39] Article 51 requires that states report to the Security Council on the measures taken by member states in their exercise of the right to self-defence, and reserves the right of the Security Council to take collective measures to uphold its primary responsibility for the maintenance or restoration of international peace and security at any time. This suspends the right of the victim state to take action in self-defence.[40]

[36] See Georg Ress and Jürgen Bröhmer, 'Article 53' in Simma et al, *The Charter of the United Nations*, vol II, 1506–24; Michael Wood, 'United Nations Charter, Enemy States Clauses' in Wolfrum, *Max Planck Encyclopedia of Pubic International Law*, vol X, 256–9.

[37] See General Assembly, A/RES/60/1 (24 Oct 2005), para 177. See also A/RES/50/52 (11 Dec 1995) and A/59/565 (2 Dec 2004), para 298.

[38] See Nicholas Tsagourias, 'Self-Defence, Protection of Humanitarian Values, and the Doctrine of Impartiality and Neutrality in Enforcement Mandates', Chapter 18 in this volume; Scott Sheeran, 'The Use of Force in United Nations Peacekeeping Operations', Chapter 16 in this volume. See also Erika de Wet, *The Chapter VII Powers of the United Nations Security Council* (Oxford: Hart, 2004) and Danesh Sarooshi, *The United Nations and the Development of Collective Security* (Oxford: Oxford University Press, 1999).

[39] See eg Sir Humphrey Waldock, 'The Regulation of the Use of Force by Individual States in International Law' (1952-II) 81 *Recueil des cours de l'Académie de droit international* 451; Derek W. Bowett, *Self-Defence in International Law* (New York: Praeger, 1958).

[40] See eg S/RES/661 concerning Kuwait/Iraq and imposing comprehensive economic and financial sanctions (6 Aug 1990). For a similar interpretation, see also Albrecht Randelzhofer and Georg Nolte,

B. Implicit Charter Exceptions

There exist two further implicit Charter-related exceptions, although both controversial and never put in practice. The first is the so-called 'Uniting for Peace' procedure, as adopted by the General Assembly in 1950. This procedure was a response to the presumed non-functioning of the Security Council.[41] Notwithstanding the division of powers between the General Assembly and the Security Council as provided under Articles 10–15 of the Charter, the General Assembly vested itself with the power to recommend military action in the case of a breach of the peace or act of aggression, should the Council fail to exercise its functions due to lack of agreement.[42] However, the General Assembly has never used this power in practice.

The second is the right of National Liberation Movements to employ all necessary means and seek international assistance in their legitimate struggle against colonialism, racist regimes, or alien occupation as referred to in Resolution 3070 (1973).[43] The struggle of peoples to liberate themselves from colonial and foreign domination was regarded as a legitimate exception to the prohibition of the use of force. Currently, this exception has lost much of its relevance.[44]

1. *Exceptions outside the Charter*

There exist two extra-Charter exceptions. The first is a proposed exception under customary international law to the prohibition on the use of force in the case of a life-threatening emergency situation abroad.[45] In such a situation, states would have the right to rescue their nationals, even by military coercion, but only if the foreign government was unable or unwilling to provide protection.[46] Customary

'Article 51' in Simma et al, *The Charter of the United Nations*, vol II, 1397, 1428. On self-defence see also Yoram Dinstein, *War, Aggression and Self-Defence* (5th edn, Cambridge: Cambridge University Press, 2012); Michael Wood, 'Self-Defence and Collective Security: Key Distinctions', Chapter 28 in this volume; Terry D. Gill, 'When Does Self-Defence End?', Chapter 33 in this volume.

[41] General Assembly, A/RES/377-A (3 Nov 1950). Text and report on debate in *United Nations Year Book 1950*, 193–5.

[42] General Assembly, A/RES/377-A (3 Nov 1950), para 1.

[43] General Assembly, A/RES/3070 (XXVIII) of 30 Nov 1973, para 2: '*Also reaffirms* the legitimacy of the peoples' struggle for liberation from colonial and foreign domination and alien subjugation by all available means, including armed struggle'. See also, ambiguously, Art 7 of the Definition of Aggression included in Annex to A/RES/3314 (XXIX) of 14 Dec 1974 which in part reads: 'right of these peoples to struggle to that end and to seek and receive support, in accordance with the principles of the Charter'. See also Randelzhofer and Dörr, 'Article 2(4)' in Simma et al, *The Charter of the United Nations*, vol I, 200, 228–9; Wil D. Verwey, 'Decolonization and the *Ius ad Bellum*: A Case Study on the Impact of the United Nations General Assembly on International Law' in Robert J. Akkerman et al (eds), *Declarations on Principles: A Quest for Universal Peace (Liber Röling)* (Leiden: Sijthoff, 1977), 121–40.

[44] Nico Schrijver, 'Article 2(4)' in Cot, Pellet, and Forteau, *La Charte des Nations Unies*, vol I, 437–64, 448.

[45] See Natalino Ronzitti, *Rescuing Nationals Abroad Through Military Coercion and Intervention on Grounds of Humanity* (Leiden: Martinus Nijhoff, 1985); Chittharanjan F. Amerasinghe, 'The Conumdrum of Recourse to Force—to Protect Persons' (2006) 3 *International Organizations Law Review* 7, 16–9.

[46] See Mathias Forteau, 'Rescuing Nationals Abroad', Chapter 44 in this volume.

international law principles, such as proportionality, necessity, and the observance of principles of international humanitarian law, have to be respected. Examples of this exception include the rescue operations by the UK in Suez in 1956, the operation by Belgium in Congo in 1960, the Entebbe Operation by Israel at Entebbe in Uganda in 1976, the attempt by the US to liberate the American hostages in Tehran in 1980, the operation by the US in Liberia in 1990, and the British military action to rescue peacekeepers in Sierra Leone in 2002.[47] These actions never raised a great deal of protest and, some 50 years later, constitute a rather consistent element of state practice. This led to an extra-Charter exception to Article 2(4) which clearly deviates from the exception in the case of self-defence owing to the absence of an armed attack against (the territory of) a state.

The concept of humanitarian intervention without Security Council authorization is often quoted as a second extra-Charter exception to the prohibition on the use of force, although it has given rise to considerable controversy in both doctrine and practice.[48] This concept does not centre on the protection of own nationals, but rather focuses on the protection of non-nationals. In the event of flagrant and mass violations of human rights, the use of force, without the consent of the government of the state in which the intervention takes place, could arguably be regarded as legitimate. Examples relating to this exception are Operation Provide Comfort in 1991, aimed at the protection of Kurds in northern Iraq, and the Shi'ites in the south,[49] and the North Atlantic Treaty Organization (NATO) action in Kosovo in 1999 under the name Operation Allied Force in response to the suppression of the Albanians in Kosovo by the Serbs.[50] In particular, the Kosovo action gave rise to considerable

[47] See eg Geoffrey Marston, 'Armed Intervention in the 1956 Suez Canal Crisis: The Legal Advice Tendered to the British Government' (1988) 37 *International and Comparative Law Quarterly* 773–817; Oscar Schachter, 'International Law in the Hostage Crisis: Implications for Future Cases' in Paul H. Kreisberg (ed), *American Hostages in Iran, The Conduct of a Crisis* (New Haven, CT: Yale University Press, 1985), 325–73; Richard B. Lillich, 'Forcible Protection of Nationals Abroad: The Liberian Incident of 1990' (1992) 35 *German Yearbook of International Law* 205–23.

[48] See Ian Brownlie, 'Thoughts on Kind-Hearted Gunmen' in Richard B. Lillich (ed), *Humanitarian Intervention*, 139–48; Peter Malanczuk, *Humanitarian Intervention and the Legitimacy of the Use of Force* (Amsterdam: Het Spinhuis, 1993); Carsten Stahn, 'Responsibility to Protect: Political Rhetoric or Emerging Legal Norm?' (2007) 101 *American Journal of International Law* 99–120; Nigel Rodley, 'Humanitarian Intervention', Chapter 35 in this volume.

[49] See Security Council, S/RES/688 (5 Apr 1991); Nicholas J. Wheeler, *Saving Strangers: Humanitarian Intervention and International Society* (Oxford: Oxford University Press, 2002), 141; Nigel D. White, 'Commentary on the Protection of the Kurdish Safe-Haven: Operation Desert Strike' (1996) 1 *Journal of Armed Conflict Law* 197; Oscar Schachter, 'United Nations Law in the Gulf Conflict' (1991) 85 *American Journal of International Law* 452; Peter Malanczuk, 'The Kurdish Crisis and Allied Intervention in the Aftermath of the Second Gulf War' (1991) 2 *European Journal of International Law* 114; Nico Schrijver, 'Sovereignty versus Human Rights? A Tale of UN Security Council Resolution 688 (1991) on the Protection of the Kurdish People' in Monique Castermans-Holleman et al (eds), *The Role of the Nation-State in the 21st Century: Human Rights, International Organisations, and Foreign Policy* (The Hague: Kluwer Law International, 1998), 347–57.

[50] Nicholas J. Wheeler, *Saving Strangers: Humanitarian Intervention and International Society* (Oxford: University Press, 2002), 265; Louis Henkin, Editorial comment on NATO's Kosovo

controversy. Limited state practice and the absence of a widely accepted *opinio juris* regarding the legitimacy of the use of force for humanitarian purposes not authorized by the UN Security Council, lead to the conclusion that humanitarian intervention without the authorization of the Security Council cannot be regarded as a customary international law exception to the prohibition on the use of force.[51]

V. The Interpretation of the Prohibition on the Use of Force

Throughout the existence of the UN, the prohibition on the use of force is repeatedly confirmed as a principle of international law, most importantly by reference to its application by the General Assembly, the Security Council, and the ICJ, and by its incorporation into multilateral treaties. This section discusses the interpretation of Article 2(4) in practice.

A. The General Assembly

Various resolutions of the General Assembly have clarified and elaborated on the meaning of the principle of the non-use of force. While these resolutions are not binding,[52] they can, if unambiguously and widely supported, be regarded as authoritative interpretations of the UN Charter. Important resolutions with provisions on the use of force include the Declaration on the Granting of Independence to Colonial Countries and Peoples of 14 December 1960, which states that: 'All armed action or repressive measures of all kinds directed against dependent peoples shall cease in order to enable them to exercise peacefully and freely their right to complete independence, and the integrity of their national territory shall be respected.'[53] A second important resolution is the Declaration on Principles of International Law

intervention, 'Kosovo and the Law of Humanitarian Intervention' (1999) 93 *American Journal of International Law* 824.

[51] Antonio Cassese, '*Ex inuria ius oritur*: Are We Moving Towards International Legitimation of Forcible Humanitarian Countermeasures in the World Community?' (1999) 10 *European Journal of International Law* 23–30; Anne Orford, *International Authority and the Use of Force* (Cambridge: Cambridge University Press, 2011).

[52] Charter of the United Nations, 892 UNTS 119, 26 June 1945, Arts 10–17.

[53] General Assembly, Declaration on the Granting of Independence to Colonial Countries and Peoples, A/RES/1514 (XV) (14 Dec 1960), adopted by 89 states with none against, with nine abstentions.

concerning Friendly Relations and Co-operation among States in accordance with the Charter of the United Nations of 1970, which reflects the consensus among member states as to the meaning and elaboration of the principles of the UN Charter.[54] Principle 1 of that Declaration specifies that the threat or use of force constitutes a violation of international law and the UN Charter. In addition, it provides for the duty not to use force in conflicts over international boundaries and not to forcibly deprive peoples of their rights in reprisal actions, and to refrain from encouraging or organizing irregular forces or terrorist acts.[55] Various other resolutions of the General Assembly elaborate on the prohibition to use force, such as the Essentials of Peace Resolution,[56] the Declaration on the Inadmissibility of Intervention in the Domestic Affairs of States and the Protection of Their Independence and Sovereignty,[57] the Definition of Aggression,[58] the Declaration on the Enhancement of the Effectiveness of the Principle of Refraining from the Threat or Use of Force in International Relations,[59] and the Resolution on the Conclusion of a world treaty on the non-use of force in international relations, a Soviet initiative which did not bear fruit.[60]

In 2005 the World Summit Outcome Document reiterated the General Assembly's determination to establish a just and lasting international peace and to refrain from the threat or use of force in international relations in conformity with the purposes and principles of the UN.[61] The General Assembly also expressed its determination to uphold the resolution of disputes by peaceful means in conformity with the principles of justice and international law.[62] Furthermore, according to the World Summit Outcome Document, peace and security, development, and human rights are the pillars of the UN system and the foundations for collective security and well-being.[63] In addition, it expressed the view that the relevant provisions of the Charter are sufficient to address the full range of threats to international peace and security and it reaffirmed the authority of the Security Council to mandate coercive action to maintain and restore international peace and security, while noting the role of the General Assembly relating to the maintenance of international peace and security.[64] The General Assembly recognized that UN peacekeeping plays a vital role in helping the parties to a conflict to end hostilities, but stressed the need to

[54] General Assembly, Declaration on Principles of International Law concerning Friendly Relations and Co-operation among States in accordance with the Charter of the United Nations, A/RES/2625 (XXV) (24 Oct 1970).

[55] *Declaration on Principles of International Law concerning Friendly Relations and Co-operation among States in accordance with the Charter of the United Nations*, Principle 1.

[56] A/RES/290 (IV), Essentials of Peace (1 Dec 1949). [57] A/RES/2131 (XX) (21 Dec 1965).

[58] A/RES/3314 (XXIX) (14 Dec 1974). [59] A/RES/42/22 (18 Nov 1987).

[60] A/RES/31/9 (8 Nov 1976).

[61] World Summit Outcome Document, A/RES/60/1 (2005), para 5.

[62] World Summit Outcome Document (2005), para 5.

[63] World Summit Outcome Document (2005), para 9.

[64] World Summit Outcome Document (2005), paras 79, 80.

mount operations with adequate capacity to counter hostilities and to fulfil their mandates effectively.[65]

B. The Security Council

During the Cold War, the collective security system with the prohibition of the use of force was paralysed. The Security Council could not address the use of force in the case of the Soviet interventions in Hungary (1956) and Czechoslovakia (1968), the invasion of Goa by India in 1961, the quarantine imposed on Cuba (1962), the armed intervention in the Dominican Republic in 1965, nor in the Vietnam War (1964–75).[66] The inaction in these cases demonstrated that the collective security system could only work if the permanent members reached agreement and engaged in cooperation. Consequently, most practice by the Security Council relating to Article 2(4) stems from the period after the Cold War. Nevertheless, there are a few early examples of action by the Security Council in response to a breach of peace or a threat to international peace and security. In 1950, the Security Council declared that the armed attack on the Republic of Korea by forces of North Korea was a breach of the peace and demanded the immediate cessation of hostilities.[67] Two days later, the Security Council, having noted that the authorities in North Korea did not cease hostilities nor withdraw its forces, recommended that 'the Members of the United Nations furnish such assistance to the Republic of Korea as may be necessary to repel the armed attack and to restore international peace and security in the area'.[68] This is one of the first instances in which the Security Council called for a coalition of the able and willing to repel an armed attack against one of the members of the UN.

A second example is the situation in Congo, where the Security Council first authorized a UN operation to use force by urging that 'the United Nations take immediately all appropriate measures to prevent the occurrence of civil war in the Congo, including arrangements for cease-fires, the halting of all military operations, the prevention of clashes, and the use of force, if necessary, in the last resort'.[69]

A third pre-1990 example from that period concerns the oil supplies to Southern Rhodesia, notwithstanding the call of the Security Council for all states to apply an oil embargo against the territory. In Resolution 221 (1966), the Security Council called upon the government of the UK to 'prevent, by the use of force if necessary,

[65] World Summit Outcome Document (2005), para 92.

[66] Bernardus V. A. Röling, 'International Law and the Maintenance of Peace' (1973) 4 *Netherlands Yearbook of International Law* 1–103. For a post-Cold War account, see Kofi Annan, *Interventions* (New York: Penguin Press, 2012).

[67] Security Council, S/RES/82 (25 June 1950).

[68] Security Council, S/RES/83 (27 June 1950).

[69] Security Council, S/RES/161 (21 Feb 1961).

the arrival at Beira of vessels reasonably believed to be carrying oil destined for Southern Rhodesia.'[70]

During the 25 years after the Cold War, the Security Council adopted three times as many resolutions as during its first 45 years, with quite a large number adopted under Chapter VII. The Security Council started to interpret the concept of 'a threat to the peace' more extensively and, for example, came to view internal conflicts as a threat to international peace. The Security Council imposed a wide variety of sanctions and also intervened several times militarily, although it often left the actual action to a coalition of able and willing member states. The phrase 'all necessary means' evolved as the standard formula by which the Security Council authorized the use of military force if necessary to maintain or restore international peace and security. Situations in which the Security Council authorized the use of force include the cases of Kuwait/Iraq, Somalia, Haiti, East Timor, Afghanistan, Libya, Côte d'Ivoire, and Mali.[71]

Apart from the authorization to use force in such specific cases, the Security Council regularly addressed the substance of the prohibition of Article 2(4). It is important to note that the Council only occasionally referred *expressis verbis* to Article 2(4). These cases include the armed conflict between Greece and Turkey regarding Cyprus,[72] the attack by the Israeli Air Force against the Iraqi nuclear installations near Baghdad,[73] the acts of aggression by South Africa against Angola,[74] and Israel's raid on the PLO headquarters in Tunis.[75] More often, the Council employed language similar to the wording of Article 2(4) or included a general reference to Article 2. An example of the latter can be found in Resolution 242 (1967), adopted in response to the Six Day War.[76]

Only seldom has the Security Council engaged in a constitutional discussion on the content and status of the prohibition of the threat or use of force. Grenada, Nicaragua, and Iraq are pertinent examples. In the case of Grenada, the military regime of Grenada was deposed by an armed intervention by a multinational task force composed of members of the Organisation of Eastern Caribbean States

70 Security Council, S/RES/221 (9 Apr 1966).

71 Kuwait, S/RES/678 (1990); Somalia, S/RES/794 (1992); Haiti, S/RES/940 (1994); East Timor, S/RES/1264 (1999); Afghanistan, S/RES/1386 (2001) and S/RES/1563 (2004); Iraq, S/RES/1546 (2004); Libya, S/RES/1973 (2011); Côte d'Ivoire, S/RES/1975 (2011); and Mali, S/RES/2085 (2012). See Niels N. Blokker, 'Is the Authorization Authorized? Powers and Practice of the UN Security Council to Authorize the Use of Force by "Coalitions of the Able and Willing"' (2000) 11 *European Journal of International Law* 541 and his 'Outsourcing the Use of Force: Towards More Security Council Control of Authorized Operations?', Chapter 9 in this volume.

72 Security Council, S/RES/186 (1964).

73 Security Council, S/RES/487 (1981).

74 Security Council, S/RES/545 (1983).

75 Security Council, S/RES/573 (1985).

76 S/RES/242 (1967): '*Emphasizing further* that all Member States in their acceptance of the Charter of the United Nations have undertaken a commitment to act in accordance with Article 2 of the Charter' (preamble). See also Sydney D. Bailey, *The Making of Resolution 242* (Dordrecht: Martinus Nijhoff, 1985).

(OECS) and other invited states in 1983.[77] Proponents advocated that the action by the task force was legal and that the Charter prohibition of the use of force was contextual and not absolute since there were provisions, even within the Charter, that justified the use of force in pursuit of other values such as freedom, democracy, and peace.[78] The Charter, according to those proponents, did not require peoples to submit to terror, nor their neighbours to be indifferent to their terrorization.[79] A draft resolution, referring to Article 2(4), deploring the armed intervention and calling for the immediate withdrawal of the foreign troops from Grenada, received 11 votes in favour, three abstentions, and only one negative vote by the US, and it was consequently not adopted. The air strikes by the US on Tripoli and Benghazi in 1986 also raised questions regarding the delineation between the general rule of Article 2(4) and the exception under Article 51 of the Charter. Primarily, the question was raised whether there existed a right to pre-emptive self-defence against terrorist acts, and whether terrorist acts could be attributed to a state. Again, a draft resolution condemning the attack by the US as well as condemning all terrorist activities was vetoed by the US.[80] In the case of Iraq, a discussion arose as to whether Resolution 1441 (2002) included authorization of the use of force in the case of non-compliance by Iraq with the resolution. Given that Resolution 1441 (2002) did not include the standard authorization 'to use all necessary measures', it cannot reasonably be interpreted as authorizing individual member states to use military force to compel Iraq to comply with Security Council resolutions.[81] Occasionally, members of the Security Council want to make it explicitly clear that a certain resolution does

[77] See Ved P. Nanda, 'The United States Armed Intervention in Grenada–Impact on World Order' (1984) 14 *California Western International Law Journal* 395–424; Louise Doswald-Beck, 'The Legality of the United States Intervention in Grenada' (1984) 24 *Indian Journal of International Law* 200–23; Robert J. Beck, 'International Law and the Decision to Invade Grenada: A Ten-Year Retrospective' (1993) 33 *Virginia Journal of International Law* 765–817.

[78] See Michael Byers and Simon Chesterman, '"You, the People": Pro-Democratic Intervention in International Law' in Gregory H. Fox and Brad R. Roth (eds), *Democratic Governance and International Law* (Cambridge: Cambridge University Press, 2000), 259–92; Jeremy I. Levitt, 'Pro-Democratic Intervention in Africa' in Jeremy I. Levitt (ed), *Africa: Mapping New Boundaries in International Law* (Oxford: Hart, 2008), 103–47; Simone van den Driest, '"Pro-Democratic Intervention and the Right to Political Self-Determination: The Case of Operation Iraqi Freedom' (2010) 57 *Netherlands International Law Review* 29–72.

[79] *Repertoire of the Practice of the UN Security Council 1981–1984, Supplement*, 343.

[80] *Supplement 1985–1988*, 443–4.

[81] See also the statement by US Ambassador Negroponte that this resolution does not contain 'hidden triggers' and 'no automaticity' with respect to the use of force, S/PV 466 (8 Nov 2002), 3. See also ch 8 of the *Report of the Dutch Committee of Inquiry on the War in Iraq*, 'The Basis in International Law for the Military Intervention in Iraq', published in (2010) 57 *Netherlands International Law Review* 137–210. For academic analyses, see Oliver Corten, 'Opération Iraqi Freedom: peut-on admettre l'argument de l'"autorisation implicite" du Conseil de Sécurité?' (2003) 36 *Revue Belge de Droit International* 205–47; 'Agora' (2003) 97 *American Journal of International Law* 553–642; Michael Byers, 'Agreeing to Disagree: Security Council Resolution 1441 and Intentional Ambiguity' (2004) 10 *Global Governance* 2; Marc Weller, *Iraq and the Use of Force in International Law* (Oxford: Oxford University Press, 2010).

not contain an authorization to use of force. In an effort to attract the votes of China and Russia, in 2012 Morocco submitted a draft resolution on the question of Syria in which it was stated that 'nothing in this resolution authorizes measures under article 42 of the Charter'. However, the two permanent members still considered the draft to be a too far-reaching infringement of the principle of non-intervention and the sovereignty and territorial integrity of Syria and exercised their veto.[82]

c. The International Court of Justice

Several judgments of the ICJ have contributed to the consolidation of the prohibition of the use of force in international relations.[83] The most important decision is the judgment in the case of Nicaragua against the US. Due to a limitation of jurisdiction, the ICJ had to base its judgment on customary international law. The Court held that the prohibition on the use of force under customary international law is in essence similar to the provision in Article 2(4) with respect to both practice and *opinio juris*. The Court justified this decision by reference to the attitude of the parties to the conflict and those of other states. Consent to various General Assembly resolutions relating to the prohibition of the use of force, in particular to the Declaration on Principles of International Law Concerning Friendly Relations and Co-operation among States, is an expression of the *opinio juris* that non-use of force constitutes a principle of international law.[84] Consequently, the Court concluded that the US had acted in breach of its obligation under customary international law not to use force against another state.[85] The Court in this case also made clear that self-defence can only be exercised in response to an armed attack, and that under customary international law there is no rule permitting the exercise of collective self-defence in the absence of a request by the country in which the alleged attack occurred, or even in the absence of a declaration by the respective state that it has been attacked.[86] The Court refers to the principle of non-use of force as a cardinal principle that has been the pivotal point of a time-honoured legal philosophy that has evolved particularly after the two world wars of the 20th century.[87]

[82] See text of the draft resolution in S/2012/77 (11 Feb 2012).

[83] See also Guillaume Etienne, 'L'emploi de la force armée devant la Cour internationale de justice' (2002) III *Annuaire Français de Relations Internationales* 215–49; Claus Kreß, 'The International Court of Justice and the "Principle of Non-Use of Force"', Chapter 25 in this volume.

[84] *Military and Paramilitary Activities in and against Nicaragua (Nicaragua v. US)*, Merits, Judgment, ICJ Rep 1986, 90, paras 189–90. Pierre-Michel Eiseman, 'L'arret de la CIJ du 27 juin (fond) dans l'affaire des activités militaires et paramilitaries au Nicaragua et contre celui-ci' (1987) 32 *Annuaire Français de Droit International* 153–91; Joe Verhoeven, 'Le droit, le juge et la violence' (1987) 91 *Revue Générale de Droit International Public* 1159–239.

[85] *Nicaragua*, Merits, 147, para 292.

[86] *Nicaragua*, Merits, 147, para 195.

[87] *Nicaragua*, Merits, 147, para 190.

Other authoritative interpretations by the ICJ of the prohibition of the use of force include the *Corfu Channel* case (1949),[88] the advisory opinion on the issue of the *Legality of the Use of Nuclear Weapons* (1996),[89] the *Oil Platforms* case (2003) and the *Armed Activities* case (2005). In the *Oil Platforms* case, the Court repeated that self-defence is only allowed in response to an armed attack, as specified in Article 51 of the UN Charter and customary international law, and that it has to be necessary and proportionate, and that the envisaged target must be a legitimate military target, open to attack in the exercise of self-defence.[90] In its advisory opinion on the *Legality of the Threat or Use of Nuclear Weapons*, the Court held that Article 2(4) and other provisions on the use of force do not refer to specific weapons, and that those provisions neither prohibit nor permit the use of any specific weapon. In the advisory opinion, the Court clarifies that any threat to use force is also impermissible, if the actual use of force in the same situation is illegal.[91]

The *Case Concerning Armed Activities on the Territory of the Congo (DRC v. Uganda)* dealt with the question whether Uganda had violated the prohibition to use force by engaging in military and paramilitary activities against the Democratic Republic of the Congo (DRC). The case was somewhat complicated, because prior to August 1998 the DRC had not objected to the military presence of Uganda in its eastern border region, and in fact both countries agreed that their armies would cooperate to ensure the security and peace in that region. The Court held that the consent of the DRC to the foreign presence in its territory was not open-ended and that Uganda had expanded the scope and nature of its activities, while the DRC had withdrawn its consent by accusing Uganda of invading its territory.[92] Given that the DRC no longer consented to the military presence of Uganda on its territory, the Court had to determine whether the acts of Uganda were permitted as self-defence. This was not the case, since Uganda never claimed that it had been subjected to an armed attack by the armed forces of the DRC and did not report any acts to the Security Council that required Uganda to act in self-defence. Consequently, the Court concluded that the Republic of Uganda, by engaging in military activities against and on the territory of the DRC, by occupying Ituri, and by extending support to irregular forces operating on the territory of the DRC, had violated the prohibition on the use of force expressed in Article 2(4) of the UN Charter, as well as the principle of non-intervention.[93]

In the advisory opinion on *Kosovo* the Court also made a cursory reference to Article 2(4), where it stated that: 'The Court recalls that the principle of territorial

[88] *Corfu Channel*, Judgment of 9 April 1949, ICJ Rep 1949, 4.

[89] *Legality of the Threat or Use of Nuclear Weapons*, Advisory Opinion, ICJ Rep 1996, 226.

[90] *Oil Platforms (Iran v. US)*, Judgment, ICJ Rep 2003, para 51.

[91] *Legality of the Threat or Use of Nuclear Weapons*, Advisory Opinion, paras 37–50.

[92] *Armed Activities on the Territory of the Congo (DRC v. Uganda)*, Judgment, ICJ Rep 2005, 168, paras 42–54.

[93] *Armed Activities*, Judgment, paras 42–165 and 345.

integrity is an important part of the international legal order and is enshrined in the Charter of the United Nations, in particular in Article 2, paragraph 4'.[94]

In addition to these cases, the Court has occasionally imposed provisional measures with the aim of preventing the escalation of a conflict and to avoid incidents, and has demanded withdrawal of armed forces and the suspension of military support. Recent examples are *Costa Rica v. Nicaragua*[95] and *Georgia v. Russia*.[96]

D. Multilateral Treaties

The substance of Article 2(4) has also been incorporated in different multilateral treaties since 1945, primarily in treaties establishing defence organizations or political institutions. Both the North Atlantic Treaty and the Warsaw Security Pact of 1955 incorporate almost verbatim the text of Article 2(4) of the UN Charter, while obliging states to settle their disputes by peaceful means.[97] Similarly, the Pact of the League of Arab States,[98] the Inter-American Treaty of Reciprocal Assistance,[99] and the Southeast Asia Collective Defense Treaty[100] explicitly prohibit the use of force. This applies equally to the United Nations Convention on the Law of the Sea[101] and the Rome Statute of the International Criminal Court.[102] More recently, the African Union in its Constitutive Pact incorporated the principle of the prohibition of the use of force or threat to use force among member states of the Union.[103]

In addition, the International Law Commission addressed the issue of the use of force in two provisions in its 2001 Articles on State Responsibility. Article 21 reads: 'The wrongfulness of an act of a State is precluded if the act constitutes a lawful measure of self-defence taken in conformity with the Charter of the United Nations'. Furthermore, Article 50 provides that 'Countermeasures shall not affect the obligation to refrain from the threat or use of force as embodied in the Charter of the United Nations'.[104]

[94] *Accordance with International Law of the Unilateral Declaration of Independence in Respect of Kosovo*, Advisory Opinion, ICJ Rep 2010, 18, para 80.

[95] *Dispute Regarding Navigational and Related Rights (Costa Rica v. Nicaragua)*, ICJ Rep 2009, 213.

[96] *Application of the International Convention on the Elimination of All Forms of Racial Discrimination (Georgia v. Russian Federation)*, Preliminary Objections, Judgment, ICJ Rep 2011, 70.

[97] Warsaw Security Pact of 14 May 1955; North Atlantic Treaty, 4 Apr 1949, Art 1.

[98] Pact of the League of Arab States, 22 Mar 1945, Art 5.

[99] Inter-American Treaty of Reciprocal Assistance, 2 Sept 1947, Art 1. See also the Charter of the Organization of American States, 1948, Arts 15 and 16.

[100] Southeast Asia Collective Defense Treaty (Manila Pact), 8 Sept 1954, Art I.

[101] United Nations Convention on the Law of the Sea, 10 Dec 1982, Art 301.

[102] Rome Statute of the International Criminal Court, 17 July 1998, Preamble.

[103] Constitutive Act of the African Union, 11 July 2000, Art 4(f). Art 4(h) reads: 'the right of the Union to intervene in a Member State pursuant to a decision of the Assembly in respect of grave circumstances, namely: war crimes, genocide and crimes against humanity.'

[104] Responsibility of States for Internationally Wrongful Acts, *Yearbook of the International Law Commission*, 2001, vol II (2); GA Res 56/83 (12 Dec 2001), corrected by A/56/49, (Vol. I)/Corr. 4.

These references to the prohibition to use force in multilateral treaties and other principal legal documents contribute to the firm establishment of this principle in international law.

VI. The Legal Status of Article 2(4) of the UN Charter

There can be little doubt that the prohibition to use force is a fundamental principle of international law, which has achieved a firm status in contemporary public international law. It is prominently recorded in the UN Charter, included as the first of seven main principles of international law in the Declaration on Friendly Relations of 1970, and frequently incorporated in multilateral treaties, judicial decisions, and declarations of states. Yet, armed force is still resorted to on numerous occasions, as the annual reports of the Stockholm International Peace Research Institute show.[105]

Nevertheless, the principle of the prohibition to use force as enshrined in Article 2(4) of the UN Charter is frequently identified as a norm of *jus cogens*, often referring to the commentary of the International Law Commission (ILC) on the Draft Articles on the Law of Treaties, in which the ILC expressed the opinion that 'the law of the Charter concerning the prohibition to use force constitutes a conspicuous example of a rule in international law having the character of *ius cogens*'.[106] The ICJ quoted this passage of the ILC in its judgment in the *Nicaragua* case, but it did not itself confirm the legal status of the prohibition. The Court held only that the prohibition to use force was a fundamental or cardinal principle of law.[107] It also

[105] See eg 59 major armed conflicts reported for the period between 1990 and 2003, *Stockholm International Peace Research Institute Yearbook 2004: Armaments, Disarmament and International Security* (2004), 132.

[106] *Yearbook of the International Law Commission*, 1966, vol II, 270, para 1. See also eg Joe Verhoeven, *Droit International Public* (Paris: Larcier, 2000), 671 ('elle revêt un caractère d'ordre public, ce qui entache de nullité toute convention qui la méconnaîtrait,... et que ça violation est constitutive d'un 'crime international', quelle que soit la portée exacte'); Patrick Daillier and Alain Pellet, *Droit international public* (7th edn, Paris: LGDJ, 2002), 967, para 576 ('l'interdiction de recourir à la force armée... constitue une norme impérative'). Ian Brownlie includes the prohibition of the use of force among the 'least controversial examples' of *jus cogens* in his *Principles of Public International Law* (6th edn, Oxford: Oxford University Press, 2003), 489. See also James Crawford, *Brownlie's Principles of Public International Law* (8th edn, Oxford: Oxford University Press, 2012), 595–6; Jochen A. Frowein, 'Jus Cogens' in Wolfrum, *Max Planck Encyclopedia of Pubic International Law*, vol III, 443–6; André de Hoogh, '*Jus Cogens* and the Use of Armed Force', Chapter 54 in this volume.

[107] *Nicaragua*, Merits, para 190. See also the Separate Opinion of Judge Sette-Camara, 199–200 ('I firmly believe that the non-use of force as well as non-intervention... are not only cardinal principles

confirmed that the norm coincided with customary international law.[108] In its advisory opinion on *Kosovo* the Court left unclear, among some other issues, whether the principle enshrined in Article 2(4) is of a *jus cogens* nature. It stated: 'the illegality attached to the declarations of independence thus stemmed not from the unilateral character of these declarations as such, but from the fact that they were, or would have been, connected with the unlawful use of force or other egregious violations of norms of general international law, in particular those of a peremptory character (*jus cogens*)'. While the Court includes here the prohibition to use force among the norms of general international law, it remains unclear from this formulation whether the Court includes the unlawful use of force among the *jus cogens* norms.[109] Furthermore, opinions on the primordial legal status of the principle of the non-use of force do not apply to the prohibition of the threat to use force.

What are the merits of attaching peremptory status to the norm not to use force? Article 53 of the 1969 Vienna Convention on the Law of Treaties gives a description of the concept of *jus cogens*, equating it in the title of the article to 'a peremptory norm of general international law'. Article 53 defines such a peremptory norm as 'a norm accepted and recognized by the international community of States as a whole as a norm from which no derogation is permitted and which can be modified only by a subsequent norm of general international law having the same character'.[110] From this article it can first of all be derived that only widely accepted and recognized norms of general international law can potentially gain the status of *jus cogens*. In addition, a very large majority of states must have accepted and recognized a norm as 'peremptory'. The norm does not have to be accepted by all states: from the *travaux préparatoires* of the Vienna Convention it can be derived that 'no individual state should have the right of veto in determining what were and what were not peremptory norms'.[111] The third criterion for a norm to become a norm of *jus cogens* specifies that no derogation from the norm is permitted.[112] Does the prohibition to use force meet those three criteria? First, it amply meets the test of being widely accepted and recognized. Secondly, from the almost universal membership of the UN and the frequent pronouncements of adherence to the UN Charter, it can be

of customary international law but could in addition be recognized as peremptory rules of customary international law which impose obligations on all States').

[108] *Nicaragua*, Merits, paras 189–90, 292.

[109] *Accordance with International Law of the Unilateral Declaration of Independence in Respect of Kosovo*, Advisory Opinion, ICJ Rep 2010, 18, para 81.

[110] Vienna Convention on the Law of Treaties, 1155 UNTS 331, 22 May 1969, Art 53.

[111] Ian Sinclair, *The Vienna Convention on the Law of Treaties* (2nd edn, Manchester: Manchester University Press, 1984), 214.

[112] See Eric Suy, 'Article 53' in Oliver Corten and Pierre Klein (eds), *Vienna Conventions on the Law of Treaties. Commentary Article by Article* (Oxford: Oxford University Press, 2011), vol II, 1224–33; Paul Reuter and Philippe Cahier, *Introduction au droit des traités* (3rd edn, Paris: Presses Universitaires de France, 1995), 127, para 221; Tamslin Olawale Elias, *The Modern Law of Treaties* (New York: Oceana Publications, 1974), 177–87.

safely concluded that a very large majority of states, if not all, accept and still recognize the prohibition to use force in very general terms as a 'peremptory norm'.

It is the third criterion which is the more problematic, also in the light of the increasing number of claims of new exceptions to the prohibition to use force. The two main exceptions provided in the text of the Charter (collective enforcement action and self-defence) have always been part and parcel of the law of the UN with respect to the use of force, and are therefore not problematic. Expansive interpretations of the right of self-defence, including the claimed legality of pre-emptive and even preventive self-defence,[113] and the invoked right to use armed force unilaterally, in cases of humanitarian emergencies, the 'global war' against terrorism, and the proliferation of weapons of mass destruction, do infringe, each on their own but certainly in combination, on the legal status of the prohibition on the use of force, especially when the practice of leading states frequently deviates from the general norm of the Charter. In the post-11 September world, it is all too frequently held that the struggle against terrorism has to be fought with all necessary means, including armed force with or without authorization by the UN.[114] Obviously, the international community has to be careful with all too expansive interpretations of exceptions to the principle on the prohibition of the use of force as so prominently enshrined in the UN Charter. No cause would be served by opening the gates and returning to the nearly unqualified pre-Charter *jus ad bellum*. Consequently, the maintenance of *jus cogens* status calls for constant care and alertness as regards additional extra-Charter loopholes and for faithful observance by states in international affairs. In this respect, it is of the utmost importance to interpret the newly evolving principle of the 'Responsibility to Protect', which confers on the international community a secondary responsibility to protect civilians in life-threatening situations wherever they may be, in the sense in which the General Assembly did in the Word Summit Outcome, where it stated that: 'we are prepared to take collective action, in a timely and decisive manner, through the Security Council, in accordance with the Charter, including Chapter VII, on a case-by-case basis and in co-operation with relevant regional organisations as appropriate, should peaceful means be inadequate and national authorities are manifestly failing to protect their populations from genocide, war crimes, ethnic cleansing and crimes against humanity'.[115]

[113] See *The National Security Strategy of the United States*, Washington DC, Sept 2002 available at <http://www.whitehouse.gov/nsc/nss.pdf>.

[114] See Helen Duffy, *The 'War on Terror' and the Framework of International Law* (2nd edn, Cambridge: Cambridge University Press, forthcoming); Larissa J. van den Herik and Nico Schrijver (eds), *Counter-Terrorism Strategies in a Fragmented International Legal Order: Meeting the Challenges* (Cambridge: Cambridge University Press, 2013).

[115] World Summit Outcome Document (2005), paras 138–9. See also International Commission on Intervention and State Sovereignty, *The Responsibility to Protect* (2001) and the subsequent endorsement of the concept of the responsibility to protect in the High-Level Panel Report, 'A More Secure World', A/59/565 (2004), paras 202–3, the Secretary-General's Report, 'In Larger Freedom', A/59/2005

VII. Concluding Remarks

Article 2(4) is the crystallization of a very long process of regulating the *jus ad bellum*. The inclusion of the prohibition on the use of force in the UN Charter was certainly somewhat of a revolutionary step.[116] Without doubt, the prohibition to use force has become a fundamental principle of international law that has achieved a firm status in contemporary public international law and it can perhaps even be accorded the character of *jus cogens*. However, in view of both the frequent violations of the principle and the numerous outcries to halt serious violations of human rights, to respond to humanitarian catastrophes and to terrorism, and to stop the proliferation of weapons of mass destruction, the principle enshrined in Article 2(4) is constantly under attack. It is important to realize that Article 2(4) functions as the backbone of the Charter system of collective security, both in a normative sense and as the foundation for the institutionalized facilities for the pacific settlement of international disputes and the ultimate, supranational authority of the Security Council to take effective measures for the maintenance or restoration of international peace and security. The task is to uphold rather than to bend the rules of Article 2(4) and to effectuate this through a collective security system which maintains international peace and security and equally restores it by taking timely and decisive action under the auspices of the Security Council, whenever necessary.

(2005), paras 132, 135. For recent academic reviews, see Ramesh Thakur, *The United Nations, Peace and Security: From Collective Security to the Responsibility to Protect* (Cambridge: Cambridge University Press, 2006); Thomas G. Weiss, *Humanitarian Intervention: Ideas in Action* (2nd edn, Cambridge: Polity, 2012); Mindia Vaskakmadze, 'Responsibility to Protect' in Simma et al, *The Charter of the United Nations*, vol I, 1201–36.

[116] Virally referred to it as 'une veritable mutation du droit international, un changement qu'il n'est pas excessif de qualifier de révolutionnaire'. See Michel Virally, 'Article 2 paragraphe 4' in Cot and Pellet, *La Charte des Nations Unies* (2nd edn, 1991), 115.

CHAPTER 22

INTERVENTION, ARMED INTERVENTION, ARMED ATTACK, THREAT TO PEACE, ACT OF AGGRESSION, AND THREAT OR USE OF FORCE: WHAT'S THE DIFFERENCE?

JAN KLABBERS

I. Introduction

LAWYERS are often accused of having a fixation on words and language, and justifiably so. Part of the skill of being an investment lawyer is to realize the difference between 'prompt, adequate and effective compensation' and alternative standards of compensation which, inevitably, will be cast in different words.[1] Part of the skill of being a UN lawyer is to realize that the word 'concurring' in Article 27(3) of the Charter has received a different meaning in practice than its dictionary meaning would suggest.[2] Much of the discussion on self-defence in international law revolves around the question how seriously one ought to take the phrase 'if an armed attack occurs', to be found in Article 51 of the Charter.[3]

In the light of this, it is hardly a coincidence that international lawyers have come to pay great attention to rules of interpretation. If words are of great relevance, then it stands to reason that there should be rules on how to read and understand those words—whether to excavate the original intentions of their drafters, whether to focus on the aim a specific combination of words was thought to achieve, or whether to stay close to the accepted meaning of words in their ordinary usage, with further debates raging on how much context to take into account and, indeed, what exactly establishes the context of a provision or treaty. International lawyers engage in these debates with great gusto when it comes to interpreting treaties (there are, after all, recognized rules on treaty interpretation, laid down in Articles 31–3 of the Vienna Convention on the Law of Treaties), and increasingly also when it comes to interpreting and understanding other documents, such as resolutions adopted by the UN Security Council.[4]

Yet, there is one branch of international law where somehow this verbal precision and attention for legal detail and nuance seems to be largely lacking, and that is the use of force. Whenever force is used in interstate relations, the labelling takes on widely varying dimensions, with a number of different terms being eagerly used without, or so it seems, too much attention for legal subtleties—and without paying much attention to any rules on interpretation either. Terms such as 'invasion', 'intervention', 'armed attack', 'breach of the peace', 'threat or use of force', and 'aggression' appear to be used interchangeably and rather indiscriminately, both in popular parlance and in professional legal discussions.

A swift perusal of the literature suggests that leading and reasonable international lawyers characterize the same act or set of acts using widely different terms. Thus, the US military action in Iraq, which commenced in 2003, is characterized by Sean Murphy as an 'intervention'.[5] Vaughan Lowe, on the other hand, mostly classifies

[1] See Jan Klabbers, 'The Meaning of Rules' (2006) 20 *International Relations* 295–301.

[2] See *Legal Consequences for States of the Continued Presence of South Africa in Namibia (South West Africa) Notwithstanding Security Council Resolution 276 (1970)*, Advisory Opinion, ICJ Rep 1971, 16.

[3] Franck famously referred to the literal reading of Art 51 as an 'idiot rule'. See Thomas M. Franck, *The Power of Legitimacy Among Nations* (Oxford: Oxford University Press, 1990), 75.

[4] See generally (and sceptically) Jan Klabbers, 'Virtuous Interpretation' in Malgosia Fitzmaurice, Olufemi Elias, and Panos Merkouris (eds), *Treaty Interpretation and the Vienna Convention on the Law of Treaties: 30 Years On* (The Hague: Martinus Nijhoff, 2010), 17–37.

[5] See Sean Murphy, *Principles of International Law* (St Paul, MN: Thomson/West, 2006), 453.

the action as an 'invasion',[6] although he also uses the term 'intervention'.[7] Yoram Dinstein uses the term 'occupation',[8] while Tarcisio Gazzini mostly uses 'intervention', but also speaks of a 'massive military campaign', 'outbreak of hostilities', and 'occupation'.[9] Andrew Clapham speaks of 'war' and while adding that he does so in a non-technical sense, nonetheless suggests that the war is largely the responsibility of the US and the UK and their allies.[10] Christine Gray, finally, deftly avoids characterizing the action by consistently referring to its given name of Operation Iraqi Freedom.[11]

While this suggests an undisciplined discourse, appearances may deceive: there is a sense in which such characterizations are as subtle and sensitive as in any other branch of international law—or perhaps even more so. It is just that the subtleties are different in nature than the ones usually informing legal discussion. In this chapter, I aim to take stock of the different ways in which the use of force can be classified, and aim to present an explanation for the ways in which this occurs. Section II provides a rough overview of the relevant practice of states when concluding agreements on the topic (Sections II.A and II.E), sandwiching an overview of the practice of the Security Council when confronted with interstate conflicts.[12] The overview is neither complete nor very systematic, but does provide a general picture. Section III ties these overviews together, while Section IV contains a brief discussion of the practice of the ICJ; again, the data are not gathered in a highly systematic fashion, but again, they confirm the proposition that precise classifications are not the main priority when it comes to issues of war and peace. Section V sets out some thoughts on the relationship between language and law when the use of force is concerned, while Section VI concludes.

[6] See Vaughan Lowe, *International Law* (Oxford: Clarendon Press, 2007), 57.

[7] Lowe, *International Law*, 108.

[8] See Yoram Dinstein, *War, Aggression and Self-Defence* (4th edn, Cambridge: Cambridge University Press, 2005), 297.

[9] See Tarcisio Gazzini, *The Changing Rules on the Use of Force in International Law* (Manchester: Manchester University Press, 2005), 78–81.

[10] See Andrew Clapham, *Brierly's Law of Nations* (7th edn, Oxford: Oxford University Press, 2012), 486–7.

[11] See Christine Gray, 'The Use of Force and the International Legal Order' in Malcolm D. Evans (ed), *International Law* (3rd edn, Oxford: Oxford University Press, 2010), 615, 637–8.

[12] And some other instances as well, where considered relevant for the discussion.

II. An Infinite Variety

The law on the use of force, such as it is, is itself not characterized by conceptual or linguistic clarity, and probably for good reason: after all, a clear definition not only includes certain acts, but will also exclude certain others that perhaps, on second thought, ought to be included as well. The problem is familiar to students of jurisprudence, with Hart's classic example 'No vehicles in the park' giving rise to heated debates as to what counts as a vehicle: while obviously cars are covered, are toy cars also covered?[13] Or wheelchairs? Or immobilized, defunct, cars that have become part of a monument? There may be relative certainty at the core of rules (or definitions or classifications), as Hart proclaimed, but there is bound to be uncertainty at the penumbra.

A. The UN Charter and Other Security Arrangements

The UN Charter alone uses a variety of terms. It speaks of 'threats to the peace', 'acts of aggression', and 'other breaches of the peace' in Article 1(1) and refers to 'the threat or use of force' in Article 2(4). The possibility that certain situations 'endanger international peace and security' is mentioned in Article 11(3), whereas disputes that are likely to 'endanger the maintenance of international peace and security' are mentioned in Article 33(1) and in Articles 34 and 37(2). Article 39 harks back to the formula of Article 1(1), but places the terms in different order, speaking of 'any threat to the peace, breach of the peace, or act of aggression', while Article 51 speaks of an 'armed attack'. Finally, Article 99 authorizes the Secretary-General to call the Security Council's attention to matters which may 'threaten the maintenance of international peace and security'.

This linguistic diversity is mirrored in other treaties. The constituent treaty of the North Atlantic Treaty Organization (NATO), for example, alternates between 'armed attack' (Arts 3, 5, and 6), the 'threat or use of force' (Art 1), and threats to the 'territorial integrity, political independence or security' of any of its parties (Art 4). The same applies to the Australia, New Zealand, United States Security (ANZUS) Treaty, which mostly speaks of 'armed attack' (Art II, IV, and V) but also mentions the 'threat or use of force' (Art I) and threats to the 'territorial integrity, political independence or security' of its parties (Art III).

The erstwhile South East Asia Treaty Organization (SEATO) Treaty used different terms still.[14] While it too mentioned 'armed attack', it also spoke of 'subversive

[13] See H. L. A. Hart, *The Concept of Law* (Oxford: Clarendon Press, 1961), 122.

[14] SEATO was set up in 1954, and dissolved in 1977.

activities against the territorial integrity and political stability' of its parties (Art II), and further specified that 'armed attack' was to be conceptualized as a means of aggression (Art IV). A similar conceptualization can be found in the Organization of American States (OAS) Charter, which speaks of 'armed attacks' and of 'an act of aggression that is not an armed attack' (Art 29). Such acts must be directed at the territorial integrity of a party 'or the inviolability of the territory' or 'against the sovereignty or political independence' of American states (Art 28). And to conclude this brief survey, the constitution of the African Union (AU) prohibits 'the use of force or threat to use force' (Art 4(f)) as well as 'interference' in the internal affairs of the members (Art 4(g)), and seems to reserve the term 'intervention' to denote action by the Union itself (Art 4(h) and (j)).

The former Warsaw Pact[15] also utilized various terms. Its member states promised 'to refrain in their international relations from the threat or use of force', and to settle their disputes peacefully 'so as not to endanger international peace and security' (Art 1). They also promised to participate in activities 'to safeguard international peace and security' (Art 2). In case one of the members fell victim to an 'armed attack', the other members pledged to come to its rescue by whatever means necessary, 'including the use of armed force' (Art 4). More generally, cooperation between members was warranted in part 'to provide safeguards against possible aggression' (Art 5). It is unlikely that the Pact envisaged aggression amongst members, but nonetheless it urged members to respect the principle of 'non-interference in... internal affairs' (Art 8).

B. The Security Council's Early Practice

The first time it was asked to deal with something potentially constituting use of force, the Security Council proved highly hesitant. Confronted with tensions in northern Greece in late 1946, the Council mentioned that it had been made aware of 'disturbed conditions', and resolved to set up a Commission of Investigation into 'alleged border violations'.[16] Likewise, when the incidents making up the celebrated *Corfu Channel* case took place, the Council's first response was to set up a mechanism for investigations.[17]

The next incident was also cast in neutral terms, with the Council noting the conduct of 'hostilities in progress' between the Netherlands and Indonesia, but without specifying who the aggressor was.[18] A subsequent resolution though, adopted less than four weeks later, hinted at Dutch responsibility, speaking of the 'military

[15] The Warsaw Pact was concluded in 1955, and terminated in 1991.

[16] The Greek Question, SC Res 15 (1946).

[17] The Corfu Channel incidents, SC Res 19 (1947).

[18] The Indonesian Question, SC Res 27 (1947).

occupation' of Indonesia.[19] Later resolutions nonetheless still used relatively neutral terms, urging both parties to 'cease hostilities',[20] until in 1949 the Council made clear that the Netherlands were engaged in a 'continued occupation' of Indonesia's territory.[21] In 1950, Indonesia was admitted to the UN, having been judged to be a 'peace-loving state'.[22]

A similar even-handedness characterized the Council's first dealings with the dispute between India and Pakistan over Kashmir. Yet, a little later the Kashmir dispute had reached new levels of intensity, and the Council's temperature too had been elevated, with the Council referring to the conduct of the parties as 'fighting', and recommending the prevention of further 'intrusions'.[23]

The Palestine question raised things to a new level of urgency. Resolution 43 (1948) observed 'increasing violence and disorder', with the Council calling on Arab and Jewish groups to 'cease acts of violence' immediately. Its next resolution called upon all governments to abstain from 'hostile military action'.[24] A week later, on 29 May 1948, the Council went further. It called upon governments to cease 'all acts of armed force', and threatened to start thinking of the matter as one coming within the scope of Chapter VII of the Charter.[25]

On 15 July 1948, the Council took the historical step of launching its first ever Chapter VII decision when it held that the Palestine question constituted a 'threat to the peace'.[26] The main operative reason for doing so, it seems, was the renewed outbreak of hostilities following the rejection of a truce by member states of the Arab League. Indeed, in March 1949 Israel was admitted as a new UN member, having explicitly been deemed a 'peace-loving State' by the Council.[27] In 1951, when violence flared up around the Syrian border, the Council noted in neutral terms that 'fighting had broken out'.[28] Still, in a later resolution, it seemed to condemn Israeli aerial action as a violation of its obligations under Article 2(4) of the Charter, albeit in a roundabout way.[29] Likewise, a later incident for which Israel was deemed responsible was classified, somewhat imprecisely, as being 'inconsistent' with obligations

[19] The Indonesian Question, SC Res 30 (1947).

[20] The Indonesian Question, SC Res 36 (1947), eg urging the cessation of 'activities' not in conformity with earlier resolutions.

[21] The Indonesian Question, SC Res 67 (1949).

[22] Admission of new Members to the UN: Indonesia, SC Res 86 (1950).

[23] The India–Pakistan Question, SC Res 47 (1948), preamble and para A1(a), respectively.

[24] The Palestine Question, SC Res 49 (1948).

[25] The Palestine Question, SC Res 50 (1948), paras 1 and 11, respectively.

[26] The Palestine Question, SC Res 54 (1948).

[27] Admission of New Members to the UN: Israel, SC Res 69 (1949).

[28] The Palestine Question, SC Res 92 (1951).

[29] The Palestine Question, SC Res 93 (1951). The Council first recalled that Israel and Syria had obligations under Art 2(4) of the Charter, and went on to clarify that a specified Israeli action had violated 'obligations assumed under the Charter', without being specific as to which obligations were violated. It seems reasonable to assume though that the Council must have had Art 2(4) in mind.

assumed under an armistice agreement and under the UN Charter, without highlighting which obligations it concerned.[30]

Famously, in 1950 the Council condemned North Korea for its 'armed attack' (later also classified as an 'unlawful attack'[31]) on the Republic of Korea, and held that this constituted a 'breach of the peace'.[32] Less well known perhaps is that as early as January 1951, the Council unanimously resolved to terminate its involvement: the item was dropped from the Council's agenda.[33] In September 1950, the Council was seized after allegations that there had been an 'armed invasion' of Taiwan by the People's Republic of China,[34] but this item too lived a short existence: it was not to recur on the Council's agenda, without being formally removed. In 1954, moreover, following a request by Guatemala (embroiled in unfriendliness with Honduras and Nicaragua), the Council called for the termination of any action 'likely to cause bloodshed'.[35]

c. Subsequent Security Council Practice

The 1950s were quiet years for the Council, at least in terms of the number of resolutions adopted. Between 1951 and 1956, it only adopted a few handfuls of resolutions, and even fewer between 1957 and 1959, with quite a large proportion of these being devoted to institutional matters. By contrast, 1956 was a relatively busy year. The Suez crisis was characterized as a 'grave situation'—France and the UK's involvement clearly precluded the Council from going any further.[36] Similarly, the Soviet action in Hungary was deemed to have created a 'grave situation'.[37]

In the Congo question, the Council authorized the Secretary-General to 'take the necessary steps... to provide the [Congolese] Government with such military assistance as may be necessary'.[38] This then proved to constitute Chapter VII action, but without following Article 39 of the Charter in any strict manner: at no point did the Council establish that there had been a threat to the peace, breach of the peace, or act of aggression. Resolution 146 urged the UN member states to 'accept and carry out' the Council's decisions in accordance with Articles 25 and 49 of the Charter,[39] and a later resolution recalled that the absence of unity among the

[30] The Palestine Question, SC Res 101 (1953).

[31] Complaint of Aggression upon the Republic of Korea, SC Res 85 (1950).

[32] Complaint of Aggression upon the Republic of Korea, SC Res 82 (1950).

[33] Complaint of Aggression upon the Republic of Korea, SC Res 90 (1951).

[34] Complaint of armed invasion of Taiwan (Formosa), SC Res 87 (1950).

[35] Question submitted by Guatemala, SC Res 104 (1954).

[36] Complaint by Egypt against France and the United Kingdom, SC Res 119 (1956).

[37] Complaint by France and the United Kingdom against Egypt, SC Res 120 (1956).

[38] SC Res 143 (1960). For an excellent discussion of the UN's involvement in Congo, see Georges Abi-Saab, *The United Nations Operation in the Congo 1960–1964* (Oxford: Oxford University Press, 1978).

[39] The Congo Question, SC Res 146 (1960).

permanent members prevented the Council from realizing its primary responsibility for the maintenance of international peace and security, all of which suggests that the initial action was taken under Chapter VII.[40]

During the next few years, too, the Council was rarely very specific. Border skirmishes between Senegal and Portuguese Guinea were referred to as 'incidents';[41] some of Portugal's colonial practices were seen as 'acts of repression';[42] South Africa's apartheid system was regarded as 'seriously disturbing' international peace and security;[43] and Vietnamese boundary incursions into Cambodia were qualified as 'penetration of units'.[44]

During the 1960s and 1970s the Council slowly also adopted more forceful language. It condemned, for instance, the 'invasion' of Portugal into Guinea,[45] having already labelled it an 'armed attack'.[46] It also held that Portugal had been guilty of 'acts of violence' against Senegal[47] and condemned a later 'attack' on a Senegalese post,[48] and suggested that South Africa's incursions into Zambia could be seen as a 'threat or use of force'.[49]

Some of the UN's long-standing involvements date back to political crises of the 1960s, none more so perhaps than its continued presence in Cyprus. Its first resolution on the topic, adopted in 1964, recalled verbatim the provisions of Article 2(4).[50] Still, it refrained from qualifying the behaviour of Turkey, limiting itself to rather factual qualifications: Turkey was to stop its 'bombardment' and 'the use of military force'.[51]

While the situation in the Middle East generated a number of Security Council resolutions, it did not generate strong language. In Resolution 233 (1967) the Council merely noted the 'outbreak of fighting' and a 'menacing situation' including 'military activities'.[52] The next resolution upped the ante by speaking of an 'even more menacing situation',[53] whereas the one after that referred to 'hostilities'.[54] After a ceasefire had provided temporary relief and the conflict flared up again, the Council expressed its concern over 'prohibited military activities'.[55]

Four weeks later, the Council's language showed remarkable development. The situation had become a 'grave situation' and, more importantly, the Council

[40] The Congo Question, SC Res 157 (1960). [41] Complaint by Senegal, SC Res 178 (1963).

[42] Question relating to Territories under Portuguese administration, SC Res 180 (1963).

[43] Question relating to the policies of apartheid of the Government of the Republic of South Africa, SC Res 181(1963) and 182 (1963).

[44] Question relating to the policies of apartheid of the Government of the Republic of South Africa, SC Res 189 (1964).

[45] Complaint by Guinea, SC Res 290 (1970). [46] Complaint by Guinea, SC Res 289 (1970).

[47] Complaint by Senegal SC Res 294 (1971). In later resolutions, it would speak of 'acts of violence and destruction': SC Res 302 (1971) and 321 (1972).

[48] Complaint by Senegal, SC Res 321 (1972). [49] Complaint by Zambia, SC Res 300 (1971).

[50] The Cyprus Question, SC Res 186 (1964). [51] The Cyprus Question, SC Res 193 (1964).

[52] Middle East, SC Res 233 (1967). [53] Middle East, SC Res 234 (1967).

[54] Middle East, SC Res 235 (1967). [55] Middle East, SC Res 240 (1967).

reminded the parties to the conflict of the 'inadmissibility of the acquisition of territory by war' and of their commitments under Article 2 of the Charter.[56] Subsequent resolutions continued the new hard-nosed language, with the Council no longer beating around the bush. Resolution 248 condemned 'the military action launched by Israel in flagrant violation of the United Nations Charter' and spoke of 'actions of military reprisal',[57] whereas later ones reaffirmed the inadmissibility of territorial acquisition by 'military conquest'[58] and roundly condemned Israel's 'massive air attacks' as well as 'premeditated and repeated military attacks'.[59] Israel's bombing of the airport of Beirut, later in 1968, was also met with strong words as 'premeditated military action in violation of [Israel's] obligations under the Charter'.[60]

Having earlier found a 'breach of the peace' to exist when North Korea invaded South Korea,[61] one of the rare later occasions where the Council drew the same conclusion occurred on the outbreak of the Falklands War. The Council noted an Argentinian 'invasion' which, so it held, constituted a 'breach of the peace'.[62]

D. The Security Council After the Cold War

When the conflict between Iraq and Kuwait broke out, the Security Council did not mince its words. It immediately qualified the action as an 'invasion',[63] later adding the term 'occupation'.[64] The Council also activated Chapter VII of the Charter, although without classifying Iraq's invasion in terms of Article 39: the Council refrained from speaking of threat or breach of the peace or act of aggression, and merely noted that it was acting 'under chapter VII'.[65]

The dissolution of Yugoslavia was, however, cast in terms close to those of Article 39, albeit in a curious manner. In Resolution 713 (1992), the Council stated that the fighting in Yugoslavia, and the consequences it entailed for neighbouring countries, were a matter of deep concern and added that 'the continuation of this situation constitutes a threat to international peace and security'. Arguably then, and strictly speaking, such a threat to international peace (not 'threat to the peace') did not yet exist, but was prospective: conditional upon a continuation of the situation. Nonetheless, acting under Chapter VII of the Charter, the Council imposed an arms embargo. Resolution 721 (1991) likewise provided that the 'continuation and aggravation' of the situation constitute a threat to international peace and security—again, therewith, speaking in prospective terms.[66]

56 Middle East, SC Res 242 (1967).
57 Middle East, SC Res 248 (1968).
58 Middle East, SC Res 252 (1968).
59 Middle East, SC Res 256 (1968).
60 Middle East, SC Res 262 (1968). Similar wordings were used regarding air attacks in SC Res 265 (1969) and SC Res 270 (1969), and with respect to an attack on a mosque in Jerusalem in SC Res 271 (1969).
61 Complaint of aggression upon the Republic of Korea, SC Res 82 (1950).
62 Falkland Islands (Malvinas), SC Res 502 (1982).
63 Iraq–Kuwait, SC Res 660 (1990).
64 Iraq–Kuwait, SC Res 661 (1991).
65 Iraq–Kuwait, SC Res 661 (1991).
66 Socialist Federal Republic of Yugoslavia, SC Res 721 (1991).

The prospective formula would be used on a limited number of later occasions as well. Thus, the continuation of the conflict in Somalia was deemed to constitute a threat to international peace and security,[67] as was the ousting of President Aristide in Haiti.[68] Nonetheless, a strong argument can be made that the prospective formula ought not be taken too literally: it can hardly have been the intention of the Council to stipulate that behaviour would be acceptable on Monday, but unacceptable if continued on Tuesday, and the more natural reading is that 'continuation' would include 'current existence'. The use of 'continuation' *simpliciter* does suggest, however, that it is difficult to find the right words to capture unwarranted behaviour, partly due to the limits of language, partly no doubt also due to diplomatic sensitivities. It is not unlikely that a proposed resolution could only muster a relevant majority precisely by not condemning the behaviour outright.

This would help to explain why in other cases, playing out during roughly the same period, the prospective formula was not used. With respect to Liberia, for instance, it was the 'deterioration' of the situation which constituted a threat to international peace and security,[69] whereas Libya's refusal to hand over terrorism suspects was deemed to constitute a 'threat to international peace and security'.[70]

In the meantime, in situations not calling for Chapter VII action, the Council's classifications remained varied. Thus, the Nagorno-Karabakh conflict was described as 'armed hostilities', although the Council also noted an 'invasion', seemingly as part thereof, by Armenia.[71] The conflict concerning the political status of Abkhazia was designed as, indeed, a 'conflict',[72] as was the war between Ethiopia and Eritrea, although the Council also spoke of 'hostilities' and 'use of force'.[73]

The Kosovo situation gave rise to concerted action under Chapter VII, but initially without the invocation of the terms of Article 39. Instead, the Serbian police were accused of 'excessive force', while the Kosovo Liberation Army was held to have engaged in 'acts of terrorism'.[74] The Council subsequently made clear that the Kosovo situation constituted a 'threat to peace and security in the region'.[75] The term is reminiscent of Article 39, but without actually being part of Article 39.

The events of 11 September 2001 were characterized by the Council as 'horrifying terrorist attacks', and regarded by the Council as 'a threat to international peace and security'.[76] This would give rise, as is well known, to Chapter VII action, through Resolution 1373, targeting in particular the financing of terrorism.[77]

[67] Somalia, SC Res 733 (1992). [68] Haiti, SC Res 841 (1993).

[69] Liberia, SC Res 788 (1992). [70] Libyan Arab Jamahiriya, SC Res 748 (1992).

[71] Armenia-Azerbaijan, SC Res 822 (1993). [72] Georgia, SC Res 1036 (1996).

[73] On the situation between Eritrea and Ethiopia, SC Res 1177 (1998).

[74] On the letters from the UK (S/1998/223) and the US (S/1998/272), SC Res 1160 (1998).

[75] Kosovo (FRY), SC Res 1199 (1998).

[76] Threats to international peace and security caused by terrorist acts, SC Res 1368 (2001).

[77] Threats to international peace and security caused by terrorist acts, SC Res 1373 (2001). Its relevance is discussed in Ian Johnstone, *The Power of Deliberation: International Law, Politics and Organizations* (Oxford: Oxford University Press, 2011), esp 95–9.

Occasionally, the Council has also explored the possibility that phenomena not involving the direct use of force may nonetheless come within the Council's remit. In a high-level meeting in 1992, it stipulated that threats to the peace could possibly arise from economic, social, humanitarian, and ecological crises.[78] In 2000, it made a careful link between the HIV/AIDS pandemic and peace, stressing that the pandemic, 'if unchecked, may pose a risk to stability and security',[79] and a few years later it made a connection between the proliferation of small arms and light weapons and their impact on peace and security in West Africa. While it stopped short of characterizing this proliferation in terms of the use of force, it nonetheless found that these weapons 'contribute to serious violations of human rights and international humanitarian law'.[80] Similarly, the proliferation of nuclear, biological, and chemical weapons was characterized as a 'threat to international peace and security'.[81]

E. Defining Aggression

Inspired by the desire to assist the Security Council in its work on maintaining international peace and security, the General Assembly of the UN decided as early as 1952 to define aggression. After several attempts had come to naught, a Special Committee of the Assembly, comprising 35 member states, was created for the task at hand in 1967, and managed in 1974 to reach agreement, resulting in General Assembly Resolution 3314 (XXIX).[82]

Aggression is defined in Article 1 in broad terms as the use of armed force, against the sovereignty, territorial integrity, or political independence of a state, or in any other manner inconsistent with the UN Charter. Article 2 then stipulates that the first use of armed force is prima facie evidence of aggression—hence, again armed force is seen as a species of aggression. Article 3 continues by listing activities that shall qualify as acts of aggression. These include invasions, attacks on territory and military occupation; annexation; bombardment 'or the use of any weapons' against the territory of a state; blockades; and attacks on the troops of a state. Such acts can be committed not just by regular armed force, but also by sending armed bands, irregulars, insurgents, or mercenaries, or from bases outside one's own territory.

Whilst the definition aims to cast a strong net around aggression by listing acts that qualify as such and by stating that 'no consideration of whatever nature…may serve as a justification for aggression' (Art 5(1)), the definition ends up presenting

[78] S/23500 (31 Jan 1992), reproduced in (1992) 31 ILM 758–62.

[79] HIV/AIDS and International Peacekeeping Operations, SC Res 1308 (2000).

[80] Proliferation of small arms and light weapons and mercenary activities: threats to peace and security in West Africa, SC Res 1467 (2003).

[81] Non-proliferation of weapons of mass destruction, SC Res 1540 (2004).

[82] See Bengt Broms, *The United Nations* (Helsinki: Suomalainen Tiedeakademia, 1990), 307–11. Broms had chaired the General Assembly's Special Committee to Define Aggression.

precisely such justifications. Article 6 provides that the definition is without prejudice to the Charter, including its provisions on the lawful use of force (presumably, this relates first of all to self-defence), and Article 7 explicitly withdraws independence struggles from the scope of aggression. In other words, aggression is bad, unless done for good reasons, and those reasons themselves remain relatively open-ended.[83]

The gist of the 1974 General Assembly definition was followed, by and large, by the meeting of the parties to the International Criminal Court (ICC) in Kampala, in 2010, with a view to defining aggression. While the ICC Statute focuses on individual responsibility, an 'act of aggression' involves a 'manifest violation' of the UN Charter, and is further defined as the use of armed force against the sovereignty, territorial integrity, or political dependence of states or otherwise 'inconsistent' with the UN Charter. And like the 1974 definition, the Kampala text lists a number of activities which will be deemed to constitute aggression, including bombardments, blockades, invasion of territory, and attacks on troops.[84]

III. Bringing Some Strands Together

The previous survey is neither comprehensive nor systematic, but nonetheless suggests a few important things. A first conclusion to draw is that the terminology is immensely varied, ranging from the blandly descriptive ('hostilities') to the accusatory 'armed attack'. Secondly, the survey of Security Council practice suggests that the Council never was overly concerned when classifying acts to do so in the terms of the Charter: there are relatively few straightforward cases where the Council utilized the language of Article 39 of the Charter and first identified a threat to the peace, breach of the peace, or act of aggression before authorizing measures under Chapter VII. Thirdly, the Council has sometimes employed language relating to the use of force to describe non-forcible acts (eg the refusal to hand over terrorism suspects), or acts taking place within a single state (Somalia, Haiti). Fourthly, and much more important perhaps, is that the classifications often do their best to remain neutral, with a few noted exceptions. Most often, at least in the practice of the Security Council, care is taken to find non-offensive phrases, phrases which do not blame one side or the other and which leave diplomatic wriggle room.

[83] For a strong critique, see Julius Stone, 'Hopes and Loopholes in the 1974 Definition of Aggression' (1977) 71 *American Journal of International Law* 224–46.

[84] Kampala Review Conference Resolution RC/Res 6, Annex 1.

The main exceptions seem to be threefold. First, the Council has been outspoken in the face of colonial aggression, as Portugal has experienced a few times. Secondly, the Council has been outspoken when blatant and one-sided aggression was presumed, as when North Korea invaded South Korea and when Iraq invaded Kuwait. Thirdly, the Council tried out neutral language at early stages of a conflict, but became more explicit as the question (or the politics) of culpability became clearer: this happened to the occupation of Indonesia by the Netherlands, as well as to the position of Israel in the Middle East.

This survey suggests that the Council is usually very careful in the language it employs, working from the clear desire not to prejudice or aggravate the situation. This is logical: the Council is a political organ, endowed with a political task, and while its decisions will inevitably be accompanied by legal fall-out, it is not for the Council to assume the role of judicial body or lawmaker.

Nonetheless, some terms seem to have received more or less clarified meanings. Intervention, for example, is not usually used in a pejorative sense. The AU Charter, for example, refers to intervention as collective action by the AU, and the Security Council does not appear to resort to the term when discussing one-sided violence. When the Council wants to voice its disapproval, it tends to use a term such as 'invasion' or, if the situation is prolonged, 'occupation', and variations thereof.

Perhaps remarkably, given the central place of Article 39 in the framework of the UN's collective security mechanism, its language is hardly utilized, not even when the Council authorizes collective action. Partly this finds its cause in the circumstance that notions of peace and security may have broadened in the years since 1945, when the Charter was drafted: it would have been unorthodox, in 1945, to think of designating economic crises or ecological disasters as threats to the peace, let alone as breaches of the peace or acts of aggression. Likewise, internal conflicts may have been far from the minds of the drafters; hence, it may somehow feel more secure not to capture these habitually in the precise terms of Article 39, but use related, more circumspect designations, such as 'threats to peace and security', or 'threats to regional security'. Arguably, in the light of the discretion enjoyed by the Security Council, this is legally not all that relevant, even if it may make a political difference.[85] But even in cases involving interstate conflicts, the language of the Charter has rarely been used with the precision one would perhaps expect from an administrative organ, endowed with the task to apply the law to particular cases. The Council's practice has been much more circumspect: utilizing whatever term it sees fit without worrying too much whether that makes sense in terms of the provisions of the Charter.

[85] In similar vein, Jochen A. Frowein and Nico Krisch, 'Article 39' in Bruno Simma et al (eds), *The Charter of the United Nations: A Commentary* (2nd edn, Oxford: Oxford University Press, 2002), 717–29.

IV. The ICJ

It would seem that the ICJ, too, in its judicial practice on the use of force, has not been terribly concerned about the possible legal nuances of the language it uses or, put differently, that the ICJ too has utilized a wide variety of terms and given them roughly the same meaning. Generally speaking, the Court has been more concerned with finding out whether behaviour crossed the threshold of legality or not, than with exactly how the behaviour ought to be qualified.

This was already visible in the ICJ's first relevant decision in *Corfu Channel*, where the Court discussed shots fired by Albania on UK ships but did not consider whether this would have to be deemed an armed attack or an act of aggression.[86] Likewise, while the Court found that the UK's minesweeping operation (Operation Retail) constituted an 'intervention' and manifested a 'policy of force',[87] there is no argument as to why exactly these terms were chosen, and why Operation Retail did not, for example, constitute an armed attack. The precise classification of the act was considered less relevant than the conclusion as to its legality, and in its *dispositif*, the Court concluded that the UK violated the sovereignty of Albania, without being more specific.[88]

Other relevant ICJ decisions likewise do not place a great premium on the precise legal characterization of activities, despite the ICJ's occasional exhortations in this direction.[89] Typically, what concerns the Court is not the precise difference between an invasion and an armed attack or an act of aggression, but rather whether one of the parties to the conflict crossed the threshold of legality. Small boundary skirmishes tend not to be regarded as amounting to an armed attack or suchlike,[90] and mostly the concern has been with issues of attribution. After all, many conflicts are being fought by irregular troops, giving rise to the question whether the actions of those groups can be attributed to the state concerned.[91]

In this light, it should probably come as no surprise that one of the main legal controversies on the topic in recent years has crystallized around precisely this issue of the standard of attribution, with the ICJ in the *Nicaragua* case applying a different standard ('effective control' by the state[92]) from the International

[86] *Corfu Channel*, Merits, ICJ Rep 1949, 4, 27 ff. The Court seems to suggest that Albania's action was difficult to reconcile with the right of innocent passage, but does not draw any firm conclusion on this point.

[87] *Corfu Channel*, Merits, 35. [88] *Corfu Channel*, Merits, 36.

[89] See eg *Case Concerning Armed Activities on the Territory of the Congo (DRC v. Uganda)*, ICJ Rep 2005, 168, para 72.

[90] See *Nicaragua Military and Paramilitary Activities in and against Nicaragua (Nicaragua v. US)*, Merits, ICJ Rep 1986, 14.

[91] See eg *Armed Activities (DRC v. Uganda)*. [92] See *Nicaragua*.

Criminal Tribunal for the former Yugoslavia (ICTY) (endorsing the lower standard of 'overall control'[93]), and being able to distinguish this in terms of the situations coming before both tribunals.[94]

The Court's laconic attitude to legal characterizations of the use of force is partly explained by the circumstance that some uses of force are to be considered legal. This applies, for example, to force used in self-defence; hence, the question before the Court is not whether force can be classified as 'aggression' or 'invasion', but rather whether the use of force, if established, could be legally justified. The Court, in other words, will be looking for a possible justification, and this implies that the Court is interested in whether the use of force was legal or illegal: since aggression, armed attack, invasion, etc, are all considered illegal, the precise differences between them are considered less relevant. Perhaps the clearest illustration of this methodology is the *dispositif* in *Oil Platforms*, with the Court finding that the actions of the US 'cannot be justified' under the 1955 Iran–US Amity Treaty as interpreted in the light of the international law on the use of force, and adding that this did not mean that the US acts amounted to a violation of US obligations under the same treaty.[95]

The consideration that the Court is not looking for precise classifications, but rather looks for the threshold of legality, is further strengthened by the structure of the parties' submissions. The typical submission asks the Court to adjudge and declare that the other side has violated its obligations under international law. The Court is rarely asked to adjudge and declare that the other side committed 'aggression' or engaged in an 'armed attack' (though sometimes submissions come close to this type of question[96]). Hence, the relevant issue is whether the threshold of legality has been transgressed: whether the behaviour ought to be characterized in a more specific manner therewith becomes a relatively moot point.

As a result, the Court's findings tend to be fairly general rather than specific. In *Nicaragua*, it held that the US had violated its obligation 'not to use force against another State'.[97] Likewise, in *DRC v. Uganda*, it concluded that Uganda had violated the 'principle of non-use of force' and the 'principle of non-intervention'.[98]

93 See ICTY, Case IT-94-1-A, *Prosecutor v. Duško Tadić*.

94 See *Application of the Convention on the Prevention and Punishment of the Crime of Genocide (Bosnia and Herzegovina v. Serbia and Montenegro)*, ICJ Rep 2007, 43.

95 See *Case Concerning Oil Platforms (Iran v. US)*, ICJ Rep 2003, 161, para 125(1).

96 In *Armed Activities*, eg the Court was asked to find that Uganda had committed aggression within the meaning of the General Assembly's Definition of Aggression (para 23), later amended to the less specific charge that Uganda had violated 'the principle of the non-use of force, including the prohibition of aggression' (para 24).

97 See *Nicaragua*, Merits, para 292(4).

98 See *Armed Activities*, para 345(1).

v. The Language of Law and the Use of Force

It is a well-known feature of language generally that descriptions inevitably tend to come with an evaluation. Labelling a work of art as 'beautiful' entails not merely (or not so much) a description, but also implies an evaluation; classifying a walk through a meadow as 'trespass' likewise entails an evaluation as to the propriety of the action. In recent years, few illustrations of the power of words have been as clear as that pertaining to the construction of a wall by Israel through its occupied territory. While often described as a wall, with the negative associations this provokes of exclusion, Israel itself consistently referred to it as a 'fence', therewith using a term with less negative connotations and perhaps even in the hope of evoking the positive association according to which fences are not exclusionary devices but, instead, contribute to security. Israel also used the term 'wall' in inverted commas, so as to underline its disagreement with the characterization.[99] As Friedrich Kratochwil puts the general point, 'the characterisation of actions whether in the legal or in the practical discourse is not a description at all, but rather an *appraisal*; it is an evaluation of "facts" in terms of some normative considerations.'[100]

Earlier generations of international lawyers found this out the hard way after attempting to render 'war' illegal. Through a succession of treaties, war was outlawed, and needed even to be declared.[101] As a result, arguments arose that certain activities stopped short of being 'war' in any legal sense, or were not 'really' war, all the more so as few wars were actually declared.[102] And while 'war' is still used in everyday speech and popular culture, the term has largely vanished from the legal discussion.[103]

This is not untypical: as soon as a legal category exists, activities are represented in such a way as to either fit in or not fit in, and some claim that this is inevitable: rules (and therewith also categories and definitions) tend to be over-inclusive

[99] See *Legal Consequences of the Construction of a Wall in the Occupied Palestinian Territory*, Advisory Opinion, ICJ Rep 2004, 136, and in particular the statement submitted by Israel's foreign minister and government, dated 29 and 30 Jan 2004.

[100] See Friedrich V. Kratochwil, *Rules, Norms, and Decisions: On the Conditions of Practical and Legal Reasoning in International Relations and Domestic Affairs* (Cambridge: Cambridge University Press, 1989), 229.

[101] See generally Stephen C. Neff, *War and the Law of Nations: A General History* (Cambridge: Cambridge University Press, 2005).

[102] It has been argued, rather cogently (if, alas, in Dutch), that the 1907 Convention has been terminated by virtue of *desuetudo*. See E. W. Vierdag, 'Oorlogsverklaring', inaugural address, University of Amsterdam, 1992.

[103] Although the ICJ, if somewhat in passing, spoke of the 1980s conflict between Iraq and Iran as 'war'. See *Oil Platforms*, para 23.

and under-exclusive, always covering things they were never intended to cover, while missing things they were actually intended to cover.[104] For most purposes, this is perfectly acceptable, although on occasion it may lead to a deactivation of moral intuitions, losing something of value in the process. Thus, it has been suggested that the international legal prohibition of genocide or of the use of nuclear weapons has turned a strong moral norm into a technical issue, with people spending their time debating whether behaviour meets with the definition instead of being outraged, and therewith making the activity somehow more *salonfähig*, or respectable.[105]

The point that emerges from the previous discussion, then, is not so much that linguistic concerns are considered irrelevant or beside the point, but largely that interpretative communities[106] in the field of security and the use of force are all too well aware of the implications that may stem from precise classifications and qualifications. Referring to 'hostilities' can still be considered a fairly neutral act, as it leaves unsaid who started them; by contrast, accusing another state of 'aggression' or an 'invasion' is not. 'Intervention' too is relatively neutral, albeit for different reasons: 'intervention', so its usage suggests, can take place by military means, but also by non-military means, in which case it can be considered more benign. Hence, usage of the term leaves open the possibility of reaching a diplomatic settlement, in ways that do not apply quite as easily when the same act is classified as 'use of force' or 'invasion'.

The instrumental rationality typically underlying law gives way to a certain (for want of a better term) political rationality. Instrumental rationality typically involves the idea that drafters aim to reach a certain goal, for example the banning of chemical weapons, and utilize the terms they deem most suitable to achieve that goal: under the Chemical Weapons Convention, for instance, states agree 'never under any circumstances' to use or develop chemical weapons.[107] Here there is little wriggle room, and little wriggle room is needed: if a state party nonetheless develops or stockpiles chemical weapons, it is clearly in violation, and something must be done. The important thing to note though is that its violation does not necessarily immediately affect others, except in an abstract sense. If a state develops chemical weapons, it violates the Chemical Weapons Convention, but no one is directly injured, and there is no urgent need for the behaviour to stop.[108] The

[104] See generally Frederick Schauer, *Playing by the Rules: A Philosophical Examination of Rule-based Decision-making in Law and in Life* (Oxford: Clarendon Press, 1991), esp 31–44.

[105] See Martti Koskenniemi, 'Faith, Identity, and the Killing of the Innocent: International Lawyers and Nuclear Weapons' (1997) 10 *Leiden Journal of International Law* 137–62.

[106] On the notion of interpretative communities generally, see the work of literary theorist Stanley Fish, in particular perhaps his *Doing what Comes Naturally: Change, Rhetoric, and the Practice of Theory in Literary and Legal Studies* (Oxford: Clarendon Press, 1989). The notion is usefully applied to international law by Johnstone, *The Power of Deliberation*.

[107] See the 1993 Convention on the Prohibition of the Development, Production, Stockpiling and Use of Chemical Weapons and on their Destruction, Art 1.

[108] The example implodes when a state actually uses chemical weapons, but in that case it can most likely be accused of aggression as well.

first—and only—priority, in other words, is to get the state concerned to respect its commitments.

This is different when force is actually used. Inasmuch as the concern rests with getting the state concerned to stop, the prior concern must be to bring an end to hostilities, no matter who started them. In this respect, the law on the use of force faces a particular problem other branches of international law do not face: delays kill people. While obviously in some other branches, violations of the law also tend to immediately affect the other party directly (eg an import prohibition in trade law), nonetheless these do not tend to result in immediate loss of life. The law on the use of force therewith carries a special responsibility: its violations create direct victims, and often those victims may die while the violations persist. Hence, there is a strong moral imperative to hold that priority number one must be to bring an end to hostilities, and for that purpose it does not matter too much whether an act is described as 'invasion' or 'aggression', as 'armed attack' or as 'use of force'.

What does matter though is whether the classification leaves open the possibility of a diplomatic or judicial settlement: strongly stigmatizing terms tend not to do so, and are accordingly only sparingly used. While they play a role in the drafting of security arrangements (it could hardly be otherwise), they play but a minor role once hostilities have actually taken place, that is, in the practice of the Security Council and the ICJ.

VI. By Way of Conclusion

In an important sense, all this is how it should be. Political actors mediating or deciding over conflicts (eg the Security Council) need to be able to keep wriggle room available for political settlements; outright characterizations of behaviour as 'aggression' or 'armed attack' may not be all too helpful on that score, and it seems reasonably clear that the Security Council is well aware of this. Likewise, the tasks of judicial institutions include coming to a judgement whether behaviour was legally justifiable or not. In this light, it is more relevant to establish whether behaviour actually was justifiable under international law or not than to present a precise classification, all the more so if the legal consequences attached to the various possible classifications do not themselves differ dramatically. And that still seems to be the case in international law, where the law on responsibility does not provide much room for attaching different consequences to different wrongful acts. In other words, if the punishment for 'aggression' or 'invasion' is the same, then why bother to make a distinction between the two when it comes to classifying the act?

More than other branches of international law, the law on the use of force needs to be able to accommodate the imperative of peace-making. Given the circumstance that language often comes with evaluative characteristics, it makes some sense that classifications of behaviour often forego legal precision, and replace it by political precision, whose rationale is the desire to bring a conflict to a speedy end and prevent further suffering. After all, this, typically, can only be done by political means.

CHAPTER 23

THE PROHIBITION OF THE USE OF FORCE AND NON-INTERVENTION: AMBITION AND PRACTICE IN THE OAS REGION

JEAN MICHEL ARRIGHI

I. Introduction

The end of the wars of independence in Latin America in the first decades of the 19th century ushered in the states that would later constitute the inter-American system. From the British Empire arose the United States of America, which remained united only at the cost of a civil war. The Portuguese Empire took a different track, when its imperial authorities transferred their seat of power from their European capital to their great American colony and set up in Rio de Janeiro, turning the colonial city into their capital. Eventually, independence from Spain and the constitution of the Republic preserved the unity of Brazilian territory. In contrast, the former Spanish colonies split into multiple states pitted against one another in border disputes and rent internally by conflicts, fights among local strongmen, civil wars, and endless political instability.

From that time on, border delimitation and demarcation issues constituted the principal cause of clashes among the countries of the Americas. They arose mainly between former Spanish colonies as a result of poorly defined boundaries or, following independence, as a consequence of fratricidal wars. More recently, the need to establish maritime limits has triggered fresh conflicts.

Several such disputes persist[1] and, to this day, prompt serious tensions among states in the region. One such dispute is that between Bolivia and Chile, which dates back to the War of the Pacific at the start of the 20th century.[2] Others, the majority, were settled in the course of the 19th and 20th centuries through some peaceful mechanism for the peaceful resolution of disputes, be it a bilateral agreement, an arbitration award, or a judicial ruling. Some are still being examined by the International Court of Justice (ICJ) in The Hague and others, such as the border dispute between Guatemala and Belize[3] are likely to be submitted to it soon. In the past, there were also conflicts between the US and Mexico and between Brazil and its neighbours, which allowed the US and Brazil to expand their borders at the expense of the former Hispanic colonies, sometimes through conquest and at times through clever negotiation of agreements that took advantage of authorities weakened by internal wrangling.

Foreseeing the fratricidal clashes that would occur within the former Spanish colonies and weaken each of the countries that could arise out of them, Bolívar attempted in vain to forge a confederation to avoid that break-up of the former empire.[4]

[1] Jorge I. Dominguez, 'Conflictos territoriales y limítrofes en América Latina y el Caribe' in *Conflictos territoriales y democracia en América Latina* (Buenos Aires: XXI Siglo Editora, 2003), 15.

[2] This refers to Bolivia's ongoing claim against Chile for the loss of its access to the sea following the War of the Pacific and the Treaty of 1904. The two countries do not maintain diplomatic relations. Bolivia regularly repeats its claim in international, especially inter-American, fora, in particular at each regular session of the OAS General Assembly.

[3] The Court in The Hague has examined and made the delimitations in the Territorial and Maritime Disputes between Nicaragua and Colombia (ICJ Rep 2012, 624) and between Peru and Chile (ICJ, Judgment of 27 Jan 2014). Owing to the good offices of the OAS Secretary General, in Dec 2008 Guatemala and Belize signed a Special Agreement to Submit Guatemala's Territorial, Insular, and Maritime Claim to the International Court of Justice and agreed to hold a referendum in both countries on 6 Oct 2013 aiming to elicit the population's consent to the procedure. The date of the referendum was postponed and a new date is not yet established. All the documents and details relating to this process undertaken by the OAS with a view to facilitating agreement between the two countries are available at <http://www.oas.org/sap/peacefund/belizeandguatemala/>.

[4] In 1826 Bolívar convened the Congress of Panama which adopted the Treaty of Union, League, and Perpetual Confederation, ratified only by Gran Colombia (comprising today's Colombia, Ecuador, Panama, and Venezuela). For a recent study of the extensive bibliography on Bolívar and the Congress of Panama, see John Lynch, *Simon Bolívar* (New Haven, CT: Yale University Press, 2006), 212.

At the same time, the European powers still maintained colonies in the Americas and threatened to intervene in multiple ways, ranging from the dispatching of a European prince to Mexico to the presence of fleets off the Venezuelan coast to enforce debt collection.

President Monroe of the US gave voice to the desire to keep the Americas free of interference from outside the hemisphere, which at that time had to be construed to mean free of European encroachment.[5] Although it was unilateral, that declaration was reflected in Article 21 of the Covenant of the League of Nations,[6] an organization that the US ultimately did not join.[7] Later on, the Monroe Doctrine was interpreted and applied by US presidents to justify US intervention in the internal affairs of the countries of the region, first with the pretext that putting order into their institutions and enforcement of their international obligations would eliminate the grounds for their possible involvement in extra-hemispheric conflicts, and later, more blatantly, to overthrow regimes deemed contrary to North American interests.[8]

In 1902, the Argentine Minister of Foreign Affairs, Luis Drago, strongly opposed the use of force to collect debts from a state, and particularly the deployment of European fleets against Venezuela. That stance of objection to such measures as contravening international law, while allowing certain exceptions authorizing recourse to force when no agreement was reached on submitting to arbitration, was built into the 'Drago-Porter' Convention adopted at the Second Hague Peace Conference of 1907.[9]

At the sub-regional level, the first efforts to achieve a shared legal framework began with the convocation of the Lima Conferences on Andean integration in 1847 and 1864 and the Montevideo Conference of 1888 on codification of international private law,[10] which sought to avoid tensions in such matters as execution of sentences, extradition, and the law applicable to international contracts.

[5] Jay Sexton, *The Monroe Doctrine: Empire and Nation in Nineteenth-Century America* (New York: Hill and Wang, 2011).

[6] 'Nothing in this Covenant shall be deemed to affect the validity of international engagements, such as treaties of arbitration or regional understandings like the Monroe doctrine, for securing the maintenance of peace'. All the Latin American countries were members of the League of Nations, some for its entire duration and others for shorter periods.

[7] 'The inclusion in the Covenant of a specific reference to the Monroe Doctrine was disliked by nearly all the Latin American Members of the League': Francis P. Walters, *A History of the League of Nations* (Oxford: Oxford University Press, 1952), 56.

[8] Camilo Barcia Trelles, 'La doctrine Monroe dans son développement historique' (1930) 32 *Recueil des cours de l'Académie de droit international* 557; Gaddis Smith, *The Last Years of the Monroe Doctrine* (New York: Hill and Wang, 1994).

[9] Georges Abi-Saab, 'Evolution dans le règlement pacifique des différends économiques depuis la Convention Drago-Porter' in Yves Daudet (ed), *Actualité de la Conférence de La Haye de 1907, Deuxième Conférence de la Paix* (The Hague: Académie de Droit International de La Haye, 2008), 177.

[10] F. V. García Amador, *The Inter-American System*, vol 1 (New York: Oceana Publications, 1983), 19.

After overcoming numerous hurdles and thanks to the enormous efforts of Secretary of State Blaine to elicit the approval of the US Senate[11] and secure the participation of the American states,[12] the US government invited the independent American states to meet in Washington 'for the purpose of discussing and recommending for adoption to their respective governments some plan of arbitration for the settlement of disagreements and disputes that may hereafter arise between them, and for considering questions relating to the improvement of Business intercourse and means of direct Communications between said countries, and to encourage such reciprocal commercial relations'.[13] For trade to develop in the region, it was necessary to ensure peace among states, cooperation, and domestic stability.[14] For cooperation, a vast network of shared institutions and legal agreements was forged in a wide range of fields. To ensure peace, mechanisms were gradually established for the peaceful settlement of disputes. To achieve domestic stability, however, a variety of approaches were adopted, ranging from illegitimate intervention to the pretext of self-defence, to protection of its citizens, by what was initially a great regional power and then one of the global powers caught up in the Cold War. In the early years of the 20th century, that scenario was what shaped the history of Central America, particularly that of Nicaragua, and, in the Caribbean, that of the Dominican Republic and Haiti.[15]

Common defence of the region, the consolidation of peaceful means of settling disputes as the only way to resolve still existing international conflicts,[16] defence of the principle of non-intervention,[17] which was now threatened from within the hemisphere, and respect for the legal equality of states within a single organization

[11] David Healy, *James G. Blaine and Latin America* (Columbia, MO: University of Missouri Press, 2001), 138.

[12] Thomas F. McGann, *Argentina, the United States and the Inter-American System* (Cambridge, MA: Harvard University Press, 1957), 120.

[13] James Brown Scott (ed), *The International Conferences of American States 1889–1928* (Oxford: Oxford University Press, 1931), 5.

[14] Laurence Boisson de Chazournes, 'Les relations entre organisations régionales et organisations universelles' (2010) 347 *Recueil des cours de l'Académie de droit international* 142.

[15] See eg the cases in which US troops intervened to install 'friendly' governments or even governments formed entirely of US officials in the Dominican Republic (1916–24), Nicaragua (1927–33), and Haiti (1915–34). Robert L. Scheina, *Latin America's War*, vol 2 (Washington DC: Brassey's Inc, 2003), 48–72; Suzy Castor, *L'occupation américaine d'Haïti* (Port-au-Prince: CRESDEF, 1988).

[16] Thus, to cite just one sub-regional example, in Rio de Janeiro in 1933 Argentina, Brazil, Chile, Mexico, Paraguay, and Uruguay adopted the Anti-War Treaty of Non-Aggression and Conciliation (the Saavedra Lamas Treaty), Art I of which reads: 'The high contracting parties solemnly declare that they condemn wars of aggression in their mutual relations or in those with other states, and that the settlement of disputes and controversies of any kind that may arise among them shall be effected only by pacific means which have the sanction of international law.'

[17] In 1936, at the Inter-American Conference for the Maintenance of Peace, the American states adopted and appended an Additional Protocol Relative to Non-Intervention to the Convention for the Maintenance, Preservation and Reestablishment of Peace.

when the UN was being created,[18] led, albeit with conflicting interests, to the adoption of the Inter-American Treaty of Reciprocal Assistance in 1947, and, in 1948, to the establishment of the Organization of American States (OAS) and to the adoption of the American Treaty on Pacific Settlement (the Pact of Bogotá).

II. The OAS Region

A. Principles Governing Relations Among OAS Member States

As of the 1889 Conference, a number of principles began to govern inter-American relations and would eventually be built into the OAS Charter of 1948. Thus, rejection of conquest as a way to acquire territories,[19] the legal equality of states expressed in practice by each state having one vote with the organization's decisions being adopted by a simple majority with all member states participating, and condemnation of aggression in international relations[20] were some of the principles agreed upon at the First International Conference of American States.[21] Establishing the principle of non-intervention proved to be more difficult. It was finally recognized by all the American states at their Seventh International Conference (Montevideo, 1933). There they adopted the Convention on Rights and Duties of States,[22] which would later influence other regions, and even the UN, in a number of aspects, such as the definition of elements (qualifications) comprising a state (Art 1), the juridical equality of states (Art 4), and matters relating to their recognition (Arts 6 and 7). Finally, Article 8 stipulates that 'no State has the right to intervene in the internal or external affairs of another'.[23] The

[18] On the participation of the American states in the drafting of provisions relating to regional agreements on the maintenance of international peace and security, see Jean Salmon, 'Les accords régionaux dans les travaux préparatoires de la Charte des Nations-Unies' in Jorge Cardona Llorens (ed), *La ONU y el mantenimiento de la paz en el siglo XXI* (Valencia: CEDRI, 2008), 405.

[19] Recommendation 'The Right of Conquest' of the First International Conference of American States in Scott, *The International Conferences of American States 1889–1928*, 44.

[20] Resolution 'Aggression', Sixth International Conference of American States (La Havana, 1928) in Scott, *The International Conferences of American States 1889–1928*, 441 ('The war of aggression constitutes an international crime against the human species').

[21] Julio Barberis, 'Les règles spécifiques du droit international en Amérique Latine' (1992) 235 *Recueil des cours de l'Académie de droit international* 176.

[22] *The International Conferences of American States, first supplement 1933–1940* (New York: Carnegie Endowment for Peace, 1940), 121.

[23] Similar articles had previously been proposed and had always been opposed by the US delegation. On this occasion, on express instructions from President Franklin D. Roosevelt, the US

Inter-American Conference for the Maintenance of Peace (Buenos Aires, 1936), convened at the end of the Chaco War between Paraguay and Bolivia (1932–5)— the longest and bloodiest war anywhere in the region during the 20th century[24]—adopted, with no reservations by any American state, the Declaration of Principles of Inter-American Solidarity and Cooperation, Article 3 of which reads as follows:

> 3. That the following principles are accepted by the American community of Nations:
> (a) Proscription of territorial conquest and that, in consequence, no acquisition made through violence shall be recognised;
> (b) Intervention by one State in the internal or external affairs of another State is condemned;
> (c) Forcible collection of pecuniary debts is illegal; and
> (d) Any difference or dispute between the American nations, whatever its nature or origin, shall be settled by the methods of conciliation, or unrestricted arbitration, or through operation of international justice.[25]

Finally, when the Charter of the OAS was adopted in 1948, these principles were spelt out. After a series of amendments to the Charter, especially those of 1967 and 1985, they were addressed in separate paragraphs of what is today Article 3:

> (e) Every State has the right to choose without external interference, its political, economic and social system and to organise itself in the way best suited to it, and has the duty to abstain from intervening in the affairs of another State…
> (h) An act of aggression against one American State is an act of aggression against all the other American States;
> (i) Controversies of an international character arising between two or more American States shall be settled by peaceful procedures…

And, in the Chapter on Collective Security, Article 29 states:

> If the inviolability of the integrity of the territory or the sovereignty or political independence of any American State should be affected by an armed attack or by an act of aggression that is not an armed attack, or by an extracontinental conflict, or by a conflict between two or more American States, or by any other fact or situation that might endanger the peace of America, the American States, in furtherance of the principles of continental solidarity or collective self-defence, shall apply the measures and procedures established in the special treaties on the subject.

For its part, at the end of the first paragraph, Article 1 specifies that:

> Within the United Nations, the Organization of American States is a regional agency.

delegation joined the consensus, albeit with major reservations. Ann Thomas and Aaron J. Thomas Jr, *Non-Intervention* (University Park, TX: Southern Methodist University Press, 1956), 61.

[24] Bruce W. Farcau, *The Chaco War* (New York: Praeger, 1996). This was one of the few conflicts in the Americas that was brought before the League of Nations, Fabián Herrera, *La política mexicana en la Sociedad de Naciones ante la Guerra del Chaco* (Mexico City: Secretariat of Foreign Affairs, 2009).

[25] *The International Conferences of American States, first supplement 1933–1940*, 160.

Abstention from the use of force, the peaceful settlement of disputes, reciprocal assistance in the event of aggression, collective self-defence as authorized by the UN Charter, and non-intervention in the affairs of another member state are principles embodied in the OAS Charter and, even before it, in numerous inter-American resolutions and agreements. The main intergovernmental bodies responsible for applying these principles are the General Assembly—the highest organ of the UN, meeting annually—the Permanent Council composed of representatives of all the member states at the organization's headquarters in Washington DC, and the Meeting of Consultation of Ministers of Foreign Affairs.

B. The Member States

Attending the 1889 Conference were the US, the Hispanic American states, Haiti, and Brazil. When the OAS was established in 1948, 21 states participated: almost 40 per cent of those that had founded the UN three years earlier. The nine English-speaking Caribbean countries began joining in the 1970s, and Canada finally became a member in 1990.[26] Although Article 143 of the OAS Charter provides for its denunciation, so far no country has done so.[27] Currently, there are 35 member states. Countries, large and small, the leading world power, and some of the most powerful nations[28] along with some of the poorest countries, live together in the OAS region.

In 1964, the First Special Inter-American Conference adopted the Act of Washington, whereby no new member could be admitted if its territory was wholly or partly the object of claims that were not in the process of being settled by peaceful means. That meant that Belize and Guyana could not be admitted until 1991, because at the time of their independence from a power outside the hemisphere, namely the UK, their territories were the object of claims by Venezuela and Guatemala, respectively. In 1991, both Venezuela and Guatemala withdrew their objection to

[26] Jean-Paul Hubert, 'Les raisons qui ont poussé le Canada à devenir membre de l'Organisation des États Américains' in *Jornadas de Derecho Internacional, Ottawa 2005* (Washington DC: OEA, 2006), 583.

[27] In 1962, the Cuban government was prohibited from participating in the institutions of the inter-American system, including the OAS organs, by a resolution of the Meeting of Ministers of Foreign Affairs of the Inter-American Treaty of Reciprocal Assistance. Cuba participated in that meeting and voted against the resolution; it did not denounce either the Treaty or the OAS Charter. It maintained at the time that it entailed coercive measures that could only be adopted by the UN Security Council. Finally, in 2009, the OAS General Assembly revoked the resolution and decided that 'the participation of the Republic of Cuba in the OAS will be the result of a process of dialogue initiated at the request of the government of Cuba, and in accordance with the practices, purposes, and principles of the OAS', AG/RES.2438 (XXXIX-O/09).

[28] Today, five OAS member states form part of the G20: Argentina, Brazil, Canada, Mexico, and the US.

membership of the two new states and, since then, there have been peaceful negotiations to resolve their differences.

Finally, in 1985, a clause was inserted in Article 8 of the OAS Charter stating that:

Membership in the Organization shall be confined to independent States of the Hemisphere that were Members of the United Nations as of December 10, 1985, and the non autonomous territories mentioned in document OEA/Serv.P. AG/doc.1939/85 of November 5, 1985, when they become independent.

The document referred to makes no mention of the Malvinas (Falkland) Islands, so that, were they to become an independent state, they could not be admitted as an OAS member state.

III. The Use of Force, Provisions Regulating it, and Reality

A. Regional Agreements on Reciprocal Assistance and Abstention from the Use of Force

Dating back to the days of independence, a major concern of the new countries to emerge from the colonial empires was to agree on mechanisms for collective defence against possible attacks and intervention by powers outside the hemisphere. However, that quickly deteriorated into military interventions with no more political justification than the need to restore order in countries bordering on the emerging regional superpower, with an array of juridical pretexts, especially the need to protect nationals.

The threat of an attack from outside loomed again during the Second World War, when the fighting in Europe divided the hemisphere into countries that were neutral and those that supported the Allies. In 1939, at the First Meeting of Consultation of Ministers of Foreign Affairs, held in Panama, the American states declared themselves neutral and established an Inter-American Neutrality Committee.[29] One year later, the ministers declared that 'Any attempt on the part of a non-American State against the integrity or inviolability of the territory, the sovereignty or the political independence of an American State shall be considered as an act of aggression against the States which sign this declaration.'[30] As the war progressed, from

[29] General Declaration of Neutrality in *The International Conferences of American States, first supplement 1933–1940*, 326.

[30] 'Reciprocal assistance and cooperation for the defense of the Nations of the Americas', resolution of the Second Meeting of Ministers of Foreign Affairs of the American Republics (Habana, 1940) in *The International Conferences of American States, first supplement 1933–1940*, 360.

North to South, the various American states began supporting the Allies' efforts and declared war on the Axis powers. In March 1945, when the process of establishing the UN was already under way, the American countries, meeting in Mexico, agreed to draw up a treaty for their collective defence in the event of an act of aggression against any of them, based on the provisions of the new 'general international organisation, when established'.[31] In 1947, in Rio de Janeiro, the member states of what was then the Pan American Union, and which one year later was to give rise to the OAS, adopted the Inter-American Treaty of Reciprocal Assistance (Rio Treaty).[32] Currently, 22 countries are parties to the Treaty.[33]

This treaty, which predates the establishment of the regional organization, was conceived, pursuant to Article 51 of the UN Charter, as an agreement on collective self-defence in the event of an attack against an American state.[34] For that reason, it encompassed an area covering the entire territory of the Americas, including countries that, like Canada, are not parties to it, as well as a maritime zone extending approximately 300 miles from the coast. The Treaty provides for several scenarios: (1) an armed attack against an American state within the geographical area set by the Treaty; (2) an armed attack against an American state outside that area; and (3) a scenario in which 'the integrity of the territory or the sovereignty or political independence of any American State should be affected by an aggression which is not an armed attack or by an extra-continental or intra-continental conflict, or by any other fact or situation [that] might endanger the peace of America. . . .' (Art 6). The first scenario, in turn, covers two eventualities: that the armed attack against an American state comes from a state outside the hemisphere or from another American state. The first eventuality had long since been addressed by the founding provisions and principles of the inter-American system providing for joint defence way before it was established in the UN Charter. If such a scenario were to arise, it is to be

[31] Inter-American Conference on Problems of War and Peace, Mexico City, 21 Feb–8 Mar 1945, *The International Conferences of American States, second supplement* (Washington DC: Pan American Union, 1958), 68.

[32] Jean-Michel Arrighi, 'The Inter-American Treaty of Reciprocal Assistance' in Rüdiger Wolfrum (ed), *Max Planck Encyclopedia of Public International Law* (Oxford: Oxford University Press, 2012), vol V.

[33] Argentina, Bahamas, Bolivia, Brazil, Chile, Colombia, Costa Rica, Cuba, Dominican Republic, Ecuador, El Salvador, Guatemala, Haiti, Honduras, Nicaragua, Panama, Paraguay, Peru, Trinidad and Tobago, the US, Uruguay, and Venezuela. In 1990 Peru denounced the Treaty but withdrew its denunciation one year later. Mexico denounced the Treaty in 2002. During the last regular session of the OAS General Assembly in June 2012 the governments of Bolivia, Ecuador, Nicaragua, and Venezuela announced their intention to denounce the Treaty. The text of the Treaty and the status of signatures and ratifications are available at <http://www.oas.org/juridico/english/treaties/b-29.html>.

[34] Art 3(1): 'The High Contracting Parties agree that an armed attack by any State against an American State shall be considered as an attack against all the American States and, consequently, each one of the said Contracting Parties undertakes to assist in meeting the attack in the exercise of the inherent right of individual or collective self-defense recognised by Article 51 of the Charter of the United Nations.'

considered an attack against all the American states and the organ of consultation established by the Treaty, the Meeting of Ministers of Foreign Affairs,[35] will adopt any necessary measures until the matter is discussed in the UN Security Council. In the second eventuality, of an attack by another American state, the organ of consultation is to take steps to restore peace, and foster a solution to the conflict by peaceful means. If it determines that one state is the aggressor, it must apply measures against it.[36] When an armed attack against an American state occurs outside the area determined by Article 4 of the Treaty, the organ of consultation may adopt measures in support of the attacked state, but collective security does not apply. Finally, in a situation that does not constitute an armed attack, as provided for in the aforementioned Article 6 and as in the majority of cases in which the Treaty has been invoked, 'the Organ of Consultation shall meet immediately in order to agree on the measures which must be taken in case of aggression to assist the victim of the aggression or, in any case, the measures which should be taken for the common defense and for the maintenance of the peace and security of the Continent'. This lack of precision regarding the measures to be adopted and the broad scope of the grounds on which they may be requested gave rise to a wide variety of inappropriate interpretations from the mid-1950s to the 1970s, during the Cold War, when the UN Security Council was hamstrung.[37] The protection of nationals, self-defence, and the threat to regional peace posed by the election of governments with tendencies deemed to be too close to Communist ideology were the reasons invoked to request truly interventionist measures, in some cases involving the use of force not authorized by the UN Security Council. Decisions by the Organ of Consultation require a two-thirds majority of the states parties to the Treaty. When the OAS Charter was adopted one year later, it was agreed (current Art 29[38]) that collective security would

[35] Today, the OAS Permanent Council, the successor to the Governing Board of the Pan American Union, acts provisionally as an organ of consultation until the Ministers of Foreign Affairs meet.

[36] Art 7: 'In the case of a conflict between two or more American States, without prejudice to the right of self-defense in conformity with Article 51 of the Charter of the United Nations, the High Contracting Parties, meeting in consultation shall call upon the contending States to suspend hostilities and restore matters to the *status quo ante bellum*, and shall take in addition all other necessary measures to reestablish or maintain inter-American peace and security and for the solution of the conflict by peaceful means. The rejection of the pacifying action will be considered in the determination of the aggressor and in the application of the measures which the consultative meeting may agree upon.'

Art 8: 'For the purposes of this Treaty, the measures on which the Organ of Consultation may agree will comprise one or more of the following: recall of chiefs of diplomatic missions; breaking of diplomatic relations; breaking of consular relations; partial or complete interruption of economic relations or of rail, sea, air, postal, telegraphic, telephonic, and radiotelephonic or radiotelegraphic communications; and use of armed force.'

[37] Antonio Remiro Brotons, *La Hegemonía americana, factor de crisis en la OEA* (Bolonia: Publicaciones del Real Colegio de España en Bolonia, 1972).

[38] See Charter of the Organization of American States (Concluded 30/04/1948, Entry into Force 13/12/1951) 119 UNTS 3. For most recent version of Charter Amended by the Protocol of Buenos Aires of February 27, 1967, the Protocol of Cartagena de Indias of November 16, 1985 and Protocol of Managua of 6 October, 1993 (entered into force 29 January 1996) see: <http://www.oas.org/dil/treaties_A-41_Charter_of_the_Organization_of_American_States.htm>.

be governed by the 1947 Treaty. However, today 13 OAS member states are not parties to the Treaty of Reciprocal Assistance. In contrast, all of the member states are governed by the corresponding provisions of Chapter IV, 'Fundamental Rights and Duties of States', and, in particular, by the provisions of Articles 19–22. In the event of one of those scenarios occurring without the Rio Treaty being invoked, the competent organ is the Meeting of Consultation of Ministers of Foreign Affairs of the OAS. Exceptionally, in one particular case, both instruments (the Treaty and the OAS Charter) were invoked and both Meetings of Consultation were held.[39]

In 1975, an additional protocol was agreed,[40] introducing the concept of 'collective economic security'. That protocol is not in force and all the signs suggest that it never will be.

The threat of nuclear war, which loomed over the world after the Second World War, led the Latin American states to ban nuclear weapons. In 1967, they adopted the Nuclear Non-Proliferation Treaty (Tlatelolco, Mexico),[41] which has been ratified by 33 of the 35 OAS member states.[42] The OAS has established a new regional organization, OPANAL (Agency for the Prohibition of Nuclear Weapons in Latin America and the Caribbean), whose secretariat is located in Mexico City. So far, Latin America has remained free of nuclear weapons.

Reflecting the fact that there are now numerous OAS member states that have not ratified the Rio Treaty, the OAS Charter established the Meeting of Consultation of Ministers of Foreign Affairs as one of its principal organs. It meets 'in order to consider problems of an urgent nature' (Art 61) and also addresses matters relating to any armed attacks arising in the region 'without prejudice to the provisions of the Inter-American Treaty of Reciprocal Assistance with regard to the States parties to that instrument' (Art 65).

B. From Provisions to Actual Practice

The agreements on reciprocal assistance in the event of attack, which were supposed to be rules for preventing repercussions in the American states of a possible new conflict in Europe, soon turned into Cold War tools in the region.[43] The Inter-American Treaty

[39] That occurred following the terrorist attacks on US soil on 9/11. Brazil requested convocation of the Meeting provided for in the Rio Treaty, while Mexico requested convocation of the Meeting of Consultation under the OAS Charter.

[40] Antonio Gomez-Robledo, 'El Protocolo adicional al Tratado Interamericano de Asistencia Recíproca' in *III Curso de Derecho Internacional. Rio de Janeiro 1976* (Washington DC: OAS, 1977), 131.

[41] Alfonso Garcia-Robles, 'Mesures de désarmement dans des zones particulières: le traité visant l'interdiction des armes nucléaires en Amérique Latine' (1971) 133 *Recueil des cours de l'Académie de droit international* 43.

[42] The US, along with France, the Netherlands, and the UK is not party to the Treaty. They are all nonetheless parties to the additional protocols under which they undertake to observe the Treaty in the territories under their control in the nuclear weapons-free zone established by the Treaty.

[43] John Lewis Gaddis, *We Now Know: Rethinking Cold War History* (Oxford: Oxford University Press, 1997), 177.

of Reciprocal Assistance was invoked 20 times to address internal hemispheric concerns and only twice in response to external conflicts. The former occurred between 1948 and 1967; the latter in 1982 and 2001.[44] The majority of the cases within the hemisphere were in Central America and the Caribbean.

The first case in which the Treaty was invoked, in 1948, involved a complaint by Costa Rica against an invasion by Nicaraguan troops. A fact-finding commission was appointed and a friendly settlement agreement was signed. However, it turned out to be the first in a long series of border conflicts between the two countries[45] that are still being considered, albeit with reference to other inter-American treaties,[46] by the ICJ.

The second case involved a clash between Haiti and the Dominican Republic. Relations between the two countries sharing the same island have always been difficult, since the time of independence and the creation of the two states.[47] The massive presence of Haitian workers on Dominican territory and the plight of the inhabitants of both countries during bloody dictatorships and widespread violation of human rights have strained relations between them. In 1950, Haiti set the Treaty's mechanisms in motion in response to the invasion of its territory by Dominican troops. Confidence-building measures adopted by the Ministers of Foreign Affairs managed to quell the conflict. Years later, in 1963, the Meeting of Ministers of Foreign Affairs was convened once again, this time at the behest of the Dominican Republic, to address its complaint that Haitian authorities had attempted to enter the Dominican embassy in Port-au-Prince to detain Haitian asylum-seekers fleeing persecution by the Duvalier government. As a result of the actions undertaken by the OAS, the asylum-seekers were able to leave Haiti.

In 1954, in the midst of the Cold War, several countries ruled by military dictatorships requested convocation of the Meeting of Ministers of Foreign Affairs to review the situation created by the presence of a 'communist' regime in Guatemala, that of President Arbenz.[48] A US military invasion overthrew him and the ministers said nothing. Nor, however, did the UN Security Council pronounce on the matter when Guatemala protested at the aggression and invasion of its territory. The Council said that it considered that the question should be settled at the regional level.[49] Never

[44] For background on all these instances, see *Inter-American Treaty of Reciprocal Assistance, Applications* (Washington DC: General Secretariat of the OAS), vol I (1948–9), 1973; vol II (1960–72), 1973; vol III part 1 (1973–6), 1977; vol III part 2 (1977–81), 1982; vol IV (1982–2003), 2004.

[45] René-Jean Dupuy, 'L'application du traité d'assistance mutuelle de Rio de Janeiro dans l'affaire Costa Rica-Nicaragua' (1955) 1 *Annuaire français de droit international* 99.

[46] In 1978, Costa Rica once again set the Treaty's mechanisms in motion, against Nicaragua.

[47] Laurent Dubois, *Haiti: The Aftershocks of History* (New York: Metropolitan Books, 2012), 303.

[48] *Inter-American Treaty of Reciprocal Assistance, Applications*, vol I, 165

[49] Eduardo Jimenez de Aréghaga, 'Le traitement des différends internationaux par le Conseil de Sécurité' (1954-I) 85 *Recueil des cours de l'Académie de droit international* 83

again did the Security Council maintain that position in future cases brought before it,[50] even though they were also reviewed at the regional level. It even agreed that they could be brought before it directly, without first exhausting regional remedies.[51] However, it must be said that the Cold War and the veto system precluded effective cooperation between the universal body and the regional organization.

In 1955, Ecuador and Peru clashed over demarcation of the border between them, which had been drawn up by a treaty in 1942 which appointed four countries as guarantors.[52] Thanks to the guarantors, an agreement was reached. However, the same dispute arose 40 years later, in early 1995, with violent clashes between the two countries' troops. Once again, the guarantors managed to restore peace and, in 1998, the Brasilia Agreement finally put an end to the dispute and paved the way for a definitive demarcation of the border.

There was also a clash between Bolivia and Chile: one of the few instances in which disputes between South American countries were brought before the Rio Treaty's organ of consultation. It occurred in 1962, when Bolivia denounced the Chilean authorities for diverting the course of the Luaca River. The Permanent Council restricted itself to requesting that both governments seek a peaceful solution to their dispute using the mechanisms devised for that purpose.

In 1961, the government of Venezuela accused the government of the Dominican Republic, headed by the dictator Trujillo, of supporting an attempt to assassinate the Venezuelan president. The Ministers of Foreign Affairs requested from the members of the inter-American system, among other measures, the 'breaking off of diplomatic relations of all the member states with the Dominican Republic.'[53] It was the first time those measures had been adopted under the Treaty and they triggered immense debate regarding whether a regional organization was competent to adopt measures of that nature.[54] The measures were lifted two years later. When the matter was brought before the UN Security Council, it simply took note of the decisions taken by the OAS.[55]

[50] Eduardo Jimenez de Aréghaga, 'La coordination des systèmes de l'ONU et de l'Organisation des Etats Américains pour le règlement pacifique des différends et la sécurité collective' (1964-I) 111 *Recueil des cours de l'Académie de droit international* 429.

[51] Despite the fact that Art 2 of the Rio Treaty provides that 'the High Contracting Parties undertake to submit every controversy which may arise between them to methods of peaceful settlement and to endeavor to settle any such controversy among themselves by means of the procedures in force in the Inter-American System before referring it to the General Assembly or the Security Council of the United Nations.'

[52] The 'Protocol of Peace, Friendship and Boundaries' known as the 'Rio de Janeiro Protocol', in Article 5 establishes that the guarantors are Argentina, Brazil, Chile, and the US.

[53] *Inter-American Treaty of Reciprocal Assistance, Applications*, vol II, 9.

[54] Felipe Paolillo, 'Nuevas reflexiones en torno a una debatida cuestión: facultades de las entidades regionales en materia de acción coercitiva', 1964, *Anuario Uruguayo de Derecho Internacional, Montevideo* (1965), 173.

[55] Ademola Abass, *Regional Organisations and the Development of Collective Security* (Oxford: Hart, 2004), 44.

A situation that persisted throughout the late 1950s and early 1960s involved relations between Cuba and other member states in the inter-American system, after Fidel Castro took power on the island and declared his adherence to Communist ideology. In 1959, the government of Panama denounced the Cuban government for supporting a revolutionary group on its territory, a denunciation that was withdrawn when the group ceased to exist. Then, in 1961, the Colombian government denounced the Cuban authorities for supporting illegal activities on Colombian soil and for disseminating what it called 'Marxist-Leninist' ideology, which it considered a threat to governments in the region. Convened under the Rio Treaty, the Meeting of Ministers of Foreign Affairs resolved in early 1962 to exclude 'the present government of Cuba from participation in the inter-American system'.[56] At the time, the Cuban government argued that that amounted to coercive measures that could only be adopted by the UN Security Council. Nevertheless, the measures were adopted by a majority vote of the states parties to the Treaty and the Cuban government saw its right to participate in the various institutions in the system withdrawn[57] without the Security Council pronouncing on the matter. It was not until 2009 that the OAS General Assembly[58] lifted the sanction.[59] In October 1962, the US government denounced the installation of launch pads for Soviet missiles on Cuban territory and requested convocation by the OAS of the Rio Treaty's Organ of Consultation along with the convocation of a meeting of the UN Security Council. Acting provisionally as an inter-American organ of consultation, the OAS Permanent Council agreed to authorize the states parties to 'take all measures, individually and collectively, including the use of armed force,...to ensure that the government of Cuba cannot continue to receive...military materials'.[60] For its part, the UN Security Council restricted itself to recommending that the UN Secretary-General act as an intermediary to put an end to the matter. One day after the resolution of the provisional

[56] *Inter-American Treaty of Reciprocal Assistance, Applications*, vol II, 76.

[57] It only maintained its right to participate in the Pan American Health Organisation, as this is a regional agency of the World Health Organization which pertains to the UN.

[58] Whilst it is true that it would have been up to the Meeting of Ministers of Foreign Affairs of the Rio Treaty to lift the sanction as it had imposed it, nevertheless the OAS General Assembly was chosen for one simple reason: nowadays, the states comprising the inter-American system to which Cuba has been reincorporated are more numerous than those that are parties to the Rio Treaty. As the resolution was adopted unanimously, it enshrines the will of all the governments that, regardless of whether they are parties to the Treaty, are to interact with the Cuban government in the regional institutions.

[59] AG/RES.2438 (XXXIX-O/09) resolves: '1. That Resolution VI, adopted on January 31, 1962, at the Eighth Meeting of Consultation of Ministers of Foreign Affairs, which excluded the Government of Cuba from its participation in the inter-American system, hereby ceases to have effect in the Organisation of American States (OAS). 2. That the participation of the Republic of Cuba in the OAS will be the result of a process of dialogue initiated at the request of the government of Cuba, and in accordance with the practices, purposes, and principles of the OAS.'

[60] *Inter-American Treaty of Reciprocal Assistance, Applications*, vol II, 112. This decision was taken on 23 Oct 1962.

organ of consultation, the US president issued a proclamation announcing the decision 'to interdict...the delivery of offensive weapons.... To enforce this order, the Secretary of Defense shall take appropriate measures'. This was later referred to as the 'quarantine' of Cuba. Relations between the US and the Soviet Union were very tense for a number of hours thereafter.[61] In the end, an understanding reached on 27 October between the two superpowers of the time resolved the crisis. One undertook to withdraw its installations in Cuba, the other its installations in Turkey. Much has been written about that crisis, the first to involve nuclear arms. Most experts, like some OAS member states, did not accept that the Organ of Consultation was competent to authorize the use of force, a competence reserved exclusively for the Security Council. Some justified it by invoking collective self-defence, one of the *raisons d'être* of the Rio Treaty. For that, they had to argue that installing missile pads constituted an armed attack or else invoke the moot and mostly rejected argument of 'preventive self-defence'. Finally, others discerned a tacit agreement in the attitude adopted by the two superpowers that justified both the measures and their consequences.[62] In 1963, Cuba was again denounced to the Organ of Consultation, this time by Venezuela denouncing the Cuban authorities for committing terrorist acts against its president. It was agreed, by a slight majority, to ask the member states of the inter-American system to break off diplomatic relations with Cuba. That decision was not respected by several countries, which considered that there were insufficient legal grounds for it in the regional framework and they maintained relations with the government in Havana.[63] In 1975, that decision was set aside, so that the states of the Americas were free to maintain whatever relations they wished with the Cuban government.

In 1964, the government of Panama accused the US of ordering the entry into its territory of troops stationed in the Panama Canal Zone, which at the time was administered by the US. That led to breaking off diplomatic relations and convocation of the Organ of Consultation of the Rio Treaty. That organ requested the two states to negotiate a new treaty establishing new rules governing administration of the canal.[64] The process would eventually lead to the 'Torrijos-Carter' treaty, which, in 1977, repealed the 'Hay-Bunau Vanilla' Treaty of 1903 and allowed Panama to resume control of the Canal Zone as of 1999.

In 1969, Honduras and El Salvador referred the matter of an armed clash to the Organ of Consultation, initiating a series of disputes between the two countries regarding territorial differences, which were finally resolved by the ICJ.

[61] For a detailed account, see Michael Dobbs, *One Minute to Midnight: Kennedy, Khrushchev and Castro on the Brink of Nuclear War* (New York: Knopf, 2008).

[62] Eduardo Jimenez de Arégha, 'Los acontecimientos de octubre de 1962 y el derecho internacional', *1963 Anuario Uruguayo de Derecho Internacional* (Montevideo, 1964), 104.

[63] See the statements by Chile and Mexico in *Inter-American Treaty of Reciprocal Assistance, Applications*, vol II, 218.

[64] *Inter-American Treaty of Reciprocal Assistance, Applications*, vol II, 258.

The last two cases in which the Rio Treaty was applied involved actions outside the hemisphere. The first concerned the Malvinas (Falkland) Islands. These islands, which are located within the geographic zone covered by the Treaty, have been occupied by the UK since 1833 and have been claimed ever since by Argentina. On 2 April 1982, Argentine troops disembarked on the islands. The UN Security Council immediately requested 'an immediate cessation of hostilities' and 'an immediate withdrawal of all Argentine forces'.[65] US Secretary of State Alexander Haig attempted to mediate, but failed. British troops were dispatched to the islands. On 19 April, the Argentine government requested the convocation of the Rio Treaty's Organ of Consultation. The Permanent Council urged that a peaceful solution to the conflict be found. The Ministers of Foreign Affairs met on 26 April and it became clear that they differed in their positions: some considered that collective self-defence should be invoked given the advance of the British armed forces; others considered that the decision should be left to the UN Security Council; and still others, while accepting Argentina's rights to the islands, considered that by resorting to arms to recover them it had forfeited its right to invoke the Rio Treaty.[66] In the end, the meeting simply adopted a resolution calling for an end to hostilities, a truce, and voicing its support for a peaceful settlement taking into account Argentina's sovereign rights. The stationing of British troops on the islands led to fierce clashes between the armed forces of the two countries. The Meeting of Consultation issued several more pronouncements along the same lines as that issued at its first meeting, without taking any other decision. The intermediation efforts entrusted to the UN Secretary-General by the Security Council also failed[67] as did the intermediation initiated by Pope John Paul II. Finally, on 14 June the Argentine troops surrendered to the British commander, without any measure being implemented within the framework of the inter-American system.[68]

The second case—that of the terrorist attacks of 11 September 2001 on US soil—produced statements of condemnation from the UN Security Council, the Rio Treaty's Organ of Consultation, and the Meeting of Consultation of Ministers of Foreign Affairs under the OAS Charter.[69]

The last time the Rio Treaty was invoked in connection with disputes between American states was in 1978. The immense majority of disputes arising since then

[65] Falkland Islands (Malvinas), UN Security Council Resolution 502 (3 Apr 1982).

[66] For a detailed account of the positions expressed by each of the states parties to the treaty, see *Inter-American Treaty of Reciprocal Assistance, Applications*, vol IV, 14–26.

[67] Falkland Islands (Malvinas), UN Security Council Resolution 505 (26 May 1982).

[68] Every year the OAS General Assembly adopts a resolution in which it 'reaffirms the need for the governments of the Argentine Republic and the United Kingdom of Great Britain and Northern Ireland to resume, as soon as possible, negotiations on the sovereignty dispute, in order to find a peaceful solution to this protracted controversy' (eg, in the last session, Res AG/DEC.70 (XLII-O/12)).

[69] In the case of the OAS, after the events had taken place, the government of Brazil requested convocation of the Organ of Consultation of the Rio Treaty and the government of Mexico, which

have been, or are in the process of being, resolved through procedures established in the American Treaty on Pacific Settlement (Pact of Bogotá) and taken before the ICJ.[70]

Other conflicts between OAS member states were settled by applying bilateral treaties. To cite two recent instances, this was the case with the previously mentioned border dispute between Peru and Ecuador in 1995, which was settled by diplomatic moves by the guarantors of the Treaty, and with the dispute between Argentina and Uruguay regarding the construction of pulp mills on the River Uruguay, which was brought before the Court, as required under the Statute of the River Uruguay, a bilateral treaty signed in 1975.[71]

However, apart from the Rio Treaty and the Pact of Bogotá—another treaty to which not all the current OAS member states are party—there is also the possibility of resorting to the Meeting of Consultation of Ministers of Foreign Affairs under the OAS Charter, which provides for the participation of all the states in the inter-American system, regardless of whether they are a party to the Rio Treaty or the Pact of Bogotá. This option was chosen, unfortunately, in 1965, in order for the Tenth Meeting of the Consultation of Ministers of Foreign Affairs to authorize, without any legal justification (because no such legal grounds existed) 'the formation of an inter-American force [which] will signify *ipso facto* the transformation of the forces presently in Dominican territory', that is, the US troops stationed in the Dominican Republic, in clear violation of the principle of non-intervention, at a time when demonstrators were calling for the return of President Bosch, who had been elected in 1962 and deposed shortly thereafter.[72] The Meeting of Consultation merely conveyed its decision to the UN Security Council. The affair was, undoubtedly, one of the worst moments of the inter-American system, in which it reneged on its fundamental principles.

had announced just a few days before that it would denounce that Treaty, called for a Meeting of Consultation of Ministers of Foreign Affairs under the OAS Charter. The two organs met one after the other and adopted identical resolutions.

[70] Between 1986 and 2014: *Border and Transborder Armed Actions (Nicaragua v. Costa Rica)*, removed from the list in 1987; *Border and Transborder Armed Actions (Nicaragua v. Honduras)*, removed from the list in 1992; *Territorial and Maritime Dispute between Nicaragua and Honduras in the Caribbean Sea (Nicaragua v. Honduras)*, Judgment of 8 Oct 2007, ICJ Rep 2007, 659; *Territorial and Maritime Dispute (Nicaragua v. Colombia)*, Judgment of 19 Nov 2012, ICJ Rep 2012, 614; *Dispute regarding Navigational and Related Rights (Costa Rica v. Nicaragua)*, Judgment of 13 July 2009, ICJ Rep 2009, 213; *Maritime Dispute (Peru v. Chile)*, Judgment of 13 July 2009, ICJ Rep 2009, 213; *Aerial Herbicide Spraying (Ecuador v. Colombia)*, removed from the list in 2013; *Certain questions concerning diplomatic relations (Honduras v. Brazil)*, removed from the list in 2010; *Certain Activities carried out by Nicaragua in the Border Area (Costa Rica v. Nicaragua)*, provisional measures decided by the Court in 2013; *Construction of a Road in Costa Rica along the San Juan River (Nicaragua v. Costa Rica)*, pending and more recently, also pending, Obligation to Negotiate Access to the Pacific Ocean *(Bolivia v. Chile)*; Question of the Delimitation of the Continental Shelf between Nicaragua and Colombia beyond 200 nautical miles from the Nicaraguan Coast *(Nicaragua v. Colombia)*; Alleged Violations of Sovereign Rights and Maritime Spaces in the Caribbean Sea *(Nicaragua v. Colombia)*; and Maritime Delimitation in the Caribbean Sea and the Pacific Ocean *(Costa Rica v. Nicaragua)*.

[71] Judgment of 20 April 2010, ICJ Rep 2010, 14.

[72] Abraham F. Lowenthal, *The Dominican Intervention* (2nd edn, Baltimore, MD: Johns Hopkins University Press, 1995).

A more recent case in which the Meeting of Consultation of Ministers of Foreign Affairs was convened, this time in accordance with law, was 1 March 2008 when Colombian troops bombarded a camp established by the Colombian terrorist group, the Revolutionary Armed Forces of Colombia (FARC), on Ecuadorian soil. The rebel leader Raúl Reyes was killed in the attack and his body, along with computers found at the site, was taken by the Colombian troops back to Colombia. At Ecuador's request, the Permanent Council immediately convened the Meeting of Consultation and dispatched the Secretary General to the site of the attack, together with a group of ambassador members of the Permanent Council, to report on the events which had occurred. Based on their report when they got back, Colombia's acknowledgement of the facts, and the statements of its president apologizing to the Ecuadorian government, the Meeting of Consultation resolved 'to reject the incursion by Colombian military forces and police personnel into the territory of Ecuador…to take note of the full apology for the events that occurred…by Colombia' and 'to instruct the Secretary General to use his good offices to implement a mechanism for…the restoration of an atmosphere of trust between the two Parties.'[73] Only the US delegation disagreed with the arguments adduced in the resolution, on the ground that Colombia had acted in self-defence, a position that, as noted earlier, was not shared by the Colombian delegation, whose president had apologized to the Ecuadorian government and had undertaken that it 'would not be repeated under any circumstances'. Owing to the Secretary General's good offices, confidence-building measures were implemented to enhance cooperation on the border between the two countries, leading eventually to the restoration of diplomatic relations, which had been suspended since 1 March 2008.

Although, as noted at several points in the previous discussion and especially during the Cold War, the regional body has sometimes been used for actions bordering on the edge of, or even clearly beyond, those permitted under international law, in other instances the need to protect nationals or requests for help from a government or a sub-regional grouping were adduced to justify unilateral actions that were condemned by regional or universal bodies and occasionally by the ICJ itself. This last instance was triggered by support for the 'Contras' against the Nicaraguan government, which prompted the Court to reaffirm the still binding nature of the principle of non-intervention, to underscore its origins in the inter-American system,[74] and to rule that the US government had acted 'in breach of its obligation under customary law not to intervene in the affairs of another State.'[75]

[73] Twenty-fifth Meeting of Consultation of Ministers of Foreign Affairs, RC.25/RES.1/08 rev.1, 17 Mar 2008.

[74] *Case Concerning Military and Paramilitary Activities in and against Nicaragua (Nicaragua v. US)*, Merits, 27 June 1986, para 204.

[75] For an analysis of this case, see Christine Gray, *International Law and the Use of Force* (3rd edn, Oxford: Oxford University Press, 2008), 171.

In 1983, American troops invaded Grenada, invoking a request for it to do so by the Organisation of Eastern Caribbean States (OECS), without any involvement by the UN and without obtaining agreement from the OAS.[76]

In contrast, when US troops entered Panamanian territory in 1989 and, after fierce fighting, arrested General Noriega and removed him to the US[77] arguing that it was acting in defence of US citizens, the OAS Permanent Council issued a vigorous condemnation.

The regional organization has also condemned the abduction of a person by agents of a foreign government as occurred in 1990 when agents of the US Drug Enforcement Administration (DEA) forcibly abducted the physician, Dr Alvarez Machaín, from Mexico to the US to be tried for the murder, on Mexican soil, of a US agent. When the competence of the US courts was challenged because of the manner in which the accused was brought before it, the US Supreme Court concluded that 'the fact of respondent's forcible abduction does not therefore prohibit his trial in a court of the United States'. The OAS Permanent Council asked the Inter-American Juridical Committee—a consultative organ of the organization—to issue its opinion 'on the international legality of the decision of the Supreme Court of the United States.' The Juridical Committee concluded that there had been 'a serious violation of international law.'[78]

Finally, the organization also cooperated with the restoration of peace in Central America and the subsequent demobilization of the parties to the conflict,[79] even though its efforts, and especially those of its Secretary General, were not readily accepted by various groups of American states involved, which preferred the involvement of ad hoc bodies to that of the regional organization.[80] These pacification activities laid the foundations for the first OAS missions to support and observe electoral processes and to assist judicial institutions in those countries.

[76] Olivier Corten, *The Law against War* (Oxford: Hart, 2012), 265 and 338.

[77] Louis Henkin, 'The Invasion of Panama under International Law: A Gross Violation' (1991) 29 *Columbia Journal of Transnational Law* 293.

[78] CJI/RES.II-15/92, in 1992 Annual Report of the Inter-American Juridical Committee to the General Assembly, OAS, Washington DC, 8.

[79] Antonio Augusto Cançado Trindade, 'Mécanismes de règlement pacifique des différends en Amérique Centrale: de Contadora à Esquipulas II' (1967) XXXIII *Annuaire français de droit international* 816.

[80] That led the Secretary General to propose that he be given wider ranging powers, a request that was finally approved in the 1985 amendment to the OAS Charter, which introduced para 2 of Art 110, which reads: 'The Secretary General may bring to the attention of the General Assembly or the Permanent Council any matter which in his opinion might threaten the peace and security of the Hemisphere or the development of the Member States'.

IV. The Principle of Non-Intervention and the Defence of Democracy

It was no easy task to embody the principle of non-intervention in the inter-American legal framework. Despite its embodiment in legal provisions, it was violated on numerous occasions, on such pretexts as collective self-defence, protection of a country's nationals, or the struggle against ideologies deemed to pose a threat to security.

Once the Cold War was over and with the end of the region's dictatorships, representative democracy began to be consolidated as a form of government throughout the hemisphere and inter-American provisions were adopted to prevent interruptions of that order. As with the provisions designed to maintain peace in the first half of the 20th century, these new provisions also harbour a risk of violation of the principle of non-intervention.[81]

A. Provisions for the Defence of Democracy in the OAS Charter and in Sub-Regional Bodies

Once the republic had been consolidated as a form of state and all attempts to install kings or establish new empires had been discarded, the desire emerged to consolidate the democratic form of government as a system providing for separation of powers, rotation of authorities, and respect for minorities. Following the example of the US Constitution and the doctrines of Locke and Montesquieu, the Latin American constitutions began to establish those precepts. Nevertheless, personal rivalry, local interests, strong-man politics, and authoritarian leaders meant that *coups d'état*, civil wars, and dictatorships were, in practice, the most common form of government.

Internationally, a few rulers here and there proposed in vain to the other American states that they should not recognize governments arising from *coups d'état*.[82] Most states rejected such proposals as violating the principle of non-intervention and as contrary to international law,[83] or at least the international law of the time.[84]

[81] Edmundo Vargas Carreño, 'El principio de no intervención' in *XXX Curso de Derecho Internacional. Rio de Janeiro 2003* (Washington DC: OAS, 2004), 162.

[82] eg the proposals put forward by Ecuador's Minister of Foreign Affairs, Carlos Tobar, in 1907, by the Uruguayan Minister of Foreign Affairs, Eduardo Rodríguez Larreta, in 1945, and by President Betancourt of Venezuela in 1963.

[83] The position taken by the Mexican Minister of Foreign Affairs, Genaro Estrada, in 1930.

[84] In 1945, during the Inter-American Conference on Problems of War and Peace, Guatemala asked that it be established that governments arising out of *coups d'état* would not be recognized. The Inter-American Juridical Committee was asked to give its opinion and, in 1946, stated that under

In 1936, the Inter-American Conference for the Maintenance of Peace, held at the end of the Chaco War, adopted (in Resolution XXVII) a Declaration of Principles of Inter-American Solidarity and Co-operation, the first declarative paragraph of which reads:

That the American Nations, true to their republican institutions, proclaim their absolute juridical liberty, their unqualified respect for their respective sovereignties and the existence of a common democracy throughout America.

This was the first time that a document adopted by all the American states mentioned the idea of democracy, without further specification of what was understood by that term. Two years later, the Eighth International Conference of American States requested that the states of the hemisphere promote the teaching of democratic principles in their educational establishments.[85]

In 1948, the American states established the OAS and mentioned democracy twice in the Preamble to its Charter[86] and once in Article 5(d) (now Art 3(d)). This article, which lists the principles governing relations between the American states, reads as follows:

The solidarity of the American States and the high aims which are sought through it require the political organisation of those States on the basis of the effective exercise of representative democracy.

This time the reference is to 'representative democracy'. What such a democracy comprises was to be spelt out at the Fifth Meeting of Consultation of Ministers of Foreign Affairs in Santiago, Chile, in 1959.[87] All these were pioneering provisions in

international law at that time Guatemala's proposal would have to be rejected, but it added, with certain powers of premonition, that 'no descartamos la hipótesis de que un caso que hoy es doméstico pueda mañana volverse internacional' ('we do not rule out the hypothesis that what today is a domestic issue may become international tomorrow'), Inter-American Juridical Committee, *Recomendaciones e informes 1945–1947* (Rio de Janeiro: Imprenta Nacional, 1950), 117–27. In the inter-American system, the Juridical Committee has been a pioneer in positing the obligation of American states to respect the democratic form of government, as testified to in numerous resolutions and reports since the early 1990s. See also *La democracia en los trabajos del Comité Jurídico Interamericano, 1946–2010* (Washington DC, OEA, 2011).

[85] Resolution LXXII, 'Teaching of Democracy' in *The International Conferences of American States, first supplement 1933–1940*, 284.

[86] The Preamble states that: 'the true significance of American solidarity and good neighborliness can only mean the consolidation on this continent, within the framework of democratic institutions, of a system of individual liberty and social justice based on respect for the essential rights of man…' and 'representative democracy is an indispensable condition for the stability, peace and development of the region'.

[87] The Fifth Meeting of Consultation of Ministers of Foreign states declare:

1. The principle of the rule of law should be assured by the separation of powers, and by the control of the legality of governmental acts by competent organs of the state.
2. The governments of the American republics should be the result of free elections.
3. Perpetuation in power, or the exercise of power without a fixed term and with the manifest intent of perpetuation, is incompatible with the effective exercise of democracy.

international law. Unfortunately, however, they were all followed in practice by prolonged periods of civil war, dictatorships, human rights violations, and clashes and interventions in the context of the Cold War. The peace process in Central America in the 1980s, which led to the establishment of democratically elected authorities, and the end to the dictatorships in the Southern Cone enabled the regional organization once again to debate 'representative democracy' as a form of government in the Americas.[88] The 1985 amendment of the OAS Charter incorporated current Article 2(b), which established that one of the purposes of the organization (no longer just a principle that the states must abide by) is to:

> promote and consolidate representative democracy, with due respect for the principle of nonintervention.

Here, therefore, we find the link between the defence of representative democracy and the principle of non-intervention.

Under that authorization, which of course included the General Secretariat, and with the countries agreeing on the principle of non-intervention, the OAS organized the first missions in support of peace, reconciliation, and democratization processes, including the first electoral observation missions, technical and legislative assistance, and cooperation for institution-building (electoral rosters, the judicial system). Nicaragua in 1990 was a case in point. In the throes of the restoration of democracy and the momentum provided by the English-speaking Caribbean states that had just won their independence and had joined the OAS, and the incorporation of Canada, in 1991 the General Assembly adopted Resolution 1080,[89] which avowed that:

4. The governments of the American states should maintain a system of freedom for the individual and of social justice based on respect for fundamental human rights.
5. The human rights incorporated into the legislation of the American states should be protected by effective judicial procedures.
6. The systematic use of political proscription is contrary to American democratic order.
7. Freedom of the press, radio, and television, and, in general, freedom of information and expression are essential conditions for the existence of a democratic regime.
8. The American states, in order to strengthen democratic institutions, should cooperate among themselves within the limits of their resources and the framework of their laws so as to strengthen and develop their economic structure, and achieve just and humane living conditions for their peoples.

Text in *Reuniones de Consulta de Ministros de Relaciones Exteriores, t.I* (Washington DC: OAS, 1984), 202. English translation available at <http://www.oas.org/consejo/MEETINGS%20OF%20CONSULTATION/Actas/Acta%205.pdf>.

[88] There was one exception during the period of the dictatorships when a political organ of the OAS pronounced in favour of democracy. In 1979, the Seventeenth Meeting of Consultation of Ministers of Foreign Affairs resolved that it was necessary to replace the dictatorial regime of the Somoza family in Nicaragua and to install a democratic government: Resolution II of 23 June 1979. By that time, the Inter-American Commission on Human Rights, a body comprised of independent members, had already pronounced on violations of human rights in a number of countries in the region.

[89] OAS General Assembly Res AG/RES.1080 (XXI-O/91).

in the event of any occurrences giving rise to the sudden or irregular interruption of the democratic political institutional process or of the legitimate exercise of power by the democratically elected government in any of the Organisation's member states.

An ad hoc meeting of the Ministers of Foreign Affairs or a special session of the General Assembly would be convened to

look into the events collectively and adopt any decisions deemed appropriate, in accordance with the Charter and international law.

This vague formula was rendered more precise in another amendment to the OAS Charter, which incorporated today's Article 9, which specifies that a member of the organization whose democratically constituted government has been overthrown by force may be suspended from the exercise of the right to participate in the organs of the organization. This Protocol of amendments to the Charter (Washington, 1992) was not ratified by all the states, especially by those that considered that it authorized the OAS to violate the principle of non-intervention in internal affairs.[90] New circumstances, other than military coups, such as those brought about by violations of the constitutional order fostered by the democratically elected executive or cases of electoral fraud in which it was impossible to determine which new authority had been elected, led in 2001 to the adoption of another General Assembly resolution, entitled Inter-American Democratic Charter. This new resolution not only seeks to ensure that the OAS organs can adopt measures aimed at preventing potential crisis scenarios, but also reaffirms the ties between democracy and human rights and between democracy and economic development.[91]

The various sub-regional organizations and Presidential Summit bodies adopted similar provisions, which, generally speaking, required suspending a state from participating in their activities.[92]

B. Cases

So far, there have been applications of Resolution 1080 of 1991 and of the Inter-American Democratic Charter of 2001, and, on two occasions, generic invocations of the OAS Charter. On the other hand, Article 9 of the OAS Charter, incorporated by the Washington Protocol of 1992, has never been invoked.

Shortly after the 1991 OAS General Assembly resolution had been adopted, the situation that it contemplated and for which it had been adopted actually occurred,

[90] Among other grounds for not being party to this amendment, the government of Mexico declared that 'it is unacceptable that the regional body be given supranational powers and instruments for intervening in the internal affairs of our states.'

[91] Jean-Michel Arrighi, 'L'Organisation des Etats Américains et le droit international' (2011) 355 *Recueil des cours de l'Académie de droit international* 361.

[92] As in the Summits of the Americas, MERCOSUR, UNASUR, and others.

namely a classical military coup overthrowing democratically elected authorities, which occurred in Haiti when the military ousted President Aristide. The first decision taken by the Meeting of Consultation of the Ministers of Foreign Affairs of the OAS was to not recognize the de facto authorities and to continue to recognize President Aristide and his officials, starting with his ambassador to the organization.[93] Other measures followed, such as the request to the American states that they break off commercial, diplomatic, and consular relations. All these measures were reported to the UN Security Council, which was proceeding to adopt similar measures of an obligatory and universal nature and which authorized coordination between the two organizations regarding the appointment of a joint representative of the two secretaries general. Finally, when negotiations for the peaceful withdrawal of the military junta and the return of President Aristide failed, the Security Council authorized the use of force.[94] It was avoided at the last minute when the military stepped down, the coup leaders were exiled, and President Aristide returned to Port-au-Prince. This was the first case in which the OAS applied the provisions on the defence of democracy and was a test case of how far the powers of the organization could go without violating the principle of non-intervention. It was not always easy, particularly when the OAS Permanent Council established a committee to monitor measures adopted with respect to breaking off economic relations. The Dominican Republic, the only country to share a border with Haiti, was particularly emphatic that the measures had been recommendations and it rejected any interpretation of them as binding.

There were also situations in which it was the democratically elected government that violated the constitutional order, a very different scenario from that of the traditional coup d'état.[95] In the Peruvian case, which required a very broad interpretation of Resolution 1080, it was agreed, after diplomatic moves by a group of ministers of foreign affairs, that a constituent assembly should be convened. In the Guatemalan case, rejection of the situation engendered by the President of the Republic quickly led to his departure and replacement.

In 2000, there were two cases of electoral fraud denounced by OAS observation missions.[96] In those cases, in which it was impossible to invoke Resolution 1080 because the situation it addressed did not apply, Article 2(b) of the OAS Charter was used. With the government's consent, hence with respect for the principle of non-intervention mentioned in that provision, missions were dispatched

[93] MRE/RES.1/91 of 3 Oct 1991.

[94] Res 940 of 31 July 1994. At no time was it proposed (as it had been, incorrectly, in earlier decades) that the regional organization could be empowered to use force.

[95] This occurred in Peru in 1992 and in Guatemala in 1993.

[96] Peru during presidential elections, and Haiti during elections to the Senate.

to resolve the crisis through dialogue with the different forces participating in the elections.

In 2001, the General Assembly adopted the resolution entitled Inter-American Democratic Charter, which addresses scenarios ranging from a possible crisis which could be prevented, and in respect of which the government concerned requests assistance from the regional organization, to interruption of the democratic order, a scenario in which the only option open to the OAS is to suspend the state from participation in it by a vote of two-thirds of its members. This Charter has been used on various occasions when governments have asked for the organization's support to resolve institutional crises pitching their executive against the legislature[97] or the judiciary.[98] In 2002, a military commando detained President Chávez of Venezuela. The crisis lasted for 48 hours, after which the president resumed control of the country. Applying the Democratic Charter, the Council decided, after the crisis had been resolved, to support round table discussions among the various sectors involved with a view to leading to an electoral process.[99]

In 2009, the military overthrew President Zelaya of Honduras, arrested him, and deported him, and a de facto president gained control of the country. Pursuant to Article 21 of the Democratic Charter, and unanimously, the General Assembly agreed in a special session to suspend the state's participation in the OAS. Two year later, after extensive negotiations, many of them conducted by the OAS Secretary General, President Zelaya's return to the country led to the suspension being lifted.[100]

These are the cases to which the regional organization has thus far applied the provisions allowing it, since 1985, to defend 'representative democracy'. In all these instances, decisions were taken unanimously or with the consensus of all members. For their part, the sub-regional organizations have also adopted similar measures and included democratic clauses in their provisions.[101]

This marks a fundamental change in the history of inter-American relations in which institutional crises were either triggered or ineffectively settled by unilateral military action, albeit under cover of some pretence of legality, as was the case during the Cold War in Central America or in Panama and Grenada: actions that were condemned by the majority of OAS member states as clearly violating the principle of non-intervention.

[97] Nicaragua in 2004 and 2005. [98] Ecuador in 2005.

[99] CP/RES.811(1315/02) of 18 Apr 2002. [100] AG/RES.1(XLI-E/11) of 1 June 2011.

[101] Jean-Michel Arrighi, 'Las normas interamericanas para la defensa de la democracia' in *XXXVIII Curso de Derecho Internacional. Rio de Janeiro 2011* (Washington DC: OAS, 2012), 228.

V. Conclusion

The region encompassed by the OAS was, with very few exceptions, practically devoid of wars between its states throughout the 20th century.[102] However, the most powerful state in the region did deploy a wide range of excuses to intervene in the internal affairs of some of the OAS member states, often availing itself of majorities or vetoes in the regional or universal bodies. Such situations have not recurred for some time and the last were widely condemned in the region. Today, it is a question of strengthening the democratic system. While much remains to be done, the situation today is very different from that of a few decades earlier[103] and in the various scenarios in which the provisions have been invoked no one has argued on the basis of violation of the principle of non-intervention, even in the case of Honduras when harsh sanctions were imposed.

[102] Eric Hobsbawm wrote, in an overview of the 20th century, 'we tend to forget that there are regions, like Latin America, where no army ever crossed the border of an enemy state throughout the twentieth century, with the one exception of the Chaco War' in *On the Edge of the New Century* (New York: New Press, 2000), 9.

[103] Peter H. Smith, *Democracy in Latin America* (Oxford: Oxford University Press, 2005), 78.

CHAPTER 24

THE CRIME OF AGGRESSION AT THE INTERNATIONAL CRIMINAL COURT

SEAN D. MURPHY

I. Introduction

Those seeking to uphold the international prohibition on the use of force by one state against the territorial integrity or political independence of another often favour the idea of criminally punishing governmental leaders who initiate such force. Indeed, at least since the prosecution of the major political and military leaders at the Nuremberg and Tokyo war crimes tribunals, many states and individuals have sought to establish a global criminal tribunal for prosecuting government officials who plan and unleash interstate aggression. Throughout most of the 20th century, that aspiration remained unfulfilled, but in 1998 120 states adopted the Rome Statute establishing the International Criminal Court (ICC).[1] The Rome Statute, to which 122 states are a party as of September 2014,[2] contemplated the activation of ICC

[1] Rome Statute of the International Criminal Court, 17 July 1998, 2187 UNTS 3.

[2] The states parties to the Rome Statute may be found at: <http://www.icc-cpi.int/en_menus/asp/states%20parties/Pages/the%20states%20parties%20to%20the%20rome%20statute.aspx/>.

jurisdiction over the crime of aggression, but only at a future point when the crime would be defined and the conditions for its operation would be elaborated.

At the ICC Review Conference, held in 2010 at Kampala, Uganda, the states parties reached major decisions towards that end, settling upon definitions for 'act of aggression' and 'crime of aggression', and making the jurisdiction potentially available even in the absence of a referral from the Security Council. At the same time, the states parties decided that the ICC's jurisdiction over this crime will not become operative until sometime after 1 January 2017 pursuant to a further decision by the states parties. Even then, the ICC's jurisdiction will be limited over this crime, since there are exceptions available for states parties that wish to avoid exposure to such jurisdiction and the jurisdiction will not extend to states that are not parties to the Rome Statute.[3] Moreover, considerable uncertainties and ambiguities exist concerning the exact process for activating the jurisdiction, the manner in which the jurisdiction operates once it is activated, its institutional effects on the Security Council and the ICC itself, and its long-term implications for the *jus ad bellum*.

II. Antecedents: From Versailles to Kampala

As noted elsewhere in this volume and discussed in depth in specialized treatises,[4] individuals were first held criminally accountable for waging a *war of aggression* at the International Military Tribunal convened at Nuremberg in the aftermath of the Second World War. The road to Nuremberg was an uneven one. The 1919 Treaty of Versailles after the First World War called for the arrest and trial of German officials,[5] notably Kaiser Wilhelm II, but the Kaiser lived out his life comfortably in the Netherlands and the 1921 'Leipzig trials' of other officials before the German Supreme Court were inconsequential.[6] Such trials were for violations of the laws

[3] For the sake of simplicity, this chapter will refer to a *state* (or *state party*) being exposed to the ICC's jurisdiction over the crime of aggression, though what is actually meant is exposure for a *national* of that state or a *person* accused of committing the crime on the territory of that state.

[4] See eg Randall Lesaffer, 'Too Much History: From War as Sanction to the Sanctioning of War', Chapter 1 in this volume, at 35; Nico Schrijver, 'The Ban on the Use of Force in the UN Charter', Chapter 21 in this volume, at 465; Telford Taylor, *The Anatomy of the Nuremberg Trials: A Personal Memoir* (Boston, MA: Little Brown & Co, 1992).

[5] Treaty of Versailles, Arts 227–30, in Lawrence Martin (ed), *I Treaties of Peace, 1919–1923* (New York: Carnegie Endowment for International Peace, 2007), 121–2.

[6] See Claud Mullins, *The Leipzig Trials* (Livingston: H. F. & G. Witherby, 1921); Kirsten Sellers, 'Delegitimizing Aggression: First Steps and False Starts after the First World War' (2012) 10 *Journal of International Criminal Justice* 7. The Kaiser died in the Netherlands in 1941.

and customs of war, not for aggression or any other unlawful use of force, though the unconsummated trial of the Kaiser would have been 'for a supreme offence against international morality and the sanctity of treaties.'[7]

In the 1928 Kellogg–Briand Pact (or Pact of Paris), the states parties solemnly declared 'that they condemn recourse to war for the solution of international controversies and renounce it as an instrument of national policy in their relations with one another.'[8] The Pact, however, did not specify criminal liability either for states or for individuals in the event of a violation of the Pact; whether the norm set forth in the Pact reflected a general rule of international law or one binding solely upon those states that had ratified the Pact was uncertain. As such, after the outbreak of the Second World War, many believed that no 'international agreement criminalising wars of aggression was in force in 1939, and therefore, on the basis of the *nullum crimen sine lege* principle, the Allies were not legally entitled to prosecute the top Nazi leaders for aggression.'[9]

Nevertheless, at the San Francisco conference in April 1945, the 'enforcement arrangements' committee asserted that:

> It being the original intent and meaning of the Kellogg-Briand Pact... that any person in the service of any Party-State who violated its provisions... should be held individually responsible for these acts, it is declared that the aggressions of the Axis states since the signing of the Pact violated its provisions and that the persons in the service of such Axis states are individually responsible for such acts and may be brought to trial and punishment before any United Nations court or other tribunal of competent jurisdiction which may secure custody of such persons or any of them.[10]

As such, when the Charter establishing the International Military Tribunal to prosecute major war criminals of the European Axis powers was adopted in August 1945, it provided jurisdiction to the Tribunal over:

> Crimes Against Peace: namely, planning, preparation, initiation or waging of a war of aggression, or a war in violation of international treaties, agreements or assurances, or preparation in a common plan or conspiracy for the accomplishment of any of the foregoing. ...[11]

In implementation of the Charter, and with reliance on the Kellogg–Briand Pact and other treaties and agreements, the first trial of the major war criminals proceeded in Nuremberg to prosecute and convict eight defendants for crimes against

[7] Treaty of Versailles, Art 227 in *Treaties of Peace*, 121.

[8] General Treaty for the Renunciation of War, 27 Aug 1928, 46 Stat 2343, 94 LNTS 57.

[9] Page Wilson, *Aggression, Crime and International Security: Moral, Political and Legal Dimensions of International Relations* (Abingdon: Routledge, 2009), 55; see at 50 ('the UK, Soviet Union and France raised many of the same objections to the criminality of aggression which had been played out earlier within US bureaucratic circles').

[10] UN Conference on International Organisation 104 (4 Apr 1945). The 'enforcement arrangements' committee at San Francisco was a technical committee set up under Commission III, which addressed Security Council measures.

[11] See Agreement for the Prosecution of the Major War Criminals of the European Axis Powers and Charter of the International Military Tribunal, Charter, Art 6(1), 8 Aug 1945, 82 UNTS 279.

peace. Although invited to do so by the prosecution, the Tribunal did not convict any defendants for 'a war in violation of international treaties, agreements or assurances.'[12] Rather, the Tribunal only convicted defendants for conducting (or conspiring to conduct) a 'war of aggression', although it took into account pre-war international agreements in finding that aggression had been outlawed. When parsing the facts, the Tribunal characterized the *Anschluss* in Austria and the German administration in parts of Czechoslovakia as 'aggressive actions', inasmuch as they were shown to be part of a plan for aggressive wars against other countries.[13] By contrast, the Tribunal characterized the uses of force against Belgium, Denmark, Greece, Luxembourg, the Netherlands, Norway, Poland, the Soviet Union, the US, and Yugoslavia as 'aggressive wars'.[14] The convicted defendants were found to have been knowingly involved in activities 'not too far removed from the time of decision and of action', and all to have 'contributed to the initiation of the war in an important and "aggressive" role.'[15]

When judging the culpability of the defendants for such conduct, the Tribunal developed two counts relating to the crime of aggression. Count one concerned the conduct of broadly engaging in a common plan to prepare, initiate, and wage aggression. This count could be shown, for instance, by establishing that the defendant participated in four secret conferences from 1937 to 1939 at which Adolph Hitler revealed his plans for invading other countries.[16] Count two concerned the conduct of planning or waging a particular war of aggression, such as the conviction of Admiral Karl Doenitz for the waging of submarine warfare.[17] Eight of the defendants at the first trial were convicted of counts one and two, while four were convicted only of count two.

The International Military Tribunal for the Far East (Tokyo Tribunal), established by a special proclamation issued by the Supreme Commander of the Allied Powers in the East (General Douglas MacArthur), also possessed jurisdiction over crimes against peace.[18] Twenty-eight Japanese senior political and military leaders were brought before the Tribunal; count one charged them as 'leaders, organisers, instigators, or accomplices in the formulation or execution of a common plan or conspiracy... to wage wars of aggression, and war or wars in violation of international

[12] Wilson, *Aggression, Crime and International Security*, 52; see generally George Ginsburgs and Vladimir N. Kudriavtsev (eds), *The Nuremberg Trial and International Law* (Leiden: Martinus Nijhoff, 1990).

[13] International Military Tribunal Proceedings, vol XXII, 433, 536, 555.

[14] International Military Tribunal Proceedings, vol XXII, 427, 445–58, 562. At the first trial, the tribunal did not address whether the wars against France and the UK were aggression.

[15] Thomas Weigend, '"In General a Principle of Justice": The Debate on the "Crime against Peace" in the Wake of the Nuremberg Judgment' (2012) 10 *Journal of International Criminal Justice* 41, 43.

[16] International Military Tribunal Proceedings, vol XXII, 467–8.

[17] International Military Tribunal Proceedings, vol XXII, 554–7.

[18] See Special Proclamation: Establishment of an International Military Tribunal for the Far East, in The Tokyo War Crimes Trial, Vol I: Pre-Trial Documents, Transcript of the Proceedings in Open Session, 1–2.

law', while other counts concerned waging unprovoked war specifically against the British Commonwealth, China, France (in Indochina), the Netherlands, the Soviet Union, and the US. Though two died and one was declared incompetent, the remaining defendants were all convicted of crimes against peace.[19]

The UN General Assembly in 1946 affirmed the principles of international law set forth in both the Charter of the Nuremberg Tribunal and its judgment of the major war criminals.[20] Moreover, in 1950 the International Law Commission codified a series of principles reflecting that charter and judgment, including with respect to the crime of aggression.[21] Some saw these steps as a prelude to the creation of a permanent international criminal court, but international criminal tribunals disappeared after Nuremberg and Tokyo. The political divide of the Cold War, the resistance of the major powers to scrutiny of their uses of force, and the slowly evolving structures in international law for addressing rights and obligations of individuals held those aspirations in check.

Perhaps the most important development in this period was the adoption in 1974 by the UN General Assembly of a resolution, to which was annexed a document entitled 'Definition of Aggression'.[22] Though generally referred to as a 'definition', the resolution is probably best understood as a series of factors set forth by the General Assembly as guidance for the Security Council when considering whether an act of 'aggression' has occurred; no single factor standing alone was meant to be determinative, but had to be weighed by the Council in the context of all relevant circumstances. Article 1 of the annex stated: 'Aggression is the use of armed force by a State against the sovereignty, territorial integrity or political independence of another State, or in any other manner inconsistent with the Charter of the United Nations, as set out in this Definition.'[23] Article 2 then asserted that a first use of force was prima facie an act of aggression, 'although the Security Council may, in conformity with the Charter, conclude that a determination that an act of aggression has been committed would not be justified in the light of other relevant circumstances, including the fact that the acts concerned or their consequences are not of sufficient gravity.'[24] Article 3 provided a non-exhaustive list of seven types of act that a state

[19] See Yuma Totani, *The Tokyo War Crimes Trial: The Pursuit of Justice in the Wake of World War II* (Cambridge, MA: Harvard University Press, 2009); Neil Boister and Robert Cryer, *The Tokyo International Tribunal: A Reappraisal* (Oxford: Oxford University Press, 2008); Timothy P. Maga, *Judgment at Tokyo: The Japanese War Crimes Trials* (Lexington, KY: University Press of Kentucky, 2001).

[20] GA Res 95 (I), A/236 (1946), 1144.

[21] 'Principles of International Law Recognized in the Charter of the Nürnberg Tribunal and in the Judgment of the Tribunal, with Commentaries', Report of the International Law Commission on the Work of its Second Session, UN GAOR, 5th Sess, Supp No 12, A/1316 (1950), reprinted in *Yearbook of the International Law Commission*, 1950, vol II (2), 374.

[22] Definition of Aggression, GA Res 3314 (XXIX) (1974); see Bengt Broms, 'The Definition of Aggression' (1977-I) 154 *Recueil des cours de l'Académie de droit international de la Haye* 348; Julius Stone, 'Holes and Loopholes in the 1974 Definition of Aggression' (1977) 71 *American Journal of International Law* 224.

[23] GA Res 3314 (XXIX), Art 1. [24] GA Res 3314 (XXIX), Art 2.

might commit that would presumptively constitute aggression, but reiterated that a determination in each case was to be made by the Security Council.[25] As such, the resolution's annex did not directly equate all uses of force that violated Article 2(4) of the UN Charter with 'aggression'. Rather, it provided in Article 1 that 'aggression' might consist of the types of force 'as set out in this Definition', identified in Articles 2 and 3 certain illustrative acts, and then left it to the Security Council to decide for any given incident whether 'aggression' in fact had occurred.

Importantly for present purposes, the resolution was focused on state responsibility for aggression, not on the criminal responsibility of individuals; it principally 'deals with aggression by States, not with the crimes of individuals, and is designed as a guide for the Security Council, not as a definition for judicial use.'[26] The only reference to 'crime' appears in Article 5(1) of the annex, which (echoing Nuremberg) asserted that a '*war of* aggression is a crime against international peace.'[27] As such, the 'drafters of the Definition thereby signaled clearly that not every act of aggression constitutes a crime against peace; only war of aggression does.'[28]

After the end of the Cold War, some thought was given to the prosecution of Iraqi leaders for war crimes during Iraq's 1990 invasion of Kuwait,[29] but no steps were taken to do so. Nevertheless, having begun in that crisis to exercise more robustly its Chapter VII powers, the Security Council did establish in 1993 the International Criminal Tribunal for the former Yugoslavia (ICTY)[30] and in 1994 the International Criminal Tribunal for Rwanda (ICTR)[31] for the prosecution of persons who committed war crimes, crimes against humanity, or genocide in those conflicts. Neither tribunal possessed jurisdiction over the crime of aggression, nor did other ad hoc tribunals or special courts that emerged relating to atrocities in Cambodia, East Timor, Kosovo, Lebanon, or Sierra Leone,[32] usually because the circumstances of the crisis were largely internal in nature.

The creation of the ICTY and ICTR, however, helped to break through the political log-jam holding back the creation of a permanent International Criminal Court, which was founded with the adoption of the Rome Statute in 1998 and its entry into

[25] GA Res 3314 (XXIX), Art 3 ('Any of the following acts, regardless of a declaration of war, shall, *subject to and in accordance with the provisions of article 2*, qualify as an act of aggression…') (emphasis added).

[26] Report of the International Law Commission on the Work of its Forty-Sixth Session, A/49/10 (1994), 38.

[27] ILC, Report 1994, Art 5(1) (emphasis added).

[28] Yoram Dinstein, *War, Aggression and Self-Defence* (5th edn, Cambridge: Cambridge University Press, 2011), 135.

[29] See SC Res 674 (29 Oct 1990), paras 1–2 (referring to Iraq's accountability for war crimes and calling upon states to collect information regarding such conduct).

[30] SC Res 827 (1993); see Jean-Paul Bazelaire and Thierry Cretin, *La justice internationale, son évolution, son avenir, de Nuremberg à La Haye* (Paris: Presses universitaires de France, 2000).

[31] SC Res 955 (1994).

[32] See Guénaël Mettraux, *International Crimes and the Ad-Hoc Tribunals* (Oxford: Oxford University Press, 2006); Cesare P. R. Romano et al (eds), *Internationalized Criminal Courts and Tribunals: Sierra Leone, East Timor, Kosovo, and Cambodia* (Oxford: Oxford University Press, 2004).

force in 2002. While sufficient consensus existed in 1998 regarding the operation of the ICC's jurisdiction over war crimes, crimes against humanity, and genocide, agreement could not be reached on what was meant by the 'crime of aggression' or on what the role should be for the Security Council in determining whether an act of aggression had occurred prior to the ICC exercising its criminal jurisdiction.[33] Ultimately, a compromise was reached in 1998: while Article 5(1) of the Rome Statute provided that the Court would have jurisdiction over all four types of crime—war crimes, crimes against humanity, genocide, and 'the crime of aggression'—Article 5(2) stated that the Court would only exercise jurisdiction over the latter crime 'once a provision is adopted in accordance with articles 121 and 123 defining the crime and setting out the conditions under which the Court shall exercise jurisdiction with respect to this crime.'[34]

Article 121 of the Rome Statute concerns the amendment process, while Article 123 provides that seven years after entry into force of the Rome Statute a 'review conference' shall be convened to consider such amendments, including to 'the list of crimes contained in Article 5.'[35] The Rome Statute entered into force on 1 July 2002, such that by late 2009 the time was ripe for convening the review conference, which was held in Kampala, Uganda from 31 May to 11 June 2010.

III. The Kampala Amendments

In the years preceding Kampala, a Special Working Group on the Crime of Aggression met and prepared documents for adoption at the review conference.[36] After difficult negotiations,[37] the review conference adopted a resolution on the crime of aggression (Resolution RC/Res 6), to which was annexed four amendments to the Rome Statute (Annex I), as well as certain amendments to the 'Elements of Crimes' previously adopted by the Assembly of States Parties (Annex II), and certain interpretive understandings (Annex III).[38]

[33] See Mahnoush H. Arsanjani, 'The Rome Statute of the International Criminal Court' (1999) 93 *American Journal of International Law* 22, 29–30.

[34] Rome Statute, Art 5. [35] Rome Statute, Art 123.

[36] For a compendium, see Stefan Barriga, Wolfgang Danspeckgruber, and Christian Wenaweser (eds), *The Princeton Process on the Crime of Aggression: Materials of the Special Working Group on the Crime of Aggression, 2003-2009* (Boulder, CO: Lynne Rienner, 2009).

[37] For a compendium of documents concerning the negotiations leading up to and at Kampala, see Stefan Barriga and Claus Kreß (eds), *The Travaux Préparatoires of the Crime of Aggression* (Cambridge: Cambridge University Press, 2012).

[38] International Criminal Court Assembly of States Parties, Review Conference, Resolution RC/Res 6 (11 June 2010) (hereinafter 'RC/Res 6').

Of particular interest are the four amendments. The first amendment simply deletes Article 5(2) from the Rome Statute.[39] The second amendment creates a new Article 8*bis*, which defines both an 'act of aggression' and the 'crime of aggression', derived verbatim from the definitions proposed by the Special Working Group. Under Article 8*bis*(2), 'act of aggression' means:

> the use of armed force by a State against the sovereignty, territorial integrity or political independence of another State, or in any other manner inconsistent with the Charter of the United Nations. Any of the following acts, regardless of a declaration of war, shall in accordance with the United Nations General Assembly resolution 3314 (XXIX) of 14 December 1974, qualify as an act of aggression: [the amendment then lists the seven types of act identified in that resolution].[40]

Under Article 8*bis*(1), 'crime of aggression' means:

> the planning, preparation, initiation or execution, by a person in a position effectively to exercise control over or to direct the political or military action of a State, of an act of aggression which, by its character, gravity and scale, constitutes a manifest violation of the Charter of the United Nations.[41]

The ICC's definition of 'act of aggression' draws heavily on the General Assembly's 1974 resolution, but in ways not provided for in that resolution. The first sentence of Article 8*bis*(2) essentially equates aggression with *any* violation of Article 2(4) of the UN Charter. The second sentence of Article 8*bis*(2) appears to assert, without qualification, that all the acts enumerated in the 1974 resolution constitute aggression. As noted previously, this was not the approach taken in the 1974 General Assembly definition, which viewed such acts as presumptively constituting aggression, but subject to a determination of the Security Council, which might conclude that 'relevant circumstances, including the fact that the acts concerned or their consequences are not of sufficient gravity', indicated that 'aggression' had not occurred.[42]

Kampala's 'crime of aggression' by its terms is a leadership crime; the defendant must hold a position by which he or she 'effectively…exercise[s] control over or…direct[s] the political or military action of a State.'[43] The language adopted excludes non-governmental actors, such as persons leading a terrorist group (eg Al Qaeda), leaders of an insurgency, or industrialists in a country even if they have substantial

39 RC/Resolution 6, Annex I, para 1 ('*Article 5, paragraph 2, of the Statute is deleted*'). The final documents of the Review Conference may be found at (2010) 49 ILM 1325 and in Barriga and Kreß, *The Travaux Préparatoires of the Crime of Aggression*, 99.

40 RC/Res 6, Annex I, Art 8*bis*, para 2.

41 RC/Res 6, Annex I, Art 8*bis*, para 1.

42 For a discussion of the alteration at Kampala of the 1974 language, see Stefan Barriga, 'Negotiating the Amendments on the Crime of Aggression' in Barraga and Kreß, *The Travaux Préparatoires of the Crime of Aggression*, 3, 26.

43 See Roger S. Clark, 'Amendments to the Rome Statute of the International Criminal Court Considered at the first Review Conference on the Court, Kampala, 31 May–11 June 2010' (2010) 2 *Goettingen Journal of International Law* 689, 696–7.

involvement in and influence upon governmental conduct.[44] Like Nuremberg, the 'planning', 'preparation', or 'initiation' of an act of aggression falls within the scope of the crime; the term 'execution' is used in place of Nuremberg's 'waging' of a war. Unlike Nuremberg, there is no requirement that the conduct relate to a 'war of aggression.' Rather, all acts falling within the scope of Article 2(4) of the UN Charter, including those set forth in Resolution 3314 (XXIX), may serve as a basis for finding a crime of aggression, as long as they are a 'manifest' violation of the Charter. The requirement of a 'manifest' violation is not found in the UN Charter or in the General Assembly's 1974 resolution, so it presents a new standard that will be discussed later in this chapter.

The third amendment creates a new Article 15*bis*, which addresses the ability of the ICC to exercise jurisdiction over the crime of aggression in a given situation based on either a referral by a state or the prosecutor's own initiative (*proprio motu*).[45] The fourth amendment provides for exercise of such jurisdiction when the Security Council refers to the ICC a situation in which the crime of aggression appears to have been committed.[46]

These amendments addressed several outstanding issues concerning how the crime of aggression would operate before the ICC, but leave open many others, both in terms of procedure and substance.

IV. Procedural Issues

A. Rome Statute Article 121(5) Provides the Process for Entry into Force

According to the resolution on aggression that was adopted at Kampala, all the amendments concerning the crime of aggression 'are subject to ratification or acceptance and shall enter into force in accordance with article 121, paragraph 5' of the Rome Statute.[47] Article 121(5) was apparently regarded as the relevant basis for bringing the amendments into force because, as previously noted, one of the Kampala amendments formally alters Article 5 of the Rome Statute,[48] and Article 121(5) applies to 'any' amendment to Article 5.[49] Article 121(5) provides:

> Any amendment to Articles 5, 6, 7, and 8 of this Statute shall enter into force for those States Parties which have accepted the amendment one year after the deposit of

[44] Mauro Politi, 'The ICC and the Crime of Aggression' (2012) 10 *Journal of International Criminal Justice* 267, 285–7.

[45] RC/Res 6, Annex I, Art 15*bis*.

[46] RC/Res 6, Annex I, Art 15*ter*.

[47] RC/Res 6, Annex I, para 1.

[48] RC/Res 6, Annex I, para 1.

[49] Rome Statute, Art 121, para 5.

their instruments of ratification or acceptance. In respect of a State Party which has not accepted the amendment, the Court shall not exercise its jurisdiction regarding a crime covered by the amendment when committed by that State Party's nationals or on its territory.

Arguably not all the amendments adopted at Kampala concerning the crime of aggression had to be brought into force pursuant to Article 121(5), since most of the amendments do not amend Articles 5, 6, 7, and 8. The selection of a single process for all the amendments appears to reflect a conclusion by the states parties that it was appropriate to proceed *in toto* either under Article 121(5) or under an alternative procedure set forth in Article 121(4). That conclusion may have been reached because the amendments, as a whole, activate a new form of ICC criminal jurisdiction (the basic concern of Art 121(5)) and thus it was appropriate for all the amendments to be 'subject to ratification or acceptance [and to] enter into force in accordance with article [121(5)].'[50]

B. A Package Deal?

At present, states are deciding whether to ratify or accept the amendments; 15 had done so as of September 2014.[51] Whether states parties must ratify these amendments as a package or can pick and choose as among them may be debated. On the one hand, the package consists of four amendments and other decisions that were orchestrated all at once as part of a series of compromises. On the other hand, there is not a single amendment, but four amendments, and there is no prohibition or restriction within the package requiring that these amendments be ratified or accepted by a state *in toto*.

Article 121(5) provides that amendments to Article 5 of the Statute enter into force for any state party one year after the deposit of the instrument of ratification or acceptance.[52] However, embedded within these amendments are two additional requirements that must be met before the ICC can actually exercise jurisdiction over an alleged crime of aggression. First, the ICC can only exercise jurisdiction

[50] See Beth Van Schaack, 'Negotiating at the Interface of Power and Law: The Crime of Aggression' (2011) 49 *Columbia Journal of Transnational Law* 505, 531 ('the legislative history of the ICC Statute somewhat favoured considering Article 121(5) as the *lex specialis* for any amendments to the substantive criminal provisions'). For a cogent discussion of the ambiguities that existed in the Rome Statute prior to Kampala for how to bring into operation the crime of aggression, see Roger S. Clark, 'Ambiguities in Articles 5(2), 121 and 123 of the Rome Statute' (2009) 41 *Case Western Reserve Journal of International Law* 413.

[51] For information on the states that have ratified the amendments, see <http://treaties.un.org/pages/ViewDetails.aspx?src=TREATY&mtdsg_no=XVIII-10-b&chapter=18&lang=en>.

[52] Rome Statute, Art 121, para 5.

over an alleged crime that occurs more than one year after 30 states have ratified or accepted the amendments.[53]

Second, the ICC may only exercise jurisdiction 'subject to a decision to be taken after 1 January 2017 by the same majority of states parties as is required for the adoption of an amendment to the Statute.'[54] While that language is a bit ambiguous in meaning, it is best understood to mean that jurisdiction may not be exercised until after a decision by at least a two-thirds majority of the Assembly of States Parties, occurring sometime in 2017 or thereafter, expressing approval of the ICC exercising such jurisdiction. It is not clear whether the states parties must take a decision with respect to all of these amendments as a package or can take a decision only with respect to some portions of that package, but it seems likely that the states parties will proceed on them together.

C. Temporal Exercise of Jurisdiction by the ICC

One uncertainty that arises concerns the ICC's temporal jurisdiction: can the ICC only exercise jurisdiction over an alleged crime that is temporally committed after both of the previously mentioned requirements are met? The language of the amendments does not say as much and, indeed, could be read as allowing ICC jurisdiction in, for example, 2017 over a crime committed in 2015, if at that point one year had elapsed since 30 states had ratified or accepted the amendments. The Kampala Review Conference, however, adopted an understanding on this issue.[55] The language of the understanding appears to provide that any alleged crime of aggression must occur after *both* of the two requirements are met. Only crimes occurring after the further decision of the states parties in 2017 (or thereafter) could fall within the scope of the ICC's jurisdiction, not crimes that occur in earlier years, even if 30 states had ratified or accepted the amendments before 2017.[56]

D. Jurisdiction of the ICC over States Parties that Do Not Ratify/Accept

Assuming that the Security Council has not acted, an important issue is whether a state party that does not ratify or accept the amendments is exposed to the ICC's

[53] RC/Res 6, Annex I, Art 15*bis*, para 2; Art 15*ter*, para 2.

[54] RC/Res 6, Annex I, Art 15*bis*, para 3; Art 15*ter*, para 3.

[55] RC/Res 6, Annex III, Understanding No 3.

[56] For an analysis of the legal effects of the understandings, finding that they are supplementary means of interpretation, see Kevin Jon Heller, 'The Uncertain Legal Status of the Aggression Understandings' (2012) 10 *Journal of International Criminal Justice* 229.

jurisdiction over the crime of aggression. In other words, does the failure to ratify the amendments mean that the state party is not exposed or must the state party affirmatively opt out if it wishes to avoid the ICC's jurisdiction?

As noted earlier, Article 121(5) of the Rome Statute provides in its second sentence that, for a state party that has not ratified or accepted an amendment, 'the Court shall not exercise its jurisdiction regarding a crime covered by the amendment when committed by that state party's nationals or on its territory.'[57] The ordinary meaning of that sentence is that if a state party does not ratify or accept the amendments adopted at Kampala, then the ICC has no Article 15*bis* jurisdiction over that state party's nationals.[58] The language in French, which is equally authentic, seems even clearer: 'La Court n'exerce pas sa competence á l'égard d'un crime…'[59]

That interpretation might be bolstered by comparison to an analogous provision of the Rome Statute. Article 124 is a 'transitional provision' that allows a state party to declare (in language similar to Art 121(5)) that, for a period of seven years, 'it does not accept the jurisdiction of the Court with respect to the category of crimes referred to in article 8 when a crime is alleged to have been committed by its nationals or on its territory.'[60] To the extent that Article 124 is interpreted as placing the state party entirely outside the scope of the ICC's jurisdiction during that time, then it would seem that a comparable result should operate for Article 121(5).[61]

This interpretation comports with background rules on the amendment of treaties, which provide that an 'amending agreement does not bind any State already a party to the treaty which does not become a party to the amending agreement',[62] and which otherwise accord protections for a treaty party from amendments.[63] Arguably, exposure of a state's *nationals* (or persons who commit the crime in the territory of the state) to the ICC's jurisdiction is not the same as the state *itself* being bound by the amendment, but presumably the state's obligations under the Rome Statute to cooperate with the ICC would be viewed as applying to the investigation and surrender of such nationals (or persons), and in that sense the amendments are altering the *state's* treaty obligations.

An alternative interpretation advanced during the period leading up to and at Kampala maintained that, once the ICC's 'aggression' jurisdiction is activated, it has certain effects for *every* state party (unless that state party affirmatively opts out of the jurisdiction, as permitted by the amendments[64]). This interpretation, which

[57] Rome Statute, Art 121, para 5.

[58] At Kampala, this interpretation was referred to as the 'negative understanding'.

[59] See Andreas Zimmermann, 'Amending the Amendment Provisions of the Rome Statute' (2012) 10 *Journal of International Criminal Justice* 209, 217.

[60] Rome Statute, Art 124.

[61] Zimmermann, 'Amending the Amendment Provisions of the Rome Statute', 217.

[62] Vienna Convention on the Law of Treaties, Art 40(4), 1155 UNTS 331.

[63] Zimmermann, 'Amending the Amendment Provisions of the Rome Statute', 210–11.

[64] See RC/Res 6, Annex I, Art 15*bis*, para 4.

became known as the 'positive understanding',[65] argued that the second sentence of Article 121(5) only precludes ICC jurisdiction arising under a new amendment over the non-ratifying state party when the jurisdiction is predicated solely on the conduct having occurred in the territory of the non-ratifying state party or by a national of that state party. Yet, under this interpretation, the second sentence does not prevent the Court from exercising jurisdiction over a national of the non-ratifying state party when that national's conduct was taken against or occurred within the territory of a state party that *has* ratified or accepted the amendment. The lynchpin of this theory is Article 12(2) of the Rome Statute, which allows the Court to exercise its jurisdiction over the nationals of states that are not party to the Statute whenever their conduct occurs on the territory of a state party.

In essence, this interpretation places the state party that fails to ratify the Kampala amendments in a position (with respect to the crime of aggression) analogous to that of a state that fails to ratify the Rome Statute (with respect to war crimes, crimes against humanity, and genocide); neither state's nationals are exposed to the Court's jurisdiction by virtue of that state's consent, but those nationals are exposed when they take action that falls within the ambit of another state's consent to the Court's jurisdiction. Thus, even a state party that has not ratified or accepted the Kampala amendments may find its leaders exposed to prosecution for the crime of aggression, as long as the aggression occurs in the territory of a state party that has ratified or accepted the amendments (just as the nationals of a non-state party can be exposed to the Court's other forms of jurisdiction under Art 12).

Proponents of the 'positive understanding' relied in part on the fact that there is an 'opt-out' procedure in new Article 15*bis*(4).[66] Arguably no such procedure is needed if a state party can effectively opt out of the ICC's jurisdiction simply by not ratifying the new amendments. In the first instance, this argument assumes that the amendments were carefully drafted, with a coherent legal theory understood and accepted by all states parties, which may not have been the case.[67] In any event, there are reasons why a state party might ratify the amendments, but then opt out of Article 15*bis*, including: (1) a desire to support the overall scheme, including the definition of aggression and the role of the Security Council, but a desire not to expose itself to the ICC's jurisdiction under Article 15*bis*; (2) a potential interest in

[65] See Claus Kreß and Leonie von Holtzendorff, 'The Kampala Compromise on the Crime of Aggression' (2010) 8 *Journal of International Criminal Justice* 1179, 1197–8; Van Schaack, 'Negotiating at the Interface of Power and Law', 528.

[66] Art 15*bis* provides that the Court may not exercise jurisdiction over a crime arising from the conduct of that state party if the 'State Party has previously declared that it does not accept such jurisdiction by lodging a declaration with the Registrar' of the ICC. RC/Res 6, Annex I, Art 15*bis*, para 4.

[67] Robert Heinsch, 'The Crime of Aggression After Kampala: Success or Burden for the Future?' (2010) 2 *Goettingen Journal of International Law* 713, 739. ('In the end, one could get the impression that paragraph 4 has been hastily inserted in Article 15*bis* without bringing it completely in coherence with the articles dealing with the amendment procedure'); see Barriga, 'Negotiating the Amendments', 53–7.

exposing itself to Article 15*bis*, but with a short-term preference for waiting to see how the ICC will begin exercising its jurisdiction before doing so; and (3) a desire only to expose itself partially to the ICC's jurisdiction and thus use the opt-out declaration to carve out some areas where the state party would not be exposed (discussed later in the chapter).[68]

The 'positive understanding' was contentious at Kampala for various reasons.[69] Japan, in particular, argued forcefully at Kampala that such an interpretation of the Article 121 amendment procedures effectively amends Article 121, a step not possible except through the amendment procedures set forth in Article 121(4).[70]

A second objection was that such an interpretation technically appeared to open the door for the Assembly of States Parties, at any time it could secure a two-thirds vote, to adopt amendments modifying Article 5 of the Rome Statute, so as to add new crimes pursuant to whatever amendment procedures it so chose, thereby exposing the nationals of even dissenting states parties to those crimes based on the states parties' prior acceptance of Article 12. Indeed, if the 'positive understanding' theory of Article 121(5) was correct, it would seem to apply equally to the 'Belgian' Amendment adopted at Kampala criminalizing the use of certain weapons in a non-international armed conflict (meaning that nationals of states parties that do not ratify or accept that amendment may nevertheless be prosecuted for that crime).[71]

Due to such concerns, a different interpretation (referred to by some as the 'softened consent-based regime') has been advanced as an explanation of how best to understand the outcome from Kampala.[72] This interpretation focuses on the purported combined effects of Articles 5(2), 12(1), and 121(3), as well as the ability of non-ratifying states parties to 'opt out' of the ICC's jurisdiction under new Article 15 *bis*. In essence, this interpretation argues that every state party to the Rome Statute *has* accepted, in Article 5, that the ICC has jurisdiction over the crime of aggression (as opposed to other possible crimes). Further, every state party *has* accepted that such jurisdiction may be exercised 'once a provision is adopted in accordance with articles 121 and 123 defining the crime and setting out the conditions under which

[68] See van Schaack, 'Negotiating at the Interface of Power and Law', 586.

[69] See eg Kreß and von Holtzendorff, 'The Kampala Compromise on the Crime of Aggression', 1198 ('one can hardly deny that the "positive understanding" of [para 121]'s second sentence does not naturally flow from its wording'); Politi, 'The ICC and the Crime of Aggression', 280 ('The main issue is whether the States Parties [at Kampala] were legally entitled to establish a new regime that would, in substance, modify the provisions in Article 121 without having recourse to the formal procedure for amending the Statute').

[70] See Politi, 'The ICC and the Crime of Aggression', 281; Kreß and von Holtzendorff, 'The Kampala Compromise on the Crime of Aggression', 1212.

[71] International Criminal Court Assembly of States Parties, Review Conference, Resolution RC/Res 5 (11 June 2010).

[72] Kreß and von Holtzendorff, 'The Kampala Compromise on the Crime of Aggression', 1212–16; Politi, 'The ICC and the Crime of Aggression', 278–83.

the Court shall exercise jurisdiction with respect to this crime.' That decision now having been made at Kampala, all states parties are exposed to the effects of the amendments *relating to aggression* and their nationals may be subject to the ICC's 'aggression' jurisdiction if they commit the crime of aggression in the territory of a state party that has ratified or accepted the amendments. At the same time, the delegates at Kampala chose to allow states parties to opt out of the amendments by lodging an affirmative declaration to that effect. By grounding itself in Article 5(2), this interpretation is responsive to the second objection noted earlier to the 'positive understanding', by limiting the interpretation solely to the crime of aggression.

Yet the first objection noted previously appears to remain valid; it is hard to see how this variation could be the amendment process for the crime of aggression that the states meeting in Rome had in mind. Why would states in Rome establish an amendment process that strongly protected their interests for any changes relating to crimes *other* than aggression (allowing them to avoid exposure to those crimes by non-ratification), but create an amendment process for the crime of aggression that leaves them vulnerable to whatever conditions thought desirable by a two-thirds decision of the Assembly? If anything, the unusual nature of the crime of aggression, as compared with other possible ICC crimes, suggests the need for *greater* deference to state consent concerning exposure to that crime, since the crime of aggression has very important and inescapable implications for the responsibility of the state itself, not just the individual.[73] Thus, while the idea of a 'softened consent-based regime' may well have been a 'creative' political compromise that sought to 'bridge the gap' at Kampala,[74] it remains to be seen whether the states parties and the ICC itself regard such an interpretation of the Rome Statute as correct.

E. The Ability of States Parties to Opt Out of ICC Jurisdiction

Assuming that a state party is exposed to the effects of the amendment, a further issue arises with respect to the 'opt-out' procedure under Article 15*bis*, which

[73] See Dapo Akande, 'Prosecuting Aggression: The Consent Problem and the Role of the Security Council', Oxford Legal Studies Research Paper No 10/2011, 15–17 (Feb 2011), available at <http://ssrn.com/abstract=1762806> (arguing that in the lead-up to Kampala, because a determination that an individual has committed the crime of aggression requires a prior determination that a state has committed an act of aggression and a breach of the UN Charter, the ICC would act in violation of the consent principle in cases where the alleged aggressor state has not provided prior consent to the Court's jurisdiction); see also Report of the International Law Commission on the Work of its Forty-Eighth Session, A/51/10 (1996), 30 ('An individual cannot incur responsibility for this crime in the absence of aggression committed by a State. Thus, a court cannot determine the question of individual criminal responsibility for this crime without considering as a preliminary matter the question of aggression by a State').

[74] Kreß and von Holtzendorff, 'The Kampala Compromise on the Crime of Aggression', 1213–14.

provides that the Court may not exercise jurisdiction over a crime arising from the conduct of a national of that state party if the 'State Party has previously declared that it does not accept such jurisdiction by lodging a declaration with the Registrar' of the ICC.[75]

Such language leads to an obvious question: the declaration must be lodged 'previous' to what? How late in the game can the state party file such a declaration? Must the declaration be lodged prior to the date on which the alleged aggression occurred, including the planning and preparation for such aggression? Or can it be lodged at any point up until the date that a state party refers the matter to the ICC or that the Prosecutor initiates an investigation *proprio motu*? How about up until the issuance of an ICC arrest warrant? Obviously, the answer is rather important in terms of the ability of a state party to shield its leaders from ICC prosecutions.

One answer might be that the Declaration must be filed prior to a state party's ratification or acceptance of the amendments. The Kampala resolution seems to suggest this approach, when it 'notes that any State Party may lodge a declaration referred to in Article 15 *bis* prior to ratification or acceptance.'[76] Indeed, that language may confirm that the 'positive understanding' or 'softened consent-based regime' interpretations are incorrect, since the scheme appears to link the issue of 'opting out' to the situation where a state party *has* ratified or accepted the amendments and does not link it to some other situation, such as opting out in the absence of ratification or acceptance. Seen in this way, the scheme has a certain coherence: a state party is not exposed to the Court's jurisdiction over the crime of aggression until it ratifies or accepts the amendment and, if it seeks to opt out of Article 15*bis* jurisdiction in whole or in part, it must so declare before its ratification or acceptance.

A different question is whether a state party faces a binary choice of 'opt in' or 'opt out', or whether there are intermediate positions where a state party can opt out with respect to certain circumstances. A state party might seek to opt out of the ICC's jurisdiction solely with respect to crimes of aggression arising from that state's military operations against a specified country, such as a neighbour. More broadly, a state party might seek to opt out solely with respect to actions against a class of countries, such as any country that is not a state party to the Rome Statute or any country that is a state party but has opted out of the crime of aggression. Perhaps a state party would seek to opt out from the ICC's jurisdiction for a specified time period or a specified subject matter area, such as uses of force over maritime resources. For example, a state party might seek to opt out of the ICC's 'aggression' jurisdiction solely with respect to alleged crimes arising from that state's involvement in a military operation of the North Atlantic Treaty Organization (NATO). One need look

[75] RC/Res 6, Annex I, Art 15*bis*, para 4. [76] RC/Res 6, para 1.

no further than the practice of states' acceptance of the compulsory jurisdiction of the International Court of Justice (ICJ) to find ample evidence of temporal, geographic, and subject-matter carve-outs to jurisdiction; nothing in the text of Article 15*bis* forbids doing the same.

F. The Problem of a Lack of Reciprocity

A different concern arises given that the structure of this 'opt-out' does not carry with it a coherent notion of reciprocity. Assume that state X and state Y both ratify the amendments, but state X lodges a declaration by which it opts out of the crime of aggression, while state Y does not file any such declaration. If state X invades state Y, the ICC will not have jurisdiction to investigate and indict state X's leaders, but if state Y invades state X, state Y's leaders will be exposed to the ICC's jurisdiction. If an armed conflict breaks out between the two states with both sides claiming that the other is the aggressor, apparently the ICC can investigate the leaders of state Y but not the leaders of state X.

At first glance, this lack of reciprocity seems inconsistent with jurisdiction as it normally operates before international courts and tribunals. In that context, the standard rule is that any step taken by one state to restrict its exposure to the tribunal's jurisdiction can be invoked by the other state in the event that a bilateral dispute arises. Yet in this instance, the lack of reciprocity for ICC jurisdiction may be explained on the basis that the ICC is not adjudicating bilateral disputes between states; rather, it is prosecuting individuals for wrongful conduct because the state of which those individuals are leaders accepted the possibility of such prosecutions. According to this argument, there is no problem of reciprocity because this does not concern an interstate relationship.

Yet there may be a political problem, in that the absence of reciprocity when an armed conflict erupts seems inherently unfair and could undermine the ICC's appearance as an even-handed institution. In any event, this lack of reciprocity may provide a strong incentive for states parties to opt out of the Court's jurisdiction over this crime at least vis-à-vis other states parties that have opted out. The theory behind reciprocity (eg as part of the compulsory jurisdiction system of the ICJ) is, in part, that a state will be induced to join the system, since otherwise it cannot benefit from that system. By contrast, with the ICC's jurisdiction over the crime of aggression, states parties do not automatically benefit by accepting the ICC's jurisdiction over this crime (in this sense, it differs from the ICC's other heads of jurisdiction, for which there is no opt-out). Time will tell whether ratifying states refrain from opting out vis-à-vis other states parties that have opted out simply because they see it as the right thing to do; yet unconditional acceptance of the ICC's jurisdiction appears to provide no automatic benefits with respect to foreign invaders.

G. The Position of Non-State Parties

The part of the amendments that probably received the most immediate public attention concerned the treatment of non-state parties. Article 15*bis* provides that the Court has no jurisdiction over the crime of aggression with respect to a state that is not a party to the Rome Statute 'when committed by that State's nationals or on its territory.'[77] This provision forecloses exercise of Article 15*bis* jurisdiction over nationals of states that are not parties to the Rome Statute, including at present China, Russia, and the US.

While many lament this carve-out from the Court's jurisdiction as drastically scaling back the scope of the regime, the decision to do so ultimately may be in the best interests of the Court. The crime of aggression is more than just a crime associated with a particular individual; as noted previously, it is a crime that relates much more closely to the state and state policy as a whole. When adjudicating the wrongfulness of state conduct before international courts and tribunals, the international legal system is built upon the idea of express state consent, because dispute settlement institutions only operate effectively when they are premised upon such acceptance *ab initio* by states. The compulsory jurisdiction of the ICJ, although only accepted by some 70 states, has historically operated quite effectively in terms of participation and compliance, precisely because those states have affirmatively chosen to opt in to the system. Had this exemption not been included, the legitimacy of the ICC might have been seriously damaged, especially if states parties were provided the ability to opt out of this new jurisdiction, while non-state parties were not.

H. The Problem of Alleged Aggression by a Coalition

The existence of ICC jurisdiction over some states but not over other states, however, may well raise a dilemma for the ICC if faced with alleged aggression by a group or coalition of states. Assume that a group of four states engages in alleged aggression against a fifth state. State A is a state party to the Rome Statute that has ratified the amendments without reservation, state B is a state party that has ratified the amendments but opted out of the ICC's jurisdiction, state C is a state party that has not ratified the amendments, and state D is a non-state party. In the absence of a Security Council referral, the ICC presumably only has jurisdiction over action by the leaders of state A (if the 'positive understanding' or 'softened consent-based regime' interpretations is correct, it would also have jurisdiction over state C). Yet when investigating and prosecuting that alleged aggression, it seems inevitable that the ICC, in essence, would have to assess the culpability of states B, C, and D. The leaders of those states presumably would not be defendants in the ICC's courtroom

[77] RC/Res 6, Annex I, Art 15*bis*, para 5.

but, given the nature of the crime at issue, the ICC in effect would be discussing and passing upon the conduct of those other leaders.

There is precedent in other settings, such as the ICJ, for the international tribunal to decline to pass upon the merits of the case because of a lack of jurisdiction over other parties whose rights and obligations are inextricably woven into the case.[78] Given that the ICC will no doubt confront this difficult issue in situations where alleged aggression involves a group of states, the Assembly of States Parties would do well to consider, in advance of the matter reaching the Court, the best approach legally and politically that the Court should take.

1. Security Council Referral of a Situation of Aggression

A further conundrum concerns Article 15*ter*, which addresses the ICC's jurisdiction over the crime of aggression based upon Security Council referral. Once the hurdles previously discussed concerning the ratification of 30 states and the further decision of the Assembly after 2016 are met, a question arises as to whether Article 15 *ter* operates even as against states parties that have not ratified or accepted the amendments.

As noted earlier, Article 121(5) indicates that the Court shall not exercise jurisdiction regarding a crime covered by an amendment when committed by nationals (or on the territory) of a state that has not ratified or accepted the amendment. Consequently, it would appear that the process for Security Council referral established under Article 15*ter* might not operate with respect to states parties that do not ratify or accept the amendments.

At Kampala, however, the states parties adopted an Understanding that 'the Court shall exercise jurisdiction over the crime of aggression on the basis of a Security Council referral in accordance with Article 13, paragraph b, of the Statute irrespective of whether the State concerned has accepted the Court's jurisdiction in this regard.'[79] The legal theory here appears to be that Article 15*ter* is principally addressing the capacity of the ICC, as an institution, to receive Security Council referrals and is consistent with the view that the Council has the power to confer authority upon the ICC to so act. Once the amendment enters into force and this

[78] See *Monetary Gold Removed from Rome in 1943 (Italy v. France, United Kingdom of Great Britain and Northern Ireland, United States of America)*, Preliminary Question, ICJ (15 June 1954), 19 (absence of Albania precluded a decision by the Court); *East Timor (Portugal v. Australia)*, ICJ (30 June 1995), 90 (absence of Indonesia precluded decision by the Court); see also *Advisory Opinion on the Status of Eastern Carelia*, PCIJ, Ser B, No 5 (23 July 1923) (absence of Russia precludes provision of advisory opinion); but see *Certain Phosphate Lands in Nauru (Nauru v. Australia)*, Preliminary Objections, ICJ (26 June 1992), 240, 255–62 (no bar to the proceedings unless the Court has to determine the responsibility of the non-consenting state as a prerequisite to determining the claims before it).

[79] RC/Res 6, Annex III, Understanding No 2.

capacity is activated, then the ICC can receive referrals from the Security Council with respect to any situation involving any country that the Council, in the exercise of its Chapter VII authority, deems appropriate for ICC scrutiny.[80]

V. Substantive and Institutional Issues

A. The Contours of 'Act' and 'Crime' of Aggression

Turning to more substantive issues, the contours of what constitutes an 'act' and 'crime' of aggression are not well defined in the Kampala amendments. As noted previously, the 'act of aggression' in Article 8*bis* essentially is equated with a violation of Article 2(4) of the UN Charter, and further illuminated by the types of acts identified in the General Assembly's 1974 resolution.[81] The 'crime of aggression' is the 'planning, preparation, initiation or execution' of an act of aggression by a senior leader, but only in situations where the act 'by its character, gravity and scale' constitutes a 'manifest violation' of the UN Charter.[82] Since these same definitions had been developed by the Special Working Group in advance of Kampala, many commentators raised concerns even at that time about the uncertain and difficult line-drawing that arises from the vagueness of the definitions. Some of the concerns related to the principle of *nullum crimen sine lege*, which requires that a criminal law be reasonably clear to a defendant at the time he commits his allegedly wrongful conduct,[83] while other concerns focused on the institutional burdens that such definitions may place upon the ICC.[84]

[80] Clark, *Amendments to the Rome Statute*, 702–3.

[81] RC/Res 6, Annex I, Art 8*bis*, para 2. [82] RC/Res 6, Annex I, Art 8*bis*, para 1.

[83] See Andreas Paulus, 'Second Thoughts on the Crime of Aggression' (2010) 20 *European Journal of International Law* 1117, 1123; Michael Glennon, 'The Blank-Prose Crime of Aggression' (2010) 35 *Yale Journal of International Law* 71; Sean D. Murphy, 'Aggression, Legitimacy and the International Criminal Court' (2009) 20 *European Journal of International Law* 1147; but see Marko Milanovic, 'Aggression and Legality: Custom in Kampala' (2012) 10 *Journal of International Criminal Justice* 165, 170–1, 184 (finding the definition vague but not so vague as to violate the principle of legality); Heinsch, 'The Crime of Aggression After Kampala', 724–6 (same).

[84] See eg Sean D. Murphy, 'Criminalizing Humanitarian Intervention' (2009) 41 *Case Western Reserve Journal of International Law* 241; David Scheffer, 'A Pragmatic Approach to Jurisdictional and Definitional Requirements for the Crime of Aggression in the Rome Statute' (2009) 41 *Case Western Reserve Journal of International Law* 397; Claus Kreß, 'The Crime of Aggression Before the First Review of the ICC Statute' (2007) 20 *Leiden Journal of International Law* 851; Mauro Politi and Giuseppe Nesi (eds), *The International Criminal Court and the Crime of Aggression* (Farnham: Ashgate, 2004);

Two of the Understandings adopted at Kampala are responsive to such concerns. One provides that 'aggression is the most serious and dangerous form of illegal use of force', and a determination that aggression has occurred 'requires consideration of all the circumstances of each particular case, including the gravity of the acts concerned and their consequences, in accordance with the Charter of the United Nations.'[85] The other clarifies that determining the existence of a 'manifest' violation of the Charter requires findings with respect to *each* of the three elements identified in the definition of the crime: character, gravity, and scale.[86] Specifically, the Understanding provides that 'No one component can be significant enough to satisfy the manifest standard by itself.'

Such clarifications are very useful, but some very basic questions remain. For example, it is unclear exactly what kinds of action, by their 'character, gravity, and scale', rise to the level of a 'manifest violation' of the UN Charter. One possibility is that the standard will be interpreted as encompassing only unlawful uses of force undertaken at a very high level of coercion. If so, then the unprovoked and massive invasion by one state of another state would presumably fall within the scope of the crime of aggression, such as Iraq's August 1990 invasion of Kuwait. By contrast, the sinking by a North Korean submarine of a South Korean warship, the *Cheonan*, in March 2010, even though resulting in the death of 46 sailors, might not fall under the crime of aggression if the Court concluded that—even though such conduct might violate the UN Charter—the gravity and scale of the conduct were insufficient.[87]

If the 'manifest violation' standard is interpreted in this way, there may be few prosecutions for crimes of aggression before the ICC since aggression of that scale very rarely happens. For that reason, such an interpretation might be attractive to the ICC Prosecutor and judges, at least initially, as it may allow them to avoid the ICC becoming entangled in numerous incidents of alleged aggression. At the same time, the non-prosecution of cases under such a high standard might have the unfortunate effect of *sub silentio* condoning lesser uses of force. Every time the ICC announces that a particular transnational use of force does not fall within the scope of its jurisdiction over the crime of aggression (eg the sinking of the *Cheonan*), the state whose conduct is in question may seek to exploit that decision to promote the idea that its conduct was not wrongful.[88]

Andreas Paulus, 'Peace Through Justice? The Future of the Crime of Aggression in a Time of Crisis' (2004) 50 *Wayne Law Review* 1.

[85] RC/Res 6, Annex III, Understanding No 6.

[86] RC/Res 6, Annex III, Understanding No 7.

[87] On 20 May, South Korea formally accused North Korea of sinking the *Cheonan*, based on an investigation that it conducted in conjunction with Australia, Canada, Sweden, and the UK. See Choe Sang-Hun, 'South Korea Publicly Blames the North for Ship's Sinking', *New York Times*, 19 May 2010, A1; Choe Sang-Hun, 'North Korea Denies Sinking Navy Ship', *New York Times*, 17 Apr 2010, A8.

[88] See Mary Ellen O'Connell and Mirakmal Niyazmatov, 'What is Aggression?' (2012) 10 *Journal of International Criminal Justice* 189, 191 ('it is imperative that what international law prohibits as

Another possibility is that the 'manifest violation' standard will be interpreted as emphasizing not the magnitude of the coercion but, rather, whether regarding the conduct as unlawful is clear or obvious to all relevant observers.[89] Under such a standard, perhaps both Iraq's invasion of Kuwait and North Korea's sinking of the *Cheonan* would be viewed as 'manifest' violations of the UN Charter, since they were generally condemned by states as unlawful, whereas more contested actions would not be viewed as 'manifest' violations. Thus, NATO's bombing campaign against Serbia in 1999 might not fall within the Kampala definition of an act of aggression because 'reasonable' people disagreed about whether that intervention was lawful, with some arguing that it was permissible in order to protect the fundamental human rights of Kosovar Albanians. Such an interpretation may also have an attraction for the ICC Prosecutor and Judges, as it would allow for ICC action in a range of situations large and small, but only when, as a political matter, virtually the entire international community views the conduct as unlawful. Such an approach might trigger highly spirited, public debates by states over the legality of the relevant conduct, as a means of signalling to the Court their views on the matter. A problem with this approach, however, is that it casts the Court in the role of bending to the political will of the international community, rather than adhering to more objective standards of law. Further, since there will often be considerable differences of views about the legality of a use of force, here too the Court's jurisdiction may rarely be triggered.[90]

A third possibility is that the 'manifest violation' standard will be viewed as encompassing less coercive and less blatantly unlawful transnational uses of force. Here, 'manifest' might be viewed as excluding small-scale skirmishes or 'frontier incidents', but other uses of force could constitute a crime of aggression. If so, then the ICC may be confronted with passing upon some very difficult factual scenarios. In addition to the Kosovo and North Korea incidents, the ICC might need to assess incidents such as the intervention in Liberia of the Economic Community of West African States (ECOWAS) in 1990, the series of wars that has plagued the Great Lakes region of Africa for the past 20 years, Ethiopia's 2007 and 2011 interventions

aggression not be undermined by the political realities of the Review Conference'); but see Heinsch, 'The Crime of Aggression After Kampala', 731 ('There is no danger that the prohibition of the use of the use of force laid down in Article 2(4) of the UN Charter will be undermined by this construction. Rather, any kind of penalisation of only a certain (manifest) form of aggression will in the long run strengthen the general norm as well').

89 The amended 'elements of crimes' provide that the 'term "manifest" is an objective qualification.' RC/Res 6, Annex II, Introduction, para 3. See James Potter, 'The Threshold in the Proposed Definition of the Crime of Aggression' (2008) 6 *New Zealand Yearbook of International Law* 155; Heinsch, 'The Crime of Aggression After Kampala', 730 ('If one has a look at the *travaux préparatoires*, it becomes clear that the idea behind this qualifier is to exclude all violations of the prohibition of the use of force which are controversial').

90 Paulus, 'Second Thoughts on the Crime of Aggression', 1121 ('What... is obvious for one is completely obscure to the other, in particular in international law').

in Somalia (which highlight the difficulty of assessing an 'invitation' for intervention by an authority that no longer governs the relevant territory), or Colombia's 2008 attack in Ecuador upon guerrillas of the Revolutionary Armed Forces of Colombia (FARC), to name just a few. Even in a situation where the Security Council has authorized a use of force, there may well be calls for the ICC to assess the circumstances, such as whether NATO's air campaign against the government of Libya in 2011 constituted an act of aggression because it exceeded the authorization issued by the UN Security Council. At the time of all these actions, there were differing views about their permissibility under the UN Charter, with the positions taken by governments and observers often driven more by political concerns than by well-defined legal criteria.[91]

B. Institutional Integrity of the Court

The typical answer to the dilemma of imprecise definitions seems to be that those definitions will be refined in practice by the ICC Prosecutor and Judges (at least absent Security Council involvement), who by prosecuting and convicting defendants (or by not doing so) will sketch out over time what is meant by an 'act' and 'crime' of aggression. Considerable uncertainties with respect to the Nuremberg and Tokyo Charters were refined in practice, including with respect to crimes against the peace.

Even so, refinement of these concepts will pose a considerable challenge for the ICC.[92] How exactly can prosecutors and judges form a view as to whether a state is acting in self-defence, in the often complicated context of inchoate threats, indirect action, and reactions that span time and space? How does the ICC gauge whether that defence was necessary or proportionate? Whether that defence was properly undertaken in anticipation of an attack? Whether a use of force to protect human rights is consistent with the UN Charter? What legal standards, of the kind necessary for pursuing criminal charges, will the Court rely upon?

Given the lack of bright lines in this area, given the extraordinary publicity attendant to transnational uses of force, and given the inescapable focus on senior government officials with respect to the crime of aggression, it appears possible that the Court will be an enormous lightning rod for intense political scrutiny with

[91] According to Kreß, 'The Crime of Aggression Before the First Review of the ICC Statute', 858 ('One essential albeit regrettable aspect of this reality is the existence of a grey area in the international legal framework. Reasonable international lawyers may legitimately disagree in their assessment of the *lex lata* for this crime, depending *inter alia* on how recent international practice is seen and weighed').

[92] Politi, 'The ICC and the Crime of Aggression', 284 ('the task that the Chambers are due to face in dealing with the questions raised by an alleged state aggression appear to be quite complex both in substance and at different procedural junctures, especially when determinations by the Security Council or the [ICC's Pre-Trial Division] have taken place').

respect to any transnational use of force that falls within the scope of its jurisdiction. To the extent that some observers think the current ICC case against Sudan's President Omar al-Bashir or Kenya's President Uhuru Kenyatta, and the adverse reaction of many states parties to those cases,[93] is damaging the Court, one can imagine the same scenario potentially playing out multiple times in the context of demands for criminal charges against sitting heads of state or government across the globe for aggression.

c. Collateral Effects on the *Jus ad Bellum*

Adoption of the definitions on 'act' and 'crime' of aggression may have collateral implications outside the criminal context, especially on rules relating to the *jus ad bellum*. As previously noted, the definition of 'act of aggression' is equated with any use of force in violation of the UN Charter. As such, the notion in the *jus ad bellum* of 'aggression' as a particularly egregious violation of Article 2(4)—worse than a threat to or breach of the peace[94]—may be diminished, allowing for less variegation in methods of condemnation and response. Cognizant of such possibilities, the states parties at Kampala adopted an understanding which may blunt the crossover effects of these definitions upon general international law:

> It is understood that the amendments that address the definition of the act of aggression and the crime of aggression do so for the purpose of this Statute only. The amendments shall, in accordance with article 10 of the Rome Statute, not be interpreted as limiting or prejudicing in any way existing or developing rules of international law for purposes other than this Statute.[95]

Even so, the long-term practice of the ICC in prosecuting or not prosecuting particular conduct as a 'crime of aggression' may affect conventional understandings as to what are permissible and impermissible uses of force. As suggested earlier, adoption of a high standard for what constitutes a crime of aggression within the jurisdiction of the ICC might serve to condone lesser uses of unlawful force. A low standard for what constitutes a crime of aggression could end up deterring low levels of undesirable coercion, but it might also inhibit lawful uses of force that help to keep aggressors in check. Since the line dividing permissible force and impermissible aggression is not clear, any deterrent effect upon wrongful uses of force might affect lawful uses of force, at least on the margin where a state is contemplating using force to help another state or to end atrocities.

[93] See eg Neil MacFarquhar and Marlise Simons, 'Bashir Defies War Crime Arrest Order', *New York Times*, 6 Mar 2009, A10 (reporting that 'China joined the African Union and the Arab League in calling on the United Nations Security Council to use its powers to suspend the [al-Bashir] indictment for a year, lest it stymie peace talks between the government and the rebels in Darfur').

[94] See eg UN Charter, Art 39.

[95] RC/Res 6, Annex III, Understanding No 4.

For example, assume that NATO's 1999 intervention was lawful, but Ethiopia's 2007 intervention in Somalia was not. Both NATO and Ethiopia asserted that they were intervening lawfully and for good purposes. But how are the leaders of the two interventions to know that their use of force is permissible or impermissible under the criminal standards of the ICC? Assuming that there is a deterrent effect, then, in the absence of bright lines, both uses of force may well be deterred, even though only one of them is unlawful. The worst-case scenario would be if unlawful uses of force are *not* deterred by the ICC's jurisdiction (on a theory that law is simply not effective against aggressor governments), while lawful uses of force are deterred.

D. Effects upon the Exercise of National Jurisdiction

A different concern arises with respect to the effects of the amendments upon the exercise of national jurisdiction. The Rome Statute is predicated on the notion that the ICC is not the primary avenue for prosecutions. Rather, states parties are expected to prosecute the crimes identified in the Rome Statute and the ICC is only 'complementary' to that jurisdiction by acting when a given state party in a given situation is unable or unwilling to act.[96]

Activation of the crime of aggression may have the effect of encouraging states parties to criminalize aggression in their national laws. While in the abstract that may be regarded as an important means for stigmatizing aggression, making it less likely that a leader will resort to it, there may also be adverse repercussions. If such conduct is criminalized in national law then, when a conflict erupts, each side might have no political choice but to indict and prosecute *in absentia* the leaders of the other side for aggression. Doing so may serve simply to raise the stakes for both sides, making it harder for them to find a political solution to the crisis. To avoid self-interested prosecutions, more impartial third states might be expected to pursue the prosecutions, but third states may not wish to assume that role.

Perhaps with that in mind, the Kampala Review Conference adopted an Understanding that 'the amendments shall not be interpreted as creating the right or obligation to exercise domestic jurisdiction with respect to an act of aggression committed by another State.'[97] That Understanding might help in discouraging states from adopting national laws that allow for the prosecution of foreign leaders, leaving it more likely that, if such laws are adopted, they will focus only on potential prosecution of domestic leaders. However, the Understanding does not preclude national laws that encompass crimes of aggression by foreign leaders, and a state may be inclined to adopt such a law if it is thought necessary to maintain ICC

[96] Rome Statute, Preamble and Arts 1, 17; see Mohammed El Zeidy, *The Principle of Complementarity in International Criminal Law* (Leiden: Martinus Nijhoff, 2008).

[97] RC/Res 6, Annex III, Understanding No 5.

deference to its courts in situations that involve a mixture of ICC crimes.[98] If such laws are enacted, they may have the unfortunate effect of entrenching nationalist passions within relatively inflexible legal proceedings, making it harder to resolve inter-state conflict.

E. Institutional Role of the Security Council

Finally, there are concerns about the effects of this new ICC jurisdiction upon the Security Council. Arguments that the Council should be the exclusive 'trigger' for the ICC's jurisdiction on the crime of aggression failed to garner sufficient support in Kampala. The Council has a role under both Article 15*bis* and Article 15*ter*, but not an exclusive role.

One possibility is that the outcome at Kampala will help to promote a partnership between the Council and the ICC. The Council has in two cases regarded the ICC as a useful means for addressing certain conflicts (Darfur in 2005[99] and Libya in 2011[100]). In addition to its existing options for responding to aggression, such as imposing economic sanctions or authorizing the use of military force, there will now be an option for the Council to refer a situation of possible aggression to the ICC under Article 15*ter*. Perhaps the ease with which the Council may refer a situation involving aggression to the ICC will play a role in helping to deter aggression, though it remains unclear whether the Council's current ability to refer situations involving non-aggression crimes has helped to deter such crimes.

One uncertainty is whether, after the ICC's 'aggression' jurisdiction is activated, the Council can limit a referral (legally or politically) to just crimes *other* than aggression, or whether the referral must allow the ICC to pursue all possible crimes relating to that situation. If the latter is the case, then perhaps establishment of Article 15*ter* will have the unfortunate effect of inhibiting Security Council referrals that would have occurred prior to activation of 'aggression' jurisdiction, if the Council cannot agree on allowing the ICC to pursue the crime of aggression for that particular situation.

Another unfortunate outcome would be for the Council to refer a situation to the ICC simply to avoid otherwise dealing with the matter. Confronted with a difficult situation of transnational armed conflict, the Council might find it attractive to send the matter to the ICC so as to simply move it off the Council's agenda—'burying' it in a years-long legal process at the ICC. In other words, it is possible that the Council might use the referral process as a means of escaping its responsibility to address aggression.

[98] See Beth Van Schaack, 'Par in Parem Imperium Non Habet: Complementarity and the Crime of Aggression' (2012) 10 *Journal of International Criminal Justice* 133.

[99] SC Res 1593 (2005). [100] SC Res 1970 (2011).

Further problems may arise if the Council and the ICC are acting not as partners, but at cross-purposes, such as when the Council is actively engaged in trying to resolve an armed conflict and the ICC injects itself uninvited into the situation by means of Article 15*bis*. The Council might have decided not to declare a certain crisis as involving an act of aggression, perhaps out of a sense that it would aggravate the situation, only to have the ICC bring charges against senior leaders involved in the crisis for the crime of aggression. For example, there is some support for the proposition that when NATO commenced its bombing campaign of Serbia in 1999, NATO leaders contemplated simply extracting a bilateral settlement with President Milošević not unlike that which occurred in 1995 with the Dayton Accords. However, in the midst of the bombing campaign, the ICTY indicted several senior Serbian leaders, including Milošević. Marc Weller has suggested that the issuance of the indictment during the hostilities 'triggered a strategic shift', one in which the nature of the hostilities transformed from mere 'coercive diplomacy' into outright 'war',[101] a transformation not anticipated by NATO states. According to Weller, after issuance of the indictment

> President Slobodan Milosevic, the most prominent of the indictees, and his close associates were no longer an indispensable element to a resolution of the Kosovo conflict. Instead, they were to be considered as probable war criminals that needed to be defeated militarily. Indeed, this fact was reflected in the fact that at the end of the conflict, no peace settlement as such was concluded with the Belgrade leadership. Instead, the peace terms were established by way of... Security Council resolution...[102]

If that is correct, then a further worry is that the Security Council's ability to manage a situation of armed conflict, which may already be compromised by existing ICC jurisdiction, might be even more affected through further expansion of the ICC's jurisdiction. Though unlikely, it is even possible that, when a war breaks out between states A and B, the Council might declare that state A has committed an act of aggression, while the ICC brings charges against leaders of state B for a crime of aggression. Article 15*bis* expressly provides that a 'determination of an act of aggression by an organ outside the Court shall be without prejudice to the Court's own findings under this Statute.'[103]

This problem may be ameliorated by the fact that some states will not be exposed to the ICC's jurisdiction. It might also benefit from the Security Council's ability to postpone, on a year-by-year basis, action by the ICC with respect to a particular situation.[104] But relying on Council deferral forces the Council to extend a benefit to the aggressor (by turning off ICC jurisdiction) right at the point where the Council is attempting to place pressure on that aggressor, which may prove to be a difficult if not impossible balancing act. And, since the

[101] Marc Weller, *Contested Statehood: Kosovo's Struggle for Independence* (Oxford: Oxford University Press, 2009), 167.

[102] Weller, *Contested Statehood*, 74.

[103] RC/Res 6, Annex I, Art 15*bis*, para 9.

[104] RC/Res 6, Annex I, Art 15*bis*, paras 8 and 16.

leaders of the aggressor can never be certain that the Council will postpone prosecutions indefinitely, they will have to react in a manner that discounts the certainty of such deferrals.

VI. Conclusion

Whether the activation of jurisdiction at the ICC over the crime of aggression ultimately serves to deter aggression or to punish those who initiate it remains to be seen.[105] For now, despite its successes, there emerged from Kampala considerable uncertainties concerning procedural and substantive aspects of how the crime of aggression at the ICC will actually operate. Prior to 2017, there remain opportunities for resolving some of these issues. Greater clarity as to the procedural aspects of the Court's jurisdiction may occur as states parties ratify or accept the amendments, as some opt out of the jurisdiction, and as other states parties that do not ratify or accept the amendments make known their views as to the effects of non-ratification. Further, at the meeting of the Assembly of States Parties after 2016, there will be an opportunity in the course of its decision to clarify matters further. As such, those interested in the effective functioning of the ICC's jurisdiction over the crime of aggression, and in the efficacy of international norms on the use of force generally, should not view Kampala as the final word on the crime of aggression, but as an opportunity to continue to grapple with the very real and very challenging issues that still remain.

[105] Marko Milanovic, 'Aggression and Legality: Custom in Kampala' (2012) 10 *Journal of International Criminal Justice* 165, 166 ('It may turn out to be nothing more than a diplomatic dud, a waste of everybody's time. The ICC's ponderous progress in dealing even with "ordinary" crimes in its jurisdiction does not inspire much confidence').

CHAPTER 25

THE INTERNATIONAL COURT OF JUSTICE AND THE 'PRINCIPLE OF NON-USE OF FORCE'

CLAUS KREß

I. Introduction

The international law on the use of force underwent significant developments in the inter-war period, most significantly through the renunciation of war as an instrument of national policy, as enshrined in Article I of the 1928 Kellogg–Briand Pact.[1] Yet, the law preceding the United Nations Charter[2] remained fraught with uncertainties due, perhaps most importantly, to the notoriously ambiguous concept of war and the possible scope for certain lawful forcible measures short of war.[3] The

[1] General Treaty for Renunciation of War as an Instrument of National Policy of 27 Aug 1928, LNTS XCIV (1929), 58.

[2] Charter of the United Nations and Statute of the International Court of Justice, 26 June 1945.

[3] For one important exposition of the complexities of the pre-Charter law on the use of force, see Ian Brownlie, *International Law and the Use of Force by States* (Oxford: Oxford University Press, 1963), 19–111, 214–50; Sir Humphrey Waldock, 'The Regulation of the Use of Force by Individual States in International Law' (1952-II) 81 *Receuil des cours de l'Académie de droit international* 455.

Permanent Court of International Justice (PCIJ) had not developed a case law on those matters[4] and only limited light was shed on them by the International Military Tribunals immediately after the Second World War.[5] Since 1945, the International Court of Justice (ICJ) has been called upon to interpret the UN Charter provisions on the use of force in international relations against this international law background full of obscurities. It was clear from the outset that the ICJ's mandate to construe the new provisions went far beyond a technical legal exercise. The new provisions on the use of force were to form one of the main pillars of the new international legal order. As the new body of law consists of just a few rules, ambiguities were almost certain to come to light on closer inspection and in the course of the subsequent practice of states. Controversies about the correct interpretation of the new law were thus to emerge almost inevitably and those controversies would almost necessarily involve 'high' principles laden with political sensitivity. The challenge posed to the Court was therefore a formidable one.

The first opportunity for the ICJ to confront this challenge presented itself as early as 1949 in the *Corfu Channel* case. This arose out of the mining of the Corfu Channel in Albanian territorial waters, which had affected the British navy, and the latter's minesweeping operation without Albanian consent. In its judgment of 9 April 1949, the Court avoided a direct reference to Article 2(4) of the UN Charter, but the pertinent parts of its reasoning foreshadowed its subsequent jurisprudence in an important respect.[6] After this early encounter, the Court had to wait almost four decades before it could again turn its attention to the international law on the use of force.

After having devoted, in passing, a brief *obiter dictum* on the attempted 1980 rescue operation by US forces in its judgment in 1980 in the *Case Concerning United States Diplomatic and Consular Staff in Tehran*,[7] the prohibition on the use of force was central to the Court's judgment in 1986 in the *Case Concerning Military and*

[4] For a recent appraisal of the work of the PCIJ, see Christian J. Tams and Malgosia Fitzmaurice (eds), *Legacies of the Permanent Court of International Justice* (Leiden: Martinus Nijhoff, 2013).

[5] For the text of the main judgment at Nuremberg, see (1947) 41 *American Journal of International Law* 172; for an appraisal, see Oscar Solera, *Defining the Crime of Aggression* (London: Cameron May, 2007), 247–51; for the texts of the judgments in the subsequent Nuremberg trials in the *High Command*, *Ministries*, *Farben*, and *Krupp* cases, which all dealt with crimes against peace, see respectively Trials of War Criminals before the Nuremberg Military Tribunals under Control Council Law No 10, vol XI, 462, vol XIV, 314, vol VIII, 1081; vol IX, 390 (Opinion of the Tribunal concerning the Dismissal of the Charges of Crimes Against Peace); for an appraisal, see Kevin Jon Heller, *The Nuremberg Military Tribunals and the Origins of International Criminal Law* (Oxford: Oxford University Press, 2011), 179–202; for the text of the judgment in the Tokyo war crimes trial, see Neil Boister and Robert Cryer (eds), *Documents on the Tokyo International Military Tribunal. Indictment and Judgment* (Oxford: Oxford University Press, 2008), 70; for an appraisal, see Neil Boister and Robert Cryer, *The Tokyo International Military Tribunal: A Reappraisal* (Oxford: Oxford University Press, 2008), 115.

[6] *Corfu Channel*, Merits, Judgment of 9 Apr 1949, ICJ Rep 1949, 4.

[7] *Case Concerning United States Diplomatic and Consular Staff in Tehran (US v. Iran)*, Judgment of 24 May 1980, ICJ Rep 1980, 3.

Paramilitary Activities in and against Nicaragua.[8] The most important aspect of the case—and rather typical of the Cold War era—was the vast military and financial support given by the US between 1981 and 1984 to the Contras, a rebel force fighting against the government of Nicaragua, support which the US had justified as a lawful exercise of the right of collective self-defence in view of hostile action of Nicaragua against El Salvador. The Court decided that it lacked competence to decide the case on the basis of UN Charter law and it therefore rendered its judgment in the *Nicaragua* case essentially on the basis of customary international law. From a substantive perspective, however, the Court dealt with the international law on the use of force as a whole and made pronouncements that have shaped the ICJ's jurisprudence on this body of law until today.

The prohibition on the use of force also played a role in the ICJ's advisory opinion in 1996 in the *Legality of the Threat or Use of Nuclear Weapons*.[9] Owing to the abstract nature of the question posed, the Court, in this opinion, made general pronouncements. The ICJ was again much more specific in its judgment of 2003 in the *Case Concerning Oil Platforms*, which Iran brought against the US.[10] The proceedings were about the destruction by the US of certain Iranian oil platforms which the US claimed to have been a lawful exercise of the right of individual self-defence against Iranian attacks on US-flagged merchant vessels and war ships in the Persian Gulf within the context of the 1980–8 international armed conflict between Iran and Iraq. The Court, in the light of its findings on other issues, could have easily avoided dealing with the prohibition of the use of force. The ICJ, however, placed the international law on the use of force, albeit being an ancillary issue from a procedural perspective, in the foreground of its judgment.

In its advisory opinion in 2004 on the *Legal Consequences of the Construction of a Wall in the Occupied Palestinian Territory*, the ICJ devoted only a single paragraph to the international law on the use of force (and more specifically to the right of self-defence in the case of transnational violence by non-state actors).[11] But due to its rather opaque formulation, this paragraph has given rise to a significant amount of commentary.

The judgment in 2005 in the *Case Concerning Armed Activities on the Territory of the Congo*[12] contains the last substantial engagement to date by the ICJ with the international law on the use of force. The Democratic Republic of the Congo

[8] *Case Concerning Military and Paramilitary Activities in and against Nicaragua (Nicaragua v. US)*, Merits, Judgment of 27 June 1986, ICJ Rep 1986, 14.

[9] *Legality of the Threat or Use of Nuclear Weapons*, Advisory Opinion of 8 July 1996, ICJ Rep 1996, 226.

[10] *Case Concerning Oil Platforms (Iran v. US)*, Judgment of 6 Nov 2003, ICJ Rep 2003, 161.

[11] *Legal Consequences of the Construction of a Wall in the Occupied Palestinian Territory*, Advisory Opinion of 9 July 2004, ICJ Rep 2004, 136.

[12] *Case Concerning Armed Activities on the Territory of the Congo (DRC v. Uganda)*, Judgment of 19 Dec 2005, ICJ Rep 2005, 168.

(DRC) brought a case against Uganda because of the latter's extensive military operations in the DRC between 1998 and 2003. Uganda had justified those operations partly on the basis of a consent allegedly given by the DRC to the Ugandan military presence and partly on the basis of the need both to defend Uganda against cross-border violence carried out by anti-Ugandan non-state actors and to meet some other less specified legitimate security interests. Uganda also counterclaimed that the DRC was illegally involved in cross-border armed activity against Uganda. The *Armed Activities* case has provided the ICJ with the only occasion to date to pronounce, in a contentious case, directly on Article 2(4) of the UN Charter.

This chapter is divided into two sections. Section II sets out the ICJ's jurisprudence in some detail. It will be shown that the Court has touched (but not necessarily elaborated) upon an impressive number of relevant legal issues pertaining to the use of force. For the sake of clarity, the review of the case law will be structured under four subsections: Section II.A with certain basic issues, Section II.B with the prohibition of the use of force, Section II.C with the exceptions to that prohibition, and Section II.D with the prohibition of the threat of force. The section aims to present and to explain the ICJ's case law as comprehensively as possible. The references to state practice and to scholarly writings are therefore selective and only serve the limited purpose of elucidating the background against which the Court has developed its legal views on the subject.

The purpose of Section III is no more than an attempt to shed light on the *overall* picture of the Court's case law.

In concluding, the chapter offers suggestions regarding the desirable development of the ICJ's future case law.

II. The Case Law of the Court

A. Basic Issues

The core of the ICJ's case law on the use of force directly addresses the prohibition of the use of force and the exceptions to it as well as the prohibition of the threat of force. Before the Court's views on those matters are set out, it is useful to review what the ICJ decided on some issues concerning the law on the use of force more broadly. In a way, those views build the framework for the Court's more specific legal findings, and perhaps some of those findings were even influenced in a subtle manner by this framework.

1. *Terminology*

The international law on the use of force is widely referred to as the *jus ad bellum* (as contrasted with the *jus in bello*).[13] This term has also been used by individual ICJ judges.[14] The Court, however, has avoided the term and has instead used the language of Article 2(4), such as the 'area of the regulation of the use of force in international relations'.[15] In the *Nicaragua* case, the ICJ repeatedly referred to the 'principle of non-use of force' which, according to the Court, includes the prohibition of the threat of force.[16] This use of terms has become so firmly entrenched in the ICJ case law that, in the *Armed Activities* case, the Court, while being competent to adjudicate on the basis of Article 2(4) of the UN Charter, found Uganda to have violated 'the principle of non-use of force in international relations'.[17] The Court's preference for this expression over the generic term *jus ad bellum* may imply a subtle inclination towards the tendency (which is apparent from some of the more recent literature on the subject[18]) to replace the generic term *jus ad bellum* with that of *jus contra bellum*.

2. *No political question doctrine*

In the *Nicaragua* case, the ICJ explicitly rejected the idea that it could be prevented from dealing with the international law on the use of force by virtue of some kind of international political question doctrine. The Court stated:

> It must be remembered that, as the *Corfu Channel* case... shows, the Court has never shied away from a case brought before it merely because it had political implications or because it involved serious elements of the use of force.[19]

The Court specifically recognized the 'legal dimension' of the right to self-defence.[20] The ICJ hereby implicitly endorsed the famous statement made by the International Military Tribunal at Nuremberg that:

> whether action taken under the claim of self-defense was in fact aggressive or defensive must ultimately be subject to investigation and adjudication if international law is ever to be enforced.[21]

[13] See eg Tom Ruys, *'Armed Attack' and Article 51 of the UN Charter. Evolutions in Customary Law and Practice* (Cambridge: Cambridge University Press, 2010), 1; Keiichiro Okimoto, *The Distinction and Relationship between* Jus ad Bellum *and* Jus in Bello (Oxford: Hart, 2011).

[14] For most recent examples, see *Armed Activities*, Judgment, Declaration of Judge Koroma, para 7; Separate Opinion of Judge Kooijmans, paras 58 ff.

[15] *Nicaragua*, Merits, para 176.

[16] *Nicaragua*, Merits, para 227.

[17] *Armed Activities*, Judgment, para 345(1).

[18] See, most notably, Robert Kolb, *Ius contra bellum. Le droit international relatif au maintien de la paix internationale* (2nd edn, Basel: Helbing Lichtenhahn, 2009); see also Olivier Corten, *Le droit contre la guerre* (Paris: Pédone, 2008).

[19] *Case Concerning Military and Paramilitary Activities in and against Nicaragua*, Judgment, Jurisdiction of the Court and Admissibility of Application of 26 Nov 1984, para 96.

[20] *Nicaragua*, Judgment, Jurisdiction of the Court and Admissibility of Application, para 98.

[21] (1947) 41 *American Journal of International Law* 207.

The Court made these statements, although the US had not raised a fully-fledged political question objection in the *Nicaragua* case. The argument advanced by the latter state was more specific in that it referred to the unsuitability of the ICJ becoming involved in an *ongoing* armed conflict.[22] The Court's response was as follows:

A situation of armed conflict is not the only one in which evidence of fact may be difficult to come by, and the Court has in the past recognized and made allowance for it (*Corfu Channel, I.C.J. Reports, p. 18; United States Diplomatic and Consular Staff in Tehran, I.C.J. Reports 1980, p. 10, para. 13*).[23]

3. *No Security Council monopoly*

In the *Nicaragua* case, the US had also argued that the claim that a member state of the UN had unlawfully resorted to the use of armed force constituted a matter that the UN Charter confined to the political organs of the organization and essentially to the Security Council.[24] The Court considered:

the fact that a matter is before the Security Council should not prevent it being dealt with by the Court and that both proceedings could be pursued *pari passu*.[25]

More specifically, the Court emphasized that Article 24 of the UN Charter entrusts the Security Council with *primary* instead of *exclusive* responsibility for the maintenance of international peace and security and that no provision such as Article 12 demarcates between the competences of the Security Council and the Court. In the light of this, the Court concluded that:

both organs can . . . perform their separate but complementary functions with respect to the same events.[26]

It should be added that the ICJ has not yet indicated its position on possible conflicts between its judicial findings and Security Council action with respect to one and the same armed conflict. In fact, the Court emphasized in the *Nicaragua* case that it was 'not asked to say that the Security Council was wrong in its decision, nor that there was anything inconsistent with law in the way in which members of the Council employed their right to vote'.[27]

In the *Armed Activities* case, the Court avoided a determination as to whether Uganda's vast military operation in the DRC constituted an *act of aggression*. The Court instead characterized Uganda's armed activities as 'grave violations of Article 2,

[22] *Nicaragua*, Judgment, Jurisdiction of the Court and Admissibility of Application, para 99; cf also the observation in n 24.

[23] *Nicaragua*, Judgment, Jurisdiction of the Court and Admissibility of Application, para 101.

[24] *Nicaragua*, Judgment, Jurisdiction of the Court and Admissibility of Application, para 89; this, again, goes some way towards formulating (a kind of) political question argument.

[25] *Nicaragua*, Judgment, Jurisdiction of the Court and Admissibility of Application, para 93.

[26] *Nicaragua*, Judgment, Jurisdiction of the Court and Admissibility of Application, para 95.

[27] *Nicaragua*, Judgment, Jurisdiction of the Court and Admissibility of Application, para 98.

paragraph 4, of the Charter'.[28] The ICJ's caution with respect to the use of the term 'act of aggression' is perhaps explained by the fact that the Security Council had refrained from making a determination pursuant to Article 39 of the UN Charter that Uganda had committed an act of aggression. By omitting a judicial finding to that effect, the Court may have wished to avoid any impression of disharmony in the approach of both UN organs to the same conflict. This judicial restraint was criticized by Judges Elaraby[29] and Simma in their respective separate opinions.[30]

4. *Treaty and custom*

In the *Nicaragua* case the customary international law on the use of force gained prominence in the Court's case law. The Court established that both the prohibition of the use of force and the right of self-defence form part of customary international law alongside Articles 2(4) and 51.[31] The precise meaning of the ICJ's views, as expressed in the *Nicaragua* judgment, on the sources of the right to self-defence, is not entirely free from ambiguity:

> the Charter, having itself recognized the existence of this right [ie the customary right to self-defence] does not go on to regulate directly all aspects of its content. For example, it does not contain any specific rule whereby self-defence would warrant only measures which are proportional to the armed attack and necessary to respond to it, a rule well-established in customary international law. Moreover, a definition of the 'armed attack' which, if found to exist, authorizes the exercise of the 'inherent right' of self-defence, is not provided in the Charter, and is not part of treaty law.[32]

In the light of the fact that the Court had stated that 'the right to self-defence is of course *enshrined* in the United Nations Charter',[33] it would probably go too far to interpret this passage as saying that the right of self-defence exists only in customary international law and that Article 51 of the UN Charter does no more than refer to this customary right as an exception to the (treaty and customary) prohibition on the use of force. Yet, one wonders whether the Court considers the right to self-defence, *as enshrined in Article 51*, to constitute an incomplete treaty rule which, in order to be properly applied, requires referring to certain parts of the (supposedly complete) customary right to self-defence. While the above citation creates this impression, a second (and perhaps more natural) construction of the

[28] *Armed Activities*, Judgment, para 153.

[29] *Armed Activities*, Judgment, Separate Opinion of Judge Elaraby, paras 9–20.

[30] The latter stated (Separate Opinion of Judge Simma, *Armed Activities*, para 3): 'The Council will have had its own—political—reasons for refraining from such a determination. But the Court, as the principal *judicial* organ of the United Nations, does not have to follow that course. Its very *raison d'être* is to arrive at decisions based on law and nothing but law, keeping the political context before it in mind, of course, but not desisting from stating what is manifest out of regard for such non-legal considerations. This is not the division of labour between the Court and the political organs of the United Nations envisaged by the Charter!'.

[31] *Nicaragua*, Merits, paras 172–86.

[32] *Nicaragua*, Merits para 176.

[33] *Nicaragua*, Merits, para 48 (emphasis added).

Court's position would be that the latter components of the right of self-defence (the definition of the term 'armed attack' as well as the limitations of necessity and proportionality), while having been of a purely customary nature in the first place, have been incorporated into the treaty rule in Article 51 on the right to self-defence. Seen this way, a complete treaty regulation on the right to self-defence exists alongside its customary corollary.

In the *Nuclear Weapons* advisory opinion, the Court did not eliminate the ambiguity. On the one hand, the Court reaffirmed the customary law nature of the requirements of necessity and proportionality, but on the other hand the Court stated that:

> The entitlement to resort to self-defence under Article 51 is subject to certain constraints. Some of these constraints are inherent in the very concept of self-defence. Other requirements are specified in Article 51.[34]

According to the ICJ, the 'dual condition' of necessity and proportionality 'applies equally to Art. 51 of the UN Charter';[35] this can mean that the treaty rule on self-defence must be completed by reference to the customary 'dual condition' of necessity and proportionality or that those requirements are 'inherent' in the very concept of self-defence so that they form part of the treaty right to self-defence enshrined in Article 51 even without the need of any incorporation of customary law.

The ICJ's recognition of customary rules on the prohibition of the use of force and the right of self-defence raised the question whether the content of those rules is identical or (partly) different from their UN Charter counterparts. In the *Nicaragua* judgment, the ICJ held: 'The areas governed by the two sources of law thus do not overlap exactly, and the rules do not have the same contents'.[36] While this general statement leaves room for rather significant differences between the UN Charter and the customary law regulation of the use of force, the subsequent more specific passages of the *Nicaragua* judgment make it clear that the Court, quite to the contrary, construes the treaty and customary regulation on the prohibition of the use of force and on the right to self-defence in a largely identical manner.[37]

In fact, upon closer inspection the non-existence under customary law of the duty to report the exercise of the right to self-defence to the Security Council as contained in Article 51 turns out to be the only difference identified by the Court.[38] In its subsequent case law, the ICJ has at no point departed from this essentially 'harmonious construction'. In the *Armed Activities* case, the Court went as far as to base (the relevant part of) its judgment on 'the principle of non-use of force in international relations' without specifying this principle's source.[39] It can therefore be concluded that, in the view of the Court, the international legal regime governing the use of force by states—outside the UN Charter's collective security system—is

[34] *Nuclear Weapons*, Advisory Opinion, para 40.

[35] *Nuclear Weapons*, Advisory Opinion, para 41.

[36] *Nicaragua*, Merits, para 176.

[37] *Nicaragua*, Merits, paras 181, 188.

[38] *Nicaragua*, Merits, para 200.

[39] *Armed Activities*, Judgment, para 345(1).

based on essentially identical rules of treaty and customary law existing alongside each other.

This 'harmonious construction' has been criticized within the Court. In his dissenting opinion in *Nicaragua*, Judge Jennings rejected the idea that Articles 2(4) and 51 merely codified existing customary law rules and he further disputed the idea that the UN Charter, in conjunction with consonant state practice, had subsequently generated a body of customary law with a content essentially mirroring that of the treaty rules. According to Judge Jennings, the few states that were not parties to the Charter had not been in a position to produce a sufficiently significant amount of state practice to such an effect, while the post-1945 practice of UN member states had to be explained by their being bound by the Charter itself.[40] The passage where the Court came closest to explaining its contrary view reads:

> far from having constituted a marked departure from a customary international law which still exists unmodified, the Charter gave expression in this field to principles already present in customary international law, and that law has in the subsequent four decades developed under the influence of the Charter to such an extent that a number of rules contained in the Charter have acquired a status independent of it. The essential consideration is that both the Charter and the customary international law flow from a common fundamental principle outlawing the use of force in international relations.[41]

In this statement, the Court refrained from making an attempt to elucidate the pre-Charter state of customary law on the use of force.[42] While the passage signals the Court's readiness to accept the view, as articulated perhaps most prominently by Ian Brownlie,[43] that the pre-1945 customary law had already been developing in the direction of the new restrictive Charter rules on the use of force, the Court did not consider the Charter regime on the prohibition of the use of force and the right to self-defence as a mere codification of pre-existing customary international law. Instead, the Court held that the almost complete convergence between Article 2(4) and 51 and customary law came about 'under the influence of the Charter'. This implies that the ICJ, contrary to Judge Jennings' view, did not feel that, with respect to the 'principle of the non-use of force', the famous 'Baxter paradox', prevented it from recognizing the development of customary international law through treaty rules that enjoy widespread ratification.[44] While the Court does not justify this approach explicitly, it would seem that it was guided by two considerations. First, the Court stressed that it considered the international regulation of the use of force to flow from a 'fundamental principle'. This may be taken to suggest that the

[40] *Nicaragua*, Merits, Dissenting Opinion of Judge Jennings, 530–1.

[41] *Nicaragua*, Merits, para 181.

[42] This holds true for the whole *Nicaragua* judgment and for the ICJ's jurisprudence in general.

[43] Brownlie, *International Law and the Use of Force by States*, 110–11.

[44] Richard S. Baxter, 'Treaties and Custom' (1970-I) 129 *Recueil des cours de l'Académie de droit international* 64, 73.

Court did not see the need to subject customary law developments pertaining to the 'principle of the non-use of force' to the most stringent 'inductive' test because of this body of law's paramount importance for the international legal order as a whole. In addition, however, the Court relied on the consideration that:

apart from the treaty commitments binding the Parties to the rules in question, there are various instances of their having expressed recognition of the validity thereof as customary international law in other ways.[45]

Given the heavy reliance,[46] on General Assembly Resolution 2625,[47] this document, in the view of the Court, probably constituted the most important instance of UN member states expressing their recognition of the 'principle of non-use of force' as part of customary international law.

5. *No 'death' of the 'principle of the use of force'*

In 1970, Thomas M. Franck famously proclaimed the death of Article 2(4) of the UN Charter because of widely diverging state practice and because of the ineffectiveness of the collective security system.[48] The Court, however, never alluded to the possibility that the 'principle of non-use of force' might have lost its legal validity. In the *Nicaragua* judgment, the Court implicitly dealt with the argument of widely diverging state practice in the context of its analysis of the emergence of a rule of customary international law and held:

In order to deduce the existence of customary rules, the Court deems it sufficient that the conduct of States should, in general, be consistent with such rules, and that instances of State conduct inconsistent with a given rule should generally have been treated as breaches of that rule, not as indications of the recognition of a new rule. If a State acts in a way prima facie incompatible with a recognized rule, but defends its conduct by appealing to exceptions or justifications contained within the rule itself, then whether or not the State's conduct is in fact justifiable on that basis, the significance of the attitude is to confirm rather than to weaken the rule.[49]

This argument had already been addressed in passing in the judgment in the *Corfu Channel* case where the possible defects in international organization had been considered to constitute an irrelevant consideration with respect to forms of forcible intervention as practised in the pre-Charter era.[50] In its *Nicaragua* judgment, the ICJ returned to the issue in a much more explicit form and found:

[45] *Nicaragua*, Merits, para 185. [46] *Nicaragua*, Merits, para 188.

[47] Declaration on Principles of International Law concerning Friendly Relations and Co-operation among States in accordance with the Charter of the United Nations, GA Res 2615 (XXV) (24 Oct 1970).

[48] Thomas M. Franck, 'Who Killed Article 2(4)?' (1970) 64 *American Journal of International Law* 809; Georg Schwarzenberger had made an argument pointing in the same direction as early as 1955 in his study 'The Fundamental Principles of International Law' 87 (1955-I) *Recueil des cours de l'Académie de droit international* 338–9.

[49] *Nicaragua*, Merits, para 186. [50] *Corfu Channel*, Merits, 35.

The principle of non-use of force, for example, may thus be regarded as a principle of customary international law, not as such conditioned by provisions relating to collective security, or to the facilities or armed contingents to be provided under Article 43 of the Charter.[51]

While this argument is situated at the customary law level, one would be surprised if, under the Court's vision of an essentially identical corpus of customary and treaty law, the reliance on the argument were allowed with respect to Articles 2(4) and 51. In fact, the Court has never suggested that such reliance might be possible.

6. Jus cogens *and obligation* erga omnes

The *Nicaragua* judgment recalled that the International Law Commission (ILC) had in 1966 expressed the view that the prohibition of the use of force constitutes *jus cogens*.[52] This may indicate an inclination itself to move in that direction, but it does not constitute a determination to that effect. It is worth noting that, as yet, no such determination has been made by the Court.[53]

The concept of 'obligation *erga omnes*' has not played any role in the ICJ's judgments which specifically deal with the use of force. This may perhaps partly be explained by the existence of the right to *collective* self-defence, which specifically deals with the legal position of third states. Be this as it may, in its judgment in the *Barcelona Traction* case, where the Court famously introduced the concept of obligation *erga omnes* into its case law, it was recognized that such an obligation was to be derived from the 'outlawing of acts of aggression'.[54]

7. *Legal consequences of an unlawful use of force*

In its *Nicaragua* and *Armed Activities* judgments, the ICJ recognized that a violation of the 'principle of the non-use of force', in accordance with the law of state responsibility for internationally wrongful acts, resulted in the obligation of the offending state to make reparation to the victim state.[55] The Court has not, however, had the occasion to go into any legal detail on this point. In its *Wall* advisory opinion, the ICJ further held that the illegality of territorial acquisition resulting from the threat or use of force constituted a corollary of the principle of the non-use of force.[56] In

[51] *Nicaragua*, Merits, para 188.

[52] *Nicaragua*, Merits, para 190.

[53] In particular, the Court again stopped short of such a determination in *Accordance with International Law of the Unilateral Declaration of Independence in Respect of Kosovo*, Advisory Opinion of 22 July 2010, ICJ Rep 2010, para 81, where it notes 'the unlawful use of force or other egregious violations of norms of general international law, in particular those of a peremptory character (*jus cogens*)'.

[54] *Case Concerning the Barcelona Traction, Light and Power Co, Ltd (New Application: 1962) (Belgium v. Spain)*, Second Phase, Judgment of 5 Feb 1970, ICJ Rep 1970, para 34.

[55] *Nicaragua*, Merits, para 292(13); *Armed Activities*, Judgment, paras 259–60, 345(5).

[56] *Wall*, Advisory Opinion, para 87; where the Court held that '*all* States were under the obligation not to recognize the illegal situation resulting from the construction of the wall in the Occupied Palestinian Territory, it did not return to the obligation not to use force, but it based this statement on the *erga omnes* effect of the obligation to respect the right to self-determination and of certain obligations under international humanitarian law' (paras 155, 159).

none of its judgments has the ICJ alluded to the possibility that the unlawful use of force could give rise to international rights of *individuals* to reparation vis-à-vis the offending state. Finally, the Court, unsurprisingly in the light of its interstate jurisdiction, has not touched upon matters of *individual* criminal responsibility under international law for the participation in (certain) breaches of the prohibition of the use of force.[57]

B. The Prohibition of the Use of Force

The prohibition of the use of force raises a number of legal issues beginning with its addressees and its geographical scope, including the question of possible 'in-built limitations' of the material scope of the prohibition and ending with the very concept of 'use of force'. This section structures the ICJ's views around those various issues.

1. *The use of force* by states *in their* international relations

There is nothing in the ICJ's case law to suggest that the 'principle of non-use of force' could, as a result of a more recent development, have become binding on *non*-state actors.[58] To the contrary, in its 2010 advisory opinion on the *Accordance with International Law of the Unilateral Declaration of Independence in Respect of Kosovo*, the Court determined that the prohibition of the use of force as a particular aspect of the obligation to respect the territorial integrity of states is confined to 'the sphere of relations between States'.[59]

In its advisory opinion in *Nuclear Weapons*, the ICJ was careful to distinguish the use of force by a state 'within its own boundaries' from the prohibition of the use of force.[60] It would probably overstate the significance of the Court drawing this broad demarcation line in *Nuclear Weapons* to deduce therefrom that the Court would *never* be prepared to characterize the use of force by a state on its own territory as unlawful under the 'principle of the non-use use of force *in the international relations*'. But the Court would certainly not so qualify the use of force by a state *against its own population* on its own soil.

[57] In his separate opinion in the *Armed Activities* judgment, Judge Elaraby criticized the Court's avoidance of the issue of 'aggression' (cf the text accompanying n 29) also for a missed opportunity to contribute to overcoming 'the culture of impunity'; *Armed Activities*, Judgment, separate opinion of Judge Elaraby, para 20.

[58] For a (perhaps) different position, see Anne-Marie Slaughter and William Burke White, 'An International Constitutional Moment' (2002) 43 *Harvard International Law Journal* 1.

[59] *Accordance with International Law of the Unilateral Declaration of Independence in Respect of Kosovo*, Advisory Opinion of 22 July 2010, ICJ Rep 2010, para 80.

[60] *Nuclear Weapons*, Advisory Opinion, para 50.

2. *The 'all-inclusive' nature of the prohibition of the use of force*

In the *Corfu Channel* case, the UK justified its minesweeping action as a lawful measure of self-help responding to unlawful behaviour by Albania and, more specifically, as a limited intervention in order to secure possession of evidence to be submitted to an international tribunal.[61] In the course of its oral argument, the UK explicitly addressed Article 2(4) of the UN Charter and argued that its action 'threatened neither the territorial integrity nor the political independence of Albania'.[62] It was implicit in the argument that the operation was also 'not in any other manner inconsistent with the purposes of the United Nations Charter' because it was directed towards facilitating the work of an international tribunal. The UK thus anticipated a legal argument, which was later to be developed in much greater detail and sophistication by legal scholars: that the Article 2(4) prohibition is subject to an exception for certain 'non-aggressive' uses of force.[63]

In the judgment in the *Corfu Channel* case, the ICJ, while recognizing 'the Albanian Government's complete failure to carry out its duties', rejected the UK's line of reasoning and stated:

> The Court can only regard the alleged right of intervention as the manifestation of a policy of force, such as has, in the past, given rise to most serious abuses and such as cannot, whatever be the present defects in international organization, find a place in international law.[64]

The legal significance of this determination suffers somewhat from the fact that the Court, following the language used in the Special Agreement between the UK and Albania, did not specifically relate it to the prohibition of the use of force.[65] Yet, had the Court wished to reject the UK's argument of a 'limited right to intervention for a benign purpose' even without qualifying the latter's action in Albanian waters as a use of force, it would be surprising if the same Court accepted such an argument in the case of a more serious action that did amount to a use of force within

[61] In its judgment, the Court treats the UK's line of reasoning as consisting of the two distinct arguments of a limited right of intervention to secure evidence and of a limited right to self-help (*Corfu Channel*, Merits, 34), but, in fact, those arguments are too closely intertwined to be separated; for a close analysis of the UK's pleadings in *Corfu Channel*, see Christine Gray, 'A Policy of Force' in Karine Bannelier, Theodore Christakis, and Sarah Heathcote (eds), *The ICJ and the Evolution of International Law. The Enduring Impact of the Corfu Channel Case* (Abingdon: Routledge, 2012), 234–5.

[62] Oral Statement of 12 Nov 1948, *Corfu Channel*, ICJ, Pleadings, Oral Arguments, Documents, Oral Proceedings (First Part), 296.

[63] For an early exposition of this view, see Julius Stone, *Aggression and World Order* (Berkeley, CA: University of California Press, 1958), 95–6; for a prominent later variation, see Michael Reisman, 'Coercion and Self-Determination: Construing Charter Article 2(4)' (1984) 78 *American Journal of International Law* 642.

[64] *Corfu Channel*, Merits, 35.

[65] A number of judges, however, did address Art 2(4) directly in their individual opinions attached to the judgment; *Corfu Channel*, Merits, Individual Opinions of: Judge Alvarez, 42; Judge Krylow, 77; and Judge ad hoc Ečer, 130; for a cautious appraisal that reflects the ambiguity of the majority's approach, see Hersch Lauterpacht, *The Development of International Law by the International Court* (London: Stevens & Sons, 1958; repr Cambridge: Cambridge University Press, 1982), 317.

its technical legal meaning. It is therefore plausible to read the Court's judgment in *Corfu Channel* as the judicial rejection of the idea that the words 'against the territorial integrity or political independence of any state, or in any other manner inconsistent with the purposes of the UN Charter' subject the prohibition of the use of force to an exception for certain 'non-aggressive' uses of force.[66] There is nothing in the subsequent jurisprudence of the ICJ to suggest that the Court has subsequently developed a different opinion on that question.

3. *'Indirect' use of force*

In the *Nicaragua* case, the ICJ considered the *arming* and *training* of non-state actors fighting on the territory of another state against the latter's governmental forces as violating the prohibition of the use of force.[67] The Court based this broad interpretation of the prohibition of the use of force on the formulation of the eighth and ninth paragraphs of General Assembly Resolution 2625, but it added that 'the mere supply of funds' was not covered. The Court again referred to Resolution 2625 in the *Armed Activities* case, this time to consider the *toleration* by a state of non-state actors who make use of that state's territory for cross-border armed action.[68] This decision strongly suggests that the ICJ also considers this form of state involvement into forcible non-state action to constitute (an indirect) use of force by the respective state. There is no suggestion in the Court's jurisprudence that the inclusion of the two aforementioned forms of state conduct in the prohibition of the use of force is based on the idea that, in those cases, the use of force *of the non-state actors* can be *attributed* to the involved state. It is rather the arming, the training, and the toleration as such that, according to the Court, constitute instances of a use of force by the state concerned.

4. *'Use of force'*

A closer look into state practice and scholarly writing reveals that in a number of situations the question whether the legal threshold for the use of force has been passed by state action is open to argument.[69] It is the subject of debate, for example, under what conditions the intrusion or otherwise uninvited presence of military (or even police organs) on foreign soil without actual fighting amounts to a use of

[66] For the same view, see Gray, 'A Policy of Force' in Bannelier, Christakis, and Heathcote, *The ICJ and the Evolution of International Law*, 237; and Christopher Greenwood, 'The International Court of Justice and the Use of Force' in Vaughan Lowe and Malgosia Fitzmaurice (eds), *Fifty Years of the International Court of Justice. Essays in Honour of Sir Robert Jennings* (Cambridge: Cambridge University Press, 1996), 378–9.

[67] *Nicaragua*, Merits, para 228; oddly, the authoritative English version of this paragraph contains an ambiguity in that it says that 'the arming and training of the *contras* can certainly be said to involve the *threat or* use of force' (first emphasis in the original, second emphasis added), while the French version uses only the word 'l'emploi de la force'.

[68] *Armed Activities*, Judgment, para 300.

[69] For a fairly recent detailed account, see Corten, *Le droit contre la guerre*, 65–121.

force, and, to mention another example, whether a minimal use of coercion, such as the arrest of a person, the seizure of a foreign fishing vessel, or the opening of a diplomatic bag,[70] could constitute a use of force. A more recent discussion focuses on whether state use of computer malware with detrimental cross-border consequences may be qualified as a use of force.[71] Those debates refer back to the very concept of 'use of force'.

The Court could have shed light on this concept as early as the *Corfu Channel* case where the state conduct in issue was the UK's 'assembl[ing] of a large number of warships in the territorial waters of another State . . . to carry out minesweeping in those waters',[72] such sweeping resulting in no physical harm to persons or property. The ICJ, however, failed to use this early occasion to specify whether and why the mere presence, in foreign territorial waters, of a large number of warships adopting a threatening posture amounted to a use of force and whether such use must pass a certain minimal threshold of intensity in order to fall within the prohibitive scope of the 'principle of the non-use of force'. The ICJ did not explicitly refer to this principle or even more precisely to Article 2(4) of the UN Charter, but chose instead to condemn, without any conceptual elaboration, the UK's Operation Retail as a policy of force.[73] This left room for divergent interpretations and the subsequent case law did nothing to dispel the ambiguity. While the use of the term 'force' may be taken to suggest that the ICJ *implicitly* qualified Operation Retail as an unlawful use of force,[74] it is also *possible* to interpret the Court's avoidance of any explicit reference to Article 2(4) as implying the view that the threshold for a use of force in its technical legal meaning had not been reached.[75]

The ICJ has also on no subsequent occasion set out to define the concept of a use of force. Yet, a number of elements of the use of force with some indicative value can be discerned from the case law of the ICJ. In the *Oil Platforms* case, the

[70] In *Fisheries Jurisdiction (Spain v. Canada)*, Spain characterized the seizure by Canadian authorities of a Spanish fishing vessel and the arrest by the same authorities of the ship's master as a 'violation of Article 2, paragraph 4, of the Charter'; the ICJ found that it lacked jurisdiction and therefore abstained from dealing with the matter; *Fisheries Jurisdiction (Spain v. Canada)*, Judgment, Jurisdiction of the Court of 4 Dec 1998, paras 19–20 (for the factual allegation), para 78 (for Spain's legal characterization), and para 84 (for the Court's abstention from dealing with the legal issue); the other two examples mentioned in the previous text are inspired by Yoram Dinstein, *War, Aggression and Self-Defence* (5th edn, Cambridge: Cambridge University Press, 2011), 208.

[71] Michael N. Schmitt (ed), *Tallinn Manual on the International Law Applicable to Cyber Warfare* (Cambridge: Cambridge University Press, 2013), 42–52.

[72] *Corfu Channel*, Merits, 33–4.

[73] cf citation accompanying n 64.

[74] This would seem to be the inference drawn by Robert Jennings, 'International Force and the International Court of Justice' in Antonio Cassese (ed), *The Current Legal Regulation of the Use of Force* (Leiden: Martinus Nijhoff, 1986), 332–3, and (probably) also by Lauterpacht, *The Development of International Law by the International Court*, 317.

[75] For such a view, see Theodore Christakis, 'Intervention and Self-Help' in Bannelier, Christakis, and Heathcote, *The ICJ and the Evolution of International Laws*, 220 ff; Corten, *Le droit contre la guerre*, 91.

ICJ emphasized that 'The United States never denied that its actions against the Iranian platforms amounted to a use of *armed* force'.[76] This indicates the Court's view that the concept of use of force only covers *armed* force. Yet, in its advisory opinion in *Nuclear Weapons*, the ICJ had made it clear that the prohibition of the use of force applies 'regardless of the weapon employed'[77] and, within the context of the 'principle of the non-use of force', the Court has never confined the concept of weapons to those traditionally used by the military. This would allow the Court to place emphasis rather on the (potential) *effect* of the conduct concerned than on the *means* used to decide borderline cases. As far as the requisite effect is concerned, it is worth noting that in the *Nicaragua* case the ICJ had highlighted 'the element of coercion' as forming 'the essence' of unlawful *intervention*,[78] while clarifying at the same time that not every such unlawful intervention amounts to a *use of force*. This may be taken to imply the requirement, in the view of the Court, for a *qualified* form of coercion as forming 'the essence' of the use of force and such qualified form of coercion could exist in *physical* harm to a person or *physical* damage to objects.

As regards the question whether state conduct must be liable to produce physical harm to persons or physical damage to objects of *a certain intensity*, the ICJ has also not yet pronounced a definitive view. While the Court made it clear in the *Nicaragua* case that the prohibition of the use of force covers 'less grave forms' of such use[79] and it had no difficulty in the *Oil Platforms* case in qualifying US military action that was limited in time and space as a use of force, the Court's jurisprudence does not seem to categorically rule out the possibility of setting a *de minimis* threshold.

The ICJ's judgment in the *Armed Activities* case adds a final element to the 'use of force' picture. In that judgment, the Court went as far as to qualify Uganda's (unlawful) *military occupation* of part of the territory of the DRC *as such* as a violation of the principle of the non-use of force.[80] In the same judgment, the ICJ refrained from characterizing the *un*lawful presence of Ugandan troops during the withdrawal period as a use of force.[81]

In the light of all this, it is difficult to avoid the impression that the Court has yet to fully clarify its understanding of the concept of the 'use of force'. It might be safely concluded from the ICJ's reference to *armed* force in the *Oil Platforms* case (and perhaps also from the exclusion of the 'mere supply of funds' from the concept of an 'indirect' use of force in the *Nicaragua* case[82]) that the Court would not

[76] *Oil Platforms*, Judgment, para 45 (emphasis added).

[77] *Nuclear Weapons*, Advisory Opinion, para 39.

[78] *Nicaragua*, Merits, para 205.

[79] *Nicaragua*, Merits, para 191.

[80] *Armed Activities*, Judgment, para 345(1); in paras 56–64 of his Separate Opinion, Judge Kooijmans dissented from this finding by the Court.

[81] *Armed Activities*, Judgment, para 99, in conjunction with para 345(1).

[82] cf Section II.C.

consider the mere infliction of *economic* harm (eg sanctions) to amount to a use of force. However, it cannot be predicted with certainty if, and at what point, the ICJ would characterize the use of computer malware with detrimental cross-border effects as a use of force. It is also not clear under what precise circumstances it would regard the mere uninvited presence of military or police organs of a state on foreign soil as a use of force, and it finally remains an open question whether the Court would require the state conduct to have (or to be capable of having) a minimum degree of physical impact for it to violate the 'principle of non-use of force'.

5. *Consent*

The ICJ touched upon the issue of consent in the *Nicaragua* case when it stated that a foreign intervention is 'allowable at the request of the government of a state'.[83] While this *dictum* forms part of a passage of the *Nicaragua* judgment that deals with unlawful *intervention*, it is difficult not to extend it to the *use of force*. This is because the Court had made it clear that the most important forms of US intervention in the internal affairs of Nicaragua, such as the arming and training the Contras, constituted an intervention *amounting to the use of force*. Interestingly, the ICJ did not qualify its *dictum*. The Court therefore did not indicate the possibility that a non-international armed conflict, as has been argued in the literature,[84] might be of a nature or might reach a point that precludes the government from expressing legally valid consent. Yet one should probably not consider this question to have been settled by this one sentence that the Court included, somewhat in passing, in its *Nicaragua* judgment.

The issue of consent was much more prominent in the *Armed Activities* case.[85] In its judgment, the ICJ assumed that the use of force by a state on foreign soil is not unlawful if it is based on the consent of the territorial state. The Court did not address the issue of consent as an *exception* to the prohibition of the use of force. It rather (implicitly) held that the valid consent expressed by the territorial state precludes the existence of use of force within the meaning of the principle of the non-use of force if the invited state acts within the parameters of such consent. The ICJ did not exclude the possibility that valid consent may by expressed *implicitly* and emphasized at the same time that such consent may, as a rule, be withdrawn explicitly or implicitly and at any time.[86]

[83] *Nicaragua*, Merits, para 246.

[84] Louise Doswald-Beck, 'The Legal Validity of Military Intervention by Invitation of the Government' (1985) 56 *British Yearbook of International Law* 189.

[85] *Armed Activities*, Judgment, paras 42 ff.

[86] *Armed Activities*, Judgment, paras 46–7.

C. Exceptions to the Prohibition of the Use of Force

The following section on the (possible) exceptions to the use of force is subdivided between the use of force *within* and *outside* the collective security system and it begins with the former.

1. *The use of force within the collective security system*

The ICJ has not yet pronounced on any legal question surrounding the UN Charter's collective security system in a contentious case, but one can make an attempt to draw a measure of support from two advisory opinions for the 'authorization model' on the use of force under Chapter VII of the UN Charter. This model has been developing in practice since the adoption of Security Council Resolution 678[87] after Iraq's invasion of Kuwait.[88] In *Certain Expenses of the United Nations (Article 17, Paragraph 2, of the Charter)*, the Court stated that it 'cannot be said that the Charter has left the Security Council impotent in the face of an emergency situation when agreements under Article 43 have not been concluded'.[89] This, of course, was stated with a view to peacekeeping rather than to (fully-fledged) enforcement action. The latter kind of action was directly addressed by the Court only in the *Nuclear Weapons* advisory opinion where it held in the most general terms that 'a further lawful use of force is envisaged in Article 42, whereby the Security Council may take military enforcement measures in conformity with Chapter VII of the Charter'.[90] In the light of the fact that this statement was made a couple of years after the practice on the 'authorization model' had begun, it may perhaps be read as implying the Court's inclination towards seeing that model in a legally favourable light. Be that as it may, the ICJ certainly did not go any further in the *Nuclear Weapons* advisory opinion, and it explicitly abstained from addressing 'questions which might, in a given case, arise from the application of Chapter VII'.[91]

2. *The unilateral use of force*

For the purposes of the following considerations, the term 'unilateral' simply means 'outside the collective security system' and it does not therefore generally exclude forcible action taken *collectively*, such as collective self-defence.

The ICJ's views on the one exception to the prohibition of the use of force, the *existence* of which is uncontroversial, will be set out first.

[87] S/678 (29 Nov 1990).

[88] On this practice, see Thomas M. Franck, *Recourse to Force. State Action Against Threats and Armed Attacks* (Cambridge: Cambridge University Press, 2002), 24 ff; Erika de Wet, *The Chapter VII Powers of the United Nations Security Council* (Oxford: Hart, 2004), 260 ff.

[89] *Certain Expenses of the United Nations (Article 17, Paragraph 2, of the Charter)*, Advisory Opinion of 20 July 1962, ICJ Rep 1962, 167.

[90] *Nuclear Weapons*, Advisory Opinion, para 38.

[91] *Nuclear Weapons*, Advisory Opinion, para 49.

1. Individual *self-defence*

For the sake of clarity, the ICJ's views on *individual* self-defence will be presented initially. The right of collective self-defence, in the view of the Court, is accessory to the right of individual self-defence and subject to certain *additional* conditions. The latter will be set out in a separate subsection.

a) An (actual or imminent) armed attack as a *conditio sine qua non*

The question whether the right of individual self-defence, as recognized in Article 51 of the UN Charter, requires an armed attack, has perhaps given rise to the most famous controversy surrounding this provision. As early as 1952, Waldock argued that Article 51, despite its reference to an armed attack, did not limit the wider 'inherent' customary right of self-defence as it had existed at the time of the entry into force of the UN Charter. This included, for example, the right of *anticipatory* self-defence in case of an *imminent* armed attack.[92]

In 1958, this position was taken up and developed further by Bowett who listed the right to protect nationals abroad and the defence of certain economic interests as important aspects of this wider customary right of self-defence.[93] The contrary position, whereby an armed attack constitutes a *conditio sine qua non* of the right of individual self-defence under the UN Charter was most prominently defended by Brownlie in 1963.[94] Leaving the special question of *anticipatory* self-defence (to which we shall turn specifically in the next subsection) aside, it is certainly fair to say that the position requiring an (actual or perhaps imminent) *armed attack* has become the prevailing one in the international scholarly discourse.[95]

Since the *Nicaragua* case, the ICJ has been following this majority view.[96] The Court categorically stated that in 'the case of individual self-defence, the exercise of this right is subject to the state concerned having been the victim of an *armed attack*'.[97] While the *Nicaragua* Court decided the matter under customary international law, it was clear that, in that very respect, its view on the customary nature of the law of individual self-defence was based on the restrictive interpretation of Article 51.[98] This position has not changed since.[99]

[92] Waldock, 'The Regulation of the Use of Force by Individual States in International Law', 463–4 in connection with 496 ff.

[93] Derek W. Bowett, *Self-Defence in International Law* (Manchester: Manchester University Press, 1958), 87 ff, and 106 ff, each time in connection with 182 ff.

[94] Brownlie, *International Law and the Use of Force by States*, 270 ff.

[95] For two recent treatments of the matter in the sense of the predominant position, see Ruys, '*Armed Attack' and Article 51 of the UN Charter*, 55 ff; Albrecht Randelzhofer and Georg Nolte, 'Article 51' in Bruno Simma et al (eds), *The Charter of the United Nations. A Commentary*, vol II (3rd edn, Oxford: Oxford University Press, 2012), 1403 ff (marginal notes 9 ff).

[96] Randelzhofer and Nolte, 'Article 51' in Simma et al, *The Charter of the United Nations*, 1404 (marginal note 13).

[97] *Nicaragua*, Merits, para 195 (emphasis added). [98] cf Section II.A.4.

[99] eg in *Oil Platforms* the ICJ held: 'in order to establish that it was legally justified in attacking the Iranian platforms in exercise of the right to self-defence, the United States has to show that attacks had

It was primarily due to Judge Schwebel that the expansive reading of the right of individual self-defence under the UN Charter and customary international law did not go completely unnoticed by the ICJ. In his voluminous dissent in the *Nicaragua* case, Judge Schwebel questioned whether the ICJ had actually wished to decide the matter, and stated, before explicitly referring to Waldock's earlier article, the following:

[The] Judgment may be open to the interpretation of inferring that a State may react in self-defence, only if an armed attack occurs... I wish, *ex abundanti cautela,* to make clear that, for my part, I do not agree with a construction of the United Nations Charter which would read Article 51 as if it were worded: 'Nothing in the present Charter shall impair the inherent right of individual or collective self-defence if, and only if, an armed attack occurs...'. I do not agree that the terms or intent of Article 51 eliminate the right of self-defence under customary international law, or confine its entire scope to the express terms of Article 51.[100]

Judge Schwebel was right to question whether the ICJ had decided the question of *anticipatory* self-defence, as we shall see in the next subsection, but it is impossible to deny that the Court rejected the idea that Article 51 recognizes a pre-Charter right of self-defence that goes beyond the case of an actual or perhaps imminent *armed attack*.

b) The case of an *imminent* armed attack

Another classical controversy focuses on the question whether the contemporaneous international law on the use of force leaves room for anticipatory self-defence.[101] This debate has been an important part of the controversy as to whether the armed attack constitutes a *conditio sine qua non* for the right of self-defence. The latter fact explains why some of the formulations of the ICJ on the requirement of an armed attack read *as if* the Court had ruled out any scope for anticipatory self-defence. Such a construction of the jurisprudence would, however, go too far in the light of two explicit statements by the Court to the effect that it did *not* wish to decide that matter. In its judgment in the *Nicaragua* case, the ICJ found as follows:

In view of the circumstances in which the dispute has arisen, reliance is placed by the Parties only on the right of self-defence in the case of an armed attack which has already occurred, and the issue of the lawfulness of a response to the imminent threat of armed attack has not been raised. Accordingly, the Court expresses no view on that issue.[102]

been made upon it for which Iran was responsible; and that those attacks were of such a nature as to be qualified as "armed attacks" within the meaning of that expression in Article 51 of the United Nations Charter, and as understood in customary law on the use of force'; Judgment, para 51.

[100] *Nicaragua*, Merits, Dissenting Opinion of Judge Schwebel, para 173.

[101] Björn Schiffbauer, *Vorbeugende Selbstverteidigung im Völkerrecht. Eine systematische Ermittlung des gegenwärtigen friedenssicherungsrechtlichen Besitzstands aus völkerrechtsdogmatischer und praxisanalytischer Sicht* (Berlin: Duncker & Humblot, 2012).

[102] *Nicaragua*, Merits, para 194.

This caveat was reiterated in the *Armed Activities* case.[103] While the ICJ has therefore refrained from deciding the question of anticipatory self-defence, it has made clear its view that such anticipatory self-defence is conceivable only in a case where an armed attack is *imminent*. The following statement in the *Armed Activities* case may be read as a firm rejection of any legal claims of anticipatory self-defence exceeding the situation of an imminent armed attack:

> Article 51 of the Charter may justify a use of force in self-defence only within the strict confines there laid down. It does not allow the use of force to protect perceived security interests beyond these parameters. Other means are available, including, in particular, recourse to the Security Council.[104]

c) The concept of armed attack *ratione materiae*

In the *Nicaragua* case, the ICJ opined: 'There appears now to be general agreement on the nature of the acts which can be treated as constituting armed attacks'.[105] Yet, the Court did not specify that nature either in the abstract or by a list of acts. In particular, the ICJ has at no point in its jurisprudence suggested that the concept of *armed* attack implies the use of *weapons* generally recognized as *military* in nature. Again in the *Nicaragua* case, the ICJ made reference to Article 3(g) of the Definition of Aggression annexed to General Assembly Resolution 3314[106] in order to give meaning to the concept of armed attack in the case before the Court. Importantly, however, the ICJ did not state that the concepts 'armed attack' (within the meaning of Art 51) and 'act of aggression' (within the meaning of Art 39) have the same meaning. The Court also refrained from establishing any other conceptual relationship between those two terms. While the ICJ has thus not yet defined the concept of armed attack (and it did not have to), its case law, in a similar manner as regards the concept of a 'use of force' (within the meaning of Art 2(4) and customary international law), provides a number of elements that shed light on the Court's understanding of the concept *ratione materiae*.

In the *Nicaragua* case, the ICJ found it necessary 'to distinguish the *most grave forms of the use of force* (those constituting an armed attack) from other less grave forms'.[107] A gravity threshold for the concept of 'armed attack' and a gap between that concept and the one of use of force were thus established. While the formulation 'most grave' might be taken to indicate a high threshold, the subsequent reference to a 'frontier incident'[108] as an example of a case where the gravity threshold is not reached reads somewhat differently.[109] The ICJ confirmed the existence of a

[103] *Armed Activities*, Judgment, para 143. [104] *Armed Activities*, Judgment, para 148.

[105] *Nicaragua*, Merits, para 195. [106] GA Res 3314 (XXIX) (14 Dec 1974).

[107] *Nicaragua*, Merits, para 191 (emphasis added). [108] *Nicaragua*, Merits, para 195.

[109] The same is true for the fact that the ICJ did not rule out the possibility that a *single* 'trans-border incursion' may amount to an armed attack; *Nicaragua*, Merits, para 231.

gravity threshold in the *Oil Platforms* case and repeated the *Nicaragua* distinction between 'most grave' and 'less grave forms' of the use of force.[110] Subsequently in the same judgment, the Court became much more specific and declared that it did 'not rule out the possibility that the mining of a single military vessel might be sufficient to bring into play the "inherent right of self-defence" '.[111] The judgment in the *Oil Platforms* case also contains a new element pertaining to the gravity threshold in that the ICJ alludes to the possibility of considering a *series of attacks* 'in combination' in order to determine whether an armed attack was committed.[112] The Court displayed a similar openness to regard certain attacks as 'cumulative in nature' in its judgment in the *Armed Activities* case.[113] In both instances, however, the ICJ did not decide that question and did not specify any conditions for accepting an 'accumulation of events' for the purpose of determining whether the gravity requirement of the concept of armed attack has been fulfilled in a given case.[114] It may be concluded that the ICJ has posed a gravity requirement for the concept of armed attack within the meaning of Article 51 and customary international law. While the Court's abstract description of armed attacks as 'the most grave forms' of a use of force may suggest a stringent threshold, the recognition of the possibility of a use of force against a single military vessel amounting to an armed attack appears to nuance that impression. The question would lose some practical significance were the ICJ to finally endorse, as it seemed inclined to do in the *Oil Platforms* case as well as in the *Armed Activities* case, some form of accumulation of events doctrine for the purpose of measuring gravity in cases of a series of attacks.

The armed attack within the meaning of Article 51 and customary international law must be directed *against a state*. This is clearly the case where the attack is against the *territory* of such a state. It is less clear whether armed attacks may also be directed against (certain) *extraterritorial manifestations* of another state.[115] In the *Oil Platforms* case the ICJ recognized the possibility of an armed attack against *one military vessel* of a state outside that state's territorial waters. Interestingly, the Court, in the same case, did not seem to exclude the possibility of an armed attack being directed against a *merchant* vessel of a state. The ICJ may thus be prepared to extend the concept of 'armed attack' beyond the confines of Article 3(d) of the General Assembly's Resolution on the Definition of Aggression. In that context, it is perhaps also noteworthy that the ICJ, while not directly addressing the right of

[110] *Oil Platforms*, Judgment, para 51. [111] *Oil Platforms*, Judgment, para 72.

[112] *Oil Platforms*, Judgment, para 64; to be precise, this element was foreshadowed in *Nicaragua* where the Court, in passing, alluded to the possibility that 'trans-border incursions' could amount 'singly or *collectively*' to an armed attack; *Nicaragua*, Merits, para 231.

[113] *Armed Activities*, Judgment, para 146.

[114] For a critical stance vis-à-vis the use of the accumulation of events doctrine in this context, see *Oil Platforms*, Judgment, Separate Opinion of Judge Simma, para 14.

[115] Ruys, *'Armed Attack' and Article 51 of the UN Charter*, 199 ff.

self-defence, repeatedly used the term 'armed attack' in the *Tehran Hostages* case to label the seizure of the US embassy in Tehran.[116]

Finally, the question arises whether an armed attack within the meaning of Article 51 of the UN Charter requires some kind of *intent*. In the *Oil Platforms* case, the ICJ, when examining whether the minelaying could have amounted to an armed attack, considered the issue of intent. It noted that it had not been established that this action 'aimed specifically' at the US and that the mine struck by one of the ships in question, 'was laid with the specific intention of harming that ship'.[117] This reads as if the ICJ had wished to establish the requirement of an attacker's *intent specifically directed* against the victim state. While such a rather odd requirement would perhaps constitute too far-reaching an inference from this one passage,[118] the same passage would, however, at least seem to signal the Court's inclination to exclude *mistaken action* from the concept of armed attack.

d) The concept of armed attack *ratione personae*

aa) Armed attack *by a state*

In the *Nicaragua* case, the ICJ found that an armed attack by a state does not require action by de jure organs of that state. Instead, and relying on Article 3(g) of the Definition of Aggression, the ICJ determined:

> that an armed attack must be understood as including not merely action by regular armed forces across an international border, but also 'the sending by or on behalf of a State of armed bands, groups irregulars or mercenaries, which carry out acts of armed force against another State of such gravity as to amount to' (*inter alia*) an actual armed attack conducted by regular forces, 'or its substantial involvement therein'.[119]

In the same paragraph, the Court formed the view that the 'assistance to rebels in the form of the provision of weapons or logistical or other support' did not amount to an armed attack. The *Nicaragua* Court avoided establishing a direct connection between the idea of an armed attack by a state through irregular forces and the customary international law rules on attribution. However, it would seem fair to infer that the Court accepted the possibility of extending the concept of an armed attack by a state beyond the conduct of de jure state organs to all those cases where the use of armed force by persons can be otherwise *attributed* to a state under customary international law. It is also clear that there is, according to the Court, a (second) gap between the concepts of 'armed attack' and 'use of force'.

[116] *Tehran Hostages*, Judgment, paras 57, 64, 91. [117] *Oil Platforms*, Judgment, para 64.

[118] For a similar expression of caution, see 'The Chatham House Principles of International Law on the Use of Force in Self-Defence' (2006) 55 *International and Comparative Law Quarterly* 966; the unexplained reference to 'motivations' in *Nicaragua*, Merits, para 231, is too vague to enable one to infer a clear-cut position adopted by the Court on the matter of intent.

[119] *Nicaragua*, Merits, para 195.

This is because the (mere) arming and training by a state of non-state actors fighting the government of another state on the latter's territory, while constituting a(n indirect) use of force by the supporting state,[120] does not amount to an armed attack. The remaining grey area concerns forms of state involvement into the use of force by persons, which go beyond the mere arming or training of rebels fighting in another state, but which are insufficiently intense to justify the attribution of that use of force to the involved state under the strict requirements, as they have eventually come to be clarified by the Court in its judgment in the *Genocide* case.[121] Those requirements are, in the alternative, the *complete dependence* of a group of violent non-state actors on the support of the state concerned or the latter's *effective* control over the specific forcible actions carried out from within such a group.[122] The 'harbouring' by a state of transnationally violent non-state actors on its territory, to take one specific and recently much discussed example, would seem to fall into that grey area. There are two legal avenues through which the ICJ could proceed to construe the concept of armed attack by a state so as to cover this form of state involvement (and similar ones). The Court could recognize the emergence of a *lex specialis* on attribution within the specific context of the law on the use of force[123] or it could accept some limited room for the concept of an *indirect* armed attack consisting in the *substantial* (though insufficient for purposes of attribution) involvement of a state in the (transnational) use of force by non-state actors. As yet, there is, however, very little in the case law of the ICJ that would suggest that the Court is inclined to use either of those avenues. The ICJ has, in particular, refrained completely from indicating whether the concept of 'substantial involvement', as contained in Article 3(g) of the Definition of Aggression, possesses a scope of application exceeding that covered by the general requirements of attribution, as understood by the Court.[124]

[120] cf Section II.B.3.

[121] *Case Concerning Application of the Convention on the Prevention and Punishment of the Crime of Genocide (Bosnia and Herzegovina v. Serbia and Montenegro)*, Judgment of 26 Feb 2007, ICJ Rep 2007, paras 385–415.

[122] Jérôme Reymond, *L'attribution de comportements d'organes de facto et d'agents de l'Etat en droit international. Étude sur la responsabilité internationale des Etats* (Zurich: Editions Schulthess, 2013).

[123] This question has been the subject of much discussion; see eg Tal Becker, *Terrorism and the State. Rethinking the Rules of State Responsibility* (Oxford: Hart, 2006), 285 ff; Christian Henderson, *The Persistent Advocate and the Use of Force. The Impact of the United States upon the* Jus ad Bellum *in the Post-Cold War Era* (Farnham: Ashgate, 2010), 137 ff; for the suggestion that a particularly far-reaching *lex specialis* has emerged, see Randelzhofer and Nolte, 'Article 51' in Simma et al, *The Charter of the United Nations*, 1418–19 (marginal note 41).

[124] For an analysis of *Nicaragua* in the light of the alternative of 'substantial involvement', see *Nicaragua*, Merits, Dissenting Opinion of Judge Schwebel, paras 165 ff.

bb) Non-state *armed attack*

One of the most important current debates on the right to self-defence concerns the question whether the armed attack within the meaning of Article 51 of the UN Charter must be carried out *by a state*. While the predominant scholarly view before the terror attacks of 11 September 2001 was perhaps to insist on such a requirement,[125] there has since been a growing trend to accept the possibility of *non-state* armed attacks.[126] In the *Nicaragua* case, the ICJ confined the concept of armed attack to *state* conduct.[127] The Court followed this line in the *Oil Platforms* case, where it required the US to show that attacks had been made upon it '*for which Iran was responsible*'.[128]

The picture becomes less clear with the ICJ's *Wall* advisory opinion. The pertinent passage of the opinion reads:

> Article 51 of the Charter...recognizes the existence of an inherent right of self-defence in the case of an armed attack *by one State* against another State. However, Israel does not claim that the attacks against it are *imputable to a foreign State*. The Court also notes that Israel exercises control in the Occupied Palestinian Territory and that, as Israel itself states, the threat which it regards as justifying the construction of the wall originates within, and not outside, that territory. The situation is thus different from that contemplated by Security Council resolutions 1368 (2001) and 1373 (2001), and therefore Israel could not in any event invoke those resolutions in support of its claim to be exercising the right of self-defence.[129]

It would be an understatement to say that this passage is not entirely clear. In the first two sentences of the citation, the ICJ appeared to follow its prior case law and seemed to require, in the most explicit terms, *state* action. Then, however, the Court made a reference to Resolutions 1368 and 1373, adopted in the wake of the attacks of 9/11, the preambular references of which to the right of self-defence are often taken as evidence for the Security Council's recognition of the possibility of *non*-state armed attacks falling within the meaning of Article 51. The ICJ did not clarify the significance of its reference to those two resolutions. Instead, it distinguished the situation before it from that addressed by those resolutions. The very fact, though, that the Court felt the need to engage in that distinguishing exercise casts doubt on the rigour with which the Court wished to adhere to the requirement of state action despite its seemingly clear articulation of that requirement at the beginning of that paragraph.

[125] For an earlier view to the contrary, see Claus Kreß, *Gewaltverbot und Selbstverteidigungsrecht nach der Satzung der Vereinten Nationen bei staatlicher Verwicklung in Gewaltakte Privater* (Berlin: Duncker & Humblot, 1995), 206–35.

[126] See eg para 10 of the 2007 resolution of the Institut de Droit International on Self-Defence; 'The Chatham House Principles', 969; for a thorough more recent account of the debate with numerous references, see Ruys, *'Armed Attack' and Article 51 of the UN Charter*, 419 ff.

[127] *Nicaragua*, Merits, para 195; for the same interpretation of this passage, see *Wall*, Advisory Opinion, Separate Opinion of Judge Higgins, para 33.

[128] *Oil Platforms*, Judgment, para 51 (emphasis added).

[129] *Wall*, Advisory Opinion, para 139 (emphasis added).

The ICJ returned to the question of non-state armed attacks in the *Armed Activities* case. In that case, the Court was asked to determine whether Uganda could justify part of its military operations in the DRC by reference to the right of individual self-defence because of cross-border armed action having emanated from the territory of the DRC and having been directed against Uganda. The Court examined the possibility of attributing that armed action to the DRC and rejected the possibility. The Court continued its analysis as follows:

For all these reasons, the Court finds that the legal and factual circumstances for the exercise of a right of self-defence by Uganda against the DRC were not present. Accordingly, the Court has no need to respond to the contentions of the Parties as to whether and under what conditions contemporary international law provides for a right of self-defence against large-scale attacks by irregular forces.[130]

In his separate opinion, Judge Kooijmans drew upon his diplomatic skills when he characterized this passage as 'not altogether clear'.[131] In fact, it remains a matter of speculation why the ICJ did not feel the need to address the issue of *non*-state armed attacks *after having rejected the possibility of attributing the armed action* in question to a state. Whatever the reasons were, it is worth noting that the ICJ has addressed the issue of a *non*-state armed attack as an *open question* rather than considering the matter to have been conclusively dealt with in the negative in its prior jurisprudence. This may be taken as a signal by the Court that it is willing to (re) consider the issue on a future occasion.

Judges Higgins, Kooijmans, and Buergenthal (in the *Wall* advisory opinion), and Judges Kooijmans and Simma (in the *Armed Activities* case) have been less reluctant than the Court and have all expressed their preference for recognizing the possibility of non-state armed attacks within the meaning of Article 51.[132]

cc) The requirements of necessity and proportionality

There would seem to be a broad consensus that the exercise of the right of self-defence under international law is governed by the principles of necessity and proportionality. Reference is generally made to the famous 1837 *Caroline* incident in support of that position.[133] The content of those two principles turns out to be remarkably controversial[134] and the situation is further complicated by the fact that there is uncertainty about the preliminary question whether the halting or repelling of the

[130] *Armed Activities*, Judgment, para 147.

[131] *Armed Activities*, Judgment, Separate Opinion of Judge Kooijmans, para 20.

[132] *Wall*, Advisory Opinion, Separate Opinion of Judge Higgins, para 33; Separate Opinion of Judge Kooijmans, para 35; Declaration of Judge Buergenthal, para 6; *Armed Activities*, Judgment, Separate Opinion of Judge Kooijmans, paras 28 ff; Separate Opinion of Judge Simma, para 11.

[133] Ruys, *'Armed Attack' and Article 51 of the UN Charter*, 92 ff.

[134] Thorough scholarly treatises of the relevant legal issues are rare; for one exception, see Judith Gardam, *Necessity, Proportionality and the Use of Force by States* (Cambridge: Cambridge University Press, 2004).

armed attack constitutes the only legally admissible goal of self-defence action apart from the specific case of anticipatory self-defence.[135]

With respect to the content of the principle of necessity, it is unclear whether it imposes a *temporal* restraint on the defensive use of force often referred to as the requirement of *immediacy*. With respect to proportionality, there is a more fundamental uncertainty about the legal point of reference. Proportionality may be understood to require 'some sort of equation between the gravity of the armed attack and the defensive response'.[136] Alternatively (or cumulatively), proportionality is measured against the aim of the defensive action. This second view on proportionality, which is sometimes referred to as the *functional* approach,[137] follows an often-cited statement by Roberto Ago, Special Rapporteur of the ILC on state responsibility for internationally wrongful acts, which reads:

> The action ... may well have to assume dimensions disproportionate to those of the attack suffered. What matters in this respect is the result to be achieved by the 'defensive' action, and not the forms, substance and strength of the action itself.[138]

Such an understanding of the concept of proportionality reduces its practical relevance to an examination which could also be conducted under the requirement of necessity. In the light of those and other questions, it is interesting to see what the Court has had to say on such matters.

Beginning with its judgment in the *Nicaragua* case, the ICJ has left no doubt that it considers the right of self-defence to be subject to the requirements of necessity and proportionality. The Court, without ever specifically referring to the *Caroline* incident, considers those requirements to be rooted in customary international law and, perhaps, even to be inherent in the very concept of self-defence.[139] Regarding the more precise content of those principles, the ICJ has refrained from defining them in the abstract so that it is necessary to look at how the Court applied them to the concrete cases before it. In that respect, however, one important general caveat is in place. None of the ICJ judgments in question actually hinged on the question of necessity or proportionality. The Court has therefore addressed those questions indirectly, rather briefly, and more as marginal issues, in particular in the *Nicaragua* and *Armed Activities* cases.[140] This cautions against drawing far-reaching conclusions from the relevant parts of the judgments.

[135] For an intriguing recent argument to broaden the list of possible aims of self-defence action beyond 'halting and repelling', see David Kretzmer, 'The Inherent Rights to Self-Defence and Proportionality in *Jus ad Bellum*' (2013) 24 *European Journal of International Law* 260; for a response, see Georg Nolte, 'Multipurpose Self-Defence, Proportionality Disoriented: A Response to David Kretzmer' (2013) 24 *European Journal of International Law* 283.

[136] Ruys, *'Armed Attack' and Article 51 of the UN Charter*, 111, calls this a 'quantitative approach'.

[137] Ruys, *'Armed Attack' and Article 51 of the UN Charter*, 112.

[138] Roberto Ago, 'Addendum to the 8th Report on State Responsibility', *Yearbook of the International Law Commission*, 1980, vol II (1), 69.

[139] cf Section II.A.4.

[140] *Nicaragua*, Merits, para 237; *Armed Activities*, Judgment, para 147.

In the *Nicaragua* case, the ICJ rejected the necessity of the use of force by the US because the 'major offensive of the armed opposition against the Government of El Salvador had been completely repulsed, and the actions of the opposition considerably reduced in consequence'. 'Thus', the Court continued, 'it was possible to eliminate the danger to the Salvadorian Government without the United States embarking on activities in and against Nicaragua'.[141] In this passage, the Court alluded to the temporal aspect of the necessity requirement and its formulation may be read to suggest that forcible measures of self-defence are no longer necessary when the armed attack has ended. For the reasons stated previously, it would seem problematic, though, to interpret this one and rather broad reference to the 'elimination of the danger' as precluding the possibility for a state (such as the US after 9/11) to act in self-defence in order to prevent the reoccurrence in the near future of an armed attack emanating from the same source from which an armed attack had recently emanated. Even if one interprets the previously cited passage in the *Nicaragua* judgment as the endorsement of the view that the only admissible aim of self-defence action is to halt and repel an ongoing armed attack, its application requires a clear understanding of when an armed attack ends, and such a determination may well be controversial in the light of the fact that, here again, there may be room to resort to the concept of a continuing armed attack based on the idea of an accumulation of events.

While the Court has yet to pronounce clearly on those legal questions, it is important to recall that the ICJ has already, albeit implicitly, dealt with another aspect of the question of when an armed attack ends. The Court qualified Uganda's military occupation of parts of the DRC, resulting from an unlawful use of force against that state, to constitute as such an (unlawful) use of force.[142] If this reasoning were transferred to the level of an armed attack, it would mean that an armed attack continues as long as the attacker militarily occupies (parts of) the victim state.[143] The implications for the application of the necessity requirement in its temporal dimension are obvious and only an additional requirement of immediacy could then limit the temporal scope of defensive action. Whether the ICJ would accept such a requirement, either as an independent condition or as part of the principle of necessity, is impossible to tell from its case law so far.

In the *Oil Platforms* case, the ICJ observed, as part of its analysis of the necessity of the use of force in question 'that there is no evidence that the United States complained to Iran of the military activities of the platforms'[144] before bombarding them. This may be understood as implying that the use of force must be a measure of *last resort* in order for it to qualify as a necessary measure of self-defence. While this principle would again hardly seem problematic, if stated in the abstract, it would appear imprudent for the ICJ to require a state, that is actually under attack,

[141] *Nicaragua*, Merits, para 237. [142] cf Section II.B.4.

[143] For such a view, see Okimoto, *The Distinction and Relationship between* Jus ad Bellum *and* Jus in Bello, 52.

[144] *Oil Platforms*, Judgment, para 76.

invariably to attempt a diplomatic solution before adopting defensive measures. The Court's brief statement in the *Oil Platforms* case, which concerned a claim of self-defence against an alleged series of minor uses of force, would therefore be better interpreted in not such a sweeping manner.[145]

In the *Oil Platforms* case, the ICJ also alluded to the possibility that the necessity requirement could limit the scope of lawful targets—independently and perhaps beyond the limitations imposed by the applicable law of armed conflict—to such objects that directly contribute to the ongoing armed attack.[146] The Court was not, however, very specific in this respect and did not elaborate upon this point so that, here again, it would seem appropriate to confine the significance of the reasoning to the particularities of an alleged series of relatively low-scale attacks.

With respect to the proportionality principle, it is even more difficult to identify the ICJ's position in abstract terms, perhaps with one exception. The Court makes it fairly clear in the *Oil Platforms* case that the proportionality of an exercise of the right of self-defence must—other than the proportionality of an attack under the law of armed conflict—be assessed in the light of the defensive operation and the armed attack, both taken as a whole.[147]

The ICJ has not specified explicitly at any point in its jurisprudence whether it prefers the 'functional' or the 'quantitative' approach to proportionality. Yet, it would seem clear that the Court would not accept as lawful a forceful response to an armed attack that does not even meet the requirements of the functional approach, meaning a forceful response which exceeds that necessary to halt and repel the armed attack. Whether the Court would base its rejection of such a forceful response on *necessity* or on *proportionality* or on some sort of combination thereof is unclear. But this is more of analytical than practical relevance. What matters in practice is whether the Court, in addition, recognizes some quantitative limitation of the forceful response to an armed attack despite the necessity of the latter response. The pertinent passages in the *Nicaragua*[148] and *Armed Activities* cases[149] suggest that the ICJ indeed assumes the existence of such a limitation, but as the Court's findings were not supported by reasons it is impossible to derive any criteria that could guide the identification of the quantitative threshold in question. While the Court was somewhat more elaborate in

[145] For a more circumspect formulation of the same principle, see 'The Chatham House Principles', 966.

[146] 'The Chatham House Principles', para 74.

[147] 'The Chatham House Principles', para 77: 'the Court cannot assess in isolation the proportionality of that action to the armed attack to which it was said to be a response; it cannot close its eyes to the scale of the whole operation…'; for the same interpretation of this passage, see the Principles, 969.

[148] *Nicaragua*, Merits, para 237: 'Whatever uncertainty may exist as to the exact scale of the aid received by the Salvadorian opposition from Nicaragua, it is clear that these latter United States activities in question could not have been proportionate to that aid.'

[149] *Armed Activities*, Judgment, para 147: 'The Court cannot fail to observe, however, that the taking of airports and towns many hundreds of kilometres from Uganda's border would not seem proportionate to the series of transborder attacks it claimed had given rise to the right of self-defence, nor to be necessary to that end.'

the *Oil Platforms* case, the considerations contained in that judgment, in the end, do not elucidate the matter. In that case, the ICJ held that the destruction of two Iranian oil platforms in response to the mining of a single military vessel was disproportionate, while the destruction of two other oil platforms in response to a missile attack on a single merchant vessel might have been proportionate.[150] It is not easy to make sense of this distinction.[151] In conclusion, all that can be said in the abstract is that the ICJ is inclined to recognize the possibility that a forceful defensive measure is *dis*proportionate because its intensity is in *excess* of the gravity of the armed attack. The jurisprudence offers no real guidance, however, as to *when* an action taken in self-defence can be said to become excessive in that quantitative sense.

e) Self-defence and Security Council action

The ICJ has yet to address the words 'until the Security Council has taken the measures necessary to maintain international peace and security'.[152] In *Nuclear Weapons*, the ICJ simply ignored that part of Article 51 of the UN Charter and instead restated the rest of the provision.[153]

f) The duty to report to the Security Council

The ICJ has consistently referred to the UN Charter[154] requirement to report immediately any exercise of the right of self-defence to the Security Council.[155] In the *Nicaragua* case, the ICJ treated the failure of the US to report its alleged collective self-defence action as an indication that the US was perhaps itself not convinced of the strength of its legal claim.[156] In the *Armed Activities* case, the ICJ, in the light of Uganda's omission, could have specified the legal consequence, under the UN Charter, of a failure to report. But it did not. As the Court did not say that Uganda's self-defence claim failed because of its failure to report,[157] it may be assumed that the Court does not consider this requirement to be a condition for the lawfulness of self-defence, but rather as an independent procedural obligation.

g) Self-defence and military occupation

In the *Wall* advisory opinion, the ICJ rejected Israel's claim that the security barrier it erected was an act of individual self-defence against (non-)state armed attacks against Israel's territory emanating from occupied territory. The ICJ noted that Israel,

150 *Oil Platforms*, Judgment, para 77.

151 James A. Green, *The International Court of Justice and Self-Defence in International Law* (Oxford: Hart, 2009), 86 ff.

152 But see Nico Krisch, *Selbstverteidigung und Kollektive Sicherheit* (Berlin: Springer, 2001).

153 *Nuclear Weapons*, Advisory Opinion, para 44.

154 On the Court's position that no such requirement exists under *customary* international law, see Section II.A.4.

155 *Nicaragua*, Merits, para 200; *Nuclear Weapons*, Advisory Opinion, para 44; *Armed Activities*, Judgment, para 145.

156 *Nicaragua*, Merits, para 235.

157 For the relevant passage, see *Armed Activities*, Judgment, para 145.

as the occupying force, exercised control in the territory from which the alleged armed attack originated.[158] This can be taken to mean that the Court prefers not to qualify individual forcible measures adopted by an occupying force within the occupied territory as a use of force within the meaning of the 'principle of the non-use of force in the international relations', but rather as measures to be examined exclusively under the law of military occupation.[159] At the same time it should be recalled that the ICJ in the subsequent *Armed Activities* case, found Uganda's military occupation of parts of the DRC to constitute such a use of force.[160] The ICJ could therefore hardly deem the right of self-defence as irrelevant with respect to the question whether the use of force, which consists in a military occupation as such, can be justified. The distinction between the military occupation itself and an individual forcible measure adopted by the occupying power during such occupation, is a fine one, but it is submitted that this distinction would allow the reconciliation of what the ICJ had to say on 'the principle of non-use of force' and military occupation in the *Wall* advisory opinion, on the one hand, and in the *Armed Activities* case, on the other hand.

II. *Collective self-defence*

The very concept of the right of *collective* self-defence (the existence of which in pre-Charter customary international law is less clear than the ICJ assumed in the *Nicaragua* case)[161] has long been the subject of two conflicting views. According to the first, the right in question entitles a state, which is not itself the victim of an armed attack, to come to the assistance of such a victim.[162] The second position has been articulated most clearly by Bowett who stated:

> The requirements of the right of collective self-defence are two in number; firstly that each participating state has an individual right of self-defence, and secondly that there exists an agreement between the participating states to exercise their rights collectively.[163]

In the *Nicaragua* case, the ICJ implicitly rejected Bowett's position and sided with the concept of collective self-defence as the 'defence of another State'. Starting from that premise, the Court subjected the right of collective self-defence to the following specific conditions:

> The Court concludes that the requirement of a request by the State which is the victim of the alleged attack is additional to the requirement that such State should have declared itself to have been attacked.[164]

[158] cf the citation accompanying n 122.

[159] For a thoughtful treatment of this difficult question, see Iris Canor, 'When *Jus ad Bellum* Meets *Jus in Bello*: The Occupier's Right of Self-Defence against Terrorism Stemming from Occupied Territories' (2006) 19 *Leiden Journal of International Law* 139.

[160] Section II.B.4.

[161] *Nicaragua*, Merits, para 193; for the contrary view, see Dissenting Opinion of Judge Jennings, 530–1.

[162] Brownlie, *International Law and the Use of Force by States*, 330–1.

[163] Bowett, *Self-Defence in International Law*, 207; Bowett's view was followed by Judge Jennings in his Dissenting Opinion in the ICJ's judgment in *Nicaragua*, Merits, 545.

[164] *Nicaragua*, Merits, para 199.

Judge Jennings criticized this formulation of a specific double requirement as 'somewhat formalistic'.[165] Perhaps the ICJ took that observation into account when it formulated somewhat more generously in the *Oil Platforms* case. Here the Court cited only part of the relevant passage in the *Nicaragua* judgment and held that the right of collective self-defence required 'the existence of a request "by the State which *regards* itself as the victim of an armed attack"'.[166]

a) Exceptions to the prohibition of the use of force other than self-defence?

The ICJ has at no point unambiguously stated that the right to self-defence constitutes the *only* exception to the prohibition of the use of force outside the collective security system. Instead, the Court said in the *Nicaragua* case that the 'general rule prohibiting force allows for *certain* exceptions'.[167] And in *Nuclear Weapons*, after mentioning Article 51 of the UN Charter, it referred to Article 42 as the legal basis for '[a] further lawful use of force'[168] instead of calling it the only further exception. At the same time, the ICJ has not to date recognized any exception to the prohibition of the use of force, apart from self-defence and collective security, in its existing jurisprudence.

aa) Individual *forcible countermeasures against less grave uses of force*

The point where the ICJ perhaps came closest to recognizing another (and very limited) exception is in the *Nicaragua* case, where the Court addressed in some detail the gap that exists, in its view, between the prohibition of an *indirect* use of force[169] and the narrower concept of armed attack.[170] In that respect, the ICJ wondered:

> whether a State has a right to respond to intervention with intervention going so far as to justify a use of force in reaction to measures which do not constitute an armed attack but may nevertheless involve a use of force.[171]

The Court did not answer this question because it held that it was inconceivable that such a right to adopt 'counter-measures' involving a 'less grave' use of force could be relied upon by a *third* state as analogous to the right to *collective* self-defence.[172]

In the *Oil Platforms* case, the ICJ did not revisit the matter despite the relatively small-scale nature of the Iranian uses of force, as alleged by the US, and despite the difficulties the Court was facing in establishing whether the threshold of an armed attack had been passed. This was criticized by Judge Simma. Where a state has been subject to an unlawful use of force that falls short of an armed attack, Judge Simma argued that this victim state has the right to take individual 'defensive action by

165 *Nicaragua*, Merits, Dissenting Opinion of Judge Jennings, 544.
166 *Oil Platforms*, Judgment, para 51 (emphasis added).
167 *Nicaragua*, Merits, para 193 (emphasis added).
168 *Nuclear Weapons*, Advisory Opinion, para 38.
169 cf Section II.B.3.
170 cf Section II.C.2.i(a)(cc).
171 *Nicaragua*, Merits, para 210.
172 *Nicaragua*, Merits, paras 210, 249.

force also short of Article 51'.[173] It is somewhat tempting briefly to speculate why the idea of a right to individual forcible countermeasures 'short of Article 51', as Judge Simma put it, was not taken up by the ICJ in the *Oil Platforms* case. The most straightforward reason is that when the Court found that the evidence did not bear out on an Iranian armed attack, it implicitly also found no 'less grave' Iranian use of force thereby rendering moot any consideration of forcible individual countermeasures by the US 'short of Article 51'. Yet, in the *Nicaragua* case the ICJ had also flagged the same issue by way of an *obiter dictum* so that one might have expected the Court to recall it, had it attributed great significance to it. Perhaps, therefore, the ICJ's silence in the *Oil Platforms* case suggests that the Court was not too eager to confirm the question that it had asked in the *Nicaragua* case, and instead chose to lower the gravity threshold for the concept of armed attack[174] in order to reduce the gap between Article 2(4) and Article 51.[175]

On a final terminological note, it is worth mentioning that it was surprising to see the ICJ using the term 'countermeasures' in that specific context. This is because the term came into use through the ILC as a modern term replacing that of *reprisals* within the legal framework of state responsibility,[176] and the ICJ would observe in *Nuclear Weapons* that 'armed reprisals in time of peace...are considered to be unlawful'.[177]

bb) The use of force in an anti-colonial struggle

In the *Nicaragua* case, the ICJ explicitly left open the possibility that an exception to the prohibition of the use of force could have come into existence within the context of 'decolonization'[178] and this *obiter dictum* met with the criticism of Judge Schwebel.[179] In the light of the near completion of the decolonization process, it is unlikely that this controversy will have any bearing on the future jurisprudence of the Court.

cc) The state of necessity

In 1980, and again as Special Rapporteur of the ILC, Roberto Ago had expressed an open mind to the possibility that, under certain limited conditions, the state of necessity could serve as an independent exception from the prohibition of the use of force.[180] Subsequently, a few writers have gone further and have explicitly argued

173 *Oil Platforms*, Judgment, Separate Opinion of Judge Simma, para 12.

174 cf Section II.C.2.i(c).

175 For an observation pointing in that direction, see Ruys, *'Armed Attack' and Article 51 of the UN Charter*, 143.

176 Hubert Lesaffre, 'Countermeasures' in James Crawford, Alain Pellet, and Simon Olleson (eds), *The Law of International Responsibility* (Oxford: Oxford University Press, 2010), 471.

177 *Nuclear Weapons*, Advisory Opinion, para 46.

178 *Nicaragua*, Merits, para 206.

179 *Nicaragua*, Merits, Dissenting Opinion of Judge Schwebel, paras 179–81.

180 Roberto Ago, 'Addendum to the 8th Report on State Responsibility', *Yearbook of the International Law Commission*, 1980, vol II (1), 39 ff (paras 56 ff).

in favour of such an exception.[181] There is nothing in the jurisprudence of the ICJ suggesting that the Court would be amenable to accept such an exception. In the *Armed Activities* case, for example, one would have expected the ICJ, after having rejected the claim of self-defence, to deal with such an exception had it been inclined to recognize it in principle.[182]

dd) Forcible rescue actions abroad

In the *Tehran Hostages* case, the ICJ stated that it could not 'let pass without comment the incursion into the territory of Iran made by the United States military units on 24–25 April 1980' in order to liberate US nationals taken hostage at the time and the Court went on to express 'its concern' regarding this failed rescue attempt.[183] This has been the only encounter the ICJ has had with the controversial question whether there is a right of states to use (limited) force to protect their nationals abroad.[184] While it is clear that the ICJ's critical observation in the *Tehran Hostages* case is very far from indicating a willingness to favourably consider the possibility of such a right, it would go too far to treat this cursory remark as the rejection of such right.[185] This is because the ICJ recognized explicitly that it did not have jurisdiction to rule upon the 'legality of the operation... under the Charter of the United Nations and under general international law',[186] and it also explained its criticism on the ground that, under the specific circumstances of the case, the operation would 'undermine respect for the judicial process in international relations'.[187]

ee) Humanitarian intervention

In the *Nicaragua* case, the ICJ held:

In any event, while the United States might form its own appraisal of the situation as to respect for human rights in Nicaragua, the use of force could not be the appropriate method

[181] See eg Andreas Laursen, 'The Use of Force and (the State of) Necessity' (2004) 37 *Vanderbilt Journal of Transnational Law* 485; for two more recent examples, see (in the context of anticipatory self-defence) Andrea Bianchi and Yasmin Naqvi, *International Humanitarian Law and Terrorism* (Oxford: Hart, 2011), 19; and (albeit much more cautiously and in the context of humanitarian intervention); Michael Wood, 'The Law on the Use of Force: Current Challenges' (2007) 11 *Singapore Year Book of International Law* 11; the ILC eventually abstained from explicitly deciding the question either directly in Art 25 of its Articles on State Responsibility or in its commentary thereon; see Sarah Heathcote, 'Necessity' in Crawford, Pellet, and Olleson, *The Law of International Responsibility*, 498–9.

[182] The reference to the state of necessity in *Wall*, Advisory Opinion, is not situated in the context of possible justification of use of force.

[183] *Tehran Hostages*, Judgment, para 93.

[184] In *Wall*, Advisory Opinion, para 141, the Court held that Israel had 'the right, and indeed the duty to respond [to numerous indiscriminate and deadly acts of violence against its civilian population] in order to protect the life of its citizens. The measures taken are bound nonetheless to remain in conformity with applicable international law'; this statement is not only phrased in very general terms, but it is also not placed in the context of the specific legal question as to whether use of force could be justified.

[185] For the same view, Jennings, 'International Force and the International Court of Justice' in Cassese, *The Current Legal Regulation of the Use of Force*, 330–1.

[186] *Tehran Hostages*, Judgment, para 94.

[187] *Tehran Hostages*, Judgment, para 93.

to monitor or ensure such respect. With regard to the steps actually taken, the protection of human rights, a strictly humanitarian objective, cannot be compatible with the mining of ports, the destruction of oil installations, or again with the training, arming and equipping of the *contras*. The Court concludes that the argument derived from the preservation of human rights cannot afford a legal justification for the conduct of the United States, and cannot in any event be reconciled with the legal strategy of the respondent State, which is based on the right of collective self-defence.[188]

In the light of this statement, it would seem impossible to suggest that in *Nicaragua* the Court saw any place for the use of force to end serious human rights violations in another state. Yet, as the ICJ itself pointed out, the 'legal strategy of the respondent State' was not to claim a right to use force to avert a 'humanitarian catastrophe'. Accordingly, the Court dealt with the matter only cursorily.

The legal claim that a state is entitled, under certain circumstances, to use force unilaterally to avert a humanitarian catastrophe in another state was subsequently brought before the ICJ in 1999 by Belgium in the *Case Concerning Legality of Use of Force (Serbia and Montenegro v. Belgium)*.[189] The ICJ was, however, precluded from addressing this justification of the 'Kosovo intervention' in the various *Legality of Use of Force* cases for lack of jurisdiction.[190]

In the *Genocide case*, the ICJ recognized the duty of states to prevent genocide even beyond their own borders. When the Court specified the parameters of that duty, it was careful to add that states 'may only act within the limits permitted by international law'.[191] The ICJ thus precluded the possibility of relying on its judgment in support of a right to (forcible unilateral) humanitarian intervention to prevent *genocide*.[192]

ff) On the possible emergence of new exceptions through subsequent practice

The ICJ has not directly addressed the question of whether a new exception to the prohibition of the use of force could come into existence through state practice. In the context of the prohibition of intervention, however, the Court stated in the *Nicaragua* case that 'reliance by a State on a novel right or an unprecedented exception to the principle might, if shared in principle by other States, tend towards a modification of customary international law'.[193] While this sentence was directly concerned only with the prohibition of intervention and the change of *customary*

188 *Nicaragua*, Merits, para 268.

189 *Case Concerning Legality of Force (Serbia and Montenegro v. Belgium)*, Provisional Measures of 10 May 1999, CR 99/15.

190 See eg *Case Concerning Legality of Force (Serbia and Montenegro v. Belgium)*, Judgment, Preliminary Objections of 15 Dec 2004, para 129.

191 *Case concerning the Application of the Convention on the Prevention and Punishment of the Crime of Genocide (Bosnia and Herzegovina v. Serbia and Montenegro)*, Judgment of 26 Feb 2007, para 437.

192 This is emphasized by Bruno Simma, 'Genocide and the International Court of Justice' in Christoph Safferling and Eckart Conze (eds), *The Genocide Convention Sixty Years after its Adoption* (The Hague: TMC Asser Press, 2010), 262.

193 *Nicaragua*, Merits, para 207.

international law, it can perhaps also be read as an indication that the Court does not wish to exclude the possibility that a new exception to the prohibition of the use of force might emerge.[194] In that regard, in the *Nicaragua* case, the ICJ had dealt with a case of forcible intervention so that it had to apply the two prohibitions in a closely intertwined manner. Also in the *Nicaragua* case, the Court developed its vision of an essentially identical corpus of international law on the use of force based on both the UN Charter and customary international law. Accordingly, one would expect the Court not to confine the relevance of the emergence of a new exception to the prohibition of the use of force to the realm of custom.

D. The Prohibition of the *Threat* of Force

The prohibition of the *threat* of use of force has received comparatively little attention in state practice and international legal scholarship and this is mirrored in the case law of the ICJ.[195] The Court explicitly dealt with this aspect of 'the principle of the non-use of force' only on the occasion of the *Nuclear Weapons* case and, due to the nature of the proceedings, in the abstract. The one substantial statement made by the Court in that advisory opinion is brief, though of considerable importance. The ICJ held that 'if it is to be lawful, the declared readiness of a state to use force must be a use of force that is in conformity of the Charter'.[196]

[194] For the same view, see Christine Gray, *International Law and the Use of Force* (3rd edn, Oxford: Oxford University Press, 2008), 8.

[195] But see Francis Grimal, *Threats of Force: International Law and Strategy* (Abingdon: Routledge, 2012); and Nikolas Stürchler, *The Threat of Force in International Law* (Cambridge: Cambridge University Press, 2007); see also Michael Wood, 'Use of Force, Prohibition of Threat' in Rüdiger Wolfrum (ed), *Max Planck Encyclopedia of Public International Law*, vol X (Oxford: Oxford University Press, 2012), 620.

[196] *Nuclear Weapons*, Advisory Opinion, para 47; for an analysis of this statement, see James A. Green and Francis Grimal, 'The Threat of Force as Action in Self-Defense Under International Law' (2011) 44 *Vanderbilt Journal of Transnational Law* 292; those authors also argue that the ICJ addressed the prohibition of the threat of force *implicitly* in *Corfu Channel* in two respects. They observe (at 292–3) that the Court, after having qualified Operation Retail 'as the manifestation of a policy of force' (cf Section II.B.4), went on to say that it 'did not consider that the action of the British Navy was a demonstration of force for the purpose of exercising political pressure on Albania' (*Corfu Channel*, Merits, 35), and they infer from that remark that the ICJ recognized the possibility of breaching the prohibition of the use of force without at the same time breaching the prohibition of the threat of force. This may be a possible inference, but the precise significance of the whole passage remains uncertain as pointed out in Section II.B.4). Green and Grimal also argue that the ICJ implicitly accepted the possibility of justifying an otherwise unlawful threat of force as a measure of self-defence. This inference is drawn from another passage of the judgment in *Corfu Channel* in which the Court said about an earlier passage of UK warships through the Corfu Channel that, in the light of the fact that the warships had been 'at action stations', the intention of the UK had to be taken 'to demonstrate such force that she [Albania] would abstain from firing again on passing ships' (*Corfu Channel*, Merits, 31). As the ICJ did not 'characterize these measures taken by the United Kingdom authorities as a violation of Albania's sovereignty' (ibid), the Court, according to Green and Grimal, must have considered the otherwise unlawful threat of force by the UK as a legitimate

III. Some Reflections on the Overall Picture of the Jurisprudence of the Court

The ICJ has addressed a broad range of legal issues concerning the legality of the unilateral use of force by states in their international relations. Perhaps the most striking feature of the Court's rich jurisprudence on 'the principle of non-use of force' is its apodictic style. The ICJ has stated the law as if neither ambiguities nor controversies existed. It has accordingly almost never entered into an exegesis (which would deserve that term) of the *texts* of Articles 2(4) and 51 of the UN Charter, nor has it had a closer look at the practice of states as it has evolved in the course of particular incidents[197] involving the use of force. The Court's general approach finds its most remarkable expression in the statement made in the *Nicaragua* case that there 'appears now to be *general* agreement on the nature of the acts which can be treated as constituting armed attacks'.[198] In the light of the many (and at times quite heated) controversies surrounding the concept of an armed attack[199] (and some of those controversies had already come to light through dissenting judicial opinions),[200] the ICJ's claim of a 'general agreement' had an almost unintended irony.

Yet, and this holds true irrespective of the many criticisms voiced in international legal scholarship on various aspects of the ICJ's jurisprudence on the use of force,[201] it is fair to assume that the Court, be it only by virtue of its institutional prominence, was remarkably successful in clarifying the law and in influencing state practice in accordance with its interpretations.[202] The ICJ is likely to have contributed to the

measure of self-defence 'because of the preceding use of force by Albania'. With respect, this reads much into a passage in which the ICJ did not even use the term 'threat of force'. Besides, if one absolutely wishes to read this part of the judgment in *Corfu Channel* as implicitly dealing with the prohibition of the threat of force, it would be much more natural to read it as foreshadowing the *Court's* approach in *Nuclear Weapons*: the threat of force by the UK was lawful because it did no more than signal the intention to defend itself in the case of (renewed) armed attacks against their warships.

197 On the considerable legal significance of that part of state practice, see Michael Reisman, 'The Incident as a Decisional Unit in International Law (1984–5) 10 *Yale Journal of International Law* 1.

198 *Nicaragua*, Merits, para 195 (emphasis added).

199 Ruys, *'Armed Attack' and Article 51 of the UN Charter*.

200 *Nicaragua*, Merits, Dissenting Opinion of Judge Schwebel, paras 162–71; Dissenting Opinion of Judge Jennings, 542–4.

201 James A. Green arrives at the following rather grim conclusion: 'in the cases that have reached the Court, it has demonstrated itself to be unsuitable to deal with the crucial question of self-defence in international law'; Green, *The International Court of Justice and Self-Defence in International Law*, 210.

202 These reflections are concerned with the ICJ's function to ascertain and to prudently develop the law. While a detailed assessment of the Court's success in exercising its dispute settlement function in the field currently under discussion is beyond the ambit of this text, it may at least be said that it will probably pose quite a challenge to recognize more than limited success in that latter respect.

firm entrenchment of a modern law governing (and so limiting) the use of force in international relations. (The 'death' of Article 2(4) may have occasionally been declared by scholars in the heat of the moment,[203] but not by states.) The Court has probably also had an effect upon the consolidation of the understanding of the prohibition of the use of force as being 'all-inclusive' in nature.[204] It has certainly provided a powerful incentive for states increasingly to frame their justifications for the unilateral use of force as measures of *self-defence*[205] against *armed attacks*.[206] Finally, it would seem that the ICJ's view on the concept of collective self-defence[207] has by and large been accepted in state practice[208] and that the Court has increasingly induced states to comply with the duty to report their use of force in (alleged) self-defence to the Security Council.[209]

On the other hand, it is impossible to ignore the significant extent to which ambiguities and controversies continue to characterize the international law on the use of force. This is partly due to a lack of occasions on which the ICJ is able to state the law in certain important respects. But significant controversies also continue to surround legal questions that the Court has already sought to clarify. The uncertainties begin at the most fundamental level and concern the very concept of 'force'.[210] The Court has made it clear that 'economic coercion' does not, as such, amount to a use of force, and this position appears to enjoy almost universal acceptance by states. However, the ICJ's jurisprudence does little to guide the emerging debate as to whether hostile cyber operations may reach the level of a use of force, and the existing uncertainty in that respect necessarily also affects the concept of 'armed attack'.[211] As regards the ICJ's construction of the concept of 'armed attack' *ratione materiae*,[212] the US, for its part, has declared in the clearest possible terms its dissent from the Court's recognition of a gravity threshold.[213] Indeed, the same critical position has been adopted in the Chatham House Principles.[214] In that context, the

[203] cf Section II.A.5. [204] cf Section II.B.2.

[205] On the ICJ's reserved position on possible other exceptions, see Section II.C.2.ii.

[206] cf Section II.C.2.i(a)(aa); this is not to say, however, that *all* states have *necessarily* abandoned any claim to self-defence rights exceeding the case of an (imminent) armed attack; international legal *scholarship* has always been predominantly in favour of seeing an (actual or imminent) armed attack as a *conditio sine qua non* for the right of self-defence; interestingly, however, there would now also seem to be widespread endorsement of this position among *Anglo-American* international lawyers; see the 'Chatham House Principles', 965; and Schmitt, *Tallinn Manual on the International Law Applicable to Cyber Warfare*, 54.

[207] cf Section II.C.2.i(b). [208] Gray, *International Law and the Use of Force*, 188.

[209] Gray, *International Law and the Use of Force*, 121. [210] cf Section II.B.4.

[211] Schmitt, *Tallinn Manual on the International Law Applicable to Cyber Warfare*, 54 ff.

[212] cf Section II.C.2.i(c)(aa).

[213] William H. Taft, IV, 'Self-Defense and the *Oil Platforms* Decision' (2004) 29 *Yale Journal of International Law* 302: 'For its part, if the United States is attacked with deadly force by the military personnel of another State, it reserves its inherent right preserved by the U.N. Charter to defend itself and its citizens'; for the *ambiguous* practice of other states, see Green, *The International Court of Justice and Self-Defence in International Law*, 121 ff.

[214] At 966.

ICJ has not only been unsuccessful in coming up with an interpretation of the law that commands general agreement, but it has even contributed to confusing the state of the law. This confusion was caused by alluding, in one of the most problematic aspects of its entire jurisprudence on the use of force,[215] to the possibility of a right to adopt individual forcible countermeasures 'short of Article 51',[216] in order to alleviate the consequences that might otherwise result from the gap which, according to the ICJ, exists between Articles 2(4) and 51 of the UN Charter. With a view to the concept of 'armed attack' *ratione personae*, the present state of the Court's jurisprudence is difficult to define with precision. As yet, the ICJ's jurisprudence does not provide anything close to *clear* authority for a right of self-defence which would go beyond the case of an armed attack attributable (under the Court's very stringent standard) to the state on whose territory the defensive operation is to take place. Such a restrictive view of the right of self-defence has, to put it mildly, never been uncontroversial. Indeed, state practice after 9/11 has certainly not been moving in this direction.[217] Apart from the concept of 'armed attack', it is also difficult to say that the Court has been successful in clarifying the legally possible goal (or goals?) of self-defence action as well as the precise meaning of the requirements of *necessity* and *proportionality*.[218] Finally, the ICJ has explicitly left open the question of *anticipatory* self-defence,[219] and has yet squarely to address the hotly disputed cases of a use of force to protect nationals in acute physical danger abroad[220] or to avert a humanitarian catastrophe.[221] The existence of this grey area, which the ICJ has, to date, not had the occasion to eliminate, forms an important part of the background against which the states parties to the Statute of the International Criminal Court have qualified the act of aggression for the purposes of the definition of the crime of aggression. They have qualified it using the words 'which, by its character, gravity and scale, constitutes a manifest violation of the Charter of the United Nations'.[222]

[215] For just a few examples of the widespread scholarly critique, see, Dinstein, *War, Aggression and Self-Defence*, 209 and 254; Greenwood, 'The International Court of Justice and the Use of Force' in Lowe and Fitzmaurice, *Fifty Years of the International Court of Justice*, 380 ff; Ruys, *'Armed Attack' and Article 51 of the UN Charter*, 141.

[216] It would be preferable had the Court, at least, called those measures 'limited measures of *self-defence*' instead of 'countermeasures' to clearly separate them from unlawful armed *reprisals*.

[217] Ruys, *'Armed Attack' and Article 51 of the UN Charter*, 394 ff, 447 ff; for a 'collective scholarly dissent' from the restrictive position referred to in the previous text, see the 'Chatham House Principles', 969.

[218] Suffice it to refer to the critical response by the then legal adviser of the US, William Taft, IV, to the ICJ's proportionality and necessity analysis in *Oil Platforms*; Taft, 'Self-Defense and the *Oil Platforms* Decision', 303 ff.

[219] cf Section II.C.2.i(a)(bb). [220] cf Section II.C.2.ii(d). [221] cf Section II.C.2.ii(d).

[222] Emphasis added; Art 8*bis* of the Statute of the International Criminal Court; Review Conference RC/Res 6, 11 June 2010, *Review Conference Official Records*, RC/11, part II, 17; for the connection between the 'grey area' of international law on the use of force and the requirement of a 'manifest' violation of the UN Charter in the definition of the crime of aggression, see Stefan Barriga, 'Negotiating

It remains to be seen how the ICJ in the future deals with a case of anticipatory self-defence, a cross-border use of force in defence of a non-state armed attack, a forcible rescue mission abroad, and a use of force to avert an impending humanitarian catastrophe. With respect to the latter, it may be predicted that the Court would rather frame the legal issue as one of the emergence (or not) of a new exception to the prohibition of the use of force rather than recognizing a residual legal relevance for the state of necessity to preclude the wrongfulness of state use of force. In a case of genuine humanitarian intervention, the ICJ is therefore likely to apply the standard for legal change through state practice as set out in the *Nicaragua* case.[223] While this standard is undoubtedly a stringent one, the ICJ was wise enough *not* to elevate the threshold even further through a determination that the prohibition of the use of force is not only 'all-inclusive', but also forms in its entirety part of *jus cogens*.[224] The considerable challenge in dealing with the remaining 'hard cases' of anticipatory self-defence, defensive action against a non-state armed attack, and the forcible protection of nationals abroad results from the fact that, in their respective ways, the text of both Articles 2(4) and 51 of the UN Charter and subsequent state practice are fraught with ambiguity. The ICJ has yet to recognize that such an ambiguity exists and it has therefore yet to reveal a method that would allow it convincingly to address such an ambiguity. At the present time, no more can be said than the ICJ has not closed the door to accommodating the controversial legal claims to anticipatory self-defence, to the use of cross-border force necessary to repel a non-state armed attack, and to conduct, under well-defined and stringent conditions, a forcible rescue mission abroad within the legal framework as it was established by (and under the influence of) Articles 2(4) and 51 of the UN Charter.[225]

IV. Conclusion

> The power, position and prestige of the United States had been challenged by another state; and law simply does not deal with

the Amendments on the Crime of Aggression' in Stefan Barriga and Claus Kreß (eds), *The Travaux Préparatoires of the Crime of Aggression* (Cambridge: Cambridge University Press, 2012), 29; Claus Kreß and Leonie von Holtzendorff, 'The Kampala Compromise on the Crime of Aggression' (2010) 8 *Journal of International Criminal Justice* 1192–3.

[223] cf Section II.C.2.ii(f).

[224] cf Section II.A.5; for a thoughtful analysis of this point, see Ruys, *'Armed Attack' and Article 51 of the UN Charter*, 24 ff.

[225] The alternative for the ICJ would be to ask (as it would probably do in the case of a genuine humanitarian intervention) whether state practice has given rise to a new exception to the prohibition of the use of

> such questions of ultimate power—power that comes close to the sources of sovereignty.[226]

This famous statement, made by Dean Acheson looking back on the Cuban Missile Crisis, may serve as a useful reminder of the challenge of overcoming effectively the idea of a sovereign *jus ad bellum* that was so firmly entrenched in 19th-century legal and political discourse on this subject matter. In the light of the powerful historical legacy and the realities of power struggles within a decentralized international legal order, the ICJ may well have felt that the UN Charter's provisions on the use of force remained vulnerable in practice for the foreseeable future. At the same time, the early judgment in the *Corfu Channel* case had already made it clear that the Court believed its mandate to bring the prohibition of the use of force from the books into practice to be of central importance. In the same vein, the ICJ, in the *Nicaragua* case, stated that the law on the use of force is based on the '*fundamental* principle outlawing the use of force in international relations'.[227] In the *Armed Activities* case, the ICJ made explicit its basic conviction that 'The prohibition of the use of force is a *cornerstone* of the United Nations Charter'.[228] The ICJ has not elaborated on this determination, but it is fair to assume that it implies recognition of the fact that the prohibition of the use of force (irrespective of the well-defined exceptions to it, of course) is constitutive for the very existence of (an international) legal order in the full meaning of the term.

The sense of a judicial duty to consolidate a vulnerable rule of paramount importance to the international legal order would explain why the ICJ has not only firmly rejected a political question doctrine with respect of the use of force[229] and has insisted on its competence to conduct judicial proceedings *pari passu* with the political deliberations within the Security Council.[230] It would also explain why the ICJ, in both the *Nicaragua* and *Oil Platforms* cases, resorted to a rather broad interpretation of its jurisdiction to deal with the legality of the use of force by a powerful[231] state[232] and why the Court has not demonstrated much hesitance in expressing its legal views on the regulation of the use of force through *obiter dicta*.

force; for a legal view pointing in this direction for 'certain forms of evacuation operations', see Randelzhofer and Nolte, 'Article 51' Simma et al, *The Charter of the United Nations*, 1413 (marginal note 28 *in fine*).

[226] Dean Acheson, *Proceedings of the American Society of International Law* (1963), 14.

[227] *Nicaragua*, Merits, para 181 (emphasis added).

[228] *Armed Activities*, Judgment, para 148 (emphasis added).

[229] cf Section II.A.2.

[230] cf Section II.A.3.

[231] In another famous sentence in *Corfu Channel* (Merits, 35), the ICJ explicitly assumed the role of a guardian against possible abuses of 'the most powerful States'; against the background of that pronouncement, it is interesting to note that the ICJ was perhaps more reluctant than necessary to deal with the use of force in *Land and Maritime Boundary between Cameroon and Nigeria (Cameroon v. Nigeria: Equatorial Guinea intervening)*, Merits, Judgment of 10 Oct 2002, paras 308–24; Green (*The International Court of Justice and Self-Defence in International Law*, 206) takes this inconsistency as pointing towards the possibility that the Court might have been 'too eager to pronounce upon disputes involving superpower states'.

[232] The Court's rather liberal approach to its jurisdiction in *Oil Platforms*, met with the more general critical observation by Judge Owada: 'The general problem of self-defence under international law is

Much more importantly, the sense of a duty to consolidate a vulnerable rule of paramount importance may also provide one reason for the fact that, overall, the ICJ has adopted a markedly prohibitive stance on the unilateral use of force by states. In the *Nicaragua* case, in particular, the ICJ chose the more prohibitive legal view wherever the law was arguably open to conflicting interpretations.[233] As a result, the *Nicaragua* judgment reads a little bit as if the Court, at the time of its first major encounter with the modern international law on the use of force, felt the need to strengthen the paradigm shift on the use of force brought about through the UN Charter by pronouncing in favour of the most prohibitive conceivable legal framework.

As has been shown, none of those legal findings have been overturned in the ICJ's subsequent jurisprudence. Yet, there are subtle indications in both the *Oil Platforms* and *Armed Activities* cases that the Court may have begun to reconsider certain legal issues in a manner that nuances the *Nicaragua* Court's prohibitive rigour. Those indications concern the concept of an 'armed attack'. *Ratione materiae*, the ICJ signalled in the *Oil Platforms* case that the gravity threshold for an armed attack (by a state) may well be lower than one would have assumed on the basis of the *Nicaragua* judgment.[234] And in both the *Oil Platforms* and *Armed Activities* cases the Court expressed (at least more clearly than before) an inclination to recognize the relevance of an *accumulation* of uses of force in this specific context.[235] Perhaps even more importantly, the one sentence that the ICJ devoted to the problem of non-state armed attacks in the *Armed Activities* case,[236] may (with all due caution in the light of its sibylline nature) be taken to express the Court's awareness that there is a need to squarely address the matter should an appropriate occasion arise in the future. Perhaps, those very few and still barely visible elements pointing towards a little less prohibitive rigour indicate the ICJ's recognition of the fact that the 'principle of the non-use of force', despite occasional violations, has now reached a stage of considerable consolidation and that the remaining grey area, though being significant in scope (and comprising anticipatory self-defence, defence against non-state

an extremely complex and even controversial subject both in terms of theory and practice... [W]hile it is of utmost importance for the Court to pronounce its authoritative position on this general problem in a proper context, it should do so in a context where it should be possible for the Court to deal with the problem squarely in a full-fledged manner, with all its ramifications both in terms of the law and the facts involved' (*Oil Platforms*, Judgment, Separate Opinion of Judge Owada, para 38); this critique has been taken up and elaborated upon by Green, *The International Court of Justice and Self-Defence in International Law*, 199 ff. There may be some merit in this line of criticism, though it would not seem that any questionable legal position adopted by the ICJ in its jurisprudence can be easily explained on the ground that its jurisdiction rested on shaky ground or was partial only.

[233] The *dictum* concerning a possible right to individual forcible countermeasures 'short of Article 51' (cf Section II.C.2.ii(a)) constitutes the only exception.

[234] cf Section II.B.2.i(a) and Section II.B.4.i; citation accompanying n 111.

[235] cf Section II.B.2.i(a) and Section II.B.4.i; citations accompanying nn 112 and 113.

[236] cf Section II.C.2.i(a) and Section II.C.4.ii; citation accompanying n 126.

armed attacks, forcible rescue missions, and genuine humanitarian interventions), is not one which can be satisfactorily dealt with by a simple presumption in favour of prohibition.

If this were the ICJ's evolving position, it should be welcomed. International law has come an extremely long way from the 19th-century idea of a *jus ad bellum* to the present-day situation of a firmly entrenched prohibition of the use of force. There would now seem to be 'general agreement'[237] among states not only about the elimination of a 'sovereign right to go to war', but also about the prohibition to use force in self-help to secure or enforce legal rights, and even about the impossibility of invoking a state of *necessity* (as distinct from a situation of *self-defence*) in order to forcibly avert a serious threat. This constitutes a remarkable development for a legal order without reliable centralized enforcement powers and the ICJ deserves credit for having contributed to that state of affairs.

The remaining grey area on the international law on the use of force is of a different kind. This grey area, for the most part, covers cases where states are confronted with (imminent) illegal physical violence, which is being directed against their own territory or their own extraterritorial emanations, and where the use of force may constitute the only effective protection against such violence.[238] In order to deal with the undisputable legal ambiguities governing these cases, the ICJ could (explicitly or implicitly) state the one 'paramount background principle of a *Dworkinian* kind'[239] to have the use of force in international relations reduced to the greatest possible extent in order to derive from that principle the general interpretative presumption against the admission of exceptions to the prohibition of the use of force. Such an approach would be profoundly questionable, though. It must already be doubted whether such a principle exists (or, at least, that exists without any competitor) and apart from that such a principle would not necessarily justify the interpretive presumption in question. It should rather be recognized that imminent armed attacks, massive transnational violence by non-state actors, and life-threatening violence against nationals abroad constitute very serious threats to powerful and weak states alike. To postulate a Dworkinian principle that requires states only passively

[237] This is to use the words of the ICJ in *Nicaragua* (cf Section II.C.2.i(a) and Section II.C.4.i citation accompanying n 105, but in their proper context (for the critique of the context in which those words were used by the Court, cf text accompanying n 200).

[238] The case of genuine humanitarian intervention is different because such an *international* use of force aims at ending (massive) *internal* violence. It may thus be said that the acceptance of genuine humanitarian intervention implies a shift at the level of the '*Dworkinian* principles' (to which the following text will allude) which underlie the modern international legal order as established in 1945. In the light of the evolution of the practice under the UN's collective security system, it is difficult to deny that such a shift is underway. The hard question is whether the shift has reached a point that would justify even *unilateral* humanitarian intervention as a measure of last resort.

[239] For a stimulating reflection about the fundamental controversies haunting international law on the use of force in the light of '*Dworkinian* principles', see Green, *The International Court of Justice and Self-Defence in International Law*, 182 ff.

to endure such a threat if the use of force constitutes the only effective remedy, is therefore open to serious argument. What is more, to overstretch the rigour of the prohibition of the use of force would mean to lose an instrument to *deter* transnational violence from occurring in the first place. It is therefore also open to serious question whether an overly restrictive view on the lawful use of force effectively contributes to keeping the use of force in international relations to a minimum. Be that as it may, quite a few subjects of the largely decentralized international legal order would certainly regard the loss of this instrument of deterrence as a luxury which they cannot afford.

In conclusion, neither the effectiveness of the prohibition of the use of force nor the ICJ's authority would suffer from the Court adopting a somewhat less prohibitive approach in dealing with anticipatory self-defence, with the defensive use of force against massive transnational non-state violence and with the forcible protection of nationals abroad under well-defined conditions. Perhaps quite a number of states, be they more or less powerful, would then even reconsider their decision to qualify their submission to the ICJ's jurisdiction by some type of 'war exclusion clause'.[240] It would be somewhat simplistic to question the 'peace-loving' nature of those many states that have thus far decided *not* to accept the ICJ's jurisdiction over the use of force. This decision is much more likely to have been animated by the fear that the state concerned could, in a future case, be compelled to use force to avert an imminent armed attack, to defend itself against massive transnational non-state violence, or to forcibly rescue nationals who have come under an acute threat to their lives abroad. In view of the sad but real possibility that such a case may indeed arise, those many states that do not currently accept the ICJ's jurisdiction, simply do not wish to be subjected by the ICJ to a degree of prohibitive rigour which they—legitimately—deem unreasonable.

[240] On this clause, see Shabtai Rosenne, *The Law and Practice of the International Court—1920–2005. Vol II: Jurisdiction* (Leiden: Martinus Nijhoff, 2006), 772.

CHAPTER 26

THE PROHIBITION OF THE USE OF FORCE IN ARBITRATIONS AND FACT-FINDING REPORTS

VAIOS KOUTROULIS

I. Introduction

THE case law of the International Court of Justice (ICJ) occupies a central part in the analysis of the rules relating to the prohibition of the use of force.[1] However, aside from the ICJ, some arbitral tribunals, as well as commissions of inquiry or fact-finding missions, have also been called to examine these rules. This chapter analyses how these bodies have interpreted and applied *jus contra bellum*, that is, the prohibition of the use of force in international relations and its exceptions after the adoption in 1945 of the UN Charter.[2]

[1] See Claus Kreß, 'The International Court of Justice and the 'Principle of Non-Use of Force', Chapter 25 in this volume.

[2] The rules relating to the prohibition of the use of force in international relations are designated by the terms *jus ad bellum* or *jus contra bellum*. The term *jus contra bellum* is preferred here because it reflects more accurately the content of the legal regime governing the use of force in international law after the adoption of the UN Charter; Olivier Corten, *The Law Against War: The Prohibition on the Use of Force in Contemporary International Law* (Oxford: Hart, 2010), 2.

According to the ICJ, 'the word arbitration, for purposes of public international law, usually refers to "the settlement of differences between States by judges of their own choice, and on the basis of respect for law"'.[3] Along with judicial settlement, arbitration is cited in Article 33 of the UN Charter as a means of pacific settlement of disputes.[4] They both fall under what is termed 'legal settlement of disputes, meaning one in which the disputing parties submit their differences to a third party who renders a binding decision based exclusively on the application of legal principles.'[5] Leaving aside international commercial arbitration (or private international arbitration)[6]—which, given the nature of the parties and the disputes involved, is of very limited interest to this study[7]—I will focus on two prominent arbitration precedents.[8] The first is the

[3] *Case concerning Maritime Delimitation and Territorial Questions between Qatar and Bahrain (Qatar v. Bahrain)*, Merits, Judgment of 16 Mar 2001, ICJ Rep 2001, 40, 76, para 113. The citation is from Art XV of the 1899 Hague Convention for the Peaceful Adjustment of International Differences. Further sources are cited by the Court in its judgment.

[4] UN Charter, Art 33, adopted on 26 June 1945, available at <http://www.un.org/en/documents/charter/chapter6.shtml>.

[5] Charles H. Brower II, 'Arbitration' in Rüdiger Wolfrum (ed), *Max Planck Encyclopedia of Public International Law* (Oxford: Oxford University Press, 2012), vol I, 531, 532, para 3. See also John G. Merrills, *International Dispute Settlement* (5th edn, Cambridge: Cambridge University Press, 2011), 83. The criterion of the binding character of the award excludes precedents such as the Badinter Arbitration Commission for the Former Yugoslavia whose opinions did not possess such a character and thus cannot be considered as an arbitral award; see Malgosia Fitzmaurice, 'Badinter Commission (for the Former Yugoslavia)' in Wolfrum, *Max Planck Encyclopedia of Public International Law*, vol I, 775, 784, para 37.

[6] Merrills, *International Dispute Settlement*, 106–11; see generally Richard H. Kreindler and Rita Heinemann, 'Commercial Arbitration, International' in Wolfrum, *Max Planck Encyclopedia of Public International Law*, vol II, 386.

[7] Only very few incidental references to *jus contra bellum* can be found in international commercial arbitration cases. See *Corn Products International Inc. v. United Mexican States*, Decision on Responsibility, 15 Jan 2008, North American Free Trade Agreement (NAFTA) Arbitration Tribunal, ICSID Case No ARB(AF)/04/1, 146 ILR 581, 625, para 149, and 629, para 158 (confirming that countermeasures cannot affect the prohibition of the use of force and citing Art 50 of the 2001 Draft Articles on Responsibility of States for Internationally Wrongful Acts). See also *Damia Cement Ltd v. National Bank of Pakistan*, Award on Jurisdiction, 18 Dec 1976, International Chamber of Commerce, Arbitration Tribunal, 67 ILR 611. In this case, the main question was whether the Sept 1985 hostilities between India and Pakistan amounted to a state of war terminating the bank guarantee and with it the arbitration clause which was the basis for the arbitrator's jurisdiction. The Arbitrator decided that this was not the case. Among other reasons, he held that the consequence of the obligation not to resort to the threat or use of force for UN member states was that '*in case of doubt* as to the answer to be given to th[e] question [on the existence of a state of war], the answer should be negative rather than affirmative, for the existence of a state of war can certainly *not be presumed* between members of the UNO.' At 619, para 27 (emphasis in original).

[8] The award in the boundary dispute between the Emirate of Dubai and the Emirate of Sharjah also contains limited references to *jus contra bellum*; *Dubai–Sharjah Border Arbitration*, Award, 19 Oct 1981, Court of Arbitration, 91 ILR 543. The award was concerned with the delimitation of the land and maritime boundary between the two federate entities of the United Arab Emirates. It referred briefly to *jus contra bellum* rules, in relation to Arts 51 and 52 of the Vienna Convention on the Law of Treaties and the notion of coercion. The Court affirmed that in the 1930s 'there was no firmly established rule of international law which prohibited the threat of the use of force' (at 570). Moreover, referring to

Commission established to deal with claims between Eritrea and Ethiopia (Eritrea–Ethiopia Claims Commission (EECC), in connection with the conflict that took place between the two states in 1998–2000.[9] Between 2005 and 2009, the Commission has dealt with *jus contra bellum* issues with respect to claims by Ethiopia that Eritrea had violated the prohibition to use force.[10] The second is the 2007 award of an arbitral tribunal constituted under Annex VII to the United Nations Convention on the Law of the Sea (UNCLOS)[11] in a maritime boundary dispute that arose between Guyana and Suriname.[12]

Aside from the legal means of settlement of international disputes, Article 33 of the UN Charter sets out a number of diplomatic ones, namely negotiation, inquiry, mediation, and conciliation.[13] Inquiry or fact-finding is defined as a

> form of international dispute settlement...aimed primarily at clarifying the disputed facts through impartial investigation, which would then facilitate the parties' objective of identifying the final solution to the dispute....The fact-finding process may involve an impartial and neutral body carrying out the inquiry...or a joint body consisting of the representatives of the disputing parties which conducts the fact-finding activities. Additionally, the same body charged with the establishment of the facts may be required by the parties to evaluate the facts, including a legal assessment of the responsibility and relevant recommendations for the future resolution of the dispute.[14]

The creation of commissions of inquiry or fact-finding commissions was set out in the 1899 Hague Convention on the pacific settlement of disputes[15] and the relevant articles were put to use only five years later in the Dogger Bank incident, concerning the Russian fleet firing at British trawlers in the North Sea.[16] In its report, the Dogger Bank commission of inquiry held that it was unjustifiable for the Russian fleet to

the special declaration on economic coercion adopted by the 1969 Vienna Conference on the Law of Treaties, the Court held that 'the expression "threat or use of force" could not have, earlier in 1956, comprehended the use of economic coercion' (at 569).

[9] Established by the Agreement between the Government of the Federal Democratic Republic of Ethiopia and the Government of the State of Eritrea, Art 5 para 1, Algiers, 5 Dec 2000, 2138 UNTS 94, 97.

[10] EECC, Jus Ad Bellum: *Ethiopia's Claims 1–8*, Partial Award, 19 Dec 2005 (2009) XXVI RIAA 457; EECC, *Ethiopia's Damages Claims, Final Award*, 17 Aug 2009 (2009) XXVI RIAA 631; EECC, *Decision Number 7: Guidance Regarding* Jus ad Bellum *Liability*, 27 July 2007 (2009) XXVI RIAA 10.

[11] UNCLOS, Annex VII, Montego Bay, 10 Dec 1982, 1833 UNTS 3, 571.

[12] Arbitral Tribunal Constituted Pursuant to Article 287, and in Accordance with Annex VII of UNCLOS, *Guyana/Suriname*, Award of 17 Sept 2007 (2008) 47 ILM 166.

[13] UN Charter, Art 33. According to Merrills, the principal characteristic of these means of dispute settlement is that 'the parties retain control of the dispute and may accept or reject a proposed settlement as they see fit', Merrills, *International Dispute Settlement*, 83.

[14] Agnieszka Jacheć-Neale, 'Fact-Finding' in Wolfrum, *Max Planck Encyclopedia of Public International Law*, vol III, 1077, 1077–8, paras 1–2.

[15] Convention for the Peaceful Adjustment of International Differences, The Hague, 29 July 1899, reproduced in (1907) 1 *American Journal of International Law* 107, 112–14 (Arts IX–XIV).

[16] Tobias H. Irmscher, 'Dogger Bank Incident (1904)' in Wolfrum, *Max Planck Encyclopedia of Public International Law*, vol III, 190.

open fire and that the Russian admiral was responsible.[17] Since then, there have been many examples of commissions, missions, and panels established in order to investigate events and alleged violations of international law.[18] The fact-finding missions[19] that will be examined here are international missions established as impartial bodies by organs of international organizations. Thus, national fact-finding commissions,[20] reports by non-governmental organizations (NGOs), and reports by commissions established by initiatives from private individuals[21] are excluded from the scope of the chapter.[22]

Compared to the overall number of fact-finding missions, especially in the UN context, there are few which have touched upon questions of *jus contra bellum*, with four particular missions standing out. Two of them relate to the same incident: the interception on 31 May 2010 by Israeli armed forces of a flotilla of ships transporting humanitarian aid to the blockaded Gaza Strip.[23] On 27 September 2010, a fact-finding mission

[17] Finding of the International Commission of Inquiry organized under Article 9 of the Convention for the Pacific Settlement of International Disputes, of July 29, 1899, Report of the Commissioners, drawn up in accordance with Article VI of the declaration of St. Petersburg of the 12th (25th) November, 1904, reproduced in (1908) 2 *American Journal of International Law* 931. The 'unjustifiable' character of the Russian admiral's actions was founded on the fact that the trawlers did not commit any hostile act and that there were no torpedo boats in the vicinity, as the admiral had thought. However, the report offers no further legal analysis of the subject.

[18] See the references in Jacheć-Neale, 'Fact-Finding' in Wolfrum, *Max Planck Encyclopedia of Public International Law*, 1077–81, paras 3–16; Alain Pellet, 'Peaceful Settlement of International Disputes' in Wolfrum, *Max Planck Encyclopedia of Public International Law*, vol VIII, 201, 214, paras 49–51.

[19] Terminology varies widely with respect to fact-finding bodies; compare the denominations of the various bodies cited in nn 24–7. In this chapter, the term 'fact-finding missions' will be used.

[20] eg Turkish National Commission of Inquiry, 'Report on the Israeli Attack on the Humanitarian Aid and Convoy to Gaza on 31 May 2010', Feb 2011, Ankara, available at <http://www.mfa.gov.tr/data/Turkish%20Report%20Final%20-%20UN%20Copy.pdf>; the Public Commission to Examine the Maritime Incident of 31 May 2010: The Turkel Commission, Report: Part One, Jan 2011, available at <http://www.turkel-committee.gov.il/files/wordocs/8707200211english.pdf>.

[21] eg the commission established in 1982 by six lawyers and professors considered Israel's invasion in Lebanon. The commission published a report, *Israel in Lebanon: Report of the International Commission to Enquire into Reported Violations of International Law by Israel During its Invasion of Lebanon* (Reading: Ithaca Press, 1983).

[22] Cases where international experts were consulted but no distinct body of inquiry was established are also excluded. One relevant precedent exists in relation to the conflict between Iran and Iraq in 1980–8. Although the UN Security Council contemplated the creation by the Secretary-General of an impartial body entrusted with inquiring into responsibility for the conflict (see SC Res 598 (20 July 1987), para 6), no such body was officially created. The Secretary-General directly contacted the two states asking for their 'detailed views' on the subject and, in parallel, 'decided to consult separately some independent experts'. On the basis of the available information, in 1991 the Secretary-General submitted a report to the Security Council asserting that it was Iraq which violated the prohibition of the use of force; see Security Council, Further Report of the Secretary-General of the Implementation of Security Council Resolution 598 (1987), S/23273 (9 Dec 1991), 1–2, paras 4, 6–7.

[23] For an account of the relevant facts, see 'Palestine–Israeli attack on aid flotilla' (2010) 56 *Keesing's Record of World Events* 49865.

established by the UN Human Rights Council (HRC) delivered the first report on the incident[24] and the second report, on the same incident, was handed down in September 2011[25] by a panel of inquiry established by the UN Secretary-General. The third report was the outcome of an international fact-finding mission established by the Council of the European Union in relation to the 2008 conflict in Georgia.[26] Finally, the fourth report which will be analysed here was delivered by the independent fact-finding committee on Gaza established by the League of Arab States (LAS) in relation to the military offensive launched by Israel against Gaza from 27 December 2008 to 18 January 2009 (Operation Cast Lead).[27] Aside from these four cases, where necessary reference will also be made to other fact-finding missions, whose reports can shed some light on *jus contra bellum* rules. The 1962 report of the commission of inquiry established to determine the facts in the *Red Crusader* incident (when a Danish frigate arrested and opened fire when in pursuit on the British trawler *Red Crusader* in 1961) is a relevant example in this respect.[28]

The purpose of this chapter is to evaluate the approach of arbitral tribunals and fact-finding missions with respect to post-1945 rules regulating the use of force in international relations and to identify their contribution in determining the scope and content of those rules (Section III). However, this cannot be accurately appreciated without a clear understanding of the legal character and value of arbitral awards and fact-finding reports as such which are discussed in the following section.

[24] HRC, 'Report of the international fact-finding mission to investigate violations of international law, including international humanitarian and human rights law, resulting from the Israeli attacks on the flotilla of ships carrying humanitarian assistance', 27 Sept 2010, A/HRC/15/21 (hereafter HRC Flotilla Report).

[25] UN Secretary-General, Report of the Secretary-General's Panel of Inquiry on the 31 May 2010 Flotilla Incident, Sept 2011, available at <http://www.un.org/News/dh/infocus/middle_east/Gaza_Flotilla_Panel_Report.pdf> (hereafter Secretary-General's Panel Report). To the best of the author's knowledge, the report has not been given an official UN document number. The report was submitted to the Secretary-General on 2 Sept 2010; see 'Statement attributable to the Spokesperson for the Secretary-General of the Panel of Inquiry on the 31 May 2010 Flotilla Incident', 2 Sept 2011, available at <http://www.un.org/sg/statements/index.asp?nid=5482>.

[26] Independent International Fact-Finding Mission on the Conflict in Georgia, Report, vols I, II, III, Sept 2009, available at <http://www.ceiig.ch> (hereafter IIFFMCG Report).

[27] Security Council, Letter dated 1 October 2009 from the Permanent Observer of the League of Arab States to the United Nations addressed to the President of the Security Council, Annex, 'Report of the Independent Fact-Finding Committee on Gaza: No Safe Place', S/2009/537 (14 Oct 2009), 18 and 230 (hereafter LAS Gaza Report).

[28] Commission of Enquiry (Denmark–UK), *The Red Crusader*, 23 Mar 1962 (1967) 35 ILR 485. For another example of a report by a fact-finding mission with *jus contra bellum* considerations, see HRC, 'Implementation of General Assembly Resolution 60/251 of 15 March 2006 Entitled "Human Rights Council": Report of the Commission of Inquiry on Lebanon pursuant to Human Rights Council resolution S-2/1', A/HRC/3/2 (23 Nov 2006) (hereafter HRC Lebanon Report).

II. Legal Significance of Arbitral Awards and Fact-Finding Reports

As has already been pointed out, the findings of arbitral tribunals on *jus contra bellum* are binding upon the parties. Therefore, in the context of a specific international dispute, arbitral tribunals have a direct impact on the application of *jus contra bellum* rules. On the other hand, fact-finding reports are not legally binding, as the Secretary-General's panel of inquiry readily admits.[29] Looking beyond the limits of a specific dispute, it is important not only to evaluate the *jus contra bellum* findings of such decisions and reports but also to appreciate their influence more broadly on the interpretation and application of the rules on the prohibition of the use of force. Naturally, it is difficult to measure the extent of such an influence objectively. However, evidence can be found in the invocation of the awards and reports by states or by international tribunals in *jus contra bellum*-related cases.

Decisions by arbitral tribunals are 'judicial decisions' within the meaning of Article 38(1)(d) of the ICJ Statute and as such constitute subsidiary means for the determination of international law.[30] Although the control of the parties over the composition of arbitral tribunals is a key element of arbitration, the arbitrators are expected to be impartial and independent from the parties that appointed them.[31] These features add to the judicial value of the awards' findings. Nevertheless, the ad hoc nature of arbitral tribunals and their dispute-resolution role should be borne in mind when evaluating the interpretations advanced by arbitral awards:

> As ad hoc tribunals with no continuing existence, no institutional affiliation, and no capacity to affect legal interests of third States, arbitral tribunals may see the disputing parties as their sole audience and the resolution of the dispute as their sole task. . . . [W]hereas judicial settlement must view individual interests through the lens of community interests, arbitration may focus more directly on the particular interests of disputing parties.[32]

[29] Secretary-General's Panel Report, 10, para 14.

[30] Gilbert Guillaume, 'Can Arbitral Awards Constitute a Source of International Law under Article 38 of the Statute of the International Court of Justice?' in Yas Banifatemi and Emmanuel Gaillard (eds), *Precedent in International Arbitration* (New York: Juris Publishing, 2008), 105; Eric De Brabandere, 'Arbitral Decisions as a Source of International Investment Law' in Tarcisio Gazzini and Eric De Brabandere (eds), *International Investment Law: The Sources of Rights and Obligations* (Leiden: Martinus Nijhoff, 2012), 245, 247–50.

[31] Brower, 'Arbitration' in Wolfrum, *Max Planck Encyclopedia of Public International Law*, 541, para 50. For a recent example of a challenge against an arbitrator for lack of impartiality and independence, see Arbitral Tribunal constituted under Annex VII of the 1982 United Nations Convention on the Law of the Sea, *The Republic of Mauritius v. The United Kingdom of Great Britain and Northern Ireland*, Reasoned Decision on Challenge, 30 Nov 2011, available at <http://www.pca-cpa.org/showpage.asp?pag_id=1429>.

[32] Brower, 'Arbitration' in Wolfrum, *Max Planck Encyclopedia of Public International Law*, 533 and 546, paras 5 and 91 respectively.

Even so, arbitration does 'affect legal interests of third States' to some extent through the influence that arbitral awards exercise on the development of international law rules, in our case *jus contra bellum*. This has given rise to concerns that 'dispositive appreciations of variable quality ultimately inform the development of the law' while third states for various reasons remain silent on these 'appreciations'.[33] However, such influence, especially on *jus contra bellum* rules, should not be overestimated. Although there is no formal hierarchy between arbitral decisions and judicial decisions of international courts, in practice arbitral awards are adversely affected by the ad hoc nature of arbitration. International courts have a tendency to refer to their own case law and value the idea of consistency of jurisprudence, even without an obligation to do so,[34] thereby confirming, consolidating, and in some cases correcting previous findings. This is not easily transposable to arbitral tribunals in view of their ad hoc character. References to arbitral decisions by international courts, namely the ICJ, are relatively rare,[35] although some progress has been observed in recent years in this respect.[36] Given this reluctance, it seems that the value of each arbitral award as a precedent is determined on a case-by-case basis. As far as the arbitral findings on *jus contra bellum* are concerned, it is still too early to appreciate their concrete impact on the development of the relevant rules: first, the two most explicit findings on *jus contra bellum* are fairly recent[37] and, secondly, the ICJ has not dealt with a case bearing on *jus contra bellum* since these awards were delivered. In the end, as Jan Paulsson suggests, the impact of arbitral decisions comes down to the expertise of the arbitrators,[38] the quality of the legal reasoning, and the persuasiveness of the analysis adopted by the tribunal in what he refers to

[33] Sir Daniel Bethlehem, 'The Secret Life of International Law' (2012) 1 *Cambridge Journal of International and Comparative Law* 23, 32–3.

[34] *Case concerning application of the Convention on the Prevention and Punishment of the Crime of Genocide (Croatia v. Serbia)*, Preliminary Objections, Judgment of 18 Nov 2008, ICJ Rep 2008, 412, 428–9, para 53; *Case concerning the Land and Maritime Boundary between Cameroon and Nigeria (Cameroon v. Nigeria)*, Preliminary Objections, Judgment of 11 June 1998, ICJ Rep 1998, 275, 292, para 28; International Criminal Tribunal for the Former Yugoslavia, *Prosecutor v. Zlatko Aleksovski*, Judgment of 24 Mar 2000, Appeals Chamber, IT-95-14/1-A, paras 92–111; Mohamed Shahabuddeen, *Precedent in the World Court* (Cambridge: Cambridge University Press, 1996); Gilbert Guillaume, 'The Use of Precedent by International Judges and Arbitrators' (2011) 2 *Journal of International Dispute Settlement* 5, 9–10.

[35] Christine Gray and Benedict Kingsbury, 'Inter-State Arbitration since 1945: Overview and Evaluation' in Marc W. Janis (ed), *International Courts for the Twenty-First Century* (Leiden: Martinus Nijhoff, 1992), 55, 71.

[36] Gilbert Guillaume, 'The Use of Precedent by International Judges and Arbitrators', 19; Alain Pellet, 'Article 38' in Andreas Zimmermann, Christian Tomuschat, and Karin Oellers-Frahm (eds), *The Statute of the International Court of Justice: A Commentary* (Oxford: Oxford University Press, 2006), 677, 788.

[37] The *Guyana/Suriname* award was handed down in 2007 and the awards of the Eritrea/Ethiopia Claims Commission from 2005 to 2009, see nn 10 and 12.

[38] cf Christine Gray's comments on the arbitrators of the EECC, Christine Gray, 'The Eritrea/Ethiopia Claims Commission Oversteps its Boundaries: A Partial Award?' (2006) 17 *European Journal of International Law* 699, 707.

as the 'Darwinian reality: the unfit will perish'.[39] In reality, compared to the decisions of international courts, arbitral awards have even less chance of survival. In the Darwinian world of international case law, while the former march in packs (and possibly in a specific direction), the latter are left to wander alone.

Fact-finding reports also have a place among subsidiary sources of international law as manifestations of legal doctrine. At best, they can be regarded as informed doctrine, due to the expertise of the missions' members. It should also be noted that all parts of fact-finding reports do not necessarily have the same value. For example, the report of the EU mission on the Georgian conflict is divided into three volumes. While the first volume discusses the relevant *jus contra bellum* issues in just three-and-a-half pages, the second volume contains a detailed legal analysis of these issues spanning more than 60 pages. However, the report clearly states that the only authoritative findings are those in the first volume and that 'The elaboration, findings and opinions expressed in these texts [ie those in the second volume] do not necessarily reflect the views of the Mission'.[40]

As a diplomatic means of international dispute settlement, fact-finding missions are of a predominantly political character. Indeed, even the publication of these reports can be subject to political considerations.[41] Therefore, even more so than arbitral tribunals, the value and impact of legal pronouncements by fact-finding missions depend greatly on the quality of legal reasoning as well as on the authority, impartiality, and independence of the members of the mission.[42] In fact, impartiality and independence appear to be the keystones in the acceptance of the outcome of fact-finding procedures.[43] Some of the missions examined here

[39] Jan Paulsson, 'The Role of Precedent in Investment Arbitration' in Katia Yannaca-Small (ed), *Arbitration Under International Investment Agreements: A Guide to Key Issues* (Oxford: Oxford University Press, 2010), 699, 704.

[40] IIFFMCG Report, vol II, 1.

[41] eg the publication of the report on Gaza by the Secretary-General's panel of inquiry 'was delayed several times as Turkey and Israel sought to reconcile their deteriorating relationship and perhaps avoid making the report public'; Neil MacFarquhar and Ethan Bronner, 'Report finds naval blockade by Israel legal but faults raid', *New York Times*, 1 Sept 2011, available at <http://www.nytimes.com/2011/09/02/world/middleeast/02flotilla.html?pagewanted=all&_r=0>. See also 'Turkey kicking out top Israeli diplomats over Gaza blockade', *CNN*, 3 Sept 2011, available at <http://edition.cnn.com/2011/WORLD/europe/09/02/turkey.israel/index.html> and Press statement by H. E. Mr Ahmet Davutoğlu, Minister of Foreign Affairs of the Republic of Turkey, regarding Turkish–Israeli relations, 2 Sept 2011, available at <http://www.mfa.gov.tr/press-statement-by-h_e_-mr_-ahmet-davutoglu_-minister-of-foreign-affairs-of-the-republic-of-turkey_-regarding-turkish-israeli-re.en.mfa>.

[42] See the Press statement by the Minister of Foreign Affairs of Turkey cited at n 41 criticizing the finding that Israel's blockade of Gaza is lawful: 'the controversial views put forward by the Chair and Vice-Chair of the Panel exceeding their mandates are based on political motives rather than on legal grounds. Turkey in no way accepts this approach, which jeopardizes the functioning and integrity of the panel.'

[43] See in general Thomas M. Franck and H. Scott Farley, 'Procedural Due Process in Human Rights Fact-Finding by International Agencies' (1980) 74 *American Journal of International Law* 308; Theo Boutruche, 'Credible Fact-Finding and Allegations of International Human Rights law Violations: Challenges in Theory and Practice' (2011) 16 *Journal of Conflict and Security Law* 105.

have been subject to severe criticism, focusing on their composition, methodology, and the contours of their mandate.[44] The approval of the final report by the relevant institution is also a significant element for the potential impact of fact-finding reports.

When interpreting the findings of these reports on *jus contra bellum* questions, all of the previously mentioned elements should be kept in mind. This is equally true for evaluating the influence of such reports on the development of *jus contra bellum* rules. The cautious approach to the value of legal findings in fact-finding reports is mirrored in the reluctance of international tribunals to rely on these findings, with the notable exception of the International Tribunal for the Law of the Sea, which has cited the report of the commission of inquiry into the *Red Crusader* incident.[45] It remains to be seen whether the *jus contra bellum* findings of the more recent fact-finding reports will have the same fate. Of course, these considerations diminish neither the significant political impact of fact-finding reports[46] nor their important role in dispute resolution.

III. The Application of *Jus Contra Bellum* in Arbitral Awards and Fact-Finding Reports

Clearly, in the light of the inherent limitations of this chapter, it is impossible to present a complete overview of arbitral awards and fact-finding reports with respect to all the *jus contra bellum* rules, therefore the following analysis is not exhaustive since some *jus contra bellum* pronouncements have had to be left out.[47] This

[44] See eg James G. Steward, 'The UN Commission of Inquiry on Lebanon: A Legal Appraisal' (2007) 5 *Journal of International Criminal Justice* 1039, 1041. See also n 42.

[45] *The M/V 'Saiga' (No. 2) (St Vincent and Grenadines v. Guinea)*, Judgment, International Tribunal for the Law of the Sea (ITLOS), 1 July 1999 (1999) 38 ILM 1323, 1355, para 156.

[46] Dapo Akande and Hannah Tinkin, 'International Commissions of Inquiry: A New Form of Adjudication?' in *EJIL:*Talk!, 6 Apr 2012, available at <http://www.ejiltalk.org/international-commissions-of-inquiry-a-new-form-of-adjudication/>.

[47] Cases in point are the conflicting pronouncements of the Guyana/Suriname tribunal and the EU mission on the conflict in Georgia on the threat to use force. Cf *Guyana/Suriname* arbitral award, 229–30, para 439 and IIFFMCG Report, vol I, 25–6, para 24. See François Dubuisson and Anne Lagerwall, 'The Threat of the Use of Force and Ultimata', Chapter 42 in this volume. Other examples are the pronouncements on the obligation of a state acting in self-defence to report immediately to the Security Council the measures taken; see EECC, Partial Award on *Jus ad Bellum*, 464–6, para

section focuses on findings relating to fundamental *jus contra bellum* questions, which appear problematic, controversial, or conflicting.

The section is divided into three parts. Section III.A deals with questions relating to the threshold for the application of *jus contra bellum* rules, namely Articles 2(4) and 51 of the UN Charter. Section III.B deals with the personal scope of application of *jus contra bellum* rules, mainly the much-debated question of whether such rules are applicable to actors other than states. Section III.C discusses the approach of arbitral tribunals and fact-finding missions on the exceptions to the prohibition to resort to force. Here, the main focus is on the right to self-defence and the conditions relating to exercising that right.

A. Crossing the Rubicon: Distinction Between Resort to Force Not Covered by Article 2(4) of the UN Charter, Violation of Article 2(4), and Armed Attack

The determination of the threshold for applying Articles 2(4) and 51 of the UN Charter is a salient point in *jus contra bellum*.[48] As will be shown, the arbitral tribunals and fact-finding missions stand by the distinction between actions amounting to an armed attack and less grave forms of resort to force prohibited under Article 2(4). The most problematic finding with respect to acts triggering the application of *jus contra bellum* comes from the *Guyana/Suriname* arbitral award and concerns the threshold for applying Article 2(4) itself.

The facts of the case are as follows. On 3 June 2000, two patrol boats from the Surinamese navy ordered an oil rig and a drill ship to withdraw from a maritime zone which was disputed between Guyana and Suriname.[49] Suriname characterized the operation as 'a law enforcement measure'.[50] Guyana, on the other hand, claimed that Suriname 'has breached Article 2(4) of the UN Charter'.[51] While 'accept[ing] the argument that in international law force may be used in law enforcement activities provided that such force is unavoidable, reasonable and necessary', the Tribunal held that 'in the circumstances of the present case' Suriname's operation 'seemed

11 (with respect to Eritrea); IIFFMCG Report, vol II, 246–7 and 269; Secretary-General's Panel Report, 5, recommendation (vi), 72, para 160, and 73, para 164; HRC Lebanon Report, 131, note 37.

[48] See, among many, Christine Gray, *International Law and the Use of Force* (3rd edn, Oxford: Oxford University Press, 2008); Yoram Dinstein, *War, Aggression and Self-Defence* (5th edn, Cambridge: Cambridge University Press, 2011); Corten, *The Law Against War*; Tom Ruys, *'Armed Attack' and Article 51 of the UN Charter: Evolutions in Customary Law and Practice* (Cambridge: Cambridge University Press, 2010). See also Nico Schrijver, 'The Ban on the Use of Force in the UN Charter', Chapter 21 in this volume and Jan Klabbers, 'Intervention, Armed Intervention, Armed Attack, Threat to Peace, Act of Aggression, and Threat or Use of Force—What's the Difference?', Chapter 22 in this volume.

[49] *Guyana/Suriname* arbitral award, 184, para 151.

[50] At 202, para 270.

[51] At 201, para 263.

more akin to a threat of military action rather than a mere law enforcement activity' and as such amounted to a threat to resort to force contrary to international law.[52]

The Tribunal confirmed that some cases of use of force are classified as law enforcement activities, falling outside the scope of Article 2(4). However, based on 'the circumstances of the present case', it seemed to set a particularly low threshold for applying Article 2(4). The Tribunal's elliptic reasoning makes it difficult to decipher these 'circumstances'. One possible interpretation is that they refer to the gravity of the threat to use force. The Tribunal attributed particular weight to the fact that the Surinamese order to withdraw was accompanied by the phrase that, should the rig and drill ship not conform to the order, 'the consequences would be theirs'. This phrase was interpreted by the rig supervisor and the rig area manager as a threat that armed force would be used against them.[53] If these are indeed the 'circumstances' referred to by the Tribunal, they stretch the criterion of gravity for the application of Article 2(4) beyond breaking point. Despite voices to the contrary,[54] several incidents of resort to force at sea attest to the fact that resort to force by a state against private vessels flying the flag of another state has generally been treated as law enforcement activity. For example, in the *Fisheries Jurisdiction* case between Spain and Canada before the ICJ, Spain claimed that the arrest on the high seas of a Spanish fishing vessel by Canada pursuant to Canadian legislation on fisheries protection violated, among others, Article 2(4) of the UN Charter.[55] The ICJ refused to accept the Spanish argument and viewed the Canadian use of force as an 'enforcement measure'.[56] The 1961 *Red Crusader* incident concerning the arrest by the Danish navy of the British trawler *Red Crusader* for illegal fishing in an area where fishing was prohibited for British vessels is another case in point. The 1962 report of the commission of inquiry established by the UK and Denmark in relation to the incident appeared to consider the force used by the Danish navy as a case of law enforcement and none of the parties seems to have invoked *jus contra bellum*.[57]

[52] At 231, para 445. [53] At 184, para 151.

[54] cf the claims to self-defence raised by the US and the UK in the context of the 1980–8 Iran–Iraq war; Christine Gray, 'The British Position in Regard to the Gulf Conflict' (1988) 37 *International and Comparative Law Quarterly* 420 and Christine Gray, 'The British Position with Regard to the Gulf Conflict (Iran–Iraq): Part 2' (1991) 40 *International and Comparative Law Quarterly* 464. See also, Douglas Guilfoyle, *Shipping Interdiction and the Law of the Sea* (Cambridge: Cambridge University Press, 2009), 272–7. For the ambiguity in the UK position in the Gulf conflict, see Vaughan Lowe, 'The Impact of the Law of the Sea on Naval Warfare—Commentary' (1987–8) 14 *Syracuse Journal of International Law and Commerce* 657, 679.

[55] *Fisheries Jurisdiction (Spain v. Canada)*, Judgment on Jurisdiction of the Court of 4 Dec 1998, ICJ Rep 1998, 432, 465, para 78.

[56] *Fisheries Jurisdiction*, Judgment on Jurisdiction of the Court, 466, para 84. It should be noted that the Court's finding was not on the merits of the case; it was made in the context of interpreting the scope of Canada's reservation to the ICJ's jurisdiction. See also ITLOS, *The M/V 'Saiga' (No. 2)*, Judgment, 1355–6, paras 153–9. For more examples and analysis, see Ruys, *'Armed Attack' and Article 51 of the UN Charter*, 204–13; Corten, *The Law Against War*, 55–60.

[57] Commission of Enquiry (Denmark–UK), *The Red Crusader*, 499.

While the Tribunal refers to the relevant precedents in support of its finding relating to the possibility to use force in law enforcement activities,[58] it does not confront them directly nor does it explain the distinction between them and the *Guyana/Suriname* case.

Another possible interpretation of the 'circumstances of the case' is that they point to the context of the incident in question, in this case the existence of a territorial dispute between Guyana and Suriname. Indeed, in its submission Guyana insisted on this point.[59] The context plays a significant role in determining whether a threat or use of force comes under Article 2(4), mainly as an indication that a state has the intent to resort to force against another state.[60] However, in the case at hand, there were no other material hostile acts by Suriname. If the 'circumstances of the case' do indeed refer to the Guyana/Suriname border dispute, then the Tribunal appears to be implying that, in the context of territorial disputes, any resort to force would cross the threshold of Article 2(4). This appears to be a broad reading of Article 2(4). In the words of Olivier Corten, 'each border dispute gives rise to claims to sovereignty that are sometimes materialised by the ephemeral despatching of a few troops into the disputed territory, without that implying for the other State an accusation of violation of article 2(4).'[61]

The orthodox view on the threshold of Article 2(4) is confirmed by the experts of the fact-finding mission on the conflict in Georgia. The experts affirmed that 'very small incidents lie below this threshold, for instance the targeted killing of single individuals, forcible abductions of individual persons, or the interception of a single aircraft.'[62] According to the experts, such incidents also include a small-scale operation by a state in order to rescue its nationals.[63] This seems to be in accordance with state practice, as shown by the US operation conducted in Liberia in 1990 in order to evacuate their nationals from the US embassy in Monrovia.[64]

Turning to the distinction between armed attack and 'less grave forms' of resort to force prohibited under Article 2(4), both the arbitral tribunals and the fact-finding

[58] *Guyana/Suriname* arbitral award, 253, note 518 (the Tribunal cites the report on the *Red Crusader* incident, the ITLOS judgment on the *M/V Saiga* case, and the 1933 joint report of the commissioners in the *SS I'm Alone* incident); see also *Guyana/Suriname* arbitral award, 230–1, paras 442–4 (reference by the parties to the *Fisheries Jurisdiction* and the *M/V Saiga* cases).

[59] *Guyana/Suriname* arbitral award, 228, paras 429–30.

[60] Corten, *The Law Against War*, 73–84; Raphaël van Steenberghe, *La légitime défense en droit international public* (Brussels: Larcier, 2012), 228 ff.

[61] Corten, *The Law Against War*, 83; van Steenberghe, *La légitime défense en droit international public*, 228.

[62] IIFFMCG Report, vol II, 242 and fn 49.

[63] IIFFMCG Report, vol II, 286. However, the experts' reference to the Entebbe incident between Israel and Uganda as a relevant precedent is incorrect; see Olivier Corten, 'Le rapport de la mission d'enquête internationale sur le conflit en Géorgie: quel apport au *jus contra bellum*?' (2010) 114 *Revue générale de droit international public* 35, 39–40.

[64] Marc Weller (ed), *Regional Peace-Keeping and International Enforcement: The Liberian Crisis* (Cambridge: Cambridge University Press, 1994).

missions uphold the relevant ICJ case law and confirm the distinction.[65] The findings of fact-finding missions in favour of the existence of an armed attack in the relevant conflicts do not appear controversial in view of the sufficient gravity of the actions at hand. This is true for the Israeli attack against Lebanese territory in 2006,[66] the attack by Georgian forces against South Ossetia,[67] the Russian military action in Georgia,[68] as well as the attack of the Abkhaz forces against Georgia in the Kodori valley.[69]

In this respect, the EECC awards on *jus contra bellum* merit further analysis. Ethiopia accused Eritrea of carrying out a series of armed attacks and launching a full-scale invasion against Ethiopia from 12 May to 11 June 1998.[70] Eritrea responded that its actions of 12 May were acts of self-defence in response to previous forcible incursions by Ethiopia into its territory as well as to the use of force against Eritrean soldiers in early May 1998 (mainly on 6 and 7 May).[71] The Commission held that:

> Localized border encounters between small infantry units, even those involving the loss of life, do not constitute an armed attack for purposes of the Charter.... [T]he events... involved geographically limited clashes between small Eritrean and Ethiopian patrols along a remote, unmarked and disputed border. The Commission is satisfied that these relatively minor incidents were not of a magnitude to constitute an armed attack by either State against the other within the meaning of Article 51 of the UN Charter.[72]

The EECC followed the strict view on armed attack that the ICJ had adopted in its *Nicaragua* judgment.[73] However, the Commission limited its appreciation of armed attack to the incidents of early May 1998. By doing so, it failed to take into account Eritrea's claim that Ethiopia was unlawfully occupying its territory.[74] Also, the Commission did not specify whether Ethiopia's actions constituted 'less grave forms' of resort to force in violation of Article 2(4) or whether they fell outside the

[65] *Guyana/Suriname* arbitral award, 230, para 440; IIFFMCG Report, vol II, 242, 245. The award refers to the ICJ judgment on the merits in the *Nicaragua* case, see *Case concerning Military and Paramilitary Activities in and Against Nicaragua*, Merits, Judgment of 27 June 1986, ICJ Rep 1986, 14, 101, para 190. The IIFFMCG Report refers to the same judgment and to the judgment in the *Oil Platforms* case, see *Case concerning Oil Platforms (Iran v. US)*, Merits, Judgment of 6 Nov 2003, ICJ Rep 2003, 161, 187, para 51.

[66] HRC Lebanon Report, 23, paras 58, 61.

[67] IIFFMCG Report, vol I, at 22–23, para 19 and vol II, 242–3 and 263.

[68] IIFFMCG Report, vol I, 24, para 21.

[69] IIFFMCG Report, vol I, 25, para 24 and vol II, 212, 291.

[70] EECC, Partial Award on *Jus ad Bellum*, 464, paras 6, 8. [71] At 464–5, para 9.

[72] At 465–6, paras 11, 12.

[73] The Commission did not use the possibility for a more extensive approach left open by the ICJ in the *Oil Platforms* judgment; ICJ, *Oil Platforms*, Judgment, 195, para 72.

[74] Christine Gray, 'The Eritrea/Ethiopia Claims Commission Oversteps its Boundaries', 710–12. Based on the presentation of Eritrean submissions in the 2005 partial award, Eritrea's self-defence plea was not linked to the occupation of its territory by Ethiopia; see EECC, Partial Award on *Jus ad Bellum*, 464–5, para 9. The parties' submissions to the Commission have not been made public. The temporal limit of May 1998 has its source in the Algiers Agreement, see n 9.

scope of the prohibition altogether.[75] Given the context of the situation between the two states and the gravity of the clashes, it would be plausible to suggest that they do in fact come under Article 2(4).[76] The Commission's statement that Eritrea did not bear 'sole legal responsibility for all that happened throughout the two years of the conflict'[77] may also point in this direction.

The Commission found that Eritrea had committed an armed attack in violation of Article 2(4) 'by resorting to armed force on May 12, 1998 and the immediately following days to attack and occupy the town of Badme, then under peaceful administration by [Eritrea] as well as other [Eritrean] territory'.[78] It rejected for lack of proof Ethiopia's claim that Eritrea's armed attack included all subsequent attacks in May and June 1998.[79]

Interestingly, in determining Eritrea's liability to pay damages for the violation, the EECC distinguished Eritrea's armed attack from aggression and 'aggressive war'. According to the Commission, its finding on the violation of *jus contra bellum* by Eritrea was 'limited as to place and time;[80] and

> did not include a finding that Eritrea had waged an aggressive war, had occupied large parts of Ethiopia or otherwise engaged in the sort of widespread lawlessness that the Security Council identified in the case of the invasion and occupation of Kuwait.[81]

Moreover, the Commission 'did not find that Eritrea bore sole legal responsibility for all that happened throughout the two years of the conflict.'[82]

Thus, the Commission appears to introduce a distinction between an armed attack limited in time and space and full-scale aggression, at least for the purposes of state responsibility. It seems to suggest that, while in a war of aggression the state having violated *jus contra bellum* is responsible for everything that ensues, this would not be the case with respect to a limited armed attack.[83] In the latter case, the armed attack triggering the war is distinct from the rest of the conflict. At least, this is how the Commission treated Eritrea's resort to force.[84] This is problematic in that it gives the impression that the *jus contra bellum* did not apply to subsequent hostilities.[85]

[75] Eritrea did not file a *jus ad bellum* claim against Ethiopia therefore the EECC felt no need to examine this question.

[76] This seems to be the position adopted by Ruys, *'Armed Attack' and Article 51 of the UN Charter*, 179.

[77] EECC, Final Award, 719, para 282.

[78] EECC, Partial Award on *Jus ad Bellum*, 469, para B.1 of the operative part of the award. See also 468, para 19.

[79] EECC, Partial Award on *Jus ad Bellum*, 468, para 18.

[80] EECC, Final Award, 719, para 282.

[81] EECC, Decision Number 7, 20, para 32.

[82] EECC, Final Award, 719, para 282.

[83] It is not, however, clear whether the extensive responsibility of the state in the 'aggressive war' scenario of the 1990–1 Gulf War was due to Security Council powers; EECC, Decision Number 7, 20, para 32: 'Moreover, this Commission did not—nor could it—alter the international law rules defining the extent of compensable damages that follow from the breach of international law that it identified.'

[84] EECC, Partial Award on *Jus ad Bellum*, 468, para 19.

[85] For the position that *jus contra bellum* continues to apply during a conflict, see Christopher Greenwood, 'The Relationship Between *Ius ad Bellum* and *Ius in Bello*' (1983) 9 *Review of International Studies* 221, 222–3.

B. The Personal Scope of Application of *Jus Contra Bellum*: Non-State Actors and the Prohibition to Use of Force

Given the interstate nature of the disputes brought before them, the arbitral tribunals studied here were not confronted with the sensitive issue of the application of *jus contra bellum* to actors other than states.[86] That said, two fact-finding missions have dealt with the issue specifically. This resulted in findings which are not exempt from controversy.

The first is the Secretary-General's panel of inquiry on the flotilla incident.[87] The panel accepted that the imposition of a naval blockade constituted a measure adopted in the exercise of Israel's right to self-defence against attacks from the Gaza Strip, explicitly recognizing that a state is entitled to act in self-defence against attacks by non-state actors.[88] The members of the panel did not engage in a substantial discussion of the issue. In support of their finding, they invoked the *Caroline* case and recent practice, although no actual practice is stated or analysed in the report.[89] Therefore, the absence of relevant state practice and the cursory reasoning undermine the persuasiveness of the panel's finding, especially in view of the significant controversy that this particular question has raised among scholars and the negative stance of the ICJ case law on the matter.[90]

The most controversial pronouncement on the application of *jus contra bellum* to non-state actors comes from the fact-finding mission of the European Union (EU) on the conflict in Georgia. Despite voicing doubts about whether South Ossetia and Abkhazia can be considered to be states,[91] the mission's report asserts that the UN

[86] On this issue, see Kimberley N. Trapp, 'Can Non-State Actors Mount an Armed Attack?', Chapter 30 in this volume.

[87] The HRC report on the 2006 conflict in Lebanon does not answer the question whether Israel could invoke its right to self-defence against Hezbollah; HRC Lebanon Report, 23, para 61.

[88] Secretary-General's Panel Report, 39–41, paras 71–2 and 91, para 41.

[89] Secretary-General's Panel Report, 91, para 41 (in fn 145, the members of the Panel point to the analysis of two scholars and the practice cited therein).

[90] Indeed, the ICJ has not been receptive to arguments pleading in favour of applying *jus contra bellum* to non-state actors; *Nicaragua*, Judgment, 103, para 195; *Legal Consequences of the Construction of a Wall in the Occupied Palestinian Territory*, Advisory Opinion of 9 July 2004, ICJ Rep 2004, 136, 194, para 139; *Case Concerning Armed Activities on the Territory of the Congo (DRC v. Uganda)*, Merits, Judgment of 19 Dec 2005, ICJ Rep 2005, 168, 222–3, paras 146–7. This approach has been criticized by some of the Court's judges; see *Wall*, Advisory Opinion, 215, para 33 (Separate Opinion of Judge Higgins) and 242, paras 5–6 (Declaration of Judge Buergenthal); *Armed Activities*, Judgment, 337–8, paras 11–13 (Separate Opinion of Judge Simma) and 313–15, paras 26–31 (Separate Opinion of Judge Kooijmans). The members of the Panel cite the views of Judges Higgins and Buergenthal in the *Wall* advisory opinion in support of their position; Secretary-General's Panel Report, 91, para 41, fn 145. Moreover, they reject the Court's conclusion to the contrary because 'there is no extensive reasoning by the Court on the point and no analysis of the customary law or State practice'. This is a rather bold criticism given that the Panel's report itself suffers from exactly the same shortcomings.

[91] IIFFMCG Report, vol II, 134–5.

Charter rules on *jus contra bellum* were applicable to the conflicts between Georgia, South Ossetia, and Abkhazia: for example, Georgia's attack against South Ossetia and Abkhazia's attack on Georgia were considered violations of Article 2(4) thereby triggering the application of the opposite side's right to self-defence.[92] However, the report refused to apply the *jus contra bellum* in its entirety. The experts of the mission did not recognize South Ossetia's right to collective self-defence in response to the armed attack by Georgia.[93]

The fact-finding mission's pronouncements are unpersuasive for two reasons. First, none of parties argued that Articles 2(4) and 51 of the Charter were applicable to the relations between Georgia, South Ossetia, and Abkhazia, not even South Ossetia and Abkhazia themselves.[94] This undermined the mission's finding in favour of the direct application of the UN Charter to the relevant conflict.[95] Secondly, if one accepts the applicability of the Charter rules on *jus contra bellum* in this case, it is difficult to understand the exclusion of collective self-defence in favour of South Ossetia. The need to avoid an escalation of the conflict[96] is a policy argument and does not explain why collective self-defence would be admitted in favour of Georgia. All the more so since this exclusion runs counter to the experts' own admission that the personal scope of application of Articles 2(4) and 51 must be identical for both sides of a conflict.[97] It should be noted, however, that this controversial point is found only in the second volume of the report, which, as mentioned earlier, does not necessarily reflect the views of the mission as such.[98] The authoritative first volume of the report, on the other hand, does not mention the exclusion of South Ossetia's right to collective self-defence.

C. Self-Defence

Turning to the substance of the right to self-defence, the more interesting material comes from fact-finding reports. The various commissions of inquiry have produced conflicting pronouncements concerning the possibility of invoking self-defence against future attacks (Section III.C.1) as well as the impact of occupation on the exercise of a state's right to self-defence (Section III.C.2). On the other hand, the reports follow a more classical approach concerning the application of the conditions of necessity and proportionality (Section III.C.3).

[92] IIFFMCG Report, vol I, 23, para 19 and 25, para 24. [93] IIFFMCG Report, vol II, 282.

[94] IIFFMCG Report, vol III, 135–209 and 228–67 (Georgia), 437–38 (Russia), 506 and 518–22 (South Ossetia), 531–2 and 547–57 (Abkhazia). Both South Ossetia and Abkhazia characterized Georgian operations as 'aggression'. However, they did not explicitly invoke the UN Charter in this respect. They only referred to the ceasefire agreements concluded by the parties.

[95] For a general critical appraisal of this finding, see Corten, 'Le rapport de la mission d'enquête internationale sur le conflit en Géorgie', 54–7.

[96] IIFFMCG Report, vol II, 282. [97] IIFFMCG Report, vol II, 242.

[98] See n 40 and related text.

1. *The case of preventive self-defence*

The controversy over the question of the legality of invoking self-defence against a future armed attack is reflected in the fact-finding reports that took up the issue. The experts of the EU mission on the 2008 conflict in Georgia examined whether Georgia's military operation could be justified as self-defence against a future armed attack by Russia. They distinguished between self-defence against 'an objectively verifiable, concretely imminent attack' and 'a potential or abstract threat which might amount to an imminent attack, as determined in a subjective manner by the state which feels threatened'.[99] In consonance with the majority of scholarly opinion, self-defence in the second scenario was unequivocally rejected as contrary to the UN Charter and customary international law.[100] As for the first scenario, the experts pointed to the existing controversy among scholars as to the legality of self-defence against imminent attack and avoided a clear finding on the question since the factual situation could not substantiate the existence of an imminent attack.[101] Contrary to the caution expressed by the experts of the EU fact-finding mission, the members of the Secretary-General's panel of inquiry on the flotilla incident were much more direct in recognizing the legality of self-defence against an imminent armed attack in favour of Israel.[102] However, aside from the *Caroline* incident,[103] the members of the panel do not point to any other elements substantiating their finding. It should be noted in this respect that neither Georgia nor Israel appear to have relied on the argument of preventive self-defence with respect to the situations under scrutiny by the missions.[104] Therefore, actual state practice relating to the reports does not support the position in favour of preventive or pre-emptive self-defence.

2. *Self-defence and occupation*

Another issue on which there have been conflicting pronouncements from fact-finding missions is the possibility of exercising the right to self-defence against attacks stemming from occupied territory. Having determined that Gaza remained under Israeli occupation even after the 2005 disengagement,[105] the fact-finding

[99] IIFFMCG Report, vol II, 254. For a similar distinction, see Dinstein, *War, Aggression and Self-Defence*, 194–205.

[100] IIFFMCG Report, vol II, 254–5.

[101] IIFFMCG Report, vol II, 255–6 (by Russia against Georgia) and 293–4 (by Georgia against Abkhazia). For an overview of the controversy, see Robert Kolb, Ius contra bellum—*Le droit international relatif au maintien de la paix* (Brussels: Helbing & Lichtenhahn/Bruylant, 2003), 192–5.

[102] Secretary-General's Panel Report, 90–1, para 41.

[103] Secretary-General's Panel Report, 90, para 41. For the *Caroline* incident, see John Basset Moore II (ed), *Digest of international Law* (Washington DC: United States Printing Office, 1906), 409 and Christopher Greenwood, 'Caroline, The' in Wolfrum, *Max Planck Encyclopedia of Public International Law*, vol I, 1141.

[104] At least, there is no indication of such a claim in any of the two reports analysed here. Only Abkhazia appears to have explicitly relied on preventive self-defence against Georgia, IIFFMCG Report, vol II, 292.

[105] LAS Gaza Report, 109–10, paras 400–4.

mission established by the LAS on Operation Cast Lead held that Israel could not invoke its right to self-defence with respect to that operation. Among other reasons, the mission suggested that military operations against an occupied population 'should rather be categorized as police or enforcement action against resistance action by the occupied people.'[106] On the other hand, the Secretary-General's panel of inquiry asserted that 'the uncertain legal status of Gaza under international law cannot mean that Israel has no right to self-defence against armed attacks directed towards its territory.'[107] These two positions reflect the debate surrounding the relevant ICJ finding in the *Wall* advisory opinion. In this opinion, the Court rejected Israel's claim of self-defence as justification for the construction of the wall, invoking, inter alia, the control exercised by Israel over the occupied Palestinian territory.[108] Judges Higgins and Buergenthal were highly critical of the Court's position.[109]

Much of the controversy on this question is due to the fact that it is linked to the debate on the exercise of the right to self-defence against attacks by non-state actors, which was analysed earlier.[110] However, not all cases of use of force against groups operating within an occupied territory are cases of use of force against non-state actors. In this respect, a distinction should be made depending on whether these groups belong to[111] or are under the control of[112] the occupied state. The first scenario is not problematic as no separate *jus contra bellum* issue arises between the rebel group and the occupying power. If the occupation constitutes an armed attack by the occupying power against the occupied state, then the latter has the right to self-defence and the rebel group is in reality exercising that right. Therefore, the occupying power cannot invoke its own right to react in self-defence against the actions of the group. The second scenario, where the resistance group has no link to the occupied state, is more problematic. In this respect, two questions arise. The first is whether a state can invoke its right to self-defence against a non-state actor. Provided that the answer to this question is in the affirmative, the second question is whether a state can also invoke this right when the non-state actor is operating from within the occupied territory. In this respect, states seem hesitant to recognize the occupying power's right to self-defence and thus support the finding of the LAS mission.[113]

[106] LAS Gaza Report, 111, para 409.

[107] Secretary-General's Panel Report, 40, para 72. The reference to the 'uncertain status' of Gaza seems to point to the controversy of whether Gaza remained occupied after the 2005 Israeli disengagement.

[108] *Wall*, Advisory Opinion, 194, para 139.

[109] *Wall*, Advisory Opinion, 215, para 34 (Separate Opinion of Judge Huggins) and 241–3, paras 5–6 (Declaration of Judge Buergenthal).

[110] See Section III.B.

[111] Geneva Convention relative to the treatment of prisoners of war of August 12, 1949 (entered into force 21 Oct 1950), 75 UNTS 135, 138.

[112] cf Art 8 of the Draft Articles on State Responsibility, see Draft Articles on the Responsibility of States for Internationally Wrongful Acts in Report of the International Law Commission to the General Assembly on its Fifty-Third Session A/56/10 (2001), 103–9.

[113] Vaios Koutroulis, 'Of Occupation, *Jus ad Bellum* and *Jus in Bello*: A Reply to Solon Solomon's "The Great Oxymoron: *Jus In Bello* Violations as Legitimate Non-Forcible Measures of Self-Defense: The

In his separate opinion, Judge Kooijmans seems to accept a state's right to self-defence against a non-state actor, while denying this right when it is exercised against groups operating from within an occupied territory.[114] The criticism levelled against this position is that it leaves the occupying power with no means of protecting itself and its citizens against rebel attacks.[115] It is submitted that this is not the case. The occupying power has several coercive options, stemming from both law enforcement rules and *jus in bello* (be they rules applicable during belligerent occupation such as Article 43 of the Hague Regulations, or rules relating to the conduct of hostilities[116]).

Moreover, the added value of invoking *jus contra bellum* with respect to armed groups operating in an occupied territory is not clear. In cases where an armed group attacks state A from the territory of state B, the reason for state A to invoke self-defence is to be able to conduct a military operation against the armed group in state B without violating international law. In cases where the group attacks state A from within an occupied territory, the legality under *jus contra bellum* of the occupation as such is linked to the legal relationship between the occupying power and the occupied state. It will not be affected by the distinct legal relationship under *jus contra bellum* between the occupying power and the armed group. For the rest, the occupying power does not need specific authorization under general international law in order to conduct military operations in the occupied territory.

3. *The conditions of necessity and proportionality in the exercise of the right to self-defence*

For the most part, the pronouncements of fact-finding reports on necessity and proportionality confirm the classical reading of the two criteria for the exercise of the right to self-defence.[117] A critical issue in evaluating the necessary and proportionate character of defensive military operations is the purpose of self-defence. The report by the EU mission on the conflict in Georgia follows the traditional view: the purpose of self-defence is to repel the initial armed attack[118] and to prevent the occurrence of future attacks.[119] Punitive operations go beyond this scope.[120] In this respect, the HRC mission on Operation Cast Lead seems to reject Israel's

Post-Disengagement Israeli Measures towards Gaza as a Case Study"' (2011) 10 *Chinese Journal of International Law* 897, 906–8.

114 *Wall*, Advisory Opinion, 229–30, para 35–6 (Separate Opinion of Judge Kooijmans).

115 *Wall*, Advisory Opinion, 215, para 34 (Separate Opinion of Judge Higgins).

116 The application of international humanitarian law rules on the conduct of hostilities will depend on whether an armed conflict exists between the rebel group and the occupying power.

117 See Olivier Corten, 'Necessity', Chapter 39 in this volume; Theodora Christodoulidou and Kalliopi Chainoglou, 'The Principle of Proportionality from a *Jus ad Bellum* Perspective', Chapter 55 in this volume.

118 IIFFMCG Report, vol I, 22–3, para 19.

119 IIFFMCG Report, vol I, 24, para 21. See Ruys, *'Armed Attack' and Article 51 of the UN Charter*, 518–19;

120 IIFFMCG Report, vol II, 250 and 271.

claim to self-defence because the attack was directed against the civilian population as a whole.[121] Along the same lines, the HRC flotilla report refers to its finding that the blockade constituted an act of collective punishment in order to reject Israel's justification of the blockade 'on security grounds'.[122] These findings confirm that *jus in bello* is among the elements to be taken into account in evaluating the necessary and proportionate character of a self-defence action.[123] They are also in line with ICJ case law[124] and scholarly opinion.[125]

As for the concrete evaluation of necessity and proportionality with respect to operations conducted in self-defence, the main emphasis is given to the extent of the operations as compared to the actual armed attack or the threat of future attack that must be prevented. Thus, for example, while recognizing that the initial phase of the Russian response to Georgia's attacks against Russian peacekeepers was in line with the conditions of self-defence, the mission found that the subsequent Russian military campaign 'went far beyond the reasonable limits of defence…[and] cannot be regarded as even remotely commensurate with the threat to Russian peacekeepers'.[126] To substantiate this conclusion, the mission referred to the massive and extended character of Russia's military operations.[127]

This last finding of the EU mission is quite revolutionary. In the ICJ case law, necessity and proportionality tend to have an accessory role:

> the Court each time dismissed the argument of self-defence primarily because the State invoking it had failed to prove that it had previously been the victim of an armed attack, and only incidentally because its riposte did not prove 'necessary' or 'proportionate' under the circumstances of the case.[128]

The EU mission provides an explicit precedent where military action starts out as a case of legitimate self-defence but is subsequently transformed into an armed attack because of its unnecessary and disproportionate character. This armed attack, in turn, gives the former aggressor state the right to react in self-defence.[129]

[121] HRC, 'Human rights in Palestine and other occupied Arab territories: Report of the United Nations fact-finding mission on the Gaza conflict', A/HRC/12/48 (25 Sept 2009), 406, para 1883.

[122] HRC Flotilla Report, 53, para 263.

[123] See also IIFFMCG Report, vol II, 271.

[124] *Oil Platforms*, Judgment, 187, para 51 and 196, para 74.

[125] Keiichiro Okimoto, 'The Relationship Between *Jus ad Bellum* and *Jus in Bello*', Chapter 56 in this volume; Vaios Koutroulis, '*Jus ad/contra Bellum*' in Raphaël van Steenberghe (ed), *Le droit international humanitaire en tant que régime spécial du droit international* (Brussels: Larcier, 2013), 149, 175–9.

[126] IIFFMCG Report, vol I, 24, para 21.

[127] IIFFMCG Report, vol I, 24, para 21. The mission cited 'the bombing of the upper Kodori valley', 'the deployment of armoured units to reach extensive parts of Georgia', 'the setting up of positions in and nearby major Georgian towns as well as to control major highways', and 'the deployment of navy units on the Black Sea.' See also, with respect to Georgia's attack against South Ossetia, vol I, 22–3, para 19.

[128] Corten, *The Law against War*, 471–2. See also Gray, *International Law and the Use of Force*, 151–4.

[129] IIFFMCG Report, vol I, 24, para 21. The HRC Lebanon Report seems to offer another, less explicit, precedent; HRC Lebanon Report, 23, para 61 and 131, fn 37.

IV. Conclusion

The analysis of the pronouncements of arbitral decisions and fact-finding reports bearing on *jus contra bellum* revealed that both findings follow an 'orthodox' approach to relevant rules and cases of highly controversial interpretations. It is mainly the findings of the second category that raise concerns of the impact of arbitral awards and fact-finding reports on the development of *jus contra bellum*. Keeping in mind what was said earlier about the value of such awards and reports,[130] three additional comments can be made in this respect.

First, the key role of state practice in the development of international law should not be underestimated. Aside from the reluctance of international tribunals to reproduce legal findings by arbitral awards and fact-finding reports,[131] the impact of such findings on *jus contra bellum* will be measured against their invocation by states. Although it is still too soon to draw any conclusions in this respect, it can be expected that a state will refer to arbitral awards and fact-finding reports when their pronouncements support its position.[132] Of course, this does not mean that the state will endorse all the findings of the relevant awards or reports,[133] or that it will hesitate to ignore findings contrary to its view. In the end, any development of *jus contra bellum* will be the result of the views expressed by states, the awards and reports being at best elements meant to render the state's position more persuasive.

Secondly, some of the controversial *jus contra bellum* issues analysed by the various awards and reports have given rise to conflicting pronouncements. The application of the right to self-defence against actions by non-state actors is a case in point.[134] In such cases, if one award or report is invoked in defence of a particular interpretation by state A, another may equally be invoked in support of the contrary one by state B. This diminishes the risk of unwarranted developments in the scope and content of the relevant rules.

[130] See Section II. [131] See nn 35, 36, and 45 and related text.

[132] eg in its written statement on preliminary objections in the case concerning the *Application of the International Convention on the Elimination of All Forms of Racial Discrimination (Georgia v. Russian Federation)* before the ICJ, the Russian Federation cited with approval the EU fact-finding mission's *jus contra bellum* conclusion according to which the attack launched by Georgia on 7 Aug 2008 was unlawful under international law; *Case Concerning Application of the International Convention on the Elimination of All Forms of Racial Discrimination (Georgia v. Russian Federation)*, Preliminary Objections of the Russian Federation, 1 Dec 2009, vol I, 1, para 1.1, 6, para 15, available at <http://www.icj-cij.org/docket/files/140/16099.pdf>.

[133] *Case Concerning Application of the International Convention on the Elimination of All Forms of Racial Discrimination*, Preliminary Objections, 1, fn 2 (the Russian Federation does not endorse all the findings of the EU fact-finding mission).

[134] See the pronouncements on the possibility of the occupying power to invoke self-defence against actions stemming from the territory it occupies, at nn 106 and 107 and related text. Another example are the pronouncements on the threat to use force, see n 47.

Thirdly, it should be noted that the most recurrent problem with the material studied here lies in the lack of detailed legal reasoning substantiating the relevant findings. As it was seen previously, the most thorough analysis of *jus contra bellum* rules was that of the second volume of the EU mission on the conflict in Georgia, that is, in a non-authoritative text that does not express the views of the mission itself. One possible explanation resides in the inherent controversy surrounding many of the salient issues on *jus contra bellum*. Another explanation, at least with respect to fact-finding missions, may be found in the absence of an explicit mandate bearing on *jus contra bellum* and in a conscious focus on behalf of the members on the dispute settlement function of the mission. However, this last explanation is less relevant for arbitral tribunals, with the caveat of limitations stemming from their constitutive instruments. This lack of in-depth analysis adversely affects the persuasiveness of the awards and reports, their value as precedents, and, *in fine*, also their chances of 'survival' in the 'Darwinian' legal universe.

CHAPTER 27

THE RESILIENCE OF THE RESTRICTIVE RULES ON SELF-DEFENCE

JÖRG KAMMERHOFER*

I. Introduction

Law is, as Philip Allott wrote in his path-breaking *Eunomia*, 'a reality transmitted from the past of society to the future of society with a view to determining the content of that future' and 'pre-forms the future by willing it in advance'.[1] By its very idea—the idea of the ideal[2]—it is a counter-point to reality, what Niklas Luhmann called 'counter-factually stabilised expectation of behaviour'.[3] It could not even begin to will to determine the future otherwise. Law is also, however, responsive to changes (at least the so-called 'positive law' is); past willing seeks to determine the future; future willing

* Senior Research Fellow, University of Freiburg, Germany. The author would like to thank his former research assistant, Clarissa Henle, for her help in analysing the vast literature on the use of force and the participants at the ILA British Branch Spring Conference 2012 in Nottingham for their helpful comments.

[1] Philip Allott, *Eunomia. New Order for a New World* (Oxford: Oxford University Press, 1990, 2001), 114.

[2] Allott, *Eunomia*, xxii (preface to the paperback edition); Philip Allott, *The Health of Nations: Society and Law beyond the State* (Cambridge: Cambridge University Press, 2002), 33.

[3] 'Normen sind demnach kontrafaktisch stabilisierte Verhaltenserwartungen', Niklas Luhmann, *Rechtssoziologie* (Reinbek: Rowohlt, 1974), 43; Niklas Luhmann, *Das Recht der Gesellschaft* (Frankfurt: Suhrkamp, 1993), 134.

will seek to determine an even more distant future. Law seems resilient and malleable at the same time, like a corn-starch suspension:[4] hit it and it will feel like a solid mass; stir it gently and it will feel like a fluid. This 'non-Newtonian nature' of positive law is most marked in legal orders largely based on customary norms such as international law: any particular breach of a customary prohibition shows law's resilience to change, a change in state practice shows its malleableness.

And the point where theoretical abstraction meets practical observation is a particularly puzzling phenomenon in the law on self-defence since 2001. On the one hand, the pendulum of international security law in recent years seems firmly to have swung towards the less restrictive side, both in scholarship and state practice. On the other hand, however, the International Court of Justice's (ICJ's) post-2001 jurisprudence and other practice have reaffirmed the restrictive reading. Trivially, but crucially, the UN Charter has not been amended. The law—at least Charter law, but perhaps also customary law—seems resilient to change, but perceptions of the law seem to have changed. What has happened and what are the dynamics at play? What is 'resilience' when it comes to the *jus ad bellum*? How can law be resilient vis-à-vis changing circumstance, opinions, interpretation, and state practice?

This chapter will proceed in two steps. Section II will cast a glance on the indicators for and against resilience in an as yet un-theoretical and somewhat phenomenological 'pathology' of post-2001 developments. By contrast, Section III will engage in a theoretical analysis of what 'resilience' can and cannot be and how the law and its perceptions change—or remain static.

II. A Pathology of Resilience and Change since 2001

Legal scholarship deals with thought-objects.[5] Thus, even a pathological account, a diagnosis, is laden with a lot of presuppositions, not the least of which is an

[4] This non-Newtonian liquid is shear thickening: apparent viscosity increases with increased stress, see eg Abdoulaye Fall et al, 'Shear Thickening of Cornstarch Suspensions' (2012) 56 *Journal of Rheology* 575–91.

[5] See the very contentious debate regarding the nature of the 'sciences of the mind' (*Geisteswissenschaften*), expressed inter alia in the so-called *Positivismusstreit* in sociology in the early 1960s (Theodor W. Adorno et al, *Der Positivismusstreit in der deutschen Soziologie* (Neuwied/Berlin: Luchterhand, 1969)). One might note, however, that the 'real' objects of natural sciences are just as much (re)constructed in the scientist's mind as the thought-objects are in the sociologist's or legal scholar's.

assumption of where the law stood on the morning of 11 September 2001. Just as we disagree significantly over the possibility that (and, possibly, the extent to which) the law has changed since then, the state of the law on the relevant date—our very starting point—is equally unclear and disputed. Who is to tell whether the law has changed when those who prefer an extensive reading of the right to self-defence claim that this has been the law since approximately 1842?[6] This is true and there is no good answer to such a challenge. For the purposes of the present argument which describes trends and perception, rather than seeking to provide an 'objective' or quasi-empirical account of the state of the law, however, this does not matter much. The chapter will proceed on the pragmatic assumption that a perceived pre-2001 orthodoxy[7] on the law on self-defence is the yardstick. This orthodoxy incorporates what could be called the '*Nicaragua* consensus' (the view that the judgment on the merits in *Nicaragua* accurately reflects the law), but goes further than that; it is the majority view amongst international lawyers on this area before 9/11. Again, this terminology is inaccurate, as majorities within national contexts—particularly amongst US international lawyers—differed from the *Nicaragua* consensus even before 2001, but for the global community of scholars the majority was probably and roughly in favour of a relatively restrictive reading. With all possible caution, one might outline major positions of a global pre-2001 orthodoxy on self-defence law (at least under Art 51) as follows:

- self-defence is only allowed if and as long as an 'armed attack' occurs and only to end it;
- the armed attack has to have 'begun' for self-defence to be validly exercised;
- an armed attack is a qualified use of force; not every use of force amounts to an armed attack;
- armed attacks can only be committed by a state; actions by non-state entities have to be attributed to a state to count as armed attacks.

A brief overview of the indicators that lead to the perception of change and those that make us perceive stability in self-defence law will follow. It is the indicators—at

[6] eg regarding anticipatory self-defence and without mentioning the *Caroline* incident: High-Level Panel on Threats, Challenges and Change, 'A More Secure World. Our Shared Responsibility', A/59/565 (2004), 54, para 188: 'a threatened State, according to long established international law, can take military action as long as the threatened attack is imminent, no other means would deflect it and the action is proportionate'; regarding non-state armed attacks: Christopher Greenwood, 'Self-Defence' in Rüdiger Wolfrum (ed), *Max Planck Encyclopedia of Public International Law* (Oxford: Oxford University Press, 2012), vol 9, 103, 107 (para 17); Sean D. Murphy, 'Terrorism and the Concept of "Armed Attack" in Article 51 of the U.N. Charter' (2002) 43 *Harvard International Law Journal* 41, 50–1.

[7] The notion of 'orthodoxy' as used here does not imply that the views held are undisputed, merely 'maintaining opinions or practices in accordance with those prevailing or officially sanctioned in one's profession, discipline, party, etc.; conventional, conservative' ('orthodox', adj.,n., A.2.b, *Oxford English Dictionary* (3rd edn, Oxford: Oxford University Press, 2004); online version June 2012, <http://www.oed.com/view/entry/132801>.

best: the so-called 'material sources of law'—we are looking for. Accordingly, selected indicators in three areas will be presented here: jurisprudence, scholarly literature, and state and institutional practice.

A. Jurisprudence

The ICJ has made pronouncements on and partial clarifications of important aspects of the law on self-defence in several major cases since 2001. These are well known and the following will serve as a reminder of salient points only, rather than as an exhaustive analysis.[8]

(1) In its 6 November 2003 judgment in *Oil Platforms*, the ICJ reaffirmed—against certain expansionist voices and citing *Nicaragua*[9]—that the presence of an armed attack is required for the exercise of self-defence and, more indirectly, that these attacks needed to be attributed to a state, viz. Iran.[10]

(2) Eight months later, on 9 July 2004, the ICJ in the *Wall* advisory opinion reaffirmed the conditionality of self-defence under Article 51 on an armed attack, but arguably went much further. Framing the right, it characterized the condition as 'armed attack *by one State* against another State'[11]—pertinently and pointedly disavowing the possibility of non-state armed attacks. On this point, however, the ICJ's 'economy of argument' meant that its reasoning only went as far as was necessary to refute the argument and no further ('Israel does not claim that the attacks against it are imputable to a foreign State').[12]

(3) Most importantly, however, the *Armed Activities* judgment of 19 December 2005 clarified and reaffirmed the *Nicaragua* consensus in a case where the salient facts were eerily reminiscent of *Nicaragua* and where for the first time Articles 2(4) and 51 of the UN Charter were directly applicable in a contentious proceeding. Again, the Court reaffirmed a restrictive right of self-defence under Article 51 after 9/11. The Court's decisions on the law on self-defence is much more complex than those in *Oil Platforms* and *Wall* and, indeed, somewhat reminiscent of *Nicaragua* even with its partially over-complex reasoning. In *Armed Activities*, the Court also did not follow

[8] Chapter 25 deals with ICJ jurisprudence in greater detail.

[9] *Military and Paramilitary Activities in and against Nicaragua (Nicaragua v. US)*, Merits, Judgment of 27 June 1986, ICJ Rep 1986 14, 103, para 195.

[10] *Oil Platforms (Iran v. US)*, Merits, Judgment of 6 Nov 2003, ICJ Rep 2003, 161, 186–7, para 51: 'the United States has to show that attacks had been made upon it for which Iran was responsible; and that those attacks were of such a nature as to be qualified as "armed attacks" within the meaning of that expression in Article 51 UN Charter, and as understood in customary law on the use of force.'

[11] *Legal Consequences of the Construction of a Wall in the Occupied Palestinian Territory*, Advisory Opinion of 9 June 2004, ICJ Rep 2004 136, 194, para 139 (emphasis added).

[12] *Wall*, Advisory Opinion, 194, para 139.

the alleged relaxation of the requirements for self-defence under the Charter. Uganda's actions on the territory of the Democratic Republic of the Congo (DRC) could be justified as self-defence only if there was 'satisfactory proof of the involvement in these attacks, direct or indirect, of the Government of the DRC...the attacks did not emanate from armed bands or irregulars sent by the DRC or on behalf of the DRC',[13] as laid down in Article 3(g) of the Definition of Aggression 1974.[14] The actions of the ADF (a non-state armed group) were classified as an 'armed attack' only in quotes; such attacks 'remained non-attributable to the DRC'.[15] It thus clearly denied self-defence against non-attributable 'armed attacks'. Equally, in deciding whether the actions of two other groups were attributable to Uganda, the Court applied Articles 4, 5, and 8 of the International Law Commission (ILC) Articles on State Responsibility 2001,[16] which seem to be 'the requisite tests...for sufficiency of control of paramilitaries'.[17]

However, the reasoning of the Court is over-complex at several points in the judgment and this muddies the water somewhat; in this specific case, while the Court does not find the actions of pro-Uganda groups attributable *stricto sensu*, Ugandan support had consequences nonetheless; it amounted only to unlawful intervention and (somewhat incoherently argued) also indirectly to a breach of the prohibition of the use of force.[18] At another point, the Court discussed a possible breach of the DRC's 'duty of vigilance by tolerating anti-Ugandan rebels on its territory',[19] but it is unclear whether that passage refers to the expansionist 'unable and unwilling' doctrine,[20] or whether it does not, which is more likely, as the Court found that 'Neither Zaire nor Uganda were in a position to put an end to [rebel groups'] activities...the absence of action by Zaire[]...is [not] tantamount to "tolerating" or "acquiescing" in their activities.'[21]

(4) As an aside, in the judgment in *Bosnia Genocide* of 26 February 2007, the Court even dismissed the *Tadić* standard of 'overall control' for attribution of actions

[13] *Armed Activities on the Territory of the Congo (DRC v. Uganda)*, Merits, Judgment of 19 Dec 2005, ICJ Rep 2005 168, 222–3, para 146.
[14] Definition of Aggression, Art 3(g), A/RES/3314 XXIX (1974), Annex.
[15] *Armed Activities*, Merits, 223, para 146.
[16] Articles on Responsibility of States for Internationally Wrongful Acts, A/RES/56/83 (2001), Annex.
[17] *Armed Activities*, Merits, 226, para 160, citing *Nicaragua*, Merits, 62–5, paras 109–15.
[18] *Armed Activities*, Merits, 226–7, paras 161–5.
[19] *Armed Activities*, Merits, 268, para 300.
[20] eg Davis Brown, 'Use of Force Against Terrorism after September 11th: State Responsibility, Self-Defense and other Responses' (2003) 11 *Cardozo Journal of International and Comparative Law* 1, 30–1; Barry A. Feinstein, 'A Paradigm for Analysis of the Legality of the Use of Armed Force Against Terrorists and States that Aid and Abet Them' (2004) 17 *Transnational Lawyer* 51, 67; Elizabeth Wilmshurst, 'The Chatham House Principles of International Law on the Use of Force in Self-Defence' (2006) 55 *International and Comparative Law Quarterly* 963, 969.
[21] *Armed Activities*, Merits, 268, para 301.

of non-state armed groups—'In this context, the argument in favour of that test is unpersuasive'[22]—and favoured the *Nicaragua* standard.[23]

With minor qualifications and subject always to *caveats*—the Court primarily decides the case before it; its judgments are not meant to be scholarly statements of the law and sometimes lack clarity—the ICJ's post-2001 jurisprudence is truly an indicator for the resilience of the orthodoxy as previously defined. This is also how it has been perceived by many commentators.

1. *Scholarship*

These commentators, the legal scholars, are the opinion leaders in both senses of the word: their opinions are privileged by being published and reasoned and scholarly opinion is more often the avant-garde when it comes to perceiving or claiming changes. However, in contrast to jurisprudence, scholarly literature in international law is far more difficult to survey, for a number of reasons. (1) The debates in international legal scholarship are to a surprisingly large extent still confined within national or linguistic boundaries. German-language contributions, for example, even those published in leading journals such as the *Zeitschrift für ausländisches öfffentliches Recht und Völkerrecht* or the *Archiv für Völkerrecht*, are hardly read outside German-speaking countries. Even within English-language publications hailing from the Anglo-Saxon countries, the US debate, for example, is clearly more self-referential than others and develops its own dynamics. (2) Many scholars keep cover and do not give a clear opinion in their writings whether the law has changed. Others argue, as mentioned previously, that the law has not changed at all and has always supported a relaxed reading.[24] (3) A significant amount of time has passed since 2001 and a generational change among scholars writing on this topic has taken place. While some authors have published before and after September 2001,[25] many of those surveyed later in the chapter started publishing only after that date.[26] Indeed, few of those who have published both before and after the watershed moment have been clear in responding to perceived changes in the law.[27]

[22] *Application of the Convention on the Prevention and Punishment of the Crime of Genocide (Bosnia and Herzegovina v. Serbia and Montenegro)*, Judgment of 26 Feb 2007, ICJ Rep 2007, 43, 210, para 404.

[23] *Bosnia Genocide*, Judgment, 207–9, paras 398–401.

[24] eg Brian Finucane, 'Fictitious States, Effective Control, and the Use of Force Against Non-State Actors' (2012) 30 *Berkeley Journal of International Law* 35, 60–82; Noam Lubell, *Extraterritorial Use of Force Against Non-State Actors* (Oxford: Oxford University Press, 2010) 35; Murphy, 'Terrorism and the Concept of "Armed Attack" in Article 51 of the U.N. Charter', 50.

[25] See eg the books by Christine Gray and Yoram Dinstein spanning the divide: Christine Gray, *International Law and the Use of Force* (Oxford: Oxford University Press, 2000; 2nd edn, 2004; 3rd edn, 2008); Yoram Dinstein, *War, Aggression and Self-Defence* (Cambridge: Cambridge University Press, 1988; 2nd edn, 1994; 3rd edn, 2001; 4th edn, 2005; 5th edn, 2011).

[26] eg Raphaël Van Steenberghe, 'Self-Defence in Response to Attacks by Non-State Actors in the Light of Recent State Practice' (2010) 23 *Leiden Journal of International Law* 183; Andrew C. Orr, 'Unmanned, Unprecedented, and Unresolved' (2011) 44 *Cornell International Law Journal* 729.

[27] See later in this section for Albrecht Randelzhofer's commentary on Art 51 as an example.

In the light of the mass of publications and the complexity of drawing an in any way 'representative' cross-section of scholarly opinion, a random sample[28] of 61 English- and German-language articles, chapters, and books published by 53 authors in the period 2001–12 has been taken here. This sample will be analysed for their authors' position on one aspect of the orthodox opinion arguably subject to change since 2001: the possibility, degree, and shape of a 'delinkage' of armed attacks from the 'host' state. The criterion for delinkage is, roughly, whether the author in question requires that *somehow* the non-state entity's actions be attributed in the sense of 'legally being made a state's actions', even if the required standard of attribution is relatively weak.

On this standard, 39 authors in the sample support a wide reading, 13 do not, and one is too close to call. Unsurprisingly, of 15 authors identifiable as 'US scholars', only one comes even close to a narrow reading of the right of self-defence. However, the tally without 'US scholars' (38 authors) is still significantly in favour of a wide reading: 25 for, 12 against, one unclear. There was no time to draw a similar sample of pre-2001 literature, but a reasonable assumption is that among non-US scholars, the proportion of wide to narrow readings would have been at least reversed. The impression is that pre-2001 the vast majority required attribution to a state within relatively tight parameters à la 'sent by or on behalf of'.[29] For fairness' sake, it must be pointed out that this statement—even if it is echoed in vast parts of the literature on the topic—may be an example of hindsight bias, as a considerable minority of authors in the period 1945–2001 did support a wide reading.[30]

It is significantly more difficult to say which of the authors canvassed believe that the law (or its interpretation) has changed[31] to a wider notion of self-defence in the years immediately preceding, at the time of, due to, or after the 9/11 attacks. With

[28] The sample was drawn from a search in the Heidelberg Max Planck Institute's OPAC (at <http://aleph.mpg.de>) of papers with the classification VR 30.2 (use of force, self-defence), 2001–12 (1,064 as of 24 July 2012), taking such publications which contain significant information on the question of non-state actors in self-defence law and were accessible to the author at the University of Freiburg. The present author is aware of the very real possibility of a sampling bias, as it is possible that the percentage of those who support self-defence against non-state entities is significantly higher amongst authors who write on this topic, simply because scholars who hold such views are more likely to write about them. Conversely, it is also possible that those who do not support this view are less likely to write specifically on this topic. In his own writings, however, the author has dealt explicitly with the topic while holding a restrictivist view (eg Jörg Kammerhofer, 'The *Armed Activities* Case and Non-State Actors in Self-Defence Law' (2007) 20 *Leiden Journal of International Law* 89–113) and therefore does not believe that such a bias can be established beyond doubt.

[29] Definition of Aggression, Art 3(g).

[30] The pre-2001 literature, including the streams of expansionist reading current before the events of 9/11, has been analysed by the present author in Jörg Kammerhofer, 'Uncertainties of the Law on Self-Defence in the United Nations Charter' (2005) 35 *Netherlands Yearbook of International Law 2004* 143–204; Jörg Kammerhofer, *Uncertainty in International Law. A Kelsenian Perspective* (Abingdon: Routledge, 2010), 5–57.

[31] The exact nature of what has changed or not will be deferred to Section III; the reference to 'the law' in this section is only colloquial usage and should not be understood as prejudging the legal-theoretical analysis later in the chapter.

attendant caveats regarding the accuracy of sometimes rather ambiguous phrases, one can say that 23 think that *something* has changed and 30 think that the legal landscape has not significantly shifted or do not give a position. Among non-US authors only, the majorities are reversed: 20 are pro change and 18 are contra or silent. Also interesting is the correlation of wide or narrow readings with the opinions on post-2001 change: of the 39 authors supporting a wide reading of self-defence in this context, a narrow majority (20) think that 'the law' has changed, while 18 authors do not believe in change (one is silent). Of the supporters of a narrower reading, nine do not believe in change and two do.[32] Among US scholars supporting a wide reading, however, ten do *not* believe in significant legal change after 2001, only three do. This may simply be due to the prevalence of wide readings in US scholarly debate pre-2001 which makes the events of 9/11 not an agent of change, but an application of a wider right earlier established. Also, it is tactically less advantageous to argue for a change in the law than to claim that the law has always allowed the actions claimed to be legal by a proponent.

These numbers support the anecdotal evidence[33] that (particularly continental European) non-US writings have changed to a significant degree because of the impact of the events on and following 9/11 on society, including scholars. Even writers in countries where restrictive readings used to be prevalent, for example Germany, have now moved to an expansionist position. A well-known example where the movement is manifested in one author is Albrecht Randelzhofer's commentary on Article 51 in Bruno Simma's *The Charter of the United Nations*. In its first two emanations (the German 1991 and first English 1994 editions), Randelzhofer criticizes *Nicaragua* for relying in its discussion of non-state armed attacks on Article 3(g) of the Definition of Aggression 'as a whole, i.e. [that] apart from the sending itself, the "substantial involvement" in the sending of armed groups is also supposed to come within the notion of an "armed attack"'. The Court's position, he argues, can only be accepted if 'the ambiguous term "substantial involvement" ... is interpreted restrictively';[34] thus, in 1991/4 he supports a position even more restrictive than the '*Nicaragua* consensus'. In 2002, however, we find Randelzhofer's position changed. While still requiring attribution to a state,

[32] Four authors were silent on one or the other category and a correlation could not be made.

[33] The pre-2001 literature is often portrayed, perhaps a little too conveniently uniformly, as having adhered to the narrow reading. Statements like Hannes Hofmeister's are perhaps a little too categorical to be true: 'Consensus existed only over the observation that armed attacks could only be committed by states. If private groups committed an attack, it had to be attributable to a state for Article 51 to apply' (Hannes Hofmeister, 'When is it Right to Attack So-Called "Host States"?' (2007) 11 *Singapore Yearbook of International Law* 75, 76).

[34] Albrecht Randelzhofer, 'Article 51' in Bruno Simma (ed), *Charta der Vereinten Nationen. Kommentar* (Munich: C. H. Beck, 1991), 617, 631–2 (para 31); Albrecht Randelzhofer, 'Article 51' in Brunno Simma (ed), *The Charter of the United Nations: A Commentary* (Oxford: Oxford University Press, 1995), 661, 674 (para 31).

the standard he holds necessary comes close to the expansionist positions now orthodox:

> they are also attributable to a State if they have been committed by private persons and the State has encouraged these acts, has given direct support to them, planned or prepared them at least partly within its territory, or was reluctant to impede these acts. The same is true, if a State gives shelter to terrorists after they have committed an act of terrorism within another State.[35]

The last variant goes beyond what even some expansionist scholars would regard as sufficient and was clearly a response to the specific situation following the 9/11 attacks. In the third edition 2013, however, Randelzhofer (now co-authoring with Georg Nolte) backtracks a little on the expansionist rhetoric in the light of the ICJ's post-2001 jurisprudence. The examples cited previously are still there, even if the last sentence is modified by adding the following words: 'in a situation in which the attack can still be regarded as ongoing'.[36] The framework, however, is significantly less wide, for example: 'the preferable view still seems to be that attacks by organized armed groups need to be attributed to a State in order to enable the affected State to exercise its right of self-defence' or 'It would go too far, however, to potentially expose any State, from the territory of which organized armed groups operate, to forcible measures of self-defence'.[37]

Thus, while the academic debate on the law on the use of force, in particular regarding the modalities of the right to self-defence is as controversial and vibrant as ever, and while scholars disagree as fundamentally about the issues at stake as before 2001, the 'smallest common denominator', the orthodoxy, seems to have shifted markedly in favour of a wider reading of the right in the last 13 years. Measured by the expressions of academic opinion, then, 'the law' has—the restrictive rules on self-defence have—not been resilient, but has changed with changing circumstances.

2. *State and Security Council practice*

Even on a spuriously cursive view, events seem to be accumulating where a less restrictive reading of the right to self-defence would result in its conformity, in other words: state practice seems to be favouring a wider right. In contrast, the instances of *opinio juris* (eg on non-state armed attacks or a wide anticipatory self-defence) seem a little less prevalent and they seem to be confined to a few states. States have also not decided to change Article 51 of the UN Charter. Lastly, of course, the

[35] Albrecht Randelzhofer, 'Article 51' in Bruno Simma et al (eds), *The Charter of the United Nations: A Commentary* (2nd edn, Oxford: Oxford University Press, 2002), 788, 802 (para 34).

[36] Albrecht Randelzhofer and Georg Nolte, 'Article 51' in Bruno Simma et al (eds), *The Charter of the United Nations: A Commentary* (3rd edn, Oxford: Oxford University Press, 2012), 1397, 1418 (para 38).

[37] Randelzhofer 'Article 51' in Bruno Simma et al (eds), *The Charter of the United Nations: A Commentary* (3rd edn, 2012), 1417 (para 37).

Security Council's response to the 9/11 attacks in S/RES/1368 and 1373 has variously been read as endorsing a wide notion of self-defence.[38]

III. What is Resilient and What Does Resilience Mean?

We have, then, a number of partially contradicting 'indicators' for and against the resilience of 'the law'. It would be illusory to try to pronounce a winner based on a quasi-metrization of these along the lines of: 'one instance of state practice equals 0.545 ICJ judgments equals 64.83 scholarly papers'. An answer to the question '*How* resilient is "the law" on a given point?' cannot even be attempted, however, without elucidating some of the underlying theoretical issues in tandem with an analysis of the various 'factors' mentioned in Section II for changing 'the law'. The use of the colloquialism 'the law' in combination with resilience and change is already one of the key questions, for *what* is resilient (or not) in this context. Another question, inextricably bound up with the first, is: what does it mean to say that 'the law' (whatever that is) is resilient or has changed? Whereas the first question asks what has changed, the second question asks what the change looks like; inevitably, this will depend on the object of change.

Most doctrinal writings on the law on self-defence are not extraordinarily concerned with clarifying such theoretical issues; those who believe that 'self-defence law' has changed since 2001 do not tell us, for example, precisely

[38] *Wall*, Advisory Opinion, Separate Opinion of Judge Kooijmans, 229–230, para 35, Declaration of Judge Buergenthal, 244, para 6; *Armed Activities*, Merits, Separate Opinion of Judge Simma, 337, para 11, Separate Opinion of Judge Kooijmans, 313, para 26; Daniel Bethlehem, 'International Law and the Use of Force: The Law as it Is and as it Should Be' in UK House of Commons Select Committee on Foreign Affairs, *Foreign Policy Aspects of the War against Terrorism, Seventh Report of Session 2003–04* (2004), Written evidence (Ev 100), para 17, available at <http://www.publications.parliament.uk/pa/cm200304/cmselect/cmfaff/441/4060808.htm>; Wilmshurst, 'The Chatham House Principles', 970; Randelzhofer, 'Article 51' in Simma et al (eds), *The Charter of the United Nations: A Commentary* (2nd edn, 2002), 802 (para 35); Dinstein, *War, Aggression and Self-Defence*, 228; Thomas M. Franck, 'Terrorism and the Right of Self-Defense' (2001) 95 *American Journal of International Law* 839, 839–40; Pieter H. Kooijmans, 'The Legality of the Use of Force in the Recent Case Law of the International Court of Justice' in Sienho Yee and Jacques-Yvan Morin (eds), *Multiculturalism and International Law: Essays in Honour of Edward McWhinney* (Leiden: Martinus Nijhoff, 2009), 455, 465; Christian J. Tams, 'The Use of Force Against Terrorists' (2009) 20 *European Journal of International Law* 359, 377; Kimberley N. Trapp, 'Back to Basics: Necessity, Proportionality, and the Right of Self-Defence against Non-State Terrorist Actors' (2007) 56 *International and Comparative Law Quarterly* 141, 143, 151.

what has changed and how. Oftentimes, it is a pragmatic mixture of *ab inconvenienti* arguments,[39] change of customary law, and a quasi-officious reinterpretation. A random example may serve as an illustration of this point. Hannes Hofmeister argues: 'The military response to the 9/11 attacks undoubtedly had an impact on international law.... In this regard, the collective response to those terrorist attacks can be constructed as a jurisgenerative event'.[40] The arguments used will be analysed in greater detail later; however, two broad lines of argument can be discerned: first, that somehow Article 51 and/or a parallel (or uniquely) customary norm is changed (Section III.B); second, that something other than the norm is affected, mostly that a 'reinterpretation' has taken place or has to take place (Section III.C). These are also the two theoretically most promising avenues on the question of what is resilient: either the norm or its interpretation (perception), whatever that may mean.

A. What Can Cause Change?

Before we can tackle these questions, however, we need to clarify what the factor is that can change or has changed 'the law' for those who propound such change. *How* do scholars—or judges in their individual opinions—envisage that change in this area of the law can take or has taken place? Let us take the three manifestations or indicators of change and resilience examined in Section II.

- *Scholarship*. It may implicitly ascribe to itself the power to make law by virtue of its unique insights,[41] but this is usually not voiced openly. The UN Charter does not specify that it can be changed by scholarly opinion and neither do the rules on customary international lawmaking, this much is clear. But that is not the claim that is sometimes made by scholars when they imply that scholarship has some influence upon change and resilience;[42] the claim is rather that scholarship can influence the 'interpretation' of the law and that this means something. But this depends on what 'the interpretation' is and what it can do (Section III.C).

[39] eg Tom Ruys and Sten Verhoeven, 'Attacks by Private Actors and the Right of Self-Defence' (2005) 10 *Journal of Conflict and Security Law* 289, 310; Benjamin Langille, 'It's "Instant Custom": How the Bush Doctrine Became a Law After the Terrorist Attacks of September 11, 2001' (2003) 26 *Boston College International and Comparative Law Review* 145, 156.

[40] Hofmeister, 'When is it Right to Attack So-Called "Host States"?', 83.

[41] Jörg Kammerhofer, 'Law-Making by Scholarship? The Dark Side of 21st Century International Legal "Methodology"' in James Crawford and Sarah Nouwen (eds), *Select Proceedings of the European Society of International Law. Third Volume: International Law 1989–2010: A Performance Appraisal. Cambridge, 2–4 September 2010* (Oxford: Hart, 2012), 115.

[42] Possibly Michael Byers, 'Terrorism, the Use of Force and International Law after 11 September' (2002) 51 *International and Comparative Law Quarterly* 401, 409–10.

- *Jurisprudence*. In a non-common law legal system such as the international legal order, judicial pronouncements in judgments and advisory opinions are at most individual norms binding on the parties. ICJ judgments do not directly (on the level of the hierarchy of lawmaking) make or change treaty or customary norms. Here again, it is the interpretation of Article 51 or a judgment's factual influence upon customary lawmaking processes that is deemed to be constituted by jurisprudence.
- *Practice*. Overwhelmingly, nearly uniformly and irrespectively of whether the author in question claims change in the law or its interpretations, it is the actual practice, the circumstances, a 'change in fact',[43] post-2001 state practice[44] (possibly including *opinio juris*),[45] or institutional practice, that has changed. Implicit is the claim that 'practice'—whatever that may mean precisely—can effect change in the law or its interpretation(s).

Hence, it is clear that the two possibilities of where change happens will have to be analysed (on the legal-theoretical level) on the basis of the assumption that it is primarily 'practice' that can do this. As mentioned, many authors subconsciously or deliberately leave open exactly what has changed or exactly how this change happens or can happen. They leave this to the theoretical debates and believe that doctrinal writings need not address these points. We will therefore seek to reintegrate the generalist debates into the law on self-defence.

B. Practice Changes 'the Law'

'The law' for the purposes of this argument is taken to mean the sum totality of positive norms of the legal order 'international law'. In our case, the right of self-defence, as an exception to the prohibition of the use of force, is a positive norm of international treaty law and/or customary international law. How can these norms be changed through state and institutional practice—that is, how can the 'existence' (validity) of one or more norms have a different form (or content)?

1. *Change in the UN Charter as treaty norm*

Article 51 of the UN Charter specifies the right to self-defence as a norm of an international legal treaty. The relevant articles of the Charter have not been amended by

[43] Carsten Stahn, 'Terrorist Acts as "Armed Attack"' (2003) 27 *Fletcher Forum of World Affairs* 35, 36.

[44] James A. Green, *The International Court of Justice and Self-Defence in International Law* (Oxford: Hart, 2009), 47, 157; Greenwood, 'Self-Defence' in Wolfrum, *Max Planck Encyclopedia of Public International Law*, 107 (para 18); Theresa Reinold, 'State Weakness, Irregular Warfare, and the Right to Self-Defense post-9/11' (2011) 105 *American Journal of International Law* 244, 245, 284; Tom Ruys, *'Armed Attack' and Article 51 of the UN Charter* (Cambridge: Cambridge University Press, 2010), 486–7; Steenberghe, 'Self-Defence in Response to Attacks by Non-State Actors in the Light of Recent State Practice', 184, 199; Tams, 'The Use of Force Against Terrorists', 378, 384–5.

[45] Ruys, *'Armed Attack' and Article 51 of the UN Charter*, 486.

contrarius actus or through the procedure for amendments under Articles 108 and 109. The claim, therefore, can only be that the Charter has been changed by subsequent practice. While in the debate canvassed here this specific claim seems not to have been used much,[46] the question of role and power of subsequent practice to change treaty law is a standard debate amongst international lawyers. Proponents of a wide reading prefer to argue on different grounds, but we will briefly touch upon the arguments here. Raphaël van Steenberghe summarizes the argument:

> as has been correctly underlined in the legal literature, treaty modification based on subsequent state practice is generally admitted in jurisprudence, scholarship, and state practice. The general condition agreed on is that the practice of states parties to a treaty must clearly evidence an agreement between these states to modify the treaty.[47]

This short statement contains the three arguments that have been used to justify the (rather counter-intuitive) idea that practice, that is, facts alone, can change treaties.

(1) Steenberghe points to 'state practice' that 'generally admit[s]' modification by subsequent practice.[48] This begs the question, proving the conclusion by inserting it in the premise; it is also a breach of the Is–Ought dichotomy. If the behaviour of the subjects of law *alone* determines the law applicable to them at every moment and without the law's authorization, breaches of treaty norms would be impossible. Restricting this to a widespread or common practice does not alleviate the breach. Practice alone, without being authorized to do so by the law, cannot modify the law.

(2) The two main arguments are that either subsequent practice is evidence of a tacit treaty purporting to modify the written treaty, or that it forms part of a customary international law norm modifying or abrogating the treaty. In contradistinction to the opinions canvassed here, in the general debate a justification as a subsequent and informal agreement is by far the most popular.[49] However, this is not unproblematic either: where is the meeting of wills as a necessary condition for

[46] Of the papers used here, only Steenberghe, 'Self-Defence in Response to Attacks by Non-State Actors in the Light of Recent State Practice' discusses this option outright and comes to the conclusion that it has not happened (yet) with respect to self-defence against non-state entities.

[47] Steenberghe, 'Self-Defence in Response to Attacks by Non-State Actors in the Light of Recent State Practice', 186.

[48] Within the generalist debate, Salo Engel can also be quoted: 'in the daily practice of Members and organs, the Charter has undergone far-reaching changes even without the adoption of formal amendments.' Salo Engel, 'Procedures for de facto Revision of the Charter' (1965) 59 *American Society of International Law Proceedings* 108, 108.

[49] C. F. Amerasinghe, 'Interpretation of Texts in Open International Organizations' (1995) 65 *British Yearbook of International Law 1994* 175, 200; Rudolf Bernhardt, *Die Auslegung völkerrechtlicher Verträge insbesondere in der neueren Rechtsprechung internationaler Gerichte* (Cologne: Heymanns, 1963), 126–7; Rudolf Bernhardt, 'Interpretation and Implied (Tacit) Modification of Treaties. Comments on Arts. 27, 28, 29 and 38 of the ILC's 1966 Draft Articles on the Law of Treaties' (1967) 25 *Zeitschrift für ausländisches öffentliches Recht und Völkerrecht* 491, 498–9; Gerald G. Fitzmaurice, 'The Law and Procedure of

lawmaking? How do we prove that this has taken place? Similar behaviour may be motivated by a range of factors, particularly in the law on the use of force, and an agreement to make new (treaty) law is surely one of the least likely interpretations. To presume this will from the uniformity of practice—hardly the case with self-defence against non-state entities anyway—is highly fictitious. If it is to be a legal fiction, then proof that this is part of the rules on lawmaking is required; this has so far not been established.

(3) What of the argument that a norm of customary international law (of which state practice is a constituent part) can modify a treaty?[50] If orthodox generalists—even proponents of the modifiability of treaties by subsequent custom[51]—are correct that all sources of international law are hierarchically equal,[52] then a mutual derogability, as is also claimed,[53] cannot be the consequence. For if customary international law and treaty law on the same topic can exist side by side, as the Court held in *Nicaragua*,[54] why should two equal sources be able to modify one another? Derogability requires specific regulation; non-derogability does not. Who would argue in the realm of domestic private law that an earlier contract between parties A to R can be amended by the later practices of B, E, and G? Derogation is a specific norm function, requiring the presence of a derogating norm which needs to be higher law. This is a very complex and problematic topic and it is not entirely clear that it can work in non-hierarchically ordered normative systems such as international law.[55]

the International Court of Justice 1951–4: Treaty Interpretation and other Treaty Points' (1958) 33 *British Yearbook of International Law 1957* 203, 212.

[50] In generalist literature this is proposed inter alia in: Michael Byers, *Custom, Power and the Power of Rules. International Relations and Customary International Law* (Cambridge: Cambridge University Press, 1999), 177–80; Wolfram Karl, *Vertrag und spätere Praxis im Völkerrecht* (Berlin: Springer, 1983), 86–110, 248–68; Nancy Kontou, *The Termination and Revision of Treaties in the Light of New Customary International Law* (Oxford: Oxford University Press, 1994); Hugh Thirlway, *International Customary Law and Codification* (Leiden: Sijthoff, 1972), 130–2.

[51] Karl, *Vertrag und spätere Praxis im Völkerrecht*, 86–7, 109, 249.

[52] eg Maarten Bos, 'The Recognized Manifestations of International Law. A New Theory of "Sources"' (1977) 20 *German Yearbook of International Law* 9, 73–4; Torsten Gihl, 'The Legal Character and Sources of International Law' (1957) 1 *Scandinavian Studies in Law* 51, 75.

[53] eg Malcolm N. Shaw, *International Law* (6th edn, Cambridge: Cambridge University Press, 2008), 123.

[54] *Nicaragua*, Merits, 93–6, paras 174–9.

[55] The present author has previously tried to spell out some aspects of this problem in international law: Kammerhofer, *Uncertainty in International Law*, 139–94; on general jurisprudential aspects see also: Jörg Kammerhofer, 'Robert Walter, die Normkonflikte und der zweite Stufenbau des Rechts' in Clemens Jabloner et al (eds), *Gedenkschrift für Robert Walter* (Vienna: Manz, 2013), 237, 251–5.

2. *Change in Article 51, seen as merely incorporating an external (customary) standard*

Several of the authors canvassed argue that the *customary* right of self-defence has changed after 2001.[56] Again, Steenberghe's analysis is a good starting point. He points out, in line with *Nicaragua*, 'that the right to act in self-defence is regulated by both customary and conventional norms', but he finds it 'difficult to identify which of these two sources, customary or conventional law, are invoked by states'.[57] One is tempted to object that even if there are two norms, a customary right to self-defence does not justify a breach under Article 2(4) of the UN Charter *stricto sensu* and Article 51 cannot justify a breach of the customary prohibition. Hence, claiming a customary right that is possibly wider than the Charter right does not help in justifying a prima facie breach of Article 2(4). But Steenberghe, in line with a significant part of the scholarly community, believes that:

> Article 51 itself refers to customary law... [this] may be clearly inferred from the words with which Art. 51 begins—'Nothing in the present Charter shall impair...'. These words logically imply that the right of self-defence existed prior to the UN Charter and, as a result, is of a customary nature.[58]

This is a reference to what the present author has called the 'black hole' theory.[59] A number of writers have maintained that 'The effect of this article is not to create the right but explicitly to recognize its existence',[60] that is, that the Charter itself does not regulate the right of self-defence. If this were true in the way these authors claim, Article 51 would leave a hole in the normative framework of the Charter. The most common variant of this theory, both in pre-2001 literature[61] and amongst the authors canvassed here,[62] is that Article 51 refers to the current state of the customary

[56] eg Dinstein, *War, Aggression and Self-Defence*, 227–8; Christian Henderson, 'The Bush Doctrine: from Theory to Practice' (2004) 9 *Journal of Conflict and Security Law* 3, 5; Langille, 'It's "Instant Custom"', 154; possibly: Green, *The International Court of Justice and Self-Defence in International Law*, 47, 157; Ruys, *'Armed Attack' and Article 51 of the UN Charter*, 486–7.

[57] Steenberghe, 'Self-Defence in Response to Attacks by Non-State Actors in the Light of Recent State Practice', 185.

[58] Steenberghe, 'Self-Defence in Response to Attacks by Non-State Actors in the Light of Recent State Practice', 185.

[59] Kammerhofer, *Uncertainty in International Law*, 7.

[60] Leland M. Goodrich, Edvard Hambro, and Anne P. Simmons, *Charter of the United Nations: Commentary and Documents* (3rd edn, New York: Columbia University Press, 1969), 344.

[61] eg Derek W. Bowett, *Self-Defence in International Law* (Manchester: Manchester University Press, 1958), 184–8; Myres S. McDougal and Florentino P. Feliciano, *Law and Minimum World Public Order* (New Haven, CT: Yale University Press, 1961), 235; Stephen M. Schwebel, 'Aggression, Intervention and Self-Defence in Modern International Law' (1972-II) 136 *Recueil des cours de l'Académie de droit international* 411, 480; Sir Humphrey Waldock, 'The Regulation of the Use of Force by Individual States in International Law' (1952-II) 81 *Recueil des cours de l'Académie de droit international* 451, 497.

[62] eg Finucane, 'Fictitious States, Effective Control, and the Use of Force Against Non-State Actors', 40; David McKeever, 'The Contribution of the International Court of Justice to the Law on the Use of Force' (2009) 78 *Nordic Journal of International Law* 361, 367; Norman G. Printer, 'The Use of Force Against Non-State Actors under International Law' (2003) 8 *UCLA Journal of International Law and Foreign Affairs* 331, 338.

international right of self-defence.[63] The Charter, on this view, seems not to want to regulate self-defence—yet this is exactly what it does. This is so for two reasons.

A conventional reason is that on a systematic interpretation, the Charter established a complete system of collective security, of which the pacification of inter-member relations and the prohibition of force between members is an integral part. The general prohibition of force in Article 2(4) seems to prohibit all threats or uses of force—whether allowed by pre-Charter customary law or not—and exceptions need to be found in the Charter. The word 'nothing' in Article 51 refers, after all, to 'in this Charter'. The *Armed Activities* judgment supports this reading: 'Article 51 of the Charter may justify a use of force in self-defence only within the strict confines there laid down. It does not allow the use of force by a State…beyond these parameters.'[64]

A more theoretical argument is that even if Article 51 is intended as a sort of 'hole' in the Charter's tapestry, this cannot work as envisaged. Simply by having Article 51 there, the matter is being regulated by the Charter. As an incorporation clause, it does not establish a connection between the referring norm and the norm referred to and does not cut a hole in the Charter through which we pull another cloth, that of customary law. Rather, it is a shortcut to lawmaking: Article 51 creates self-defence law in shorthand form and Article 51 is filled with treaty-law content. But this conception is not unproblematic, for if a treaty norm is its text, non-written norms such as customary law cannot form part of that norm: the incorporation fails and anything that the applying organ believes to be 'the law' can be taken as the basis for that organ's decision. Where no organ is empowered to decide, as in the case of Article 51, no one can make that decision.

If the present state of customary international law includes a right to defend against non-state entities and if Article 51 incorporates this wide customary right, this incorporation would be severely limited in how far it can change the Charter as a treaty norm. In other words, Article 51 cannot function like a true black hole and it cannot devour the Charter regulation of the use of force. Since Article 51 is part of the Charter, the content of Article 51 as a treaty norm is dependent upon the Charter system of regulation. Most obvious are the conditions for the valid exercise of the right in Article 51 itself: 'if an armed attack occurs' and 'until the Security Council has taken measures necessary'. Whatever the two conditions mean exactly, no one can deny that they are *conditiones sine qua non* for the exercise of self-defence under Charter law.

Let us assume that Article 51 allows for self-defence against non-state entities' armed attacks as well as against state armed attacks; it can thus justify prima facie

[63] See also *Nicaragua*, Merits, 94, para 176: 'The Court therefore finds that Article 51 of the Charter is only meaningful on the basis that there is a "natural" or "inherent" right of self-defence, and it is hard to see how this can be other than of a customary nature, even if its present content has been confirmed and influenced by the Charter.'

[64] *Armed Activities*, Merits, 223, para 148.

breaches of various norms of the Charter—'Nothing *in the present Charter* shall impair'—by the defending state. However, the defender will not breach Article 2(4) by using military force against individuals or groups, since they are not protected by that prohibition. However, if the individuals are present on another state's territory, the defender will have prima facie violated Article 2(4), but only vis-à-vis the territorial state. As the Chatham House Principles correctly note: 'it must be conceded that an attack against a non-state actor within a State will inevitably constitute the use of force on the territorial State.'[65] Hence, the defender (normally) needs to justify the breach of Article 2(4) vis-à-vis the territorial state. Only vis-à-vis the territorial state is Article 2(4) violated and only against it must the defender's actions be justified. The only pertinent justification in the Charter is Article 51. Thus, even if Article 51's 'armed attack' criterion is not bound to state action, it does clearly establish that it works as a justification only vis-à-vis the 'entity' having authored the armed attack.[66] (The rather unconvincing way out is to argue that unwillingness or inability to suppress these private groups constitutes an armed attack by the territorial state in its own right.[67]) This specific argument can be countered, but the point to be made here is not about the doctrinal specifics. Rather, it is that the 'black hole' argument can in no case work as intended, because even an incorporated norm is not an alien norm, but properly part of the incorporating treaty.

3. *Change in customary international law*

What of the possibilities of change and resilience of the parallel customary international right of self-defence *sans* Charter? The customary law norm on self-defence can be changed by state practice accompanied by *opinio juris* rising (as it arguably has to change a *jus cogens* norm) to a very high level. There is some practice, but, *pace* Tom Ruys,[68] rather little *opinio juris*, possibly too little to change normal customary law,[69] certainly not a *jus cogens* norm. In addition, an arguably wide customary right is limited in its import upon the Charter regime, because, as mentioned earlier, only Articles 51 and 42, not customary norms, can justify a prima facie breach of Article 2(4). A second limitation is that the systemic argument

[65] Wilmshurst, 'The Chatham House Principles', 670.

[66] This argument has been made in more detail, pointing also to its potential weaknesses, in Kammerhofer, 'The *Armed Activities* Case and Non-State Actors in Self-Defence Law', 105–6; Kammerhofer, *Uncertainty in International Law*, 36–43. For similar arguments, see also Constantine Antonopoulos, 'Force by Armed Groups as Armed Attack and the Broadening of Self-Defence' (2008) 55 *Netherlands International Law Review* 159, 169; Tams, 'The Use of Force Against Terrorists', 385.

[67] Natalino Ronzitti, 'The Expanding Law of Self-Defence' (2006) 11 *Journal of Conflict and Security Law* 343, 349; possibly: Randelzhofer, 'Article 51' in Simma et al, *The Charter of the United Nations: A Commentary* (2nd edn, 2002), 802 (para 34).

[68] Ruys, *'Armed Attack' and Article 51 of the UN Charter*, 486.

[69] Kalliopi Chainoglou, 'Reconceptualising Self-Defence in International Law' (2007) 18 *King's Law Journal* 61, 94.

in Section III.B.2—of the relationship between the author of the armed attack as a condition for self-defence and the 'victim' of the defender's prima facie breach of the prohibition—may find a parallel in customary law.

Whether and to what extent later state practice and *opinio juris* have changed customary international law is rather less important, however, than whether—as is sometimes and implicitly argued[70]—developments in practice alone can change and have changed the law on self-defence. Among the authors canvassed here, this is typically expressed by arguing that 'the law' has changed, yet this change has taken place through the new 'reality', the new 'practice' on the ground. Again, the idea that customary international lawmaking requires practice only is not new or restricted to the law on the use of force. In theoretical writings on international law, 'single element' theories of customary law-creation are sometimes voiced[71] and discussed,[72] although the bulk of these designs originate in specialist writings. Arguments that presuppose a theory of custom-creation just requiring practice tend to be prevalent in the field at issue in this chapter; theories with an *opinio juris* bias tend to be found mainly in writings on humanitarian and human rights law. Well-developed arguments, not to mention a rigorously coherent theoretical groundwork, are usually missing in both fields.[73]

Of the writings canvassed, two statements voice the idea that customary law can be changed by subsequent practice alone. Kalliopi Chainoglou argues that 'new rules on the use of force are being shaped and it is likely that it will take some more time and some more state practice before they are codified'[74] and for Davis Brown: 'State practice has clearly established that an attack of the scale and effect of September 11th is an armed attack against a state'.[75] Neither statement is clear, but this is not surprising, since it is far more common and convenient to argue in favour of a change of 'the interpretation' through state practice (Section III.C) and since a theoretical analysis shows that one-element theories are untenable. Practice alone cannot create law if law is a rule, a norm in any sense of the word, if law is more than a simple description of what happens. A collection of facts cannot be *pre*scriptive in its own

[70] Eustace Chikere Azubuike, 'Probing the Scope of Self Defense in International Law' (2011) 17 *Golden Gate University School of Law Annual Survey of International and Comparative Law* 129, 159; Hofmeister, 'When is it Right to Attack So-Called "Host States"?', 83; Jerzy Kranz, 'Die völkerrechtliche Verantwortlichkeit für die Anwendung militärischer Gewalt' (2010) 48 *Archiv des Völkerrechts*, 281, 304; possibly: Green, *The International Court of Justice and Self-Defence in International Law*, 157.

[71] Lazare Kopelmanas, 'Custom as a Means of the Creation of International Law' (1937) 18 *British Yearbook of International Law* 127–51; Hans Kelsen, 'Théorie du droit international coutumier' (1939) 1 (NS) *Revue internationale de la théorie du droit* 253.

[72] Jason Beckett, *The End of Customary International Law? A Purposive Analysis of Structural Indeterminacy* (Saarbrucken: VDM, 2008); Kammerhofer, *Uncertainty in International Law*, 61–2.

[73] This is not particularly surprising, given the politico-moralist instrumentalization of these fields; see Jörg Kammerhofer, 'Orthodox Generalists and Political Activists in International Legal Scholarship' in Matthew Happold (ed), *International Law in a Multipolar World* (Abingdon: Routledge, 2011), 138–57.

[74] Chainoglou, 'Reconceptualising Self-Defence in International Law', 94.

[75] Brown, 'Use of Force Against Terrorism after September 11th', 29.

right—this would be a custom, not customary *law*. Accordingly, it is not surprising that (generalist) orthodoxy has, for the past 120–200 years, required *opinio juris sive necessitatis*.[76] In generalist scholarship, important examples for one-element theories based on practice are Maurice Mendelson's Hague Academy course of 1998 and the International Law Association's 2000 report on customary international law,[77] which, to some degree, both argue that the subjective element is not a necessary condition for the coming-into-existence of a customary norm.[78] This view is, however, crucially short of a complete disavowal of the subjective element, as the presence of that element is presumed.[79] The subjective element is not eliminated under these theories, because certain conceptions of state practice can contain expressions of a will/belief that something is/be law.

c. Practice Changes 'the Interpretation'

But for the majority of writers, the claim to change is much softer and, in their eyes, much more sustainable.[80] 'The law' on self-defence, it is argued, can change through its interpretation, through a change in the way 'we' (scholars, practitioners, subjects of law) 'view' the law.[81] Among the writers canvassed, typical statements

[76] For a retracing of this element, see inter alia: Peter Benson, 'François Gény's Doctrine on Customary Law' (1983) 20 *Canadian Yearbook of International Law* 267; Jörg Kammerhofer, [Book Review:] 'Amanda Perreau-Saussine, James Bernard Murphy (eds), *The Nature of Customary Law. Legal, Historical and Philosophical Perspectives* (2009)' (2012) 23 *European Journal of International Law* 589.

[77] Maurice H. Mendelson, 'The Subjective Element in Customary International Law' (1996) 66 *British Yearbook of International Law 1995* 177; Maurice H. Mendelson, 'The Formation of Customary International Law' (1999) 272 *Recueil des cours de l'Académie de droit international 1998* 155; International Law Association (ILA), Committee on the Formation of Rules of Customary (General) International Law, *Final Report of the Committee: Statement of Principles Applicable to the Formation of General Customary International Law* (2000).

[78] Mendelson, 'The Subjective Element in Customary International Law', 188.

[79] ILA, *Final Report of the Committee: Statement of Principles*, 32.

[80] Further on present writer's arguments on the proper limits of interpretation: Jörg Kammerhofer, 'Systemic Integration, Legal Theory and the ILC' (2010) 19 *Finnish Yearbook of International Law 2008* 157.

[81] eg: Thomas Bruha, 'Gewaltverbot und humanitäres Völkerrecht nach dem 11. September 2001' (2002) 40 *Archiv des Völkerrechts* 383; Thomas Bruha, 'Kampf gegen den Terrorismus als neue Rechtfertigungsfigur für die Anwendung militärischer Gewalt' in Thomas Bruha (ed), *Legalität, Legitimität und Moral* (Tubingen: Mohr Siebeck, 2008), 157; Byers, 'Terrorism, the Use of Force and International Law after 11 September'; Rein Müllerson, '*Jus ad Bellum* and International Terrorism' (2002) 32 *Israel Yearbook on Human Rights* 1; Reinold, 'State Weakness, Irregular Warfare, and the Right to Self-Defense post-9/11'; Christian Schaller, 'Operation Enduring Freedom und das Recht auf Selbstverteidigung gegen Terroristen' (2011) 86 *Die Friedens-Warte* 111; Michael N. Schmitt, 'Counter-Terrorism and the Use of Force in International Law' (2002) 32 *Israel Yearbook on Human Rights* 53; Rüdiger Wolfrum, 'The Attack of September 11, 2001, the Wars Against the Taliban and Iraq' (2003) 7 *Max Planck Yearbook of United Nations Law* 1, 36; possibly/unclear: James A. Green, 'Docking the Caroline' (2006) 14 *Cardozo Journal of International and Comparative Law* 429; Markus Krajewski,

are: 'The post-9/11 environment provides fertile ground for developing a broader interpretation of the concept of armed attack',[82] or: 'the understandings of the precise parameters of the law evolve[]...international law is understood in light of the circumstances in which it finds itself'.[83] On the issue of non-state entities' armed attacks, the argument that interpretation has changed is also combined with the position that the law has always recognized this form: '[this] should not be seen as a modification of the law of self-defence, but at most as an interpretation of this law which had never been excluded.'[84] That such a change of 'understanding' is not, strictly speaking, a change of law, is recognized even by those who promote the change: 'The apparent change...was in many ways a change in fact, rather than a change in the law....it is the circumstances rather than the legal matrix that has changed.'[85] That subsequent practice can change the interpretation of Article 51 is the most common claim amongst scholars and is certainly most practically relevant. However, on a thorough legal-theoretical analysis, this claim is the least theoretically sustainable of those alleging that the law in this area is not resilient.

Article 31(3)(b) of the Vienna Convention on the Law of Treaties 1969 provides that subsequent practice is a factor in the interpretation of treaties and this provision has been taken by generalist orthodoxy to mean that the behaviour of parties to an international treaty after its entry into force and/or of international organs vis-à-vis their constituting instruments is in some way determinative of what the treaty 'means'. Generalist writings frequently point to the difficulty in distinguishing interpretation from change. Where does determination of the meaning end and the change begin? However, even if interpretation is difficult or impossible to distinguish from change,[86] we thus only show that we experience difficulty in ascertaining a borderline, not that it does not exist. Yet the question persists in a more ontological form: is the law the provision or its interpretation? In the deceptively easy case of the treaty norm at issue here: 'Nothing in the present Charter shall

'Selbstverteidigung gegen bewaffnete Angriffe nicht-staatlicher Organisationen' (2002) 40 *Archiv des Völkerrechts* 183; Stahn, 'Terrorist Acts as "Armed Attack"'; Steenberghe, 'Self-Defence in Response to Attacks by Non-State Actors in the Light of Recent State Practice', 199; Tams, 'The Use of Force Against Terrorists', 384–5.

[82] Reinold, 'State Weakness, Irregular Warfare, and the Right to Self-Defense post-9/11', 248.

[83] Schmitt, 'Counter-Terrorism and the Use of Force in International Law', 102.

[84] Steenberghe, 'Self-Defence in Response to Attacks by Non-State Actors in the Light of Recent State Practice', 199.

[85] Stahn, 'Terrorist Acts as "Armed Attack"', 36.

[86] Bernhardt, 'Interpretation and Implied (Tacit) Modification of Treaties', 499; Karl, *Vertrag und spätere Praxis im Völkerrecht*, 39; Georg Ress, 'Die Bedeutung der nachfolgenden Praxis für die Vertragsinterpretation nach der Wiener Vertragsrechtskonvention (WVRK)' in Roland Bieber and Georg Ress (eds), *Die Dynamik des europäischen Gemeinschaftsrechts. Die Auslegung des europäischen Gemeinschaftsrechts im Lichte nachfolgender Praxis der Mitgliedstaaten und der EG-Organe* (Baden-Baden: Nomos, 1987), 49, 61, 64; Ian Sinclair, *The Vienna Convention on the Law of Treaties* (2nd edn, Manchester: Manchester University Press, 1984), 138; Sir Humphrey Waldock, Third Report on the Law of Treaties, A.CN.4/167, A.CN.4/167/Add.1–3, reprinted in 16 *Yearbook of the International Law Commission*, 1964, vol II, 1, 60, para 25.

impair...' it can validly be asked whether these words are the norm—or the various meanings that may be accorded to these words. If the latter, as one may instinctively feel, then in the last instance nothing was decided in San Francisco. We now know of the radical indeterminacy of natural languages[87]—and radically speaking, anything could mean anything. Yet the act of positive norm-creation did create *something* and something did become Charter law. This is not the place for an exhaustive discussion and a few paragraphs must suffice.

For written norms, it can be argued that they are made of language and are formulated as words and sentences.[88] If that is the case, the words, the text are the norm itself. The opposite viewpoint is held by some legal philosophers, for example Riccardo Guastini: 'As a matter of course, norms should not be confused with norm-formulations.... norms (as opposed to norm-formulations) are but the result of interpretation.'[89] This is unconvincing: if Kelsen and modern linguists are correct that there is the possibility of multiple and equally possible meanings,[90] the view of norms as different from their formulation makes no sense. Norms are no more precise than their text, while single 'meaning-contents' are narrower than their respective norms. Interpretation is a hermeneutic process, a process of cognition of norms, which include the sum total of possible meaning-contents. That means that neither time nor changing majority opinions can change the totality of possible meaning-contents. The possible meanings of a norm—the 'frame of possible meanings'[91]—are therefore not determined, expanded, or restricted by factors not amounting to a change of the norm—by factors outside the meta-law on law-creation. Since interpretation is about finding the meanings of a treaty, even when we use subsequent practice, it can only ever be a method to help discover meanings. Because practice can at best be evidence of possible meanings,[92] it must be established that subsequent practice is helpful in this regard. But this is doubtful: practice can be observance just as likely as it can be a breach. Who is to say that the actions, even if they happen also to be lawmakers, will reflect (or determine) what is required? This would be like taking the private behaviour of parliamentarians as a guide to what the law says—who would claim that?

If the 'changes in interpretation' were to occur in a manner that would support the non-state nature of armed attacks, this interpretation could still not be part of

[87] Ludwig Wittgenstein, *The Blue and Brown Books* (Oxford: Basil Blackwell, 1958), 25.

[88] Michael Thaler, *Mehrdeutigkeit und juristische Auslegung* (Vienna: Springer, 1982), 10, fn 12.

[89] Riccardo Guastini, 'Kelsen on Legal Knowledge and Scientific Interpretation' in Letizia Gianformaggio and Stanley L. Paulson (eds), *Cognition and Interpretation of Law* (Turin: Giappichelli, 1995), 107, 108.

[90] Hans Kelsen, *Reine Rechtslehre* (2nd edn, Vienna: Deuticke, 1960), 348–9.

[91] Kelsen, *Reine Rechtslehre*, 348.

[92] Gerald G. Fitzmaurice, 'The Law and Procedure of the International Court of Justice: Treaty Interpretation and Certain other Treaty Points' (1952) 28 *British Yearbook of International Law 1951* 1, 21; Fitzmaurice, 'The Law and Procedure of the International Court of Justice 1951–4', 224; Arnold Duncan McNair, *The Law of Treaties* (Oxford: Clarendon Press, 1961), 364, 424.

the law if they were not part of the possible meanings before the change. However, this also means that even an earlier restrictive reading of Article 51 (if, *arguendo*, both extensive and restrictive readings are possible) would not have restricted the law. The law, the norm, would still have included wider readings. This, however, is not to deny the immense practical effect of the change of an orthodoxy. If everyone—scholars, states, practitioners, courts—agrees that a given norm has only certain meanings and that other (on a linguistic analysis of the norm) possible meanings are excluded, this may not change the law, but for all *practical* purposes everyone will act accordingly.

IV. Conclusion

The confusion caused by the apparent resilience of a changing law on self-defence can be explained by a legal scholarship overly reliant on practical changes and overly concerned with 'interpretations' rather than the law. While strictly speaking the law has not changed, the practical dealings of many persons connected with this area of international law have changed. On a theoretically founded analysis, therefore, the law itself is indeed significantly more resilient than is commonly assumed. However, the interpretations of the law are responsive to changes in reality. But interpretations are significantly less authoritative than commonly thought and cannot determine the law in a legal manner, only 'determine' it as a matter of pragmatic facts. Over-reliance on 'interpretation' by legal scholarship means that it is in danger of becoming a branch of political science.

What does that mean for us? The importance of majority interpretations of the law, of an 'orthodoxy' lies on a different level. This 'commonality of views' is not the law, it is an expectation of future behaviour, it is what legal realists do right to study and would falsely call the law. If there is a clear orthodoxy, one can expect the subjects of law to behave accordingly. It is a factual, an empirical importance, not one of the law itself. Thus also, the unity of opinion is more important than in proper legal scholarship. If the streams of interpretation diverge, as is the case at the moment, the context matters more than it usually does. If, say, one is presenting a case before the ICJ, the law is indeed resiliently restrictive and counsel would be unwise to claim otherwise. If one were asked to present a paper before a US academic audience, this does not apply. Thus it is all the more important for us to recognize the limits of our craft: to cognize the law and, with it, all possible meaning-contents of any given norm.

CHAPTER 28

SELF-DEFENCE AND COLLECTIVE SECURITY: KEY DISTINCTIONS

SIR MICHAEL WOOD

I. Introduction

THERE is an elementary distinction between the two principal exceptions to the prohibition of the use of force in international law: the exercise of the right of self-defence (including collective self-defence), recognized by Article 51 of the UN Charter, and the taking of measures involving the use of force by or authorized by the UN Security Council under Chapter VII of the Charter.[1]

[1] Hans Kelsen, 'Collective Security and Collective Self-Defence under the Charter of the United Nations' (1948) 41 *American Journal of International Law* 783; Eugene V. Rostow, 'Until What? Enforcement Action or Collective Self-Defence?' (1991) 85 *American Journal of International Law* 506; Burns H. Weston, 'Security Council Resolution 678 and Persian Gulf Decision Making: Precarious Legitimacy' (1991) 85 *American Journal of International Law* 516; Christopher Greenwood, 'New World Order or Old? The Invasion of Iraq and the Rule of Law' (1992) 55 *Modern Law Review* 153, reproduced in Christopher Greenwood, *Essays on War in International Law* (London: Cameron May, 2006), 517; Derek W. Bowett, 'Collective Security and Collective Self-Defence: The Errors and Risks of Identification' in Manuel Rama Montaldo (ed), *El derecho internacional en un mundo en transformación: liber amicorum en homenaje al profesor Eduardo Jiménez de Aréchaga*, vol I (Montevideo: Fundación de Cultura Universitaria, 1994), 425; Terry D. Gill, 'Legal and Some Political

The latter are sometimes referred to as collective security measures.[2]

Dinstein summed up the distinction with characteristic pithiness:

> Collective security postulates the institutionalization of the lawful use of force in the international community... Collective security shares with collective self-defence the fundamental premise that recourse to force against aggression can (and perhaps must) be made by those who are not the immediate victims. But self-defence, either individual or collective, is exercised at the discretion of a single State or a group of States. Collective security operates on the strength of an authoritative decision made by a central organ of the international community.[3]

The present chapter aims to do no more than recall the distinction between collective self-defence and 'collective security', and their interrelations, and to do so principally by reference to an article by Bowett published in 1994.[4]

II. The Debate in 1990–1

It is worth briefly recalling earlier cases in which the distinction was discussed, since they may go some way towards explaining the academic debate and confusion in 1990–1. In particular, the controversy regarding the legal basis of the use of force over Korea in

Limitations on the Power of the UN Security Council to Exercise its Enforcement Powers under Chapter VII of the Charter' (1995) XXVI *Netherlands Yearbook of International Law* 90; Nico Krisch, *Selbstverteidigung und kollektive Sicherheit* (Berlin: Springer, 2001); Frank Berman, 'The Authorization Model: Resolution 678 and Its Effects' in David Malone (ed), *The UN Security Council. From the Cold War to the 21st Century* (Boulder, CO: Lynne Rienner, 2004), 153; Alexander Orakhelashvili, *Collective Security* (Oxford: Oxford University Press, 2010), 277–87; Marc Weller, *Iraq and the Use of Force in International Law* (Oxford: Oxford University Press, 2010), 34–40; Yoram Dinstein, *War, Aggression and Self-Defence* (5th edn, Cambridge: Cambridge University Press, 2011), 287–350.

[2] 'It is true that "collective security" is not a term of art': Bowett, 'Collective Security and Collective Self-Defence' in Rama Montaldo, *El derecho internacional*, 427. The term does not have a clear legal meaning, and is more popular in the discourse of international relations than of law. It is often used to refer to enforcement measures under the UN Charter, but the term is not used in the Charter and it is sometimes doubted—though nothing turns on it—whether the UN system is properly to be described as a collective security system: see Erika de Wet and Michael Wood, 'Collective Security' in Rüdiger Wolfrum (ed), *The Max Planck Encyclopedia of Public International Law* (Oxford: Oxford University Press, updated July 2013); Vaughan Lowe et al, *The United Nations Security Council and War: The Evolution of Thought and Practice Since 1945* (Oxford: Oxford University Press, 2008); Dinstein, *War, Aggression and Self-Defence*, 303–50.

[3] Dinstein, *War, Aggression and Self-Defence*, 303, para 806. There are two minor changes from the first (1988) edition cited by Bowett's article: omission of 'and direct' from the phrase 'not the immediate and direct victims', and use of the term 'a central organ' instead of simply 'an organ'.

[4] Bowett, 'Collective Security and Collective Self-Defence' in Rama Montaldo, *El derecho internacional*.

1950 was no doubt at the back of people's minds on the later occasion.[5] Two days after the North Korean attack on 25 June 1950, the Security Council:

> Recommend[ed] that the Members of the United Nations furnish such assistance to the Republic of Korea as may be necessary to repel the armed attack and to restore international peace and security in the area.[6]

This does not look like an authorization to use force; in terms it is a recommendation to assist the Republic of Korea, that is, a recommendation to join in collective self-defence. On the other hand, the reference (which found an echo in 1990) to restoring international peace and security in the area, on its face goes beyond self-defence. And the fact that those acting in self-defence were under a Unified Command under the US,[7] with authorization to use the UN flag, may be seen to point to a collective security operation. These matters were much discussed at the time, but in reality the case had many special factors, not least the prior UN involvement in the situation in the Korean peninsula.[8] In fact, the only clear authorization to use force prior to 1990 was in 1966, when the Security Council 'call[ed] upon the United Kingdom to prevent, by the use force if necessary, the arrival at Beira' of the *Joanna V* and other vessels carrying oil for the illegal regime in Southern Rhodesia.[9]

Notwithstanding the ambiguous, 'hybrid' Korean precedent, it is hard to fathom why the distinction was ever regarded as unclear. But such appears to have been the case, particularly at the time of the operation to eject Iraq from Kuwait in 1991–2 (referred to by its American code name, 'Desert Storm'). In his 1994 article,[10] Bowett urged the need to distinguish between collective self-defence and collective measures under Chapter VII in the light of what he saw as ambiguous statements from, among others, the UK government, about Security Council resolution 678 (1990) of 29 November 1990.[11] In particular, Bowett expressed misgivings relating to 'the possibility of a future misuse of the precedent of the Gulf action, if the view that resolution 678 endorsed action in collective self-defence prevails'.[12] These are referred to further in Section IV.

[5] William Stueck, 'The United Nations, the Security Council, and the Korean War' in Lowe et al, *The United Nations Security Council and War*, 265–79.

[6] SC Res 83 (1950) of 27 June 1950.

[7] SC Res 84 (1950) of 7 July 1950.

[8] See Dana Constantin, 'Korean War (1950–53)' in Wolfrum, *The Max Planck Encyclopedia of Public International Law* (2012), with bibliography; Weller, *Iraq and the Use of Force in International Law*, 35–7.

[9] SC Res 221 (1966) of 9 April 1966.

[10] Bowett, 'Collective Security and Collective Self-Defence' in Rama Montaldo, *El derecho internacional*.

[11] In para 2 of SC Res 678 (1990), the Security Council '*Authorizes* Member States co-operating with the Government of Kuwait, unless Iraq on or before 15 January 1991 fully implements, as set forth in paragraph 1 above, the foregoing resolutions, to use all necessary means to uphold and implement resolution 660 (1990) and all subsequent relevant resolutions and to restore international peace and security in the area.'

[12] Bowett, 'Collective Security and Collective Self-Defence' in Rama Montaldo, *El derecho internacional*, 427.

Bowett identified six differences between collective self-defence and collective measures under Chapter VII:

(1) Collective self-defence needs no authorization from the Security Council. '[A] salient and fundamental difference between collective measures of the kind contemplated in Chapter VII, and collective self-defence, is that only the Security Council can authorise the former, but the latter needs no authorisation.'[13]
(2) The circumstances which 'trigger' the Council's powers under Chapter VII (a threat to the peace, breach of the peace, or act of aggression under Article 39) are not identical to an 'armed attack' which is a precondition for the exercise of the right of self-defence as recognized in Article 51. 'Thus collective measures under Chapter VII could be taken when no possibility of collective self-defence existed.'[14]
(3) '[I]n collective measures under Chapter VII it is for the Security Council to determine which Member State may participate.' In the case of collective self-defence 'it is essentially for the victim State to determine which States shall participate'.[15]
(4) Measures in self-defence must be proportionate. The limitations on the choice of collective measures are quite different, and are governed by the aim of maintaining and restoring international peace and security.[16]
(5) The aims of self-defence (the protection of the state) and collective security (maintenance and restoration of international peace and security) are very different, with the latter permitting measures of 'far greater scope'.[17]
(6) The timing of the response differs, in that action in self-defence depends on proof of immediacy.[18]

Bowett goes on to consider in some detail whether the 1991 operation to eject Iraq from Kuwait (Desert Storm) was an action in self-defence or a collective security

[13] Bowett, 'Collective Security and Collective Self-Defence' in Rama Montaldo, *El derecho internacional*, 427–8.

[14] Bowett, 'Collective Security and Collective Self-Defence' in Rama Montaldo, *El derecho internacional*, 428–9.

[15] Bowett, 'Collective Security and Collective Self-Defence' in Rama Montaldo, *El derecho internacional*, 429. Bowett may have included the word 'essentially' because of his regret (see his fn 9) that the International Court of Justice (ICJ) had effectively said it was up to the victim state to determine who participates. It is not clear why Bowett thought this inevitably blurred the borderline between collective self-defence and collective security.

[16] Bowett, 'Collective Security and Collective Self-Defence' in Rama Montaldo, *El derecho internacional*, 429–30.

[17] Bowett, 'Collective Security and Collective Self-Defence' in Rama Montaldo, *El derecho internacional*, 430.

[18] Bowett, 'Collective Security and Collective Self-Defence' in Rama Montaldo, *El derecho internacional*, 430. Weller gives a similar, though not identical, list: *Iraq and the Use of Force in International Law*, 35.

measure.[19] He gives an extensive list of objectives for which force was authorized, not only to ensure the withdrawal of Iraqi forces from Kuwait but all the other objectives set out in the Security Council resolutions passed before (and possibly after) resolution 678 (1990).[20] He submits that 'the aims for which force was authorised under resolution 678 exceeded the aims which were legitimate for self-defence.'[21] And he concludes, in general terms, that 'much more may be permitted in the interests of maintaining or restoring international peace and security than is permitted in self-defence.'[22]

III. A Clear Distinction

The rules of international law on the use of force are relatively easy to state. They are to be found in the Charter and in customary international law. The Charter contains, among the Principles of the United Nations, a prohibition of the threat or use of force under Article 2(4). The Charter refers to two not unrelated circumstances in which the prohibition does not apply. First, forcible measures may be taken or authorized by the Security Council, acting under Chapter VII of the Charter. Second, force may be used in the exercise of the right of individual and collective self-defence, as recognized in Article 51 of the Charter. A further possible exception is the use of force to avert an overwhelming humanitarian catastrophe (sometimes referred to as 'humanitarian intervention'). It has limited support. It is not mentioned in the Charter, and so must be found, if at all, in customary international law.[23] A recent example of this argument being deployed is the UK government's legal advice in relation to a possible use of force against Syria in August 2013.[24]

[19] Bowett, 'Collective Security and Collective Self-Defence' in Rama Montaldo, *El derecho internacional*, 430–5.

[20] Interestingly, in view of the emphasis placed on it years later in connection with the 2003 invasion of Iraq, Bowett does not list the aim 'to restore peace and security in the area', though he does mention it later in the article (at 438).

[21] Bowett, 'Collective Security and Collective Self-Defence' in Rama Montaldo, *El derecho internacional*, 432.

[22] Bowett, 'Collective Security and Collective Self-Defence' in Rama Montaldo, *El derecho internacional*, 438.

[23] For the present author's view, see 'The Law on the Use of Force: Current Challenges' (2007) 11 *Singapore Year Book of International Law* 1, 11: 'it may be best to view the claims made in 1991 and 1999 [relating to the safe havens in northern Iraq and over Kosovo] as based on some exceptional defence or justification of necessity, such as is found in domestic legal systems, rather than on a positive rule of law'.

[24] 'Chemical weapons use by Syrian regime—UK Government legal advice', 29 Aug 2013, available at <https://www.gov.uk/government/publications/chemical-weapon-use-by-syrian-regime-uk-government-legal-position/chemical-weapon-use-by-syrian-regime-uk-government-legal-position-html-version>.

Force used at the request or with the consent, duly given, of the government of the territorial state does not give rise to an issue under the *jus ad bellum*.[25] The use of force in retaliation (punishment, revenge, or reprisals) is illegal.[26]

While aspects of the right of self-defence remain controversial,[27] for present purposes the following propositions would seem to be generally accepted. The right of individual or collective self-defence is inherent. It is an exception to the general prohibition on the use of force set forth in Article 2(4) of the UN Charter.[28] As such it is recognized (but not granted) by Article 51 the Charter.[29] The exercise of the right of self-defence does not require authorization by the Security Council, though the Council may endorse such exercise. It may only be exercised 'if an armed attack occurs', and its purpose is to repel or reverse such attack; it does not have broader purposes. Action taken must be necessary and proportionate. The right to exercise self-defence lasts only 'until the Security Council has taken the measures necessary to maintain international peace and security.'

For the lawful exercise of collective self-defence[30] three conditions must be met. As with individual self-defence, there must be an armed attack. The state which is attacked must declare that it has been attacked. And that state must request the third state for assistance.[31]

Perhaps two related issues led to what Bowett saw as ambiguous statements by UK ministers (which were not in fact particularly ambiguous), and to what has been described as 'a considerable doctrinal debate'.[32] First, whether Security Council

[25] (2011) 74 *Yearbook of the Institute of International Law, Rhodes Session* 181 (report by Gerhard Hafner).

[26] See art 50(1)(a) of the 2001 Articles on the Responsibility of States for Internationally Wrongful Acts: James Crawford, *State Responsibility: The General Part* (Cambridge: Cambridge University Press, 2013), 690–1.

[27] Christopher Greenwood, 'Self-Defence' in Wolfrum, *The Max Planck Encyclopedia of Public International* (2012); James Crawford, *Brownlie's Principles of Public International Law* (8th edn, Oxford: Oxford University Press, 2012), 747–57.

[28] Art 2(4) reads: 'All Members shall refrain in their international relations from the threat or use of force against the territorial integrity or political independence of any state, or in any other manner inconsistent with the Purposes of the United Nations.'

[29] Art 51 reads: 'Nothing in the present Charter shall impair the inherent right of individual or collective self-defense if an armed attack occurs against a Member of the United Nations, until the Security Council has taken the measures necessary to maintain international peace and security. Measures taken by Members in the exercise of this right of self-defense shall be immediately reported to the Security Council and shall not in any way affect the authority and responsibility of the Security Council under the present Charter to take at any time such action as it deems necessary in order to maintain or restore international peace and security.' (The original signed version of the Charter has the American spelling 'self-defense', though in later publications the UN, as is its practice, uses English spelling—'self-defence'.)

[30] Greenwood, 'Self-Defence' in Wolfrum, *The Max Planck Encyclopedia of Public International Law* (2012), paras 35–40; Dinstein, *War, Aggression and Self-Defence*, 278–302.

[31] *Military and Paramilitary Activities in and against Nicaragua (Nicaragua v. US)*, Merits, Judgment, ICJ Rep 1986, 14, 102–5, paras 193–200. Dinstein, *War, Aggression and Self-Defence*, 278–302; Greenwood, 'Self-Defence' in Wolfrum, *The Max Planck Encyclopedia of Public International Law* (2012), paras 35–40.

[32] Orakhelashvili, *Collective Security*, 281.

involvement was such that the right of self-defence had terminated because, in the words of Article 51, the Council has 'taken measures necessary to maintain international peace and security'. And second, whether a use of force may at one and the same time be both an exercise of the right of (collective) self-defence and a (collective security) measure under Chapter VII of the Charter.

Greenwood considered whether resolution 678 (1990) authorized the use of force as a collective security measure or merely gave Security Council approval to action by way of collective self-defence. While admitting that 'It is difficult to escape the conclusion that there was a degree of deliberate ambiguity' he regarded the resolution 'as providing for enforcement action rather than giving a blessing (of political, not legal, significance) to an action in self-defence which could lawfully have been mounted without the authorisation of the Council.'[33]

Berman has also addressed the relationship between collective self-defence and collective security in connection with resolution 678 (1990).[34] He noted that 'the proper characterization of this resolution is still not wholly resolved', and explained:

> One school holds that Resolution 678 was essentially an endorsement of the right of collective self-defense with the legitimate government of Kuwait. The other holds the resolution to have been an exercise of the powers reserved to the Security Council under the Charter, albeit in an innovative form not expressly foreseen in the Charter.[35]

Berman convincingly demonstrates nevertheless that:

> the self-defense thesis offers a poor explanation of what the Security Council conceived itself to be doing in Resolution 678. The basis implicitly underlying the thesis is that self-defence and collective security are mutually exclusive, but is this in fact the case?... There is no reason in principle why... the relationship between self-defence and collective security should not also have a dynamic element—as long as the continuing claim to self-defence is, and remains, in support of the Council's objectives and measures. The crux is surely that, under the last sentence of Article 51, the Council has the unfettered right to assume control.[36]

In the course of his argument, Berman states the following:

> when the Council authorized the collective use of force under Resolution 678, this must surely be construed under Article 51 as 'measures necessary to maintain international peace and security,' which therefore displaced the right to use force in self-defence.[37]

[33] Greenwood, *Essays on War in International Law*, 541.

[34] Berman, 'The Authorization Model' in Malone, *The UN Security Council*.

[35] Berman, 'The Authorization Model' in Malone, *The UN Security Council*, 154.

[36] Berman, 'The Authorization Model' in Malone, *The UN Security Council*, 154–5. It has to be noted that Dinstein asserts at some length, unconvincingly, and without actually examining the text of resolution 678 (1990), that Operation Desert Storm was an exercise of collective self-defence, not collective security: Dinstein, *War, Aggression and Self-Defence*, paras 796–805.

[37] Berman, 'The Authorization Model' in Malone, *The UN Security Council*, 154.

This may well be the better interpretation of resolution 678 (1990), but it is not the only one. As Randolzhofer and Nolte write:

> The wording and the purpose of [Article 51] suggest that the answer depends on a proper interpretation of the resolution concerned, in particular on whether there are indications that the SC considered the measures it took as being sufficient to deal with the situation and as implying a full or partial limitation of the exercise of the right to self-defence.[38]

The question of determining whether 'the Security Council has taken the measures necessary to maintain international peace and security' is fact-specific and depends on the circumstances of the particular case. It 'can only be taken to refer to measures which are actually effective to bring about the stated objective'.[39] As Matheson has written:

> self-defence is suspended only when the Council has taken actions that effectively restore and maintain international peace and security, or that are inconsistent with separate national military action. For example, where the Council authorises major military operations under unified command, it would be reasonable to conclude that States may not conduct separate military operations that would interfere with or compromise those directed by the Council.[40]

It follows that states must take the greatest care when drafting Security Council resolutions authorizing forcible measures (and indeed any measures) under Chapter VII if they wish to preserve unaffected their right to use force in exercise of individual or collective self-defence.

There is no reason in principle why a state using force may not be doing so with a double or multiple legal basis. Of course, the aims will differ, and as Bowett explained the Security Council basis is likely to be broader than the self-defence one. The former may mask the latter, but that does not mean that the latter may not subsist in parallel. And the continuance of the right of self-defence may well be regarded as of vital importance for the victim state. Therefore, the need to ensure that action by the Security Council does not terminate that right is paramount.

There may be many reasons for seeking action by the Security Council, even including authorization, when the circumstances are such that the right to self-defence exists. Matheson refers to the political benefit of authorization by the international community, the fact that such authorization may override contrary legal obligations, and assist in overcoming concerns about neutrality and special treaty provisions (such as those governing passage though international canals and rivers).[41]

[38] Albrecht Randolzhofer and Georg Nolte, 'Article 51' in Bruno Simma et al (eds), *The Charter of the United Nations: A Commentary* (3rd edn, Oxford: Oxford University Press, 2012), 1428.

[39] United Kingdom letter to the President of the Security Council, 30 April 1982, S/15016, reproduced in (1982) 53 *British Yearbook of International Law* 544.

[40] Michael Matheson, *Council Unbound. The Growth of UN Decision Making on Conflict and Postconflict Issues after the Cold War* (Washington DC: United States Institute of Peace Press, 2006), 133.

[41] Matheson, *Council Unbound*, 137.

Nevertheless, in the past most uses of force have had one basis or the other, self-defence or Security Council authorization. Thus the UK's use of force to recover the Falkland Islands after the Argentine invasion of 2 April 1982 was carried out exclusively in exercise of the right of self-defence. The Security Council was involved, but care was taken to ensure that such involvement, and in particular resolutions 502 (1982) of 3 April 1982 and 505 (1982) of 26 May 1982, did not affect the right of self-defence. While there was some discussion as to whether the measures taken by the Council in resolution 502 (1982) were such as to terminate the UK's right of self-defence,[42] this was not a serious issue; indeed, resolution 502 (1982) was seen to give important political support to the UK's action in self-defence.

An example, albeit highly controversial, of action that, according to those involved, was based exclusively on Security Council authorization was the intervention in Iraq in 2003. As the UK Attorney General's now public advice of 7 March 2003 indicates, for the UK, the legality of the invasion turned solely on whether it had been authorized by the Security Council. It is clear that the Security Council may authorize the use of force. The only question was: had it done so? That turned on the interpretation of a series of Security Council resolutions. The present writer's own views have been given to the Chilcot Inquiry:

20.... The series of resolutions at issue in relation to the use of force against Iraq in 2003 were complex. Their interpretation was not straightforward. I agreed with most of what was said in the Attorney General's advice of 7 March 2003....

21.... Where I had a different view was on whether a 'reasonable case' could be made for saying that, by adopting SCR 1441, the Security Council had already made a finding of material breach which had the effect of reviving the authorization in SCR 678 for some future use of force, without the need for a further decision by the Council. In other words, I did not consider that the Council, by adopting SCR 1441, had left to individual States the decision whether at some point in the future a material breach had occurred sufficient to revive the authorization to use force. I reached this conclusion after considering the wording of SCR 1441, its negotiating history, the circumstances of its adoption, subsequent developments in the Council, and the Council's practice.

...

23. My reading was that the Council had decided in paragraph 12 to convene upon a certain event (the submission of a report) for the purpose of considering certain matters (the situation and the need for full compliance with all relevant SCRs). Paragraph 4 spoke of a material breach being referred to the Council 'for assessment'. In my view, the ordinary meaning to be given to the terms of these provisions in their context was that the Council would consider the situation, and assess the nature of any breach. Paragraph 12 made no express mention of subsequent Council action. But neither did it clearly indicate that no such action was needed before the Council's authorization of the use of force revived. In my view, the natural reading of the provisions in question, in context, was that the purpose of

[42] S/PV.3260, S/PV/3262; United Kingdom letter to the President of the Security Council, 30 April 1982, S/15016, reproduced in (1982) 53 *British Yearbook of International Law* 544–5.

Council consideration and assessment was for the Council to decide what measures were needed in the light of the circumstances at the time. Among such circumstances, as it turned out, was the ongoing work of UNMOVIC [the United Nations Monitoring, Verification and Inspection Commission] and the view strongly held by many that the inspectors should be given more time. A strong hint of what might come was given in paragraph 13. This reading of the text was not, in my view, contradicted by anything in the preparatory work of the resolution. If anything it was reinforced by the preparatory work. And many statements made in connection with the adoption of SCR 1441 pointed towards this view set out in the present paragraph.[43]

The action over Libya in 2011 is another recent example of a use of force based exclusively on Security Council authorization under Chapter VII.[44] That was viewed, by some, as an example of Council implementation of the 'responsibility to protect', sometimes referred to, obscurely, as 'an emerging norm'. Security Council resolution 1973 (2011) of 17 March 2011 authorized states to use force with two principal objectives: to protect civilians and civilian-populated areas, and to enforce compliance with a no-fly zone. The resolution is noteworthy for the clarity of its drafting, relative clarity at any rate. Gareth Evans wrote a few days after its adoption, in the *Sydney Morning Herald*, that 'a hugely important precedent has been set'. Even if the text of Resolution 1973 might have appeared to be a model for 'responsibility to protect', as envisaged by the UN General Assembly in 2005, the question has been raised as to whether, in the words of the headline to the Gareth Evans' article, the intervening states have 'stuck to the UN script'.[45]

IV. An Important Distinction

The distinction between collective self-defence and collective security, while elementary, is undoubtedly important for the reasons given by Bowett (Section II above). In addition to the six reasons listed by him there is the fact that the right to act in self-defence, including in collective self-defence, is subject to a possible temporal limitation under Article 51, by reference to the operation of the 'collective security' system under the UN Charter. And the reporting requirements, which are increasingly seen as important for 'accountability' to the Council, may well

[43] Iraq Inquiry: (First) Statement by Sir Michael Wood, 15 Jan 2010, available at <http://www.iraqinquiry.org.uk/>.

[44] Christian Henderson, 'International Measures for the Protection of Civilians in Libya and Côte d'Ivoire' (2011) 60 *International and Comparative Law Quarterly* 767.

[45] Gareth Evans, 'When intervening in a conflict, stick to UN script', *Sydney Morning Herald*, 24 Mar 2011.

differ significantly. They are likely to be more precise, and more onerous, in the case of authorization, at least if the Security Council is doing its job properly.

In 1994, Bowett saw the importance of upholding the distinction in the following terms:

> There is a slight risk that Member States might see in resolution 678 a justification for extending U.N. control over self-defence, in the sense that, if prior 'authorisation' was sought on that occasion, it should be sought on future occasions.
>
> Far more serious is the risk that States exercising the right of self-defence will argue for a very extensive interpretation of self-defence, using 'Desert Storm' as a precedent.[46]

Neither of these perceived risks has in fact materialized. States generally have not had doubts about the distinction between self-defence (including collective self-defence, and measures authorized by the Security Council under Chapter VII), either in theory or in practice. In relation to the second, 'far more serious' risk, Bowett posits a series of ways in which resolution 678 (1990) might set a dangerous precedent for self-defence,[47] but no one else seems to have imagined any such precedent.

In practice, what matters most, in this author's view, is that those using force, and states and commentators more generally, should be clear as to legal basis for the use of force. They should be clear in their own minds, and the general public should be clear, whether they are acting in exercise of the right of collective self-defence or under a Security Council authorization. There is no longer the excuse that the law of the Charter is new, untested, and unclear. Any temptation to 'fudge' the legal issue, which sometimes seems to amount to little more than putting forward an 'accumulation of bad arguments', should be resisted. To do so is usually to signal a weak legal case.

V. Conclusion

Some surprise was expressed at the beginning of this chapter that the distinction between collective security and collective self-defence was ever regarded as unclear. The fact that both concepts include the word 'collective' can hardly be an explanation. More plausible, perhaps, is the fact—now hard to recall—that, with the end

[46] Bowett, 'Collective Security and Collective Self-Defence' in Rama Montaldo, *El derecho internacional*, 438.

[47] Bowett, 'Collective Security and Collective Self-Defence' in Rama Montaldo, *El derecho internacional*, 438–40.

of the Cold War and the revival of the Security Council, circumstances in 1990–1 were quite novel. Questions were raised about concepts (such as Security Council authorization) that had lain largely dormant for decades. In this as in other fields, new thinking was required, and required instantly. These new circumstances arose in 1990–1 in a situation in which different bases for the use of force were successively in play (first self-defence, then Security Council authorization). This perhaps explains the confused thinking at the time, even if it does not excuse it. But it hardly explains the continuing confusion that we find in some writings, though not, it is submitted, on the part of states. The practice since 1990–1 seems clear enough.

CHAPTER 29

TAMING THE DOCTRINE OF PRE-EMPTION

ASHLEY S. DEEKS

I. Introduction

One of the most contested questions in the *jus ad bellum* is whether and when it is lawful for a state to use force unilaterally *before* it suffers an armed attack. The question took on particular salience in 2002, when the US claimed—more clearly and assertively than before—that a state could use force to forestall certain hostile acts by its adversaries.[1] Twelve years after that controversial assertion, it is well worth assessing where the debate currently stands and where it is heading.

Because states and scholars use a variety of poorly defined terms to discuss acts of self-defence in advance of an attack, Section II sorts through the terminology. Section III lays down the basic positions in the historical debate about the legality of such self-defence. Section IV turns to new pressures on self-defence brought on by new actors, new threats, and new technologies. Section V considers the future of pre-emption. It concludes that recent trends in state practice and in scholarship reveal that the timing of a state's right to use force in self-defence continues to evolve, particularly when the fact patterns implicate terrorist groups or weapons of

[1] National Security Council, *The National Security Strategy of the United States of America* (2002). The 2010 National Security Strategy does not discuss use of force in advance of an attack. National Security Council, *The National Security Strategy of the United States of America* (2010), 21.

mass destruction (WMD). Yet certain technological developments make it difficult to predict the degree to which this evolution will continue.

II. Terminology

States and scholars tend to use three different terms when discussing the use of force in self-defence in advance of an armed attack: anticipatory self-defence, pre-emptive self-defence, and preventive self-defence. Yet these terms defy crisp definition.[2] For instance, some use 'anticipatory self-defence' as a catch-all description for any self-defence that precedes an attack.[3] Others use 'anticipatory self-defence' to describe only the narrowest and least-controversial form of pre-attack self-defence—that which meets the requirements set forth in the exchange of notes between the US and the UK in the wake of the *Caroline* incident.[4] This chapter uses the terms as follows:

Anticipatory self-defence means the use of force in self-defence to halt an imminent armed attack by a state or a non-state actor. This approach adheres to the *Caroline* principle that a state may respond to an attack before it is completed, but only where the need to respond is 'instant, overwhelming, and leaving no choice of means, and no moment for deliberation.'[5] Although the potential victim state has not yet suffered a completed armed attack, it perceives the attack to be temporally imminent—as when the enemy is about to launch missiles towards the victim state.

Pre-emptive self-defence means the use of force in self-defence to halt a particular tangible course of action that the potential victim state perceives will shortly evolve into an armed attack against it.[6] The potential attack appears more distant in time than an attack forestalled by anticipatory self-defence, but the potential victim state

[2] See Christopher Greenwood, 'International Law and the Pre-Emptive Use of Force: Afghanistan, al Qaida, and Iraq' (2003) 4 *San Diego Journal International Law Journal* 7, 9 (describing terminological confusion). See also Yoram Dinstein, *War, Aggression and Self-Defence* (3rd edn, Cambridge: Cambridge University Press, 2001), 172 ('interceptive self-defense'); Matthew Waxman, 'The Use of Force Against States That Might Have Weapons of Mass Destruction' (2009) 31 *Michigan Journal of International Law* 7 ('precautionary self-defense').

[3] Michael Doyle, *Striking First: Preemption and Prevention in International Conflict* (Princeton, NJ: Princeton University Press, 2008), 5.

[4] Sean Murphy, 'The Doctrine of Preemptive Self-Defense' (2005) 50 *Villanova Law Review* 699, 703.

[5] Letter from Daniel Webster, US Secretary of State, to Lord Ashburton, British Plenipotentiary (6 Aug 1842), quoted in John Bassett Moore, *A Digest of International Law*, vol 2 (Princeton, NJ: Princeton University Press, 1906), § 217, at 412.

[6] See Murphy, 'The Doctrine of Preemptive Self-Defense', 704.

has good reasons to believe that the attack is likely, is near at hand, and, if it takes place, will result in significant harm.

Preventive self-defence means the use of force in self-defence to halt a serious future threat of an armed attack, without clarity about when or where that attack may emerge.[7] Its advocates focus on the quantum of the threat to be avoided and the difficulty in ascertaining precisely when and how that threat will manifest itself as an armed attack. A state's use of force may also be viewed as preventive when it purports to respond to a state's or group's threatening behaviour in the absence of credible evidence that the state or group has the capacity and intent to attack.

These terms describe uses of force on a temporal continuum, with anticipatory self-defence closest to the full manifestation of the armed attack and preventive self-defence the furthest away. Anticipatory self-defence requires a state to be virtually certain about the time, place, author, and fact of the future attack; preventive self-defence requires no such certainty about those factors.

III. Representative Positions in the Debate

States, international organizations, and scholars hold a wide range of views on when international law permits a state to use force unilaterally before it has suffered an armed attack.[8] Many international actors express comfort with the legality of anticipatory self-defence, with some states and scholars defending pre-emptive self-defence. The view that a state must wait to suffer an armed attack before being able to respond forcibly now appears to be a minority view,[9] as does the view that preventive self-defence is lawful. The following discussion articulates the arguments in favour of distinct positions on the temporal continuum.

Before describing key positions in the debate, it is worth identifying a larger point about the nature of self-defence. To some extent, all uses of force in self-defence in

[7] US National Security Strategy, 1 (asserting a right to take defensive action 'even if uncertainty exists as to the time and place of the enemy attack'); Waxman, 'The Use of Force Against States That Might Have Weapons of Mass Destruction', 13 ('Prevention refers to the use of force to avoid an emerging state of affairs in which a threat would be more likely or increasingly dire').

[8] The International Court of Justice (ICJ) has declined to opine on the lawfulness of a 'response to the imminent threat of armed attack'. *Case Concerning Military and Paramilitary Activities in and against Nicaragua (Nicaragua v. US)*, Merits, ICJ Rep 1986, 14, 102–6.

[9] See eg Report of the Secretary-General, 'In Larger Freedom: Towards Development, Security and Human Rights for All', A/59/2005, para 124 ('Imminent threats are fully covered by Article 51 ... Lawyers have long recognized that this covers an imminent attack as well as one that has already happened').

response to a completed armed attack have an anticipatory element in them. That is, for force to be 'necessary', the victim state must anticipate that the attacker has the capacity and intent to strike again.[10] The difference is plain between self-defence after and in advance of an attack: in the former situation, the attacker has already demonstrated an intent and willingness to attack. Nevertheless, self-defence in response to a completed armed attack contains a predictive element similar to that of anticipatory and pre-emptive self-defence.

A. Requirement of an Armed Attack

One school of thought holds that a state may not use force in self-defence unless and until it suffers an armed attack.[11] Those who defend this view cite the plain language of Article 51 of the UN Charter, which states, 'Nothing in the present Charter shall impair the inherent right of individual or collective self-defense *if an armed attack occurs*...'[12] By their reading, the right to self-defence does not exist if an armed attack has not yet occurred. Adherents to this view include Ian Brownlie,[13] Louis Henkin,[14] and Philip Jessup.[15] Policies underlying this position include a concern about replacing a bright-line rule with a hazy one;[16] a fear of minimizing the importance of resorting to the Security Council to adjudge threats to international peace and security before those threats materialize; and a desire maximally to enforce the comprehensive prohibition on interstate uses of force in Article 2(4) of the UN Charter. Further, a rule that allows a state to use force in advance of an armed attack may lead states to pre-empt each other's pre-emptive acts of self-defence.[17] Yet even scholars such as Brownlie concede that in some circumstances a potential victim

[10] Murphy, 'The Doctrine of Preemptive Self-Defense', 735 ('there is an idea, embedded within standard notions of self-defence, that a state, having been attacked, may ward off future similar attacks through the defensive action. Granted, the likelihood of future attacks is much more apparent when an attack already has occurred, but nevertheless the defensive response focuses on preventing future attacks, not simply repulsing the prior attack').

[11] See Murphy, 'The Doctrine of Preemptive Self-Defense', 706 (terming this the 'strict constructionist' view).

[12] UN Charter, Art 51 (emphasis added).

[13] Ian Brownlie, *International Law and the Use of Force by States* (Oxford: Clarendon Press, 1963), 278.

[14] Louis Henkin, *International Law: Politics, Values and Functions* (Leiden: Martinus Nijhoff, 1990), 156.

[15] Philip Jessup, *A Modern Law of Nations* (Hamden, CT: Archon Books, 1968), 166.

[16] An actual armed attack is 'clear, unambiguous, subject to proof, and not easily open to misinterpretation or fabrication.' Louis Henkin, *How Nations Behave: Law and Foreign Policy* (New York: Columbia University Press, 1979), 142. See also Brownlie, *International Law and the Use of Force by States*, 259 (noting difficulty in assessing the certainty of a forthcoming attack and the intention of another government).

[17] Doyle, *Striking First*, 26 ('Unless all states agree on what constitutes a specific threat... every state will be preempting every other state's preventive strikes').

state may respond with force to apparently offensive operations that have not yet resulted in an attack.[18]

B. Anticipatory Self-Defence

Others find it legally and strategically untenable to require a state to suffer an armed attack before it may respond, and believe that international law allows a state to resort to force in anticipatory self-defence.[19] Members of this school argue that Article 51 specifically preserves the 'inherent' right of self-defence, which they interpret to mean the right as it existed before states drafted the Charter.[20] That right embraced the rule captured most clearly in the famous *Caroline* incident of 1837: a state may use force in anticipation of an imminent armed attack. The international military tribunals at Nuremberg and Tokyo cited the *Caroline* test, which this group sees as evidence that the right of anticipatory self-defence clearly existed pre-Charter.[21]

Several states have invoked anticipatory self-defence to justify their own uses of force or that of other states.[22] A number of scholars identify Israel's use of force against Egypt in 1967—where Israel attacked Egypt's air force after Egypt massed its forces on the Israeli border and closed the Straits of Tiran—as a classic example of anticipatory self-defence.[23] Israel came under little criticism in the UN Security Council or General Assembly for its actions.[24] Several UN-related reports also

[18] See Brownlie, *International Law and the Use of Force by States*, 368 ('Thus a naval force of a state which had stated its intention to attack, approaching territorial waters, might be regarded as offensive and intercepted on the high seas').

[19] See eg Derek W. Bowett, 'The Use of Force for the Protection of Nationals Abroad' in Antonio Cassese (ed), *The Current Legal Regulation of the Use of Force* (Leiden: Martinus Nijhoff, 1986), 40; Dinstein, *War, Aggression and Self-Defence*, 191 ('It would be absurd to require that the defending State should sustain and absorb a devastating (perhaps a fatal) blow, only to prove the immaculate conception of self-defense'); Greenwood, 'International Law and the Pre-Emptive Use of Force', 14–15 (listing Franck, Waldock, Fitzmaurice, Bowett, Schwebel, Jennings, Watts, and Higgins as supporting anticipatory self-defence).

[20] Murphy, 'The Doctrine of Preemptive Self-Defense', 711.

[21] International Military Tribunal (Nuremberg), Judgment and Sentences (1947) 41 *American Journal of International Law* 172, 205; 'International Military Tribunal at Tokyo (1948)' in Leon Friedman (ed), *The Law of War: A Documentary History*, vol 2 (London: Random House, 1972), 1029, 1157–9.

[22] This includes the UK, Israel, and the US. See eg 'Statement by the UK Government about the 1986 U.S. attack on Libya' (1986) 57 *British Yearbook of International Law* 494, 639–41; Thomas Franck, *Recourse to Force* (Cambridge: Cambridge University Press, 2004), 103 (arguing that Israel's 'words and actions [in striking Egypt's airfields in 1967] clearly asserted a right to anticipatory self-defense against imminent armed attack').

[23] Dinstein, *War, Aggression and Self-Defence*, 173; William O'Brien, *The Conduct of Just and Limited War* (Westport, CT: Greenwood Publishing, 1981), 133. Others cite the Dutch declaration of war against Japan on 8 Dec 1941 (before any attack had occurred against the Dutch West Indies) as an example of anticipatory self-defence, given that the Japanese planned to attack those islands on that date. Brownlie, *International Law and the Use of Force by States*, 258.

[24] Rosalyn Higgins, 'The Attitude of Western States Towards Legal Aspects of the Use of Force' in Cassese, *The Current Legal Regulation of the Use of Force*, 443.

embrace this approach to self-defence. In 2004, for instance, the Secretary-General's High-Level Panel on Threats, Challenges and Change stated, '[A] threatened State, according to long established international law, can take military action as long as the threatened attack is *imminent*, no other means would deflect it and the action is proportionate.'[25]

Those who embrace anticipatory self-defence but reject pre-emptive self-defence reveal a commitment to limit self-defence only to situations in which the forthcoming armed attack is both very close at hand and virtually certain. This stems from a desire to cabin the 'slippery slope' of pre-attack self-defence while acknowledging the reality that no state, given the means, would stand by to suffer a first blow.[26] As Matthew Waxman explains, 'Requiring that a specific attack be about to occur helps ensure that a defender exhaust other, non-forcible means, and it reduces the likelihood of mistakes, insofar as waiting until that point is more likely to expose an adversary's true intentions.'[27]

C. Pre-Emptive Self-Defence

Increasingly, some states and scholars argue that the *Caroline* requirements are too restrictive. Michael Doyle points out that there is virtually no historical use of force that meets those rigorous factors.[28] In general, this group seeks to redefine and expand the 'imminence' requirement to deal with new threats.[29] Instead of forcing a state to wait until the attack is underway, or about to commence, this school deems lawful a response that takes place in the last window of opportunity in which a state may act effectively to defend itself against an entity that has both the intent and capacity to attack.[30] This might mean that a state may attack a WMD storage facility

[25] High-Level Panel on Threats, Challenges and Change, 'A More Secure World' (2004), 63, para 188 (emphasis in original).

[26] Mary Ellen O'Connell, 'The Myth of Pre-Emptive Self-Defence' (2002) 8 *American Society of International Law Task Force* ('based on the practice of states... as well as simple logic, international lawyers generally agree that a state need not wait to suffer the actual blow before defending itself, so long as it is certain the blow is coming').

[27] Waxman, 'The Use of Force Against States That Might Have Weapons of Mass Destruction', 8.

[28] Doyle, *Striking First*, 14–15 (noting that extreme *Caroline*-type conditions are rarely found in reality). See also Higgins, 'The Attitude of Western States Towards Legal Aspects of the Use of Force' in Cassese, *The Current Legal Regulation of the Use of Force*, 442; Michael Walzer, *Just and Unjust Wars* (New York: Basic Books, 1977), 76–9.

[29] See eg John Brennan, 'Strengthening Our Security By Adhering to Our Values and Laws', Remarks at Harvard Law School, 16 Sept 2011; High-Level Panel, 'A More Secure World', para 189 (accepting 'pre-emptive' self-defence as lawful defence against 'an imminent or proximate threat', but rejecting preventive self-defence, defined as action against a non-imminent or non-proximate threat).

[30] Michael Schmitt, 'Responding to Transnational Terrorism Under the *Jus Ad Bellum*: A Normative Framework' (2008) 56 *Naval Law Review* 1, 21; Kalliopi Chainoglou, *Reconceptualising the Law of Self-Defence* (Brussels: Ant. N. Sakkoulas, 2008), 334–5.

in another state where it has concrete intelligence that the latter state is about to transfer nuclear weapons to a terrorist group. In contrast, it would not be lawful for the state to attack that facility if it only had generalized concerns that the other state someday may transfer WMD to those terrorists.[31]

At the same time, this school demands a significant level of certainty about the risk of the incoming attack and a short time horizon in which the threat will materialize. For those who deem pre-emptive self-defence lawful, drawing a credible line between pre-emptive self-defence and (unlawful) preventive self-defence is a challenge, implicating questions about what types of intelligence should be required and what degree of confidence a state must have about the accuracy of that intelligence. Section IV discusses how scholars have proposed to cabin the potential misuse of pre-emptive self-defence.

A number of states defend the lawfulness of pre-emptive self-defence. Indeed, some of their statements might be read to support preventive self-defence, a concept discussed in the following section. Most famously, in 2002 the US produced a National Security Strategy that clearly argued for the propriety of pre-emptive self-defence.[32] The document stated, 'If necessary, however, under long-standing principles of self-defense, we do not rule out the use of force before attacks occur, even if uncertainty remains as to the time and place of the enemy's attack. When the consequences of an attack with WMD are potentially so devastating, we cannot afford to stand idly by as grave dangers materialise. This is the principle and logic of pre-emption.'[33] Australia, Japan, and the UK have also defended their right to use force in certain situations to prevent terrorist or WMD threats from materializing.[34] Japan, for example, has publicly contemplated using pre-emptive force against North Korea if it has strong evidence that North Korea is planning a missile attack against it.[35] In 2012, Russia suggested that it was prepared to use 'pre-emptive force'

[31] Schmitt, 'Responding to Transnational Terrorism Under the *Jus Ad Bellum*: A Normative Framework', 21.

[32] 2002 US National Security Strategy, 15. Several scholars characterize this argument as one in support of preventive—not merely pre-emptive—self-defence. Doyle, *Striking First*, 25; Ivo Daalder and James Steinberg, 'The Future of Preemption' (Winter 2005) *American Interest* 1 fn 1.

[33] 2002 US National Security Strategy, 15.

[34] 'PM warns of continuing global terror threat', 10 Downing Street, 5 Mar 2004 ('Containment will not work in the face of the global threat that confronts us. The terrorists have no intention of being contained. The states that proliferate or acquire WMD illegally are doing so precisely to avoid containment. Emphatically I am not saying that every situation leads to military action. But we surely have a duty and a right to prevent the threat materialising'); Phil Mercer, 'Tensions Rise Over Australia's Pre-Emptive Strike Policy Ahead of ASEAN Summit', *Epoch Times*, 26 Nov 2004 ('[Then Prime Minister] Howard repeatedly has said his government would attack militants overseas if they were planning to strike Australian interests and the host country refused to act…').

[35] 'Japan Threatens Force Against North Korea', *BBC News*, 14 Feb 2003 ('Japan has warned it would launch a pre-emptive military action against North Korea if it had firm evidence Pyongyang was planning a missile attack'); Anthony Faiola, 'In Japan, Tough Talk About Preemptive Capability', *Washington Post*, 11 July 2006 ('Japanese officials on Monday called for a debate on whether Japan should pursue military capabilities that would enable preemptive strikes at North Korean missile

against missile-defence sites in Poland, though its statements provided no detail about the precise type of threat it believed would trigger that right.[36]

D. Preventive Self-Defence

It is uncontroverted that preventive use of force is lawful when the UN Security Council authorizes it. The Security Council clearly may allow states to take forcible measures against a 'threat to the peace'.[37] The High-Level Panel Report reflected this understanding when it rejected arguments for unilateral acts of preventive self-defence but stated, 'if there are good arguments for preventive military action, with good evidence to support them, they should be put to the Security Council, which can authorise such action if it chooses to.'[38] In this view, the Council serves as a 'jurying or adjudicative process' through which to assess claims that another state's actions pose a threat to international peace and security.[39]

Unilateral use of force in preventive self-defence is far more controversial than Council-authorized preventive uses of force. Yet it has its supporters. First, the US position is often characterized as favouring preventive self-defence; the US has articulated a right to use force in the face of perceived threats posed by WMD 'even if uncertainty remains as to the time and place of the enemy's attack.'[40] The US view is driven by a concern that restricting state action until the threat of attack looms large may mean foregoing the opportunity to respond to the attack at all—an unacceptable outcome when that threat involves terrorists, WMD, or both. Secondly, several scholars accept preventive (and other) uses of force because they see the UN Charter as defunct.[41]

Those who support anticipatory or pre-emptive self-defence but reject preventive self-defence believe that 'the risk to the global order and the norm of non-intervention on which it continues to be based is simply too great for the legality of unilateral preventive action... to be accepted.'[42] One reason Israel's attack on

bases.... The Japanese parliament has previously ruled that a preemptive strike on missiles about to be fired at Japan may fall under the definition of self-defense. In recent days, Japanese leaders have been citing such interpretations').

[36] Andrew Kramer, 'Russian General Makes Threat on Missile-Defense Sites', *New York Times*, 3 May 2012.

[37] See UN Charter, Arts 39, 42.

[38] High-Level Panel, 'A More Secure World', para 190.

[39] Thomas Franck, 'The Power of Legitimacy and the Legitimacy of Power: International Law in an Age of Power Disequilibrium' (2006) 100 *American Journal of International Law* 88, 104.

[40] 2002 US National Security Strategy, 15. See also UK Attorney General's speech in the House of Lords, HL Deb, 21 Apr 2004, vol 660 cols 369–72 (stating that states may act in self-defence where there is evidence of further imminent attacks by terrorist groups, even if there is no specific evidence of where such an attack will take place or of the precise nature of the attack).

[41] This includes Michael Glennon and Anthony Clark Arend. See Murphy, 'The Doctrine of Preemptive Self-Defense', 717–19 (describing the 'Charter-is-Dead' school).

[42] High-Level Panel, 'A More Secure World', paras 189–90.

the Osirak reactor in Iraq in 1981 was roundly criticized was because it appeared preventive. That is, states did not believe that Iraq's nuclear programme had ripened into a tangible threat to use force, let alone a threat of imminent attack.[43]

Parsing different legal views on the use of force in self-defence before an attack transpires helps to identify key areas of disagreement. Some disagreement flows from the imprecise use of language. Further, various players start with distinct pre-existing moral commitments: some seek to limit—to the greatest extent possible—the use of force in the international community, while others give relative priority to a state's security.[44] These actors also possess different intelligence about the threats and evaluate the evidence differently. Other disagreement may stem from the dearth of actual practice in this area. Given a relatively narrow range of fact patterns, it is harder to compile systematic state responses to different situations or to ascertain whether and how the law is evolving.[45] Finally, the various schools take distinct methodological approaches, including by paying more or less attention to treaty language and different types of state practice.[46] In short, wide substantive and rhetorical disagreement remains about the lawfulness of using force in situations other than manifestly imminent attacks.

IV. New Pressures on the Law

Three geopolitical and technological developments place additional pressure on the legal framework. First, the spread of WMD (particularly nuclear) technology to rogue states raises concerns about how those states may use those weapons and whether the states may proliferate the technology.[47] Secondly, the methods of transnational

[43] Higgins, 'The Attitude of Western States Towards Legal Aspects of the Use of Force' in Cassese, *The Current Legal Regulation of the Use of Force*, 443; Franck, *Recourse to Force*, 108; Terence Taylor, 'The End of Imminence?' (2004) 27 *Washington Quarterly* 57, 58.

[44] Compare Leland Goodrich and Edvard Hambro, *Charter of the United Nations: Commentary and Documents* (London: Stevens, 1949), 44–5 (arguing that Art 2(4) was designed to prevent armed conflict and allows very few exceptions to that goal), with Waxman, 'The Use of Force Against States That Might Have Weapons of Mass Destruction', 7 ('The basic policy behind international self-defense doctrine is to promote global order by permitting states sufficient leeway to respond to expected security threats while not creating an exception so broad to the baseline prohibition of force that it swallows the rule...').

[45] Murphy, 'The Doctrine of Preemptive Self-Defense', 738. Murphy notes that it is not clear whether state practice is relevant here as evidence of states' interpretations of the Charter language, or as evidence of an emerging norm of customary international law on the use of force that supersedes the Charter (at 710).

[46] Murphy, 'The Doctrine of Preemptive Self-Defense', 720–1.

[47] Waxman, 'The Use of Force Against States That Might Have Weapons of Mass Destruction', 9–10.

terrorist groups bent on conducting spectacular attacks means that the traditional military signals forecasting an imminent attack often will be absent. Thirdly, there is a looming possibility that cyber tools may be used to conduct armed attacks. Given the speed and complexity of cyber attacks, requiring a state to wait until there is 'no moment for deliberation'[48] before responding with force increasingly looks like a requirement that a state should stand by and suffer an attack. These developments place new pressures on the doctrine of pre-attack self-defence because of the nature of the threat and the quantum of harm that would result from an attack; the probable stealth of delivery; and the speed at which attack could arrive once launched. This section explores the impact of these new threats on the law and the limited state practice in responding to these developments.

A. WMD

Certain scholars and states deem it imperative to update the self-defence concept of imminence in response to efforts by rogue states (and potentially non-state actors) to acquire WMD.[49] Indeed, the self-defence posture in the 2002 US National Security Strategy appears to have been driven by concerns about the use of WMD against the US. It states, 'Our immediate focus will be those terrorist organisations of global reach and any terrorist or state sponsor of terrorism which attempts to gain or use weapons of mass destruction (WMD) or their precursors.'[50] Adversaries with WMD may be 'able to strike with little or no notice' and, once they have initiated a WMD attack, 'the targeted state is likely have limited options for protecting its population.'[51] In this view, WMD capabilities produce a very different type of threat than that posed by conventional weapons—that is, from the type of threat from which the *Caroline* test emerged.[52] Sir Christopher Greenwood believes that a WMD attack 'can reasonably be treated as imminent in circumstances where an attack by conventional means would not be so regarded' because of the extreme risk to a state forced to wait until the attack takes place and the impossibility of affording that state's population any effective protection after the attack has been launched.[53] That said, in most cases the potential victim state will face significant uncertainty both about the potential aggressor state's capacity and its intent to use

[48] Letter from Daniel Webster (see n 5).

[49] Waxman, 'The Use of Force Against States That Might Have Weapons of Mass Destruction', 12 (describing the 'widespread belief that legal doctrine, and the concept of imminence in particular, needs to be updated in light of contemporary threats such as the proliferation of WMD').

[50] 2002 US National Security Strategy, 6.

[51] Waxman, 'The Use of Force Against States That Might Have Weapons of Mass Destruction', 8–9.

[52] Waxman, 'The Use of Force Against States That Might Have Weapons of Mass Destruction', 11; Doyle, *Striking First*, 11–17; Greenwood, 'International Law and the Pre-Emptive Use of Force', 16

[53] Greenwood, 'International Law and the Pre-Emptive Use of Force', 16.

WMD.[54] Thus, the cost of failing to pre-empt an attack that uses WMD is extremely high, but it is particularly hard to predict their use accurately.

One recent example of state practice causes us to consider whether states are changing their views on the legality of pre-emptive self-defence, at least in the WMD context. On 6 September 2007, Israel bombed an industrial facility near al Kibar, Syria.[55] The CIA later identified the target as a nearly complete nuclear reactor, likely built with North Korean assistance to produce plutonium. As Leonard Spector and Avner Cohen put it, 'What was particularly notable about this attack was what occurred afterward: the near total lack of international comment or criticism of Israel's actions. The lack of reaction contrasted starkly to the international outcry that followed Israel's preventive strike in 1981 that destroyed Iraq's Osiraq reactor.'[56] Yet it was clear that the presence of the Syrian reactor hardly met the *Caroline* factors: Syria was some time away from producing fissile material for nuclear weapons and further from producing the weapons themselves.[57] Only if Israel's use of force met the *Caroline* test would there be a clear explanation for the lack of an international reaction.

Several factual differences between the Osirak and al Kibar bombings may explain the radically different reactions to them. Iraq, which was building its facilities publicly, allowed the International Atomic Energy Agency (IAEA) to visit those facilities. Syria, out of favour with the international community, was building the reactor secretly with the aid of another disfavoured state.[58] Shortly after the Syrian bombing, the CIA provided a 12-minute video and an extensive briefing, making a strong case that the target was a North Korean-built reactor designed to produce weapons-usable plutonium (unlike Iraq's in 1981, which could have been used for peaceful purposes).[59] The IAEA later discovered uranium particles at the site.[60] Yet the different facts do not seem to entirely account for dramatically different state reactions.

One hypothesis is that the threat of WMD in the hands of states with a track record of unpredictable behaviour has caused states to shift their views of the propriety of pre-emptive self-defence against such a threat.[61] A single example of

[54] Waxman, 'The Use of Force Against States That Might Have Weapons of Mass Destruction', 4.

[55] Leonard Spector and Avner Cohen, *Israel's Airstrike on Syria's Reactor: Implications for the Non-Proliferation Regime* (Washington DC: Arms Control Association, 2008).

[56] Spector and Cohen, *Israel's Airstrike on Syria's Reactor*.

[57] Spector and Cohen, *Israel's Airstrike on Syria's Reactor*. See also Andrew Garwood-Gowers, 'Israel's Airstrike on Syria's Al-Kibar Facility: A Test Case for the Doctrine of Pre-emptive Self-Defence?' (2011) 16 *Journal of Conflict and Security Law* 263, 268.

[58] Spector and Cohen, *Israel's Airstrike on Syria's Reactor*.

[59] Spector and Cohen, *Israel's Airstrike on Syria's Reactor*.

[60] Garwood-Gowers, 'Israel's Airstrike on Syria's Al-Kibar Facility', 264; IAEA, *Implementation of the NPT Safeguards Agreement in the Syrian Arab Republic*, GOV/2010/29.

[61] Another hypothesis is that states' non-response to the al Kibar bombing reflected political support for Israel's action rather than collective acceptance that such an act was legal. Garwood-Gowers, 'Israel's Airstrike on Syria's Al-Kibar Facility', 290.

state practice cannot prove such a shift; only time (and future cases of pre-emptive self-defence) can do so. Nevertheless, there appears to be a growing recognition that the threat posed by WMD is distinctive in ways that affect how states analyse pre-emptive self-defence.

B. Terrorist Groups

A second development is the rise of hostile terrorist groups that operate across state borders. Assuming that non-state actors can commit armed attacks that trigger a state's right to self-defence,[62] the attacks that these non-state actors commit also challenge notions of imminence.[63] Terrorist attacks inherently rely on unpredictability, stealth, and concealment. Greenwood writes: 'it is far more difficult to determine the time scale within which a threat of attack by terrorist means would materialise than it is with threats posed by, for example, regular armed forces.'[64] Secondly, many terrorist groups exist exclusively to conduct violent attacks on states and civil society; there is little question that they intend to undertake attacks when they have the means to do so.[65] Finally, efforts by terrorist groups to obtain WMD technology are particularly problematic because, unlike with states, these groups are very hard to deter.[66] Relatedly, because states often deem it unpalatable or fruitless to negotiate with terrorist groups, the requirement that states exhaust other avenues (eg diplomacy or sanctions) before resorting to force fits imperfectly into the traditional doctrine. In short, terrorist organizations (such as Al Qaeda and Hezbollah) have proved their ability to conduct extensive attacks against states across sovereign borders, and their tactics and goals suggest a strong need—in certain circumstances—to use force against those groups before they initiate an armed attack.

[62] See eg Schmitt, 'Responding to Transnational Terrorism Under the *Jus Ad Bellum*', 6–7.

[63] Judith Gardam, 'A Role for Proportionality in the War on Terror' (2005) 74 *Nordic Journal of International Law* 3, 11 (conceding that the *Caroline* requirement of immediacy 'may no longer prevail in the face of the threat of terrorism' but demanding a 'distinct quantifiable threat' before a state may act); Philippe Sands, 'International Law and the Use of Force', Written Evidence to Select Committee on Foreign Affairs, (2004), para 15 (concept of imminence must be 'flexibly interpreted in an age in which technology allows great devastation to be wrought in a very short period of time').

[64] Greenwood, 'International Law and the Pre-Emptive Use of Force', 16; see also Doyle, *Striking First*, 21 (noting that the rise of belligerent non-state actors makes evidence of 'active preparation' very hard to identify in time to pre-empt the threat).

[65] Schmitt, 'Responding to Transnational Terrorism Under the *Jus Ad Bellum*', 10 ('Even though the timing and location of an attack may be uncertain, there is near certainty that an attack will be conducted since that is the group's very purpose').

[66] Doyle, *Striking First*, 21, 93.

c. Cyber

Scholars have started to consider seriously whether and what type of cyber attack may rise to the level of an armed attack that triggers a state's right of self-defence.[67] They have spent less time examining when that right is triggered temporally. If cyber attacks can constitute armed attacks, this raises at least two questions relevant to pre-attack self-defence. First, how should one determine when an attack has been initiated, in a world in which a bad actor can plant delayed-release time bombs or logic bombs in another actor's computer system?[68] Secondly, when a cyber attack can hit its target in less than a second and when it may be impossible to determine in advance what level of damage an attack will inflict, does it make sense to require a state to refrain from responding to anything other than a threat of an 'imminent' attack, or even to act only in the 'last clear window' before an attack? These questions are compounded by the more general questions raised by cyber weapons: how to attribute attacks; where the line falls between 'active defence' and offence; how to gauge proportionality; and whether ideas of sovereignty limit how a state may respond to attacks that pass through neutral territory. Each of these developments challenges the traditional understanding of imminence. When the threat of an armed attack comes from entities that possess WMD, a state may be unable to respond if it waits for the armed attack to become 'imminent' in the *Caroline* sense. With terrorist groups, a state will often have little indication that the group is about to initiate an attack. And for cyber weapons, not only may a state not be aware that its opponent has initiated an attack, but there will also rarely be a 'build up' phase to put the state on notice that an armed attack is temporally imminent.

D. Guiding the Pre-Emptive Application of Force

In response to these three developments, some states and scholars have articulated dissatisfaction with a legal rule that prevents a state from acting until an attack is virtually upon it. Then-senior White House official John Brennan recently asserted that both the US and other states increasingly recognize that:

> a more flexible understanding of 'imminence' may be appropriate when dealing with terrorist groups, in part because threats posed by non-state actors do not present themselves in the ways that evidenced imminence in more traditional conflicts.... [A]n increasing number of our international counterterrorism partners have begun to recognise that the traditional conception of what constitutes an 'imminent' attack should be broadened in

[67] See eg Michael N. Schmitt (ed), *Tallinn Manual on the International Law Applicable to Cyber Warfare* (Cambridge: Cambridge University Press, 2013); Oona Hathaway et al, 'The Law of Cyber-Attack' (2012) 100 *California Law Review* 817.

[68] Marco Roscini, 'World Wide Warfare—*Jus ad Bellum* and the Use of Cyber Force' (2010) 14 *Max Planck Yearbook of International Law* 85, 120.

light of the modern-day capabilities, techniques, and technological innovations of terrorist organisations.[69]

States have not yet set forth in greater detail how they would redefine 'imminence' to meet today's threats.

Yet even those who argue for increased flexibility recognize the need to cabin it. Scholars have done more work than states in this regard: some scholars have proffered factors for states to use when assessing whether they may lawfully use force in advance of an armed attack. Michael Doyle, for instance, would require states to assess four factors before using force: the lethality of the threat the potential victim state would suffer; the likelihood that the threatened attack will materialize; the legitimacy of the victim state's proposed action (assessed using just war principles); and the legality of the target state's domestic and international behaviour and the victim state's response.[70] Doyle would require the potential victim state to attempt to resort to the Security Council, but would not deem authorization necessary.[71] Abraham Sofaer offers four comparable factors or steps that a potential victim state would need to consider or undertake: the magnitude of the threat faced by that state; the probability that the threatened attack will occur; the exhaustion of peaceful alternatives; and the consistency of that state's action with the purposes underlying the UN Charter.[72]

Christopher Greenwood would revisit conventional understandings of imminence, arguing that a state assessing imminence today may take into account the gravity and method of delivery of the threat.[73] He would also demand evidence that the state (or non-state actor) possesses weapons and intends to use them.[74] Likewise, a Chatham House project on the use of force in international law states that, in interpreting the criterion of imminence in the face of current threats, 'reference may be made to the gravity of the attack, the capability of the attacker, and the nature of the threat, for example if the attack is likely to come without warning.'[75]

[69] Remarks of John Brennan, 'Strengthening Our Security By Adhering to Our Values and Laws'. See also James Steinberg, 'Preventive Force in U.S. National Security Strategy' (2005–6) 47 *Survival* 55, 58–9 ('according to the President and his national security team, there are three reasons for a more expansive use of preventive force—the changing *nature of the actors* who threaten the United States (rogue states and terrorists vs traditional state adversaries); the *threat* (clandestine weapons programmes) and the *inadequacy of relying on collective action* through the Security Council').

[70] Doyle, *Striking First*, 46.

[71] Doyle, *Striking First*, 61–2. See also Ivo Daalder and James Steinberg, 'The Future of Preemption' (calling for the creation of 'coalitions of like-minded states to legitimate decision-making on the preventive use of force' where the UN or regional route has failed and noting that 'if it proves impossible to convince one's democratic peers that intervention is justified, that should in and of itself give any national leadership pause about proceeding').

[72] Abraham Sofaer, 'On the Necessity of Pre-Emption' (2003) 14 *European Journal of International Law* 209, 220.

[73] Greenwood, 'International Law and the Pre-Emptive Use of Force', 16.

[74] Greenwood, 'International Law and the Pre-Emptive Use of Force', 16.

[75] Elizabeth Wilmshurst, *Principles of International Law on the Use of Force by States in Self-Defence* (London: Chatham House, 2005). See also Schmitt, 'Responding to Transnational Terrorism Under the *Jus Ad Bellum*', 11 (accepting pre-attack self-defence 'when a terrorist group harbors both the intent and

In sum, virtually every scholar who offers factors to limit pre-emptive self-defence considers the nature and quantum of the threat at issue; the harm that would likely result from an attack; the urgency and specificity of the particular threat; and whether the state contemplating action has exhausted viable alternatives—in particular, resort to the Security Council. Yet the real problem in this area of the law may lie not in achieving agreement on basic principles, but in applying those principles to real-world facts: how serious and realistic is a particular threat of an armed attack, and what constitutes a reasonable response to that threat.[76] The way out of the endless debate may turn more on wider disclosures of intelligence by the state using force (of the type that took place after Israel's attack on the Syrian nuclear facility) and less on the law.

Those who object to pre-attack force reject any and all factors that would guide a state's reliance on pre-emptive self-defence. Rather than establish malleable factors such as those just discussed, some critics would prefer instead that a state that acts before suffering an armed attack asks forgiveness afterwards, based on the claimed rightness of its cause.[77] Others question whether such factors really would impose limits on a state determined to act.[78] In any case, the recent work on pre-emption suggests some level of consensus by those scholars about what alignment of factors renders pre-emptive force lawful and legitimate.

V. Taming Pre-Emption?

The title of this chapter invites an antecedent question: does pre-emption need to be tamed? There is a good argument that the doctrine of pre-emption has more bark than bite. States have only infrequently relied on anticipatory or pre-emptive self-defence to justify legally their uses of force.[79] The US, for instance, defended its

means to carry out attacks, there is no effective alternative for preventing them, and the State must act now or risk missing the opportunity to thwart the attacks').

[76] Richard Tuck, 'Comment' in Doyle, *Striking First*, xxi; Greenwood, 'International Law and the Pre-Emptive Use of Force', 14 (noting that states condemned the Osirak attack on the facts, not because they rejected the concept of anticipatory self-defence); Schmitt, 'Responding to Transnational Terrorism Under the *Jus Ad Bellum*', 4 (stating that criticism of the US bombing in Sudan was driven by concern that the attack was based on faulty intelligence, not on resistance to self-defence against terrorist acts).

[77] Harold Koh, 'Comment' in Doyle, *Striking First*, 117.

[78] Tuck, 'Comment' in Doyle, *Striking First*, 126.

[79] Doyle, *Striking First*, 17 fn 18 (noting that genuine cases of pre-emptive war have been rare); Murphy, 'The Doctrine of Preemptive Self-Defense', 710 (noting that 'strict constructionists' believe that invocations of anticipatory self-defence have been rare and that other states have resisted those invocations).

invasion of Iraq in 2003 on the basis of several UN Security Council resolutions, not pre-emptive self-defence.[80] The US missile strikes in Afghanistan and Sudan in 1998 against suspected Al Qaeda targets arguably constituted self-defence in response to a previous armed attack. The US legal basis for contemporary drone strikes against members of Al Qaeda and associated forces in Yemen, Pakistan, and Somalia is that they are discrete military operations in the context of an ongoing armed conflict.[81] There clearly have been cases in which anticipatory self-defence is either the best or the only explanation for a state's action—for instance, Israel's bombing of the Egyptian air force in 1967 or its strike on the Osirak reactor in 1981. But these cases are infrequent. Additionally, the backlash against the highly controversial US invasion of Iraq—which many viewed as an exercise in pre-emptive (or preventive) self-defence—may have led US officials to adopt a cautious posture towards future military activity that relies on such a legal justification.

Why, then, do states continue to press for the legal acceptance of pre-emptive self-defence, if they rarely intend to rely on it and incur political costs in doing so? One reason may be that states favouring pre-emption believe that the argument itself serves as a deterrent: it signals to other states that they should be very cautious about undertaking actions that could credibly be construed as pre-cursors to an armed attack. Another reason may be strategic: repeated public assertions about the need for a robust doctrine of pre-emption may make the invocation of narrower claims of anticipatory self-defence more palatable.[82] A third reason—the one most worrying to those concerned about pre-emption—is that states believe they will need to rely on such a legal justification in the fast-approaching future, given the technological developments discussed previously. In this view, these public defences of pre-emption lay the groundwork for probable uses of force to come. In short, it is easy to overstate the importance of periodic state claims about the lawfulness of pre-emption, but states are far from abandoning those claims.

As a substantive matter, *has* the international doctrine of self-defence evolved to embrace uses of force that take place in situations further removed from 'imminent' attacks on the temporal continuum? Possibly, though there is insufficient evidence to say with certainty. Sean Murphy suggests that 11 September 2001 may have marked a turning point in how states view defensive uses of force. He notes: 'there appear to be significant historical periods where global politics have dramatically influenced the way states think about uses of force, whether it be the bipolar confrontation of the Cold War... or the post-September 11 period in which we now find

[80] William Taft IV and Todd Buchwald, 'Preemption, Iraq, and International Law' (2003) 97 *American Journal of International Law* 557.

[81] Remarks of John Brennan, 'Strengthening Our Security By Adhering to Our Values and Laws'.

[82] Garwood-Gowers, 'Israel's Airstrike on Syria's Al-Kibar Facility', 276 ('While the notion of pre-emptive force against non-imminent threats has not been accepted, a by-product of the Bush doctrine appears to be greater explicit support for the more limited right of anticipatory self-defence in relation to imminent threats').

ourselves.'[83] Michael Schmitt has argued: 'ultimately, law must be construed in the context in which it is to be applied if it is to remain relevant; and in the twenty-first century security environment, insistence on a passé restrictive application of international legal principles to strategies of preemption would quickly impel States at risk to ignore them.'[84] Even scholars who are sympathetic to narrow readings of self-defence suggest that we are seeing a trend towards increased tolerance of certain pre-attack uses of force, particularly where the force is intended to suppress terrorist acts or the proliferation of WMD.[85]

Wherever the law stands now, current technological changes virtually guarantee that the law will not stand still for long. Some technological developments seem poised to drive the concept of imminence even further from its roots in the *Caroline* test. The speed and stealth of incoming cyber attacks, for example, suggest that the 'last window of opportunity' to act may necessarily be far removed from certainty about an impending attack in order for self-defence to remain meaningful. Other developments pull in the other direction. The ability of satellites and drones to hover for days or weeks over targets and acquire detailed imagery of WMD facilities, for instance, may vastly improve a potential victim state's capacity to gauge correctly its opponent's capacity and intent.[86] That intelligence collection capacity may also diminish the danger of waiting until the last possible moment to act, at least in some cases. Advancing cyber technologies may endow states with a wider range of responses that fall below the level of force, allowing those states to avoid the self-defence debate entirely. The international community is likely to hold high expectations that any state using force in advance of an attack will share the intelligence that led the state to act pre-emptively (such as the CIA did after Israel's al Kibar strike). This expectation will put pressure on such states not to act in the absence of such intelligence.

[83] Murphy, 'The Doctrine of Preemptive Self-Defense', 745.

[84] Michael Schmitt, 'Pre-Emptive Strategies in International Law' (2003) 24 *Michigan Journal of International Law* 513, 546.

[85] Garwood-Gowers, 'Israel's Airstrike on Syria's Al-Kibar Facility', 290; Christine Gray, 'The Use of Force to Prevent the Proliferation of Nuclear Weapons' (2009) 52 *Japanese Yearbook of International Law* 101, 126.

[86] See eg William Broad and Mark Mazzetti, 'Yet Another Photo of Site in Syria, Yet More Questions', *New York Times*, 27 Oct 2007 (quoting a senior US intelligence official as stating that US spy satellites had observed Syria's site for years).

VI. Conclusion

Pre-emptive self-defence remains one of the most hotly contested principles in the *jus ad bellum*. In some ways, the stakes are high: the further international law moves (or is viewed by powerful states as moving) away from *Caroline*-type principles, the more likely we are to see objectively unnecessary uses of force that could destabilize the international regime. In other ways, the stakes are manageable: there are few historical instances of pre-emptive self-defence, and the clear trend in scholarship is to offer critical limiting factors, many of which states would likely accept as relevant to their pre-attack actions today. The speed with which relevant technologies are developing—and the physical speed of action that those technologies allow—ensure that future conversations about pre-emption will implicate issues beyond our current collective imagination.

CHAPTER 30

CAN NON-STATE ACTORS MOUNT AN ARMED ATTACK?

KIMBERLEY N. TRAPP

I. Introduction

ARTICLE 2(4) of the UN Charter[1] prohibits the use of force *between states*, but that prohibition does not 'impair the inherent right of individual or collective self-defence if an *armed attack* occurs against a Member of the United Nations'.[2] In its Charter incarnation, the prohibition of the use of force is situated in a strictly inter-state context, and does not speak to the phenomenon of uses of force by non-state actors (NSAs). The question examined in this chapter is whether the exception to that prohibition—the right to use force in self-defence—is nevertheless responsive to the war-making capacity of NSAs or whether it is limited to a snapshot of the right as it may have been conceptualized in the immediate aftermath of a global conflict between states. Otherwise put, is the definition of 'armed attack' in Article 51 of the UN Charter (and related customary international law) conditioned on the attacker being a state?[3]

[1] UN Charter, 26 June 1945, 1 UNTS XVI. [2] UN Charter, Art 51 (emphasis added).

[3] This chapter only addresses the definition of 'armed attack' and the conditions for the applicability of Art 51 of the UN Charter in terms of the *identity* of the attacker. Further elements of the definition of 'armed attack', including whether the use of force is of sufficient gravity to amount to

On a cursory examination, the logic of the UN Charter might suggest that an armed attack to which states can respond with defensive force in reliance on Article 51 *must* be attributable to a state. This is because Article 2(4) of the UN Charter prohibits the threat or use of force against the territorial integrity or political independence of any state. Using defensive force against the base of operations of NSAs within a foreign host state's territory, even if that defensive force only targets the NSAs which have launched an attack, still amounts to a violation of the host state's territorial integrity. If Article 51 is to be a true exception to the prohibition on the use of force as set forth in Article 2(4) (and a circumstance precluding wrongfulness with respect thereto[4]), it should respond in some way to the violation of the host state's territorial integrity. The legal mechanism which has traditionally been relied on to preserve an inter-state reading of Article 51, yet accommodate the need to respond to attacks by NSAs, is that of attribution. As will be examined in Section II, attribution is certainly a sufficient condition (in *ratione personae* terms) for the applicability of Article 51 of the UN Charter.

The difficulty, however, with an *exclusively* attribution-based definition of 'armed attack' is that it fails to account for recent uses of defensive force in response to attacks carried out by NSAs (which were *not* attributable to the host state on the basis of Article 3(g) of the UN Definition of Aggression[5] or the ILC Articles on State Responsibility) that were widely accepted as legitimate by the international community. In addition, a definition of 'armed attack' that is limited to attributable force fails to respond to the security concerns of states which may be the victim of un-attributable armed attacks. Section III explores the extent to which attribution is a necessary element of the right to respond to armed attacks by NSAs with defensive force in foreign territory through an examination of: (III.A) the language of the UN Charter (and the *travaux préparatoires*); (III.B) the jurisprudence of the International Court of Justice (ICJ); and (III.C) state practice. Section III further considers whether there is an alternative framework (to that of attribution) available that preserves an inter-state reading of Article 51, consistent with the logic of the UN Charter, but which accommodates the security needs of states to defend themselves against armed attacks by NSAs.

an armed attack within the meaning of Art 51, are addressed in Jan Klabbers, 'Intervention, Armed Intervention, Armed Attack, Threat to Peace, Act of Aggression, and Threat or Use of Force: What's the Difference', Chapter 22 in this volume. See also *Military and Paramilitary Activities in and against Nicaragua (Nicaragua v. US)*, Merits, Judgment, ICJ Rep 1986, 14, para 195; *Oil Platforms (Iran v. US)*, Judgment, ICJ Rep 2003, 161, para 51.

[4] See Art 21, Commentary to Part Two, Chapter I, Draft Articles on Responsibility of States for Internationally Wrongful Acts, with Commentaries in Report of the International Law Commission on the work of its Fifty-Third Session, A/56/10 (2001), 31 (hereinafter 'ILC Articles on State Responsibility').

[5] UN Definition of Aggression, GA Res 3314 (1974), Annex.

II. Aggression and Attributable Attacks by Non-State Actors

While the use of armed force by NSAs has been the subject of increasing (perhaps overwhelming) academic attention, it is not an entirely modern phenomenon. The capacity and willingness of states to wage war by proxy, through reliance on fighters associated with, but outside the formal structures of the state, has long been a source of concern to the international community.[6] Such 'indirect' use of force was addressed extensively during negotiation of the UN Definition of Aggression, finally adopted by the General Assembly in 1974.[7] The Special Committee on the Question of Defining Aggression spent much time debating whether uses of force by NSAs, with which the state had *some* involvement, should be included in the definition of aggression.[8] It was generally agreed that state involvement in the activities of NSAs would amount to a breach of the peace or an illegal intervention in the domestic affairs of another state.[9] Western states, however, insisted that the 'organization or instigation of or assistance or participation in' attacks by NSAs should figure in the definition of aggression.[10] The Soviet Union preferred to distinguish between aggression and indirect aggression,[11] while members of the Non-Aligned Movement (NAM) raised objections to the concept of indirect aggression altogether.[12]

Representatives of NAM states were preoccupied with the relationship between the definition of aggression and the definition of 'armed attack' under Article 51 of the UN Charter. In particular, NAM states were concerned that a failure to limit the definition of aggression to direct state action raised the possibility of powerful states disingenuously accusing weaker states of acquiescing in or supporting armed bands operating from their territory to justify an aggressive use of force (under the guise of self-defence) against that weaker state.[13] As a result, the proposed definition of aggression supported by NAM members expressly excluded the right to use force in

[6] See eg Czechoslovakia's and the Philippine's observations on the Dumbarton Oaks proposals, both of which suggest that 'aggression' should be defined (for the purposes of triggering the Security Council's powers) to include supporting armed bands. Doc 2, G/14(b) (1 May 1945), United Nations Conference on International Organization Documents (UNCIO), vol III, 469 (Czechoslovakia); Doc 2, G/14(k) (5 May 1945), UNCIO, vol III, 538 (the Philippines).

[7] UN Definition of Aggression.

[8] See Report of the Special Committee on the Question of Defining Aggression, A/8019 (1970), paras 26–30.

[9] A/8019 (1970), para 127.

[10] See Report of the Special Committee on the Question of Defining Aggression, A/8719 (1972), App B, Section A.

[11] See A/8019 (1970), para IV.B(7).

[12] See Reports of the Special Committee on the Question of Defining Aggression, A/7620, paras 26–9, 62, and 69–72; A/8019 (1970), Annex I, para 7; A/8419 (1971), paras 27–8; A/8719 (1972), Section C.

[13] See A/7620 (1969), para 127.

self-defence, in reliance on Article 51 of the UN Charter, in response to 'subversive and/or terrorist acts by irregular, volunteer or armed bands organized or supported by another State…'[14] In general, Western states rejected NAM's treatment of 'aggression' and 'armed attack' as coextensive,[15] did not accept as a matter of principle that defensive force in reliance on Article 51 could not be used in response to armed attacks by armed bands,[16] and argued that failing to include indirect aggression in the definition would encourage states to engage in wars by proxy, through active or passive support of NSAs.[17]

The compromise between these positions, which allowed the UN Definition of Aggression to be adopted by consensus, operated on several fronts. First, the definition was adopted for the purposes of guiding the Security Council in the exercise of its powers under Article 39 of the UN Charter[18] and was independent of any agreement on the definition of 'armed attack' under Article 51. Secondly, in respect of indirect aggression, the position seems to have been to accept that acts of aggression could be carried out by NSAs, but to require their attributability. Article 1 of the UN Definition of Aggression defines aggression as 'the use of armed force *by a State* against the sovereignty, territorial integrity or political independence of another State…'[19] The use of armed force, however, need not be carried out by a state's military forces: Article 3(g) of the UN Definition of Aggression provides that 'sending by or on behalf of a State of armed bands, groups, irregulars or mercenaries, which carry out acts [amounting to aggression], or its substantial involvement therein' also amounts to aggression.[20] Article 3 is intended to provide a non-exhaustive list of acts that amount to aggression within the meaning of Article 1. As such, the 'sending by or on behalf of a State of armed bands…, or…substantial involvement therein' in paragraph (g) must be interpreted as a *lex specialis* threshold for

[14] Draft proposal submitted by Colombia, Cyprus, Ecuador, Ghana, Guyana, Haiti, Iran, Madagascar, Mexico, Spain, Uganda, Uruguay, and Yugoslavia, A/AC.134/L.16 and Add.1 and 2, para 7 in Report of the Special Committee on the Question of Defining Aggression, A/9019 (1973), 9.

[15] See Special Committee on the Question of Defining Aggression, Third Session, vol II, A/AC.134/SR.67 (19 Oct 1970), 6 (UK); A/8019 (1970), para 69,

[16] See eg A/AC.134/SR.67 (n 15), 106–7 (UK), 7 (Japan). See further, A/8019 (1970), paras 27 and 128. See further Derek W. Bowett, *Self-Defence in International Law* (Manchester: Manchester University Press, 1958), 256–60 and Sean D. Murphy, 'The Crime of Aggression at the International Criminal Court', Chapter 24 in this volume for a discussion of the concepts of 'aggression' and 'armed attack'.

[17] A/7620 (1969), para 128. See also Benjamin Ferencz, 'A Proposed Definition of Aggression: By Compromise and Consensus' (1973) 22 *International and Comparative Law Quarterly* 407, 419–21, for a summary of the debate.

[18] See Special Committee on the Question of Defining Aggression, Seventh Session, UN A/AC.134/SR.110–113 (18 July 1974), 39 (UK).

[19] UN Definition of Aggression, Art 1 (emphasis added). See Julius Stone, 'Hopes and Loopholes in the 1974 Definition of Aggression' (1977) 71 *American Journal of International Law* 224, 232.

[20] UN Definition of Aggression, Art 3(g).

attributing the acts amounting to aggression carried out by the armed bands to the state sending them,[21] thereby maintaining the Article 1 requirement that an act of aggression be a 'use of armed force *by a State*'.[22] Indeed, proposals to minimize the level of state involvement required for NSA force to amount to an act of aggression, including 'assistance to', 'knowing acquiescence in', or 'collaboration in',[23] were rejected in favour of the 'sending by or on behalf of' and 'substantial involvement therein' standard.[24]

The ICJ has implicitly linked the concepts of 'aggression' and 'armed attack' through its reliance on the UN Definition of Aggression to determine the legitimacy of a use of force in self-defence.[25] At a minimum, the UN Definition of Aggression recognizes that acts of aggression can be carried out by NSAs (if attributable to a state), and the ICJ has consistently treated the Article 3(g) standard of 'sending by or on behalf of' as a basis for attributing those acts to states when determining the scope of the Article 51 right to use force in self-defence.[26] As discussed later, however, the circumstances of those cases do not suggest that the definition of 'armed attack' is subject to all the same conditions as the definition of 'aggression'. Nor should they, given that states did not accept that the concepts of 'aggression' and 'armed attack' are coextensive in their negotiation of the UN Definition of Aggression and left the definition of 'armed attack' to its Charter and customary international law development.

III. Non-Attributable Attacks by Non-State Actors

The fact that the UN Definition of Aggression restricts acts of aggression by NSAs to attributable force does not preclude the possibility that armed attacks might be

[21] 'Sending by or on behalf of a State' is not a basis of attribution specifically set forth in the ILC Articles on State Responsibility, and therefore can be regarded as a *lex specialis* basis of attribution, although it closely tracks the attribution threshold in Art 8 of the ILC Articles.

[22] UN Definition of Aggression, Art 1 (emphasis added).

[23] See A/9019 (1973).

[24] In keeping with this negotiating history, the Court has not accepted assistance to or collaboration with NSAs as a basis for attributing their armed attacks to a state, focusing instead on the 'sending by or on behalf of' element of Art 3(g). *Nicaragua*, Merits, para 195. Indeed, in *Armed Activities on the Territory of the Congo (DRC v. Uganda)*, Judgment, ICJ Rep 2007, 43, the Court did not even mention 'substantial involvement', focusing entirely on the 'sending by or on behalf of' standard. The resulting interpretation of Art 3(g) is that 'substantial involvement' qualifies 'sending by or on behalf of' and, having been interpreted restrictively by the Court, does not admit very much less than actual sending.

[25] See nn 37–50 and accompanying text.

[26] See *Nicaragua*, Merits, para 195; *Armed Activities*, Judgment, para 146, each as discussed in nn 41, 48, and 49 and accompanying text.

un-attributable—although it does make clear that attribution is at least a sufficient condition for the applicability of Article 51 of the UN Charter (in *ratione personae* terms). The question remains whether it is a necessary one.

A. Article 51 of the UN Charter and the *Travaux Préparatoires*

While Article 2(4) is clearly the progeny of its World War parents, prohibiting *inter-state* uses of force, there is nothing in the language of Article 51 which restricts 'armed attacks' to attacks carried out *by* or *on behalf of* states.[27] Nor does the negotiating history of the UN Charter suggest that such a restriction should be read into Article 51. The initial Dumbarton Oaks proposals contained no reference to self-defence[28]—it was only in San Francisco that states proposed to expressly include reference to a right of self-defence in the Charter. These proposals were concerned with the possibility of an ineffective Security Council and were principally focused on the interim rights and responsibilities of regional security organizations (eg under the Act of Chapultepec[29]). As a result, the right of self-defence was addressed in the US Diplomatic Papers under the headings 'Regional Arrangements' or the 'Regional Problem'.[30]

Some initial proposals regarding the right of self-defence referred to 'an attack *by any State*' against a member state[31]—suggesting that attribution was at least

[27] See *Legal Consequences of the Construction of a Wall in the Occupied Palestinian Territory*, Advisory Opinion, ICJ Rep 2004, 136, Separate Opinion of Judge Higgins, para 33, questioning the ICJ's having required that armed attacks be attributed to a state in its *Nicaragua* decision, given that there is nothing in the language of the Charter itself that restricts 'armed attacks' to uses of force by a state.

[28] See 'Proposals for the Establishment of a General International Organization', *The Department of State Bulletin*, vol XI, No 375 (1 Oct 1944), 368–74. There is nevertheless some suggestion in US materials relating to the United Nations Conference that some Dumbarton Oaks delegations had considered the right to use force in self-defence to be implicit in the proposed collective security framework. See eg *Foreign Relations of the United States*, Diplomatic Papers (1945), vol I, 776, 781.

[29] The Act of Chapultepec was a declaration of reciprocal assistance and US solidarity, adopted at the Inter-American Conference on War and Peace in 1945 (*The Department of State Bulletin*, vol XII, No. 297 (4 Mar 1945), 339) and formalized in the Inter-American Treaty of Reciprocal Assistance (21 UNTS 324 (9 Feb 1947)).

[30] See eg *Foreign Relations of the United States* (1945), vol I, 662–4, 674, 719.

[31] *Foreign Relations of the United States* (1945), vol I, 659 (emphasis added). See also ibid, 674. A separate (and informal) US proposal responding to Latin American concerns (and expressly mentioning the Act of Chapultepec) relied on 'aggression' as the trigger for the right of self-defence: 'Should the Security Council not succeed in preventing aggression, and should aggression occur *by any state* against any member state, such member state possesses the inherent right to take necessary measures for self-defence' (emphasis added). *Foreign Relations of the United States* (1945), vol I, 685–6, 691. Turkey also proposed that 'it would be useful to insert in the Charter a provision justifying legitimate defence against a surprise attack *by another state*' (emphasis added). Doc 2, G/14(e) (1 May 1945), UNCIO, vol III, 483.

implicitly contemplated by sponsoring states. Other proposals, however, were without regard to the source of the attack which triggered the right of self-defence.[32] In any event, discussions in regard to these proposals, concentrated as they were on the continued availability of regional security arrangements, never focused on the *source of* the attack (state or non-state). Indeed, reference to an attack '*by any State*' was dropped from later proposals. The two proposals which formed the basis of the final text of Article 51 each conditioned the right of self-defence on an armed attack (without specifying the source of any such attack) and the Security Council's inaction (whether characterizing that inaction as a 'failure' or not).[33] The move from an 'attack *by any State*' to 'armed attack' (without reference to its source) was not the subject of minuted discussion.[34] While deletion of the words 'by any State' might be interpreted as supporting the argument that attribution is *not* a necessary condition of reliance on Article 51, it might also be the case that 'by any State' was considered implicit. Without any discussion of the change in language (and whether the change was intended to convey meaning)—the *travaux préparatoires* are at best ambiguous on this issue. And given that ambiguity, there is no interpretive basis for augmenting the language of Article 51 by reading in the words 'by any State' following 'armed attack'.

B. The ICJ's Jurisprudence

The ICJ's decisions in *Case Concerning Military and Paramilitary Activities in and against Nicaragua*, *Legal Consequences of the Construction of a Wall in the Occupied Palestinian Territory Wall*, and *Case Concerning Armed Activities on the Territory of*

[32] A UK proposal relied on 'a breach of the peace' as the trigger for the right of self-defence (*Foreign Relations of the United States* (1945), vol I, 699), while a French proposal was without reference to any trigger (other than Security Council inaction). The French proposal had member states reserving a 'right to act as they may consider necessary in the interest of peace, right and justice' in the event of Security Council deadlock. Doc 2, G/7(o) (21 Mar 1945), UNCIO, vol III, 385 (as discussed in *Foreign Relations of the United States* (1945), vol I, 691, 698).

[33] The proposals were (1) 'Nothing in this Charter impairs the inherent right of self-defence, either individual or collective, in the event that the Security Council has failed to maintain international peace and security and an armed attack against a member state has occurred' (*Foreign Relations of the United States* (1945), vol I, 705 (UK/US)); and (2) 'Nothing in this Charter impairs the inherent right of self-defence, either individual or collective, if prior to undertaking the measures for the maintenance of international peace and security by the Security Council an armed attack against a member state occurs' (at, 813 (USSR)). The second proposal was largely in keeping with the UK/US draft, but responded to the view that it would be better not to mention the possibility of Security Council failure (at 713, 836). See also the US's formal proposal on self-defence, substantially in line with Art 51 as adopted. Doc 510 G/62 (23 May 1945), UNCIO, vol III, 635.

[34] Post-vote comments on the provision as adopted unanimously by the Fourth Subcommittee were principally regarding its consistency with regional security arrangements. See UNCIO, vol XII (Commission III; Security Council), 680–1 (statement by Colombia with which South American states associated themselves).

the Congo (DRC v. Uganda) might be interpreted as limiting 'armed attacks' to uses of force by or attributable to a state.[35] There is, however, an alternative interpretation of the Court's decisions, informed by judicial economy, which does not condition the right to use defensive force in reliance on Article 51 of the UN Charter on the attributability of an armed attack. Such an interpretation does not treat the Court's pronouncements as generally applicable statements of law, but rather as determinations made in reference to (and constrained by) very particular factual contexts and the submissions of the parties—mindful of and limited by the facts relating to the alleged armed attacks and responsive uses of defensive force addressed by the Court in its decisions.

A majority of the ICJ has consistently held that uses of defensive force *against the state* from whose territory NSAs operate, in response to an armed attack by those NSAs, would only be a legitimate exercise of rights under Article 51 of the UN Charter if the armed attack was attributable to the state in whose territory (and against which) defensive force was used. To situate these judgments within their proper factual context, two separate forms of the use of force in self-defence, in response to armed attacks by NSAs, must be distinguished. The first involves a use of force which only targets the NSAs and their bases of operation in the foreign (host) state's territory. The second is where the use of force also, or perhaps only, targets the foreign host state from whose territory the NSAs operate. The fact that the ICJ has required armed attacks launched by NSAs to be attributable to the state from whose territory they were supported or operated could be understood as a direct consequence of the fact that, in each contentious case to come before the ICJ, the host state was the target of defensive force. The ICJ's refusal to address the circumstances under which a state has a right to use force in self-defence against (and only against) NSAs, however much lamented in the separate opinions,[36] would therefore be justified on the basis of judicial economy and the facts of each case and should not be read as precluding such uses of defensive force.

[35] Arguing that attribution is a necessary element of 'armed attack', see eg Antonio Cassese, 'The International Community's "Legal" Response to Terrorism' (1989) 38 *International and Comparative Law Quarterly* 589, 596–9 (requiring attributability under the law of state responsibility, but, in line with the dissents in *Nicaragua*, describing state support and acquiescence in terrorism as a 'grey' area in the law that might form the basis of attribution); Pierluigi Lamberti Zanardi, 'Indirect Military Aggression' in Antonio Cassese (ed), *The Current Legal Regulation of the Use of Force* (Leiden: Martinus Nijhoff, 1986), 111, 112–16; Luigi Condorelli, 'Les attentats du 11 septembre et leur suites: où va le droit international?' (2001) 105 *Revue Générale de Droit International Public* 829, 838; Olivier Corten, 'Opération "liberté immutable": Une éxtension abusive du concept de légitime defence' (2002) 106 *Revue Générale de Droit International Public* 51, 55. But see eg Thomas Franck, 'Terrorism and the Right of Self-Defence' (2000) 95 *American Journal of International Law* 839, 840; Sean D. Murphy, 'Terrorism and the Concept of "Armed Attack" in Article 51 of the UN Charter' (2002) 43 *Harvard Journal of International Law* 41, 50; Christopher Greenwood, 'War, Terrorism and International Law' (2003) 56 *Current Legal Problems* 505, 419–21; Carsten Stahn, 'Terrorist Acts as "Armed Attack": The Right to Self-Defence, Article 51(1/2) of the UN Charter, and International Terrorism' (2003) 27 *Fletcher Forum of World Affairs* 35, 42.

[36] See eg *Armed Activities*, Judgment, Separate Opinion of Judge Simma, para 8; Separate Opinion of Judge Kooijmans, para 25.

In *Nicaragua*, the ICJ considered whether US assistance to the Nicaraguan Contra forces[37] amounted to a legitimate exercise of the right of collective self-defence. The US claimed to be acting (primarily) in defence of El Salvador, which was the victim of armed attacks by NSAs allegedly supplied with arms through Nicaragua (with the active support, or at the very least complicity, of the Sandinista government).[38] The Contras did not use force against the NSAs attacking El Salvador. Instead, the Contras' main target was Sandinista troops.[39] The ICJ noted that, to defend El Salvador, the US might have arranged for a strong patrol force along El Salvador's frontiers, and that 'it is difficult to accept that [the US] should have continued to carry out military and paramilitary activities against Nicaragua if their only purpose was, as alleged, to serve as a riposte in the exercise of the right of collective self-defence.'[40]

Given that the US-supported Contras were directly targeting the Nicaraguan government and military, the circumstances under which a state could legitimately use force in response to armed attacks by NSAs *against and only against those NSAs* was not in issue. And the Court did not decide it. Instead, the Court had to consider the circumstances under which a state could legitimately respond to armed attacks by NSAs with a use of defensive force *against the state from whose territory the NSAs were allegedly supported.* And on this limited question, the Court held that the conditions for a legitimate use of defensive force were not met because the armed attacks by the NSAs were not attributable to the state against which defensive force was used (relying on Art 3(g) of the UN Definition of Aggression as a basis of attribution).[41] The Court also held that Nicaragua's alleged assistance to NSAs (in the form of provision of weapons and logistical support) did not in itself

[37] The ICJ held that the US was responsible for financing, training, and providing logistical support to the Contras (including the supply of weapons and intelligence as to Nicaraguan troop movements). *Nicaragua*, Judgment, paras 100–8.

[38] An affidavit attached to the US Counter-Memorial on jurisdiction declared that Nicaragua was providing El Salvador rebels 'with sites in Nicaragua for communications facilities, command and control headquarters, training and logistics support[, that the] Government of Nicaragua [was] directly engaged with these armed groups in planning ongoing military and paramilitary activities conducted in and against El Salvador', and that the Nicaraguan government supplied the rebels with arms through its territory. *Nicaragua*, Judgment, para 128. The Court focused principally on the allegations relating to arms traffic, and held that 'it has not... been able to satisfy itself that any continuing flow [of arms] on a significant scale took place after the early months of 1981', and that, in any event, it had not been proven that Nicaragua should be held responsible for any arms traffic (Judgment, paras 153–5).

[39] There were also numerous reports of attacks on non-combatants (*Nicaragua*, Judgment, para 113) and Nicaragua alleged a US-devised strategy for the Contras to attack 'economic targets like electrical plants and storage facilities' in Nicaragua (Judgment, para 105).

[40] *Nicaragua*, Judgment, para 156. The ICJ's argument is effectively a commentary on the necessity of the US operation. See Louis B. Sohn, 'The International Court of Justice and the Scope of the Right of Self-Defence and the Duty of Non-Intervention' in Yoram Dinstein (ed), *International Law at a Time of Perplexity: Essays in Honour of Shabtai Rosenne* (Leiden: Martinus Nijhoff, 1989), 869, 874.

[41] *Nicaragua*, Judgment, para 195.

amount to an armed attack.[42] As a result, the wrongfulness of the US use of force (through its support of the Contras) was not precluded on the basis of Article 51 of the UN Charter.

In the *Wall* advisory opinion, Israel submitted a written statement to the Court addressing questions of jurisdiction and justiciability, but did not participate in the oral phase of the proceedings. The Court therefore relied on Israel's justifications of the wall as submitted to the Secretary-General and General Assembly—namely that construction of the wall was consistent with Article 51 of the UN Charter and Security Council Resolutions 1368 (2001) and 1373 (2001) which 'recognized the right of States to use force in self-defence against terrorist attacks'.[43] The Court held that 'Article 51 of the Charter... recognizes the existence of an inherent right of self-defence in the case of an armed attack by one State against another State. However Israel does not claim that the attacks against it are imputable to a foreign State.'[44] One interpretation of this statement might be that international law conditions the right to use force in self-defence on the attributability of an armed attack. But given that such a condition would be at odds with the Security Council resolutions in regard to 11 September 2001 which the Court draws on,[45] and its subsequent decision in *Armed Activities* (discussed later), this interpretation is not very convincing. The Court should instead be understood to be merely reaffirming the very conditions for the applicability of Article 51 of the UN Charter. Article 51 serves to justify a use of force that would *otherwise* be prohibited by Article 2(4) of the UN Charter. As the Court considered the West Bank to be occupied territory, Israel's construction of the wall could not engage the Article 2(4) prohibition which only applies as between sovereign states. As Article 2(4) is inapplicable, Article 51 is equally inapplicable. The Court's refusal to genuinely engage with the justification of self-defence has subjected it to severe criticism,[46] but is arguably defensible based on the occupied status of the Palestinian territories and the resulting availability of an alternative legal framework within which to assess Israeli conduct.

In *Armed Activities*, the ICJ held that the attacks carried out by NSAs against Uganda were 'non-attributable to the DRC' (on the basis of Art 3(g) of the UN

[42] *Nicaragua*, Judgment, para 195. [43] *Wall*, Advisory Opinion, para 138.

[44] *Wall*, Advisory Opinion, para 139. [45] See further Section III.C.

[46] See Christian J. Tams, 'Light Treatment of a Complex Problem: The Law of Self-Defence in the Wall Case' (2005) 16 *European Journal of International Law* 965; Sean D. Murphy, 'Self-Defense and the Israeli Wall Advisory Opinion: An *Ipse Dixit* from the ICJ?' (2005) 99 *American Journal of International Law* 62. But note that the ICJ's opinion has been interpreted as at least implicitly recognizing a right to use force in self-defence against non-state terrorist actors in foreign territory, even though refusing to accept such a right as applicable in the circumstances based on the occupied status of the territory from which the terrorist attacks emanated. See Iris Canor, 'When *Jus ad Bellum* Meets *Jus in Bello*: The Occupier's Right of Self-Defence against Terrorism Stemming from Occupied Territories' (2006) 19 *Leiden Journal of International Law* 29, 132.

Definition of Aggression),[47] and that the legal and factual circumstances giving rise to a right to use defensive force were therefore not satisfied. In its decision, the Court emphasized that Uganda's defensive measures were carried out *against the DRC*,[48] particularly noting the fact that Ugandan military action was directed against towns and villages far removed from the border region from which anti-Ugandan rebels launched attacks.[49] Again, the Court's decision reflects the distinction discussed previously between defensive force legitimately used *against the state from whose territory NSAs operate* (which—according to the Court—would require that the armed attacks are attributable to the territorial state on the basis of Art 3(g) of the UN Definition of Aggression), and defensive force against NSAs *within* the territorial state, while expressly refusing to address the conditions under which the latter use of force would be legitimate. Indeed, given that Uganda's defensive force targeted the DRC, the Court held that it had 'no need to respond to the contentions of the Parties as to whether and under what conditions contemporary international law provides for a right of self-defence against large-scale attacks by irregular forces.'[50] By leaving the legitimacy of defensive force against NSAs expressly open, the Court can be understood to be responding to critiques of its *Wall* advisory opinion, confirming that the question was not settled in that decision (or even backtracking to the extent that it subsequently considered the question to have been wrongly settled). The statement also highlights the Court's judicial economy—namely, that the Court does not decide more than it needs to, and should not be understood to have done so.

Taken together, these interpretations of the Court's decisions suggest that attribution is only a necessary condition for the applicability of Article 51 of the UN Charter if a use of defensive force is targeted *against the state* from whose territory NSAs operate. The Court's decisions do not preclude uses of defensive force against (and only against) NSAs in foreign territory, in response to un-attributable armed attacks carried out by those NSAs.

c. State Practice

There is room—in the language of the UN Charter, *travaux préparatoires*, and the ICJ's jurisprudence—for the right to use defensive force in foreign territory against NSAs which have launched an un-attributable armed attack. That said, the growing recognition of such a right has not been entirely linear—not least because

[47] *Armed Activities*, Judgment, para 146. The Court did not elaborate on the standard of 'sending of armed bands' as a basis for attribution because it did not consider there to be 'satisfactory proof of the involvement in [the attacks by anti-Ugandan rebel forces against Uganda], direct or indirect, of the Government of the DRC.' Ibid.

[48] *Armed Activities*, Judgment, paras 118 and 147.

[49] *Armed Activities*, Judgment, paras 81–6.

[50] *Armed Activities*, Judgment, para 147.

translating the declarations and practice of states into the elements of customary international law is not often a straightforward exercise. This is particularly the case in the intensely political settings of the General Assembly and Security Council, where states may adopt legalistic arguments for political effect.[51] In addition, individuals speaking on behalf of states are not necessarily legally trained (and therefore may not situate their comments within recognized legal frameworks) or are sometimes too well trained (profiting from the ambiguities of language to keep options open). These challenges certainly should not prevent the search for *opinio juris*—but suggest that any such interpretive exercise needs to proceed carefully and be sensitive to factual context.

At one end of the spectrum—where relatively clear support for a right to use defensive force in response to un-attributable armed attacks by NSAs is evident—there is Operating Enduring Freedom and the 2006 Israeli/Hezbollah conflict. In the case of Operation Enduring Freedom, the US-led coalition responded to the 9/11 terrorist attacks with force, in express reliance on Article 51 of the UN Charter.[52] The right to do so was recognized in Security Council Resolutions 1368 (2001) and 1373 (2001) and by the majority of the international community.[53] The armed attacks carried out by Al Qaeda were not attributable to Afghanistan or its de facto Taliban government,[54] but states (and the Security Council) nevertheless situated the response within the Charter framework, in particular Article 51. While the use of force against the Taliban (rather than merely against the Al Qaeda source of the armed attacks) remains controversial and the subject of much debate,[55] at the very least the 9/11-related practice suggests broad acceptance of a right to use force in response to un-attributable armed attack by NSAs in reliance on Article 51 of the UN Charter.

[51] Consider eg US statements regarding the Turkish and Iranian rights to use defensive force in Iraqi territory in response to cross-border armed attacks by the PKK—supporting the Turkish efforts to protect their border while condemning the Iranian response as without justification whatsoever, and justifying the difference in treatment on the basis of Iran being an outlaw state. See Tom Ruys, *'Armed Attack' and Article 51 of the UN Charter* (Cambridge: Cambridge University Press, 2010), 432–3.

[52] See eg Letter dated 7 October 2001 from the Permanent Representative of the United States of America to the United Nations addressed to the President of the Security Council, S/2001/946; Letter dated 9 October 2001 from the Permanent Representative of Belgium to the United Nations addressed to the Secretary-General, S/2001/967; Letter dated 24 October 2001 from the Chargé D'Affaires a.i. of the Permanent Mission of Canada to the United Nations addressed to the President of the Security Council, S/2001/1005; Letter dated 29 November 2001 from the Permanent Representative of Germany to the United Nations addressed to The President of the Security Council, S/2001/1127; Letter dated 17 December 2001 from the Permanent Representative of New Zealand to the United Nations addressed to the Secretary-General, S/2001/1193.

[53] See Ruys, *'Armed Attack' and Article 51 of the UN Charter*, 435–6.

[54] See Kimberley N. Trapp, *State Responsibility for International Terrorism* (Oxford: Oxford University Press, 2011), 53–54.

[55] See Ruys, *'Armed Attack' and Article 51 of the UN Charter*, 442–3. For a discussion of the right to use defensive force against terrorist host states, see Lindsay Moir, 'Action Against Host States of Terrorist Groups', Chapter 32 in this volume.

In July 2006, Israel launched a large-scale military campaign against Hezbollah in Lebanese territory. The campaign was in response to Hezbollah's abduction of two Israeli soldiers and a number of rocket attacks they launched from southern Lebanon into northern Israeli towns. Not without some ambiguity, Israel claimed to be acting not against the territorial host state, but primarily against NSAs[56] whose conduct was un-attributable to Lebanon.[57] A majority of Security Council members, as well as the UN Secretary-General, recognized Israel's right to defend itself.[58] But the scale of Israel's use of force in Lebanese territory, particularly as regards the destruction of all three runways at Beirut International Airport[59] and the tragic number of civilian deaths,[60] meant that all but one of the states recognizing Israel's right to act in self-defence also characterized Israel's use of force in July 2006 as disproportionate or excessive.[61] By evaluating the use of defensive force on the basis of its proportionality—a criterion which limits the legitimate exercise of the right of self-defence—these states implicitly confirmed Article 51 of the UN Charter as the applicable framework for assessing the lawfulness of Israel's response. The logical implication of such an evaluation is that un-attributable armed attacks by NSAs fall within the scope of Article 51.

At the other end of the spectrum are uses of defensive force which have an impact on regional peace and security and are broadly condemned on at least that basis—for instance, Israel's response to the terrorist attack against a Haifa café by Islamic Jihad in 2003. Following the attack, Israel launched a guided missile attack in Syrian

[56] Israel claimed that it 'has repeatedly been compelled to act not against Lebanon, but against the forces and the monstrosity which Lebanon has allowed itself to be taken hostage by', S/PV.5503 (31 July 2006), 4. Israel also suggested that Lebanon, Iran, and Syria were responsible for Hezbollah's activities, but did not appear to be suggesting that Hezbollah's attacks were attributable to any of those states for the purposes of a defensive use of force. See S/PV.5489 (14 July 2006), 6; Identical letters dated 12 July 2006 from the Permanent Representative of Israel to the United Nations addressed to the Secretary-General and the President of the Security Council, S/206/515 (in which Israel claimed that responsibility for the attacks lay with the government of Lebanon but tied that responsibility to the fact that the attacks were launched from Lebanese territory).

[57] See Ruys, *'Armed Attack' and Article 51 of the UN Charter*, 453–4.

[58] See S/PV.5489 (14 July 2006), 9–17; S/PV.5493 (21 July 2006), 17; S/PV.5492 (20 July 2006), 3; S/PV.5498 (30 July 2006), 3.

[59] See BBC, 'Israel Imposes Lebanon Blockade', 13 July 2006, available at <http://news.bbc.co.uk/2/hi/middle_east/5175160.stm>.

[60] See BBC, 'Q&A: Mid-East War Crimes', 21 July 2006, available at <http://news.bbc.co.uk/2/hi/middle_east/5198342.stm>; Human Rights Watch, 'Fatal Strikes; Israel's Indiscriminate Attacks against Civilians in Lebanon', available at <http://hrw.org/reports/2006/lebanon 0806/>; Amnesty International, 'Deliberate destruction or 'collateral damage'? Israeli attacks on civilian infrastructure', at <http://web.amnesty.org/library/print/ENGMDE180072006>.

[61] S/PV.5489 (14 July 2006), 9 (Argentina), 12 (Japan), 12 (UK), 13–14 (Tanzania considered Israel's use of force as disproportionate without expressly characterizing Israel's use of force as in self-defence), 14 (Peru), 15 (Denmark), 16 (Slovakia), 16 (Greece), 17 (France). The US is the only state to have explicitly recognized Israel's right to defend itself without characterizing Israel's defensive measures as disproportionate or excessive. The Secretary-General also condemned Israel's excessive use of force: S/PV5492 (20 July 2006), 3; S/PV.5498 (30 July 2006), 3.

territory, targeting what it claimed to be Islamic Jihad's base of operations.[62] All but one state appearing before the Security Council condemned Israel's response.[63] Many states firmly situated their condemnation of both the terrorist attack in Haifa and the Israeli response within the broader framework of the Middle East peace process.[64] Their expressions of condemnation were based on the effect both attacks would have on the implementation of the road map devised by the Quartet,[65] which was released in between the attack in Haifa and Israel's military campaign in Syria. Other states, characterizing the Israeli response as aggression, did not address allegations of Syrian complicity in terrorist activities from its territory, but made statements in support of Syria which suggested that they did not accept the factual basis on which Israel claimed to act in self-defence in Syrian territory.[66] None of the delegations making presentations before the Security Council addressed the legality of defensive force specifically targeting terrorist bases in foreign territory given an inability to rely on that state to prevent armed attacks planned or launched from its territory. While the expressions of condemnation before the Security Council have been interpreted as an absence of general support for a wide right to use force against terrorist training camps in foreign territory,[67] it is very difficult to extract any such *opinio juris* from the statements made.

More recently, Colombia conducted military operations against the Revolutionary Armed Forces of Colombia (FARC) training camp in Ecuador, two miles from the Colombian border.[68] Colombia claimed to be acting in self-defence, and partly invoked Ecuadorian support for FARC as justification for its violation of Ecuadorian sovereignty.[69] In response, the Organization of American States adopted a resolution recognizing every state's right to defend itself, but positioning the right in the context of the principles of sovereignty and non-intervention. The resolution considered that Colombia's incursion constituted 'a violation of the sovereignty and territorial integrity of Ecuador and of principles of international law'[70], for which Colombia issued an

[62] S/PV.4836 (5 Oct 2003), 5.

[63] See S/PV.4836 (5 Oct 2003). Only the US did not condemn the Israeli attack, and instead admonished Syria for 'harbouring and supporting the groups that perpetrate terrorist acts' (at 13–14). The Secretary-General also condemned the Israeli response in Syria, while also condemning the preceding terrorist attack in Haifa: SG/SM/8918 (2003).

[64] S/PV.4836 (5 Oct 2003), 9 (Spain, China, UK, Russia), 10 (France, Bulgaria), 11 (Chile, Mexico), 12 (Angola, Guinea), 13 (Cameroon). But see ibid, 14 (League of Arab States).

[65] In April 2003, the United Nations, European Union, the US, and Russia (the 'Quartet') presented a 'performance-based roadmap to a permanent two-state solution to the Israeli-Palestinian conflict' to Palestinian and Israeli leaders. See <http://www.un.org/News/dh/mideast/roadmap122002.pdf>.

[66] S/PV.4836 (5 Oct 2003), 15 (Lebanon), 16 (Algeria), 18 (Egypt), 19 (Tunisia), 19–20 (Kuwait), 20 (Saudi Arabia), 21 (Iran), 22 (Bahrain), 23 (Libya, Yemen), 24 (Qatar).

[67] See Christine Gray, *International Law and the Use of Armed Force* (3rd edn, Oxford: Oxford University Press, 2008), 237.

[68] (March 2008) 54 *Keesing's Record of World Events* 48456.

[69] (March 2008) 54 *Keesing's Record of World Events* 48456.

[70] OAS, Convocation of the Meeting of Consultation of Ministers of Foreign Affairs and Appointment of a Commission, 5 Mar 2008, CP/RES.930 (1632/08).

apology.[71] The swift South American condemnations and Colombian apology, both of which took place in the broader context of the inter-American system, highlight the lack of a broad acceptance, on the facts, of Ecuadorian support for FARC.

In the middle of this spectrum are uses of defensive force in response to un-attributable armed attacks by NSAs that are supported by some segments of the international community and condemned by others, or are not the subject of any reaction at all. In such cases, the precise legal basis for support or condemnation is not clearly articulated (or is not articulated in legal terms), or the facts on the basis of which a right to use defensive force is claimed are contested.

For example, in response to the 1998 terrorist attacks on its embassies in Tanzania and Kenya, the US attacked terrorist training camps in Afghanistan and a pharmaceutical plant in Sudan. The US notified the Security Council of its use of force in self-defence. In particular, the US highlighted that its use of force was only directed against installations and training camps used by the Bin Laden organization and was 'carried out only after repeated efforts to convince the Government of the Sudan and the Taliban regime in Afghanistan to shut these terrorist activities down and to cease their cooperation with the Bin Laden organization.'[72] In effect, the US justification for a use of defensive force is based on a right to target NSAs in foreign territory where there is an inability to rely on the host states' counterterrorism efforts. The US attack on the pharmaceutical plant in the Sudan was widely condemned—primarily based on an absence of evidence that it was used for anything other than civilian purposes.[73] There was no similar condemnation of the use of force in Afghanistan, which was directed solely against Al Qaeda facilities, and not against the Taliban.[74] The failure to condemn should not necessarily be viewed as indicating broad support for the US military operation in Afghanistan. But given the abundant state practice of expressly condemning notified uses of defensive force in letters to the Security Council, the muted reaction (most particularly of the League

[71] Speech of Colombian Ambassador to OAS, 4 Mar 2008, available at <http://www.oas.org/speeches/speech.asp?sCodigo=08-0021>.

[72] Letter dated 20 August 1998 from the Permanent Representative of the United States of America to the United Nations addressed to the President of the Security Council, S/1998/780.

[73] The Sudan, in a letter to the Security Council, denied that the pharmaceutical plant in Khartoum was used for terrorist purposes. Letter dated 21 August 1998 from the Permanent Representative of The Sudan to the United Nations addressed to the President of the Security Council, S/1998/786. The League of Arab States and Non-Aligned Movement condemned the US for its attack on the Sudan. Letter dated 21 August 1998 from the Charge D'Affaires A.I. of the Permanent Mission of Kuwait to the United Nations addressed to the President of the Security Council, S/1998/789; Letter dated 24 August 1998 from the Charge D'Affaires A.I. of the Permanent Mission of Kuwait to the United Nations addressed to the President of the Security Council, S/1998/800; Letter dated 21 September 1998 from the Permanent Representative of the Sudan to the United Nations Addressed to the President of the Security Council, S/1998/879.

[74] The US position at the time was that Al Qaeda operated on its own, without having to depend on a state sponsor for support (although depending on state acquiescence). See Sean D. Murphy (ed), 'Contemporary Practice of the United States' (2000) 94 *American Journal of International Law* 348, 367.

of Arab States and the NAM) to the US operation in Afghanistan is significant and certainly signals the beginning of the emerging consensus that uses of force specifically targeting non-state terrorist actors, in response to armed attacks they launch from foreign territory, is a legitimate exercise of the right of self-defence.

The examples of a claimed right to use defensive force examined earlier are consistently articulated in terms of an inability to rely on the host state to prevent its territory from being used as a base of operations from which NSAs launch armed attacks.[75] Where the complicity or failure to prevent territory from being used as a base of NSA operations was broadly accepted as fact, states have expressed their support for the right to use defensive force in response to un-attributable armed attacks by NSAs. This was particularly the case in regard to Operation Enduring Freedom and the Israel/Hezbollah conflict. Having supported those uses of defensive force, states should not be understood to be rejecting a right to respond to un-attributable armed attacks *in principle* in later cases (eg in regard to Colombia's use of force against FARC training camps in Ecuador) merely because they reject its invocation in the particular circumstances. But the range of reactions to such invocations certainly indicates that the parameters of the right to respond to un-attributable attacks by NSAs are still being worked out in practice.

D. Reconciling Defensive Force against Non-State Actors and the Inter-state Prohibition of Article 2(4)

Article 51 is one of the UN Charter exceptions to the prohibition on the inter-state use of force, as set forth in Article 2(4). If Article 51 is to truly excuse, or preclude the wrongfulness of, a use of force that is otherwise in breach of a state's territorial integrity, Article 51 should respond in some way to the inter-state context of Article 2(4). The ICJ has consistently conditioned the legitimacy of defensive force *against* the state from which NSAs operate on the attributability of the armed attacks carried out by those NSAs. The Court has, however, never ruled out defensive force against (and only against) NSAs operating from foreign territory in response to *un-attributable* armed attacks. While state practice suggests support for the legitimacy of such a right in principle (as discussed previously), commentators continue to gravitate towards attribution as the fuel powering an inter-state reading of Article 51. But, if we understand that attribution is nothing more than a mechanism for ensuring that Article 51 speaks to the prohibition on the use of force against the territorial integrity or political independence of another state, an alternative to attribution which accommodates recent state practice and is consistent with the logic of the

[75] See Kimberley N. Trapp, 'Back to Basics: Necessity, Proportionality, and the Right of Self-Defence against Non-State Terrorist Actors' (2007) 56 *International and Comparative Law Quarterly* 141, 147–55; Ruys, *'Armed Attack' and Article 51 of the UN Charter*, 494–5.

UN Charter emerges. That alternative is based on the customary international law requirement that defensive force be necessary.[76]

If a host state is doing everything possible to prevent its territory from being used as a base of attacks by NSAs, then a use of defensive force in that state's territory (against NSAs) is simply not necessary. Instead, the matter should be addressed through cooperative arrangements with the host state. If, however, a state is complicit in its territory being used as a base of NSA operations (and is therefore unwilling to prevent its territory from being used as a base of terrorist operations), or is unable to prevent its territory from being so used,[77] then a use of defensive force in response to armed attacks by NSAs is indeed necessary, and the unwillingness or inability accounts for the limited and targeted violation of the host state's territorial integrity. A state's complicity in the activities of NSAs operating from its territory, which threaten the security of other states, is an internationally wrongful act for which the complicit state bears responsibility.[78] Similarly, states are under an obligation to cooperate in the prevention of at least terrorist activities from their territory.[79] A refusal to cooperate, in circumstances where the host state is otherwise unable to prevent its territory from being used as a base of such activities, would equally amount to an internationally wrongful act for which the host state would bear responsibility.

Host state wrongfulness does not of course, in itself, justify a use of force that is otherwise inconsistent with Article 2(4) of the UN Charter. A use of defensive force is justified by virtue of an armed attack by NSAs under the terms of Article 51. But necessity is a condition for the lawfulness of any such use of defensive force. And necessity is established by virtue of the host state's complicity or failure to cooperate—both of which are wrongful. This element of host state wrongfulness simultaneously meets the conditions for lawful self-defence and accounts for the breach of the host state's territorial integrity. Effectively, where defensive force responds to non-state armed attacks, necessity serves as the bridge between Article 51 and the inter-state prohibition of the use of force in Article 2(4).

[76] For a discussion, see Olivier Corten, 'Necessity', Chapter 39 in this volume.

[77] In regard to the Israel/Lebanon 2006 war, states which recognized Israel's right to defend itself also underlined the need for Lebanon to extend its exclusive control over all of its territory and to act in prevention of Hezbollah's attacks against Israel (S/PV.5489 (14 July 2006), 9–17. See also S/PV.5492 (20 July 2006), 4; SC Res 1559 (2004), paras 1–3; SC Res 1583 (2005), paras 3–4; SC Res 1655 (2006), paras 3, 6, 8; SC Res 1680 (2006), preamble; and SC Res 1701 (2006), para 3). By accepting a right to use defensive force in response to attacks by NSAs, and calling on Lebanon to control its territory, states in effect recognized that defensive force in foreign territory against NSAs is sometimes necessary given the host state's inability (rather than its unwillingness) to prevent its territory from being used as a base of NSA operations. See further *Armed Activities*, Judgment, Separate Opinion of Judge Kooijmans, paras 27–31.

[78] See Trapp, *State Responsibility for International Terrorism*, 61.

[79] See Trapp, *State Responsibility for International Terrorism*, section 3.1.

IV. Conclusion

The ever increasing military capacity of NSAs calls for a modern assessment of the definition of 'armed attack' and the conditions for lawful self-defence. As early as 1974, when the UN Definition of Aggression was adopted, states were mindful of the security threats posed by NSAs and were weary of restricting their right to respond to such threats through overly heavy reliance on an inter-state paradigm. As a result, states left the definition of 'armed attack' open to customary international law development, and state practice in the 21st century suggests that the attributability of armed attacks by NSAs is no longer (if ever it was) a necessary condition of the right to use force in self-defence. That said, the precise parameters of the right to respond to an armed attack by NSAs with a use of force in foreign territory are still being worked out in practice. While states are quick to invoke the 'unwilling or unable' doctrine in their justifications of defensive force against attacks by NSAs, the international community has, quite rightly, refused to accept this 'ritual incantation of a magic formula'[80] without evidence of host state wrongfulness as a measure of the necessity of the defensive force. Territorial integrity therefore remains a cornerstone of the international legal system—with the right to use force in foreign territory in response to an un-attributable armed attack by NSAs at the fault line of the Charter's prohibition of the use of force in Article 2(4) and recognition of states' security interests in Article 51.

[80] See Gray, *International Law and the Use of Armed Force*, 119.

CHAPTER 31

THE PROBLEM OF IMMINENCE IN AN UNCERTAIN WORLD

NOAM LUBELL*

I. Introduction

ALMOST any discussion of self-defence under international law inevitably includes the debate over anticipatory self-defence. This is true not only in modern writings, but also throughout the centuries of legal and philosophical examinations of the matter. Most arguments supporting anticipatory action invariably turn at some point to requiring a criterion of imminence, whether stating it specifically, or in another guise. Whether or not anticipatory self-defence should be allowed is a question that encompasses numerous legal, moral, and political conundrums. The current examination does not aim to resolve the wider debate on anticipatory self-debate. Rather, it focuses on one particular and crucial component of the debate: the concept of imminence. The following examination proceeds, therefore, on the assumption that anticipatory self-defence may be a legitimate option for action. Based on this premise, it sets out to analyse the meaning of imminence in this context, how it is to be

* Thanks are due to Charlotte Pier for her research assistance.

interpreted, what it might justify and what it might exclude, and whether it is in fact a criterion that can be upheld in the light of modern challenges.

II. The Requirement of Imminence

The requirement of imminence can be traced back to early discussions of anticipatory self-defence. Hugo Grotius recognized the need to include a restriction of this kind, noting that 'The danger must be immediate, which is one necessary point.'[1] The incident of the *Caroline*, just over two centuries later, has become a seminal reference point for the requirement of imminence, and continues to be turned to in modern discussion and debate.[2] This revolved around circumstances in 1837 during which the British and US governments exchanged correspondence over the legality of action taken by the UK, which included British forces forcibly boarding a ship (the *Caroline*), said to be supplying Canadian rebels, setting it on fire and sending it over the Niagara Falls.[3] The following is quoted from this exchange:

> Undoubtedly it is just, that while it is admitted that exceptions growing out of the great law of self-defence do exist, those exceptions should be confined to cases in which the 'necessity of that self-defence is instant, overwhelming, and leaving no choice of means, and no moment for deliberation.'[4]

The customary right to anticipatory self-defence, which many trace back to the *Caroline*, came under challenge with the emergence of the United Nations Charter. When the provision on self-defence in Article 51 of the Charter was drafted, the possibility for anticipatory self-defence appeared to have been excluded, by only allowing for a right of self-defence if 'an armed attack occurs'. However, even in the process of this act of exclusion, imminence remained at the forefront of discussion. In the ensuing debates, the centrality of imminence to any justification

[1] Hugo Grotius, *On the Law of War and Peace. De Jure Belli ac Pacis* (trans A. C. Campbell, London: 1814), Book II, ch 1, V.

[2] eg the UK Attorney General traced the customary international law definition of self-defence to the *Caroline*, when noting that this definition 'included the right to use force in anticipation of an imminent armed attack'. Lord Goldsmith, Attorney General of the UK, House of Lords, Hansard, 21 Apr 2004, col 370; see also 'Judgement, Part 18, The Invasion of Denmark and Norway: Conclusion' in *Trial of the Major War Criminals before the International Military Tribunal. Vol I: Official Documents* [Official text in the English language], Nuremberg: IMT, 1947, 206–9.

[3] Robert Jennings 'The Caroline and McLeod Cases' (1938) 32 *American Journal of International Law* 82.

[4] Letter from Mr Webster to Lord Ashburton, Department of State, Washington, 6 Aug 1842, available at <http://www.yale.edu/lawweb/avalon/diplomacy/britain/br-1842d.htm>.

of anticipatory self-defence was reflected in the arguments of both detractors and supporters of such action. Kunz, for example, noted in 1947, 'The "imminent" armed attack does not suffice under Art. 51'.[5] Bowett, conversely, stated that 'It is not believed, therefore, that Art. 51 restricts the traditional right of self-defence so as to exclude action taken against an imminent danger but before "an armed attack occurs"'.[6]

While it is the UN Charter's apparent renunciation of anticipatory self-defence which supplies the opponents of such action with their most potent ammunition, it is also through developments under the UN auspices which provide support for a limited form of anticipatory self-defence. The 2004 Report of the Secretary General's High-Level Panel on Threats, Challenges and Change declared that:

> a threatened State, according to long established international law, can take military action as long as the threatened attack is *imminent*, no other means would deflect it and the action is proportionate. The problem arises where the threat in question is not imminent but still claimed to be real.[7]

Notably, once again the key criterion and primary restriction imposed on anticipatory self-defence, is that it can only be launched against an imminent attack. Imminence appears here as an additional requirement, on top of necessity (stated in the previous quotation as 'no other means would deflect it') and proportionality. The latter two criteria are considered fundamental to legitimizing any claim of self-defence,[8] not only anticipatory action. Imminence, however, is less relevant when dealing with an existing armed attack that has already occurred or is ongoing. By definition, it relates to a future event. It therefore comes into play once we begin considering anticipatory self-defence. It is traditionally used as a temporal description,[9] pointing to a specific impending attack.[10] The imminence of the said attack can present a useful test when measuring the necessity and proportionality of

[5] Josef Kunz, Editorial Comment, 'Individual and Collective Self-Defense in Article 51 of the Charter of the United Nations' (1947) *American Journal of International Law* 872, 878.

[6] Derek W. Bowett, *Self-Defence in International Law* (Manchester: Manchester University Press, 1958), 191–2.

[7] Report of the Secretary General's High-Level Panel on Threats, Challenges and Change, 'A More Secure World: Our Shared Responsibility' (2004), para 188. The given example of *not* imminent is 'for example the acquisition, with allegedly hostile intent, of nuclear weapons-making capability'; see also 'Imminent threats are fully covered by Article 51, which safeguards the inherent right of sovereign States to defend themselves against armed attack. Lawyers have long recognized that this covers an imminent attack as well as one that has already happened.' Report of the Secretary-General, delivered to the General Assembly, 'In Larger Freedom: Towards Development, Security and Human Rights for All', A/59/2005 (21 Mar 2005), para 124.

[8] *Case Concerning Military and Paramilitary Activities in and against Nicaragua (Nicaragua v. US)*, Merits, ICJ Rep 1986, 14, para 194; *Oil Platforms (Iran v. US)*, Judgment, ICJ Rep 2003, para 51; *Legality of the Threat or Use of Nuclear Weapons*, Advisory Opinion, 8 July 1996, ICJ Rep 1996, paras 41–3.

[9] Onder Bakircioglu, *Self-Defence in International and Criminal Law: The Doctrine of Imminence* (Abingdon: Routledge, 2011), 196; but see next section on modern threats for an examination of the viability of the temporal aspect.

[10] See Section III on meaning of imminence.

any self-defence action.[11] Imminence can therefore be described as a third requirement, in addition to necessity and proportionality.[12] It remains separate from necessity: an armed attack may be imminent, but self-defence is not necessary because there are non-forcible alternatives to prevent it striking the state or due to the Security Council already mobilizing to preclude the need for self-defence action. Conversely, and controversially, one might argue that there is necessity to take action in self-defence against a future attack that is not imminent. The latter argument is at the heart of some of the more contentious areas of anticipatory self-defence.[13]

The practice of states and views of commentators clearly demonstrate that the presence of imminence will often be a major factor in their position on anticipatory action. This is true both with regard to the general position taken on this issue as a matter of law, as well as the reaction to particular events. The Independent International Fact-Finding Mission on the Conflict in Georgia provides some of the most recent examples of the relevance of imminence in the views of states.[14] The Georgian government noted that in the absence of an imminent attack by Georgia, Russia had no right to self-defence;[15] the Russian argument included the alleged danger of an imminent attack by Georgia on Abkhazia.[16]

Two of the most commonly referred to cases in the debates over anticipatory self-defence have involved the State of Israel, and the criterion of imminence was central to them both. While there are differing interpretations of the events and positions surrounding the 1967 Israeli–Arab war,[17] it has been argued that most of the international community perceived this as a case of self-defence taken in the face of an imminent attack, and consequently viewed it as an acceptable course of action.[18] Conversely, Israel's attack on the Iraqi nuclear reactor in 1981 was condemned due to the lack of an imminent threat.[19] Tellingly, in an exchange at the Security Council, after the Israeli representative cited the position of Sir Humphrey Waldock as support for anticipatory action, the Iraqi representative responded by pointing out that the Israeli quotation had conveniently left out Waldock's reference to the

[11] Bakircioglu, *Self-Defence in International and Criminal Law*, 213.

[12] The UK Attorney General, after discussing the imminence requirement, proceeds to discuss the 'Two further conditions' of necessity and proportionality, House of Lords, Hansard, 21 Apr 2004, col 370.

[13] See Section IV on modern challenges.

[14] Independent International Fact-Finding Mission on the Conflict in Georgia, Sept 2009, vol II, available at <http://www.ceiig.ch/Report.html>.

[15] Independent International Fact-Finding Mission on the Conflict in Georgia, para 186.

[16] Independent International Fact-Finding Mission on the Conflict in Georgia, para 222; Abkhazia also claimed to have a right of self-defence against an imminent Georgian attack, para 292.

[17] Compare eg: Thomas Franck, *Recourse to Force: State Action Against Threats and Armed Attacks* (Cambridge: Cambridge University Press, 2002), 101–5; Christine Gray, *International Law and the Use of Force* (Oxford: Oxford University Press, 2008), 161.

[18] Franck, *Recourse to Force*.

[19] As noted by the UK at the time, 'There was no instant or overwhelming necessity for self-defence' (1981) 20 ILM 970, paras 199–201.

anticipated attack being *imminent*.[20] The International Court of Justice (ICJ) has refrained from taking an explicit position on anticipatory self-defence.[21] However, the International Military Tribunal at Nuremberg relied on the *Caroline* formula, ruling that Germany's invasion of Norway was not taken in the face of an imminent Allied landing.[22] The requirement of imminence arises not only in relation to specific cases, but also as a general rule. According to the UK Attorney General: 'it has been the consistent position of successive United Kingdom Governments over many years that the right of self-defence under international law includes the right to use force where an armed attack is imminent.'[23]

As for the community of legal commentators, while they continue to be engaged in a debate that has persisted for decades over the legitimacy of anticipatory self-defence—and it is difficult to pinpoint a majority of opinion either way at any given time—there does appear to be a growing number of views that support pre-emptive action when limited to imminent attacks.[24] Even while presenting the lack of agreement and the critique of anticipatory self-defence, the majority of opinion does note that if anticipatory self-defence were to be accepted, then it must only be in relation to imminent attacks.[25]

There are many reasons to consider anticipatory self-defence as unlawful, regardless of impending attacks, and to maintain a strict requirement that self-defence can only take place after an attack has occurred.[26] Indeed, the legal, textual, ethical, and political cases against any form of anticipatory self-defence all have merit. Notwithstanding, it is equally clear that there is also support for the argument that a state facing an impending devastating attack cannot be expected to have to wait for it to actually strike its cities before engaging in forcible self-defence. Arguments for anticipatory self-defence of some form or another have been continuously presented by both commentators and states.[27] As seen previously, the requirement of imminence is a common theme running through most of these arguments and is, in fact, often the key factor upon which the legitimacy of such action will turn.

[20] SCOR, 36th Sess, 2288th mtg, S/PV.2288 (19 June 1981).

[21] '... the issue of the lawfulness of a response to the imminent threat of armed attack has not been raised. Accordingly the Court expresses no view on that issue.' ICJ, *Nicaragua*, Merits, para 194; this was later repeated in *Case Concerning Armed Activities on the Territory of the Congo (DRC v. Uganda)*, 'So it is in the present case', Judgment, ICJ Rep 2005, para 143.

[22] Nuremberg IMT, 206–9.

[23] Attorney General, House of Lords, Hansard, 21 Apr 2004, col 370.

[24] 'A More Secure World'; 'In Larger Freedom'; Attorney General, House of Lords, Hansard, 21 Apr 2004, col 370; 'The Chatham House Principles of International Law on the Use of Force by States in Self-Defence' (2006) 55 *International and Comparative Law Quarterly* 963, 965; Bowett, *Self-Defence in International Law*; Christopher Greenwood et al in Elizabeth Wilmshurst, 'Principles of International Law on the Use of Force by States in Self-Defence', working paper, Royal Institute of International Affairs, Oct 2005; see also the analysis of views in Tom Ruys, *'Armed Attack' and Article 51 of the UN Charter* (Cambridge: Cambridge University Press, 2010), 324–42.

[25] See analysis in Fact-Finding Mission on the Conflict in Georgia, 254–56; for an examination, and critique, of anticipatory self-defence, see Gray, *International Law and the Use of Force*, 160–6, 212.

[26] See general discussion of anticipatory self-defence, Gray, *International Law and the Use of Force*.

[27] See n 24.

Assuming that we wish to accept a right to anticipatory self-defence, the requirement of imminence demands further clarification.

III. The Meaning of Imminence

The plain English-language definition of 'imminent' reveals some of the difficulties that arise in the legal interpretation in the context of self-defence. Note the differences between the following definitions: according to the Oxford English dictionary an imminent event is one which is 'about to happen'.[28] The Cambridge dictionary defines it as 'coming or likely to happen very soon';[29] according to the Merriam-Webster dictionary it is an event which is 'ready to take place' or 'hanging threateningly over one's head'.[30] Most strikingly, the first of these might be read as describing a definite impending event, while the second definition introduces the notion of 'likely'—that is, not definite and might not occur—and the third definition remains equivocal, since something that is 'ready to take place' tells us nothing as to the certainty or timing of its future occurrence. When attempting to implement the requirement for imminence in practice, both the temporal aspect and the gap between certainty and likelihood, prove to be the primary areas of debate and concern.

The imminence criterion is a regular feature in discussions of anticipatory self-defence, and is usually presented as a requirement for legitimizing the action. However, setting aside the dictionary definition, there is no legal definition of this notion. There are, nonetheless, certain characteristics that can be deduced from state practice, cases, and commentators' opinions. Two particular elements repeatedly found in this context, are the temporal aspect of imminence as referring to an immediate threat; and the requirement that the threat be specific and identifiable.

The temporal aspect was already evident in the early treatment of the subject by Grotius, who required the danger to be 'immediate'.[31] This immediacy of the threat is also apparent in the treatment of the subject by a large number of commentators.[32] State practice provides further evidence for such an approach, which differentiates between potentially legitimate anticipatory self-defence, as opposed to the

[28] <http://oxforddictionaries.com/definition/english/imminent?region=uk&q=imminent>.

[29] <http://dictionary.cambridge.org/dictionary/british/imminent?q=imminent>.

[30] <http://www.merriam-webster.com/dictionary/imminent>.

[31] Grotius, *On the Law of War and Peace*, ch 1, V.

[32] See analysis of views by Fact-Finding Mission on the Conflict in Georgia, paras 254–6; see analysis of views in Ruys, *'Armed Attack' and Article 51 of the UN Charter*, 322–4.

vaguer notion of preventive self-defence against threats further into the future.[33] Indeed, when force was used in circumstances perceived as lacking an immediate threat, this has led to condemnation.[34] This apparent correlation between imminence and an immediate threat notwithstanding, in the *Case Concerning the Gabčíkovo-Nagymaros Project*, the ICJ appeared to take a slightly different approach to imminence, noting:

> 'Imminence' is synonymous with 'immediacy' or 'proximity' and goes far beyond the concept of 'possibility'. As the International Law Commission emphasised in its commentary, the 'extremely grave and imminent' peril must 'have been a threat to the interest at the actual time'... That does not exclude, in the view of the Court, that a 'peril' appearing in the long term might be held to be 'imminent' as soon as it is established, at the relevant point in time, that the realisation of that peril, however far off it might be, is not thereby any less certain and inevitable.[35]

While this might appear to delink the notion of imminence from immediacy, it must also be read in context: the case was not one of self-defence and use of force, and the Court might therefore have felt less concerned over taking a more lax interpretation of imminence. Furthermore, the case dealt with an environmental threat subjected to scientific standards, rather than guessing future political and military intentions of another party.[36] As will be seen in a later section, the inability to achieve certainty in the prediction of future attacks is a key factor in the assessment of imminence. Moreover, this statement by the Court also highlights the second characteristic of imminence: that it is in relation to a specific and identifiable threat.

While the ICJ has not explicitly ruled on anticipatory self-defence, it has declared that self-defence cannot be taken in order to 'protect perceived security interests' outside of Article 51 of the Charter.[37] The notion of imminence requires a specific

[33] 'It is therefore the Government's view that international law permits the use of force in self-defence against an imminent attack but does not authorise the use of force to mount a pre-emptive strike against a threat that is more remote.' Attorney General, House of Lords, Hansard, 21 Apr 2004, col 370; Nuremberg IMT; condemnation of Israeli strike (1981) 20 ILM 971; see also Fact-Finding Mission on the Conflict in Georgia, nn 14–22 and accompanying text.

[34] The UK condemned the Israeli attack on the Iraqi nuclear reactor, since 'There was no instant or overwhelming necessity for self-defence' (1981) 20 ILM 970; German action was unjustified since 'they were not made for the purpose of forestalling an imminent Allied landing, but, at the most, that they might prevent an Allied occupation at some future date.' Nuremberg IMT, 206–9; contrast these cases with the 1967 Israeli–Arab war, in relation to which it has been argued that Israel was taking action to prevent what was perceived as an imminent attack about to occur, and that most of the international community even if not explicitly endorsing it, did view this as acceptable action. Franck, *Recourse to Force*, 101–5.

[35] *Case Concerning the Gabčíkovo-Nagymaros Project (Hungary/Slovakia)*, ICJ Rep 1997, 7, para 54.

[36] See Section V on certainty and Section IV on the last window of opportunity; see view on the factual approach to imminence in Constantine Antonopoulos, 'Force by Armed Groups as Armed Attack and the Broadening of Self-Defence' (2008) 55 *Netherlands International Law Review* 159, 177.

[37] *Armed Activities*, Judgment, para 148.

anticipated attack. This must go beyond vague suspicions,[38] and requires a threat of an identifiable actual attack which is being prepared, rather than the unformed potential of attack,[39] or a threat which has not yet materialized.[40] There must be a 'concrete danger of an imminent attack' which is 'objectively verifiable',[41] and there is wide agreement by states and writers that force in self-defence cannot be taken to counter 'potential or abstract' threats.[42]

These characteristics of imminence are linked to the concept of 'interceptive self-defence'.[43] The use of the word 'interceptive' suggests circumstances in which the incoming attack is a definite occurrence—indeed, it may have already begun—and the state is able, in the nick of time, to step in and stop it before the damage is done. This is an enticing proposition for a solution which some may view as bridging the gap between an attack that has already occurred, and a future one which may or may not take place. At closer examination, it is however unclear whether this concept in fact clarifies the situation. Interception can be presented in one of two ways: either as referring to an armed attack which is physically occurring and cannot be undone, and in which we are speaking of circumstances such as intercepting rockets in flight;[44] or as referring to situations in which the opposing state has 'embarked upon an *apparently* irreversible course of action'[45] such as sending troops towards the border. This juxtaposition means that we are, in fact, back to the starting point. There are only two possibilities: either the attack has begun and is occurring, in which case self-defence can take place under the strict requirements of Article 51; or, however 'apparently irreversible' it might seem, it has not physically begun and there is at least a theoretical chance of it never occurring (eg troops can be called back before crossing the border), in which case we are in the familiar territory of anticipatory self-defence. The concept revolves around the possibility of defining the occurrence of an armed attack based on when it begins, rather than when the effect of the first strike is experienced.[46] But once we are willing to consider that an attack has begun even in situations in which it can conceivably be stopped before it actually affects the

[38] Emer de Vattel, *The Law of Nations*, from the new edn, by Joseph Chitty (Philadelphia: Johnson & Co, 1883), Book II, ch IV, 50.

[39] Note the differentiation made in the Report of the UN Secretary General, between an imminent attack for which anticipatory self-defence is supported, as opposed to a latent threat. 'In Larger Freedom', paras 124–5.

[40] Chatham House Principles, 968.

[41] Fact-Finding Mission on the Conflict in Georgia, paras 254–6.

[42] Fact-Finding Mission on the Conflict in Georgia, paras 254–6.

[43] Yoram Dinstein, *War, Aggression and Self-Defence* (Cambridge: Cambridge University Press, 2012), 203; see also discussion of possibility of intercepting rockets in flight, in Ian Brownlie, *International Law and the Use of Force by States* (Oxford: Oxford University Press, 1963), 367–8.

[44] Brownlie, *International Law and the Use of Force by States*, 367–8.

[45] Dinstein, *War, Aggression and Self-Defence*, 204 (emphasis added).

[46] 'The crux of the issue, therefore, is not who fired the first shot but who embarked upon an apparently irreversible course of action, thereby crossing the legal Rubicon. The casting of the die, rather than the actual opening of fire, is what starts the armed attack.' Dinstein, *War, Aggression and Self-Defence*, 204.

target state, then we are back to asking the same questions that arise in the context of anticipatory self-defence. Interceptive self-defence is not therefore a 'third way' between strict non-anticipatory and anticipatory self-defence; depending on how one presents the notion, it is either part of the former or the latter. It can, on the one hand, be understood as pointing to the possibility of considering an armed attack to have occurred from the first moment a truly irreversible act has taken place (eg missiles are in flight and cannot be aborted), even if the strike has not yet been felt.[47] If imminence would thereby be equated with this interpretation of interceptive action, the imminence criterion would itself be redundant, since it would be understood as covering only those cases in which the armed attack is already occurring; as such it can fit well within the framework of Article 51. On the other hand, interceptive action could be understood as allowing for self-defence from the moment it *seems* that the other party has decided to attack and has begun taking steps to put the attack in place, and it *appears* inevitable from their actions that the attack will happen (eg the opposing state is amassing troops and moving them within its own territory towards the border). Since the attack has not yet materialized and could still be reversed with no harm, this interpretation is in fact a form of anticipatory self-defence. It is, however, one which adheres to as strict and narrow a requirement of imminence as can be, and would meet most tests for reasonable assumptions of an impending attack. Adhering to this and judging whether the attack is indeed inevitable, will ultimately require a process of judgement and reliance on certain indicators and proof, as will be discussed in a later section.

IV. Imminence and Modern Threats

The pre-emption doctrine advanced by the US during the Bush (G. W.) presidency, expanded the notion of anticipatory self-defence into a policy advocating preventive action to counter a range of future threats, noting the particular threats posed by weapons of mass destruction (WMD) and terrorism. According to the US National Security Strategy of 2002:

For centuries, international law recognised that nations need not suffer an attack before they can lawfully take action to defend themselves against forces that present an imminent danger of attack. Legal scholars and international jurists often conditioned the

[47] Whether and how far the notion of armed attack can be stretched in this manner will remain questionable. In a related context, Gray notes that 'In practice states prefer to argue for an extended interpretation of armed attack and to avoid the fundamental doctrine debate'. Gray, *International Law and the Use of Force*, 165.

legitimacy of preemption on the existence of an imminent threat-most often a visible mobilisation of armies, navies, and air forces preparing to attack. We must adapt the concept of imminent threat to the capabilities and objectives of today's adversaries. Rogue states and terrorists do not seek to attack us using conventional means. They know such attacks would fail. Instead, they rely on acts of terror and, potentially, the use of weapons of mass destruction...[48]

In 2006 the UK Secretary of State for Defence at the time, explicitly linked these threats to the debates over the concept of imminence, stating that: 'Another specific area of international law we perhaps need to think more about is whether the concept of imminence—i.e. the circumstances when a state can act in self-defence without waiting for an attack—is sufficiently well developed to take account of the new threats faced.'[49] Other state representatives, as well as commentators, have also pointed to a perceived need to interpret the concept of imminence in the light of terrorism, WMD, and modern threats more generally.[50] But, what is it about these specific threats that ignites the desire to rethink—and possibly bring into question—the notion of imminence, which as demonstrated earlier has been established as a fundamental component in the theories of anticipatory self-defence? To answer this, it is necessary to first distinguish between two different threats mentioned previously, and recognize the distinct challenges they present.

The threat of terrorism is rooted in the unpredictability of its source. The concept of terrorism, however, lacks a commonly agreed or legally adopted definition, and its selective use and frame of reference, are often the subject of controversy.[51] In the context of self-defence, one of the main issues at stake is the preliminary question as to the possibility for a state to invoke the right to self-defence following an attack by a non-state actor operating from outside its borders, and which cannot be attributed to

[48] *The National Security Strategy of the United States of America*, The White House, Sept 2002, 15.

[49] 'Reid addresses RUSI on "20th-Century Rules, 21st-Century Conflict"', 3 Apr 2006, available at <http://www.mod.uk/DefenceInternet/DefenceNews/DefencePolicyAndBusiness/ReidAddressesRusiOn20thcenturyRules21stcenturyConflict.htm>.

[50] Attorney General of the UK, House of Lords, Hansard, 21 Apr 2004, col 370; Jay Bybee, 'Authority of the President Under Domestic and International Law to Use Military Force Against Iraq', Memorandum Opinion for the Counsel to the President, 23 Oct 2002, 45; Anthony Arend, 'International Law and the Preemptive Use of Military Force' (2003) 26 *Washington Quarterly* 89, 97–8; Daniel Bethlehem, 'International law and the use of force: the law as it is and as it should be', written evidence submitted by Daniel Bethlehem QC, Select Committee on Foreign Affairs, Minutes of Evidence, June 2004; Philippe Sands, 'International Law and the Use of Force', 1 June 2004, written evidence submitted by Professor Philippe Sands QC, to Select Committee on Foreign Affairs, para 15.

[51] For an examination of attempts to reach a definition, see Ben Saul, 'Attempts to Define "Terrorism" in International Law' (2005) 52 *Netherlands International Law Review* 57; this debate is long-standing, see Thomas Franck and Bert Lockwood, 'Preliminary Thoughts towards an International Convention on Terrorism' (1974) 68 *American Journal of International Law* 69.

another state.[52] Assuming that self-defence may arise in the context of non-state actors, we must proceed to inquire as to how the nature of the attacking entity might affect the requirement of imminence. The challenge posed in the context of imminence is that, in effect, we are faced with a threat, for which we cannot positively identify how soon it might happen, where it will originate from, where it will strike, or even who precisely will be behind the attack. It is, as such, as far from a specific impending attack as can be. The threat of terrorism plays on the fear of the unknown, and raises the question of engaging in self-defence to prevent a possible future attack without knowledge of what it might be. As such, it challenges not so much the interpretation of imminence, but in effect calls into question the very existence of the imminence requirement. The notion of imminence, as examined earlier, is built around the need to respond with urgency to a concrete and known threat that, absent immediate action, is going to materialize into a specific and identifiable attack.[53] The idea of acting to prevent a vague and non-specific threat cannot, therefore, be covered within the concept of imminence.[54] This may lead some to consider rethinking the viability of the imminence criterion as we know it, and to allow states to act even if the threshold of imminence is not met; opinions along this line were emerging most clearly following the 11 September 2001 attacks.[55] Allowing resort to force against vague and non-specific threats is however considered by many to risk ushering in a new age of widespread unwarranted force on the pretext of self-defence, and this approach has failed to gain significant support, with the majority of opinion continuing to consider the possibility of anticipatory self-defence only in relation to imminent attacks.[56] The notion of imminence presents a brick wall through which claims of self-defence against non-specific and unidentifiable threats cannot pass. Either such claims of self-defence must fail, or the requirement of imminence must be set aside.

It may, on the other hand, be the case that there is concrete information of a specific impending terrorist attack from an identifiable source, in a manner that is similar to the claim of an imminent attack from another state. In such circumstances, the notion of imminence must be understood and applied as it is with impending attacks by another state. This approach is, however, predicated on an assumption that self-defence against non-state actors is a legitimate concept, and would be subject to any additional constraints placed upon such action (eg the need for the defending state to satisfy the necessity requirement by first allowing for the territorial state to prevent the attack).[57] All this is not without further controversy, but as for the question at hand, it means that the threat of terrorism with regard to

[52] This is a subject of debate which has been examined at length in recent years, and will not be addressed in any further detail here. See Noam Lubell, *Extraterritorial Use of Force Against Non-State Actors* (Oxford: Oxford University Press, 2010), chs 1–3.

[53] See Section III on the meaning of imminence.

[54] See nn 32–4 and accompanying text.

[55] See nn 48–50.

[56] See discussion in the previous sections.

[57] Lubell, *Extraterritorial Use of Force Against Non-State Actors*, ch 2.

identifiable specific impending attacks, does not require us to rethink the notion of imminence.

It would appear therefore, that the threat of terrorism does not modify the imminence requirement. In the case of specific and identifiable impending attacks it leaves the concept of imminence intact. Conversely, in the face of unknown, non-specific, future threats, unless we are willing to simply do away with the imminence requirement, the lack of imminence will prohibit a claim of self-defence.

The threat posed by WMD is of a different nature: it is less about the source of the threat, and more about the gravity of its consequences should it materialize. Accordingly, it requires an examination of whether the scale of the threat might affect the understanding of imminence. Even outside the question of WMD, it is clear that the scale of threat must be relevant to imminence, insofar as there must be a minimal threshold to be crossed before one can consider anticipatory self-defence. Such a threshold also goes beyond the question of imminence, and is in fact part of the broader question of the scale of attack necessary to trigger self-defence. Moreover, this is not just a matter of anticipatory self-defence, and is an issue which is debated with regards to armed attacks more generally. Without straying too far beyond the remit of the current examination, it should briefly be noted that there must exist a certain gravity to the armed attack which can trigger self-defence. Whether this should include any and all casualties or damage from cross-border force, or go beyond what some call mere 'border incidents', remains a subject of debate.[58] The discussion also tends to centre upon self-defence in response to attacks which have occurred, rather than anticipatory self-defence. With regard to the latter circumstances, any claim to engage in anticipatory self-defence must surely require that the impending attack be at least of a similar scale to an actual attack which would have triggered self-defence. Indeed, in the context of anticipatory action, it may be wise to ensure that this threshold is interpreted as being above minor incidents. If one accepts a high threshold of gravity for armed attacks in regular (that is non-anticipatory) self-defence then clearly an equally high threshold is required for anticipatory action. If, however, one considers minor incidents (eg border incidents with few casualties or damage) as constituting armed attacks, it may be prudent to refrain from taking the same position for anticipatory self-defence. This would mean creating a differentiation between the armed attack thresholds of gravity for triggering regular self-defence as opposed to anticipatory self-defence,

[58] For differing views and analysis of the issue of a threshold for armed attack, see: Kunz, 'Individual and Collective Self-Defense in Article 51', 878; *Oil Platforms (Iran v. US)*, ICJ Rep 1993, 35, paras 71–2; *Eritrea-Ethiopia Claims Commission, Partial Award Ius ad Bellum, Ethiopia's Claims 1–8* (2006) 45 ILM 430, para 11; Antonio Cassese, *International Law* (Oxford: Oxford University Press, 2005), 354, 469; Albrecht Randelzhofer, 'Article 51' in Bruno Simma (ed), *The Charter of the United Nations: A Commentary* (Oxford: Oxford University Press, 1994), 661–78, 669; James Green, *The International Court of Justice and Self-Defence in International Law* (Oxford: Hart, 2009), 31–42; Dinstein, *War, Aggression and Self-Defence*, 210–12.

with the latter being higher. No doubt this would be a contestable approach, but if we seek to keep anticipatory self-defence from becoming a pretext for unwarranted engagement in force, there may be merit in such an interpretation.

Support for a comparatively high threshold of gravity in the case of impending attacks capable of triggering anticipatory self-defence can be found in the language often used when discussing the possibility of anticipatory action. The attack which must be thwarted is described using terms such as 'an overpowering attack',[59] 'a devastating (perhaps a fatal) blow',[60] or 'potentially devastating consequences'.[61] Accordingly, discussion of anticipatory self-defence often presumes a significantly high threshold of gravity for the attack that must be thwarted. Returning to WMD, the threat of such an attack is often raised as a justification to expand the notion of anticipatory self-defence. However, this argument could equally be turned on its head and, in the light of the earlier discussion, the threat of WMD can be presented as part of an approach which in fact *restricts* the resort to anticipatory action, rather than *expands* it. The previous quotations all share an apparent need to bolster the support for anticipatory self-defence, with the use of circumstances in which there is an especially high level of threat, rather than referring to any armed attack. Circumstances of WMD attacks could therefore be presented not as evidence for a new expanded form of anticipatory self-defence, but rather as indicating the gravity of threat required for any anticipatory action.[62] Accordingly, one might argue that anticipatory self-defence, unlike 'regular' self-defence, requires a particularly high threshold of anticipated attack, such as the potentially devastating repercussions of WMD or near-existential threats. Accepting this interpretation would mean that absent an imminent threat bearing extreme consequences, anticipatory self-defence would not be justified.

Nonetheless, if an approach of this type is not pursued, and if the legitimacy of anticipatory self-defence is not dependent on a relatively high threshold, then the threat of WMD will present an additional challenge that goes beyond other lesser threats. Indeed, the threat of WMD has instigated a call for rethinking notions of self-defence. It has been noted by a growing number of commentators that the gravity of the threat must be one of the factors to be considered when assessing imminence of a threatened attack.[63] While this statement attracts support for its seemingly

[59] Franck, *Recourse to Force*, 107. [60] Dinstein, *War, Aggression and Self-Defence*, 204.

[61] Rosalyn Higgins, *Problems and Process: International Law and How We Use It* (Oxford: Oxford University Press, 1994), 242.

[62] Interestingly, following an examination of the issue of anticipatory self-defence, the UK Foreign Affairs Committee stated the following 'We recommend that in its response to this Report the Government set out how, in the event of the legitimisation of the doctrine of anticipatory self-defence, it will persuade its allies to limit the use of the doctrine to a "threat of catastrophic attack".' House of Commons, Foreign Affairs Committee, Foreign Policy Aspects of the War against Terrorism, Seventh Report of Session 2003–04, Hansard, HC 441-I, vol I, 29 July 2004, para 429.

[63] Chatham House Principles, 967; Memorandum Opinion for the Counsel to the President, 45.

realistic approach, precisely how this factor of gravity will in fact affect the imminence, is not always clear. The following analysis will attempt to discern the modalities by which the threat of WMD might cause imminence to be assessed differently, and what such an effect would—and would not—justify in practice.

'New tests' of imminence will inevitably mean applying a less strict standard than the one thus far regarded as commonly accepted.[64] In practical terms, raising the possibility of gravity being an influence on the imminence assessment is designed to allow for a looser interpretation of imminence than perhaps previously endorsed. Accordingly, a question posed by the threat of WMD is whether we might also have a sliding scale of gravity which could affect the interpretation of imminence. Such a link would entail a negative correlation between gravity and imminence, whereby the higher the gravity of the impending attack grows, the weaker the requirement of imminence becomes. Accordingly, when faced with an anticipated threat of attack by WMD, one might argue that imminence be interpreted in a loose manner, allowing for action to be taken in circumstances that might not have allowed for it had the threat been of lesser gravity. There are, however, a number of difficulties with accepting a more lenient version of imminence in the face of WMD. First and foremost, there is the near impossible task of negotiating a sliding scale of imminence. Imminence, as described earlier, often centres upon the notion that an event is impending, and is about to happen any moment in the immediate future. How does one 'relax' the concept of imminence? There are a number of ways to approach this task. The first would require loosening of the temporal 'impending' aspect, by saying that with regard to WMD, imminence should not be understood as demanding that the threat be impending, and opening up a wider temporal framework with no regard to the immediacy of the threat. If this means allowing for self-defence against future attacks with no reference whatsoever to the timescale in which it might materialize, then we would not so much be relaxing the requirement of imminence, but rather would be consigning it to oblivion.[65] This approach can, however, take a more nuanced form which requires examination, and which can be referred to as 'the last window of opportunity' in which the self-defence will still be effective.[66] Capability and/or intent of the enemy have also been raised as relevant factors in this context.[67] Nonetheless, the question remains as to what is the

[64] Greenwood, eg, speaks of 'a more generous notion of imminence if what is threatened is another "9/11" rather than the minor acts of the Caroline incident', working paper on 'Principles of International Law on the Use of Force by States in Self-Defence'.

[65] As was seen in the previous discussion on responding to non-imminent threat in the context of terrorism.

[66] For discussion of this or similar approaches: Memorandum Opinion for the Counsel to the President, 47; Thomas Anderson, 'Legitimizing the New Imminence: Bridging the Gap Between the Just War and the Bush Doctrine' (2010) 8 *Georgetown Journal of Law and Public Policy* 261, 278; Arend, 'International Law and the Preemptive Use of Military Force', 98; Michael Schmitt, 'Counter-Terrorism and the Use of Force in International Law', The Marshall Center Papers, No 5, 2002 (The George C. Marshall European Center for Security Studies), 65.

[67] Memorandum Opinion for the Counsel to the President; Chatham House Principles, 967.

precise event that must be stopped in this last window: is it the acquisition of WMD by an enemy, must there be evidence that this enemy plans to attack, should a specific attack already be in preparation, is a general animosity enough to presume intent, or is it simply the last moment it is physically possible to successfully attack and destroy the enemy's WMD capability?

These questions have been put to the test in a series of cases, ranging from the Cuban Missile Crisis through to current discussion of potential attacks by Israel/US against Iranian nuclear facilities. In the case of the former, although President Kennedy spoke of a threat to the peace,[68] and a general sense of threat may have been in place, there did not appear to be any specific attack which would have supported action in self-defence.[69] Israel justified its attack on Iraq's Osirak nuclear facility in 1981 as a case of self-defence, and that it had attacked at this point in time, since waiting would have made it too late due to the repercussions of attacking a functional reactor.[70] Israel's operation was however strongly condemned, and was not accepted as a legitimate self-defence action.[71] Notably it was, among other factors, precisely the lack of imminence that set this operation as one outside the parameters of self-defence.[72] An attack by Israel in 2007 against a suspected nuclear facility in Syria received far less attention,[73] the lack of which can be attributed to a number of factors,[74] but which makes it difficult to draw any conclusive evidence of legal opinion. With ongoing speculation about the possibility that the US/Israel might strike Iranian nuclear facilities,[75] the debates over action of this type will not be dissipating anytime soon.

There are a number of serious obstacles to accepting the legality of self-defence in circumstances such as these. First, and most obvious, is the absence of a specific attack that must be thwarted, no matter how far into the future one is willing to look. General animosity and political rhetoric may well be disconcerting, but they are hardly evidence of an identifiable attack that must be stopped in its tracks. More is required in order to satisfy even the lowest of evidentiary thresholds.[76] The attack on the Iraqi reactor was therefore widely recognized as unlawful,[77] and an attack against Iran in similar circumstances is likely to elicit the same criticism. Secondly, these circumstances revolved around the threat of an attack at a future date, possibly years into the future. The further ahead we advance on the temporal scale, the more possibilities there are for reality to diverge from the predictions. When the

[68] John F. Kennedy, 'Soviet Missiles in Cuba', *Department of State Bulletin*, 12 Nov 1962, 715–20.

[69] See discussion in Dinstein, *War, Aggression and Self-Defence*, 199; see also Ruys, *'Armed Attack' and Article 51 of the UN Charter*, 267–72.

[70] S/PV.2280 (12 June 1981), paras 58, 95.

[71] S/RES/487 (1981), 19 June 1981.

[72] See UK statement (1981) 20 ILM 970.

[73] 'Israelis "blew apart Syrian nuclear cache"', *The Sunday Times*, 16 Sept 2007.

[74] Including Syria's own desire to avoid scrutiny over the construction of the facility, and the relative low level of damage caused by the strike.

[75] 'Netanyahu: Israel has right to pre-emptive attack on Iran', *The Independent*, 6 Mar 2012.

[76] See Section VI on proof.

[77] SC Res 487; Franck, *Recourse to Force*.

impending attack is hours, days, or perhaps even weeks away, the amount of variables that might change and cause the prediction to be faulty are far fewer than in the case of an attack that is alleged will materialize three years later. Nonetheless, a possibility might be raised of a high likelihood of a specific attack that will occur further into the future, and that it is not possible to wait until the last minute when it would become imminent (ie now is the 'last window of opportunity'). In such circumstances, despite the fact that this scenario might fall foul of the imminence requirement, might it be legitimately argued that self-defence at this early stage is nevertheless necessary? Such an argument is theoretically possible, but unlikely to hold in practice. First, it could be argued that imminence is a requirement additional to necessity. While non-anticipatory self-defence requires necessity and proportionality,[78] the very notion of anticipatory self-defence was developed in the context of imminent attacks, and the requirement of imminence may have become a third, additional, criterion.[79] Any such argument would therefore have to reinvent the understanding of imminence. Secondly, the premise itself is flawed when considering scenarios far into the future, as the infinite possibilities for unforeseen developments, including the prospects of preventing the materialization of the threat through other, non-forcible, avenues, will mean that the accuracy of prediction will take a nosedive far below any reasonable threshold that could be presented as close to certain. It would then mean arguing that it is necessary to use force right now to prevent an event that may well never happen, and no possibility to credibly make this assessment.[80] The two key elements of imminence are linked: the further we venture into the future and away from 'impending', the less possible it becomes to identify a specific threatened attack as opposed to a vague concern over the possibility. As such, the lack of imminence will most likely deliver a fatal blow to the credibility of an argument based on necessity. The imminence criterion cannot be met in the context of desiring to prevent the acquisition or development of WMD in order to negate the potential that they might, or might not, be used at an indeterminate date in the far future. Arguing that imminence can be understood as allowing a right to use force in circumstances where there is no evidence of a specific attack in the foreseeable future, is in fact no more than paying lip service to the imminence criterion while bending it so far out of shape it becomes unrecognizable. It would be more coherent an approach to simply advocate the removal of the imminence requirement altogether, and either develop new ways to keep anticipatory self-defence within safe bounds, or be prepared for the dangerous consequences of a less restrictive approach to use of force.

[78] *Legality of the Threat or Use of Nuclear Weapons*, Advisory Opinion of 8 July 1996, ICJ Rep 1996, para 41.

[79] See Section II on the requirement of imminence.

[80] 'Imminence provides an objective yardstick against which the necessity of private force can be measured . . .', Bakircioglu, *Self-Defence in International and Criminal Law*, 213.

Finally, there is however one more option that might be taken with regard to a possible new approach to imminence in the light of WMD. While maintaining the insistence that imminence requires that there be a specific impending attack we are seeking to prevent, we might nevertheless allow in certain circumstances, such as WMD threats, for variance in the accepted level of likelihood of the attack materializing. It must still centre upon a threat of a specific impending attack to be thwarted, but given the higher risk posed by this type of attack, one might argue for a less stringent demand for absolute certainty that it will occur.[81] Once again, such an approach is likely to be highly controversial, as it opens the door towards an acceptance of anticipatory self-defence and use of force in circumstances in which it is uncertain whether the threat was ever really going to materialize. As such, it would appear to negate the very premise of anticipatory self-defence as a necessary course of action in the face of an incoming attack. Anticipatory self-defence, it can been argued, should be limited only to those circumstances in which we are certain of the imminent attack, and losing our grip on this certainty leads down a dangerous path of use of force based on nothing but speculation. This criticism reflects a sound approach, requiring definitive notions of certainty as a safeguard from abuse of the law. But it also opens up room for another question: what does certainty mean in this context, and is it ever appropriate to claim that an imminent attack is *certain* to happen?

V. Certainty

Centuries ago, Grotius cautioned that 'to maintain that the bare probability of some remote, or future annoyance from a neighbouring state affords a just ground of hostile aggression, is a doctrine repugnant to every principle of equity.'[82] Indeed, the idea of going to war on the basis of probabilities is one that likely continues to appear repugnant to many up to this day. Probabilities are, however, the only reality we can realistically work with, despite any inclinations to fall under the alluring spell of illusions of certainty. Definitive language is commonly used with an assumption that we can require certainty as a categorical and unwavering test, rather than realizing the fluid and indeterminate challenge posed by such a requirement. Simply put, as long as we are talking about an attack that has not yet happened—and this is the essence

[81] eg see the reference to balancing a low probability against a high degree of harm, in Memorandum Opinion for the Counsel to the President, 47.

[82] Grotius, *On the Law of War and Peace*, Book II, ch 1, XVII.

of anticipatory self-defence—then we can never be *certain* of its future materialization. Troops marching towards a border can be ordered to turn back; missiles being loaded might not be fired; and orders to carry out attacks can be rescinded in the final moment before an attack takes place. In fact, unless states (or individuals) are claiming the clairvoyant powers to predict the future, the one thing they can never do, is claim that a future attack is certain. We are, therefore, left playing the game of probabilities and trying to settle upon a notion of being 'certain enough' that an attack is imminent. If that is the case, a serious investigation of the required certainty of an imminent attack necessitates a better understanding of the relationship between certainly, likelihood, and decision making processes. Judgement in the face of uncertainty is a daily necessity cutting across all paths of life and all areas of policy, ranging from medical decisions, criminal law convictions, economic policy, and more.[83] Rarely are we afforded the luxury of making a decision with all the facts pertaining not only to the past but also the future. To combat uncertainty, a number of principles can be employed to assist the decision-making process. The starting point is an assumption that the government of a state is presented with information concerning a possible attack against them from another state, and assuming also that other options have been explored, so that the only way to avoid being struck by such an attack, would be to engage in anticipatory self-defence. To justify such action, the feared attack must be imminent. However, there can be no foolproof certainty that this impending attack will indeed happen. The decision makers at the head of government will therefore, whether they realize it or not, be engaging in a process of statistical analysis, balancing values, probabilities, risk, and the law. Much of this can be encapsulated in a model which lays bare the consequences of false positives and false negatives.[84] If the question is whether there really is an imminent attack approaching, then false positives are decisions which proceed on the basis of an imminent attack which in fact would not have happened, whereas false negatives would be decisions to erroneously assume there is no imminent attack that requires immediate action and neglect to thwart it. Each of these has its consequences: false positives will lead to unnecessary use of force by the state, resulting in casualties and damage, increasing the chances of further escalation of conflict, and carrying potential repercussions in terms of international politics and the perceived disregard for international law. Conversely, false negatives would mean failing to act and

[83] For a detailed analysis of the notion of uncertainty in decision making, see Kenneth Hammond, *Human Judgment and Social Policy: Irreducible Uncertainty, Inevitable Error, Unavoidable Injustice* (Oxford: Oxford University Press, 1996).

[84] For an analysis combining fields of psychology and policy decisions in this context, see Philip Dunwoody and Kenneth Hammond, 'The Policy of Preemption and Its Consequences: Iraq and Beyond' (2006) 12 *Journal of Peace Psychology* 19. The authors use Brunswik's lens model and the Taylor-Russell diagram, to analyse the decision-making process on the topic of pre-emptive military action; for general discussion of false positives and negatives, see Hammond, *Human Judgment and Social Policy*, ch 1.

suffering an attack against the state, with the casualties and damage that this may entail. A simplistic assessment would rely on the 'duality of error' approach, choosing between the lesser of two evils—would we rather be wrong and endure a false positive, or a false negative.[85] The balance in this case may well shift towards preferring false positives on the basis of perceived self-interest, since this would mean that any unnecessary casualties will mount up higher on the other side of the border, rather than risking being seen as falling asleep on guard and allowing an attack to proceed on home soil. But such an appraisal would ignore the additional ramifications that may come from engaging in an unnecessary attack, including the human, political, and legal costs. More importantly, this would be an overly simplified analysis, which treats the likelihood of false positives and false negatives as being equal. A better reasoned decision would need to include some measurement of probabilities for each of the possible outcomes—if a false positive is far more likely than a false negative, then this could tilt the balance. Furthermore, in the choice between false negatives and false positives, the risk calculation will include consideration of the specific details of the perceived threat.

This is the point at which the earlier discussion of WMD may become relevant. A decision resulting in a false negative would mean incorrectly assuming that the circumstances do not amount to an imminent attack requiring anticipatory action and as a result, suffering the consequences of an attack that might have been prevented. If these consequences entail being subjected to a nuclear attack, then the repercussions of a false negative will leap to the top of the scale. The risks of a false positive might, at this point, be seen as a more palatable outcome despite its own repercussions.[86] In other words, once we acknowledge that any decisions on imminent attacks will inherently include a need to predict the likelihood of an uncertain event, we must also accept that this necessitates engaging in a decision-making process that is not a precise science, and which can be affected by the variables of the formula. The potential devastation caused by a WMD attack is one such variable. The need to make a judgement within a realm of uncertainty could, therefore, mean that the higher perception of risk calls for the toleration of a lower level of certainty. This lower threshold of certainty could manifest in one of two ways: first, it might affect the level of evidence on the basis of which the decision is made (the 'decision criterion').[87] As much as we might wish it to be so, there will never be 100 per cent certainty in assessing future events. Therefore, if, for example, for a non-WMD

[85] One of the first and most well-known examples is known as 'Pascal's Wager' in which the 17th-century French philosopher and mathematician queried whether one would be safer in believing that there is a god even if that might be incorrect, or living as if there is no god, and the risks entailed if that were false. See Hammond on this and for an examination of duality of error and how this affects decision-making across a number of fields. *Human Judgment and Social Policy*, chs 1–2.

[86] 'The greater the threat, the greater is the risk of inaction', National Security Strategy of the US (2002), 15.

[87] See Section VI on proof.

case the state might only have engaged in anticipatory self-defence when it is 95 per cent certain that a specific enemy attack is imminent, when faced with WMD it might decide to move ahead when it is 80 per cent certain, as a result of the higher projected damage entailed by false negative decisions. Secondly, since the accuracy of assessing likelihood of a specific threat materializing will diminish the further it is into the future, the temporal aspect of imminence could also be affected. Lowering the threshold of certainty would result in allowing for consideration of thwarting attacks that are less certain to happen since they are expected to occur slightly further down the line. However, the temporal scale can be traversed only so far. If, in the circumstances of the case, the time frame opens up the realistic possibility for preventing the attack by other means, then the necessity requirement is less likely to be satisfied. Moreover, as the earlier analysis demonstrated, advancing along the temporal scale not only reduces the likelihood of a future attack, it also makes it more and more difficult to credibly claim that there are plans for a specific attack rather than the vague fear of a threat. In the latter circumstances, this is no longer just a question of a reduced certainty as to whether the attack will happen, but it becomes a situation in which there is no specific attack to be thwarted, and is therefore removed from the realm of justification through imminence.

Accordingly, if we are to perceive anticipatory self-defence as a legitimate course of action taken to prevent an imminent attack, it may be unavoidable that faced with information about a possible specific attack by way of WMD, decision-makers will be more likely to engage in anticipatory self-defence than when they are faced with a lesser gravity of repercussion for inaction. Lastly, it should be stressed that this decision-making process must be restricted to those cases in which the possible attack over which self-defence is contemplated is specific and identifiable; this is not an open door to justifying self-defence against vague concerns over acquisition of WMD or fear of attack due to general animosity between nations.

VI. Proving the Existence of an Imminent Attack

Assessing the likelihood of an imminent attack will rest on the use of reliable evidence. Indeed, it has been noted that 'evidence, rather than abstract principle, seems to determine the response to each instance in which a state claims the right to use force in anticipatory self-defense.'[88] Proving the existence of an imminent attack will

[88] Franck, *Recourse to Force*, 107; indeed, such an approach echoes the words of Vattel who spoke of the need to provide proof, so as to justify action in the eyes of all mankind. Vattel, *Of The Mode of Terminating Disputes Between Nations*, ch XVIII, 334.

therefore require evidence; this inevitably requires a decision that a given amount of evidence be regarded as constituting sufficient grounds for assuming that the prediction is correct. This factor regarding the required level of evidence can be described as the 'decision criterion'.[89] This choice of threshold for considering that the evidence is sufficient will have a direct effect on the balance between correct decisions and disastrous mistakes: 'Given a particular level of uncertainty, reducing false negatives by lowering the decision criteria must increase false positives and vice versa'.[90] In other words, a high threshold for the level of evidence would lead to fewer unwarranted uses of force (false positives), but raise the risk of inaction due to insufficient proof of an imminent attack that does materialize (false negatives). Conversely, a lower threshold of evidence would more easily allow for use of force and therefore reduce the chances of negligent inaction (false negatives), but increase the chance of unnecessary force (false positives). The understanding of what might constitute acceptable proof of an imminent attack is therefore a crucial concern.

There has been relatively little attention to discerning the type of evidence that would be considered sufficient for such purposes.[91] It is said that evidence to support the use of force must be objective, and 'clear and convincing'.[92] The reliability of the evidence will be a crucial matter.[93] Examining Uganda's claim to self-defence, the ICJ rejected unsupported internal political reports,[94] statements by Ugandan politicians,[95] 'news reports of variable reliability',[96] and 'internal documents, often with no authenticating features, and containing unsigned, unauthenticated and sometimes illegible witness statements'.[97] Moreover, proving an imminent attack creates particular difficulties as it will, as discussed earlier, require an element of prediction. In the context of self-defence, a state cannot rely on 'supposed intention',[98] 'assumptions, expectations or fear of what is sometimes called a "latent" threat',[99] nor mere propensities of another state.[100] The Fact-Finding Mission to the conflict in Georgia

[89] Dunwoody and Hammond, 'The Policy of Preemption and Its Consequences', 26.

[90] Dunwoody and Hammond, 'The Policy of Preemption and Its Consequences', 26.

[91] Among the few related examples is an examination of the evidence necessary in the context of self-defence against terrorism, in Mary Ellen O'Connell, 'Evidence of Terror' (2002) 7 *Journal of Conflict and Security Law* 19; for an examination of the ICJ's 'gathering, evaluation and disposition of evidentiary material' see Keith Highet, 'Evidence, the Court, and the Nicaragua Case' (1987) 81 *American Journal of International Law* 1.

[92] 'The alternatives to the clear and convincing standard include standards both lower and higher than clear and convincing. Lower standard requires only a preponderance of the evidence; the higher standard mandates proof beyond a reasonable doubt.' O'Connell (but note that this was said in a different context), 'Evidence of Terror'.

[93] *Armed Activities*, Judgment, para 120.

[94] *Armed Activities*, Judgment, paras 122, 123.

[95] *Armed Activities*, Judgment, paras 124, 129.

[96] *Armed Activities*, Judgment, para 136.

[97] *Armed Activities*, Judgment, para 134.

[98] Grotius, *On the Law of War and Peace*, Book II, ch 1, V.

[99] Dinstein, *War, Aggression and Self-Defence*, 206.

[100] 'Propensities, however, are obdurately unamenable to conclusive proof.' Franck, *Recourse to Force*, 106–7.

was of the view that the presence of Russian troops near the Georgian border may have indicated an abstract danger, but there was 'not enough evidence to ascertain such an imminent attack by Russia.'[101]

Ultimately, when dealing with assessing an imminent event (as opposed to a past occurrence), the judgement of evidence will include a measure of subjectivity and reliance on a combination of factors some of which are more susceptible to fault than others (eg opinions provided by intelligence analysts).[102] It is virtually impossible to define an objective watertight definition of proof for future attacks. Each case will be examined in the light of a different combination of varying indicators, and the determination may well be influenced by subjective interpretation by the eyes which behold them. If we are to reduce the risk of unnecessary force while allowing anticipatory self-defence, then we must require that the evidentiary threshold be as stringent as possible. But, such an approach can only be taken if accepting that this also carries its own risks of failing to act, due to the high evidentiary threshold, against attacks which would materialize. The acceptance of risks is a necessary result of engaging with uncertainty. Ultimately, we are dealing with 'threat assessment based on the integration of multiple fallible indicators under conditions of irreducible uncertainty.'[103]

VII. Conclusion

The question of whether or not a particular attack is imminent will never be able to generate the same level of agreement as cases in which the armed attack has already occurred. Controversy will almost always follow use of self-defence in this context. However, an examination of the concept of imminence in relation to self-defence does reveal certain characteristics that must be satisfied for an attack to be imminent: it must be an impending attack over which there is a reasonable level of certainty that it will occur in the foreseeable future; and it must be a specific and identifiable attack, rather than a vague threat of unknown form. A majority of opinion supports this notion of imminence. Although this understanding has been questioned in

[101] Fact-Finding Mission on the Conflict in Georgia, 254–6.

[102] 'All of the best satellite imagery, electronic interception, and human intelligence afforded by modern technology does not change the basic fact that at the end of the day some analyst somewhere has to make a guess about what an adversary is doing. Sophisticated technology makes that guess a highly educated one, but a guess it remains.' Anderson, 'Legitimizing the New Imminence', 282; 'assessments are inherently subjective and contextual', Schmitt, 'Counter-Terrorism and the Use of Force in International Law', 69; views of evidence can change with time Franck, *Recourse to Force*, 106–7.

[103] Dunwoody and Hammond, 'The Policy of Preemption and Its Consequences', 23–4.

light of modern threats, it remains largely unchanged. Accommodating the arguments made over the threat of unpredictable terrorism could mean relinquishing the notion of imminence, and allowing for self-defence against vague unknown threats in a manner that renders the concept of self-defence open to unconscionable abuse. As for the concern over attacks by WMD, it has been demonstrated that the gravity of the perceived threat might understandably influence the decision-making process in relation to the level of certainty to be demanded, but that this must be kept within the strict confines of a threat of a specific attack. Moreover, there will remain a threshold of evidence to be met in order to establish the existence of the threat. While the threat of WMD has also led to some calls for flexibility on the temporal element so as to counter attacks further into the future, the danger is that in practice this would lead to allowing self-defence not only against non-temporally impending attacks, but also against unspecified future threats based on fear and suspicion rather than evidence. The wider temporal framework might also mean that other, non-forcible, options are available. For both these reasons, the temporal scale cannot be stretched if it results not only in negating the imminence criterion, but also in discrediting any argument of necessity. Bearing this in mind, the analysis of decision-making in the face of uncertainty has revealed that the potential devastation via an attack of WMD might allow for a slight shift away from demanding that the threatened attack be immediate. However, this cannot allow for ignoring non-forcible viable alternatives, and it cannot go beyond the reasonably foreseeable future in a manner which transitions from thwarting a specific approaching attack into action to prevent a generalized threat.

Ultimately, the only way to completely avoid these dilemmas is to take a position that precludes variable standards of proof, probability assessments, and risk calculation, by demanding absolute certainty as a prerequisite for anticipatory action. The flaw in such an approach is that, as presented earlier, certainty of a future event is simply impossible. If it is absolute certainty of an attack that we require, then the attack would not be an imminent future event, but rather a present occurrence. As such, the concept of imminence would not be relevant, and self-defence would rule out anticipatory action. Clearly, therefore, one possibility is to reject the legitimacy of anticipatory self-defence and thereby avoid the challenges in applying the criterion of imminence. Another option is to reject the imminence criterion and allow for use of force against non-specific threats further into the future. This opens the door to a dangerous new world of preventive self-defence against vague threats, and can lead to abuse of the notion of self-defence on a massive scale. If, however, our wish is to maintain a position that endorses anticipatory self-defence while limiting it to absolute emergencies, then it is precisely the criterion of imminence, with all the challenges addressed earlier, that serves as the strongest barrier to an expansive notion of preventive operations, while allowing anticipatory self-defence in those circumstances in which it is more likely to be viewed as an appropriate course of action.

CHAPTER 32

ACTION AGAINST HOST STATES OF TERRORIST GROUPS

LINDSAY MOIR

I. Introduction

ARTICLE 51 of the UN Charter does not indicate what constitutes an armed attack, or who can carry one out. It preserves the inherent right of self-defence in the case of an 'armed attack' per se, and not in relation to 'any particular kind of attacker'.[1] Self-defence may have tended to be used in the context of attacks by one state against another, but 'there is no *a priori* reason why the term should be so confined'.[2] Given the emergence of non-state actors capable of launching significant attacks abroad, the ability of target states to respond lawfully against such armed groups and states in which they are located is an important question, which has attracted widespread attention since the 11 September 2001 terrorist attacks. It would be a mistake, however, to believe that it had received little consideration before then.[3] In 1963, Brownlie argued that 'a co-ordinated

[1] Thomas Franck, 'Terrorism and the Right of Self-Defense' (2001) 95 *American Journal of International Law* 839, 840.

[2] Christopher Greenwood, 'International Law and the "War Against Terrorism"' (2002) 78 *International Affairs* 301, 307.

[3] The *Caroline* dispute, widely considered the *locus classicus* regarding self-defence in customary international law, concerned the activities of Canadian rebels, rather than regular state forces. See

and general campaign by powerful bands of irregulars, with obvious or easily proven complicity of the government of a state from which they operate, would constitute an "armed attack"';[4] and that, 'In so far as there is a use of force by forces controlled by a foreign state, this may be met by lawful measures of self-defence'.[5] However, the precise scope and extent of such defensive action is complex. With considerable foresight, Brownlie cautioned that 'delicate problems' could arise in such circumstances,[6] and it is to these problems that we now turn.

II. Indirect Attack: State Control and Attribution

Action against armed groups is not a recent phenomenon—a (relatively small) number of states had consistently asserted the right to respond forcibly to such attacks over many years.[7] Strikes tended to be limited to terrorist bases within host states, with some level of host state responsibility asserted, whilst the 'self-defence' claimed more often closely resembled armed reprisals. International reaction was mixed at best.[8] Thus, Israel's 1968 strike on Beirut airport in response to attacks by Arab groups within Lebanon was condemned unanimously by the Security Council,[9] whereas US strikes on Al Qaeda targets in Afghanistan and Sudan in 1998,

Greenwood, 'International Law and the "War Against Terrorism"', 308; Jordan J. Paust, 'Use of Armed Force Against Terrorists in Afghanistan, Iraq, and Beyond' (2002) 35 *Cornell International Law Journal* 533, 535; Derek Jinks, 'Self-Defense in an Age of Terrorism' (2003) *Proceedings of the American Society of International Law* 141, 146.

[4] Ian Brownlie, *International Law and the Use of Force by States* (Oxford: Oxford University Press, 1963), 279.

[5] Brownlie, *International Law and the Use of Force by States*, 372.

[6] Brownlie, *International Law and the Use of Force by States*, 372–3.

[7] Perhaps most extensively Israel, Portugal, South Africa, and the US. See Antonio Cassese, 'Terrorism is Also Disrupting Some Crucial Legal Categories of International Law' (2001) 12 *European Journal of International Law* 993, 996; Christine Gray, *International Law and the Use of Force* (3rd edn, Oxford: Oxford University Press, 2008), 195–8; Lindsay Moir, *Reappraising the Resort to Force: International Law, Jus ad Bellum and the War on Terror* (Oxford: Hart, 2010), 25–31; Tom Ruys and Sten Verhoeven, 'Attacks by Private Actors and the Right of Self-Defence' (2005) *Journal of Conflict and Security Law* 289, 292–6.

[8] Although condemnation or otherwise often hinged upon issues such as perceived responsibility for the attack, the proportionality of any response, armed struggles in the context of self-determination, etc, rather than discussion as to the scope of self-defence.

[9] SC Res 262 (1968), 31 Dec 1968. See also Gray, *International Law and the Use of Force*, 195; Richard A. Falk, 'The Beirut Raid and the International Law of Retaliation' (1969) 63 *American Journal of International Law* 415.

following terrorist attacks on its embassies in Kenya and Tanzania, were received more favourably.[10]

Some clarity was provided in the *Nicaragua* case, where the International Court of Justice (ICJ) confirmed that attacks need not be carried out by a state's regular armed forces to trigger the right of self-defence. Relying on the General Assembly's Definition of Aggression,[11] it held that 'armed attack' for the purposes of self-defence included:

not merely action by regular armed forces across an international border, but also 'the sending by or on behalf of a State of armed bands, groups, irregulars or mercenaries, which carry out acts of armed force against another State of such gravity as to amount to' *(inter alia)* an actual armed attack conducted by regular forces, 'or its substantial involvement therein'.[12]

Given that 'states may not evade responsibility... when they, instead of acting through their own officials, *use* groups of individuals to undertake actions that are intended to damage... other states',[13] the Court's use of the Definition of Aggression to cover indirect armed attack seems appropriate. It continued, however, to set an exacting threshold for attribution, finding the provision of weapons or of logistical or other support to be insufficient,[14] and insisting that an armed attack (and hence self-defence) required 'effective control' of military operations on the part of the state.[15]

Equating 'substantial involvement' with 'effective control' was controversial, and the Court was not unanimous in its approach. Judge Schwebel found it too restrictive, and a departure from 'accepted—and desirable—law',[16] whilst Judge Jennings believed that assistance falling short of control could, in combination with additional involvement, form an important element of armed attack: 'to say that the provision of arms, coupled with "logistical or other support" is not armed attack is going much too far'.[17] Nonetheless, the judgment echoed Brownlie's support for self-defence where armed groups are *controlled* by a foreign state.

The International Criminal Tribunal for the former Yugoslavia (ICTY) subsequently used an alternative test to determine when armed forces act on behalf of

[10] Sean D. Murphy, 'Contemporary Practice of the United States relating to International Law' (1999) 93 *American Journal of International Law* 161; Gray, *International Law and the Use of Force*, 197.

[11] GA Res 3314 (XXIX), Definition of Aggression, 14 Dec 1974, para 3(g).

[12] *Case Concerning Military and Paramilitary Activities in and against Nicaragua (Nicaragua v. US)*, Merits, Judgment of 27 June 1986, ICJ Rep 1986, para 195.

[13] Antonio Cassese, 'The *Nicaragua* and *Tadić* Tests Revisited in Light of the ICJ Judgment on Genocide in Bosnia' (2007) 18 *European Journal of International Law* 649, 654.

[14] *Nicaragua*, Merits, para 195. It could, however, constitute a violation of Art 2(4).

[15] *Nicaragua*, Merits, para 115. No explanation was provided as to *why* this was so, nor reference to state practice or other authorities. See Cassese, 'The *Nicaragua* and *Tadić* Tests Revisited', 653.

[16] *Nicaragua*, Merits, Dissenting Opinion of Judge Schwebel, para 155. He argued, paras 162–71, that provision of 'arms, munitions, other supplies, training, command-and-control facilities, sanctuary and lesser forms of assistance' represented 'substantial involvement', and should permit an armed response in self-defence.

[17] *Nicaragua*, Merits, Dissenting Opinion of Judge Jennings, 528, 543.

a state. Distinguishing between the activities of individuals and those of organized armed groups, it held that attribution could be demonstrated in the latter case where a state exercises 'overall control' of the group as a whole.[18] This slightly lower threshold is crossed where a state equips and finances the armed group, *and* assists in the coordination or planning of its activities. Nevertheless, it still requires more than mere assistance, providing a territorial base, or condoning its actions.[19]

Although it has been suggested that the 'overall control' test better reflects state practice and is more appropriate in the context of international terrorism,[20] subsequent ICJ jurisprudence has seen the Court entrench its *Nicaragua* approach. Thus, in the *Wall* advisory opinion, the Court simply held that Article 51 recognizes the right of self-defence 'in the case of armed attack by one State against another State' and that, since Israel had not asserted the imputability of attacks launched from the West Bank to another state, self-defence was not relevant.[21] Similarly, in the *Armed Activities* case, it held that Uganda had failed to prove the necessary involvement of the DRC in the activities of Allied Democratic Forces (ADF) and that, consequently, self-defence was not available as the attacks 'did not emanate from armed bands or irregulars sent by the DRC or on behalf of the DRC, within the sense of... resolution 3314'.[22] Neither case discussed the 'overall control' test, whilst the Court firmly dismissed its relevance in the *Bosnia Genocide* case.[23]

The clarity provided by *Nicaragua* (namely, that self-defence is permissible against a host state in effective control of an armed group) is, however, of limited value. First, both the *Nicaragua* and *Armed Activities* cases concerned defensive action against the host state itself, rather than against armed groups located therein. In such circumstances, it is 'far less incredible' that the ICJ required attribution of the attacks to the state against which force was being used,[24] but this fails to address the more common (and more difficult) situation where force is limited to terrorist

[18] *Prosecutor v. Tadić*, Appeals Chamber Judgment of 15 July 1999, para 120.

[19] *Tadić*, Appeals Chamber Judgment, paras 130–1.

[20] Cassese, 'The *Nicaragua* and *Tadić* Tests Revisited', 657–63, 665–7.

[21] *Legal Consequences of the Construction of a Wall in the Occupied Palestinian Territory*, Advisory Opinion, 9 July 2004, ICJ Rep 2004, para 139. Clearly a higher threshold than 'substantial involvement', this position was described as 'remarkable', and contrary to *Nicaragua* and state practice. See Ruys and Verhoeven, 'Attacks by Private Actors and the Right of Self-Defence', 304–5; Christian Tams, 'Light Treatment of a Complex Problem: The Law of Self-Defence in the *Wall* Case' (2006) 16 *European Journal of International Law* 963, 978.

[22] *Case Concerning Armed Activities on the Territory of the Congo (DRC v. Uganda)*, Judgment of 19 Dec 2005, ICJ Rep 2005, para 146.

[23] *Application of the Convention on the Prevention and Punishment of the Crime of Genocide (Bosnia and Herzegovina v. Serbia and Montenegro)*, Judgment of 26 Feb 2007, ICJ Rep 2007, paras 402–6. See Raphaël van Steenberghe, 'Self-Defence in Response to Attacks by Non-State Actors in the Light of Recent State Practice: A Step Forward?' (2010) 23 *Leiden Journal of International Law* 183, 195–6; and strong criticism of the Court's approach by Cassese, 'The *Nicaragua* and *Tadić* Tests Revisited'.

[24] Kimberley N. Trapp, 'Back to Basics: Necessity, Proportionality, and the Right of Self-Defence Against Non-State Terrorist Actors' (2007) 56 *International and Comparative Law Quarterly* 141, 142.

targets. Secondly, it fails to appreciate that effective control is likely to be difficult to demonstrate:

> How could one prove that a particular terrorist group has acted upon instructions or directions or under the specific control of a state in such a manner as to imply that the state has…directed the perpetration of individual terrorist actions? The hidden nature of those groups, their being divided up into small and closely-knit units, the secretive contacts of officials of some specific states with terrorist groups, all this would make it virtually impossible…[25]

Far more likely, but not yet addressed by the ICJ, is that host state involvement comprises support for armed groups falling short of control, or else an inability to prevent attacks from its territory.

III. State Involvement Short of Control

It seems unclear whether, prior to 9/11, international law accepted that an armed attack could occur, permitting a forcible response, without attribution to a state. The international response to Operation Enduring Freedom (as a lawful exercise of self-defence), and its impact on the *jus ad bellum* is therefore important—and pivotal is the nature of the relationship between Al Qaeda and Afghanistan's governing Taliban regime.

It was to be expected that Security Council Resolution 1368, adopted the day after 9/11, condemned the attacks. Perhaps more surprising was that, without any evidence as to the perpetrators and the extent of any state involvement, it also recognized the inherent right of self-defence in accordance with the UN Charter.[26] Granted, it refers to the attacks as a 'threat to international peace and security' rather than an 'armed attack' per se, but the terms are not mutually exclusive.[27]

[25] Cassese, 'The *Nicaragua* and *Tadić* Tests Revisited', 666. See also Carsten Stahn, 'International Law at a Crossroads? The Impact of September 11' (2002) *Zeitschrift für ausländisches öffentliches Recht und Völkerrecht* 183, 219.

[26] SC Res 1373 (2001), 28 Sept 2001, reaffirmed the characterization of the attacks as a threat to international peace and security, recognized the right of self-defence and reiterated the duty upon all states to 'refrain from organizing, instigating, assisting or participating in terrorist acts in another State or in acquiescing in organized activities within its territory directed towards the commission of such acts'.

[27] See Greenwood, 'International Law and the "War Against Terrorism"', 307, outlining that Iraq's 1990 invasion of Kuwait—clearly an armed attack—was also referred to by the Security Council in the context of (a breach of) international peace and security.

Furthermore, whilst it has been argued that the Security Council did not 'recognize the right of self-defence to act against private actors without attribution to a state, but only generally reaffirmed the right of self-defence irrespective of context',[28] Resolution 1368 (2001) cannot sensibly be considered independently from the 9/11 paradigm. As such, it is difficult to escape the conclusion that the events of 9/11 were considered an armed attack in the context of Article 51,[29] and that, moreover, 'those responsible for aiding, supporting or harbouring the perpetrators, organizers and sponsors of these acts' were to be 'held accountable'.[30] To the extent that this envisaged forcible action against a state 'harbouring' terrorists but not controlling their activities as per *Nicaragua*, it would seem to have exceeded the parameters of the *jus ad bellum* as accepted at the time.[31] This was the US view, however,[32] and the response launched on 7 October 2001, based explicitly on self-defence,[33] struck both Al Qaeda and Taliban targets.

[28] Jörg Kammerhofer, 'The *Armed Activities* Case and Non-State Actors in Self-Defence Law' (2007) 20 *Leiden Journal of International Law* 89, 99.

[29] Greenwood, 'International Law and the "War Against Terrorism"', 308; Franck, 'Terrorism and the Right of Self-Defense', 840.

[30] SC Res 1368 (2001), para 3. The US apparently considered this as authorization to use force. See William Taft, 'International Law and the "War on Terror": A Look Back' (2009) *Proceedings of the American Society of International Law* 345, 352. Ralph Zacklin, 'The United Nations Secretariat and the Use of Force in a Unipolar World', Hersch Lauterpacht Memorial Lectures, Lecture III, University of Cambridge, 24 Jan 2008, available at <www.lcil.cam.ac.uk/Media/lectures/pdf/2008_Hersch_Lectures/2008_Lecture_3.pdf>, highlights concern by senior UN officials that Art 51 was being 'distorted' and that the Security Council 'had acted in the emotion of the moment rather than with calm deliberation…instead of assuming a responsible position of leadership it had in effect provided the United States with a green light to take any action it deemed appropriate'.

[31] See eg Paust, 'Use of Armed Force Against Terrorists in Afghanistan, Iraq, and Beyond', 540: 'Absent U.N. Security Council or regional organization authorization to use military force against a state that merely harbors terrorists or is unable to control misuse of its territory, and absent direct involvement by such state in a process of armed attack that triggers the right of self-defense…the use of military force against such a state would be impermissible'.

[32] President Bush stated that the US would make 'no distinction between the terrorists who committed these acts and those who harbor them' and, on 18 Sept, Congress authorized action against 'those nations, organizations or persons [found to have] planned, authorized, committed, or aided the terrorist attacks that occurred on September 11, 2001, or harboured such organizations or persons'. See 'Address to the Nation on the Terrorist Attacks' (11 Sept 2001), 37 *Weekly Compilation of Presidential Documents* 1301 (17 Sept 2001); 'Authorization for Use of Military Force', Public Law No 107–140, 115 Stat 224 (18 Sept 2001), para 2(a).

[33] The US informed the Security Council that it was acting pursuant to Art 51, and that the 9/11 attacks and ongoing threat from Al Qaeda resulted from 'the decision of the Taliban regime to allow the parts of Afghanistan that it controls to be used by this organization as a base of operation'. See Letter dated 7 October 2001 from the Permanent Representative of the United States of America to the United Nations addressed to the President of the Security Council, S/2001/946 (7 Oct 2001). The UK indicated that it too was acting under Art 51 against 'Usama Bin Laden's Al-Qaeda terrorist organization and the Taliban regime that is supporting it'. See Letter dated 7 October 2001 from the Chargé d'Affaires a.i. of the Permanent Mission of the United Kingdom of Great Britain and Northern Ireland to the United Nations addressed to the President of the Security Council, S/2001/947 (7 Oct 2001).

Complicity between Al Qaeda and the Taliban seemed certain, as did Afghanistan's failure to 'refrain from organizing, instigating, assisting or participating in . . . terrorist acts in another State or acquiescing in organized activities within its territory directed towards the commission of such acts when the acts . . . involve a threat or use of force'.[34] This provision relates to the interpretation of Article 2(4), however, and it is an armed attack rather than an unlawful use of force, that triggers the right of self-defence.[35] Three options therefore remain. The first is that Afghanistan was seen as responsible for 9/11 through its effective control of Al Qaeda. This seemed unlikely.[36] Although the UK asserted that the attacks were only possible due to Al Qaeda's 'close alliance with the Taleban regime',[37] neither the UK nor the US suggested that it was subject to Afghan control.

Secondly, is that Afghanistan was deemed responsible for the attacks, and susceptible to defensive measures, on some other ground—most likely that its refusal to surrender Osama bin Laden to the US (or any suitable third state), to instigate its own investigation, or to close Al Qaeda training camps, represented an official endorsement of Al Qaeda's activities and adoption of these as its own, as per the *Tehran Hostages* case and Article 11 of the International Law Commission's (ILC's) Articles on State Responsibility.[38] The Security Council had called for Bin Laden's surrender and the closure of all terrorist training facilities in Afghanistan,[39] and the Taliban's failure to comply may have represented 'encouragement and assistance'—especially after Al Qaeda attacks on US embassies in 1999 and the *USS Cole* in 2000, when it was 'foreseeable . . . that further actions would take place . . . controlled by

[34] GA Res 2625 (XXV), Declaration on Principles of International Law Concerning Friendly Relations and Cooperation among States in Accordance with the Charter of the United Nations, 24 Oct 1970.

[35] Albrecht Randelzhofer, 'Article 51' in Bruno Simma et al (ed), *The Charter of the United Nations: A Commentary* (2nd edn, Oxford: Oxford University Press, 2002), vol I, 788, 790–2.

[36] It was suggested that the Taliban was more dependent upon Al Qaeda than vice versa. See Michael N. Schmitt, 'Deconstructing October 7th: A Case Study in the Lawfulness of Counterterrorist Military Operations' in Michael N. Schmitt and Gian Luca Beruto (eds), *Terrorism and International Law: Challenges and Responses* (Sanremo: International Institute of Humanitarian Law, 2003) 39, 45–6.

[37] UK Government, 'Responsibility for the Terrorist Atrocities in the United States', available at <http://www.number-10.gov.uk/output/page3682.asp>. Indeed, there was agreement that responsibility 'had to be laid partly at the door of the Taliban Government'. See Peter Rowe, 'Responses to Terror: The New "War"' (2002) 3 *Melbourne Journal of International Law* 301, 307–8.

[38] *United States Diplomatic and Consular Staff in Tehran (US v. Iran)*, Judgment of 24 May 1980, ICJ Rep 1980, paras 73–4; Annex to GA Res 56/83 (12 Dec 2001), International Law Commission Articles on Responsibility of States for Internationally Wrongful Acts (2001). See Sean D. Murphy, 'Terrorism and the Concept of "Armed Attack" in Article 51 of the UN Charter' (2002) 43 *Harvard International Law Journal* 41, 50–1.

[39] SC Res 1267 (1999), 15 Oct 1999, demanded that the Taliban 'turn over Usama bin Laden without further delay to appropriate authorities in a country where he has been indicted, or to appropriate authorities in a country where he will be returned to such a country, or to appropriate authorities in a country where he will be arrested and effectively brought to justice'; SC Res 1333 (2000), 19 Dec 2000, repeated this, further demanding that the Taliban 'close all camps where terrorists are trained within the territory under its control'.

Osama bin Laden and his associates from bases on the territory of Afghanistan'.[40] The UN Secretary-General's Personal Representative had even 'exhorted the Taliban to hand over Bin Laden in compliance with [Security Council resolutions], and repeatedly spelled out the consequences that were likely to ensue from their continued refusal to do so'.[41] Nonetheless, it was difficult to evidence Taliban approval for 9/11, 'Nor could they *perpetuate* the acts of al Qaeda members in the same way as the *Tehran Hostages Case*'.[42] Afghanistan's adoption of Al Qaeda's conduct as its own was, therefore, 'questionable'.[43]

The final option is that the response was prima facie inconsistent with the prevailing rules.[44] Given the difficulty in placing Operation Enduring Freedom within the *Nicaragua* framework, and yet virtually universal approval (based upon acceptance that the relationship between Al Qaeda and the Taliban exposed the latter to forcible measures),[45] it may have reflected a move towards more flexibility regarding the state involvement necessary to constitute an armed attack. This would have been a significant development, and arguments to that effect were certainly common. Schmitt, for example, believed that 'Without any doubt, the degree of support necessary to constitute an armed attack has dropped precipitously',[46] whilst numerous commentators suggested that the level of support required had, almost overnight, become that of 'harbouring' the group responsible.[47] Cassese suggested that a broad spectrum of situations and varying levels of control or other involvement should

[40] Rowe, 'Responses to Terror', 309.

[41] Report of the Secretary-General to the General Assembly and Security Council, The Situation in Afghanistan and its Implications for International Peace and Security, A/56/681–S/2001/1157 (6 Dec 2001), para 90. See also Taft, 'International Law and the "War on Terror"', 351.

[42] Rowe, 'Responses to Terror', 308. [43] Stahn, 'International Law at a Crossroads?', 220–1.

[44] Paust, 'Use of Armed Force Against Terrorists in Afghanistan, Iraq, and Beyond', 542–3.

[45] See Malcom Shaw, 'War View: Keep the Response Legal', 9 Oct 2001, available at <http://news.bbc.co.uk/hi/english/uk/newsid_1587000/1587034.stm>, indicating that, 'governments . . . around the globe' found the responsibility of Afghanistan to have been 'adequately demonstrated'. Antonio Cassese, *International Law* (2nd edn, Oxford: Oxford University Press, 2005), 474, suggested that 'practically all states' had accepted the legitimacy of action in response to the attacks based on Art 51. See also Gray, *International Law and the Use of Force*, 193; Sean D. Murphy, 'Terrorist Attacks on the World Trade Center and Pentagon' (2002) 96 *American Journal of International Law* 237, 248.

[46] Michael N. Schmitt, 'The Legality of Operation Iraqi Freedom under International Law' (2004) *Journal of Military Ethics* 82, 88. See also Michael N. Schmitt, 'US Security Strategies: A Legal Assessment' (2004) 27 *Harvard Journal of Law and Public Policy* 737, 762.

[47] See eg Ronli Sifris, 'Operation Iraqi Freedom: United States v Iraq—The Legality of the War' (2003) 4 *Melbourne Journal of International Law* 521, 534; Devika Hovell, 'Chinks in the Armour: International Law, Terrorism and the Use of Force' (2004) 27 *University of New South Wales Law Journal* 398, 414; Christian Henderson, 'The Bush Doctrine: From Theory to Practice' (2004) 9 *Journal of Conflict and Security Law* 3, 5; Ruys and Verhoeven, 'Attacks by Private Actors and the Right of Self-Defence', 319; Olivier Corten, 'The Controversies over the Customary Prohibition on the Use of Force: A Methodological Debate' (2006) 16 *European Journal of International Law* 803, 810; Cassese, 'Terrorism is Also Disrupting Some Crucial Legal Categories of International Law', 996–7; Christine Gray, 'The Use of Force and the International Legal Order' in Malcolm D. Evans (ed), *International Law* (2nd edn, Oxford: Oxford University Press, 2006), 589, 602.

be considered on a case-by-case basis, and that 'the training, moving, lodging, and equipping of an insurgent or terrorist army, or simply giving sanctuary to rebels or terrorists... should engage the State's responsibility for attacks', whereas lesser forms of acquiescence should not.[48] Similarly, the 2002 *Commentary on the UN Charter* saw the *Nicaragua* test as inadequate to protect states from indirect attack, suggesting that the extent to which state support has 'enabled private groups to commit private acts of military force which, committed by a State, have to be qualified as "armed attack"' should be decisive.[49]

Consistent with such an approach, Israel has been keen to claim the right to respond in self-defence against Hezbollah attacks launched from Lebanon. Asserting that Hezbollah was being harboured by Lebanon (and Syria), and that it was receiving support from those states (as well as from Iran), Israel clearly stopped short of claiming that the *Nicaragua* threshold had been crossed, and that Hezbollah was acting on behalf of, or controlled by, Lebanon. Nonetheless, it argued that without 'financial, political and logistical support [from Syria, Lebanon and Iran], including the supply of weapons', Hezbollah's attacks would be impossible.[50] Given that this was precisely the type of support envisaged by Resolution 1373 (2001) (which reaffirmed the right of self-defence in the context of terrorist attacks), Israel explicitly justified its actions as self-defence.[51]

When, following a 2003 Islamic Jihad terrorist attack, Israel extended its military operations beyond Lebanon into Syria, striking a terrorist base north-west of Damascus,[52] Syria was accused of complicity by providing 'encouragement, safe harbour, training facilities and logistical support'.[53] Again referring to Resolution 1373 (2001), Israel claimed that its 'measured' response was 'a clear act of self-defence in accordance with Article 51'.[54] It found little support in the Security Council. Only the US insisted that Syria was 'on the wrong side in the war on terrorism', and that

[48] Cassese, *International Law*, 471–2.

[49] Randelzhofer, 'Article 51' in Simma et al, *The Charter of the United Nations: A Commentary*, 801: where a state 'places its territory at the disposal of [an armed] group to train its members and to offer them a safe haven... it is hardly to be understood why this should be a lesser participation in the acts of the group than the mere sending of it. It is not adequate to exclude generally certain types of supporting terrorism from being qualified as "substantial involvement" and consequently "armed attack".'

[50] Letter dated 10 April 2002 from the Chargé d'Affaires a.i. of the Permanent Mission of Israel to the United Nations addressed to the Secretary-General, A/56/913–S/2002/374.

[51] Letter dated 5 September 2002 from the Permanent Representative of Israel to the United Nations addressed to the Secretary-General, A/56/1032–S/2002/986; Letter dated 27 January 2003 from the Permanent Representative of Israel to the United Nations addressed to the Secretary-General, A/57/717–S/2003/96; Identical Letters dated 11 August 2003 from the Permanent Representative of Israel to the United Nations addressed to the Secretary-General and the President of the Security Council, A/57/857–S/2003/806.

[52] See discussion in Trapp, 'Back to Basics', 152–3; Gray, *International Law and the Use of Force*, 236–7.

[53] SCOR, 4836th mtg, S/PV.4836 (5 Oct 2003), 5–6.

[54] SCOR, 4836th mtg, S/PV.4836 (5 Oct 2003), 7.

it must 'stop harbouring and supporting the groups that perpetrate terrorist acts',[55] although condemnation was not framed in terms of a discussion of the lawfulness of action against armed groups and/or host states.[56]

The ICJ declined the opportunity to provide greater clarity in the *Armed Activities* case,[57] where Uganda characterized its actions against the DRC as lawful self-defence, triggered by the support of the DRC for, as evidenced by its *tolerance* of, the activities of the ADF.[58] Instead, the Court simply reaffirmed its *Nicaragua* judgment, holding that the ADF had not been sent 'by or on behalf of' DRC—rejecting, at least implicitly, the notion that tolerance of armed groups by a state triggers self-defence.[59] The longer term implications of Operation Enduring Freedom are therefore unclear and, by 2005, suggestions of rapid developments in customary law were treated more cautiously. Cassese, for example, argued that what may at the time have appeared to indicate widespread acceptance of a broader right of self-defence had been 'motivated by the emotional reaction to the horrific terrorist action of 11 September, [and] may not amount to the consistent practice and *opinio juris* required for a customary change'.[60]

Nonetheless, continued reliance on the *Nicaragua* test seems unpalatable, in that the consequences are:

(1) a state may provide weapons, logistical support and safe haven to a terrorist group; (2) that group may then inflict violence of any level of gravity on another state, even with

[55] SCOR, 4836th mtg, S/PV.4836 (5 Oct 2003), 14. Pakistan, Spain, China, France, Bulgaria, Chile, Mexico, and Cameroon, SCOR, 4836th mtg, S/PV.4836 (5 Oct 2003), 8–11, 13, all agreed that the Israeli response violated international law; Mexico and Guinea suggested that it was an armed reprisal.

[56] The UK and Germany, SCOR, 4836th mtg, S/PV.4836 (5 Oct 2003), 9–10, made no reference to international law, simply describing Israel's actions as 'unacceptable', whilst most members considered things in the broader context of the Middle East peace process.

[57] *Armed Activities*, Judgment, Separate Opinion of Judge Simma, para 11. Judge Kooijmans believed that, in refusing to consider the continuing relevance of *Nicaragua*, the Court had 'missed the chance to fine-tune the position it took 20 years ago in spite of the explicit invitation by one of the Parties to do so'. See *Armed Activities*, Judgment, Separate Opinion of Judge Kooijmans, para 25; Dissenting Opinion of Judge Kateka, para 13.

[58] It argued that tolerance on the part of the DRC served to 'generate legal responsibility' such that the activities of the ADF represented 'armed attacks for the purpose of Article 51'. See Counsel for Uganda, Oral Pleadings, CR 2005/7, 30, para 80. Counsel for the DRC countered that this was contrary to *Nicaragua* and therefore to 'established principles'. See Oral Pleadings, CR 2005/12, 26, para 6.

[59] The ICJ in the *Armed Activities* case, at para 147, saw 'no need to respond to the contentions of the Parties as to whether and under what conditions contemporary international law provides for a right of self-defence against large-scale attacks by irregular forces' although, having decided that Uganda's military action was not self-defence because ADF attacks could not be *attributed* to the DRC, it would seem to have resolved the issue. See also Separate Opinion of Judge Kooijmans, para 22.

[60] Cassese, *International Law*, 475. Gilbert Guillaume, 'Terrorism and International Law' (2004) 53 *International and Comparative Law Quarterly* 537, 547, also argued that 'this evolution would amount to such a radical change in international law that it would require clearer practice and a more constant *opinio juris*'; whilst Gery Simpson, *Great Powers and Outlaw States* (Cambridge: Cambridge University Press, 2004), 335–6, suspected that any such 'instant custom' would 'dissolve as quickly as it appeared' when more expansive self-defence was claimed by other states.

weapons of mass destruction; (3) the second state has no right to respond in self-defense against the first state because the first state's provision of such assistance is not an 'armed attack' within the meaning of Article 51; and (4) the second state has no right to respond in self-defense against the terrorist group because its conduct cannot be imputed to the first state, absent a showing that the first state 'sent' the terrorist group on its mission.[61]

As Murphy concludes, 'Such a legal construct, if intended, seems unlikely to endure'.[62] It is suggested that it has not—although it is, admittedly, disappointing that the Court was unable to assess the legality of a Ugandan response limited to proportionate strikes against ADF, rather than DRC, targets.

IV. Absence of Attribution: Failure/Inability to Prevent Attacks

Beyond the question of state support for armed groups operating from their territory, and a consequent unwillingness to prevent their attacks as required by international law, it is also possible that armed groups are free to launch cross-border attacks due to the host state's lack of control over the entirety of its territory—and hence an inability, rather than an unwillingness, to prevent the attacks. This is clearly yet further removed from the *Nicaragua* threshold, in that the host state does not condone the group's activities, let alone direct or control them. In the *Wall* advisory opinion, however, Judges Kooijmans and Buergenthal saw Resolutions 1368 (2001) and 1373 (2001) as demonstrating a new approach, recognizing the right to respond in self-defence without requiring that an armed attack be imputed to another state.[63]

As such, attribution as per *Nicaragua* would no longer be necessary for an armed attack to occur. The host state would not be responsible for the attack, and hence could not be targeted in response—but its inability to prevent terrorist attacks would leave its territorial integrity susceptible to 'breach' by the target state, with defensive action limited to terrorist targets.[64] Yet again, Brownlie foresaw this possibility in 1963, although cautioning that the legitimacy of such a response must be based on

[61] Sean D. Murphy, 'Self-Defense and the *Israeli Wall* Advisory Opinion: An *Ipse Dixit* from the Court?' (2005) 99 *American Journal of International Law* 62, 66.

[62] Murphy, 'Self-Defense and the *Israeli Wall* Advisory Opinion', 66.

[63] *Wall*, Advisory Opinion, Separate Opinion of Judge Kooijmans, para 35; Declaration of Judge Buergenthal, para 6.

[64] Kammerhofer, 'The *Armed Activities* Case and Non-State Actors in Self-Defence Law', 105; 'The Chatham House Principles of International Law on the Use of Force in Self-Defence' (2006) 55 *International and Comparative Law Quarterly* 963, 970.

'principle and policy since the legal materials relating to self-defence in international law contemplate action against states only'.[65]

It may well be, however, that at least one impact of 9/11 has been to permit states to contemplate defensive action against armed groups. After all, 9/11 clearly demonstrated the capacity of terrorists to cause significant damage, comparable to more 'traditional' attacks by regular armed forces, even without the control or complicity of any state.[66] In the light of this, it would be a 'strange formalism which regarded the right to take military action against those who caused or threatened such consequences as dependent upon whether their acts could somehow be imputed to a state'.[67] Indeed, to hold otherwise would make terrorists operating from a 'failed state' incapable of launching an armed attack in the context of Article 51, denying the target state a lawful defensive response.[68] This is neither reasonable nor realistic. Instead, rather than require attribution to a state to constitute an armed attack, attribution should determine the permissible target(s) of a defensive response.[69] Thus, an inability to prevent 9/11 would not have made Afghanistan responsible for an indirect armed attack, but it would have rendered lawful a forcible response by the US and its allies against Al Qaeda.[70]

This view has gained credence post-9/11 in the opinion of numerous commentators,[71] and in state practice. Russia, for example, claimed the right to respond against Chechen rebels in Georgia on the basis that Georgia was unwilling and unable to prevent their incursions into Russian territory. Asserting that 'responsibility for the consequences of the armed incursion [therefore lay] fully with the Georgian side',[72]

[65] Brownlie, *International Law and the Use of Force By States*, 375.

[66] Greenwood, 'International Law and the "War Against Terrorism"', 307.

[67] Greenwood, 'International Law and the "War Against Terrorism"', 307.

[68] Stahn, 'International Law at a Crossroads?', 214–15.

[69] Jackson N. Maogoto, 'War on the Enemy: Self-Defence and State-Sponsored Terrorism' (2003) 4 *Melbourne Journal of International Law* 406, 431. Shaw similarly argued ('War View: Keep the Response Legal'), that the 9/11 attacks could not 'constitute anything other than an "armed attack"', but 'more difficult to answer is the question of responsibility'.

[70] Schmitt, 'Deconstructing October 7th', 45. Paust, 'Use of Armed Force Against Terrorists in Afghanistan, Iraq, and Beyond', 540, maintained that 'unless the state is organizing, fomenting, directing, or otherwise directly participating in armed attacks by non-state terrorists, the use of military force against the state, *as opposed to only the non-state terrorists*, would be impermissible' (emphasis added). Although the Taliban seemed unwilling rather than unable, limiting the response in this way would have avoided controversy in that, whilst the Taliban had indicated that it would 'vigorously oppose any foreign forces entering its territory to root out Al-Qaida bases', Taliban targets were attacked 'before they had the chance to resist'. See Christopher Greenwood, 'International Law and the Preemptive Use of Force: Afghanistan, Al-Qaida, and Iraq' (2003) 4 *San Diego Journal of International Law* 7, 25; Schmitt, 'US Security Strategies', 760.

[71] See eg Angus Martyn, 'The Right of Self-Defence under International Law—the Response to the Terrorist Attacks of 11 September', Parliament of Australia Current Issues Brief No 8, 2001–02, 12 Feb 2002, available at <http://www.aph.gov.au/library/pubs/CIB/2001-02/02cib08.htm>: 'terrorist groups with the means to reach across international borders to inflict significant damage... must represent the sort of threat against which self-defence is legitimate if the doctrine is to have any practical contemporary value'; Guillaume, 'Terrorism and International Law', 546.

[72] Letter dated 31 July 2002 from the Chargé d'Affaires a.i. of the Permanent Mission of the Russian Federation to the United Nations addressed to the Secretary-General, A/57/269–S/2002/854.

Russia reserved 'the right to act in accordance with Article 51'.[73] Similarly, Uganda argued in *Armed Activities* that the DRC had been unable to control the whole of its territory so as to prevent insurgent attacks, and in favour of a 'standard of responsibility, according to which a failure to control the activities of armed bands, creates a susceptibility to action in self-defence'.[74] The ICJ accepted that there had been a lack of control over the activities of rebels in the border region but, in the context of Uganda's response against the DRC, held that this was not 'tantamount to "tolerating" or "acquiescing" in their activities', even if this lower standard was sufficient for attribution, and thereby constituted neither unlawful intervention in, nor armed attack against, Uganda.[75]

Judge Kooijmans agreed that an inability to control the activities of armed bands did not result in attribution, but refused to accept that this ruled out self-defence altogether as the Court had not considered the lawful response to action by armed groups which, '"because of its scale and effects, would have been classified as an armed attack…had it been carried out by regular armed forces"…but [where] no involvement of the "host government" can be proved'.[76] Reiterating that Article 51 was not limited to attacks by one state on another,[77] and again influenced by Security Council Resolutions 1368 and 1373, he argued that:

> If the activities of armed bands present on a State's territory cannot be attributed to that State, the victim State is not the object of an armed attack by it. But if the attacks by the irregulars would, because of their scale and effects, have had to be classified as an armed attack had they been carried out by regular armed forces, there is nothing in the language of Article 51…that prevents the victim State from exercising its *inherent* right of self-defence.[78]

Agreeing that terrorist acts can constitute armed attacks without attribution, Judge Simma believed that it 'would be unreasonable to deny the attacked State the right to self-defence merely because there is no attacker State and the Charter does not require so'.[79]

By 2006, a group of leading British international lawyers adopted a set of principles outlining their view that 'the right of States to defend themselves against ongoing attacks, even by private groups of non-state actors, is not generally questioned', and that:

[73] Letter dated 11 September 2002 from the Permanent Representative of the Russian Federation to the United Nations addressed to the Secretary-General, S/2002/1012. US opposition to the Russian position should, however, be noted for its potential impact on the development of a customary rule. See Gray, *International Law and the Use of Force*, 230–1.

[74] *Armed Activities*, Oral Pleadings, Counsel for Uganda, para 80.

[75] *Wall*, Advisory Opinion, paras 300–1.

[76] *Armed Activities*, Separate Opinion of Judge Kooijmans, para 26.

[77] *Wall*, Advisory Opinion, Separate Opinion of Judge Kooijmans, para 35.

[78] *Armed Activities*, Separate Opinion of Judge Kooijmans, para 29.

[79] *Armed Activities*, Separate Opinion of Judge Simma, para 12, quoting Yoram Dinstein, *War, Aggression and Self-Defence* (3rd edn, Cambridge: Cambridge University Press, 2002), 216.

The right to use force in self-defence... is not dependent upon any prior breach of international law by the State in the territory of which defensive force is used.

Thus, where a State is unable or unwilling to assert control over a terrorist organization located in its territory, the State which is a victim of the terrorist attacks would, as a last resort, be permitted to act in self-defence against the terrorist organization in the State in which it is located.[80]

When, in the same year, Israel took further military action against Hezbollah targets in Lebanon,[81] it again asserted that it was acting in self-defence and argued that responsibility lay with 'Lebanon, from whose territory these acts have been launched into Israel'.[82] Rather than claim active support or participation in the attacks, however, Israel asserted that Lebanon had been unable to exercise appropriate jurisdiction over its own territory due to 'ineptitude and inaction'.[83] Its response, limited to 'Hizbollah strongholds, positions and infrastructure',[84] met with significant criticism (primarily for lack of proportionality),[85] although the Security Council stressed that Lebanon had a responsibility to exercise effective control over its territory, preventing further Hezbollah attacks, and most Council members did accept that Israel had the right to take defensive action in the circumstances.[86]

Similarly, Turkish attacks on PKK targets in northern Iraq have received little to no international condemnation.[87] At least since 2007, a clear legal justification for these actions has not been easily discerned,[88] nor have these Turkish actions been reported to the Security Council as required by Article 51.[89] Nonetheless, Turkey clearly did not consider the attacks imputable to Iraq,[90] and the international community has

80 Chatham House Principles, 970.

81 See Trapp, 'Back to Basics', 153–5; Gray, *International Law and the Use of Force*, 237–44.

82 Identical letters dated 12 July 2006 from the Permanent Representative of Israel to the United Nations addressed to the Secretary-General and the President of the Security Council, A/60/937–S/2006/515.

83 A/60/937–S/2006/515. Lebanon denied responsibility, insisting that it had been unaware of the incident and did not endorse it. See SCOR, 5489th mtg, S/PV.5489 (14 July 2006), 4.

84 S/PV.5489, 6.

85 S/PV.5489, 7, 9, 11–15, and 17; SCOR, 5492nd mtg, S/PV.5492 (20 July 2006), 3; SCOR, 5493rd mtg, S/PV.5493 (21 July 2006), 14; SCOR, 5498th mtg, S/PV.5498 (30 July 2006), 3.

86 S/PV.5489, 9, 12, and 14–16; S/PV.5493, 17 and 19. The UN Secretary-General also explicitly recognized the right of Israel to take action under Art 51. See S/PV.5492, 3; S/PV.5498, 3.

87 On the 2007–8 operations in particular, see Tom Ruys, '*Quo Vadit Jus ad Bellum?* A Legal Analysis of Turkey's Military Operations Against the PKK in Northern Iraq' (2008) 9 *Melbourne Journal of International Law* 334; Van Steenberghe, 'Self-Defence in Response to Attacks by Non-State Actors in the Light of Recent State Practice', 187–9.

88 Although see statements by Turkish Prime Minister Erdogan referred to in Van Steenberghe, 'Self-Defence in Response to Attacks by Non-State Actors in the Light of Recent State Practice', 188.

89 This is probably a procedural/evidential rather than substantive requirement, however, which may weaken the case for lawful self-defence—but which does not extinguish it. See Donald W. Greig, 'Self-Defence and the Security Council: What Does Article 51 Require?' (1991) 40 *International and Comparative Law Quarterly* 366.

90 It is perhaps unclear whether Iraq was unable or unwilling to prevent the attacks, but it did take steps aimed at preventing PKK activities, and received advance warning of Turkish operations in Feb 2008. See Ruys, '*Quo Vadit Jus ad Bellum*?', 341–2.

done little to cast doubt upon the availability of self-defence in such circumstances. Indeed, whilst many states were equivocal in their response,[91] the Dutch foreign minister asserted in 2008 that, 'Kurdish attacks from Iraq have taken place on Turkish territory, and since the UN Security Council has not yet taken any measures against these attacks, Turkey can invoke the right of self-defence'.[92] This position was reiterated, and supported by the US, following similar operations in 2011.[93]

V. Conclusion

As Judge Higgins explained, 'nothing in the text of Article 51 ... stipulates that self-defence is available only when an armed attack is made by a State. *That* qualification is rather a result of the Court so determining in [the *Nicaragua* case]'.[94] The *Nicaragua* judgment has, however, been subjected to consistent criticism, and its continuing efficacy has been questioned.[95] If the concept of self-defence is to retain any modern value, states must be permitted to defend themselves against armed attacks, irrespective of the perpetrators. As Lowe indicates, 'Self-defence is an inherent right; and the right exists whenever one is attacked, whether by a State army or by an individual terrorist'.[96] To suggest that states may not lawfully defend themselves because state control over, or substantial involvement in, the activities of armed groups cannot be demonstrated seems unfair, 'lacks correspondence with the realities of international politics and, more importantly, cannot explain states' overwhelming approval of the US action in Afghanistan'.[97]

[91] See eg 'EU Presidency Statement on the Terrorist Attacks of the PKK in Turkey over the Weekend', Press release, 22 Oct 2007, supporting 'Turkey's efforts to protect its population and fight terrorism, while... refraining from taking any disproportionate military action'.

[92] Ministerial Statement, 3 Mar 2008, as cited and translated in Ruys, '*Quo Vadit Jus ad Bellum?*', 356.

[93] Ministerial Statement, 3 Oct 2011: see 'Dutch Foreign Minister Supports Turkish Cross Border Raids', available at <http://www.rudaw.net/english/world/4042.html>. See also US Department of State Press Briefings, 18 Aug 2011, at <http://www.state.gov/r/pa/prs/dpb/2011/08/170709.htm#TURKEY>, and 20 Oct 2011, at <http://www.state.gov/r/pa/prs/dpb/2011/10/175929.htm#TURKEY>, outlining US support for Turkey's right of self-defence against terrorist attacks.

[94] *Wall*, Advisory Opinion, Separate Opinion of Judge Higgins, para 33. See also Declaration of Judge Buergenthal, para 5.

[95] See n 25; Rein Müllerson, 'Jus ad Bellum and International Terrorism' in Fred L. Borch and Paul S. Wilson (eds), *International Law Studies, Vol 79: International Law and the War on Terror* (Newport, RI: US Naval War College, 2003), 75, 112; Dinstein, *War, Aggression and Self-Defence* (4th edn, 2005), 193–6, and 219.

[96] Vaughan Lowe, *International Law* (Oxford: Oxford University Press, 2007), 278.

[97] Simpson, *Great Powers and Outlaw States*, 334.

The relationship between Afghanistan and Al Qaeda was probably unique in the context of an international system predicated on the superiority of states, and the 9/11 attacks were accordingly difficult to assess through the prevailing rules requiring effective control. Equally, support for the extension of military operations beyond Al Qaeda to the Taliban could probably be explained by reasons that were as political as they were legal.[98] Nonetheless, bolstered by the effect of Security Council Resolutions 1368 and 1373, there does seem to be a trend towards accepting the possibility of lawful self-defence without attribution to the host state. A strict requirement to demonstrate imputability would, after all, severely limit the ability of states to take defensive action in a situation which is '*per definitionem* so urgent that it does not logically allow a state victim of an armed attack to wait to raise questions of responsibility'.[99] State practice does, however, also tend to indicate that some responsibility on the part of the host state is still asserted—from harbouring or otherwise supporting/assisting the armed group in question to simply being unable to prevent its activities. Attribution of an armed attack to a state is, therefore, more relevant to the question of who may be targeted by the defensive response than to the question of whether the victim state has been subjected to an armed attack per se.

Armed action against armed groups where the host state cannot take preventive action certainly appears to meet the 'necessity' criteria for lawful self-defence in that, given the host state's failure to control its own territory, there is no reasonable and/or effective alternative to the use of force.[100] As such, a host state's inability to take effective measures against armed groups operating from its territory is probably now tantamount to the level of involvement necessary to render action against *those armed groups* lawful. Clearly, then, a forcible response is equally necessary where the host state is, due to its tolerance of and support for the presence and activities of an armed group, unwilling, rather than unable, to prevent its military activities. Defensive action against the *host state itself* would, however, only be necessary where attribution is present and there has actually been an indirect armed attack by that state, acting through an armed group as per *Nicaragua*, or else where it actively resists lawful measures taken against armed groups on its territory.

[98] See Moir, *Reappraising the Resort to Force*, 154–5. Schmitt, eg, suggested that one factor in assessing the lawfulness of defensive action against a host state should be 'the extent to which the state is perceived as generally law-abiding and legitimate', and that the unpopularity of the Taliban regime 'made striking them even more palatable'. See Schmitt, 'Counter-Terrorism and the Use of Force in International Law' in Borch and Wilson (eds), *International Law and the War on Terror*, 69–70; Schmitt, 'The Legality of Operation Iraqi Freedom', 88.

[99] Van Steenberghe, 'Self-Defence in Response to Attacks by Non-State Actors in the Light of Recent State Practice', 195–6.

[100] Van Steenberghe, 'Self-Defence in Response to Attacks by Non-State Actors in the Light of Recent State Practice', 199–202; Trapp, 'Back to Basics', 146–7 and 154–5.

The *Nicaragua* and *Armed Activities* cases both concerned action against host states, and it is important not to broaden their scope beyond reason. It must also be borne in mind that most claims of self-defence against terrorist attacks have asserted the right *only* against terrorist targets. Recent developments probably indicate the availability and acceptance of defensive measures against armed groups where the host state is unwilling or unable to prevent their activities, but to permit action against the host state in such situations would 'too readily justify the robust use of military force [and]...set dangerous precedents'.[101] International law does not do so.

[101] Maogoto, 'War on the Enemy', 438. As Greenwood warned, 'we do not want to give credence to a theory that as soon as any state has a group of terrorists which have operated from its territory, it exposes itself to armed attack. That very broad brush approach opens up the most horrific possibilities because at some time or other virtually every state however hard it tried otherwise, had ended up with terrorists operating from its territory'. See 'Panel I Discussion—Jus ad Bellum' in Borch and Wilson, *International Law and the War on Terror*, 145.

CHAPTER 33

WHEN DOES SELF-DEFENCE END?

T. D. GILL

I. Introduction

The exercise of the right of self-defence has a beginning and an end. However, while considerable attention has been devoted to the question when the right to exercise self-defence commences, particularly in relation to the question whether an incipient or potential attack activates the right of self-defence, much less attention has been given to the question when the right terminates. In view of, inter alia, the continued reliance by the US on the right of self-defence in response to the attack by Al Qaeda on the World Trade Center and Pentagon over a decade ago, the question can reasonably be posed as to how long reliance upon self-defence remains operative. Does the right to exercise self-defence cease once an initial attack has been responded to or does the effectiveness of the response enter into the equation in the sense that until the threat has been neutralized the right to exercise self-defence remains operative? If the latter is the case, how should the existence of a continuing threat be assessed? Is it sufficient that the original attacker still has the capacity to launch a renewed attack and has not clearly demonstrated an intention to cease further attacks, or must there be concrete indications that a renewed attack is imminent or ongoing? Can a series of attacks carried out over a stretch of time be seen as a valid reason to prolong the right to exercise self-defence? If this is accepted, what are the conditions attached to treating a series of attacks as an ongoing attack still in progress? Must there be a demonstrable level of organization, coordination, and temporal and geographical connection between separate attacks to treat them as forming a whole, or is a relatively loose degree of shared ideology, methodology, and purpose sufficient to treat a number of discrete actors as one actor and separate incidents as a single attack, which would justify measures of self-defence directed against all of them until all threat of recurrence had ceased or been terminated?

This chapter will attempt to stimulate further reflection and discussion and hopefully provide some answers to these and other questions related to the suspension and termination of the right of self-defence. The latter set of questions relates to the nature and duration of the initial attack and possible subsequent attacks, to the principles of necessity and proportionality in the context of the ongoing exercise of self-defence, and to the effect that Security Council action to restore international peace and security might have upon the continued exercise of the right of self-defence. It will, first, examine the nature of the right of self-defence and the modalities of armed attack in relation to the influence these might have upon the duration of the right of self-defence. Secondly, it will discuss the relationship of the principles of necessity, proportionality, and immediacy to the duration of the exercise of self-defence. Thirdly, attention will be given to the question of the effect of collective security measures adopted by the Security Council upon the continued exercise of self-defence. Finally, a number of general conclusions will be presented in an attempt to provide an overall answer to the question: 'when does self-defence end?'

II. The Nature of Self-Defence and the Modalities of Armed Attack in Relation to the Duration of the Exercise of the Right of Self-Defence

While controversy exists in relation to certain aspects of the right of self-defence under international law, there is nevertheless a considerable degree of agreement regarding its core nature as a legally sanctioned forceful response to an unlawful resort to force and the requirement of a prior or imminent armed attack as a threshold for its exercise.[1] Self-defence is a right grounded both in the UN Charter and in

[1] On self-defence as a right to respond to illegal force, see Yoram Dinstein, *War, Aggression and Self-Defence* (4th edn, Cambridge: Cambridge University Press, 2005), 178.

customary international law,[2] which provides a state the right to forcibly respond to an armed attack in order to repel the attack and, if necessary forestall the continuation of further attacks. This is what separates it from other modalities of the use of force, whether legal or illegal. It is essentially reactive in that it is a response to a prior, ongoing, or imminent threat of attack. It has a recognized legal basis, which sets it apart from uses of force which do not. Its purpose is the repelling of an armed attack and the forestalling of further attacks. This is distinct from responses to threats to international peace and security, which are not restricted to responding to armed attacks and which are the sole prerogative of the UN Security Council.[3] The dual legal basis of the right in both Charter and customary law implies that the exercise of the right must conform to the requirements laid down in both sources. With regard to the Charter, these are essentially the incorporation of the right within the context of the prohibition of the use of force and with respect to the powers and primacy of the Security Council in the maintenance and restoration of peace and security. The Charter also requires the occurrence of an armed attack, although it is silent as to what constitutes an armed attack and when it can be said to commence and terminate, other than the use of the rather open-ended phrase 'if an armed attack occurs'. In short, the Charter recognizes self-defence as an exception to the prohibition of the use of force and requires that its exercise is in response to an armed attack and is subject to the overall primacy of the Security Council. Both of these Charter-based aspects of the right of self-defence have relevance to the question of the duration of the right.

The question of the relationship of the exercise of self-defence to action taken by the Council and the impact of the customary requirements of necessity, proportionality, and immediacy will be dealt with subsequently. Nevertheless, the question now before us is the relationship between the occurrence of an armed attack and the duration of the exercise of self-defence. The starting point is, while the Charter requires an armed attack, it is not specified or clarified what constitutes an armed attack or when it begins or ends. Since we are primarily concerned with the question of when self-defence ends, we will only refer to the other aspects insofar as necessary to shed light on the duration of the right. However, since the Charter does not provide any real insight into the nature or modality of an armed attack, we must look to customary international law to provide some indication of the forms an armed attack can take. This will enable us to then turn to the question how this influences and partially determines the duration of the right of self-defence.

[2] The dual legal basis for self-defence is generally recognized and was acknowledged by the Court in *Military and Paramilitary Activities in and against Nicaragua*, Merits, ICJ Rep 1986, 14, 94.

[3] The place of the Security Council in maintaining international peace and security is dealt with inter alia, by Dinstein, *War, Aggression and Self-Defence*, 278 ff; Rüdiger Wolfrum, 'Preamble' in Bruno Simma et al (eds), *The Charter of the United Nations: A Commentary* (2nd edn, Oxford: Oxford University Press, 2002), vol 1, 33–44; and Leland M. Goodrich, Evans Hambro, and Anne P. Simons, *Charter of the United Nations* (3rd revd edn, Medford, MA: World Peace Foundation, 1969), 25–9.

An armed attack can take various forms and can be undertaken by different authors. In the *Nicaragua* case, the International Court of Justice referred to two distinct types of armed attack: direct and indirect. In the context of that case, these were respectively armed attacks directly carried out by the armed forces of one state against another state and actions carried out by armed bands, irregulars, and so forth, which were either under the effective control of a state, or in which a state was substantially involved. Such an indirect attack was deemed potentially capable of constituting an armed attack if its scale and effects were comparable to those resulting from a direct armed attack carried out by state armed forces.[4] On the basis of this rendition of the law, an attack would have to rise to a certain level of gravity before it could be qualified as an armed attack and could be carried out by state agents acting directly, or through proxies acting under the control or substantial influence of a state. The Court has more or less stuck to this interpretation in subsequent decisions, albeit not without a certain degree of criticism from both within and from outside it.[5]

In recent years a significant amount of practice has emerged which points strongly in the direction of the possibility of an armed attack additionally being potentially conducted by an organized armed group, which is not acting under the direction or significant influence of any particular state. While there is still a degree of controversy regarding this last named possibility, it has become increasingly accepted since the events of 11 September 2001 and the international reaction thereto.[6] Hence, for our purposes, possible authorship will be included alongside the other two mentioned by the Court. Without going further into the controversy regarding the

[4] *Nicaragua*, Merits, paras 195, 104–5.

[5] The Court repeated its position in subsequent decisions such as *Oil Platforms (Iran v. US)*, Merits, ICJ Rep 2003, 161, reproduced in (2003) 42 ILM 1334 paras 55–72 and *Case Concerning Armed Activities on the Territory of the Congo (DRC v. Uganda)*, ICJ Rep 2005, 168, paras 144–7. In both cases, there were significant differences of opinion within the Court relating to its interpretation of the law related to self-defence, including in particular the threshold of an armed attack and, in the latter case, whether self-defence was confined to attacks initiated by or under the control of a state.

[6] The applicability of self-defence was asserted by the US in response to the 9/11 attacks, by Turkey in relation to its repeated cross-border incursions into northern Iraq in pursuit of PKK rebels, by Colombia in response to the presence of FARC rebels in neighbouring Ecuador, by Israel in relation to attacks by Hezbollah and Hamas from Lebanon and Gaza, to name several examples. The Security Council has acknowledged the applicability of self-defence in relation to the 9/11 attacks (SC Res 1368 and 1373 (2001)). While there has been criticism of some aspects related to the examples referred to, this has not been directed against the application of self-defence in response to attacks by armed groups, but rather to questions of proportionality and necessity and considerations not related directly to self-defence, such as allegations of violations of humanitarian law. The Court refrained from ruling on the question in *Armed Activities*, but several judges expressed their opinion that self-defence was potentially applicable in such situations. Likewise, the international community at large does not seem to rule out this possibility in its reactions to 9/11 and other examples cited, provided the other conditions relating to the exercise of self-defence are met. For an extensive analysis of self-defence in relation to attacks launched by non-state actors, see Kinga Tibori Szabo, *Anticipatory Action in Self-Defence* (The Hague: TMC Asser Press, 2011), 203 ff.

nature and gravity of the use of force required to constitute an armed attack, it will also be assumed for the sake of our discussion that an armed attack must rise above the level of criminal violence or an isolated small-scale armed intrusion or incident.

Taking these as starting points for our discussion, we can then turn to the question of which forms an armed attack can take. Essentially, this involves both elements of gravity and duration. Put simply, an armed attack can, first, consist of a single reasonably significant use of force, which lasts only for a limited period of time and is closed once both parties refrain from further action. An example of this would be a one-off use of force by one party, which is answered by the other and is limited in both geographical and temporal scope to a particular location and does not cause further armed action by either party.[7] An example of this would be a border skirmish between opposing forces of two states, which lasts several hours or days, and which is serious enough to constitute an armed attack on the part of one of the parties and justify self-defence by the other. The party initiating hostilities or otherwise engaging in an unlawful incursion would normally be designated as the author of the armed attack and the other party would then be justified in countering the attack by measures aimed at repelling it. The more serious the incident was, the more likely it would result in recurrent incidents and/or possibly even escalation into full-scale hostilities. Another example of such a one-off use of force, (possibly) amounting to an armed attack justifying a quick one-off defensive response, might also be found in certain types of rescue actions aimed at ending a grave threat to the lives and physical safety of a state's citizens located abroad of the type Israel carried out in its rescue action in Entebbe in 1976. The legality of such operations is somewhat controversial, but assuming they can be legal within certain conditions and circumstances, then the duration of the right of rescue (usually linked to self-defence) would necessarily be limited in time to what was strictly required to put an end to the illegal situation and evacuate those concerned to safety.[8]

If we move up the scale in terms of both gravity and duration, we come to a second *modus* for an armed attack, namely a series of relatively small-scale armed incidents, which are conducted by the same author and are reasonably connected geographically and temporally. This possibility has been recognized in both practice and elsewhere and is often referred to as the 'accumulation of events' theory. This enables a state confronted with what is in effect a phased armed attack, to treat a number of related incidents as a single armed attack and to gauge its response accordingly. In principle, the gravity and duration of the series of acts constituting an armed attack would determine the duration of the response. If the response

[7] Dinstein refers to this *modus* of self-defence as an 'on the spot reaction', see *War, Aggression and Self-Defence*, 219–21.

[8] For an overview of the controversies relating to the rescue of nationals, see Terry D. Gill and Paul A. L. Ducheine, 'Rescue of Nationals' in Terry D. Gill and Dieter Fleck (eds), *The Handbook of the International Law of Military Operations* (Oxford: Oxford University Press, 2010), 217–19.

succeeded in ending further repetition of attack, the right of self-defence would terminate once it were clear that no repetition was likely in the reasonably immediate future. If a significant period of time passed and a new (series of) incident(s) occurred, it would be more realistic to treat it as a new armed attack rather than as part of an ongoing attack, simply because self-defence is predicated upon the occurrence of an armed attack and reaction thereto within a reasonably proximate time frame, and it does not allow for the possibility of treating incidents divided by significant intervals of time and/or geographical location as a single armed attack. For example, the recurrent hostilities between Indian and Pakistani forces along the 'line of control' in disputed Kashmir over an extended period of time have been generally regarded as discrete uses of force over time and not as one ongoing armed attack and exercise of self-defence, notwithstanding the fact that they relate to the same territorial dispute which dates back for decades since independence and subsequent partition of the territory. The same applies to repeated outbreaks of hostilities between Israel and Hamas militants located in Gaza or between Israel and Hezbollah in southern Lebanon.[9] While the underlying causes of tension and hostility may well have a common root, this does not mean that all uses of force over a period of years between the opposing sides can be lumped together and treated as a single attack and response thereto, since there have been significant intervals of time between separate (series of) incidents and uses of force.

A third *modus* for an armed attack is that of initiating a war through invasion and (attempted) occupation of (part of) another state's territory, or other large-scale use of force directed against its territory, population, or armed forces of a state which triggered a corresponding right of the defending state (and possibly by states assisting it) to engage in a war based on self-defence, with the object of repelling the attack and forestalling future attacks, which can require in some cases the defeat of the attacking party. Two examples of such a use of force rising to the level of full-scale war were the war between Iraq and Iran in the period 1980–8 and the subsequent invasion by Iraq of Kuwait and the reaction thereto by the international community in 1990–1. In such cases, the right of self-defence will, in principle, last until a peace agreement or ceasefire has been reached or ordered by the Security Council, or one side has been defeated and no further action is undertaken by either side or by the international community acting in assistance of the defending state and/or under Security Council mandate.

[9] There have been several discrete armed conflicts (1947, 1965, and 1971) between India and Pakistan since partition and independence, two of which were directly linked to Kashmir. There are also intermittent skirmishes along the 'line of control' from time to time. In Gaza, there have been several larger scale conflicts, most notably in 2008–9, interspersed with exchanges of fire, cross-border incursions, and tenuous ceasefire agreements. The situation in southern Lebanon was essentially similar, with intermittent exchanges of fire and incursions by both sides preceding the 2006 Israel/Hezbollah armed conflict and subsequent UN ceasefire agreement and deployment of UN peacekeeping troops into the border area.

It should be clear from the preceding discussion that while the impact of the mode of armed attack and corresponding right of self-defence have an independent significance in partially influencing the duration of the right of self-defence, they are closely tied to the notions of necessity, proportionality, and immediacy, which are part of the customary dimension of the right of self-defence. We will turn to those and how they relate to the duration of self-defence now.

III. Necessity, Proportionality, and Immediacy as Factors Determining the Duration of the Right of Self-Defence

The customary principles of necessity, proportionality, and immediacy are integral parts of the normative framework governing the exercise of self-defence.[10] They act alongside the Charter provisions relating to the legal basis of the right and they will inevitably play a crucial role in determining the modalities of self-defence, including how long the right remains operative. They are universally recognized as being of cardinal importance in regulating the exercise of the right of self-defence. While capable of a general definition, they must be applied in the light of the relevant factual circumstances in order to take on meaning.

Necessity in the context of self-defence usually refers to two separate, but related, aspects of the right. First, it refers to the existence of an ongoing armed attack or imminent and manifest threat of an armed attack, which is on the point of being launched within the proximate future. Secondly, it refers to the lack of feasible alternatives for the taking of action in self-defence. Such alternatives can range from the realistic possibility of resolving a crisis situation by peaceful measures of dispute settlement through the possibility of resorting to alternative measures not involving the use of transboundary armed force, to action undertaken by the UN Security Council which has the object of precluding the exercise of self-defence and which succeeds in providing an effective alternative to self-defence (which will be dealt with separately later). An example of transboundary armed force is resort to international cooperation relating to law enforcement in relation to combating

[10] On necessity and proportionality, see eg Oscar Schachter, *International Law in Theory and Practice* (Leiden: Martinus Nijhoff, 1991), 152–5, Judith Gardam, *Necessity, Proportionality and the Use of Force by States* (Cambridge: Cambridge University Press, 2004), 148–53 and Dinstein, *War, Aggression and Self-Defence*, 208–10.

international terrorism or other military or non-military measures falling short of actual use of force in self-defence.

In short, the principle of necessity requires that an armed attack be in progress or on the point of being launched in the proximate future, and that there are no feasible alternatives to the taking of armed action across international frontiers in order to forestall, repel, or overcome the attack. As stated, it must be seen in relation to the available evidence and factual circumstances, which are at the disposal of the defending state at the relevant time. For example, a situation of heightened crisis, whereby a potential adversary has both the capacity and a demonstrated will to launch an armed attack would, in principle, qualify as a situation in which self-defence could be qualified as necessary much earlier than in a situation in which both parties have adequate time to resort to alternatives to resorting to armed force. Another example would be if a terrorist group is known to be actively operating on another state's territory and poses a threat to (an)other state(s), the normal course of action would be to inform the state where the group is located of the threat in question, request it to take adequate measures to forestall or halt (further) terrorist action, and, in cooperation with it, to take measures of law enforcement to prevent terrorist acts from being undertaken from that state's territory. Only in the event that a state was unwilling or unable to take adequate measures and there was a clear threat of a terrorist act, which likely reached the threshold of an armed attack, would action in self-defence be necessary and justified, provided the other requirements relating to its exercise were met. Simply stated, necessity must be seen in the context of the relevant factual situation in order to determine whether feasible alternatives to armed action exist in a particular situation.

Proportionality is both a legal principle, in a general sense with application to various legal regimes and a customary rule which has a specific meaning in relation to self-defence. It must also be linked to factual considerations to be capable of being meaningfully applied. As a principle, it is generally taken to have both a quantitative element (force used in self-defence must be roughly commensurate with the scale of the armed attack or threat of impending attack) and a qualitative element (force used in self-defence must not exceed what is required under the circumstances to repel the attack and forestall future attacks within the proximate future), with the latter being the more important of the two. However, it is clear that any determination regarding proportionality is likewise subject to factual and other relevant considerations, such as what is the scale of the attack, what is the probable threat of future attacks within the reasonably immediate future, what means are available to repel the attack, etc. Proportionality does not translate into a sort of *lex taliones*, whereby a reaction must be equivalent in kind or level of harm imposed, nor is it a prescription of how self-defence must be carried out. If, for example, a state uses a proxy armed group under its control or substantial influence to carry out attacks against another state, it could well be justified to react against both the armed group and the state on whose behalf it was operating, without necessarily violating the principle of proportionality.

Immediacy is generally linked to the requirement that a state acting in self-defence does so within a reasonable time frame and it does not unduly postpone the taking of measures.[11] The primary reasoning behind this principle is that self-defence is a type of emergency action which has as its purpose the repelling of an attack or forestalling of an imminent threat of attack and it is therefore to be distinguished from a retaliatory measure of reprisal, which has the purpose of exacting retribution for a wrong which has been committed. Hence, undue delay could be seen as being retaliatory rather than defensive in nature. Nevertheless, the relevant factual circumstances must be taken into account. These can include the necessity of gathering of intelligence and evidence relating to the author/source of the attack (particularly relevant to attacks by non-state actors acting either in collusion with a state or on their own volition), the geographical location of an attack (an attack against a remote part of a state's territory may require longer preparations to enable a response), the level of military preparedness of the defending state, the need to comply with constitutional requirements relating to the use of force, the need to obtain diplomatic and/or military support from third states, and so forth. As long as action is undertaken within a reasonable time frame and no undue delay occurs in resorting to measures aimed at providing for an adequate response, taking into account relevant circumstances, there is no forfeiture of the right to exercise self-defence simply on the basis of the fact that a state does not have the means or necessary evidence to enable an instant response to be undertaken.

How do the previously mentioned considerations of a more general nature relate to the duration of the right of self-defence? In a nutshell, as long as a necessity of self–defence continues to exist in the sense of an ongoing attack, which can include occupation of (part of) a state's territory or ongoing military operations aimed at facilitating an attack, or clear evidence of threat of attack in the proximate future persists, the right of self-defence will remain operative. Conversely, if the necessity of self-defence ceases, for example because the attacking state or entity no longer poses a threat or other alternatives have proven to provide an adequate solution (eg an attacking state accepts a ceasefire order from the Security Council and proceeds to withdraw forces and gives adequate assurances of non-repetition), there is no justification for continuing the exercise of self-defence. Considerations relating to proportionality will also play a role. The greater in scale the attack or threat of attack, the more likely that action in self-defence will be of a longer duration in order to counter it. Conversely, a small-scale one-off incident rising to the level of an armed attack will normally not require action in self-defence any longer than is required to repel the attack and would normally be limited in temporal terms to

[11] For a more extensive discussion of the principle of immediacy, see Terry D. Gill, 'The Temporal Dimension of Self-Defence: Anticipation, Preemption, Prevention and Immediacy' in Michael Schmitt and Jelena Pejic (eds), *International Law and Armed Conflict: Exploring the Faultlines* (Leiden: Martinus Nijhoff, 2007), 113, 151–5.

a short duration. Finally, immediacy could play a role in limiting the duration of self-defence to responses carried out within a reasonable period of time after an attack has occurred, taking into account relevant circumstances of the type referred to earlier.

The customary requirements of necessity, proportionality, and immediacy also have a direct relevance to the (continued) legality of any exercise of self-defence in terms of the duration of the exercise of the right. Action taken in the absence of necessity or which is disproportionate in the sense of exceeding what is required to repel an attack and forestall future attack within the proximate future, or which because of undue delay without reasonable grounds thereby extends the exercise of self-defence in temporal terms beyond what is required to repel the attack, loses its legality, and becomes an unlawful use of force, irrespective of whether it was legal at the outset. Self-defence is an inherent right, but one which is subject to legal considerations and the violation of one or more of those considerations can divest the state of its right to continue to exercise it.

IV. The Primacy of the Security Council and the Duration of Self-Defence

The Charter provides for a clear primacy of the Security Council in the maintenance and restoration of international peace and security.[12] This obviously can have a direct impact upon the duration of the (continued) exercise of self-defence, and it is an integral part of the contemporary right of self-defence. This is clear from both the text and underlying purpose of Article 51 of the Charter, as well as from the entire system of collective security laid down in various provisions elsewhere in the Charter. Taken together, these provide the Council with a wide discretion to take the action it deems necessary to react to threats to the peace, breaches of the peace, or acts of aggression. This regulatory framework lays down the maintenance and restoration of peace as the primary objective of the UN, provides the Council with primary responsibility to carry out this objective, and further provides the Council with an array of possible measures it can choose to employ to carry out

[12] UN Charter, Art 24 provides for this role of primacy and should be read in conjunction with Arts 1(1), 27, and Chapter VII. For analysis of this provision, see Simma et al, *The Charter of the United Nations: A Commentary*, 445–9.

this responsibility. In direct relation to the exercise of self-defence, Article 51 provides that this primacy translates into an incorporation of self-defence into the overall regulatory framework relating to the maintenance and restoration of peace and security, specifically in the form of limiting the exercise of self-defence to situations pending an adequate response by the Council, assuming that one is forthcoming.[13]

This means that while it is the prerogative of a state which deems itself to be the object of an armed attack to invoke self-defence, the Security Council has the ultimate authority regarding the taking of measures which may remove the necessity of exercising self-defence. In practice, this does not mean that any measure the Council may choose to take will have that effect, but if the Council's action results in removing the necessity for the exercise of self-defence, there would be no legal basis for continuing its exercise. This raises the question as to who or what decides whether a particular measure taken by the Security Council has the effect of terminating the exercise of self-defence. The short answer is that the Council has the final say. In practice, the Council can endorse an invocation of self-defence, simply take note of such an invocation, or order a state to stand down and cease action. It can also ignore it, which during the first 40 years of its history was what happened most often, but has since become less prevalent. In the situation the Council implicitly or explicitly endorses a particular invocation of self-defence, it is clear that measures it may take will not stand in the way of the exercise of self-defence. The same applies to a situation where the Council either simply takes note of a particular situation, or ignores it. In all of those cases, the right is not affected by the Council's (in)action. Nor does the fact that the Council may choose to take measures aimed at alleviating the situation—such as enforcement measures of a non-military character or the mandating of a UN force or authorization to member states to take 'all necessary measures'—necessarily have the effect of terminating the right of self-defence. Such measures can well be seen as complementary to the exercise of self-defence by one or more states, as was the case in relation to the Kuwait crisis of 1990–1, or the situation in Afghanistan, where the Council implicitly endorsed the (continued) exercise of (collective) self-defence by the US and a number of its allies in response to the 9/11 attacks, while at the same time taking a number of measures not involving the use of force and providing a mandate for the International Security Assistance Force (ISAF)

[13] On the relationship between self-defence and collective security, see inter alia, Schachter, *International Law in Theory and Practice*, 401–4; Dinstein, *War, Aggression and Self-Defence*, 211–16; Rosalyn Higgins, *Problems and Process: International Law and How We Use It* (Oxford: Oxford University Press, 1994), 239–240; Sir Humphrey Waldock, 'The Regulation of the Use of Force by Individual States in International Law' in (1952) 41 *Recueil des cours de l'Académie de droit international* 487–8. The present author's views are set out in more detail in 'Legal and Some Political Limitations on the Power of the UN Security Council to Exercise its Enforcement Powers under Chapter VII of the Charter' in (1995) XXVI *Netherlands Yearbook of International Law* 90–106.

coalition. At no time in either of these situations did the Council indicate or decide that the exercise of self-defence was no longer necessary, much less order the state(s) concerned to stand down. While this can partially be ascribed to the fact that one or more permanent members of the Council were involved in exercising self-defence, this does not mean the Council was prevented from taking such a decision simply by the (threat of) the use of the veto. Indeed, in both cases, the Council repeatedly made clear that the exercise of self-defence was compatible with the measures it had taken, by referring directly or indirectly to the right of self-defence in the relevant resolutions, including the renewal of the mandate for ISAF.[14] It is not plausible to assume that such (implicit) endorsement would be forthcoming if it were simply a question of the Council being unable to issue a stand down order to a permanent member because of the veto. On the other hand, where the Council views the (continued) exercise of self-defence to be incompatible with international peace and security, it does so explicitly, as it did in its ceasefire order to both parties to the Iran/Iraq War in 1987 after six years of warfare had elapsed.[15]

Neither does the endorsement of self-defence in relation to the situation in Afghanistan imply that the Council necessarily endorses (or disapproves) of its exercise in other situations, such as in relation to counter terrorist strikes in Yemen, Somalia, or elsewhere on the basis of an (alleged) connection between the threats posed in these various locations and temporal settings.[16] Since the Council has not (yet) taken a position in relation to those other situations, it is left to the member states and the international community as a whole to determine whether invocations of self-defence in relation to those situations is justified. This depends, in the first instance, upon how one views the organizational and temporal link between the various actors and threats. If they are seen as essentially pursuing a common strategy and engaging in a coordinated series of attacks originating from different locations, but forming a whole, then the possibility of treating them as a single actor and source of threat is opened. If they are seen as separate actors with certain common overall objectives and ideology, but without sufficient coordination and cohesion, it would be stretching self-defence beyond the reasonable to treat them as a common actor. However, assuming for the sake of argument that the former situation were correct, it would then essentially depend upon whether in each case the requirements of necessity, proportionality, and immediacy had been met. If there were feasible alternatives to action in self-defence, such as law

[14] SC Res 2120 (10 October 2013). [15] SC Res 598 (20 July 1987).

[16] The Security Council referred to the right of self-defence in its Resolutions 1368 and 1373 (2001) in connection with the armed attacks of 9/11. It has subsequently referred to all previous resolutions, including these, in its periodic renewal of the mandate for the ISAF, starting with SC Res 1386 (2001) to the most recent, SC Res 2120 (2013).

enforcement, if the reaction was excessive, or the response unduly delayed, the action taken would be unjustified in terms of self-defence. Conversely, if the threat was ongoing, alternatives were unavailable, the actions taken within the confines of what was required to repel or neutralize the threat and were undertaken within a reasonable time frame, the response could be justified in terms of the law of self-defence, which does not automatically equate into compliance or otherwise with other relevant legal considerations, such as the humanitarian law of armed conflict, or human rights law if either or both were applicable, which is outside the scope of our discussion.[17]

In sum, the Council's action can either complement the exercise of self-defence or remove the necessity of its continued exercise. It is the Council which ultimately determines whether a particular measure has removed the necessity, but this will only occur if the Council explicitly so determines. In any case, the Council can also order a cessation of the exercise of self-defence, even in the absence of further action on its part, aside from ordering a general cessation of hostilities and deeming further use of force a threat to or breach of the peace. In the event the ceasefire order has the desired effect, no further exercise of the right of self-defence would be justified. If either side were to ignore the order, this would constitute a new or renewed attack and justify the other party in taking measures of self-defence until the Council had implemented enforcement measures which were adequate under the circumstances to restore the situation. In other words, the Council has the ultimate authority but, as a consequence, also the responsibility to ensure its measures are adequate to address the situation. If it is unable to take such adequate measures, it cannot divest a state which is the object of an ongoing or renewed attack of the right to defend itself, or for that matter disallow third states which elect to assist the defending state from doing so.

[17] The legality of the US counter-terrorist strategy aimed at neutralizing the ability of Al Qaeda and its affiliates to conduct strikes through targeted killings carried out by unmanned aerial vehicles (drones) against suspected terrorist cells located in Pakistan, Yemen, Somalia, and elsewhere, is controversial in a number of ways. In terms of reliance upon self-defence, it would hinge in large measure upon whether the affiliate groups of Al Qaeda acting outside the context of the operations in Afghanistan were seen as part of the same organization which authored both the attacks of 9/11 and subsequent actions directed against US, Afghan, and allied forces operating there, or were instead separate organizations with no clear links to the attacks of 9/11 and subsequent operations in Afghanistan, unless there was clear evidence of separate armed attack(s) launched by all of them which could justify action in self-defence. For a discussion of some of the legal issues involved, see Michael Schmitt, 'Drone Attacks under the *Jus ad Bellum* and *Jus in Bello*: Clearing the "Fog of Law"' (2010) 13 *Yearbook of International Humanitarian Law* 311.

V. Conclusions

Our examination leads to a number of conclusions, which provide a general set of criteria. However, they do not remove the need to review the question of how long reliance upon self-defence may last within a factual context. This takes into account considerations relating to the nature of a particular attack, the existence or lack thereof of feasible alternatives, the scale of the attack and corresponding required scale of a response to repel or neutralize it, and the effects and objectives of any enforcement measures the Security Council may elect to take.

First, the mode of attack will be relevant in determining how long action in self-defence is justified and is closely related to considerations related to necessity and proportionality. Isolated or small-scale attacks will not require prolonged responses, whereas a series of attacks, which have a common source and are carried out over a longer time period, can justify reliance upon self-defence over a long(er) period, provided the attacks are sufficiently interconnected to justify treating them as a whole. Larger scale attacks will probably require a more prolonged response in order to neutralize the threat of continuation or repetition in the proximate future and, if they take the form of initiating a war of aggression, may indeed require a quite prolonged response extending over several months or even years, depending upon the relative strength of the opponents. That was the case with the historical examples of the Second World War and the Korean War and more recently with the Iran–Iraq War. In the response to the invasion of Kuwait, the required response time was shorter (since the opponents were less evenly matched), but nevertheless took a period of several months, from the outset of the initial armed attack until the Security Council-imposed ceasefire was accepted and in place.

Secondly, the customary requirements of necessity, proportionality, and immediacy will have a major influence upon the permissible duration of the response in self-defence. As long as the necessity of self-defence persists, the right of self-defence remains operative. Once the necessity ceases, the right to exercise self-defence terminates. This is true both in relation to the existence of an ongoing attack or manifest threat of attack in the proximate future and the availability, or lack thereof, of feasible alternatives to the exercise of self-defence. Likewise, the scale of the attack, or threat of attack, will have an influence upon the modality of self-defence in terms of duration as stated in the first proposition above and the requirement to undertake self-defence within a reasonable time frame will also influence the duration of its justified exercise, subject to factual and other considerations.

Thirdly, the action or inaction of the Security Council in taking measures of enforcement aimed at restoring the situation will impact upon the duration of the exercise of self-defence, especially in terms of necessity. To the extent that they have the object of precluding further exercise of self-defence, they will terminate the exercise of self-defence provided they have the desired effect and are adequate under the circumstances to remove the necessity of the further exercise of self-defence. If they either do not have the explicit intention of precluding self-defence, or one or both sides fail to comply and engage in further attack, the right of self-defence will remain operative until such time as the Council succeeds in restoring the situation, or the necessity of self-defence no longer exists.

CHAPTER 34

THEATRE OF OPERATIONS

JEAN-CHRISTOPHE MARTIN*

I. Introduction

THE concept of 'theatre of operations'—which replaces in military vocabulary the term 'battlefield', a legal concept not defined in international law—refers in a narrow sense to areas of combat operations, areas or places in which combat operations occur or are progressing, in any kind of armed conflicts.[1] It can be defined in a broad sense as that portion of an area of war necessary for *military operations* and for the administration of such operations. The notion of 'theatre of operations' is used in actual military vocabulary to mean the geographical areas in which military forces conduct any kind of operations, including peace or humanitarian operations (and not only combat operations).[2]

* The author would like warmly to thank his colleague Anne Millet-Devalle for her support in writing this chapter.

[1] An armed conflict exists 'wherever there is a resort to armed force between States or protracted armed violence between governmental authorities and organised armed groups or between such groups within a State': *Prosecutor v. Duško Tadić*, Decision of the Appeals Chamber, 2 Oct 1999, para 70. It should be noted that the character of some military operations (especially those of a counter-terrorist nature) unconnected to an ongoing armed conflict is controversial.

[2] For a definition of the concept of 'military operations', see Terry D. Gill and Dieter Fleck, 'Concept and Sources of the International Law of Military Operations' in Terry D. Gill and Dieter Fleck (eds), *The Handbook of the International Law of Military Operations* (Oxford: Oxford University Press, 2011), 3–4. On the applicability of international humanitarian law to peace operations, see Robert Kolb, Gabriele Porretto, and Sylvain Vité (eds), *L'application du droit international humanitaire et des droits de l'homme aux organisations internationals* (Brussels: Bruylant, 2005), 117–232; Philippe Lagrange, 'Forces des Nations Unies et respect du droit international humanitaire. De l'importance de la notion

This implies that this chapter focuses on the geographical limitation to the use of force by belligerents, what could be called the 'boundaries of the battlefield'. The question is of great interest, according to many recent developments that tend to extend the concept of 'theatre of operations': military use of drones (or Unmanned Aerial Vehicles),[3] or the doctrines of 'war on terrorism'[4] and 'targeted killings'[5] raise questions, among others, on the locus of military operations. In the same way, developing concern about 'cyber warfare' introduces the evanescent concept of 'cyber theatre of operations'.[6]

The question of how the 'theatre of operations' is defined encompasses two main legal issues. The first is to determine where the parties to an armed conflict have the right to conduct military operations; and the second relates to the applicable law to armed operations conducted beyond the borders of a state and, more precisely, whether the law of armed conflicts applies to the operations in question. In a first approach, it can be affirmed that a 'theatre of operations' must take place in the 'area of war', where military operations can be exclusively conducted. During an armed conflict, the belligerents do not have the right to conduct military operations wherever they want; the scope of the area of war is not unlimited and therefore belligerents do not have the right to extend the theatre of operations beyond those geographic limits. It must be emphasized that this geographic parameter is a question of right/obligation of the parties to the conflict, and not a question of the scope of application *ratione loci* of the international law of armed conflicts, that applies

de participation aux hostilités' in Abdelwahab Biad and Paul Tavernier (eds), *Le droit international humanitaire face aux défis du XXI siècle* (Brussels: Bruylant, 2012), 291–311.

[3] See Jordan J. Paust, 'Remotely Piloted Warfare as a Challenge to the *Jus ad Bellum*', Chapter 51 in this volume. A drone or 'UAV' is a pilotless aircraft, designed to be remotely controlled, used for reconnaissance, and, more recently, for launching aerial attacks. 'When a drone strike occurs within a recognized and accepted theater of active arm conflict, such as Afghanistan or Irak, there is virtually no question that the attack is covered by the *lex specialis* of armed conflict by virtue of geography. However, when such an attack occurs in areas outside the traditional, geographically limited "hot" battlefield, reasonable people disagree on whether the operation is or should be covered by the law of armed conflict': Ryan J. Vogel, 'Drone Warfare and the Law of Armed Conflict' (2010) 39 *Denver Journal of International Law and Policy* 130. See also Michael W. Lewis, 'Drones and the Boundaries of the Battlefield' (2012) 47 *Texas International Law Journal* 293.

[4] See Marco Sassoli, 'Use and Abuse of the Laws of War in the "War on Terrorism"' (2004) 22 *Law and Inequality* 195; Anne-Marie Slaughter and William Burke-White, 'An International Constitutional Moment' (2002) 43 *Harvard International Law Journal* 1.

[5] See Nils Melzer, *Targeted Killing in International Law* (Oxford: Oxford University Press, 2008), 468; Gabriella Blum and Philip Heymann, 'Law and Policy of Targeted Killings' (2010) *Harvard Law School National Security Journal*, available at <http://harvardnsj.org/2010/06/law-and-policy-of-targeted-killing/> and Jean-Christophe Martin, 'Les assassinats ciblés de terroristes présumés et l'argument de la nécessité', SFDI, *La nécessité en droit international*, Actes du Colloque de Grenoble (Paris: Pedone, 2007), 297–306.

[6] See Michael N. Schmitt, 'The Use of Cyber Force and International Law', Chapter 52 in this volume. 'Cyber theatre of operations' has been presented for instance as another theatre of operations for the US military, Declaration of the Vice Chairman of the Joint Chiefs of Staff (2009); see Jim Garamone, American Forces Press Service, Questions Abound in Cyber Theater of Operations, Washington DC, 9 June 2009, available at <http://www.defense.gov/news/newsarticle.aspx?id=54709>.

even to 'illicit' theatres of operation, that is, even if the attacks take place in a zone where military operations should not be conducted. The international law of armed conflict applies to those attacks, wherever they occur.[7]

As military operations have been conducted on land, at sea, and in the air, rules have been progressively defined to apply to ground warfare, sea warfare, and aerial warfare. The basic rules and principles of international humanitarian law apply to all theatres of operations be they land, sea, or air, and certainly also apply, *mutatis mutandis*, to attacks conducted in outer space and cyberspace. This chapter does not suppose to present these rules but it can, however, be emphasized that it is a fundamental principle of international law of armed conflicts that a 'theatre of operations' is not a free-fire zone; and the rights of the parties to the conflict to choose methods or means of warfare, as well as the objectives of attack, are not unlimited. Military operations, wherever they take place, can only be conducted against military objectives, excluding both the civilian population and civilian property; a principal distinction which applies to sea, land, and aerial warfare. The concept of 'total war', meaning that the means and objectives of warfare are unlimited since the territory of the enemy constitutes a military objective as a whole (ie all nationals and property participate in the nation's effort for the prosecution of war through complete mobilization of its population and resources), has been applied during the 20th century. This conception, which blurs the fundamental principle of the distinction between military and non-military objectives, was abandoned as such after the Second World War (although it appears by devious means in certain contemporary doctrinal attempts to enlarge the definition of a military objective[8]).

Furthermore, if 'theatres of operation' must be portions of an 'area of war', combat operations cannot take place anywhere inside that area; indeed, 'protected zones' can be established in an area of war. As attacks are prohibited in such zones according to the international law of armed conflicts, they constitute limitations to the theatre of operations (*ratione loci* criterium). Linked to the question of the locus of military operations (but, rather, constituting a *ratione materiae* criterium),

[7] Robert Kolb, *Ius in bello. Le droit international des conflits armés* (Brussels: Helding & Lichtenhahn/Bruylant, 2003), 106, § 222. It can be added that the international law of armed conflicts also applies to the entire territory of the belligerent states, even those parts where no hostile acts are conducted, ie beyond the theatre of operations. More precisely, 'Although the Geneva Conventions are silent as to the geographical scope of international "armed conflicts," the provisions suggest that at least some of the provisions of the Conventions apply to the entire territory of the Parties to the conflict, not just to the vicinity of actual hostilities. Certainly, some of the provisions are clearly bound up with the hostilities and the geographical scope of those provisions should be so limited. Others, particularly those relating to the protection of prisoners of war and civilians, are not so limited... the rules contained in Article 3 (of Protocol I to the Geneva Conventions) also apply outside the narrow geographical context of the actual theatre of combat operations': ICTY, Appeals Chamber, Decision on the Defence Motion for Interlocutory Appeal on Jurisdiction, 2 Oct 1995, *Tadić* case, § 68.

[8] Robert Kolb, *Ius in bello*, 67–8.

it should also be noted that some property—monuments of architectural, artistic, or historical interest, whether religious or secular; groups of buildings which, as a whole, are of historical or artistic interest; archaeological sites, etc[9]—whilst located in the area of warfare, where combat operations can take place, are given special protection. As such, they enjoy immunity and as a consequence are excluded from the theatre of operations. States parties to the Convention for the Protection of Cultural Property in the Event of Armed Conflict (1954) 'undertake to ensure the immunity of cultural property under special protection by refraining, from the time of entry in the International Register, from any act of hostility directed against such property'.[10] The restatement of existing rules of customary law of armed conflicts does not contain a general prohibition of attacks on those properties, which can be military objectives or objects of attacks if this is imperative as a result of military necessity.[11] However, 'all... destruction or wilful damage done to institutions dedicated to religion, charity, education, the arts and sciences, historic monuments and works of art and science is prohibited'.[12] In the same way, it should be underlined that under the general principles of the conduct of hostilities 'No part of the natural environment may be attacked, unless it is a military objective' and 'destruction of any part of the natural environment is prohibited, unless required by imperative military necessity'.[13]

This question of the areas of warfare primarily concerns the *jus in bello*[14] but considerations relating to *jus ad bellum* (authorization to use force by the Security

[9] The notion of 'cultural property' is defined in Art 1 of the Convention for the Protection of Cultural Property in the Event of Armed Conflict (1954) as: 'movable or immovable property of great importance to the cultural heritage of every people, such as monuments of architecture, art or history, whether religious or secular; archaeological sites; groups of buildings which, as a whole, are of historical or artistic interest; works of art; manuscripts, books and other objects of artistic, historical or archaeological interest; as well as scientific collections and important collections of books or archives or of reproductions of the property defined above'.

[10] Art 9 of the Convention of 1954. See also Arts 7 and 9 of the Second Protocol of 26 Mar 1999 to the Hague Convention of 1954. This Second Protocol (Arts 10–14) also establishes a different system of protection not relying on the criterion of military necessity: cultural property of the greatest importance for humanity can be placed under 'enhanced protection' provided it is adequately protected by domestic law and not used for military purposes or to shield military sites. This protection is granted from the moment of entry in the List of Cultural Property Under Enhanced Protection. Art 12 states: 'The Parties to a conflict shall ensure the immunity of cultural property under enhanced protection by refraining from making such property the object of attack from any use of the property or its immediate surroundings in support of military action'.

[11] Rule 38 of the ICRC Handbook on *Customary International Humanitarian Law*: 'Special care must be taken in military operations to avoid damage to buildings dedicated to religion, art, science, education or charitable purposes and historic monuments unless they are military objectives'; 'Property of great importance to the cultural heritage of every people must not be the object of attack unless imperatively required by military necessity'. See rules 39 and 40.

[12] Rule 40 of the ICRC Handbook. [13] Rule 43 of the ICRC Handbook.

[14] The relevant sources of law are the First and Fourth Geneva Conventions of 1949 and Additional Protocols I and II, and customary international law applicable to armed conflicts. Identification of the customary rules has been realized by four main private codification projects (which may include a

Council and self-defence) and even actions taken by the Security Council in reaction to armed conflicts (creation of 'security zones') have to be taken into account. As *jus in bello* and security zones established by the Security Council will be analysed in this chapter, two other points should be made at this juncture. When the Security Council authorizes states, under Chapter VII of the UN Charter, to conduct military operations, it can decide on the geographical scope of that authorization. Therefore the theatre of those operations is expressly limited in the authorization and armed forces of the states participating in the implementation of the resolution are not allowed to conduct attacks in any other location. Such attacks would, as a consequence, constitute violations of international law. When a state uses armed force against another in a situation considered to be in self-defence, the international law of armed conflict applies. But the specific regime of self-defence will produce repercussions for the theatre of operations. Armed operations taken by a state in self-defence must respect the principles of necessity and proportionality, and these principles may certainly limit the area where military attacks can take place. The nature of the target and the scale of the operations of self-defence—both aspects of the criteria of necessity and proportionality[15]—are in fact parameters that limit the 'theatre of operations'. This also results from the aim that actions in self-defence must follow: to terminate the armed attack.

The following sections will consider three issues relating to the 'theatre of operations': the geographical extent of the areas of military operations (Section II), the 'protected zones' in which military operations are excluded under the international law of armed conflicts (Section III), and security zones defined by the Security Council as zones excluded from the area of war, that cannot be classified as part of the theatre of operations (Section IV).

dimension of progressive development that must eventually be taken into account). Weighty authority is attached to these restatements, which are of great interest for this study:

- *San Remo Manual on International Law Applicable to Armed Conflicts at Sea* (Cambridge: International Institute of Humanitarian Law/Cambridge University Press, 1994);
- The 'Harvard Manual' on International Law Applicable to Air and Missile Warfare (Program on Humanitarian Policy and Conflict Research at Harvard University), 15 May 2009;
- The ICRC Handbook: Jean-Marie Henckaerts and Louise Doswald-Beck (eds), *Customary International Humanitarian Law* (Cambridge: ICRC/Cambridge University Press, 2006 (French version) and 2009 (English version));
- Michael N. Schmitt (ed), *Tallinn Manual on the International Law Applicable to Cyber Warfare* (Cambridge: Cambridge University Press, 2013).

[15] *Oil Platforms (Iran v. US)*, Judgment of 6 Nov 2003, ICJ Rep 2003, paras 74 and 77.

II. Geographical Extent of the Areas of Military Operations

During an armed conflict, the area of war where military operations can take place is limited and we can affirm as a first approach that military operations cannot be conducted on the territory of states not parties to the armed conflict and the territory of neutral states. Zones located in the territory of belligerent states can even be excluded from the theatre of operations, which is not the case with so-called 'exclusion zones', that are zones of warfare.

A. Warfare Area

As a starting point, 'the answer for how the boundaries of the battlefield and the scope of IHL's [international humanitarian law's] application can be properly determined is found in neutrality law'.[16] The geographical limitations of the area of war is a result of the status of neutrality of states. This classification has been extended to states not taking part in the conflict,[17] and international law includes a general prohibition of conducting hostilities in neutral territory (in the sense of territory of states that are not parties to the conflict). The territory of neutral/non-belligerent states—in respect of land but also in their internal and territorial waters and in the airspace above their territory—is excluded from the area of warfare. There is, however, a general exception to this principle: if a neutral/non-belligerent state allows one of the belligerents to conduct military operations on its territory, other belligerents have the right to conduct military operations in that territory in order to stop the operations permitted by the neutral/non-belligerent state.

In principle, military forces can only conduct combat operations on the territories of the parties to the conflict and, during non-international armed conflicts, military operations must also be limited to the territory (including the territorial sea and national airspace) of the state in which the conflict is taking place. This traditional view is, however, debatable and, in the light of the conflict in Afghanistan and the transnational military operations conducted against terrorists, many commentators and even states now tend to affirm that the theatre of operations of such conflicts can be extended beyond the boundaries of that state, 'arguing this is the status of the actors, not geography, which is the determinative factor in classification

[16] Michael W. Lewis, 'Drones and the Boundaries of the Battlefield' (2012) 47 *Texas International Law Journal* 314.

[17] On the erosion of the status of neutral states, see Maurice Torrelli, 'La neutralité' (1991) 35 *Annales de Droit International Medical* 25.

of conflict'.[18] At present, this question is controversial.[19] It is, nevertheless, rather difficult to admit as a principle that, even if persons planning or conducting attacks are located in the territory of a 'third' state (as in the case of Pakistan in relation to the conflict in Afghanistan), an area of war could be de jure extended to portions of the territory of that state and, as a consequence, permitting the conduct of operations within those areas without the consent of that state.

That said, the area of war is traditionally limited to the territories of the parties to the conflict, including the maritime and aerial elements, to the high seas, and the exclusive economic zones (EEZs) and international airspace.[20] The question of the limits of the theatre of operations has moreover to be addressed in the context of space warfare and cyber warfare.

1. *On land*

As a principle resulting from the concept of state sovereignty, the territories of neutral/non-belligerent states are excluded from the area of war (cf the previous discussion). Belligerents are not permitted to conduct hostile operations beyond the borders of the states parties to an international armed conflict, or beyond the borders of the state in which a non-international armed conflict is taking place. On land, the area of war is thus limited to the terrestrial territory of the belligerent states, delimited by their boundaries and including rivers and landlocked lakes. Within these borders, all the territory of the parties to the conflict (every area, wherever located, belonging to the jurisdiction of those states) can constitute an area of military operations.

Beyond this principle, states can decide through contractual agreements[21] to keep so-called 'neutralized zones' outside the area of warfare. Thus, no operations may take place in these zones even during an armed conflict and 'even if the state to whose area of jurisdiction they belong is a party to the conflict'.[22] Spitsbergen, the

[18] *Tallinn Manual*, 71.

[19] Vogel, 'Drone Warfare and the Law of Armed Conflict', 130–3. For this author: 'The argument that a conflict with a non-state actor must be confined to a geographical boundary may seem appealing to some, but it is not supported by law or custom and it becomes dangerously illogical when applied to conflicts that by their nature cross borders and by definition are not between or among territorially limited states'.

[20] See Dieter Fleck and Michael Bothe (eds), *The Handbook of Humanitarian Law in Armed Conflicts* (New York: Oxford University Press, 1995), paras 215–20.

[21] The 1921 Convention on the Demilitarisation and Neutralisation of the Åland Islands, concluded by ten states, or the 1959 Antarctic Treaty, binding upon 50 states parties (Art I, para 1) are examples.

[22] Christopher Greenwood, 'Scope of Application of Humanitarian Law' in Fleck and Bothe, *The Handbook of Humanitarian Law in Armed Conflicts*, 52, para 219. 'However, if an attack is made against, or an invasion into, the neutralised territory, or if there is a danger of such an attack or invasion, the State exercising sovereignty over the neutralised territory is permitted to take military measures to defend the territory': Lauri Hannikainen, 'The Continued Validity of the Demilitarised and Neutralised Status of the Åland Islands' (1994) 54 *Zeitschrift für ausländisches öffentliches Recht und Völkerrecht* 616.

Åland islands, the Suez Canal, the Panama Canal, and the Antarctic regions are, for instance, neutralized zones.

2. *At sea*

At sea, the area of war includes zones under the sovereignty of the states parties to the conflict; that is, internal and territorial waters. It also extends to maritime areas that are not under the sovereignty of any state. In the application of this principle, military operations can take place on the high seas, and also in the EEZs, even of neutral states.[23] In effect, the EEZs of neutral states are not considered to be an element of their territory, and are in consequence part of the area of war. According to rule 10 of the *San Remo Manual on International Law Applicable to Armed Conflicts at Sea* (12 June 1994):

hostile actions by naval forces may be conducted in, on or over:

(a) the territorial sea and internal waters, the land territories, the exclusive economic zone and continental shelf and, where applicable, the archipelagic waters, of belligerent States;
(b) the high seas; and
(c) subject to paragraphs 34 and 35, the exclusive economic zone and the continental shelf of neutral States.

Where hostile action takes place on the high seas, in the EEZ of a neutral state, or a state not party to the conflict, belligerents are under an obligation to have due regard to the rights of other states: 'exercise by neutral states of rights of exploration and exploitation of the natural resources of the sea-bed, and ocean floor, and the subsoil thereof'[24] on the high seas; and in the case of operations in the EEZ of a neutral state or a state not party to the conflict, 'exploration and exploitation of the economic resources of the exclusive economic zone and the continental shelf and the protection and preservation of the marine environment'.[25]

3. *In the air*

The airspace above the terrestrial and maritime territory of belligerent states is a zone of air and missile warfare. Likewise, the airspace above the high seas, contiguous zones, EEZs, and territories not subject to the sovereignty of any state (eg Antarctica and the Arctic)—the so-called 'international airspace'—can also be a warfare zone. Customary international law prohibits belligerent parties from conducting hostilities in the airspace of states not taking part in the armed hostilities. According to rule 167(a) of the Program on Humanitarian Policy and Conflict Research (HCPR), Manual on

[23] On EEZs, see Art 58 of the United Nations Convention on the Law of the Sea of 10 December 1982, 1833 UNTS 3.

[24] Rule 36 of the *San Remo Manual.*

[25] See rules 34 and 35 of the *San Remo Manual.*

International Law Applicable to Air and Missile Warfare:[26] 'Belligerent Parties are prohibited in neutral territory to conduct any hostile actions, establish bases of operations or use such territory as a sanctuary. Furthermore, neutral territory must not be used by Belligerent Parties for the movement of troops or supplies, including overflights by military aircraft or missiles, or for the operation of military communication systems.' In principle, a belligerent military aircraft may not even enter the airspace of neutral states and 'any incursion or transit by a belligerent military aircraft (including a UAV/UCAV [unmanned aerial vehicle/unmanned combat air vehicle]) or missile into or through neutral airspace is prohibited' (rule 170(a)).[27]

4. *In outer space*

The theatre of operations could potentially be extended in the future to outer space, and 'space warfare', meaning combat that takes place outside the atmosphere,[28] could become reality. The 1967 Outer Space Treaty, that provides for the demilitarization of celestial bodies and their utilization only for peaceful purposes, 'does not limit military activities in the space between celestial bodies, the outer void space, except for the prohibition of weapons of mass destruction and the application of general international law, including the UN Charter'.[29] The rules of general international law certainly apply to the use of force in outer void space, not only those of the UN Charter but also the law of armed conflict.[30] No legal instrument has been adopted to develop international law of armed conflict to encompass space warfare, as no armed conflict has yet occurred in space. Thus, there is still uncertainty about the applicable legal rules to a military confrontation in outer space. We can, however, assume, according to the specificities of outer space, that 'it cannot be held beforehand that the corpus of the law of armed conflicts applies *in toto* to armed conflict in outer void space because of the unique

[26] Section X (rules 166–75) of the manual is dedicated to 'neutrality', a notion that means the status of a state not a belligerent party in an international armed conflict. See the commentary, 305 ff. See also Anne-Sophie Millet, 'La neutralité aérienne' (1991) 35 *Annales de Droit International Médical* 63–81.

[27] This principle has the following exception: rule 172 of the HCPR Manual.

[28] The vertical limit between the airspace constituting the national territory of a state and outer space is defined as the altitude at which the density of the air permits the employment of satellites. According to the commentary of the HCPR Manual, 'Air' or 'airspace' means the air up to the highest altitude at which an aircraft can fly and below the lowest possible perigee of an earth satellite in orbit. On the topics of definition and status of outer space, see Bin Cheng, 'The Legal Status of Outer Space and Relevant Issues: Delimitation of Outer Space and Definition of Peaceful Use' (1983) 11 *Journal of Space Law* 89 and Bin Cheng, *Studies in International Space Law* (Oxford: Clarendon Press, 1997).

[29] Arjen Vermeer, 'The Laws of War in Outer Space: Some Legal Implications for the *Jus ad Bellum* and the *Jus in Bello* of the Militarisation and Weaponisation of Outer Space' in Julia Boll (ed), *War: Interdisciplinary Investigations* (Oxford: Inter-disciplinary Press, 2008) available at <http://inter-disciplinary.net/ptb/wvw/wvw4/Vermeer%20paper.pdf>.

[30] See Michael N. Schmitt, 'Targeting in Operational Law' in Terry D. Gill and Dieter Fleck (eds), *The Handbook of the International Law of Military Operations* (Oxford: Oxford University Press, 2011), 245–6.

environment it presents'.[31] This question remains debatable but, owing especially to the specificities of the space environment and the dual use of most satellites, the applicability of many fundamental principles of international law of armed conflict (proportionality of attacks, military necessity, reduction or avoidance of collateral damage to the environment and to civilians or civilian objects) is problematic. For instance, in warfare the issue of fragments resulting from destruction of objects (mainly satellites)—that can remain orbiting the Earth as space debris—is of particular concern according to the rules of international law of armed conflicts prohibiting attacks the effects of which are indiscriminate[32] and/or disproportionate,[33] and to the rule prohibiting the use of methods or means of warfare that are 'intended, or may be expected, to cause widespread, long-term and severe damage to the natural environment'.[34]

5. *In cyberspace*

Cyber warfare raises a number of complex issues relating to the applicability of classic provisions of *jus ad bellum* and *jus in bello*. The *Tallinn Manual on the International Law Applicable to Cyber Warfare* tackles cyber warfare issues.[35] Rule 20 of the Manual provides that the law of armed conflict applies to cyber operations executed in the context of an armed conflict. Rule 21 of the Manual provides that 'cyber operations are subject to geographical limitations imposed by the relevant provisions of international law applicable during an armed conflict'. The Manual defends the application of the classical rules of international law of armed conflict to cyber warfare: 'as a rule, cyber operations may be conducted from, on or with effects in the entire territory of the parties to the conflict, international waters or airspace and, subject to certain limitations, outer space. Cyber operations are generally prohibited elsewhere. Of particular importance in this regard is the law of neutrality because cyber operations can transit neutral territory and may have unintended effects therein'.[36] This rule is intended to apply the 'cyber theatre of operations'

[31] Gill and Fleck, *The Handbook of the International Law of Military Operations*, 7. See also P. J. Blount, 'Targeting in Outer Space: Legal Aspects of Operational Military Actions in Space', Harvard National Security Journal Features (2012), available at <http://harvardnsj.org/wp-content/uploads/2012/11/Targeting-in-Outer-Space-Blount-Final.pdf>.

[32] See rule 12 of the ICRC Handbook on 'indiscriminate attacks' that defines indiscriminate attacks as those which 'employ a method or means of combat the effects of which cannot be limited as required by' international law.

[33] See rule 14 of the ICRC Handbook on 'proportionality in attack': 'Launching an attack which may be expected to cause incidental loss of civilian life, injury to civilians, damage to civilian objects, or a combination thereof, which would be excessive in relation to the concrete and direct military advantage anticipated, is prohibited'.

[34] Rule 45 of the ICRC Handbook; rule 44 states that 'Methods and means of warfare must be employed with due regard to the protection and preservation of the natural environment. In the conduct of military operations, all feasible precautions must be taken to avoid, and in any event to minimize, incidental damage to the environment'.

[35] At 300. The handbook was written at the invitation of the NATO Cooperative Cyber Defence Centre of Excellence.

[36] *Tallinn Manual*, 71.

strictly to the same geographical limits that international law applies to the dimensions (land, sea, air) of warfare, without permitting any exception. The matter is therefore quite complex due to the different types and methods of cyber operations. And it is noteworthy that rule 167(b) of the HCPR Manual on International Law Applicable to Air and Missile Warfare, dedicated to the use of networks such as the Internet, affirms that: 'when Belligerent Parties use for military purposes a public, internationally and openly accessible network such as the Internet, the fact that part of this infrastructure is situated within the jurisdiction of a Neutral does not constitute a violation of neutrality'.

B. Aerial and Maritime 'Exclusion Zones'

It is worth drawing attention to the concept of 'exclusion zones' which should not be misunderstood. So-called 'exclusion zones' are not zones in which attacks are excluded; on the contrary, in such zones parties to an armed conflict unilaterally decide to limit or even prohibit sailing or flying and, in fact, this limitation or prohibition is intended to permit the use of force against ships or planes entering the zone notwithstanding the prohibition.[37] It is indeed clear that such zones are part of the theatre of operations under the control of military forces.

A belligerent state can declare a 'maritime exclusion zone', where ships and planes entering the zone can be attacked. For example, the UK declared such zones during the Falklands/Malvinas war in 1982.[38] The belligerent can neither declare that the exclusion zone is too large an area, nor decide that the law of armed conflicts will not be applied in the zone.[39] The same rules apply when such zones are established in airspace: a belligerent state can unilaterally establish 'exclusion zones' in international airspace or no-fly zones in its own, or in enemy, national airspace.[40] In both cases, the belligerent party is not absolved of its obligations under the law of international armed conflict by establishing 'exclusion zones' or 'no-fly zones' and

[37] 'Subject to the Rules set out in Sections D and G of this Manual, aircraft entering a no-fly zone without specific permission are liable to be attacked': rule 110 of the HCPR Manual.

[38] See Sylvie-Stoyanka Junod, *La protection des victimes du conflit armé des îles Falkland-Malvinas (1982): droit international humanitaire et action humanitaire* (Geneva: International Committee of the Red Cross, 1985), 45; L. F. E. Goldie, 'Maritime War Zones & Exclusion Zones' (1991) 64 *International Law Studies* 171–4; Wolff Heintschel von Heinegg, 'Current Legal Issues in Maritime Operations: Maritime Interception Operations in the Global War on Terrorism, Exclusion Zones, Hospital Ships and Maritime Neutrality' (2006) 80 *International Law Studies* 216–17.

[39] See rules 105–8 of the *San Remo Manual*. According to rule 106, 'the extent, location and duration of the zone and the measures imposed shall not exceed what is strictly required by military necessity and the principle of proportionality'.

[40] Arts 105–10 of the HCPR Manual. According to rule 107, 'The extent, location and duration of the "exclusion zone" and the measures imposed must not exceed what is reasonably required by military necessity'. According to rule 109, 'The commencement, duration, location and extent of the no-fly zones must be appropriately notified to all concerned'.

'Zones designated for unrestricted air or missile attacks are prohibited' (rule 105 of the HCPR Manual), as emphasized by rule 107(a): 'The same rules of the law of international armed conflict will apply both inside and outside the "exclusion zone".'

III. Zones in Which Military Operations are Excluded: 'Protected Zones'

The international law of armed conflict prohibits military operations in certain zones of protection, which constitute enclaves in the area of war that cannot be theatres of operation. Norms excluding attacks against such zones are defined in treaties and also in customary laws of war. Four types of protected zones can be distinguished. Three types of which can only be created by the conclusion of an agreement between the parties to the conflict. A 'non-defended locality', that remains an area of war but under a specific protection status, can be created by a unilateral declaration of a belligerent.

A. Zones Created by Agreement Between the Parties to the Conflict

Zones located in the territory of parties to a conflict may be excluded from the area of war if the parties agree to such exclusion. These zones are removed from the theatre of operations by the parties themselves, through the conclusion of an agreement (written or even verbal); however, a unilateral declaration by one party does not result in the creation of a protected zone, without the formal acceptance of other belligerents. Draft agreements are attached to the Geneva Conventions to serve as a model and facilitate the conclusion of such agreements.[41] However, in practice there are few examples of such agreements.

1. *Hospital and safety zones*

The First and Fourth Geneva Conventions provide for the possibility of setting up hospital and safety zones.

[41] Draft agreement relating to hospital zones and localities, Annex I, First Geneva Convention; Draft agreement relating to hospital and safety zones and localities, Annex I, Fourth Geneva Convention.

Article 23 of the First Geneva Convention for the Amelioration of the Condition of the Wounded and Sick in Armed Forces in the Field provides: 'In time of peace, the High Contracting Parties and, after the outbreak of hostilities, the Parties thereto, may establish *in their own territory and, if the need arises, in occupied areas*, hospital zones and localities so organized as to protect the wounded and sick from the effects of war, as well as the personnel entrusted with the organization and administration of these zones and localities and with the care of the persons therein assembled'.

Article 14 of the Fourth Geneva Convention relative to the Protection of Civilian Persons in Time of War extends this rule to the protection from the effects of war of 'wounded, sick and aged persons, children under fifteen, expectant mothers and mothers of children under seven'.

To this end, parties to an armed conflict may, on the outbreak and during the course of hostilities, as per Article 14, 'conclude agreements on mutual recognition of the hospital zones and localities they have created'. Furthermore, 'The Protecting Powers and the International Committee of the Red Cross (ICRC) are invited to lend their good offices in order to facilitate the institution and recognition of these hospital zones and localities'.

According to the ICRC Handbook: 'Directing an attack against a zone established to shelter the wounded, the sick and civilians from the effects of hostilities is prohibited' (rule 35). Customary law prohibits attacks on hospital and safety zones.

2. *Neutralized zones*

The prohibition of attacks on neutralized zones—which is a customary rule[42]—was set up by Article 15 of the Fourth Geneva Convention. A neutralized zone is a zone established in the regions where fighting is taking place and 'intended to shelter from the effects of war the following persons, without distinction: (a) wounded and sick combatants or non-combatants; (b) civilian persons who take no part in hostilities, and who, while they reside in the zones, perform no work of a military character'. The two key differences between 'neutralized zones' and 'hospital and safety zones' are, first, that all civilians have access to neutralized zones, if they do not take part in hostilities, whereas hospital and safety zones only concern certain types of person with a more restrictive scope; and, secondly, that neutralized zones should be created in areas of combat operations, whereas hospital and safety zones can be remote from such areas.

Neutralized zones are established by the conclusion of a written agreement by the parties to the conflict, fixing the beginning and the duration of the neutralization of the zone. The agreement supposes that parties 'have agreed upon the geographical position, administration, food supply and supervision of the proposed neutralized

[42] Rule 35 of the ICRC Handbook (cf the previous discussion) encompasses neutralized zones.

zone'. Such zones had been established by Croatia and the Socialist Federal Republic of Yugoslavia in agreements concluded in 1991: the Memorandum of Understanding on the application of IHL established neutralized zones at the Franciscan monastery and the New Hospital in Dubrovnik. An agreement had also been specifically concluded to establish a protected zone around the hospital in Osijek.[43] These zones were all placed under the supervision of the ICRC. It should be noted that, during the Falklands/Malvinas war, belligerent parties concluded an agreement creating neutralized zones in the high seas (called Red Cross Box) in order to protect both states' hospital ships. This constitutes an interesting innovation in the law of armed conflicts.[44]

3. *Demilitarized zones*

The prohibition of extending military operations to demilitarized zones is defined in Article 60 of Additional Protocol I to the Geneva Conventions relating to the Protection of Victims of Non-International Armed Conflicts. This article, inspired by the concept of safety zones defined in Article 14 of the Fourth Geneva Convention, states in its first paragraph that 'it is prohibited for the Parties to the conflict to extend their military operations to zones on which they have conferred by agreement the status of a demilitarised zone, if such extension is contrary to the terms of this agreement'.[45] A demilitarized zone, opened to any non-combatant, is defined as 'any zone which fulfils the following conditions: (a) all combatants, as well as mobile weapons and mobile military equipment, must have been evacuated; (b) no hostile use shall be made of fixed military installations or establishments;(c) no acts of hostility shall be committed by the authorities or by the population; and (d) any activity linked to the military effort must have ceased'. It is mentioned in paragraph 2 that the agreement (which shall be an express agreement, concluded verbally or in writing), whenever it is concluded (in peacetime, as well as after the outbreak of hostilities) 'should define and describe, as precisely as possible, the limits of the demilitarized zone and, if necessary, lay down the methods of supervision'. Paragraph 5 also provides that the party which is in control of such a zone shall mark it, as far as possible, by such signs as may be agreed upon with the other party, which shall be displayed where they are clearly visible, especially on its perimeter and limits, and on highways. The demilitarized zone loses its status if one of the parties to the conflict commits a material breach of the provisions of paragraph 3 or 6; that is, the other party is released from its obligations under the agreement conferring on the zone the status

[43] Jean-Marie Henckaerts and Louise Doswald-Beck (eds), *Customary International Humanitarian Law, Vol II: Practice, Part 1* (Cambridge: ICRC/Cambridge University Press, 2005), 672.

[44] Eric David, *Principes de droit des conflits armés* (4th edn, Brussels: Bruylant, 2002), 319.

[45] According to para 6: 'If the fighting draws near to a demilitarized zone, and if the Parties to the conflict have so agreed, none of them may use the zone for purposes related to the conduct of military operations or unilaterally revoke its status'.

of a demilitarized zone. Although the zone loses its specific protection status but, in this case, the other rules of international law applicable in armed conflict obviously apply to the zone. It should be added that making a demilitarized zone the object of an attack is a grave breach of Additional Protocol I (Art 85(3)(d) I).

Rule 36 of the handbook on *Customary International Law of Armed Conflicts*, presented as a norm of customary international law applicable in both international and non-international armed conflicts, reads as follows: 'Directing an attack against a demilitarized zone agreed upon between the parties to the conflict is prohibited'. According to the commentary on this rule, 'A demilitarized zone is generally understood to be an area, agreed upon between the parties to the conflict, which cannot be occupied or used for military purposes by any party to the conflict'.

B. Non-Defended Localities

Non-defended localities (the modern expression for 'open towns'[46]), unilaterally defined as such by a belligerent without agreement,[47] are parts of the warfare area but are under a special protection status. A party to the conflict declares that the particular locality is non-defended and that no hostile acts will be perpetrated from the area. As a consequence of the concept of military necessity and the principle which prohibits destruction that is not absolutely necessary, international law prohibits an attack on a non-defended locality—that is, a locality of which an enemy could take possession without conducting any hostilities. Attacks against such zones are prohibited even if military objectives are located within the territory. Although military operations are totally excluded, the locality can be occupied by the armed forces,[48] without any resistance. This is the object of Article 59 of Additional Protocol I (reiterating Art 25 of the Regulations Respecting the Laws and Customs of War on Land) that prohibits 'for the Parties to the conflict to attack, by any means whatsoever, non-defended localities' (para 1). According to rule 37 of the *Handbook on Customary Law*, 'Directing an attack against a non-defended locality is prohibited' which is applicable in both international and non-international armed conflicts. A party to the conflict may declare as a non-defended locality 'any inhabited place

[46] R. Y. Jennings, 'Open Towns' (1945) 22 *British Yearbook of International Law* 258–63.

[47] Art 59(5) of Additional Protocol I recognizes the right for belligerents to establish a non-defended locality by agreement: 'The Parties to the conflict may agree on the establishment of non-defended localities even if such localities do not fulfil the conditions laid down in paragraph 2. The agreement should define and describe, as precisely as possible, the limits of the non-defended locality; if necessary, it may lay down the methods of supervision'. Art 59(6) defines exactly the same duty for the party which is in control of a locality governed by such an agreement to mark it by signs agreed upon with the other Party.

[48] Fleck and Bothe, *The Handbook of Humanitarian Law in Armed Conflicts*, 52, para 218.

near or in a zone where armed forces are in contact which is open for occupation by an adverse Party', provided four cumulative conditions are fulfilled:

(a) all combatants, as well as mobile weapons and mobile military equipment must have been evacuated;
(b) no hostile use shall be made of fixed military installations or establishments;
(c) no acts of hostility shall be committed by the authorities or by the population; and
(d) no activities in support of military operations shall be undertaken.

When a locality ceases to fulfil these conditions, it loses its status as a non-defended locality. Furthermore, according to paragraph 4, the unilateral declaration of a non-defended locality 'shall be addressed to the adverse Party and shall define and describe, as precisely as possible, the limits of the non-defended locality'.

It should be noted that making a non-defended locality the object of an attack is a grave breach according to Additional Protocol I (Arts 59(1) and 85(3)(d)) and a war crime under the Statute of the International Criminal Court (Art 8(2)(b)(v), which makes 'intentionally attacking towns, villages, dwellings or buildings which are undefended and which are not military objectives' in international armed conflicts a war crime).[49]

IV. Safety and Exclusion Zones Defined by the Security Council

In order to protect populations targeted during many particularly brutal armed conflicts, the Security Council has defined safety zones,[50] within which hostile acts are strictly forbidden, and has also more recently established no-fly zones, in which it imposes a ban on all flights in the airspace of a state, as such reducing the aerial dimension of the theatre of operations.

It should be noted that, in doing so, the Security Council on the one hand removes zones from the area of war thereby excluding military operations by the parties to

[49] Art 3(c) of the Statute of the International Criminal Tribunal for the former Yugoslavia (adopted by the UN Security Council on 25 May 1993, in SC Res 827) also defines as a war crime within the jurisdiction of the tribunal 'attack, or bombardment, by whatever means, of undefended towns, villages, dwellings, or buildings'.

[50] In SC Res 1296 (2000) on the protection of victims of armed conflict, the Security Council 'Indicates its willingness to consider the appropriateness and feasibility of temporary security zones and safe corridors for the protection of civilians and the delivery of assistance in situations characterized by the threat of genocide, crimes against humanity and war crimes against the civilian population' (para 15).

the conflict within those zones and authorizing other states to oversee that the relevant parties do not use the zones as theatres of operation. On the other hand, by authorizing states to use all necessary means to ensure that military operations are not conducted in these zones, the Security Council defines a theatre of operations for those states that participate in the implementation of the resolution and conduct military operations to that end.

A. Safety Zones

Since the beginning of the 1990s, the Security Council has created 'safety zones' (also called 'security zones') in many conflicts,[51] that are to be distinguished from the different types of protected zones defined by the law of armed conflict.

A specific status applies to these zones which were created to provide protection for civilians who are being deliberately targeted during armed conflicts. The zones are relevant for the question of the boundaries of the 'theatre of operations' since hostile acts, military activities (operations in direct support of the use of force), and armed incursions are forbidden in these safe areas. For example, the situation in Bosnia and Herzegovina led the Security Council to resolve that 'all the parties and others concerned treat Srebrenica and its surroundings as a safe area which should be free from any armed attack or any other hostile act'.[52] In Resolution 824 (1993) it stipulated 'the immediate cessation of armed attacks or any hostile act against the safe areas, and the withdrawal of all Bosnian Serb military or paramilitary units from these towns to a distance wherefrom they cease to constitute a menace to their security and that of their inhabitants to be monitored by United Nations military observers'. It additionally requested full respect by all parties of the rights of the UNPROFOR [United Nations Protection Force] and the international humanitarian agencies to 'free and unimpeded access to all safe-areas' in Bosnia and Herzegovina (para 4).

The use of force by other actors can be authorized by the Security Council in these areas in order to implement the prohibition of armed attacks and other hostile acts. In practice, the Security Council has mandated peace operations to control security zones. For example, the Security Council authorized UNPROFOR 'to take the necessary measures, including the use of force, in reply to bombardments against the safe areas by any of the parties or to armed incursions into them or in the event of any deliberate obstruction in or around those areas to the freedom of

[51] See Bruce M. Oswald, 'The Creation and Control of Places of Protection During United Nations Peace Operations' (2001) 844 *International Review of the Red Cross* 1013; Maurice Torelli, 'Les zones de sécurité' (1995) 99 *Revue Générale de Droit International Public* 787.

[52] S/RES/819 (1993), 16 April 1993, para 1. The concept of safe areas was applied to 'Sarajevo, and other such threatened areas, in particular the towns of Tuzla, Zepa, Gorazde, [and] Bihac...': S/RES/824 (1993), 6 May 1993, para 3.

movement of the Force or of protected humanitarian convoys'[53]. Furthermore, the Security Council can authorize states to use force in order to protect a safe area and implement the prohibition to conduct military activities. Resolution 836 (1993) authorized member states (acting nationally or through regional organizations), in coordination with the Secretary-General and UNPROFOR, to take 'all necessary measures, through the use of air power, in and around the safe areas... to support [UNPROFOR]... in the performance of its mandate'.[54]. That was also the case for Rwanda: the Security Council authorized under Chapter VII of the Charter the member states cooperating with the Secretary-General to conduct an humanitarian operation and to use 'all necessary means to achieve humanitarian objectives set out in paragraphs 4(a) and (b) of Resolution 925(1994)',[55] which include to 'contribute to the security and protection of displaced persons, refugees and civilians at risk in Rwanda, including through the establishment and maintenance, where feasible, of secure humanitarian areas'. States were therefore mandated to create safe areas and to use force to protect them.

These considerations raise a question about the need for states for an authorization by the Security Council to create security zones where military activities are forbidden and, more broadly, of the conditions for the creation of such zones. Two situations must be distinguished.

On the one hand, if parties to the conflict agree to the creation of a safe area, this area can be created and located by the Security Council (even acting under Chapter VI of the Charter) and enforced by UN operations and states. That said, it is usual in practice for belligerents to agree to the creation of such a place of protection, as was the case with the establishment of safe areas in Croatia.[56]

On the other hand, if parties to the conflict do not agree to the creation of a safe area, the Security Council can only authorize the creation of a security zone by acting under Chapter VII,[57] qualifying a situation as a threat to the international peace

[53] S/RES/836 (1993), 4 June 1993, para 9. According to para 5, its mandate was to 'deter attacks against the safe areas, to monitor the cease-fire, to promote the withdrawal of military or paramilitary units other than those of the Government of Bosnia and Herzegovina and to occupy some key points on the ground, in addition to participating in the delivery of humanitarian relief to the population'.

[54] S/RES/836 (1993), 4 June 1993, para 10.

[55] S/RES/929 (1994), 22 June 1994, para 3.

[56] SC Res 743 (1992), SC Res 749 (1992), SC Res 824 (1993), and SC Res 836 (1993). The renewal of the mandate of UNPROFOR has, however, been formally accepted by the parties. In SC Res 959 (1994), the Security Council requested 'the Secretary-General to update his recommendations on modalities of the implementation of the concept of safe areas and to encourage UNPROFOR, in cooperation with the Bosnian parties, to continue their efforts to achieve agreements on strengthening the regimes of safe areas taking into account the specific situation in each case' (para 5).

[57] In the same way, 'A more legally controversial situation arises when the Security Council has not made a Chapter VII determination and a UN Force witnesses gross violations of human rights being committed by the belligerents. As discussed above, in such a case the Force will be acting under Chapter VI and will not have a mandate to create places of protection without the belligerents' consent': Oswald, 'The Creation and Control of Places of Protection During United Nations Peace Operations', 1021.

and security. In this case, we know that there is no need to obtain the consent of some or all the belligerents. The Security Council has thus authorized the establishment of security zones in Bosnia and Herzegovina in 1992[58] and also authorized the creation of a humanitarian security zone in Rwanda without the consent of the belligerents.[59] France was duly authorized to create, within the framework of its Operation Turquoise, on 2 July 1994, a 'humanitarian protected zone' in the Cyangugu-Kibuye-Gikongoro triangle in south-western Rwanda, covering approximately one-fifth of Rwandese territory.

It should be added that the legality of creating places of protection in the absence of the consent of parties and of an explicit Chapter VII authorization is highly controversial. An example can be found in the practice of many states that created safe havens in northern Iraq to protect the Kurds at the end of the Gulf War in 1991 (protected through an aerial exclusion zone), invoking an implicit authorization in Security Council Resolution 688 (1991). It is, however, difficult to admit this legal basis, and the argument has been criticized.[60] Those particular states preferred to invoke an interpretation of Resolution 688 rather than refer to the concept of humanitarian intervention, which reveals that they probably considered that, in international law, humanitarian intervention does not constitute a customary exception to the rule prohibiting the use of force against a state and the principle of sovereignty.

B. 'Exclusion Zones' Established by the Security Council

The Security Council can also decide not to create a security zone as such but to prohibit (or restrict) flights over portions of the territories of state(s)—or even in international airspace—in order to protect a civilian population against aerial attack. A ban can be limited to portions of the airspace of a state or cover the entire airspace. The theatre of operations is restricted only in its aerial component; military operations can be conducted by belligerent parties on the ground. The purpose of this ban on flights in a delimited airspace is to exclude the use of aerial means of warfare and weapons to conduct air or missile attacks against civilians; it can also contribute to the safety of the delivery of humanitarian assistance and constitutes a decisive step for the cessation of hostilities.

The Security Council established an air exclusion zone for the first time in October 1992 in Bosnia and Herzegovina. In Resolution 781 (1992), it decided 'to establish a

[58] SC Res 757 (1992), SC Res 758 (1992), SC Res 787 (1992), SC Res 819 (1993), SC Res 824 (1993). The Security Council refers to agreements signed at Geneva on 22 May 1992.

[59] SC Res 929 (1994), para 3, referring to subparas 4(a) and (b) of SC Res 925 (1994).

[60] See Torrelli, 'La neutralité', 824.

ban on military flights in the airspace of Bosnia and Herzegovina, this ban not to apply to United Nations Force flights or to other flights in support of United Nations operations, including humanitarian assistance' (para 1). In Resolution 816 (1993), it decided to extend the ban established by Resolution 781 to cover 'flights by all fixed wing and rotary-wing aircraft in the airspace of the Bosnia and Herzegovina', excluding from this prohibition flights authorized by UNPROFOR (para 1). As a consequence, the Operation Deny Flight conducted by the North Atlantic Treaty Organization (NATO) from April 1993 to December 1995 on the basis of Resolution 816 was explicitly authorized by the Security Council.

In reaction to the situation in Libya, in March 2011 the Security Council created a so-called no-fly zone.[61] In Resolution 1973 (2011), it 'decides to establish a ban on all flights in the airspace of the Libyan Arab Jamahiriya in order to help protect civilians' (para 6), not to apply to flights the sole purpose of which are humanitarian,[62] and 'Authorizes Member States that have notified the Secretary-General and the Secretary-General of the League of Arab States, acting nationally or through regional organizations or arrangements, to take all necessary measures to enforce compliance with the ban on flights imposed by paragraph 6 above, as necessary' (para 8). This no-fly zone, which ended on 31 October 2011,[63] was particularly strong in its geographical extent and the scope of the authorization of implementation.[64]

The Security Council can therefore limit or extend the scope of the aerial exclusion zone and therefore the operations conducted by a state to implement it are legal only if that state respects the limits defined in the Security Council's resolution, which can prohibit only military flights (as in the case of Bosnia and Herzegovina) or limit the ban on a portion of the airspace.

[61] In the HCPR Manual a semantic distinction is made between 'exclusion zones', established by a belligerent party in international airspace during an international armed conflict (rule 107) and 'no-fly zones' that are established and enforced by a belligerent party in its own or in enemy territory during international or non-international armed conflict (rule 108).

[62] Para 7, that mentions flights such as 'delivering or facilitating the delivery of assistance, including medical supplies, food, humanitarian workers and related assistance, or evacuating foreign nationals from the Libyan Arab Jamahiriya'. The ban does not apply to flights organized by member states to protect civilians and civilian-populated areas under threat of attack in Libya.

[63] In Res 2016 (2011) of 27 Oct 2011, the Security Council decided that the no-fly zone 'shall be terminated from 23.59 Libyan local time on 31 October 2011'.

[64] Michael N. Schmitt, 'Wings over Libya: The No-Fly Zone in Legal Perspective' (2011) *Yale Journal of International Law Online* 46, available at <http://www.yjil.org/docs/pub/o-36-schmitt-wings-over-libya.pdf>.

V. Conclusion

The concept of 'theatre of operations', not defined as such by international law but used in military vocabulary, is relevant within the framework of this volume as it raises the question of where military operations can be conducted by the parties to an armed conflict.

The parties do not have the right to extend the theatre of operations beyond the geographic limits of the 'warfare area', on land, at sea, and in the air. Indeed, the hostilities can only take place on the territories of the parties to the conflict (including the territorial sea and national airspace, but excluding 'exclusion zones' defined by agreements), and also on the high seas, the EEZs, international airspace, and outer space. According to a general principle of international law, the theatre of operations shall not be extended to the territory of a state not party to the armed conflict, without its consent. This principle applies even to 'cyber theatres of operations', as the law of armed conflict encompasses cyber operations executed in the context of an armed conflict.

Even inside a 'warfare area', theatres of operations cannot be established in any location: according to the international law of armed conflicts, four types of 'protected zones' can be established by the parties to the conflict. Military operations are thus excluded in these zones of protection, which thus constitute enclaves in the area of war. Furthermore, limitations on the geographical scope of military operations can be decided by the Security Council with the consent of territorial state or/and acting under Chapter VII of the UN Charter. In many conflicts, it has established 'safety zones' within which attacks and military activities by the belligerents are strictly forbidden. It has also established no-fly zones, that is, bans on flights over the territory (or even portions) of a state: military operations are not prohibited on the ground, but the theatre of operations is restricted in its aerial component. In both cases, the Security Council can authorize other states to conduct military operations in order to implement the prohibition for belligerents in these areas. It thus defines a theatre of operations for those states.

Finally, the international law of armed conflicts applies to any 'theatre of operations', even if the attacks take place in a zone where military operations should not be conducted. Thus, a 'theatre of operations' is not a free-fire zone, where methods or means of warfare and objectives of attacks are unlimited.

PART IV

ACTION ON BEHALF OF PEOPLES AND POPULATIONS

CHAPTER 35

'HUMANITARIAN INTERVENTION'

SIR NIGEL RODLEY

I. Introduction

This chapter addresses the question of whether, beyond the right of individual and collective self-defence and the power of collective enforcement action undertaken or authorized by the UN Security Council, there is a further exception to the international law prohibition on resort to armed force. The asserted doctrine of humanitarian intervention would represent such an exception.

The doctrine, with origins in 19th-century European interventions in situations of perceived persecution of Christians in territories under Ottoman Turkish rule, claims a right to rescue populations undergoing grave persecution or, in current terminology, widespread and/or systematic violations of basic human rights.[1] The question is whether, to the extent that it existed at all, it survived the advent of the UN Charter, Article 2(4) of which introduced a global obligation on states not to threaten or use force against each other. From the earliest days of the Charter, the preponderant view of

[1] Thomas M. Franck and Nigel S. Rodley, 'After Bangladesh: The Law of Humanitarian Intervention by Military Force' (1973) 67 *American Journal of International Law* 275; Thomas M. Franck, *Recourse to Force: State Action against Threats and Armed Attacks* (Cambridge: Cambridge University Press, 2002), ch 9; Christine Gray, *International Law and the Use of Force* (3rd edn, Oxford: Oxford University Press, 2008), 30–59.

publicists, including the present writer, has been that there simply is no such exception.[2] That is why the title of this chapter is in quotation marks. The opposite view has been defended by a minority of (highly respected) scholars, with legal argument substantially buttressed by potent moral considerations.[3] An event that took place on the eve of the second millennium, the North Atlantic Treaty Organization (NATO) action in favour of the population of Kosovo, led some of the sceptics to wonder whether a norm change might be emerging (*de lege ferenda*).[4] Others remained sceptical.[5]

Meanwhile, at the universal level, a paradigm change has been acknowledged, in the form of the so-called 'responsibility to protect' (commonly, though informally, known as R2P). Enshrined in the UN General Assembly's 2005 World Summit Outcome Document,[6] and reaffirmed in Security Council Resolution 1674 (2006) on 'protection of civilians in armed conflict', is the notion that grave human rights violations that would amount to genocide, ethnic cleansing, war crimes, or crimes against

[2] Franck and Rodley, 'After Bangladesh'; Ian Brownlie, 'Thoughts on Kind-Hearted Gunmen' in Richard B. Lillich (ed), *Humanitarian Intervention and the United Nations* (Charlottesville, VA: University Press of Virginia, 1973), 139; and 'Humanitarian Intervention' in John Norton Moore (ed), *Law and Civil War in the Modern World* (Baltimore, MD: Johns Hopkins University Press, 1974), 217; Natalino Ronzitti, *Rescuing Nationals Abroad through Military Coercion and Intervention on Grounds of Humanity* (Leiden: Martinus Nijhoff, 1985), ch 4; Sean D. Murphy, *Humanitarian Intervention: the United Nations in an Evolving World Order* (Philadelphia, PA: University of Pennsylvania Press, 1996); Simon Chesterman, *Just War or Just Peace: Humanitarian Intervention and International Law* (Oxford: Oxford University Press, 2001); Brian D. Lepard, *Rethinking Humanitarian Intervention* (University Park, PA: Pennsylvania State University Press, 2002).

[3] Richard B. Lillich, 'Intervention to Protect Human Rights' (1969) 15 *McGill Law Journal* 205 and 'Humanitarian Intervention: A Reply to Ian Brownlie and a Plea for Constructive Alternatives' in Moore, *Law and Civil War in the Modern World*, 229; W. Michael Reisman, 'Sovereignty and Human Rights in Contemporary International Law' (1990) 84 *American Journal of International Law* 866; Ved P. Nanda, 'Tragedies in Northern Iraq, Liberia, Yugoslavia, and Haiti—Revisiting the Validity of Humanitarian Intervention under International Law—Part I' (1992) 20 *Denver Journal of International Law and Policy* 305; Fernando Tesón, *Humanitarian Intervention: An Inquiry into Law and Morality* (3rd edn, Ardsley, NY: Transnational, 2005); Ved. P. Nanda, Thomas F. Muther Jr, and Amy E. Eckert, 'Tragedies in Somalia, Yugoslavia, Haiti, Rwanda and Liberia—Revisiting the Validity of Humanitarian Intervention under International Law—Part II' (1998) 26 *Denver Journal of International Law and Policy* 827; Nicholas J. Wheeler, *Saving Strangers: Humanitarian Intervention in International Society* (Oxford: Oxford University Press, 2000).

[4] Michael F. Glennon, 'The New Interventionism: The Search for a Just International Law' (May/June 1999) 78 *Foreign Affairs* 2; Antonio Cassese, '*Ex iniuria ius oritur*: are we moving towards International Legitimation of Forcible Humanitarian Countermeasures in the World Community?' (1999) 10 *European Journal of International Law* 23; Antonio Cassese, 'A Follow-Up: Forcible Humanitarian Countermeasures and *Opinio Necessitatis*' (1999) 10 *European Journal of International Law* 791; Vaughan Lowe, 'International Legal Issues Arising in the Kosovo Crisis' (2000) 49 *International and Comparative Law Quarterly* 934; Sean D. Murphy, 'The Intervention in Kosovo: A Law-Shaping Incident?' (2000) *American Society of International Law Proceedings* 302; Ralph Zacklin, 'Beyond Kosovo: The United Nations and Humanitarian Intervention' (2000) 41 *Virginia Journal of International Law* 923; Michael J. Glennon, *Limits of Law, Prerogatives of Power: Interventionism after Kosovo* (New York/Basingstoke: Palgrave Macmillan, 2001).

[5] eg Franck, *Recourse to Force*, ch 9; Nigel S. Rodley and Basak Çalı, 'Kosovo Revisited: Humanitarian Intervention on the Fault Lines of International Law' (2007) 7 *Human Rights Law Review* 275.

[6] GA Res 60/1 (2005).

humanity are susceptible of attracting coercive action under Chapter VII of the UN Charter. That means that implicitly such practices even when taking place within national frontiers may be considered as a threat to or breach of international peace and security within the meaning of Article 39 of the UN Charter. This is the threshold that must be passed before the Security Council may take enforcement actions.

This overdue, but still politically controversial development—at least, when it comes to implementation—will be taken as a given, a normative *acquis*. The present chapter limits itself to addressing whether action taken by one state or a group of states without a Security Council mandate under Chapter VII may nevertheless be legally justifiable. Where R2P is directly relevant is in the identification of the phenomena that could begin to be pertinent. Earlier discussions had to cope with the problem of what types or levels of human rights violation or abuse could justify 'humanitarian intervention' if it were permitted at all. While problems of scope and intensity remain, the notions of genocide, ethnic cleansing, war crimes, and crimes against humanity offer sufficient criteria of seriousness to avoid or, at any rate, permit exposure of abusive invocations of human rights problems as spurious justification of unlawful intervention in the sovereign independence of another state.

First, there will be an examination of the relevant provisions of the UN Charter. These provisions will generally be seen to reflect rules, not just for the parties to the particular treaty that is the UN Charter, but as part of general international law and, in their essence, *jus cogens*. This will be followed by a review of state practice that will be seen to be relevant, both to establishing the existence of a rule of customary international law and to the proper interpretation of uncertain treaty provisions. This will lead to a discussion of criteria that would be relevant to determining the legality of any action claiming to be justified under the purported doctrine of humanitarian intervention. In any event, these same criteria would be pertinent to assessments of circumstances that could be considered as mitigating a finding of unlawfulness. A conclusion will reaffirm the present author's view that there is no humanitarian exception to the prohibition of the use of force in international law.

II. The Terms of the Prohibition on the Use of Force

Article 2(4) of the UN Charter contains the following obligations on UN member states:

> All Members shall refrain in the international relations from the threat or use of force against the territorial integrity or political independence of any State, or in any other manner inconsistent with the Purposes of the UN.

By these words, the founding members—the states gathered at San Francisco in 1945—believed they were closing a gap that had been left open by the Covenant of the League of Nations and had only partially been closed by the 1928 Kellogg–Briand Pact, which outlawed resort to war.[7] That treaty only bound those states party to it and prohibited resort to 'war', a formal status, the existence of which had to be declared by the parties. Much violence could be done by recourse to armed force short of such war. That violence too was to be out of bounds to the UN, whose membership aspired to universality. The references to political independence and territorial integrity evidently aimed at describing the fundamental elements of sovereignty while avoiding the vagueness associated with that volatile notion.

The norm was reinforced by the reaffirmation in Article 2(7) of the principle of non-intervention 'in matters which are essentially within the domestic jurisdiction of any State', and human rights were indeed at that stage understood to be matters 'essentially' within states' domestic jurisdiction.[8]

The position of those who deny the existence (or survival) of the doctrine of humanitarian intervention rely on this original understanding of the Charter. That understanding, they maintain, was bolstered by recent history. While it was true and to be welcomed that the promotion of human rights was now a purpose of the Charter,[9] an achievement justified by the inescapable link between oppression at home and aggression abroad displayed by Nazi Germany, it was also remembered that the beginnings of the Second World War were characterized by Germany's invasion of neighbours, which was justified by spurious claims of oppression of people of German ethnic origin.[10]

It was evident that not all the 'purposes' of the UN were of equal status. To be sure, Article 1 includes among the purposes of the organization both 'to maintain international peace and security' and 'to achieve international cooperation … in promoting and encouraging respect for human rights and fundamental freedoms for all …'[11] Overlooking the difference in directness of the language of the two purposes, it is clear that the 'principles' articulated in Article 2 have no comparable counterpart in respect of human rights to the use of force prohibition in Article 2(4). The avoidance and repression of international armed conflict was the dominant gene in the UN's genetic code.

The interpretation of the Charter that would on the contrary defend the existence of a doctrine of humanitarian intervention is similarly both textual and contextual. As regards the text of Article 2(4), the limited purpose of rescuing a population from extreme persecution would not be seen as infringing the political

[7] The Pact of Paris, the General Treaty for Renunciation of War as an Instrument of National Policy.

[8] cf the parallel language of the Covenant of the League of Nations that had excluded from consideration matters '*solely* within the domestic jurisdiction' of states: Art 15(8); the UN Charter was evidently aiming to exclude more activity than a narrow technical reading of the principle would have contemplated.

[9] UN Charter, Art 1(c). [10] Franck and Rodley, 'After Bangladesh', 284.

[11] UN Charter, Art 1(a) and (c) respectively.

independence or the territorial integrity of the state intervened in. It would not aim at regime change and, so, would leave intact the state's political independence. It would not involve territorial changes, thus preserving the state's territorial integrity. Moreover, Article 2(7) would not be offended, since a humanitarian intervention would not be inconsistent with the purposes of the UN, given that the advancement of human rights was a purpose stipulated in Article 1(c). Accordingly, the provision would offer no obstacle to coercive action, since Article 2(7) contains the warning that it may not 'prejudice the application of enforcement measures under Chapter VII'.

Contextually, it must surely have been unthinkable that the drafters of the UN Charter could have expected that, after the Nazi-perpetrated genocides, the world would again have to stand by if widespread atrocities were being committed behind the veil of national sovereignty. The world could not have unlearned the lesson so soon. In any event, if it was not the case at first, since it has come to be accepted that there is now not only a right, but a responsibility to protect against the major atrocities that scarred the conscience of the world, it is unconscionable to leave the fate of populations to the will of the Security Council, especially when that will is determined by a veto that may be cast for reasons having nothing to do with the clarity of the call and the need for rescue of those in danger.

III. State Practice

As will be discussed later, the prohibition on the use of force is not only a treaty rule. The UN Charter is, of course, a treaty, but it is also commonly held to be a world constitutional instrument and so should not necessarily be interpreted in the same way as might some tax treaty or even a multilateral treaty dealing with such traditional issues as the law of the sea or diplomatic privileges and immunities. Moreover, the prohibition of the use of force is a rule of general or customary international law and a rule of *jus cogens* at that, indeed the archetypal such rule.[12]

State practice is relevant to treaty interpretation.[13] When dealing with rules of customary international law, state practice is central to the existence and content of the rule. Does state practice acknowledge any exception to the prohibition in favour of populations being the object of widespread atrocity?

[12] See André de Hoogh, '*Jus Cogens* and the Use of Armed Force', Chapter 54 in this volume.
[13] See Art 31(3)(b) of the 1969 Vienna Convention on the Law of Treaties.

Again it will only be the more evident that candidacies for the title of example of humanitarian intervention are hard to come by. It is not intended to consider rescues of the intervening state's national (or other foreign nationals) abroad.[14] To the (questionable) extent that such interventions may be lawful,[15] they are rarely if ever justified as being undertaken pursuant to a general right of humanitarian intervention, that would protect all those in the territory of the state in question, but only for the more limited right to protect foreign nationals; sometimes self-defence is advanced as an underlying justification. Certainly, such a defence is the only one consistent with the original notion that the only exceptions to the prohibition on the use of force were self-defence and Security Council-authorized action under Chapter VIII of the UN Charter.

The pre-Charter interventions said to be in the name of humanitarian objectives are of limited relevance. They consist mainly of the Western European intervention in favour of Christian inhabitants under Ottoman rule.[16] The hands of the Christians were not always devoid of bloodstains. Strategic and other commercial interests were rarely, if ever, absent.[17] Occasionally, self-determination could be an issue, as with the 1823 intervention in favour of Greek independence,[18] but this was hardly a principle that was generally asserted as a right, much less a right justifying foreign intervention (even apart from the colonial mote in the eye). The strategic convenience of the interests was hardly accidental or incidental. Only one other pre-1945 intervention could be invoked with any credibility, namely, the US intervention that secured Cuban independence from Spanish colonization. Historic US neuralgia about European colonization, as manifested by this Spanish possession 90 miles off Key West, Florida, gave this 'humanitarian' initiative a particularly self-interested tint.[19] In any event, whatever the reality of the existence of the doctrine, it was asserted in an international legal system that did not outlaw resort to war. Any inhibition on the use of force, short of resort to outright war, must inevitably have had more than a trace of flimsiness about it, thus creating space for the possibility of armed action for many politically convenient purposes. It is after the advent of the universal prohibition on the use of force that state practice becomes especially important.

[14] eg the US intervention in Grenada, allegedly to rescue US students in the wake of a military coup, and itself condemned by the UN General Assembly: Res 38/7 (1983).

[15] Mathias Forteau, 'Rescuing Nationals Abroad', Chapter 44 in this volume.

[16] Franck and Rodley, 'After Bangladesh', 279–83.

[17] Franck and Rodley, 'After Bangladesh', 279–83.

[18] Franck and Rodley, 'After Bangladesh', 279–83.

[19] Contemporaneous US removal of Spain from the Philippines led to a US occupation that only finally ended with independence in 1946; see also Franck and Rodley, 'After Bangladesh', 283–5.

A. The Cold War Period

1. *Bangladesh 1971*

India's invasion of Pakistan has been considered a possible instance of humanitarian intervention.[20] Certainly, the Pakistani central government, recently relocated from Lahore to Islamabad, West Pakistan, responded to an East Pakistan attempt at secession from its western counterpart over 1,000 miles away, with extreme brutality and widespread shedding of blood.[21] India invaded, defeated the Pakistani army, and presided over the establishment in East Pakistan (East Bengal, geographically) of the new state of Bangladesh.

As far as appears from the debates in the UN, India's primary defence was based on the notion of self-determination.[22] This may well be the only case in which India has embraced an interpretation of the right to self-determination that would apply to a territory that had already emerged from colonialism.[23] India also invoked the humanitarian situation, albeit not clearly in terms propounding a legal claim. Again, it would be anomalous Indian practice. There has been no sign of a similar interest when serious bloodshed of Tamils in Sri Lanka on various occasions in the past 30 years could have been expected to arouse that interest. Meanwhile, the hostility between India and Pakistan—sometimes cold, sometimes hot—has been the central strategic issue for the Subcontinent[24] and it is likely that the opportunity to inflict a decisive strategic advantage dictated the decision to invade.

What particularly deprives the action of any serious precedential value for the notion of humanitarian intervention is the reaction of the international community, which was no more moved by the flow of millions of refugees than it was by the carnage of those who remained. Paralysed by the Soviet veto exercised on behalf of India, the Council itself referred the situation to the General Assembly.[25] The Assembly, in turn, firmly called for a ceasefire with an overwhelming majority,[26] with only India, the Soviet Union, its traditional allies, plus Bhutan, voting against. Far from suggesting a world *opinio juris* in favour of humanitarian intervention this reaction is more forceful evidence of the opposite.

As the 1970s began with the intervention that gave birth to Bangladesh, it ended with four major foreign military interventions that led to the ouster of the sort of regimes whose methods of exerting and remaining in power could not have made

[20] eg Ved P. Nanda, 'A Critique of the United Nations Inaction in the Bangladesh Crisis' (1972–3) 49 *Denver Law Journal* 53; Lillich, 'Humanitarian Intervention: A Reply to Ian Brownlie'.

[21] Nanda, 'A Critique of the United Nations Inaction in the Bangladesh Crisis'.

[22] See Franck and Rodley, 'After Bangladesh', 276–7.

[23] India is notoriously touchy about possible secessionist movements of its own, *vide* the Punjab.

[24] China/US were generally allied with Pakistan, while the Soviet Union tended to align with India.

[25] SC Res 303 (1971).

[26] GA Res 2793 (1971); 104 for, 11 against, 10 abstentions (A/PV.2003).

them more suitable candidates as exemplars of the doctrine. All were at the extreme ends of even the kinds of despotisms that scarred the 20th century.

2. *Uganda*

After a period of cross-border tensions, involving Ugandan dissidents seeking safe haven in Tanzania from the atrocities of the regime led by Idi Amin Dada, Uganda declared war on Tanzania in 1978 and occupied part of the Kagera region of Tanzania.[27] Tanzania then led a successful invasion of Uganda in 1979 with the support of dissidents supporting former Ugandan President Dr Milton Obote, whom Amin had overthrown in a 1971 coup. Obote was reinstalled as president. Few regimes had been responsible for as much brutality as that of Amin, whose regime became a byword for the grossest violations of human rights, characterized by torture, murder, and enforced disappearance of any perceived enemy, as well as (very early in his rule), the mass expulsion of Asians with British nationality. The invasion was characterized by Tanzania as an exercise in self-defence, not as a belated intervention justified on humanitarian grounds against a regime whose support was anyway beginning to erode. Interestingly, the Organisation for African Unity (OAU—now the African Union) did condemn the invasion as a violation of Uganda's sovereignty.[28] Consultations in the UN yielded no will to condemn Tanzania, in either the Security Council or the General Assembly. This may have had to do with the fact that the self-defence notion was reasonably applicable to the situation and the lack of will to seem to support a blatantly illegitimate regime.[29]

3. *Kampuchea*

The Pol Pot-led Khmer Rouge regime of what was called Democratic Kampuchea (now restored to the earlier Cambodia), was ousted by Vietnamese forces in 1979.[30] This was after several years of border incursions. A pro- (or at least not anti-) Vietnamese regime was installed. The principal justification for the invasions invoked by Vietnam was self-defence, albeit it made propaganda about the atrocities of the Khmer Rouge regime, whose imposition of 'year zero' on Cambodia involved mass murder of genocidal proportions on 'class enemies'. The response of the international community was clear. Again the Security Council

[27] Franck, *Recourse to Force*, 143–5.

[28] While consistent with the rigid non-intervention line of the OAU, which also embraced total lack of concern for the human rights of its members' populations, it may be speculated that the shockwaves generated by the impunity achieved by Tanzania for its invasion led the organization to embrace human rights concerns by adopting the African Charter on Human and Peoples' Rights; perhaps non-coercive human rights action could forestall coercive action on whatever grounds.

[29] At the time, Africa was not as much of a fulcrum of East–West competition as other regions, so neither side was identified with one of the two power blocs; this may have made Tanzania's action less likely to excite political opposition.

[30] Franck, *Recourse to Force*, 145–51.

was paralysed by a pro-Vietnamese Soviet veto (China had supported the Khmer Rouge) and the General Assembly took over consideration of the situation. In unambiguous terms, the Assembly called for 'the immediate withdrawal of all foreign forces from Kampuchea' and called on 'all states to refrain from all acts and threats of aggression and all forms of interference in the internal affairs of States in South-East Asia'.[31]

4. *Afghanistan*

At around the same time, another brutal clique was murdering and disappearing thousands of perceived opponents.[32] This time the neighbouring Soviet Union intervened directly on behalf of the competing faction of the ruling party, restoring a decidedly less brutal, albeit pro-Soviet authoritarian regime. The humanitarian relief brought about by this action once more led to a paralysed Security Council (as a result of a Soviet veto) calling for General Assembly action.[33] Five days later in an emergency session, the General Assembly by a large majority, adopted a resolution that 'Strongly deplore[d] the recent armed intervention in Afghanistan' and 'call[ed] for the immediate unconditional and total withdrawal of the foreign troops from Afghanistan'.[34]

5. *Central African Empire*

In 1979 France gave military support to a 'coup' in the Central African Empire that overthrew 'Emperor' Bokassa and reinstated as head of state David Dacko, the constitutional president, who had been ousted in a coup by then Colonel Jean-Bédel Bokassa in 1966.[35] Bokassa had been responsible for many deaths of opponents. In January 1979, in clashes between anti-regime students and government security forces, some 150 people lost their lives. In May 1979 Amnesty International issued a report alleging that in March some 100 children had been arrested and killed by government troops. This explosive allegation led to a commission of inquiry set up by French–African heads of state and government. The Commission confirmed the allegations and even concluded that Bokassa had participated in the killings, an allegation that Amnesty International had refrained from making public.[36] France did not justify its intervention on humanitarian grounds. After first denying involvement, it eventually accepted that it had 'aided' an indigenous coup attempt. While the USSR and a few African countries criticized France for its involvement, no action was taken by, nor even initiated at, the UN.

[31] GA Res 34/22 of 14 Nov 1979, para 7; votes 91–22–29.

[32] Under presidents Taraki and Hafizullah Amin.

[33] SC Res 462 (1980) of 9 Jan 1980.

[34] GA Res ES-6/2(1980) of 14 Nov 1980.

[35] Franck, *Recourse to Force*, 151–2.

[36] The Commission visited Amnesty International and took testimony from its regional experts: author's recollection; he was the organization's Legal Adviser at the time.

6. *Summary*

The condemnations by the UN General Assembly of the interventions in Bangladesh, Kampuchea, and Afghanistan are sufficient to deny these interventions the status of evidence of state practice qualifying as custom. The Ugandan intervention, justified by Tanzania on ground of self-defence and, still condemned by the OAU, at best could be offered as an example of the mitigating circumstances principle at work. The same conclusion is the better explanation of the non-condemnation of France's intervention, again not justified on the basis of a doctrine of humanitarian intervention.

B. The Post-Cold War Period

1. *Liberia*

In 1990 a brutal civil war was taking place in Liberia between the armed forces of Liberia under the regime of President Samuel Doe, who had come to power ten years earlier by a military coup led by then Sergeant Samuel Doe and insurrectionary armed forces that had entered the country from Côte d'Ivoire and had themselves split into two factions.[37] Extreme brutality characterized the activities of both sides with thousands of civilians losing their lives. The Economic Community of West African States (ECOWAS) decided in August 1990 to establish a joint military intervention force, the Economic Community Monitoring Group (ECOMOG). It acted unilaterally, without prior authorization of the Security Council. In principle, the UN Charter in its Chapter VIII acknowledges a collective role for regional bodies, in the monitoring of international peace and security. However, Article 53 of the UN Charter is clear: 'no enforcement action shall be taken under regional arrangements or by regional agencies without the authorization of the Security Council'. No such authorization was granted, as none had been sought. On the other hand, neither the Security Council nor the General Assembly condemned it.

Two years later the Security Council appeared to ratify the intervention *ex post facto*. In fact, ECOMOG had had limited success in achieving or enforcing a resolution of the conflict. In 1992, it turned to the UN for help. Help was forthcoming, beginning with Security Council Resolution 788 (1992). That resolution, which eventually led to the establishment of a UN presence in the country,[38] specifically commended 'ECOWAS for its efforts to restore peace, security and stability in Liberia'.[39] Moreover, it imposed an arms embargo on the parties under Chapter VII. In a preambular paragraph, it recalled 'the provisions of Chapter VIII' of the Charter.[40] This may suggest that Article 53 can be read as requiring either prior or subsequent authorization for

[37] Franck, *Recourse to Force*, 155–63.

[38] United Nations Observer Mission in Liberia (UNOMIL), Sept 1993–Sept 1997.

[39] SC Res 788 (1992), para 1.

[40] SC Res 788 (1992), preambular para 6.

the regional enforcement action, alternatively, it may be understood as the application of a general international law rule of recognition that allows the international community to convert an apparently illegal act into a legal one.[41] A further alternative espoused by Professor Franck was that it was simply a question of the actual necessity and partly positive outcome conducing to a mitigation of the illegality rather than a determination of legality.[42]

In any event, what might be considered an unlawful unilateral intervention (albeit collective) may in retrospect be considered, if not lawful, at least devoid of adverse legal consequences. A relevant dimension, of course, was that the Council, if only formally, stressed the transnational (ie non-internal) dimensions of the situation, the deterioration of which it determined to be 'a threat to international peace and security, particularly in West Africa as a whole'.[43]

2. *Kurdish North Iraq*

In the wake of the first Gulf War that, with UN Security Council support (as enforcement action or collective self-defence), led to the forced removal of Iraq from occupied Kuwait (1991), unrest in the Kurdish area of northern Iraq attracted typically brutal repression[44] from Iraqi President Saddam Hussein, whose regime used massive political imprisonment, torture, murder, and enforced disappearance as regular tools of governance. This led to a refugee flow of some 400,000 towards Turkey in the north and Iran in the east.[45] The humanitarian situation of those in the mountains near or over the border with Turkey, together with Turkey's unwillingness to host large numbers of refugees indefinitely, led the West, notably France, the UK, and the US, to establish in mid-April 1991 and enforce a no-fly zone in northern Iraq for Saddam's forces. This would permit the delivery of aid and the voluntary return of the refugees to the protected enclaves (called save havens). The effect was to create an autonomous Kurdish zone in northern Iraq.[46]

The three states expressed the view that their action was 'consistent with' or 'in support of' Security Council Resolution 688 (1991).[47] That resolution had been adopted

[41] Georg Schwarzenberger and E. D. Brown, *A Manual of International Law* (6th edn, London: Stevens, 1976), 54–6.

[42] Franck, *Recourse to Force*, 139.

[43] SC Res 788 (1992), preambular para 5. Indeed, the regional implications included the descent of Sierra Leone into a brutal civil war that was only resolved by Security Council-authorized British intervention in support of UNAMSIL, a failing UN peace mission.

[44] As did the similar Shi'ite unrest in the South.

[45] See generally Lawrence Freedman and David Boren, 'Safe Havens for Kurds in Post-War Iraq' in Nigel S. Rodley (ed), *To Loose the Bands of Wickedness: International Intervention in Defence of Human Rights* (London: David Davis Memorial Institute of International Studies/Brassey's, 1992), 43, 48–52.

[46] Freedman and Boren, 'Safe Havens for Kurds in Post-War Iraq' in Rodley, *To Loose the Bands of Wickedness*, 63–8.

[47] See Freedman and Boren, 'Safe Havens for Kurds in Post-War Iraq' in Rodley, *To Loose the Bands of Wickedness*, 54; Franck, *Recourse to Force*, 154 fn 101.

a week and a half earlier. It is no accident that the interveners did not attempt to claim that their action was legally contemplated by Resolution 688 (1991). It was not. While the resolution condemned 'the repression of the Iraqi civilian population..., including most recently in Kurdish-populated areas'[48] that had led to 'massive refugee flows',[49] as well as its being 'Deeply disturbed by the magnitude of the human suffering involved',[50] it did not authorize enforcement action to resist it. Nor, untypically of resolutions on Iraq before and during Operation Desert Storm, did it invoke Chapter VII of the Charter. Certainly, it considered there was a threat to regional peace and security,[51] at least as concerned the 'massive flow of refugees towards and across international frontiers'[52] and 'cross-border incursions',[53] seemingly implying the relevance of Chapter VII. It also 'demanded' that Iraq cease the repression.[54] But its only request to member states other than Iraq was an appeal to 'all Member States and to all humanitarian organizations to contribute to ... humanitarian relief efforts'. This is not language by which enforcement action is authorized.[55]

Indeed, had it been otherwise, it would not have been necessary to include this case in the present chapter. Moreover, again, there was no negative reaction from either the Security Council or the General Assembly which reacted with 'benevolent silence'.[56]

3. *Kosovo*

The NATO intervention in what had until 1989 been the Serbian autonomous territory of Kosovo was to be the last paroxysm of the collapse of Yugoslavia.[57] Kosovan resistance to the attempted annexation by Slobodan Milošović's Serbia was for a number of years non-violent, then, as protests were repressed, became violent with the creation of a Kosovo Liberation Army (KLA). Killings and bombardments by the Belgrade authorities led to a massive refugee flight to its mountains. The Security Council condemned the repression and imposed an arms embargo[58] and on 24 March 1999 the NATO bombing campaign began. NATO did not seek to base its legal justification directly on the earlier Security Council resolutions, as it was clear that they did not authorize this enforcement action.[59] It was also clear that the Soviet Union would have vetoed any Security Council resolution that would authorize an armed intervention.[60] Although NATO was a regional organization, Chapter VIII was also of no avail. While the situation in Kosovo, with its massive

[48] SC Res 688 (1991), para 1. [49] Preambular para 3. [50] Preambular para 4.

[51] Para 1. [52] Preambular para 3. [53] Preambular para 3. [54] Para 2.

[55] Nigel S. Rodley, 'Collective Intervention to Protect Human Rights and Civilian Populations' in Rodley, *To Loose the Bands of Wickedness*, 14, 28–34.

[56] Franck, *Recourse to Force*, 154.

[57] The wealth of literature spawned by this incident is enormous; a fair sampling of it is cited in Rodley and Çalı, 'Kosovo Revisited', fns 7 (illegal), 8 (legal), and 9 (illegal, but a potential harbinger of future legality).

[58] SC Res 1160 of 31 Mar 1998. [59] Albeit they were invoked to provide at least political legitimacy.

[60] See the Russian attempt to have the intervention condemned, below.

export of refugees, could be and was considered by the Council as a threat to international peace and security, it clearly was not an armed attack, justifying resort to (regional) self-defence. Moreover, none of the republics of ex-Yugoslavia, including Serbia, were members of NATO and so legitimately under the discipline of that or any other regional organization. Indeed, the only justification NATO itself could agree on was one of overwhelming necessity.

In the words of the UK Permanent Representative, it was justified as 'an exceptional measure to prevent an overwhelming humanitarian catastrophe'.[61] A Russian attempt to have the Security Council condemn NATO's intervention was rejected by 12 votes to three, with only China, the Soviet Union, and Namibia voting in favour.[62] There was no attempt to take the issue to the General Assembly, which would have been expected to follow the majority in the Security Council. After all, here we had an alliance of states, all but one of which had a majority Christian population,[63] intervening against a state similarly composed (Serbia) on behalf of a predominately Muslim population, sympathy for which was widespread in the global South that constitutes the General Assembly majority. Instead, Russia participated in brokering an agreement that restored a measure of autonomy to Kosovo, endorsed by the Security Council.[64] It is disputed whether the Security Council was thereby ratifying the intervention.

4. *Summary*

The post-Cold War incidents provide better evidence of a possibly emerging doctrine of humanitarian intervention. Liberia's credentials are ambivalent. Clearly, the ECOWAS intervention was not condemned. There was an evident issue of regional peace and security. Prior authorization by the Security Council, even had it taken place 15 years before R2P was formally consecrated, would have put the intervention beyond challenge to its legal legitimacy. Security Council Resolution 788 (1992), in any event, seems to rectify the omission.

The intervention in northern Iraq, where the situation also had regional peace and security implications, including major refugee flows, under the political umbrella of Resolution 688 (1991), cannot be ruled out as possible evidence for an emerging norm, but is more plausibly consistent with the 'mitigating circumstances' approach.

Kosovo is evidently on the borderline. Certainly, the transnational elements of regional destabilization, not just involving massive refugee flows, as confirmed by Security Council resolutions, put the issue beyond simply intervening in a brutal internal situation. There is no doubt that, had the Security Council authorized the action, its legal legitimacy would have been watertight. From a legal analytical

[61] Franck, *Recourse to Force*, 167. [62] S/PV/3989 (1999).
[63] Turkey; a second Muslim majority state, Albania, joined NATO in 2009.
[64] SC Res 1244 (1999).

perspective, the hard issue would have crystallized if a draft resolution had been put to the vote and then been blocked by a Russian veto. From a political perspective, given that there appears to have been no doubt that such a veto would have been deployed, it may have been felt that it was better to act under the political cover of the earlier resolutions, rather than in the wake of a defeated resolution. Insofar as there was no serious doubt that there would have been a veto cast on a draft that would otherwise have secured the required majority of nine votes, it is reasonable to see the intervention as indeed posing the problem of what may be done after an unreasonably deployed veto.

IV. Threshold Criteria for Legality or Mitigation of Illegality

There is general agreement that, if a doctrine of humanitarian intervention (however denominated) were to be acknowledged as a lawful exception to the prohibition of the use of force, any particular intervention would have to pass a number of tests. The same tests would be applicable to any argument involving mitigation of blameworthiness. Before a brief concluding defence of the view that there is no such exception to the prohibition, these tests of legal or at least political legitimacy are considered.

A. Gravity of the Situation

It is suggested that the first criterion would be that there be a substantive threshold of gravity that would, in principle, be the same as that for triggering R2P, namely, the existence of genocide, ethnic cleansing, crimes against humanity, or war crimes. The implication is that there is a substantial level of oppression, characterized normally by widespread bloodshed.

This would seem to rule out the sort of US-led intervention as was authorized in Haiti to restore democracy after a coup overturning a UN-observed 1990 election.[65] Alternatively, a distinction could be drawn between the *responsibility* to protect,[66] denoting an obligation to act, and a *right* to protect that could permit a more flexible threshold. If this latter perspective were to prevail, it would be

[65] SC Res 940 (1994).

[66] See André Nollkaemper, '"Failures to Protect" in International Law', Chapter 20 in this volume.

even more appropriate that the decision be taken only pursuant to the discipline of obtaining Security Council blessing.

B. Political Neutrality

One of the strongest arguments in the hands of the opponents of the idea of legal humanitarian intervention is the tendency of the interveners to be seen to be as much, if not more, motivated by national self-interest than international solidarity with the victims of oppression. The Indian intervention in Bangladesh offers a vivid example. It is rare enough for states to act wholly out of humanitarian motives, whatever the action or its cause, nevertheless, the 'CNN factor' can play a role. That is, governments may be prodded into action by a population unable to stomach atrocity that it feels its government could help to prevent. The Kosovo intervention was a case in point. It would be too much to demand immaculate selflessness, but that any external political advantage should be outweighed by the humanitarian motive. A fair test could be whether the intervention would not have happened, *but for* the humanitarian exigency.

Neutrality does not necessarily mean consistency or uniformity. Regrettable as it most indisputably is, not every situation whose oppressed population may be crying out for rescue will be able to attract the needed intervention. Many factors may conduce to inconsistency. Firstly, the resources of potential interveners are not inexhaustible and may simply be too stretched. They cannot be everywhere, especially if they are also involved in other (non-primarily-humanitarian) military activities. Secondly, national populations will only have a limited stomach for sacrificing their own personnel in the role of 'world policeman'. The CNN factor raises its head here. Thirdly, not every situation will be amenable to a rapid military solution and, even those that may at first blush appear to be apt for a military fix may also require the sort of long-term military, political, and economic commitment that would deter the initial reflex to want to help.[67] Fourthly, it has to be recognized that some states are simply too militarily powerful to be restrained by outside intervention, however brutal their governments' repression of their own population.

C. Security Council Paralysis

The condition that the Security Council should be unable to act because the (already qualified) majority required for decision-making is prevented from acting by

[67] The failure of successive interventions in Afghanistan, unilateral, multilateral, or mixed, to bring stable rule-of-law-based government to that country is instructive, as is the comparable situation of the Democratic Republic of the Congo.

deployment of the veto is self-explanatory. During the Cold War period, very little happened in the world (outside Sub-Saharan Africa) that was not characterized by East–West competition and so the veto was an ever-present problem. In the 1990s, after the dissolution of the Soviet Union in 1991, there was a window in which a weak Russia seemed to be moving westward politically and the first President Bush could speak hopefully of a 'new world order'.[68] A decade later, with Russia reasserting a major (if not super-) power posture, an increasingly less cooperative Security Council appeared. Still as late as 2011, neither Russia nor China felt able to veto what became Resolution 1973 (2011) that paved the way for an Arab-League-sponsored, European-led intervention in a Libya that was brutally repressing attempts to secure Arab-Spring-type freedom. The nature of the actual intervention that brought about regime change was portrayed by China, Russia, and others as going beyond what Resolution 1973 (2011) authorized, constituting the backdrop for future paralysis, as evidenced by the inability of the Council to agree to Arab League demands to apply sanctions to Syria in 2012–13. The stage may be set for further appeals for interventions to protect against widespread grave human rights violations, without Security Council authorization. The key factor will be the genuineness in any given situation of the veto-induced paralysis. Moreover, it would be preferable for a draft resolution authorizing military intervention to have been presented and actually blocked by a veto, rather than leaving the matter to tacit understanding. An explicit threat by a permanent member of the Security Council to veto any such draft, should it be presented, would probably be sufficient to justify dispensing with an incontrovertibly foredoomed formality.

D. Necessity

The famous definition of the threshold for self-defence—the necessity being 'instant, overwhelming, leaving no choice of means, and no moment for deliberation'—should apply a fortiori to humanitarian intervention, since it would hardly be plausible to consider that states had adopted a lower threshold of acceptability for 'humanitarian intervention' than is required to justify measures of self-defence. It follows that all other tools of diplomacy—political and economic, bilateral and multilateral—are considered ruled out as a means of successfully addressing the harm.

Further, it also means that armed intervention needs to be the only *coercive* measure capable of achieving the objective. If there were a reasonable possibility that Article 41-type sanctions could be effective, then they should be undertaken. Evidently, the greater the level of bloodshed, the less likely will be the prospects for effective non-military intervention. So, while a graduated coercive response, culminating in

[68] Address Before a Joint Session of the Congress on the Persian Gulf Crisis and the Federal Budget Deficit (11 Sept 1990) by George H. W. Bush.

military force only after exhaustion of other measures, is the model to be aspired to, it cannot be expected that a box-ticking formalism of graduation be followed to the evident detriment of assisting those at risk. For example, once it was clear that the United Nations Assistance Mission for Rwanda (UNAMIR) was not going to be willing to prevent the 1994 genocide in Rwanda, any intervention, whether by the Security Council or by any single country or group of countries, could not have tried all the lesser alternatives. To do so would have ensured the success of the genocide.[69]

Finally, the test of necessity requires, in addition to the exclusion of non-coercive measures and of coercive measures short of armed force, that the military force actually deployed be the minimum necessary to secure a cessation of the violations. For instance, if it is reasonably foreseeable that the mere insertion of foreign military would cause them to stop, then that would be the course to adopt, rather than violently attacking the forces perpetrating or sustaining the violations.[70]

E. Proportionality

The latter test of necessity could also be considered a manifestation of the principle of proportionality. Here, the notion is used in a more substantive sense. Whatever the level of force used, however scrupulously hewing to the rule that it be the minimum necessary, it must also be proportionate to the goal.[71] If the goal is to stop a certain level of bloodshed, for example, then a 'humanitarian' response that results in as much or even more bloodshed would be patently disproportionate. It does not follow that proportionality requires an anodyne comparative body count. The range of situations that may be characterized by, say, crimes against humanity or war crimes is extensive and elastic. The point is that the interventionist prescription cures, rather than aggravates, the malady, much less kills the patient.[72]

F. Accountability

The modern notion of accountability, usually considered in the context of institutional and democratic constraints on domestic decision-making, is no less applicable to the international system.[73] Even before the creation of universal organizations,

[69] In the end, the successful Rwanda Patriotic Front did what had to be done, defeating the Rwandan Armed Forces and the *genocidaires*.

[70] As occurred with the 1994 US intervention in Haiti, pursuant to SC Res 940 (1994).

[71] See Franck, 'On Proportionality of Countermeasures in International Law' (2008) 102 *American Journal of International Law* 715.

[72] The fate of Iraq after the US-led imposition of 'regime change' comes to mind.

[73] Rodley and Çalı, 'Kosovo Revisited', 294–7; Charlotte Ku, 'Transparency, Accountability, and Responsibility for Internationally Mandated Operations', Chapter 19 in this volume.

the decentralized system had a rudimentary system of accountability in the form of 'recognition' or acquiescence. Indeed, the reaction of other states acting individually to the behaviour in question was arguably the core test of whether a legal claim could be evaluated as valid or invalid.[74]

With the advent of the UN, there emerged at the *universal* level fora that could facilitate the collective expression of the previously atomized responses. For present purposes, the two key bodies are the Security Council and the General Assembly, of which the former is the more authoritative. As already seen, the Security Council has the power to authorize the use of force, including in the context of R2P. If it authorizes an action to prevent or repress grave and widespread human rights violations, characterized by genocide, ethnic cleansing, war crimes, and crimes against humanity, then that will render the action lawful. The Council provides the system of accountability for the UN and the international community of states as a whole. Whatever may be the 'democratic deficit' in the Council's composition, it still represents a substantial proportion of the world's population and distribution of power. It is an accountability system that offers full legal and a significant measure of political legitimacy.

Where the Council is veto-paralysed, the General Assembly remains. In the past, it has tended to be used to condemn interventions that the Council could not condemn because of the veto. For reasons that cannot be explored here, Uniting for Peace—the system of referral to the General Assembly when the Council failed to exercise its 'primary responsibility' to monitor international peace and security—has fallen into desuetude.[75] Still, the Assembly can discuss what it wants to discuss and inferences may (cautiously) be drawn from its silence.

In broad democratic terms, the Assembly too has a voting structure that is not beyond democratic challenge. Its one-state-one-vote structure is democratic, only insofar as the legal fiction of the sovereign equality of states is wholly respected. In terms of population or power, the 'democratic deficit' is palpable. There is little real democracy when the vote of the Marshall Islands (population around 55,000) is of equal value to that of the People Republic of China (population around 1.3 billion). On the other hand, the General Assembly majority may genuinely comprise enough states to reflect a general world consensus and in this sense it provides a plausible forum of accountability.

This does not mean that the General Assembly can replace the Security Council in its power to authorize or refuse to authorize the use of armed force against the wishes of the object state. It cannot grant legal legitimacy. It can, however, grant political legitimacy.

While the UN is the universal *locus* of accountability, there are also *regional* such *loci*. The role of the sub-regional ECOWAS in Liberia has been noted. It has also

[74] Schwarzenberger and Brown, *A Manual of International Law*, 54–6.

[75] GA Res 377A (1950).

intervened in problems such as those affecting Sierra Leone (1997). Similarly, the larger, regional African Union has intervened in certain situations, such as that of Somalia with a view to rebuilding the previously collapsed state and has also supported others, notably, in Mali (2013).[76] While the legal validity of regional organizations' interventions is subject to Security Council authorization under Article 53 of the UN Charter, these organizations have a certain degree of legitimacy insofar as they are acting in respect of members that have voluntarily submitted themselves to their authority. As such they are repositories of a quantum of political legitimacy.

On the other hand, the world should not be too hasty to overlook the abuse of regional organizations during the Cold War, as typified by the Warsaw Pact interventions in Hungary (1956) and Czechoslovakia (1968) or those of the inter-American system in Guatemala (1954) and the Dominican Republic (1965).[77] At the present time, there are no relevant recognized regional organizations that are amenable to the global superpower hegemony of the Cold War period. However, within the regions themselves there are powers of greater or lesser political, economic, and military might, that could find themselves tempted to exert abusive authority within their regional organizations. Also, a clear distinction needs to be drawn between regional organizations which intervene against their own members and those which intervene in respect of non-member states, such as NATO in the former Yugoslavia or even further afield as in Afghanistan and Libya. Here whatever limited accountability *inter se* may be found in their decision-making processes,[78] they are incapable of being a source of accountability, either globally or more crucially *as regards the object state*. By definition, that state will have had no say in the process that has led to the intervention. Whatever the legal or political legitimacy of such an intervention, it does not arise from the 'regional' character of the organization.

V. 'Humanitarian Intervention': Lawful or Pardonable?

It is now necessary to offer a conclusion as to whether armed interventions to rescue populations from widespread grave human rights violations, without authorization

[76] It opposed the Western intervention in Libya.

[77] Thomas M. Franck and Edward Weisband, *Word Politics: Verbal Strategy Among the Superpowers* (Oxford: Oxford University Press, 1971). Of course, while membership of the OAS and NATO was, by any standards, voluntary, the same could not be said of the Warsaw Pact.

[78] They are not negligible in NATO, Art 4 of whose Charter requires consultation and is interpreted as requiring consensus before action can be taken.

from the Security Council, can be considered lawful. It remains the present writer's view that they cannot.

The challenge of interpreting state practice in this field is that it stands on the fault lines of international law.[79] At any given moment, state behaviour may, when set against previous expectations, be an example of unlawfulness or a harbinger of future lawfulness, or both. This is inherent in assessing the existence or content of a rule of customary international law and it is still a problem when state practice is examined as an aid to treaty interpretation. The problem is accentuated when issues of *jus cogens* arise.[80] The prohibition of the use of force is the most secure *jus cogens* norm. The prohibitions of committing crimes against humanity and war crimes enjoy the same status. After all, any type of torture undoubtedly enjoys that status.[81] We are left with the conundrum that a rule of *jus cogens*, a rule so important that it cannot be varied by treaty, has to be breached to pave the way for an alternative rule. Such a paradigmatic paroxysm should not be lightly presumed.

The primacy of the norm prohibiting the use of force was at the heart of the UN at its birth. While internal conflict has tended to characterize the Charter period, full-scale international armed conflict can still happen (*vide* the Argentinian invasions of the Falklands/Malvinas, the Iraq invasion of Kuwait, the NATO invasion of Afghanistan in response to the 9/11 attack on the US and the US/UK-led invasion of Iraq). The bloodshed during these conflicts and (possibly, as in the latter two of these examples) arising from consequent institutional collapse can be cataclysmic.

At a less portentous level, we might also ask ourselves how, if regional enforcement action can only be lawful when authorized by the Security Council, unilateral intervention can be lawful absent the same authorization. Surely, a fortiori the latter, not contemplated by the Charter, needs at least the same authority as the former?

Those who deny the existence—or the desirability—of a legal doctrine of humanitarian intervention are not blind to the possibility that rescuing a foreign population from the depredations of their own governments may be the lesser evil in terms of moral responsibility, as opposed to legal responsibility. The Liberia and Kosovo interventions are probably cases in point. Such a conclusion is not unknown to law—even the most justice-oriented law imaginable. It is in the nature of the normative exercise, that is the discipline of law, that it cannot deliver perfect justice in every individual case. That is why legal systems have developed techniques to temper the rigours of the law with mercy.

79 Rodley and Çalı, 'Kosovo Revisited', 289–91.

80 See André de Hoogh, '*Jus Cogens* and the Use of Armed Force', Chapter 54 in this volume.

81 See most recently *Questions Relating to the Obligation to Prosecute or Extradite (Belgium v. Senegal)*, Judgment of 20 July 2012, ICJ Rep 2012, para 99.

The way it is generally achieved in national law is by the notion of mitigation. Professor Franck explored an iconic cannibalism case in which stranded seamen who survived only by eating the flesh of a dying cabin boy, after they killed him, were found guilty of murder, but then pardoned.[82] The reason for the law's rigidity is the fear that exceptions that would either permit killing one who does no harm so that others survive, or permit someone to help another to die by removing otherwise irremediable pain, would be exploited and abused because of the limits of the law in getting at the truth and to protect the vulnerable from improper moral pressure. It is how rule utilitarianism is reconciled with act utilitarianism.[83]

Such an approach is even more required by the relatively decentralized system of international law. Indeed, international law itself can seemingly require states to take such an approach. This may well be the case as regards the prohibition of torture. It is generally accepted that torture, as defined in the UN Convention against Torture or Other Cruel, Inhuman or Degrading Treatment or Punishment, can never, as a matter of law, be permitted or justified.[84] It is a crime engaging the concerned states' responsibility, which requires the state to ensure prosecution of perpetrators with no defence, not even the defence of necessity.[85] Nevertheless, it has been argued that where the torture may have been inflicted in good faith to prevent grave harm, it may be appropriate to contemplate a role for mitigation of punishment.[86]

As far as humanitarian intervention is concerned, there is rarely a judicial forum available to establish guilt and apply the legal consequences.[87] Thus, the nearest equivalent of a sanction will typically be the intensity of international condemnation. As has been seen, in some cases—those closely resembling the paradigm of 'lawful' humanitarian intervention, complying with the conditions of legality that would be required of such an intervention—the level of universal or regional institutional condemnation has been muted or non-existent, as in the Kosovo case.

[82] Franck, *Recourse to Force*, ch 10; see generally A. W. Brian Simpson, *Cannibalism and the Common Law: The Story of the Tragic Last Voyage of the Mignonette and the Strange Legal Proceedings to Which It Gave Rise* (Chicago, IL: University of Chicago Press, 1984).

[83] Act utilitarianism assesses any individual act against the test of the happiness of the greatest possible number: see Wolfgang Friedmann, *Legal Theory* (4th edn, London: Stevens, 1960), 270; whereas rule utilitarianism posits a rule capable of delivering the same goal, with acts conforming to the rule being right and those departing from it being wrong: see Richard T. Garner and Bernard Rosen, *Moral Philosophy: A Systematic Introduction to Normative Ethics and Meta-ethics* (Basingstoke: Macmillan, 1967), 70.

[84] See Nigel S. Rodley, *The Treatment of Prisoners under International Law* (2nd edn, Oxford: Oxford University Press, 1999), 78–84; Yuval Ginbar, *Why Not Torture Terrorists?: Moral, Practical and Legal Aspects of the Ticking Bomb Justification for Torture* (Oxford: Oxford University Press, 2008), esp 269–348.

[85] See *Gaefgen v. Germany* (App no 22978/05), ECtHR, Judgment (GC), 1 June 2010.

[86] eg Oren Gross, 'Lecture Commentary (on Nigel S. Rodley, "Torture Violence and the Global War on Terror")' (2005) *American Society of International Law Proceedings* 407–10.

[87] For a rare exception, see *Military and Paramilitary Activities in and against Nicaragua (Nicaragua v. US)*, Merits, Judgment, ICJ Rep 1986, 14, paras 257–68.

It is possible, however, that a phenomenon other than mitigation is in play, that is, the doctrine of acquiescence or recognition, as may have been the case with the ECOWAS intervention in Liberia. This, it will be recalled, is the process by which a decentralized legal system allows for a measure of legal acceptance. This could only be satisfactory explanation if, as in the Liberia case, it were the Security Council itself offering the *post hoc* absolution.

Just as the prohibition of murder in domestic law could not easily survive an exception for euthanasia or assisted suicide, the prohibition on the use of force in international law could even less easily survive a humanitarian exception.

CHAPTER 36

PRO-DEMOCRATIC INTERVENTION

DAVID WIPPMAN

I. Introduction

DEBATES about pro-democratic intervention have a dated feel, but they were all the rage in the recent past. In the 1990s, the end of the Cold War opened the door to new possibilities for the use of force in international relations. With the collapse of the Soviet Union, the Western liberal democratic model seemed to have little competition, leading Francis Fukuyama to proclaim famously, 'What we may be witnessing is not just the end of the Cold War, or the passing of a particular period of post-war history, but the end of history as such: that is, the end point of mankind's ideological evolution and the universalization of Western liberal democracy as the final form of human government.'[1] Fukuyama's thesis, often oversimplified or distorted, has since been showered with criticism, but it captured an extraordinary moment in international politics, when a 'new world order' based on liberal democratic norms seemed tantalizingly within reach.

International organizations after 1990 increasingly insisted on democratic governance or, more narrowly, periodic free and fair elections, as conditions for membership, benefits of various kinds, or even recognition of new states or governments. The trend became so pronounced that Professor Tom Franck, in a famous

[1] Francis Fukuyama, 'The End of History?' (Summer 1989) 16 *The National Interest* 4.

1992 article, heralded the notion of an emerging 'democratic entitlement'.[2] Citing provisions in human rights treaties protecting the rights to self-determination, free expression, and periodic elections, Franck concluded that democratic governance was becoming an enforceable legal right.[3]

Although Franck expressly disavowed a right to use military force to promote democracy, others were not so reticent. In a 1984 editorial in the *American Journal of International Law*, Michael Reisman sketched an elegant argument for reinterpreting the general prohibition on the use of force in international relations found in Article 2(4) of the UN Charter. That prohibition, Reisman argued, was historically and politically contingent on a collective security system that never functioned as hoped. In the absence of an effective global sheriff, Reisman suggested, states would necessarily resort to coercion, but rather than condemn all interstate uses of force, each particular use of force should be judged by two criteria: first, whether it enhances or undermines world order and, secondly, whether it 'serve[s], in terms of aggregate consequences, to increase the probability of the free choice of peoples about their government and political structure'.[4] In subsequent writings, Reisman elaborated on this argument. Citing human rights instruments providing that 'the will of the people shall be the basis of the authority of government', UN monitoring of elections and periodic insistence that only democratic elections could legitimize new governments, and instances of pro-democratic intervention in Haiti, Sierra Leone, and elsewhere, Reisman argued that military intervention to reinstate an ousted democratically elected government following a coup that is clearly against the popular will should not be deemed a violation of national sovereignty.[5] Reisman was careful to qualify his argument, noting that the legality of pro-democratic military intervention should 'turn on many contextual factors',[6] including the reasons for intervention, the availability of alternatives to the use of force, the level of force required, and more. But in clear cases, such as Haiti or Sierra Leone, pro-democratic intervention should, he argued, be accepted as lawful.

Reisman's arguments never gained wide acceptance and, in recent years, the focus of attention has shifted. The heady days of the 1990s, and its notions of a democratic peace and a new world order with a triumphalist US in the lead, have

[2] Thomas Franck, 'The Emerging Right to Democratic Governance' (1992) 86 *American Journal of International Law* 46.

[3] Franck, 'The Emerging Right to Democratic Governance'. See also Susan Marks, 'What has Become of the Emerging Right to Democratic Governance?' (2011) 22 *European Journal of International Law* 507, 509.

[4] Michael Reisman, 'Coercion and Self-Determination: Construing Charter Art. 2(4)' (1984) 78 *American Journal of International Law* 642.

[5] Michael Reisman, 'Sovereignty and Human Rights in Contemporary International Law' in Gregory H. Fox and Brad Roth (eds), *Democratic Governance and International Law* (Cambridge: Cambridge University Press, 2000), 239.

[6] Reisman, 'Sovereignty and Human Rights in Contemporary International Law' in Fox and Roth, *Democratic Governance and International Law*, 249.

yielded to a multi-polar world in which an undemocratic China is extending its global influence, a less dominant US focuses on a national security agenda dominated by terrorism and nuclear proliferation, and Europe struggles with economic stagnation and increasingly intolerant right-wing political parties. Even the much vaunted Arab Spring, which might suggest a democratic trend in one of the world's least democratic regions, struggles to make headway against entrenched militaries and Islamist politics.

In this context, discussion of pro-democratic intervention may seem a little out of place. But few trends are uniform, and the notion that governmental legitimacy matters in assessing intervention remains a potent one. Governments and international organizations routinely condemn coups that oust democratically elected governments and sometimes employ sanctions and even force to restore elected leaders to office. We are still far from accepting a legal regime in which states may intervene unilaterally to oust an undemocratic regime, even if that regime has itself ousted a democratically elected government. But pro-democratic intervention takes many forms, and assessments of their legality vary. These forms include Security Council-authorized interventions, interventions by contemporaneous invitation of sitting or recently ousted officials, interventions by regional organizations, interventions authorized in advance by treaty, and interventions combining two or more of these forms. In many instances, interventions that may be deemed illegal under traditional interpretations of the UN Charter attract little or no condemnation and sometimes explicit commendation from international organizations and individual governments.

Assessments of legality are complicated further by an apparent general relaxation in the norms governing the use of force.[7] This is not a new phenomenon. In 1970, for example, Tom Franck famously asked 'Who Killed Article 2(4)?' in a lead article in the *American Journal of International Law*.[8] But the North Atlantic Treaty Organization's (NATO's) 1998 intervention in Kosovo, intervention in Iraq in 2003 by the US and its coalition partners, US drone strikes in multiple countries, and a host of other military interventions of questionable legality under traditional understandings of the UN Charter in general raise continuing questions about the vitality of Article 2(4). Those questions may have a penumbra effect when assessing pro-democratic intervention.

In this confused and shifting landscape, judgments about legality necessarily depend on the facts of specific cases, especially since promotion of democracy is typically only one of multiple justifications offered for the use of force in any given

[7] See Jean d'Aspremont, 'Mapping the Concepts Behind the Contemporary Liberalization of the Use of Force in International Law' (2010) 31 *University of Pennsylvania Journal of International Law* 1089.

[8] Tom Franck, 'Who Killed Article 2(4)? Or Changing Norms Governing the Use of Force by States' (1970) 64 *American Journal of International Law* 809. Michael Glennon takes up that theme in 'The Limitations of Traditional Rules and Institutions Relating to the Use of Force', Chapter 3 in this volume.

case. But, it is possible to locate most cases along a spectrum of legality, with UN Security Council-authorized interventions at the generally accepted end and unilateral action on the generally condemned end of the spectrum. Harder cases involve intervention based on the consent of an ousted but democratically elected government, particularly when that consent is provided in advance by treaty.

II. Evolving Attitudes towards Governmental Legitimacy

Part of the problem in assessing pro-democratic intervention lies in continued disagreement over the nature of governmental legitimacy. For most of the modern era, international law has treated any group of nationals in effective control of the state as the government of that state, without regard to the manner by which that government attained or secured its hold on power.[9] Although international instruments dating back to the Universal Declaration of Human Rights insisted that 'the will of the people shall be the basis of the authority of government' and that 'this will shall be expressed in periodic and genuine elections',[10] the notion of a legal right to democratic governance came much later. The International Covenant on Civil and Political Rights, for example, although it speaks of the right to genuine and periodic elections, does not condition governmental authority on respect for the will of the people.[11] As a result, even Soviet bloc states felt free to ratify the Covenant.[12]

The contending political philosophies of the Cold War made movement towards a broadly shared understanding of the connection between democracy and governmental legitimacy impossible, with one exception. UN member states gradually coalesced around the view that denial of majority rule in the colonial territories of Africa and Asia violated the principle of self-determination, justifying economic and diplomatic sanctions and, for some states, support for wars of national liberation. But apartheid regimes were seen as a special case; similar scrutiny was not

[9] See eg Legal Aspects of Problems of Representation in the United Nations, S/1466 (1950) (recognition turns on 'whether the new government exercises effective authority within the territory of the State and is habitually obeyed by the bulk of the population'); Montevideo Convention on the Rights and Duties of States (1933) 165 LNTS 19 (articulating a declarative theory of statehood).

[10] Universal Declaration of Human Rights, Art 21, GA Res 217A(III), A/810 (1948).

[11] International Covenant on Civil and Political Rights (1966) 999 UNTS 171.

[12] See Henry Steiner, 'Political Participation as a Human Right' (1988) 1 *Harvard Human Rights Yearbook* 77, 91.

applied to undemocratic regimes elsewhere and no shared understanding of either the desirability or the meaning of a democratic entitlement emerged.[13]

The end of the Cold War opened the floodgates to new treaties, resolutions, and declarations expressing support for democratic governance and, in some cases, explicitly tying governmental legitimacy to respect for political participation norms. This flowering of pro-democratic instruments and practices reflected 'the spread of democratic politics to Eastern Europe, Latin America, parts of South-East Asia, and parts of Africa', the increasing reliance by international organizations on promotion of democratic institutions as part of post-conflict settlement processes, and the rapid spread of election monitoring by international organizations.[14]

Regional systems went furthest in seeking to define the essentials of democratic governance. Various regional organizations conditioned recognition of new states and membership in the organizations on respect for democratic principles, and both the Organization for Security and Co-operation in Europe (OSCE) and the Organization of American States (OAS) pledged to take action to oppose unconstitutional seizures of power in member states.[15] Ironically, given the frequency with which outside states have intervened in Africa in the past, it is the African Union (AU) and African sub-regional organizations, particularly the Economic Community of West African States (ECOWAS), that have gone the farthest in committing themselves to oppose unconstitutional seizures of power, by force if necessary.

Nonetheless, no international consensus has emerged either on the content of a right to democratic governance or the circumstances under which military intervention to promote democracy is desirable. In fact, there is considerable debate on whether a general right to democratic governance (as opposed to a regional norm) is, or should be, emerging.[16] Part of the problem rests with continued disagreements over the content of such a right. As Greg Fox observes, most international organizations and instruments have focused on the procedural aspects of democratic governance, especially free and fair elections and rights of political participation.[17] But procedural definitions have been 'criticized in the name of a "substantive"

[13] See Gregory H. Fox, 'Democracy, Right to, International Protection' in Rüdiger Wolfrum (ed), *Max Planck Encylopedia of Public International Law* (Oxford: Oxford University Press, 2008), para 1.

[14] Fox, 'Democracy, Right to, International Protection' in Wolfrum, *Max Planck Encylopedia of Public International Law*, para 2.

[15] In the Document of the Copenhagen Meeting of the Conference on the Human Dimension, June 29, 1990 (1990) 29 ILM 1305, the then Conference on Security and Cooperation in Europe declared that member states would 'defend and protect' the 'democratic order' in any participating state against a violent overthrow. Similarly, the OAS pledged that the OAS Permanent Council would meet 'to examine the situation' in the event of an unconstitutional seizure of power. Res 1080, OAS General Assembly, 5th Plen Sess, OEA/ser P/XXI.O.2 (1991).

[16] See Marks, 'What has Become of the Emerging Right to Democratic Governance?', 511–12.

[17] Fox, 'Democracy, Right to, International Protection' in Wolfrum, *Max Planck Encylopedia of Public International Law*, para 9.

conception which includes protection of minorities, equality guarantees, and economic and social rights.'[18] The result is 'an uncertain foundation for a global norm'.[19]

More broadly, many states, particularly in Asia and in much of the Islamic world, still do not share the enthusiasm of the West for democratic governance. Even when states can agree on whether a particular government is democratic, or on the related but different question of whether it secured power through democratic means, states still often disagree on whether or to what extent a state's right to be free of external intervention should turn on the character of its government. For most states, effective control remains a powerful determinant of a government's right to control the territory and population of a state. Accordingly, while states that suffer unconstitutional seizures of power or otherwise abandon democratic principles can expect broad condemnation and often diplomatic and even economic sanctions, military intervention remains an infrequent consequence. When it does occur, its legality is often contested.

III. Legal Bases for Pro-Democratic Intervention

When states or international organizations wish to respond to a threat to or absence of democracy in a particular state, they have a wide range of tools, ranging from diplomatic pressure to economic sanctions to military action. But responses that do not entail coercion do not constitute prohibited intervention under international law. My focus here is therefore on military intervention to promote democracy.

A. Security Council-Authorized Pro-Democratic Intervention

Security Council authorization remains the most compelling and, many would argue, the only legal basis for the use of force to reinstate an ousted democratically elected government or otherwise give effect to notions of the democratic entitlement. For a time, even this basis for intervention was contested. When the end of the Cold War relieved Security Council gridlock, the newly activist Council authorized military intervention to stop

[18] Marks, 'What has Become of the Emerging Right to Democratic Governance?', 512.

[19] Fox, 'Democracy, Right to, International Protection' in Wolfrum, *Max Planck Encyclopedia of Public International Law*, para 36.

repression of Kurds in Iraq,[20] create a safe environment for food aid in famine-stricken Somalia,[21] restore democracy in Haiti,[22] stop ethnic cleansing in Bosnia,[23] and (belatedly) oppose genocide in Rwanda,[24] among others. In each case, the Security Council found internal disorder (with its attendant cross-border effects) a sufficient threat to international peace and security to justify invocation of the Council's Chapter VII coercive powers. But in most of these cases, the disorder at issue did not represent the 'aggressive use of force across a boundary' that had previously been understood to constitute the kind of threat to international peace necessary for a military response. As a result, international lawyers debated whether the Council had exceeded its authority under the Charter or whether the Council effectively had unlimited discretion to decide whether particular circumstances constituted a threat to international peace.[25]

As a practical matter, concerns over *ultra vires* action have had no discernible impact on the Council's decision-making. Moreover, questions about the Security Council's legal authority to act in such cases have largely subsided. In short, the Security Council can almost invariably find sufficient transboundary effects in cases of significant internal disorder, including the disorder caused by a coup or other unconstitutional seizure of power, to justify a decision to authorize force. Nonetheless, the Council remains extremely reluctant to authorize military intervention against a sitting government, even one widely deemed illegitimate; the authorization to use force to restore Jean Bertrand Aristide to power in Haiti in 1994,[26] and to protect civilians in Libya from attacks by the government of Mu'ammer Gaddafi in 2011,[27] remain rare exceptions to the general rule.

A more difficult question is whether the Security Council can authorize military intervention retroactively and, if so, whether Security Council acquiescence in military action by states or regional organizations can itself be treated as authorization. In late 1989, Liberia slid into civil war; by July 1990, all semblance of civil authority had disappeared and the human toll was mounting rapidly. In August 1990, armed forces from five ECOWAS member states, acting as the ECOWAS Monitoring Group (ECOMOG), intervened to stop the fighting and to help to install an interim government in Monrovia. ECOMOG acted only after appeals to the US and the UN failed. The US insisted that an 'African solution' should be found, and the UN Security Council, preoccupied with other matters and reluctant to get drawn into the conflict, refused even to discuss the situation.[28] Most of the francophone

[20] SC Res 688 (1991). [21] SC Res 733 (1992); SC Res 746 (1992).

[22] SC Res 940 (1994). [23] SC Res 941 (1994). [24] SC Res 918 (1994).

[25] A related question was whether the International Court of Justice could review the Council's decisions on such matters. For a review of the debate between 'legalists' and 'realists,' see José E. Alvarez, 'Judging the Security Council' (1996) 90 *American Journal of International Law* 1–40.

[26] SC Res 940 (1994). [27] SC Res 1973 (2011).

[28] David Wippman, 'Enforcing the Peace: ECOWAS and the Liberian Civil War' in Lori Damrosch (ed), *Enforcing Restraint: Collective Intervention in Internal Conflicts* (New York: Council on Foreign Relations Press, 1993), 157, 159.

members of ECOWAS initially expressed concern that ECOMOG had overstepped its bounds, but as the conflict wore on, ECOWAS largely coalesced around military action aimed at stabilizing Liberia and creating conditions for the establishment of an elected government.[29]

The UN Security Council did not publicly address the situation in Liberia until January 1991, after ECOWAS had forced a ceasefire on the warring parties. In a general statement, the Council lauded ECOWAS for helping to restore peace to Liberia and encouraged all parties to cooperate with ECOWAS. Seventeen months later, the Council again praised ECOWAS for its efforts to bring peace to Liberia. Only Burkina Faso expressed reservations.[30] Most delegates treated ECOMOG as a peacekeeping force and avoided awkward questions about its initial authority to intervene. But it is hard to read the Council's statements as anything other than tacit approval of ECOWAS military action.[31] It appears that Council members, while not wishing to get drawn into the conflict themselves, felt relieved that ECOWAS had taken responsibility for one of the many costly and protracted conflicts then multiplying around the world.

In the past, most scholars have argued that only express, prior Security Council authorization can justify military intervention that is not in self-defence. During the Cuban Missile Crisis, the US argued that the failure of the Security Council to condemn the naval blockade of Cuba amounted to its implicit authorization.[32] Most states rejected this argument. Accepting implicit, after-the-fact approval might encourage regional organizations or individual states to act without authorization in the hope that the Council will be induced, in the light of changes in the parties' positions stemming from the intervention itself, to acquiesce or tacitly endorse the action. This risk, however, has to be set against the danger of discouraging desirable interventions that might receive tacit approval but which would be rendered ineffective if forced to await prior authorization.[33]

In 1996, ECOWAS again used force without prior Security Council authorization, this time to restore to office the ousted government of the president of Sierra Leone,

[29] Wippman, 'Enforcing the Peace: ECOWAS and the Liberian Civil War' in Damrosch, *Enforcing Restraint*, 173.

[30] Wippman, 'Enforcing the Peace: ECOWAS and the Liberian Civil War' in Damrosch, *Enforcing Restraint*, 185.

[31] See Jeremy Levitt, 'Humanitarian Intervention by Regional Actors in Internal Conflicts: The Cases of ECOWAS in Liberia and Sierra Leone' (1998) 12 *Temple International and Comparative Law Journal* 333, 342–3. But see Monica Hakimi, 'To Condone or Condemn? Regional Enforcement Actions in the Absence of Security Council Authorization', Working Paper No 198 (2007), available at <http://ssrn.comb/abstract=1010359> (arguing that the Security Council did not retroactively authorize but 'simply overlooked ECOWAS's deviation from Article 53').

[32] Wippman, 'Enforcing the Peace: ECOWAS and the Liberian Civil War' in Damrosch, *Enforcing Restraint*, 187.

[33] Wippman, 'Enforcing the Peace: ECOWAS and the Liberian Civil War' in Damrosch, *Enforcing Restraint*, 187.

Ahmad Tejan Kabbah. Again, the Security Council tacitly endorsed the intervention after the fact. More recent regional interventions in West Africa and elsewhere have followed a similar pattern. While such cases still fall at best into a grey area of legality, as a practical matter the states involved pay little or no price for what might be deemed technical violations of the UN Charter. Both the Council and the international community seem willing to tolerate and even welcome interventions seen as genuinely or at least predominantly pro-democratic and/or humanitarian, particularly if they are undertaken by multilateral organizations in areas that do not implicate critical strategic interests of major powers.[34] In this sense, such actions may represent a form of 'acceptable breach', a term describing interventions that are unauthorized but widely viewed as desirable,[35] at least when tacit Security Council authorization follows.

B. Consent

A state may use force on the territory of another state provided it acts with the consent of that state and in ways that the consenting state could lawfully act itself. It is 'dictatorial interference' in the internal affairs of another state that is impermissible, not intervention per se.[36] In general, any indigenous government in effective control of the state is deemed entitled to grant or withhold consent to intervention, whether or not the government at issue is democratically elected or popularly supported. The consent of the population is inferred from the fact of effective control. Accordingly, external intervention against the will of a government in effective control is generally deemed illegal, even if the goal is to replace a dictatorship with a democracy.[37]

On occasion, however, states or international organizations seek to rely on the consent of an ousted but democratically constituted government as the legal basis for intervention to restore that government to power. Interveners sometimes also seek to rely on consent that has been given in advance, by treaty. Both forms of consent are legally problematic, but sometimes accepted or, in any event, tolerated.

[34] See Hakimi, 'To Condone or Condemn?', fn 10 ('Many legal scholars now accept that, at least in certain circumstances, the Security Council may retroactively authorize a regional enforcement action') (citing Simon Chesterman, *Just War or Just Peace? Humanitarian Intervention and International Law* (Oxford: Oxford University Press, 2001), 123.

[35] See generally Jean-Pierre L. Fonteyne, 'The Customary International Law Doctrine of Humanitarian Intervention: Its Current Validity Under the UN Charter' (1974) 4 *California Western International Law Journal* 203 (discussing the pros and cons of acceptable breaches).

[36] Lassa Oppenheim, *International Law* (ed Hersch Lauterpacht, 8th edn, London: Longmans, 1955), 305 (defining prohibited intervention).

[37] David Wippman, 'Pro-Democratic Intervention by Invitation' in Fox and Roth, *Democratic Governance and International Law*, 293, 295.

1. *Consent of an ousted government*

During the Cold War, and to a limited extent thereafter, both France and the UK intervened periodically in former colonies to support friendly governments against small-scale rebellions or palace coups. Most states accepted such interventions, even when the inviting government had already lost its hold on power when it extended the invitation. As long as the interventions were swift and small in scale, the coup-makers were treated as temporary usurpers, whose brief control of the state did not fundamentally alter the de jure government's claim to represent the state in its international relations.[38] This attitude may reflect a sense that the former colonial powers should have some leeway in assisting their former colonial territories to maintain order, even if the same sort of intervention might not be seen as acceptable elsewhere.

The more difficult question is whether the consent of a democratically constituted government will suffice to override the claim of a usurping government that holds control for an extended period and seems likely to retain control absent external intervention. The two cases most directly on point involve Haiti in 1990 and Sierra Leone in 1996.[39]

Jean Bertrand Aristide became president of Haiti in 1990, following internationally monitored elections. But a few months later, the Haitian military seized power and forced Aristide to flee the country. If Aristide had immediately invited and obtained external military intervention to restore him to office, the case may have seemed unremarkable. But Aristide was extremely reluctant to invite intervention, and did so only after months of economic sanctions and international pressure failed to force the military junta from office. Moreover, this was not the typical palace coup; the military had significant, though minority, Haitian popular support. Thus, the coup-makers could not be viewed simply as transient occupiers of the presidential mansion.

Should Aristide's invitation by itself suffice to justify military intervention? Aristide remained the internationally recognized head of state; both the UN and the OAS repeatedly reaffirmed his status and demanded his reinstatement. By contrast, the military junta took power by force and retained it by terrorizing much of the country. For most states, 'there was no contest over the mandate to articulate the will of the "legitimate government" '.[40] Accordingly, one could make a strong argument that Aristide's consent alone constituted sufficient warrant for external intervention.

[38] Wippman, 'Pro-Democratic Intervention by Invitation' in Fox and Roth, *Democratic Governance and International Law*, 295, 300.

[39] The discussion of Haiti and Sierra Leone that follows is drawn from Wippman, 'Pro-Democratic Intervention by Invitation' in Fox and Roth, *Democratic Governance and International Law*, 301–11.

[40] Brad R. Roth, 'Governmental Illegitimacy Revisited: "Pro-Democratic" Armed Intervention in the Post-Bipolar World' (1993) 3 *Transnational Law and Contemporary Problems* 481, 511–12.

But when the Security Council finally acted, it relied principally on its own authority under Chapter VII of the UN Charter to authorize military intervention. The Council's authorizing resolution took note of Aristide's consent,[41] but the Council was unwilling to treat that consent as either a necessary or a sufficient legal basis for intervention.[42] The Council's reluctance appears to reflect in part the continuing importance of effective control as an indicator of a government's authority to speak for the state. In Haiti, effective control and democratic legitimacy were divided between the military junta and the ousted president; in that context, the Council seemed unwilling to let either acting alone express the will of the state. Instead, the Council asserted, not entirely persuasively, that the junta's refusal to reinstate Aristide constituted a threat to international peace and security that warranted a military response. As a result, Haiti remains an ambiguous precedent.

Sierra Leone offers another, somewhat sharper but still ambiguous, precedent. In 1996, after years of military rule, internal conflict, and general instability, Sierra Leone elected Ahmad Tejan Kabbah as president in internationally monitored elections. But six months later, a group of low-level military officers seized power, leading to the general collapse of law and order, widespread violence, and gross human rights violations. Internal opposition to the coup was broad and deep, in almost all sectors of Sierra Leonean society. Similarly, international opposition was prompt and near universal. The UN, OAU, ECOWAS, Commonwealth, and the European Union (EU) all condemned the coup and demanded the immediate reinstatement of Kabbah's government. No state recognized the military junta, known as the Armed Forces Revolutionary Council (AFRC).

ECOWAS, on its own authority, imposed an embargo on Sierra Leone and engaged in sporadic attacks on the AFRC. ECOWAS action was generally supported or at least condoned; the Security Council, for example, applauded ECOWAS efforts to obtain 'a peaceful resolution' of the crisis[43] and eventually imposed its own economic sanctions and authorized ECOWAS to help to enforce them.[44] Only the Russian Federation expressed any misgivings, noting that 'enforcement measures should not be taken by regional organizations without Security Council authorization.'[45]

When a subsequent peace plan with the AFRC broke down, ECOWAS again took matters into its own hands. In February 1998, ECOMOG troops seized Freetown after a week of sometimes intense fighting. ECOWAS neither sought not received Security Council authorization before launching its offensive, claiming among

[41] SC Res 940 (1994) (citing letters from Aristide and Haiti's Permanent Representative to the UN implicitly supporting military intervention).

[42] During the Council debate over the resolution, several states' representatives referenced Aristide's consent as an important factor behind their support for the resolution, but none treated it as sufficient by itself. See UN Provisional Verbatim Record, 3413th mtg, S/PV.3413 (31 July 1994), 17, 19, 23, 24.

[43] Statement by the President of the Security Council, S/PRST/1997/42 (6 Aug 1997).

[44] SC Res 1132 (1997).

[45] Security Council Press Release 6425 (8 Oct 1997).

other things that it was acting in self-defence and pursuant to a mutual assistance treaty with Sierra Leone.

The question for our purposes is whether Kabbah's consent by itself justified ECOMOG's military intervention. The argument is much the same as with Aristide. Kabbah was the elected head of state and retained broad popular support. The international community continued to recognize his government and demand its reinstatement. The AFRC had little popular support and no international legitimacy. When ECOMOG took the capital, the populace celebrated.[46]

In this context, reliance on effective control preserves few interests other than the integrity of the rule itself. Although Nigeria played the lead role, the decision to intervene was multilateral. There was little risk of inciting a broader regional conflict. The people of Sierra Leone welcomed the intervention and so did most states and international organizations. On the other hand, the ECOMOG intervention constituted an end run around the Security Council, which raised systemic concerns not fully addressed by Kabbah's consent and popular support for the intervention. ECOMOG's failure even to seek Security Council authorization transferred decision-making authority from the Council to a sub-regional organization, leaving the Council with limited options.

The Security Council was evidently troubled by the offensive but unwilling to condemn or even directly criticize it. Instead, the Council simply called for the combatants to avoid harm to civilians and to reach a ceasefire.[47] Nonetheless, a few weeks later, the Council 'welcome[d] the fact that the rule of the military junta has been brought to an end' and commended ECOWAS for its contributions to a 'peaceful resolution of this crisis'.[48] In short, the Council, and most states, tacitly approved or at least acquiesced in ECOMOG's decision, treating it more or less as another instance of an acceptable—or at least accepted—breach.

2. *Treaty-based consent*

The most interesting development in recent years, and the one that poses the greatest challenge to the effective control standard and the UN Charter framework governing the use of force, is the use of treaties by regional and sub-regional organizations to authorize military intervention in advance under specified circumstances. These circumstances include gross human rights violations, internal disorder, and the unconstitutional overthrow of a democratically constituted government. These treaties now appear most prominently in Africa but have occasionally been used elsewhere.

[46] See Howard French, 'Nigerians Take Capital of Sierra Leone as Junta Flees', *New York Times*, 14 Feb 1998, A3.

[47] French, 'Nigerians Take Capital of Sierra Leone as Junta Flees'; Press Release SG/SM/6462 AFR/38 (11 Feb 1998).

[48] S/PRST/1998/5 (26 Feb 1998).

In the pre-UN Charter era, treaties of guarantee were not uncommon. Such treaties provided that one or more states might intervene forcibly in another signatory state to maintain a particular state of affairs as stipulated in the treaty. The 1960 Cyprus Treaty of Guarantee, which authorized the UK, Turkey, and Greece to 'take action' in Cyprus to maintain the constitutional order established by the contemporaneously adopted Cypriot Constitution, is the best modern example.[49]

The UN Charter, however, seems to leave little room for such treaties. Article 103 of the Charter provides that states' obligations under the Charter override any inconsistent obligations in other treaties. Similarly, under customary international law, states cannot by treaty contract out of, or around, peremptory norms. Since the prohibition on the use of force in Article 2(4) of the Charter is widely recognized as a peremptory norm, states cannot by treaty circumvent their obligation to use force only in self-defence or pursuant to Security Council authorization. Accordingly, critics of treaties of guarantee and similar treaty arrangements contend that any such treaties are void *ab initio*.[50]

1. *Post-Charter treaties of guarantee*

Until recently, post-Charter instances of such treaties, other than the Cyprus Treaty of Guarantee, have been rare. One possible exception is a 1995 agreement contained in the Dayton Accords, a set of agreements intended to end the conflict in Bosnia. The Dayton agreements created a complex set of arrangements for power-sharing among Bosnian Serbs, Croats, and Muslims.[51] Annex I-A of the Dayton Accords, the Agreement on the Military Aspects of the Peace Settlement, authorized outside states to enforce key aspects of the accords by any means necessary, 'including the use of necessary force'.[52] Annex I-A 'invited' the Security Council to adopt a

[49] Treaty of Guarantee, Art 4 (1960) 382 UNTS 3. Nevertheless, some argue that the Treaty of Guarantee is contrary to international law. See eg Andrew J. Jacovides, *Treaties Conflicting with Peremptory Norms of International Law and the Zurich–London 'Agreements'* (Nicosia 1966), 21 (stating that their combined effect 'was to arrest the constitutional and political development of the Republic by putting it into a straight jacket at its infancy as a sovereign entity, and to subject it to the will of three outside powers [thus creating] a state of affairs inconsistent with the basic elements of the principles of sovereign equality and non-intervention...'). For contrasting perspectives on the legality of the Treaty, see Lawrence Hargrove et al, 'Cyprus: International Law and the Prospects for Settlement' (1984) 78 *Proceedings of the Annual Meeting (American Society of International Law)* 107–32.

[50] See eg Brad R. Roth, 'The Illegality of "Pro-Democratic" Invasion Pacts' in Fox and Roth, *Democratic Governance and International Law*, 328.

[51] The Dayton agreements consist of a single General Framework Agreement with a set of 12 annexes containing separate agreements among the Republic of Bosnia and Herzegovina, the Federation of Bosnia and Herzegovina, and the Republika Srpska. The agreement and its annexes are reprinted at (1996) 35 ILM 75. While the agreements are not treaties in the Vienna Convention sense because they are not between two or more states but rather between a state and political communities within the state, such communities, as belligerent entities, have been treated as possessing sufficient international legal personality to enter binding commitments. Wippman, 'Pro-Democratic Intervention by Invitation' in Fox and Roth, *Democratic Governance and International Law*, 318 fn 83.

[52] Annex I-A, Art 2(b).

resolution authorizing such use of force, which the Security Council promptly did.[53] But if agreements authorizing the use of force outside the Charter framework are void *ab initio*, then one might conclude that Annex I-A, the linchpin of the Dayton settlement, was void. Neither the parties nor outside states took that position.

Standing by itself, Annex I-A might be dismissed as an anomaly. But in recent years, several new treaties authorizing military intervention have appeared, all of them in Africa. These treaties raise fundamental questions regarding the legality of attempts to authorize military intervention in advance and absent the contemporaneous consent of an effective government, whether to reinstate an ousted government or for some other potentially laudable purpose. They also raise basic questions about the proper relationship between the UN Security Council and regional organizations.

II. *A pro-democratic security pact?*

A version of contemporary pro-democratic intervention treaties was first suggested by Tom Farer in a prescient 1988 article.[54] Farer posited a hypothetical agreement among Caribbean countries and interested NATO members to safeguard democracy in the signatory states. In the event of a coup, treaty signatories could use force to restore the ousted constitutional government, either at the request of the deposed government officials or, if they were unable to communicate with pact members, at the initiative of two-thirds of the treaty's signatories.[55] Farer argued that such a treaty would permit pro-democratic military intervention even in the absence of Security Council authorization, 'since such an action is carried out with the previously expressed consent of the target state…'[56]

As Farer noted, the difficult question 'is whether, despite ceding to others a right to intervene under stated circumstances, the state retains, by virtue of its continuing existence as a sovereign entity, an absolute right to revoke the ceded authority.'[57] In short, does intervention absent the contemporaneous consent of a government in effective control require Security Council authorization? Elsewhere, I have analysed this question in terms of possible divisions in the authority of a government to speak for the state.[58]

Ordinarily, a government in effective control alone represents the political community of the state in its international relations. That government generally remains free to withdraw previously expressed consent to intervention, whether the consent

[53] SC Res 1031 (1995).

[54] Tom J. Farer, 'The United States as Guarantor of Democracy in the Caribbean Basin: Is There a Legal Way?' (1988) 10 *Human Rights Quarterly* 157.

[55] Farer, 'The United States as Guarantor of Democracy in the Caribbean Basin', 332.

[56] Farer, 'The United States as Guarantor of Democracy in the Caribbean Basin', 332.

[57] Farer, 'The United States as Guarantor of Democracy in the Caribbean Basin', 332.

[58] Wippman, 'Pro-Democratic Intervention by Invitation' in Fox and Roth, *Democratic Governance and International Law*, 324–6.

is expressed in a treaty or otherwise.[59] During the course of the long-running conflict in the Democratic Republic of the Congo (DRC), Laurent Kabila, the DRC president, at one point consented by treaty to Ugandan military action against anti-Ugandan forces operating in the DRC. The International Court of Justice concluded that the DRC's consent had been withdrawn by August 1998, and that the continued presence of Ugandan troops on DRC territory after that date constituted a violation of the DRC's sovereignty.[60] Thus, consent to military intervention is ordinarily revocable by the government in effective control of the state.

At times, however, questions may arise as to the authority of a particular government, even one in control of the territory of the state, to speak for the state as a whole. In extreme cases, such as in Sierra Leone, the ousted government, widely recognized as the continuing legitimate government and retaining substantial popular support, might still be deemed to possess at least some authority to speak for the state, arguably enough to overcome the competing claim of the de facto authorities. In other cases, if a de facto government can demonstrate significant popular support, or the ousted government no longer exists, the strength of the ousted government's claim to speak for the state will be less evident. My conclusion was that it would be appropriate to adopt a rebuttable presumption treating a coup against an elected government as a break in the political unity of the state sufficient to prevent the new government from unilaterally revoking the consent of its democratic predecessor to the treaty of guarantee.[61]

III. *Pro-democratic intervention pacts in Africa*

But we now have several actual treaties of guarantee to consider. Jeremy Levitt in particular has chronicled the development and importance of these treaties.[62] As Levitt notes, the UN security system 'has not offered a viable strategy to reduce armed conflict and human suffering and solidify democracy in Africa.'[63] As a result, African states and organizations 'have sought to fashion African solutions to African problems by creating innovative rules and mechanisms for pro-democracy and human rights-based intervention.'[64] Levitt views the developments in Africa as driving regional customary international law, and perhaps even general customary international law, towards greater acceptance of treaty-based pro-democratic intervention. But the solution adopted by ECOWAS, the AU, and other sub-regional organizations in Africa remains deeply problematic under the UN Charter.

[59] See eg Yoram Dinstein, *War, Aggression and Self-Defence* (Cambridge: Cambridge University Press, 2005), 116.

[60] *Case Concerning Armed Activities on the Territory of the Congo (DRC v. Uganda)*, Judgment of 19 Dec 2005, ICJ Rep 2005, 165.

[61] Wippman, 'Pro-Democratic Intervention by Invitation', 325.

[62] See generally Jeremy Levitt, 'Pro-Democratic Intervention in Africa' (2006) 24 *Wisconsin International Law Journal* 785.

[63] Levitt, 'Pro-Democratic Intervention in Africa', 786.

[64] Levitt, 'Pro-Democratic Intervention in Africa', 786.

a) The ECOWAS security system

ECOWAS began as a regional economic community but gradually morphed into a sub-regional collective security system. A 1978 ECOWAS Protocol prohibited aggression between member states[65] and a 1981 defence pact committed ECOWAS members to provide mutual assistance for defence in the case of any external (ie extra-regional) aggression.[66] But ECOWAS's experiences in Liberia and Sierra Leone persuaded ECOWAS members that political stability and economic growth could best be promoted by a stronger regional security system, particularly given the reluctance of the UN to become involved in African conflicts. In 1999, just a few years after its intervention in Sierra Leone, ECOWAS adopted a Protocol Relating to the Mechanism for Conflict Prevention, Management, Resolution, Peace-keeping and Security. The Protocol established a nine-member Mediation and Security Council, empowered to decide by a 2/3 vote on ECOWAS responses to conflicts in member states. Among other things, the Mediation and Security Council is permitted to 'authorise all forms of intervention' as necessary to manage 'serious and massive violation of human rights and the rule of law'; 'an overthrow or attempted overthrow of a democratically elected government'; and 'Any other situation as may be decided by the Mediation and Security Council.' A key goal of the Protocol is to promote 'constitutional convergence,' that is, to insist on internal succession processes that do not threaten member states with coups or other unconstitutional seizures of power.[67] As altruistic as the provisions of the Protocol might sound, it is clear that self-interest—the desire of existing governments to protect themselves from coups—played a key role in member states' decisions to create the Protocol.[68]

On its face, the ECOWAS Protocol challenges the primacy of the UN Security Council[69] and seems to run afoul of Article 103 of the UN Charter. ECOWAS has arrogated the right to decide for itself when to authorize military intervention in member states, with or without the contemporaneous consent of an affected state. Yet, so far, neither the Security Council nor individual states have lined up to declare the Protocol void; in fact, the Protocol has attracted surprisingly little international attention.

Following adoption of the Protocol, ECOWAS has on several occasions deployed troops to restore order or assist an elected government in a member state, but not under circumstances that pose a direct challenge to the Security Council. In Côte

[65] Protocol on Non-Aggression, reprinted in *West Africa*, 25 May 1981, 1153.

[66] Protocol Relating to Mutual Assistance on Defence, A/SP3/5/81, reprinted in Official Journal of the ECOWAS, June 1981, 9.

[67] Frederick Cowell, 'The Impact of the ECOWAS Protocol on Good Governance and Democracy' (2011) 19 *African Journal of International and Comparative Law* 331, 333.

[68] Cowell, 'The Impact of the ECOWAS Protocol on Good Governance and Democracy', 335.

[69] See Eliav Lieblich, 'Intervention and Consent: Consensual Forcible Intervention in Internal Armed Conflicts as International Agreements' (2011) 29 *Boston University International Law Journal* 337, 369–70.

d'Ivoire, following an unconstitutional overthrow of the elected government by disgruntled soldiers, ECOWAS did threaten to intervene militarily if contending parties did not restore the constitutional order.[70] When a settlement was reached, ECOWAS joined France in deploying a peacekeeping force, with UN Security Council support. Similarly, in 2005, ECOWAS imposed sanctions on Togo, following a military coup against the elected government that was condemned by the UN, the AU, and ECOWAS itself. The sanctions, supported by the AU, helped to force new elections (which, ironically, were won by supporters of the coup).[71]

b) The AU security system

The AU has followed a path much like that of ECOWAS, setting up in the AU Peace and Security Council a mini-UN Security Council, and conferring upon itself a right to intervene militarily in African conflicts. Article 4(h) of the African Union Constitutive Act of 2000 identifies as one of the Union's operative principles 'the right of the Union to intervene in a Member State pursuant to a decision of the Assembly in respect of grave circumstances, namely: war crimes, genocide and crimes against humanity.'[72] A planned amendment would add 'a serious threat to legitimate order' to the list. The subsequent Protocol Relating to the Establishment of the Peace and Security Council of the African Union contains provisions establishing an AU Peace and Security Council that may among other things 'authorize the mounting and deployment of peace support missions' and 'institute sanctions whenever an unconstitutional change of Government takes place in a Member State.'[73] Moreover, the African Charter on Democracy, Elections and Governance, which entered into force in early 2012, directs the AU Peace and Security Council, when confronted with a threat to the constitutional order in a member state, to 'exercise its responsibilities in order to maintain the constitutional order in accordance with relevant provisions of the Protocol.'[74]

Like ECOWAS, the AU has not yet exercised its claimed powers in ways that directly challenge the primacy of the UN Security Council. The AU has, however, joined the UN and other actors in using sanctions to reverse coups in Mauritania, São Tomé and Príncipe, Guinea, and elsewhere.[75] While action to preserve democracy generally accords with the international principles that give rise to claims of

[70] Levitt, 'Pro-Democratic Intervention in Africa', 809–10.

[71] Levitt, 'Pro-Democratic Intervention in Africa', 811–12.

[72] Constitutive Act of the African Union, Art 4(h), 11 July 2000, available at <http://www.africa-union.org/root/au/aboutau/constitutive_act_en.htm>.

[73] Protocol, Arts 7c and 7g, available at <http://www.africa-union.org/root/au/organs/psc/Protocol_peace%20and%20security.pdf>.

[74] African Charter on Democracy, Elections, and Good Governance, Art 24, available at <http://www.africa-union.org/root/AU/Documents/Treaties/text/Charter%20on%20Democracy.pdf>.

[75] See Eki Yemisi Omorogbe, 'A Club of Incumbents? The African Union and Coups d'Etat' (2011) 44 *Vanderbilt Journal of Transnational Law* 123, 131.

a democratic entitlement, ECOWAS and the AU have acted principally with the goal of preserving order rather than fostering any substantive conception of democracy. As Eki Omorogbe puts it, 'When responding to *coups*, the AU has consistently favored the constitutional order, irrespective of incumbent regimes, the claims made by those challenging them, or the likelihood that the *coup* might advance democracy. As a result, the AU's actions have generally protected incumbent governments.'[76] In Niger, Mauritania, and elsewhere, AU actions may have undermined efforts to displace democratically elected governments that behaved undemocratically once in office.[77]

c) Treaty-based intervention revisited

Both ECOWAS and the AU have claimed the authority to authorize military intervention in circumstances that the UN Charter appears to reserve for the Security Council. By setting up their own mini-Security Councils, ECOWAS and the AU have exceeded the authority that the Charter grants to regional organizations. Under Article 53 of the Charter, 'no enforcement action shall be taken under regional arrangements or by regional agencies without the authorization of the Security Council.' Absent extraordinary circumstances, such as existed in Sierra Leone for example, it is hard to reconcile these arrangements with Article 53 or *jus cogens* provisions relating to the use of force.

But at the same time, neither the UN nor individual states have denounced the treaties or challenged the ECOWAS and AU assertions of authority in any significant way. One option would be to conclude, as Jeremy Levitt does, that multilateral pro-democratic intervention is now accepted, at least on a regional basis.[78] But it is not clear how regional practice, even if tolerated and perhaps tacitly welcomed by the UN, can modify the UN Charter or *jus cogens* norms on the use of force. At the same time, it seems problematic simply to dismiss the ECOWAS and AU security regimes as straightforward violations of the UN Charter framework. Accordingly, pro-democratic intervention by treaty seems destined to remain awkwardly poised between condoned practice and accepted law.

[76] Omorogbe, 'A Club of Incumbents?', 138. [77] Omorogbe, 'A Club of Incumbents?', 153.
[78] Levitt, 'Pro-Democratic Intervention in Africa', 787–8.

IV. Conclusion

The uncertain status of pro-democratic intervention seems likely to persist indefinitely, for the simple reason that pro-democratic intervention almost invariably brings important values of the international legal system into conflict. The norms that collectively support the 'democratic entitlement'—self-determination, free expression, political participation—remain core values of the international legal order. But respect for the principle of non-intervention (understood as deference to the will of a government in effective control of the state on matters internal to that state) also remains a core value, even if the government at issue is undemocratic.

If the UN Security Council could be relied upon to address coups and other manifest threats to democratic governance whenever they arose, the uncertainty might resolve. Security Council-authorized intervention in this context is widely accepted, and if the Security Council took action in appropriate cases and condemned unauthorized interventions by others, the legal status of pro-democratic intervention would be considerably clearer. But the Security Council often prefers to remain on the sidelines and, as we have seen, frequently acquiesces in or even commends regional or sub-regional organizations that take matters into their own hands.

To condemn interventions which the Council commends seems problematic. International law rests fundamentally on state practice. If multilateral organizations intervene with general approbation, then declaring the intervention illegal carries little weight.[79] The acting states incur little or no reputational cost and may even gain in stature.

But such interventions do risk undermining the UN Charter framework governing the use of force, even if only modestly. This is the dilemma of the 'acceptable breach' theory. Actions contrary to formal treaty rules but desirable on humanitarian or other grounds and accepted by most states promote some international values while undermining others. As Ian Brownlie suggested many years ago with reference to humanitarian intervention, some actions may be tolerated as on balance desirable in particular cases, but not formally legalized for fear of eroding core legal principles.[80] The degree of erosion will vary with the circumstances and the plausibility of a particular government's claim to speak for the state, but absent Security Council authorization, some erosion will occur.

[79] For a similar argument in connection with NATO's intervention in Kosovo, see David Wippman, 'Kosovo and the Limits of International Law' (2001) 25 *Fordham International Law Journal* 129, 135–7.

[80] Ian Brownlie, 'Thoughts on Kind-Hearted Gunmen' in Richard B. Lillich (ed), *Humanitarian Intervention and the United Nations* (Charlottesville, VA: University Press of Virginia, 1973), 139.

CHAPTER 37

INTERVENTION BY INVITATION

GREGORY H. FOX

I. Introduction

STATES have frequently justified interventions in internal armed conflicts by claiming they were invited to assist one of the belligerent parties. In most cases the invitation is said to come from the government. Much less frequently states rely on an invitation from a rebel group fighting against the government. As a general matter, invitations from governments provide a lawful basis for intervention. If a target state holds rights against foreign intervention and that state, through its government, waives those rights by consenting to the presence of foreign troops on its territory, no claim remains that a right against intervention has been violated. Such mitigation through consent is consistent with principles of state responsibility, which provide that consent to an otherwise unlawful act precludes the wrongfulness of that act. Conversely, because the state holds the right against foreign intervention, consent issued by a rebel group does not mitigate the wrongfulness of intervention *against* the representative of the state: its government. The primary value at stake in this rather straightforward conception of intervention by invitation, in other words, is the territorial integrity of the state as defined and invoked by its incumbent government.

Even taken on its own terms this scenario is incomplete, for it assumes a clarity in the status of the actors and the nature of the consent that is often lacking. First, the government issuing the invitation may control only a portion of the national territory, thus calling into question its capacity to consent on behalf of the state. Secondly, and relatedly, the invitation may seek assistance in fighting a civil war that has so torn the country and its population that outside intervention on the government side might be the decisive factor in a struggle for power that should be decided by the people themselves. Thirdly, questions may arise about the invitation itself: was it issued by officials with proper authority, did it come before or after the intervention, or, indeed, was it issued at all? Fourthly, what if the invitation comes in response to a prior intervention by a third state against the incumbent government? Finally, what if prior to the outbreak of the conflict the state had entered into a treaty consenting to intervention under certain defined circumstances? Can another party to the treaty intervene even though the government then in power in the target state objects?

Each of these questions has engaged international law since the early 19th century when norms concerning outside involvement in civil wars began to emerge. The answers have varied over time as the broader regime of peace and security norms evolved and eventually coalesced into the collective security system of the UN Charter. But there was also a remarkable consistency when the factual variables represented by these questions were not contested. The view that 'international law treats civil wars as purely an internal matter'[1] appears constant over a remarkable period of history. International law traditionally had no qualitative criteria on questions of national governance and the legitimate acquisition of political power. Who may legitimately govern a state, how regimes come to power, whether citizens have a right to depose odious regimes, and whether any given regime can defend itself against an armed insurrection were all questions that did not engage international law. As a result, the question of whether and when other states can intervene in civil wars was not answered by reference to matters such as the human rights practices of the incumbent regime or the democratic bona fides of the armed opposition. The answer turned rather on wholly pragmatic questions of effective control over territory. A government in control of its territory could invite outside assistance to counter a rebel movement and the rebels could not.

In the post-Cold War era, however, international law in a variety of areas has begun to develop qualitative criteria on questions of governance. These developments pose a challenge for rules on intervention by invitation. If a regime has demonstrated its legitimacy according to these emerging criteria, should it not always be permitted to invite outside assistance to counter rebels who are less legitimate or illegitimate according to those same criteria? Conversely, should an 'illegitimate' regime be permitted to invite assistance to counter rebels who promise to reverse its disregard for human rights or democratic institutions? If international law has

[1] Malcolm Shaw, *International Law* (6th edn, Cambridge: Cambridge University Press, 2008), 1148.

started to formulate norms on the nature of national government, in other words, why should national actors be prevented from inviting third parties to give effect to those norms? Has this qualitative view of governance begun to remove civil wars from the protected sphere of domestic jurisdiction and refocused the question on whether an invitation for outside intervention will or will not advance these qualitative values?

This chapter will examine both the variable factual questions that typified discussions of the traditional view of intervention by invitation and the recent challenges to that traditional view.

II. The Traditional Framework

A. Framing the Issue: The Nature of Prohibited Intervention

Norms on intervention by invitation have traditionally been linked to international law's approach to notions of political authority within a state. As an abstract entity a state can function only through human agents—its government. If a government unquestionably represents a state then it has been seen as possessing the authority to seek outside assistance to retain its authority in the face of internal rebellion. Questions arise, however, when the government's representative capacity is called into question. Some scholars have suggested a sliding scale of authority to issue invitations: at some point, when a regime's control over its territory and population is significantly diminished, its capacity to issue invitations will terminate. But this view is disputed. Moreover, focusing the legal question on the regime's agency relationship to the state implicates a host of other doctrines and emerging ideas concerning the legitimacy of governmental authority.

Analysis of these questions largely involves understanding exceptions to exceptions to a general rule. International law broadly prohibits states from intervening on the territory of other states, a rule primarily embodied in Article 2(4) of the UN Charter but also in the many General Assembly resolutions and other sources contributing to a parallel norm of customary international law.[2] There are several well-recognized exceptions to this rule: actions in self-defence (individual

[2] See Christine Gray, *International Law and the Use of Force* (3rd edn, Oxford: Oxford University Press, 2008); Thomas M. Franck, *Recourse to Force* (Cambridge: Cambridge University Press, 2002).

and collective), authorization by the Security Council under Chapter VII of the Charter, actions by regional organizations approved by the Council, and an invitation from an incumbent government. As discussed previously, however, several factors may render an invitation insufficient, such as lack of territorial control or, more controversially, abusive policies by the government. That is, the exceptions to the non-intervention rule themselves have exceptions.

The overarching prohibition is a relative concept: the degree of latitude permitted by the 'intervening' state depends on the legal capacity of the target state to keep aspects of its society free from external intervention. The prohibition is not against all forms of external involvement in domestic matters, only against those that international law reserves to states for their own autonomous decision-making. In the *Nicaragua* case, the International Court of Justice (ICJ) observed that intervention is prohibited when it bears 'on matters in which each State is permitted, by the principle of State sovereignty, to decide freely … Intervention is wrongful when it uses methods of coercion in regard to such choices, which must remain free ones.'[3] One such area is 'the choice of a political, economic, social and cultural system, and the formulation of foreign policy.'[4] Efforts to coerce the choice of a national government seek to prevent states from exercising a prerogative that is rightfully theirs and theirs alone.[5] The Court drew upon widely supported General Assembly resolutions such as the Friendly Relations Declaration and other sources of custom to hold that lethal assistance to a rebel force seeking to overthrow an incumbent government was prohibited.[6]

Traditionally, then, other states had no interest in the outcome of civil wars unless they received a valid invitation from the government to intervene. Governments faced no limitations on their ability to quell internal uprisings and anti-government rebels held no international legal entitlement to displace incumbent governments (with a limited and controversial exception for self-determination conflicts). As detailed later, the success of insurgents might require third parties to accord them certain rights under international law. But these obligations, which arose when other states interacted with parties to a civil war on the high seas, in prize proceedings, and elsewhere, did not turn on the merits of the conflict between a regime and its internal opponents.[7]

[3] *Military and Paramilitary Activities in and against Nicaragua (Nicaragua v. US)*, Judgment of 27 June 1986, ICJ Rep 1986, 14, para 205.

[4] *Nicaragua*, Judgment, para 205.

[5] Christopher C. Joyner and Michael A. Grimaldi, 'The United States and Nicaragua: Reflections on the Lawfulness of Contemporary Intervention' (1984–5) 25 *Vanderbilt Journal of International Law* 621, 643 ('international law supports the fundamental right of states to create a government, adopt a constitution and establish internal laws without external suasion or coercion of any sort').

[6] *Nicaragua*, Judgment, para 242.

[7] See Richard Falk, 'Introduction' in Richard Falk (ed), *The International Law of Civil War* (Baltimore, MD: Johns Hopkins Press, 1971), 11.

B. Evolution of Norms on Invitations to Intervene

The UN Charter's rules on the use of force significantly altered prior international law. But those rules, grounded in Article 2(4), deal exclusively with interstate conflicts. Engaging those rules here requires understanding that external intervention in civil wars internationalizes the conflict for purposes of international law, even though the dominant players and issues at stake may remain primarily domestic. In a series of important resolutions, the General Assembly equated assistance to rebel forces with prohibited interstate aggression.[8] For example, the 1970 Friendly Relations Declaration provides that 'no state shall organize, assist, foment, finance, incite or tolerate subversive terrorist or armed activities directed towards the violent overthrow of the regime of another state, or interfere in civil strife in another state.'[9]

But the Declaration left two critical issues unaddressed: the lawfulness of assistance to governments and the status of regimes being targeted with external assistance. The ICJ addressed the first question in its 1986 *Nicaragua* judgment. The US had provided direct and indirect assistance to rebel forces that were seeking to overthrow the Sandanista government. The ICJ, citing the Friendly Relations Declaration, held that these actions constituted prohibited intervention, since no 'general right of intervention, in support of an opposition within another State, exists in contemporary international law.'[10] The ICJ rejected the suggestion that an invitation from a rebel group might nevertheless justify external assistance. The prohibition on intervention, the Court observed:

> would certainly lose its effectiveness as a principle of law if intervention were to be justified by a mere request for assistance made by an opposition group in another State—supposing such a request to have actually been made by an opposition to the régime in Nicaragua in this instance. Indeed. it is difficult to see what would remain of the principle of non-intervention in international law if intervention, *which is already allowable at the request of the government of a State*, were also to be allowed at the request of the opposition. This would permit any State to intervene at any moment in the interna1 affairs of another State, whether at the request of the government or at the request of its opposition. Such a situation does not in the Court's view correspond to the present state of international law.[11]

The Court's remark in passing that intervention at the request of a government 'is already allowable' is a remarkably blunt statement. It can be read to hold in all cases. The Court does not qualify the right based on the government's control over territory, its record in power, or the nature of the opposition it seeks aid in resisting. The Court has not expanded on this cryptic passage, though in the *Armed Activities* case

[8] Declaration on the Principles of International Law Concerning Friendly Relations, GA Res 2625 (XXV) (1970); Inadmissibility of Intervention, GA Res 2131 (1965); Declaration on the Rights and Duties of States, GA Res 375 (1949).

[9] Friendly Relations Declaration.

[10] *Nicaragua*, Judgment, para 209.

[11] *Nicaragua*, Judgment, para 246 (emphasis added).

it assumed without discussion that a government could consent to the presence of foreign troops on its territory, and instead focused all its attention on whether, how, and when consent could be withdrawn.[12] The Court also reaffirmed its main holding in *Nicaragua* that the prohibition on assisting rebel forces is a matter of customary law and that the prohibition applies with special (though not exclusive) force to rebels seeking to overthrow the government.[13]

The basis for the *Nicaragua* rule is fairly straightforward. States are entitled to have their territory free from foreign interventions and they are free to consent to intervention that might otherwise violate that independence. Article 20 of the International Law Commission's (ILC's) Draft Articles on State Responsibility provides that 'Valid consent by a State to the commission of a given act by another State precludes the wrongfulness of that act in relation to the former State to the extent that the act remains within the limits of that consent.'[14] In general, governments have the capacity to consent on behalf of the state and opposition forces do not. Indeed, 'the very ability to make such a request reinforces the inviting state's authority.'[15] Because of the controversy surrounding invited interventions, however, ILC members suggested during the discussion of Article 20 that the secondary rule on consent would not be dispositive of the issue and would instead give way to primary rules on the use of force.[16]

The second question left unanswered by the Friendly Relations Declaration concerns the status of the government issuing the invitation. Does it matter that the regime is winning a civil war, at an impasse with rebels, or has lost substantial portions of its territory to rebel control? International law on this point is less than a model of clarity. On the one hand, pre-Charter rules on this aspect of civil wars have likely fallen into desuetude.[17] On the other hand, the critical factor at the centre of the traditional rules—the degree of rebel control over territory—is also central to contemporary approaches to evaluating government invitations. Understanding the opacity of law on governmental invitations requires a review of its change over time.

The pre-Charter norms on civil wars emerged following the American Revolution and the Latin American struggles for independence in the early 19th century. Disputes arose when the rebelling colonies sought both neutral rights on the high

[12] *Armed Activities on the Territory of the Congo (DRC v. Uganda)*, Judgment of 19 Dec 2005, ICJ Rep 2005, 168, paras 42–54.

[13] *Armed Activities*, Judgment, paras 162–3.

[14] Draft Articles on Responsibility of States for Internationally Wrongful Acts, Report of the International Law Commission on its 53rd Session, 23 April–1 June, 2 July–10 Aug, Art 20, reprinted in *Yearbook of the International Law Commission*, 2001, vol II (2).

[15] Christopher J. LeMon, 'Unilateral Intervention by Invitation in Civil Wars: The Effective Control Test Tested' (2003) 35 *NYU Journal of International Law and Policy* 741, 743.

[16] Georg Nolte, *Eingreifen auf Einladung: Zur völkerrechtlichen Zulässigkeit des Einsatzes fremder Truppen im internen Konflikt auf Einladung der Regierung* (Berlin: Springer, 1999).

[17] Falk, *The International Law of Civil War*, 15 (describing 'a virtual abandonment of the traditional categories used to regulate outside participation in civil wars'); see text accompanying nn 28–32.

seas and to condemn captured prizes in neutral ports. The questions became even more pointed during the American Civil War, when the rebelling south issued letters of Marque to privateers, forcing European states to take a position on the status of the confederacy. Similar issues arose during the Crimean War.[18]

By the mid-19th century, treatise writers were generally in agreement on a set of rules on how third parties should relate to civil wars.[19] These turned largely on the degree of territorial control and political authority exercised by the government and the rebels; in other words, the questions were almost exclusively factual. There were three categories of uprisings: rebellion, insurgency, and belligerency.[20] A rebellion involved low-level hostilities and was almost entirely a matter of domestic jurisdiction. No international rights accrued to opposition forces. A conflict became an insurgency when violence escalated and rebels acquired control over significant portions of territory. An insurgency was no mere group of lawbreakers, but the consequences of recognition by other states was 'at best, uncertain and indefinite'[21] since insurgents acquired no rights under international law and states were still prohibited from providing them assistance. The third stage, belligerency, came about when four criteria[22] were met, most importantly when the rebels' 'degree of control matched or exceeded that of the previously-recognised government.'[23] Because belligerents were assumed to function like the territorial government of a state, international law both granted the belligerents *jus in bello* rights and created obligations for third parties. The two parties effectively became co-equal sovereigns for the purposes of the conflict.

But scholars diverged on whether belligerency was a matter of fact or came about only upon formal recognition.[24] More fundamentally, they disagreed on the consequences of belligerency for third parties. Continuing the analogy to an interstate

[18] See Sam Foster Halabi, 'Traditions of Belligerent Recognition: The Libyan Intervention in Historical and Theoretical Context' (2012) 27 *American University International Law Review* 321, 330–46; Yair M. Lootsteen, 'The Concept of Belligerency in International Law' (2000) 166 *Military Law Review* 109; Rosalyn Higgins, 'International Law and Civil War' in Evan Luard (ed), *The International Regulation of Civil War* (London: Thames & Hudson, 1972), 169.

[19] Halabi, 'Traditions of Belligerent Recognition', 351–71.

[20] Lootsteen, 'The Concept of Belligerency in International Law', 113–14 (citing numerous sources).

[21] Falk, *The International Law of Civil War*, 12.

[22] Hersch Lauterpacht, *Recognition in International Law* (1947, reissue Cambridge: Cambridge University Press, 2012), 176–8.

> First, there must exist within the State an armed conflict of a general (as distinguished from a purely local) character; secondly, the insurgents must occupy and administer a substantial portion of national territory; thirdly, they must conduct the hostilities in accordance with the rules of war and through organized armed forces acting under a responsible authority; fourthly, there must exist circumstances which make it necessary for outside States to define their attitude by means of recognition of belligerency.

[23] LeMon, 'Unilateral Intervention by Invitation in Civil Wars', 747.

[24] Lootsteen, 'The Concept of Belligerency in International Law', 117–18.

conflict, some asserted that third parties could assist either the government or belligerency upon a valid invitation.[25] Others asserted an obligation to remain neutral.[26]

The first significant test of the belligerency doctrine in the 20th century came in the Spanish Civil War. The Nationalist forces clearly met the standards of a belligerency yet no government recognized the conflict as such and belligerent rights were not extended until quite late.[27] The failure of belligerency norms during the Spanish Civil War marked their long, slow decline in international discourse. In the years since few states have made formal declarations of recognition, and the myriad civil wars of the Cold War era and beyond passed without the traditional categories having any impact whatsoever on the international legal response.[28] When the ICJ discussed external assistance to rebel movements in the *Nicaragua* case it made no reference to the belligerency doctrine.

Two additional factors have contributed to the view among scholars that the 19th-century belligerency doctrine had fallen into desuetude.[29] First, especially after the onset of the Cold War, states provided such an enormous and varied quantity of assistance to both sides in internal conflicts of all types that it became virtually impossible to reconcile state practice with the gradations of the traditional rules.[30] Often the same states took opposing positions on the legitimacy of intervention

[25] Robert W. Gomulkiewicz, 'International Law Governing Aid to Opposition Groups in Civil War: Resurrecting the Standards of Belligerency' (1988) 63 *Washington Law Review* 43, 47 ('When a state of belligerency exists, an outside government may give formal diplomatic recognition to the belligerent group and may give it military or economic aid'); LeMon, 'Unilateral Intervention by Invitation in Civil Wars', 747 ('Once a state of belligerency was recognised, an invitation to intervene or offer assistance was legally valid, regardless of whether the inviting party was the previously-recognised government or the anti-government forces'); Richard Falk, 'Janus Tormented: The International Law of Internal War' in James N. Rosenau (ed), *International Aspects of Civil Strife* (Princeton, NJ: Princeton University Press, 1964), 203 ('International law treats an internal war with the status of belligerency as essentially identical to a war between sovereign states. This also means that an interventionary participation on behalf of either the incumbent or the insurgent is an act of war against the other. That is, as with a truly international war, a state is given the formal option of joining with one of the belligerents against the other or remaining impartial').

[26] Lindsay Moir, *The Law of Internal Armed Conflict* (Cambridge: Cambridge University Press, 2001), 7, 8 ('Recognition of belligerency by third States rendered the customary international law of neutrality applicable between those States and the parties to the conflict … Third States were prohibited from providing assistance to the legitimate government, eliminating to some degree the latent inequality between the parties to the conflict'); Louise Doswald-Beck, 'The Legal Validity of Military Intervention by Invitation of the Government' (1985) 56 *British Yearbook of International Law* 189, 196 ('The only situation where traditional texts require neutrality on the part of third States is on recognition of belligerency').

[27] Halabi, 'Traditions of Belligerent Recognition', 347–9.

[28] Doswald-Beck, 'The Legal Validity of Military Intervention by Invitation of the Government', 197.

[29] See Yoram Dinstein, *War, Aggression and Self-Defence* (5th edn, Cambridge: Cambridge University Press, 2011), 110 ('Notwithstanding its implicit utilitarian advantages, the doctrine of belligerency has fallen into disuse').

[30] Falk, *The International Law of Civil War*, 15 ('There has been no pretense of impartiality or neutrality on the part of principal governments and no consistent willingness to endorse either the legitimacy of the constituted government or the legitimacy of revolutionary change').

depending on the political setting.[31] 'Foreign military interventions in civil wars have been so common in our day that the proclaimed rule of non-intervention may seem to have been stood on its head.'[32] Secondly, the traditional rules' careful delineation between internal conflicts that implicated international concern and those that did not has been wholly undermined by the Security Council's aggressive involvement in the prevention, management, and termination of those conflicts.[33] Since the end of the Cold War the Council has regularly invoked its Chapter VII powers by describing all varieties of internal conflicts as a threat to the peace, with no discernible consideration of the traditional criteria.[34] The Council has demanded the cessation of hostilities,[35] it has decried human rights violations and the commission of international crimes,[36] it has endorsed agreements ending conflicts,[37] and dispatched countless post-conflict missions to oversee implementation of peace accords and transition to stable governance.[38]

The example of the 2012–13 conflict in Mali is illustrative. The Council began its involvement by invoking Chapter VII to condemn 'the forcible seizure of power

[31] Edwin Brown, 'Firmage, Summary and Interpretation' in Falk, *The International Law of Civil War*, 405.

[32] Oscar Schachter, 'The Right of States to Use Armed Force' (1983–4) 82 *Michigan Law Review* 1620, 1641.

[33] *Prosecutor v. Tadić*, Case No IT-94-1-AR72, Decision on Jurisdiction, 2 Oct 1995, para 30 ('the practice of the Security Council is rich with cases of civil war or internal strife which it classified as a "threat to the peace" and dealt with under Chapter VII ... It can thus be said that there is a common understanding, manifested by the "subsequent practice" of the membership of the United Nations at large, that the "threat to the peace" of Article 39 may include, as one of its species, internal armed conflicts'). See the detailed discussion and case studies in Vaughan Lowe et al (eds), *The Security Council and War* (Oxford: Oxford University Press, 2010).

[34] The Council's justifying resolutions under Chapter VII focus on a wide range of triggers for its involvement, none of which connect to the traditional factors. See eg SC Res 751 (24 Apr 1992) ('deterioration of the humanitarian situation' in Somalia); SC Res 940 (31 July 1994) (failure of democratic governance in Haiti); SC Res 1173 (12 June 1998) (failure of peace process in Angola); SC Res 1445 (26 Apr 2006) ('the importance of elections as the foundation for the longer term restoration of peace and stability, national reconciliation and establishment of the rule of law in the Democratic Republic of the Congo'); SC Res 2048 (18 May 2012) (military coup in Guinea Bissau); SC Res 1962 (20 Dec 2010) ('attempts to usurp the will of the people and undermine the integrity of the electoral process and any progress in the peace process in Côte d'Ivoire'); SC Res 1545 (21 May 2004) (ongoing internal conflict in Burundi).

[35] See, eg SC Res 2139 (22 Feb 2014) (demanding all parties to Syrian civil war 'immediately put an end to all forms of violence, irrespective of where it comes from'); SC Res 1769 (31 July, 2007) (demanding 'an immediate cessation of hostilities and attacks' in Darfur).

[36] SC Res 2042 (14 Apr 2012) (condemning human rights violations in Syrian civil war); SC Res 1970 (26 Feb 2011) (condemning widespread attacks in Libyan civil war that 'may amount to crimes against humanity').

[37] SC Res 2092 (22 Feb 2013) (welcoming peace agreement in Guinea Bissau); SC Res 1574 (19 Nov 2004) (welcoming peace agreements for Sudan); SC Res 1031 (15 Dec 1995) (welcoming Dayton Peace Accords for Bosnia and Herzogovina).

[38] SC Res 1031 (15 Dec 1995) (creating mission for Bosnia and Herzogovina): SC Res 1023 (22 Nov 1995) (creating mission for Eastern Slavonia); SC Res 1072 (25 Oct 1999) (creating mission for East Timor). See generally, Ray Murphy (ed), *Post-Conflict Rebuilding and International Law* (Farnham: Ashgate, 2012).

from the democratically elected Government of Mali by some members of the Armed Forces of Mali' in March 2012.[39] The Council refused to recognize the usurping junta and endorsed the work of the Economic Community of West African States (ECOWAS) to restore constitutional order, including the deployment of a stabilization force.[40] It demanded 'the full, immediate and unconditional cessation of hostilities by rebel groups in the North of Mali.'[41] And it called upon all the warring parties 'to cease all abuses of human rights and violations of international humanitarian law', warning that violators of those norms 'shall be brought to justice'.[42] When the situation had not improved late in the year, the Council approved a stabilization force to be jointly led by ECOWAS and the African Union (AU).[43] It also escalated its condemnation of the northern rebels and support of the incumbent transitional regime by 'demanding' that Malian rebels sever all ties to terrorists.[44] More importantly, it authorized the deployment of an African-led military mission to 'support the Malian authorities in recovering the areas in the north of its territory under the control of terrorist, extremist and armed groups and in reducing the threat posed by terrorist organizations' among other tasks.[45] It urged member states and regional and international organizations to support the mission.[46]

Nevertheless, the African-led force failed to deploy in time to stop the rebels from making significant advances in the north. In response to a request from the transitional (but incumbent and recognized) government, on 11 January 2013 France began airstrikes against the rebels and deployed troops to Mali.[47] On 25 April 2013 the Council welcomed 'the swift action by the French forces, at the request of the transitional authorities of Mali, to stop the offensive of terrorist, extremist and armed groups towards the south of Mali.'[48] With the rebel threat receding, the Council authorized the creation of a peacekeeping mission with a mandate to use 'all necessary means' to consolidate stability throughout the country and to assist in implementing a 'transitional roadmap' that included holding elections and promoting human rights.[49]

The mission's broad objectives included assisting in an investigation opened by the International Criminal Court (ICC) into the situation in Mali in a response to a request by the Malian government.[50] Remaining French troops were authorized to use 'all necessary means' to support the mission in times of crisis, upon request of the Secretary-General.[51] Mali's political future, the Security Council emphasized,

[39] SC Res 2056 (5 July 2012). [40] SC Res 2056. [41] SC Res 2056, para 9.

[42] SC Res 2056, para. 11. [43] SC Res 2085 (20 Dec 2012). [44] SC Res 2085, para 2.

[45] SC Res 2085, para 9. [46] SC Res 2085, paras 13, 14.

[47] Stephen Erlanger and Scott Sayare, 'French Airstrikes in Mali Deter Islamist Rebels', *New York Times*, 11 Jan 2013; Statement of Malian Representative, S/PV.6905, 6 (22 Jan 2013) (describing Malian president's appeal for assistance to France).

[48] SC Res 2100 (25 Apr 2013). [49] SC Res 2100, para 16(b).

[50] SC Res 2100, para 16(g); Letter from Malian Minster of Justice to ICC Prosecutor (13 July 2012), available at <http://www.icc-cpi.int/NR/rdonlyres/A245A47F-BFD1-45B6-891C-3BCB5B173F57/0/ReferralLetterMali130712.pdf>.

[51] SC Res 2100, para 18.

depended upon a political transition that would begin with 'the restoration of democratic governance and constitutional order, including through the holding of free, fair, transparent and inclusive presidential and legislative elections.'[52]

The Council thus addressed almost every aspect of the Malian conflict: its descent into strife (numerous calls for a ceasefire and efforts at mediation), the merits of the conflict (decidedly favouring the incumbent regime), the tactics used by both sides (invoking human rights and humanitarian law and supporting an ICC investigation), the prospect of a rebel victory (authorizing national, regional, and global forces to defeat the rebels and secure the peace), and the nature of the post-conflict state (prescribing liberal democratic institutions).

With the Security Council omnipresent in domestic conflicts, what can be left of the 19th-century rules' distinction between conflicts solely of domestic concern and those that engage international law? And what remains of international law's self-imposed isolation from the causes, means of prosecution, and solutions to civil wars? The Mali case shows the Council deeply immersed in the internal architecture and stability of single nations, seeking to engage both state and non-state actors in order to achieve a political equilibrium. Much of its attention goes well beyond the *jus ad bellum* of which the traditional rules were a part. But the Council appears to have disregarded doctrinal boundaries in taking a holistic approach to civil wars, and its directives to apply humanitarian law, human rights law, and international criminal law to conflicts like Mali should make clear that viewing *any* aspect of civil wars as wholly domestic is increasingly untenable.

The Council obviously does not give every civil war this degree of attention. One might therefore argue that we now have at least two classes of internal conflict: those unaddressed by the Council that are regulated by whatever remains of the pre-Charter rules and those that the Council regulates directly through its Chapter VII powers, which are increasingly deployed to authorize intervention and to apply the full range of human rights, humanitarian, and democratic norms.[53] Conflicts falling in between these two categories—that is, those that the Council regulates only partially—would be subject to the old norms in the areas unaddressed by the Council. This typology assumes the Council's actions do not themselves affect customary law, a proposition that may become increasingly fragile as fewer and fewer civil wars remain wholly immune to its scrutiny.

[52] SC Res 2100, para 18.

[53] To take two illustrative cases, the Security Council apparently passed no resolutions on the Sri Lankan civil war during the entirety of the almost 30-year conflict. By contrast, the Council mandated that the United Nations Multidimensional Integrated Stabilization Mission in Mali (MINUSMA), authorized in April 2013, would protect civilians, investigate human rights abuses, 'take fully into account gender considerations as a cross cutting issue throughout its mandate', and called on MINUSMA 'to abide by international humanitarian, human rights and refugee law'. SC Res 2100 (25 Apr 2103).

c. Intervention in Civil Wars: The Negative Equality Principle

If the pre-Charter rules are now barely a presence in discussions of intervention by invitation, their focus on territorial control has lived on. Many contemporary scholars argue that if a conflict has reached the level of a civil war, intervention on the government side, permitted without qualification by the *Nicaragua* case, is in fact prohibited.[54] One report has described this doctrine of 'negative equality'—each side being equally unable to invite outside assistance—as 'the most recent trend in scholarship'.[55] The view is that where a society is fully divided about its political future, meaning the government cannot plausibly claim to represent the entire population, external assistance on the government's behalf would interfere with the people's right to determine their own future.[56] If a country is sufficiently divided, identifying the 'legitimate' government may be difficult, even according to supposedly objective criteria such as effective control.[57] Negative equality has also been justified for the practical reason that it avoids the question of whether an invitation from either side has been properly issued and thus 'relieves lawyers of the difficult task of identifying and proving a valid invitation.'[58] Others argue that the principle can help to avoid escalating a civil war into an international conflict.[59]

What conflicts would be subject to the negative equality principle? Whether a conflict has become a 'civil war' is as difficult a question as identifying the difference between an insurgency and a belligerency.[60] No generally accepted definition exists, largely because 'civil war' is not a critical term of art in international instruments. Christine Gray argues that the restrictive definition of a 'non-international armed conflict' in Additional Protocol II to the Geneva Conventions is an appropriate

[54] The Institut de Droit International's widely cited 1975 resolution provides that 'third States shall refrain from giving assistance to parties to a civil war which is being fought in the territory of another state.' Institut de Droit International, 'The Principle of Non-Intervention in Civil Wars' (1975), available at <http://www.idi-iil.org/idiE/resolutionsE/1975_wies_03_en.pdf>. See also, Rein Mullerson, 'Intervention by Invitation' in Lori Damrosch and David Scheffer (eds), *Law and Force in the New International Order* (Boulder, CO: Westview Press, 1991), 127, 132; Gray, *International Law and the Use of Force*, 81.

[55] II Report of the Independent International Fact-Finding Mission on the Conflict in Georgia 277 (2009), available at <http://www.ceiig.ch/pdf/IIFFMCG_Volume_II.pdf> (Georgia Report).

[56] Gray, *International Law and the Use of Force*, 81.

[57] David Wippman, 'Pro-Democratic Intervention by Invitation' in Fox and Roth, *Democratic Governance and International Law*, 293, 299.

[58] Georgia Report, 279.

[59] Joyner and Grimaldi, 'The United States and Nicaragua', 644.

[60] A 2007 legal opinion of the UN Secretariat could not identify an accepted definition of 'civil war' in international law but noted that describing a conflict as civil war presupposes that 'the Government has lost control of part of its territory'. Note to the Assistant Secretary-General for Political Affairs, Regarding the Usage of the term 'Civil War' (30 Jan 2007) (2007) *United Nations Juridical Yearbook* 458, 459. Of course, this is precisely the metric used by belligerency doctrine.

point of reference.[61] But the definition, while containing the familiar requirement of territorial control and several other factors, has been criticized as vague and difficult to apply in practice.[62]

Negative equality does not share the pre-Charter rules' complete indifference to the political dynamic of civil wars. Instead of analogizing the two sides to warring sovereign states, it recognizes the reality of single societies in which political consensus has dissolved and a single 'legitimate' leadership cannot be identified. But one may well ask whether this is a distinction without a difference. By focusing largely on territorial control, the negative equality principle reaffirms the old rules' indifference to the policies and practices of the competing factions. Later we will ask whether ascendant ideas of democratic legitimacy have or should alter this continuing obsession with effective control.

Negative equality has not yet attracted a consensus among scholars and indeed remains controversial, for it is vulnerable to the same criticism of disjunction from state practice used to criticize pre-Charter belligerency doctrine. Governments that have lost substantial portions of their territory to rebel insurgencies have continued to receive external assistance.[63] In the Mali episode discussed earlier, the rebels had captured the entire northern portion of the country, proclaimed its independence from the central government, and were advancing less than 300 miles from the capital when France intervened at the government's invitation.[64] Addressing the Security Council, the Malian ambassador admitted that the 'northern part of the country' was 'controlled' by the rebels and that just prior to the French intervention the president had appealed 'for a general mobilization and imposed a state of emergency throughout the country.'[65] He described the French response to the invitation as 'making it possible to save Mali as a State'.[66] Others also described pre-intervention Mali as under the control of two separate factions.[67] Yet no state raised the negative equality principle or spoke in opposition to the French intervention.

[61] Gray, *International Law and the Use of Force*, 81 fn 70. Art 1(1) applies the Protocol to conflicts 'which take place in the territory of a High Contracting Party between its armed forces and dissident armed forces or other organized armed groups which, under responsible command, exercise such control over a part of its territory as to enable them to carry out sustained and concerted military operations and to implement this Protocol.' Protocol Relating to the Protection of Victims of Non-international Armed Conflicts, 8 June 1977, 1125 UNTS 610. Additional Protocol II's definition is narrower than that in Common Article 3 to the main Conventions and would subject fewer internal conflicts to the negative equality principle. Moir, *The Law of Internal Armed Conflict*, 101 (Additional Protocol II 's definition encompasses 'only the most intense and large-scale conflicts').

[62] Moir, *The Law of Internal Armed Conflict*, 103–9.

[63] Dinstein, *War, Aggression and Self-Defence*, 119.

[64] Al Jazeera, 'Tuaregs Claim Independence From Mali', 6 Apr 2012, available at <http://www.aljazeera.com/news/africa/2012/04/20124644412359539.html>; Adam Nossiter and Eric Schmitt, 'France Battling Islamists in Mali', *New York Times*, 11 Jan 2013.

[65] S/PV.6905 (22 Jan 2013), 5, 6. [66] S/PV.6905, 6.

[67] See S/PV.6905, 14 (representative of Benin describes northern Mali as 'under the control of fundamentalist groups').

A final criticism of negative equality was raised by developing countries in the aftermath of decolonization: a prohibition on aid to both sides necessarily benefits the stronger party, which is in almost all cases the incumbent regime. The result is a doctrine effectively in service of the political status quo. This critique becomes all the more poignant if one accepts Quincy Wright's observation that successful revolutions 'have usually depended to some extent upon such outside contacts and assistance'.[68] Like negative equality itself, this criticism makes no reference to the actual ideology or political record of the parties, evidently assuming that a more level playing field would lead to more victories by rebel forces, which would be a desirable outcome. While the politics of the 1960s and 1970s may have been more favourable to this argument, it seemed quite unlikely even then that most governments would support a doctrine that could, under the right circumstances, lead to their own demise. The Mali episode indeed demonstrates that the international community has not in fact accepted this view.

III. Points of Tension in Traditional Doctrine

In addition to the deep cleavages over the broad parameters of invitations to intervene, uncertainty also marks discussion of specific elements of invitations. This section reviews the most prominent of these issues.[69]

A. Legitimacy of an Invitation

If a legitimate invitation is fundamentally grounded in state consent, questions will inevitably arise about whether that consent was properly given. Cases in which invitations were given by officials with doubtful authority to speak for the state,[70] likely

[68] Quincy Wright, 'Subversive Intervention' (1960) 54 *American Journal of International Law* 521, 530.

[69] One question not discussed in detail here is whether groups engaged in self-determination struggles are entitled to invite external assistance. This issue has lost much of its salience since the end of decolonization. Gray, *International Law and the Use of Force*, 59–64. At least one claim for an invitation to support a self-determination struggle outside the decolonization setting (ie secession) has been rejected. See Georgia Report, 279 ('a secessionist party cannot validly invite a foreign state to use force against the army of the metropolitan state').

[70] The 1983 US invasion of Grenada was justified in part by an invitation by the Governor-General. Many doubted his authority to speak for the state. See Shaw, *International Law*, 1151. The 1965 US

manufactured by the intervener[71] or given after the fact, are not uncommon.[72] The disputes in these and other situations mostly involve wildly divergent versions of the facts involved rather than disagreements over legal standards. The rules on procedural aspects of state consent 'are regulated by firmly established norms of international law'.[73] Apart from the ICJ's holding that withdrawal of consent to the presence of foreign forces need not follow any particular formalities, the law of consent is dispersed over a variety of regimes unrelated to the use of force.[74] The general framework is a matter of state responsibility, though as the ILC noted in its commentary to Article 20 of its Draft Articles, 'Whether consent has been validly given is a matter addressed by international law rules outside the framework of State responsibility.'[75] Questions of whether a particular official may consent on behalf of a state and whether consent has been coerced are addressed by treaty law,[76] whether a particular regime represents the state is a matter of recognition law,[77] and some circumstances surrounding the withdrawal of consent are now covered by international criminal law.[78]

B. Prior Intervention

Even if one accepts the negative equality doctrine, the legal calculus changes if a foreign state has previously intervened on behalf of a rebel group. Many states have justified assistance to governments on the ground that they were responding to prior interventions[79] and this justification is widely accepted by scholars.[80] The exception can be justified on two grounds. First, prior intervention effectively

intervention in the Dominican Republic raised similar issues. See LeMon, 'Unilateral Intervention by Invitation in Civil Wars', 762–8.

71 Iraq's claim that its 1990 invasion of Kuwait was requested by a Free Provisional Government of Kuwait likely falls into this category. See Gray, *International Law and the Use of Force*, 87–8.

72 While the facts surrounding the invitation cited by the Soviet Union in its 1979 invasion of Afghanistan are not clear, it seems unlikely the invitation was issued prior to the intervention. See Doswald-Beck, 'The Legal Validity of Military Intervention by Invitation of the Government', 230–4.

73 Eliav Leiblich, 'Intervention and Consent: Consensual Forcible Interventions in Internal Armed Conflicts as International Agreements' (2011) 29 *Boston University International Law Journal* 337, 341.

74 See *Armed Activities*, Judgment, para 51.

75 Draft Articles on Responsibility of States for Internationally Wrongful Acts, 73. See generally, Affef Ben Mansour, 'Circumstances Precluding Wrongfulness in the ILC Articles on State Responsibility: Consent' in James Crawford, Alain Pellet, and Simon Olleson (eds), *The International Law of Responsibility* (Oxford: Oxford University Press, 2010), 439.

76 Vienna Convention on the Law of Treaties, 23 May 1969, 1155 UNTS 311, Art 7 (officials with full powers to bind state), Art 51 (coercion of a state representative).

77 See generally, Stefan Talmon, *Recognition in International Law* (Leiden: Martinus Nijhoff, 2000).

78 Review Conference of the Rome Statute, Amendments to the Rome Statute of the International Criminal Court on the Crime of Aggression, Resolution RC/Res 6, Annex I, RC/Res 6 (11 June 2010) (crime of aggression includes failure to withdraw troops from territory after withdrawal of consent by host state).

79 Schachter, 'The Right of States to Use Armed Force', 1641.

80 Gray, *International Law and the Use of Force*, 94; Doswald-Beck, 'The Legal Validity of Military Intervention by Invitation of the Government', 251; Shaw, *International Law*, 1153.

internationalizes the conflict and the negative equality principle, which applies only to civil wars, is no longer relevant. Secondly, external assistance to rebels can be viewed as an armed attack giving rise to a right of collective self-defence on the part of the government. Neither argument is particularly controversial.

But the claim of prior intervention is also one of the most abused exceptions to the non-intervention principle. From the Soviet interventions in Czechoslovakia and Afghanistan to the US interventions in the Dominican Republic and Grenada, the factual predicate for some interventions has been thin or non-existent.[81] In some cases, such as Cyprus, the Security Council has been able to pass resolutions condemning the intervention and at least implicitly rejecting reliance on prior intervention.[82] But in the US and Soviet cases cited above, the Council did not act and the claims remained essentially self-judging.

c. Treaty-Based Invitation

All of the invitations examined so far have come in reaction to conflicts already underway in target states. But in some cases states enter into forward-looking treaty commitments that authorize intervention in advance under a defined set of circumstances. Such 'pro-invasion pacts' change the calculus of the negative equality principle. Third parties are no longer left to wonder whether the rebels or the government in a civil war legitimately speak for the state. That question will have been stipulated in advance by the treaty, which would indicate which party to a conflict is entitled to secure its authority with outside support and which is to be regarded as an illegitimate usurper.

The debate over such agreements has traditionally been polarized between two strongly held positions.[83] Those supporting the agreements argue that a state is entitled to alienate any aspect of its sovereign autonomy through a treaty, since entering into international agreements is a quintessentially sovereign act.[84] Indeed, a state might enter into an agreement to terminate its own existence, for example through merger with another state. If a state can extinguish all its sovereignty presumably it can cede authority over particular aspects of its statehood, the greater presumably including the lesser. The *Nicaragua* case long ago held that no principle of sovereignty prevents a state from binding itself by treaty to hold free and fair elections, thereby limiting its ability to choose its leaders by other means.[85] From a

[81] See Doswald-Beck, 'The Legal Validity of Military Intervention by Invitation of the Government', 239–42 (detailing Soviet and US cases).

[82] See eg SC Res (16 Aug 1974).

[83] See David Wippman, 'Treaty-Based Intervention: Who Can Say No?' (1995) 62 *University of Chicago Law Review* 607.

[84] *The SS Wimbledon*, 1923 PCIJ, Ser A, No 1, 25 (28 June) (entering into international agreements is 'an attribute of state sovereignty').

[85] *Nicaragua*, Judgment, para 259:

The Court cannot discover, within the range of subjects open to international agreement, any obstacle or provision to hinder a State from making a commitment of this kind [to holding free and fair

policy perspective, an additional instrument seeking to protect elected governments against coups and other domestic disruptions seems a logical next step. Opponents argue that the non-intervention norm has attained *jus cogens* status and no agreement can permit what that superior norm forbids.[86]

David Wippman has offered a nuanced compromise between these polar views. Wippman argues that the essential problem with pro-invasion pacts is that while they may represent the views of a government and by extension its citizens at the time of the treaty's execution, there is no guarantee that support will exist at the time an intervention occurs.[87] This is almost certainly true when the treaty is invoked in the midst of a civil war in which a state has effectively divided into separate political communities. If the incumbent regime seeks to perpetuate itself by denouncing the treaty in those circumstances, Wippman argues, the decision should not be theirs alone. Rather, 'the concurrent will of each of the relevant communities should be necessary to rescind the treaty.'[88] Other commentators have accepted Wippman's view that a regime in a deeply divided state cannot unilaterally claim to represent the state in order to renounce a prior consent to intervention.[89]

Wippman's view seems particularly appropriate to two innovative regimes in Africa that pre-authorize intervention in member states. First, Article 4(h) of the Constitutive Act of the African Union establishes 'the right of the Union to intervene in a Member State pursuant to a decision of the Assembly in respect of grave circumstances, namely war crimes, genocide and crimes against humanity.'[90] Intervention is initiated by the AU Assembly upon recommendation of the Peace and Security Council.[91] While the precise procedures triggering intervention are not specified, no additional consent by the target state is necessary.[92] Secondly, the

elections]. A State, which is free to decide upon the principle and methods of popular consultation within its domestic order, is sovereign for the purpose of accepting a limitation of its sovereignty in this field.

[86] See Brad R. Roth, 'The Illegality of "Pro-Democratic" Invasion Pacts' in Fox and Roth, *Democratic Governance and International Law*, 328.

[87] Wippman, 'Pro-Democratic Intervention by Invitation' in Fox and Roth, *Democratic Governance and International Law*.

[88] Wippman, 'Pro-Democratic Intervention by Invitation' in Fox and Roth, *Democratic Governance and International Law*, 315.

[89] Dinstein, *War, Aggression and Self-Defence*, 123.

[90] Constitutive Act of the African Union, Art 4(h), 26 May 2001, 2158 UNTS 3.

[91] Protocol Relating to the Establishment of the Peace and Security Council of the African Union, Art 4(f), 9 July 2002, available at <http://www.africaunion.org/root/au/auc/departments/psc/asf/doc/PSC%20protocol.pdf>. (Council guided by 'the right of the Union to intervene in a Member State pursuant to a decision of the Assembly in respect of grave circumstances, namely war crimes, genocide and crimes against humanity, in accordance with Article 4(h) of the Constitutive Act').

[92] Ntombizozuko Dyani-Mhango, 'Reflections on the African Union's Right to Intervene' (2012) 38 *Brooklyn Journal of International Law* 1, 14–17. That the target state need not consent to intervention under Art 4(h) is made clear by subsection 4(j), which establishes 'the right of Member States to request intervention from the Union in order to restore peace and security.'

ECOWAS Lomé Protocol of 1999 establishes a standing intervention force to be used in a variety of situations, including an 'internal conflict that threatens to trigger a humanitarian disaster, or that poses a serious threat to peace and security in the sub-region', 'serious and massive violations of human rights and the rule of law', and 'an overthrow or attempted overthrow of a democratically elected government.'[93] In these circumstances, a Mediation and Security Council may 'authorise all forms of intervention and decide particularly on the deployment of political and military missions.'[94] The ECOWAS Protocol also makes no provision for additional prior consent by the target state.[95]

In Wippman's view, a regime committing the acts triggering AU or ECOWAS intervention could not in good faith renounce these treaties on the ground that a legitimate political division existed within the state.[96] The regime would have demonstrated its illegitimacy by committing mass violence against its citizens (human rights violations) or thwarting the will of electoral majorities or pluralities (interruption of democratic governance). In either case, the targets of these acts would be quite unlikely to agree to renounce the treaties. In Wippman's correct estimation, this failure would validate the grounds for treaty-based intervention.

IV. Recent Practice: The Emergence of Qualitative Factors?

The pre-Charter belligerency standards and the negative equality principle are united by a common focus on a question of agency: does a regime issuing an invitation to intervene properly speak for the state? Both answer the question largely (though not exclusively) by focusing on control of territory. Whether or not a regime is in effective control has traditionally been the most important factor in the law of recognition, and so it is not surprising that the idea was incorporated wholesale into this aspect of the *jus ad bellum*. But since the end of the Cold War, questions of recognition have increasingly revolved around democratic criteria, specifically whether a regime has been chosen in free and fair elections.[97] The rise of

[93] Protocol Relating to the Mechanism for Conflict Prevention, Management, Resolution, Peace-Keeping and Security, 12 Dec 1999, ECOWAS Doc A/P10/12/99, available at <http://www.oecd.org/dataoecd/55/62/388735 20.pdf>.

[94] ECOWAS Protocol, Art 10. [95] Lieblich, 'Intervention and Consent', 368–9.

[96] David Wippman, 'Treaty-Based Intervention: Who Can Say No?', 630–2.

[97] See Gregory H. Fox, 'Democracy, Right to, International Protection' in Rüdiger Wolfrum (ed), *Max Planck Encyclopedia of Public International Law* (Oxford: Oxford University Press, 2008), available

a democratic legitimacy principle, while still controversial, has introduced qualitative factors into the question of which group is to be regarded as 'the government'. The implications are critical, for if taken seriously the principle might validate an invitation to intervene by a government in exile that controls no territory.[98] Even further, it might validate requests by rebel factions that have never held power, but which promise a democratic future for the state, or at least one that is less undemocratic than the prospects under the incumbent regime.[99]

A. Invitations and Theories of Legitimate Government

Ideas of democratic legitimacy appeared only sporadically in international law prior to the end of the Cold War.[100] This was no less true when the legitimacy of an invitation to intervene was at issue. Many regimes with no demonstrable democratic credentials sought and received outside assistance without objection from other states.[101] But after 1989, the situation changed considerably. The individual right to political participation emerged from dormancy in human rights law, spawning an elaborate jurisprudence that clarified many aspects of how elections are to be administered and their relation to other individual rights.[102] An increasing number of international organizations require member states to be 'democratic' and have created elaborate democracy-protection regimes.[103] Election monitors from

at <http://opil.ouplaw.com/home/epil>; Sean D. Murphy, 'Democratic Legitimacy and the Recognition of States and Governments' (1999) 48 *International and Comparative Law Quarterly* 545.

[98] Several writers take this view. See eg Julie Dubé Gagnon, 'ECOWAS's Right to Intervene in Côte D'Ivoire to Install Alassane Ouattara as President Elect' (2013) 3 *Notre Dame Journal of International and Comparative Law* 51, 67 ('democratic governments, which do not exercise an effective control over the territory of the state, seem to be entitled to validly invite another state to forcefully intervene'); Jeremy Levitt, 'Pro-Democratic Intervention in Africa' (2006–7) 24 *Wisconsin International Law Journal* 785, 793 ('even ousted regimes lacking effective control can make a valid request for intervention').

[99] Where none of the parties to a civil war has professed democratic leanings these questions will be largely irrelevant. Louise Doswald-Beck notes of the situation in Afghanistan at the time of the Soviet intervention, for example, that 'Not only was the government in power at the time of the invasion a dictatorship, but there is also no indication whatever that the various groups fighting against the government had any democratic leanings.' Doswald-Beck, 'The Legal Validity of Military Intervention by Invitation of the Government', 206.

[100] See generally, Hilary Charlesworth, *Designing Democracy in International Law* (forthcoming 2015); Fox and Roth, *Democratic Governance and International Law*.

[101] See Institut de Droit International, Report of Sub-Group on Intervention by Invitation (25 July 2007), available at <http://www.idi-iil.org/idiF/annuaireF/10th_commission_d.pdf> ('even authorities which acceded to power in a non-democratic way and were subsequently not confirmed by general elections, and still did not meet with objections concerning the exercise of the functions of government, were seen as entitled to issue a request for military assistance').

[102] Gregory H. Fox, 'The Right to Political Participation in International Law' in Fox and Roth, *Democratic Governance and International Law*, 48–90.

[103] See Gregory H. Fox, 'Democracy, International Right to, Protection' in Wolfrum, *Max Planck Encyclopedia of Public International Law*, available at <http://opil.ouplaw.com/home/EPIL>.

intergovernmental and non-governmental organizations are now omnipresent in new and emerging democracies.[104] The Security Council regularly calls on states to enact democratic reforms and its frequent missions to assist in the reconstruction of post-conflict states have advanced a variety of democratic institutions.[105] Perhaps most importantly, debates on recognition of governments have increasingly focused on electoral mandates, with the Security Council on several occasions declaring a regime in effective control to be illegitimate based on its defiance of clear election results.[106]

These developments have three consequences for the evaluation of invitations to intervene. First, because many have been multilateral initiatives, the Security Council and other intergovernmental bodies have slowly supplanted individual states as the critical decision-makers. Secondly, when disputes arise over regime legitimacy, a faction with effective control but without democratic bona fides has had difficulty convincing international organizations that it nonetheless merits recognition. This is certainly true for regional organizations, such as the OAS and AU, that require the virtually automatic suspension of member states in which democratic government is interrupted.[107] UN practice has been less uniform, though when two factions claim to represent a state and one has a clear electoral mandate, the organization is increasingly unlikely to prefer effective control to democratic legitimacy.[108]

Thirdly, in three cases the Security Council has applied democratic criteria in responding to requests for assistance from elected leaders to depose factions that refused to honour election results.

- In the case of Haiti, President Jean-Bertrand Aristide was elected president in a UN-monitored vote and then deposed by the Haitian military in 1991. The Security Council described the coup as illegal and continued to recognize Aristide as the country's legitimate leader.[109] Aristide asked the international community to take 'prompt and decisive action' to restore him to office.[110] The Security Council,

[104] Judith G. Kelly, *When International Election Observation Works, and Why It Often Fails* (Princeton, NJ: Princeton University Press, 2012) 16–42; Eric C. Bjornland, *Beyond Free and Fair: Monitoring Elections and Building Democracy* (Baltimore, MD: Johns Hopkins University Press, 2004).

[105] Gregory H. Fox, 'The Security Council and Democratization' in David Malone (ed), *The United Nations Security Council in the 21st Century* (Boulder, CO: Lynne Riener, 2003).

[106] See Talmon, *Recognition in International Law*.

[107] For a detailed discussion of regional democracy-protection mechanisms, see Jacob P. Wobig, 'Regional Regimes for the Defense of Democracy and Coups d'Etat', Dissertation, Department of Political Science, University of Nebraska, Lincoln, 19 April 2013, available at <http://digitalcommons.unl.edu/cgi/viewcontent.cgi?article=1023&context=poliscitheses>. For a more critical analysis, see Brad R. Roth, 'Secessions, Coups and the International Rule of Law: Assessing the Decline of the Effective Control Doctrine' (2010) 11 *Melbourne Journal of International Law* 393.

[108] See Alexander Downer, 'Towards a Declaratory School of Government Recognition' (2013) 46 *Vanderbilt Journal of Transnational Law* 581, 600–9.

[109] SC Res 841 (16 June 1993).

[110] S/1994/905 (Annex) (Aristide letter to UN Secretary-General).

taking note of Aristide's request, authorized a multinational force to remove the usurping junta that had deposed elected President Aristide.[111] The junta leaders left the country before the use of force became necessary.

- In the case of Sierra Leone, a May 1997 military coup deposing President Tejan Kabbah was met with immediate condemnation by the Organisation of African Unity and later the Security Council, which invoked Chapter VII to impose sanctions.[112] From exile, President Kabbah appealed to Nigeria, then heading ECOWAS, to restore him to power. An ECOWAS force deposed the junta in February 1998, and the Security Council praised the action and indicated its approval.[113]
- In the case of Côte d'Ivoire, the Security Council recognized Alassane Ouattara as the winner of elections held in November 2010, prevailing over Laurent Gbagbo, the incumbent, who disputed the result and refused to leave office.[114] Shortly thereafter, Ouattara requested that the regional organization ECOWAS intervene to remove Gbagbo from power.[115] The Security Council did not respond directly to this request (not surprisingly, since it was directed to another body) but on 30 March 2011, with Gbagbo still holding out, it passed Resolution 1975 authorizing a peacekeeping mission already in the country to 'use all necessary means' to protect civilians, including by 'prevent[ing] the use of heavy weapons against the civilian population.'[116] On 4 April UN and French forces attacked Gbagbo's camps and destroyed heavy weapons and munitions stockpiles. Gbagbo capitulated one week later.[117] The Security Council welcomed Ouattara's ascent to power but political divisions marked debate over the propriety of the peacekeepers' actions.[118]

In Sierra Leone and Côte d'Ivoire, leaders with electoral mandates but holding no actual power or territory requested assistance from a regional organization. In Sierra Leone, ECOWAS responded and the Security Council approved its actions. In Côte d'Ivoire, UN peacekeepers and French troops took military action that all but ensured the ousted leader's return. The Council then approved Ouattara's return

[111] SC Res 940 (31 July 1994).

[112] SC Res (8 Oct 1997); Karsten Nowrot and Emily W. Schbacker, 'The Use of Force to Restore Democracy: International Legal Implications of the ECOWAS Intervention in Sierra Leone' (1998) 14 *American University International Law Review* 321, 328 (regional reaction).

[113] Statement by the President of the Security Council, S/PRST/1998/5 (1998).

[114] See SC Res 1962 (20 Dec 2010); Alex J. Bellamy and Paul J. Williams, 'The New Politics of Protection? Côte d'Ivoire, Libya and the Responsibility to Protect' (2011) 87 *International Affairs* 825, 829–36.

[115] Gagnon, 'ECOWAS's Right to Intervene in Côte D'Ivoire', 52.

[116] SC Res 1975 (30 Mar 2011).

[117] Bellamy and Williams, 'The New Politics of Protection?', 834–5.

[118] SC Res 1980 (28 Apr 2011) (Council welcomes 'that President Alassane Dramane Ouattara of Côte d'Ivoire is now able to assume all his responsibilities as Head of State, in accordance with the will of the Ivorian people expressed at the presidential elections of 28 November 2010 and as recognised by the international community').

but did not comment on the means. In Haiti, the ousted president made a request directly to the Council, which cited the invitation in a resolution authorizing the use of force to oust the junta. Each of these cases, in its own way, contains only an indirect connection between the requesting leader's democratic bona fides and the organization's decision to intervene. At the same time, none of the organizations demonstrated the sort of reluctance to credit those invitations that negative equality or other traditional doctrines would have counselled.

It is important not to over-read these cases. All involved elections that were monitored by international organizations and whose outcome they certified. When the invitations were issued each of the inviting factions had been recognized by the Security Council and a regional organization as the legitimate government of the state. Applying the democratic legitimacy principle beyond these limited circumstances courts some danger. Without the empirical validation of a monitored election or an international organization's collective recognition, the democratic credentials of opposition groups would become a subjective determination for individual states. Opportunities for abuse would be abound.

B. Recognition of the Opposition as a 'Legitimate Representative'

A second front on which the negative equality principle may be under challenge is the recent practice of recognizing opposition groups as the 'legitimate representative' of the people of a state. During the Cold War, the General Assembly occasionally granted such recognitions but the political context of those acts limited their precedential value.[119] In two recent cases the practice has been revived in ways that have implications for contemporary invitations by opposition groups.

In Libya, President Mu'ammer Gaddafi's harsh response to a rebel uprising in early 2011 led the Security Council to pass Resolution 1970, which condemned the regime's human rights abuses, referred the situation to the ICC, demanded 'steps to fulfill the legitimate demands of the population', and imposed a variety of sanctions on the Gaddafi government.[120] The situation worsened in early March when President Gaddafi threatened harsh reprisals against the city of Benghazi, a rebel stronghold. On 10 March, France surprised even its allies by recognizing the Libyan National Council as the 'legitimate representative of the Libyan people'.[121] On 17 March 2011, the Security Council passed Resolution 1973 imposing a no-fly zone on Libya and authorizing 'Member States that have notified the Secretary-General

[119] See Stefan Talmon, 'Recognition of Opposition Groups as the Legitimate Representative of a People', Bonn Research Papers on Public International Law, 3 Mar 2013, at 9, available at <http://papers.ssrn.com/sol3/papers.cfm?abstract_id=2227615>.

[120] SC Res 1970 (26 Feb 2011).

[121] Halabi, 'Traditions of Belligerent Recognition', 375.

... to take all necessary measures ... to protect civilians and civilian populated areas under threat of attack in the Libyan Arab Jamahiriya, including Benghazi, while excluding a foreign occupation force of any form on any part of Libyan territory.'[122] In late March, the six members of the Gulf Cooperation Council recognized the Libyan Council in the same terms as France, as did Italy in early April, the US and the UK in late July, and other states shortly thereafter.[123] Several of these states clearly intended to substitute the Council for the Gaddafi regime as the recognized government of Libya and their statements reflected that decision.[124]

The Syrian civil war led to similar actions. In late 2012 a series of states and one sub-regional organization issued statements supportive of Syrian opposition groups. The wording of these statements varied widely, however, as Stefan Talmon has shown in a compilation of the differing phraseologies used by the 'recognizing' states:

(i) a legitimate representative for [of] the aspirations of the Syrian people
(ii) legitimate representatives of the aspirations of the Syrian people
(iii) a legitimate representative of the Syrian people
(iv) legitimate representatives of the Syrian people
(v) the legitimate representative of the Syrian people
(vi) the sole legitimate representative of the Syrian people.[125]

Further, not all these states in fact 'recognized' the Syrian groups. Some stated that they were 'accepting', 'acknowledging', or 'considering' them as legitimate representatives.[126] Finally, the statements differed on whether they were recognizing one group or many groups as representing the Syrian people.[127]

The legal effect of these statements is unclear. The historical antecedents are so sparse that it may be that we are witnessing the emergence of a new category of quasi-state entities. But some of the states made clear that their statements were intended for political rather than legal purposes. If the Libyan and Syrian groups were in fact recognized as the governments of the two states, other consequences would have followed, such as the closure of embassies in the two capitals, since the recognized governments did not reside there. In addition, several states issuing the declarations have for some time abandoned the formal recognition of new governments, and they gave no indication that these statements deviated from that policy.[128] One view of the new category, then, is that while the statements underline the international community's dislike for an incumbent regime and might serve to

[122] SC Res 1975 (17 Mar 2011). [123] Halabi, 'Traditions of Belligerent Recognition', 367–77.

[124] See Stefan Talmon, 'Recognition of the Libyan Transitional National Council', Oxford Legal Research Paper, June 2011, at 3–4, available at <http://papers.ssrn.com/sol3/papers.cfm? abstract_id= 1868032>.

[125] Talmon, 'Recognition of Opposition Groups', 9.

[126] Talmon, 'Recognition of Opposition Groups', 8.

[127] Talmon, 'Recognition of Opposition Groups', 4.

[128] Talmon, 'Recognition of Opposition Groups', 7.

encourage assistance to rebels within the limits of international law, they do not have legal effect.[129] They are more in the nature of rhetorical tropes. Alternatively, the statements could be understood to have a limited legal effect. One factor motivating the Libya recognitions, for example, was to grant the rebels access to state funds.[130] But a line could be drawn between a legal capacity to perform discrete ministerial functions of government such as drawing on state assets and the ability to make significant changes in national foreign policy. Finally, while in theory the recognitions could legitimize assistance upon invitation, the intervention in Libya occurred pursuant to a Chapter VII resolution and not an invitation. To date, neither individual states nor the Security Council has responded to an invitation in Syria in a way that would implicate the negative equality principle.

V. Conclusions

Traditional rules on intervention by invitation reflected 19th-century international law in all its statist glory. Because civil wars occurred entirely within national territories they were reserved to domestic jurisdiction. The government could invite outside assistance and maintain its authority without any consideration of its policies or those of the rebels. The rules changed if rebels controlled substantial portions of territory, in which case they qualified as belligerents and the factions were analogized to two states at war. Rules applicable to interstate conflict thereby came into play. But international law protected the government as long as it maintained effective control and denied rebels assistance under any circumstances. Contrary acts were condemned as intervention.

This view of states as black boxes that are properly represented by whatever faction can maintain itself in power has begun to recede. Not surprisingly, norms on invitations to intervene have changed as well. The negative equality principle, while not clearly ascendant, has attracted much support. While it shares the traditional rules' focus on territorial control, in the case of civil wars negative equality has abandoned the strained analogy to interstate conflict—a formalistic concession to statist assumptions—in favour of more policy-based responses. Its prohibition on assistance to either side is premised on the inability of outsiders to determine which

[129] Talmon, 'Recognition of Opposition Groups', 20 ('legitimacy is not to be confused with legality in the sense of enjoying a certain legal status or representative capacity under international law. The fact that a government loses its legitimacy does not mean that it also automatically loses its government status').

[130] Talmon, 'Recognition of Opposition Groups', 30.

faction commanded popular support (or more popular support) and a desire not to internationalize what might otherwise remain a local conflict.

Negative equality appears remarkably insulated from developments in other areas of international law that have aggressively examined governments' policies towards their citizens, taken seriously the claims of dissident groups, and cast a pall of illegitimacy over unelected regimes.[131] In particular, the UN and regional organizations have developed mechanisms to test the actual popular support of member state governments and to respond when regimes appear to defy the popular will. In three cases, the UN has acted on such empirical findings and authorized (or in the case of Côte d'Ivoire, possibly authorized) the use of force to bring elected leaders to power. In these areas, in other words, international law is increasingly abandoning the view that outsiders cannot understand whether a regime is supported by its citizens (and to what degree) and that even to undertake such an inquiry would be presumptuous.

Whether and how these developments will alter negative equality or the *Nicaragua* rule is unknown. One possible vehicle would be the recognition of rebel groups as the 'legitimate representatives' of a state's citizens. But apart from there only being two such cases in the post-Cold War era, real dangers abound. Absent an authoritative statement by the Security Council (not present in either the Libyan or Syrian cases (to date)), recognition will default to individual states. Politics and not empirical grounding in citizen support or respect for human rights will likely guide their decisions. If so, the danger identified by the *Nicaragua* case could well come to pass: 'it is difficult to see what would remain of the principle of non-intervention in international law if intervention, which is already allowable at the request of the government of a state, were also to be allowed at the request of the opposition. This would permit any state to intervene at any moment in the internal affairs of another state.'[132]

[131] The *Nicaragua* judgment, which on its face permits intervention in response to a government invitation in all cases, is even more remote from these developments.

[132] *Nicaragua*, Judgment, para 246.

CHAPTER 38

NATIONAL LIBERATION IN THE CONTEXT OF POST- AND NON-COLONIAL STRUGGLES FOR SELF-DETERMINATION

ELIZABETH CHADWICK

> I know not what course others may take; but as for me, give me liberty or give me death![1]

I. Introduction

REVOLUTION remains an exceptional event.[2] Moreover, revolutions differ as to their 'cause': liberation wars are fought to force an invader to leave, while internal

[1] Excerpt of speech made by Patrick Henry on 23 March 1775, at St John's Church, Richmond, Virginia.

[2] See *Accordance with International Law of the Unilateral Declaration of Independence in Respect of Kosovo*, Advisory Opinion of 22 July 2010, ICJ, General List No 141, paras 82–3 (entitlement to self-determination, and 'rights of revolution', expressly sidestepped).

struggles for regime change are fratricidal. In turn, the international community cannot impose one single framework of governance on states: 'legitimate' governance may not be 'representative', while 'legitimate' territorial consolidation does not prevent discrimination, racial myths, or fantasies of genetic difference, the struggles for or against which convey nationalist content. Accordingly, revolutions simply change, and continue to change, the international landscape. For example, only 51 UN member states existed in 1945, while a third of the world's population was dependent on colonial states.[3] Today, there are 193 UN members[4]—a costly statistic nonetheless, as over 80 per cent of casualties in post-1945 armed conflicts have been caused in non-international armed conflicts, most fought for self-determination.[5]

As violent struggle can create future difficulties, and as 'channels [are] dug by one generation of activists [and] kept open, sometimes quietly, by future ones',[6] the use of force has become fundamental in anchoring self-determination in the modern consciousness. For this reason, the contemporary viability of self-determination and liberation conflicts can be gauged in terms of the use of force and the limits placed on that force, as to frame the issues otherwise is to put the cart before the horse.[7] The normative and legal limits placed on force between states are much less flexible than are the limits on force utilized within states between governments and non-state actors. The extent of juridical space reserved in the contemporary legal environment for internal force thus goes quite some way in exposing the degree to which international support for 'legitimate' revolutionary armed conflicts for self-determination continues to affect existing rules. As such, this discussion will highlight the central role played by force when seeking self-determination, by means of the parameters of restraint developed in humanitarian and human rights laws, as those laws apply to conflicts for self-determination.

[3] See the declaration of a first UN International Decade for the Eradication of Colonialism in 1990, a second in 2001, and a third in 2011.

[4] 'UN at a Glance', available at <http://www.un.org/en/aboutun/index.shtml>.

[5] International Committee of the Red Cross (ICRC), 'Introduction: Additional Protocol II of 1977', available at <http://www.icrc.org/ihl.nsf/INTRO/475?OpenDocument>.

[6] John M. Owen, IV, 'Why Islamism Is Winning', *NY Times.com*, 6 Jan 2012. Phrased another way, 'Spring is a seasonal thing. It keeps coming back'. Ian Black, 'Regime prays spring will not arrive soon', *The Saturday Guardian*, 12 May 2012, 31.

[7] Captain Dale Stephens (Australia), 'Military involvement in law enforcement' (June 2010) 92(878) *International Review of the Red Cross* 453, 468.

II. The Essential Role of Coercion in the Internal Affairs of States

The UN Charter prohibits states from utilizing force or the threat of force against each other.[8] Exceptions include the right of self-defence, as per Article 51,[9] or action taken by the UN Security Council,[10] or by regional associations such as the North Atlantic Treaty Organization (NATO).[11] The Charter regulates domestic force only minimally,[12] as states control their own populations. Equally, sovereign states domestically implement the international laws to which each consents,[13] to the extent each wishes,[14] while 'the criminal jurisdiction exercised by a state within its territory [remains] the product of a long development whereby the state has gained sovereignty within that territory'.[15] The UN conditions its 'hands-off' approach to state domestic order largely through obligations on states to respect equal rights,[16] including rules on procedural fairness, equal protection norms, and rights of judicial defence.[17] However, inasmuch as governments retain control over the mechanisms of enforcement in domestic law, a population may experience gaps in rights coverage, at which point wider solutions and methods may be sought at the international level, in international humanitarian law (IHL) and international human rights, to name two areas relevant to rights of self-determination.

One consequence of the dual aspect of sovereignty is that few areas of human existence are immune from coercion,[18] such that mutual exchanges of force during a struggle for self-determination may prove beneficial to help in developing the conditions for negotiation, to resolve matters. For example, the post-war independence

[8] UN Charter, Art 2(4). 'Aggression' is perpetrated only between states. GA Res 3314 (XXIX) of 14 December 1974; the 1998 Rome Statute for an International Criminal Court, Art 8*bis*.

[9] See eg 'The Chatham House Principles of International Law on the Use of Force in Self-Defence, sec. F' (2006) 55 *International and Comparative Law Quarterly* 963, 969–71.

[10] UN Charter, Chapter VII. [11] UN Charter, Chapter VIII.

[12] UN Charter, Art 2(7). [13] UN Charter, Art 2(1).

[14] See eg Hans Kelsen, *The Communist Theory of Law* (New York: Frederic A. Praeger, 1976 [1955]), 102.

[15] 'Question of International Criminal Jurisdiction', A/CN.4/20 (1950), reprinted in *Yearbook of the International Law Commission*, 1950, vol ii, 20, para 15.

[16] See *Legality of the Threat or Use of Nuclear Weapons*, Advisory Opinion, ICJ Rep 1996, para 25; *Legal Consequences of the Construction of a Wall in the Occupied Palestinian Territory*, Advisory Opinion, ICJ Rep 2004, para 106; *Armed Activities on the Territory of the Congo (DRC v. Uganda)*, Judgment, ICJ Rep 2005, para 216.

[17] All of which affect the right to life. See Yasmin Naqvi, 'Doubtful prisoner-of-war status' (Sept 2002) 847 *International Review of the Red Cross*, available at <http://www.icrc.org/eng/resources/documents/misc/5flbzk.htm>.

[18] See eg Wendy Brown, *Walled States, Waning Sovereignty* (Cambridge, MA: Zone Books, The MIT Press, 2010); M. Cherif Bassiouni, 'Universal Jurisdiction for International Crimes: Historical Perspectives and Contemporary Practice' (2001) 42 *Virginia Journal of International Law* 81.

in 1991 of Eritrea from Ethiopia was followed by international recognition, and a UN-supervised referendum in 1993.[19] The Kurdistan Autonomous Region of Iraq established in 1970 achieved de facto independence in 1991, constituting an Iraqi federal entity since 2005.[20] Armenian secessionists in the South Caucasus region of Nagorno-Karabakh achieved de facto independence in 1994, although final settlement negotiations are ongoing.[21] After two civil wars, the final North/South Comprehensive Peace Agreement between Sudan and Southern Sudan was signed in January 2005, after which a successful referendum on South Sudan independence in January 2011 was formalized later on 9 July.[22] Other concrete options, such as the gradual transfer of home rule powers to Greenland by Denmark since 2008, conditional autonomy for Bougainville in Papua New Guinea since 2004, and deferred self-determination pending final settlement under international supervision for Kosovo,[23] illustrate that a measure of self-help can be effective in securing negotiation.

Nonetheless, coercion invites struggle, and struggle can cause conflict, so self-determination 'causes' generate an inherent instability in interaction between the international legal community and the political aspects of state sovereignty. As struggles for self-determination have become the main type of armed conflict during the Charter era, doctrinal disagreement has increased regarding the international recognition to be afforded to new states, governments, and other entities and situations.[24] Moreover, as the pressures of international attention during liberation conflicts have grown, a seismic shift has occurred in the traditional dual aspect of sovereignty, such that the central prohibitions against inter-state uses of force and against interference on state domestic affairs have been further holed.[25] Put simply,

[19] 'Eritrea: Background', available at <https://www.cia.gov/library/publications/the-world-factbook/geos/er.html>.

[20] Tim Arango, 'In Uprooting of Kurds, Iraq Tests a Fragile National Unity', *NY Times.com*, 21 Apr 2012.

[21] 'Regions and territories: Nagorno-Karabak', available at <http://news.bbc.co.uk/1/hi/world/europe/country_profiles/3658938.stm>.

[22] 'Sudan: Background', available at <https://www.cia.gov/library/publications/the-world-factbook/geos/su.html>.

[23] See, respectively, 'The Greenland Self-Government Arrangement', available at <http://www.stm.dk/_p_13090.html>; 'The Constitution of the Autonomous Region of Bougainville', adopted by the Bougainville Constituent Assembly at Buin on 12 Nov 2004, available at <http://www.paclii.org/pg/constitution-bougainville-2004.html>; SC Res 1244 (10 June 1999) (placing Kosovo under a transitional UN Interim Administration Mission (UNMIK) pending final determination of Kosovo's future status) and 'Kosovo Declaration of Independence', of 17 Feb 2008, available at <http://www.assembly-kosova.org/?cid=2,128,1635>.

[24] See eg James Crawford, *The Creation of States in International Law* (2nd edn, Oxford: Oxford University Press, 2007), discussing, inter alia, the final phases of decolonization, the status of Israel and Palestine, the dissolution of Yugoslavia and the USSR, the reunification of Germany, and self-determination for Chechnya and Kosovo.

[25] See eg Edward A. Laing, 'The Norm of Self-Determination, 1941–1991' (1993) 22 *International Relations* 209, 222, citing Ian Brownlie (1973): 'self-determination [is] a legal principle, and UN organs do not permit Article 2(7) to impede discretion and decision when the principle is in issue' (citation omitted).

today, 'international law treats civil wars as purely internal matters, *with the possible exception of self-determination conflicts*'.[26] This shift in the spheres of sovereign power not only has blurred the non-interference principle by creating a further inroad in the presumed illegality of third state assistance to 'rebels', but further, it has also blurred the legal distinction between 'peacetime' contexts of police action (against domestic riots, isolated acts of violence, and the like), and domestic force used militarily in an internal armed conflict.

As noted by the ICRC:

> The principle [of self-determination], which was proclaimed by the French Revolution, and was subsequently often denied, has from the outset constantly come up against the legal order; this did not prevent it from being applied with increasing frequency and from growing in strength ... [as] a guiding principle in politics and a rule of exception in international law.[27]

Non-international armed conflicts in general are the least regulated by international law, and the question arises as to how struggles for self-determination should be viewed. One Islamic school of thought, for example, posits that all 'rebels', both Muslim and non-Muslim, are 'privileged' combatants, for whom all laws of war are applicable.[28] Another hypothesis finds 'fractionation', whereby the relations between the government authorities and the rebel group retain a purely internal character,[29] while a third view holds that the 'cause' of a conflict determines the applicable law, for example 'if the authorities (representing a people in conflict), are seeking, *in fine*, the creation of a new state, a conflict could formally be qualified as international even though one of the belligerents is not (yet) established as a sovereign entity'.[30] Similar transformations in the agreed parameters on non-interference and force due to self-determination have slowed somewhat in the

See also Antony Lewis, 'The Responsibility to Protect: a new response to humanitarian suffering?', *e-International Relations*, 6 July 2010; Ramesh Thakur, 'Humanitarian Intervention' in Thomas G. Weiss and Sam Daws (eds), *The Oxford Handbook on the United Nations* (Oxford: Oxford University Press, 2008), ch 22. Consider the following Security Council resolutions: SC Res 1674 of 28 Apr 2006, para 4 (responsibility to protect), SC Res 1973 of 17 Mar 2011, para 4 (Libya), and SC Res 2043 of 21 Apr 2012 (Syria).

[26] Emphasis added. Malcolm N. Shaw, *International Law* (6th edn, Cambridge: Cambridge University Press, 2008), 1148. See also GA Res 60/145 of 14 Feb 2006, on the 'universal realisation of the right of peoples to self-determination', para 2.

[27] Yves Sandoz, Christophe Swinarski, and Bruno Zimmermann, *Commentary on the Additional Protocols of 8 June 1977* (Leiden: Martinus Nijhoff, 1987), 42 (citations omitted).

[28] Sadia Tabassum, 'Combatants, not bandits: the status of rebels in Islamic law' (Mar 2011) 93 *International Review of the Red Cross* 121, 132. Of interest also, see the ISISC and NATO School, 2012 Seminar on Sharia Law and Military Operations, 18–24 Nov 2012, Siracusa, regarding the possible implications on military operations of Sharia law in Islamic states.

[29] Supplemental Report to the International Institute of Humanitarian Law, ICRC, XXVIIth Round Table on Current Problems of IHL, 'International humanitarian law and other legal regimes: interplay in situations of violence' (Nov 2003), San Remo, Italy, 4, available at <http://www.icrc.org/eng/resources/documents/misc/5ubcvx.htm>.

[30] ICRC, 'International humanitarian law and other legal regimes: interplay in situations of violence'.

era since 11 September 2001,[31] but as force impacts heavily on civilians,[32] and compounds jurisprudential perplexities surrounding what law to apply, the current readiness of states to use armed force represents a worrying trend.

III. Self-Determination and the *Jus in Bello*

'Civilized' European states sought early to restrain new war technologies, and in 1868, agreed that:

> The only legitimate object which states should endeavour to accomplish during war is to weaken the military forces of the enemy;
>
> That for this purpose it is sufficient to disable the greatest possible number of men;
>
> That this object would be exceeded by the employment of arms which uselessly aggravate the sufferings of disabled men, or render their death inevitable;...[33]

However, such practical and humanitarian sentiments held little weight for long against 19th-century German commentary on *Kriegsrecht* (the law of war), a dominant strain of which favoured *Kriegsraison* (conduct dictated by 'necessity of war') over *Kriegsmanier* (the lawful conduct of war), and which has fuelled armed conflicts ever since. Once demobbed soldiers returned home after both World Wars,[34] the efficacies of terror tactics were passed on to their revolutionary allies,[35] and an increasing resort to indiscriminate violence generally has been the result.[36] Walzer attributes 'the breakdown of a political code first worked out in the second half of the nineteenth century and roughly analogous to the laws of war worked out at the same time', to the removal of 'a line that we will have little difficulty recognising as the political parallel of the line that marks off combatants from non-combatants'.[37] While a weakening dichotomy

[31] Elizabeth Chadwick, *Self-Determination in the Post-9/11 Era* (Abingdon: Routledge, 2011); Elizabeth Chadwick, 'It's war Jim, but not as we know it: A "reality check" for international laws of war?' (2003) 39 *Crime, Law and Social Change* 233.

[32] See eg 'ICRC survey on the impact of armed conflict on civilians: views from Lebanon' (ICRC, 2010), available at <http://www.icrc.org/eng/resources/documents/report/views-from-field-report-lebanon-230609.htm>.

[33] Preamble, Saint Petersburg Declaration 1868.

[34] See eg Ryan Devereaux, 'Academy taught US officers to prepare for "total war" with Islam', *The Saturday Guardian*, 12 May 2012, 12 (Dresden, Tokyo, Hiroshima, and Nagasaki considered as precedents).

[35] Michael Walzer, *Just and Unjust Wars: A Moral Argument* (2nd edn, New York: Basic Books, 1977), 198.

[36] See generally Alexander L. George (ed), *Western State Terrorism* (Cambridge: Polity Press, 1991).

[37] Walzer, *Just and Unjust Wars*. See also Michael Howard, '*Temperamenta Belli*: Can War Be Controlled?' in Jean B. Elshtain (ed), *Just War Theory* (Oxford: Blackwell, 1992), 23, 30–3.

between 'war' and 'peace' in a 'just cause' does not release either side from their respective humanitarian responsibilities, it does make protecting civilians, whether under IHL, human rights laws, refugee law, and/or anti-terror laws, much more problematic.

A. Non-International Uses of Force and Self-Determination

The exceptional nature of self-determination is reflected in modern laws of armed conflict at the most basic level. In 1949, the Geneva Conventions were revised and supplemented, and Article 3 common to the four Geneva Conventions was inserted to provide basic humanitarian protections in non-international armed conflicts for non-participants and those placed *hors de combat*. Termed 'a convention within a convention', Common Article 3 constituted a legal breakthrough in traditional laws on armed conflict which previously had applied formally only between states. Human rights laws were yet to be developed, and the rationale behind Common Article 3 in particular was to restrain governments. Common Article 3 provides:

In the case of armed conflict not of an international character occurring in the territory of one of the High Contracting Parties, each Party to the conflict shall be bound to apply, as a minimum, the following provisions:

(1) Persons taking no active part in the hostilities, including members of armed forces who have laid down their arms and those placed *hors de combat* by sickness, wounds, detention, or any other cause, shall in all circumstances be treated humanely, without any adverse distinction founded on race, colour, religion or faith, sex, birth or wealth, or any other similar criteria.

To this end, the following acts are and shall remain prohibited at any time and in any place whatsoever with respect to the above-mentioned persons:

(a) violence to life and person, in particular murder of all kinds, mutilation, cruel treatment and torture;
(b) taking of hostages;
(c) outrages upon personal dignity, in particular, humiliating and degrading treatment;
(d) the passing of sentences and the carrying out of executions without previous judgement pronounced by a regularly constituted court affording all the judicial guarantees which are recognised as indispensable by civilised peoples.

(2) The wounded and sick shall be collected and cared for.

An impartial humanitarian body, such as the International Committee of the Red Cross, may offer its services to the parties to the conflict.

The Parties to the conflict should further endeavour to bring into force, by means of special agreements, all or part of the other provisions of the present Convention.

The application of the preceding provisions shall not affect the legal status of the Parties to the conflict.

The trigger for implementing Common Article 3 is 'armed conflict'. Nonetheless, many states in 1949 were reluctant to accept obligations of restraint in conflicts against 'rebels' and 'bandits', unless forced to do so by battlefield conditions,[38] and the following agreed conditions proved influential in formalizing Common Article 3:

- That the *de jure* government has recognised the insurgents as belligerents; or
- that it has claimed for itself the rights of a belligerent; or
- that it has accorded the insurgents recognition as belligerents for the purposes only of the present Convention; or
- that the dispute has been admitted to the agenda of the UN Security Council or the General Assembly as being a threat to international peace, a breach of the peace, or an act of aggression.[39]

These points simply acknowledge certain behavioural patterns in 'armed conflict',[40] while it was not yet anticipated that equal rights and the self-determination of peoples, or the use of force for a 'cause', might generate 'special cases' such that a civil war 'should' be recognized once the military is called out.[41] The Algerian 'War of Independence' from France (1954–62) is a case in point.[42] France preferred to characterize that conflict—which was both a decolonization war, and a true 'civil' war between loyalist French Algerians and pro-independence insurrectionists—as 'terrorism' throughout. France also employed torture widely, because 'The struggle against terrorism makes it necessary to resort to certain questioning techniques as the only way of saving human life and avoiding new attacks'.[43] At no point did France acknowledge the de jure applicability of the Geneva regime—not even of Common Article 3, but it was ultimately forced to apply certain Geneva provisions, de facto, to its battlefield behaviour and treatment of prisoners.

[38] And, remain so. See eg Notes and Comments, Theodore Meron, 'On the Inadequate Reach of Humanitarian and Human Rights Law and the Need for a New Instrument' (1983) 77 *American Journal of International Law* 589.

[39] ICRC, 'Commentary: Common Article 3', available at <http://www.icrc.org/ihl.nsf/COM/365-570006?OpenDocument>.

[40] See eg Luc Reydams, 'A la guerre comme à la guerre: patterns of armed conflict, humanitarian law responses and new challenges' (2006) 864 *International Review of the Red Cross*, available at <http://www.icrc.org/eng/resources/documents/article/review/review-864-p729.htm>.

[41] See generally the ILA Use of Force Committee, 'Final Report on the Meaning of Armed Conflict in International Law', submitted at The Hague, 15–20 Aug 2010, available at <http://www.ila-hq.org>.

[42] See eg Arnold Fraleigh, 'The Algerian Revolution as a Case Study in International Law' in Richard A. Falk (ed), *The International Law of Civil War* (Baltimore, MD: Johns Hopkins Press, 1971), 179; Recent Publications, Meyer (1989) 4 *Interights Bulletin* 13 (attempt by the Algerian Provisional Government in 1960 to accede to the 1949 Geneva Conventions).

[43] Luis Lema, 'Torture in Algeria. The report that was to change everything', *Le Temps*, 19 Aug 2005, available at <http://www.icrc.org/eng/resources/documents/misc/algeria-history-190805.htm>.

B. 'Internationalized' Uses of Force and Self-Determination

The peace–war dichotomy was further weakened by General Assembly Resolution 2625 (XXV) of 24 October 1970 (the 'Friendly Relations' Declaration), which provides:

> the territory of a colony or other non-self-governing territory has … *a status separate and distinct* from the territory of the state administering it; and such separate and distinct status under the Charter shall exist until the people of the colony or non-self-governing territory have exercised their right of self-determination in accordance with the Charter …[44]

Resolution 2625 (XXV) appears to assume that international rules of armed conflict apply in struggles for self-determination, and conditions the non-interference principle, as follows:

> Nothing … shall be construed as authorising or encouraging any action which would dismember or impair, totally or in part, the territorial integrity or political unity of sovereign and independent states *conducting themselves in compliance with the principle of equal rights and self-determination of peoples … and thus possessed of a government representing the whole people belonging to the territory without distinction as to race, creed or colour.*[45]

This 'clarification' led many, including Friedrich, to argue that Resolution 2625 (XXV) provides strong support for the transformation of the denial of internal rights entitlements into external, secessionist rights.[46] Nonetheless, caution should remain. Resolution 2625 (XXV) does not equate 'representative' and 'democratic' governance. The exhortation to preserve only those states the governments of which represent the people 'belonging' to the land hearkens back to colonial contexts of traditional national liberation theory to oust invaders.[47] Resolution 2625 also undermines the doctrine of *uti possidetis*,[48] which had explosive consequences once the UN General Assembly, in Resolutions 3070 (XXVIII) of 30 November 1973 and 3246 (XXIX) of 29 November 1974, approved the right of peoples to use 'all available means' to achieve their self-determination, such that these and other developments required the further modernization of IHL, which occurred in 1977: Additional Protocol I regulates international armed conflicts, and Additional Protocol II, non-international armed conflicts.

44 Emphasis added. 45 Emphasis added.

46 Jürgen Friedrich, 'UNMIK in Kosovo: Struggling with Uncertainty' (2005) 9 *Max Planck Yearbook of United Nations Law* 225, 248 (citations omitted).

47 See eg Gene Currivan, 'Zionists Proclaim New State of Israel', *NY Times.com*, 15 May 1948 (a 'self-evident right of the Jewish people to be a … sovereign state').

48 The doctrine of *uti possidetis* conveys the international law principle that only he who possesses territory (and other property) at the end of a war may keep it, subject to any contrary treaty provision. See *Case concerning the Frontier Dispute (Burkina Faso v. Republic of Mali)*, ICJ Rep 1986, paras 20–6.

As states determine order within their borders, one main advantage for governments during civil wars remains: domestic law continues to apply. In other words, IHL does not operate as the *lex specialis* in internal armed hostilities.[49] Additional Protocol I, Article 1(4), circumvents this state of affairs by following the nod given by Resolution 2625 (XXV) regarding the separate status of certain liberation conflicts, as follows:

[International armed conflicts] include armed conflicts in which peoples are fighting against colonial domination and alien occupation and against racist regimes in the exercise of their right of self-determination.

In automatically catapulting the nominated liberation conflicts from the internal to the international plane, for regulation by the *lex specialis* of IHL, the parameters of Resolution 2625 (XXV) were expanded greatly in relation to struggles for self-determination. As noted by the ICRC:[50]

The expression 'colonial domination' certainly covers the most frequently occurring case in recent years … The expression 'alien occupation' … covers cases of partial or total occupation of a territory which has not yet been fully formed as a state. Finally, *the expression 'racist regimes' covers cases of regimes founded on racist criteria*. The first two situations imply the existence of distinct peoples.[51] *The third implies, if not the existence of two completely distinct peoples, at least a rift within a people which ensures hegemony of one section in accordance with racist ideas.*[52]

This extension in coverage proved somewhat costly in terms of state ratification, which occurred slowly.[53] Certain key states, concerned that a 'just cause' or a 'terrorist charter' was deemed appropriate for regulation under international rules,[54] pressured the ICRC to elucidate the provision further, which it did, in clarifying that 'the mere existence of a government or resistance movement is not sufficient evidence of the international character of the conflict, nor does it establish that

[49] But see *Prosecutor v. Duško Tadić*, Case No IT-91-1-AR72, Decision on the Defence Motion for Interlocutory Appeal on Jurisdiction (Appeals Chamber), 2 Oct 1995, paras 113–18 (discussing the premise that 'international humanitarian law includes principles or general rules protecting civilians from hostilities in the course of internal armed conflicts'), and 134 ('customary international law imposes criminal liability for serious violations of Common Article 3').

[50] Sandoz, Swinarski, and Zimmermann, *Commentary on the Additional Protocols of 8 June 1977*, 54.

[51] Regarding 'peoples', the ICRC adopts both an 'ethnic' or 'minority' approach, and a common 'civic' or political dimension. Sandoz, Swinarski, and Zimmermann, *Commentary on the Additional Protocols of 8 June 1977*, 52–5.

[52] Emphasis added. A racist/ethnic conflict can also constitute genocide. See eg the *Application of the Convention on the Prevention and Punishment of the Crime of Genocide (Bosnia and Herzegovina v. Serbia and Montenegro)*, Judgment of 26 February 2007, ICJ Rep 2007, 43 (Srebrenica massacre constituted genocide).

[53] As of July 2014, the ICRC lists 174 states parties to Additional Protocol I, and 167 to Additional Protocol II.

[54] See eg Judith Gardam, 'Protocol 1 to the Geneva Conventions: A Victim of Short-Sighted Political Considerations?' (1989) 17 *Melbourne University Law Review* 107.

character'.[55] However, Additional Protocol I may not alter the status of either party to a conflict, but it does encourage a people to adopt forceful means, in order to attract regulation by IHL and thus a measure of recognition as an international armed conflict.

Additional Protocol II, in contrast, updates and supplements Common Article 3, the central concern being to extend more international restraints to civil wars generally. The material field of application of Additional Protocol II is narrow, and applies to conflicts which:

> take place in the territory of a High Contracting Party between its armed forces and dissident armed forces or other organised armed groups which, under responsible command, exercise such control over a part of its territory as to enable them to carry out sustained and concerted military operations and to implement this Protocol.[56]

A lower threshold of intensity also applies: 'internal disturbances and tensions, such as riots, isolated and sporadic acts of violence and other acts of a similar nature' are not covered.[57] Additional Protocol II, Article 3, preserves governmental responsibility to re-establish law and order, and the protocol cannot justify external intervention. Should neither protocol be applicable, there remains Common Article 3 of the 1949 Geneva Conventions.[58] Most importantly, as noted by the International Law Association's (ILA's) Use of Force Committee in 2010:

> States may not, consistently with international law, simply declare that a situation is or is not an armed conflict based on policy preferences.[59]

IV. Self-Determination and the *Jus ad Bellum*

Force impacts on the interrelationship between human rights standards and IHL obligations in terms of the respective social costs. Specifically, peacetime uses of

[55] Sandoz, Swinarski, and Zimmermann, *Commentary on the Additional Protocols of 8 June 1977*, 508 (citation omitted). See Sonja Boelaert-Suominen, 'The ICTY and the Kosovo conflict' (2000) 82 *International Review of the Red Cross* 217.

[56] Additional Protocol II, Art 1(2). See Konstantin Obradovic, 'International humanitarian law and the Kosovo crisis' (Sept 2000) 839 *International Review of the Red Cross*, available at <http://www.icrc.org/eng/resources/documents/misc/57jqqb.htm> (KLA/Serbian conflict as an Additional Protocol II situation rather than 'terrorism'). For case law concerning 'responsible command' and capacity to implement Additional Protocol II, see the ILA Use of Force Committee, 'Final Report on the Meaning of Armed Conflict in International Law', 20–1.

[57] The 1998 Rome Statute, Art 8(2)(d) and (f) ('war crimes'), applies this threshold to all non-international armed conflicts.

[58] See eg *Hamdan v. Rumsfeld*, 548 US 66 (2006) (Common Art 3 applicable to the Afghan conflict between the US and Al Qaeda).

[59] ILA Use of Force Committee, 'Final Report on the Meaning of Armed Conflict in International Law', 2.

armed force by governments are expected to be necessary, proportionate, and sparing, and to exhibit the parameters of governmental legitimacy. The institutional and legal frameworks in place to restrain force in peacetime should operate within a non-discriminatory environment, while legitimate civilian authority over the use of force should accord with the rule of law,[60] particularly as the rule of law component provides the institutional reference point for a number of preferred outcomes, including the state monopoly on the use of force, and such human rights and fundamental freedoms as permit individuals to plan and live their lives. Accordingly, the meaning and function of 'proportionality' in law enforcement as opposed to military operations are quite different,[61] and peacetime law enforcement tasks are not ordinarily undertaken by military force.[62]

The ending of the Cold War provided fresh opportunities in which to seek the peaceful solution of many struggles for self-determination,[63] while the modern-day 'security-industrial complex' makes it much more difficult to argue for persuasive content in liberation theories which depend for their effectiveness on the use of force.[64] Nonetheless, the 9/11 era has afforded a general permissiveness to states to direct their *military* operations against both civil disorder and 'terrorist' actors (however defined),[65] and states which opt to do so implicitly acknowledge that they consider certain domestic criminal matters to have metamorphosed into national security issues.[66] It is also of note that neither self-determination nor terrorism is defined at the global level,[67] while the exceptionalism carved by self-determination into

[60] A view approved by Stephens, 'Military involvement in law enforcement', citing Christian Tomuschat (citation omitted), 503 fn 52.

[61] See Kenneth Watkin, 'Controlling the Use of Force: A Role for Human Rights Norms in Contemporary Armed Conflict' (2004) 98 *American Journal of International Law* 17.

[62] See eg Stephens, 'Military involvement in law enforcement'.

[63] At least 32 new self-determination settlements have been achieved since 1988, with many more in the pipeline: Marc Weller, *Escaping the Self-Determination Trap* (Leiden: Martinus Nijhoff, 2008), 20.

[64] See eg Colin Bennett and Kevin Haggerty (eds), *Security Games: Surveillance and Control at Mega-Events* (Abingdon: Routledge, 2011) (transnational cooperation between corporate, governmental, and military actors). Consider also 'Times Topics: Blackwater Worldwide', *NY Times.com*, 25 Apr 2011 (now called Xe Services).

[65] See eg Christian J. Tams, 'The Use of Force against Terrorists' (2009) 20 *European Journal of International Law* 359; Jude McCulloch and Sharon Pickering, 'Pre-crime and counter-terrorism: imagining future crime in the "war on terror"' (2009) 49 *British Journal of Criminology* 628.

[66] Stephens, 'Military involvement in law enforcement', 456. See also David Weisburd et al, 'Terrorist threats and police performance: a study of Israeli communities' (2010) 50 *British Journal of Criminology* 725. Cf Clive Walker, 'Conscripting the Public in Terrorism Policing: Towards Safer Communities or a Police State?' [2010] *Criminal Law Review* 441.

[67] But see Report of the Ad Hoc Committee to the General Assembly, A/65/37, 14th Sess, 14–16 Apr 2010, 7; GA Doc A/59/894, App II: 'Draft comprehensive convention against international terrorism: Consolidated text', available at <http://www.un.org/en/ga/search/view_doc.asp?symbol=A/59/894>; 'Background, etc', Draft Comprehensive Convention on International Terrorism, available at <http://cns.miis.edu/inventory/pdfs/intlterr.pdf>. See also Mahmoud Hmoud, 'Negotiating the Draft Comprehensive Convention on International Terrorism: Major Bones of Contention' (2006) 4 *Journal of International Criminal Justice* 1031.

IHL finds little parallel content in anti-terrorist provisions. As state strategic choices have always necessitated a certain degree of tactical disparity from the rule of law,[68] ongoing challenges to the rule of law can only intensify the consequential spirals of state repression/public reaction/force, as have occurred between Serbia and Kosovo in the 1990s,[69] and throughout the Middle East today.[70]

A. Terrorism and Self-Determination

During the Cold War, the bipolar East and West avoided open confrontation with each other by sponsoring proxy liberation struggles. Examples include Indonesia (1945–8), the Israeli War of Independence in 1948, the Cuban revolution (1953–9), Goa's annexation by India in 1961 (ending Portuguese colonial rule), Biafra's failure to secede from Nigeria (1960–70), Bangladesh's secession from Pakistan in 1971, the post-colonial conflicts in Angola and Mozambique after independence from Portugal in 1975, and the Vietnam Wars.[71] Equally, major coups, dictatorships, and military invasions were also engineered. Weller points in 2008 to at least 26 conflicts then being waged which had already lasted an average of 27 years,[72] while civilians continue to be killed in the Middle East and beyond, 'anti-terror' assassinations increase, and violence of many descriptions proliferates.[73] In turn, the completely different strain of resistance theory

[68] See Peter Beaumont, 'Egypt's generals wait in wings as the revolution turns messy', *The Observer*, 6 May 2012, 26–7 (transition to democracy undermined at every turn).

[69] See eg Obradovic, 'International humanitarian law and the Kosovo crisis'.

[70] See eg UNHRC, 'Report of the independent international commission of inquiry on the Syrian Arab Republic', A/HRC/25/65, 25th Sess, 12 Feb 2014, agenda item 4 (investigation of ongoing criminal acts by government and non-state armed forces).

[71] See eg 'Oversight of Covert Action', available at <https://www.cia.gov/library/center-for-the-study-of-intelligence/csi-publications/books-and-monographs/agency-and-the-hill/12-The%20Agency%20and%20the%20Hill_Part2-Chapter9.pdf>; Historical Milestones: 'Entrenchment of a Bi-Polar Foreign Policy, 1953–1960', at <http://history.state.gov/milestones/1953-1960/foreword>, 'Entangling Alliances, 1961–1968', at <https://history.state.gov/milestones/1961-1968/foreword>, 'Decolonization of Asia and Africa, 1945–1960', at <http://history.state.gov/milestones/1945-1952/AsiaandAfrica>, and 'The Arab–Israeli War of 1948', at <http://history.state.gov/milestones/1945-1952/ArabIsraeliWar>. See also 'Bangladesh: Introduction', at <https://www.cia.gov/library/publications/the-world-factbook/geos/bg.html>; Borgna Brunner, 'Portugal: End of an Empire: The Portuguese colonial empire comes to a close', at <http://www.infoplease.com/spot/macao.html>; Book Review, Laurie, 'Takes on Intelligence and the Vietnam War' (2011) 55 *Studies in Intelligence* 73; Crawford, *The Creation of States in International Law*.

[72] Weller, *Escaping the Self-Determination Trap*, 19–20.

[73] See eg Christian Henderson, 'International measures for the protection of civilians in Libya and Côte d'Ivoire' (2011) 60 *International and Comparative Law Quarterly* 767; A. P. V. Rogers and Dominic McGoldrick, 'Assassination and Targeted Killing—The Killing of Osama Bin Laden' (2011) 60 *International and Comparative Law Quarterly* 778; Shane Darcy and John Reynolds, '"Otherwise Occupied": The Status of the Gaza Strip from the Perspective of International Humanitarian Law' (2010) 15 *Journal of Conflict and Security Law* 211; Danio Campanelli, 'The law of military occupation put to the test of human rights law' (2008) 871 *International Review of the Red Cross*, available at <http://www.icrc.org/eng/resources/documents/article/review/review-871-p653.htm>; James Ross, 'Black letter

represented by Islamic Jihad, which appeared in the 1970s,[74] only muddies the 'legitimate' self-determination waters further.[75]

The 'fact' of revolution, and the spread of religious extremism and intolerance in the contemporary geopolitical environment, each illustrate that a government monopoly over force cannot operate in isolation from the social effects of that force, particularly as regards the social and political alienation generated by overly repressive government. As noted by Ulfelder:

> Since 1955, the average life span for a democratic regime is just 16 years, and a substantial majority of the democratic episodes that began in the past half century have ended with a return to some form of autocracy.[76]

Shenker notes more specifically that 'In the Arab world … the focus and self-awareness that comes from [their] recent history of anti-colonial struggle has been transmitted from one generation to the next.'[77] While the origins of the current spate of Middle Eastern revolutionary upheaval can be traced back to the period referred to by Ulfelder, the violence displayed remains clearly separable, in law and in fact,[78] from the violence perpetrated by groups such as Al Qaeda.[79] The point that is missed concerns instead the crucial difference between today's liberation wars and those of former decades: their funding sources. The near-automatic linkage found in UN Security Council and General Assembly resolutions,[80] between terrorism or unauthorized violence of any description and crime, means that any infusion of funds into a people's struggle by local extremist and/or criminal networks can sabotage a people's chances of achieving self-determination 'legitimately' in the eyes of the world,

abuse: the US legal response to torture since 9/11' (Sept 2007) 867 *International Review of the Red Cross*, available at <http://www.icrc.org/eng/resources/documents/article/review/review-867-p561.htm>.

[74] See eg Harry J. Benda, 'Elites' in Frank Tachau (ed), *The Developing Nations: What Path to Modernization?* (New York: Harper & Row, 1972), 105, 107–9; Jason Burke, *Al-Qaeda: Casting a Shadow of Terror* (London: I.B. Tauris, 2003), 5.

[75] See eg the following Security Council resolutions in 1998: SC Res 1189 of 13 Aug, SC Res 1193 of 28 Aug, and SC Res 1214 of 8 Dec. See also SC Res 1267 of 15 Oct 1999, imposing a sanctions regime on the Taliban, and establishing a sanctions monitoring committee.

[76] Shashank Joshi, 'The Arab Spring Redux? The Egyptian Revolution returns with a vengeance' (RUSI, 2011), quoting Jay Ulfelder, 'Prospects for New Democracies in the Arab World: Chronicles of Deaths (and Rebirths) Foretold' (citation omitted), available at <http://www.rusi.org/analysis/commentary/ref:C4ECE6A5C6E644/>.

[77] Jack Shenker, 'How youth-led revolts shook elites around the world', *The Guardian.co.uk*, 12 Aug 2011, quoting Cambridge Professor Priyamvada Gopal. See also Jack Shenker, 'Scratching away Mubarak's legacy, one map at a time', *The Saturday Guardian*, 21 May 2011, 24.

[78] Antonio Cassese, 'The Multifaceted Criminal Notion of Terrorism in International Law' (2006) 4 *Journal of International Criminal Justice* 933.

[79] See Thomas L. Friedman, 'The Bin Laden Decade', *NY Times.com*, 31 May 2011. See also Rogers and McGoldrick, 'Assassination and targeted killing—the killing of Osama Bin Laden'.

[80] See eg ICPO Interpol-General Assembly, Resolution No. AGN/53/RES/6 concerning 'violent crime commonly referred to as terrorism', 53rd session, Luxembourg, 4–11 Sept 2004 ('considering that: (a) in many countries there are organized groups engaging in violent criminal activities designed, by spreading terror or fear, to enable them to attain allegedly political objectives').

as has been evidenced in the struggles of Muslim peoples as diverse as the Chechens,[81] Bosnians, Kosovars,[82] and Algerians.[83]

Moreover, as governments today are afforded a free hand to tar their opponents as 'criminal' and 'terrorist' at the international level, monitor the actions or movements of 'terrorists', maintain international and regional 'terror lists', and assist Interpol in such tasks,[84] the historical, social, and economic causes of terrorism are generally ignored.[85] 'Terror lists', for example, do not differentiate between the purposes or causes of violence,[86] while a 'liberation' motive need never be considered during a prosecution for terrorism under domestic criminal laws which can be applied far more broadly to 'terrorist' cases than to those for 'war crimes'.[87] To the extent that 'mutual' state enforcement action remains decentralized in an anarchic international system in which the political will to enforce state accountability directly is lacking,[88] it remains

[81] Ekaterina Stepanova, 'Islamist Terrorism in the Caucasus and Central Asia' in Alex P. Schmid and Garry F. Hindle (eds), *After the War on Terror: Regional and Multilateral Perspectives on Counter-Terrorism Strategy* (London: RUSI Books, 2009), 104.

[82] James Summers (ed), *Kosovo: A Precedent?* (Leiden: Martinus Nijhoff, 2011).

[83] 'Algeria: Introduction' (2006 merger of Algerian Salafist GSPC, to form Al Qaeda in the Lands of the Islamic Maghreb), available at <https://www.cia.gov/library/publications/the-world-factbook/geos/ag.html>; 'Algeria profile: timeline', available at <http://www.bbc.co.uk/news/world-africa-14118856> (last updated 18 Apr 2014); Adam Nossiter, 'Algerian Election Results Draw Disbelief', *NY Times.com*, 12 May 2012.

[84] See eg SC Res 1333 of 19 Dec 2000: [Sanctions Monitoring Committee] to maintain updated lists of people, organisations and relief agencies providing humanitarian assistance to Afghanistan. See also Interpol, '"Best Practices" in Combating Terrorism, Executive Summary', Report submitted to the UNSC–C-TED, Oct 2006.

[85] But see UN Secretary-General, 'Report to the General Assembly: Uniting Against Terrorism: Recommendations for a Global Counter-Terrorism Strategy', A/60/825 (27 Apr 2006), paras 20–37.

[86] See eg *Bouyahia Maher Ben Abdelaziz, et al* (20 Sept 2007) Supreme Court of Cassation (Italy), available at <http://www.geneva-academy.ch/RULAC/pdf_state/Abdelaziz.pdf>; Lucia Aleni, 'Distinguishing Terrorism from Wars of National Liberation in the Light of International Law: A View from Italian Courts' (2008) 6 *Journal of International Criminal Justice* 525. Cf Antonio Cassese, 'The multifaceted criminal notion of terrorism in international law' (2006) 4 *Journal of International Criminal Justice* 933; Chadwick, *Self-Determination in the Post-9/11 Era*, 112–15.

[87] See eg *SOS Home Dept v. DD (Afghanistan)* [2010] EWCA Civ 1407 (direct military action against UN forces contrary to UN purposes and principles); *KJ (Sri Lanka) v. SOS Home Dept* [2009] EWCA Civ 292 (armed action by Tamil Tigers against Sri Lankan forces part terrorist, part military). Cf *AH (Algeria) v. SOS Home Dept* [2012] EWCA Civ 395 (conviction by foreign court not conclusive of status under the 1951 UN Convention on Refugees, Art 1F). See also Ian Cobain, 'Police to investigate MI6 over rendition and torture of Libyans', *The Guardian.co.uk*, 12 Jan 2012; University of Reading, 'Law, Terrorism and the Right to Know: List of Potential Cases that Could Be Affected', available at <http://www.reading.ac.uk/LTRK/Securitysecrecyandcivilproceedings/ltrk-JusticeandSecurityPotentialCases.aspx>. Contrast Case Comment, Nathan Rasiah, 'The Court-Martial of Corporal Payne and Others and the Future Landscape of International Criminal Justice' (2009) 7 *Journal of International Criminal Justice* 177; Peter Rowe, 'Military Misconduct during International Armed Operations: "Bad Apples" or Systemic Failure?' (2008) 13 *Journal of Conflict and Security Law* 165.

[88] See eg the 1998 Rome Statute, Art 98, and the 1945 Statute of the International Court of Justice, Chapter II.

doubtful whether a non-international *jus ad bellum* exists.[89] In turn, the 1948 Universal Declaration of Human Rights does not even refer explicitly to self-determination,[90] and concrete action must ordinarily await diplomacy, international legal pressure, and the progressive development of international law.[91]

B. Human Rights and Self-Determination

An 'emergency' situation caused by civil disorder may require governments to derogate from certain individual rights. The measures adopted should be 'necessary' and 'proportionate' to the exigencies of the situation and the 'general interests in society'—the latter phrase originating in Article 29(2) of the Universal Declaration of Human Rights, to permit rights limitations in accordance with 'the just requirements of morality, public order and the general welfare in a democratic society'. The margin of appreciation retained by states when derogating is malleable, but the deprivation of the individual right to life attracts a particularly stringent standard—that of 'absolute necessity'.[92] This led the International Criminal Tribunal for the former Yugoslavia (ICTY) to state that 'what is inhumane, and consequently proscribed, in international wars, cannot but be inhuman and inadmissible in civil strife'.[93] In turn, since 1999, the UN Security Council has adopted resolutions which refer both to the 'protection of civilians in armed conflict' and to 'respect for human rights in armed conflicts'.[94] The European Court of Human Rights concentrates on peacetime standards when adjudicating deprivations of life during conflict, as in the *Isayeva* cases, in which the Court awarded compensation against the use of indiscriminate force by the Russian Federation during the Chechen wars of secession.[95]

[89] William Abresch, 'A Human Rights Law of Internal Armed Conflict: The European Court of Human Rights in Chechnya' (2005) 16 *European Journal of International Law* 741, 765 ('whether there is really any such body of law as the "*jus ad bellum* of internal conflict" may be doubted').

[90] The principle appears subsequently in Art 1 common to the two International Covenants on Human Rights of 1966, on civil and political rights, and on economic, social, and cultural rights. Other human rights instruments either add to this basic provision or further delimit it. Cf Ross, 'Black letter abuse'.

[91] See eg UN News Centre, 'Security Council strongly condemns massacre of civilians in Syria', 27 May 2012, available at <http://www.un.org/apps/news/story.asp?NewsID=42095&Cr=syria&Cr1=>.

[92] See eg the 1950 European Convention of Human Rights (ECHR), Art 2. Consider *Al Skeini and Others v. UK* [2011] 53 EHRR 589; *Smith and Others (No. 2) v. The MOD* [2013] UKSC 41, [2013] 3 WLR 69; *Hassan v. the UK*, ECtHR (Grand Chamber) (App no 29750/09), Judgment of 16 September 2014, available at <http://hudoc.echr.coe.int/sites/eng/Pages/search.aspx" \l " {"http://hudoc.echr.coe.int/sites/eng/Pages/search.aspx#{"documentcollectionid2":["GRANDCHAMBER","CHAMBER"],"itemid":["001-146501"]}>. Cf Andrew Clapham, 'Human Rights Obligations of Non-State Actors in Conflict Situations' (Sept 2006) 88(863) *International Review of the Red Cross* 491 (options for private military company accountability).

[93] *Prosecutor v. Tadić*, Appeal, 2 Oct 1995, para 119.

[94] See eg SC Res(s) 1265 of 17 Sept 1999 and 1296 of 17 Apr 2000. See also GA Res 3319 (XXIX) of 14 Dec 1974.

[95] *Isayeva, Yusopova and Bazayeva v. Russia* (App nos 57947/00, 57948/00, and 57949/00), ECtHR, 24 Feb 2005; *Isayeva v. Russia* (App no 57950/00), 24 Feb 2005. The Russian Federation had not sought

Differing legal standards and doctrinal disagreement mean, however, that the lack of congruence between the *jus ad bellum* and the *jus in bello* at the international and non-international levels is likely to remain in place, particularly in asymmetric conflicts,[96] which causes cases such as *Tadić* to be so contentious. Specifically, the ICTY stretched the minimal threshold of humanitarian law in that case, by diluting the adjective 'sustained', as found in Additional Protocol II to mean 'protracted' hostilities,[97] so as to include within IHL coverage periods of interruption in the hostilities, and to impose individual criminal responsibility on the participants in a conflict far earlier. States and liberation groups which choose to disregard IHL restraints on their reciprocal uses of force thus should not escape liability by relying on legal uncertainties, even as the civilians being killed in the 'Arab Spring' in Tunisia, Egypt, Bahrain, Libya, Syria, Lebanon, and Yemen, and elsewhere, continue to be characterized, not as the victims of self-determination conflicts, but instead, as 'criminals' and/or 'terrorists'. As each uprising casts its own government's forceful overreactions under the spotlight of international opinion,[98] and Al Qaeda 'spokespersons' try to take the credit for any and all uprisings in Muslim countries around the world,[99] the pursuit of greater rights entitlements can become quite forgotten, leaving only an impression of the privileging of force over law.

derogation from ECHR, Art 2(c), which permits 'action lawfully taken for the purpose of quelling a riot or insurrection', or from Art 15(2), which permits derogation from Art 2 'in respect of deaths resulting from lawful acts of war'.

[96] A category which may include episodes in the 'war on terror'. Andreas Paulus and Mindia Vashakmadze, 'Asymmetrical war and the notion of armed conflict—An attempt at a conceptualization' (2009) 873 *International Review for the Red Cross*, available at <http://www.icrc.org/eng/resources/documents/article/review/review-873-p95.htm>. See also ILA Use of Force Committee, 'Final Report on the Meaning of Armed Conflict in International Law', 32 ('States rarely recognize armed conflict beyond the zone of intense fighting'), citing Christopher Greenwood, 'Scope of Application of Humanitarian Law' in Dieter Fleck (ed), *The Handbook of Humanitarian Law in Armed Conflicts* (2nd edn, Oxford: Oxford University Press, 2008), 54, 61–2.

[97] *Prosecutor v. Tadić*, Appeal, 2 Oct 1995, para 70. See also *Prosecutor v. Tadić*, Case No IT-94, Opinion and Judgment (Trial Chamber), 7 May 1997, para 562 (criteria of intensity and organization distinguish 'an armed conflict from banditry, unorganised and short-lived insurrections, or terrorist activities'); *Prosecutor v. Milosević*, Case No IT-02-54-T, Decision on Motion for Judgement of Acquittal Under Rule 98 bis, 16 June 2004, paras 14–22 (unsuccessful argument of *amici curiae* to the effect that Serbia's conflict with Kosovo involved *only* 'acts of banditry, unorganised and short-lived insurrections or terrorist activities' prior to the NATO bombing campaign of late Mar 1999); *Prosecutor v. Kordić and Čerkez*, Case No IT-95-14/2-A, Judgement (Appeals Chamber), 17 Dec 2004, para 341 ('protracted' fighting prior to Apr 1993).

[98] See eg Rachel Martin, 'CIA Tracks Public Information for the Private Eye', *NPR*, 22 Jan 2012 (lawmakers on Capitol Hill blame CIA for 'missing' Arab Spring), available at <http://www.npr.org/2012/01/22/145587161/cia-tracks-public-information-for-the-private-eye>; 'Syria: Introduction', at <https://www.cia.gov/library/publications/the-world-factbook/geos/sy.html>.

[99] ICSR Insight, Alexander Meleagrou-Hitchens, 'Al-Qaeda interpretations of the Libyan Uprising', available at <http://icsr.info/2011/04/icsr-insight-al-qaeda-interpretations-of-the-libyan-uprising/>; Owen, IV, 'Why Islamism Is Winning'. See also Valentina Soria, 'Global Jihad Sustained Through Africa', RUSI UK Terrorism Analysis No 2, Apr 2012, at <http://rusi.org/analysis/commentary/ref:C4F7BDEE390DBB/>.

V. Conclusion

The Westphalian system of states established in 1648 may have institutionalized 'effective' control over territory as the key to successful assertions of statehood, as is mirrored in the 1933 Montevideo Convention on Rights and Duties of States,[100] but territorial control alone has never sufficed to resolve wider issues of legitimacy. Resolution 2625 indeed proved influential, and once peoples were encouraged to utilize *all available means* to achieve their self-determination, the proverbial horse bolted.

The fact that a people might feel compelled to seek their rights through force provides evidence, if any were needed, that contemporary international society can only seek at best to restrain the first use of force. Furthermore, the answer to any question whether traditional national liberation theory still retains vitality and meaning in modern struggles against autocratic government, inequality, high unemployment, a lack of rights, and official corruption, is undoubtedly 'yes'. However, this response is valid only so long as restraint over force is exercised, and only so long as all persons, whether in victorious governments, or insurrectionists who succeed in forming new governments, are held responsible for their unlawful acts committed while seeking to wield power.[101]

Whenever prohibitions on force are left simply to fall away without sanction, the international legal community of states and other entities risk appearing as either unable or unwilling to reconcile the balance between the twin imperatives of peace *and* security by working beyond existing political interrelationships.[102] They instead reinforce the use of superior force to decide political matters, to the detriment of lawful rules on force.[103] Therefore, the more extremist parameters of 'national security', the mutual hostility and contempt between government and the governed, and the inter-ethnic tensions and/or fratricidal conflagrations which fuel conflict,[104] are likely to continue coming together in struggles for self-determination, which, '[as] a guiding principle in politics and a rule of exception in international law',[105] will continue to ensure geopolitical change.

[100] The essential requirements for which are a permanent population, a defined territory, a government, and capacity to conduct diplomatic relations. Supplementary criteria are that independence is achieved in accordance with self-determination, and not for racist policies. David J. Harris, *Cases and Materials on International Law* (3rd edn, London: Sweet & Maxwell, 1983), 81.

[101] ILC, 'Articles on State Responsibility for Internationally Wrongful Acts', A/Res/56/83 (12 Dec 2001), Art 10(2).

[102] Hans Kelsen, *The Law of Nations* (London: Stevens and Sons Ltd, 1951), xiii.

[103] Elizabeth Chadwick, *Traditional Neutrality Revisited: Law, Theory and Case Studies* (Alphen aan den Rijn: Kluwer Law International, 2002), 266.

[104] See eg Christina Pantazis and Simon Pemberton, 'From the "Old" to the "New" Suspect Community: Examining the Impacts of Recent UK Counter-Terrorist Legislation' (2009) 49 *British Journal of Criminology* 646.

[105] Sandoz, Swinarski, and Zimmermann, *Commentary on the Additional Protocols of 8 June 1977*.

PART V

REVIVAL OF CLASSICAL CONCEPTS?

CHAPTER 39

NECESSITY

OLIVIER CORTEN

I. Introduction

According to the well-known Webster formula, a use of force can be admissible if there is 'a necessity of self-defence, instant, over-whelming, leaving no choice of means, and no moment for deliberation'. Moreover, 'the act, justified by the necessity of self-defence, must be limited by that necessity, and kept clearly within it'.[1] This classical dictum perfectly illustrates the importance, as well as the ambiguity, of the concept of necessity. On the one hand, the *Caroline* precedent is often used to broaden the possibilities of using force.[2] As such, it is commonly invoked as the legal basis of anticipatory self-defence in the case of an 'imminent' attack.[3] And it is sometimes evoked more generally as a topical precedent reducing the question of the legality of a use of force to a condition of necessity, even if in that latter case the authors consider that the Webster formula must be adapted to the current characteristics of international relations (existence of nuclear weapons, rise of terrorist

[1] Correspondence between Great Britain and the United States, respecting the Arrest and Imprisonment of Mr McLeod, for the Destruction of the Steamboat Caroline (Mar, Apr 1841, text in J. B. Moore, *Digest of International Law* (1906), 412). See Robert Jennings, 'The Caroline and McLeod Cases' (1938) 32 *American Journal of International Law* 82–99.

[2] See eg Derek W. Bowett, *Self-Defence in International Law* (Manchester: Manchester University Press, 1958), 59–60; Michael N. Schmitt, *Counter-Terrorism and the Use of Force in International Law* (Garmisch-Partenkirchen: The Marshall Center Papers, No 5, 2002), 22–3.

[3] Michael Wood, 'Nécessité et légitime défense dans la lutte contre le terrorisme: quelle est la pertinence de l'affaire de la *Caroline* aujourd'hui?' in Société française pour le droit international, *La nécessité en droit international* (Paris: Pedone, 2007), 281–6.

organizations, complicity of 'rogue states', etc).[4] Following this doctrinal trend, as an 'inherent' right, self-defence is legal if, and to the extent that, it is necessary in a given situation.[5] More generally, necessity should be used to assess the legality of every use of force, including those extending beyond the case of self-defence, like a 'humanitarian intervention' or a measure of armed reprisal. Against this background, necessity would be more than a simple legal concept. It would offer a fundamental criterion allowing the adaptation of international law to the evolution and particularities of international relations: 'in the end, each use of force must find legitimacy in the facts and circumstances that the states believe made it necessary. Each should be judged not on abstract concepts, but on the particular events that gave rise to it'.[6] On the other hand, the *Caroline* formula can also be used to limit the possibilities of a use of force.[7] In that case, 'necessity' constitutes a rather strict condition, reducing the leeway of the intervening state. After all, Webster himself used the concept of necessity to establish the illegality of the British action. More recently, necessity was commonly considered as a customary condition, closely linked to the condition of proportionality, limiting (and not founding) the right of self-defence.[8] Far from constituting an extra-legal criterion reminiscent of some kind of natural law, necessity should thus be used in accordance with the relevant rule of positive international law. In other words, it should not be misused as a tool to circumvent existing legal obligations, like the existence of a previous 'armed attack' in the case of self-defence. Ultimately, necessity should not be assimilated to a general principle, but rather to a simple element among others of an existing rule of international law.[9]

As it can be noticed, studying necessity highlights the diversity of the interpretations of the existing *jus ad/contra bellum* and more deeply of the general conceptions of the international legal order.[10] More specifically, this chapter aims to present different forms of the doctrine of necessity and to assess them critically. In Section II, the thesis of necessity as a general justification of use of force will be tested, in the light of the international law of responsibility. In the following sections, necessity will be contemplated as a condition enshrined in particular exceptions to the prohibition of the use of force, namely self-defence (Section III) and collective

[4] Abraham D. Sofaer, *The Best Defense? Legitimacy & Preventive Force* (Stanford, CA: Hoover Institution Press, Pub No 576, 2010), 89 ff.

[5] Abraham D. Sofaer, 'On the Necessity of Pre-Emption' (2003) 14 *American Journal of International Law* 209–26.

[6] William Taft IV and Todd Buchwald, 'Preemption, Iraq and International Law' (2003) 97 *American Journal of International Law* 557.

[7] Oscar Schachter, *International Law in Theory and Practice* (Dordrecht: Martinus Nijhoff, 1991), 151.

[8] See Section III.

[9] See generally Olivier Corten, 'La nécessité et le *jus ad bellum*' in Société française pour le droit international, *La nécessité en droit international*, 127–50.

[10] Olivier Corten, 'The Controversies Over the Customary Prohibition on the Use of Force: A Methodological Debate' (2005) 16 *European Journal of International Law* 803–22.

security (Section IV). Lastly, we will turn to the methodological problems raised by any interpretation of the concept of necessity, particularly in the realm of the use of force (Section V).

II. Is 'Necessity' a General Justification to the Use of Force?

Some authors understand necessity as a general concept able to justify a military action. As briefly stated earlier, this argument elevates necessity to a legal basis to an action in self-defence, an act of reprisal, or a humanitarian intervention. A good example of this doctrinal trend can be found in Abraham Sofaer's article appropriately entitled 'the necessity of pre-emption', that tends to legally justify American interventionism after 11 September 2001.[11] In his paper, the author supports an extensive conception of the use of force founded both on 'pre-emption' and 'necessity': 'The standard generally applicable to pre-emptive self-defence is, rather, the *same general rule applicable to all uses of force: necessity to act under the relevant circumstances, together with the requirement that any action be proportionate to the threat addressed*'.[12] Even if it is formally linked to the legal institution of self-defence, necessity appears in this context as a general justification to use force. As such, it could be examined in connection with Article 25 of the International Law Commission (ILC) Articles on State Responsibility, which mentions 'state of necessity' as a general circumstance precluding wrongfulness.[13] The Commission expressly cites the *Caroline* precedent as an illustration[14] and it seems that this article could be applied to some military interventions.[15] Therefore, can we consider necessity as a general legal basis for the use of force in international law?

In view of the existing texts and practice, this is far from certain.[16] First, it must be pointed out that state of necessity 'can only be invoked on an exceptional basis'.[17]

[11] Sofaer, 'On the Necessity of Pre-Emption'.

[12] Sofaer, 'On the Necessity of Pre-Emption', 220 (emphasis added).

[13] Annexed to GA Res 56/83 of 13 Dec 2001, adopted by consensus.

[14] *Yearbook of the International Law Commission*, 2001, vol II (2), 81, para 5.

[15] Andreas Laursen, 'The Use of Force and (the State of) Necessity' (2004) 37 *Vanderbilt Journal of Transnational Law* 485–526; Jean Raby, 'The State of Necessity and the Use of Force to Protect Nationals' (1988) 26 *Canadian Yearbook of International Law* 253–72.

[16] Olivier Corten, 'L'état de nécessité peut-il justifier un recours à la force non constitutif d'agression?' (2004) *The Global Community Yearbook of International Law and Jurisprudence* 1, 11–50; Tom Ruys, *'Armed Attack' and Article 51 of the UN Charter. Evolutions in Customary Law and Practice* (Cambridge: Cambridge University Press, 2010), 379–82.

[17] *Case concerning the Gabčíkovo-Nagymaros Project (Hungary/Slovakia)*, ICJ Rep 1997, 40, para 51.

Necessity was considered by the ILC as a circumstance that must be interpreted narrowly and certainly not as a revival of previous doctrines such as 'self-protection' or 'self-preservation'.[18] For that reason, the ILC insisted that necessity may constitute a circumstance precluding wrongfulness only 'under certain very limited conditions'.[19] The only means to make this controversial notion acceptable was to guarantee from the outset that 'it had been agreed that a state of necessity could in no event justify recourse to armed force'.[20] One of the relevant guarantees in this regard was the introduction in the final text of Article 26 of the Articles on State Responsibility which provides that: 'Nothing in this chapter precludes the wrongfulness of any act of a State which is not in conformity with an obligation arising under a peremptory norm of general international law.' As noted by the ICJ in the *Nicaragua* case,[21] the ILC had already recognized that 'the law of the Charter concerning the prohibition of the use of force in itself constitutes a conspicuous example of a rule in international law having the character of *jus cogens*'.[22] States reached the same conclusion in various contexts: elaboration of the concept of *jus cogens* itself,[23] discussions preceding the elaboration of General Assembly resolutions on the use of force (2625 (XXV),[24] 3314 (XXIX),[25] 42/22[26]), comments on the state of necessity during the

[18] Julio Barboza, 'Necessity (Revisited) in International Law' in Jerzy Makarczyk (ed), *Essays in International Law in Honour of Judge Manfred Lachs* (Leiden: Martinus Nijhoff, 1984), 28.

[19] *Yearbook of the International Law Commission*, 2001, vol II (2), 83, para 14.

[20] *Yearbook of the International Law Commission*, 1980, vol I, 1618th mtg, 181, para 27.

[21] ICJ Rep 1986, 100, para 190.

[22] Draft Articles on the Law of Treaties with Commentaries, *Yearbook of the International Law Commission*, 1966, vol II, 247.

[23] See eg UN Conference on the Law of Treaties, 1st session; Greece, 52nd mtg, 4 May 1968, para 18; Kenya, para 31; Nigeria, para 48; Uruguay, 53rd mtg, 6 May 1968, 329, para 48; UK, para 59; Cyprus, para 69; FGR, 55th mtg, 7 May 1968, para 31; Ecuador, para 42; Tanzania, 56th mtg, 7 May 1968, 349, para 2; Ukraine, para 6; Philippines, para 20; Switzerland, para 26; Norway, para 39; Malaysia, para 51. See also FGR (UN Conference on the Law of Treaties, 2nd session, 9 Apr–22 May 1969, para 26); Ecuador, paras 35 and 39; Italy, para 39; Belarus, para 48; Nepal, para 70; Cuba, para 42.

[24] See eg Ukraine (A/C.6/S.R.757, 12 Nov 1962, para 13); UK (A/C.6/S.R.761, 16 Nov 1962, para 5); Czechoslovakia (A/C.6/S.R.802, 29 Oct 1963, para 12); Hungary (A/C.6/S.R.806, 6 Nov 1963, para 4, A/C.6/S.R.999, 16 Nov 1967, para 6); Mexico (A/C.6/S.R.806, 6 Nov 1963, para 12); US (A/C.6/S.R.808, 11 Nov 1963, para 15); Bolivia (A/C.6/S.R.814, 19 Nov 1963, para 6); Cyprus (A/C.6/S.R.822, 29 Nov 1963, para 7, A/C.6/S.R.892, 7 Dec 1965, para 19); Madagascar (A/AC.119/SR.9, 3 Sept 1964); Tanzania (A/C.6/S.R.882, 24 Nov 1965, para 8); Iran (para 18); Ecuador (A/C.6/S.R.1003, 20 Nov 1967, para 53); Thailand (A/C.6/S.R.1093, 12 Dec 1968, para 1); Romania (para 7); Iraq (A/C.6/S.R.1163, 29 Nov 1969, para 6); Venezuela (Report of the Special Committee on Principles of International Law concerning Friendly Relations and Co-operation among States, Supp no 18, A/8018, 1970, 77, para 109); and Ethiopia (A/C.6/S.R.1182, 25 Sept 1970, para 49).

[25] See eg Ecuador (A/AC.134/SR.10, 17 June 1968 in A/AC.134/SR.1-24; A/C.6/SR.1078, 22 Nov 1968, para 36; A/AC.134/SR.35, 14 Mar 1969 in A/AC.134/SR.25-51; A/AC.134/SR.58, 21 July 1970 in A/AC.134/SR.52-66; A/C.6/SR.1209, 28 Oct 1970, para 36); DRC (A/AC.134/SR.35, 14 Mar 1969 in A/AC.134/SR.25-51); Argentina (A/C.6/S.R.888, 2 Dec 1965, para 37).

[26] Report of the Special Committee on Enhancing the Effectiveness of the Principle of Non-Use of Force in International Relations, General Assembly, 34th mtg, Supp no 41, A/34/41 (4 June 1979), para 31; see also paras 57, 72, and 104. The Committee was composed of representatives of the FRG, Belgium, Benin, Bulgaria, Cyprus, Cuba, Egypt, Ecuador, Spain, US, Finland, France, Greece,

works of the ILC,[27] and participation in judicial proceedings.[28] Another guarantee was introduced in Article 25 itself, which stipulates: 'in any case, necessity may not be invoked by a state as a ground for precluding wrongfulness if: a) The international obligation in question excludes the possibility of invoking necessity'. The ILC gave the example of the 'military necessities' in the law of war: when the relevant primary rule already takes into account the necessity criterion to make a balance between the different values at hand, it implicitly excludes the possibility to invoke a general 'state of necessity' as a circumstance precluding wrongfulness.[29] The same reasoning can be transposed to *jus contra bellum*, as the commentary of the ILC clearly suggests.[30] By allowing the possibility to use force to riposte against an armed attack, self-defence appears as a particular expression of the concept of necessity.[31] In the *Nuclear Weapons* case, the International Court of Justice (ICJ) evoked 'an extreme circumstance of self-defence, in which the very survival of a State would be at stake'.[32] Significantly, the Court never raised the possibility to invoke a general 'state of necessity' to justify a use of military force (nor did the states during the written and oral proceedings dedicated to the case). In the same vein, the states included in the General Assembly Definition of Aggression a safeguard clause stating that: 'no consideration of whatever nature, whether political, economic, military

Guinea, Hungary, India, Iraq, Italy, Japan, Morocco, Mexico, Mongolia, Nepal, Nicaragua, Uganda, Panama, Peru, Poland, Romania, UK, Senegal, Somalia, Togo, Turkey, and the USSR. See also Report of the Special Committee on Enhancing the Effectiveness of the Principle of Non-Use of Force in International Relations, General Assembly, 38th mtg, Supp no 41, A/38/41 (1983), paras 20, 46, and 54; Report of the Special Committee on Enhancing the Effectiveness of the Principle of Non-Use of Force in International Relations, General Assembly, 39th mtg, Supp no 41, A/39/41 (4 Apr 1984), paras 27, 44, and 100; Report of the Special Committee on Enhancing the Effectiveness of the Principle of Non-Use of Force in International Relations, General Assembly, 41st mtg, Supp no 41, A/41/41 (13 Mar 1986), paras 82, 84, and 89; Report of the Special Committee on Enhancing the Effectiveness of the Principle of Non-Use of Force in International Relations, General Assembly, 42nd mtg, Supp no 41, A/42/41 (20 May 1987), para 26. See many other examples in Olivier Corten, *The Law against War* (Oxford: Hart, 2010), 204–7.

[27] See eg Mexico (A/C.6/54/SR.23, 2 Nov 1999, 4, para 20); Cuba (A/C.6/54/SR.28, 5 Nov 1999, 11, para 93).

[28] See eg *Military and Paramilitary Activities*, ICJ Rep 1986, 101, para 190; *Legality of the Threat or Use of Nuclear Weapons* (Malaysia, Note Verbale of 19 June 1995, 4; India, Letter dated 20 June 1995 from the Ambassador of India, together with written Statement of the Government of India, 1; Indonesia, CR 95/25, 3 Nov 1995, 19, para 13; New Zealand, CR 95/28, 9 Nov 1995, 42; Philippines, CR 95/28, 9 Nov 1995, 56 and 60), *Land and Maritime Boundary between Cameroon and Nigeria (Cameroon v. Nigeria: Equatorial Guinea intervening)* (Reply of Cameroon, 4 Apr 2000, 469, para 10.24); *Oil Platforms (Iran v. US)* (Memorial of the Government Submitted by the Islamic Republic of Iran, 8 June 1993, 94, paras 4.05–4.06; see also Counter-Memorial and Counter-Claim Submitted by the USA, 23 June 1997, 154–5, paras 4.58–4.61); *Armed Activities (DRC v. Uganda)* (Memorial of the DRC July 2000, paras 3.08 and 3.12–3.13).

[29] *Yearbook of the International Law Commission*, 2001, vol II (2), 84, para 21.

[30] *Yearbook of the International Law Commission*, 2001, vol II (2), 84, para 21.

[31] Barboza, 'Necessity (Revisited) in International Law', 34–6.

[32] ICJ Rep 1996, 265, para 105.

or otherwise, may serve as a justification for aggression'[33] and added a few years later that: 'no consideration of whatever nature may be invoked to warrant resorting to the threat or use of force in violation of the Charter'.[34] If necessity can be assessed as an element of the relevant primary rules (especially self-defence), it cannot be used as a general cause, possibly justifying a violation of those rules.[35]

Against this background, it is not surprising that practice reveals a general reluctance to invoke necessity as a circumstance precluding the wrongfulness of any use of force. In fact, in the vast majority of cases in which necessity could have been invoked to justify a military action limited in scope and duration, the intervening states preferred to rely on self-defence according to Article 51 of the UN Charter. Various examples could be cited, particularly the Israeli Operation at Entebbe (1976),[36] the unsuccessful raid to rescue hostages in Iran (1980),[37] or the US military actions against Sudan and Afghanistan (1998).[38]

The only example of an explicit and clear invocation of the state of necessity can be found in the context of the war against Yugoslavia in 1999.[39] During the proceedings before the ICJ in relation to the provisional measures requested by Yugoslavia, a Belgian counsel asserted the following: 'if we have failed to convince you that what has been taking place is armed humanitarian intervention justified by international law, the Government of the Kingdom of Belgium will also plead, in the alternative, that there is a state of necessity'.[40] Belgium was, however, the only state to do so; all the other intervening states relied on other legal arguments, like an implied authorization of the Security Council or an alleged 'right of humanitarian intervention'.[41] The ICJ did not make any pronouncement on the merits, as it denied having jurisdiction prima facie. Nevertheless, the Court was 'profoundly concerned with the use of force in Yugoslavia [and that] under the present circumstances such use raise[d] very serious issues of international law'.[42] Moreover, a great number of states condemned the action as a violation of the UN Charter.[43] In sum, practice shows that necessity can be used as a particular element of an existing legal

[33] Art 5(1) of the Definition of Aggression annexed to GA Res 3314 (XXIX), adopted without a vote.

[34] Principle I.3 of the Declaration of the Enhancement of the Effectiveness of the Principle of Refraining from the Threat or Use of Force in International Relations, 18 Nov 1987, annexed to GA Res 42/22, adopted without a vote.

[35] This is also confirmed by a review of the discussions of the General Assembly Sixth Commission; see Corten, *The Law against War*, 217–20.

[36] S/PV.1939 (9 July 1976), para 115.

[37] Letter dated 25 April 1980 from the Permanent Representative of the USA to the UN addressed to the President of the Security Council, S/13908 (25 Apr 1980).

[38] Letter dated 25 April 1998 from the Permanent Representative of the USA to the UN addressed to the President of the Security Council, S/1998/780 (20 Aug 1998).

[39] Attila Tanzi, 'Necessity, State of' in Rüdiger Wolfrum (ed), *Max Planck Encyclopedia of Public International Law* (Oxford: Oxford University Press, 2012), vol VII, 586, para 13.

[40] Ergec, CR 99/15 (10 May 1999).

[41] Corten, *The Law against War*, 541–4.

[42] ICJ Rep 1999, 132, para 17.

[43] See eg the 'Rio Group' Declaration, 15 Mar 1999, A/53/884–S/1999/347.

justification (self-defence, in the vast majority of cases). It cannot, however, be used as a justification, as such, to use force.

In this regard, some authors contend that a difference should be made between grave uses of force (equivalent to an act of aggression), on the one hand, and limited uses of force, on the other.[44] In the former case, necessity could not be invoked, as the prohibition of aggression is a peremptory rule. By contrast, necessity could be used in the latter case, as Rapporteur Ago seemed to suggest when he initially introduced the state of necessity as a circumstance precluding wrongfulness.[45] However, this subtle distinction has not been made by states, either in relevant texts or in practice. Indeed, it is the prohibition of the threat or a use of force as a whole that has been recognized as having a peremptory character, not only the prohibition of aggression. This explains why states prefer to invoke self-defence rather than a 'state of necessity' when they resort to force, even when the military action in question is very limited. This does not mean that the scope of a measure is fully irrelevant when assessing its legality. It must be recalled in this regard that Article 2(4) of the UN Charter only prohibits the use or a threat to use 'force', but does not apply to every kind of extraterritorial coercive measure.[46] In the *Eichmann* case, for example, Israel's action was considered as a violation of Argentina's sovereignty, not as a breach of *jus contra bellum* as such.[47] In the *Saiga* case, the International Tribunal for the Law of the Sea (ITLOS) qualified an excessive use of force as a violation of the law of the sea, not of Article 2(4) of the Charter.[48] The same distinction was debated in other precedents, like the *Fisheries* case (*Spain v. Canada*)[49] or the *Guyana/Suriname* case.[50] In this context, if the threshold of the use of force according to the UN Charter is not reached, a coercive measure must be assessed in relation to other sets of rules. As a matter of principle, nothing precludes a state from invoking a 'state of necessity' in those particular cases, if the conditions laid down in Article 25 of the ILC project are met. *A contrario*, no use or threat to use 'force' according to the Charter can be justified by necessity, unless necessity constitutes an element of another legal justification provided for by the relevant primary rules, as is the case, in particular, with self-defence (and within the limits of the said justification).

[44] Theodore Christakis, 'Unilatéralisme et multilatéralisme dans la lutte contre la terreur: l'exemple du terrorisme biologique et chimique' in Karine Bannelier et al (eds), *Le droit international face au terrorisme* (Paris: Pedone, 2002), 173–6.

[45] A/CN.4/318/Add.5-8, *Yearbook of the International Law Commission*, 1980, vol II (1), 39, paras 56, 40–1, 58–9, 44, and 66 and *Yearbook of the International Law Commission*, 1980, vol II (2), 43–5.

[46] Corten, *The Law against War*, 51–92.

[47] SC Res 138 (1960) of 23 June 1960, para 1.

[48] ITLOS, *The M/V Saiga (Saint Vincent and the Grenadines v. Guinea)*, Judgment of 4 Dec 1997, paras 155–6.

[49] ICJ Rep 1998, 466, para 84.

[50] Arbitral Tribunal Constituted Pursuant to Article 287, and in Accordance with Annex VII of the UN Convention on the Law of the Sea (Guyana and Suriname), (2007) 139 ILR 566, para 445.

III. Necessity as a Condition of Self-Defence

In its resolution on self-defence adopted in 2007, the Institut de Droit International stated that 'necessity and proportionality are essential components of the normative framework of self-defence'.[51] This assertion can also be found in case law, notably in the *Nuclear Weapons* case, the ICJ recalling that 'the submission of the exercise of the right to self-defence to the conditions of necessity and proportionality is a rule of customary international law [which] applies equally to Article 51 of the Charter...'[52] As regards existing practice, on numerous occasions states have criticized military actions as not fulfilling the conditions of necessity and proportionality governing a measure of self-defence. In many situations, such as the Lebanon war that took place in summer 2006, the criticism on necessity and proportionality even appears as a means to avoid the debate on the difficult question of the determination of the aggressor.[53] Against this backdrop, some authors seem to reduce the legality of a measure of self-defence to its necessity or its proportionality, two criteria which tend to be closely linked.[54] Following this line of reasoning, a preventive or pre-emptive measure of self-defence would be legal, if it was necessary in the circumstances of the case.[55] Likewise, the legality of a use of force against a state harbouring terrorists should be resolved with regard to its necessity; it should not depend on the determination of a previous armed attack by the targeted state.[56] In sum, necessity becomes the only relevant criterion of a measure of self-defence, and this criterion would allow a broad interpretation of self-defence supporting notions like 'preventive war' or 'war against terror'.

In my opinion, this interpretation of existing law is far from convincing, for several reasons. First and foremost, an overview of the existing case law confirms that necessity is only one of the various criteria determining the legality of a measure of self-defence. And this criterion is obviously not the most decisive, especially in comparison to the core question of the existence of an 'armed attack' according to Article 51 of the Charter. In *Nicaragua*, *Oil Platforms*, and *Armed Activities*, the ICJ indeed focused on the determination of an armed attack by the respondent state.[57] It thus rejected the claim of self-defence by the US (in the two former cases) and

[51] 27 Oct 2007, Santiago Session; see <http://www.idi-iil.org/idiE/navig_chon2003.html>.

[52] ICJ Rep 1996, 245, para 41.

[53] S/PV.5488 (13 July 2006), S/PV.5489 (14 July 2006), S/PV.5493 and S/PV.5493 (Resumption 1) (21 July 2006).

[54] Kimberly N. Trapp, 'Back to Basics: Necessity, Proportionality and the Right to Self-Defence Against Non-State Terrorist Actors' (2007) 56 *International and Comparative Law Quarterly* 141–56.

[55] Sofaer, 'On the Necessity of Pre-Emption'.

[56] Trapp, 'Back to Basics'.

[57] ICJ Rep 1986, 70 ff, paras 126 ff, ICJ Rep 2003, 186 ff, paras 50 ff, ICJ Rep 2005, 199 ff, paras 55 ff.

by Uganda (in the latter) because those states had not proven themselves to be victims of an armed attack by the applicant state (respectively Nicaragua, Iran, and the Democratic Republic of the Congo (DRC)). In addition, the Court noticed that the respondent state did not succeed in establishing that its measures were necessary and proportionate under the circumstances.[58] But, taking each of the three judgments as a whole, this second question clearly appears as incidental or subsidiary. If we go beyond the case law of the ICJ to look at the general practice of states, no precedent is known as having given rise to a dispute focusing exclusively on the question of necessity or proportionality of a riposte. During the 2006 war, for example, many states denounced the invasion of Lebanon by the Israeli army as an aggression violating the UN Charter.[59] These states did not limit their criticism to the question of necessity or proportionality. All in all, the main problem remains the determination of the aggressor.

Secondly, it must be pointed out that necessity, far from being conceived as a means to elude the strictness of the law, has generally been interpreted restrictively, in theory as well as in practice. In his 1980 report on state responsibility, Roberto Ago considered that 'the reason for stressing that action in self-defence must be necessary is that the state attacked...must not, in the particular circumstances, have had any means of halting the attack other than recourse to armed force'.[60] This conception is shared by many scholars[61] and states.[62] A restrictive interpretation is also reflected in the existing cases. In *Oil Platforms*, the Court asserted that 'the requirement of international law that measures taken avowedly in self-defence must have been necessary for that purpose is strict and objective, leaving no room for any "measure of discretion"'.[63] In the *Armed Activities* case, the Court pointed out that 'Article 51 of the Charter may justify a use of force in self-defence only within the strict confines there laid down. It does not allow the use of force by a State to protect perceived security interests...'[64] *A contrario*, the Court strongly rejected the conceptions of the respondent states arguing that 'a measure of discretion should

[58] See the details later in the chapter.

[59] S/PV.5493 (Resumption 1) (21 July 2006), 26–7 (League of Arab States), Final Communiqué of the Annual Coordination Meeting of Ministers of Foreign Affairs of Member States of the OIC, UN Headquarters, New York, 25 Sept 2006; A/61/622-/2006/959, para 32, Fourteenth Summit Conference of Heads of State or Government of the Non-Aligned Movement, Havana, 11–16 Sept 2006, Final Document, A/61/472–S/2006/780 (29 Sept 2006), paras 142–3.

[60] *Yearbook of the International Law Commission*, 1980, vol II (1), 69, paras 12–21.

[61] See eg Rosalyn Higgins, *The Development of International Law Through the Political Organs of the United Nations* (London: Oxford University Press, 1963), 205; Elisabeth Wilmshurst, 'The Chatham House Principles of International Law on the Use of Force on the Use of Self-Defence' (2006) 55 *International and Comparative Law Quarterly* 967; see also Judge Schwebel, Dissenting Opinion, *Military and Paramilitary Activities*, ICJ Rep 1986, paras 201 and 204.

[62] France in ICJ, *Legality of the Threat or Use of Nuclear Weapons*, Perrin de Brichambaut, CR 95/23, 1 Nov 1995, 66, US in *Oil Platforms*, Counter-Memorial, 137, UK in 'United Kingdom Materials on International Law' (1995) 66 *British Yearbook of International Law* 726.

[63] ICJ Rep 2006, 196, para 73. [64] ICJ Rep 2005, 223, para 148.

be afforded to a party's good faith application of measures to protect its essential interests',[65] or that 'it is surely the view of the victim States and its nationals which must prevail'.[66] In practice, the Court condemned as unnecessary various measures purportedly taken in self-defence. In the *Nicaragua* case, it rejected the US claim based on collective self-defence in support of El Salvador because the military measures 'were only taken, and began to produce their effects, several months after the major offensive of the armed opposition in El Salvador had been completely repulsed'.[67] It thus focused on a *temporal* criterion. In the *Armed Activities* case, the Court incidentally observed that 'the taking of airports and towns many hundreds of kilometres from Uganda's border would not seem proportionate to the series of transborder attacks it claimed had given rise to the right of self-defence, nor to be necessary to that end'.[68] In this case, a *spatial* or *geographical* criterion was considered as relevant. In the *Oil Platforms* case, the Court found unnecessary some US actions because the US had not previously complained to Iran about the military activities conducted on the oil rig, 'which does not suggest that the targeting of the platforms was seen as a necessary act'.[69] In this case, the decision was founded on a *coherence* criterion; that is, the absence of any military benefit from the action undertaken in respect of its stated aim.

Thirdly, it must be kept in mind that the necessity of a measure of self-defence can be limited by the action of the Security Council. Article 51 of the Charter stipulates that self-defence 'shall not in any way affect the authority and the responsibility to take at any time such action it deems necessary in order to maintain or restore international peace and security'. Consequently, the exercise of the right of self-defence cannot be considered as 'necessary' if and to the extent that it would be in violation of a Security Council resolution applicable in the case at hand. The Council may adopt a resolution establishing a ceasefire mandatory for all parties, as happened in the Iraq/Iran war, the Falklands War, the DRC war, the Ethiopia/Eritrea war or the Sudan/South Sudan war precedents.[70] In such cases, even the aggressed state cannot invoke self-defence to use military force against the aggressor, such a means not being considered as 'necessary', according to both customary law and to the law of the Charter. Necessity could only be invoked if the aggressor state does not respect the resolution, and launches additional military actions after its adoption. In that particular case, the attacked state could invoke the very necessity of a riposte, at least if the Council does not take additional measures. This can explain the precedent of the DRC, whose military riposte to violations of the existing resolutions by Rwanda was not considered to be unlawful either by the ICJ or

[65] ICJ Rep 2003, 196, para 73; see Matheson, CR 2003/12 (26 Feb 2003), 54, para 18.64.

[66] Uganda, Brownlie, CR 2005/7 (18 Apr 2005), 34, para 92.

[67] ICJ Rep 1986, 122, para 237. [68] ICJ Rep 2005, 223, para 147.

[69] ICJ Rep 2003, 198, para 76.

[70] See respectively SC Res 598 (1987) of 20 July 1987, SC Res 502 (1982) of 3 Apr 1982, SC Res 1258 (1999) of 6 Aug 1999, SC Res 1177 (1998) of 26 June 1998, SC Res 2046 (2012) of 2 May 2012.

by the Security Council itself, even if a ceasefire had previously been established.[71] In other cases, the Security Council may impose an arms embargo in order to avoid the spread of a conflict.

A topical example is the war that took place in Bosnia and Herzegovina between 1992 and 1995. Bosnia and Herzegovina invoked its right to self-defence in order to claim the right to obtain military support, despite the arms embargo laid down by the Security Council in 1991.[72] However, this claim was clearly not accepted by the international community of states as a whole.[73] In 1994–5, when NATO states intervened militarily in the conflict, they invoked Security Council authorizations included in several resolutions.[74] None of these states relied on a right of collective self-defence that would have overridden the resolutions adopted by the Security Council.

In other cases, Security Council resolutions may implicitly, but clearly, exclude the use of force. Following the invasion of Kuwait by Iraq in August 1990, the Council adopted a resolution authorizing states to use force if certain conditions were not met on 15 January 1991. This implies that such a use would not be admissible before that date.[75] In a similar vein, when the Council decides to impose economic measures against a state, it seems *a contrario* to exclude a military option. This can explain why, in the 1990–1 Gulf War, the Council deemed it necessary to authorize a use of force after, but only after, the failure of the economic and diplomatic sanctions decided previously.

Nevertheless, some issues are more difficult to address. In certain cases, it may appear difficult to determine if, and to what extent, the Council has prevented a state from using its right to self-defence. What, for example, about Resolution 1368 (2001), which recognizes in its preamble the US' right of self-defence and 'unequivocally condemns' the 'terrorist attacks'? As the Council did not actually take any measure to restore international peace, it can be considered that it did not prevent the US from acting in self-defence. A fortiori, if the Council does not adopt any resolution in a particular case—a situation very common during the Cold War—nothing precludes a state victim from considering a riposte by military means as being 'necessary'.

[71] ICJ Rep 2005, 269, para 304.

[72] See ICJ, Application instituting proceedings, 20 Mar 1993 and Boyle, CR 1993/12 (1 Apr 1993), 41 ff and CR 1993/13 (2 Apr 1993), 47; Craig Scott et al, 'A Memorial for Bosnia: Framework of Legal Arguments Concerning the Lawfulness of the Maintenance of the United Nations Security Council's Arms Embargo on Bosnia and Herzegovina' (2004) 16 *Michigan Journal of International Law* 1–140.

[73] See eg 'United Kingdom Material on International Law' (1994) 65 *British Yearbook of International Law* 691–2 and Théodore Christakis, *L'ONU, le Chapitre VII et la Crise Yougoslave* (Paris: Montechrestien, 1996), 48 ff.

[74] See eg 'Pratique française du droit international' (1993) 39 *Annuaire Français de Droit International* 1023, (1994) 40 *Annuaire Français de Droit International* 1039.

[75] SC Res 678 (1990) of 29 Nov 1990.

In sum, necessity is a legal notion conditioning the exercise of the right to self-defence that must be interpreted narrowly with regard to the existing texts, case law, and practice. This does not mean that no margin of appreciation subsists in assessing this legal condition.[76] At this point, several clarifications can be made. First, an aggressed state is not obliged to prove that it has exhausted all the peaceful means before reacting in self-defence. In its resolution on self-defence, the Institut de Droit International stated that this right 'may be exercised only when there is no lawful alternative in practice in order to forestall, stop or repel the armed attack'.[77] Nevertheless, one must concede that, in the various cases previously mentioned, the ICJ did not request the respondent states to prove that this condition was met. As shown, the Court developed more specific arguments, using a temporal, geographical, or 'coherence' criterion. In fact, it seems that the state concerned has to show that the military measures were motivated by a defensive purpose, more specifically, repelling an act of aggression. *A contrario*, the military action undertaken cannot pursue objectives such as a change in a border, the appropriation of resources, the punishment of a state, or even a general and vague defence of security interests. To be considered necessary, a measure must be shown to be fully efficient in achieving its only legitimate aim: to put an end to an armed attack. If this is the case, and no Security Council resolution is infringed, the condition will be fulfilled, even if the state has not proven to have exhausted all peaceful means.

This pattern is confirmed by state practice. When the US launched the war against Afghanistan in October 2001, some authors considered the military option was premature, as some peaceful options (in particular recourse to the Security Council for appropriate measures) had not been explored.[78] Nevertheless, the war was widely supported by states from many regions, indicating that the necessity of self-defence was not really challenged.[79] Even if it raises certain ambiguities regarding its very particular circumstances,[80] this precedent shows that if a state is really the victim

[76] Schachter, *International Law in Theory and Practice*, 152 ff.

[77] Art 3 of the Santiago resolution.

[78] Antonio Remiro Brotons, 'Terrorismo, Mantenimiento de la paz y nuevo orden' (2001) 53 *Revista Española de Derecho Internacional* 150–60; Joaquín Alcaide Fernandez, 'La "guerra contra el terrorismo": una "OPA hostil" al derecho de la comunidad internacional' (2001) 53 *Revista Española de Derecho Internacional* 300–1; Olivier Corten and François Dubuisson, 'Opération "liberté immuable": une extension abusive du concept de légitime défense' (2002) 106 *Revue Générale de Droit International Public* 74–5.

[79] EU (Statement by General Affairs Council of the EU, 8 Oct 2001, available at <http://www.europa.eu.int/>; Military operations in Afghanistan—Declaration by the EU Presidency, 7 Oct 2001, at <http://www.eu2001.be/>), OAS (CP/RES.796 (1293/01), 19 Sept 2001, at <http://www.oas.org/>), NATO (12 Sept 2001, Press Release (2001) 124, at <http://www.nato.int/>).

[80] Marcelo Kohen, 'The Use of Force by the United States After the End of the Cold War, and its Impact on International Law' in Michael Byers and Georg Nolte (eds), *United States Hegemony and the Foundations of International Law* (Cambridge: Cambridge University Press, 2003), 224, Pierre Klein, 'Le droit international à l'épreuve du terrorisme' (2006) 321 *Recueil des Cours de l'Académie de Droit International* ch IV.

of an armed attack it benefits from a certain leeway in how to react. The same can be said of the debate on the timing of the reaction. Certain authors consider that self-defence cannot be exercised after an attack has ended.[81] This seems logical, as 'defence' cannot lead to punitive action, since it is supposed to put an end to an ongoing attack. The question is simple enough if the attack consists of an armed occupation; that is, an ongoing unlawful act. But what about a succession of isolated acts of war: air strikes, land operations, shelling, etc? In the *Legality of Use of Force* case, the Court refused to isolate every act, and considered instead that the different military actions were to be 'taken as a whole'.[82] In the *Oil Platforms* case, the ICJ did not criticize the US actions as unnecessary because they took place after the end of the attacks, to which these actions were supposed to respond.[83] In the Afghanistan war, no state considered the US riposte as unnecessary for the sole reason that the 9/11 attacks had ended. Case law and practice seem therefore to support the 'accumulation of events' theory, according to which a use of force must be considered as a whole.[84] The necessity of self-defence means that the aim of the riposte must be limited to putting an end to the armed attack, whatever form the latter takes. This obviously involves a careful evaluation of the situation at hand. If it is clear that an attack has ended and that other peaceful means are at the disposal of the state attacked, it will be difficult to prove the 'necessity' of the military option. If, conversely, it is far from certain that the armed attack has ended, for example because a succession of military actions has taken place in the recent past, it will be difficult to challenge the necessity of the riposte. No rigid conception of timing (limiting the riposte to a fixed period) is to be taken into account.[85]

Finally, the decisive question regarding self-defence is: who is the aggressor? We are thus faced with one of two alternatives: either the state that invokes self-defence can prove that it has previously been the victim of an armed attack or it cannot. In the first instance, the state will benefit from a certain margin of appreciation in deciding how to retaliate, the only imperative limit being the obligation to respect a Security Council resolution, if any such resolution exists. In the second alternative, the necessity question will appear as subsidiary, as it will be clear that *jus contra bellum* has been infringed. In this particular instance, however, it is common for the state to be criticized not only as the author of the initial armed attack, but also as having adopted measures exceeding the condition of necessity. As shown previously, this second alternative is illustrated by existing case law. In the *Nicaragua*, *Oil*

[81] Avra Constantinou, *The Right of Self-Defense under Customary International Law and Article 51 of the UN Charter* (Athens: Ant. N. Sakkoulas/Brussels: Bruylant, 2000), 159–61.

[82] ICJ Rep 1999, 134, para 28. [83] ICJ Rep 2003, 198, para 76.

[84] Roberto Ago, Addendum to the Eight Report on State Responsibility, *Yearbook of the International Law Commission*, 1980, vol II (1), 70, para 122; see also Judge Schwebel, Dissenting Opinion, *Military and Paramilitary Activities*, ICJ Rep 1986, 368–9, para 213.

[85] Judith Gardam, *Necessity, Proportionality and the Use of Force by States* (Cambridge: Cambridge University Press, 2004), 150–3.

Platforms, and *Armed Activities* judgments, the self-defence claim of the respondent states was rejected both because no armed attack had been established and because the measures taken were not necessary under the circumstances. On the other hand, the first alternative seems to be reflected in practice. When a state is recognized as having been the victim of an armed attack, there is no known precedent of the victim state being criticized on the sole ground of the unnecessary character of its riposte. The precedent of the DRC, after the attacks launched by Rwanda and Uganda in August 1998, or the precedent of the war against Afghanistan after the 9/11 attacks, seem to support this interpretation. By contrast, considering necessity as the sole or decisive criterion justifying self-defence is clearly incompatible with existing law and practice. Necessity appears as a legal and subsidiary notion, not as a justification as such. This conclusion also finds support in the existing system of collective security.

IV. Necessity as an Element of the UN Collective Security System

Necessity can also be interpreted as a relevant criterion within the framework of the collective security system enshrined in the UN Charter.[86] First, the wording of the Charter itself refers to the concept of necessity, particularly in Articles 42 and 51. Secondly, the Security Council often uses it in its resolutions authorizing the use of force. In both cases, the problem is in interpreting what is considered to be 'necessary' under the circumstances at hand. Generally, it can be stated that, in this context, necessity certainly has a broader sense than the one it has as a (restrictive) condition of self-defence, particularly since it is supposed to limit the powers of the Security Council.

In this first hypothesis, the relevant legal terms seem to have been conceived as allowing a very broad margin of appreciation. According to Article 42, the Council 'may take such action by air, sea, or land forces *as may be necessary* to maintain or restore international peace and security', whereas Article 51 states that self-defence 'shall not in any way affect the authority and responsibility of the Security Council, under the present Charter, to take at any time such action *as it deems necessary* in order to maintain or restore international peace and security'.[87] In view of such a

[86] Gardam, *Necessity, Proportionality and the Use of Force by States*, 188–229.

[87] Emphasis added.

wording, it is hard to imagine how the Security Council could exceed its powers by adopting (or by failing to adopt) military measures.[88] The Charter terms are clear: it is the Council which determines whether the measures to be taken are opportune (ie whether non-military measures 'would be inadequate or have proved to be inadequate') and which consequently decides which measures are 'necessary'. In 2005, the Secretary-General recommended that the Security Council adopt a resolution setting out the principles it relied on in authorizing the use of force.[89] Some states seemed to support this proposition.[90] However, the final document of the 2005 World Summit only contains a vague reference to 'the importance of acting in accordance with the purposes and principles of the Charter',[91] and the Council never adopted a resolution exposing any principles guiding (and limiting) its faculty to use force. In view of existing practice, the only legal limits seem to be the following. First, it is the Security Council itself that must, according to the text of the Charter, 'take' action.[92] *A contrario*, the Council cannot generally delegate its responsibility to a state or a group of states, thus giving them the power to determine whether there is a threat to peace and to authorize a use of force in a particular case.[93] Similarly, once action has been taken, it must been overseen by the Security Council. The military measures must, according to the Charter, be taken 'under its authority'.[94] This is how practice can be interpreted, the Security Council having effectively coupled its authorization with guarantees to prevent excessive decentralization of the use of force.[95] Those limitations aside, the Security Council keeps a discretionary competence in assessing the situation and choosing the measures it deems necessary.

The conclusion appears somewhat different if we consider a second hypothesis: a Security Council resolution authorizing states to take 'necessary measures' to achieve certain objectives. This type of formula was used in the Gulf War,[96] and was

[88] Corten, *The Law against War*, 322–3, Gardam, *Necessity, Proportionality and the Use of Force by States*, 189.

[89] 'In Larger Freedom: Towards Development, Security and Human Rights For All', Report of the Secretary-General, A/59/2005 (24 Mar 2005), 39, para 126.

[90] Special Meeting of the Ministers of Foreign Affairs of the Non-Aligned Movement, Doha, Qatar, 13 June 2005, NAM/2005/SFMM/05, 13 June 2005, paras 13 and 14; text available at <http://www.un.int/malaysia>; Proposed Amendments by the NAM to the Draft Outcome Document of the High-Level Plenary Meeting of the G.A., A/59/HLPM/CRP.1/Resee2, paras 55 and 134; at <http://www.reformtheun.org>.

[91] 2005 World Summit Outcome Document, A/RES/60/1 (24 Oct 2005), para 79.

[92] UN Charter, Art 42.

[93] Erica de Wet, *The Chapter VII Powers of the United Nations Security Council* (Oxford: Hart, 2004), 295; Dan Sarooshi, *The United Nations and the Development of Collective Security. The Delegation by the United Nations Security Council of its Chapter VII Powers* (Oxford: Clarendon Press, 1999), 33–42; Linos-Alexandre Sicilianos, 'L'autorisation par le Conseil de sécurité de recourir à la force: une tentative d'évaluation' (2002) 106 *Revue Générale de Droit International Public* 89.

[94] UN Charter, Art 53.

[95] Théodore Christakis and Karine Bannelier, 'Acteur vigilant ou spectateur impuissant? Le contrôle exercé par le Conseil de sécurité sur les Etats autorisés à recourir à la force' (2004) 37 *Revue Belge de Droit International* 498–527.

[96] SC Res 678 (1990) of 29 Nov 1990, para 2.

later reproduced in various cases: Somalia,[97] Bosnia and Herzegovina,[98] Haiti,[99] East Timor,[100] Côte d'Ivoire,[101], Libya,[102] etc.[103] In this sort of case, what is the margin of appreciation of the member states? In *Nicaragua*, the ICJ, referring to a conventional clause containing the term, stated that: 'whether a measure is necessary [is not] purely a question for the subjective judgment of the party; the text does not refer to what the party "considers necessary"'.[104] Similarly, the European Court of Human Rights considered that 'the adjective "necessary"... is not synonymous with "indispensable"... neither has it the flexibility of such expressions as "admissible", "ordinary"..., "useful"..., "reasonable"... or "desirable"'.[105] The ordinary meaning of the word seems here to confer a certain leeway, even if it requires a state to show that the measures taken are able to reach the legitimate aims enounced in the relevant resolution.[106] A general overview of existing practice reveals the difficulty of an application of those theoretical guidelines on a case-by-case basis. During the Gulf crisis, the French government specified that 'it goes without saying that the resolution must not be understood as a blanket authorisation for the indiscriminate use of force... this naturally must take place only as a last resort and be limited to what is strictly necessary'.[107] Several months later, some states refused to interfere in the internal conflict between the Iraqi government and the Kurdish rebels because such an intervention would not be 'necessary' in the light of the terms of Resolution 678 (1990).[108]

On the other hand, France, as well as some of its allies, supported a remarkably broad interpretation of necessity in 2011, in the context of the Libyan crisis. In Resolution 1973 (2011), the Security Council authorized member states to take 'all necessary measures... to protect civilians and civilian populated areas under threat of attack in the Libyan Arab Jamahiriya' and 'to enforce compliance with the ban on flights...' imposed by the Council.[109] After a few weeks, some of the states implementing this resolution contended that they were entitled not only to protect civilians threatened, but also to interfere in the internal conflict by fighting the Libyan government and supporting the rebels.[110] This interpretation was strongly criticized by other states, including some

97 SC Res 794 (1992) of 3 Dec 1992, para 10.

98 SC Res 836 (1993) of 4 June 1993, para 10.

99 SC Res 940 (1994) of 31 July 1994, para 4, and SC Res 1529 (2004) of 29 Feb 2004, para 6.

100 SC Res 1264 (1999) of 15 Sept 1999, para 3.

101 SC Res 1464 (2003) of 4 Feb 2003, para 9; see also SC Res 1527 (2004) of 4 Feb 2004, para 2 and SC Res 1528 (2004) of 27 Feb 2004, para 16.

102 SC Res 1973 (2011) of 1 Mar 2011, para 4.

103 Corten, *The Law against War*, 312 ff.

104 ICJ Rep 1986, para 282.

105 *Handyside v. UK*, ECtHR, 7 Dec 1976, Ser A, No 24, para 48 (references to articles of the Convention omitted).

106 Corten, *The Law against War*, 327–9.

107 S/PV.2938 (25 Aug 1990), 32.

108 See the US ((1991) *Keesing's Contemporary Archives* 38081 and 38127), France ('Pratique française du droit international' (1991) 37 *Annuaire Français de Droit International* 1012), UK ('United Kingdom Materials on International Law' (2003) 74 *British Yearbook of International Law* 786).

109 SC Res 1973 (2011), paras 4 and 8.

110 See eg France (<http://www.elysee.fr/president/les-actualites/conferences-de-presse/2011/sommet-du-g8-de-deauville-conference-de-presse.11462.html>).

having voted in favour of Resolution 1973 (2011).[111] The Libyan precedent thus confirms that, once an authorization to take all 'necessary measures' has taken place, it will become difficult to limit the interpretation of the UN member states, even if some critiques will be possible in some extreme cases.

All in all, necessity plays a different role in the collective security system than as an element of the right to self-defence. Given the existing texts and relevant practice, the meaning is obviously broader in the former case than in the latter. This is particularly true when necessity is an element of the UN Charter articles enouncing the powers of the Security Council, whose discretionary powers are recognized. Necessity remains open to various interpretations when used in particular Security Council resolutions authorizing states to use force, even if the debate appears somewhat more open in this case. In any event, we are far from the strict conception of necessity as an essential limit of the right to self-defence according to Article 51 of the Charter. Such a difference is far from surprising. When the use of force is decided collectively, according to Chapters VII and VIII of the Charter, the use of force can be interpreted less strictly than when it is unilaterally decided by a state or a group of states. This line of reasoning rests on a rather restrictive methodology, which leads us to conclude with some more general comments.

V. Conclusion: Back to Methodology

Finally, it is difficult to appraise necessity without returning to a fundamental interrogation about the essence of the international legal order. A first option is to conceive necessity as an extra-legal concept, which would prevail over formal requirements in the name of some 'objective' ones. Following this line of reasoning, necessity can justify a use of force in a large variety of cases, particularly in the name of the fight against terrorism or of the values of the 'international community'. Necessity enables every state to make a proper assessment of the values at hand in order to decide if a use of force is 'necessary' on a case-by-case basis. A second option is to consider that necessity must not prevail over law, but it is rather a particular element of existing legal rules. If this is true, its content must be determined according to the relevant rules, and following the legal principles of interpretation. Necessity, like other similar notions, such as reasonableness or proportionality, has

[111] See eg Russia (<http://eng.kremlin.ru/transcripts/2076>, S/PV.6709 (26 Jan 2012), 7), China (<http://www.mfa.gov.cn/eng/xwfw/s2510/2511/t809578.htm>, S/PV.6528 (4 May 2011), 10), and South Africa (S/PV.6702 (12 Jan 2012), 3).

an axiological dimension. Its application implies a balance of values and facts able to adapt the law to the particular situation at hand. But, if it is appraised as an element of the prohibition of the use of force, it must be interpreted narrowly and in conformity with the object and purpose of the existing *jus contra bellum*. This can lead to various conclusions, depending on the legal and factual context. As a subsidiary condition of the legality of self-defence, necessity must be strictly interpreted, particularly with respect to the aggressor state. As an element of the system of collective security, necessity is open to a broader margin of appreciation, especially in favour of the Security Council. By contrast, necessity has never been recognized as a general justification to use force, neither by the ILC or the ICJ, nor by state practice. This second line of reasoning, grounded on a restrictive conception of the international legal order, has been followed in this chapter. One must be aware, however, that certain authors do not share this view and tend to rely on a broader conception of necessity that, in the present author's view, appears like a contemporary expression of the classical concept of self-help.[112]

[112] Gardam, *Necessity, Proportionality and the Use of Force by States*, 28 ff.

CHAPTER 40

RETALIATION AND REPRISAL

SHANE DARCY*

I. Introduction

The concepts of retaliation and reprisal have had a peripheral presence in the law governing the use of force in international relations. Their exact meaning and scope has often proved elusive and despite the apparent silence on the matter of relevant international treaties, the overwhelming weight of opinion is that a use of force by way of retaliation or reprisal is generally unlawful. This has not prevented occasional scholarly attempts to justify unilateral uses of force by resort to these legal doctrines. Reprisals in particular are a traditional act of self-help under international law, consisting of a breach of international law in response to a prior violation by another state and undertaken for the purpose of enforcing compliance. They are 'unlawful acts that become lawful in that they constitute a reaction to a delinquency by another State'.[1] Retaliation is a broader concept, which tends to evade precise definition. The general prohibition on the use of force in the UN Charter outlaws any threat or use of force and prohibits such unless authorized by the Security Council or when states act in self-defence under Article 51.[2] Whether this prohibition covers

* The author wishes to acknowledge the research assistance provided by Natia Mueller and Menaka Nayer.

[1] Antonio Cassese, *International Law* (2nd edn, Oxford: Oxford University Press, 2005), 299.

[2] UN Charter, Art 2(4), 24 Oct 1945, 1 UNTS XVI.

reprisals or retaliatory action was seemingly clarified by the UN General Assembly in 1970, when it declared in Resolution 2625 that 'States have a duty to refrain from acts of reprisal involving the use of force'.[3]

This chapter will explore the evolution of the law on the use of force as it relates to armed reprisals and retaliation, particularly since the adoption of the UN Charter in 1945. While the preponderance of scholars, and indeed states, view armed reprisals or countermeasures involving force as prohibited under international law, the doctrine would seem to retain appeal for those seeking to legitimize force not falling within the Charter's exceptions. The counterpart applicable in times of armed conflict, belligerent reprisal, has been restricted but not completely outlawed under international humanitarian law.[4] The chapter will examine the evolution of international law on the use of force relating to reprisals and consider claimed instances of state practice, as well as judicial and scholarly consideration of the lawfulness of such reprisals. It will conclude with a look at calls for the revival of reprisals or retaliation as permitted exceptions to the prohibition on the use of force. First, it is necessary to define the concepts of retaliation and reprisal as understood in international law.

II. Defining Retaliation and Reprisals

Reprisals are a recognized yet controversial concept within international law, whereas retaliation is a term often employed in a broader non-legal sense and generally referring to 'an attack or assault in return for a similar attack'.[5] The *Max Planck Encyclopedia of Public International Law* has a detailed entry for reprisals, but makes no mention of retaliation.[6] Kelsen defined reprisals as 'acts, which although normally illegal, are exceptionally permitted as reaction of one state against a violation of its right by another state'.[7] The aspect of unlawfulness is an essential element of reprisals, whereas retaliation can be used more broadly to include reprisals[8] or other

[3] GA Res 2625 (XXV) of 24 Oct 1970.

[4] See Shane Darcy, 'The Evolution of the Law of Belligerent Reprisals' (2003) 175 *Military Law Review* 184–251; Shane Darcy, 'What Future for the Doctrine of Belligerent Reprisals?' (2002) 5 *Yearbook of International Humanitarian Law* 107.

[5] *The Oxford Compact English Dictionary* (2nd edn, Oxford: Oxford University Press, 2003), 974.

[6] Rüdiger Wolfrum (ed), *The Max Planck Encyclopedia of Public International Law* (Oxford: Oxford University Press, 2012), 927–30.

[7] Hans Kelsen, *Principles of International Law* (New York: Rinehart & Co, 1952), 23.

[8] See eg Evelyn Speyer Colbert, *Retaliation in International Law* (New York: King's Crown Press, 1948); Richard A. Falk, 'The Beirut Raid and the International Law of Retaliation' (1969) 63 *American Journal of International Law* 415.

unfriendly or hostile, yet lawful acts of retorsion.[9] Reprisals taken during a situation of armed conflict are described as belligerent reprisals,[10] while those resorted to during peacetime are referred to as peacetime, pacific, or armed reprisals. Such reprisals are the primary focus of this chapter and can be considered as acts of forcible self-help, involving an unlawful use of force falling short of war, by one state in response to a prior violation of international law by another. 'Armed reprisals' is the most suitable label for such actions,[11] given that they amount to 'modes of putting stress upon an offending state which are of a violent nature, though they fall short of actual war'.[12]

The interchangeable and overlapping uses of the terms reprisal and retaliation is a notable feature of scholarship on these subjects.[13] Evelyn Speyer Colbert, in what remains the sole monograph on this topic, used retaliation as a general term which also covered reprisals.[14] She observed that the meaning given to the concepts of retaliation, reprisal, and retorsion 'seem at times to be as varied as the writers dealing with them'.[15] T. J. Lawrence wrote in 1915 that reprisal 'is used in a bewildering variety of senses'.[16] Reprisals are often defined as certain acts of retaliation,[17] given that they are a response to a previous act, and in this broad sense, retaliation could also cover lawful acts of self-defence taken in response to an armed attack. The terms retaliation and reprisal were used interchangeably in the *Naulilaa* arbitration, discussed in Section III, although it is clear that reprisals in a narrow legal sense is what was being addressed. The 1863 Lieber Code referred only to retaliation yet it is the precursor to many subsequent developments in international law concerning belligerent reprisals. The Code stated that 'The law of war can no more wholly dispense with retaliation than can the law of nations'.[18] International law has indeed sought to dispense with retaliation both

[9] See eg Hubert Lesaffre, 'Circumstances Precluding Wrongfulness in the Articles on State Resonsibility: Countermeasures' in James Crawford, Alain Pellet, and Simon Olleson (eds), *The Law of International Responsibility* (Oxford: Oxford University Press, 2010), 469, 471–2; Joseph G. Starke, *Introduction to International Law* (8th edn, London: Butterworths, 1977), 549.

[10] See generally Frits Kalshoven, *Belligerent Reprisals* (Leiden: Martinus Nijhoff, 1971).

[11] Yoram Dinstein, *War, Aggression and Self-Defence* (5th edn, Cambridge: Cambridge University Press, 2011), 244.

[12] Thomas J. Lawrence, *The Principles of International Law* (6th edn, Lexington, MA: D. C. Heath & Co, 1915), 334.

[13] See eg Roberto Barsotti, 'Armed Reprisals' in Antonio Cassese (ed), *The Current Legal Regulation of the Use of Force* (Leiden: Martinus Nijhoff, 1986), 79; Richard A. Falk, 'The Beirut Raid and the International Law of Retaliation', 425–6.

[14] Speyer Colbert, *Retaliation in International Law*, 2–3 fn 1.

[15] Speyer Colbert, *Retaliation in International Law*, 2–3 fn 1.

[16] Lawrence, *The Principles of International Law*, 334.

[17] J. L. Brierly, *The Law of Nations* (Oxford: Clarendon Press, 1963), 399; William V. O'Brien, 'Reprisals, Deterrence and Self-Defense in Counter-Terror Operations' (1989–90) 30 *Virginia Journal of International Law* 421 fn 1.

[18] Instructions for the Government of Armies of the United States in the Field, prepared by Francis Lieber, promulgated as General Orders No 100 by President Lincoln, 24 Apr 1863.

as a term of art and as a legal concept where this involves a use of force by way of armed reprisals. This chapter principally focuses on the more legally recognizable concept of armed reprisals.

The purpose of armed reprisals is law enforcement, as they are a mode of self-help for the protection of a state's interests.[19] According to a 1934 resolution of the Institut de Droit International:

> Reprisals are measures of coercion, derogating from the ordinary rules of international law, decided and taken by a State, in response to wrongful acts committed against it, by another State, and intended to impose on it, by pressure exerted through injury, the return to legality.[20]

Other purposes have been ascribed to armed reprisals, although it is 'open to doubt whether these other purposes (such as punishment, retaliation, deterrence) are legitimate'.[21] Some view armed reprisals as punitive actions,[22] others exclude punishment as a rationale,[23] whereas Antonio Cassese considered that reprisals 'were aimed at either impelling the delinquent state to discontinue the wrongdoing, or at punishing it, or both'.[24] Frits Kalshoven noted how the law enforcement function of reprisals can sit alongside the goals of punishment, redress, enforcing compliance, and prevention, but subject to an important caveat:

> It is submitted that reprisals can serve and actually are used to achieve all of these purposes including the prevention of future wrongs—with the sole exception, that is, of punishment in the narrow sense of revenge pure and simple: if that is the real purpose of a retaliatory action, it does not have the function of coercion characteristic of reprisals.[25]

A state seeking the cloak of legality once offered by armed reprisals would of course deny that the motivation behind a retaliatory use of armed force is revenge.

[19] Hans Kelsen, 'Collective Security and Collective Self-Defence under the Charter of the United Nations' (1948) 42 *American Journal of International Law* 783.

[20] Institut de Droit International, Session de Paris 1934, *Régime de répresaillies en temps de paix*, Article 1 (author's translation).

[21] Karl Josef Partsch, 'Reprisals' in Rudolf Bernhardt (ed), *Encyclopedia of Public International Law*, vol IV (Amsterdam: North-Holland, 1992), 201.

[22] Kinga Tibori Szabó, *Anticipatory Action in Self-Defence* (The Hague: TMC Asser Press, 2011), 313; Derek W. Bowett, 'Reprisals Involving Recourse to Armed Force' (1972) 66 *American Journal of International Law* 1, 3; Nina H. B. Jørgsenson, *The Responsibility of States for International Crimes* (Oxford: Oxford University Press, 2000), 173.

[23] Richard B. Lillich, 'Forcible Self-Help under International Law' (1980) 62 *International Law Studies Ser. US Naval War College* 129, 131.

[24] Cassese, *International Law*, 299.

[25] Kalshoven, *Belligerent Reprisals*, 25–6. See also Bowett, 'Reprisals Involving Recourse to Armed Force', 3; David Kretzmer, 'The Inherent Right to Self-Defence and Proportionality in Ius ad Bellum' (2013) 24 *European Journal of International Law* 235, 251.

III. The Evolving International Law Regarding Reprisals

Positive international law addressing armed reprisals remains relatively thin on the ground. While the 20th century saw several important legal developments concerning reprisals, the law prior to then was 'shrouded in doubt'.[26] T. J. Lawrence considered there to be 'a great need of international legislation on the subject of reprisals',[27] despite the reprisal doctrine's lengthy history, the beginning of which lay in the practice of private reprisals.[28]

During the Middle Ages, private individuals were indemnified 'for injuries and losses inflicted on them by subjects of other nations. Letters of marque were issued by the sovereign to those who had been wronged, and they were thereby authorized to recoup themselves by capturing vessels and cargoes of the offending nationality'.[29] Evelyn Speyer Colbert considered that until the end of the 17th century, 'peace time retaliation was a weapon used for the most part to remedy the grievances of private men, was subject to fairly strict and uniform regulation, and was limited to the attainment of compensation for damages to the extent of damages received'.[30] The US Constitution reflects this practice, conferring on Congress the authority to 'declare War, grant Letters of marque and reprisal'.[31]

Private reprisals became less tolerable with the increasing role of the state and the emergence of state responsibility,[32] with public reprisals emerging as a coercive tool 'to force the offending state to do justice'.[33] These armed reprisals comprised seizure of property or ships on the high seas, and even bombardment or occupation of territory in response to a previous wrong, such measures being classified as falling short of war.[34] Ian Brownlie considered that their value 'lay in the possibility of gaining redress without creating a formal state of war'.[35] The actions comprising the reprisals were considered to be prima facie unlawful but justified for being taken in response to a prior unlawful act:

> it is assumed that a State has committed an international tort and, on request, refuses to make due reparation. Then, the State which has suffered the wrong is entitled to retaliate by

[26] Georg Schwarzenberger, *International Law as applied by International Courts and Tribunals, Vol. II: The Laws of Armed Conflict* (London: Stevens & Sons, 1968), 39.

[27] Lawrence, *The Principles of International Law*, 344.

[28] Brierly, *The Law of Nations*, 399. See further Emer de Vattel, *The Law of Nations* (ed Béla Kapossy and Richard Whatmore, Indianapolis, IN: Liberty Fund, 2008), 460–7.

[29] Lawrence, *The Principles of International Law*, 335.

[30] Speyer Colbert, *Retaliation in International Law*, 3–4. [31] US Constitution, Art 1, Section 8(11).

[32] Lawrence, *The Principles of International Law*, 335.

[33] Speyer Colbert, *Retaliation in International Law*, 4.

[34] Speyer Colbert, *Retaliation in International Law*, 4.

[35] Ian Brownlie, *International Law and the Use of Force by States* (Oxford: Oxford University Press, 1963), 220 (footnote omitted).

way of measures which, in themselves, would also be tortious, but receive their legality from the unredressed prior wrong.[36]

While there was an absence of clear positive or customary rules governing reprisals, the law on the use of force was itself also underdeveloped, which adds complexity to the question of a reprisal's inherent unlawfulness. As Georg Schwarzenberger observed, 'So long as the right to resort to war was unlimited, it was hard to be dogmatic on rules limiting resort to compulsory measures short of war'.[37]

The rudimentary nature of international law on the use of force has prompted some scholars to question the legal basis of the institution of armed reprisals. Roberto Barsotti, for example, considered that 'the features which distinguish the customary right of reprisal are anything but clear and unambiguous'.[38] He explains:

> at the time when resort to war was unconditionally permitted, the need to define and distinguish between the single measures short of war was not felt, since their lawfulness was never in doubt. Thus when the necessity to make this distinction arose (in consequence of the prohibition of war and even of the threat of use of force), it became apparent that there was some uncertainty as to the essential characteristic of the reprisal.[39]

Antonio Cassese has commented similarly that:

> the requirement whereby armed reprisals are lawful only to the extent that they constitute a reaction to a wrong committed by another State presupposes the emergence of a rule prohibiting forcible intervention, that is, any interference in another State by the threat or use of force... So long as such intervention was admitted, armed reprisals hardly made up a separate category, for it did not matter very much whether forcible measures short of war were to be labelled 'intervention' or 'reprisal'.[40]

The permissiveness of the law on the use of force saw actions incorrectly labelled as reprisals,[41] with categorizations usually being made by jurists retrospectively.[42] J. L. Brierly was prompted to comment that even leading international law scholars 'seem conscious of a certain unreality in the profession of the law to regulate reprisals'.[43]

The *Naulilaa* arbitration represents the only noteworthy judicial application of the concept of armed reprisals. Germany and Portugal had set up a Special Arbitral Tribunal after an incident in 1914 in which the Governor of German South-West Africa ordered reprisal attacks on Portuguese forts and posts after two German officers and an official were killed by Portuguese soldiers. The Tribunal found the

[36] Schwarzenberger, *International Law as applied by International Courts and Tribunals*, 48.

[37] Schwarzenberger, *International Law as applied by International Courts and Tribunals*, 38.

[38] Barsotti, 'Armed Reprisals', 84.

[39] Barsotti, 'Armed Reprisals', 84.

[40] Cassese, *International Law*, 300.

[41] Barsotti, 'Armed Reprisals', 84.

[42] Brownlie, *International Law and the Use of Force by States*, 220.

[43] J. L. Brierly, 'International Law and Resort to Armed Force' (1932) 4 *The Cambridge Law Journal* 308, 309.

killings were due to a misunderstanding,[44] which did not qualify as a 'violation of a rule of international law by the State against which the reprisals are directed'.[45] The Tribunal set out the following criteria governing resort to reprisals:

Reprisals are illegal if they are not preceded by a request to remedy the alleged wrong. There is no justification for using force except in cases of necessity.... Reprisals which are altogether out of proportion with the act that prompted them are excessive and therefore illegal. This is so even if it is not admitted that international law requires that reprisals should be approximately of the same degree as the injury to which they are meant to answer.[46]

The Tribunal also noted the 'tendency to restrict the notion of legitimate reprisals and to prohibit any excess of their use'.[47] The *Naulilaa* arbitral award is seen as setting out the established customary criteria for armed reprisals, including a prior violation of international law, an unmet demand for reparation, and proportionality,[48] although its interpretation of the latter requirement has been queried.[49] Of course, the backdrop to the arbitration was Germany having been found internationally responsible for the First World War and obliged to make reparations under the Treaty of Versailles and accordingly, 'It was not accidental that the Tribunal dealt so confidently with reprisals as a legal institution'.[50]

The permissiveness of international law towards the use of force was progressively restricted during the 20th century.[51] Limitations on the use of force were notably set out in the Covenant of the League of Nations and the Kellogg–Briand Pact,[52] although it is unclear whether these new rules limited resort to reprisals, given that no express prohibition was included in these instruments.[53] A Special Committee of Jurists created by the Council of the League of Nations to examine the 1923 Corfu incident, where Italy had bombed and occupied Corfu as a reprisal for the assassination of Italian officials in Greece, concluded, quite unhelpfully, that 'Coercive measures which are not intended to constitute acts of war may or may

[44] *Portugal v. Germany (The Naulilaa Case)*, Special Arbitral Tribunal, 31 July 1928 (1927–8) *Annual Digest of Public International Law Cases* 526.

[45] *The Naulilaa Case*, 527.

[46] *The Naulilaa Case*, 527. [47] *The Naulilaa Case*, 527.

[48] Malcolm Shaw, *International Law* (6th edn, Cambridge: Cambridge University Press, 2008), 1129–30; Anthony Arend Clark and Robert J. Beck, *International Law and the Use of Force* (Abingdon: Routledge, 1993), 17.

[49] Partsch, 'Reprisals', 202.

[50] Schwarzenberger, *International Law as applied by International Courts and Tribunals*, 48.

[51] See eg Hague Convention II: Convention Respecting the Limitation of the Employment of Force for the Recovery of Contract Debts, 18 Oct 1907.

[52] Covenant of the League of Nations, 28 Apr 1919, Arts 10–16; Treaty between the United States and other Powers providing for the renunciation of war as an instrument of national policy, 27 Aug 1928, Arts I–II.

[53] Brownlie, *International Law and the Use of Force by States*, 220. See also Brierly, 'International Law and Resort to Armed Force', 315–16. See, however, Schwarzenberger, *International Law as applied by International Courts and Tribunals*, 45; Kelsen, 'Collective Security and Collective Self-Defence under the Charter of the United Nations', 787.

not be consistent with the provisions of Articles 12 to 15 of the Covenant'.[54] The obligation in the Covenant to settle disputes by pacific means could arguably have precluded armed reprisals where a peaceful resolution was not sought first, according to Brierly, although he considered that reprisals might remain permissible in response to a breach of either the Covenant or the Pact themselves.[55] In 1931, the Permanent Court of International Justice referred to the general concept of pacific reprisals as an 'alleged right'.[56] The aforementioned Institut de Droit International resolution in 1934 on armed reprisals declared that they were forbidden in the same way as recourse to war was.[57]

The developments in international law at the end of the Second World War fundamentally altered the legal landscape for states with regard to the use of force, as well as the permissible conduct of armed forces during wartime and the domestic protection of human rights. The Nuremberg Tribunal convicted leading Nazis in 1946 for waging wars of aggression, in addition to war crimes and crimes against humanity.[58] At the London Conference on Military Trials leading to the creation of the Nuremberg Tribunal, the French delegate took issue with a proposed definition of aggression, for it would 'dispose of the whole question of reprisals—the question of reprisals in international law is one existing for the last 500 years and you cannot wipe it out in just one word'.[59] The parallel process of creating an international organization aimed at ensuring global peace and security, the United Nations, saw the adoption of a treaty incorporating the most far-reaching restrictions to date on the use of force.

The UN Charter is of course the key international treaty governing the use of force in international relations and it is largely viewed as having prohibited resort to the doctrine of armed reprisals. The Charter obliges states parties to settle international disputes by peaceful means, 'in such a manner that international peace and security, and justice, are not endangered'.[60] Moreover, Article 2(4) sets out the related rule:

> All Members shall refrain in their international relations from the threat or use of force against the territorial integrity or political independence of any state, or in any other manner inconsistent with the Purposes of the United Nations.

[54] See Kalshoven, *Belligerent Reprisals*, 5–6. See however Tibori Szabó, *Anticpatory Action in Self-Defence*, 86.

[55] Brierly, *The Law of Nations*, 412 (footnote omitted).

[56] Permanent Court of International Justice, *Railway Traffic Between Lithuania and Poland*, Advisory Opinion of 15 October 1931, General List No 39, 114.

[57] Institut de Droit International, Session de Paris 1934, *Régime de répresaillies en temps de paix*, Art 4.

[58] International Military Tribunal (Nuremberg), Judgment and Sentences, 1 Oct 1946, reprinted in (1947) 41 *American Journal of International Law* 172.

[59] 'Minutes of 25 July 1945', Report of Robert H. Jackson United States Representative to the International Conference on Military Trials, London, 1945 (Washington DC: United States Department of State, 1949), 381.

[60] UN Charter, Art 2(3).

With Security Council-authorized force under Article 42 and self-defence under Article 51 being the only exceptions to Article 2(4), a plain reading of the Charter rules would strongly suggest that reprisals involving force were prohibited by this new legal regime. This is the most accepted interpretation of states, UN bodies, international courts, and the majority of scholars, as discussed later. A 1946 Commentary on the Charter states that the obligation in Article 2(3) is such that 'It is obvious that this rules out recourse to certain measures short of war which involve the use of force, such as armed reprisals.'[61]

The records of the diplomatic conferences leading to the adoption of the Charter do not reveal any overt discussion of the question of armed reprisals. The doctrine does not seem to have even been discussed at either Dumbarton Oaks or San Francisco, even though the proposed rules on the use of force were obviously subjected to detailed negotiations.[62] The Charter provisions on the use of force largely mirror the Dumbarton Oaks proposals and the obligation of states to settle disputes by peaceful means was 'not controversial' at the 1944 Dumbarton Oaks conference.[63] The Norwegian delegation to the San Francisco conference had suggested that the Dumbarton Oaks formulation on the prohibition on the use of force should make it clear that the prohibition of the threat or use of force extended to actions 'not approved by the Security Council as a means of implementing the purposes of the organization.'[64] The reasons given by the delegation were that:

> The plea might be put forward that force or threat of force used by a member state in order to secure the fulfilment of a final international award or a recommendation by the Security Council would not be inconsistent with the purpose of the Organization.[65]

At San Francisco, the US delegate clarified that 'the intention of the authors of the original text was to state in the broadest terms an absolute all-inclusive prohibition; the phrase "or in any other manner" was designed to insure that there should be no loopholes.'[66] The relevant rapporteur confirmed that the Norwegian view, that 'the unilateral use of force or similar coercive measures is not authorised or admitted',

[61] Leland M. Goodrich and Edvard Hambro, *Charter of the United Nations; Commentary and Documents* (Boston, MA: World Peace Foundation, 1946), 67.

[62] On the powers of the Security Council, eg, see Robert C. Hilderbrand, *Dumbarton Oaks: The Origins of the United Nations and the Search for Postwar Security* (Chapel Hill, NC: University of North Carolina Press, 1990), 122–58.

[63] Hilderbrand, *Dumbarton Oaks*, 85.

[64] Amendments and Observations on the Dumbarton Oaks Proposals, Submitted by the Norwegian Delegation, May 3, 1945, Doc 2 G/7(n)(1), *Documents of the United Nations Conference on International Organization, San Francisco, 1945*, vol III (New York: United Nations Information Organization, 1945), 366.

[65] Amendments and Observations on the Dumbarton Oaks Proposals, Submitted by the Norwegian Delegation. See also Summary Report of Seventh Meeting of Committee I/1, 16 May 1945, Doc 382, I/1/19, *Documents of the United Nations Conference on International Organization*, vol VI, 304.

[66] Summary Report of Eleventh Meeting of Committee I/1, 4 June 1945, Doc 784, I/1/27, *Documents of the United Nations Conference on International Organization*, vol VI, 334–5.

was covered in the final text adopted,[67] which is as appears in the final Article 2(4) of the Charter. With regard to the absence of any provision explicitly directed at armed reprisals, Michael J. Kelly considers that the pre-eminence given to the maintenance of international peace and security meant that 'it seemed unnecessary to specifically issue a death sentence on the old reprisal doctrine'.[68]

Leading scholars of international law are unhesitatingly of the view that reprisals involving the use of force are prohibited by the Charter. For Brierly, 'it is beyond argument that armed reprisals…would be a flagrant violation of international law'.[69] Ian Brownlie was of the opinion that the 'Unambiguous prohibition of forcible reprisals was finally accomplished by the Charter of the United Nations'.[70] Armed reprisals are 'considered indisputably contrary to Art. 2(4)', according to Antonio Cassese,[71] while Georg Schwarzenberger asserted that 'The formulation chosen was intended to remove any doubt that, in future, not only wars in the technical sense, but also *de facto* wars and forcible measures short of war should be illegal'.[72] Frits Kalshoven was a little more circumspect:

> while it is saying too much that the coming into force of the Charter has removed any uncertainty concerning the legitimacy or illegitimacy of reprisals involving the use of armed force in time of peace, it cannot be denied that the Principles laid down in Article 2, sections 3 and 4, point strongly towards the prohibition of such use.[73]

The *Commentary on the Charter of the United Nations* considers it to be particularly important 'that reprisal, once the most frequently used form of force, is today likewise only admissible in so far as it does not involve the use of armed force'.[74] Even though armed reprisals are viewed as outlawed under the Charter,[75] non-forcible

[67] Report of Rapporteur of Committee 1 to Commission I, Doc 885, I/1/34, 9 June 1945, *Documents of the United Nations Conference on International Organization*, vol VI, 400. The rapporteur's report was adopted by 36 votes to 0, see Summary Report of Fifteenth Meeting of Committee I/1, 11 June 1945, Doc 926, I/1/36, *Documents of the United Nations Conference on International Organization*, vol VI, 423.

[68] Michael J. Kelly, 'Time Warp to 1945—Resurrection of the Reprisal and Anticipatory Self-Defense Doctrines in International Law' (2003) 13 *Journal of Transnational Law and Policy* 1, 12.

[69] Brierly, *The Law of Nations*, 415.

[70] Brownlie, *International Law and the Use of Force by States*, 223. See also at 281, 348, 431; Ian Brownlie, *Principles of Public International Law* (7th edn, Oxford: Oxford University Press, 2008), 466.

[71] Antonio Cassese, 'Return to Westphalia? Considerations on the Gradual Erosion of the Charter System' in Cassese, *The Current Legal Regulation of the Use of Force*, 514.

[72] Schwarzenberger, *International Law as applied by International Courts and Tribunals*, 51.

[73] Kalshoven, *Belligerent Reprisals*, 6–7.

[74] Bruno Simma et al (eds), *The Charter of the United Nations: A Commentary*, vol I (3rd edn, Oxford: Oxford University Press, 2012), 794.

[75] See also Kelsen, 'Collective Security and Collective Self-Defence under the Charter of the United Nations', 784; Szabó, *Anticpatory Action in Self-Defence*, 113; Stephen C. Neff, *War and the Law of Nations* (Cambridge: Cambridge University Press, 2005), 318; Oscar Schachter, *International Law in Theory and Practice* (Leiden: Martinus Nijhoff, 1991), 127.

reprisals or countermeasures are permitted 'when carried out by economic, financial or other peaceful means'.[76]

The practice of international organizations would seem to support this 'most widely-accepted interpretation' of the Charter.[77] In 1964, the Security Council adopted a resolution regarding British military action in Yemen, in which it 'condemns reprisals as incompatible with the purposes and principles of the United Nations'.[78] The UK did not dispute the unlawfulness of reprisals, but rather challenged the categorization of the military action in question as either a reprisal or retaliation.[79] The Security Council condemned an attack by Israel on villages in southern Lebanon in 1969 as a violation of the Charter and of previous resolutions, and declared that:

> such actions of military reprisal and other grave violations of the cease-fire cannot be tolerated and that the Security Council would have to consider further and more effective steps as envisaged in the Charter to ensure against repetition of such acts.[80]

The General Assembly has also viewed armed reprisals as inconsistent with the UN Charter in a resolution adopted 25 years to the day after the entry into force of the Charter. The 1970 Declaration on Principles of International Law Concerning Friendly Relations and Cooperation among States sets out that 'states have a duty to refrain from acts of reprisal involving the use of force'.[81] The General Assembly's 1981 Declaration on the Inadmissibility of Intervention and Interference in the Internal Affairs of States proclaimed that the duty of states to refrain from armed intervention and interference also covers 'acts of reprisal involving the use of force'.[82] The Final Act of the Conference on Security and Co-operation in Europe obliges participating states to 'refrain in their mutual relations from any act of reprisal by force'.[83]

The International Court of Justice (ICJ) has occasionally commented on the legality of armed reprisals. In the *Nuclear Weapons* advisory opinion, the Court observed that:

> Certain States asserted that the use of nuclear weapons in the conduct of reprisals would be lawful. The Court does not have to examine, in this context, the question of armed reprisals in time of peace, which are considered to be unlawful.[84]

[76] Partsch, 'Reprisals', 202. See also Brierly, *The Law of Nations*, 416; Schwarzenberger, *International Law as applied by International Courts and Tribunals*, 58; Neff, *War and the Law of Nations*, 318; Schachter, *International Law in Theory and Practice*, 185–6.

[77] Barsotti, 'Armed Reprisals', 79.

[78] SC Res 188, S/RES/188 (9 Apr 1964).

[79] Barsotti, 'Armed Reprisals', 91.

[80] SC Res 270, S/RES/270 (26 Aug 1969), para 4. See also SC Res 111, S/3538 (19 Jan 1956), para 2; SC Res 171, S/5111 (9 Apr 1962), para 2.

[81] GA Res 2625 (XXV) (24 Oct 1970).

[82] GA Res 36/103 (9 Dec 1981), Section II(c).

[83] Final Act, Conference on Security and Co-operation in Europe, Helsinki, 1 Aug 1975.

[84] *Legality of the Threat or Use of Nuclear Weapons*, Advisory Opinion of 8 July 1996, General List No 95, para 46. India in its submission to the Court seemed to consider reprisals as not being unlawful ('when a State commits such a wrongful act or delict, the use of force by way of reprisal would have to be proportionate'), although it also argued that 'reprisals could not involve acts which are *malum*

This statement has been criticized for not explicitly declaring armed reprisals to be unlawful,[85] although the Court's statement can be interpreted as doing so. In *Nicaragua*, the Court drew on Resolution 2625 (XXV), finding that it 'affords an indication of [States'] *opinio juris* as to customary international law', and it identifies reprisals as a prohibited 'less grave form of the use of force'.[86] The Court addressed the meaning of an armed attack in the context of self-defence and held that 'a use of force of a lesser gravity cannot...produce any entitlement to take collective counter-measures involving the use of force', and that such acts 'could only have justified proportionate counter-measures on the part of the State which had been the victim of these'.[87] It held in particular, that such action 'could not justify intervention involving the use of force'.[88]

The *Oil Platforms* case is probably the closest the Court could have come to date to addressing armed reprisals, and although the final majority judgment is silent on the subject, several of the judges broached the issue.[89] Alain Pellet raised reprisals when he addressed the Court on behalf of Iran:

> You could never accept that, on the pretext that one of the Parties has violated (even by force) the obligation to respect freedom of commerce in their mutual relations, the other Party is entitled to do likewise: these are the very foundations of contemporary international law, built on the prohibition of the use of force in international relations, which you would undermine, thus resurrecting the old right of armed reprisal and at the same time enshrining the right of the strongest to take the 'law' into its own hands, a so-called law which is off-limits to the weak. That cannot be the position of the principal judicial organ of the United Nations.

Judge Elaraby viewed the US action as military reprisals and felt that the Court should have addressed the 'illegality of reprisals in international law'.[90] He felt that an ICJ pronouncement on the matter 'would have, no doubt, added authority to the illegality of such practice', and he considered that the judgment was a missed opportunity 'to reaffirm, clarify, and, if possible develop, the law on the use of force in all manifestations'.[91] Judge Simma lamented the Court's failure to address countermeasures involving force.[92] He addressed the question of how

in se such as certain violations of human rights, certain breaches of the laws of war and rules in the nature of *jus cogens*'. See Letter dated 20 June 1995 from the Ambassador of India, together with Written Statement of the Government of India, 2.

[85] Cassese, *International Law*, 303.

[86] *Case Concerning Military and Paramilitary Activities in and against Nicaragua (Nicaragua v. US)*, Merits, Judgment of 27 June 1986, General List No 70, para 191.

[87] *Nicaragua*, Merits, para 249.

[88] *Nicaragua*, Merits, para 249.

[89] *Case Concerning Oil Platforms (Iran v. US)*, Judgment of 6 Nov 2003, ICJ Rep 2003, 161. It has been argued that the judgment implicitly finds the US military action to be unlawful reprisals, see Christine Gray, *International Law and the Use of Force* (3rd edn, Oxford: Oxford University Press, 2008), 153.

[90] Dissenting Opinion of Judge Elaraby, para 1.2.

[91] Dissenting Opinion of Judge Elaraby, para 1.2.

[92] Separate Opinion of Judge Simma, para 12.

a state might respond to a use of force not rising to the level of armed attack, taking the view that when this was addressed in *Nicaragua*, 'by such proportionate counter-measures the Court cannot have understood mere pacific reprisals'.[93] He advocates a concept of defensive military action that falls short of 'full-scale self-defence'.[94]

The International Law Commission (ILC) has had to address armed reprisals when preparing the Articles on State Responsibility, given the continued validity of non-forcible reprisals, now renamed countermeasures.[95] The Commission was persuaded that developments since 1945 confirmed that the prohibition of armed reprisals or forcible countermeasures had 'acquired the status of a customary rule of international law'.[96] Accordingly, the regime of countermeasures in the Articles excludes measures affecting 'The obligation to refrain from the threat or use of force as embodied in the Charter of the United Nations'.[97] This prohibition on the use of force includes armed reprisals and 'definitively consolidates the inclusion of their peaceful character in the definition of countermeasures'.[98] During the preparatory work of the Articles, the Commission observed, and dismissed, a line of thinking which has claimed the continuing legitimacy or indeed legality of armed reprisals as part of self-defence. The Commission stated:

> The contrary trend, aimed at justifying the noted practice of circumventing the prohibition by qualifying resort to armed reprisals as self-defence, does not find any plausible legal justification and is considered unacceptable by the Commission. Indeed, armed reprisals do not present those requirements of immediacy and necessity which would only justify a plea of self-defence.[99]

The final section of this chapter addresses the attempts, by scholars primarily, to revive the doctrine of reprisals and to challenge the accepted view that the Charter's rules do not tolerate such a use of force.

[93] Separate Opinion of Judge Simma, para 12.

[94] See also Dinstein, *War, Aggression and Self-Defence*, 254. See, however, James Green, *The International Court of Justice and Self-Defence in International Law* (Oxford: Hart, 2009), 54–6, where he seeks to distinguish forcible countermeasures and armed reprisals.

[95] Third Report on State Responsibility, by Mr Gaetano Arango-Ruiz, Special Rapporteur, A/CN.4/440 and Add.1 (19 July 1991), 11–12.

[96] ILC, Summary Record of the 2424th Meeting, 21 July 1995, *Yearbook of the International Law Commission*, 1995, vol I, 297. See also ILC, Draft Articles on Responsibility of States for Internationally Wrongful Acts with commentaries, *Yearbook of the International Law Commission*, 2001, vol II (2), 132.

[97] Art 50(1)(a). See also Lesaffre, 'Circumstances Precluding Wrongfulness', 469.

[98] Denis Alland, 'The Definition of Countermeasures' in Crawford, Pellet, and Olleson, *The Law of International Responsibility*, 1130. See, however, Kretzmer, 'The Inherent Right to Self-Defence and Proportionality in *Ius ad Bellum*', 22.

[99] ILC, Summary Record of the 2424th Meeting, 21 July 1995, *Yearbook of the International Law Commission*, 1995, vol I, 297 (footnotes omitted).

IV. The Futile Case for Revival

From the time of the adoption of the Charter, scholars have occasionally claimed that armed reprisals are not absolutely prohibited by the treaty's rules on the use of force and pacific settlement of disputes.[100] Armed reprisals might be seen as a 'necessary evil'[101] or even a 'desirable tool',[102] with one argument being that it would be 'preferable to maintain legal standards to govern the resort to coercion short of war, rather than abandon all such resort to force to a blanket condemnation'.[103] Such positions are taken, it is claimed, because of 'U.N. impotence to provide its members with protection against illegal uses of force'.[104] Derek Bowett's 1972 *American Journal of International Law* article has been particularly influential in the revival debate.[105] Bowett suggested a 'credibility gap' between state practice and the norm prohibiting reprisals, and argued that 'a total outlawry of armed reprisals, such as the drafters of the Charter intended, presupposed a degree of community cohesiveness and, with it, a capacity for collective action to suppress any resort to unlawful force which has simply not been achieved'.[106] He asserted that 'The law of reprisals is, because of its divorce from actual practice, rapidly degenerating to a stage where its normative character is in question'.[107] The Security Council has condemned retaliatory actions, but often for different reasons, which is problematic for Bowett, 'if the principle is that *all* reprisals are illegal'.[108] There may be scope for 'reasonable' legitimate armed reprisals he claims, 'that certain reprisals will, even if not accepted as justified, at least avoid condemnation'.[109] He was clear to point out that '*if this trend continues*, we shall achieve a position in which, while reprisals remain illegal *de jure*, they become accepted *de facto*'.[110] He added, however, that:

[100] See eg Speyer Colbert, *Retaliation in International Law*, 200; Barry Levenfeld, 'Israel's Counter-*Fedayeen* Tactics in Lebanon: Self-Defense and Reprisal Under Modern International Law' (1982–3) 21 *Columbia Journal of Transnational Law* 1, 35; Alberto R. Coll, 'Legal and Moral Adequacy of Military Responses to Terrorism' (1987) 81 *American Society of International Law Proceedings* 297, 302–3; O'Brien, 'Reprisals, Deterrence and Self-Defense in Counter-Terror Operations', 470; Arend Clark and Beck, *International Law and the Use of Force*, 186.

[101] Partsch, 'Reprisals', 201.

[102] Levenfeld, 'Israel's Counter-*Fedayeen* Tactics in Lebanon', 35.

[103] Levenfeld, 'Israel's Counter-*Fedayeen* Tactics in Lebanon', 35. See also Lillich, 'Forcible Self-Help under International Law', 133; Speyer Colbert, *Retaliation in International Law*, 201.

[104] Coll, 'Legal and Moral Adequacy of Military Responses to Terrorism', 302–3. See also Falk, 'The Beirut Raid and the International Law of Retaliation', 428; Lillich, 'Forcible Self-Help under International Law', 130–2; Colbert, *Retaliation in International Law*, 1; Thomas M. Franck, *Recourse to Force; State Action Against Threats and Armed Attacks* (Cambridge: Cambridge University Press, 2002), 110, 132–3; O'Brien, 'Reprisals, Deterrence and Self-Defense in Counter-Terror Operations', 470.

[105] Bowett, 'Reprisals Involving Recourse to Armed Force', 1.

[106] Bowett, 'Reprisals Involving Recourse to Armed Force', 1–2.

[107] Bowett, 'Reprisals Involving Recourse to Armed Force', 2.

[108] Bowett, 'Reprisals Involving Recourse to Armed Force', 7.

[109] Bowett, 'Reprisals Involving Recourse to Armed Force', 10, 20.

[110] Bowett, 'Reprisals Involving Recourse to Armed Force', 10–11 (emphasis added).

it is possibly premature to suggest that the principle is now jeopardized. The principle as part of the broader prohibition of the use of force, is *jus cogens*, and no spasmodic, inconsistent practice of one organ of the United Nations could change a norm of this character.[111]

As a member of the ILC, Bowett articulated the similar view in later years that armed reprisals were 'not admissible countermeasures', because of the peremptory status of the prohibition on the use of force in Article 2(4).[112]

Claims of state practice sit at the crux of Bowett's article and others arguing that the prohibition of armed reprisals is out of step with how states actually use force.[113] It is argued that customary international law,[114] or at least state practice,[115] serves to weaken the norm prohibiting reprisals. Clearly absent from these assertions has been the element of *opinio juris*, with states almost never labelling military actions as reprisals. The 1923 Italian bombardment stands as one of the few 20th-century examples of a state representative unambiguously categorizing action as an armed reprisal.[116] There are a few isolated examples,[117] but nothing approaching widespread practice, and states invariably justify unilateral actions under self-defence, rather than reprisals. Barsotti considers that the frequent recourse to self-defence suggests that states 'are aware of the illegality of their conduct if it is described in any other way'.[118] Moreover, scholars have noted that Israeli military operations against neighbouring states 'are generally taken to constitute the main nucleus of modern practice on armed reprisals'.[119] Employment of the language of reprisals or retaliation, as with self-defence (which is seemingly favoured by Israel), may serve to portray military action as being responsive in nature.[120] The Security Council itself, as well as individual members, has frequently condemned Israeli actions as unlawful reprisals or retaliation contrary to the UN Charter.[121] Roberto Barsotti provides

[111] Bowett, 'Reprisals Involving Recourse to Armed Force', 22.

[112] ILC, Summary Record of the 2423rd Meeting, 20 July 1995, *Yearbook of the International Law Commission*, 1995, vol I, 295.

[113] See also Kelly, 'Time Warp to 1945', 12–19; Dinstein, *War, Aggression and Self-Defence*, 252.

[114] Levenfeld, 'Israel's Counter-*Fedayeen* Tactics in Lebanon', 46.

[115] Coll, 'Legal and Moral Adequacy of Military Responses to Terrorism', 302–3.

[116] Kalshoven, *Belligerent Reprisals*, 4–5.

[117] For the sole examples of reprisals, as opposed to retaliation, referred to by Falk and Bowett see Falk, 'The Beirut Raid and the International Law of Retaliation', 429; Bowett, 'Reprisals Involving Recourse to Armed Force', 13 fn 48. See, however, Barsotti, 'Armed Reprisals', 87, 91.

[118] Barsotti, 'Armed Reprisals', 91.

[119] Barsotti, 'Armed Reprisals', 88. See also Lillich, 'Forcible Self-Help under International Law', 131; O'Brien, 'Reprisals, Deterrence and Self-Defense in Counter-Terror Operations', 421; Dinstein, *War, Aggression and Self-Defence*, 254.

[120] eg see O'Brien, 'Reprisals, Deterrence and Self-Defense in Counter-Terror Operations', 426–33, 441, 443, describing reactive measures as 'counterterror' and 'counterforce' actions. See, however, the example at 432–3, where an action was viewed as preventive, but that 'political considerations may have been more influential in determining the timing and character of the raids'.

[121] See eg Security Council, 1502nd mtg, S/PV.1502 (18 Aug 1969), para 74. See also Bowett, 'Reprisals Involving Recourse to Armed Force'; Gray, *International Law and the Use of Force*, 236–7; O'Brien, 'Reprisals, Deterrence and Self-Defense in Counter-Terror Operations', 435–7.

a most persuasive rebuttal to Bowett's 'reasonable' reprisals suggestion,[122] and holds that there is 'absolutely no sign of an *opinio juris* in the conduct of the States in question, but there is even evidence of an awareness of the unlawfulness of reprisals, which is stated explicitly above all when other States carry out retaliatory action'.[123]

As noted by the ILC, there have been claims that reprisals are permitted under the rubric of self-defence,[124] although this is not a well-supported contention given the clear distinctions between the two concepts.[125] The Acting US Secretary of State, Kenneth Rush, touched on this in 1974 while endorsing the norm prohibiting reprisals in Resolution 2625 (XXV):

> The United States has supported and supports the foregoing principle. Of course, we recognized that the practice of States is not always consistent with this principle and that it may sometimes be difficult to distinguish the exercise of proportionate self-defence from an act of reprisal. Yet, essentially for reasons of the abuse to which the doctrine of reprisals particularly lends itself, we think it desirable to endeavor to maintain the distinction between lawful self-defense and unlawful reprisals.[126]

It is argued that overlap between the concepts in practice is primarily a matter of fact rather than law.[127] The matter is complicated by the broadening of self-defence by some states in an attempt to shelter unilateral uses of force going beyond what is acceptable under the Charter.[128] Yoram Dinstein contends that his controversial concept of 'defensive armed reprisals' is permitted under Article 51 and customary international law, while accepting the general rule that armed reprisals are themselves unlawful.[129] These defensive armed reprisals are justified in response to an armed attack, 'in circumstances satisfying all the requirements of valid self-defence', including necessity, proportionality, and immediacy.[130] The issues of immediacy and appropriate targets are, however, treated more flexibly by Dinstein in his conception of armed reprisals than would be generally accepted under self-defence. With defensive armed reprisals, 'the responding State strikes at a time and a place different from those of the original armed attack',[131] the target of military action 'may be

[122] Barsotti, 'Armed Reprisals', 94–7. [123] Barsotti, 'Armed Reprisals', 92.

[124] See eg Franck, *Recourse to Force*, 65–8; O'Brien, 'Reprisals, Deterrence and Self-Defense in Counter-Terror Operations', 470.

[125] Kalshoven, *Belligerent Reprisals*, 27. See, however, Kretzmer, 'The Inherent Right to Self-Defence and Proportionality in *Ius ad Bellum*', 23; Gray, *International Law and the Use of Force*, 150–1; Neff, *War and the Law of Nations*, 330.

[126] Department of State File No P74 0071-1935, reprinted in (1978) 68 *American Journal of International Law* 736. See also American Law Institute, Third Restatement of the Law; *The Foreign Relations Law of the United States*, vol II (1987), 383.

[127] Kalshoven, *Belligerent Reprisals*, 27.

[128] See eg Gray, *International Law and the Use of Force*, 197–8. See also Bowett, 'Reprisals Involving Recourse to Armed Force', 2–10; Kretzmer, 'The Inherent Right to Self-Defence and Proportionality in Ius ad Bellum', 29; Noam Lubell, *Extraterritorial Use of Force Against Non-State Actors* (Oxford: Oxford University Press, 2010), 52; Simma et al, *The Charter of the United Nations: A Commentary*, 794.

[129] Dinstein, *War, Aggression and Self-Defence*, 245, 250.

[130] Dinstein, *War, Aggression and Self-Defence*, 245, 247.

[131] Dinstein, *War, Aggression and Self-Defence*, 245. See also 249.

entirely different and far away',[132] while proportionality remains the 'quintessential' or 'decisive' factor in assessing legality.[133]

Aside from the lack of convincing legal grounds underpinning the argument that armed reprisals are not contrary to the UN Charter, there are other reasons why the case for a revival of armed reprisals is weak. The reprisals doctrine holds obvious appeal for states seeking to subvert the strictures of the Charter, for it 'provides justification on legal grounds for acts ordinary illegal'.[134] Reprisals or retaliatory action have invariably been the preserve of more powerful and usually Western states,[135] which highlights the inherent risks of shaping an international legal doctrine solely in the light of the interests of the major military powers. Militarily strong states are unlikely to 'give way under violent and coercive pressure' in the form of a reprisal, and armed reprisals 'may be used to inflict injury on small states, and extort from them compliance with unreasonable demands',[136] to create a *casus belli* or gain a military advantage over an enemy before war breaks out.[137] Ian Brownlie described reprisals as a weapon of the Great Powers for pursuit of national policy and considered it doubtful that 'any non-European state or small power has resorted to forcible reprisal or pacific blockade'.[138] The unilateral nature of armed reprisals means that 'an aggrieved state is the judge in its own case' and there is thus a significant potential for abuse of the doctrine, not to mention further retaliation and greater instability.[139] Derek Bowett found that the strongest argument against armed reprisals is their 'degenerating effect',[140] and firmly concluded that 'reprisals have proved to be productive of greater violence rather than a deterrent to violence'.[141]

There are, of course, imperfect alternatives available, including non-forcible countermeasures and sanctions, which are less likely to be counterproductive.[142] A reinstatement of the doctrine of armed reprisals would undermine the established rules of international law on the use of military force and facilitate unilateral resort to force that would actually threaten international peace and security. Reprisals would comprise 'a regression to the "just war" theory',[143] and hark back

[132] Dinstein, *War, Aggression and Self-Defence*, 245.

[133] Dinstein, *War, Aggression and Self-Defence*, 248, 254. See further Cassese, *International Law*, 301–3, 371–3; Arend Clark and Beck, *International Law and the Use of Force*, 186; O'Brien, 'Reprisals, Deterrence and Self-Defense in Counter-Terror Operations', 476; Neff, *War and the Law of Nations*, 330; Kretzmer, 'The Inherent Right to Self-Defence and Proportionality in *Ius ad Bellum*', 30; *Oil Platforms*, Separate Opinion of Judge Simma, para 13.

[134] Colbert, *Retaliation in International Law*, 1.

[135] Barsotti, 'Armed Reprisals', 90.

[136] Lawrence, *The Principles of International Law*, 343–4. See also Brierly, *The Law of Nations*, 400.

[137] Colbert, *Retaliation in International Law*, 55.

[138] Brownlie, *International Law and the Use of Force by States*, 220. See also Colbert, *Retaliation in International Law*, 200.

[139] Colbert, *Retaliation in International Law*, 200–1. See also Lesaffre, 'Circumstances Precluding Wrongfulness', 469; Alland, 'The Definition of Countermeasures', 1129.

[140] Bowett, 'Reprisals Involving Recourse to Armed Force', 16.

[141] Bowett, 'Reprisals Involving Recourse to Armed Force', 32.

[142] Barsotti, 'Armed Reprisals', 101. See also Kalshoven, *Belligerent Reprisals*, 10.

[143] Jackson Nyamuya Maogoto, 'War on the Enemy: Self-Defense and State Sponsored Terrorism' (2003) 4 *Melbourne Journal of International Law* 406, 428.

to a 'primitive model of society from which the spirit of cooperation and a growing belief in the importance of social values have progressively brought us further away'.[144] The case for the revival of armed reprisals remains unpersuasive, and its failure to gain any significant acceptance by states serves in fact to reinforce the widespread support for the established norms on the use of force.

[144] Barsotti, 'Armed Reprisals', 102.

CHAPTER 41

HOT PURSUIT

WILLIAM C. GILMORE

I. Introduction

In the modern law of nations the term 'hot pursuit' is generally taken to connote the projection of the coercive powers of the state beyond national territory for law enforcement purposes. As Poulantzas has noted: 'the objective of the right of hot pursuit is to bring escaping wrong-doers before the jurisdictions of the injured State. As the doctrine is justified by the need for the effective administration of justice of the injured State, hot pursuit is not a panacea to cover cases which have nothing to do with the strict legal conditions of this right and should be clearly distinguished from other institutions of international law such as self-defence and reprisals.'[1] The chapter adopts this orthodox approach in its analysis of the law and practice of such pursuit by sea, land, and air.

This stance finds additional justification in that efforts over time to carve out a separate place for a doctrine of 'hot pursuit' as a legal justification for cross-border military incursions independent of the right of self-defence[2] have proved to be highly controversial and have been generally rejected.[3] The term 'hot pursuit' has been

[1] Nicholas Poulantzas, *The Right of Hot Pursuit in International Law* (2nd edn, The Hague: Martinus Nijhoff, 2002), 2–3.

[2] See eg Christine Gray, *International Law and the Use of Force* (3rd edn, Oxford: Oxford University Press, 2008), 137.

[3] See eg Yoram Dinstein, *War, Aggression and Self-Defence* (5th edn, Cambridge: Cambridge University Press, 2011), 270–1; Marco Roscini, 'Neighbourhood Watch? The African Great Lakes Pact and the *ius ad bellum*' (2009) 69 *Zeitschrift für Ausländisches öffentliches Recht und Völkerrecht* 931, 945–7.

formally utilized in a use of force context, such as with the November 2006 Protocol on Non-Aggression and Mutual Defence in the Great Lakes Region.[4] However, even in such cases, there is a compelling case for legal analysis to be conducted through a use of force rather than an extraterritorial criminal law enforcement prism.

II. Sea

It is a long established principle of international law that 'Vessels on the high seas are subject to no authority except that of the State whose flag they fly'.[5] In the course of time, however, a number of exceptions were carved out, including arrest in the course of hot pursuit.[6] As the Supreme Court of Canada was to state in the 1906 case of *The North*: 'by the law of nations when a vessel within foreign territory commits an infraction of its laws either for the protection of its fisheries or its revenues or coasts she may be immediately pursued into the open sea beyond the territorial limits and there taken'.[7] This right of hot pursuit is said to be justified by the need for the effective administration of justice and as a continuation of an act of jurisdiction already commenced.[8]

Although this right was firmly established in the Anglo-American practice of the 19th century,[9] it was not until the Hague Codification Conference of 1930, sponsored by the League of Nations, that it was unequivocally accepted in international law. For these reasons the doctrine was selected, without difficulty, for inclusion in the draft articles to be presented to the First UN Conference on the Law of the Sea.[10]

[4] Art 8, entitled 'measures against armed groups', is worded, in relevant part as follows: '6. A Member State whose armed forces are engaged in the hot pursuit of armed groups shall inform and notify Member States towards whose territory the armed groups are fleeing, and shall request any such Member States to intercept, apprehend and disarm them; 7. A Member State unable or unwilling to intercept armed groups in flight or operating on its territory shall be encouraged to enter into bilateral agreements which specify the conditions under which the armed forces of another Member State may undertake the hot pursuit of the said armed groups, provided that such agreements shall be consistent with the objectives of this Protocol.' See also, eg Art 8(10) which makes reference to the failure, after notification or request, to intercept and disarm such groups, in the context of the articulation of a self-defence non-derogation clause.

[5] *The SS Lotus*, 1927 PCIJ, Ser A, No 10, 25.

[6] See eg Ivan Shearer, 'Problems of Jurisdiction and Law Enforcement against Delinquent Vessels' (1986) 35 *International and Comparative Law Quarterly* 320, 336–9.

[7] [1906] 37 SCR 385.

[8] See eg Susan Maidment, 'Historical Aspects of the Doctrine of Hot Pursuit' (1972–3) *British Yearbook of International and Comparative Law* 365, 369 fn 8.

[9] See eg Lord McNair, *International Law Opinions* (Cambridge: Cambridge University Press, 1956), vol I, 253–5.

[10] See eg UN Conference on the Law of the Sea, Official Records, vol IV, Second Committee (High Seas: General Regime), A/CONF.13/40, 79–92.

The right of hot pursuit was there enshrined in the detailed provisions of Article 23 of the Geneva Convention on the High Seas of 1958.[11]

A very similar formulation was carried forward into Article 111 of the 1982 UN Convention on the Law of the Sea. The most significant difference between them is that the latter had to take account of the increased zonal complexity of ocean space recognized elsewhere in the text. Thus, while the 1958 Convention had as its focus pursuit from the territorial sea or contiguous zone,[12] Article 111(2) stipulates that 'The right of hot pursuit shall apply *mutatis mutandis* to violations in the exclusive economic zone or on the continental shelf, including safety zones around continental shelf installations, of the laws and regulations of the coastal State applicable in accordance with this Convention to the exclusive economic zone or the continental shelf, including such safety zones'.

The two Convention texts in question adopt near identical approaches to the detailed criteria governing the proper exercise of this right. As the International Tribunal for the Law of the Sea (ITLOS) was to stress in its 1 July 1999 judgment in *The M/V 'Saiga' (No 2)* case, these conditions 'are cumulative; each of them has to be satisfied for the pursuit to be legitimate under the Convention'.[13] The central conditions are:

(1) there must be 'good reason to believe' that the vessel in question has violated a relevant law or regulation of the coastal state. Mere 'suspicion' of a violation is insufficient;[14]
(2) pursuit must be commenced when the foreign ship or one of its boats is within a relevant zone of costal state jurisdiction;[15]
(3) the pursuit 'may only be commenced after a visual or auditory signal to stop has been given at a distance which enables it to be seen or heard by the foreign ship';[16]
(4) the right may only be exercised by warships or military aircraft, or by other ships and aircraft 'clearly marked and identifiable as being on government service and authorized to that effect';[17]
(5) the pursuit once commenced must be continuous and uninterrupted;[18] and
(6) the right of pursuit ceases when the foreign vessel in question enters the territorial sea of its own or a third state;[19] it is not otherwise restricted in terms of time or distance.[20]

[11] 450 UNTS 82. [12] See Art 23(1). [13] ITLOS Reports 1999, para 146.
[14] See ITLOS Reports 1999, para 147. See also Art 111(1). [15] See Art 111(1) and (4).
[16] See Art 111(4). [17] See Art 111(5). [18] See Art 111(1). [19] See Art 111(3).
[20] See eg David Anderson, 'Freedom of the High Seas in the Modern Law of the Sea' in David Freestone et al (eds), *The Law of the Sea: Progress and Prospects* (Oxford: Oxford University Press, 2006), 327, 343–4. For a detailed discussion of all of the criteria, see Robert Reuland, 'The Customary Right of Hot Pursuit onto the High Seas' (1993) 33 *Virginia Journal of International Law* 557–89.

While the basic thrust of the right of hot pursuit is relatively clear and straightforward, two particular issues of difficulty have emerged in practice. First, the extent to which all of the detailed rules contained in the 1958 and 1982 texts can be properly regarded as codifying customary international law. Secondly, the proper interpretation of these detailed rules. Both can be well illustrated by reference to the controversy over the concept of constructive presence.

Coastal state law enforcement has for long been facilitated by the acceptance of this doctrine in international law. As McNair has explained, 'When a foreign ship outside territorial waters sends boats into territorial waters which commit offences there, the mother ship renders herself liable to seizure by reason of these vicarious operations.'[21] It is thus broadly similar in nature to the universally accepted notion of objective territorial jurisdiction.

Difficulties have, however, surrounded the question of the scope of this doctrine. As O'Connell has stated: '[A] distinction is drawn between simple and extensive constructive presence, the former being the case where the ship's own boats are used to establish the nexus, and the latter being the case where other boats are used.'[22] Simple constructive presence has long been accepted in state practice and in the case law.[23] It was also adopted by the Hague Codification Conference of 1930. Similarly, the concept of simple constructive presence commanded broad support in the International Law Commission which undertook the preparatory work for the 1958 Geneva Diplomatic Conference. Indeed, in the final draft articles prepared by the Commission in 1956, the doctrine of simple constructive presence alone was embraced. Draft Article 47(3) stated, in relevant part: 'Hot pursuit is not deemed to have begun unless . . . the ship pursued *or one of its boats* is within the limits of the territorial sea or, as the case may be, within the continuous zone.'[24]

By way of contrast, no such broad consensus surrounded the acceptability of extensive constructive presence. In such instances the nexus is said to exist even when the foreign ship uses boats other than its own as, for example, when cargo is transhipped to boats coming from the coastal state by prearrangement.

When the doctrine of constructive presence was debated by the International Law Commission, acceptance of its 'extensive' version was vigorously opposed by certain of its most influential members. At the Commission's 125th meeting on 16 July 1951, J. P. François stated:

that, to justify pursuit, the boats used in committing the offences must be the boats of the offending vessel itself. As to the other cases, he had rejected the concept of constructive

[21] McNair, *International Law Opinions*, 245.

[22] Daniel P. O'Connell, *The International Law of the Sea* (Oxford: Clarendon Press, 1984), vol II, 1093.

[23] See eg McNair, *International Law Opinions*, 245; and Poulantzas, *The Right of Hot Pursuit in International Law*, 71–4.

[24] *Yearbook of the International Law Commission*, 1956, vol II, 284 (emphasis added).

presence. He had stated in his report that he felt 'that this opinion had not received enough support to entitle it to appear in the text to be adopted by the Commission....'[25]

In this stance he was supported by the chairman J. L. Brierly.[26] Consequently it was the 'simple' version of constructive presence which was incorporated into the final draft articles of 1956. In the attached Commentary the following explanation appears:

The article also applies to ships which lie outside the territorial sea and cause their boats to commit unlawful acts in that sea. The Commission, however, refused to assimilate to such cases that of a ship staying outside the territorial sea and using, not its own boats, but other craft.[27]

At the Conference, the draft article on hot pursuit was examined, on a section-by-section basis, by the Second Committee at its 28th meeting held on 9 April 1958. At that time, Mexico proposed an amendment which called for the insertion of the words 'or other craft working as a team and using the ship pursued as a mother ship' after 'or one of its boats'.[28] According to the Mexican delegate, his proposal was intended to confer 'on the coastal State the right of hot pursuit in respect of ships which, though not themselves actually within the State's territorial sea or contiguous zone, or sending any of their boats into those areas, were none the less engaging in illicit acts therein for which boats other than their own were being used'.[29] A roll-call vote was held on this amendment on 11 April and it was adopted by 35 votes to 13, with 16 abstentions.[30] It appears in the 1958 Convention in this form in Article 23(3) and was thereafter carried forward to Article 111(4) of the 1982 text.

Notwithstanding the above, national courts, including those of Canada, have been generally ready to accept that the formulation of extended constructive presence in these multilateral instruments is reflective of customary law.[31] The case law has also tended to adopt interpretations of the doctrine which are sensitive to the needs of the law enforcement community. For instance, notwithstanding specific reference in Article 23(3) and Article 111(4) to team work and the existence of a

[25] *Yearbook of the International Law Commission*, 1951, vol I, 365.

[26] *Yearbook of the International Law Commission*, 1951, vol I, 365.

[27] *Yearbook of the International Law Commission*, 1951, vol I, 285.

[28] Marjorie M. Whiteman, *Digest of International Law* (Washington DC: US Department of State, 1965), vol 4, 682.

[29] UN Conference on the Law of the Sea: Official Records, vol IV, 81.

[30] See UN Conference on the Law of the Sea: Official Records, vol IV, 91.

[31] See eg the Canadian decisions *R v. Sunila and Soleyman* (1986) 28 DLR (4th) 450; and *The Queen v. Rumbaut*, Court of Queen's Bench of New Brunswick, Trial Division, 2 July 1998. In the latter, the judge engages with some of the relevant academic literature including William Gilmore, 'Hot Pursuit and Constructive Presence in Canadian Law Enforcement' (1988) *Marine Policy* 105–11 and Craig Allen, 'Doctrine of Hot Pursuit: A Functional Interpretation Adaptable to Emerging Maritime Law Enforcement Technologies and Practices' (1989) 20 *Ocean Development and International Law* 309–41. For an Italian decision along similar lines, see *Re Pulos and others* (1976) 77 *International Law Reports* 587–92. See also William Gilmore, 'Hot Pursuit: The Case of *R v Mills and others*' (1995) 44 *International and Comparative Law Quarterly* 949.

mother-ship relationship, the courts have provided strong support for the view that the doctrine of extended constructive presence embraces one-off instances of the unloading of contraband by prearrangement.[32] Law enforcement friendly interpretations are also evident in other areas such as in the use of radio transmissions to give the initial order to stop and in relation to the requirement that the pursuit must be continuous and uninterrupted.[33] Reflecting this philosophy, Churchill and Lowe have concluded: 'it seems both inevitable and desirable that the conditions for the exercise of the right of hot pursuit be given a flexible interpretation in order to permit the effective exercise of police powers on the high seas'.[34]

On occasion, additional flexibility for law enforcement authorities flows from bilateral or multilateral treaty practice. Of particular interest in this regard has been the emergence of a network of so-called ship-rider agreements. These were pioneered by the US in a series of bilateral narcotics agreements with certain of the states of Latin America and the Caribbean and the concept was mutilateralized for the first time in a Caribbean Area treaty in 2003.[35]

As Guilfoyle has noted, these 'involve placing a designated law enforcement officer from one party ("the ship-rider") aboard the vessel of another party ("the host State"). The ship-rider is then able to board the vessels of their flag state and enforce flag-state law once aboard, possibly with the assistance of host-state officers'.[36] By way of illustration, under Article 9 of the Caribbean Area Agreement a ship-rider (known as an 'embarked law enforcement official') may, inter alia, authorize the entry of the foreign vessel on which he or she is located to the territorial waters of the designating party. A ship-rider may also enforce national law within his or her national waters and seaward of the territorial sea 'in the exercise of the right of hot pursuit or otherwise in accordance with international law'.[37] While such agreements are most common in a drugs context they are not confined to that sphere:[38] these agreements have also been concluded in a number of different parts of the world. Interestingly the UN Security Council has encouraged the conclusion of 'ship-rider' agreements in the context of its efforts to combat piracy and armed robbery at sea off the coast of Somalia.[39]

[32] See eg Gilmore, 'Hot Pursuit: The Case of *R v Mills and others*', 954–5.

[33] See eg Gilmore, 'Hot Pursuit: The Case of *R v Mills and others*', 955–7.

[34] Robin R. Churchill and Alan V. Lowe, *The Law of the Sea* (3rd edn, Manchester: Manchester University Press, 1999), 216.

[35] See Agreement Concerning Co-operation in Suppressing Illicit Maritime and Air Trafficking in Narcotic Drugs and Psychotropic Substances in the Caribbean Area, 2003.

[36] Douglas Guilfoyle, *Shipping Interdiction and the Law of the Sea* (Cambridge: Cambridge University Press, 2009), 72.

[37] Art 9(3)(6).

[38] See eg Guilfoyle, *Shipping Interdiction and the Law of the Sea*, 119–20 and 196–7. See also the May 2009 Framework Agreement on Integrated Cross-Border Maritime Law Enforcement Operations between the US and Canada. While this applies to an unusually broad range of offences (Art 1) it is restricted to action in 'shared waterways'. See Art 2(5).

[39] See eg SC Res 1851 (2008), operative para 3.

While the 1958 and 1982 Conventions set out in some detail the criteria governing the proper exercise of the right of hot pursuit at sea they remain almost totally silent on the important issue of restrictions upon the use of force in this context.[40] As Shearer has noted, 'It was assumed that customary international law already governed the exercise of force—including force in a peace time police role—at sea and that the customary rules would, for the most part, be sufficient'.[41]

ITLOS provided some clarifications on this issue in its 1999 judgment in *The M/V 'Saiga' (No. 2)* case. It noted that: 'although the Convention does not contain express provisions on the use of force in the arrest of ships, international law, which is applicable by virtue of article 293 of the Convention, requires that the use of force must be avoided as far as possible and, where force is unavoidable, it must not go beyond what is reasonable and necessary in the circumstances'. In its view 'Considerations of humanity must apply in the law of the sea, as they do in other areas of international law'.[42]

The Tribunal went on to stress that international law and practice required resort to a graduated response in such law enforcement operations. The 'normal practice' was to first give an auditory or visual signal to the pursued vessel to stop. Where this fails to bring about the required response 'a variety of actions may be taken, including the firing of shots across the bows of the ship'. Only thereafter and 'as a last resort' may force be used against the pursued ship. In its words: 'even then, appropriate warning must be issued to the ship and all efforts should be made to ensure that life is not endangered'.[43] In the instant case, the officials of Guinea had failed to abide by these limitations. In addition they were also found to have used excessive force whilst on board the *Saiga* in that 'they fired indiscriminately while on the deck and used gunfire to stop the engine of the ship'.[44] In both contexts, that is before and after boarding the vessel, Guinea had violated the rights of the flag state under international law.[45]

III. Land

Hot pursuit involves the projection of the coercive power of the state beyond national territory for law enforcement purposes. In the case of pursuit on land,

[40] But see 1982 Convention, Art 225. By way of contrast, 'ship-rider' agreements tend to engage with this matter in some detail. See eg Agreement Concerning Co-operation in Suppressing Illicit Maritime and Air Trafficking in Narcotic Drugs and Psychotropic Substances in the Caribbean Area, Art 22, and Guilfoyle, *Shipping Interdiction and the Law of the Sea*, 285–6.

[41] Shearer, 'Problems of Jurisdiction and Law Enforcement against Delinquent Vessels', 341.

[42] ITLOS Reports 1999, para 155.

[43] ITLOS Reports 1999, para 156.

[44] ITLOS Reports 1999, para 158.

[45] See ITLOS Reports 1999, para 159.

it follows that any such law enforcement operations will be consummated on the territory of a third state. Where this is done in a manner consistent with international law it constitutes an exception to the foundational principle of the law of nations that enforcement jurisdiction is strictly territorial in nature. As the Permanent Court of International Justice was to state in *The Lotus* case in 1927: 'the first and foremost restriction imposed by international law upon a State is that—failing the existence of a permissive rule to the contrary—it may not exercise its power in any form in the territory of another State. In this sense jurisdiction is certainly territorial; it cannot be exercised by a State outside its territory except by virtue of a permissive rule derived from international custom or from a convention'.[46]

Given national sensitivities concerning issues of sovereignty, it is perhaps unsurprising that exceptions to the exclusively territorial nature of enforcement jurisdictions are relatively rare. In particular for present purposes there is near universal acceptance that pursuit across a national border by land has 'not succeeded in acquiring the character of a right in customary international law…'[47] Even as a matter of treaty law, it is safe to say that the normal mechanism for obtaining jurisdiction over a person located on the territory of a third state is through extradition.[48]

Agreements concerning hot pursuit on land are far from unknown. For example, Daman has noted that 'From the 19th century onwards, many European states concluded bilateral agreements which, on a reciprocal basis, laid down the conditions for hot pursuit over land'.[49] Similarly Poulantzas has drawn attention to the early treaty practice in the Americas and in particular to that involving the US and Mexico.[50] That of 4 June 1896 concerning the 'close pursuit of Kid's band of hostile Indians…' is one such interesting example.[51] However, in contrast to the position in relation to the law of the sea no treaty of universal reach has yet been concluded which touches upon this subject and none is in prospect.

[46] *The SS Lotus*, 18. See also Robert Jennings and Arthur Watts (eds), *Oppenheim's International Law* (9th edn, London: Longman, 1992), 385–90.

[47] See eg Poulantzas, *The Right of Hot Pursuit in International Law*, 11–12; and Hugo Caminos, 'Hot Pursuit' in Rüdiger Wolfrum (ed), *Max Planck Encyclopedia of Public International Law* (online), para 3.

[48] See generally eg Torsten Stein, 'Extradition' in Wolfrum, *Max Planck Encyclopedia of Public International Law* (online).

[49] Maarten Daman, 'Cross-Border Hot Pursuit in the EU' (2008) 16 *European Journal of Crime, Criminal Law and Criminal Justice* 171, 173.

[50] See Poulantzas, *The Right of Hot Pursuit in International Law*, 13–16. See also Amos Hershey, 'Incursions into Mexico and the Doctrine of Hot Pursuit' (1919) 13 *American Journal of International Law* 557–69.

[51] Art I. Perhaps uniquely this treaty contains a 'genocide' clause; Art IX indicating that it 'shall remain in force until Kid's band of hostile Indians shall be wholly exterminated or rendered obedient to one of the two Governments'.

To date, multilateral practice has been concentrated within continental Europe. This flows in part from the challenge to effective policing posed by the realities of local political geography. By way of illustration, Germany alone borders upon nine separate states. However, of greater significance is the enhanced mobility of individuals and the decreasing significance of national frontiers brought about by economic and political integration movements. This is most obviously the case for the member states of the European Union as they have sought to come to terms with the criminal justice implications flowing from the creation of a single market and the free movement of goods, people, services, and capital which it ensures.[52]

The facilitation of hot pursuit over land borders has been one of the compensatory law enforcement measures, which emerged in this context.[53] The best known and most important multilateral arrangement covering this topic is the Schengen Convention on Border Controls of 1990 (often known as Schengen II).[54] Though able to draw upon the experience of the Benelux countries (Belgium, Luxembourg, and the Netherlands) and in particular the 1962 treaty between them[55] in this respect, the negotiations proved to be difficult; the resulting scheme complex and highly circumscribed.

Article 41 is central to the approach adopted. It provides that the officers of one party who are pursuing an individual found in the act of committing or participating in the commission of any of a list of specified criminal offences of a serious character or, alternatively and more liberally, any extraditable offence[56] 'shall be authorised to continue the pursuit without prior authorisation in the territory of another Contracting Party if that Party's competent authorities cannot be given advance warning of entry to their territory, by reason of special urgency, by one of the means of communication provided for in Article 44 or if such authorities are unable to reach the spot in time to take over the pursuit. The same applies if the person pursued escapes while under temporary arrest or while serving a period of

[52] On the gradual evolution of the EU as an actor in the criminal justice sphere, see eg Valsamis Mitsilegas, *EU Criminal Law* (Oxford: Hart, 2009).

[53] Other measures to facilitate operational cross-border policing have also been agreed within the EU. Schengen II, eg, contains provision on controlled delivery (Art 73) and cross-border observation (Art 40). Subsequent initiatives have extended the range of such possibilities. The May 2000 EU Convention on Mutual Assistance in Criminal Matters, eg, envisages the establishment of joint investigation teams (Art 13) and the use of covert investigations (Art 14). These EU precedents have influenced wider European practice. The 2001 2nd Additional Protocol of the Council of Europe's European Convention on Mutual Assistance in Criminal Matters addresses all of these forms of police cooperation but, importantly, does not extend to hot pursuit by land. See eg Arts 17–20. Analysis of these issues falls beyond the scope of this chapter.

[54] See Daman, 'Cross-border Hot Pursuit in the EU', 175 for a discussion of the subsequent incorporation of the Schengen *acquis* within the Union.

[55] Treaty of 27 June 1962 between Belgium, Luxembourg, and the Netherlands concerning extradition and mutual assistance in criminal matters, as amended.

[56] See Art 41(4)(a) and (b).

detention or imprisonment'.[57] The officers giving effect to the pursuit[58] are required, prior to the actual crossing of the border, to 'apply to the competent authorities' of the third country in question who are, in turn, empowered to order that the operation be discontinued. It is further provided that: 'the competent local authorities shall, on request by the pursuing officers, apprehend the person pursued in order to establish his identity or arrest him.'[59]

The above approach, which lacks the simplicity and clarity which characterized the earlier Benelux provisions, is further complicated by the failure of the parties to agree on uniform provisions for implementation. In contrast, they elected to introduce what den Boer has described as 'a national differentiated approach'.[60] Thus, at the time of signature of the convention each contracting state must, by declaration, elect between three specific sets of options relating to important aspects of this operational technique. First, each party must opt either to provide the pursuing officers with a limited power to question the individual concerned or to deny 'the right of interrogation'.[61] Secondly, and as noted previously, they must choose between a list of specified serious offences or all extraditable offences as providing the required basis for intervention.[62] Finally, they must elect to permit hot pursuit either 'without limitation as to area or time' or to restrict its proper use by specific reference to one or other of such factors.[63]

Within the limits thus established, all pursuit operations are subject to a number of conditions which include:

(1) the need for compliance with the law of the territory in question and with orders issued by the local authorities;
(2) that pursuit may only take place across land frontiers;
(3) that pursuing officers must be identifiable through the wearing of a uniform or armband or by 'devices' attached to their vehicle;
(4) that the officers in question must be able at all times to provide proof that they are acting in an official capacity;
(5) that, while foreign officers may carry their service weapons these may only be used in self-defence;
(6) that such officers may not enter private homes or places not accessible to the public; and
(7) that following each operation the pursuing officers must appear before the local authorities to render a report on their mission and, upon request, 'remain available until the circumstances of their action have been adequately clarified'.[64]

[57] See Art 41(1).

[58] The right attaches to specified officers only and the listing does not extend to members of the military forces of the parties.

[59] Art 41(1). See also Art 41(6).

[60] Monica den Boer, *Schengen: Intergovernmental Scenario for European Police Cooperation* (Edinburgh: Department of Politics, University of Edinburgh, 1991), 6.

[61] Art 41(2). [62] Art 41(4). [63] Art 41(3). [64] Art 41(5)(g).

The coverage of hot pursuit is completed by a series of provisions designed to ensure the cooperation of the pursuing authorities in subsequent inquiries and judicial proceedings,[65] the regulation of the formal legal position of the foreign officers,[66] and the resolution of issues relating to liability and compensation.[67] It is of importance to emphasize, in contrast to the situation in a law of the sea context, that persons apprehended in the course of a hot pursuit under Schengen are not to be returned directly to the territory from which the pursuit commenced. As Peers has stated: 'it is implicit that if the pursuing police catch the person they are chasing, they cannot simply take him or her back across the border, but must hand the person they have caught over to the host State authorities and arrange to issue an extradition request (or presumably now issue a European Arrest Warrant, in most cases)'.[68] It should be noted that Article 41(10) permits the conclusion of supplementary agreements and some parties, including the Benelux countries, have taken advantage of this possibility.[69] Schengen has also had the effect of stimulating further relevant treaty practice on hot pursuit extending to neighbouring non-EU member countries. The trilateral agreement of April 1999 between Switzerland, Austria, and Liechtenstein[70] is one such example.

Finally, within the context of the EU, it should be noted that hot pursuit is also addressed in the 1997 convention on mutual assistance and cooperation between customs administrations (often known as Naples II). While not identical to Schengen, the drafting approach adopted was heavily influenced by that earlier instrument.[71] Naples II contains a specific provision on pursuit at sea thus addressing a loophole in the Schengen text which, under Article 41(5)(b), is restricted to pursuit 'over land frontiers only'. Article 20(4)(b) of Naples II is worded as follows:

> when the pursuit takes place on the sea, it shall, where it extends to the high sea or the exclusive economic zone, be carried out in conformity with the international law of the sea as reflected in the United Nations Convention on the Law of the Sea, and, when it takes place in the territory of another Member State, it shall be carried out in accordance with the provisions of this Article.

The wording utilized is, inter alia, such as to authorize pursuit into and through the territorial sea as well as the internal and inland waters of neighbouring states. The continuation of such a pursuit on land territory is not precluded and, in theory at least, would appear to be permissible.[72]

[65] Art 41(5)(h). [66] See Art 42.

[67] See Art 43. The treatment of criminal and civil liability in Schengen II has also influenced subsequent treaty practice on liability in the context of operational police cooperation. See eg the 2000 EU Convention on Mutual Assistance in Criminal Matters, Arts 15 and 16; the 2001 2nd Additional Protocol to the European Convention on Mutual Assistance in Criminal Matters, Arts 21 and 22.

[68] Steve Peers, *EU Justice and Home Affairs Law* (3rd edn, Oxford: Oxford University Press, 2011), 935.

[69] See generally Daman, 'Cross-border Hot Pursuit in the EU'.

[70] See 1999 Treaty on Collaboration of Police and Customs Authorities across the National Borders, Art 11.

[71] See eg Peers, *EU Justice and Home Affairs Law*, 936 and 185–6 fn 49.

[72] For a specific authorization of this kind, see eg the 2009 Framework Agreement on Integrated Cross-Border Maritime Law Enforcement Operations between the US and Canada, Art 3(3), (4), and (5).

IV. Air

The international law and practice concerning hot pursuit is at its least developed in relation to pursuit by air. In particular, it is to be doubted that a convincing case can be made for the existence of a rule of customary international law which permits the pursuit of a foreign aircraft beyond national air space for law enforcement purposes. Nor is provision for such a right included in relevant multilateral treaties of global reach. By way of illustration Article 3*bis* of the Chicago Convention on International Civil Aviation addresses the right of every state to require civil aircraft flying above national territory without authority to land. It also treats related matters including the imposition of significant restraints on the use of weapons against such aircraft in flight.[73] However, in contrast to the UN Convention on the Law of the Sea, its provisions do not directly contemplate law enforcement action furth of national air space. As Caminos has remarked, as of today 'a right of aerial hot pursuit is not recognised in international law'.[74]

Somewhat curiously, however, the right to utilize aircraft in maritime hot pursuit operations is now well entrenched. Thus, in its 1956 draft articles the International Law Commission—though not unanimously—felt able to recognize the right of pursuit of a ship by an aircraft.[75] This innovative position was accepted by the subsequent diplomatic conference and was incorporated in Article 23 of the Geneva Convention on the High Seas of 1958. It was, in turn, carried forward into the wording of Article 111 of the 1982 UN Convention on the Law of the Sea. Neither text, however, permits the pursuit of one aircraft by another.

Importantly Article 111 paragraph 6(a) is fully in line with the policy articulated by the International Law Commission in 1956 that the lawfulness of such a practice should be recognized 'provided it is exercised in accordance with the principles governing its exercise by ships…'[76] The Convention also explicitly permits aircraft to operate in combination with relevant vessels in giving effect to the pursuit and subsequent arrest.[77] The term 'aircraft' is not defined in the 1982 Convention and can be taken to comprise 'any kind of flying machines such as seaplanes and helicopters'.[78]

It is also not uncommon for so-called ship-rider agreements to address the issue of 'suspect aircraft'. For instance, the 2003 Caribbean Area Agreement seeks to

[73] 1984 Protocol Relating to an Amendment to the Convention on International Civil Aviation (1984) 23 ILM 705.

[74] Caminos, 'Hot Pursuit' in Wolfrum, *Max Planck Encyclopedia of Public International Law*, para 3. See also Jennings and Watts, *Oppenheim's International Law*, 386.

[75] See *Yearbook of the International Law Commission*, 1951, vol I, 285.

[76] *Yearbook of the International Law Commission*, 1951, vol I, 285.

[77] Art 111(6)(b).

[78] Caminos, 'Hot Pursuit' in Wolfrum, *Max Planck Encyclopedia of Public International Law*, para 13. See also the discussion in Allen, 'Doctrine of Hot Pursuit', 324–5.

promote cooperation to the fullest extent possible in combating illicit maritime and air traffic in narcotic drugs 'with a view to ensuring that suspect vessels and suspect aircraft are detected, identified, continuously monitored, and where evidence of illicit traffic is found, suspect vessels are detained for appropriate law enforcement action by responsible law enforcement authorities'.[79] In incorporating this dimension the negotiators were concerned to ensure that the final text should provide in a full and appropriate manner for the safety of civil aviation. This is particularly evident in the wording of Article 13 and in the terms of Article 22(8) which explicitly prohibits the use of force against civil aircraft in flight.

V. Conclusions

While 'hot pursuit', in the sense of the projection of the coercive power of the state beyond national boundaries for law enforcement purposes, is well recognized in the customary international law of the sea it has yet to achieve that form of normative recognition in relation to pursuit on land or by air. In these spheres, deep-rooted sensitivities concerning territorial sovereignty (and indeed public safety) have restricted acceptance of the concept to a patchwork of bilateral and regional agreements in treaty form. In all instances, the exercise of the right has been tightly circumscribed by numerous conditions.

While the restrictive formulation of the right of pursuit, especially by land and air, might be such as to limit the possibility that it will be resorted to with any great frequency, in practice the international community has nonetheless sent a valuable message to the criminal fraternity that the protection to be obtained by the mere expedient of crossing international boundaries is by no means absolute.

[79] Art 2.

CHAPTER 42

THE THREAT OF THE USE OF FORCE AND ULTIMATA

FRANÇOIS DUBUISSON
ANNE LAGERWALL

I. Introduction

There is no doubt that the UN Charter requires that states refrain not only from the use of force but also from the threat of force.[1] The principle embodied in Article 2(4) is generally recognized as customary[2] and peremptory.[3] The disposition stipulates that 'all members shall refrain in their international relations from the threat or use of force against the territorial integrity or political independence of any state, or in any other manner inconsistent with the Purposes of the United Nations'. The Charter prohibits the threat of force in the same way as it prohibits the actual use of force.

[1] *Legality of the Threat or Use of Nuclear Weapons*, Advisory Opinion of 8 July 1996, ICJ Rep 1996, 244, para 38.

[2] Krysztof Skubiszewski, 'Use of Force by States. Collective Security. Law of War and Neutrality' in Max Sorensen (ed), *Manual of Public International Law* (New York: Macmillan, 1968), 745. *Contra*, Romana Sadurska, 'Threats of Force' (1988) 82 *American Journal of International Law* 248.

[3] International Law Commission, *Yearbook of the International Law Commission*, 1966, vol II, 270; Individual Opinion of Judge Bruno Simma, *Case Concerning Oil Platforms (Iran v. US)*, ICJ Rep 2003, 161, para 6.

The threat of force has not been given a great deal of attention in international law; rather, authors have studied the prohibition of the use of force and its exceptions, such as self-defence.[4] The threat of force has sometimes been analysed in the context of the right to pre-emptive defence, which supposedly allows a state to react, not to an effective armed attack but to a simple threat to trigger an armed attack.[5] But monographs[6] and articles[7] devoted specifically to the threat of force remain scarce. Yet, instances where states complain about unlawful threats of force are not as rare as one might think. For example, in a letter sent to the President of the Security Council in 2008, Thailand affirmed that 'the Prime Minister of Cambodia publicly issued an ultimatum against Thailand to withdraw by 1200 hours of 14 October 2008 or Cambodia would turn the border area into a "death zone"', in contradiction with the prohibition of the threat of force enshrined in the Article 2(4) of the UN Charter.[8] During the oral proceedings of the International Court of Justice (ICJ) in the case concerning *Certain activities carried out by Nicaragua in the Border Area*, the agent of the Republic of Nicaragua recalled that the Security Minister of Costa Rica had stated that 'these people will withdraw either through reason or by force...'[9] Media have reported threatening discourses from Iran and Israel[10] as well as from North Korea and the US.[11] These examples illustrate the practical importance of the subject. This chapter aims at clarifying the exact conditions under which an act may qualify as a threat of force contrary to the UN Charter (Section II) and unveils the trends adopted in different instances where states, arbitrators, or experts

[4] See eg Josef Mrazek, 'Prohibition of the Use and Threat of Force: Self-Defence and Self-Help in International Law' (1989) 27 *Canadian Yearbook of International Law* 81.

[5] See Thomas M. Franck, *Recourse to Force. State Action Against Threats and Armed Attacks* (Cambridge: Cambridge University Press, 2002), 99 ff; Belatchew Asrat, *Prohibition of Force under the UN Charter. A Study of Art. 2(4)* (Uppsala: Iustus Forlag, 1991), 222 ff.

[6] Nicolas Stürchler, *The Threat of Force in International Law* (Cambridge: Cambridge University Press, 2007); Francis Grimal, *Threats of Force. International Law and Strategy* (London/New York: Routledge, 2013).

[7] Sadurska, 'Threats of Force'; Major Matthew A. Myers Sr, 'Deterrence and the Threat of Force Ban: Does the UN Charter Prohibit some Military Exercises?' (1999) 162 *Military Law Review* 132; François Dubuisson and Anne Lagerwall, 'Que signifie encore l'interdiction de recourir à la menace de la force?' in Karine Bannelier et al (eds), *L'intervention en Iraq et le droit international* (Paris: Pedone, 2004), 83; Mario Roscini, 'Threats of Armed Force and Contemporary International Law' (2007) 54 *Netherlands International Law Review* 229; Dino Kritsiotis, 'Close Encounters of a Sovereign Kind' (2009) 20 *European Journal of International Law* 299; James A. Green and Francis Grimal, 'The Threat of Force as an Action in Self-Defense Under International Law' (2011) 44 *Vanderbilt Journal of Transnational Law* 285.

[8] Letter dated 16 October 2008 from the Permanent Representative of Thailand to the United Nations addressed to the President of the Security Council, S/2008/657 (17 Oct 2008), para 2.

[9] *Certain activities carried out by Nicaragua in the Border Area (Costa-Rica v. Nicaragua)*, CR 2011/2, 11 Jan 2011, 4, para 30.

[10] 'Iran's leader threatens to level cities if Israel attacks, criticizes US nuclear talks', *Fox News*, 21 Mar 2013. See Kritsiotis, 'Close Encounters of a Sovereign Kind', 316–22.

[11] 'North Korea threatens to strike without warning', *CNN*, 15 Apr 2013.

have commented on certain acts in relation to the prohibition of the threat of force (Section II).

In addition, there have been a number of quite spectacular instances of formal ultimata. For instance, NATO threatened the use of air power in Bosnia and Herzegovina, in relation to the demand made to ethnic Serb forces to withdraw heavy weapons from exclusion zones surrounding the so-called safe areas by a specified date and time. Most spectacularly, NATO threatened the use of force against Serbia or alternatively the Kosovo Liberation Army in the run-up to the Rambouillet negotiations on Kosovo. It threatened to use force against whichever side would obstruct reaching an interim settlement for Kosovo within a short, concentrated time frame. When the Kosovo negotiations produced no result, it actually employed force in accordance with that threat on a large scale.[12] However, as the cases of Bosnia and Herzegovina and Kosovo were, at least in part, linked to demands made through the UN Security Council, they will not be considered in any detail in this chapter, which focuses on the threat of force outside of the context of collective security.

II. What Constitutes a Threat of Force Contrary to the United Nations Charter?

Article 2(4) raises two main questions. What particular acts may qualify as 'threats' of force (Section II.A)? And under what conditions are these acts unlawful (Section II.B)?

A. What Acts Qualify as a 'Threat' of Force?

It is generally admitted that 'force' in Article 2(4) of the Charter means *armed* force.[13] The threat which the Charter prohibits can therefore only be an armed threat.[14]

[12] See Marc Weller, *Contested Statehood* (Oxford: Oxford University Press, 2009), 111 f.

[13] See Bert V. A. Röling, 'The Ban of the Use of Force and the U.N. Charter' in Antonio Cassese (ed), *The Current Regulation of the Use of Force* (Dordrecht: Martinus Nijhof, 1986), 4 and Antonio Tanca, 'The Prohibition of Force in the U.N. Declaration of Friendly Relations of 1970' in Cassese, 400–2; Yoram Dinstein, *War, Aggression and Self-Defence* (5th edn, Cambridge: Cambridge University Press, 2011), 88; Asrat, *Prohibition of Force under the UN Charter*, 40; Albrecht Randelzhofer and Oliver Dörr, 'Article 2(4)' in Bruno Simma et al (eds), *The Charter of the United Nations: A Commentary* (3rd edn, Oxford: Oxford University Press, 2012), 208–210.

[14] Kritsiotis, 'Close Encounters of a Sovereign Kind', 304–5.

According to Ian Brownlie: 'A threat of force consists in an express or implied promise by a government of a resort to force conditional on non-acceptance of certain demands of that government'.[15] In a more flexible fashion, Romana Sadurska considers that the mere conclusion of collective defence treaties, such as the North Atlantic Treaty, may be seen as a threat to resort to armed measures.[16] Most authors agree, however, that the threat should be formulated in precise and direct terms to the attention of a clearly identifiable state or group of states, hence excluding threats which are too vague or general.[17] Moreover, the threat should be coercive[18] and accompanied by specific demands for the targeted state(s) to adopt a particular conduct.[19] Examples of threats frequently include, under certain circumstances, rearmament,[20] military manoeuvres,[21] establishment of military bases on the territory of a foreign state,[22] bellicose declarations,[23] concentration of troops along the borders,[24] general mobilization,[25] and propaganda in favour of a war of aggression.[26]

[15] Ian Brownlie, *International Law and the Use of Force by States* (Oxford: Clarendon Press, 1963), 364.

[16] Sadurska, 'Threats of Force', 243. See also Randelzhofer and Dörr, 'Article 2(4)' in Simma et al, *The Charter of the United Nations: A Commentary*, 218; Grimal, *Threats of Force*, 43; Green and Grimal, 'The Threat of Force as an Action in Self-Defense Under International Law', 296.

[17] See Asrat, *Prohibition of Force under the UN Charter*, 140; Randelzhofer and Dörr, 'Article 2(4)' in Simma et al, *The Charter of the United Nations: A Commentary*, 218; Olivier Corten, *Le droit contre la guerre* (Paris: Pedone, 2008), 125–50; Olivier Corten, *The Law against War. The Prohibition on the Use of Force in Contemporary International Law* (Oxford: Hart, 2010), 94–111; Robert Kolb, *Ius contra bellum. Le droit international relatif au droit de la paix* (2nd edn, Brussels: Bâle, Bruylant, Helbing Lichtenhahn, 2009), 243; Stürchler, *The Threat of Force in International Law*, 258–60.

[18] See Dinstein, *War, Aggression and Self-Defence*, 89; Randelzhofer and Dörr, 'Article 2(4)' in Simma et al, *The Charter of the United Nations: A Commentary*, 218; Sadurska, 'Threats of Force', 245.

[19] See Randelzhofer and Dörr, 'Article 2(4)' in Simma et al, *The Charter of the United Nations: A Commentary*, 218; Corten, *Le droit contre la guerre*, 145–6; Eduardo Jiménez de Aréchaga, 'International Law in the Past Third of a Century' (1978) 159 *Recueil des cours de l'Académie de droit international* 88. *Contra*, Dinstein, *War, Aggression and Self-Defence*, 89.

[20] See Randelzhofer and Dörr, 'Article 2(4)' in Simma et al, *The Charter of the United Nations: A Commentary*, 218; Jean-Gabriel Castel, *International Law* (3rd edn, Toronto: Butterworths, 1976), 1220.

[21] Skubiszewski, 'Use of Force by States', 780; Jiménez de Aréchaga, 'International Law in the Past Third of a Century', 88; Sadurska, 'Threats of Force', 243; Grimal, *Threats of Force*, 43–4; Stürchler, *The Threat of Force in International Law*, 172–217; Roscini, 'Threats of Armed Force and Contemporary International Law', 239–40; Myers, 'Deterrence and the Threat of Force Ban'.

[22] Castel, *International Law*, 1220.

[23] Jiménez de Aréchaga, 'International Law in the Past Third of a Century', 88; Grimal, *Threats of Force*, 42–3.

[24] Jiménez de Aréchaga, 'International Law in the Past Third of a Century', 88; Sadurska, 'Threats of Force', 243; Asrat, *Prohibition of Force under the UN Charter*, 140.

[25] Jiménez de Aréchaga, 'International Law in the Past Third of a Century', 88.

[26] Asrat, *Prohibition of Force under the UN Charter*, 139.

The ICJ's case law clarifies the definition of a 'threat' of force. In the *Corfu Channel* case, the Court had to decide whether minesweeping operations led by UK vessels were carried out in conformity with international law.[27] Albania underlined that it had not consented to the operation which therefore violated its sovereignty and argued that the presence of military vessels escorting the minesweepers constituted 'an unnecessarily large display of force, out of proportion to the requirements of the sweep'.[28] Condemning the minesweeping operation, the Court nevertheless rejected Albania's contentions on this particular aspect:

> The Court thinks that this criticism is not justified. It does not consider that the action of the British Navy was a demonstration of force for the purpose of exercising political pressure on Albania. The responsible naval commander, who kept his ships at a distance from the coast, cannot be reproached for having employed an important covering force in a region where twice within a few months his ships had been the object of serious outrages.[29]

In the *Nicaragua* case, the Court had to determine the conditions under which military manoeuvres or rearmament could be constitutive of threats of force.[30] Between 1982 and 1985, the US had conducted troop movements in Honduran regions located close to Nicaraguan borders and deployed vessels off the Nicaraguan coast.[31] Nicaragua contended that these operations were unlawful threats of force. The Court, however, was not satisfied that 'the manoeuvres complained of, in the circumstances in which they were held, constituted on the part of the United States a breach, as against Nicaragua, of the principle forbidding recourse to the threat or use of force'.[32] Moreover, the US maintained that its operations were justified owing to the 'excessive militarization' of Nicaragua 'such as to prove its aggressive intent'. The Court held that such justification could not stand:

> It is irrelevant and inappropriate, in the Court's opinion to pass upon this allegation of the United States, since in international law there are no rules, other than such rules as may be accepted by the State concerned, by treaty or otherwise, whereby the level of armaments of a sovereign State can be limited, and this principle is valid for all States without exception.[33]

In its advisory opinion in the *Legality of the Threat or Use of Nuclear Weapons*, the Court explained that the threat of force is characterized by 'a signalled intention to use force if certain events occur' or if there was a 'stated readiness to use it'.[34] As an example, the Court affirmed that 'it would be illegal for a State to threaten force

[27] Grimal, *Threats of Force*, 54–7; Stürchler, *The Threat of Force in International Law*, 68–74; Kritsiotis, 'Close Encounters of a Sovereign Kind', 322–9.

[28] *Corfu Channel (UK v. Albania)*, ICJ Rep 1949, 35.

[29] *Corfu Channel (UK v. Albania)*, ICJ Rep 1949, 35.

[30] See Grimal, *Threats of Force*, 58–9; Stürchler, *The Threat of Force in International Law*, 74–9; Corten, *The Law against War*, 101–3.

[31] *Military and Paramilitary Activities in and against Nicaragua (Nicaragua v. US)*, ICJ Rep 1986, 53, para 92.

[32] *Nicaragua*, 118, para 227. [33] *Nicaragua*, 135, para 269.

[34] ICJ Rep 1996, para 47. On this case, see Stürchler, *The Threat of Force in International Law*, 79–90.

to secure territory from another State, or to cause it to follow or not follow certain political or economic paths'.[35]

In sum, the threat of force is defined in strict terms by the ICJ. To qualify as a threat, demonstrations of force must be accompanied by particular circumstances showing that these demonstrations amount to political pressure in order to obtain something from the targeted state by declaring a willingness to react if certain events occur.[36] For conduct to be considered as a threat of force, a signalled intention or a declaration stating these aims is required.[37] Implicit terms should not, in principle, be considered as threats of force,[38] unless particular circumstances so justify.[39]

B. Under What Conditions is a Threat of Force Unlawful?

Article 2(4) of the UN Charter implies that a threat is unlawful when the use of force contemplated by the threat would itself be unlawful. The threat of force is contrary to the Charter when the use of force cannot be justified, either because no authorization has been granted by the Security Council or the conditions required by the Charter's Article 51 with regard to self-defence are not met.[40] In that respect, the prohibition of the threat of force is symmetrical to that of the use of force.[41]

Some authors have questioned this symmetry by asserting that the threat of force is accepted in broader[42] or stricter[43] terms than the corresponding use of force in practice. The prohibition of the threat of force has also been said to have no autonomy from the prohibition of the use of force; any distinction between the two remaining 'virtual' as only threats which have been implemented are generally condemned.[44] Romana Sadurska even considers that a state may sometimes threaten

[35] ICJ Rep 1996, para 47.

[36] Dubuisson and Lagerwall, 'Que signifie encore l'interdiction de recourir à la menace de la force?' in Bannelier et al, *L'intervention en Iraq et le droit international*, 85–8.

[37] Kritsiotis, 'Close Encounters of a Sovereign Kind', 306; Corten, *The Law against War*, 108.

[38] *Contra* Stürchler, *The Threat of Force in International Law*, 260–1.

[39] Corten, *The Law against War*, 108–9.

[40] See Dinstein, *War, Aggression and Self-Defence*, 88; Brownlie, *International Law and the Use of Force by States*, 364; Bruno Simma, 'NATO, the UN and the Use of Force: Legal Aspects' (1999) 10 *European Journal of International Law* 10–11; Grimal, *Threats of Force*, 37–8; Kolb, *Ius contra bellum*, 243, Roscini, 'Threats of Armed Force and Contemporary International Law', 254–8; Kritsiotis, 'Close Encounters of a Sovereign Kind', 305; Green and Grimal, 'The Threat of Force as an Action in Self-Defense Under International Law', 292–5.

[41] See Dubuisson and Lagerwall, 'Que signifie encore l'interdiction de recourir à la menace de la force?' in Bannelier et al, *L'intervention en Iraq et le droit international*, 88–93; Corten, *The Law against War*, 111–24.

[42] Randelzhofer and Dörr, 'Article 2(4)' in Simma et al, *The Charter of the United Nations: A Commentary*, 218.

[43] Stürchler, *The Threat of Force in International Law*, 273.

[44] Jean Combacau and Serge Sur, *Droit International Public* (5th edn, Paris: Montchrestien, 2001), 629.

force, despite the use of force contemplated being unlawful, as such threats prove to be effective tools in facilitating the resolution of certain disputes and form symbolic substitutes to effective recourses to force.[45] When the threat is exercised reasonably and carefully, in order to maintain peace and security within the parameters of the UN objectives or to sustain the legitimate right of a state, it is not unlawful.[46]

These different stances are difficult to support. State practice, since the adoption of the UN Charter, as well as the case law of the ICJ, show that the prohibition of the threat of force has frequently been reaffirmed as an autonomous obligation and that the prohibition is conceived in similar terms, whether the conduct is a threat or a recourse to force.[47] The Security Council has adopted numerous resolutions condemning threats of force or demanding that states refrain from such threats, as in Resolutions 186 and 187 (Cyprus),[48] Resolutions 326 and 411 (Southern Rhodesia),[49] Resolution 487 (Iraq/Israel),[50] and Resolution 573 (Tunisia/Israel).[51] Without referring explicitly to the prohibition of the threat of force, other resolutions adopted by the Security Council have called on concerned states to restrain themselves in extremely tense situations and avoid any incident or provocative declaration which could aggravate the situation, in conformity with the principle of peaceful resolution of disputes.[52] In addition, the symmetrical prohibition of the threat and the use of force has been reaffirmed in general international instruments, such as resolutions adopted by the General Assembly,[53] the United Nations Convention on the Law of the Sea,[54] the Final Act of Helsinki,[55] and the Charter of Paris for a New Europe adopted by the Organization for Security and Co-operation in Europe (OSCE) in 1990.[56] The advisory opinion rendered by the ICJ in the *Nuclear Weapons*

[45] Sadurska, 'Threats of Force', 246. [46] Sadurska, 'Threats of Force', 260–6.

[47] See Dubuisson and Lagerwall, 'Que signifie encore l'interdiction de recourir à la menace de la force?' in Bannelier et al, *L'intervention en Iraq et le droit international.*

[48] S/RES/186 (1964), Preamble and para 1; S/RES/187 (1964), Preamble and para 1.

[49] S/RES/326 (1973), para 1: 'The Security Council condemns all the acts of provocation and harassment, including economic blockade, blackmail and military threats, against Zambia by the illegal regime in collusion with the racist regime of South Africa'; S/RES/411 (1977), paras 1–2.

[50] S/RES/487 (1981), paras 1–2: 'The Security Council strongly condemns the military attack by Israel in clear violation of the Charter of the United Nations and the norms of international conduct; calls upon Israel to refrain in the future from any such acts or threats thereof'.

[51] S/RES/573 (1985), paras 1–2: 'The Security Council condemns vigorously the act of armed aggression perpetrated by Israel against Tunisian territory in flagrant violation of the Charter of the United Nations, international law and norms of conduct; demands that Israel refrain from perpetrating such acts of aggression or from threatening to do so'.

[52] S/RES/395 (1976); S/RES/1177 (1998); S/RES/1226 (1999).

[53] See eg Declaration on the Inadmissibility of Intervention in the Domestic Affairs of States and the Protection of Their Independence and Sovereignty, A/RES/20/2131 (21 Dec 1965); Declaration on Principles of International Law Concerning Friendly Relations and Cooperation among States in accordance with the Charter of the United Nations, A/RES/25/2625 (24 Oct 1970); Peaceful settlement of disputes between States, A/RES/37/10 (15 Nov 1982).

[54] Convention, Art 301.

[55] OSCE, Helsinki Final Act, 1 Aug 1975, available at <http://www.osce.org/node/39501>, Principle II.

[56] OSCE, Charter of Paris for a New Europe, 1990, available at <http://www.osce.org/mc/39516>.

case provides an even clearer illustration of the perfectly symmetrical prohibition of both the threat and the use of force:

> The notions of 'threat' and 'use' of force under Article 2, paragraph 4, of the Charter stand together in the sense that if the use of force itself in a given case is illegal—for whatever reason—the threat to use such force will likewise be illegal. In short, if it is to be lawful, the declared readiness of a State to use force must be a use of force that is in conformity with the Charter.[57]

On this particular matter, the Court has underlined that 'no State... suggested to the Court that it would be lawful to threaten to use force if the use of force contemplated would be illegal.'[58] The principle of symmetry is again reaffirmed in unequivocal terms with regard to the threat of using nuclear weapons:

> Whether this is a 'threat' contrary to Article 2, paragraph 4, depends upon whether the particular use of force envisaged would be directed against the territorial integrity or political independence of a State, or against the Purposes of the United Nations or whether, in the event that it were intended as a means of defence, it would necessarily violate the principles of necessity and proportionality. In any of these circumstances the use of force, and the threat to use it, would be unlawful under the law of the Charter.[59]

Authors who doubt such symmetry sometimes ground their position on the Cuban Missile Crisis and the *Corfu Channel* case. But in the case of the Cuban quarantine, the US justified its blockade by referring to the authorization supposedly obtained from the Organization of American States (OAS) by virtue of Chapter VIII of the UN Charter. Whether or not the argument is valid, suffice to say that the US did not intend to dissociate the appreciation of the legality of the threat of force from that of the effective use of force, both in their view being justified under the Charter.[60] In the *Corfu Channel* case, it is highly questionable whether it can be inferred from the Court's decision that the Court accepted the legality of a threat of force from the circumstance that the threat was intended to strengthen a recognized right. If the Court decided that the passage of British warships through the channel did not violate Albania's sovereignty, it was because their conduct could qualify as an *innocent passage*[61] and because the UK's demonstration of force was intended to prevent Albania from continuing to fire at the vessels.[62] From the perspective of the prohibition of the threat of force—which was not the angle chosen by the ICJ—it may be said that if such a threat existed, it could be considered as formulated in relation to self-defence.[63] The Court did not examine the admissibility of the use of force to compel a state to admit or execute an existing right.[64]

[57] ICJ Rep 1996, 246, para 47. [58] *Nuclear Weapons*, Advisory Opinion, para 47.

[59] *Nuclear Weapons*, Advisory Opinion, 246–7, para 48.

[60] See Leonard C. Meeker, 'Defensive Quarantine and the Law' (1963) 57 *American Journal of International Law* 515–24.

[61] ICJ Rep 1949, 31. [62] *Corfu Channel*, 31.

[63] In diplomatic correspondence, the UK warned the Albanian government that 'if Albanian coastal batteries in the future opened fire on any British warship passing through the Corfu Channel, the fire would be returned' (ICJ Rep 1949, 27).

[64] See Article 50 of the Articles on the Responsibility of States for Internationally Wrongful Acts, International Law Commission, Annex to GA Res 56/83, A/RES/56/83: 'Countermeasures shall not

III. The Application of the Rule Prohibiting the Threat of Force in Particular Cases

Given that the ICJ case law suggests that the prohibition of the threat of force is interpreted in rather strict terms, it could be questioned whether such a classical interpretation has been adopted in instances where particular acts have been commented on in relation to this prohibition. Three specific cases have been studied in that respect: state practice with regard to the US and British threats of force against Iraq in 2002 and 2003 (Section III.A), the Permanent Court of Arbitration's findings in the case between Suriname and Guyana in 2007 (Section III.B), and the Report issued by the Independent International Fact-Finding Mission on the conflict in Georgia in 2009 (Section III.C).

A. Iraq (2002–3)

During the Gulf crisis, both British and US authorities frequently signalled their intention to use force against Iraq if Saddam Hussein did not leave the country or disarmament was not duly pursued.[65] This readiness to use force became clearly apparent when the US Congress adopted 'the authorization for use of military force against Iraq resolution of 2002'.[66] Commenting on the resolution, President Bush affirmed that 'Iraq must disarm and comply with all existing UN resolutions, or it will be forced to comply'.[67] In similar terms, Tony Blair declared that 'Saddam must now make his choice. My message to him is this: disarm or you face force'.[68] The US and the UK then deployed troops in countries surrounding or close to Iraq. The pressure finally reached its peak when President Bush declared his country's readiness to launch a military operation unless Saddam Hussein and his sons left the territory within 48 hours.[69] Such declarations and acts made abundantly clear that the

affect…the obligation to refrain from the threat or use of force as embodied in the Charter of the United Nations'.

[65] *New York Times*, 16 Feb 2002.

[66] *Authorization for Use of Military Force Against Iraq Resolution of 2002*, Public Law No 107–243, 116 Stat 1498 (16 Oct 2002), HJRes 114.

[67] 'Bush Says Confronting Iraq Is *Matter of National Security*', radio address to the nation, 12 Oct 2002, available at <http://iipdigital.usembassy.gov>.

[68] 'Prime Minister statement on Iraq following UN Security Council resolution', 8 Nov 2002, available at <http://webarchive.nationalarchives.gov.uk>.

[69] 'Bush Gives Saddam Hussein and Sons 48 Hours to Leave Iraq', 17 Mar 2003, available at <http://iipdigital.usembassy.gov>.

two states intended to use force in the event that Iraq did not conform with certain conditions and can therefore be qualified as a 'threat of force' under Article 2(4) of the Charter.[70] Its lawfulness depends on the use of force contemplated. If the US and British threats had been formulated in similar terms to those expressed by Security Council's Resolution 1441 (2002) which warned Iraq 'that it will face serious consequences as a result of its continued violations of its obligations'[71]—consequences to be decided by the Security Council[72]—the threats would have been lawful. However, the declarations expressed the intent to use force even in the absence of Security Council authorization.[73] The US representative to the Security Council affirmed that: 'We hope and expect that the Council will act and play its proper role as a safeguard of our common security. If it fails to do so, then we and other States will be forced to act.'[74] For that reason, the threat of force formulated was in violation of the UN Charter as the unilateral use of force contemplated was contrary to Article 2(4).[75]

States remained relatively silent with regard to such bellicose declarations, and such silence may support the hypothesis that the threat of use of force was not generally condemned as such. It should be recalled that a number of states explicitly disapproved of the intention of the US and the UK to operate unilaterally. The 118 states of the Non-Aligned Movement (NAM) reiterated 'their firm condemnation... of threats of military action against the sovereignty, territorial integrity and independence of Member States of the Movement which constitute acts of aggression and blatant violations of the principle of non-intervention and non-interference.'[76] The Organisation of the Islamic Conference, counting 57 member states, expressed 'its categorical rejection of any... threat to the security and safety of any Islamic State and emphasized the need to settle the Iraqi question by peaceful means within the framework of the United Nations'[77]. However, a number of states did admit—not

[70] 'U.S. Stands Behind UN Inspectors, Says Powell', 31 Oct 2002, available at <http://iipdigital.usembassy.gov>; 'Prime Minister statement opening Iraq debate', 18 Mar 2003, at <http://webarchive.nationalarchives.gov.uk>.

[71] S/RES/1441 (2002); See Olivier Corten, 'Opération *Iraqi Freedom:* peut-on admettre l'argument de l'"autorisation implicite" du Conseil de sécurité?' (2003) 36 *Belgian Review of International Law* 211–12.

[72] See eg Declarations of the representatives of France, the UK, Mexico, Russia, Norway, Syria, Cameroon, China, and Colombia, S/PV.4644 (8 Nov 2002); Chile, Angola, Bulgaria, and Pakistan, S/PV.4714 (7 Mar 2003); and Malaysia, South Africa, League of Arab States, Algeria, Egypt, India, Libya, Iran, Australia, and Brazil, S/PV.4717 (11 Mar 2003). See Serge Sur, 'La résolution 1441 du Conseil de sécurité et l'affaire iraquienne: un destin manqué' (2003) *Dalloz* 836; Corten, 'Opération *Iraqi Freedom*', 205 ff.

[73] A/57/PV.2 (12 Sept 2002), 10.

[74] S/PV.4625 (Resumption 3) (17 Oct 2002), 13.

[75] See 'Appeal by international jurists concerning the use of force against Iraq' (2003) 36 *Belgian Review of International Law* 271.

[76] Final document of the XIII Conference of Heads of State or Government of the Non-Aligned Movement, Kuala Lumpur, 24–25 Feb 2003, available at <http://www.nam.gov.za/media/030227e.htm>.

[77] Second extraordinary session of the Organisation of the Islamic Conference, Doha, 5 Mar 2003, available at <http://www.oic-oci.org>.

to say encourage—the threat of force formulated by the US and the UK as a tool capable of persuading Iraq to disarm. Nevertheless, this may be explained by the fact that until February 2003 the threats referred to Security Council action as well as to Resolution 1441[78] and did not clearly present themselves as threats to use force unilaterally. France declared that 'the American and British military presence in the region lends support to our collective resolve. We all recognize the effectiveness of the pressure that is being exerted by the international community'.[79] Similarly, Canada affirmed that

> The record leaves no doubt that the Iraqi authorities have begun to cooperate only because they face heavy outside pressure, including the indispensable build-up of military force by the United States, the United Kingdom, Australia and others, and the willingness of the international community to back diplomacy with force if necessary.[80]

In other words, states that welcomed the threat of force generally understood the threat as being a multilateral one decided within the context of the UN. For that reason, it seems rather difficult to view their behaviour as showing a tendency to apprehend threats independently from the uses of force that such threats contemplate. The Iraq crisis cannot therefore be interpreted as a sign of flexibility towards the threat of force. On the contrary, it shows rather that the prohibition of the threat of force is reaffirmed and still envisaged autonomously and symmetrically to the prohibition of the use of force, in conformity with the classical approach retained by the ICJ.[81]

B. *Guyana/Suriname* Award (2007)

The arbitral tribunal constituted for the *Guyana/Suriname* case also examined certain acts in relation to the prohibition of the threat to use force. Guyana claimed that Suriname had resorted to the use of force on 3 June 2000 to expel a Canadian oil exploration company's rig and drill ship named *C.E. Thornton* from a disputed maritime area and had threatened other licencees.[82] The rig supervisor described the incident:

> Shortly after midnight on 4 June 2000, while this coring process (drilling for core samples) was underway, gunboats from the Surinamese Navy arrived at our location. The gunboats

[78] UK, S/PV.4707 (14 Feb 2003), 20; US, S/PV.4707 (14 Feb 2003), 22–3.

[79] Declaration of the representative of France, S/PV.4714 (7 Mar 2003). See also Declarations of the representatives of Spain, S/PV.4714 (7 Mar 2003), Cameroon, S/PV.4707 (14 Feb 2003), Angola, S/PV.4707 (14 Feb 2003), Greece, S/PV.4709 (18 Feb 2003), Argentina, S/PV.4709 (18 Feb 2003), Macedonia, S/PV.4709 (Resumption 1) (19 Feb 2003).

[80] Declaration of the representative of Canada, S/PV.4717 (10 Mar 2003).

[81] Corten, *The Law against War*, 123–4.

[82] Arbitral Tribunal Constituted Pursuant to Article 287, and in Accordance with Annex VII of the UN Convention on the Law of the Sea (Guyana and Suriname) (2007) 139 ILR 566, 140, para 426.

established radio contact with the C.E. Thornton and its service vessels, and ordered us to 'leave the area in 12 hours,' warning that if we did not comply 'the consequences will be yours.' The Surinamese Navy repeated this order several times. I understood this to mean that if the C.E. Thornton and its support vessels did not leave the area within twelve hours, the gunboats would be unconstrained to use armed force against the rig and its service vessels.[83]

The Tribunal also considered a testimony from Major Jones, the Commander Staff Support of the Suriname Air Force and Navy who recorded his exchange with the drilling platform:

This is the Suriname navy. You are in Suriname waters without authority of the Suriname Government to conduct economic activities here. I order you to stop immediately with these activities and leave the Suriname waters. The answer to this from the platform was: 'we are unaware of being in Suriname waters'. I persisted saying that they were in Suriname waters and that they had to leave these waters within 12 hours. And if they would not do so, the consequences would be theirs. They then asked where they should move to. I said that they should retreat to Guyanese waters. He reacted by saying that they needed time to start up their departure. I then allowed them 24 hours to leave the Suriname waters. We then hung around for some time and after about one hour we left for New Nickerie.[84]

Given that the commander and two captains of Surinamese patrol boats clearly specified that they had no intention nor instructions to use force,[85] it is somehow difficult to understand the reasons justifying that the Tribunal 'is of the view that the order given by Major Jones to the rig constituted an explicit threat that force might be used if the order was not complied with'.[86] All the more so when the Tribunal makes explicit references to the *Nicaragua* case together with the *Nuclear weapons* case, where the ICJ adopted a rather restrictive approach to what constitutes a threat of force contrary to the UN Charter. More specifically, the Tribunal did not determine the conditions under which a threat directed at a private company could fall within the scope of application of Article 2(4) of the Charter which only prohibits threats formulated by one state against another. To Suriname, the measures were of the nature of law enforcement measures adopted to preclude unauthorized drilling in the disputed area. Suriname argued that their lawfulness could be grounded on the case law of international courts and tribunals such as the *Fisheries Jurisdiction* cases[87] and *Saiga* case.[88] Without providing any specific argument, the Tribunal only stated that:

the action mounted by Suriname on 3 June 2000 seemed more akin to a threat of military action rather than a mere law enforcement activity. This Tribunal has based this finding

[83] Award, 142, para 433. [84] Award, 142, para 436. [85] Award, 143, paras 437–8.
[86] Award, 143, para 438. [87] *Fisheries Jurisdiction (Spain v. Canada)*, ICJ Rep 1998.
[88] *The M/V 'Saiga' (No 2) (Saint Vincent and the Grenadines v. Guinea)*, Judgment of 1 July 1999, available at <https://www.itlos.org>.

primarily on the testimony of witnesses to the incident, in particular the testimony of Messrs Netterville and Barber. Suriname's action therefore constituted a threat of the use of force in contravention of the Convention, the UN Charter and general international law.[89]

In the absence of clear motivation, it is not easy to make sense of the Award in relation to the prohibition of the threat of force. One could say, however, that the Tribunal adopted an interpretation of Article 2(4) which is much more extensive than that traditionally used by the ICJ.

c. Russia/Georgia Report (2009)

The outbreak of hostilities between Georgia and the Russian Federation in August 2008 was preceded by an escalation of tensions involving all actors in the conflict.[90] These facts were analysed in great detail by the Independent International Fact-Finding Mission on the Conflict in Georgia in the report the Mission delivered in September 2009.[91] It follows from the report that the Mission contemplates what might constitute an unlawful threat of force in broad terms, underlining that such a threat might be implicit and result from the context as long as it appears credible.[92] The report makes clear that a threat is not required to adopt the form of an ultimatum.[93] Concerning Georgia, the following acts were taken into account:

(1) launched air surveillance over the Abkhaz conflict zone in spring 2008, (2) participated in repeated exchanges of fire in South Ossetia, and (3) had engaged in a comprehensive military build-up with the assistance of third parties such as the US, including the acquisition of modern weaponry.[94]

In the Mission's opinion, these elements taken together constituted a threat of force contrary to Article 2(4) of the Charter:

Taken together, Georgia's actions amounted to a threat of force. That Georgia was hardly in a position to substantially harm Russian political and territorial integrity by military means is not relevant. It suffices that Georgia signalled a readiness to use force against its adversaries, which may have included Russian troops on Georgian soil, if they were not withdrawn.[95]

[89] Award, 147, para 445.

[90] See Vaios Koutroulis, 'The Prohibition of the Use of Force in Arbitrations and Fact-Finding Reports', Chapter 26 in this volume.

[91] Report of the Independent International Fact-Finding Mission on the Conflict in Georgia, Sept 2009, vol II, ch 6, 'Use of force', available at <http://www.ceiig.ch/Report.html>. See François Dubuisson and Anne Lagerwall, 'Le conflit en Géorgie de 2008 au regard du *jus contra bellum* et à la lumière du rapport de la mission d'enquête internationale de 2009' (2009) 42 *Belgian Review of International Law* 448–98; Olivier Corten, 'Le rapport de la mission d'enquête internationale indépendante sur le conflit en Géorgie: quel apport au *jus contra bellum*?' (2010) 114 *Revue Générale de Droit International Public* 35–62.

[92] Report, 231–2. [93] Report, 232–3. [94] Report, 233. [95] Report, 233.

With regard to Russia, the report mentions the following acts:

(1) In April, Russia warned Tbilisi that Georgian NATO membership would result in the permanent loss of its breakaway territories and that Russian military bases would be established there. (2) Also in April, the Russian Foreign Ministry issued a warning stating that Moscow was prepared to use military force if Georgia started an armed conflict with Abkhazia and South Ossetia. (3) Russian warplanes repeatedly flew over Abkhaz and South Ossetian territory in a clear warning to Tbilisi. Moscow claimed a right to conduct the flights, while denying Georgia the right to fly reconnaissance drones in the same area. At least one Georgian drone was shot down by a Russian combat plane. (4) In May, Russia increased its troop levels in Abkhazia and sent railway construction troops on a 'humanitarian mission' into the region, without permission of Georgia. In July, Russian troops performed the 'Kavkaz 2008' military exercise. Although it was declared as a regular exercise, numerous features made it appear an extraordinary threat. Moreover, after completion of the exercise, some Russian troops remained in the area and on increased levels of alert.[96]

Taken together, these facts were also considered as an unlawful threat of force:

By any reasonable definition, the sum of actions undertaken by Russia by mid-2008 amounted to a threat of force vis-à-vis Georgia. For Tbilisi, both official statements by Moscow and the military operations it authorised on the border and within Georgian territory generated a definite sense that, within the context of earlier experiences and of the latest developments, Georgia ran a substantial risk of Russian military intervention. This risk involved the de facto partition of Georgia and thus a re-definition of its territorial boundaries. While some of the political steps undertaken by Russia, such as the granting of Russian nationality, did not in and of themselves constitute a threat of force because they lacked a specific reference to the use of force, they contributed to a perception of a threat and to crisis escalation. The Russian side did not limit its threats to the exclusive objective of discouraging an armed attack, but sought to gain additional political concessions.[97]

These conclusions appear to be grounded on a definition of the conditions under which a threat of force is unlawful which is more extensive than that derived from the case law of the ICJ. Moreover, they do not seem to differentiate between the multiple facts taken into account. The overall approach adopted by the Mission makes it hard to understand what acts do specifically qualify as a threat of force. A clarification would have been of great help since military surveillance or overflights, arms acquisitions or military exercises are not traditionally considered to be threats of force unless accompanied by a clear and precise intention to use force. Other elements (eg the warning from Moscow on the eventuality of force) could have been studied individually to verify if they met the relevant criteria (terminology used, context of the declaration, on the ground situation, credibility of the threat, etc). Besides and more importantly, the report suggests that the threats referred to could not have been lawful even though the use of force contemplated was lawful: 'in situations of severe crisis between longstanding adversaries, governments must refrain

[96] Report, 234. [97] Report, 235.

from any kind of military threat, even when their actual use of force might be justified'.[98] According to the report, this is so because in a prolonged conflict 'no real distinction between aggressor and victim of aggression can be made and thus no scenario exists where the justification of self-defence can meaningfully be applied'.[99] On this particular point, the report also adopts an approach to the prohibition of the threat of force which is very different from the classical approach adopted by the ICJ.[100]

IV. Conclusion

Even though the prohibition of the threat of force has not been frequently subject to judicial or doctrinal attention, its substance has been clearly defined in the few instances where the ICJ was invited to apply it. The level which should be reached in order for acts to be qualified as threats is high as it should leave no doubt as to the determination of a state to resort to force if the targeted state does not adopt certain conduct. The ultimate criteria will be the existence of coercion. The conditions under which the threat is unlawful are in perfect symmetry to those of the use of force. A threat is legal only if the envisaged force is conceived as a response to aggression or authorized by the UN Security Council. In this regard, state practice shows no tendency towards a change in the rule. Given the principles set by the ICJ, it is surprising that the majority of authors consider that the criteria are very unclear and difficult to apply to particular cases. It should be also noted that the international bodies, which had to apply the principle of the prohibition of the threat of use of force, as was the case of the Arbitral Tribunal and the European Union Inquiry Mission in Georgia, did it in a very confused way, departing from the criteria set by the ICJ.

[98] Report, 235. [99] Report, 237.

[100] See also Corten, 'Le rapport de la mission d'enquête internationale indépendante sur le conflit en Géorgie', 51–3.

CHAPTER 43

BLOCKADES AND INTERDICTIONS

WOLFF HEINTSCHEL VON HEINEGG

I. Introduction

STATING that blockades and interdictions are a 'revival of classic concepts' seems to suggest that the concepts, while certainly valid in a distant past, are no longer compatible with the current international legal regime governing the use of force or contemporary public international law in general. Indeed, one might argue that international navigation and aviation may not be interfered with, unless the UN Security Council has expressly authorized such interference or if it is necessary for self-defence purposes.

The mere characterization of a concept as 'classic' does not mean it has fallen into desuetude. This certainly holds true for blockades, interdictions, and other methods by which states interfere with international navigation and aviation. On the one hand, blockade is expressly referred to in Article 42 of the UN Charter and, according to a long-standing treaty,[1] military manuals,[2] and other

[1] Declaration Respecting Maritime Law, Paris, 30 Mar 1856.

[2] *The Commander's Handbook on the Law of Naval Operations* (Newport, RI: US Naval War College, 2007), NWP 1-14M, para 7.7; Federal Ministry of Defence of the Federal Republic of Germany, *Humanitarian Law in Armed Conflicts—Manual* (Bonn: Federal Ministry of Defence of the Federal Republic of Germany, 1992), paras 1051–3; UK Ministry of Defence, *The Manual of the Law of Armed Conflict* (Oxford: Oxford University Press, 2004), paras 13.65–13.76.

documents[3] continues to be a recognized method of naval and aerial warfare. On the other hand, the practice of the UN Security Council,[4] state practice,[5] and the progressive development of international treaty law[6] provide sufficient evidence of the legality of interdiction operations if they serve a recognized purpose. This does not mean that states are at an almost unlimited liberty. Rather, the principle of flag state sovereignty and the freedom of navigation and aviation—either for economic, or for security policy, reasons—continue to be of overall importance. Therefore, states agree that interdiction operations taken against foreign vessels and aircraft would constitute a violation of the exclusive jurisdiction and sovereignty of the flag state or state of registry, if there is no valid legal basis or the operations do not remain within the rather strict limits of the applicable rules and principles of international law.[7]

The purpose of the present chapter is to identify those rules and principles that allow for a naval or aerial blockade or some other form of interference with foreign vessels and aircraft, without the explicit authorization by the UN Security Council. It may be added in this context that an authorization by the Security Council, although highly desirable, will in most cases not serve as a perfect legal basis. Even if the Council authorizes the use of 'all necessary means' or the use of force in order to enforce an embargo,[8] for instance, there will be numerous unresolved legal issues with regard to the status of persons and objects, the scope of lawful enforcement measures, and the relevance of other branches of international law, such as human rights.[9]

[3] Louise Doswald-Beck (ed), *San Remo Manual on International Law Applicable to Armed Conflicts at Sea* (Cambridge: Cambridge University Press, 1995), paras 93–104; Harvard Program on Humanitarian Policy and Conflict Research (HPCR), *Manual on International Law Applicable to Air and Missile Warfare* (Cambridge, MA: HPCR, 2009), Section V; International Law Association, 'Helsinki Principles on the Law of Maritime Neutrality', Report of the 68th Conference, Taipei, 1998, para 5.2.10.

[4] See the references in n 8.

[5] eg the counterterrorism operations Operation Enduring Freedom and Operation Active Endeavour, and the operations of states relying on an authorization by the UN Security Council resolutions referred to in n 8.

[6] See eg Art 8*bis* of the Protocol of 2005 to the Convention for the Suppression of Unlawful Acts Against the Safety of Maritime Navigation, London, 14 Oct 2005, IMO Doc LEG/CONF. 15/21.

[7] See Anglo-American claims Commission, Award, *The Jessie, The Thomas F. Bayard and The Pescawha* (1926) Nielsen's Report 479 ff: '[It] is a fundamental principle of international maritime law that, except by special convention or in time of war, interference by a cruiser with a foreign vessel pursuing a lawful avocation on the high seas is unwarranted and illegal and constitutes a violation of the sovereignty of the country whose flag the vessel flies.'

[8] See SC Res 221, 9 Apr 1966 (Rhodesia); SC Res 665, 25 Aug 1990 (Iraq); SC Res 875, 16 Oct 1993 (Haiti); SC Res 713, 25 Sept 1991; SC Res 757, 30 May 1992; SC Res 787, 16 Nov 1992; SC Res 820, 17 Apr 1993 (Former Yugoslavia); SC Res 1701, 11 Aug 2006 (UNIFIL); SC Res 1970, 26 Feb 2011; SC Res 1973, 17 Mar 2011 (Libya).

[9] See Martin D. Fink, 'The Right of Visit for Warships: Some Challenges in Applying the Law of Maritime Interdiction on the High Seas' (2010) 49 *The Military Law and the Law of War Review* 7–45. Further Lois E. Fielding, *Maritime Interception and U.N. Sanctions* (San Francisco, CA: Austin & Winfield, 1997).

While the focus will be on the *jus ad bellum*, the *jus in bello* will also be taken into consideration in order to clarify the concept of blockade. Moreover, some states parties to a non-international armed conflict or to an armed conflict whose classification is contested have interfered with foreign vessels and aircraft and have justified their measures by reference to the *jus in bello*.

II. Blockade Under the *Jus ad Bellum* and the *Jus in Bello*

A. Concept and Distinction

The term 'blockade' is all too often used for measures that do not qualify as a blockade proper, such as sieges on land or the barring of passage through an international strait or an international canal.[10] Sometimes the use of the term is cautiously avoided because states are unwilling to admit that they are indeed establishing and enforcing a blockade against another state.[11] Neither the erroneous use of the term nor the refusal of its use are relevant to the legal concept of blockade. A blockade is a military operation to prevent all vessels and/or aircraft from entering or exiting specified ports, airports, or coastal areas belonging to or under the control of another state.[12] Hence, a blockade by its very nature can only be established off the coast of another state and not within the territory of another state or within a sea area that is not geographically connected with land territory, that is, on the high seas. A blockade will regularly affect freedom of navigation and aviation in

[10] Egypt's closure of the Suez Canal in 1956 did not qualify as a blockade *stricto sensu*. Findings to the contrary are not based upon the law of blockade but upon the prohibition, under Art 1 of the 1888 Convention of Constantinople, to 'subject the Canal to the exercise of the right of blockade'. Only if that distinction is observed is it correct to state that Egypt had 'subjected the Canal to a blockade against Israeli ships within the meaning of... Article 1 of the Constantinople Convention' because the 'normal meaning of blockade would, in any event, not make much sense in connection with that clause'; Leo Gross, 'Passage Through the Suez Canal of Israeli-Bound Cargo and Israel Ships' (1957) 51 *American Journal of International Law* 530, 541.

[11] The most prominent case in the post-1945 era was the 'Cuban Quarantine'—a term invented to distract from the fact that a blockade proper had been established around Cuba. See, inter alia, Carl Q. Christol and Charles R. Davies, 'Maritime Quarantine: The Naval Interdiction of Offensive Weapons and Associated Matériel to Cuba, 1962' (1963) 57 *American Journal of International Law* 525; Quincy Wright, 'The Cuban Quarantine', ibid, 546; Charles G. Fenwick, 'The Quarantine Against Cuba: Legal or Illegal?', ibid, 587; Myres S. McDougal, 'The Soviet-Cuban Quarantine and Self-Defense', ibid, 597.

[12] See, inter alia, Wolff Heintschel von Heinegg, 'Blockade' in Rüdiger Wolfrum (ed), *Max Planck Encyclopedia of Public International Law* (Oxford: Oxford University Press, 2012), vol I, 960, 960.

sea areas and beyond the outer limit of the territorial sea and in the airspace above. A blockade must be distinguished from other measures interfering with navigation or aviation, such as contraband control, exclusion or no-fly zones, naval minefields, embargoes, or maritime interdiction operations.[13]

B. Conditions of Legality

The maintenance and enforcement of a blockade is achieved by the use of the armed forces and, if necessary, by the use of military force against vessels and/or aircraft breaching, or attempting to breach, the blockade. While it may be doubtful whether and to what extent the use of force against merchant vessels and civil aircraft is to be measured in the light of Article 2(4) of the UN Charter,[14] the establishment and maintenance of a blockade by the use of armed forces qualifies as an act of aggression[15] and, a fortiori, use of force prohibited under that provision, unless justified by another rule of international law.

There seems to be general agreement among states and international lawyers on the legality of a naval or aerial blockade during an international armed conflict.[16] In view of the principle of equal application of the *jus in bello*, it is irrelevant whether one of the parties to the conflict has resorted to the use of force in violation of the *jus ad bellum* or whether the establishment of the blockade as such constitutes a prohibited use of force under Article 2(4) of the UN Charter.[17] Namely, the illegality or legality under *jus ad bellum* has no impact on the illegality or legality under the *jus in bello*. The efforts to limit the *in bello* legality in the light of the *jus ad bellum*[18] have been futile and cannot be considered as reflecting the general consensus of

[13] Heintschel von Heinegg, 'Blockade' in Wolfrum, *Max Planck Encyclopedia of Public International Law*, 960.

[14] While some states are prepared to resort to the right of self-defence if a merchant vessel flying its flag has been attacked, other states do not share that position. Under the Definition of Aggression (Annex to GA Res 3314 [XXIX] of 14 Dec 1974) an attack on an individual merchant vessel does not constitute an 'act of aggression'.

[15] GA Res 3314, Art 3(c).

[16] See the references in nn 2 and 3. Further Robert W. Tucker, *The Law of War and Neutrality at Sea* (Washington DC: US Government Printing Office, 1957), 283; C. John Colombos, *International Law of the Sea* (6th rev edn, London: McKay Co., 1967), 714; Lance Edwin Davis and Stanley L. Engerman, *Naval Blockades in Peace and War: An Economic History Since 1750* (Cambridge: Cambridge University Press, 2006); Bruce A. Elleman and S. C. M. Paine, *Naval Blockades and Seapower. Strategies and Counter-Strategies, 1805–2005* (London: Routledge, 2006).

[17] See Henri Meyrowitz, *Le principe de l'égalité des belligérants devant la droit de la guerre* (Paris: Pedone, 1970); Yoram Dinstein, *The Conduct of Hostilities under the Law of International Armed Conflict* (2nd edn, Cambridge: Cambridge University Press, 2010), 3.

[18] For a critical analysis of the approach by the UK, see Wolff Heintschel von Heinegg, 'Manoeuvring in Rough Waters: The UK Manual of the Law of Armed Conflict and the Law of Naval Warfare' in A. Fischer-Lescano et al, *Frieden in Freiheit. Peace in Liberty. Paix en liberté, Festschrift für Michael Bothe zum 70. Geburtstag* (Baden-Baden: Nomos, 2008), 428, 429 ff.

states. Hence, if, during an international armed conflict, a blockade is in compliance with the rules and principles of the law of air or naval warfare,[19] its legality may not be doubted. This is without prejudice to the powers of the UN Security Council to determine a wide-ranging obligation of the aggressor state, under the *jus ad bellum*, to compensate all losses suffered by other states and by individuals during the armed conflict.[20]

Finally, the international law of the sea does not restrict the exercise of belligerent rights at sea. According to the third sentence of the first paragraph of Article 87 of the 1982 UN Convention on the Law of the Sea (UNCLOS),[21] inter alia, the list of high seas freedoms in list a)–f) is not exhaustive. Accordingly, the freedom of the high seas also comprises other uses. Moreover, it is emphasized in the second sentence of Article 87(1) of UNCLOS that the freedom of the high seas is to be exercised not only 'under the conditions laid down by this Convention' but also 'by other rules of international law'. Hence, the admissibility and legality of military uses follows from either the law of naval warfare and neutrality at sea[22] or from other rules and principles of customary international law.[23]

C. Blockade Authorized as a Military Enforcement Measure

Article 42 of the UN Charter provides, inter alia, that the UN Security Council may decide on the establishment and enforcement of a blockade as a military enforcement measure. Nowadays, it is undisputed that the Council is entitled to authorize states to take such measures, by either specifically referring to blockade or by merely authorizing the use of 'all necessary means'.[24] Then, an individual state or a

[19] See *San Remo Manual*, paras 93–104; *HPCR Manual*, Section V.

[20] See SC Res 687 of 3 April 1991, para 16, in which the Security Council, inter alia, reaffirmed that 'Iraq…is liable under international law for any direct loss, damage—including environmental damage and the depletion of natural resources—or injury to foreign Governments, nationals or corporations as a result of its unlawful invasion and occupation of Kuwait'.

[21] A/CONF.62/121 (10 Dec 1982); 1833 UNTS 396.

[22] For an analysis of that law, see George P. Politakis, *Modern Aspects of the Laws of Naval Warfare and Maritime Neutrality* (London: Kegan Paul, 1998); Wolff Heintschel von Heinegg, *Seekriegsrecht und Neutralität im Seekrieg* (Berlin: Duncker & Humblot, 1995).

[23] Hence, it is made clear in the commentary to the ILA Helsinki Principles (at 498) that 'Although UNCLOS does not explicitly address questions arising out of wartime situations, its clauses on "other rules of international law" (e.g., Article 87, para. 1) include the law of armed conflict.'

[24] Jochen A. Frowein and Nico Krisch, 'Article 42' in Bruno Simma et al (eds), *The Charter of the United Nations: A Commentary* (2nd edn, Oxford: Oxford University Press, 2002), vol I, paras 20 ff. On the possible limits of an authorization, see Erika de Wet, *The Chapter VII Powers of the United Nations Security Council* (Oxford: Hart, 2004), 256 ff.

coalition of states would be provided with a sufficient legal basis for the establishment and enforcement[25] of an aerial and/or naval blockade.

In such instances, the armed forces of member states wishing to make use of the authorization will regularly not be UN personnel, as defined in the 1994 Convention on the Safety of United Nations and Associated Personnel.[26] The question thus arises whether and to what extent the law of blockade, as part of the *jus in bello*, governs the respective blockade. It would not suffice to merely refer to the national, that is, non-UN, status of the armed forces or to the existence of an international armed conflict and to apply the respective rules in an unmodified manner, if the Security Council has not expressly provided for exceptions.

On the one hand, there is no room for the traditional rules of neutrality if the Security Council has taken action under Chapter VII of the Charter.[27] Therefore, states not actively taking part in the enforcement measures cannot rely on their impartial stance and claim to remain unmolested by the measures taken. Rather, they are obliged to refrain from any activities that could jeopardize the effectiveness of such measures. On the other hand, the unmodified application of the *jus in bello* rules on blockade would jeopardize the very object and purpose of enforcement measures under Chapter VII—maintaining or restoring international peace and security. Therefore it is not possible to consider a blockade authorized by the Security Council void because it no longer complies with the principle of effectiveness. It must be stressed, however, that the principle of humanity and the ensuing obligations of the blockading power with a view to protecting the civilian population in the blockaded area continue to apply.[28]

D. Contested or Unresolved Legal Issues

While the foregoing findings most likely reflect the general consensus of states, there are some unresolved or even contested issues regarding the legality of blockades.

1. *Blockades in situations other than international armed conflict*

A highly contested issue relates to blockades established and enforced in situations not amounting to an international armed conflict. In this context it is important to distinguish two situations.

[25] With regard to the admissibility of the use of force, see Rob McLaughlin, 'The Legal Regime Applicable to Use of Lethal Force When Operating Under a United Nations Security Council Chapter VII Mandate Authorizing "All Necessary Means"' (2007) 12 *Journal of Conflict and Security Law* 389.

[26] Convention on the Safety of United Nations and Associated Personnel, Art 1(a), A749/49 (1994).

[27] See only *San Remo Manual*, paras 7–9; *HPCR Manual*, Rule 165.

[28] The practice of the Security Council provides sufficient evidence that humanitarian considerations have an impact on the scope of measures taken under Chapter VII of the Charter. See, inter alia, SC Res 661 of 6 August 1990. Further Heintschel von Heinegg, 'Blockade' in Wolfrum, *Max Planck Encyclopedia of Public International Law*, 973.

The first relates to the establishment of a blockade on the basis of the right of self-defence in response to an imminent armed attack by another state. In principle, the mere fact that a state exercises the right of self-defence by resorting to the use of armed force does not in and of itself bring into existence an international armed conflict.[29] However, if it is agreed that the law of international armed conflict becomes applicable 'whenever there is a resort to armed force between States'[30] it would be rather difficult to deny the existence of an international armed conflict if a state responds to an imminent armed attack by establishing a blockade against another state. However, if there existed no international armed conflict, the measures taken would have to comply with the recognized limitations, that is, necessity, proportionality, and imminence.[31] Measures aimed at preventing exit and entry of foreign neutral vessels and/or aircraft would be lawful under the right of self-defence in exceptional circumstances only because there would have to be a clear nexus to the armed attack. Enforcement measures taken against all vessels, that is, regardless of such a nexus, would most probably be contrary to the principles of necessity and proportionality. The state exercising the right of self-defence would be obliged to allow vessels that cannot be associated with the self-defence situation to leave or enter the coastal area in question. The measure in question would thus no longer qualify as a blockade but would have to be characterized as some form of interdiction operation.

The second situation relates to blockades established in the course of a non-international armed conflict. While there is general agreement that non-states parties to such a conflict are not entitled to make use of that method of warfare, it is less clear whether states parties would have the right to establish and enforce a blockade that is primarily directed against their opponent. According to the position taken here, there is no doubt that states are entitled to close parts of their territorial sea to foreign ships as long as the relevant provisions of the law of the sea are observed.[32] Entry into national airspace has always been dependent upon prior approval by the authorities of the state. If such conduct is admissible in peacetime it is, a fortiori, lawful in a situation of non-international armed conflict, which constitutes a threat to the security of the state. However, the measures taken must be strictly limited to the territorial sea and, to the extent Article 33 of UNCLOS is observed, the contiguous zone. Then, the closure of parts of a state's territorial sea no longer qualifies as

[29] See, inter alia, Terry D. Gill, *The 11th of September and the International Law of Military Operations* (Amsterdam: Vossiuspers, 2002), 22.

[30] International Criminal Tribunal for the Former Yugoslavia, *Prosecutor v. Tadić*, Decision on the Defence Motion for Interlocutory Appeal on Jurisdiction of 2 Oct 1995, IT-94-1-AR72, para 70.

[31] Yoram Dinstein, *War, Aggression and Self-Defence* (5th edn, Cambridge: Cambridge University Press, 2011), 230 ff.

[32] See esp UNCLOS, Art 25(3). On the wide margin of discretion enjoyed by the coastal states, see Robin R. Churchill and Vaughan Lowe, *The Law of the Sea* (3rd edn, Manchester: Manchester University Press, 1999), 87 ff.

a blockade. In sum, 'there is no consistent state practice and *opinio juris* suggesting blockade is available outside an [international armed conflict]'.[33]

Whether the establishment of a blockade is lawful in a non-international armed conflict is an issue that arose in the context of Israel's blockade of the Gaza Strip and its measures against the so-called Gaza Flotilla in 2010.[34] Those who considered Israel's blockade as contrary to international law argue, inter alia, that the conflict was non-international in character.[35] There are convincing arguments either in favour of the international character of the conflict or of the applicability of the law of international armed conflict and, thus, of the law of blockade.[36] If the law of international armed conflict was applicable to the Gaza blockade, neutral vessels and aircraft were obliged to respect the blockade and to comply with all legitimate orders by the blockade force.[37] Forcible resistance is considered an 'act of hostility' that renders the vessel or aircraft liable to attack.[38]

2. *Proportionality and humanity*

If a blockade constitutes a method of warfare, there is, in principle, no room for applying a general principle of proportionality. Rather, proportionality is to be assessed in the light of the *jus in bello*, that is, of the prohibition of excessive civilian casualties in relation to the military advantage anticipated and of starvation as a method of warfare.[39] The mere fact that a blockade has a negative impact on the supply of the civilian population in the blockaded area does not render a blockade unlawful. Of course, the blockading power is obliged to provide for relief consignments, if the civilian population of the blockaded area is no longer adequately provided with goods essential for its survival, that is, with food, water, and medical supplies.[40] It is, however, contested whether the facts on the ground justify the

[33] Douglas Guilfoyle, 'The *Mavi Marmara* Incident and Blockade in Armed Conflict' (2011) 81 *British Yearbook of International Law* 171, 217.

[34] For the facts, see Report of the Secretary-General's Panel of Inquiry on the 31 May 2010 Flotilla Incident, paras 83 ff (Sept 2011) (the 'Palmer Report').

[35] Guilfoyle, 'The *Mavi Marmara* Incident and Blockade in Armed Conflict', 176 ff; Andrew Sanger, 'The Contemporary Law of Blockade and the Gaza Freedom Flotilla' (2010) 13 *Yearbook of International Humanitarian Law* 397, 426 ff; Russell Buchan, 'The International Law of Naval Blockade and Israel's Interception of the *Mavi Marmara*' (2011) 58 *Netherlands International Law Review* 209, 216 ff.

[36] See Yoram Dinstein, *The International Law of Belligerent Occupation* (Cambridge: Cambridge University Press, 2009), 276 ff; HCJ 769/02 *Public Committee Against Torture v. Government* (2006); 2 IsrLR 459 (2006); The Public Commission to Examine the Maritime Incident of 31 May 2010, The Turkel Commission (Jan 2010), para 44; Palmer Report, para. 73. It should be noted that the authors referred to in n 35 are hesitant to bluntly deny the existence of an international armed conflict.

[37] See only Tucker, *The Law of War and Neutrality at Sea*, 335 fn 1; Colombos, *International Law of the Sea*, 769 ff.

[38] *San Remo Manual*, paras 98, 146, 153; Declaration concerning the Laws of Naval War, Art 63, London, 26 Feb 1909. See also Tucker, *The Law of War and Neutrality at Sea*, 336; Colombos, *International Law of the Sea*, 770.

[39] *San Remo Manual*, para 102; *HPCR Manual*, Rule 153.

[40] *San Remo Manual*, para 103; *HPCR Manual*, Rule 158.

conclusion that the civilian population is in fact no longer supplied with goods essential for its survival or that the civilian casualties are excessive in relation to the military advantage anticipated.[41]

It would fall short of the applicable law if the general principle of proportionality were disregarded altogether. Vessels and aircraft breaching or attempting to breach a blockade are liable to capture, not to attack.[42] They only lose their protection against attack if they effectively contribute to the enemy's military action or if they are actively resisting interception and capture.[43] Hence, the mere fact that vessels or aircraft endeavour to escape interception or capture does not mean that they may be sunk or shot down on sight. However, the blockading force may use all proportionate measures, including the use of force, with a view to stop a vessel or to force an aircraft to land on a designated airfield.[44] The permissible use of force may range from warning shots to disabling fire but must at all times be proportionate.

The same standards apply to measures taken against passengers and crew who actively resist enforcement measures taken by the blockade forces.[45] Again, as shown in the case of the Gaza blockade, establishing and analysing the facts in the light of proportionality is a most difficult undertaking and will only in exceptional cases result in a generally accepted legal evaluation.[46]

E. Further Observations on Blockade

The establishment, maintenance, and enforcement of a naval and/or aerial blockade are highly challenging tasks for the blockading power. In view of the principle of effectiveness there must be a high probability that vessels and/or aircraft are in fact prevented from entering or exiting the blockaded area. This presupposes that the blockading power exercises a considerable degree of superiority and that it applies the blockade in a strictly impartial manner. If those conditions are met, the blockading power is entitled to interfere not only with enemy but also with neutral

[41] With regard to the different evaluations of the situation in Gaza, see Guilfoyle, 'The *Mavi Marmara* Incident and Blockade in Armed Conflict', 198 ff; Buchan, 'The International Law of Naval Blockade and Israel's Interception of the *Mavi Marmara*', 232 ff; Sanger, 'The Contemporary Law of Blockade and the Gaza Freedom Flotilla', 435 ff; Palmer Report, 68 ff. It needs to be emphasized that the blockading power may prescribe the technical arrangements, including search, under which relief consignments are permitted. Moreover, it may be recalled that, in 2010, the Israeli government was prepared to allow the shipment of the flotilla's cargo to Gaza under the condition that it was unloaded in an Israeli port and that its distribution was entrusted to the UN. That proposal was well in accordance with the applicable law.

[42] *San Remo Manual*, para 98.

[43] *San Remo Manual*, para 98. See also *HPCR Manual*, Rule 174.

[44] See the references in nn 37 and 38.

[45] See the references in nn 37 and 38.

[46] Sanger, 'The Contemporary Law of Blockade and the Gaza Freedom Flotilla', 438 ff; Buchan, 'The International Law of Naval Blockade and Israel's Interception of the *Mavi Marmara*', 237 ff; Palmer Report, 61; Turkel Report, 263 ff.

navigation and aviation. It may be added that blockade is the only method of warfare by which a belligerent is entitled to prevent the exports of goods from enemy territory.

By its very nature, a blockade will very often have far-reaching effects on maritime and air traffic. Naturally, neutral states will not easily be prepared to accept belligerent measures interfering with their vessels and aircraft. The history of blockade gives ample examples of protests and other measures by which neutral states have doubted the legality of blockades as such or of enforcement measures taken by the blockading power.[47] It is, however, most doubtful whether such statements and measures may be understood as expressions of *opinio juris*. All too often, they have been merely political in character or guided by extralegal considerations. Under the law of blockade that is limited to situations of international armed conflict,[48] neutral states are obliged to tolerate interference with their shipping and aviation if the blockade is in compliance with the applicable *jus in bello*. If a neutral state decides to prevent the blockading power from exercising its rights, it either violates its obligations under the law of neutrality or it becomes a party to the conflict.

III. Interdiction Operations

Whereas blockade is a well-established legal concept, 'interdiction operations' is an operational term of art used for describing a variety of measures. Those measures have in common that, although to a varying degree, they have an impact on the freedom of navigation and/or overflight enjoyed by foreign aircraft and vessels. Moreover, they serve a common purpose insofar as they are to protect security interests either of individual states or of the international community. These common features may not distract from the fact that there are several distinct legal bases for interdiction operations. Those legal bases are exceptional in character insofar as they allow interference with foreign vessels and aircraft that, in principle, constitutes an infringement of the sovereignty of the flag state or the state of

[47] See the contributions in Elleman and Paine, *Naval Blockades and Seapower*; further Wolff Heintschel von Heinegg, 'Naval Blockade' in Michael N. Schmitt (ed), 'International Law Across the Spectrum of Conflict: Essays in Honour of Professor L. C. Green on the Occasion of His Eightieth Birthday' (2000) 75 *International Law Studies* 203–30.

[48] The same obligation arises from Art 25 of the UN Charter in the case of a binding decision taken by the UN Security Council under Chapter VII explicitly or implicitly authorizing the establishment of a blockade.

registry.[49] Hence, the legality of interdiction operations is subject to considerable legal limitations.

If interdictions operations are based on a decision taken by the UN Security Council under Chapter VII, their legality cannot be doubted.[50] Although the respective resolutions often lack the necessary clarity as to the concrete measures that are permissible under their terms,[51] interdiction operations authorized by the Council are not dealt with in the present chapter. Likewise, counter-piracy[52] and counter-proliferation[53] operations are not addressed because they are covered by other contributions of this volume.[54] Finally, measures against foreign aircraft and vessels taken during an international armed conflict, which are governed by the law of prize as part of the *jus in bello*[55] and not by the *jus ad bellum* cannot be addressed either.

A. Scope of Interdiction Operations

In the maritime context,[56] interdiction operations 'may range from querying the master of [a] vessel to stopping, boarding, inspecting, searching, and potentially seizing the cargo or the vessel'.[57] Moreover, states may establish zones around units and warn vessels that they could be considered as showing 'hostile intent' and that they risk being subjected to certain measures. Such zones may also be established in specified sea areas for various purposes, such as weapons exercises, military

[49] See also Michael A. Becker, 'The Shifting Public Order of the Oceans: Freedom of Navigation and the Interdiction of Ships at Sea' (2005) 46 *Harvard International Law Journal* 131; Douglas Guilfoyle, *Shipping Interdiction and the Law of the Sea* (Cambridge: Cambridge University Press, 2009); Wolff Heintschel von Heinegg, 'UNCLOS and Maritime Security Operations' (2005) 48 *German Yearbook of International Law* 151.

[50] See Lois E. Fielding, *Maritime Interception and U.N. Sanctions* (San Francisco, CA: Austin & Winfield, 1997).

[51] See only Fink, 'The Right of Visit for Warships', 12 ff.

[52] See Tullio Treves, 'Piracy, Law of the Sea, and Use of Force: Developments off the Coast of Somalia' (2009) 20 *European Journal of International Law* 399; Wolff Heintschel von Heinegg, 'Repressing Piracy and Armed Robbery at Sea—Towards a New International Legal Regime?' (2010) 40 *Israel Yearbook on Human Rights* 219.

[53] Michael Byers, 'Policing the High Seas: The Proliferation Security Initiative' (2004) 98 *American Journal of International Law* 526; Wolff Heintschel von Heinegg, 'The Proliferation Security Initiative—Security vs. Freedom of Navigation?' (2005) 35 *Israel Yearbook on Human Rights* 181.

[54] See Daniel H. Joyner, 'The Implications of the Proliferation of Weapons of Mass Destruction for the Prohibition of the Use of Force', Chapter 48 and Douglas Guilfoyle, 'The Use of Force against Pirates', Chapter 49 both in this volume.

[55] *San Remo Manual*, paras 112–58; *HPCR Manual*, Section U.

[56] See Craig H. Allen, 'A Primer on the Non-Proliferation Regime for Maritime Security Operation Forces' (2007) 54 *Naval Law Review* 51, who rightly states that maritime interception operations (MIOs), have become a 'familiar element in the daily routine of units assigned to the maritime component of combined and joint forces commands' (at 51).

[57] Terry D. Gill and Dieter Fleck (eds), *The Handbook of the International Law of Military Operations* (Oxford: Oxford University Press, 2010), para 20.01.

manoeuvres, or the protection of 'high-value targets'.[58] In the aerial context, similar measures may be taken with a view to identifying an aircraft's nationality, course, cargo, or passengers, for instance by intercepting the aircraft and/or ordering it to land at a specified airfield or airport.[59] These zones will in most cases also be applied and enforced against aircraft. Finally, states may subject aircraft and vessels to restrictions, in the exercise of their right of self-defence.

If international law provides a legal basis for any such interdiction operations, the aircraft or vessels affected will regularly be obliged to comply with all legitimate orders. If they do not comply, they either operate at their own risk or they may be subjected to measures enforcing the exercise of the right in question. However, whether the right may be enforced by the use of proportionate force depends on the applicable legal basis.

B. Legal Bases under International Treaties

With regard to maritime interdiction operations (MIO) both UNCLOS and the Suppression of Unlawful Acts (SUA) Convention, as amended by the 2005 Protocol,[60] provide the legal bases necessary for an interference with foreign shipping. Further legal bases are provided by special treaties.

1. *UN Convention on the Law of the Sea*

The right of coastal states to interfere, within their territorial sea, with foreign vessels is recognized by Articles 25 and 27 of UNCLOS. According to the latter provision the coastal state may exercise its criminal jurisdiction on board a foreign ship, that is, it may arrest persons, conduct investigations, and temporarily capture the vessel, if crimes have been committed on board during passage. However, a breach of the domestic criminal law of the coastal state will justify the exercise of its criminal jurisdiction only in cases where the crime has been committed on board a ship passing through the territorial sea after having left the coastal state's internal waters

[58] With regard to the different purposes of maritime zones and their legal bases, see Richard Jacques, *Maritime Operational Zones* (Newport, RI: US Naval War College, 2006).

[59] See Michael N. Schmitt, 'Air Law and Military Operations' in Gill and Fleck, *The Handbook of the International Law of Military Operations*, paras 18.05, 18.06, 18.07, 18.12, and accompanying commentary.

[60] Convention for the Suppression of Unlawful Acts Against the Safety of Maritime Navigation (SUA Convention), Rome, 10 Mar 1988, 1678 UNTS 221; reprinted in (1988) 27 ILM 668. Protocol for the Suppression of Unlawful Acts against the Safety of Fixed Platforms Located on the Continental Shelf, Rome, 10 Mar 1988, 1678 UNTS 304; Protocol of 2005 to the Convention for the Suppression of Unlawful Acts Against the Safety of Maritime Navigation, London, 14 Oct 2005, IMO Doc LEG/CONF. 15/21; Protocol of 2005 to the Protocol for the Suppression of Unlawful Acts against the Safety of Fixed Platforms Located on the Continental Shelf, London, 14 Oct 2005, IMO Doc LEG/CONF. 15/22.

(Art 27(2)). If the vessel concerned has not left a port of the coastal state the exercise of criminal jurisdiction, according to Article 27(1), is limited. If the crime giving rise to interdiction measures has been committed before entry into the territorial sea and if the ship, proceeding from a foreign port, is only passing through the territorial sea without entering internal waters, the coastal state may not take any steps on board the ship.[61] According to Article 25(1), the coastal state 'may take the necessary steps in its territorial sea to prevent passage which is not innocent'. According to Article 19(1), passage is not innocent if it is 'prejudicial to the peace, good order or security of the coastal State' or if the vessel is engaged in one of the activities listed in Article 19(2).

Coastal states are entitled to take enforcement measures against foreign ships in sea areas beyond the outer limit of the territorial sea, if they have proclaimed a contiguous zone.[62] Such measures 'may be taken only in respect of offences committed within the territory or territorial sea of a State, not in respect of anything done within the contiguous zone itself.'[63]

Coastal states also enjoy the right of 'hot pursuit'.[64] However, an arrest after hot pursuit is legal only if pursuit has commenced within the sea areas mentioned in Article 111(1) and (2), it has been continuous, and in compliance with the further conditions laid down in that article.

Apart from 'hot pursuit', foreign vessels may only be boarded in high seas areas, if 'there is reasonable ground for suspicion' that they are engaged in one of the activities enumerated in Article 110(1). According to Article 92(2), vessels flying the 'flags of two or more States, using them according to convenience,... may be assimilated to a ship without nationality' and they may be boarded in accordance with Article 110. The right of visit is limited to the verification of 'the ship's right to fly its flag'. The intercepting warship or military aircraft may only take those measures that are necessary to verify whether the grounds for suspicion prove to be founded.[65] If suspicion remains after the documents have been checked, a further examination on board the ship may 'be carried out with all possible consideration.'[66] Article 110 gives no guidance as to the further measures that may be taken against a vessel if the suspicions prove to be founded. However, the right of visit would be futile if the vessel could not be diverted to a designated port under the command of the boarding team.

Finally, under Article 98, there is a duty to render assistance to all persons who are in distress at sea. Rendering such assistance may imply the necessity to prevent other ships or aircraft from approaching the respective area or from interfering with

[61] UNCLOS, Art 27(5). Note, however, that this restriction does not apply to cases provided for in UNCLOS Part XII on the protection of the marine environment or with respect to violations of laws and regulations adopted in accordance with Part V.

[62] UNCLOS, Art 33.

[63] Churchill and Lowe, *The Law of the Sea*, 137.

[64] UNCLOS, Art 111.

[65] According to UNCLOS, Art 110(4), 'these provisions apply mutatis mutandis to military aircraft.'

[66] UNCLOS, Art 110(2).

the rescue operation. If distress arose due to the conduct of a vessel, the only option may be to take measures against the vessel, in order to either prevent or to terminate the conduct.

2. *Convention for the Suppression of Unlawful Acts Against the Safety of Maritime Navigation (SUA Convention) of 1988 (as amended in 2005)*

According to the SUA Convention, as amended by the 2005 Protocols, foreign merchant vessels encountered on the high seas may be boarded and searched if there are grounds for suspicion that they are involved in either of the offences specified in Articles 3, 3*bis*, 3*ter*, or 3*quater*, and if the flag state has authorized those measures.[67] The necessary consent by the flag states, according to Article 8*bis*, paragraph 5, may be given in advance and in a general manner. It is important to note that, according to Article 8*bis*, paragraph 9, the use of force is allowed, 'when necessary to ensure the safety of its officials and persons on board, or where the officials are obstructed in the execution of the authorized actions.' However, 'Any use of force pursuant to this article shall not exceed the minimum degree of force which is necessary and reasonable in the circumstances.'

3. *Other treaties*

Flag states and states of registry may always consent to the boarding of their vessels or to the interception of their civil aircraft by special agreement. For instance, such agreements have been concluded by the US and various flag states with a view to preventing the proliferation of weapons of mass destruction by non-state actors.[68] Moreover, boarding is permissible under regional treaties concerning the suppression of illicit trafficking of drugs at sea or in the air.[69]

4. *Enforcing interdiction rights under existing treaties*

Apart from the 2005 SUA Convention, as amended in 2005, the treaties referred to earlier do not expressly provide for the use of force if the vessel or aircraft does not comply with the legitimate orders by the warship or military aircraft or if it actively resists visit, boarding, capture, or diversion. According to those treaties, the intercepted vessels and aircraft are obliged to tolerate the exercise of the respective

[67] See also Stuart Kaye, 'Threats from the Global Commons: Problems of Jurisdiction and Enforcement' in Michael D. Carsten (ed), 'Global Legal Challenges: Command of the Commons, Strategic Communications and Natural Disasters' (2007) 86 *International Law Studies* 69, 74 ff.

[68] The agreements are available at <http://www.state.gov/t/isn/trty/index.htm>.

[69] See, inter alia, the Agreement concerning Cooperation in Suppressing Illicit Maritime and Air Trafficking in Narcotic Drugs and Psychotropic Substances in the Caribbean Area, San Jose, 10 Apr 2003.

measures. Hence, any act of non-compliance or of active resistance triggers the right of the intercepting warship or military aircraft to resort to the use of force that is strictly necessary to enforce compliance or to overcome resistance. Only that degree of force necessary is permissible to enforce the right in question. It may therefore be in accordance with the law to fire warning shots or to apply other measures that are apt to induce the vessel or aircraft to comply with the respective orders or to desist from further resistance. However, the use of lethal force will be lawful in exceptional cases only and will most probably be limited to situations of self-defence. For instance, if an act of resistance amounts to an imminent armed attack against a boarding team, the use of deadly force, while not permissible under a law enforcement paradigm, would be lawful under the right of self-defence.[70]

c. Applicability of Prize Law During Non-International Armed Conflicts?

During an international armed conflict, belligerents are entitled to exercise prize measures, that is, to capture enemy merchant vessels and aircraft and to visit, search, and, if there are reasonable grounds for suspicion that they are engaged in the carriage of contraband, to capture neutral merchant vessels and civil aircraft.[71] States parties to a non-international armed conflict sometimes resort to the use of prize measures. It is, however, doubtful whether in the course of a non-international armed conflict foreign vessels and aircraft may be subjected to visit and search under the law of prize.

The government that is confronted with insurgents, rebels, etc is entitled to suspend the right of innocent passage through the territorial sea[72] and to prohibit access to the ports controlled by the rebels. Accordingly, it may use all necessary means, including the use of force, in order to prevent such passage or access. However, measures in the sea areas beyond the outer limit of the territorial sea and in the airspace above seem to have no basis in international law.

During the non-international armed conflicts in Spain[73], Algeria,[74] and Sri Lanka[75] the parties took the position that they were entitled to interfere with foreign

[70] For the legality of the use of force in maritime interdiction operations, see Wolff Heintschel von Heinegg, 'Maritime Interception/Interdiction Operations' in Gill and Fleck, *The Handbook of the International Law of Military Operations*, para 20.12 and accompanying commentary.

[71] *San Remo Manual*, paras 112–58; *HPCR Manual*, Section U; ILA Helsinki Principles, para 5.2.

[72] See n 32 and accompanying text.

[73] Norman J. Padelford, 'Foreign Shipping During the Spanish Civil War' (1938) 32 *American Journal of International Law* 264.

[74] Laurent Lucchini, 'Actes de contrainte exercés par la France en Haute Mer au cours des opérations en Algérie' (1966) *Annuaire Français de Droit International* 803. See also Daniel P. O'Connell, 'International Law and Contemporary Naval Operations' (1970) 44 *British Yearbook of International Law* 19, 36 ff.

[75] Guilfoyle, 'The *Mavi Marmara* Incident and Blockade in Armed Conflict', 193.

merchant vessels on the high seas in order to prevent the flow of arms and other materiel to the respective opponent. The reactions by the affected flag states were far from uniform.[76] Moreover, even those states that were not prepared to consider the Gaza conflict as an international armed conflict did not protest against Israel's exercise of the right of visit and search.[77]

Guilfoyle believes that 'On the basis of relevant state practice one can at most hazard a suggestion that irrespective of the precise classification of a conflict, states are likely to tolerate the assertion of a blockade only in cases of higher-intensity conflicts on a par with the traditional understanding of war.'[78] However, the intensity of a non-international armed conflict is but one indicator for the legality of interdiction operations by the state that is party to a non-international armed conflict. Intensity is not sufficient to justify the applicability of the law of prize that is applicable in international armed conflict only.[79]

The definition of lawful military objectives applies in non-international armed conflict.[80] There is no convincing reason that would justify its limitation to vessels and aircraft of the nationality of the state concerned. Accordingly, any vessel, regardless of the flag it is flying, and any aircraft, wherever registered, used by an organized armed group in the course of a non-international armed conflict for military purposes constitutes a lawful military objective by either nature or use. Hence, the parties to a non-international armed conflict will not refrain from attacking such vessels or aircraft as soon as they have left the territorial sea or the national airspace. It is not to be expected that other states will protest attacks on such vessels and aircraft for the sole reason that such attacks occurred in international sea areas or in international airspace. If such vessels and aircraft may be attacked, it is of course lawful to capture them (and to enforce capture by the use of force).

The intensity of armed hostilities during a non-international armed conflict may, under exceptional circumstances, constitute an element of proof for the necessity of interdiction operations in high seas areas. State practice during non-international armed conflicts seems to justify the conclusion that the state

[76] See the references in nn 73 and 74.

[77] In 2008 and until the establishment of the blockade of Gaza on 3 Jan 2009, Israel exercised the right of visit and search in order to prevent the flow of arms into the Gaza Strip. It seems that the few measures taken against foreign vessels that were suspected, on reasonable grounds, of being engaged in the transportation of arms destined to the Hamas, did not give rise to strong protests. Either the flag states implicitly recognized Israel's security interests or they simply did not want to admit that the ships flying their flags had been engaged in the smuggling of arms and ammunition.

[78] Guilfoyle, 'The *Mavi Marmara* Incident and Blockade in Armed Conflict', 193 ff.

[79] Prize measures are part of the law of neutrality that does not apply to situations of non-international armed conflict. See James Kraska, 'Prize Law' in Wolfrum, *Max Planck Encyclopedia of Public International Law*, vol VIII, 477.

[80] Jean-Marie Henckaerts and Louise Doswald-Beck (eds), *Customary International Humanitarian Law* (Cambridge: Cambridge University Press, 2005), vol I (Rules), 30 ff; Michael N. Schmitt, Charles H. B. Garraway, and Yoram Dinstein, *The Manual on the Law of Non-International Armed Conflict. With Commentary* (San Remo, Mar 2006), para 1.1.4.

party to a non-international armed conflict—not the non-state actor—is entitled to resort to interdiction operations on the high seas and in international airspace if: (1) vital security interests of the state must be at stake; (2) there are reasonable grounds for suspicion that the foreign vessels and aircraft are engaged in activities jeopardizing those security interests (eg by supplying the non-state party with arms); (3) the measures are taken in close vicinity to the conflict area; and (4) the measures are necessary and proportionate.[81] If those conditions are fulfilled, the legal basis for the interdiction operations is not prize law. Rather, the legal basis is to be seen in the right of self-defence or in the customary right of self-preservation in order to protect the territorial and political integrity of the state. The finding by the International Court of Justice that the right of self-defence does not apply if there is no transborder element[82] finds no basis in state practice.

D. Other Legal Bases?

While it is uncontested that consent by the flag state or by the state of registry constitutes a sufficient legal basis for the exercise of interdiction operations against foreign vessels and aircraft, there is less agreement with regard to other legal bases that have been asserted by states and by legal scholars.

1. *Master's consent*

States disagree as to whether the consent of the master suffices to justify the boarding and search of a foreign vessel. Indeed, the flag state principle and the underlying principle of state sovereignty seem to justify the conclusion that, absent express exceptions in international treaty or customary law, the consent of the flag state or state of registry is paramount to the legality of any act of interference. The boarding and searching of foreign vessels and aircraft constitutes an exercise of jurisdiction that by necessity violates the 'exclusive jurisdiction'[83] of the flag state.[84] Since the master is not entitled to waive the flag state's jurisdiction, his consent is legally irrelevant. Some states take the position that master's consent justifies the exercise of so-called 'consensual boarding',[85] because the 'plenary authority of the master over

[81] eg the measures taken by France in the course of the Algerian conflict and those taken by the Sri Lankan government during the long-lasting conflict with the Tamil Tigers were not protested by all states whose vessels were affected.

[82] *Legal Consequences of the Construction of a Wall in the Occupied Palestinian Territory*, Advisory Opinion, ICJ Rep 2004, para 139: 'The Court also notes that Israel exercises control in the Occupied Palestinian Territory and that...the threat which it regards as justifying the construction of the wall originates within, and not outside, that territory. The situation is thus different from that contemplated by Security Council resolutions 1368 (2001) and 1373 (2001)...Consequently, the Court concludes that Article 51 of the Charter has no relevance in this case.'

[83] See only UNCLOS, Art 92(1).

[84] See also Fink, 'The Right of Visit for Warships', 36 ff.

[85] NWP 1-14M, para 3.11.2.5.2.

all activities related to the operation of his vessel while in international waters is well established in international law and includes the authority to allow anyone to come aboard his vessel as his guest, including foreign law enforcement officials.'[86] However, this does not mean that such consent provides a legal basis for the exercise of maritime enforcement jurisdiction. Although the 'voluntary consent of the master permits the boarding,... it does not allow the assertion of law enforcement authority. A consensual boarding is not, therefore, an exercise of maritime law enforcement jurisdiction *per se*.'[87] Moreover, it may not be left out of consideration that every 'consensual boarding' is 'subject to conditions imposed by the master and may be terminated by the master at his discretion.'[88] Hence, if accepted as a legal basis, a master's consent will at best serve as a tool for verifying a vessel's true nature, its cargo, documents, and destination but not for enforcement measures that go beyond such verification.

2. *Right of individual or collective self-defence*

It is unclear whether and to what extent the right of individual or collective self-defence provides a basis for interdiction operations. Of course, in the case of an imminent armed attack the victim state is entitled to take all necessary and proportionate measures in order to eliminate the self-defence situation. If and insofar as foreign vessels and aircraft by their conduct directly contribute to the imminent armed attack, they may be made the objects of self-defence measures, including interdiction operations. The same holds true if there are reasonable grounds for suspicion that the vessels and aircraft are used in support of the imminent armed attack. Then, however, the exercise of the right of self-defence is limited to what is strictly necessary and proportionate and will only in exceptional circumstances justify the use of deadly force.[89]

According to the position taken here, the interdiction operations conducted by the US in the Persian Gulf were therefore not justified because of the rather vague wording of Security Council Resolution 661 (1990),[90] as submitted by Zeigler,[91] but rather because they were taken in response to the illegal attack by Iraq against Kuwait. It may be recalled that Security Council Resolution 661 (1990) called for the embargo of trade to and from Iraq and Kuwait, but did not specifically authorize interdiction operations.[92] Still, between 16 August and 25 August 1990 the US conducted such operations.[93] Contrary to the argument of Zeigler, a resolution

[86] NWP 1-14M, para 3.11.2.5.2. See also David G. Wilson, 'Interdiction on the High Seas: The Role and Authority of a Master in the Boarding and Searching of His Ship by Foreign Warships' (2008) 55 *Naval Law Review* 157.

[87] Wilson, 'Interdiction on the High Seas', 157.

[88] Wilson, 'Interdiction on the High Seas', 157.

[89] Heintschel von Heinegg, 'Maritime Interception/Interdiction Operations' in Gill and Fleck, *The Handbook of the International Law of Military Operations*, 375.

[90] SC Res 661 of 6 Aug 1990.

[91] Richard D. Zeigler, 'Ubi Sumus? Quo Vadimus? Charting the Course of Maritime Interception Operations', Naval War College Paper, Newport, RI, 1995, 69, also published in (1996) 43 *Naval Law Review* 1.

[92] SC Res 661, para 3.

[93] According to Zeigler, 'Ubi Sumus?, 119, 'there were, between August 17, 1990 and 28 February 1991, only eleven warning shots fired, no use of disabling fire, only eleven takedown actions, and a mere 51

only serves as a legal basis for such operations if the UN Security Council either expressly authorizes member states to that effect, as it did in Resolution 665 (1990), or if it uses the phrase 'all necessary means'. If the resolution only obliges member states to comply with an embargo, this as such does not imply the authorization of enforcement measures against foreign vessels and aircraft. It must be borne in mind that, in 1991, the use of force against Iraq did not necessarily constitute a military enforcement measure under Chapter VII of the Charter. Rather Security Council Resolution 678 (1990)[94] was an endorsement of the exercise of the right of collective self-defence. None of the resolutions adopted by the Security Council can be interpreted as limiting the exercise of the right of self-defence. Hence, the states cooperating with Kuwait were entitled to autonomously decide upon the point in time at which to exercise the right of collective self-defence.

Another problem with regard to the right of self-defence relates to interdiction operations within the framework of counterterrorism operations. For instance, states contributing to Operation Enduring Freedom based the right of visit either on the *jus in bello*, flag state consent, or the right of self-defence.[95] Operation Active Endeavour was based on Article V of the Washington Treaty but the measures taken were limited to 'compliant boardings'.[96] Obviously, none of the states claimed the right to undertake other interdiction operations. It is interesting that the right of self-defence continues to serve as a legal basis for those counterterrorism operations although states do not seem to be prepared to specify the exact nature and scope of measures they consider a lawful exercise of the right of self-defence with regard to maritime interdiction operations. This lack of clarity is certainly an obstacle to the development of a distinct legal regime applicable to interdiction operations. Moreover, it leaves the armed forces entrusted with counterterrorism operations in a legal grey area that will prevent them from taking the measures necessary to effectively eliminate the threat posed by transnational terrorism.

3. *Zones*

The 'appropriate measures' taken within safety zones provided for in Article 60(4) of UNCLOS might be considered a form of maritime interdiction operation. In view of their limited extent of 500 metres they do not pose a noteworthy obstacle to international shipping and can therefore be ignored here.

However, warning zones may have an impact on the exercise of the freedoms of navigation and overflight. Such warning zones may be established around naval units operating in an uncertain operating environment. Their object is:

> to help sort the common operational picture and ascertain the intent of inbound entities. This objective may be accomplished during peacetime while adhering to international law

diversions of vessels. Most of the warning shots were fired by U.S. vessels early in the operation, even before August 25, 1990, the effective date of U.N. Security Council Resolution 665.'

[94] SC Res 678 of 29 Nov 1990. [95] See only Fink, 'The Right of Visit for Warships', 30 ff.
[96] See only Fink, 'The Right of Visit for Warships', 30 ff.

as long as the navigational rights of other ships, submarines, and aircraft are respected. Specifically, when operating in international waters, commanders may assert notice (via NOTAMs [Notices to Airmen] and NOTMARs [Notices to Mariners]) that within a certain geographic area, for a certain period of time, dangerous military activities will be taking place. Commanders may request that entities traversing the area communicate with them and state their intentions. Moreover, such notice may include reference to the fact that if ships and aircraft traversing the area are deemed to represent an imminent threat to U.S. naval forces they may be subject to proportionate measures in self-defense. Ships and aircraft are not required to remain outside such zones and force may not be used against such entities merely because they entered the zone. Commanders may use force against such entities only to defend against a hostile act or demonstrated hostile intent, including interference with declared military activities.[97]

Hence, warning zones are a tool used for force protection purposes and should not be considered as a type of maritime interdiction operation.

Other zones, especially 'exclusion zones', may not be made use of in peacetime,[98] unless they are strictly necessary and proportionate for self-defence purposes. However, this will be the case in rather exceptional circumstances only.[99]

4. *Countermeasures*

If it is accepted that the UN Security Council may impose, in a general and abstract manner, obligations upon states with regard to, for instance, the suppression of transnational terrorism[100] or the proliferation of weapons of mass destruction, including their delivery systems,[101] states not complying with the terms of such resolutions commit an internationally wrongful act. According to the position taken here, those states that are specially affected by the internationally wrongful act are entitled to take countermeasures.[102] Such countermeasures may include the exercise of interdiction operations against the vessels flying the flag, or against aircraft registered in, the state that is in violation of its obligations under the respective resolution, if there are reasonable grounds for suspicion that the aircraft or vessels are engaged in prohibited activities.[103] It will have to be seen whether states are

[97] NWP 1-14M, para 4.4.7.

[98] For the establishment of exclusion zones under the law of international armed conflict, see *San Remo Manual*, paras 105–8; *HPCR Manual*, Section P.

[99] For a theoretical example, see Wolff Heintschel von Heinegg, 'Current Legal Issues in Maritime Operations: Maritime Interception Operations in the Global War on Terrorism, Exclusion Zones, Hospital Ships and Maritime Neutrality' in Richard B. Jaques (ed), 'Issues in International Law and Military Operations' (2006) 80 *International Law Studies* 207, 214 ff.

[100] SC Res 1373 of 28 Sept 2001.

[101] SC Res 1540 of 28 Apr 2004.

[102] International Law Commission, Responsibility of States for Internationally Wrongful Acts, Arts 22 and 49–53, GA Res 56/83 Annex, A/RES/56/83 (12 Dec 2001).

[103] See Heintschel von Heinegg, 'Current Legal Issues in Maritime Operations' in Jaques, *Issues in International Law and Military Operations*, 213.

prepared to make use of that justification and to ground interdiction operations on that legal basis.

IV. Concluding Remarks

According to well-established rules of the *jus in bello*, a naval or aerial blockade is a lawful method of warfare aimed at preventing all vessels and/or aircraft from entering or leaving the blockaded enemy port, airfield, or coastline. While the circumstances prevailing at the time may cast doubts on the legality of measures enforcing a blockade with regard to the principles of humanity and proportionality, there seems to be general agreement that the parties to an international armed conflict are entitled to make use of blockade and thus interfere considerably with the shipping and aviation of neutral states. According to the position taken here, blockade is a method of warfare that may not be applied in non-international armed conflicts. States parties to such conflict may impose those restrictions that are in accordance with general international law, especially with the law of the sea. However, those measures do not qualify as blockades proper.

If the UN Security Council, acting under Chapter VII, authorizes the establishment and enforcement of a naval or aerial blockade, the states making use of such authorization are not bound by the strict conditions of the traditional law of blockade.

The legal assessment is less clear when it comes to interdiction operations. Security Council resolutions authorizing interdiction operations are all too often vague and do not provide a satisfactory legal basis, especially with regard to the status of persons and objects and the scope of measures that may be taken. The same holds true with regard to the legal bases in international treaties and customary international law. Either they lack the necessary legal clarity or there is no sufficient agreement on their scope. Although states increasingly entrust their armed forces with the exercise of interdiction operations on the high seas or in international airspace, they seem to be unwilling to provide them with legal tools that are operable, specific, and, what is more important, based on a sufficient international consensus. Moreover, the various rules of international treaty and customary law that either directly or indirectly have an impact on the legality of interdiction operations are not applied in the necessary comprehensive manner. Hence, the law may be progressively developed in one area of international law without the other relevant areas of international law being duly taken into consideration. It is therefore important that states willing to take part in interdiction operations take a concerted approach with a view to identifying the legal issues involved and to arrive at a consented legal regime applicable to interdiction operations. However, in view of the vital importance of the freedoms of navigation and overflight, such efforts should not be too proactive and should not focus on current security interests thus ignoring the mid-term and long-term effects.

CHAPTER 44

RESCUING NATIONALS ABROAD

MATHIAS FORTEAU*

I. Introduction

DESPITE the fundamental nature in contemporary international law of the prohibition of the use of force and of the principle of territorial integrity, states (at least some of them) seem still to consider, as their practice shows, that they are not prohibited to use force unilaterally to rescue their nationals abroad when their life or security is threatened. Facts and law in that regard contradict each other, which explains to a large extent the continuing uncertainty of international law on this issue—which has not been really clarified by international courts or tribunals. As one commentator put it, the question of rescuing nationals abroad remains today 'one of the most hotly debated issues of the *Ius ad Bellum*'.[1]

Admittedly, the International Court of Justice (ICJ) in its judgment on the merits in the *Corfu Channel* case seemed to exclude any kind of military interventions, including the 'methods of self-protection or self-help', other than those expressly enshrined in the UN Charter. According to the ICJ:

> the alleged right of intervention... cannot... find a place in international law... [b]etween independent States, respect for territorial sovereignty is an essential foundation of

* This chapter benefits from the research assistance of M. Kerim Uster, Research Assistant at the UN International Law Commission during its 64th session (2012). I wish to express my thanks for his valuable aid.

[1] Tom Ruys, *'Armed Attack' and Article 51 of the UN Charter: Evolutions in Customary Law and Practice* (Cambridge: Cambridge University Press, 2010), 214.

international relations. The Court recognizes that the Albanian Government's complete failure to carry out its duties after the explosions, and the dilatory nature of its diplomatic notes, are extenuating circumstances for the action of the United Kingdom Government. But to ensure respect for international law, of which it is the organ, the Court must declare that the action of the British Navy constituted a violation of Albanian Sovereignty.[2]

But it has to be noted that the *Corfu Channel* case did not concern rescuing nationals abroad as such.

Similarly, if the ICJ 'express[ed] its concern in regard to the United States' incursion into Iran' occurring when the Court was preparing its judgment in *Diplomatic and Consular Staff* (a case which is directly relevant to rescuing nationals abroad since it involved the detention of US hostages in and by Iran), the Court did not condemn the operation on the ground of the prohibition of the use of force but rather because 'an operation undertaken in those circumstances [the Court preparing its judgment], from whatever motive, is of a kind calculated to undermine respect for the judicial process in international relations' and because, additionally, it violated the 1979 Order of the Court on provisional measures.[3] Had the Court been seized of this dispute (ie the legality of the US operation), it could have perhaps considered that the US incursion in Iranian territory was not reprehensible.[4]

The uncertainty of international law on this matter has objective grounds. It results, to a large extent, from the necessity and the difficulty to articulate two concurrent, *and equally legitimate*, state powers. Contrary to *intervention d'humanité* or Responsibility to Protect doctrines, in which states claim a right to intervene on the sole basis of the gravity of the crimes alleged to have occurred regardless of the nationality of the individuals concerned and wherever the violations take place, rescuing nationals abroad is based on a more classical and less disputable legal ground: the personal jurisdiction of the state of nationality. Hence, the relevant issue concerning rescuing nationals abroad is not to assess in the abstract whether international law allows or prohibits states to intervene, but rather to determine how personal and territorial jurisdictions must concretely be coordinated when the lives or security of nationals are threatened abroad.

In 1925, the arbitrator in the *British Property in Spanish Morocco* case, Max Huber, apparently considered that in such a case priority had to be given to personal jurisdiction over territorial jurisdiction.[5] It is not clear, however, whether this gave rise

[2] *Corfu Channel (UK v. Albania)*, Judgment of 9 Apr 1949, ICJ Rep 1949, 4, 35. See also Jean-Marie Henckaerts et al, *Customary International Humanitarian Law. Vol I: Rules* (Cambridge: ICRC/ Cambridge University Press, 2009), 513, stating that 'States cannot use force in a manner unauthorised by the Charter to ensure respect for international humanitarian law'.

[3] Judgment of 24 May 1980, ICJ Rep 1980, 43, para 93.

[4] Joseph J. Eldred, 'The Use of Force in Hostage Rescue Missions' (2008) *Naval Law Review* 265–7.

[5] *Case of British Interests in Spanish Morocco (Spain v. UK)* (1925) II RIAA 615, 641 (original in French only): 'il est incontestable qu'à un certain point l'intérêt d'un Etat de pouvoir protéger ses ressortissants

to a right to *military* intervention.[6] In any event, the award was delivered 20 years before the adoption of the UN Charter and three years before the adoption of the Kellogg–Briand Pact, hence before any prohibition of the use of force. It therefore has little relevance in contemporary international law.

As international case law is rather scarce and not entirely decisive, as noted earlier, it is of the utmost importance to look in detail at state practice, as clarified by scholars, to determine, as far as possible, the current position of international law on the permissibility of rescuing nationals abroad. As this chapter will show, such an analysis proves quite deceptive. It shows first that the notion of 'rescuing nationals abroad' is not entirely clear from a legal point of view (Section II) and, secondly, that practice since 1945 (Section III), including more recent practice (Section IV) remains ambiguous with regard to the legality of the use of force to rescue nationals abroad.

II. Definitions

At first sight, 'rescuing nationals abroad' can be defined in broad terms as meaning the use of operational resources by a state to guarantee the security of its nationals whose lives or physical integrity are threatened in the territory of another state, especially by organizing their repatriation. Such a definition, however, is not very satisfactory from a legal point of view since it is not focused on the core issue, which lies in the admissibility of the argument of the necessity of rescuing nationals abroad as a *legal justification to circumvent the prohibition of the use of force.* Given the fundamental nature of the prohibition in modern international law, it is all the more necessary to circumscribe more precisely both the legal scope of the justification (Section II.A) and its legal nature (Section II.B).

A. Legal Scope of the Justification Based on the Necessity of Rescuing Nationals Abroad

The legal scope of the justification based on the necessity of rescuing nationals abroad remains rather uncertain for three key reasons.

et leurs biens doit primer le respect de la souveraineté territoriale, et cela même en l'absence d'obligations conventionnelles. Ce droit d'intervention a été revendiqué par tous les Etats; ses limites seules peuvent être discutées. En le niant, on arriverait à des conséquences inadmissibles: on désarmerait le droit international vis-à-vis d'injustices équivalant à la négation de la personnalité humaine…'

[6] The *British Interests* case dealt with the possibility of claiming compensation, not to use force.

First, one can legitimately ask to what extent rescuing nationals abroad really concerns the use of force as such. When no force is used to rescue nationals abroad, there is no need to invoke such a justification since it implies that the consent of the host state had been given or, at least, that no measures of *constraint* took place.[7] But even when force is resorted to, the question remains whether it can be equated with 'the use of force' as prohibited under Article 2(4) of the UN Charter. As Corten put it, 'The question of the lawfulness of minor coercive acts such as international abductions or even very limited police operations remains open'.[8] In the Guyana/Suriname arbitration, the Tribunal accepted, for instance, 'the argument that in international law force [as distinguished from military action] may be used in law enforcement activities provided that such force is unavoidable, reasonable and necessary'.[9] Therefore, it could be argued that (in some circumstances at least) forcible action to rescue nationals abroad can be viewed as a (legal) limited 'police action' rather than as a (prohibited) use of force.

Secondly, the definition of 'nationals' for the purpose of assessing the legality of rescuing nationals abroad is far from clear. Can in particular a state rescue any of its nationals, including when the national possesses the nationality of the host state? In 2006, the International Law Commission (ILC) codified the principle of 'predominant nationality' according to which a state cannot exercise diplomatic protection in respect of a person against a state of which that person is also a national if the nationality of that state is predominant.[10] This rule applies only for the purpose of the law of diplomatic protection which consists in a *claim* which does not result in *executive* action.[11] One could ask, however, whether it could be applied by analogy in the field of the use of force.[12] This issue remains unsettled in contemporary international law, although it has been raised recently. Indeed, part of the justification for the Russian use of force against Georgia in August 2008 was based on the granting of Russian citizenship to South Ossetians (the granting of which, by itself,

[7] See eg the action undertaken by France in Feb 2011 when it repatriated French people from Tripoli (Libya). The same non-forcible action was undertaken in Mar 2011 following the nuclear incident in Japan and in Dec 2008 following the terrorist attacks in Bombay (see for more information the website of the French Ministry of Defence at <http://www.defense.gouv.fr>); and the evacuation of European people from Lebanon during the 2006 war between Israel and Lebanon (see the EU press release (Council/Commission of the EU) dated 25 July 2006 (more than 40,000 persons were transferred by 27 vessels to Cyprus, under the coordination of an Israeli officer and the aid of the International Organization for Migration so far as non-European people were concerned)). See also the Chinese mission launched in Libya in early 2011 when it deployed, without any shots fired, four military transport planes and a guided-missile frigate to rescue thousands of Chinese citizens working in Libya (<http://www.atimes.com/atimes/China/NI06Ad02.html>).

[8] Olivier Corten, *The Law Against War. The Prohibition of the Use of Force in Contemporary International Law* (Oxford: Hart, 2010), 551.

[9] Arbitral Award, 17 Sept 2007 (2008) ILM 164, para 445.

[10] ILC Draft Articles on Diplomatic Protection, UN GAOR, 61st Sess, Supp No 10, A/61/10, Art 7.

[11] See Draft Articles on Diplomatic Protection, Art 1 and paras 6 and 8–11 of the commentary on the article.

[12] See Ruys, *'Armed Attack' and Article 51 of the UN Charter*, 233 fn 540.

raised many legal difficulties and occurred in countries other than Georgia) and the necessity to protect them from Georgian actions.[13] Obviously, Georgian nationality seemed predominant and, therefore, if the diplomatic protection principle of predominant nationality applied in the case at hand, then the Russian claim would fail on that ground (among others).

Thirdly, the question remains open whether the use of force to rescue nationals abroad can be invoked to rescue non-nationals in the course of an operation primarily concerning nationals—that is to say, whether rescuing nationals abroad can be used, *incidentally*, for humanitarian assistance purposes. This was, for instance, the case in the action taken by Belgium and the US in 1964 in Congo[14] and by the European Union during the 2006 Israel–Lebanon war.[15] The question is twofold in fact: whether a state *can* rescue non-nationals when rescuing its nationals, but also, and perhaps more importantly, whether it can refuse to rescue non-nationals when it decides to and actually rescues its nationals. In 1986, the ICJ considered in the *Nicaragua* case that any humanitarian assistance had to be granted without discrimination.[16] Moreover, when serious violations of human rights are at stake, states are affected not only by violations of the rights of their nationals, but also by the violations suffered by any individual.[17] In 2004, Belgium, for instance, was sued before the Belgian courts for not having rescued Rwandan people when repatriating its soldiers and because these Rwandan people were then killed by Interahamwe militias as they were no longer protected by the Belgian troops.[18]

B. Legal Nature of the Justification Based on the Necessity of Rescuing Nationals Abroad

Rescuing nationals abroad can be conceptualized in two ways. It can constitute one of the instances covered by pre-existing legal justifications such a self-defence or consent; or it can itself constitute a legal justification. In the first instance, it is not an independent justification and therefore it is pointless to try to analyse it as such; a cross-reference to the relevant legal justifications is sufficient and, in fact, is in order. In the second instance, to argue that it is an authentic autonomous justification

[13] See esp Robert Chatam, 'Defense of Nationals Abroad: The Legitimacy of Russia's Invasion of Georgia' (2011) *Florida Journal of International Law* 78, 93–5 and 97.

[14] See Linos-Alexandre Sicilianos, *Les réactions décentralisées à l'illicite. Des contre-mesures à la légitime défense* (Paris: LGDJ, 1990), 456 fn 126.

[15] See text at n 7. [16] ICJ Rep 1986, 125.

[17] On this issue, see in particular Giorgio Gaja, 'Is the State Specially Affected When its Nationals' Human Rights Are Infringed?' in *Mélanges en l'honneur d'Antonio Cassese* (The Hague: Kluwer, 2003), 373–82.

[18] See the Judgment of 8 Dec 2010 of the Brussels Court of First Instance (Tribunal de première instance de Bruxelles) in case RG nos 04/4807/A and 07/15547/A. The case is still pending before the Court of Appeal, to which it has been referred.

under international law supposes being able to demonstrate that the use of force can be used *on the legal (customary) ground* that a state has to protect its nationals abroad.

To that end, it is first possible to exclude from the relevant practice cases where the use of force for the purpose of rescuing nationals abroad was based on a treaty provision.[19] Here the legal justification rests on treaty law and not on the customary 'rescuing nationals abroad' argument. Therefore the corresponding practice is not relevant when assessing customary international law (except to the extent that the multiplication of similar provisions could give rise to a new customary rule), even if, in interpreting the treaty provision, customary rules have to be taken into account under Article 31(3)(c) of the 1969 Vienna Convention on the Law of Treaties.

It is also possible to exclude forcible operations launched with the consent of the host state—provided that consent is actually given. In such a case, there is legally speaking no intervention at all and therefore no need to justify it, whether under self-defence or the rescuing of nationals abroad doctrine.[20] However, consent can be hard to obtain when the host state is a failed state and/or when no legitimate authority is able to give that consent. In such a case, it could be argued that the use of force would be prohibited, but for very limited operations, when lives are at stake. It would remain prohibited, however, to interfere in the case of civil war and, in particular, if the intervention affects 'the responsibility of the government, by all legitimate means, to maintain or re-establish law and order in the State'.[21]

It seems that in most cases states have invoked pre-existing legal justifications without claiming that the necessity to rescue nationals abroad was by itself a sufficient ground to use force or, at least, without restricting themselves to this sole justification. Self-defence and consent have been the preferred legal grounds resorted to by states, which have also occasionally invoked *force majeure*, necessity (*état de nécessité*) or countermeasures.[22] This has not precluded some states from postulating, as a general, abstract rule, that the right to rescue their nationals abroad by use of force is of a customary nature.[23] It is of particular interest to note in that respect

[19] Provided that the treaty provision really allows states to use force for the purpose of rescuing nationals abroad. See eg the debate on Art IV of the Treaty of Guarantee concluded in 1960 between Cyprus, on the one part, and Greece, Turkey, and the UK, on the other, as analysed by Natalino Ronzitti, *Rescuing Nationals Abroad through Military Coercion and Intervention on Grounds of Humanity* (Dordrecht: Martinus Nijhoff, 1985), 115–34.

[20] *Case Concerning Armed Activities on the Territory of the Congo (DRC v. Uganda)*, Judgment of 19 Dec 2005, ICJ Rep 2005, 196 ff, paras 42 ff; Karine Bannelier and Théodore Christakis, '*Volenti non fit injuria?* Les effets du consentement à l'intervention militaire' (2004) *Annuaire Français de Droit International* 121. See also the examples given by Muriel Ubéda-Saillard, 'Aspects opérationnels de la compétence personnelle' (2009) *Annuaire Français de Droit International* 166.

[21] Art 3 of the 1977 Protocol Additional to the 1949 Geneva Conventions relating to the Protection of Victims of Non-International Armed Conflicts, 8 June 1977; Theodor Schweisfurth, 'Operations to Rescue Nationals in Third States Involving the Use of Force in Relation to the Protection of Human Rights' (1980) 23 *German Yearbook of International Law* 159–60 fn 6.

[22] Sicilianos, *Les réactions décentralisées à l'illicite*, 458–62; Corten, *The Law Against War*, 225–8.

[23] See eg the Nov 1964 declaration by a British minister who stated in Parliament that 'we take the view that under international law a State has a right to land troops in foreign territory to protect

that in the course of its work on state responsibility, the ILC considered rescuing nationals abroad not as an autonomous circumstance precluding wrongfulness; but, rather, it was considered under necessity and self-defence.[24] The same can be said of the 2008 Russian armed action in the territory of Georgia. Even if Russia claimed the existence of a right to use force for the purpose of rescuing its nationals abroad, it finally subsumed it under the justification of self-defence on which it officially based its intervention when addressing the Security Council.[25]

Conversely, cases where rescuing nationals abroad has been invoked for other purposes than the one officially declared, notably to overthrow governments, are not relevant since they cannot be considered as manifesting an authentic *opinio juris*.[26]

In the light of the previous discussion, it seems rather debatable to argue that there exists in contemporary international law an autonomous justification based on the necessity to rescue nationals abroad. State practice, at first sight, does not show any great willingness to invoke it on self-sufficient legal grounds. In its Final Report, dated September 2009, the Independent International Fact-Finding Mission on the Conflict in Georgia therefore straightforwardly asserted that:

> as soon as a rescue operation exceeds a minimum intensity and thus falls within the scope of Art. 2(4), the protection of own nationals does not, according to the prevailing opinion of writers, constitute an autonomous, additional justification for the use of force. There is probably not one single instance in state practice where a state invoked an independent, standalone entitlement to rescue its nationals, without relying on one of the classic grounds of justification. In state practice, none of the arguments advanced by states in order to justify military interventions in favour of their nationals has been accepted by the entire community of states. The prevailing reactions were rather reprobation, e.g. in the case of the Congo, Grenada and Panama. From a policy perspective, the danger of abuse counsels against generous acceptance of such a principle. To conclude, the protection of nationals abroad does not constitute an independent exception to the prohibition of the use of force, and therefore does not provide a legal basis justifying a military intervention.[27]

The conclusion can be seen, however, as too clear-cut since in fact state practice, since 1945 (Section III) and still today (Section IV), reveals some persistence of the

its nationals in an emergency if necessary', Hansard, HC Deb, vol 702, col 911, quoted by Sir Robert Jennings and Sir Arthur Watts (eds), *Oppenheim's International Law. Vol 1: Peace* (London: Longman, 1996), 440 fn 5; or France, *Manuel de droit des conflits armés* (Paris: Direction des Affaires Juridiques du Ministère de la Défense, 2003), 66.

[24] See in particular ILC, Art 33 of the Draft Articles on State Responsibility adopted in first reading in 1996, commentary, paras 23–9, *Yearbook of the International Law Commission*, 1980, vol II (2), 43–6.

[25] See Christine Gray, 'The Protection of Nationals Abroad: Russia's Use of Force in Georgia' in Aristotle Constantinides and Nikos Zaikos (eds), *The Diversity of International Law: Essays in Honour of Professor Kalliopi K. Koufa* (Leiden: Martinus Nijhoff, 2010), 134–51, esp 146.

[26] See, with regard to the US actions in Dominican Republic (1965) and Panama (1989), Christine Gray, *International Law and the Use of Force* (Oxford: Oxford University Press, 2009), 64–5.

[27] Vol II, 286 (available at <http://www.ceiig.ch/Report.html>); also quoted by Corten, *The Law Against War*, 548, who agrees.

classical 'rescuing nationals abroad' justification, even if it remains highly controversial, ambiguous, and rather elusive.

III. The Practice Since 1945

Great attention has been paid to the legality of the use of force for rescuing nationals abroad since the adoption of the UN Charter in 1945. Numerous precedents were reported during the second half of the 20th century, which gave rise to many uncertainties.

This is not the appropriate place to present in great detail the various precedents which have been reported since 1945 as they are well-known and have additionally been analysed by scholarship in a very exhaustive manner. Examples are the intervention of Belgium in the Congo in 1960, of the US and Belgium again in the Congo in 1964, of Israel which launched a raid in Uganda in July 1976 at Entebbe airport to rescue detained persons from a hijacked aircraft, of Egypt which carried out a similar operation at Nicosia airport in Cyprus in 1978, of France in Mauritania (1977, 1978, and 1979), Zaire (Shaba, 1978), Chad (1978 and 1979), Gabon (1990), Central Africa (1996), or the US in Liberia in 1990. All these precedents were carefully assessed to determine to what extent they were in conformity with international law.[28]

It is not disputed that the use of force to rescue nationals abroad was not prohibited by general international law before the adoption of the UN Charter in 1945.[29] The core issue, in fact, has been to assess whether *since 1945* it remains possible to use force to that end without contravening the UN Charter and the customary principle of non-use of force.

The problem is that the UN Charter does not deal explicitly with the point. The same is true with regard to other conventions. In particular—albeit the issue was raised during the negotiations and some amendments were proposed to tackle the issue by inserting an explicit provision on the use of force as a means of rescuing hostages (following the Entebbe raid)—the 1979 Convention against the Taking of Hostages finally

[28] Ronzitti, *Rescuing Nationals Abroad through Military Coercion and Intervention on Grounds of Humanity*, 21 ff; Jennings and Watts, *Oppenheim's International Law*, 440–1; Richard Lillich, 'Forcible Protection of Nationals Abroad: the Liberian "Incident" of 1990' (1992) 35 *German Yearbook of International Law* 205–23; Thomas Wingfield and James Meyen (eds), *Lillich on the Forcible Protection of Nationals Abroad. In Memory of Professor Richard B. Lillich* (Newport, RI: Naval War College, 2002), 41–114; Ruys, *'Armed Attack' and Article 51 of the UN Charter*, 216–29.

[29] Ruys, *'Armed Attack' and Article 51 of the UN Charter*, 213.

limited itself to the adoption of a 'without prejudice' provision (Art 14) which, as it has been stated, 'left the conundrum exactly where it was before its adoption'.[30]

Scholars have been quite divided on the issue. Three approaches were dominant in the second half of the 20th century. According to some authors, the use of force for rescuing nationals abroad is prohibited by international law, except if it falls under the criteria of self-defence as codified in Article 51 of the UN Charter.[31] Others consider that it remains permitted, under some strict conditions.[32] A third category of authors considers that the use of force for rescuing nationals abroad is not really in conformity with international law but could become legitimate and could constitute a mitigating circumstance, which prevents the responsible state being considered as an aggressor,[33] or which is tolerated, even if not legally permitted.[34]

The above approaches have been based on two sets of arguments. The first set of arguments depend on the interpretation of Article 2(4) of the UN Charter: whether it has to be strictly interpreted as prohibiting any use of force other than those expressly accepted by the UN Charter (ie self-defence and collective action decided or authorized by the Security Council) or can be interpreted with more flexibility as only prohibiting the use for force against the territorial integrity or independence of the host state. Quite clearly, it seems that the first interpretation has prevailed.[35]

The second set of arguments is linked to Article 51 of the UN Charter. The pertinent question is whether an attack against the nationals of one state located abroad can be seen as an 'armed attack' against that state according to the law of self-defence. Since states are composed of a territory and a population, it could indeed be argued that an armed attack (provided that it fits the criteria of 'armed attack' under Art 51[36]) against the population is like an attack against the territory of the state, each of them being constitutive elements of a state. At the same time, the

[30] Ruys, *'Armed Attack' and Article 51 of the UN Charter*, 235; Sicilianos, *Les réactions décentralisées à l'illicite*, 467; Eldred, 'The Use of Force in Hostage Rescue Missions', 259–60.

[31] Schweisfurth, 'Operations to Rescue Nationals in Third States Involving the Use of Force in Relation to the Protection of Human Rights', 162 ff, esp 165–6; Rex Zedalis, 'Protection of Nationals Abroad: Is Consent the Basis of Legal Obligation?' (1990) *Texas International Law Journal* 221 fn 53.

[32] Jennings and Watts, *Oppenheim's International Law*, 440–2.

[33] Sicilianos, *Les réactions décentralisées à l'illicite*, 472–4; Antonio Cassese, 'Article 51' in Jean-Pierre Cot, Mathias Forteau, and Alain Pellet (eds), *La Charte des Nations Unies. Commentaire article par article* (Paris: Economica, 2005), 1347–50.

[34] Lillich, 'Forcible Protection of Nationals Abroad', 213–15 and 219–21.

[35] See Sicilianos, *Les réactions décentralisées à l'illicite*, 464–7; Ronzitti, *Rescuing Nationals Abroad through Military Coercion and Intervention on Grounds of Humanity*, Part I; Schweisfurth, 'Operations to Rescue Nationals in Third States Involving the Use of Force in Relation to the Protection of Human Rights', 162–3; Zedalis, 'Protection of Nationals Abroad', 221 ff; Lillich, 'Forcible Protection of Nationals Abroad', 215–16; Ruys, *'Armed Attack' and Article 51 of the UN Charter*, 214; Eldred, 'The Use of Force in Hostage Rescue Missions', 253 ff.

[36] On this issue, which cannot be dealt with here, see Jan Klabbers, 'Intervention, Armed Intervention, Armed Attack, Threat to Peace, Act of Aggression, and Threat or Use of Force: What's the Difference?', Chapter 22 and see also Jörg Kammerhofer, 'The Resilience of the Restrictive Rules on Self-Defence', Chapter 27 both in this volume.

analogy is not perfect so far as the attack directed against nationals abroad is not, as such, an attack against 'the population', but rather against *some* nationals, which is quite different. On the other hand, it can be claimed that no state can stay inactive when its nationals' lives are threatened abroad.[37]

It can be deduced from this that *in any case* 'rescuing nationals abroad' has not been really conceived of as sufficient by itself to justify the use of force. It has been considered either as not prohibited by Article 2(4) of the UN Charter—hence, as something which is not a justification but an exception to the rule prohibiting the use of force, or as an application of the self-defence justification.

IV. Recent Practice

The doctrine of rescuing nationals abroad has faced new challenges in recent years. Due to the multiplication of acts of terrorism, the taking of hostages, and piracy in the last decade, states have shown a greater willingness to resort to coercive means to fight these international crimes, in some cases regardless of the nationality of the persons concerned. Moreover, the necessity to protect human rights makes it more pressing to react when people's lives are threatened and when the host state does not protect those people as it is supposed to do because it is unwilling (or unable) to do so.[38] For these reasons, one would think that it has, a fortiori, become easier since 2000 to justify the use of force to rescue nationals abroad.

Nevertheless, it is undisputed today that the prohibition of aggression is a *jus cogens* rule and that violation of the rule cannot be precluded by any circumstance precluding wrongfulness.[39] Therefore, it seems from that second perspective rather impossible today to justify the use of force on grounds other than self-defence or collective security under Security Council authority.[40] Given these contradictory elements, it is not surprising that states still have recourse to forcible means to

[37] See on the concurring interpretations of Art 51 of the UN Charter: Schweisfurth, 'Operations to Rescue Nationals in Third States Involving the Use of Force in Relation to the Protection of Human Rights', 163–5; Sicilianos, *Les réactions décentralisées à l'illicite*, 467–70; Zedalis, 'Protection of Nationals Abroad', 235–48; Lillich, 'Forcible Protection of Nationals Abroad', 216–19; Ruys, *'Armed Attack' and Article 51 of the UN Charter*, 214–15; Eldred, 'The Use of Force in Hostage Rescue Missions', 253 ff.

[38] On the Responsibility to Protect and the *intervention d'humanité*, see Sir Nigel Rodley, 'Humanitarian Intervention', Chapter 35 in this volume. A 'human rights approach' to rescue operations had already been proposed by Schweisfurth, 'Operations to Rescue Nationals in Third States Involving the Use of Force in Relation to the Protection of Human Rights', 161 and 166–79.

[39] See Art 26 of the 2001 ILC Articles on State Responsibility, *Yearbook of the International Law Commission*, 2001, vol II (2), para 77.

[40] Corten, *The Law Against War*, 213 ff.

rescue nationals abroad (Section IV.A) while the legality of these actions remains disputed (Section IV.B).

A. An Ongoing Practice

Albeit they 'by and large escaped international scrutiny',[41] many rescue operations have taken place since the beginning of the third millennium. This practice reveals that the states concerned still believe that the use of force to rescue nationals abroad is not prohibited by international law or is, at least, tolerated. Admittedly, in some cases it appears in fact that the operation was launched with the approval of the host state—hence it was a legal operation per se. But even if recent practice is not entirely sufficient to conclude that there is a customary rule authorizing the use of force against the will of the host state in cases of rescue operations, this practice has not completely disappeared.

France, for instance, conducted rescue operations in many African countries such as Côte d'Ivoire in 2002–4, the Central African Republic and Liberia in 2003, Gabon in 2007, and Chad in 2008. To that end, France deployed some 300 soldiers in the Central African Republic in 2003 and 1,400 persons were evacuated from Chad in 2008, and 6,500 from Côte d'Ivoire in 2004.[42] One could also quote the French military operations launched in September 2008 off the coast of Somalia to retake the yacht *Carré d'As IV* from Somali pirates and in Niger in January 2011 when two French citizens were kidnapped in Niamey by a terrorist group operating in the western part of Africa (AMQI). Unfortunately, during the course of this last operation, the two French hostages died.

Even if French operations are the most abundant, other countries have launched similar operations in the last decades. Foreign nationals were, for instance, successfully evacuated from Lebanon in 2006 following the Israeli–Lebanese war[43] and in January 2011, 22 commandos of the Republic of Korea Navy's UDT/SEAL began a special operation off the north-eastern Somali coast in the Indian Ocean to rescue 21 abducted crewmen off a tanker hijacked by Somali pirates. All the hostages were rescued, who were not only Korean but also Indonesian and Burmese. In January 2012, US Special Forces parachuted into Somalia to free two kidnapped international (American and Danish) aid workers held hostage by nine gunmen—the hostages were unfortunately killed during the operation.[44] In March 2012, UK Special Forces also intervened in Nigeria to rescue a British hostage, who was executed as members

[41] Ruys, *'Armed Attack' and Article 51 of the UN Charter*, 229.

[42] Ruys, *'Armed Attack' and Article 51 of the UN Charter*, 229–30; and Ubéda-Saillard, 'Aspects opérationnels de la compétence personnelle', 166. On the operation in Côte d'Ivoire, see Gilles Cottereau, 'Une licorne en Côte d'Ivoire au service de la paix' (2003) *Annuaire Français de Droit International* 193–4.

[43] Ruys, *'Armed Attack' and Article 51 of the UN Charter*, 230 fn 530.

[44] See 'U.S. Swoops In to Free 2 From Pirates in Somali Raid', 25 Jan 2012, available at <http://www.nytimes.com/2012/01/26/world/africa/us-raid-frees-2-hostages-from-somali-pirates.html?pagewanted=all>.

of the UK Special Forces and Nigerian soldiers moved in on the terrorist group's hideaway. In June 2012, a British operation was conducted in Afghanistan to free a British hostage and two Afghan colleagues who had been kidnapped.[45]

Moreover, in 2008, one of the arguments put forward by Russia to justify its armed actions in Georgia was the necessity to protect its nationals abroad. In this case, however, 'the Russian operation was not aimed at the evacuation of a small group of threatened nationals, but instead took the form of a large-scale military offensive, resulting in the occupation of a substantial part of Georgian territory'.[46] Thus, it is doubtful that the operation constituted, *stricto sensu*, a rescue operation of nationals abroad given its non-limited scope. Unfortunately, no discussion took place on this argument in the Security Council during the conflict between Georgia and Russia.[47] But as a result of the arguments submitted by Russia to the ICJ in the *Case Concerning Application of the International Convention on the Elimination of All Forms of Racial Discrimination (Georgia v. Russian Federation)*, it eventually did not rely on the 'rescuing nationals abroad' doctrine, and instead officially invoked self-defence and its responsibilities as part of the Collective Peacekeeping Forces operating in Georgia.[48]

In 2008, France reiterated that from its point of view the use of force to rescue nationals abroad was permissible under contemporary international law.[49] The same position was endorsed by Russia after the break-up of the USSR,[50] which then seemed to change its mind on the legality of such interventions,[51] and also by the US after 1990.[52] A more radical view was adopted by the US in 2002 through the enactment of the American Service Members' Protection Act according to which 'The President is authorised to use all means [which include military means] necessary and appropriate to bring about the release of any person described in subsection (b) who is being detained or imprisoned by, on behalf of, or at the request of the International Criminal Court'.[53] It cannot really be said, on the other hand, that such a legislation belongs to 'rescue operations' since it is directed against a court which cannot be considered as threatening the lives of nationals abroad.

45 See 'How the British hostages were rescued in Afghanistan', 3 June 2012, available at <http://www.telegraph.co.uk/news/worldnews/asia/afghanistan/9307833/How-the-British-hostages-were-rescued-in-Afghanistan.html>. See also on the British intervention in Sierra Leone: 'UK Materials on International Law' (2000) 71 *British Yearbook of International Law* 645.

46 Ruys, *'Armed Attack' and Article 51 of the UN Charter*, 232.

47 Gray, 'The Protection of Nationals Abroad' in Constantinides and Zaikos, *The Diversity of International Law*, 147.

48 Request for the indication of provisional measures, Order of 15 Oct 2008, ICJ Rep 2008, 370–1, paras 64–6. See, on the other hand, the Judgment of the Court of 1 Apr 2011, available at <http://www.icj-cij.org>, paras 174–5, recalling that Russia accused Georgian authorities of ethnically cleansing a portion of its own population. See also Chatam, 'Defense of Nationals Abroad', 81–2.

49 Livre blanc, *Défense et sécurité nationale* (Paris: Odile Jacob, 2008), 71–2.

50 Gray, 'The Protection of Nationals Abroad' in Constantinides and Zaikos, *The Diversity of International Law*, 136.

51 Gray, 'The Protection of Nationals Abroad' in Constantinides and Zaikos, *The Diversity of International Law*, 134.

52 Eldred, 'The Use of Force in Hostage Rescue Missions', 257.

53 §2008(a).

B. Legal Assessment

Given the ongoing practice of rescuing nationals abroad, some have tried to give it a more official status. In the course of the work of the ILC on Diplomatic Protection, the Special Rapporteur, John Dugard, proposed the following article in 2000:

The threat or use of force is prohibited as a means of diplomatic protection, except in the case of rescue of nationals where:
(a) The protecting State has failed to secure the safety of its nationals by peaceful means;
(b) The injuring State is unwilling or unable to secure the safety of the nationals of the protecting State;
(c) The nationals of the protecting State are exposed to immediate danger of their persons;
(d) The use of force is proportionate in the circumstances of the situation;
(e) The use of force is terminated, and the protecting State withdraws its forces, as soon as the nationals are rescued.[54]

The rationale of the proposition was of a realistic nature. According to the Special Rapporteur, it is not disputable that the prohibition of the use of force does not extend to the protection of nationals abroad, as confirmed by the amount of state practice since 1945 in support of such military interventions.[55] On the other hand, there is 'general agreement that the right to use force in the protection of nationals has been greatly abused in the past and that it is a right that lends itself to abuse'.[56] It was therefore necessary to codify it in order better to limit it.[57] The aforementioned draft article proposed by the Special Rapporteur seemed then, in his view:

to reflect State practice more accurately than an absolute prohibition on the use of force (which is impossible to reconcile with the protests that have been made by the injured State and third States on the occasion of such interventions). From a policy perspective it is wiser to recognize the existence of such a right, but to prescribe severe limits, than to ignore its existence, which will permit States to invoke the traditional arguments in support of a broad right of intervention and lead to further abuse.[58]

Eventually the article was not accepted by the ILC because diplomatic protection had nothing to do with the use of force.[59] In the course of the debate on the article, some members of the Commission stated that this draft article was not in conformity with the prohibition of the use of force and with the principle of non-intervention in the internal affairs of states,[60] while other members (in fact, only two) pointed

[54] First Report on Diplomatic Protection, A/CN.4/506 (7 Mar 2000), para 46.
[55] First Report on Diplomatic Protection, para 58.
[56] First Report on Diplomatic Protection, para 59.
[57] This purpose is shared by Eldred, 'The Use of Force in Hostage Rescue Missions', 268 ff.
[58] Eldred, 'The Use of Force in Hostage Rescue Missions', 268 ff.
[59] See ILC Report to the General Assembly, UN GAOR, 55th Sess, Supp No 10, A/55/10, para 439; Summary Records of the First Part of the Fifty-Second Session, *Yearbook of the International Law Commission*, 2000, vol I, 93, para 3.
[60] ILC Report to the General Assembly, UN GAOR, 55th Sess, Supp No 10, A/55/10, paras 434–6.

out that the use of force can be used to rescue nationals abroad, in particular on the basis of the right of self-defence.[61] It has also been pointed out that the issue was 'controversial'[62] or created 'insuperable difficulties'.[63]

The UN General Assembly Sixth Committee was equally divided. According to Ruys, only Italy supported the legality of forcible protection of nationals. On the other hand, 13 states rejected the legality of forcible rescue operations (Argentina, Burkina Faso, China, Colombia, Cuba, Iran, Iraq, Jordan, Libya, Mexico, Poland, Slovenia, Venezuela) while many others simply refrained from taking a position, either by saying that in any event use of force fell outside the scope of diplomatic protection or by remaining silent on the issue.[64]

This 'episode' shows how the question of the legality of forcible rescue operations remains disputed today, while the possibility of evacuation of nationals without active combat engagement remains unchallenged.[65]

Some authors even consider that state practice of forcible rescue of nationals abroad has never been opposed as such by the international community. The fact that it has been abused in some cases is of course irrelevant (the rescue operation must comply in any case with the requirements of self-defence: necessity and proportionality[66]) to establish whether a bona fide rescue operation is permissible; the problem of identifying bona fide being more difficult in cases of dual-purposed operations.[67] Others prefer to stay neutral, pointing out the uncertainty of international law[68] or the controversial nature of such operations.[69]

More radically, it has been contended that 'The use of force to protect nationals abroad is a breach of international law, even if some authorities have claimed the contrary and international practice is showing a tendency to resurrect the law in existence before the UN Charter came into force'.[70] The most exhaustive recent study on the use of force concludes that there is 'no precedent in which a right of intervention in favour of nationals have been invoked in itself and autonomously

[61] ILC Report to the General Assembly, UN GAOR, 55th Sess, Supp No 10, paras 437. See also Summary Records of the First Part of the Fifty-Second Session, *Yearbook of the International Law Commission*, 2000, vol I, 42–72.

[62] See the interventions (*Yearbook of the International Law Commission*, 2000, vol I) of Mr Tomka (45, para 73), Mr Lukashuk (52, para 54), and Mr Simma (66, para 22).

[63] Interventions of Mr Baena Soares (43, para 58) and Mr Economides (44, para 65).

[64] Ruys, *'Armed Attack' and Article 51 of the UN Charter*, 237–9.

[65] Ruys, *'Armed Attack' and Article 51 of the UN Charter*, 244 ff.

[66] Chatam, 'Defense of Nationals Abroad', 88–90, who asserts in fn 103 that 'This right is recognized by the United States, the United Kingdom, France, Israel, and numerous other States and has never been contradicted by UN action'.

[67] Bannelier and Christakis, '*Volenti non fit injuria*', 122–4.

[68] See Patrick Daillier, Mathias Forteau, and Alain Pellet, *Droit international public (N'Guyen Quoc Dinh)* (Paris: LGDJ, 2009), 1048–51.

[69] Ubéda-Saillard, 'Aspects opérationnels de la compétence personnelle', 164–6.

[70] Bruno Simma (ed), *The Charter of the United Nations: A Commentary* (Oxford: Oxford University Press, 2002), 133.

outside of any connection with a classical legal ground'.[71] It also concludes that even if some states affirmed that they think it possible to use force to rescue nationals abroad, it would be 'difficult to interpret this precedent as a general acceptance of a right of protection of foreign nationals in the absence of a more specific evidence'.[72]

V. Conclusion

The international community is divided into two groups, the first one being composed of some Western states claiming that forcible protection of nationals abroad is permissible, a second one constituting a broader group of states which either reject such a right or at least do not explicitly support it. It seems, then, that it is 'impossible to assert that there exists *de lege lata* a customary right of forcible protection of nationals'.[73] One may add that it is also difficult to assert that there exists a specific *de lege lata* prohibition of such operations. The issue of the legality of the use of force to rescue nationals abroad actually remains largely undecided.

[71] Olivier Corten, *The Law Against War. The Prohibition of the Use of Force in Contemporary International Law* (Oxford: Hart, 2010), 534 and 534 ff.

[72] Corten, *The Law Against War*, 547.

[73] Ruys, *'Armed Attack' and Article 51 of the UN Charter*, 239 ff and the conclusion at 243.

CHAPTER 45

PEACE SETTLEMENTS AND THE PROHIBITION OF THE USE OF FORCE

MARTIN WÄHLISCH

I. Introduction

OVER 30 centuries ago around 1259 BC, the Egyptian-Hittite Peace Treaty ended the Battle of Qadesh between the Empire of Rameses II and the Hittite King Muwatalli II. Both kingdoms carried out a devastating military confrontation in what is nowadays known as the Syrian Arab Republic. Inscribed on two matching silver tablets and carved into one of the temple walls in Karnak, their peace treaty enshrines the promise that both royal houses will never again wage war against each other.[1] 'Since eternity the god does not permit the making of hostility', the commitment shall be 'valid forever', says the Hittite version of the text.[2] The agreement is one of the oldest recorded international peace documents intended to maintain the prohibition of the use of force.

Since then, peace settlements have been crucial instruments to mark the end of hostilities. The Peace Treaty of Versailles after the First World War in 1919, the Compiègne Armistice between France and Germany at the end of the Second World War in 1945, the Oslo Accords between Israel and the Palestine Liberation

[1] Marc Van De Mieroop, *A History of Ancient Egypt* (Oxford: Wiley-Blackwell, 2011), 222.

[2] David J. Bederman, *International Law in Antiquity* (Cambridge: Cambridge University Press, 2004), 148.

Organization (PLO) in 1993 and 1995, the Comprehensive Peace Agreement between the Sudan People's Liberation Movement and the Government of Sudan in 2005, or the recent peace deal signed between the Mali Government and two Tuareg movements in June 2013 are just some of the many contemporary pledges signed to terminate and prevent the use of force.

The purpose of this chapter is to shed light on the role of truces, armistices, ceasefires, and peace agreements, under the overall umbrella of peace settlements, in the context of the prohibition of the use of force. What function do peace treaties have for prohibiting the use of force? What are the consequences of not complying with peace settlements? What have been previous experiences in enforcing ceasefires and peace agreements? And what role does international law play in this matter?

The chapter highlights that, in order to answer those questions, interstate and intrastate aspects must be drawn together. Dogmatically, the prohibition of the use of force, as preserved in Article 2(4) of the UN Charter, is intended to secure the territorial integrity and political independence of states. Under public international law, the law of treaties sets a legal framework for peace settlements between states.[3] Since the end of the Cold War in the 1990s, the comparatively higher number of non-international armed conflicts and increasing relevance of non-state actors challenged the soundness of contemporary international law for peacemaking and the prohibition of the use of force.[4] The incorporation of provisions in intrastate peace settlements calling for an end to hostilities and a ceasing of armed force indicates that the idea of the 'prohibition of the use of force' is also treated as a sincere principle in internal affairs.[5] This notion has ultimately been amplified by the human rights obligations of states, particularly their responsibility to protect the right to life.[6] State practice reveals that the relation between the use of force and peace settlements is sometimes perplex, as force can be used to implement peace.[7] Nevertheless, peace enforcement operations safeguarding the implementation of peace agreements under the mandate of the UN and regional organizations exemplify that the prohibition of the use of force is demanded to be more than merely lip service.[8]

[3] Randall Lesaffer, 'Peace Treaties and the Formation of International Law' in Bardo Fassbender and Anne Peters (eds), *The Oxford Handbook of the History of International Law* (Oxford: Oxford University Press, 2012), 71.

[4] Olivier Corten and Pierre Klein, 'Are Agreements between States and Non-State Entities Rooted in the International Legal Order?' in Enzo Cannizzaro (ed), *The Law of Treaties Beyond the Vienna Convention* (Oxford: Oxford University Press, 2011), 3; Noam Lubell, *Extraterritorial Use of Force Against Non-State Actors* (Oxford: Oxford University Press, 2010), 14.

[5] Benedetto Conforti, *International Law and the Role of Domestic Legal Systems* (Leiden: Martinus Nijhoff, 1993), 125.

[6] Bertrand G. Ramcharan, 'The Concept and Dimensions of the Right to Life' in Bertrand G. Ramcharan (ed), *The Right to Life in International Law* (Leiden: Martinus Nijhoff, 1985), 12.

[7] Christine Gray, *International Law and the Use of Force* (Oxford: Oxford University Press, 2008), 405.

[8] See eg Tarcisio Gazzini, *The Changing Rules on the Use of Force in International Law* (Manchester: Manchester University Press, 2005), 236.

This chapter consists of three sections: Section II elaborates on the function and concept of peace settlements, touching on their inherent purpose to regulate force and to create a conducive environment for sustainable peace. Section III focuses on elements of the applicable normative framework in international law, including concrete provisions in peace settlements which prohibit the use of force, questions about the legal validity of peace treaties, as well as the legal consequences of breaches. Section IV concentrates on implementation mechanisms considering the practice of monitoring and peace enforcement missions authorized by the UN Security Council.

II. Function and Classification of Peace Settlements

The primary, although not the only, purpose of peace settlements is a straightforward one: to end or at least halt hostilities. Peace settlements are constant reminders of the prohibition of the use of force. At best, they prepare the ground for long-term stability, facilitate reconciliation, help to restore relations, and generate 'perpetual peace' for former belligerents.

The preambles of contemporary peace settlements are impressive witnesses to those aspirations. The Dayton Peace Accords (1995), for example, speak of a desire to promote 'enduring peace and stability'; the Arusha Peace and Reconciliation Agreement for Burundi (2000) expresses a determination to put aside 'differences in all their manifestations'; and the Sudanese Comprehensive Peace Agreement (2005) proclaims being mindful 'of the urgent need to bring peace and security to the people' who have endured 'conflict for far too long'.[9]

A. Termination of War and Pledges of Peace

In the past, a major effect of peace treaties was to put a formal end to war. In the 18th century, Vattel wrote that the major function of peace treaties was to concede 'claims and grievances on both sides' of the parties to the conflict, 'putting an end

[9] The General Framework Agreement for Peace in Bosnia and Herzegovina, Preamble, para 3, 14 Dec 1995, A/50/79C, S/1995/999 (30 Nov 1995); Arusha Peace and Reconciliation Agreement for Burundi, Preamble, para 5, 28 Aug 2000; Comprehensive Peace Agreement between Sudan People's Liberation Movement and the Government of Sudan, Chapeau, para 3, 9 Jan 2005, UN Peacemaker Database, available at <http://peacemaker.unlb.org/>.

to all disputes' by an agreement 'as fair and equitable as circumstances will admit of' without deciding 'on the original cause of the war'.[10] He concluded that the effect of a treaty of peace 'leaves the contracting parties no right to commit any acts of hostility', 'wherefore they cannot lawfully take up arms again for the same subject'.[11] However, while 'the contracting parties reciprocally engage to preserve perpetual peace', peace treaties were supposed 'not to be understood' as a promise 'never to make war on each other for any cause whatever', Vattel emphasized.[12] His remarks make clear that peace treaties only regulated the use of force between former belligerents as contract parties without establishing a general principle prohibiting the use of force.

Over time, peace treaties remained 'the most frequent mode of terminating a war', as Fritz Grob put it after the end of the Second World War.[13] They are negotiated either while military operations continue or after the conclusion of a general armistice. Besides peace settlements, other constellations can lead to the end of the use of force. Among others, the 'reciprocal intermission of hostilities', conquest, subjugation, or capitulation and surrender are alternative scenarios.[14]

The development of international humanitarian law and the resulting contemporary concept of armed conflicts shifted the function of peace settlements. In 1995, the International Criminal Tribunal for the former Yugoslavia (ICTY) proposed as a general definition that 'an armed conflict exists whenever there is a resort to armed force between States or protracted armed violence between governmental authorities and organised armed groups or between such groups within a State'.[15] The ICTY stated that the application of international humanitarian law applies 'from the initiation of such armed conflicts and extends beyond the cessation of hostilities until a general conclusion of peace is reached; or, in the case of internal conflicts, a peaceful settlement is achieved'.[16] Hence, the conclusion of a peace settlement does not end the applicability of international humanitarian law. This depends on whether or not actual combat takes place. Nonetheless, peace settlements remain to establish critical landmarks in peace processes. They prompt a recall of the prohibition of the use of force and eventually enable a permanent end to hostilities.

[10] Emer de Vattel, *The Law of Nations* ([1760], London: Liberty Fund, 2008), vol IV, 663, para 18.

[11] Vattel, *The Law of Nations*, 663, para 19.

[12] Vattel, *The Law of Nations*, 663, para 19.

[13] Fritz Grob, *The Relativity of War and Peace: A Study in Law, History, and Politics* (New Haven, CT: Yale University Press, 1949), 312.

[14] Coleman Philippson, *Termination of War and Treaties of Peace* (London: T. Fisher Uwin Ltd, 1916), 1. For an analysis in historical perspective, see also Joseph Peter Haas, *Die Beendigung des Krieges nach Modernem Völkerrecht* (Munster: Westfälische Vereinsdruckerei, 1918), and Ferdinand Reiner, *Beginn und Ende des Krieges nach Modernem Völkerrecht* (Greifswald: Königliche Universität, 1913).

[15] ICTY, *Prosecutor v. Duško Tadić*, Decision on the Defence Motion for Interlocutory Appeal on Jurisdiction of 2 Oct 1995, IT-94-1, para 70.

[16] *Tadić*, para 70.

B. Modus Operandi for Military Presence

Apart from ending military activities, peace settlements can also regulate the presence of foreign armed force. This permission is limited and conditional on the unambiguous consent by a state.[17] In 2005, the International Court of Justice (ICJ) decided in the *Case Concerning Armed Activities on the Territory of the Congo* on the role of peace accords and the prohibition of the use of force.[18] In this case, the Democratic Republic of the Congo (DRC) instituted judicial proceedings against the Republic of Uganda concerning alleged unlawful armed activities. Uganda contended that the DRC government had agreed to the presence of Ugandan troops by signing the Lusaka Ceasefire Agreement in 1999. The ICJ concluded that the Lusaka Ceasefire Agreement had indeed included a 'modus operandi' about 'how the parties should move forward', but that it did not constitute the consent of the DRC to the presence of Ugandan troops.[19] Only the subsequent Luanda Peace Agreement in 2000 authorized a limited presence of Ugandan troops in the border area. The case shows how essential peace accords are for specifying the use of permitted force or its prohibition in order to prevent further conflict.

C. Nomenclature of Peace Settlements: Truces, Armistices, Ceasefires, Peace Treaties, and Peace Agreements

Regarding terminology, the differentiation between armistices, truces, ceasefires, peace treaties, and peace agreements is often incoherent in present practice (see Table 45.1). Yet, there are historical and contextual particularities.[20] For the prohibition of the use of force, the difference becomes relevant for the focus on the subjects of international law, separating state and non-state actors. Moreover, the terminological distinction plays out for cases when only a temporary halt to hostilities is intended by the parties to the conflict.

In a 'truce', belligerent states temporarily abstain from warlike acts.[21] Literally meaning 'the holding of hands', truces have been concluded since the times of Ancient Greece as a prerequisite for the conclusion of peace, allowing for burial of the dead

[17] For a comprehensive analysis of interventions by consent, see Georg Nolte, *Eingreifen auf Einladung* (Berlin: Springer, 1999), 543.

[18] *Armed Activities on the Territory of the Congo (DRC v. Uganda)*, Judgment of 19 Dec 2005, ICJ Rep 2005, 168.

[19] *Armed Activities*, para 99.

[20] Yoram Dinstein, 'Armistice' in Rüdiger Wolfrum (ed), *Max Planck Encyclopedia of Public International Law* (online), para 28.

[21] Sydney D. Bailey, 'Cease-Fires, Truces, and Armistices in the Practice of the UN Security Council' (1977) 71 *American Journal of International Law* 461.

Table 45.1 Nomenclature of peace settlements

Peace settlements	
Interstate conflict	**Intrastate conflict**
Truce	Ceasefire
Armistice	
Peace treaty	Peace agreement (eg preliminary interim agreements, framework agreements, comprehensive peace agreements, implementation agreements)

or admitting the exchange and release of prisoners.[22] In the Middle Ages, it was lawful during a truce to secure a position, recruit soldiers, or evacuate the wounded until an agreement about the suspension of military operations was reached. As a long-standing rule in customary international law, a white 'flag of truce' is waved signalling a request to suspend hostilities, begin negotiation, or finally surrender.[23]

An 'armistice' is the actual 'mutual agreement between the belligerent parties' that 'suspends military operations', as defined in the Hague Conventions.[24] As such, an armistice 'provides a transitional stage between the truce and a final peace'.[25] Common Article 36 of the Hague Conventions states that if a 'duration is not fixed, the belligerent parties can resume operations at any time, provided always the enemy is warned within the time agreed upon, in accordance with the terms of the armistice'. An armistice must be 'notified officially, and in good time, to the competent authorities and the troops' whereas hostilities 'are suspended immediately after the notification or at a fixed date'.[26] Subsequent to an armistice, a 'peace treaty' cements, in written form, the commitment to end the use of force between belligerent states.[27]

[22] Richard R. Baxter, 'Armistices and Other Forms of Suspension of Hostilities' (1976) 149 *Recueil des cours de l'Académie de droit international* 353.

[23] International Committee of the Red Cross (ICRC), Customary IHL Database, Rule 58, Improper Use of the White Flag of Truce, para 1, available at <http://www.icrc.org/customary-ihl>; ICRC, Customary IHL Database, United States of America, Practice Relating to Rule 65, Perfidy, Section E, Simulation of an Intention to Negotiate under the White Flag of Truce. See also eg Convention (II) with Respect to the Laws and Customs of War on Land and its Annex: Regulations Concerning the Laws and Customs of War on Land, 29 July 1899 and Convention (IV) with Respect to the Laws and Customs of War on Land and its Annex: Regulations Concerning the Laws and Customs of War on Land, 18 Oct 1907, Art 32.

[24] Conventions II and IV, Art 36.

[25] See eg A/1367/Rev.1 (23 Oct 1950), Supplementary Report, para 2. For a historical overview of state practice, see Howard S. Levie, 'The Nature and Scope of the Armistice Agreement' (1956) 50 *American Journal of International Law* 880.

[26] Conventions II and IV, Art 38.

[27] Jann K. Kleffner, 'Peace Treaties' in Wolfrum, *Max Planck Encyclopedia of Public International Law* (online), para 1.

Facing a growing number of intrastate conflicts after the end of the Cold War, 'ceasefire agreements' have become the 'modern concept' of armistices.[28] Whereas the term armistice mainly relates to international armed conflict between states, ceasefires usually also cover non-international armed conflicts.[29] Ceasefires often lay the ground for more substantial 'peace agreements'. The nomenclature of peace agreements can range from preliminary interim agreements, framework agreements, comprehensive peace agreements, to implementation agreements. However, the classification of peace agreements does not follow an agreed systematic, either in theory or in practice.[30] Disregarding linguistic nuances, the outlined taxonomy displays a variety of instruments for settling inter- and intrastate conflicts that aim to apply the prohibition of the use of force. The continuum of conflict resolution arrangements conveys that there are multiple mechanisms to accomplish this core principle of the UN Charter.

D. The Absence of Peace Settlements and the Role of the Security Council

In the absence of an agreement, the Security Council can lock belligerents into conflict settlement frameworks (see Table 45.2).[31] After the invasion and occupation of Kuwait by Iraq, for instance, the Security Council affirmed a formal ceasefire. The Security Council resolution defined process aspects for the demarcation of the boundary of both countries, the establishment of a demilitarized zone, the deployment of international observers, and decided that Iraq should unconditionally accept the destruction or removal of all chemical and biological weapons.[32] Some legal scholars have characterized the underlying Security

[28] Christina Bell, 'Ceasefire' in Wolfrum, *Max Planck Encyclopedia of Public International Law* (online), para 26.

[29] Bell, 'Ceasefire' in Wolfrum, *Max Planck Encyclopedia of Public International Law*, paras 14–15. See also Dinstein, 'Armistic', ibid, para 1.

[30] See eg Christine Bell, *Peace Agreements and Human Rights* (Oxford: Oxford University Press, 2000), 20, who differentiates between pre-negotiation agreements, framework or substantive agreements, and implementation agreements. Others differentiate between peace agreements signed by all warring parties (comprehensive peace agreement) or only some dyads (dyadic peace agreement), as well as full, partial, and peace process agreements depending on whether one or more dyads agreed to initiate a process that aims to settle the differences. See Stina Högbladh, *UCDP Peace Agreement Dataset Codebook*, version 1.0, Uppsala Conflict Data Program (Uppsala: Uppsala University, Oct 2006), 9. For an overview of the various denotations of peace agreement in practice, see Christine Bell and Elizabeth Craig, 'Appendix: A Decade of Peace Agreements' in Christine Bell (ed), *Peace Agreements and Human Rights* (Oxford: Oxford University Press, 2000), 323–74.

[31] Christian Henderson and Noam Lubell, 'The Contemporary Legal Nature of UN Security Council Ceasefire Resolutions' (2013) 26 *Leiden Journal of International Law* 369. See also Christine Bell, *On the Law of Peace: Peace Agreements and the Lex Pacificatoria* (Oxford: Oxford University Press, 2008), 264.

[32] SC Res 687, 3 Apr 1991, paras 1–8.

Table 45.2 Examples of peace settlements

Type	Examples
Interstate conflicts	
Armistice	Second World War: Armistice Agreements between the US, UK, USSR, and Italy (1943), Bulgaria and Rumania (1944), and Hungary (1945), Compiègne Armistice between France and Germany (1945)
	First Arab–Israeli War: Armistice Agreements between Israel and Egypt (Feb 1949), Lebanon (Mar 1949), Jordan (Apr 1949), and Syria (July 1949)
	Korean War: Armistice Agreement between the Delegation of the Korean People's Army and the United Nations Command (1953)
Peace treaty	Spanish–American War: Treaty of Peace between the US and Spain (1898)
	First World War: Treaty of Brest–Litovsk between the Austro-Hungarian Empire, Kingdom of Bulgaria, German Empire, Ottoman Empire, and the Russian SFSR (1918), Treaty of Versailles (1919)
	Arab–Israeli conflict: Egypt–Israel Peace Treaty (1979), Israel–Jordan Peace Treaty (1994)
	First Chechen War: Russian–Chechen Peace Treaty between the Russian Federation and the Chechen Republic of Ichkeria (1997)
Intrastate conflicts	
Ceasefire	Rwandan Civil War: The N'Sele Ceasefire Agreement between the Government of the Rwandese Republic and the Rwandese Patriotic Front (1991)
	Burundi Civil War: Ceasefire Agreement between the Transitional Government of Burundi and the National Council for the Defense of Democracy–Forces for the Defense of Democracy (2002)
	Darfur conflict: Humanitarian Cease Fire Agreement on the Conflict in Darfur between the Sudan Liberation Movement/ Army and the Sudan Justice and Equality Movement (2004)
Peace agreement	Israeli–Palestinian Peace Process: Interim Agreement on the West Bank and the Gaza Strip (Oslo II) between the Government of the State of Israel and the Palestine Liberation Organization (1995)
	Mindanao: Framework Agreement on the Bangsamoro between the Philippine Government and the Moro Islamic Liberation Front (2012)

(Continued)

Table 45.2 (*Continued*)

Type	Examples
Peace agreement	Second Sudanese Civil War: Comprehensive Peace Agreement between Sudan People's Liberation Movement and the Government of Sudan (2005) Uganda conflict: Implementation Protocol to the Agreement on Comprehensive Solutions signed between the Government of the Republic of Uganda and the Lord's Resistance Army/ Movement (2007)

Council resolution as a replacement for a peace treaty.[33] In the case of Kosovo, the Rambouillet Accords proposed the conclusion of an agreement on substantial autonomy for Kosovo, which the Federal Republic of Yugoslavia (FRY) refused to accept.[34] Subsequently, the Security Council adopted Resolution 1244 (1999) that 'determined to resolve the grave humanitarian situation in Kosovo'.[35] Acting under Chapter VII, the Security Council established general principles on which the political solution to the Kosovo crisis should be based. Instead of demanding a peace agreement between the FRY and the North Atlantic Treaty Organization (NATO), the resolution authorized an international civil and security presence in Kosovo to deter renewed hostilities and to maintain and if necessary enforce the ceasefire.

III. Normative Framework

The legal framework of peace settlements is predominantly contractual, as ceasefires, peace agreements, or peace treaties encapsulate *inter partes* arrangements.[36] Provisions in peace settlements explicitly or implicitly address the prohibition of the use of force.[37] They detail what kind of concrete 'force' is outlawed in a specific context. As an additional layer, international law poses limits on the validity of peace settlements and provides normative rules for their breach.

[33] Oscar Schachter, 'United Nations Law in the Gulf Conflict' (1991) 85 *American Journal of International Law* 456.

[34] Rambouillet Accords, Co-Chairmen's Conclusions, 23 Feb 1999.

[35] SC Res 1244, 10 June 1999.

[36] Bell, *Peace Agreements and Human Rights*, 304.

[37] See Table 45.3.

A. Provisions in Peace Settlements for the Prohibition of the Use of Force

Examples for provisions in peace settlements that maintain the prohibition of the use of force are many (see Table 45.3). In 1949, the Armistice Agreement between Israel and Lebanon declared that no 'military force in the settlement of the Palestine question' and 'no aggressive action by armed forces—land, sea, or air—of either Party shall be undertaken, planned, or threatened against the people or the armed forces of the other'.[38] The agreement defines that 'no warlike act' or 'act of hostility' shall be conducted.[39] At the same time, the 'right of each party to its security and freedom from fear of attack by the armed forces of the other shall be fully respected' while the armistice represents 'an indispensable step toward the liquidation of armed conflict and the restoration of peace in Palestine'.[40] The armistice is intended to 'remain in force until a peace settlement between the Parties is achieved' or the agreement is 'by mutual consent' revised or suspended.[41] As the armistice agreement highlights, it is 'dictated exclusively by military considerations'.[42]

In 1994, the Israel–Jordan Peace Treaty stated in its Preamble the desire 'to ensure lasting security' for both states, in particular 'to avoid threats and the use of force between them'.[43] As a 'General Principle', it is upheld that the parties 'will apply between them the provisions of the Charter of the United Nations and the principles of international law governing relations among states in times of peace' refraining 'from the threat or use of force against each'.[44] The treaty details that threat or use of force includes the use of 'weapons, conventional, non-conventional or of any other kind', or any 'other actions or activities that adversely affect the security of the other Party'.[45] The signatories have to 'refrain from organising, instigating, inciting, assisting or participating in acts or threats of belligerency, hostility, subversion or violence' and 'take necessary and effective measures to ensure that acts or threats of belligerency, hostility, subversion or violence against the other party do not originate from, and are not committed within, through or over their territory'.[46] The treaty also envisaged 'the creation of a Middle East free from weapons of mass destruction, both conventional and non-conventional, in the context of a comprehensive, lasting and stable peace, characterised by the renunciation of the use of force, reconciliation and goodwill'.[47]

The agreements signed during the First Chechen War (December 1994–August 1996) are an illustrative example of the sequencing of truces, ceasefires, a preliminary

[38] Lebanese–Israeli General Armistice Agreement, Art 1, paras 1–2, 23 Mar 1949, see S/1296 (23 Mar 1949).

[39] Art 3, paras 2–3. [40] Art 1, paras 3–4. [41] Art 8, paras 2–3. [42] Art 1, para 2(a).

[43] Treaty of Peace Between the State of Israel and the Hashemite Kingdom of Jordan, 26 Oct 1994, Preamble, UN Peacemaker Database <http://peacemaker.un.org/sites/peacemaker.un.org/files/IL%20JO_941026_PeaceTreatyIsraelJordan.pdf>.

[44] Art 2, para 3. [45] Art 4, para 3(a). [46] Art 4, para 3(b), (c). [47] Art 4, para 7(b).

Table 45.3 The prohibition of the use of force in peace settlements

Peace settlement	Article	Provision
Interstate agreements		
The General Framework Agreement for Peace in Bosnia and Herzegovina (1995)[48]	Art 1	'[T]he Parties shall fully respect the sovereign equality of one another, shall settle disputes by peaceful means, and shall refrain from any action, by threat or use of force or otherwise, against the territorial integrity or political independence…
Good Friday Agreement (1998)[49]	Declaration of Support, para 4	'We reaffirm our total and absolute commitment to exclusively democratic and peaceful means of resolving differences on political issues, and our opposition to any use or threat of force by others for any political purpose, whether in regard to this agreement or otherwise.'
Agreement between the Government of the State of Eritrea and the Government of the Federal Democratic Republic of Ethiopia (2000)[50]	Art 1, para 1	'The parties shall permanently terminate military hostilities between themselves. Each party shall refrain from the threat or use of force against the other.'
Pact on Security, Stability and Development in the Great Lakes Region (2006)[51]	Art 5, para 1(a)	'[R]enounce the threat or the use of force as policies means or instrument aimed at settling disagreements or disputes or to achieve national objectives.'

[48] The General Framework Agreement for Peace in Bosnia and Herzegovina.

[49] The Northern Ireland Peace Agreement/The Agreement Reached in the Multi-Party Negotiations, Good Friday Agreement, 10 Apr 1998, UN Peacemaker Database <http://peacemaker.un.org/sites/peacemaker.un.org/files/IE%20GB_980410_Northern%20Ireland%20Agreement.pdf>.

[50] Agreement between the Government of the State of Eritrea and the Government of the Federal Democratic Republic of Ethiopia, 12 Dec 2000, A/55/686, S/2000/1183 (13 Dec 2000).

[51] Pact on Security, Stability and Development in the Great Lakes Region, 15 Dec 2006, UN Peacemaker Database <http://peacemaker.un.org/sites/peacemaker.un.org/files/061215_PactonSecurityStabilityDevelopmentGreatLakes.pdf>.

Peace settlement	Article	Provision
Intrastate agreements		
The Lomé Peace Agreement (1999)[52]	Preamble, para 8	'Determined to establish sustainable peace and security; to pledge forthwith, to settle all past, present and future differences and grievances by peaceful means; and to refrain from the threat and use of armed force to bring about any change…'
Peace Agreement between the Government of Liberia, the Liberians United for Reconciliation and Democracy, the Movement for Democracy in Liberia and the Political Parties (2003)[53]	Preamble, para 3	'Determined to establish sustainable peace and security, and pledging forthwith to settle all past, present and future differences by peaceful and legal means and to refrain from the threat of, or use of force…'
Darfur Peace Agreement (2006)[54]	Ch 3, Comprehensive Ceasefire and Final Security, Section A, Art 22, para 214(c)	'Undertake to refrain from acts such as mobilization, recruitment or initiatives that are likely to jeopardize the peace process including offensive military actions, movements, deployment of forces and engaging in hostile propaganda campaigns as a reaffirmation of commitment to create and maintain a conducive atmosphere'
Djibouti Agreement (2008)[55]	Para 6(a)	'Agreed on [t]he termination of all acts of armed confrontation…'

[52] The Lomé Peace Agreement, 7 July 1999, UN Peacemaker Database <http://peacemaker.un.org/sites/peacemaker.un.org/files/SL_990707_LomePeaceAgreement.pdf>.

[53] Peace Agreement between the Government of Liberia, the Liberians United for Reconciliation and Democracy, the Movement for Democracy in Liberia and the Political Parties, 18 Aug 2003, S/2003/850 (29 Aug 2003).

[54] Darfur Peace Agreement, 6 May 2006, Uppsala Conflict Data Program <http://www.ucdp.uu.se/gpdatabase/peace/Sud%2020060505.pdf>.

[55] Agreement between the Transitional Federal Government of Somalia and the Alliance for the Re-Liberation of Somalia, Djibouti Agreement, 9 June 2008, UN Political Office for Somalia <http://unpos.unmissions.org/Portals/UNPOS/Repository%20UNPOS/080818%20-%20Djibouti%20Agreement.pdf>.

and the final settlement and contain incremental references to the prohibition of the use of force. In May 1996, a truce led to the negotiation of a full ceasefire and cessation of military activities.[56] The agreement did not hold and eventually led to a nine-point ceasefire in mid-August 1996, which included technical aspects of demilitarization, the withdrawal of both sides' forces from Grozny and the creation of joint military headquarters.[57] Finally, a week later at the end of August 2006, the Khasavyurt Agreement was signed seeking 'mutually acceptable conditions for a political settlement of the armed conflict' by the end of December 2001 and 'recognising the prohibition of the use of force or threat of force in solving problems'.[58] In May 1997, the Russian–Chechen Peace Treaty declared the end of a 'centuries-long antagonism' and 'reject[s] forever the use of force or threat of force in resolving all matters of dispute'.[59]

The N'Sele Ceasefire Agreement (1991–2), which was later annexed to the Peace Agreement between the Government of the Republic of Rwanda and the Rwandese Patriotic Front (1993), exemplifies that the prohibition of the use of force in intra-state ceasefires is often framed as the 'cessation of all hostilities'.[60] The agreement details that the truce is 'the cessation of fighting', while the ceasefire shall imply 'the cessation of all hostilities' for the 'purpose of dialogue and serious negotiations between the two parties under the auspices of the mediator or a facilitator' serving as 'the first stage of a peace process which shall culminate in a Peace Agreement to be signed at the conclusion of the political negotiations'.[61] As the 'cessation of hostilities', the ceasefire defines that this 'shall mean the end of all military operations, all harmful civil operations and denigrating and unfounded propaganda through the mass media'.[62] Moreover, the ceasefire requires the suspension of 'supplies of

[56] Agreement on a Cease-Fire, the Cessation of Military Activities, and on Measures for a Settlement of the Armed Conflict on the Territory of the Chechen Republic, 27 May 1996.

[57] 'Russian Troops Begin Pullout in Chechnya: But Truce Talks on Hold', 25 Aug 1996, *CNN World News*, available at <http://edition.cnn.com/WORLD/9608/25/chechnya/>. For details, see also Liz Fuller, 'Chechnya: Khasavyurt Accords Failed To Preclude A Second War', 30 Aug 2006, RFE/RL, at <http://www.rferl.org/content/article/1070939.html>.

[58] Khasavyurt Agreement, 31 Aug 1996, Joint Statement and Principles for Determining the Fundamentals of Relations between the Russian Federation and the Chechen Republic, para 1. For the original text in Russian, see 'Khasavyurt Agreement' (3 Sept 1996) 163 *Nezavisimaja Gazeta* (author's translation).

[59] Peace Treaty and Principles of Interrelation between Russian Federation and Chechen Republic Ichkeria, 12 May 1997, para 1, Peace Agreements Database, INCORE/TJ Institute, University of Ulster, available at <http://www.peaceagreements.ulster.ac.uk/>.

[60] The N'Sele Cease-Fire Agreement between the Government of the Rwandese Republic and the Rwandese Patriotic Front, as amended at Gbadolite on 16 Sept 1991, and at Arusha on 12 July 1992, A/48/824, S/26915 (23 Dec 1993), Annex II. See also Humanitarian Cease Fire Agreement on the Conflict in Darfur between the Sudan Liberation Movement/Army and the Sudan Justice and Equality Movement, 8 Apr 2004, Art 1; Ceasefire Agreement between the Transitional Government of Burundi and the National Council for the Defense of Democracy-Forces for the Defense of Democracy, 2 Dec 2002, Art 1, para 2, UN Peacemaker Database <http://peacemaker.un.org/sites/peacemaker.un.org/files/BI_021202_CeasefireAgreementBetweenTransitionalGovernment-CNDDFDD.pdf>.

[61] Art 1, para 2; Art 2, para 1; Art 1, para 3. [62] Art 7, para 2.

ammunition and weaponry' and 'non-lethal logistical needs' to military forces in the field.[63]

B. Legal Validity of Peace Treaties and the Use of Force

The prohibition of the use of force has been a crucial condition for the validity of treaties. At the Age of Enlightenment at the end of the 18th century, Immanuel Kant advocated in his philosophical treatise *Perpetual Peace* that 'no treaty of peace shall be held valid in which there is tacitly reserved matter for future war'.[64] Kant wrote this essay in the light of the Peace of Basel, which was a series of peace treaties by France with Prussia, Spain, and the Landgraviate of Hessen-Kassel concluding the first part of the French revolutionary wars against several European states.

Nowadays, Article 53 of the Vienna Convention on the Law of Treaties (VCLT) stipulates that a 'treaty is void if, at the time of its conclusion, it conflicts with a peremptory norm of general international law'.[65] As the prohibition of the use of force is considered to belong to this set of peremptory norms (*jus cogens*), a treaty of war would be invalid.[66]

Critical are peace treaties which permit the use of force for their implementation. The Dayton Peace Agreement has been a contested treaty in this regard. Critics have argued that the political division of Bosnia and Herzegovina into the Federation of Bosnia and Herzegovina and the Republika Srpska is an 'acquisition of territory by force'.[67] Leaving aside whether the established territorial power-sharing structures truly instigated force or not, the Security Council endorsed the signing of the Dayton Accord. Acting under Chapter VII of the UN Charter, the Security Council welcomed and supported the peace agreement considering the need for restoring 'international peace and security'.[68]

The prohibition of the use of force not only impacts on the content of peace settlements but also on the process leading to their adoption. Article 52 VCLT states that 'a treaty is void if its conclusion has been procured by the threat or use of force'. Thus, a peace treaty has no legal force if it is imposed.[69] A debated case in this context is the conclusion of the Kumanovo Agreement ending the Kosovo war in 1999.

[63] Art 2, paras 2–3.

[64] Immanuel Kant, *Zum Ewigen Frieden: Ein Philosophischer Entwurf* ([1795], Leipzig: Reclam, 1996), 2.

[65] VCLT, Art 53, 23 May 1969, 1155 UNTS 331.

[66] See eg Antonio Cassese, *The Current Legal Regulation of the Use of Force* (Leiden: Martinus Nijhoff, 1986), 149. For the recent debate, see James A. Green, 'Questioning the Peremptory Status of the Prohibition of the Use of Force' (2011) 32 *Michigan Journal of International Law* 215–57.

[67] Jesenka Rešidović, 'Validity of the Dayton Peace Agreement in Light of Articles 53 and 64 of the Vienna Convention on the Law of Treaties' (2008) 1 *Bosnian Studies: Journal for Research of Bosnian Thought and Culture* 24.

[68] SC Res 1031, 15 Dec 1995, para 1.

[69] VLCT, Art 69, para 1. See also Kleffner, 'Peace Treaties' in Wolfrum, *Max Planck Encyclopedia of Public International Law*, para 9.

Designated as a 'Military Technical Agreement' between the International Security Force (KFOR) and the governments of the Federal Republic of Yugoslavia and the Republic of Serbia, the agreement established the 'cessation of hostilities' and authorized KFOR to take actions, 'including the use of necessary force', to ensure its compliance.[70] Some scholars have stated that the legal validity of the Kumanovo Agreement is 'dubious' with regard to Article 52 VCLT, as the intervention of NATO in the name of a humanitarian intervention was carried out without a UN Security Council mandate.[71] As the threat by NATO of further bombardments played a major role in the acceptance of the Kumanovo Agreement, it has been argued that the agreement is void.[72] However, none of the concerned parties has ever invoked a defect of the treaty.[73] Some authors have argued that subsequent resolutions of the Security Council referring to the Kumanovo Agreement constituted *ex post* approval, which overrides the treaty law voidance triggered by the unauthorized use of force.[74]

c. Consequences of Breached Peace Settlements

A breach of a peace treaty or peace agreement leaves the prohibition of the use of force de jure unaffected. Under international law, conflict parties have to refrain from the use of force even if parts of a peace settlement are not observed. Article 2(4) of the UN Charter is unconditional and can only be waived for the exceptions mentioned in the Charter, namely authorization by the Security Council or self-defence. As Article 43 VCLT provides that even if the provisions of a treaty are void 'this shall not in any way impair the duty' to fulfil any obligation under international law, which exists independently from the treaty. Although Article 60(1) VCLT provides that a 'material breach of a bilateral treaty by one of the parties entitles the other to invoke the breach as a ground for terminating the treaty or suspending its operation in whole or in part', paragraph 5 of the same article underscores that this rule does not apply where the protection of human persons is concerned. Consequently, breach of provisions of a peace treaty does not entitle the other party

[70] Military Technical Agreement between the International Security Force (KFOR) and the Governments of the Federal Republic of Yugoslavia and the Republic of Serbia, 9 June 1999, Art 1, para 4(a), (b), S/1999/682 (15 June 1999), Annex.

[71] Enrico Milano, 'Security Council Action in the Balkans: Reviewing the Legality of Kosovo's Territorial Status' (2003) 14 *European Journal of International Law* 1001.

[72] Marco Roscini, 'Threats of Armed Force and Contemporary International Law' (2007) 54 *Netherlands International Law Review* 259, 262.

[73] Milano, 'Security Council Action in the Balkans', 1019.

[74] Kirsten Schmalenbach, 'Art. 52: Coercion of a State by the Threat or Use of Force' in Oliver Dörr and Kirsten Schmalenbach (eds), *Vienna Convention on the Law of Treaties: A Commentary* (Berlin: Springer, 2012), 892, para 50.

to resume hostilities.[75] Where a peace settlement is breached by restarting the use of force, the other side could possibly react in self-defence depending on the circumstances of the particular case.

International humanitarian law encompasses *lex specialis* for armistices. Article 40 of the Hague Conventions establishes that any 'serious violation of the armistice by one of the parties gives the other party the right to denounce it'.[76] 'In case of urgency', belligerents have the right 'to recommence hostilities at once'. However, the practice of the Security Council emphasizes the stability of armistices and ceasefires.[77] For instance, in the case of the 1949 Israeli Armistice Agreements, the Security Council considered that an armistice regime 'is of a permanent character' as it 'has been in existence for nearly two and a half years'.[78] Despite violations of the armistice agreements, the Security Council continued to affirm their application.[79]

Another example is the Second Gulf War. In 1991, the First Gulf War concluded with a ceasefire between Iraq and Kuwait, which was formally declared by the Security Council.[80] In order to justify the invasion by the US and the UK in Iraq during the Second Gulf War in 2003 (Operation Iraqi Freedom), some scholars argued that Iraq had violated the weapons of mass destruction (WMD) disarmament clauses in the ceasefire agreement allowing the resumption of hostilities.[81] Other scholars maintained that no side ever claimed that the ceasefire ended to operate, and all sides insisted rather on continuing compliance with the ceasefire.[82] Instead of authorizing force, the Security Council initially gave Iraq a 'final opportunity to comply with its disarmament obligations' in November 2002.[83] In March 2003, the US-led 'Coalition of the Willing' invaded and occupied Iraq based on the reasoning of anticipatory self-defence and 'pre-emption'.[84] In May 2003, the Security Council recognized the US and the UK as occupying powers under international law without judging the legality of their prior military operation.[85] The 1991 ceasefire was never revoked and continued to serve as an underlying base for future resolutions.[86]

[75] Kleffner, 'Peace Treaties' in Wolfrum, *Max Planck Encyclopedia of Public International Law*, para 19.

[76] Conventions II and IV, Art 40.

[77] Marc Weller, *Iraq and the Use of Force in International Law* (Oxford: Oxford University Press, 2010), 113.

[78] Weller, *Iraq and the Use of Force in International Law*, 113. SC Res 95, 1 Sept 1951, para 5.

[79] For a chronological overview, see Baxter, 'Armistices and Other Forms of Suspension of Hostilities', 387.

[80] SC Res 687, 8 Apr 1991, para 33.

[81] Yoram Dinstein, 'The Gulf War: 1990–2004 (And Still Counting)' (2005) 35 *Israel Yearbook of Human Rights* 7.

[82] Weller, *Iraq and the Use of Force in International Law*, 114.

[83] SC Res 1441, 8 Nov 2002, para 2.

[84] Greg Travalio and John Altenburg, 'Terrorism, State Responsibility, and the Use of Military Force' (2003) 4 *Chicago Journal of International Law* 97.

[85] SC Res 1483, 22 May 2003.

[86] See eg SC Res 1546, 8 June 2004, para 22; SC Res 1762, 29 June 2007.

IV. Implementation Mechanisms

A highly difficult part of peace settlements is their implementation. Comprehensive peace agreements that ideally resolve all major root causes and grievances leading to the initial tensions are perceived to be most viable.[87] Yet, hesitation by political actors to accept change, lack of public support, internal resistance during military demobilization, and other practical constraints can easily impact on the agreed outcome of peace negotiations.[88] Regularly, peace agreements contain monitoring and supervision mechanisms to verify whether the use of force has truly been halted or is solely a declaration on paper.[89] This can include joint armistice commissions, boundaries commissions, and claims commissions.[90] In state practice, multilateral monitoring missions of regional organizations or the UN serve as whistle-blowers about the outbreak of new violence.[91] In the course of the history of peace operations, the verification of peace accords put the monitors in the line of fire, such as in Somalia and Congo at the beginning of the 1990s.[92] This led to more robust and armed missions in situations where there is a possibility that force might be used (see Table 45.4).[93]

A. Monitoring Missions

The United Nations Truce Supervision Organization (UNTSO) is the UN's longest ceasefire monitoring mission, serving since 1948. Initially, the mission was set up by the Security Council to assist the UN Mediator and the Truce Commission

[87] Report of the Secretary-General on Enhancing Mediation and its Support Activities, S/2009/189 (8 Apr 2009), para 39.

[88] Stephen John Stedman, 'Introduction' in Stephen John Stedman, Donald Rothchild, and Elizabeth M. Cousens (eds), *Ending Civil Wars: The Implementation of Peace Agreements* (Boulder, CO: Lynne Rienner, 2002), 3.

[89] Arist von Hehn, *The Internal Implementation of Peace Agreements After Violent Intrastate Conflict: Guidance for Internal Actors Responsible for Implementation* (Leiden: Martinus Nijhoff, 2011), 61.

[90] For an example of the creation of a 'joint monitoring commission' and a 'ceasefire monitoring committee', The Lomé Peace Agreement, Art 2, paras 1–2. For an example of the establishment of an 'independent boundary commission' and 'claims commission', Agreement between the Government of the State of Eritrea and the Government of the Federal Democratic Republic of Ethiopia, Art 4, para 2 and Art 5, para 1.

[91] On this, see also Scott Sheeran, 'The Use of Force in United Nations Peacekeeping Operations', Chapter 16 and Niels Blokker, 'Outsourcing the Use of Force', Chapter 9, both in this volume.

[92] Jane Boulden, *Peace Enforcement: The United Nations Experience in Congo, Somalia, and Bosnia* (New York: Praeger, 2001), 9.

[93] Jane Boulden, 'The Verification and Monitoring of Peace Accords' (2000) 3 *Disarmament Forum* 49.

Table 45.4 Examples of UN missions mandated to observe the implementation of ceasefires and peace agreements[94]

Peace settlement	Mission	Mandate
First Arab-Israeli War: Armistice Agreements between Israel and Egypt, Lebanon, Jordan, and Syria (1949)	UN Truce Supervision Mission (UNTSO) (1948–Present)	UN SC Res 73 (1949): Monitoring and reporting about armistice violations
Fourth Arab–Israeli War (Yom Kippur War): Separation of Forces Agreement Between Israel and Syria (1974)	UN Disengagement Observer Force (UNDOF) (1974–Present)	SC Res 350 (1974): monitoring of disengagement and armistice between Israeli and Syrian forces
Angolan Civil War: Multilateral Ceasefire (1990), Bicesse Accords (1991)	UN Angola Verification Mission II (UNAVEM II) (1991–5)	SC Res 696 (1991): verifying the peace agreements and monitoring of the ceasefire
El Salvador Civil War: Geneva Agreement (1990), Caracas Agenda (1990), San José Agreement (1990), Mexico Agreements (1991), Ceasefire 'Act of New York' (1991)	UN Observer Mission in El Salvador (ONUSAL) (1991–5)	SC Res 693 (1991): monitoring of all concluded agreements and verifying the compliance by the parties
Mozambique Civil War: Rome General Peace Accords, General Peace Agreement for Mozambique (1992)	UN Operation in Mozambique (ONUMOZ) (1992–4)	SC Res 797 (1992): monitoring and verifying the ceasefire, assistance in implementing the General Peace Agreement
Georgia–Abkhazia conflict: Cease-fire Agreement (1993)	UN Observer Mission in Georgia UNOMIG (1993–2009)	SC Res 858 (1993): verifying and reporting the compliance with the ceasefire agreement, investigating reports of cease-fire violations, and attempt to resolve such incidents with the parties involved

(*Continued*)

[94] For a general overview table about principal UN peacekeeping missions from 1947–2006, see Michael W. Doyle and Nicholas Sambanis, 'Peacekeeping Operations' in Thomas G. Weiss and Sam Daws (eds), *The Oxford Handbook on the United Nations* (Oxford: Oxford University Press, 2008), 328.

Table 45.4 (*Continued*)

Peace settlement	Mission	Mandate
Rwandan Civil War: Arusha Peace Agreement (1993)	UN Assistance Mission for Rwanda (UNAMIR) (1993–6)	SC Res 872 (1993): monitoring observance of the ceasefire agreement, monitoring the security situation, assisting with mine clearance, investigating instances of alleged non-compliance with the provisions of the Arusha Peace Agreement, monitoring the process of repatriation of Rwandese refugees and resettlement, assisting in the coordination of humanitarian assistance, investigating and reporting on incidents regarding the activities of the gendarmerie and police
First Liberian Civil War: Cotonou Peace Agreement (1993)	United Nations Observer Mission in Liberia (UNOMIL) (1993–7)	SC Res 866 (1993): monitoring and reporting ceasefire violations, observing and verifying the election process, supporting coordination of humanitarian assistance
Somali Civil War: Addis Ababa General Agreement (1993)	United Nations Operation in Somalia II (UNOSOM II) (1993–5)	SC Res 814 (1993): assisting in the implementation of the peace accord, including support in disarmament, mine-clearing, repatriation of refugees, accompanied by wide-ranging military permissions
Tajikistan Civil War: Agreement on a Temporary Cease-fire and the Cessation of Other Hostile Acts (1994)	UN Mission of Observers in Tajikistan (UNMOT) (1994–2002)	SC Res 968 (1994): assisting the Joint Commission to monitor the implementation of the ceasefire agreement, investigating and reporting ceasefire violations, providing good offices as stipulated in the agreement, providing political liaison and coordination services

Peace settlement	Mission	Mandate
Bosnian War: General Framework Agreement for Peace in Bosnia and Herzegovina (1995)	Implementation Force (IFOR) (1995–6), Stabilization Force (SFOR) (1998–2004), EUFOR Althea (2004–Present)	SC Res 1031 (1995): guaranteeing the implementation of the peace agreement, equipped with the authorization to use necessary force
Second Congo War: Lusaka Ceasefire Agreement (1999), Pretoria Accord (2002)	United Nations Organization Stabilisation Mission in the Democratic Republic of the Congo (MONUC) (1999–2010), United Nations Organisation Stabilization Mission in the Democratic Republic of the Congo (MONUSCO) (2010–Present)	SC Res 1279 (1999): providing technical assistance in the implementation of the ceasefire including the investigation of ceasefire violations, and facilitating the delivery of humanitarian assistance
Second Liberian Civil War: Peace Agreement (2003)	United Nations Mission in Liberia (UNMIL) (2003–Present)	SC Res 866 (1993): investigating all reports of alleged incidents of violations of the ceasefire agreement, monitoring compliance with other elements of the peace agreement, observing and verifying the election process, assisting in the coordination of humanitarian assistance, reporting on any major violations of international humanitarian law
Ivorian Civil War: Linas-Marcoussis Agreement (2003)	United Nations Mission in Côte d'Ivoire (MINUCI) (2003–4), United Nations Operation in Côte d'Ivoire (UNOCI) (2004–Present)	SC Res 1479 (2003): monitoring the military situation

(Continued)

Table 45.4 (*Continued*)

Peace settlement	Mission	Mandate
Rwandan Civil War: Arusha Peace and Reconciliation Agreement (2000)	United Nations Operation in Burundi (ONUB) (2005–7)	SC Res 1545 (2004): ensuring respect of ceasefire agreements through monitoring their implementation and investigating their violation, carrying out disarmament and demobilization, monitoring the illegal flow of arms, contributing to the successful completion of the electoral process
Border conflict between Ethiopia and Eritrea: Agreement on Cessation of Hostilities (2000)	United Nations Mission in Ethiopia and Eritrea (UNMEE) (2000–8)	SC Res 1312 (2000): verifying the cessation of hostilities, preparing for the establishment of the Military Coordination Commission provided for in the Cessation of Hostilities Agreement
Darfur conflict: Darfur Peace Agreement (2006)	United Nations Missions in Sudan (UNMIS) (2005–11)	SC Res 1706 (2006): monitoring and verifying the implementation of the cease-fire, supporting the implementation of the peace settlement with authorization to 'use all necessary means'
Abyei conflict: Comprehensive Peace Agreement (2005), Agreement on Temporary Arrangements for the Administration and Security of the Abyei Area (2011)	United Nations Interim Security Force for Abyei (UNISFA) (2011–Present)	SC Res 1990 (2011): monitoring and verifying the redeployment of any armed forces, providing de-mining assistance and technical advice, facilitating the delivery of humanitarian aid, participating in relevant Abyei Area bodies as stipulated in the Temporary Arrangements Agreement

in observing the cessation of hostilities in Palestine during the First Arab–Israeli War (1948–9).[95] The Armistice Agreements between Israel and its Arab neighbours, Egypt, Lebanon, Jordan, and Syria in 1949, led to the creation of a Mixed Armistice Commission in charge of claims and complaints in relation to the ceasefire. UNTSO remained in place to observe and maintain the ceasefire, as well as to support 'the parties to the Armistice Agreements in the supervision of the application and observance of the terms of those Agreements'.[96] To date, UNTSO has assisted and cooperated with the United Nations Disengagement Observer Force (UNDOF) on the Golan Heights and the United Nations Interim Force in Lebanon (UNIFIL).[97] UNDOF was initially established in 1974 to monitor the ceasefire between Israel and Syria in the wake of the Arab–Israeli Yom Kippur War and continues to oversee the disengagement between Israeli and Syrian forces.[98] UNIFIL was mandated five days after Israel's invasion of Lebanon in 1978 with the 'purpose of confirming the withdrawal of Israeli forces, restoring international peace and security, and assisting the Government of Lebanon in ensuring the return of its effective authority in the area'.[99] After the Israeli–Lebanese conflict in 2006, the mission also included the task to 'monitor the cessation of hostilities', 'accompany and support the Lebanese armed forces' throughout the south along the Blue Line, and secure the borders against illegal arms transfers.[100] Since that time, following an annual request by the Lebanese government and an extension of the mandate by the Security Council, UNIFIL has been stationed in the region.[101]

Another example is the complementary work of the Economic Community of West African States Monitoring Group (ECOMOG) and the United Nations Observer Mission in Liberia (UNOMIL) during the first Liberian civil war (1989–96), as well as the United Nations Mission in Liberia (UNMIL) established after the second Liberian civil war (1999–2003).[102] UNOMIL was created after the signing of the Cotonou Peace Agreement in 1993 to 'receive and investigate all reports on alleged incidents of violations of the ceasefire agreement', 'monitor compliance with other elements of the Peace Agreement', 'observe and verify the election process', support 'the coordination of humanitarian assistance', 'report on any major violations of international humanitarian law', and 'train ECOMOG engineers in mine clearance'.[103] Whereas UNOMIL was staffed with about 300 military observers, UNMIL

[95] SC Res 50, 29 May 1948, para 6; SC Res 54, 15 July 1948, para 7.

[96] SC Res 73, 11 Aug 1949, para 6.

[97] S/2012/403 (5 June 2012); S/2012/151 (12 Mar 2012).

[98] SC Res 2052, 27 June 2012; SC Res 350, 31 May 1974. See also Separation of Forces Agreement Between Israel and Syria, 31 May 1974, B para 3, UN Peacemaker Database.

[99] SC Res 425, 19 Mar 1978, para 6.

[100] SC Res 1701, 11 Aug 2006, para 11.

[101] SC Res 2064, 30 Aug 2012; S/2012/632 (14 Aug 2012).

[102] For an overview, see David Wippman, 'Enforcing The Peace: ECOWAS and the Liberian Civil War' in Lori Fisler Damrosch (ed), *Enforcing Restraint: Collective Intervention in Internal Conflicts* (New York: Council on Foreign Relations Press, 1993), 157; Dorina A. Bekoe, 'Toward a Theory of Peace Agreement Implementation: The Case of Liberia' (2003) 38 *Journal of Asian African Studies* 256.

[103] SC Res 866, 22 Sept 1993, para 3.

received a mandate for a mission of up to 15,000 UN military personnel.[104] As the first peacekeeping mission undertaken by the UN in cooperation with a peacekeeping mission already set up by another organization, in this case ECOWAS, the UN involvement was intended as a significant contribution 'to the effective implementation of the Peace Agreement'.[105] Unlike ECOMOG, a 'participation in enforcement operations' was explicitly excluded for UNOMIL.[106] In 2003, UNMIL superseded the prior observer mission and was charged with supporting the implementation of the 2003 ceasefire agreement after the resignation of President Charles Taylor.[107] The Security Council authorized the member states participating in the multinational peacekeeping force in Liberia 'to take all necessary measures to fulfil its mandate'.[108] As an ongoing primary task, UNMIL continues 'to support the Government in order to solidify peace and stability in Liberia and to protect civilians' and 'achieve a successful transition of complete security responsibility' to the Liberia National Police.[109]

B. Peace Enforcement Operations

UN peace enforcement operations are a challenge for the prohibition of the use of force, as their aim is to end hostilities and maintain peace through the use of force.[110] The idea of peace enforcement operations goes back to the 'Agenda for Peace' proposed by UN Secretary-General Boutros Boutros-Ghali in 1992, following a request by the Security Council to strengthen the UN's capacities in preventive diplomacy, peacemaking, and peacekeeping in the post-Cold War era. Boutros-Ghali highlighted that 'cease-fires have often been agreed to, but not complied with' and the United Nations has sometimes been subsequently 'called upon to send forces to restore and maintain the cease-fire'.[111]

Meanwhile, various cases have shown in practice that the demand and support for a negotiated political settlement by the UN can be reinforced through the use of coercive measures.[112] Among others, in Somalia (1994), Bosnia and Herzegovina (1995), and Darfur (2006), the UN Security Council authorized member states to

104 SC Res 1509, 19 Sept 2003, para 1. 105 SC Res 866, 22 Sept 1993, paras 5–6.

106 SC Res 866, 22 Sept 1993, para 3(h).

107 SC Res 1497, 1 Aug 2003, para 1. See also Peace Agreement between the Government of Liberia, the Liberians United for Reconciliation and Democracy, the Movement for Democracy in Liberia and the Political Parties.

108 SC Res 1497, 1 Aug 2003, para 5. 109 SC Res 2066, 17 Sept 2012, para 2.

110 For a comprehensive overview, see Trevor Findlay, *The Use of Force in UN Peace Operations* (Oxford: Oxford University Press, 2002), 3, 16.

111 An Agenda for Peace Preventive Diplomacy, Peacemaking and Peace-keeping, A/47/277, S/24111 (17 June 1992), para 44.

112 For an overview, see Table 45.4.

help to implement a peace settlement or catalyse a peace process through military action beyond the monitoring of ceasefires.[113]

A prominent example of such a peace enforcement operation is the United Nations Operation in Somalia (UNOSOM II). Previously, UNOSOM I merely deployed UN military monitors to oversee the brokered ceasefire that tried to end the Somali civil war in the early 1990s.[114] Shortly after, the UN mission was extended to 'secure an environment for humanitarian relief operations in Somalia.'[115] In 1993, Somali political leaders signed a peace agreement in Addis Ababa that declared an immediate cessation of all hostilities and called for a National Reconciliation Conference while tasking UNOSOM II with its preparation.[116] Acting under Chapter VII of the UN Charter, the Security Council subsequently expanded the peacekeeping operation to UNOSOM II adding to its mandate: disarmament, mine-clearing, assistance in the repatriation of refugees, and wide-ranging military permissions to prevent a resumption of violence and implement the Addis Ababa peace accord.[117]

In the case of Bosnia and Herzegovina, the Security Council authorized member states to take 'all necessary measures' to ensure the implementation and compliance with the Dayton Peace Agreement stressing that the parties to the peace accords 'shall be held equally responsible' for their compliance and 'shall be equally subject to such enforcement action' by the NATO-led Implementation Force (IFOR).[118] The Security Council recognized that this includes 'the use of necessary force.'[119] In 1996, IFOR was replaced by the Stabilization Force (SFOR). The Security Council maintained the mandate to allow the use of any necessary force and reaffirmed its intention to keep the implementation of the Peace Agreement and the situation in Bosnia and Herzegovina under review.[120] In 2004, the European Union Force (EUFOR) Althea took over the military oversight of the implementation of the Dayton Agreement. The Security Council resolution reassured that the mission could take actions as required, 'including the use of force', to ensure compliance with the peace agreement and relevant Security Council resolutions.[121]

Another example is the United Nations Mission in Sudan (UNMIS) and the 2006 Darfur Peace Agreement. UNMIS was mandated by the Security Council to support implementation of the peace settlement and the accompanying humanitarian ceasefire.[122] The mission was equipped with an instruction to 'use all necessary means' to support an 'early and effective implementation of the Darfur Peace Agreement.'[123]

[113] David Wippman, 'The United Nations, Peace Accords, and International Law' (Mar 1997) 5 *African Notes* 1.

[114] SC Res 751, 24 Apr 1992, para 3.
[115] SC Res 794, 3 Dec 1992, para 10.

[116] The General Agreement, 8 Jan 1993, paras 2–4, S/25168 (26 Jan 1993), Annex 2.

[117] SC Res 814, 26 Mar 1993, para 5. See also S/25354 (3 Mar 1993), paras 56–88.

[118] SC Res 1031, 15 Dec 1995, para 15.
[119] SC Res 1031, 15 Dec 1995, para 5.

[120] SC Res 1088, 12 Dec 1996, paras 1, 8.
[121] SC Res 1575, 22 Nov 2004, para 7.

[122] SC Res 1706, 31 Aug 2006, para 8.
[123] SC Res 1706, 31 Aug 2006, para 12(a).

The mandate also provided for the seizing or collection of arms or related material the presence of which in Darfur was in violation of the peace agreement. In 2011, UNMIS ended its mission transferring its authority to the United Nations Interim Security Force for Abyei (UNISFA) and the United Nations Mission in South Sudan (UNMISS).

V. Conclusion

Empirical studies estimate that over 40 per cent of all post-civil war countries relapse into conflict within five years.[124] Statistically, about half of all civil wars return to conflict during the first decade of peace.[125] It is assessed that since 2003 every new civil war has actually been a continuation of a previous civil war.[126] In terms of interstate conflicts, other research has observed that 'most agreements that renounce the use of force or restore diplomatic relations have lasted'.[127] Whereas peace agreements are more likely to last longer than ceasefires, the latter are more likely to endure than wars that end with no agreement, cases with no agreement can also be stable as long as one side surrenders.[128] As these numbers expose, peace settlements are neither a token for peace nor an insurance against re-emerging conflict. Although the statistics for the resolution of interstate wars appear promising, peace treaties can only partially protect against new conflicts.

From a legal perspective, the principle *pacta sunt servanda* has to be obeyed, which requires that promises must be kept. Otherwise, it is pointless to sign any peace commitments. A trend in contemporary international law is the authorization of enforced peace agreements through the UN Security Council. Instead of solely sending monitors, international practice has developed towards arming peacekeeping missions. This notion implies that the prohibition of the use of force is, rather oddly, achieved through the presence and threat of arms as a necessary means to achieve peace.

124 Paul Collier et al (eds), *Breaking the Conflict Trap: Civil War and Development Policy* (Oxford: Oxford University Press/World Bank, 2003), 83.

125 Paul Collier and Anke Hoeffler, 'The Challenge of Reducing the Global Incidence of Civil War', Centre for the Study of African Economies, Department of Economics, Oxford University, Mar 2004, 9.

126 Barbara Walter, *Conflict Relapse and the Sustainability of Post-Conflict Peace* (New York: World Bank, 2011), 1.

127 Virginia Page Fortna, *Peace Time: Cease-Fire Agreements and the Durability of Peace* (Princeton, NJ: Princeton University Press, 2004), 206.

128 Page Fortna, *Peace Time*, 206.

Under current international law, breach of a peace settlement does not provide a legal basis for enforcing a peace treaty by the use of armed force.[129] Yet, given the vast amount of unimplemented peace agreements, vowing to prohibit the use of force without sincere action could risk turning the principle into an empty promise. At the same time, peace can only be imposed to a limited degree. The signing of peace accords does not necessarily mark a post-conflict phase. However, they are vital vehicles for asserting the maintenance and end of hostilities. Peace settlements are not a guarantee of peace, nonetheless they are a chance to reinforce and strengthen the prohibition of the use of force.

In 2011, the former region of Qadesh in Egypt was hit by another armed conflict. The current situation in Syria, various ceasefire proposals, and the ongoing peacemaking efforts prove that achieving an end to hostilities through mutual agreement remains a difficult and often discouraging task. Meanwhile, the Egyptian–Hittite Peace Treaty survives on the southern wall of the Great Hypostyle Temple Hall in Karnak, bearing witness to the promise of peace. The peace treaty neither established perpetual peace nor prevented wars on other occasions. Nevertheless, the document is a spectator of the opportunities it preserves: the prohibition of the use of force, despite the tendency of humanity to wage war while aiming for peace.[130]

[129] Kleffner, 'Peace Treaties' in Wolfrum, *Max Planck Encyclopedia of Public International Law*, para 19.

[130] As Lotta Themnér and Peter Wallensteen stated in 2013, the number of internationalized intrastate conflicts 'continued to be at a high level for the fourth consecutive year'. Lotta Themnér and Peter Wallensteen, 'Armed Conflicts, 1946–2012' (2013) 50 *Journal of Peace Research* 509.

CHAPTER 46

THE EFFECTS OF A STATE OF WAR OR ARMED CONFLICT

MARINA MANCINI

I. Introduction

UNDER classical international law a state of war came into being between two states whenever one or both of them expressed the intention to wage war.[1] The establishment of a state of war had far-reaching effects on relations between belligerents as well as on relations between them and third states. The belligerents' subjects were also severely affected.

The concept of a state of war was premised on the assumption that states were free to go to war to pursue their interests. In the first decades of the 20th century, however, states progressively renounced such a freedom. In 1945, the UN Charter came to impose, in Article 2(4), a general prohibition on the use or threat of armed force in international relations. This prohibition is a pillar of contemporary international law. The question arises as to how it influenced the concept of a state of war

[1] In this chapter, for the sake of convenience, international law prior to the UN Charter is referred to as classical international law. The peace treaties which ended the Second World War, although concluded after the entry into force of the Charter, are also ascribed to classical international law.

and the consequences traditionally attached to it. In fact, in the UN era belligerents tend to consider themselves not in a state of war, even when involved in large-scale hostilities. They usually confine themselves to admit to being engaged in an armed conflict. Hence, the question also arises as to the effects of an armed conflict in contemporary international law.

This chapter focuses on both of the aforementioned questions. Section II will consider the modalities through which a state of war could be established under classical international law, and Section III will survey the consequences traditionally attached to it. Section IV will explore state practice regarding the creation of a state of war in the UN era, and Section V will investigate the concept of armed conflict to which today belligerents make reference. Finally, Section VI will examine the effects of an interstate armed conflict in contemporary international law.

II. The Creation of a State of War in Classical International Law

Under classical international law a state of war arose between two states whenever one or both of them manifested the intention to make war. This constituted a temporary state of affairs, in which relations between such states were governed by the law of war, while relations between each of them and third states were regulated by the law of neutrality.[2]

Interestingly, the outbreak of hostilities between two states, even on a large-scale, did not automatically entail a state of war. This came into existence only when the intent to wage war—*animus belligerandi*—was expressed by either or both of the parties. Terminology reflected the point: actual hostilities were also referred to as 'war in the material sense' or 'de facto war', while the state of war was also mentioned as 'war in the legal sense', 'war in the technical sense', 'war in the formal sense', or 'de jure war'.[3]

The intention to make war could be manifested by a declaration of war, an ultimatum with a conditional declaration of war, or some overt act considered as conclusive, such as the exercise of belligerent rights, which states only enjoyed during a state of war.[4]

[2] Quincy Wright, 'When Does War Exist?' (1932) 26 *American Journal of International Law* 362, 363.

[3] Wright, 'When Does War Exist?', 362 f; Lothar Kotzsch, *The Concept of War in Contemporary History and International Law* (Geneva: Librairie E. Droz, 1956), 54 ff; Arnold D. McNair and Arthur D. Watts, *The Legal Effects of War* (4th edn, Cambridge: Cambridge University Press, 1966), 3.

[4] Wright, 'When Does War Exist?', 363 f.

The 1907 Hague Convention III required states parties not to begin hostilities between them without a previous and explicit warning in the form either of a reasoned declaration of war or an ultimatum with conditional declaration of war (Art 1).[5] It also obliged the states parties at war to notify the existence of a state of war to third states parties without delay. The state of war took effect in regard to the latter as soon as notification was received. Third states, however, could not plead the absence of notification to escape the duties of neutrality, if it was established beyond doubt that they were in fact aware of the state of war (Art 2). The Convention, which entered into force in 1910, was breached several times in the decades following its entry into force. However, the opening of hostilities without a previous declaration of war or an ultimatum with conditional declaration of war, while constituting an internationally wrongful act by states parties, did not in itself preclude a state of war arising.[6]

The intention to wage war could also be expressed by the attacking state after the commencement of hostilities. Moreover, where the *animus belligerandi* was not manifested by the attacking state, the state of war could nevertheless be established on the initiative of the attacked state. In fact, an act of force carried out *sine animo belligerandi* could be regarded by the victim state as creating a state of war.[7]

Where an intent to make war was manifested, a state of war came into being even if no hostilities followed. For example, in both World Wars, a number of Latin American states, by declaring war on Germany, brought about a state of war with that country, although their forces never engaged in hostilities.[8] On the other hand, once it had arisen, a state of war persisted even after the suspension of hostilities, until brought to an end, often through a peace treaty.[9]

Where neither party expressed the intention to wage war, the state of war did not arise, even though protracted hostilities occurred, such as in the case of the hostilities between China and Japan in the 1930s.[10] It is worth noting, however, that although not admitted by either of the belligerents, the existence of a state of war could be recognized by a third state. Such recognition had limited effects: it amounted to an assertion by that state of the intention to abide by the law of neutrality in the

[5] On the declaration of war, see Clyde Eagleton, 'The Form and Function of the Declaration of War' (1938) 32 *American Journal of International Law* 19.

[6] McNair and Watts, *The Legal Effects of War*, 7.

[7] Wright, 'When Does War Exist?', 365; Ian Brownlie, *International Law and the Use of Force by States* (Oxford: Oxford University Press, 1963), 39; McNair and Watts, *The Legal Effects of War*, 7 f.

[8] See Kotzsch, *The Concept of War*, 246; Yoram Dinstein, *War, Aggression and Self-Defence* (5th edn, Cambridge: Cambridge University Press, 2012), 9.

[9] On the modes of termination of the state of war, see Lassa Oppenheim, *International Law. A Treatise*, vol II (7th edn, ed Hersch Lauterpacht, London: Longmans, Green and Co, 1952), 596 ff; Alfons Klafkowski, 'Les formes de cessation de l'état de guerre en droit international' (1976-I) *Recueil des cours de l'Académie de droit international* 217.

[10] See Brownlie, *International Law and the Use of Force*, 385 ff.

relations with them and precluded it from objecting to the subsequent exercise of belligerent rights by either party against it.[11]

III. The Effects of a State of War in Classical International Law

Classical international law attached far-reaching consequences to a state of war. They can be summarized as follows.

A. Application of the Law of War

When two states entered into a state of war, they were bound to abide by the law of war. According to a well-established principle of international law, the law of war applied equally to all belligerents, irrespective of which was the aggressor.

B. Application of the Law of Neutrality

Following the creation of a state of war, the law of neutrality came to apply in the relations between belligerents and third states. It constituted a set of rules aimed at ensuring a position of impartiality by third states towards belligerents. Third countries were bound to comply with the law of neutrality as soon as they were notified of the existence of a state of war or otherwise became in fact aware of it.[12] In practice, they often issued a declaration of neutrality. Such declaration, however, was not necessary for a third state to acquire neutral status.[13]

Classical international law did not recognize an intermediate position between belligerency and neutrality. When war broke out, third states could either remain neutral or themselves become belligerents.[14] In practice, however, at the outbreak of the Second World War, a number of states, including Italy, the US, Spain, and

[11] Kotzsch, *The Concept of War*, 60; McNair and Watts, *The Legal Effects of War*, 10.

[12] Oppenheim, *International Law*, 655.

[13] Titus Komarnicki, 'The Place of Neutrality in the Modern System of International Law' (1952-I) *Recueil des cours de l'Académie de droit international* 399, 404; Oppenheim, *International Law*, 654.

[14] Dietrich Schindler, 'Aspects contemporains de la neutralité' (1967-II) *Recueil des cours de l'Académie de droit international* 225, 261.

Argentina, took a position of non-belligerency or qualified neutrality, as they favoured one of the belligerents without intervening militarily.[15]

C. Severance of Diplomatic Relations

Another consequence of the establishment of a state of war was the rupture of diplomatic relations between opposing belligerents. Where they had not yet been severed, diplomatic relations were immediately broken off following the outbreak of war.[16]

D. Treatment of the Belligerents' Subjects on Enemy Territory

The creation of a state of war severely affected the condition of the subjects of belligerents on enemy territory. Belligerent states were free to adopt a wide range of measures against enemy aliens within their territory. First of all, they could expel them en masse; however, mass expulsion of enemy subjects rarely occurred during either of the World Wars.[17]

Moreover, belligerents could take restrictive measures of varying intensity depending on the danger enemy aliens posed to public order and national security. Examples of such measures were bans on possession of certain items, in particular arms and ammunition of any kind, restrictions on movements within the national territory, compulsory residence in certain areas or even internment in camps. During the World Wars, belligerents interned large numbers of enemy aliens. Often, as the hostilities progressed, they adopted a policy of general internment.[18]

Under Article 23(1)(h) of the Regulations annexed to the 1907 Hague Convention IV, belligerents were prohibited from declaring the rights and actions of enemy nationals to be terminated, suspended, or inadmissible in the courts. In practice, however, during both World Wars in a number of cases belligerents

[15] See Robert Wilson, '"Non-Belligerency" in relation to the Terminology of Neutrality' (1941) 35 *American Journal of International Law* 121; Komarnicki, 'The Place of Neutrality', 454 ff; Schindler, 'Aspects contemporains de la neutralité', 263.

[16] Oppenheim, *International Law*, 301 f; Erik Castrén, *The Present Law of War and Neutrality* (Helsinki: Suomalaisen Tiedeakatemian Toimituksia, 1954), 103 f.

[17] See Castrén, *The Present Law of War and Neutrality*, 111.

[18] On belligerent practice during the First World War, see James Garner, 'Treatment of Enemy Aliens' (1918) 13 *American Journal of International Law* 27. On belligerent practice during the Second World War, see Maximilian Koessler, 'Enemy Alien Internment: With Special Reference to Great Britain and France' (1942) 57 *Political Science Quarterly* 98; Robert Wilson, 'Treatment of Civilian Alien Enemies' (1943) 37 *American Journal of International Law* 30.

denied enemy aliens the right of access to court. For example, enemy nationals resident in enemy territory had no right to sue in the English courts, except by licence of the Crown.[19]

As regards enemy subjects' property, customary international law prohibited the belligerents from confiscating the property of enemy aliens.[20] During both World Wars, belligerents formally abided by this prohibition and abstained from confiscating enemy aliens' property. In a number of cases, however, they took measures that in fact divested enemy aliens of their property permanently: movable and immovable property was sold, companies liquidated, and the proceeds deposited in special accounts.[21]

E. Effects on Trade Relations

Trade between the subjects of belligerent states was greatly impacted by the establishment of a state of war. In fact, during both World Wars all belligerents banned trade between their own and enemy subjects, with very few exceptions, and they enacted specific legislation to that end.[22] Notably, in several cases the legislation which had been adopted during the First World War was amended or replaced when the country entered the Second World War. In the UK, the Trading with the Enemy Act 1914 was replaced by the Trading with the Enemy Act 1939[23] and, in the US, the Trading with the Enemy Act of 1917 was amended by the First War Powers Act of 1941.[24]

[19] See McNair and Watts, *The Legal Effects of War*, 78 ff.

[20] Charles Rousseau, *Le droit des conflits armés* (Paris: Pedone, 1983), 53. The prohibition of confiscating enemy subjects' property in occupied territory was enshrined in Art 46 of the Regulations annexed to the 1899 Hague Convention II and of the Regulations annexed to the 1907 Hague Convention IV.

[21] On belligerent practice during the First World War, see John Scobell Armstrong, *War and Treaty Legislation 1914–1922 Affecting British Property in Germany and Austria, and Enemy Property in the United Kingdom* (London: Hutchinson, 1922), 3 ff, 75 ff, 103 ff; Rousseau, *Le droit des conflits armés*, 55 f. On belligerent practice during the Second World War, see Mitchell Carroll, 'Legislation on Treatment of Enemy Property' (1943) 37 *American Journal of International Law* 611; Rousseau, *Le droit des conflits armés*, 59 ff.

[22] On the legislation passed by belligerent states during the First World War, see Scobell Armstrong, *War and Treaty Legislation 1914–1922*, 3 ff, 75 ff, 103 ff; Oppenheim, *International Law*, 319 f; Rousseau, *Le droit des conflits armés*, 49 f. On the legislation enacted by belligerents during the Second World War, see Oppenheim, *International Law*, 320 f; Rousseau, *Le droit des conflits armés*, 50 ff.

[23] 'Trading with the Enemy Act, 1939' (1942) 36 *American Journal of International Law Supp* 3.

[24] See the Trading with the Enemy Act, as approved on 6 Oct 1917 in (1918) 12 *American Journal of International Law Supp* 27, and the amending provisions contained in the First War Powers Act, 1941 in (1942) 36 *American Journal of International Law Supp* 56.

F. Effects on Contracts

The ban on trade had inevitable repercussions for contractual relationships between the belligerents' subjects. Depending on the circumstances, the domestic legislation of belligerent states might provide for the nullity, termination, or suspension of contracts with enemy subjects.[25]

The peace treaties concluded after both World Wars contained provisions concerning the fate of pre-war contracts between belligerents' subjects. After the First World War, the Treaties of Versailles, Saint Germain, Trianon, and Neuilly stipulated that, in principle, all pre-war contracts were dissolved from the time when any of the parties had become 'enemies'—that is, from the date when trading between them had become unlawful—except in respect of pecuniary obligations arising out of acts carried out in the performance of those contracts.[26] However, several classes of contract were exempt from dissolution.[27] Moreover, contracts were not dissolved in cases where the execution of the contract was required in the general interest by the Allied or Associated Power of which one of the parties was a national; this applied during the six months after entry into force of the treaty.[28]

After the Second World War, the peace treaties concluded by the Allied and Associated Powers with Bulgaria, Finland, Italy, Romania, and Hungary reaffirmed the principle of the dissolution of pre-war contracts from the time when any of the parties had become 'enemies' because of the ban on trade between them, but they confined the application of such principle to contracts which required interaction between the parties for their execution.[29]

G. Effects on Treaties

The establishment of a state of war also affected treaties between belligerents. Until the beginning of the 20th century, state practice supported the view that all treaties

[25] See eg the Italian legislation on the issue: Art 2 of Lieutenant Decree no 960 of 8 Aug 1916, in SIOI, CNR, *La prassi italiana di diritto internazionale, Seconda Serie (1887–1918)* (Dobbs Ferry, NY: Oceana, 1980), vol IV, 1948; Arts 332 and 333 of the Articles of War promulgated by Royal Decree no 1415 of 8 July 1938, *Gazzetta Ufficiale del Regno d'Italia*, 15 Sept 1938 no 211, Supp.

[26] Art 299(a) and Art 1 of the Annex to Part X of the Treaty of Versailles; Art 251(a) and Art 1 of the Annex to Part X of the Treaty of Saint Germain; Art 234(a) and Art 1 of the Annex to Part X of the Treaty of Trianon; Art 180(a) and Art 1 of the Annex to Part IX of the Treaty of Neuilly.

[27] Art 2 of the Annex to Part X of the Treaties of Versailles, Saint Germain, and Trianon, and Art 2 of the Annex to Part IX of the Treaty of Neuilly.

[28] Art 299(b) of the Treaty of Versailles; Art 251(b) of the Treaty of Saint Germain; Art 234(b) of the Treaty of Trianon; Art 180(b) of the Treaty of Neuilly.

[29] Arts A and D of Annex XVI to Peace Treaty between the Allied and Associated Powers and Italy; Arts A and D of Annex V to the peace treaties concluded by the Allied and Associated Powers with Bulgaria, Finland, Romania, and Hungary.

between belligerents were automatically terminated on the creation of a state of war, except for those governing the conduct of hostilities and relations with neutral states.

However, in the first years of the new century, an opposing view emerged.[30] In 1910, in the *North Atlantic Coast Fisheries* case, the Permanent Court of Arbitration held that 'international law in its modern development recognises that a great number of Treaty obligations are not annulled by war, but at most suspended by it'.[31] Two years later, the Institute of International Law argued for the survival of most treaties between belligerents.[32]

The peace treaties that ended both World Wars generally confirmed, albeit in an ambiguous way, the new trend. The Treaties of Versailles, Saint Germain, Trianon, and Neuilly distinguished between multilateral and bilateral conventions. With regard to the former, it was stipulated that as from the entry into force of the peace treaty the contracting states should apply inter se the multilateral conventions listed therein to which they had become parties before the war.[33] For bilateral conventions, it was agreed that the pre-war conventions should 'be revived'/'put in force', in cases where each of the Allied and Associated Powers had notified them to the counterpart within six months of the entry into force of the peace treaty.[34]

The 1947 peace treaties concluded by the Allied and Associated Powers with Bulgaria, Finland, Italy, Romania, and Hungary only mentioned bilateral conventions. Each of the Allied and Associated Powers was required to notify the counterpart of the pre-war conventions which they wished to 'keep in force or revive', within six months of the entry into force of the peace treaty. The pre-war conventions not so notified were regarded as being terminated.[35]

[30] ILC, The Effect of Armed Conflict on Treaties: An Examination of Practice and Doctrine, Memorandum by the Secretariat, A/CN.4/550 (1 Feb 2005), paras 14–15.

[31] Permanent Court of Arbitration, *North Atlantic Coast Fisheries (Great Britain v. US)*, Award of the Tribunal, The Hague, 7 Sept 1910, available at <http://www.pca-cpa.org/showpage.asp?pag_id=1029>.

[32] Institut de Droit International, Règlement concernant les effets de la guerre sur les traités, Session de Christiania—1912, available at <http://www.idi-iil.org/idiF/navig_chron1913.html>.

[33] Arts 282–7 of the Treaty of Versailles; Arts 234–8 of the Treaty of Saint Germain; Arts 217–21 of the Treaty of Trianon; Arts 162–4 of the Treaty of Neuilly.

[34] Art 289 of the Treaty of Versailles; Art 241 of the Treaty of Saint Germain; Art 224 of the Treaty of Trianon; Art 168 of the Treaty of Neuilly.

[35] Art 44 of the Peace Treaty between the Allied and Associated Powers and Italy; Art 8 of the Peace Treaty between the Allied and Associated Powers and Bulgaria; Art 12 of the Peace Treaty between the Allied and Associated Powers and Finland; Art 10 of the peace treaties concluded by the Allied and Associated Powers with Romania and Hungary.

IV. The Prohibition on the Use of Force and Its Influence on State Practice

The concept of a state of war was premised on the assumption that states were free to make war to pursue their interests. However, in the first decades of the 20th century states progressively renounced such freedom. The main steps in this process were the conclusion of the Covenant of the League of Nations in 1919 and the adoption of the General Treaty for the Renunciation of War in 1928. In 1945, the UN Charter laid down, in Article 2(4), a general prohibition on the use or threat of armed force in interstate relations.

The principle of non-use of force expressed in the article is a cardinal principle of contemporary international law. Nonetheless, war in the material sense remains possible. On the one hand, the prohibition on the use of force has been breached many times; on the other, states are still permitted to resort to force in self-defence, and may be authorized to use force by the Security Council. Hence, one wonders whether war in the legal sense is likewise possible.

State practice reveals that a state of war is not in itself considered incompatible with the principle of non-use of force in international relations.[36] In several cases, the existence of a state of war was admitted by one of the belligerents: for example, in the Indo-Pakistani conflict of 1965, Pakistan introduced contraband control and established prize courts, affirming that a state of war existed with India.[37] Sometimes a state of war was recognized a posteriori at the time of restoring peace: for instance, Israel admitted that a state of war existed with Egypt only when it signed the 1979 peace treaty, which included a clause on the cessation of the state of war (Art I(1)).[38] In other cases, belligerents have implicitly recognized the possibility of establishing a state of war, although they have denied an

[36] On the question of the compatibility between the establishment of a state of war and the prohibition on the use of force, see Richard Baxter, 'The Definition of War' (1960) 16 *Revue egyptienne de droit international* 1, 8 ff; McNair and Watts, *The Legal Effects of War*, 4 ff; Elihu Lauterpacht, 'The Legal Irrelevance of the 'State of War' (1968) 62 *Proceedings of the American Society of International Law* 58, 63 ff; Dietrich Schindler, 'State of War, Belligerency, Armed Conflict' in Antonio Cassese (ed), *The New Humanitarian Law of Armed Conflict* (Naples: Editoriale Scientifica, 1979), 3, 16 ff; Christopher Greenwood, 'The Concept of War in Modern International Law' (1987) 36 *International and Comparative Law Quarterly* 283, 287 ff.

[37] 'A Proclamation as to Contraband of War, published in the Gazette of Pakistan, Extraordinary, September 9, 1965' in Surya Prakash Sharma, *The Indo-Pakistan Maritime Conflict, 1965* (Bombay: Academic Books, 1970), 65 f.

[38] 'Egypt–Israel: Treaty of Peace, Washington, March 26, 1979' (1979) 18 ILM 362.

intention to do so. During the Vietnam conflict, the US disclosed the reasons why it considered it to be 'undesirable' to declare war on North Vietnam, assuming that the adoption of a declaration of war and the ensuing creation of a state of war were permitted by international law.[39]

Overall, however, in the UN era states have tended to consider themselves not to be in a state of war, even in the case of large-scale hostilities involving massive deployment of forces. In particular, belligerents acting under the Security Council authorization have never admitted the existence of a state of war.[40]

As regards the obligation not to begin hostilities without a previous declaration of war or an ultimatum with a conditional declaration of war laid down in the 1907 Hague Convention III, it is apparently still binding on states parties.[41] However, since the entry into force of the UN Charter, the beginning of hostilities has never been preceded by an unequivocal declaration of war.[42] The fear that a declaration of war could cause a misunderstanding of the real objectives of the military action and attract the accusation of violating the prohibition on the use of force, has led states parties to the 1907 Hague Convention III to overlook the aforementioned obligation.[43] Additionally, a declaration of war is in itself a threat of force. As such, it would be lawful only if the use of the threatened force were in conformity with the UN Charter.[44] Moreover, a declaration of war, even when lawful, would not entitle the issuing state to use force beyond the limits imposed by the Charter and customary international law.[45]

39 'Effects of a Formal Declaration of War: U.S. Defense Department Statement' (1966) 5 ILM 791.

40 On this point, see Marina Mancini, *Stato di guerra e conflitto armato nel diritto internazionale* (Turin: Giappichelli, 2009), 165 ff.

41 The 1907 Hague Convention III is considered to be in force by the government of the Netherlands that is the depositary. See <http://www.minbuza.nl/en/key-topics/treaties/search-the-treaty-database/1907/10/003318.html>.

42 Christopher Greenwood, 'Scope of Application of Humanitarian Law' in Dieter Fleck (ed), *The Handbook of International Humanitarian Law* (2nd edn, Oxford: Oxford University Press, 2008), 45, 49. With regard to the 1998–2000 conflict between Ethiopia and Eritrea, the Claims Commission that was established by the Algiers Peace Agreement held that the resolution of the Ethiopian Council of Ministers and Parliament of 13 May 1998, which condemned the Eritrean invasion and demanded the immediate withdrawal of Eritrean forces from Ethiopian territory, was not, as asserted by Eritrea, a declaration of war. EECC, Partial Award, Jus Ad Bellum: *Ethiopia's Claims 1–8*, The Hague, 19 Dec 2005, para 17.

43 On this point, see UK Ministry of Defence, *The Manual of the Law of Armed Conflict* (Oxford: Oxford University Press, 2004), para 3.2.2.

44 With regard to this, in its 1996 advisory opinion on the *Legality of the Threat or Use of Nuclear Weapons*, the International Court of Justice affirmed that 'the notions of "threat" and "use" of force under Article 2, paragraph 4, of the Charter stand together in the sense that if the use of force itself in a given case is illegal—for whatever reason—the threat to use such force will likewise be illegal'. *Legality of the Threat or Use of Nuclear Weapons*, Advisory Opinion, ICJ Rep 1996, 226, para 47.

45 Greenwood, 'Scope of Application of Humanitarian Law', 50.

v. The Concept of Armed Conflict in Contemporary International Law

In 2005, the High Court of Justice of England and Wales correctly described the present state of international law in *Amin v. Brown*, where it held that 'the traditional concept of war has virtually disappeared from state practice since the Second World War. Unhappily, armed conflict has continued to be an instrument of state policy. But it is almost never necessary to invoke the traditional legal concept of war'.[46]

In the UN era, belligerents have usually confined themselves to admitting being engaged in an armed conflict. In this way, they only confirm a factual situation. Nowadays, the concept of war has largely been replaced by the concept of armed conflict.[47] As illustrated later, though the phrase 'armed conflict' in itself only describes an actual fact, important legal consequences are today attached to the outbreak of an armed conflict between states.

Armed conflict was first considered a source of rights and obligations for belligerent states by the four 1949 Geneva Conventions. Under Common Article 2(1), they apply 'to all cases of declared war or of any other armed conflict which may arise between two or more of the High Contracting Parties, even if the state of war is not recognised by one of them'. On the one hand, this provision confirms the possibility of establishing a state of war, but on the other, it makes the application of the Geneva Conventions dependent on the outbreak of an armed conflict, regardless of whether a state of war arises or not. Although Common Article 2(1) does not mention the case in which a state of war is not recognized by either of the parties, it is generally held that the Conventions also apply in such cases.[48]

However, armed conflict is not defined by either the Geneva Conventions or the subsequent conventions that likewise make their application dependent on the outbreak of an armed conflict between two or more of the states parties.[49] Indeed, there is no universally agreed definition of what constitutes an armed conflict. The International Committee of the Red Cross (ICRC) Commentaries to the Second,

[46] *Amin v. Brown* [2005] EWHC 1670 (Ch), para 28.

[47] ILA Committee on the Use of Force (2005–2010), Final Report on the Meaning of Armed Conflict in International Law, The Hague Conference, 2010, available at <http://www.ila-hq.org/en/committees/index.cfm/cid/1022>, 33.

[48] See Jean Pictet (ed), *IV Geneva Convention relative to the Protection of Civilian Persons in Time of War—Commentary* (Geneva: ICRC, 1958), 21; Jean Pictet (ed), *III Geneva Convention relative to the Treatment of Prisoners of War—Commentary* (Geneva: ICRC, 1960), 23; Greenwood, 'Scope of Application of Humanitarian Law', 47.

[49] See Art 18(1) of the 1954 Hague Convention for the Protection of Cultural Property in the Event of Armed Conflict; Art 1(3) of the 1977 Additional Protocol I; Art 1(1) of the 1980 Convention on Conventional Weapons.

Third, and Fourth Geneva Conventions define armed conflict as 'any difference arising between two States and leading to the intervention of members of the armed forces', irrespective of how long it lasts, how many casualties it causes, and how numerous the deployed forces are.[50]

A broad definition of armed conflict is also found in the well-known 1995 decision of the International Criminal Tribunal for the former Yugoslavia (ICTY) Appeals Chamber in the *Tadić* case. Referring to both international and non-international armed conflicts, the Appeals Chamber held that '*an armed conflict exists whenever there is a resort to armed force between States* or protracted armed violence between governmental authorities and organized armed groups or between such groups within a State'.[51]

Almost the same definition is contained in the Draft Articles on the Effects of Armed Conflicts on Treaties, which was adopted by the International Law Commission (ILC) on second reading in 2011.[52] Article 2(b) defines armed conflict as '*a situation in which there is resort to armed force between States* or protracted resort to armed force between governmental authorities and organized armed groups'.[53]

According to a widely held view, however, an armed conflict between states can be said to exist only where hostilities reach a certain level of intensity. For instance, upon signing the 1977 Additional Protocol I, the UK declared that 'the term "armed conflict" of itself and in its context implies a certain level of intensity of military operations which must be present before the Conventions or the Protocol are to apply to any given situation'.[54] The 2004 UK *Manual of the Law of Armed Conflict* specifies that 'whether any particular intervention crosses the threshold so as to become an armed conflict will depend on all the surrounding circumstances'.[55] By way of example, it notes that 'an accidental border incursion by members of the armed forces would not, in itself, amount to an armed conflict, nor would the accidental bombing of another country'.[56]

Referring to both international and non-international armed conflicts, the International Law Association (ILA) Committee on the Use of Force (2005–10) affirmed that there is 'significant state practice and *opinio juris* establishing that as a matter of customary international law a situation of armed conflict depends on the

[50] Pictet, *IV Geneva Convention*, 20; Pictet, *III Geneva Convention*, 23; Jean Pictet (ed), *II Geneva Convention for the Amelioration of the Condition of Wounded, Sick and Shipwrecked Members of Armed Forces at Sea—Commentary* (Geneva: ICRC, 1960), 28. See also Jean Pictet (ed), *I Geneva Convention for the Amelioration of the Condition of the Wounded and Sick in Armed Forces in the Field—Commentary* (Geneva: ICRC, 1952), 32, which contains a nearly identical definition of armed conflict.

[51] ICTY Appeals Chamber, *Prosecutor v. Duško Tadić a/k/a 'Dule'*, Decision on the Defence Motion for Interlocutory Appeal on Jurisdiction of 2 Oct 1995, para 70 (emphasis added).

[52] Report of the International Law Commission on its Sixty-Third Session (26 Apr–3 June and 4 July–12 Aug 2011), A/66/10, 175.

[53] Emphasis added. [54] 1125 UNTS 432.

[55] UK Ministry of Defence, *The Manual of the Law of Armed Conflict*, para 3.3.1.

[56] UK Ministry of Defence, *The Manual of the Law of Armed Conflict*, para 3.3.1.

satisfaction of two essential minimum criteria, namely: (a) the existence of organised armed groups; (b) engaged in fighting of some intensity'.[57] Indeed, in conflicts between states the former criterion is easily met, as the opposing forces are usually their regular armed forces; what may be in question is the fulfilment of the latter.[58]

VI. The Effects of an Armed Conflict in Contemporary International Law

On the eve of the 2003 Gulf conflict, the UK Attorney General, Lord Goldsmith, asserted in the House of Lords that 'the existence or not of a legal state of war is nowadays irrelevant for most purposes of international law'.[59] Indeed, contemporary international law attaches wide-ranging consequences to the outbreak of an armed conflict between states, regardless of whether or not a state of war comes into being. These are summarized in the following sections.

A. Application of the Law of War

As soon as an armed conflict erupts between two states, the *jus in bello* becomes applicable. This body of law has been greatly expanded since the end of the Second World War, and is now also known as the law of armed conflict or international humanitarian law. The various conventions relating to the conduct of hostilities are applicable from the outbreak of the armed conflict, irrespective of whether the state of war is recognized by the belligerents.

The law of armed conflict applies equally to all belligerent states, regardless of which is the aggressor. The principle of the equal application of the law of war to all belligerents, which was a fundamental tenet of the *jus in bello* in classical international law, has not been impacted by the affirmation of the principle of non-use of force in international relations.[60] It is implicitly recognized in Common Article 1 to the Geneva Conventions. Under this article, states parties shall respect and ensure respect for each of the Conventions 'in all circumstances'. The aforementioned

[57] ILA Committee on the Use of Force (2005–2010), Final Report, 32.

[58] ILA Committee on the Use of Force (2005–2010), Final Report, 29.

[59] Declaration of War: Parliamentary Approval, Hansard, HL Deb, 19 Feb 2003, vol 644, col 1138.

[60] Brownlie, *International Law and the Use of Force*, 406 f; Christopher Greenwood, 'The Relationship between *Ius ad Bellum* and *Ius in Bello*' (1983) 9 *Review of International Studies* 221, 225; Dinstein, *War, Aggression and Self-Defence*, 170.

principle is also explicitly proclaimed in the Preamble to Additional Protocol I, which stipulates that the Conventions and the Protocol itself 'must be fully applied in all circumstances to all persons who are protected by those instruments, without any adverse distinction based on the nature or origin of the armed conflict or on the causes espoused by or attributed to the Parties to the conflict'.

B. Exercise of Belligerent Rights

As regards belligerent rights to take certain measures of economic warfare at sea, there has been an evolution in state practice since the entry into force of the UN Charter. Until the 1960s the exercise of such rights was considered dependent on the existence of a state of war. After the 1949 armistice with Israel, Egypt continued to exercise its right to visit and search merchant ships passing through the Suez Canal, on the assumption that the state of war persisted.[61] Conversely, Israel contested this practice stressing that no state of war existed.[62] In Resolution 95 (1951), the Security Council condemned this as 'an abuse of the exercise of the right of visit, search and seizure', noting inter alia that since the armistice regime had a permanent character neither of the parties could reasonably claim to be 'actively a belligerent'. In the 1965 conflict with India, Pakistan introduced contraband control and established prize courts affirming that a state of war had come into being.[63] Conversely, India opposed such measures on the ground that there was no state of war.[64]

Nowadays the existence of a state of war is no longer considered a condition for the exercise of belligerent rights.[65] During the Falklands conflict, both the UK and Argentina established maritime exclusion zones, though neither of them recognized the state of war.[66] In the 1980–8 conflict, neither Iraq nor Iran admitted that a state of war had come into being; however, they both established war zones. Moreover, Iran imposed a blockade on Iraqi ports and the Shatt-al-Arab estuary, while Iraq established a blockade of Kharg Island. As from 1985, Iran also visited and searched

[61] 'Conclusions du Gouvernement Egyptien au sujet des plaintes des Gouvernements étrangers quant à la visite des navires neutres et la saisie des objets de contrebande dans les ports égyptiens' (1951) 7 *Revue égyptienne de droit international* 235, 238 ff.

[62] SCOR, Sixth Year, 549th mtg, S/PV.549 (26 July 1951), 1, para 41.

[63] 'A Proclamation as to Contraband of War', 65 f.

[64] 'Aide Memoire, November 25, 1965' in Sharma, *The Indo-Pakistan Maritime Conflict, 1965*, 78 f.

[65] Michael Bothe, 'Neutrality in Naval Warfare' in Astrid Delissen and Gerard Tanja (eds), *Humanitarian Law of Armed Conflict: Challenges Ahead* (Leiden: Martinus Nijhoff, 1991), 387, 390; Wolff Heintschel von Heinegg, 'The Current State of International Prize Law' in Harry Post (ed), *International Economic Law and Armed Conflict* (Leiden: Martinus Nijhoff, 1994), 5, 7 f; Louise Doswald-Beck, *San Remo Manual on International Law Applicable to Armed Conflicts at Sea* (Cambridge: International Institute of Humanitarian Law/Cambridge University Press, 1995), 74.

[66] See William Fenrick, 'The Exclusion Zone Device in the Law of Naval Warfare' (1986) 24 *Canadian Yearbook of International Law* 91, 109 ff.

third states' ships in the Persian Gulf.[67] During the 2006 Israeli–Lebanese conflict, Israel imposed an air and sea blockade on Lebanon, although it did not recognize the existence of a state of war.[68]

It appears, however, that belligerent rights cannot be exercised in all armed conflicts, whatever their scale and duration.[69] State practice shows that so far belligerents have claimed them only where they have been engaged in large-scale hostilities. Moreover, it is widely accepted that the exercise of belligerent rights is lawful only insofar as it can be justified in terms of self-defence.[70] In Resolution 95 (1951), the Security Council affirmed that in the prevailing circumstances the Egyptian practice of visiting and searching ships passing through the Suez Canal could not be justified on the ground that it was necessary for self-defence. It thus implicitly recognized that visits and searches were justifiable *only* insofar as they were necessary for self-defence. During the Iran–Iraq conflict, on the occasion of the inspection of the British merchant ship *Barber Perseus* by the Iranian navy, the UK asserted that Iran was 'entitled *in exercise of its inherent right of self-defence* to stop and search a foreign merchant ship on the high seas', if there was reasonable suspicion that it was carrying arms to the enemy.[71]

In fact, usually both parties to a conflict claim to be acting in self-defence, and the Security Council does not determine which of them the aggressor is. It is believed, however, that both the attacking state and the victim state are entitled to exercise belligerent rights as long as they comply with the necessity and proportionality requirements established by customary international law for self-defence measures.[72] Including items of no direct military utility in the contraband lists, imposing a long-distance blockade, or establishing a maritime exclusion zone in areas remote from the theatre of conflict would certainly not meet those requirements.[73]

[67] See Djamchid Momtaz, 'Iran' in Andrea de Guttry and Natalino Ronzitti (eds), *The Iran–Iraq War (1980–1988) and the Law of Naval Warfare* (Cambridge: Grotius, 1993), 19, 20 ff; Gioia, 'Iraq', ibid, 57, 72 ff.

[68] See 'Israel imposes Lebanon blockade', *BBC*, 13 July 2006, available at <http://news.bbc.co.uk/2/hi/middle_east/5175160.stm>; Yoaz, 'Beilin demands gov't formally declare that Israel is at war in Lebanon', *Haaretz*, 26 July 2006, at <http://www.haaretz.com/news/beilin-demands-gov-t-formally-declare-that-israel-is-at-war-in-lebanon-1.193733>.

[69] *San Remo Manual*, 74.

[70] See, inter alia, Christopher Greenwood, 'Self-Defence and the Conduct of International Armed Conflict' in Yoram Dinstein and Mala Tabory (eds), *International Law at a Time of Perplexity* (Leiden: Martinus Nijhoff, 1989), 273, 275 ff; Natalino Ronzitti, *Diritto internazionale dei conflitti armati* (4th edn, Turin: Giappichelli, 2011), 141.

[71] 'Answer by the Secretary of State for Foreign and Commonwealth Affairs, 28 January 1986' in de Guttry and Ronzitti, *The Iran–Iraq War (1980–1988)*, 268 (emphasis added).

[72] See Natalino Ronzitti, 'The Crisis of the Traditional Law Regulating International Armed Conflicts at Sea and the Need for its Revision' in Ronzitti (ed), *The Law of Naval Warfare* (Leiden: Martinus Nijhoff, 1988), 1, 4, 7, 10; Greenwood, 'Self-Defence', 287; Andrea Gioia, 'Neutrality and Non-Belligerency' in Post, *International Economic Law and Armed Conflict*, 51, 87, 101.

[73] Greenwood, 'Self-Defence', 284.

c. Application of the Law of Neutrality

The law of neutrality has been deeply affected by the UN Charter. In fact, whenever the Security Council imposes economic sanctions against one of the parties to an armed conflict under Article 41 of the Charter, member states cannot maintain the posture of impartiality towards all parties to the conflict which is at the core of the neutral status. In such a case, they are bound to apply the economic sanctions decided by the Security Council and deviate from the rule of impartial treatment of the opposing belligerents.[74]

On the other hand, where the Security Council only recommends that member states apply economic sanctions against one of the parties to the conflict, they are allowed to choose between remaining neutral and complying with the recommendation. In this case, maintaining a neutral status is only optional.[75] The same holds true where the Security Council authorizes member states to use force against one of the belligerents. In such a scenario, member states have three options: remain neutral, use force against that belligerent within the limits established by the Security Council, or adopt discriminatory measures against it without resorting to force.[76] Finally, whenever the Security Council stays silent, third states may remain neutral or exercise the right of collective self-defence. In the exercise of such right, they may take military action to assist the attacked state or adopt discriminatory measures against the attacking state without resorting to force.[77]

In all the aforementioned cases, as long as third states choose to remain neutral, they are required to comply with the law of neutrality, irrespective of whether a state of war is recognized by the belligerents.[78] This is confirmed by state practice. For example, during the 1991 Gulf conflict, where neither of the coalition states admitted the existence of a state of war, a number of states, including Iran and India, maintained a neutral posture. Iran manifested the intent to remain neutral and, in line with the law of neutrality, it seized over 100 Iraqi aircraft which had made emergency landings on its territory.[79] Similarly, India behaved as a

[74] Dietrich Schindler, 'Transformations in the Law of Neutrality since 1945' in Delissen and Tanja, *Humanitarian Law of Armed Conflict*, 367, 372; Gioia, 'Neutrality and Non-Belligerency', 71. See also *San Remo Manual*, para 8; *The Commander's Handbook on the Law of Naval Operations* (Newport, RI: US Naval War College, 2007), NWP1-14M, para 7.2.1.

[75] Schindler, 'Transformations in the Law of Neutrality', 372; Gioia, 'Neutrality and Non-Belligerency', 71.

[76] Gioia, 'Neutrality and Non-Belligerency', 73 f.

[77] Oppenheim, *International Law*, 650 f; Derek Bowett, *Self-Defence in International Law* (Manchester: Manchester University Press, 1958), 179 f; Schindler, 'Transformations in the Law of Neutrality', 373 f.

[78] Schindler, 'Transformations in the Law of Neutrality', 375; Michael Bothe, 'The Law of Neutrality' in Fleck, *The Handbook of International Humanitarian Law*, 571, 578.

[79] See Letter dated 28 January 1991 from the Permanent Representative of the Islamic Republic of Iran to the United Nations addressed to the Secretary-General, S/22163; Letter dated 8 February 1991 from the Permanent Representative of the United States of America to the United Nations addressed to the President of the Security Council, S/22216.

neutral, denying overflight of its territory to coalition aircraft.[80] In the 2003 Gulf conflict, even though the existence of a state of war was uncertain, a number of states abided by the neutrality obligations, while others clearly deviated from them without, however, invoking the absence of a state of war in justification. Among the latter, however, only Italy officially declared itself non-belligerent.[81] As to the former, Austria and Switzerland denied overflight of their territory to British and US aircraft, with the exception of humanitarian flights, in line with their policy of permanent neutrality.[82]

While the application of the law of neutrality no longer depends on the existence of a state of war, it is doubtful whether it can be invoked in any international armed conflict, whatever its scope and duration. According to Brownlie and Bothe, the law of neutrality is applicable only in conflicts that meet a certain threshold.[83] In fact, so far the rules of neutrality have been applied only where there were extensive hostilities involving a large number of troops. On the other hand, von Heinegg is certainly right when he observes that at least the basic obligations of neutrality, such as preventing the use of neutral territory as a base of operations for the belligerents and the passage through neutral territory of belligerent troops or arms supplies, should be applied in all international conflicts.[84]

D. Severance of Diplomatic Relations

States engaged in an armed conflict usually sever their diplomatic relations. The interruption of diplomatic relations, however, is not an automatic consequence of the outbreak of a conflict. The 1980–8 conflict between Iran and Iraq and the 1998–2000 conflict between Eritrea and Ethiopia are an illustration. Iran and Iraq terminated diplomatic relations only in 1987, seven years after the beginning of hostilities.[85] Eritrea and Ethiopia maintained diplomatic relations throughout the conflict.

[80] See 'United States: Department of Defense Report to Congress on the Conduct of the Persian Gulf War—Appendix on the Role of the Law of War, April 10, 1992' (1992) 31 ILM 612, 640.

[81] 'Comunicato della Presidenza della Repubblica sulla riunione del Consiglio supremo di difesa del 19 marzo 2003' (2003) 86 *Rivista di diritto internazionale* 904.

[82] See 'Ferrero-Waldner on the Initiation of Military Action against Iraq', 20 Mar 2003, available at <http://www.bmeia.gv.at/en/foreign-ministry/news/press-releases/2003/ferrero-waldner-on-the-initiation-of-military-action-against-iraq.html>; 'Neutrality under Scrutiny in the Iraq Conflict', 2 Dec 2005, at <http://www.eda.admin.ch/eda/en/home/topics/peasec/sec/neutr.html>, 12 f.

[83] Brownlie, *International Law and the Use of Force*, 401; Bothe, 'The Law of Neutrality', 578.

[84] Wolff Heintschel von Heinegg, '"Benevolent" Third States in International Armed Conflicts: The Myth of the Irrelevance of the Law of Neutrality' in Michael Schmitt and Jelena Pejic (eds), *International Law and Armed Conflict: Exploring the Faultlines* (Leiden: Martinus Nijhoff, 2007), 543, 567.

[85] See Rousseau, 'Chronique des faits internationaux' (1991) 95 *Revue générale de droit international public* 474.

The Eritrea–Ethiopia Claims Commission (EECC), which was established by the Algiers Peace Agreement, recognized that certain core functions of the diplomatic missions, such as promoting friendly relations between the sending and receiving states, are 'incongruous' when states are engaged in armed conflict.[86] However, it held that as Eritrea and Ethiopia chose not to sever diplomatic relations, they had to comply with the basic obligations laid down in the 1961 Vienna Convention on Diplomatic Relations, in particular those concerning the inviolability of diplomatic agents and premises.[87]

E. Treatment of the Belligerents' Nationals on Enemy Territory

Belligerent states are entitled to take various measures against enemy aliens within their territory. The existence of a state of war is irrelevant for this purpose, as confirmed by the Fourth Geneva Convention. This Convention is intended to protect civilians who 'find themselves...in the hands of a Party to the conflict or Occupying Power of which they are not nationals' (Art 4(1)), and stipulates that they may be subjected to such measures of control and security 'as may be necessary as a result of the war' (Art 27(4)). Like the other 1949 Geneva Conventions, the Fourth Geneva Convention applies in all armed conflicts between states parties, regardless of whether or not a state of war is recognized by them (Art 2(1)).[88]

As pointed out by the EECC, belligerents may also expel enemy nationals from their territory; expellees, however, are entitled to the protections afforded by the pertinent rules of international humanitarian law. In particular, the minimum humanitarian standards set forth in Articles 35 and 36 of the Fourth Geneva Convention for voluntary departures are considered applicable also in cases of expulsion.[89] It is doubtful, however, whether collective expulsions of enemy aliens, which were permitted under classical international law, are prohibited by contemporary international law. The Draft Articles on the Expulsion of Aliens, which were adopted by the ILC on first reading in 2012, leave the question unresolved. Article 10 prohibits collective expulsions of aliens, but contains a 'without prejudice' clause referring to the cases in which the expelling state is engaged in an armed conflict.[90]

[86] EECC, Partial Award, *Diplomatic Claim, Eritrea's Claim 20*, The Hague, 19 Dec 2005, para 6. EECC, Partial Award, *Diplomatic Claim, Ethiopia's Claim 8*, The Hague, 19 Dec 2005, para 6.

[87] EECC, Partial Award, *Diplomatic Claim, Eritrea's Claim 20*, para 20. EECC, Partial Award, *Diplomatic Claim, Ethiopia's Claim 8*, para 24.

[88] See Section V.

[89] EECC, Partial Award, *Civilians Claims, Ethiopia's Claim 5*, The Hague, 17 Dec 2004, para 122; EECC, Partial Award, *Civilians Claims, Eritrea's Claims 15, 16, 23 & 27–32*, The Hague, 17 Dec 2004, paras 81, 82, 99.

[90] Report of the International Law Commission on its Sixty-Fourth Session (7 May–1 June and 2 July–3 Aug 2012), A/67/10, 13 and 35.

Under Article 35(1) of the Fourth Geneva Convention, enemy aliens have the right to leave the belligerent's territory at the beginning of or during the conflict; the belligerent is entitled to refuse permission to leave only where their departure is contrary to its national interests.[91]

In relation to enemy aliens who remain or are retained in the belligerent's territory, under Article 38 of the Fourth Geneva Convention their position will 'continue to be regulated, in principle, by the provisions concerning aliens in time of peace'. An exception is made only for control and security measures that the belligerent may apply to them under the Convention.[92] However, regardless of whether or not they are subject to such measures, enemy aliens will enjoy certain minimum rights listed in Article 38, such as the right to receive medical care to the same extent as the belligerent's nationals and the right to practise their religion.

In the UN era, belligerents have rarely adopted measures against enemy aliens. Registration was imposed by Egypt on British and French nationals during the 1956 Suez crisis,[93] by the UK on Iraqi nationals with leave to enter and remain in the country for a limited period of time during the 1991 Persian Gulf conflict,[94] and by Eritrea and Ethiopia on each other's nationals during the 1998–2000 conflict.[95]

Assigned residence and internment are the most severe measures that belligerents may impose on enemy aliens. Under Article 42(1) of the Fourth Geneva Convention, they may be adopted only where the security of the belligerent makes them 'absolutely necessary'.[96] As found by the EECC, during the 1998–2000 conflict, Eritrea interned several thousand Ethiopian civilians and held them in inhumane conditions in violation of Article 42 and other provisions of the Convention; while Ethiopia detained Eritrean civilians, often together with prisoners of war, and subjected them to inhumane treatment in contravention of the Convention.[97]

Among the rights of enemy aliens who remain or are retained in the belligerent's territory, the right of access to courts deserves to be mentioned. This right, which was first recognized by Article 23(1)(h) of the Regulations annexed to the 1907 Hague Convention IV, is implicitly confirmed by Article 80 of the Fourth Geneva

[91] In this regard, see Pictet, *IV Geneva Convention*, 236. See also UK Ministry of Defence, *The Manual of the Law of Armed Conflict*, para 9.25; Fleck, *The Handbook of International Humanitarian Law*, para 575.

[92] On such measures, see Pictet, *IV Geneva Convention*, 207.

[93] See *Navios Corporation v. The Ulysses II et al*, 161 FSupp 932, 1958 AMC 1925 (US Dist Ct, Dist Md, Apr 30, 1958).

[94] The Immigration (Variation of Leave) Order 1991 (SI 1991 No 77), available at <http://www.legislation.gov.uk/uksi/1991/77/contents/made>.

[95] See EECC, Partial Award, *Civilians Claims, Ethiopia's Claim* 5, paras 45, 46; EECC, Partial Award, *Civilians Claims, Eritrea's Claims 15, 16, 23 & 27–32*, paras 74, 75.

[96] In this regard, see Pictet, *IV Geneva Convention*, 258. See also UK Ministry of Defence, *The Manual of the Law of Armed Conflict*, para 9.31; Fleck, *The Handbook of International Humanitarian Law*, para 579.

[97] EECC, Partial Award, *Civilians Claims, Ethiopia's Claim* 5, paras 100–7; EECC, Partial Award, *Civilians Claims, Eritrea's Claims 15, 16, 23 & 27–32*, paras 114, 119–22.

Convention.[98] Under the latter, 'internees shall retain their full civil capacity and shall exercise such attendant rights as may be compatible with their status'. The rights in question certainly include the right to sue and defend in the courts. If such rights are to be granted—with the said reservation—to internees, a fortiori they should be recognized to persons who are not interned.

As for enemy aliens residing in enemy territory, in *Amin v. Brown* the High Court of Justice of England and Wales reaffirmed the old rule that they cannot sue in the English courts, but stressed that it applies only in the case of war in the technical sense. Consequently, it rejected the claim that an Iraqi citizen resident in Iraq, Mrs Amin, could not sue in the English courts because, owing to the 2003 UK intervention against and ensuing occupation of Iraq, she was an enemy alien.[99]

Turning to the property of enemy aliens, belligerent states are entitled to take restrictive measures regarding such property within their territory, irrespective of the existence of a state of war. This can be derived from Article 46(2) of the Fourth Geneva Convention, which stipulates that restrictive measures affecting the property of protected persons shall be revoked 'as soon as possible after the close of hostilities'. The ICRC Commentary makes it clear that 'the words "close of hostilities" ... mean the actual end of the fighting and not the official termination of a state of belligerency'.[100] Hence, the legitimacy of those measures does not depend on the existence of a state of war.

However, belligerents are forbidden from confiscating enemy aliens' property in their territory. This prohibition, which was already part of customary international law before the entry into force of the UN Charter, still stands.[101] Moreover, the prohibition on seizure of enemy property unless demanded by military necessity, which was laid down in Article 23(g) of the Regulations annexed to the 1899 Hague Convention II and of the Regulations annexed to the 1907 Hague Convention IV, nowadays has customary status.[102]

Pronouncing on the measures taken by Ethiopia with regard to the property of Eritrean expellees, the EECC recognized that belligerent states have 'broad powers to deal with the property of the nationals of their enemies, but these are not unlimited'. It remarked that 'a belligerent is bound to ensure insofar as possible that the property of protected persons and of other enemy nationals are not despoiled and wasted' and added that 'if private property of enemy nationals is to be frozen or otherwise impaired in wartime, it must be done by the state, and under conditions providing for the property's protection and its eventual disposition by return to the owners or through post-war agreement'.[103]

[98] See Section III.D. [99] *Amin v. Brown*, paras 22, 23, 46, 47.
[100] Pictet, *IV Geneva Convention*, 270. [101] See Section III.D.
[102] See EECC, Partial Award, *Civilians Claims, Eritrea's Claims 15, 16, 23 & 27–32*, para 126.
[103] EECC, Partial Award, *Civilians Claims, Eritrea's Claims 15, 16, 23 & 27–32*, para 151.

F. Effects on Trade Relations

In the UN era, belligerent states generally prohibit trade between their own and enemy nationals. However, they abstain from applying the existing war legislation on the issue. For instance, following the invasion of the Falklands by Argentina, the UK Secretary of State for Trade introduced a ban on imports from and revoked all export licences to that country. He acted under section 1 of the Import, Export and Customs Powers (Defence) Act 1939, articles 2 and 5 of the Import of Goods (Control) Order 1954, and article 8 of the Export of Goods (Control) Order 1981.[104] The Trading with the Enemy Act 1939 was not applied.[105] This was almost certainly a consequence of the non-recognition of the state of war by the UK.[106]

As noted by the EECC, the right of a belligerent to terminate or restrict trade with its adversary is clearly established and supported by extensive practice[107] and can be exercised at the outset or during the conflict. For example, Eritrea continued to allow cargo to and from Ethiopia to be handled at the Eritrean port of Assab for a number of days after the outbreak of hostilities.[108]

In any event, belligerent states are bound to allow the free passage of humanitarian relief intended for the civilian population of the adversary. This obligation was first established by Article 23(1) of the Fourth Geneva Convention and covered 'all consignments of medical and hospital stores and objects necessary for religious worship' as well as 'all consignments of essential foodstuffs, clothing and tonics intended for children under fifteen, expectant mothers and maternity cases'. It was then broadened by Article 70(2) of Additional Protocol I to cover 'all relief consignments, equipment and personnel'. The said obligation, however, is subject to a number of conditions, which are spelt out in Article 23(2) of the Convention and Article 70(3) of the Protocol. In particular, under the latter the belligerent which allows the passage of humanitarian relief has 'the right to prescribe the technical arrangements, including search, under which such passage is permitted'.

Interestingly, the right of a party to the conflict to break off trade relations with the opposing party implies the right to suspend the operation of or even to terminate the bilateral treaties and, *inter partes*, the multilateral conventions on which such relations are based. The EECC found that five bilateral agreements regulating trade and commercial relations between Eritrea and Ethiopia were at the least

[104] Marston, 'United Kingdom Materials on International Law 1982' (1982) 53 *British Yearbook of International Law* 515.

[105] See Section III.E.

[106] On the question of the applicability of the Trading with the Enemy Act 1939 in the case of an armed conflict not constituting war in the technical sense, see McNair and Watts, *The Legal Effects of War*, 363 ff.

[107] EECC, Final Award, *Ports, Ethiopia's Claim 6*, The Hague, 19 Dec 2005, para 20.

[108] EECC, Final Award, *Ports, Ethiopia's Claim 6*, para 19.

suspended because of the armed conflict. Hence, it dismissed Ethiopia's claim for economic damage suffered as a consequence of their alleged violation by Eritrea.[109]

A belligerent state may also be bound to sever trade relations with its adversary by a Security Council resolution under Article 41 of the UN Charter. The Security Council, acting under that article, may decide that member states shall interrupt economic relations with a certain state. Whenever such measure is adopted, it shall be applied first and foremost by the member states which are engaged in an armed conflict with the targeted state.

G. Effects on Contracts

The outbreak of an armed conflict between two states may entail, depending on the case, the nullity, termination, or suspension of contracts between their respective subjects, regardless of whether or not a state of war comes into being. Generally, the absence of a state of war prevents each belligerent from applying the existing war legislation that dictates such consequences. However, they are often attached to the eruption of conflict by the clauses of the contract or the law applicable.

In certain categories of contract, the parties usually anticipate the possibility of armed conflict. Sometimes the contract expressly stipulates that it shall not be operative in the case of armed conflict. For example, life and commercial insurance policies generally incorporate a clause whereby so-called war risks are excluded. In other cases, the contract gives the parties the right to cancel it if one or more specified states become involved in an armed conflict. The so-called war cancellation clause is normally included in charter parties.[110]

Contracts which do not envisage the possibility of an armed conflict may nonetheless be affected by the outbreak of hostilities. In particular, they may be declared terminated under the doctrine of *force majeure* or impossibility of performance in civil law systems or under the doctrine of frustration in common law systems.[111]

Unlike the peace treaties which ended both World Wars, those concluded since the beginning of the 1950s do not include provisions on the fate of contracts entered into by the belligerents' subjects prior to the conflict.[112]

[109] EECC, *Partial Award, Economic Loss Throughout Ethiopia, Ethiopia's Claim 7*, The Hague, 19 Dec 2005, paras 15, 18.

[110] With regard to this, see Brian Davenport, 'War Clauses in Time Charterparties' in Ewan McKendrick (ed), *Force Majeure and Frustration of Contract* (2nd edn, London: Lloyd's of London Press, 1995), 153.

[111] As for British case law on frustration of contracts following the outbreak of an international armed conflict, see *Carapanayoti & Co Ltd v. E. T. Green Ltd* [1959] 1 QB 131; *International Sea Tankers Inc v. Hemisphere Shipping Co Ltd (The 'Wenjiang' (No 2))* [1983] 1 Lloyd's Rep 400; *Finelvet AG v. Vinava Shipping Co Ltd* [1983] 1 WLR 1469. The first case regards the Suez crisis, while the others concern the Iran–Iraq conflict.

[112] See Section III.F.

Interestingly, contracts between belligerents' subjects may be impacted by Security Council resolutions imposing economic sanctions against one of the opposing belligerents. The 1991 Gulf conflict is a case in point. The termination of many contracts between subjects of the coalition states and Iraqi subjects was a consequence of Security Council Resolution 661 (1990) and not of the conflict itself, which started only on 16 January 1991. Member states were obliged to prohibit imports from and exports to Iraq or Kuwait and prevent funds from being made available to the Iraqi government or any undertaking in Iraq or Kuwait, 'notwithstanding any contract entered into or licence granted before the date of the... resolution' (para 5).

H. Effects on Treaties

State practice does not provide significant indications on the effects of armed conflicts on treaties between belligerents. During the hostilities belligerents generally avoid announcing the effects of the conflict on treaties between them.[113] On the other hand, peace treaties concluded since the beginning of the 1950s usually do not include provisions on the fate of treaties which were in force between the parties before the conflict.[114] Case law on the issue is scant. Additionally, the 1969 Vienna Convention on the Law of Treaties contains a 'without prejudice' clause referring to the effects on treaties of the 'outbreak of hostilities between States' (Art 73).

The only instruments addressing the issue are the resolution on 'The Effects of Armed Conflicts on Treaties', which was adopted by the Institute of International Law at the Helsinki Session in 1985,[115] and the 2011 Draft Articles on the Effects of Armed Conflicts on Treaties.[116] Both stipulate, in Articles 2 and 3 respectively, that an armed conflict does not *ipso facto* cause the termination or suspension of treaties between the belligerent states. Obviously, as laid down in Article 4 of the 2011 Draft Articles, a treaty continues to operate during an armed conflict where it expressly so provides. The point is what happens to the treaties that do not anticipate the possibility of an armed conflict. Both the 2011 Draft Articles and the Helsinki resolution

[113] See A/CN.4/550, 7.

[114] A remarkable exception is the 1980 General Peace Treaty between El Salvador and Honduras. See Art 6 of the Treaty.

[115] Institute of International Law, The Effects of Armed Conflicts on Treaties, Session of Helsinki—1985, available at <http://www.idi-iil.org/idiE/navig_chon1983.html>. It deals with the effects on treaties of international armed conflicts. The existence of a state of war is considered irrelevant. See the definition of armed conflict in Art 1.

[116] See Section V. The Draft Articles deal with the effects on treaties of both international and non-international armed conflicts. As to the former, it is irrelevant whether or not a state of war comes into being. See the definition of armed conflict in Art 2(b).

consider armed conflict as an additional ground for termination or suspension of treaties to those established by the 1969 Vienna Convention.[117] In practice, however, it is particularly hard to find a case in which the termination or suspension of a treaty between opposing belligerents cannot be ascribed to one of the grounds established in the Convention, in particular a material breach, supervening impossibility of performance, or a fundamental change of circumstances. The 2011 Draft Articles also regard armed conflict as an additional ground for withdrawal from treaties to those established by the 1969 Vienna Convention.

According to the 2011 Draft Articles, in order to establish whether a treaty which does not contain any provision on its operation during armed conflict is 'susceptible to termination, withdrawal or suspension' in the event of a conflict, one should first seek to ascertain its meaning by applying 'the rules of international law on treaty interpretation' (Art 5). If this proves inconclusive, one should consider 'all relevant factors, including: (a) the nature of the treaty, in particular its subject matter, its object and purpose, its content and the number of parties to the treaty; and (b) the characteristics of the armed conflict, such as its territorial extent, its scale and intensity, its duration' (Art 6). The annex to the 2011 Draft Articles contains a non-exhaustive list of categories of treaties whose subject matter implies that they continue to operate, in whole or in part, during armed conflict (Art 7).

Such list includes, inter alia, the human rights treaties. Indeed, it is now well established that belligerent states continue to be bound by the human rights treaties to which they are parties, except for the obligations that are derogated from in conformity with a derogation clause contained therein.[118] Such a clause is incorporated in Article 15 of the 1950 European Convention on Human Rights, Article 4 of the International Covenant on Civil and Political Rights (ICCPR), and Article 27 of the 1969 American Convention on Human Rights. Under each of them, in time of armed conflict, states parties may take measures derogating from the obligations laid down in the treaty. However, no derogation may be made from certain articles, including those proclaiming the right to life, the prohibition of torture, the prohibition of slavery, and the prohibition of punishment without law. The continued operation of human rights treaties in times of armed conflict except for the provisions that are derogated from has been affirmed by the International

[117] The Helsinki resolution specifies that it 'shall not prejudge the application of the provisions of the Vienna Convention on the Law of Treaties' (Preamble). The Draft Articles stipulate that they 'are without prejudice to the termination, withdrawal or suspension of treaties as a consequence of, *inter alia*: (a) a material breach; (b) supervening impossibility of performance; or (c) a fundamental change of circumstances' (Art 18). As clarified in the ILC's commentary, this provision aims to preserve the possibility of termination, withdrawal, or suspension of a treaty as a consequence of the application of other rules of international law, in particular those enshrined in the 1969 Vienna Convention. See A/66/10, 198.

[118] The Helsinki resolution stipulates that 'the existence of an armed conflict does not entitle a party unilaterally to terminate or to suspend the operation of treaty provisions relating to the protection of the human person, unless treaty otherwise provides' (Art 4).

Court of Justice. In the 1996 advisory opinion on the *Legality of the Threat or Use of Nuclear Weapons*, the Court held that 'the protection of the ICCPR does not cease in times of war, except by operation of Article 4 of the Covenant'.[119] Later, in the 2004 *Wall* advisory opinion, it stated in more general terms that 'the protection offered by human rights conventions does not cease in case of armed conflict, save through the effect of provisions for derogation of the kind to be found in Article 4 of the ICCPR'.[120]

The UN Charter has significantly influenced the effects of armed conflict on treaties. Three principles which have developed under its influence are now considered part of customary international law. First, a state exercising its right of individual or collective self-defence may suspend the operation of a treaty incompatible with the exercise of such right. This principle is enshrined in Article 7 of the Helsinki resolution and Article 14 of the 2011 Draft Articles, and it is in line with that laid down in Article 21 of the 2001 Draft Articles on State Responsibility.[121]

Secondly, where a treaty is incompatible with a Security Council decision, member states which are parties to it shall either suspend or terminate it in order to comply with the decision. This principle, which is enshrined in Article 8 of the Helsinki resolution and is implicit in Article 16 of the 2011 Draft Articles, flows from Article 103 of the UN Charter, according to which the obligations of member states under the Charter prevail over conflicting obligations under any other treaty. Therefore, if the Security Council imposes sanctions against one of the opposing belligerents, member states including its adversary shall conform to the will of the Security Council, and either suspend or terminate treaties incompatible with it.

Thirdly, a state committing aggression is precluded from invoking the ensuing armed conflict as a ground for termination or suspension of a treaty, if it would benefit from doing so. This principle is incorporated in Article 9 of the Helsinki resolution and Article 15 of the 2011 Draft Articles. The latter also prohibits the aggressor from invoking the armed conflict as a ground for withdrawal from a treaty if it would derive a benefit from doing so. This principle is in line with the Definition of Aggression annexed to General Assembly Resolution 3314 (XXIX), which specifies that 'no territorial acquisition or *special advantage* resulting from aggression is or shall be recognized as lawful' (Art 5(3)).[122]

[119] *Legality of the Threat or Use of Nuclear Weapons*, Advisory Opinion, para 25.

[120] *Legal Consequences of the Construction of a Wall in the Occupied Palestinian Territory*, Advisory Opinion, ICJ Rep 2004, 136, para 106.

[121] *Yearbook of the International Law Commission*, 2001, vol II (2), 26. Under Art 21 of the 2001 Draft Articles on State Responsibility, 'the wrongfulness of an act of State is precluded if the act constitutes a lawful measure of self-defence taken in conformity with the Charter of the United Nations'.

[122] Emphasis added.

VII. Conclusion

As illustrated, state practice shows that a state of war is not in itself considered incompatible with the prohibition on the threat or use of armed force in international relations enshrined in the UN Charter. As a matter of fact, however, the opposing belligerents generally avoid making any reference to a state of war, and simply classify the ongoing hostilities as armed conflict. No declaration of war in accordance with the 1907 Hague Convention III has been recorded in the UN era. By admitting to be engaged in an armed conflict belligerents only intend to confirm a factual situation.

However, important legal consequences are today attached to the outbreak of an armed conflict. As emerges from the previous analysis, they do not coincide with the consequences that flowed from a state of war under classical international law. The latter were significantly impacted by the UN Charter and the evolution of international law in general. The UN Charter has impacted greatly on the law of neutrality and the exercise of belligerent rights. Moreover, it has led to the development of new principles regarding suspension and termination of treaties. On the other hand, the Fourth Geneva Convention has greatly influenced the treatment of the belligerent's nationals on enemy territory. In addition, many treaties protecting human rights have been concluded since the entry into force of the UN Charter, and the principle is now established that states engaged in an armed conflict continue to be bound by the human rights treaties to which they are parties, save for the obligations that are derogated from in conformity with the provisions contained therein.

The previous analysis also reveals that the effects of an armed conflict are practically the same, whether or not a state of war comes into being. The absence of a state of war only prevents belligerent states from applying existing war legislation affecting trade and contracts between their own and enemy subjects, which in most cases dates back to the first decades of the 20th century. Trade and contractual relations between belligerents' subjects, however, are severely affected by the outbreak of an armed conflict, even if no state of war arises. Indeed, the concept of state of war has almost no practical relevance in today's international law.

PART VI

EMERGING AREAS?

CHAPTER 47

PROLIFERATION OF WEAPONS OF MASS DESTRUCTION AND SHIPPING INTERDICTION

VASCO BECKER-WEINBERG*

GUGLIELMO VERDIRAME

I. Introduction

Maritime transportation is essential for mankind, with much of the world's trade depending on it. It is a complex and interrelated activity, often involving several jurisdictions simultaneously. For over a decade the international community has been concerned about the use of maritime transportation, by states and non-state actors,[1] to facilitate the proliferation of weapons of mass destruction (WMD) and the

* The views expressed in this chapter are the personal views of the authors.

[1] In a footnote SC Res 1540 (2004) defines a 'non-State actor' as 'an individual or entity, not acting under the lawful authority of any State in conducting activities which come within the scope of this resolution.'

transportation of delivery vehicles and related materials for WMD,[2] while terrorism at sea has been a source of international concern for even longer.[3]

No single legal regime applies to the problem of seaborne WMD proliferation. The law of the sea clearly provides the main framework of reference, but international law on terrorism and WMD is also relevant. State practice has contributed to the clarification and in some cases to the evolution of the law in this area. Much of the state and multilateral practice in recent decades has been in response to two events: the hijacking of the *Achille Lauro*[4] and the terrorist attacks of 11 September 2001.[5]

Seaborne WMD proliferation presents states with legal and strategic challenges. Interception and boarding operations offer the clearest response available against this problem. However, although many flag states are unable to exercise jurisdiction effectively over ships flying their flag, they are also reluctant to allow interception and boarding by foreign ships.

Before examining these challenges, it is important to consider some conceptual issues. First, following the US-National Strategy to Combat Weapons of Mass Destruction, a distinction must be drawn between counterproliferation, non-proliferation, and response to the use of WMD.[6] Non-proliferation and counterproliferation are

[2] 'Means of delivery' include missiles, rockets, and other unmanned systems capable of delivering nuclear, chemical, or biological weapons, specially designed for such use; 'related materials' the materials, equipment, and technology covered by relevant multilateral treaties and arrangements, or included on national control lists, which could be used for the design, development, production, or use of nuclear, chemical, and biological weapons and their means of delivery; SC Res 1540.

[3] The first attempt to combat terrorism under a treaty framework was the Convention for the Prevention and Punishment of Terrorism, which was adopted by the League of Nations on 16 Nov 1937 but never entered into force (League of Nations Doc C.546M.383 (1937)). On the historical evolution of the concept of international terrorism, see Reuven Young, 'Defining Terrorism: the Evolution of Terrorism as a Legal Concept in International Law and its Influence on Definitions in Domestic Legislation' 29 (2006) *Boston College International and Comparative Law Review* 23. See also Report of the Secretary-General's High-Level Panel on Threats, Challenges and Change, 'A More Secure World: Our Shared Responsibility' (2004) 51–2, paras 157–64.

[4] The *Achille Lauro* incident was treated by the US as piracy (see José Luis Jesus, 'Protection of Foreign Ships Against Piracy and Terrorism at Sea: Legal Aspects' (2003) 18 *International Journal of Marine and Coastal Law* 363, 388). On other aspects of the *Achille Lauro* incident, see Larry A. McCullough, 'International and Domestic Criminal Law Issues in the *Achille Lauro* Incident: A Functional Analysis' (1986) 36 *Naval Law Review* 53.

[5] On the impact of 9/11 in this area, see Natalie Klein, *Maritime Security and the Law of the Sea* (Oxford: Oxford University Press, 2011), 147–51.

[6] *National Strategy to Combat Weapons of Mass Destruction* (Dec 2002), available at <http://www.state.gov/documents/organization/63562.pdf>. The Strategy also identifies four enabling functions: (1) intelligence collection and analysis on WMD, delivery systems, and related technologies; (2) research and development to improve the ability to respond to evolving threats; (3) bilateral and multilateral cooperation; and (4) targeted strategies against hostile states and terrorists. See also: Strategy to Combat Transnational Organized Crime (July 2011), and National Security Strategy (May 2010), available at <http://www.whitehouse.gov>; Remarks by President Barack Obama in Prague, 5 Apr 2009, at <http://www.whitehouse.gov/the_press_office/Remarks-By-President-Barack-Obama-In-Prague-As-Delivered/>. On the relationship between the international law on the use of force and strategy

essentially preventative strategies: the former is 'intended to slow and ideally reverse proliferation trends', while the latter aims to prevent 'specific actors from obtaining WMD-related materials and technologies, or reducing if not eliminating an actor's existing WMD capability.'[7] Response is, as the term suggests, an after-the-event strategy.

Another key concept is interdiction. A classic instrument of naval enforcement, interdiction may involve two steps: 'first, the boarding, inspection and search of a ship at sea suspected of prohibited conduct; second, where such suspicions prove justified, taking measures including any combination of arresting the vessel, arresting persons aboard or seizing the cargo.'[8] Not in all cases, therefore, does interdiction conclude with the seizure of the vessel.

Against the background of the law on the use of force, this chapter examines the legal regime applicable to interception operations by non-flag states for the purpose of combating the proliferation of WMD, delivery vehicles, and related materials. After an analysis of the general legal framework under the law of the sea, in particular the United Nations Convention on the Law of the Sea (UNCLOS),[9] the chapter examines the three main routes through which states have sought to address the gaps in the general legal framework: resolutions of the UN Security Council; multilateral treaty-making under the auspices of the International Maritime Organization (IMO); and the practice of states involved in the Proliferation Security Initiative (PSI).

II. The Law of the Sea Framework

The sea is divided into areas that are subject to some measure of jurisdiction by coastal states, and areas that are beyond it and cannot be claimed by or allocated to any state. The first group comprises the territorial sea, internal waters, international straits, archipelagic waters, the contiguous zone, the exclusive economic zone (EEZ), and the continental shelf.[10] The measure of jurisdiction enjoyed by states in these areas varies. In some cases (eg the territorial sea, internal waters) they have

(including nuclear strategy), see Guglielmo Verdirame, 'The Sinews of Peace: International Law, Strategy and the Prevention of War' (2006) 78 *British Year Book of International Law* 83.

[7] Klein, *Maritime Security and the Law of the Sea*, 149.

[8] See Douglas Guilfoyle, *Shipping Interdiction and the Law of the Sea* (Cambridge: Cambridge University Press, 2009), 4 (also at 9 on the same point).

[9] Adopted in Montego Bay on 10 Dec 1982 and entered into force on 16 Nov 1994, 1833 UNTS 3.

[10] UNCLOS, Arts 2, 8, 34, 46, 33, 55, and 76.

full rights of sovereignty; in others (eg the continental shelf, the EEZ, and, where established, the contiguous zone) they may exercise only limited sovereign and jurisdictional rights. The second group, which is beyond the permanent jurisdictional reach of any state, comprises the high seas and the Area.[11]

The rights of foreign ships also vary from one legal area of the sea to the other. Most importantly, a foreign ship enjoys the right of innocent passage through the territorial sea and archipelagic waters without being intercepted on condition that passage is innocent,[12] that is, that passage is not prejudicial to the peace, good order, or security of the coastal state and that the ship does not engage in any threat or use of force against its sovereignty, territorial integrity, or political independence, or in any other manner in violation of the principles of international law embodied in the UN Charter.[13] There is no general right of innocent passage in internal waters; there the coastal state may board a foreign ship, and enforce its laws against her and those on board.[14]

The EEZ and the continental shelf, notwithstanding certain limited rights of coastal states, are still subject to the two key principles that define the high seas: freedom of navigation and the exclusive jurisdiction of the flag state. These principles are subject to exceptions,[15] the most ancient one of which is the universal jurisdiction to seize ships engaged in piracy. Although states must cooperate in the repression of piracy, there is however no obligation, but merely a right, to intercept and board foreign ships on suspicion of being engaged in piracy.[16]

In cases of slavery and unlawful broadcasting, states have jurisdiction to arrest the ship,[17] while in the event of illicit traffic in narcotic drugs and psychotropic substances the lawful interdiction of trafficking ships depends on the request of the respective flag state.[18] Warships have a general right of visit in respect of ships

[11] UNCLOS, Arts 1(1) and 86.

[12] UNCLOS, Arts 17, 18, 24(1), 52(1), and 54. Similarly, all ships enjoy the right of transit passage in straits used for international navigation, see Arts 38, 39, and 45.

[13] UNCLOS, Art 19(1), (2)(a). On the definition of innocent passage, see Robin Rolf Churchill and Vaughan Lowe, *The Law of the Sea* (Manchester: Manchester University Press, 1999), 82–5.

[14] The exception is provided in UNCLOS, Art 8(2).

[15] UNCLOS, Arts 92(2), and 58(1) and (3), 78(2) and 87(1)(a) and (2). See also *SS Lotus (France v. Turkey)*, 1927 PCIJ, Ser A, No 9, 25 (7 Sept), paras 64–5.

[16] UNCLOS, Art 105. Early piracy cases include the *Marianna Flora* (24 US (11 Wheat) 1 (1826)). The *Marianna Flora* was a ship of Portuguese registry that was approached by a US ship. On approach, the *Marianna Flora* fired on the US ship, mistaking it for a pirate ship. As a result, the *Marianna Flora* was seized and brought into port on the grounds of piratical aggression. In this case, the US Supreme Court considered that the seizure of the *Marianna Flora* was a lawful exercise of the right to 'approach any vessels descried at sea, for the purpose of ascertaining their real characters'.

[17] UNCLOS, Arts 99, 109(3), and 110. The slavery exception emerged in the 19th century and had been definitively accepted by the beginning of the 20th century. It played an important role in the emergence of modern humanitarianism (see Guglielmo Verdirame, *The UN and Human Rights* (Cambridge: Cambridge University Press, 2011), 36–47).

[18] UNCLOS, Art 108(2) and Art 17 of the United Nations Convention against Illicit Traffic in Narcotic Drugs and Psychotropic Substances, adopted in Vienna on 20 Dec 1988 and entered into force on 11 Nov 1990, 1582 UNTS 95. Also see UNCLOS, Art 27(1)(d). See William C. Gilmore, 'Drug Trafficking

without nationality.[19] In the case of pollution or threat of pollution in the high seas, the principle is also that of flag state jurisdiction but port and coastal states may adopt some measures on foreign ships but only in certain circumstances and provided that the relevant safeguards are adopted.[20]

Another exception to the principle of exclusive flag state jurisdiction on the high seas allows a state to pursue a foreign ship suspected of having violated its laws and regulations.[21] The right of hot pursuit gives teeth to the coastal states' jurisdictional prerogatives, as non-abiding ships might otherwise find refuge upon reaching the high seas.[22]

As is evident from this brief outline, the law of the sea does not provide a basis for a general right of interdiction in respect of threats to maritime and international security posed by the transportation of WMD and WMD-related materials. First, as made explicit in UNCLOS, the exercise of rights and the performance of duties under the law of the sea is subject to the prohibition on the use of force.[23] Secondly, UNCLOS does not include a set of general principles and rules on maritime security which could be invoked to justify any general right of interdiction. Security concerns are mentioned in the context of the right of innocent passage through the territorial sea.[24] Elsewhere, UNCLOS provides that the high seas, the Area, the EEZ, and the continental shelf up to 200 nautical miles are reserved for peaceful purposes, and that marine scientific research and the use of research installations shall be exclusively 'for peaceful purposes',[25] although military uses are not within the scope of the Convention.[26] In short, these provisions support the argument that an internationally agreed framework for preventing the exploitation of shipping for

by Sea: The 1988 United Nations Convention against Illicit Traffic in Narcotic Drugs and Psychotropic Substances' (1991) 15 *Marine Policy* 183.

[19] UNCLOS, Art 110(1)(d).

[20] UNCLOS, Arts 19(2)(h), 21(1)(f), 25, 27(5), 42(1)(b) and (2), 56(1)(b)(iii) and (2), 87(2), 94(3)(a), 194(3)(b) and (4), 211, 218, 220, and 224–7.

[21] UNCLOS, Art 111(1).

[22] Robert C. Reuland, 'The Customary Right of Hot Pursuit onto the High Seas: Annotations to Article 111 of the Law of the Sea Convention' (1992–3) 33 *Virginia Journal of International Law* 557, 589. See also Craig H. Allen, 'Doctrine of Hot Pursuit: A Functional Interpretation adaptable to Emerging Maritime Law Enforcement Technologies and Practices' (1989) 20 *Ocean Development and International Law* 309, 312–21; Klein, *Maritime Security and the Law of the Sea*, 109–114. On the origin and development of the doctrine of hot pursuit, see C. John Colombos, *The International Law of the Sea* (New York: David McKay Co Inc, 1967), 168–75.

[23] UNCLOS, Art 301. [24] UNCLOS, Arts 19(1) and 25(3).

[25] UNCLOS, Arts 58(2), 88, and 141 deal, respectively, with the EEZ, the high seas, and the Area. Arts 239, 240(a), 242(1), 246(3) and 258 deal with marine scientific research. On the concept of 'peaceful purposes' and its applicability to UNCLOS, see Boselaw A. Boczek, 'Peaceful Purposes Provisions of the United Nations Convention on the Law of the Sea' (1989) 20 *Ocean Development and International Law* 359, 364, 368–81.

[26] Donald R. Rothwell and Natalie Klein, 'Maritime Security and the Law of the Sea' in Natalie Klein, Joanna Mossop, and Donald R. Rothwell (eds), *Maritime Security: International Law and Policy Perspectives from Australia and New Zealand* (London/New York: Routledge, 2010), 22, 28–9.

the purposes of WMD proliferation would accord with the spirit of the law of the sea, but do not go further than that.

III. Use of Force and Law Enforcement at Sea

Pursuit, boarding, and seizure may require the use of force when the vessel is not cooperative. Should the use of force in these cases be characterized as use of force for the purposes of Article 2(4) of the UN Charter? Or should it instead be treated as law enforcement?

The International Court of Justice (ICJ) dealt with these questions in the *Fisheries Jurisdiction* case (*Spain v. Canada*).[27] Spain submitted that the boarding of a Spanish vessel on the high seas, while pursuant to powers conferred on the Canadian Navy by Canadian legislation, contravened international law. Canada maintained that the ICJ had no jurisdiction by virtue of a reservation in the Canadian declaration of acceptance of the Court's compulsory jurisdiction, which excluded 'disputes arising out of or concerning conservation and management measures taken by Canada with respect to vessels fishing in the NAFO [Northwest Atlantic Fisheries Organization] Regulatory Area, as defined in the Convention on Future Multilateral Co-operation in the Northwest Atlantic Fisheries, 1978, and the enforcement of such measures'.[28] Spain's position was instead that the use of force against its vessel had amounted to a violation of Article 2(4) of the Charter and gave rise to a 'separate cause of action not caught by the reservation'.[29]

The ICJ ruled in favour of Canada. It held that:

> the use of force authorized by the Canadian legislation and regulations falls within the ambit of what is commonly understood as enforcement of conservation and management measures. This is so notwithstanding that the reservation does not in terms mention the use of force. Boarding, inspection, arrest and minimum use of force for those purposes are all contained within the concept of enforcement of conservation and management measures according to a 'natural and reasonable' interpretation of this concept.[30]

The use of force against foreign vessels is subject to the general criteria of necessity and reasonableness: if there are no other practicable means to board, search, seize, and bring into port the suspected ship, the state may be entitled to use reasonable

[27] *Fisheries Jurisdiction (Spain v. Canada)*, Jurisdiction of the Court, Judgment, ICJ Rep 1998, 432.

[28] *Fisheries Jurisdiction*, Judgment, para 14.

[29] *Fisheries Jurisdiction*, Judgment, para 78.

[30] *Fisheries Jurisdiction*, Judgment, para 84.

force in the light of the refusal to comply with the arrest.[31] In the *Saiga* case, the International Tribunal for the Law of the Sea (ITLOS) underlined the importance of a graduated response in trying to stop a suspected ship.[32] Other conditions include the arrest of the ship by a warship or government ship,[33] and the adoption of measures that do not exceed the legitimate use of force, such as the deliberate sinking of an unarmed ship,[34] or the endangering of human life.[35] The assessment of the necessity and reasonableness of the use of force will depend on the circumstances of each case, taking into account the alleged offence and the conduct of the ship.[36] The state will be liable for any use of unjustified force.[37]

It is true that, to use the authoritative words of Judge Treves, 'General international law, in authorising stopping and boarding for the purpose of exercising the right of visit under Article 110 of UNCLOS or the seizure of a pirate ship under Article 105, presupposes that force may be used to reach these objectives'.[38] But there is a line to be drawn between the use of force pursuant to powers recognized under the law of the sea, and the use of force that falls outside them and that will potentially be regulated by reference to the international law on the use of force proper. The question is where to draw this line.

There are two situations where the law on the use of force may be engaged: first, the manifest and forcible abuse of rights of visit and seizure provided for under the law of the sea and, secondly, the forcible exercise of these rights outside the legal bases contemplated under the law of the sea. In both of these cases, it is still important to distinguish, as the ICJ held in *Nicaragua*, 'the most grave forms of the use of force (those constituting an armed attack) from other less grave forms'.[39] The former will trigger the right of self-defence in terms of Article 51 of the UN Charter, the latter will not. Applying the *Nicaragua* principle in the *Oil Platforms* case, the ICJ held

[31] ITLOS, *The M/V 'Saiga' (No 2) (Saint Vincent and the Grenadines v. Guinea)*, 1 July 1999, para 155. See Louise de La Fayette, 'ITLOS and the Saga of the *Saiga*: Peaceful Settlement of a Law of the Sea Dispute' (2000) 15 *International Journal of Marine and Coastal Law* 355, 385–7.

[32] *The M/V 'Saiga'*, para 156.

[33] UNCLOS, Arts 107(1), 110(1) and (2), and 111(5). Also see Art 224. A definition of warships is provided in Art 29.

[34] *SS 'I'm Alone' (Canada v. US)*, Joint Final Report of the Commissioners in the Case of the 'I'm Alone', dated 5 Jan 1935, and filed with the Secretary of State at Washington and the Minister of External Affairs for Canada at Ottawa, 9 Jan 1935, 3 RIAA 1609, 1617, 1618.

[35] *The Red Crusader (Commission of Enquiry, Denmark–United Kingdom)* (1962) 35 ILR 485.

[36] Reuland, 'The Customary Right of Hot Pursuit onto the High Seas', 585.

[37] UNCLOS, Arts 110(3) and 111(8). See also UNCLOS, Art 304 and Arts 21(18), 22(1)(f), and 35 of the Agreement for the Implementation of the Provisions of the United Nations Convention on the Law of the Sea of 10 December 1982 Relating to the Conservation and Management of Straddling Fish Stocks and Highly Migratory Fish Stocks, adopted in New York on 4 Dec 1995 and entered into force on 11 Dec 2001, 2167 UNTS 3.

[38] Tullio Treves, 'Piracy, Law of the Sea, and Use of Force: Developments off the Coast of Somalia' (2009) 20 *European Journal of International Law* 399, 413.

[39] *Military and Paramilitary Activities in and against Nicaragua (Nicaragua v. US)*, ICJ Rep 1986, 14, para 191.

that the various incidents complained of by the US, including the missile attack on an oil tanker, did not constitute an armed attack.[40]

A dissonant note is the *Guyana/Suriname* award.[41] Surinamese patrol boats had ordered an oil rig and its service vessels to leave an area of the sea disputed between Guyana and Suriname. The oil rig did not fly the Surinamese flag, but it operated on the basis of a concession granted by the government of Suriname. The Tribunal accepted Guyana's argument that this situation was different from that in *Fisheries Jurisdiction*, and that the action undertaken by the Surinamese patrol boats 'seemed more akin to a threat of military action rather than a mere law enforcement activity.'[42] The *Guyana/Suriname* decision has attracted criticism because of its failure to identify the legal basis for this conclusion clearly.[43] Moreover, even accepting the basis for distinguishing this case from *Fisheries Jurisdiction*, its findings would still sit uncomfortably with the ICJ's approach to the definition of armed attack in *Nicaragua* and *Oil Platforms*.

What conclusions should be drawn about the position in general international law on the right to stop, search, and seize vessels suspected of involvement in WMD proliferation? First of all, under the law of the sea, such a right is not expressly contemplated for either terrorism or WMD proliferation. This is not to say that some of the existing powers may not be applicable in these cases. For example, a coastal state may invoke the right of hot pursuit, under Article 111 of UNCLOS, of vessels suspected of carrying WMD-related material (on the assumption that this would contravene domestic laws and regulations). This exception does not, however, make a significant difference in strategic terms given that ships carrying WMD-related material are unlikely to enter the jurisdiction of the coastal states from which they have most to fear.

The position under the general law of the sea does not therefore provide much assistance to states which unilaterally assert rights of visit of ships suspected of engagement in WMD proliferation. States that insisted on exercising these rights would expose themselves to the risk of being accused of a violation of the law of the sea and, depending on the amount of force involved, of a breach of the prohibition on the use of force under Article 2(4) of the UN Charter.

[40] *Oil Platforms (Iran v. US)*, ICJ Rep 2003, 161, para 64. This finding was premised on the attribution to Iran of the specific attack on the oil tanker and of the other incidents in question, but in the previous paragraphs of the judgment the Court had held that the evidence did not support the contentions of the US regarding attribution. In a separate finding, the Court did not exclude that the mining of a single military vessel might amount to an armed attack but, in this respect too, did not find that the evidence on Iran's responsibility was conclusive (paras 65–72).

[41] *Guyana/Suriname*, Award of the Arbitral Tribunal Constituted Pursuant to Article 287, and in accordance with Annex VII of UNCLOS (17 Sept 2007).

[42] *Guyana/Suriname*, Award, para 445.

[43] Treves, 'Piracy, Law of the Sea, and Use of Force', 414.

For states invoking self-defence to justify interdiction of foreign shipping on the high seas, the problems are those associated with self-defence and are examined elsewhere in this volume. In brief, the outcome depends on the answer to questions such as the availability of anticipatory self-defence.[44] Outside an armed conflict, and thus purely in *jus ad bellum* terms, there are significant difficulties with attempts to justify these operations on the high seas merely on the suspicion of transporting WMD.[45] It would be necessary to demonstrate, for example, that an attack was imminent.[46] States would also risk finding themselves in the same position as the US in *Oil Platforms*: the event on which they justify their resort to force is found not to constitute an armed attack, and they end up on the wrong side of the law on the use of force.

The law of the sea and the law on the use of force would thus appear to give little solace to states keen to combat proliferation. But the international legal system possesses mechanisms of evolution and adaptation to new challenges. The three legal and institutional solutions that have emerged are examined in the following sections.

IV. The Role of the United Nations in Counterproliferation of WMD

In numerous resolutions, both the Security Council and the General Assembly have recognized the proliferation of WMD as a threat to international peace and security and one that should be effectively addressed through multilateral action.[47] In the

[44] See Ashley S. Deeks, 'Taming the Doctrine of Pre-Emption', Chapter 29 and Noam Lubell, 'The Problem of Imminence in an Uncertain World', Chapter 31 both in this volume. See also Christine Gray, *International Law and the Use of Force* (Oxford: Oxford University Press, 2008), 114–66.

[45] Douglas Guilfoyle, 'The Proliferation Security Initiative: Interdicting Vessels in International Waters to Prevent the Spread of Weapons of Mass Destruction?' (2005) 29 *Melbourne University Law Review* 733, 750–1, 756–60. Guilfoyle concludes that it would be difficult to sustain that interdiction operations of WMD could be considered under Art 51 of the UN Charter by way of reinterpretation of this provision in order to include in the concept of 'armed attack' the supply of weapons of mass destruction to a hostile non-state actor.

[46] On the problem of imminence see Noam Lubell, 'The Problem of Imminence in an Uncertain World', Chapter 31 in this volume; Guilfoyle, 'The Proliferation Security Initiative', 757; Emmanuel Roucounas, 'Present Problems of the Use of Force in International Law' (2007) 72 *Annuaire de l'Institut de Droit International* 75, 113–14. See also Michael Wood, 'The Law on the Use of Force: Current Challenges' (2007) 11 *Singapore Year Book of International Law* 1, 8–9.

[47] Relevant General Assembly resolutions during 2011–13 are: GA Res 67/38; GA Res 66/49; and GA Res 66/32. Relevant Security Council resolutions in the same period are: SC Res 2555 (2012); 2049 (2012); SC Res 1984 (2012); and SC Res 1977 (2011).

wake of the terrorist attacks of 9/11, the US invited members of the UN to support the adoption of a 'new anti-proliferation resolution' that would require states to criminalize the proliferation of WMD, enacting strict export controls and securing WMD-related material within their borders.[48] The result was Resolution 1540 (2004), which the Security Council, acting under Chapter VII of the UN Charter, adopted in 2004. This Resolution is one of a number of resolutions adopted by the Security Council to deal with general problems rather than specific and geographically delimited situations.[49]

Resolution 1540 (2004) does not deal comprehensively with maritime security or with interception and boarding operations, but does include 'trans-shipment controls' among the obligations it imposes on states. Moreover, the initial paragraphs of the Resolution, which are introduced by the terms 'the Security Council *decides*' and are thus binding on all states, contain extensive obligations many of which are indirectly relevant to issues of maritime security and seaborne WMD proliferation. In particular, all states must refrain from supporting non-state actors that attempt to develop, acquire, manufacture, possess, transport, transfer, or use WMD. States must also adopt and enforce appropriate effective laws prohibiting non-state actors from doing so, and establish domestic controls to prevent proliferation of WMD by securing and preventing access to them and implement export controls to avoid their illicit trafficking.

Security Council decisions under Chapter VII offer clear advantages in comparison with the multilateral treaty route. They can be adopted more expeditiously and are binding. In principle, the Security Council can use this route to create a general right to intercept and board foreign ships suspected of carrying WMD, effectively adding a basis for rights of visit to those already provided for under UNCLOS. In practice, however, states are unlikely to agree to such a step.

An important question is whether unilateral countermeasures can be adopted against states for breach of non-proliferation obligations under Resolution 1540 (2004). Imagine, for example, the case of a state which fails to comply with its obligation to put in place trans-shipment controls. Can another state respond to the non-compliance by intercepting a ship which transited in the non-compliant state, if it has reason to believe that she is participating in WMD proliferation? The answer differs depending on the nationality of the ship in question. If she is flying the flag of the non-compliant state, the argument in favour of unilateral countermeasures

[48] President Bush Addresses United Nations General Assembly, 23 Sept 2003, available at <http://georgewbush-whitehouse.archives.gov/news/releases/2003/09/20030923-4.html>.

[49] This trend was inaugurated by SC Res 1373 (2001). See Michael C. Wood, 'The Security Council as a Law-Maker: The Adoption of (Quasi)-Judicial Decisions' in Rüdiger Wolfrum and Volker Röben (eds), *Developments of International Law in Treaty Making* (Berlin/Heidelberg/New York: Springer, 2005), 227.

of stop and search carries some weight.[50] If she is flying the flag of another state, rights of stop and search could not be asserted by way of countermeasures because, under the law on state responsibility, countermeasures may only be adopted against the state which is responsible for the internationally wrongful act. Moreover, states could not in these cases resort to robust enforcement because of the prohibition on forcible countermeasures.[51]

V. The Work of the International Maritime Organization

The *Achille Lauro* and the 9/11 incidents shaped the work of the IMO on the improvement of maritime security.[52] It was as a result of these events that, respectively, the 1988 Convention for the Suppression of Unlawful Acts against the Safety

[50] The view that states lose the right to adopt unilateral countermeasures in the event of Security Council action was put forward in the International Law Commission, but is not reflected in the final text of Arts 49–54 of the Articles on State Responsibility (N. Jansen Calamita, 'Sanctions, Countermeasures and the Iranian Nuclear Issue' (2009) 42 *Vanderbilt Journal of International Law* 1393). Among the authors who have argued that states retain such a right are N. Jansen Calamita, ibid, and Martin Dawidowicz, 'Public Law Enforcement without Public Law Safeguards? An Analysis of State Practice on Third-Party Countermeasures and their Relationship to the UN Security Council' (2007) 77 *British Yearbook of International Law* 333.

[51] Articles on State Responsibility, Art 50(1)(a).

[52] IMO Res A.584(1X), Measures to Prevent Unlawful Acts which Threaten the Safety of Ships and the Security of their Passengers and Crews; MSC/Circ 443, Measures to Prevent Unlawful Acts Against Passengers and Crew on Board Ships; IMO Res A.924(22), of 20 Nov 2001, Review of Measures and Procedures to Prevent Acts of Terrorism which Threaten the Security of Passengers and Crews and the Safety of Ships. The aim was to revise international legal and technical measures to prevent and suppress terrorist acts against ships at sea and in port, as well as to improve security on board ships and in port. The legal framework for maritime security was also further developed with the amendments to the 1974 Safety of Life at Sea Convention and in particular Chapter XI which introduced the *International Ship and Port Facility Security Code* (the ISPS Code). The objectives of the ISPS Code included the establishment of an international legal framework to detect threats and take preventive measures against security incidents affecting ships or port facilities used in international trade (Art 1.2.1). The ISPS Code does not, however, allow the boarding of vessels at sea by non-flag states. See Malvina Halberstam, 'Terrorism on the High Seas: The *Achille Lauro*, Piracy and the IMO Convention on Maritime Safety' (1988) 82 *American Journal of International Law* 269, 291–2; Hartmut G. Hesse, 'Maritime Security in a Multilateral Context: IMO Activities to Enhance Maritime Security' (2003) 18 *International Journal of Marine and Coastal Law* 327, 327–40.

of Maritime Navigation and Protocol[53] and the 2005 Protocol to the 1988 SUA Convention were adopted.[54]

The 2005 Protocol recognizes the importance of the threat of WMD and their proliferation.[55] It criminalizes the transport of WMD by sea and admits the possibility of consensual interception and boarding operations,[56] taking into account the Non-Proliferation Treaty[57] and other international legal instruments dealing with biological and chemical weapons.[58] Several states questioned whether it was proper for the IMO, rather than the International Atomic Energy Agency, to deal with these matters. The criticism came particularly from those states that are not party to the Non-Proliferation Treaty and that have not therefore accepted a treaty-based obligation to refrain from transporting nuclear weapons.[59]

The 2005 Protocol does not take into consideration the motive of the persons who knowingly and intentionally transport by sea any explosive or radioactive material, biological or chemical weapons, or any source material or equipment to be used in a nuclear explosive activity for the purpose of threatening or carrying out an act of terror. The Convention focuses on the responsibility of the persons that benefit from the use of maritime transportation, thus removing any incentive that could result from the limitation of responsibility based on motive to cause an act of terror.[60]

The 2005 Protocol also deals with interception and boarding operations of foreign ships outside the territorial sea. In essence, these operations are still only

[53] Adopted in Rome on 10 Mar 1988 and entered into force on 1 Mar 1992, 1678 UNTS 221. The 1988 SUA Convention and the 1988 Protocol for the Suppression of Unlawful Acts against the Safety of Fixed Platforms Located on the Continental Shelf (1988 SUA Convention) had the purpose of ensuring that appropriate action was taken against persons committing unlawful acts against ships and fixed platforms on the continental shelf, namely the seizure of ships by force, acts of violence against persons on board ships, and the placing of devices on board a ship to destroy or damage it. The 1988 SUA Convention followed the models of the Convention for the Suppression of Unlawful Seizure of Aircraft, adopted in The Hague on 16 Dec 1970 and entered into force on 14 Oct 1971, 860 UNTS 105, and the Convention for the Suppression of Unlawful Acts against the Safety of Civil Aviation, adopted in Montreal on 23 Sept 1971 and entered into force on 26 Jan 1973, 974 UNTS 178.

[54] Adopted in London on 14 Oct 2005 and entered into force on 28 July 2010, IMO Doc LEG/CONF.15/21 (the 2005 Protocol).

[55] 2005 Protocol, Art 3*bis*. [56] 2005 Protocol, Art 3*bis*(1)(b).

[57] 2005 Protocol, Arts 2*bis*(3) and 3*bis*(2).

[58] Convention on the Prohibition and Development, Production and Stockpiling of Bacteriological (Biological) and Toxin Weapons and on their Destruction, adopted in Washington, London, and Moscow on 10 Apr 1972 and entered into force on 26 Mar 1975, 1015 UNTS 163; Convention on the Prohibition of the Development, Production, Stockpiling, and Use of Chemical Weapons and their Destruction, adopted in Paris on 13 Jan 1993 and entered into force on 29 Apr 1997, 1974 UNTS 45.

[59] Rosalie Balkin, 'The International Maritime Organization and Maritime Security' (2006) 30 *Tulane Maritime Law Journal* 27. See also Craig H. Allen, 'Revisiting the Thames Formula: The Evolving Role of the International Maritime Organization and its Member States in Implementing the 1982 Law of the Sea Convention' (2009) 10 *San Diego International Law Journal* 265, 287.

[60] 2005 Protocol, Art 3*bis*(1)(b)(iv).

possible with the consent of the respective flag state and within certain safeguards.[61] The coastal state must request the consent of the flag state to verify the nationality of the ships flying its flag and is allowed to intervene only when having reasonable grounds to suspect that the ship or a person on board the ship has been, is, or is about to be involved in the commission of an offence. In these cases, the flag state may confirm the nationality of the ship and, subject to its conditions, grant the coastal state authorization to stop, board, and search the ship, its cargo, and persons on board. The flag state may decline authorization, or decide to undertake such operations with or without the coastal state.[62]

When evidence is found, the flag state may authorize detention and the adoption of any additional measures, except when necessary to relieve imminent danger to the lives of persons. In these cases, the use of force is subject to necessity and reasonableness.[63] In the event of excessive force, the 2005 Protocol provides for the right of compensation.[64]

In general, the rules under the 2005 Protocol are consistent with the principles governing the exercise of maritime jurisdiction and the use of force.[65] Indeed, one of the main concerns in the drafting of the 2005 Protocol was that the freedom of navigation and the principle of flag state jurisdiction should not be undermined.[66] Nevertheless, the broad safeguards included in the 2005 Protocol could offer an incentive to flag states to consent to interception and boarding operations.

VI. The PSI and Bilateral Ship-Boarding Agreements

On 10 December 2002, relying on US intelligence, the Spanish navy intercepted and boarded the *So San*, a ship suspected of carrying suspicious material from North Korea to Yemen. The Spanish navy justified this action on the grounds that the *So San* had

[61] 2005 Protocol, Art 8*bis*(10). See Natalie Klein, 'The Right of Visit and the 2005 Protocol on the Suppression of Unlawful Acts Against the Safety of Maritime Navigation' (2007) 35 *Denver Journal of International Law and Policy* 287, 326.

[62] 2005 Protocol, Art 8*bis*(5). Also see Art 8*bis*(5)(d) and (e).

[63] 2005 Protocol, Art 8*bis*(6) and (7).

[64] 2005 Protocol, Art 8*bis*(10)(b).

[65] 2005 Protocol, Art 9.

[66] Robert C. Beckman, 'The 1988 SUA Convention and 2005 SUA Protocol: Tools to Combat Piracy, Armed Robbery, and Maritime Terrorism' in Rupert Herbert-Bruns, Sam Bateman, and Peter Lehr (eds), *Lloyd's MIU Handbook of Maritime Security* (Boca Raton/London/New York: CRC Press, 2009), 187, 194–6.

not been flying any flag and could be treated as a ship without nationality.[67] The *Son San*, which turned out to be Cambodian, was indeed carrying nuclear missiles under its cement cargo. Although the ship's manifest did not mention the missiles or their destination, after the confirmation of its nationality, the Spanish navy had to release the ship.[68] The aftermath of the *So San* incident prompted the US to launch the PSI and to issue the Statement of Interdiction Principles in 2003.[69] Other states were invited to endorse the PSI and, as of July 2014, more than one hundred states have done so.[70]

The PSI did not create an entity or organization for the purpose of overseeing the actions developed within its framework, even though in 2009 President Obama announced that the US had the intention of making the PSI and the Global Initiative to Combat Nuclear Terrorism[71] into 'durable international institutions'.[72] Crucially, the PSI does not create legally binding obligations.[73] The Statement of Interdiction Principles calls upon participating states to undertake effective measures to interdict the transfer or transport of WMD at the request of a participating state that demonstrates good cause. Board and search of vessels also depend on the existence

[67] UNCLOS, Art 110(1)(d) provides that a warship may justifiably board a foreign ship in the high seas if there is reasonable ground for suspecting that the ship is without nationality.

[68] Press Briefing by Ari Fleischer, 11 Dec 2002, available at <http://www.presidency.uscsb.edu/ws/indexphp?pid=47463>. Missile Technology Control Regime, at <http://www.mtcr.info/english/partners.html>. Yemen and North Korea did not endorse the guidelines of the Missile Technology Control Regime. This is an informal and voluntary association of countries which share the goals of non-proliferation of delivery systems capable of delivering WMD, and which seek to coordinate national export licensing efforts aimed at preventing their proliferation. The purpose of these guidelines is to limit the risks of proliferation of WMD, by controlling transfers that could make a contribution to delivery systems for such weapons. See *Missile Technology Control Regime (MTCR) Annex Handbook* (2010), at <http://www.mctr.info/english/MTCT_Annex_Hanbook_ENG.pdf>.

[69] *Proliferation Security Initiative*, available at <http://www.state.gov/t/isn/c10390.htm>; and Statement of Interdiction Principles, at <http://www.state.gov/t/isn/c27726.htm>. Also see Speech of President George W. Bush in Krakow, 31 May 2003. On the *So San* incident and PSI, see Klein, *Maritime Security and the Law of the Sea*, 107–8, 193–208; Yann-Huei Song, 'The U.S.-led Proliferation Security Initiative and UNCLOS: Legality, Implementation, and an Assessment' (2007) 38 *Ocean Development and International Law* 101, 101–10, 119–22; Daniel H. Joyner, 'The Proliferation Security Initiative: Nonproliferation, Counterproliferation, and International Law' (2005) 30 *Yale Journal of International Law* 507; Michael A. Becker, 'The Shifting Public Order of the Oceans: Freedom of Navigation and the Interception of Ships at Sea' (2005) 46 *Harvard International Law Journal* 131, 147–67; Guilfoyle, 'The Proliferation Security Initiative', 735–6, 740–1; Michael Byers, 'Policing the High Seas: The Proliferation Security Initiative' (2004) 98 *American Journal of International Law* 526–45.

[70] As at July 2014, more than one hundred states had endorsed the PSI, see <http://www.state.gov/t/isn/c27732.htm>.

[71] <http://www.state.gov/t/isn/c18406.htm>; *Fact Sheet*, available at <http://www.state.gov/documents/organization/145499.pdf>.

[72] Remarks by President Barack Obama in Prague.

[73] Anthony Aust, *Modern Treaty Law and Practice* (Cambridge: Cambridge University Press, 2007), 17; Richard Gardiner, *Treaty Interpretation* (Oxford: Oxford University Press, 2008), 20. See also Ted L. McDorman, 'From the Desk of the Editor-in-Chief' (2005) 36 *Ocean Development and International Law* 381, 382; Stuart Kaye, 'Freedom of Navigation in a Post 9/11 World: Security and Creeping Jurisdiction' in David Freestone, Richard Barnes, and David Ong (eds), *The Law of the Sea* (Oxford: Oxford University Press, 2006), 347, 357.

of 'reasonable suspicion'.[74] Under the PSI, sharing of information is encouraged but is dependent on the consent of states given the non-obligatory nature of the PSI.[75]

The PSI has, however, provided a platform for binding arrangements in the form of bilateral agreements allowing interception and boarding operations.[76] Since the launch of PSI, the US has championed many such agreements. They establish boarding procedures and relevant safeguards, in addition to procedures regarding the exchange of information, the exercise of the right of visit, and the use of force.[77]

States remain liable for damages incurred by private entities as a result of actions under the PSI.[78] In these cases, private entities may seek compensation from the relevant flag state for unlawful interference with the freedom of navigation on the ground of violation of its laws.[79]

The non-binding nature of the PSI contributed to its success. The political commitments it introduced are consistent with existing international law on freedom of navigation and flag state jurisdiction.[80] For this reason, the eventual accession of the US to UNCLOS would not have a negative impact on the PSI.[81]

However, the same features that account for the success of the PSI also explain its limits. Most importantly, the PSI does not represent an evolution of the customary nature of the right of self-defence, even if the US has in the past advanced arguments for anticipatory self-defence in relation to WMD proliferation.[82] As presently

[74] Para 4(d)(1) of the Interdiction Principles for the Proliferation Security Initiative included in the Statement of Interdiction Principles, provides that states commit 'To take appropriate actions to (1) stop and/or search in their internal waters, territorial seas, or contiguous zones (when declared) vessels that are reasonably suspected of carrying such cargoes to or from states or non-state actors of proliferation concern and to seize such cargoes that are identified; and (2) to enforce conditions on vessels entering or leaving their ports, internal waters or territorial seas that are reasonably suspected of carrying such cargoes, such as requiring that such vessels be subject to boarding, search, and seizure of such cargoes prior to entry.' This provision has to be applied taking into account the regime of innocent passage outlined previously.

[75] UNCLOS, Art 303 provides that states do not have to disclose information that is contrary to the essential interests of their security.

[76] UNCLOS, Art 110(1) provides that a state may grant its consent by treaty to another state for the purpose of intercepting and boarding in the high seas ships flying its flag.

[77] In July 2014, the US had signed 11 Proliferation Security Initiative Ship Boarding Agreements, see <http://www.state.gov/t/isn/c27733.htm>.

[78] UNCLOS, Art 110(2) and (3) and 2005 Protocol, Art 8*bis*(13) and (12).

[79] Philipp Wendel, *State Responsibility for Interferences with the Freedom of Navigation in Public International Law* (Berlin/Heidelberg: Springer, 2007), 226. Wendel concludes that 'The loose framework of the [PSI] . . ., has thus enabled the member States to avoid a strict liability regime as in the more general conventions in the Law of the Sea.'

[80] Becker argues that 'behind a façade of multilateral cooperation, the PSI is ultimately a loose instrument by which to facilitate more effective unilateral action by individual states to make possible and lawful the claims of one state upon vessels of another.' Becker, 'The Shifting Public Order of the Oceans', 221. See also Guilfoyle, 'The Proliferation Security Initiative', 740; Wendel, *State Responsibility for Interferences with the Freedom of Navigation in Public International Law*.

[81] Song, 'The US-led Proliferation Security Initiative and UNCLOS', 113–19, 124–5.

[82] The National Security Strategy of the United States of America, Sept 2002, available at <http://georgewbush whitehouse.archives.gov/nsc/nss/2002/>. In referring to the right of self-defence and

conceived, the PSI cannot justify an expansion of the right of self-defence such as to provide a legal basis for interception and boarding operations aimed at preventing WMD proliferation. States participating in the PSI have not made themselves, expressly or implicitly, liable to such operations.[83] Throughout, states reaffirmed the existing rules, and characterized the PSI as an arrangement that is entirely compatible with them. There is thus no evidence of an intention to create new custom in this area.

VII. Conclusions

WMD proliferation will remain a priority for the system of collective security as well as for the national security of many states. Indeed, the arrest in July 2013 of the North Korean ship *Chong Chon Gang*, following an inspection by the authorities of Panama which revealed that the ship was potentially concealing WMD supplied by Cuba,[84] shows that the threat is real.[85] A tension has inevitably arisen between

the legitimacy of pre-emption on the existence of an imminent threat, President Bush stated that the concept of 'imminent threat' should take into consideration the capabilities and objectives of today's adversaries and in particular the potential use of WMD that can be easily concealed, delivered covertly, and used without warning. The President added that the greater the threat to national security, the greater the risk of inaction and therefore the case for taking anticipatory action would be more compelling, 'even if uncertainty remains as to the time and place of the enemy's attack' and that 'To forestall or prevent such hostile acts by our adversaries, the [US would], if necessary, act preemptively.' President Bush also stated that 'The purpose of our actions will always be to eliminate a specific threat to the [US]' and that 'The reasons for our actions will be clear, the force measured, and the cause just.'

[83] On the potential impact of PSI principles on customary international law, see Timothy C. Perry, 'Blurring the Ocean Zones: The Effect of the Proliferation Security Initiative on the Customary International Law of the Sea' (2006) 37 *Ocean Development and International Law* 44. See also Byers, 'Policing', 534, 540; Becker, 'The Shifting Public Order of the Oceans', 167; Klein, *Maritime Security and the Law of the Sea*, 203–7.

[84] Mulino pedirá cooperación internacional para determinar qué material bélico hay en el buque norcoreano, 16 July 2013, available at <http://www.minseg.gob.pa/index.php?option= com_k2&view=item&id=275:2013-07-16-21-08-48&Itemid=344>; Statement of the Permanent Mission of Panama to the United Nations, in relation to the North Korean ship MV Chong Chon Gang, 19 July 2103, at <http://www.panama-un.org/Noticias/330-Statement-of-the-Permanent-Mission-of-Panama-to-the-United-Nations,-in-relation-to-the-North-Korean-ship-MV-Chong-Chon-Gang.html>; Statement by the Ministry of Foreign Affairs (Cuba) about the North Korean ship *Chong Chon Gang* seized in the Panama Canal, 16 July 2013, at <http://www.cubaminrex.cu/en/statement-ministry-foreign-affairs-6>.

[85] The Security Council established a Committee pursuant to SC Res 1718 (2006) imposing certain measures relating to North Korea, eg, an arms embargo and a nuclear ballistic missiles and other WMD programmes-related embargo. Also see SC Res 1874 (2009). Security Council Committee established pursuant to Res 1718 (2006), available at <http://www.un.org/sc/committees/1718/index.shtml>.

collective and national security imperatives, and the principles of freedom of navigation and exclusive jurisdiction of the flag state on which the law of the sea rests. The Security Council has sought to address this problem by imposing ever more stringent obligations on states in the area of WMD proliferation. But ensuring compliance with these obligations in the *mare liberum* is no easy feat, not least because of the well-known phenomenon of flags of convenience and the limits of flag state enforcement. Nor has the treaty practice, spearheaded by the IMO particularly in the aftermath of the *Achille Lauro* incident, produced more effective results.

Yet, it would be hasty to conclude that these settled principles of the law of the sea will soon give way to the strategic necessities of powerful states and collective security. It is worth remembering that, in spite of the unchallenged supremacy of the British navy in the 19th century, Britain too struggled to change the law of the sea in the direction of the wider rights of visits that it was, at times vigorously, advocating in order to suppress the slave trade.[86] The PSI does actually have something in common with the solution that the British also adopted in the end: securing their desired strategic outcome, that is, expanded rights of visit, under the framework of the existing law rather than against it. At some point, the combined pressure from the top (ie the Security Council) and the bottom (ie the evolving practice of states) may result in a more careful and systematic rethinking of these aspects of the law of the sea.

[86] Verdirame, *The UN and Human Rights*, 36–47.

CHAPTER 48

THE IMPLICATIONS OF THE PROLIFERATION OF WEAPONS OF MASS DESTRUCTION FOR THE PROHIBITION OF THE USE OF FORCE

DANIEL H. JOYNER

I. Introduction

THIS chapter will discuss the implications for international law governing uses of force and the proliferation of weapons of mass destruction (WMD) between both states and non-state actors. It will posit that international use of force law is currently in a state of crisis, precipitated by the proliferation of WMD technologies and the revised set of national security calculations, which determine when and why states choose to use force internationally, that have been thrust upon states as a result. It will review a number of options which have been proposed for changing the substance of international laws and institutions which currently regulate this area, in order to make them responsive to this change in international security realities and more effective and useful to states. It will conclude with a review of the current situation and present challenges and a consideration of the future.

II. Proliferation, Pre-Emption, and Use of Force Law

A. Crisis? What Crisis?

The first issue for consideration in this analysis is whether in fact there is currently a crisis in international use of force law, brought about by WMD proliferation and changed security realities for states. Some would doubtless reject this as an alarmist position, and maintain that while the instruments and means of international violence have certainly changed since the founding in 1945 of the UN Charter—the primary source of governing international law in this area—the considerations which states must undertake when deciding to use force internationally have not fundamentally changed since that time, and therefore no urgent change to existing law is required. This conclusion was indeed apparently reached by the UN Secretary-General's High-Level Panel on Threats, Challenges and Change in its 2004 report entitled 'A More Secure World: Our Shared Responsibility.'[1] In its report, the High-Level Panel found that there was no need either for rewriting or reinterpreting Article 51 of the UN Charter on self-defence, or for fundamentally changing the role of the Security Council as the sole authorizer of international uses of force other than those justified by reference to Article 51, including those purposed in addressing WMD threats. To quote from the report, 'The short answer is that if there are good arguments for preventive military action, with good evidence to support them, they should be put to the Security Council, which can authorize such action if it chooses to.'[2]

However, this static approach seems at odds with the stated opinion of the Secretary-General himself, who in September 2003, expressed this crisis to the UN General Assembly as follows:

> All of us know there are new threats that must be faced—or, perhaps, old threats in new and dangerous combinations: new forms of terrorism, and the proliferation of weapons of mass

[1] Note by the Secretary-General, Follow-up to the Outcome of the Millennium Summit, A/59/565 (2 Dec 2004), available at <http://www.un.org/secureworld/report.pdf>. See also Allen S. Weiner, 'The Use of Force and Contemporary Security Threats: Old Medicine for New Ills?' (2005) 59 *Stanford Law Review* 415, 419–20.

[2] Para 190.

destruction... Where we disagree, it seems, is on how to respond to these threats. Article 51 of the Charter prescribes that all States, if attacked, retain the inherent right of self-defence. But until now it has been understood that when States go beyond that, and decide to use force to deal with broader threats to international peace and security, they need the unique legitimacy provided by the United Nations. Now, some say this understanding is no longer tenable, since an 'armed attack' with weapons of mass destruction could be launched at any time, without warning, or by a clandestine group.

Rather than wait for that to happen, they argue, States have the right and obligation to use force pre-emptively, even on the territory of other States, and even while weapons systems that might be used to attack them are still being developed. According to this argument, States are not obliged to wait until there is agreement in the Security Council. Instead, they reserve the right to act unilaterally, or in ad hoc coalitions. This logic represents a fundamental challenge to the principles on which, however imperfectly, world peace and stability have rested for the last fifty-eight years.

Excellencies, we have come to a fork in the road. This may be a moment no less decisive than 1945 itself, when the United Nations was founded.[3]

As indicated in these remarks, the fundamental challenge to UN Charter law which the Secretary-General perceived has been most saliently presented in the context of debates regarding the legality of anticipatory, or pre-emptive, self-defence in situations where states feel that they are threatened by a target state or non-state actor's development, possession, or threat of use of WMD. Former Secretary-General Annan's remarks were made during the 2003 diplomatic stand-off over whether, and on what legal justification, to use force against Iraq in order to forcibly disarm it of its suspected WMD stockpiles. However, debates regarding the use of pre-emptive force to prevent states and non-state actors 'of concern' from developing and using WMD have not been limited to the case of Iraq. Indeed, an even more recent example of such a pre-emptive use of force was presented by Israel's 6 September 2007 unilateral attack on a site in Syria which was later claimed to be a nuclear reactor site, constructed with the help of North Korea.[4]

B. Counterproliferation

The post-11 September 2001 international security climate has seen a general shift in the policy positions of the US and a number of other relatively powerful states, towards an increased emphasis on proactive and often unilateral or

[3] Secretary-General's Address to the General Assembly, 23 Sept 2003, available at <http://www.un.org/webcast/ga/58/statements/sg2eng030923>.

[4] Robin Wright, 'N. Koreans Taped At Syrian Reactor: Video Played a Role in Israeli Raid', *Washington Post*, 24 Apr 2008; David E. Sanger, 'U.S. Sees N. Korean Links to Reactor', *New York Times*, 24 Apr 2008.

small-coalition-based strategies of 'counterproliferation', and away from more multilateral and diplomacy-based efforts of 'non-proliferation'. While non-proliferation efforts have classically depended upon diplomacy and upon individual state implementation of treaty law and of rules agreed in other normative regimes of both a formal and informal character, counterproliferation efforts are generally designed to forcefully preclude specific actors from obtaining WMD-related materials and technologies or to degrade and destroy an actor's existing WMD capability. Such counterproliferation efforts include interdiction of suspected transfers of sensitive items, and pre-emptive acts of force against either actual or potential possessors of WMD.[5]

While a shift towards counterproliferation policies can be seen in the statements of officials of a number of states, notably including Russia, Japan, India, Israel, Australia, and the UK, it has been most formally adopted by the US in its stated foreign and security policy.[6] In both the September 2002 National Security Strategy document and the December 2002 National Strategy to Combat Weapons of Mass Destruction document, US policymakers signalled a significant shift in WMD-related policies towards counterproliferation principles. As stated in the latter document:

> We know from experience that we cannot always be successful in preventing and containing the proliferation of WMD to hostile states and terrorists... Because deterrence may not succeed, and because of the potentially devastating consequences of WMD use against our forces and civilian population, U.S. military forces and appropriate civilian agencies must have the capability to defend against WMD-armed adversaries, including in appropriate cases through preemptive measures.[7]

The National Security Strategy document discussed the concept of pre-emption further thus:

> The United States has long maintained the option of preemptive actions to counter a sufficient threat to our national security. The greater the threat, the greater is the risk of

[5] Daniel H. Joyner, 'The Proliferation Security Initiative: Nonproliferation, Counterproliferation & International Law' (2005) 30 *Yale Journal of International Law* 507; Jason D. Ellis, 'The Best Defense: Counterproliferation and U.S. National Security' (Spring 2003) 26 *The Washington Quarterly* 115; Robert S. Litwak, 'The New Calculus of Pre-Emption' (Winter 2002) 44 *Survival* 53.

[6] 'India Mulls "Pre-Emptive" Pakistan Strike, Cites U.S. Iraq War Precedent', *Agence France Presse*, 11 Apr 2003, available at <http://www.fromthewilderness.com/free/ww3/041403_india.html>; 'Israel's plans for Iran strikes', *Jane's*, 16 July 2004; Mari Yamaguchi, 'Japan Mulling Action over N. Korea Missiles', AP, at <http://news.yahoo.com/s/ap/20060710/ap_on_re_as/nkorea_missiles>; 'Russia Won't Rule Out Pre-Emptive Use of Force', *Los Angeles Times*, 13 Oct 2003, at <http://straitstimes.asia1.com.sg/storyprintfriendly/0,1887,214354,00.html?>; 'Prime Minister Warns of Continuing Global Terror Threat', 5 Mar 2004, speech by Tony Blair, at <http://www.number-10.gov.uk/output/page5461.asp>; Dan Murphy, 'Terror-Preemption talk Roils Asia', *Christian Science Monitor*, 5 Dec 2002, at <http://www.globalpolicy.org/wtc/analysis/2002/1205preemption.htm>.

[7] United States National Strategy to Combat Weapons of Mass Destruction (Dec 2002), available at <https://www.fas.org/irp/offdocs/nspd/nspd-17.html>.

inaction—and the more compelling the case for taking anticipatory action to defend ourselves, even if uncertainty remains as to the time and place of the enemy's attack. To forestall or prevent such hostile attacks by our adversaries, the United States will, if necessary, act preemptively... [I]n an age where the enemies of civilization openly and actively seek the world's most destructive technologies, the United States cannot remain idle while dangers gather.[8]

The place of the doctrine of pre-emption in US counterproliferation policy was confirmed in the 2006 National Security Strategy document, which specifically sought to justify the doctrine on the basis of a right to pre-emptive self-defence in international law.

Meeting WMD proliferation challenges also requires effective international action... Taking action need not involve military force... If necessary, however, under long-standing principles of self-defense, we do not rule out the use of force before attacks occur, even if uncertainty remains as to the time and place of the enemy's attack.[9]

One of the policy manifestations of this doctrinal shift towards pre-emptive action to deal with WMD threats is to be found in the Proliferation Security Initiative (PSI), a programme involving approximately 50 states at various levels of cooperation in logistic, law enforcement, and military efforts aimed at interdicting WMD-related items and technologies in transit, most often over the sea lanes.[10] The PSI is essentially a set of principles mandating proactive efforts to arrest proliferation in WMD-related materials at its most vulnerable point; during shipment and before such materials can be integrated into WMD development programmes. PSI interdictions are ongoing, and tend to involve the stopping and searching of vessels suspected of carrying WMD-related technologies from origins or to destinations of concern to PSI participants, and the confiscation of any such materials found. The PSI has been defended by its proponents, chief among whom is John Bolton, the former US Under-Secretary of State, as being justified by reference to principles of self-defence in international law.[11]

Concerns regarding state use of pre-emptive force against other states and non-state actors, however, are not limited to the actions of the West or to developed states. There are real concerns that rhetoric by major powers legitimizing counterproliferation-oriented pre-emption will strengthen the resolve of a number

[8] The National Security Strategy of the United States of America (Sept 2002), available at <http://www.state.gov/documents/organization/63562.pdf>.

[9] The National Security Strategy of the United States of America (Mar 2006), available at <http://merln.ndu.edu/whitepapers/USnss2006.pdf>.

[10] See generally Daniel H. Joyner, *International Law and the Proliferation of Weapons of Mass Destruction* (Oxford: Oxford University Press, 2009), ch 8; Daniel H. Joyner, 'The Proliferation Security Initiative: Nonproliferation, Counterproliferation & International Law' (2005) 30 *Yale Journal of International Law* 507; Michael Byers, 'Policing the High Seas: The Proliferation Security Initiative' (2004) 98 *American Journal of International Law* 526.

[11] Greg Sheridan, 'US "free" to tackle N Korea', *The Australian*, 9 July 2003.

of other states to apply the doctrine to their own regional conflicts. Indian Foreign Minister Yashwant Sinha was quoted in 2003 as stating that India had 'a much better case to go for preemptive action against Pakistan than the United States has in Iraq', referencing the threat posed to India by Pakistan's nuclear arsenal.[12] Israel has also expressed alarm over statements by Iranian President Mahmoud Ahmadinejad that Israel should be 'wiped off the map', leading to concern that Israel will act pre-emptively against Iran to degrade its capacity to produce nuclear weapons, following a pattern of pre-emptive uses of force which Israel followed in 1967 against Egypt, in 1981 against Iraq, and in 2007 against Syria.[13]

C. International Use of Force Law

However, as former UN Secretary-General Annan's comments quoted previously express, this trend in policy emphasis upon pre-emptive, forceful counterproliferation actions does not sit easily with existing international use of force law, with the UN Charter as its cornerstone. According to the system for use of force regulation established in the Charter, which for its parties comprises binding international law superseding all other treaty commitments, there are only two legal justifications for an international use of force which violates the territorial integrity of another state.[14] The first is a recognition of the 'inherent right to self-defence' under Article 51 of the Charter, and the second is authorization of force by the UN Security Council under a resolution passed using the authority granted to the Council in Chapter VII of the Charter. Since the Security Council has not been used successfully as a forum in which anticipatory or pre-emptive uses of force against WMD threats have been authorized (a subject to which consideration will return later in this chapter), the only arguable legal basis for such actions has been a reliance upon the self-defence provisions of Article 51.[15]

[12] 'India Mulls "Pre-Emptive" Pakistan Strike, Cites U.S. Iraq War Precedent', *Agence France Presse*, 11 Apr 2003, available at <http://www.fromthewilderness.com/free/ww3/041403_india.html>.

[13] 'Israel's plans for Iran strikes', *Jane's*, 16 July 2004; Robin Wright, 'N. Koreans Taped At Syrian Reactor: Video Played a Role in Israeli Raid', *Washington Post*, 24 Apr 2008; David E. Sanger, 'U.S. Sees N. Korean Links to Reactor', *New York Times*, 24 Apr 2008.

[14] Ian Brownlie, *International Law and the Use of Force by States* (Oxford: Oxford University Press, 1963); Christine Gray, *International Law and the Use of Force* (Oxford: Oxford University Press, 2000); Anthony Arend and Robert Beck, *International Law and the Use of Force: Beyond the UN Charter Paradigm* (Abingdon: Routledge, 1993); Thomas Franck, *Recourse to Force* (Cambridge: Cambridge University Press, 2002).

[15] Michael Byers, 'Preemptive Self-Defense: Hegemony, Equality and Strategies of Legal Change' (2003) 11 *Journal of Political Philosophy* 171; Richard A. Falk, 'What Future for the UN Charter System of War Prevention?' (2003) 97 *American Journal of International Law* 590; Yoram Dinstein, *War, Aggression and Self-Defence* (3rd edn, Cambridge: Cambridge University Press, 2001).

These provisions allow for temporary, unilateral recourse to force 'if an armed attack occurs' against a member of the UN. Although the plain meaning of these terms would seem to restrict such a use of force in self-defence to a case in which an armed attack by another state or non-state actor has taken place or at least has commenced,[16] the recognition that Article 51 functions simply to recognize an already existing 'inherent right' of states has led many commentators to the conclusion that this language in Article 51 worked a retention of the rights of self-defence obtaining under pre-Charter customary law for UN Charter signatories.[17]

In classical customary international law, the right of a state to use force in a pre-emptive manner, to anticipate an attack which had not yet commenced but which was imminently threatened, enjoyed broad support among states and was a firmly established legal right. However, by the mid-19th century the right of anticipatory

[16] Bruno Simma et al (eds), *The Charter of the United Nations: A Commentary* (2nd edn, Oxford: Oxford University Press, 2002); Ahmed Rifaat, *International Aggression: A Study of the Legal Concept* (Stockholm: Almqvist & Wiksell International, 1979); Brownlie, *International Law and the Use of Force by States* ('where the Charter has a specific provision relating to a particular legal category, to assert that this does not restrict the wider ambit of the customary law relating to that category or problem is to go beyond the bounds of logic. Why have treaty provisions at all?... It is submitted that a restrictive interpretation of the provisions of the Charter relating to the use of force would be more justifiable and that even as a matter of "plain" interpretation the permission in Article 51 is exceptional in the context of the Charter and exclusive of any customary right of self-defence'). The Vienna Convention on the Law of Treaties (1969), Art 31 specifies that the plain (ordinary) meaning of a treaty provision, in context and in the light of its object and purpose, is to be given pre-eminence in interpretation. Supplementary means of interpretation, including preparatory work of the treaty, can only be employed when the foregoing analysis of ordinary meaning leaves the meaning ambiguous or obscure or 'leads to a result which is manifestly absurd or unreasonable'.

[17] Myres McDougal and Florentino Feliciano, *Law and Minimum World Public Order* (New Haven, CT: Yale University Press, 1961); Derek W. Bowett, *Self-Defence in International Law* (New York: Praeger, 1958), 185 ('It is... fallacious to assume that members have only those rights which the Charter accords to them; on the contrary they have those rights which general international law accords to them except in so far as they have surrendered them under the Charter... [T]he view of Committee I at San Francisco was that this prohibition [Art 2(4)] left the right of self-defense unimpaired'). Although addressing a different substantive question at the time (*obiter dicta*?) the International Court of Justice (ICJ) in its 1986 *Nicaragua* decision held that: 'Article 51 of the Charter is only meaningful on the basis that there is a "natural" or "inherent" right of self-defence, and it is hard to see how this can be other than of a customary nature... Moreover the Charter, having itself recognized the existence of this right, does not go on to regulate directly all aspects of its content. For example, it does not contain any specific rule whereby self-defence would warrant only measures which are proportional to the armed attack and necessary to respond to it, a rule well established in customary international law. Moreover, a definition of the "armed attack" which, if found to exist, authorizes the exercise of the "inherent right" of self-defence, is not provided in the Charter, and is not part of treaty law. It cannot therefore be held that Article 51 is a provision which "subsumes and supervenes" customary international law. It rather demonstrates that in the field in question... customary international law continues to exist alongside treaty law' (para 176). However, while standing for the principle that custom influences Charter interpretation for UN members in this area, the ICJ's opinion in *Nicaragua* does not establish a rule for circumstances in which there is clear conflict between custom and treaty law. In such a situation, it could still be argued that the treaty constitutes a special and separate regime and that for treaty signatories a conflict between treaty law and customary law must be resolved with the treaty rule being given priority.

self-defence as a matter of customary international law was circumscribed by several substantive limiting principles: imminence, necessity, and proportionality.[18]

The correspondence between US Secretary of State Daniel Webster and British officials during the famous *Caroline* incident is widely understood as offering a correct iteration of customary international law pertaining at the time.

Mr. Webster to Mr. Fox (24 April 1841)

It will be for… [Her Majesty's] Government to show a necessity of self-defense, instant, overwhelming, leaving no choice of means, and no moment for deliberation. It will be for it to show, also, that the local authorities of Canada, even supposing the necessity of the moment authorised them to enter the territories of the United States at all, did nothing unreasonable or excessive; since the act, justified by the necessity of self-defense, must be limited by that necessity, and kept clearly within it.[19]

Ian Brownlie has suggested that state practice between 1841 and 1945 served to even further limit the flexibility of the principle of anticipatory self-defence, leaving it in a tenuous state of existence at the time of drafting of the UN Charter.[20] This position would seem to be supported through even more recent events, such as the 1981 pre-emptive attack by Israel against a suspected Iraqi nuclear weapons site at Osirak.[21] Resolution 487 (1981) of the UN Security Council, which was adopted unanimously, denounced the incident as a 'clear violation of the Charter of the United Nations' notwithstanding Israel's believable (and later validated) claim regarding Iraq's clandestine WMD programme and its connection to the site.[22] As Christine Gray has observed:

the actual invocation of the right to anticipatory self-defense in practice is rare. States clearly prefer to rely on self-defense in response to an armed attack if they possibly can. In practice

[18] On the principles of necessity and proportionality in customary international law, see Brownlie, *International Law and the Use of Force by States*, 257–64. See generally Malcolm Shaw, *International Law* (5th edn, Cambridge: Cambridge University Press, 2003), 1024–5. See also the Dissenting Opinion of Judge Schwebel in the *Nicaragua* case (*Military and Paramilitary Activities in and against Nicaragua*, ICJ Rep 1986, 14, para 200) in which he argues that the *Caroline* criteria are exclusively applicable to cases of anticipatory self-defence.

[19] Kenneth E. Shewmaker et al (eds), *The Papers of Daniel Webster, Diplomatic Papers, 1841–1843* (Hanover, NH: University Press of New England, 1983), 43. The *Caroline* was a US-registered steamer hired to ferry provisions across the Niagara river to supply Canadian rebels taking part in the insurrection against British colonial rule of Canada in 1837. On 29 Dec, several boatloads of British soldiers came across the river onto the US side and set fire to the *Caroline*, dragged her into the river current, and sent her blazing over Niagara Falls, killing one man in the process. The ensuing diplomatic correspondence between US and UK officials has come to be regarded as a reliable statement of contemporary customary international law on self-defence.

[20] Ian Brownlie, *Principles of Public International Law* (6th edn, Oxford: Oxford University Press, 2003), 702.

[21] See Malfrid Braut-Hegghammer, 'Revisiting Osiraq: Preventive Attacks and Nuclear Proliferation Risks' (2011) 36 *International Security* 101.

[22] Louis Rene Beres and Yoash Tsiddon-Chatto, '"Sorry" Seems to be the Hardest Word', *The Jerusalem Post*, 9 June 2003; Anthony D'Amato, 'Israel's Air Strike upon the Iraqi Nuclear Reactor' (1983) 77 *American Journal of International Law* 584. On 6 Sept 2007, Israeli warplanes attacked and destroyed a site in Syria which was later claimed to be a nuclear reactor site, constructed with the help

they prefer to take a wide view of armed attack rather than openly claim anticipatory self-defense. It is only when no conceivable case can be made that there has been an armed attack that they resort to anticipatory self-defense. This reluctance expressly to invoke anticipatory self-defense is in itself a clear indication of the doubtful status of this justification for the use of force. States take care to try to secure the widest possible support; they do not invoke a doctrine that they know will be unacceptable to the vast majority of states. Certain writers, however, ignore this choice by states and argue that if states in fact act in anticipation of an armed attack this should count as anticipatory self-defense in state practice. This is another example of certain writers going beyond what states themselves say in justification of their action in order to argue for a wide right of self defense... A few of these commentators seem prepared to treat any US action as a precedent creating new legal justification for the use of force. Thus they use US actions as shifting the Charter paradigm and extending the right of self-defense. The lack of effective action against the USA as a sanction confirms them in this view. But the vast majority of other states remained firmly attached to a narrow conception of self-defense... The clear trend in state practice before 9/11 was to try to bring the action within Article 51 and to claim the existence of an armed attack rather than to argue expressly for a wider right under customary international law.[23]

However, the right to anticipatory self-defence, as limited by imminence, necessity, and proportionality is considered by many international lawyers to remain a valid doctrine in customary international law, and to be a right upon which even UN Charter members may rely.[24]

The problem in the context of counterproliferation-oriented pre-emptive uses of force, however, is that this policy, as expressed by the US and other states, and as carried out in practice in some recent cases and threatened in still others, calls for uses of force against states and non-state actors within other states which are simply developing or are in possession of WMD, without the existence of an

of North Korea. Information about the attack and the site have been difficult for the general public to discern, as both Israel and Syria have been less than forthcoming about the incident. Some details came to public light in Apr 2008 when US intelligence services gave a briefing to the US Congress on the event. Due to the paucity of confirmed facts regarding the site and the attack, international opinion has at the time of writing been difficult to gauge. Some have argued that the absence of formal censure by states amounted to a tacit acquiescence to the strike. However, the lack of certainty regarding the details of the site and the attack likely make such assessments premature. See Robin Wright, 'N. Koreans Taped At Syrian Reactor: Video Played a Role in Israeli Raid', *Washington Post*, 24 Apr 2008; David E. Sanger, 'U.S. Sees N. Korean Links to Reactor', *New York Times*, 24 Apr 2008; Michael Gordon and Eric Schmitt, 'U.S. Says Israeli Exercise Seemed Directed at Iran', *New York Times*, 20 June 2008.

[23] Gray, *International Law and the Use of Force*, 130, 133, 134; see also Christine Gray, 'The Principle of Non-Use of Force' in Vaughan Lowe and Colin Warbrick (eds), *The United Nations and the Principles of International Law* (Abingdon: Routledge, 1994); Christine Gray, 'The Use and Abuse of the International Court of Justice: Cases concerning the Use of Force after Nicaragua' (2003) 14 *European Journal of International Law* 867. For contrasting opinions on the subject of state practice in the area of anticipatory self-defence, see Arend and Beck, *International Law and the Use of Force*; Mark Weisburd, *Use of Force* (University Park, PA: Penn State Press, 1997).

[24] 'Principles of International Law on the Use of Force by States in Self-Defense,' Chatham House International Law Programme (Oct 2005), 4, available at <http://www.chathamhouse.org.uk/pdf/research/il/ILPForce.doc>.

immediate threat that such weapons will be used against the state pursuing the policy of pre-emption. Imminence, again, is a key criterion which must be satisfied in order to justify a self-defensive action by reference to the customary law right of anticipatory self-defence. Therefore, an implementation of this policy, in which unilateral international force is used by a state prior to an actual armed attack, against state or non-state actors that simply possess or are developing WMD, without the existence of a meaningful threat to use such weapons which satisfies the criteria set out in the *Caroline* case, does not satisfy the requirements for justification under either the text of Article 51 or the customary right of anticipatory self-defence which it arguably incorporates, and therefore constitutes a violation of Article 2(4) of the UN Charter.

Notwithstanding this legal incongruity, the policy of counterproliferation-oriented pre-emption continues to be seen by a number of states as a necessary final option to be used against WMD threats when no other tools appear to be working.[25] The idea that states must, per the text of Article 51 or the restrictive interpretation of anticipatory self-defence prescribed by customary law, wait for a WMD attack to have already taken place against them, or at least for indisputable evidence of a threat of use of WMD against them, which leaves them 'no choice of means and no moment for deliberation' before they are allowed to act in self-defence, is to the minds of many policymakers a wholly unrealistic notion, and unworkable in practice.

This then exposes the heart of the problem currently facing states in their desires both to vigorously pursue policies seen as necessary to their national security, and at the same time to support and comply with international law, and comprises the cause of the current crisis in international use of force law. The UN Charter, now almost 70 years old, is in the minds of many policymakers in states that are shifting their emphasis towards counterproliferation, an anachronism; a set of norms which, if accurately reflective of the principled universe which states inhabited within the context of the evolution of military technology and geopolitics in 1945, is currently unfit for the task of providing a set of workable and supportable principles for governing this most sensitive area of international relations.

These policymakers point not only to the proliferation of WMD technologies themselves, which have worked an evolution in the instruments of violence and the amount of damage that can be done in a single 'armed attack,' but also to the emergence of sophisticated non-state actors whom, it is feared, will be able to use these weapons, changing the rules on where states must look to predict and manage threats, as well as the effectiveness of classical doctrines such as deterrence and

[25] In addition to statements supporting pre-emptive use of force made by US officials, see similar statements of officials from Russia, Australia, the UK, Japan, India, and Israel and the articles cited in n 6.

containment for managing these threats.[26] These doctrines, while employed with some success in interstate security tensions, seem likely to be largely ineffective against the fluid assets and operative networks of international non-state actors, and particularly those driven by extreme ideological motives.[27] As Daniel Poneman has explained:

> Obviously, deterrence depends on having a return address which one can target and send an opponent a response to that which has just been received. However, terrorists do not often leave return addresses. Moreover, deterrence depends on a particular view of human nature. If you read Hobbes' Leviathan, you understand that, at the least, you need a minimal sense of self-preservation to rely upon if you expect notions of deterrence to obtain. In a terrorist context—in which, if not the leaders, then certainly the cannon fodder they send in to do the suicide bombings, are not driven by the desire for self-preservation—you can no longer count on deterrence.[28]

While some observers might characterize these views regarding the threat posed by WMD and the anachronistic character of existing international use of force law as extreme and reactionary, or perhaps even paranoid, the fact remains that many policymakers in counterproliferation-oriented states genuinely believe that it is necessary for the security of their states that they are able to use force pre-emptively against these new threats before they develop the qualities of demonstrable immediacy necessary to square such actions with existing use of force law. Moreover, it is clear that a number of these states will continue to act in pursuance of these beliefs, and of counterproliferation policies of pre-emption, regardless of the formal, technical requirements of international law.

This, then, is the heart of the crisis: a significant number of states now believe that their vital national security interests require them to act in a manner that is in breach of the law governing international uses of force laid down in the UN Charter. This is not a temporary policy shift, nor are actions taken in pursuance of counterproliferation policies isolated or extraordinary events. Policies of counterproliferation-oriented pre-emptive use of force are part of a systematic rethinking within a significant number of states about the security environment in which states find themselves, and the policy options those states feel they must

[26] Remarks by U.S. President Bush in Address to the Nation, The Cross Hall, available at <http://www.whitehouse.gov/news/releases/2003/03/print/20030317-7.html>; also Speech at West Point Military Academy on 1 June 2002, at <http://www.whitehouse.gov/news/releases/2002/06/20020601-3.html>; remarks by UK Prime Minister Tony Blair in preface to the UK government's dossier on Iraq's WMD programmes, *The Guardian*, 24 Sept 2002, at <http://www.guardian.co.uk/Iraq/Story/0,,797883,00.html>.

[27] See Derek Smith, *Deterring America: Rogue States and the Proliferation of Weapons of Mass Destruction* (Cambridge: Cambridge University Press, 2006).

[28] Daniel Poneman, 'A New Bargain' in Joseph Pilat (ed), *Atoms for Peace: A Future After Fifty Years?* (Washington DC: Woodrow Wilson Center Press, 2007), 179–80.

maintain in order to defend themselves against modern threats, and to pursue their essential interests internationally.[29]

This is a revision of thought that is likely to persist and mature within these states, and it is likely that, as WMD proliferation inevitably spreads and becomes more intimately a part of the security concerns of a growing number of states, those states too will arrive at the conclusion that traditional non-proliferation efforts based in multilateralism and diplomacy, and utilizing strategies such as deterrence and containment, are not wholly sufficient to deal with these realities. They will likely conclude, as others have done, that policies of pre-emptive use of force against states and non-state actors that threaten them with WMD, and which will not sufficiently respond to or be managed by these classic strategies, are a necessary addition to the policy options at their disposal.

Therefore, at the heart of the current crisis in international use of force law is a continuing, and likely increasing, gap between the provisions of existing law and the perceptions of a significant number of important states of the realities of the international political issue area that law is meant to regulate—a classic gap between law and reality caused by the law simply lagging behind the dynamics of technological and geopolitical change.[30] Such a situation, in which the law is seen by its subjects to be out of touch with the 'on the ground' realities of the decisions and actions it is intended to govern, in any area of the law is simply unsustainable and as in any other area of law the result of this gap is decreasing confidence in the law and its institutions of maintenance, a decreasing perception of the validity of the law, increasing antagonism towards the law, and resultant non-compliance with the reason-offending rules.[31] This was, indeed, one of the fundamental reasons underlying the decision by Western powers to invade Iraq in 2003, and is the reason that

[29] Elaine Bunn, 'Force, Preemption and WMD Proliferation' in Nathan Busch and Daniel Joyner (eds), *Combating Weapons of Mass Destruction: The future of international nonproliferation policy* (Athens, GA: University of Georgia Press, 2009); Ellis, 'The Best Defense'; Litwak, 'The New Calculus of Pre-emption'; Jason D. Ellis and Geoffrey D. Kiefer, *Combatting Proliferation: Strategic Intelligence and National Policy* (Baltimore, MD: The Johns Hopkins University Press, 2003).

[30] Hans J. Morgenthau, 'Positivism, Functionalism and International Law' (1940) 34 *American Journal of International Law* 260, 260; Michael Glennon, 'The Fog of Law: Self-Defense, Inherence, and Incoherence in Article 51 of the United Nations Charter' (2002) 25 *Harvard Journal of Law and Public Policy* 540, 549; Anne-Marie Slaughter and William Burke-White, 'An International Constitutional Moment' (2002) 43 *Harvard International Law Journal* 1, 2; Robert F. Turner, 'Operation Iraqi Freedom: Legal and Policy Considerations' (2004) 27 *Harvard Journal of Law and Public Policy* 765, 793; Ruth Wedgwood, 'The Fall of Saddam Hussein: Security Council Mandates and Preemptive Self-Defense' (2003) 97 *American Journal of International Law* 576, 583; Anthony Clark Arend, 'International Law and the Preemptive Use of Military Force' (Spring 2003) *Washington Quarterly* 89; Richard N. Gardner, 'Neither Bush nor the Jurisprudes' (2003) 97 *American Journal of International Law* 585; Jane E. Stromseth, 'Law and Force After Iraq: A Transitional Moment' (2003) 97 *American Journal of International Law* 628, 629; John C. Yoo and Will Trachman, 'Less than Bargained For: The Use of Force and the Declining Relevance of the United Nations' (2005) 5 *Chicago Journal of International Law* 379, 381.

[31] See Morgenthau, 'Positivism, Functionalism and International Law'.

fears abound regarding future acts of force outside the UN Charter use of force system by counterproliferation-oriented states, in places like Iran and North Korea.

D. Disproportionate Significance?

It is true that only relatively powerful states would consider engaging in a counterproliferation-oriented pre-emptive use of force. This is because only relatively few states in the world have the capacity to project power through military force internationally, with confidence that they will be able to successfully withstand responsive uses of force against them.

Some will no doubt argue as a consequence of this fact that there are simply too few states anxiously concerned with this issue, and willing to act in furtherance of pre-emptive strike policies, for it to be cited as the cause of a 'crisis' in international use of force law.

It should be borne in mind, however, that while numerically in the minority, these powerful actors are a disproportionately important subset of states to consider with regard to the current status and future character and substance of international use of force law for a number of interconnected reasons. First, among this subset are many states which, correctly or not, feel particularly threatened by the possibility of WMD attacks against them. For some states this is due to long-standing regional interstate disputes, the parties to which have or are in the process of developing WMD arsenals.[32] For other states, this is because of aspects of their political or cultural identity, or their international influence and activity, which they perceive have increased the likelihood of asymmetric attacks against them by terrorists and other, particularly non-state, actors using WMD.[33] This fact of perceived particular threat, together with the previously mentioned capacity of such states to act internationally in pursuance of a broad understanding of their vital national interests, produces a peculiar and important subset of states that are both most likely to want to have the legal option to engage in counterproliferation-oriented pre-emptive acts of force, and at the same time are most likely to have the power and influence in international relations to either alter or opt out of treaties, as well as to employ the means of creation of customary law, in order to bring about such desired legal changes.[34]

[32] 'India Mulls "Pre-Emptive" Pakistan Strike, Cites U.S. Iraq War Precedent', *Agence France Presse*, 11 Apr 2003, available at <http://www.fromthewilderness.com/free/ww3/041403_india.html>; 'Israel's plans for Iran strikes', *Jane's*, 16 July 2004.

[33] Remarks by UK Prime Minister Tony Blair in preface to the UK government's dossier on Iraq's WMD programmes, *The Guardian*, 24 Sept 2002, at <http://www.guardian.co.uk/Iraq/Story/0,,797883,00.html>.

[34] Michael Byers, *Custom, Power, and the Power of Rules* (Cambridge: Cambridge University Press, 1999).

In addition to their disproportionate motivation for and influence in changing relevant sources of law, these powerful actors are of particular importance in considering the future of international use of force law because they are among the relatively few states in the world against whom the horizontal enforcement mechanisms of international law—that is, issue linkaging, diplomatic or economic pressuring, or direct military force—are unlikely to be effective should they alternatively decide that acting in a way that is formally in breach of the law is in their vital national interests, even if the majority of states recognize the action as illegal.[35] The 2003 Iraq intervention is, again, an apt example of this ability.

For all of these reasons, it is argued that it is possible for the perceptions and actions of a relatively small subset of powerful states to form the basis for a crisis in international use of force law. It is further submitted, in agreement with former UN Secretary-General Annan's statements, that the current state of international use of force law is indeed in a state of crisis, the resolution of which is of fundamental importance to the future of the UN and to the UN Charter system for use of force regulation.

In his September 2003 remarks to the General Assembly, the Secretary-General went on to discuss the founding ideals of the UN Charter and to conclude, 'Now we must decide whether it is possible to continue on the basis agreed then, or whether radical changes are needed. And we must not shy away from questions about the adequacy, and effectiveness, of the rules and instruments at our disposal.'[36] There are indeed a number of possibilities for reform or amendment of relevant provisions of use of force law, and the organs of the UN, many of which have been proposed and discussed at length by others as alternatives for bridging the gap and bringing the law into harmony with the realities of international security concerns, though none of the proposals have been met with generalized approval among members of the UN.[37] This chapter will proceed by reviewing the most noteworthy of these proposals, on the subjects of the composition and decision-making processes of the Security Council, and the construction and application of the law on self-defence contained in Article 51.

[35] Abram and Antonia Chayes, 'On Compliance' (1993) 47 *International Organization* 175; Andrew T. Guzman, 'A Compliance Based Theory of International Law' (2002) 90 *California Law Review* 1826; Harold H. Koh, 'Why Do Nations Obey International Law?' (1997) 106 *Yale Law Journal* 2599.

[36] Secretary-General's Address to the General Assembly, 23 Sept 2003, available at <http://www.un.org/webcast/ga/58/statements/sg2eng030923>.

[37] Yehuda Z. Blum, 'Proposals for UN Security Council Reform' (2005) 99 *American Journal of International Law* 632; Inocencio Arias, 'Humanitarian Intervention: Could the Security Council Kill the United Nations?' (2000) 23 *Fordham International Law Journal* 1005, 1026; Thomas Franck, *Recourse to Force* (Cambridge: Cambridge University Press, 2002); David Malone (ed), *The U.N. Security Council: From the Cold War to the 21st Century* (Boulder, CO: Lynne Rienner, 2004); Bardo Fassbender, *U.N. Security Council Reform and the Right of Veto* (Leiden: Martinus Nijhoff, 1998); Joachim Muller (ed), *Reforming the United Nations: The Struggle for Legitimacy and Effectiveness* (Leiden: Martinus Nijhoff, 2006).

III. Possibilities for Change

A. The Security Council

Among proposals for amendment to the provisions and procedures of the UN Charter system for use of force regulation, none has been more discussed than the idea of amending the make-up and decision-making procedures of the Security Council in order to make it a more credible, supportable, and effective body in the exercise of its authority granted under the UN Charter.[38] These proposals essentially recognize that the 1945 political accord which provided for a ten-member rotating membership of the Security Council, plus the allocation of permanent member status and special veto rights to five specific states on the Council, is both unsatisfactory for modern ideas of democratic representation in international organizations, and unreflective of modern realities of states' power and influence.

Proposals for amendment of the Security Council have been many and varied, but can be categorized in summary as proposals for changing: (1) the size of the Council; (2) the membership of the Council; (3) the identity of permanent members of the Council (if any); (4) the powers of permanent members; and (5) the procedures for Security Council decision-making.

One set of proposals for changing the size and membership of the Security Council was made by the 2004 High-Level Panel Report.[39] The Panel concluded that a decision to enlarge the Security Council's membership was 'a necessity', and that it should be guided primarily by principles of increased democratic representation of UN members, particularly from the developing world, and of accountability in decision-making. Realization of these principles, it argued, was necessary for the Council to be seen as a legitimate, credible body in taking decisions regarding international uses of force.[40]

The Panel produced two proposals for amendment to the size and composition of the Security Council, involving a distribution of seats among four regional areas: Africa, Asia and Pacific, Europe, and the Americas. Under Model A, six new permanent seats on the Council would be created along with three two-term non-permanent seats, resulting in a revised overall Council membership of 24 states, evenly divided among the four geographic regions (see Table 48.1).[41]

[38] Blum, 'Proposals for UN Security Council Reform'; Fassbender, *U.N. Security Council Reform and the Right of Veto*.

[39] Note by the Secretary-General, Follow-up to the Outcome of the Millennium Summit, A/59/565 (2 Dec 2004), available at <http://www.un.org/secureworld/report.pdf>.

[40] Para 250.

[41] Figures 48.1 and 48.2 reprinted from the UN Secretary-General's High-Level Panel on Threats, Challenges and Change, 'A More Secure World: Our Shared Responsibility' (2004).

Table 48.1 Model A

Regional area	No of states	Permanent seats (continuing)	Proposed new permanent seats	Proposed two-year seats (non-renewable)	Total
Africa	53	0	2	4	6
Asia and Pacific	56	1	2	3	6
Europe	47	3	1	2	6
Americas	35	1	1	4	6
Totals model A	191	5	6	13	24

As an alternative construction, under Model B no new permanent seats would be created, but eight four-year renewable-term seats and one two-year non-permanent seat would be created, and divided evenly among the four regions (see Table 48.2).

Although the Panel's Model A proposed the creation of new permanent seats on the Council, it did not provide for veto powers for those new permanent members, to equal the powers coincident with permanent member status under the existing Charter structure. Indeed, neither model provided for either expansion of veto powers or circumscription of the existing veto powers of permanent members. However, proposals from other sources have included alternatives for revoking the veto rights of permanent members entirely, or for establishing new decision-making rules for the Council which would mediate the effect of permanent members' veto,

Table 48.2 Model B

Regional area	No of states	Permanent seats (continuing)	Proposed four-year renewable seats	Proposed two-year seats (non-renewable)	Total
Africa	53	0	2	4	6
Asia and Pacific	56	1	2	3	6
Europe	47	3	2	1	6
Americas	35	1	2	3	6
Totals model B	191	5	8	11	24

such as by allowing a supermajority of the Security Council to override the veto of one of the permanent members, or requiring the Council to take up a measure for 'second consideration' if it was first defeated by only one permanent member's veto. In such a case of second consideration, the measure would only be defeated by the votes of two permanent members.[42] These and other proposals for amending the distribution of power among Security Council members, and for changing the Council's voting procedures, have been primarily aimed at improving the efficiency of Security Council decision-making, and at decreasing instances of stalemate in the Council and resultant inaction in the face of threats.

A number of these proposals for amendment of the Security Council and its decision-making procedures have received substantial political support, particularly on the issue of enlargement of the Security Council. A number of alternative plans have been put forward, and variously endorsed by groups of states, including some existing permanent Council members.[43] There was some significant hope that the issue of Security Council enlargement would be made part of the formal agenda for the 2005 World Summit. However, this hope, as with most hopes for progress in UN reform efforts at the World Summit, was not realized.[44]

Even if politically possible, however, the problems with this entire line of thinking in the counterproliferation-oriented pre-emption context are several and fundamental. For the Security Council to fill the role of authorizer, through its Chapter VII powers, of counterproliferation-oriented pre-emptive uses of force, it would have to be a forum in which member states were comfortable in sharing highly sensitive intelligence information, in order to convince fellow Council members to support their application for authorization. It would further have to be a body among whose members there is likely to be substantial agreement regarding the sources and characteristics of threats warranting pre-emptive uses of force, so as to make states confident that efforts to work through the Council would be likely to be successful and worth the transaction costs and inevitable risks of intelligence leaking to the target entity involved.[45]

However, the Security Council does not meet either of these criteria as it is currently structured, and, more to the point, none of the proposals which have been offered for amending it would serve to substantially address these limitations of

[42] Inocencio Arias, 'Humanitarian Intervention: Could the Security Council Kill the United Nations?' (2000) 23 *Fordham International Law Journal* 1005, 1025, 1026.

[43] 'UN Debates New Security Council: Four Countries led by Brazil have Formally Introduced a Proposal to Enlarge the UN Security Council', BBC News Online, 12 July 2005, available at <http://news.bbc.co.uk/1/hi/world/americas/4673977.stm>.

[44] 'U.N. Reform Agenda Watered Down', *CNN*, 14 Sept 2005, available at <http://edition.cnn.com/2005/us/09/14/un.reform/index.html> (quoting Secretary-General Annan: 'The big item missing is non-proliferation and disarmament. This is a real disgrace... when we are all concerned with weapons of mass destruction and that they may get into the wrong hands').

[45] Simon Chesterman, 'Shared Secrets: Intelligence and Collective Security', Lowy Institute Paper, 2006, 10, available at <http://iilj.org/research/documents/chesterman_shared_secrets_2006.pdf>.

the institutional capacity of the Council to act in such cases. The intelligence which states collect on WMD threats of a nature which causes them such serious concern as to warrant a decision to use pre-emptive military force is intelligence of the highest sensitivity, and will have been collected through means the secrecy of which the collecting state will protect at all costs. Information of this sensitivity will simply not be shared by states with a group as diverse as the Security Council, no matter who the collecting state is. Sharing of intelligence of this degree of sensitivity sometimes occurs between the closest of allies, for functional purposes, but would never be shared either openly or confidentially to the general membership of the Council or to UN staff. The risk of leakage to the target state, and general risks of divulgence of sources and methods, is simply too great with insufficient likely gain from the effort. Although there have been proposals for the establishment of safeguards and confidence-building processes for sharing of intelligence within the UN, none of these are likely to satisfy states when dealing with information of this level of sensitivity.[46] An expanded Security Council membership, made regionally even more diverse, would further decrease the likelihood of sensitive information being shared, and thus further diminish the feasibility of the Security Council's filling a meaningful role in authorizing counterproliferation-oriented pre-emptions.

The second institutional limitation the Security Council faces in this area again lies in the diversity of states comprising the Council's membership, and is the fact that members of the Security Council differ fundamentally at times in their perception and appreciation of WMD threats. Both the case of Iraq in 2003 and the ongoing case of Iran are salient examples of such a divergence of views regarding both the existence and degree of imminence of WMD threats. In both cases it became clear to those permanent members of the Council that wished to pursue forceful action under the authority of Chapter VII of the Charter, that that view was not shared by other permanent members of the Council. Thus, in both cases, those wishing to pursue such forceful action elected to pursue that action outside the Charter framework.[47]

Although the Security Council acts as a body empowered with special legal rights, such disagreements and resultant inability to act as a body and to use those rights, are reminders that the Council is primarily an international political body, made up of states with divergent and often conflicting interests and world-views. The expectation that such a group of states would in a consistent manner substantially agree in their perception of threats, so as to give states confidence that applications to the Council for pre-emptive force against WMD threats will likely find approval by nine members of the Council including all five permanent members, has little foundation. This is against the prudential soundness of the reliance placed upon the

[46] See Chesterman, 'Shared Secrets'.

[47] Dafna Linzer, 'U.S. Urges Financial Sanctions on Iran', *Washington Post*, 29 May 2006, available at <http://www.washingtonpost.com/wp-dyn/content/article/2006/05/28/AR2006052800999_pf.html>.

Security Council, as a body with the capacity to act as an authorizer of pre-emptive uses of force, by the 2004 High-Level Report as reflected in their statement quoted earlier.[48] Again, proposals for increasing the size of the Council and the number and diversity of its membership, would only serve to exacerbate this problem further, and would make the possibility of such consistent agreement less, not more, likely and thus further compromise the Council's ability to fulfil such a role.

It is argued herein that proposals for reform of the Security Council and its procedures, with a purpose in making the Council better able to function as an authorizer of counterproliferation-oriented pre-emptive uses of force, fail entirely to grasp the nettle of the serious institutional limitations upon the Council's capacity to act in this role. As shown previously, the proposals which enjoy the broadest political support, that is, those for enlarging and diversifying the Council's membership, would in fact produce effects retrograde to these aims. The 2004 High-Level Panel Report's emphasis upon such amendment, and not upon more fundamental change to the underlying rules of international use of force law, it is therefore submitted, is largely misplaced.[49]

B. Article 51

The other most frequently discussed area for possible amendment to the UN Charter system of use of force law, particularly in consideration of the concerns some states have regarding WMD proliferation and international terrorism, and the need for pre-emptive acts to address these threats, is the UN Charter law on self-defence, contained in Article 51.[50] This provision and its relevance to debates regarding counterproliferation-oriented pre-emptive uses of force, including the argued inclusion from customary law of a right of anticipatory self-defence within its broader interpretation, have been discussed earlier. As concluded through that discussion, Article 51, even with its broader interpretation to include the customary law right of anticipatory self-defence, is not sufficient to legally justify pre-emptive strikes of the sort prescribed by some powerful states' national counterproliferation policies.

The question of amendment thus becomes, is there some other formulation of the right of self-defence which might be agreed by states through amendment to the UN Charter or authoritative process of interpretation of that document, or through the development of a more expansive right of anticipatory self-defence in

[48] See n 2: 'The short answer is that if there are good arguments for preventive military action, with good evidence to support them, they should be put to the Security Council, which can authorize such action if it chooses to.'

[49] See n 2.

[50] Michael Doyle, *Striking First: Preemption and Prevention in International Conflict* (Princeton, NJ: Princeton University Press, 2008); John C. Yoo and Will Trachman, 'Less Than Bargained For', 379, 386.

customary law, which would at once allow states the normative and procedural flexibility they desire to legally justify unilateral acts of force against developing WMD threats, while at the same time preserving an objectively verifiable rule of law on the subject of self-defence in international law?

The strength of Article 51 as currently textually constructed is its clarity, in establishing a 'bright line' rule for unilateral self-defence, requiring there to be an *ex ante* 'armed attack' against a state before it may invoke its temporary right of unilateral self-defence and use force against the state or non-state actor that has attacked it in order to repel the current attack and prevent further attacks. This standard, although still controversial in the details of its interpretation and application, establishes a fairly workable standard in principle, that is capable of objective, independent determination by other states *ex ante*, and by authoritative arbiters *ex post*. However, this clarity and definition also comprise the weakness of Article 51, as its provisions are applied to the modern realities some states feel are present in their security calculations and particularly with regard to the threat of use of WMD as discussed earlier.

In considering possibilities for amendment to Article 51, states with counter proliferation-oriented pre-emptive strike policies would likely wish for either formal amendment or authoritative reinterpretation through subsequent state practice, to produce a right of anticipatory self-defence which allows for a pre-emptive attack when a state has evidence (perhaps even if only circumstantial, and likely not open to review by other states) of WMD development or possession by another state or non-state actor, and a reasonable basis in fact (perhaps comprised largely by historical antipathy, and prior examples of aggressive acts or 'ties' to terrorist organizations) to suspect that those WMD might be used to threaten them at some point in the future. This standard sounds vague and indeterminate because it is vague and indeterminate, but in reality it is the sort of normative construction that would be necessary in order to justify the pre-emptive acts of force contemplated by some national counterproliferation policies and official statements.[51] This level of vagueness and subjectivity with regard to evidentiary standards, burden of evidentiary production, perception of threat, and imminence of threat, is precisely what would be required in order to give such states the legal flexibility they would need to pursue such policies.

However, flexibility and vagueness in law on the one hand, and predictability and verifiability in law on the other, are very difficult to engineer simultaneously into the same legal provision.[52] As the vagueness and subjectivity of the right of self-defence

[51] US National Strategy to Combat Weapons of Mass Destruction (Dec 2002), available at <http://www.whitehouse.gov/nsc/nss.html> ('We must adapt the concept of imminent threat to the capabilities and objectives of today's adversaries').

[52] See generally Timothy Endicott, *Vagueness in Law* (Oxford: Oxford University Press, 2000); Brian Leiter (ed), *Objectivity in Law and Morals* (Cambridge: Cambridge University Press, 2000).

increases through such flexible construction, so the ability of other states to judge *ex ante*, and authoritative arbiters to judge *ex post* the compliance of the action with the normative standard, decreases in measure. In a similar variance, as this ability of third parties to adjudge the compliance of a self-defending state's action with the applicable international legal standard decreases, so in proportion does the character of that standard as a rule of law.[53] As conceded previously, the existing law of self-defence contained in Article 51 is, despite being an overall workable standard in principle, controversial enough in its discrete application to facts. Increasing the level of normative vagueness and subjectivity of its provisions would serve only to exacerbate this problem.

Added to this problem of effective norm construction, is the institutional problem within the international legal system of the relative absence of practical means of authoritative adjudication of disputes, including those regarding use of force law generally and self-defence law in particular.[54] This problem is, of course, essentially the product of the voluntary jurisdictional basis of international judicial bodies such as the International Court of Justice, and the election by many states not to accede to the compulsory jurisdiction of the Court.[55] This ability of states to avoid the jurisdiction of international judicial bodies on questions of self-defence law has significantly hampered the development of authoritative interpretations of the provisions of Article 51 and their consistent application, notwithstanding the fact that they are, as previously discussed, relatively straightforward. An expansive and more flexible rule of anticipatory self-defence will only increase controversies regarding the correct interpretation of the law, as an authoritative interpreter is effectively absent.

The difficulties surrounding rule construction in the area of self-defence, and the international legal system's incapacity to adjudicate self-defence rules effectively, taken together, make reliance on amendment of Article 51 to include a broader, more flexible right of anticipatory self-defence unlikely to be a broadly satisfactory answer to the crisis caused by powerful states' desires to pursue policies of counterproliferation-oriented pre-emption in disharmony with existing international use of force law.

[53] See Larry E. Ribstein, 'Law v. Trust' (2001) 81 *Boston University Law Review* 553.

[54] Charles Lipson, 'Why are Some International Agreements Informal?' (1991) 45 *International Organization* 495, 504–5; see generally Christine Gray, 'The Use and Abuse of the International Court of Justice: Cases Concerning the Use of Force after Nicaragua' (2003) 14 *European Journal of International Law* 867.

[55] Daniel Joyner, *International Law and the Proliferation of Weapons of Mass Destruction* (Oxford: Oxford University Press, 2009), ch 5. Another problem is the decision of some states, once they have acceded to the Court's jurisdiction, to subsequently withdraw their consent to jurisdiction. This occurred, eg, when the US withdrew its consent to ICJ jurisdiction during the *Nicaragua* case proceedings. See John Quigley, 'The United States' Withdrawal from International Court of Justice Jurisdiction in Consular Cases: Reasons and Consequences' (2009) 19 *Duke Journal of Comparative and International Law* 263.

IV. Summary and Considerations

In summary, this chapter has argued that there is in fact a current crisis in international law governing the use of force. It has argued that this crisis consists of a continuing, and likely increasing, gap between the provisions of existing law and the perceptions of a significant number of important states of the realities of the international political issue area that law is meant to regulate—a classic gap between law and reality caused by the law simply lagging behind the dynamics of technological and geopolitical change. It has argued that the result of this gap between law and reality has been that a significant number of states now believe that their vital national security interests require them to act in a manner that is in breach of the laws governing international uses of force laid down in the UN Charter.

The chapter has reviewed a number of the most noteworthy proposals which have been forwarded for reform or amendment of relevant provisions of use of force law, and the organs of the UN, in order to bridge this gap and bring international law into harmony with the realities of states' international security concerns. However, it has concluded that none of these proposals have the potential to effectively and satisfactorily remedy the problem, and resolve the crisis.

This, unfortunately, is the position in which the international community currently finds itself with regard to the implications of the proliferation of WMD for the prohibition of the use of force. A gap between law and reality that will likely continue and very possibly worsen in its breadth and implications, with the very real potential effect of significantly damaging the perceived credibility of international law governing uses of force, and even of international law generally. Despite a great deal of attention having been paid to this problem and potential solutions advanced by the best minds in international legal and political theory, the problem so far seems impervious to satisfactory resolution.

The current author has elsewhere proposed quite a revolutionary, though theoretically well grounded, approach for legal restructuring to address this problem.[56] However, he is the first to admit that this is an idea unlikely ever to be implemented. Realistically, it is likely that the crisis of the current situation will continue for the foreseeable future, and that powerful states will at times find it necessary, according to their independent national security judgements, to flout the rules of international law governing uses of force in the face of perceived threats of WMD proliferation. This is a prospect fundamentally unsettling for international lawyers, whose belief in the importance of international law for world order sits ill at ease with an understanding of the apparent limits of the law's effectiveness in this substantive area.

[56] Joyner, *International Law and the Proliferation of Weapons of Mass Destruction*, ch 9.

Perhaps the most likely future for international law on the specific subject of counterproliferation-oriented pre-emptive uses of force is that, over time, enough data points of state practice coupled with sufficient inferred *opinio juris*, and sufficient general acceptance by states of the necessity of the underlying principle, will emerge to establish some new rule of customary international law recognizing a right of states to act in this fashion.

This rule, if it emerges, will undoubtedly be unsatisfactory from a legal theory perspective, particularly with regard to its characteristics of predictability and objective verifiability. However, it may successfully produce what in the end is likely the only realistic outcome—that the law of self-defence be expanded to allow for such counterproliferation-oriented pre-emptive uses of force, notwithstanding the concomitant dilution of the character of the law on self-defence as a rule of law.

This will be an imperfect end result for international lawyers, who will be left to interpret and apply this expanded, yet weakened, rule of self-defence to future actions by states. Not that this will be a particularly novel challenge to international lawyers, who are frequently left to interpret and apply rules of law that have been imperfectly theorized, conceived, or drafted by their state creators. It is the current author's expectation that the area of international use of force law will continue to present significant conceptual and practical difficulties for international lawyers for the foreseeable future.

CHAPTER 49

THE USE OF FORCE AGAINST PIRATES

DOUGLAS GUILFOYLE

I. Introduction

On 15 May 2012 it was reported that the EU Naval Force, Operation Atalanta, which is tasked with counter-piracy off the coast of Somalia, had for the first time attacked a suspected pirate base:

> on the [Somali] mainland... [M]ultinational forces used helicopters in conjunction with two warships to leave five of the pirates' fast attack craft 'inoperable' [on the shore].[1]

If this is the shape of things to come, it represents a considerable shift in the use of force under international law against pirates. The rapid growth in Somali hostage-taking piracy since 2008 has spawned a considerable literature.[2] There is little merit here, however, in rehearsing the evolution of Somali piracy and the international response.[3] It is

[1] 'Somali piracy: EU forces in first mainland raid', BBC News, 15 May 2012, available at <http://www.bbc.co.uk/news/world-africa-18069685>.

[2] Pirates typically held 15 or more ships and several hundred crew at any time for ransom: 'Somali piracy', BBC News; House of Commons Foreign Affairs Committee, 'Piracy off the coast of Somalia' (HC 2010–12, 1318), 39, available at <http://www.parliament.uk/business/committees/committees-a-z/commons-select/foreign-affairs-committee/publications/>. The numbers are now much lower.

[3] Better book-length treatments include: Bibi van Ginkel and Frans-Paul van der Putten (eds), *The International Response to Somali Piracy: Challenges and Opportunities* (Leiden: Martinus Nijhoff, 2010); Robin Geiss and Anna Petrig, *The Legal Framework for Counter-Piracy Operations in Somalia*

sufficient to note that Somali pirates are now active throughout the Indian Ocean in an area encompassing the exclusive economic zones of states as distant as the Seychelles and India. Multinational naval forces involved in patrolling this vast ocean space include 'EU operation Atalanta, North Atlantic Treaty Organization operations Allied Protector and Ocean Shield, Combined Maritime Forces' Combined Task Force 151 [an offshoot of operations in Afghanistan]' as well as vessels from 'other States acting in a national capacity' including India, China, and Russia.[4] The counter-piracy activities of these forces to date have, with rare exceptions, occurred principally at sea.[5] As discussed later, these have been conducted under the applicable public international law of the sea and as law enforcement operations. Slightly different questions are raised by the use of force by private merchant vessels in self-defence, including through the use of privately contracted armed security personnel. The opening up of land operations against Somali pirates by multinational military forces raises further and different issues about the applicable law and its scope. It is appropriate to begin with a review of the relevant Security Council resolutions before turning to the legal regime applicable at sea and ashore within Somalia itself.

II. The Security Council and Somali Pirates

Since 2008 the Security Council has, remarkably, passed more resolutions concerning Somali piracy than terrorism.[6] At least eight such resolutions are

and the Gulf of Aden (Oxford: Oxford University Press, 2011). For a concise overview, see Milena Sterio et al, 'Transnational Piracy: To Pay or to Prosecute?' (2011) 105 *Proceedings of the Annual Meeting of the American Society of International Law* 543. A rich factual account is provided in relevant reports of the UN Secretary-General and his special adviser: S/2010/394 (2010), S/2011/30 (2011), S/2011/360 (2011), and S/2012/50 (2012).

[4] SC Res 2020 (2011), Preamble.

[5] In 2008, prior to any Security Council authorization to intervene in Somalia, French forces captured ashore in Somalia those suspected of hijacking the French vessel *Le Ponant*, and removed them for trial in Paris. See generally Douglas Guilfoyle, 'Counter-Piracy Law Enforcement and Human Rights' (2010) 59 *International and Comparative Law Quarterly* 141, 156; Anaïd Panossian, 'L'Affaire du Ponant et le renouveau de la lute internationale contre la piraterie' (2008) 112 *Revue Générale de Droit International Public* 661; and Tullio Treves, 'Piracy, Law of the Sea, and Use of Force: Developments off the Coast of Somalia' (2009) 20 *European Journal of International Law* 399, 404 fn 11. Their trial commenced only in 2012.

[6] The relevant terrorism-related resolutions are: SC Res 1805 (2008), 1822 (2008), 1904 (2009), 1963 (2010), 1988 (2011), 1989 (2011).

relevant for present purposes.[7] Their numerousness prevents detailed chronological discussion. The following analysis proceeds by identifying their common features usually by reference to the most recent at time of writing, Resolution 2020 (2011). In the nature of such things, it tends to restate much of the drafting of earlier resolutions.

A. The Role of the International Law of the Sea (and the 'Savings Clause')

First the relevant Security Council resolutions call upon:

> States and regional organizations that have the capacity to do so, to take part actively in the fight against piracy and armed robbery at sea off the coast of Somalia, in particular, consistent with this resolution and relevant international law, by deploying naval vessels and military aircraft . . .[8]

Thus, while calling for the use of military assets, there is no use of the phrase 'all necessary means', widely accepted as the standard Security Council language used to authorize the use of force under Chapter VII.[9] What, then, is the 'relevant international law' governing the fight against piracy? The preambles to the relevant resolutions reaffirm:

> that international law, as reflected in the United Nations Convention on the Law of the Sea of 10 December 1982 . . . [UNCLOS], sets out the legal framework applicable to combating piracy and armed robbery at sea.[10]

This appears an unequivocal assertion that UNCLOS codifies the relevant customary international law. Despite some academic assertions to the contrary,[11] there is now clearly 'widespread agreement' that this is the case.[12] However, in each resolution

[7] SC Res 1816 (2008), 1838 (2008), 1846 (2008), 1851 (2008), 1897 (2009), 1950 (2010), 1976 (2011) and 2020 (2011). See now also SC Res 2077 (2012) and SC Res 2125 (2013). One could also note SC Res 1816 (2008) dealing with the protection of humanitarian food deliveries into Somalia and various resolutions linking piracy and the political situation in Somalia including SC Res 2036 (2012).

[8] SC Res 1846 (2008), para 9.

[9] Christine Gray, 'The Use of Force and the International Legal Order' in Malcolm D. Evans (ed), *International Law* (3rd edn, Oxford: Oxford University Press, 2010), 363.

[10] SC Res 2020 (2011) and compare SC Res 1846 and 1851 (2008), 1897 (2009), 1950 (2010) and 1976 (2011); see also SC Res 1838 (2008), para 3.

[11] Alfred Rubin, *The Law of Piracy* (2nd edn., Newport, RI: US Naval War College, 1998), 331–72 and 373–96.

[12] Geiss and Petrig, *The Legal Framework for Counter-Piracy Operations in Somalia and the Gulf of Aden*, 41; Douglas Guilfoyle, *Shipping Interdiction and the Law of the Sea* (Cambridge: Cambridge University Press, 2009), 30–1 and Guilfoyle, 'Counter-Piracy Law Enforcement and Human Rights', 143; Djamchad Momtaz, 'The High Sea' in René-Jean Dupuy and Daniel Vignes (eds), *A Handbook on the New Law of the Sea* (Dordrecht: Martinus Nijhoff, 1991), vol 1, 417.

the Security Council also, curiously, affirms that the further authorizations granted in these resolutions (discussed later):

> apply only with respect to the situation in Somalia and shall not affect the rights or obligations or responsibilities of Member States under international law, including any rights or obligations, under ... [UNCLOS], with respect to any other situation, and underscores in particular that this resolution shall not be considered as establishing customary international law.[13]

This was clearly intended to meet the concerns of states, such as Indonesia, which desired 'ample safeguards' to avoid any implication that these resolutions involved any 'modification, rewriting or redefining' of UNCLOS.[14] In part this reflects a not uncommon view among some states that UNCLOS represents an exhaustively negotiated and finely balanced package deal and as a consequence *any* adjustment to it risks undermining the balance of the whole.[15] It may also echo the hostility some South East Asian coastal states have previously expressed to the idea that major naval powers might conduct counter-piracy operations within their regional waters.[16] The Security Council direction that these resolutions 'shall not be considered as establishing customary international law' is both an intriguing and question-begging proposition that cannot be further explored here.

The reference to the resolutions not applying to *any other situation* also echoes the Security Council's earlier determination(s) that:

> the incidents of piracy and armed robbery at sea off the coast of Somalia exacerbate the situation in Somalia, which continues to constitute a threat to international peace and security in the region.[17]

That is, as South Africa has stressed, it is:

> the [underlying] situation in Somalia that constitute[s] a threat to international peace and security, and *not piracy in itself*. Piracy is [only] a symptom of the situation in Somalia.[18]

The wording thus signals that piracy per se, wherever it may occur, is not to be considered a matter justifying Security Council intervention. In any event, the total effect of the savings clauses is to emphasize the primacy of UNCLOS as an authoritative statement of the applicable law.

[13] SC Res 1816 (2008), para 9; SC Res 1846 (2008), para 11; SC Res 1851 (2008), para 10; SC Res 1897 (2009), para 8; SC Res 1950 (2010), para 8; and SC Res 2020 (2011), para 10.

[14] S/PV.5902 (2 June 2008), 2–3.

[15] S/PV.5902, 4; contrast Alan Boyle, 'Further Development of the 1982 Law of the Sea Convention: Mechanisms for Change' (2005) 54 *International and Comparative Law Quarterly* 563.

[16] On the reactions of Indonesia and Malaysia to the widely misreported US Maritime Regional Security Initiative of 2004, see Guilfoyle, *Shipping Interdiction and the Law of the Sea*, 55.

[17] See the preambles to: SC Res 1816 (2008), 1838 (2008), 1846 (2008), 1851 (2008), 1897 (2009), 1950 (2010), 1976 (2011), and 2020 (2011).

[18] S/PV.5902 (2 June 2008), 2–3 (emphasis added).

2.2 'All necessary means' or 'all necessary measures' and authorisation to conduct operations in Somalia's territorial waters and on Somalia's territory.

Notwithstanding the preamble, there remains the possibility that the chain of relevant Chapter VII Security Council resolutions have widened the scope of legal force against piracy suspects in two cases. First, this may result from Resolution 1816, and its successors', repeated authorization of states to use 'all necessary means to repress acts of piracy and armed robbery' within Somalia's territorial sea. That is, states 'cooperating' with the Transitional Federal Government of Somali (TFG) 'in the fight against piracy and armed robbery at sea', where that cooperating status has been notified in advance 'by the TFG to the Secretary-General', may enter the territorial waters of Somalia and therein:

> Use…, in a manner consistent with action permitted on the high seas with respect to piracy under relevant international law, all necessary means to repress acts of piracy and armed robbery.[19]

This grant of authority (initially time-limited but frequently renewed)[20] is clearly subject to two limitations. First, there is the procedural requirement of being granted the status of a cooperating state by the TFG. This is curious: if coastal state authorization is granted, Chapter VII authorization by the Security Council is superfluous. It may obviously serve to 'pay homage to state sovereignty' and be intended to strengthen the TFG.[21] It has also been suggested that it avoids any conflict between patrolling states and Somalia over the validity of its claimed 200-nautical mile territorial sea.[22] It is not, however, generally doubted that that claim is invalid.[23] The more obvious explanation is that:

> Not every member of the Security Council recognizes the TFG…For those members that recognize the TFG, such a condition is understandable. However, for those…that do not…, the authority to conduct counterpiracy operations in the Somali territorial sea is found in the…[Chapter VII] resolutions.[24]

On the latter view, the TFG derives its authority to permit such interventions from the resolutions.

The second limitation is that the Resolution requires that action in the territorial sea be taken 'in a manner consistent with [counter-piracy] action permitted

[19] SC Res 1816 (2008), para 7(b).

[20] SC Res 1816, para 7; as renewed in: SC Res 1846, para 10; SC Res 1897, para 7; SC Res 1950, para 7; SC Res 2020, para 9.

[21] Treves, 'Piracy, Law of the Sea, and Use of Force', 407.

[22] Treves, 'Piracy, Law of the Sea, and Use of Force', 407–8.

[23] For the argument it may be reinterpreted as a (valid) exclusive economic zone, see Thilo Neumann and Tim René Salomon, 'Fishing in Troubled Waters—Somalia's Maritime Zones and the Case for Reinterpretation' (2012) 16 *American Society of International Law Insights*, available at <http://www.asil.org/pdfs/insights/insight120315.pdf>.

[24] Ashley Roach, 'Countering Piracy off Somalia: International Law and International Institutions' (2010) 104 *American Journal of International Law* 397, 401.

on the high seas' by international law. This clearly restrains the grant of authority to use 'all necessary means' to a scope of action no wider than that allowed on the high seas. As a result, and despite the difference in wording, the 'territorial sea' provisions of these resolutions go no further than those dealing with the high seas.

The second situation covered is intervention within Somalia. Commencing with Resolution 1851, successive Chapter VII resolutions have authorized states and regional organizations cooperating with the TFG (as notified to the Secretary-General) to:

> undertake all necessary measures that are appropriate *in Somalia*, for the purpose of suppressing acts of piracy and armed robbery at sea, pursuant to the request of the TFG, provided, however, that any measures undertaken...shall be...consistent with applicable international humanitarian and human rights law.[25]

This authorization to use force is, again, subject to two limitations: such measures must be expressly requested by the TFG and states must comply with 'applicable international humanitarian and human rights law'. Both limitations are somewhat ambiguous. On the first requirement, this does not contemplate the kind of comprehensive permission in advance to conduct operations envisaged in the territorial sea provisions. While the TFG could obviously confer such blanket authority, the wording appears more consistent with case-by-case authorization of operations. As to the second limitation, the application of 'applicable' human rights law is unobjectionable (although the question of the extraterritorial effect of human rights treaties for states intervening in Somalia may be complex).[26] The reference to international humanitarian law (IHL) is regrettably confusing. Some have interpreted it to suggest that the Resolution per se makes all of IHL applicable to counter-piracy operations in Somalia's land territory.[27] This is clearly wrong: the Resolution only refers to 'applicable' IHL; that is, law that would apply *irrespective* of the Resolution. The use of military force does not necessarily implicate IHL, which is applicable only in an international or non-international armed conflict. The point is taken up further later, after a discussion of the general public international law applicable to the use of force against pirates on the high seas.

[25] SC Res 1851, para 6 (emphasis added). Renewed in: SC Res 1897, para 7; SC Res 1950, para 7; SC Res 2020, para 9.

[26] See generally: Guilfoyle, 'Counter-Piracy Law Enforcement and Human Rights', 152–69; Geiss and Petrig, *The Legal Framework for Counter-Piracy Operations in Somalia and the Gulf of Aden*, 101–30.

[27] Eugene Kontorovich, 'International Legal Responses to Piracy off the Coast of Somalia' (2009) 13 *American Society of International Law Insights*, available at <http://www.asil.org/insights090206.cfm>; *contra* Michael Passman, 'Protections Afforded to Captured Pirates Under the Law of War and International Law' (2008) 33 *Tulane Maritime Law Journal* 1, 16 ff (noting that the scope for any such application is limited).

III. The Applicable Legal Framework at Sea

A. General Considerations of Public International Law

It is clear that both UNCLOS and the earlier Geneva High Seas Convention,[28]and customary international law, provide police powers to suppress piracy.[29] On the high seas (for present purposes, being all waters outside any state's territorial sea),[30] any government vessel may board a vessel suspected of piracy as an exception to the principle of exclusive flag state jurisdiction.[31] Where evidence of piracy is discovered, the state vessel may seize the suspect vessel, arrest persons on board, and subject them to the jurisdiction of that state's courts,[32] although in the Somali case interdicting navies have often transferred suspects to regional states for trial under universal jurisdiction laws.[33] These powers apply only on the high seas and do not permit pursuing pirates into foreign territorial waters.[34] Where such acts of boarding, inspection, or seizure under UNCLOS are resisted then questions regarding the use of force obviously arise.

Simply because an operation is being carried out by naval forces does not mean the applicable law must be that of the laws of war either under the UN Charter (*jus ad bello*) or IHL (*jus in bello*). '[I]t is the mission, not the uniform worn by the actor, that determines how the force should be classified and which doctrine controls that use of force.'[35] While this proposition may seem self-evident it is seldom fully explained by commentators. On one view, the proposition can be deduced from the text of UNCLOS, which stipulates that warships may, under limited circumstances,

[28] United Nations Convention on the Law of the Sea (UNCLOS) (Montego Bay, 10 Dec 1982, 1833 UNTS 397); Convention on the High Seas (HSC) (Geneva, 29 Apr 1958, 450 UNTS 82). Presently 6 states and the Holy See are parties to the HSC but not to UNCLOS (Afghanistan, Cambodia, the Holy See, Iran, Israel, US, Venezuela). A further 21 states are parties to neither (Andorra, Azerbaijan, Bhutan, Burundi, Democratic People's Republic of Korea, El Salvador, Eritrea, Ethiopia, Kazakhstan, Kyrgyzstan, Libyan Arab Jamahiriya, Liechtenstein, Peru, Rwanda, San Marino, Syrian Arab Republic, Tajikistan, Turkey, Turkmenistan, United Arab Emirates, Uzbekistan).

[29] See eg the first report of ILC Special Rapporteur JPA François on the high seas regime: *Yearbook of the International Law Commission*, 1950, vol ii, 36, 41 (using the concept of 'Police en haute mer').

[30] UNCLOS, Art 58(2). [31] UNCLOS, Arts 92(1) and 110. [32] UNCLOS, Art 105.

[33] A useful selection of cases is available via the United Nations Interregional Crime and Justice Research Institute at <http://unicri.it/maritime_piracy/db.php>. See also *'Cygnus' case (Somali Pirates)*, Rotterdam District Court (2010) 145 ILR 491; and *US v. Dire* (US Ct of Apps (4th Cir), 23 May 2012), at <http://pacer.ca4.uscourts.gov/opinion.pdf/114310.P.pdf>.

[34] Laurent Lucchini and Michel Voelckel, *Droit de la mer*, Book 2, vol 2 (Pedone: Paris, 1996), 165; Craig H. Allen, *Maritime Counterproliferation Operations and the Rule of Law* (Westport, CT: Praeger, 2007), 168.

[35] Craig H. Allen, 'Limits on the Use of Force in Maritime Operations in Support of WMD Counter-Proliferation Initiatives' (2006) 81 *International Law Studies* 77, 82.

board and search foreign flag vessels.[36] Such an operation, permitted by UNCLOS, cannot be held to be contrary to other provisions of UNCLOS reserving the high seas 'for peaceful purposes' or which re-enact the UN Charter's Article 2(4) prohibition on 'any threat or use of force against the territorial integrity or political independence of any State'.[37] Thus, the conclusion can be drawn that a maritime 'police operation' permitted by UNCLOS is something different from a *military* 'use of force' prohibited by the UN Charter.[38] This line of reasoning is at least partially convincing and appears to have been implicitly adopted in *Guyana v. Suriname*.[39]

Other analyses are, however, possible. In particular, ILC Special Rapporteur François writing in 1950 commenced from the proposition that *in times of peace* customary international law knew only one general police power on the high seas, the right of reconnaissance and/or approach (essentially, drawing near a vessel to determine its nationality).[40] Otherwise, all 'specific' powers of interference with foreign flagged vessels derived from treaty law, with the sole exception of piracy.[41] François' approach emphasizes two useful points. First, one need not make an a priori determination that certain acts are inherently *not* contrary to the prohibition on the use of force or *not* governed by the laws of war. As regards IHL, the *jus in bello* can only apply (to use an old-fashioned phrase) in times of war. The question is one of the objective existence of an armed conflict, a point returned to later. As regards the UN Charter prohibition on the threat or use of force, uses of force are not unlawful where they are consented to.

This brings us to François' second point: interferences with foreign flag vessels on the high seas which might otherwise have historically been considered a *causus belli* or (in modern terms) an act giving rise to a right of self-defence[42] may be permitted by treaty or long-established customary right. Acts of 'policing' interference with foreign vessels are not prohibited uses of force because they are somehow not force (or involve the wrong type or quantum of force) but because they are *expressly permitted* by international law.[43] However, irrespective of whether one holds that

[36] UNCLOS, Art 110. [37] UNCLOS, Arts 88 and 301.

[38] Allen, 'Limits on the Use of Force in Maritime Operations in Support of WMD Counter-Proliferation Initiatives', 89; Rosemary Rayfuse, 'Countermeasures and High Seas Fisheries Enforcement' (2004) 51 *Netherlands International Law Review* 41, 74.

[39] *Guyana v. Suriname* (2008) 47 ILM 164, para 445 (accepting a distinction between a prohibited 'threat of military action' and the permissible use 'unavoidable, reasonable and necessary' force in 'law enforcement activities', without explaining the basis of the distinction).

[40] *Yearbook of the International Law Commission*, 1950, vol ii, 36, 41.

[41] *Yearbook of the International Law Commission*, 1950, vol ii, 36, 41.

[42] Allen, 'Limits on the Use of Force in Maritime Operations in Support of WMD Counter-Proliferation Initiatives', 89; *Case Concerning Oil Platforms (Iran v. US)*, Judgment, ICJ Rep 2003, 161, para 64 (noting *obiter* that 'the *Texaco Caribbean*...was not flying a United States flag, so that an attack on the vessel is not in itself to be equated with an attack on that State'; suggesting *a contrario* that an attack on a merchant vessel can be equated with an attack on the state).

[43] For a longer version of this argument see: Guilfoyle, *Shipping Interdiction and the Law of the Sea*, 272–7.

maritime interdiction operations permitted by UNCLOS are inherently of a kind not governed by the UN Charter prohibition on the use of force or that such acts are not wrongful because they are expressly permitted, the conclusion is the same: a policing paradigm governing the use of force applies.[44]

The difficulty, of course, is determining the content of that paradigm. The UNCLOS provisions on piracy are silent regarding the use of force. One must therefore turn to general public international law governing the use of force in maritime law enforcement operations. The critical case is *M/V Saiga (No 2)*, where the International Tribunal for the Law of the Sea (ITLOS) found that in cases of 'boarding, stopping and arresting' a vessel international law:

> requires that the use of force must be avoided as far as possible and, where...unavoidable, it must not go beyond what is reasonable and necessary in the circumstances. Considerations of humanity must apply...The normal practice...is first to give an auditory or visual signal to stop,...[then to take other actions], including the firing of shots across the bows of the ship. It is only after the appropriate actions fail that the pursuing vessel may, as a last resort, use force. Even then, appropriate warning must be issued...and all efforts should be made to ensure that life is not endangered.[45]

On the question of the use of force by government agents once aboard a suspect vessel, ITLOS endorsed the view, codified in Article 22(1)(f) of the UN Fish Stocks Agreement (FSA),[46] that such agents must:

> avoid the use of force except when and to the degree necessary to ensure the[ir] safety...and where...obstructed in the execution of their duties. The degree of force used shall not exceed that reasonably required in the circumstances.[47]

In reaching these conclusions, ITLOS had little to draw on. It could cite only two cases: *Red Crusader* and *I'm Alone*.[48] The *I'm Alone* case concerned the deliberate sinking of a vessel to prevent its escape, while in *Red Crusader* 40 mm solid shot was fired into a fleeing fishing vessel. The *M/V Saiga* case itself involved the deliberate firing of large-calibre live rounds without warning shots into a slow-moving vessel suspected only of customs offences. Precisely because these cases involved such clearly disproportionate uses of force, neither leaves us with detailed guidance on the use of force in maritime law enforcement.

[44] For a discussion of when such a paradigm might apply to maritime interdiction operations in times of armed conflict, see Douglas Guilfoyle, 'The Mavi Marmara Incident and Blockade in Armed Conflict' (2011) 81 *British Yearbook of International Law* 171, 209–10.

[45] *M/V 'Saiga' (No 2) (Saint Vincent and the Grenadines v. Guinea)*, ITLOS Case No 2; (1999) 38 ILM 1323, para 155.

[46] The United Nations Agreement for the Implementation of the Provisions of the United Nations Convention on the Law of the Sea of 10 December 1982 relating to the Conservation and Management of Straddling Fish Stocks and Highly Migratory Fish Stocks 1995, opened for signature 4 Aug 1995, 2167 UNTS 88 (entered into force 11 Dec 2001).

[47] *M/V 'Saiga' (No 2)*, para 156. [48] (1935) 3 RIAA 1609 and (1962) 35 ILR 485 respectively.

A further possible point of reference is Article 9 of the United Nations Basic Principles for the Use of Force and Firearms by Law Enforcement Officials[49] (UN Basic Principles) which provides that firearms shall only be used 'in self-defense or defense of others against the imminent threat of death or serious injury, to prevent the perpetration of a particularly serious crime…and only when less extreme means are insufficient' and that 'intentional lethal use of firearms may only be made when strictly unavoidable in order to protect life.' While this provision was not referred to by ITLOS in *M/V Saiga*, there is no doubt as to its general applicability to law enforcement operations and it has influenced a number of later instruments discussed later in the chapter.

In maritime police actions, then, the use of force is a last resort—to be avoided where possible and in all cases it must be strictly limited to what is reasonable and necessary. While an 'appropriate warning must be issued' in the case of attempting to board a vessel, no such warning need necessarily be given, for example when there is an imminent and serious danger to human life (as in the *Maersk Alabama* hostage-rescue incident).[50] These standards are, however, far from providing a detailed code on the use of force. They might fairly be considered as having more to say about the outer limits at which the use of force becomes impermissible rather than providing clear guidance as to when force is permitted.[51] They may also be misleading, given their focus on the use of firearms and lethal force, when considering the position of private actors as discussed in the following section.

B. The Use of Force by Private Actors Against Pirates

In most cases, however, it will not be naval vessels that defend ships attacked by pirates but the crew of that vessel itself. This implicates the law of self-defence applicable to private actors. The issue becomes potentially controversial when Privately Contracted Armed Security Personnel (PCASP) are retained to protect a vessel (PCASP are to be contrasted with the use of marines deployed aboard a merchant vessel by its flag state, or another state, as a so-called Vessel Protection Detachment (VPD). Such state agents are clearly governed by the standards set out previously[52]).

[49] The UN Basic Principles are a soft law instrument adopted by consensus by 127 states at the Eighth UN Congress on the Prevention of Crime and Treatment of Offenders in 1990. See A/CONF.144/28/Rev.1 (7 Sept 1990), or <http://www2.ohchr.org/english/law/firearms.htm>. On their status, see the conference report: A/CONF.144/28/Rev.1, at 269 (the Basic Principles were adopted in plenary under agenda Item 7 as part of 'Sect. B, resolutions 2 and 3') and at 201 and 207 (on participating states).

[50] See 'In Rescue of Captain, Navy Kills 3 Pirates', *New York Times*, 12 Apr 2009, available at <http://www.nytimes.com/2009/04/13/world/africa/13pirates.html>.

[51] On this point, see further Guilfoyle, *Shipping Interdiction and the Law of the Sea*, 272 (a US IMO delegation once suggested that, 'Simply put, there is almost no specific guidance regarding the use of force while conducting a boarding pursuant to treaty or customary international law').

[52] That said, a VPD would likely not be able to avail itself of the powers to actively inspect suspect pirate vessels and arrest those aboard found in UNCLOS, Arts 105 and 110. Such powers may only be

The extent to which PCASP are regulated by international 'hard' or 'soft' law will be returned to later.

The starting point is that flag state law will be the principal law binding both crew and PCASP. A ship on the high seas is subject to the exclusive jurisdiction of its flag state[53] and each flag state must 'effectively exercise its jurisdiction and control in administrative, technical and social matters over ships flying its flag'.[54] PCASP will thus operate under flag state law, within any limits established by international law. The International Maritime Organization (IMO) has issued interim guidance (only) on the use of PCASP to states, shipowners, and port states.[55] The IMO guidance to states is brief, essentially suggesting that flag states should have a policy on PCASP and should consider whether PCASP would be permitted under present national legislation, how to establish an appropriate regulatory framework and minimum licensing criteria, and provide information on such matters to the IMO for circulation.[56] The IMO guidance to shipowners is discussed later.

As to the applicable law, some flag states will permit the use of lethal or deadly force by private persons in self-defence in response to an imminent danger of death or serious bodily harm. It is commonly said that many legal systems will not allow the use of deadly force to defend property,[57] but in the UK at least that may not be strictly accurate. In the UK a person may use force in self-defence (subject to common law requirements that their act is reasonable, necessary, and proportionate) or may use reasonable force to prevent a crime (including acting to defend an innocent third party).[58] In particular, in the UK '[a] witness to violent crime [involving] a continuing threat of violence may well be justified in using extreme force to remove a threat of further violence'.[59] In defence of property in particular a person may use

exercised by warships or 'other duly authorized ships or aircraft clearly marked and identifiable as being on government service': UNCLOS, Arts 107 and 110(5).

[53] UNCLOS, Art 97(1); HSC, Art 6(1). [54] UNCLOS, Art 94(1); HSC, Art 5(1).

[55] IMO, 'Revised Interim Guidance to Shipowners, Ship Operators, and Shipmasters on the Use of Privately Contracted Armed Security Personnel on board Ships in the High Risk Area', IMO Doc MSC.1/Circ.1405/Rev.2 (2012) ('IMO Shipowner Guidance (2012)'); 'Revised interim recommendations for flag States regarding the use of privately contracted armed security personnel on board ships in the High Risk Area', IMO Doc MSC.1/Circ.1406/Rev.1 (2011) ('IMO Flag State Guidance (2011)'); and 'Interim recommendations for port and coastal States regarding the use of privately contracted armed security personnel on board ships in the High Risk Area', IMO Doc MSC.1/Circ.1408/Rev.1 (2012).

[56] IMO Flag State Guidance (2011).

[57] Self-defence under the Statute of the International Criminal Court (ICC) can extend 'in the case of war crimes, [to] property which is essential for . . . survival . . . [or] for accomplishing a military mission': ICC Statute, Art 31(1)(c).

[58] Crown Prosecution Service, 'Legal Guidance on Self-Defence and the Prevention of Crime', available at <http://www.cps.gov.uk/legal/s_to_u/self_defence/>; section 76 of the UK Criminal Justice and Immigration Act 2008 (which effectively codifies the common law requirements outlined in *Palmer v. R* [1971] AC 814 at 831–2, per Lord Morris) on self-defence; and section 3 of Criminal Law Act 1967 on prevention of crime. See further paras 19–41 ff.

[59] Crown Prosecution Service, 'Legal Guidance on Self-Defence and the Prevention of Crime', available at <http://www.cps.gov.uk/legal/s_to_u/self_defence/>.

reasonable force to prevent the destruction or taking of goods, and where a trespasser uses force a person defending property 'may oppose force to force'.[60] This suggests that the legal assessment of the use of force in defence of property remains a contextual assessment rather than being subject to an absolute prohibition on the use of lethal force. Nonetheless, where confronted with Somali pirates firing rocket-propelled grenades or machine guns, an individual clearly need not 'weigh to a nicety the exact measure of [violence used in] any necessary action'.[61]

It will be a matter for flag states whether they subject the general law of individual self-defence to more stringent requirements in the case of PCASP. The UK, for example, has issued 'Interim Guidance' advising that PCASP should use the 'minimum force necessary' to prevent the illegal boarding of a vessel and to protect the lives of those on board and that PCASP rules on the use of force should allow a 'graduated response, each stage of which is considered to be reasonable and proportionate to the force being used by the attackers'.[62] The 'minimum force necessary' standard appears more restrictive than the ordinary law of self-defence and may reflect a view that those trained in using violence should be held to higher standards. No statutory scheme in the UK, however, makes such a distinction and it remains to be seen if a court would differentiate in its application of the 'reasonable force' standard between 'ordinary' seafarers and trained security personnel.

It has been widely noted that ultimate authority for the use of force aboard a merchant vessel must rest with the master.[63] Regulation 8(a) of Chapter XI-2 of the SOLAS Convention relevantly provides:[64]

> The master shall not be constrained by the Company, the charterer or any other person from taking or executing any decision which, in the professional judgement of the master, is necessary to maintain the safety and security of the ship.

The UK Interim Guidance, however, notes that an individual's inherent right of self-defence means that if a person perceives an imminent threat to human life (including their own) that 'Neither the Master nor the security team leader can command him or her . . . to not use lethal force' against that person's own judgement.[65]

[60] James Richardson (ed), *Archbold: Criminal Pleading Evidence & Practice* (60th edn, London: Sweet & Maxwell, 2012), para 19-187. On ejecting unwanted passengers from vehicles, see *R v. Burns* [2010] EWCA Crim 1023, para 14.

[61] Section 76(7)(a) of the Criminal Justice and Immigration Act 2008; *Palmer v. R* [1971] AC 814 at 831–2.

[62] Department for Transport, 'Guidance to UK Flagged Shipping on the Use of Armed Guards to Defend Against the Threat of Piracy in Exceptional Circumstances', Dec 2011, paras 8.3 and 8.5, available at <http://www.dft.gov.uk/publications/use-of-armed-guards-to-defend-against-piracy/>.

[63] See eg IMO Shipowner Guidance (2012), Annex, 6.

[64] International Convention for the Safety of Life at Sea (SOLAS) (London, 1 Nov 1974, 1184 UNTS 2).

[65] Department for Transport, 'Interim Guidance to UK Flagged Shipping on the Use of Armed Guards to Defend Against the Threat of Piracy in Exceptional Circumstances', Dec 2011, para 5.6.

Obviously, a breach of flag state law on the use of force in self-defence or to prevent serious crime may result in liability under flag state law. In addition, the use of force without adequate legal justification by PCASP against another vessel or persons on board could itself violate either:

- Article 3(1)(b) of the SUA Convention[66] ('Any person commits an offence if that person unlawfully and intentionally: ... performs an act of violence against a person on board a ship if that act is likely to endanger the safe navigation of that ship'); or
- the law of piracy (covering 'any illegal acts of violence... committed for private ends by the crew... of a private ship... against another ship [on the high seas]..., or against persons or property on board').[67]

Further, as the requirements of self-defence vary between national legal systems, a PCASP member acting in mistaken self-defence may find themselves charged with national or international law offences in a foreign jurisdiction such as that of a victim's state of nationality.[68] This has already occurred, although admittedly in the case of a state-authorized VPD rather than PCASP. In the 2012 *Enrica Lexie* affair two Italian marines allegedly wrongfully shot dead Indian fishermen, having mistaken them for pirates.[69] Curiously, Italy does not appear to have invoked state immunity in this case,[70] but sought to rely on Article 97(1) of UNCLOS to exclude Indian jurisdiction. Article 97(1) provides:

> In the event of a collision or any other incident of navigation... on the high seas, involving the... responsibility of the master or of any other person in the service of the ship, no penal or disciplinary proceedings may be instituted... except before the... authorities either of the flag State or of the [person's state of nationality].

This provision was famously first introduced in treaty law to overturn the result of the *Lotus* case.[71] While it seems unlikely it was ever intended to cover fatal shootings as 'incidents of navigation', some suggest the provision should be construed broadly

[66] Convention for the Suppression of Unlawful Acts Against the Safety of Maritime Navigation (Rome, 10 Mar 1988, 1678 UNTS 221).

[67] UNCLOS, Art 101; HSC, Art 15(1).

[68] UK guidance on this point is apt: 'In some jurisdictions killing a national may have unforeseen consequences even for a person who believes that they have acted in self-defence'. See UK Maritime and Coast Guard Agency, 'Measures to Counter Piracy, Armed Robbery and other Acts of Violence against Merchant Shipping', Marine Guidance Note MGN 298 (M), 2005, para 6.15.1, available at <http://www.dft.gov.uk/mca/298-2.pdf>.

[69] 'India charges Italian marines with murder of fishermen', BBC News, 18 May 2012, available at <http://www.bbc.co.uk/news/world-asia-india-18118790>.

[70] Guilfoyle, *Shipping Interdiction and the Law of the Sea*, ch 11 and esp at 302–4.

[71] *The SS Lotus (France v. Turkey)*, Judgment of 7 Sept 1927, PCIJ, Ser A, No 10, 4. On the history of subsequent treaty law, see Robin R. Churchill and Vaughan Lowe, *The Law of the Sea* (3rd edn, Manchester: Manchester University Press, 1999), 208; International Convention for the Unification of Certain Rules relating to Penal Jurisdiction in matters of Collisions and Other Incidents of Navigation (Brussels, 10 May 1952, 439 UNTS 233), Arts 1 and 2; and HSC, Art 11(1).

to include all 'maritime casualties' (being any 'other occurrence on board a vessel or external to it resulting in material damage... to a vessel or cargo').[72] Whether even such a broad approach could cover fatal shootings remains untested.

Finally, one should consider whether a growing body of international soft law dealing with private military contractors applies to private military and security companies (PMSCs). The first text to consider is the Montreux Document (discussed further in Chapter 53 of this volume).[73] The Montreux Document is a soft law instrument dealing with the relationship between states and PMSCs, based on the principle that 'Contracting States retain their obligations under international law, even if they contract PMSCs to perform certain activities.'[74] To this end, it outlines principles of good practice applicable to contracting states (which retain PMSCs), territorial states (where PMSCs operate), and home states (where PMSCs are incorporated, or the states of nationality of PMSC employees). It is thus not prima facie applicable to PCASP retained by shipowners. Nonetheless, it is replete with reference to the use of force, firearms, and weapons—largely in the context of providing appropriate training and internal regulations.[75] Although these standards do not apply to PCASP, when compared with ITLOS case law (discussed in Section III.A) and IMO guidance (discussed later in this section) they suggest a degree of consensus that both PMSCs or PCASP should use 'force and firearms only when necessary in self-defence or defence of third persons'.[76]

Of more relevance is the International Code of Conduct (ICoC) which builds upon the Montreux Document and contains guidance on the use of force.[77] The ICoC is only open for signature to private security companies, although it was developed in discussion with a range of governments and non-government organizations. As at 13 June 2012 it had 404 corporate signatories. It is sometimes questioned whether the ICoC addresses maritime security. There is a good case that it does. The ICoC applies to Complex Environments, including

> any areas experiencing... unrest or instability,... where the rule of law has been substantially undermined, and in which the [state's] capacity... to handle the situation is diminished, limited, or non-existent.[78]

[72] Satya N. Nandan and Shabtai Rosenne (eds), *United Nations Convention on the Law of the Sea 1982: A Commentary*, vol III (The Hague: Martinus Nijhoff, 1995), 168, referring to the UNCLOS, Art 221(2) definition.

[73] Montreux Document on Pertinent International Legal Obligations and Good Practices for States related to Operations of Private Military and Security Companies during Armed Conflict (Montreux, 17 Sept 2008), available at <http://www.icrc.org/eng/assets/files/other/icrc_002_0996.pdf> or as annexed to IMO Doc MSC 89/INF.20 (8 Mar 2011); see also Ian M. Ralby, 'Private Military Companies and the *Jus ad Bellum*', Chapter 53 in this volume.

[74] The Montreux Document, para 1.

[75] The Montreux Document, Part II, paras 10, 12, 18, 35, 37, 43, 63 (on force and firearms), and Part II, paras 6, 9, 11, 14, 32, 34, 35, 36, 44, 55, 60, 62, 64 (on weapons).

[76] The Montreux Document, Part II, para 18.

[77] See <http://www.icoc-psp.org>.

[78] International Code of Conduct for Private Security Service Providers (as annexed to IMO Doc MSC 89/INF.21 (8 Mar 2011)), para 13, and see the definitions at Section B.

Arguably, the maritime environment off Somalia is an area 'experiencing...instability' where state authority is diminished or limited. Further, the Code itself suggests that the marine environment might require 'additional' principles, not that those it currently contains are inappropriate or inapplicable.[79]

Space precludes detailed discussion of the basic ICoC rules on the use of force (found in paras 30–2) beyond noting that these refer to using only such force as is 'strictly necessary, and...proportionate to the threat and appropriate to the situation', in cases such as 'self-defence or defence of others against the imminent threat of death or serious injury, or to prevent the perpetration of a particularly serious crime involving grave threat to life'. The concepts used thus closely follow the standards applicable to state agents discussed earlier, especially those found in the UN Basic Principles.

To conclude, the only international standards directly addressing PCASP are those in the ICoC. As noted, these may require supplementary or additional principles as regards the maritime domain, but there is little to suggest the existing standards are not applicable. Indeed, the IMO guidance to shipowners appears to track the relevant ICoC paragraphs closely in advising:

> PMSC should require their personnel to take all reasonable steps to avoid the use of force. If force is used, it should be in a manner consistent with applicable law. In no case should the use of force exceed what is strictly necessary, and in all cases should be proportionate to the threat and appropriate to the situation.
>
> PMSC should require that their personnel not use firearms against persons except in self-defence or defence of others against the imminent threat of death or serious injury, or to prevent the perpetration of a particularly serious crime involving grave threat to life.[80]

The IMO and the Code thus both appear to have derived this guidance, at least in part, from the UN Basic Principles. This adoption and replication of common standards between instruments strongly suggests an emerging international consensus that the framework for permissible use of force by PCASP is governed by the principles of necessity and proportionality, and that use of firearms is generally accepted 'in self-defence or defence of others against the imminent threat of death or serious injury'.

[79] International Code of Conduct for Private Security Service Providers, para 7. See further Wilton Park, 'Countering piracy: what are the rights and obligations of states and private security providers?' (WP1150), 29 Mar 2012, paras 12–13, available at <http://www.wiltonpark.org.uk/resources/en/pdf/22290903/2012/wp1150-report>.

[80] IMO Shipowner Guidance (2012), Annex, 7.

IV. The Applicable Legal Framework in Somali Territory

The use of force against suspected Somali pirates within the territory of Somalia may occur in one of two cases: in the territorial sea, or on Somali soil. As discussed in Section II.A, in the first case states 'cooperating' with the TFG may enter Somalia's territorial sea and therein use all necessary means to repress piracy 'in a manner consistent with action permitted on the high seas'.[81] As regards the law on the latter, the Security Council has repeatedly stressed that the applicable legal framework is that of UNCLOS. As a consequence, measures taken in the Somali territorial sea cannot go beyond that allowed on the high seas under UNCLOS.

The more contentious point is the grant of authority initially given in Resolution 1851, as subsequently renewed, to states and regional organizations cooperating with the TFG to 'undertake all necessary measures... *in Somalia*' to repress piracy provided that any measures undertaken are 'consistent with applicable international humanitarian and human rights law'.[82] Further to the previous discussion, the critical point is the reference to IHL. As already noted, the use of military force does not necessarily implicate IHL,[83] which is 'applicable' only in an international or non-international armed conflict. As I have put it elsewhere:

> Somali pirates are at best several different groups acting without state sanction who have mounted a series of individual attacks against vessels of varying nationalities. These attacks are, on occasion, seen off by foreign naval vessels with (on fewer occasions still) shots being exchanged and pirates killed as a result. The actors involved are disparate private parties of Somali nationality on the one side and disparate military forces of varying nationality on the other. When pirate–naval encounters take place they are sporadic, brief and usually involve only small-scale fire.[84]

The first question then, a question of fact, is the existence of an international armed conflict (IAC) or a non-international armed conflict (NIAC) arising from these circumstances. The accepted formula was set out by the International Criminal Tribunal for the former Yugoslavia (ICTY) in *Tadić*:

[81] SC Res 1816 (2008), para 7(b).

[82] SC Res 1851, para 6 (emphasis added). Renewed in: SC Res 1897, para 7; SC Res 1950, para 7; SC Res 2020, para 9.

[83] *Contra* Kontorovich, 'International Legal Responses to Piracy off the Coast of Somalia'.

[84] Douglas Guilfoyle, 'The Laws of War and the Fight against Somali Piracy: Combatants or Criminals' (2010) 11 *Melbourne Journal of International Law* 141, 144 (footnotes omitted).

an armed conflict exists whenever there is a resort to armed force between States or protracted armed violence between governmental authorities and organized armed groups or between such groups within a State.[85]

Thus an armed conflict exists whenever there is either: (1) recourse to violence between states (an IAC); or (2) a conflict involving 'organized armed groups' and protracted armed violence (a NIAC). As Somali pirates are not state agents, the only possibility to consider is whether the present facts may constitute a NIAC involving an 'armed group'. Somali pirates do not satisfy *any* of the relevant definitions of such armed groups: they are not organized on the basis of responsible military command, they control no territory,[86] they conduct no hostilities within Somalia,[87] and their attacks are directed principally against private merchant vessels and not against other armed bands or government forces.[88] Pirates' sporadic and relatively brief attacks on private craft also do not rise to the level of 'protracted armed violence', nor do their occasional and limited exchanges of fire with naval vessels.[89] Pirate activity thus seems closest to 'situations... such as riots, [and] isolated and sporadic acts of violence'[90] falling below the threshold for the existence of any armed conflict. On the basis of ordinary IHL principles, therefore, there are no grounds to conclude that IHL applies in the use of force against pirates.

As a parenthesis, a separate question is whether the existence of armed conflict(s) in Somalia may affect the characterization of Somali pirates' crimes. Certainly, civilians or non-combatants may commit war crimes, including that of hostage taking,[91] where that crime is sufficiently closely connected to the conflict. As to that contextual or nexus requirement, it was observed in *Kunarac*: 'the existence of an armed conflict must, at a minimum, have played a substantial part in the perpetrator's ability to commit [the crime], his decision to commit it, the manner in which it was committed or the purpose for which it was committed.'[92] On this broad approach, one might think Somali pirates' activities may arguably constitute war crimes, to the

[85] ICTY, *Prosecutor v. Tadić*, Decision on the Defence Motion for Interlocutory Appeal on Jurisdiction of 2 Oct 1995, Appeals Chamber, IT-94-1-AR72, para 70.

[86] See Art 1(1), Additional Protocol to the Geneva Conventions of 12 Aug 1949, and relating to the Protection of Victims of Non-International Armed Conflicts (Protocol II), opened for signature 8 June 1977, 1125 UNTS 609 (entered into force 7 Dec 1978). This requirement is not replicated in the ICC Statute.

[87] Art 1(1), Additional Protocol to the Geneva Conventions of 12 Aug 1949, and relating to the Protection of Victims of Non-International Armed Conflicts (Protocol II).

[88] *Tadić*, Decision on the Defence Motion for Interlocutory Appeal on Jurisdiction; Art 8(2)(f), ICC Statute, opened for signature 17 July 1998, 2187 UNTS 90 (entered into force 1 July 2002).

[89] On the test for 'protracted armed violence' see ICTY, *Prosecutor v. Haradinaj*, Judgment of 3 Apr 2008, Trial Chamber I, IT-04-84-T, para 49 (the question may be one of intensity more so than duration).

[90] Additional Protocol II, Art 1(2); compare ICC Statute, Art 8(2)(d) and (f).

[91] ICC Statute, Arts 8(2)(a)(viii) and 8(2)(c)(iii).

[92] ICTY, *Prosecutor v. Kunarac*, Judgment of 12 June 2002, Appeal Chamber, IT-96-23 and IT-96-23/1-A, para 57.

extent that conflict in Somalia enables their activities. However, post-Second World War case law would suggest that some close connection between the crime and one of the parties to hostilities is also required for offences in wartime to constitute war crimes.[93]

If this analysis is wrong and the decision was taken that IHL was applicable in counter-piracy, the fundamental principles of distinction and proportionality would become applicable.[94] Distinction allows persons to be targeted based on their status as a combatant or a direct participant in hostilities. As noted earlier, Somali pirates are not participants in hostilities in any IHL sense. They would therefore remain protected civilians. It would be hard to conclude that Somali pirates were targetable as direct participants in hostilities, as there is no relevant NIAC between pirates as an organized armed group and each individually affected flag state. Under IHL, however, force may be used by combatants against civilians consistent with a law enforcement paradigm in certain cases: for example, during an IAC occupying troops may use force against rioting civilians to fulfil their duty to maintain order in occupied territory.[95] However, if this analogy is correct, applying IHL would not grant any greater powers than those ordinarily applying in law enforcement operations.

Even if this conclusion is incorrect and IHL was applicable to pirates and they could be targeted directly in combat operations, the use of military force would remain governed by the principle of proportionality. This holds that:

> Launching an attack which may be expected to cause incidental loss of civilian life, injury to civilians, damage to civilian objects, or a combination thereof, which would be excessive in relation to the concrete and direct military advantage anticipated, is prohibited.[96]

I note in this context that pirates increasingly hold hostages both aboard mother ships and in their land bases. This fact would certainly have to be taken into account in assessing the proportionality (and therefore legality) of any attack on such targets.

In conclusion, IHL does not apply in the context of counter-piracy operations ashore in Somali territory. The question that follows is what standards do apply? Such operations can only be regarded as law enforcement actions conducted with the consent (indeed, as all relevant resolutions provide, at the invitation of) the TFG. The applicable international standards would obviously include those discussed

[93] See eg the discussion of *Röchling et al* and other cases in Antonio Cassese et al, *International Criminal Law: Cases and Commentary* (Oxford: Oxford University Press, 2011), 122–32.

[94] David Turns, 'The Law of Armed Conflict (International Humanitarian Law)' in Evans, International Law, (3rd edn, Oxford: Oxford University Press, 2010), 814, 830–2.

[95] Yoram Dinstein, *The International Law of Belligerent Occupation* (Cambridge: Cambridge University Press, 2009), 89–94; The University Centre for International Humanitarian Law, Geneva (UCIHL), 'Expert Meeting on the Right to Life in Armed Conflicts and Situations of Occupation' (Meeting Record 1–2 Sept 2005), available at <http://www.adh-geneva.ch/docs/expert-meetings/2005/3rapport_droit_vie.pdf>, 26.

[96] Jean-Marie Henckaerts et al, *Customary International Humanitarian Law, Vol I: Rules* (Cambridge: International Committee of the Red Cross, 2005), 46.

earlier, especially the UN Basic Principles. However, this leads us to a curious question in relation to the incident with which this chapter commenced—the destruction of attack boats. It is not ordinary law enforcement practice to summarily destroy property suspected of being intended for use in future crimes. Indeed, one might question the consistency of such action with human rights law.[97] Where is the lawful basis for such a deprivation of property to be found? Paragraph 2 of Resolution 1851 (as renewed) authorizes states to take action to suppress Somali piracy:

> consistent with this resolution, ... and international law, by deploying naval vessels and military aircraft and through seizure and disposition of boats, vessels, arms and other related equipment used in the commission of piracy..., or for which there are reasonable grounds for suspecting such use.

The ambit of this paragraph is not limited to actions on the high seas, as it refers to actions 'consistent with this resolution'. This must include actions on land authorized by the Resolution. The paragraph also appears to create, through Chapter VII, a novel and summary power to dispose of property suspected of pirate use.

V. Conclusions

While authority to conduct counter-piracy operations at sea is found in treaty and customary law, and while authority to conduct such operations within Somalia's territorial jurisdiction (including territorial waters) is found in Security Council resolutions and the consent of the TFG, such sources have little to say directly about the applicable law on the use of force. The universally accepted position is that in either case a policing paradigm of lawful force applies. As the commander of the EU Naval Force has put it: 'we are engaged in a constabulary task, and that is the fundamental guiding principle that constrains what we can do.'[98] In such law enforcement operations:

> The principle is the use of reasonable force, ... being the minimum necessary to impose your rights ... to board, search, seize, arrest, [and] detain [suspect vessels] ... Lethal force is available where there is a threat to life ...[99]

[97] eg Protocol to the Convention for the Protection of Human Rights and Fundamental Freedoms (Paris, 20 Mar 1952, 213 UNTS 262), Art 1.

[98] UK House of Commons Foreign Affairs Committee, 'Piracy off the coast of Somalia' (HC 2010–12, 1318), 5 Jan 2012, Evidence Annex, 14 (Major General Buster Howes, Operation Commander of EU Naval Force operation Atalanta), available at <http://www.parliament.uk/business/committees/committees-a-z/commons-select/foreign-affairs-committee/publications/>.

[99] UK House of Lords European Union Committee, 'Combating Somali Piracy: the EU's Naval Operation Atalanta' (HL 2009–10, 103), 14 Apr 2010, Evidence Annex, 29 (Commander Clive Dow, Royal Navy).

The position of private actors acting in self-defence against pirate attack on the high seas is somewhat different. Principally, such actions will be governed by the law of self-defence of the flag state which will usually apply a more generous test than 'minimum necessary' force (eg the common law standard of reasonable, necessary, and proportionate force). There are signs of an emerging consensus, however, that PCASP should be subjected to a stricter standard based on necessity and proportionality. In all cases it is generally accepted that the use of firearms is permissible against the imminent threat of death or serious injury either in self-defence or defence of others, but in any event it should be a last resort.

CHAPTER 50

THE CHANGING ENVIRONMENT AND EMERGING RESOURCE CONFLICTS

MARCO PERTILE*

I. The Environment and Resource Conflicts: Assessing the Debate

The existence of a relationship between the environment and conflicts may seem intuitive. Indeed, 'environment' and 'conflicts' are so loosely defined concepts that merely acknowledging some form of interaction between them risks being considered as a truism. Suffice it to note that the environment is our 'living space',[1] the stage on which every form of human relationship—and conflicts are no exception—takes place. It is no wonder that a phenomenon can be influenced by the context in which it occurs. The debate on 'resource conflicts', however, has long gone beyond the observation that conflicts are context-related. Starting from the end of

* The author acknowledges financial support by a Marie Curie Intra European Fellowship within the 7th European Community Framework Programme.

[1] *Legality of the Threat or Use of Nuclear Weapons*, Advisory Opinion, ICJ Rep 1996, 226, para 29.

the 1980s, several authors have dissected the relationship between the environment and conflicts.[2] Political scientists and economists have led the debate whereas legal scholars have stood on the sidelines.[3]

Within the debate on the aetiology of conflicts, the environment has been mainly investigated with reference to the cognate concept of 'natural resources', the components of the environment that are perceived as having economic value. A number of studies have highlighted how natural resources, such as water, hydrocarbons, and diamonds, may influence the origin and the development of conflicts.[4] For reasons probably related to the numerical preponderance of non-international armed conflicts, attention has focused on armed conflicts occurring within states, that is, civil wars. Conversely, the linkage between natural resources and interstate conflicts has been overlooked.

The theoretical underpinnings of the debate are based on common sense. The observation of reality seems to reveal that countries that are rich in natural resources suffer from instability and underdevelopment. The reasons for the existence of an inverse relationship between the availability of natural resources and the degree of economic development have been questioned by authors, who have investigated the paradox of the 'resource curse' question.[5] A recent stream of literature points out that the scarcity of natural resources is exacerbated by the fact that the environment itself is changing.[6] Climate change is perceived as a factor amplifying the problem of resource scarcity and favouring the occurrence of conflicts over natural resources. Within this context, the assumption is made that the confrontation between human groups to gain control over natural resources may be based either on greed or on grievances generated by questions of allocation, revenue-sharing, and negative externalities.[7] However, one of the main acquisitions of the contemporary debate on resource conflicts is that monocausal theories on the origin of conflicts have been generally abandoned. The idea that natural resources can be the exclusive cause of

[2] Arthur Westing (ed), *Global Resources and International Conflict: Environmental Factors in Strategic Policy and Action* (New York: Oxford University Press, 1986); Michael T. Klare, *Resource Wars—The New Landscape of Global Conflict* (New York: Henry Holt, 2001); Ian Bannon and Paul Collier (eds), *Natural Resources and Violent Conflict—Options and Actions* (Washington DC: The World Bank, 2003).

[3] With some significant exceptions in recent times: Mara Tignino, *L'eau et la guerre—éléments pour un régime juridique* (Brussels: Bruylant, 2011); Nico Schrijver, *Development without Destruction* (Bloomington, IN: Indiana University Press, 2010).

[4] Nurit Kliot, *Water, Resources and Conflict in the Middle East* (London: Routledge, 1994); Bannon and Collier, *Natural Resources and Violent Conflict*; Michael Ross, 'A Closer Look at Oil, Diamonds, and Civil War' (2006) 9 *Annual Review of Political Science* 265.

[5] Terry L. Karl, *The Paradox of Plenty* (Berkeley, CA: University of California Press, 1997); Michael Ross, 'The Political Economy of the Resource Curse' (1999) 51 *World Politics* 297.

[6] James R. Lee, *Climate Change and Armed Conflict* (Abingdon: Routledge, 2009); Donald A. Mwiturubani et al (eds), *Climate Change and Natural Resources Conflicts in Africa* (Pretoria: Institute for Security Studies, 2010).

[7] Paul Collier and Anke Hoeffler, 'Greed and Grievance in Civil War', Policy Research Working Paper No 2355, The World Bank, 2001. For a critical analysis, see Jack S. Levy and William R. Thomson, *Causes of War* (Chichester: Wiley-Blackwell, 2010), 186–201.

a conflict is rejected in favour of more elaborated theories. Rather than merely being considered as a cause of conflicts, natural resources are also regarded as an essential element for their continuation.

Against this background, the objective of this chapter is to describe some of the international rules having a bearing on the relationship between natural resources and conflicts. Attention will be paid to the rules pertaining to the *jus ad bellum*. Resource conflicts will thus be primarily assessed in their interstate dimension, with reference to the legal framework for the use of force in international relations. It will be considered, however, that resource conflicts that can be classified as civil wars have a strong tendency to become internationalized and have been addressed by the UN Security Council.

II. The Law of International Resource Conflicts

A. The Linkage Between Natural Resources and Interstate Conflicts

The linkage between natural resources and interstate conflicts is more than evident in practice. Although the significance of the issue has been overlooked in the literature, in a number of interstate conflicts the declarations of state authorities reveal a significant inflammatory role for natural resources. The words and the behaviour of the main actors demonstrate that natural resources have been a determinant of the decision to wage war and/or an important factor in the persistence of the conflict. Some examples are the Iran–Iraq war over the Shatt-al-Arab,[8] the war between Libya and Chad over the Aouzou Strip,[9] the Iraq invasion and occupation of Kuwait,[10] the

[8] On 17 Sept 1980, in a statement addressed to the Iraqi parliament, the President of Iraq, Saddam Hussein, declared that the 1975 Algiers Agreement on the Shatt-al-Arab had to be considered null and void due to persistent Iranian violations of the sovereignty of Iraq: 'This river must have its Iraqi–Arab identity restored as it was throughout history in name and in reality with all the disposal rights emanating from full sovereignty over the river'. Quoted in Jasim M. Abdulghani, *Iraq and Iran—The Years of Crisis* (Beckenham: Croom Helm, 1984), 202.

[9] According to the authorities of Chad, the presence of uranium in the region was among the reasons for the Libyan invasion of the Aouzou Strip. *Mémoire du Gouvernement de la République du Tchad, Livre 1, Différend territorial (Jamahiriya arabe libyenne c Tchad)*, 26 Aug 1991, 28, para 49, available at <http://www.icj-cij.org/docket/files/83/6688.pdf>.

[10] Among the political rationales that motivated the Iraqi invasion of Kuwait were allegations that Kuwait and the United Arab Emirates were overproducing oil, thus driving down prices and a

Anglo-Australian-US invasion of Iraq in 2003,[11] the ongoing border conflict between Sudan and South Sudan,[12] the intervention of Uganda, Burundi, and Rwanda in the civil war in the Democratic Republic of the Congo (DRC),[13] and the Christmas war between Burkina Faso and Mali over the Agacher Strip.[14] There is an abundance of other possible examples.

Due to climate change and technological innovations, the unprecedented accessibility of natural resources in the Arctic has generated a race to the militarization of the region.[15] Tensions on sovereignty over the Falkland Islands have resurfaced when the British administration of the Islands has awarded concessions for the exploitation of offshore oil fields to private contractors.[16]

Besides traditional interstate conflicts, some of the conflicts related to decolonization, such as the Moroccan occupation of Western Sahara,[17] the Angolan civil war,[18]

boundary dispute concerning the transboundary oil fields of Rumayla. Jacob Goldberg and Joseph Kostiner, 'Kuwait' (1990) 14 *Middle East Contemporary Survey* 507.

[11] In the initial phase, the intervening states denied that the invasion of Iraq was connected to petroleum resources. Subsequently some of them acknowledged that energy security had been a political factor at the basis of their decision. See eg the statement of the Australian Defence Minister Brendan Nelson: 'Nelson: Oil a factor in Iraq deployment', *The Age*, 5 July 2007, available at <http://www.theage.com.au/news/national/howard-links-iraq-war-to-oil/2007/07/04/1183351291906.html> and the 2007 statement of Alan Greenspan, former Chairman of the US Federal Reserve: Bob Woodward, 'Greenspan: Ouster of Hussein Crucial for Oil Security', *The Washington Post*, 17 Sept 2007, available at <http://www.washingtonpost.com/wp-dyn/content/article/2007/09/16/AR2007091601287_pf.html>.

[12] The issues of contention between Sudan and South Sudan are the sharing of oil revenues and the determination of the territorial boundary. Talks between the two countries collapsed when South Sudan occupied the town and the oil fields of Heglig. Mike Pflanz, 'Sudan and South Sudan inch closer to all-out war', *The Telegraph*, 19 Apr 2012.

[13] ICJ, *Application instituting proceedings (DRC v. Burundi)*, 13, available at <http://www.icj-cij.org/docket/files/115/7127.pdf>; ICJ, *Application instituting proceedings (DRC v. Rwanda)*, 15, at <http://www.icj-cij.org/docket/files/117/7071.pdf>; ICJ, *Application instituting proceedings (DRC v. Uganda)*, 13, at <http://www.icj-cij.org/docket/files/116/7151.pdf>.

[14] *Frontier Dispute*, Judgment, Memorial of Burkina Faso, ICJ Rep 1986, 38, para 80, available at <http://www.icj-cij.org/docket/files/69/16370.pdf>: 'la zone revendiquée par le Mali se distingue peu des secteurs environnants sinon du fait de sa richesse—toute relative—en eau et de ses probable potentialités géologiques'.

[15] Roger Howard, *The Arctic Gold Rush—The New Race for Tomorrow's Natural Resources* (London: Continuum, 2009).

[16] Jude Webber, 'Argentina warns on Falklands exploration', *Financial Times*, 15 Mar 2012.

[17] Thomas M. Franck, 'The Stealing of the Sahara' (1976) 70 *American Journal of International Law* 704.

[18] The ability of the armed group UNITA to gain control of diamond-rich territories and exchange diamonds for weapons and political support was a critical factor in the prolongation of the conflict in Angola. See Report of the Panel of Experts on Violations of Security Council Sanctions against UNITA, S/2000/203 (10 Mar 2000). Conversely, the Angolan government was able to shift military power in its favour by hiring a private security company with revenues deriving from oil-resource exploitation. Khareen Pech, 'Executive Outcomes—A Corporate Conquest' in Jakkie Cilliers and Peggy Mason (eds), *Peace, Profit or Plunder? The Privatisation of Security in War-Torn African Societies* (Pretoria: Institute for Security Studies, 1999), 86.

and the South African 'border conflict'[19] were, and in the first case are, intertwined with the struggle to gain control over natural resources. Assessing how the law on the use of force interacts with this typology of conflicts is thus a significant legal issue. Before doing so, some preliminary remarks on the allocation of natural resources under international law are in order.

B. Sovereignty as the Main Criterion for the Allocation of Natural Resources Among States

When approaching the international legal regulation of resource conflicts it is worth remembering that, whereas the phenomenon of armed conflicts is thoroughly regulated, natural resources are not the object of a coherent legal regime. Traditionally, the exclusive function of international law with regard to natural resources lies in regulating their allocation among states through the medium of territorial sovereignty. As indirectly demonstrated by a consistent practice on transboundary agreements, the allocation of natural resources is regulated by territorial sovereignty and by the existence of a title to territory or to the maritime zone in which the resources are located.[20] This is confirmed by the UN General Assembly resolutions that have proclaimed the existence of the principle of Permanent Sovereignty over Natural Resources (PSNR). These resolutions clarify beyond doubt that sovereignty over natural resources is both a right of peoples and a prerogative of states: it is not only a corollary of self-determination, but also an essential component of state sovereignty.[21]

As a matter of fact, natural resources are part of the territory of a state in several cases. Territory itself, if conceived of as a physical entity—as land—is a natural resource. Even when natural resources are not strictly territorial, states may extend a claim over them by virtue of their relationship with territory. Coastal states may claim natural resources within the exclusive economic zone (EEZ) or on their continental shelf, but such claim is linked to a legal relationship with territory, a portion of the lands above the sea.[22] An exception to this default rule on the allocation of

[19] In 1975 the direct involvement of South African troops in the Angolan civil war coincided with the decision 'to secure the Cunene river hydroelectric facilities at Calueque'. Stephen L. Weigert, *Angola—A Modern Military History, 1961–2002* (New York: Palgrave Macmillan, 2011), 60.

[20] Treaties on subjects such as fluvial regimes, freshwater aquifers, environmental protection, hydrocarbons, and fisheries, and joint development agreements on trans-boundary resources are always stipulated on the assumption that each party has a legal title to the zone or the territory on which the resources are located. See also fn 66 below.

[21] A/RES/1803 (XVII) (1962), para 5; A/RES/1515 (XV) (1960), para 5; A/RES/3202 (S-VI) (1974), under Chapter VII; A/RES/3281 (XXIX) (1974), Art 2. Blaine Sloan, Study of the implications, under international law, of the United Nations resolutions on permanent sovereignty over natural resources, in the occupied Palestinian and other Arab territories and on the obligations of Israel concerning its conduct in these territories, A/38/265 (21 June 1983), 12–15.

[22] United Nations Convention on the Law of the Sea (UNCLOS) (Montego Bay, 10 Dec 1982, 1833 UNTS 397), Arts 55 and 76.

natural resources concerns the areas of the globe that are not subject to the jurisdiction of any state such as the high seas and the Antarctic region. In principle, natural resources located therein are freely appropriable.

As a consequence of this legal framework, when states entertain cooperative or conflictual relations with respect to natural resources, when they enter into economic dealings or wage war over natural resources, they do so on the assumption that the state, which has title to territory or to a maritime zone, also has title to the resources therein. It is no wonder that in a number of the boundary disputes referred to the International Court of Justice (ICJ) or to arbitrations the issue at stake is control over natural resources.[23] Under international law territorial and boundary disputes tend to subsume disputes over natural resources. Conflicts over territory and issues of delimitation are the most typical example of international resource conflicts.

C. International Resource Conflicts under the *Jus ad Bellum*

The law on the use of force in international relations does not take natural resources directly into consideration. Nonetheless, some of the very pillars of the legal framework, such as the prohibition of the use of force, the prohibition of aggression, and the prohibition of annexation, have a significant territorial dimension that can be relevant for resource conflicts.

Article 2(4) of the UN Charter specifies that the territorial integrity of member states, along with their political independence, is the value to be preserved from the use of force in interstate relations. In the light of the text and the drafting history of this provision, territorial integrity can be read as 'territorial inviolability': an absolute prohibition of any unauthorized intervention in the territory of a state.[24] Furthermore, the definition of aggression approved by the General Assembly clarifies that the occupation of foreign territory is a prominent example of aggression.[25]

[23] Among the decisions of the ICJ see eg *Territorial Dispute (Libyan Arab Jamahiriya v. Chad)*, Judgment, ICJ Rep 1994, 6; *Frontier Dispute (Burkina Faso v. Mali)*, Judgment, ICJ Rep 1986, 554; *Sovereignty over Pulau Ligitan and Pulau Sipadan (Indonesia v. Malaysia)*, Judgment, ICJ Rep 2002, 625; *Land and Maritime Boundary between Cameroon and Nigeria (Cameroon v. Nigeria: Equatorial Guinea intervening)*, Judgment, ICJ Rep 2002, 303; *Sovereignty over Pedra Branca/Pulau Batu Puteh, Middle Rocks and South Ledge (Malaysia v. Singapore)*, Judgment, ICJ Rep 2008, 12. Among arbitral decisions see eg *The Indo-Pakistan Western Boundary (Rann of Kutch) between India and Pakistan*, Award of 19 February 1968, XVII RIAA 1; *Case concerning the delimitation of maritime boundary between Guinea-Bissau and Senegal,* Decision of 31 July 1989, XX RIIA 119; *Eritrea/Yemen*, Award of the Arbitral Tribunal in the First Stage—Territorial Sovereignty and Scope of the Dispute, Award of 9 Oct 1998, available at <http://www.pca-cpa.org>. See also Schrijver, *Development without Destruction*, 188–211.

[24] Lassa Oppenheim and Hersch Lauterpacht, *International Law: A Treatise*, vol 2 (London: Longmans, 1952), 154.

[25] A/RES/3314 (XXIX) (1974), Art 3(a).

Apart from the traditional exceptions of self-defence[26] and Security Council authorization,[27] there is no legal justification for the forcible occupation of foreign territory. Territory may be occupied during an action in self-defence to repel an armed attack. The lawfulness of the occupation under the *jus ad bellum* will then be tested against the requirements of the occurrence of an armed attack, proportionality, and necessity.[28] Territory may also be occupied during an enforcement action authorized by the Security Council. The lawfulness of the occupation will then be assessed in the light of the mandate expressed by the relevant Security Council resolutions. In any case, the de facto situation created by the occupation does not establish a title to foreign territory. The General Assembly Declaration on Friendly Relations mirrors a customary rule: 'No territorial acquisition resulting from the threat or use of force shall be recognized as legal'.[29] The use of the future tense clarifies that conquest may not be cured by unilateral annexation.[30] This is so not only when a unilateral proclamation of sovereignty (annexation) perpetuates the infringement of the territorial integrity of another state and the unlawfulness of the previous use force. In this respect, the principle of self-determination constitutes an additional parameter of legality. It postulates that even in cases of lawful use of force and in cases of *debellatio*, territories may not be conquered against the will of the people.[31]

The legal framework is completed by the principle of PSNR. The essential content of the principle, even if vague, coincides with the 'prerogative of peoples to

[26] Under the UN Charter, Art 51 and customary law.

[27] Starting from the war in Korea (S/RES 83 (1950)), and then in a number of cases from the beginning of the 1990s, the UN Security Council has authorized member states or multinational forces to adopt coercive measures in situations amounting to a threat to the peace or a breach of the peace. See eg S/RES/678 (1990), para 2 (Iraq), S/RES/794 (1992), para 10 (Somalia), S/RES/940 (1994), para 4 (Haiti), S/RES/1264 (1999), para 3 (East Timor). The legal basis of such delegation of the power to take coercive action may be found in a flexible interpretation of Arts 42 and 48(1). See Erika de Wet, *The Chapter VII Powers of the United Nations Security Council* (Oxford: Hart, 2004), 260–5.

[28] In addition to the occurrence of an armed attack, the requirements of proportionality and necessity are widely considered as necessary elements of the right to self-defence. See the following decisions and opinions of the ICJ: *Case Concerning Military and Paramilitary Activities in and against Nicaragua (Nicaragua v. US)*, Judgment, ICJ Rep 1986, 94, para 176; *Legality of the Threat or Use of Nuclear Weapons*, Advisory Opinion, ICJ Rep 1996, 245, para 41; *Case concerning Oil Platforms (Iran v. US)*, Judgment, ICJ Rep 2003, 183, para 43; *Armed Activities on the Territory of the Congo (DRC v. Uganda)*, Judgment, ICJ Rep 2005, 223, para 147. In state practice, prolonged occupations 'in the name of self-defence' have been regarded as not compatible with the requirements of necessity and proportionality. See Christine Gray, *International Law and the Use of Force* (Oxford: Oxford University Press, 2008), 154–5.

[29] A/RES/2625 (XXV) (1970), under 'The principle that States shall refrain in their international relations from the threat or use of force'. See also A/RES/3314 (XXIX) (1974), Art 3(a).

[30] Roger Clark, 'The Substance of the East Timor Case in the ICJ' in Catholic Institute for International Relations and International Platform of Jurists for East Timor (eds), *International Law and the Question of East Timor* (London: CIIR/IPJET, 1995), 247.

[31] Yoram Dinstein, *War, Aggression, and Self-Defence* (Cambridge: Cambridge University Press, 2011), 181–2.

determine how their resources will be developed, used, preserved and the "inalienable" right of each State to full exercise of authority over its natural wealth with the correlative right to dispose of its resources fully and freely'.[32] In the light of the text of the codifications of the principle and of the practice of the UN Security Council, it may be argued that the principle of PSNR covers not only situations related to the process of decolonization, but also interstate conflicts where the use of force is aimed at or may result in appropriating the resources of a foreign country.[33]

It should, however, be remembered that the acquisition of physical control over foreign territory and natural resources is not the only strategic option for states. Inducing a regime change and the liberalization of investments in a foreign state and/or in an occupied territory is an alternative course of action. After the initial use of force at the interstate level—formally justified with reference to the traditional exceptions—the acquisition of control over natural resources may be the result of the action of private juridical persons in a reformed internal legal order.[34] A similar scenario occurs when the intervention of foreign states in a civil war is aimed at subverting the government to induce the liberalization of the legal order of the targeted state. Such conduct is at odds with the principle of non-intervention, the principle of self-determination, and (when applicable) the law of occupation, but the enforcement of the relevant rules is problematic.

In this respect, the occupation of Iraq by a coalition of states, after the 2003 invasion, prompted some debate on whether the reform of the economic order and the legal regime of foreign investments of the occupied territory had been authorized by the Security Council, possibly setting aside the obligation to respect the laws in force in the occupied territory and the principle of economic self-determination.[35]

[32] Sloan, Study of the implications, under international law, of the United Nations resolutions on permanent sovereignty over natural resources, 12.

[33] The addresses of the principle of PSNR (Peoples and Nations) are mentioned in general terms by the relevant General Assembly resolutions and treaties (see resolutions quoted at n 21 and the International Covenant on Civil and Political Rights, Art 1(2); International Covenant on Economic, Social and Cultural Rights, Art 1(2)). There are no consistent indications that the subjective scope of the right is limited to situations of decolonization. Moreover, the Security Council has made reference to PSNR in cases that are not related to the context of decolonization. See eg S/RES/1483 (2003): 'Stressing the right of the Iraqi people freely to determine their own political future and control their own natural resources'; S/RES/1457 (2003): 'Reaffirming also the sovereignty of the Democratic Republic of the Congo over its natural resources'.

[34] The foreign minister of Poland stated the objectives of its country in Iraq: 'We have never hidden our desire for Polish oil companies to finally have access to sources of commodities' and added that access to the oilfields 'is our ultimate objective' ('Poland seeks Iraq Oil Stakes', *BBC News*, 3 July 2003, available at <http://news.bbc.co.uk/2/hi/europe/3043330.stm>).

[35] Under Art 43 of the Hague Regulations (Convention (IV) respecting the Laws and Customs of War on Land and its annex: Regulations concerning the Laws and Customs of War on Land, The Hague, 18 October 1907) the occupying power is required to respect the laws in force in the country 'unless absolutely prevented'. See Eyal Benvenisti, *The International Law of Occupation* (Oxford: Oxford University Press, 2012), 268–75; Marco Sassoli, 'Legislation and Maintenance of Public Order and Civil Life by Occupying Powers' (2005) 16 *European Journal of International Law* 681–2; Marten Zwanenburg, 'Existentialism in Iraq: Security Council Resolution 1483 and the Law of Occupation' (2004) 86(856)

The view may be taken that the ambiguous language of the relevant Security Council resolutions, which however made reference to the principle of self-determination and to PSNR, did not authorize the adoption of sweeping economic reforms.[36] Moreover, it may be argued that the power to impose the adoption of a specific economic order on a people is scarcely compatible with the attributions of the Security Council under the UN Charter, which are essentially related to the maintenance of peace and security.

D. The Exploitation of Natural Resources in Occupied Territories: The Interaction Between *Jus ad Bellum* and *Jus in Bello*

When the use of force at the interstate level results in the de facto control of foreign territory, the law of occupation, a branch of the *jus in bello*, grants to the occupying power some limited powers of exploitation of natural resources.[37] However, the law of occupation does not transfer any sovereign rights to the occupier. Pending a final determination of the status of the territory at the end of the conflict, the latter is merely required to administer the territory on a temporary basis and to respect—unless prevented—the laws in force in the country.

In such legal framework, natural resources can be inscribed in the categories of property protected by the Hague Regulations. When they qualify as 'public immovable property'—arguably the majority of cases—the occupying power will exercise the limited powers of the 'administrator and usufructuary'.[38] Even more restrictive is the regulation of natural resources classified as private property. An absolute prohibition of confiscation[39] is complemented by the prohibition of pillage,[40] by specific provisions on requisitions in kinds and services,[41] and on the seizure of munitions of war.[42] For all of the typologies of property, the exploitation of natural resources in

International Review of the Red Cross 759; Conor McCarthy, 'The Paradox of the International Law of Military Occupation: Sovereignty and the Reformation of Iraq' (2005) 10 *Journal of Conflict and Security Law* 43.

[36] On the one hand, the resolutions reaffirmed the sovereignty and territorial integrity of Iraq, the right to self-determination of the Iraqi people and their right to control their natural resources, and demanded full respect for the law of occupation, on the other, they seemed to acknowledge in general terms the transformative agenda of the occupying powers. See S/RES/1483 (2003), Preamble, paras 1, 5, 8; S/RES/1511 (2003), Preamble, paras 1, 8, 20, 24; S/RES/1546 (2003), Preamble, paras 1–4.

[37] Iain Scobbie, 'Natural Resources and Belligerent Occupation' in Susan Musarrat Akram et al (eds), *International Law and the Israeli–Palestinian Conflict* (Abingdon: Routledge, 2011), 229–36; Yutaka Arai-Takahashi, *The Law of Occupation: Continuity and Change of International Humanitarian Law, and its Interaction with International Human Rights Law* (Leiden: Martinus Nijhoff, 2009), 209–16.

[38] Hague Regulations, Art 55. [39] Hague Regulations, Art 46(2).

[40] Hague Regulations, Art 47. [41] Hague Regulations, Art 52.

[42] Hague Regulations, Art 53(2).

occupied territories is subject to limitations related to the purpose of such activities. A systemic interpretation of the Hague Regulations demonstrates that the exploitation of natural resources in occupied territories is acceptable only for the following purposes: defraying the costs of the occupation, benefiting the population of the occupied territory, and ensuring the security of the occupying power.[43] The prohibition of exploiting the resources of the occupied territory to sustain the general war effort or for the benefit of the occupying power is well established.[44] In this perspective, the *jus in bello* mirrors the unlawfulness of wars of conquest and depredation.

It is important to note that the law of occupation does not interfere with the *jus ad bellum* qualification of the legality of an occupation. As a consequence of the principle of equal applicability of international humanitarian law, *jus ad bellum* and *jus in bello* are conceived of as two separate parameters of legality that do not interact with each other. If an occupation of foreign territory amounts to aggression under the *jus ad bellum*, the law of occupation does not influence such qualification. Conversely, the law of occupation attributes to the aggressor the same rights and duties of a state that is occupying a territory in self-defence. When it comes to the exploitation of natural resources, as an effect of such separateness of these two bodies of law, it may well be the case that the activities of the occupying power, albeit in compliance with the law of occupation, constitute nonetheless a breach of the *jus ad bellum* as they take place in a war of aggression.[45] At the end of the conflict, the aggressor will have to provide reparations also for the exploitation or the depletion of natural resources carried out in compliance with the law of occupation.[46]

This is, however, a rather theoretical point. With the exception of the Israeli occupation of the Palestinian territory and of the multinational occupation of Iraq after the invasion of 2003, the law of occupation has rarely been applied before the end

[43] Antonio Cassese, 'Powers and Duties of an Occupant in Relation to Land and Natural Resources' in Emma Playfair (ed), *International Law and the Administration of Occupied Territories* (Oxford: Clarendon Press, 1992) reprinted in Antonio Cassese, *The Human Dimension of International Law—Selected Papers* (Oxford: Oxford University Press, 2008), 257–60.

[44] *Trial of the Major War Criminals before the International Military Tribunal*, Nuremberg, 14 Nov 1945–1 Oct 1946, 238–9; *The United States of America against Friedrich Flick et al*, Trials of War Criminals before the Nuremberg Military Tribunals under Control Council Law No 10, Nuremberg, Oct 1946–Apr 1949, 1204–12.

[45] Pierre D'Argent, *Les réparations de guerre en droit international public* (Brussels: Bruylant, 2002), 476–8.

[46] S/RES/687 (1991), adopted after the conclusion of the Gulf War, did not distinguish between violations of the *jus in bello* and violations of the *jus ad bellum* and affirmed that Iraq was 'liable under international law for any direct loss, damage, including environmental damage and the depletion of natural resources, or injury to foreign governments, nationals and corporations as a result of Iraq's unlawful invasion and occupation of Kuwait' (para 16). See Hazel Fox, 'Reparations and State Responsibility: Claims Against Iraq Arising Out of the Invasion and Occupation of Kuwait' in Peter Rowe (ed), *The Gulf War 1990–91 in International and English Law* (London: Routledge, 1993), 219–21. With reference to the practice of war reparations after the Second World War: D'Argent, *Les réparations de guerre en droit international public*, 481–6; Andrea Gattini, *Le riparazioni di guerra nel diritto internazionale* (Padua: CEDAM, 2003), 533.

of the conflict as the intervening states tend to adopt alternative legal qualifications. They would claim that they are restoring their sovereignty on a territory that originally belonged to them or they would maintain that they are supporting a national liberation movement and then install a puppet government in the occupied territory. Albeit weak, these legal arguments imply a total rejection of the applicability of the law of occupation. When confronted with a strong stance of the intervening state on arguments of *jus ad bellum*, the law of occupation becomes practically irrelevant during the conflict and tends to resurface afterwards as law of individual and state responsibility. The logical consequence of these approaches is that the aggressor or the puppet government will claim the full prerogatives of sovereignty over the natural resources located in the territory. For natural resources, the most delicate phase of an interstate conflict is when an unlawful territorial situation consolidates itself. In such a situation, the prospects of enforcement of the relevant norms are mainly related to the behaviour of third parties and, more precisely, to their duty of non-recognition of unlawful territorial situations.

E. The Exploitation of Natural Resources in Unlawful Territorial Situations: The Duty of Non-Recognition and Natural Resources

Annexation does not establish a valid title to the territory forcibly seized and to the natural resources therein. However, as a matter of fact, one cannot ignore that physical control over territory makes the exploitation of natural resources possible. Morocco in Western Sahara,[47] Indonesia in East Timor,[48] South Africa in Namibia,[49] Iraq in Kuwait,[50] Israel in East Jerusalem and the Golan Heights:[51] all of those states exploited the resources of an occupied territory claiming more or less openly to

[47] Toby Shelley, 'Natural Resources and the Western Sahara' in Claes Olsson (ed), *The Western Sahara Conflict: The Role of Natural Resources in Decolonization* (Uppsala: Nordiska Afrikainstitutet, 2006), 17–21.

[48] Commission for Reception, Truth and Reconciliation in Timor-Leste, *Chega! The Report of the Commission for Reception, Truth and Reconciliation in Timor-Leste*, 2005, Part 4, para 156, available at <http://www.cavr-timorleste.org/en/chegaReport.htm>.

[49] Report of the United Nations Council for Namibia, GAOR, 38th Sess, Supp No 24, A/38/24, paras 396–434.

[50] Michael Schmitt, 'Iraq-Kuwait War (1990–1991)' in Rüdiger Wolfrum (ed), *The Max Planck Encyclopedia of Public International Law* (Oxford: Oxford University Press, 2008), available at <http://www.mpepil.com>, para 24.

[51] See eg Report prepared by the Economic and Social Commission for Western Asia on the economic and social repercussions of the Israeli occupation on the living conditions of the Palestinian people in the occupied Palestinian territory, including Jerusalem, and of the Arab population in the occupied Syrian Golan, A/64/77, paras 59–63 and A/RES/66/225 (2012).

exercise their 'sovereign rights'. Puppet governments established by Armenia in Nagorno-Karabakh[52] and by Turkey in northern Cyprus[53] have been doing the same.

Such conduct originates from unlawful territorial situations, emanating from an act of aggression, a breach of the right to self-determination of a people, or both. In addition, they constitute a violation of the PSNR of a state or a people, depending on the circumstances. The crucial issue is how the relevant norms may be enforced, when the usual pattern of unlawful territorial situations—the physical control of territory coupled with the alteration of its demographic equilibrium—perpetuates itself. In this respect, pending a potentially never-ending dispute on title to territory and in the absence of significant action by the collective security system, the attitude of third parties becomes determinant. According to Article 41(2) of the International Law Commission (ILC) Articles on State Responsibility—states are under a duty of non-recognition of de facto territorial situations originating from serious breaches of peremptory norms, such as the prohibition of aggression and the principle of self-determination.[54] As confirmed by the General Assembly resolution on the definition of aggression and by the Declaration on Friendly Relations,[55] states shall not recognize explicitly or implicitly any sovereign rights of the unlawful occupier. Given that title to natural resources is generally subsumed by title to territory and sovereignty, the duty of non-recognition of unlawful territorial situations finds in economic dealings on natural resources one of its most relevant fields of application. States shall not enter into any dealings concerning the natural resources of the territory with the unlawful occupier. Albeit with hesitations and contradictions, the essence of Article 41(2) is confirmed by some notable examples concerning natural resources. A thread in the practice connects the UN action on the South African occupation of Namibia,[56] the reaction of Portugal to the Timor Gap Treaty between Australia and Indonesia,[57] the decision of the European Parliament to temporarily reject the conclusion of a protocol implementing the European Union (EU)–Morocco Fisheries Partnership

[52] Annex to the letter dated 11 November 2004 from the Permanent Representative of Azerbaijan to the United Nations addressed to the President of the General Assembly, A/59/568 (11 Nov 2004). The Report of Azerbaijan is also based on information published by Armenian newspapers.

[53] Peter R. Hocknell, *Boundaries of Cooperation—Cyprus,* de facto *Partition, and the Delimitation of Transboundary Resource Management* (The Hague: Kluwer, 2001), 164–230.

[54] Art 41(2), Draft Articles on Responsibility of States for Internationally Wrongful Acts, *Yearbook of the International Law Commission*, 2001, vol II (2), 26 at 29. See also the commentary by James Crawford on Art 41(2), 114–15. According to Judge Skubiszewski, the duty of non-recognition of unlawful territorial situations is a 'corollary' of the principle of non-use of force and 'does protect the rights to self-determination and to permanent sovereignty over natural resources'. *East Timor (Portugal v. Australia)*, Judgment, ICJ Rep 1995, Dissenting Opinion of Judge Skubiszewski, 224, para 131. The existence of the duty was confirmed by the ICJ in two advisory opinions: *Legal Consequences of the Construction of a Wall in the Occupied Palestinian Territory*, Advisory Opinion, ICJ Rep 2004, 136, para 159; *Legal Consequences for States of the Continued Presence of South Africa in Namibia (South West Africa) notwithstanding Security Council, Resolution 276(1970)*, Advisory Opinion, ICJ Rep 1971, 16, paras 119, 125–6.

[55] See n 29.

[56] S/RES/284 (1970), paras 2, 5; S/RES/301 (1971), para 6.

[57] *East Timor (Portugal v. Australia)*, Mémoire du Gouvernement de la République Portugaise, vol 1, 18 Nov 1991, 219–21.

Agreement,[58] the non-application of the Morocco–European Free Trade Association (EFTA)[59] and the Morocco–US[60] free trade agreements to the goods originating from Western Sahara, the non-application of the Israel–EU Association Agreement to the goods produced in the Israeli settlements in the Occupied Palestinian Territory,[61] the objection of a number of states to considering the products of the Israeli settlements in the Occupied Palestinian Territory as 'made in Israel',[62] the decision of the Council of the EU to prohibit the import of goods originating from Crimea after the illegal annexation of the region to the Russian Federation.[63] The effect of the duty of non-recognition on the exploitation of natural resources in unlawful territorial situations is potentially very significant at the interstate level. Nonetheless, it is worth remembering that the activities of exploitation of natural resources are seldom carried out directly by states and that the duty of non-recognition does not bind private enterprises and individuals.

In addition, at the interstate level a treaty related to natural resources concluded with an unlawful occupier may be held to be invalid for breach of the general

[58] In 2011, the EU Parliament rejected the conclusion of the protocol, which had already entered into provisional application, on the ground that it was, among other things, incompatible with international law. In fact, such agreement did not clearly exclude from its scope the waters offshore Western Sahara, a non self-governing territory occupied by Morocco in 1975. See 2012/15/EU, Council Decision of 20 Dec 2011 repealing Council Decision 2011/491/EU, OJ L 6/1, 10/01/2011–2. However, in 2014 the EU and Morocco concluded another protocol, not substantially different from the previous one and potentially in breach of the duty of non-recognition (see OJ L 328, 07/12/2013, 2-21). It is to be added that Russia concluded similar agreements with Morocco, which, despite being formally limited to Morocco's Exclusive Economic Zone, are also applied offshore Western Sahara. An unofficial translation of the 13 February 2013 agreement is available at: <http://www.wsrw.org/files/dated/2013-04-30/russia-morocco_fisheries_agreement_2013.pdf.> On the legality of EU fisheries agreements with Morocco, see Enrico Milano, 'The New Fisheries Partnership Agreement Between the European Community and the Kingdom of Morocco: Fishing Too South?' (2006) 22 *Anuario español de derecho internacional* 413.

[59] Norway and Switzerland interpret the Morocco–EFTA agreement as non-applicable to goods originating from Western Sahara. See Email of 6 April 2007, Martin Zbinden, Head Free Trade Agreements/EFTA—State Secretariat for Economic Affairs (SECO), Switzerland, to the Swiss Western Sahara Committee, available at <http://www.vest-sahara.no/a1x1489>; Statement by the Norwegian Minister of Foreign Affairs, Mr Jonas Gahr Støre, in the Norwegian Parliament, 11 May 2010, unofficial translation at <http://www.wsrw.org/a105x1411>.

[60] Letter by R. B. Zoellick, United States Trade Representative, to Congressman Pitts of 20 July 2004, available at <http://www.vest-sahara.no/files/pdf/Zoellick_FTA_2004.pdf>.

[61] Reply to written question P-2747/00 by Alain Lipietz (Verts/ALE) to the Council, Irregular application of the EC–Israel Agreement, OJ 113 E, 18/04/2001, 163–4. See also ECJ, C-386/08, *Firma Brita GmbH v. Hauptzollamt Hamburg-Hafen*, Judgment of the Court of 25 Feb 2010, para 53.

[62] See eg the position of South Africa: Department of Trade and Industry, Notice 379 of 2012, Labelling of products originating from Occupied Palestinian Territory wrongly labelled as originating in Israel, available at <http://www.info.gov.za/view/DownloadFileAction?id=165066> and the United Kingdom: Department for Environment, Food and Rural Affairs, Technical advice: labelling of produce grown in the Occupied Palestinian Territories, 10 December 2009, at: <http://archive.defra.gov.uk/foodfarm/food/pdf/labellingpalestine.pdf>; Denmark: Phoebe Greenwood, 'Denmark and South Africa protest at "made in Israel" goods', *The Telegraph*, 21 May 2012, and Belgium: Robert-Jan Bartunek, 'Belgium advises retailers to label products from Israeli settlements', *Haaretz*, 29 July 2014.

[63] Council Decision 2014/386/CFSP concerning restrictions on goods originating in Crimea or Sevastopol, in response to the illegal annexation of Crimea and Sevastopol, OJ L 183/70, 24 June 2014.

principle *nemo dat quod non habet*.[64] According to this principle, a cession of rights over things may only be effectuated by the natural or juridical person who has an appropriate legal title to such things.[65] It is here submitted that the principle *nemo dat quod non habet* is not (only) based on 'legal logic', but is confirmed by a consistent practice of treaties over natural resources.[66] Considering that treaties on transboundary resources are predicated upon the existence of a title to territory or to a maritime zone, there is no legal basis for an agreement on natural resources over which the ceding party does not have any legal title.

III. The Initiatives of the United Nations

In recent times the linkage between natural resources and armed conflicts has aroused the interest of civil society and the issue has thus been put on the agenda of international organizations. Besides some initiatives at the regional level, the organization that has taken a lead role is the UN, where the issue has been addressed by almost all of its principal organs.[67]

[64] Roger Clark, 'The Timor Gap: The Legality of the "Treaty on the Zone of Cooperation in an Area between the Indonesian Province of East Timor and Western Australia"' (1992) 69 *Pace Yearbook of International Law* 92–4. On the principle *nemo dat quod non habet*: *Case Concerning the Land and Maritime Boundary between Cameroon and Nigeria (Cameroon v. Nigeria: Equatorial Guinea Intervening)*, Judgment of 10 October 2002, ICJ Rep 2002, para 204; *Island of Palmas (Netherlands v. US)*, 4 Apr 1928, II RIAA 842–3; Ian Brownlie, *Principles of Public International Law* (Oxford: Oxford University Press, 2008), 121–2.

[65] Olufemi Elias and Chin Lim, '"General Principles of Law", "Soft" Law and the Identification of International Law' (1997) 28 *Netherlands Yearbook of International Law* 31–2.

[66] See eg the practice of unitization agreements on hydrocarbon resources: a hydrocarbon deposit on the continental shelf of one of the parties will be exploited as a unit if it extends to the continental shelf of the other party (eg Treaty between the Kingdom of Norway and the Russian Federation concerning Maritime Delimitation and Cooperation in the Barents Sea and the Arctic Ocean, 15 Sept 2010, available at <http://www.regjeringen.no>). The agreements on trans-boundary watercourses and aquifers are based on the same logic of cooperation between states having a sovereign title on a part of the resource (eg Indus Water Treaty, India/Pakistan, 19 Sept 1960, at <http://siteresources.worldbank.org>; Agreement on the Cooperation for the Sustainable Development of the Mekong River Basin, between The Kingdom of Cambodia, The Lao People's Democratic Republic, The Kingdom of Thailand, and The Socialist Republic of Viet Nam, 5 Apr 1995, at <http://www.mrcmekong.org>). Similar considerations apply to the agreements on fisheries. In the fisheries partnership agreements stipulated by the European Community (EC) with a number of countries, eg, the EC grants financial contributions in exchange for fishing rights in the areas over which such countries exercise jurisdiction or sovereign rights (eg Fisheries Partnership Agreement between the European Community and the Republic of Cape Verde, 30 Dec 2006, OJ L 414/3).

[67] At the regional level, in May 2000 the Economic Community of West African States (ECOWAS) launched 'a regional inquiry into the illegal trade of diamonds' (S/RES/1306 (2000), Preamble).

In 2004, the Secretary-General's High-Level Panel Report on Threats, Challenges and Change suggested that a strategy for the prevention of wars should be based inter alia on 'new legal mechanisms' and on 'norms governing the management of natural resources for countries emerging from or at risk of conflict'.[68] A number of subsequent reports of the Secretary-General have dealt with specific aspects.[69] The General Assembly and the Security Council have acknowledged the problem in open debates[70] and in resolutions formulated both in general terms[71] and with reference to specific cases.[72] Moreover, they have endorsed civil society voluntary initiatives such as the Kimberley Process for the certification of 'conflict diamonds'[73] and the Extractive Industry Transparency Initiative (EITI) on the transparency of payments from natural resources.[74]

The Security Council has taken operational measures of three typologies.[75] First, it has adopted commodity sanctions[76] and targeted sanctions[77] aimed at breaking the link between armed conflicts and natural resources. Secondly, it has incorporated tasks related to natural resources in the mandate of peacekeeping operations.[78] Thirdly, it has established panels of experts, which have publicly disclosed

Moreover, the 11 African states of the International Conference on the Great Lakes adopted a Protocol on the Illegal Exploitation of Natural Resources International Conference on the Great Lakes Region and a regional initiative aimed at the creation of a certification scheme for resources such as coltan, cassiterite, wolframite, and gold. See Protocol Against the Illegal Exploitation of Natural Resources, 30 Novr 2006, available at <https://icglr.org/IMG/pdf/Protocol_against_the_Illegal_Exploitation_of_Natural_Resources.pdf>.

[68] Report of the High-Level Panel on Threats, Challenges and Change, 'A More Secure World: Our Shared Responsibility', A/59/565 (2004), 35, para 91.

[69] The causes of conflict and the promotion of durable peace and sustainable development in Africa—Report of 13 April 1998, A/66/214–S/2011/476; Climate Change and its possible security implications—Report of 11 September 2009, A/64/350; Implementation of the recommendations contained in the report of the Secretary-General on the causes of conflict and the promotion of durable peace and sustainable development in Africa—Report of 1 August 2011, A/66/214–S/ 2011/476.

[70] S/PV/4113 (2000) (Security Council debate on the situation in Angola); S/PV/5359 (2006) (Security Council debate on peace, security and development in the Great Lakes region); S/PV/5705 (2007) (Security Council debate on natural resources and conflict).

[71] A/RES/55/56 (2000); A/RES/60/223 (2006), para 5; S/RES/1625 (2005), para 6.

[72] S/RES 1306/2000, under A (Sierra Leone); S/RES/1343 (2001), paras 2(c), 6 (Liberia); S/RES/1457 (2003) (DRC), paras 3–4; S/RES/1756 (2007), Preamble (DRC); S/RES/1807 (2008), Preamble (DRC); S/RES/1856 (2008), para 3(j) (DRC); S/RES/1952 (2010), paras 7–9 (DRC).

[73] S/RES/1643 (2005), para 9(b) (Côte d'Ivoire); S/RES/1854 (2008), Preamble, paras 4(f), 8 (Liberia); S/RES/1980 (2011), para 19 (Côte d'Ivoire).

[74] S/RES/1854 (2008), Preamble; S/PRST/2007/22; A/RES/62/74 (2008), para 4.

[75] Philippe Le Billon and Eric Nicholls, 'Ending "Resource Wars": Revenue Sharing, Economic Sanction or Military Intervention?' (2007) 14 *International Peacekeeping* 613, 615–22.

[76] S/RES/1343 (2001), para 2(c) (sanctions on diamonds—Liberia); S/RES/1643 (2005), para 6 (sanctions on diamonds—Côte d'Ivoire); S/RES/864 (1993), para 19 (sanctions on oil—Angola); S/RES/1132 (1997), para 6 (sanctions on oil—Sierra Leone); S/RES/1173 (1998), para 12(b) (sanctions on diamonds—Angola); S/RES/1306 (2000), para 1 (sanctions on diamonds—Sierra Leone); S/RES/1521 (2003), paras 6–13 (sanctions on timber—Liberia).

[77] S/RES/1857 (2008), para 4(g) (DRC).

[78] S/RES/1991 (2011), para 17 (DRC); S/RES/1509 (2003), para 3(r) (Liberia); S/RES/1643 (2005), para 10 (Côte d'Ivoire); S/RES/792 (1992) (Cambodia), paras 13–14.

the names of private enterprises, governments, and individuals allegedly involved in the 'illegal exploitation of natural resources'.[79]

The most significant measures adopted by the Security Council are commodity sanctions directly related to natural resources and sanctions targeting individuals and groups involved in the exploitation of natural resources in the context of armed conflicts. In the cases of Angola,[80] Liberia,[81] Sierra Leone,[82] Côte d'Ivoire,[83] and Cambodia[84] the Council imposed bans on trade in resources such as rough diamonds, timber, and oil. In the case of the DRC, while not adopting specific measures on natural resources, the Security Council imposed targeted measures on individuals and groups involved in the trafficking of natural resources.[85]

The Security Council has frequently intervened in internationalized civil wars, taking the view that such conflicts constituted threats to the peace and acknowledging the role of natural resources in fuelling them and in favouring their continuation. Perhaps the most relevant aspect of the practice of the Council lies in the fact that sanctions over natural resources often target only one of the parties in the war, which is identified as the main obstacle to the peace. In the cases of Angola, Sierra Leone, and Côte d'Ivoire the Council adopted the sanctions with a view to favouring the implementation of peace plans by pushing the recalcitrant party to respect and implement them.[86] In the cases of Sierra Leone and Angola resources under the control of the government were excluded from the embargo and governmental authorities were invited to establish a certification scheme to ensure that trade in the resources respected the laws in force in the country.[87] In such cases, the intervention of the Security Council on natural resources aggregates the reaction of member states against one of the warring parties. Sanctions are employed to deprive one of the parties of the means to sustain the war effort, but not necessarily as a tool to bring the conflict quickly to an end. At times the ban on natural resources arguably favoured

[79] S/RES/1643 (2005), para 9(b) (Côte d'Ivoire); S/RES/1643 (2005), para 9 (Côte d'Ivoire); S/RES/1237 (1999), para 6 (Angola); S/RES/1343 (2001), para 19 (Liberia); S/RES/1306 (2000), para 19 (Sierra Leone); S/PRST/2000/20 (DRC).

[80] S/RES/864 (1993), para 19 (sanctions on oil); S/RES/1173 (1998), para 12(b) (sanctions on diamonds).

[81] S/RES/1343 (2001), para 2(c) (sanctions on diamonds); S/RES/1521 (2003), paras 6–13 (sanctions on timber).

[82] S/RES/1132 (1997), para 6 (sanctions on oil); S/RES/1306 (2000), para 1 (sanctions on diamonds).

[83] S/RES/1643 (2005), para 6 (sanctions on diamonds).

[84] S/RES/792 (1992), paras 13–14. In the case of Cambodia, the Security Council merely supported the decision of the Cambodian authorities to set a moratorium on the export of logs and requested that a similar moratorium be established 'on the export of minerals and gems'.

[85] S/RES/1857 (2008), para 4(g).

[86] S/RES/864 (1993), para 6 (sanctions on oil—Angola); S/RES/1173 (1998), paras 1–2 (sanctions on diamonds—Angola); S/RES/1306 (2000), para 1 (sanctions on diamonds—Sierra Leone); S/RES/1643 (2005), paras 2–3 (sanctions on diamonds—Côte d'Ivoire).

[87] S/RES/1173 (1998), para 12(b) (sanctions on diamonds—Angola); S/RES/1306 (2000), paras 1, 5 (sanctions on diamonds—Sierra Leone).

the weaker party, the one that was on the verge of being defeated, thus prolonging the duration of the conflict.[88]

Finally, the role of the ICJ should not be overlooked. The judicial organ of the UN has settled several territorial and boundary disputes that were clearly related to natural resources. States resorted to a judicial body to put an end to protracted resource conflicts that had become unsustainable.[89] The decision of a third party is easier to accept for domestic public opinion, especially when issues of sovereignty are at stake, overloaded with sentiments of national pride.[90] In other cases, the decisions of the ICJ have arguably prevented the eruption of a conflict over territory, boundaries, and, in the end, natural resources.[91]

The most significant decision related to international resource conflicts is undoubtedly the *Armed Activities* case, in which the ICJ made two significant statements. First, with reference to the exploitation of natural resources in occupied territories, the Court held that an occupying power has a duty of vigilance not only over its armed forces, but also over 'private persons'.[92] This is based on a teleological interpretation of Article 43 of the Hague Regulations and is unassailable.[93] Secondly, with reference to the application of the principle of PSNR in the case under consideration, the Court cryptically stated that 'there is nothing' in the General Assembly resolutions that proclaimed the principle 'which suggests that they are applicable to the specific situation of looting, pillage and exploitation of certain natural resources by members of the army of a State militarily intervening in another State'.[94] The position of the Court may be read either as an abstract rejection of the applicability of the principle of PSNR during armed conflicts or as a statement limited to the facts of the case. The second interpretation is more persuasive. In previous paragraphs, the Court found that it did not dispose of 'credible evidence to prove that there was a governmental policy of Uganda directed at the exploitation of natural resources of the DRC or that Uganda's military intervention was carried out in order to obtain access to Congolese resources'.[95] Under this perspective, only campaigns of depredations organized by governmental authorities would be covered by the principle of PSNR, whereas cases of looting attributable to the army and individual soldiers

[88] In 1992–3, when sanctions on oil against UNITA were adopted, the rebel group controlled 70 per cent of the territory of Angola. Michael Ross, 'Booty Futures', unpublished working paper, 6 May 2005, 17–18, available at <http://www.sscnet.ucla.edu/polisci/faculty/ross/bootyfutures.pdf>.

[89] *Territorial Dispute (Libyan Arab Jamahiriya v. Chad)*, Judgment, 6; *Frontier Dispute (Burkina Faso v. Republic of Mali)*, Judgment, 554.

[90] Steven Ratner, 'Land Feuds and their Solutions: Finding International Law Beyond the Tribunal Chamber' (2006) 100 *American Journal of International Law* 814.

[91] *Sovereignty over Pulau Ligitan and Pulau Sipadan (Indonesia v. Malaysia)*, Judgment, 625; *Land and Maritime Boundary between Cameroon and Nigeria*, Judgment, 303; *Sovereignty over Pedra Branca/Pulau Batu Puteh, Middle Rocks and South Ledge*, Judgment, 12.

[92] *Armed Activities*, Judgment, para 248. [93] *Armed Activities*, Judgment, para 250.

[94] *Armed Activities*, Judgment, para 247.

[95] *Armed Activities*, Judgment, para 242. In this sense see the position of the government of Uganda in the case: Public sitting held on Wednesday 27 April 2005, at 3 p.m., at the Peace Palace, CR 2005/15, 22-23.

would not. This interpretation is in line with the idea that PSNR, given its origin and function, is a principle dealing with the aggregate relationship between peoples and states and not with the micromanagement of the conduct of individuals. It is also to be considered that there are no textual elements in support of the thesis that the principle would not be applicable to situations of armed conflict. As has been said, according to the Security Council, the principle of PSNR may be relevant in conflict and post-conflict situations even beyond the context of the decolonization.[96]

IV. Concluding Remarks

The logic of violent confrontation over natural resources between human groups, be they organized in an entity called a state or not, is often the same. The statements and the behaviour of governmental authorities demonstrate that not only civil wars, but also international conflicts, may be motivated, at least in part, by the desire or the need to gain control over natural resources. Natural resources are also a determinant factor for the duration of conflicts as they can be traded for weapons and the economic needs of the warring parties.

Against these facts, international law does not address the linkage between armed conflicts and natural resources directly. The legal regulation of the *jus ad bellum* aspects of the issue is the result of the application of the traditional rules on the use of force, as complemented by the prohibition of annexation, the principle of self-determination, and the principle of PSNR. The enforcement of such rules is achieved somewhat haphazardly through the adoption of sanctions by the Security Council and the action of third parties that are bound by the duty of non-recognition of unlawful territorial situations.

Under the relevant legal framework, the appropriation of natural resources is not a valid justification for the use of force. Conquest and annexation do not transfer a title, neither to territory nor to the natural resources therein. International resource conflicts are therefore rationalized by the intervening states with reference to the traditional legal bases for the use of force, but in several cases the appropriation of natural resources is quite likely among the motives that induced them to act. In practice, there seems to be a huge gap between the legal justifications offered for the use of force and the reasons for the basis of the conduct of governmental authorities. As a result, in this context, one is left with the impression that only rarely does international law contribute *ex ante* to the elaboration of public policies. Rather, it seems to be used as a linguistic construction to legitimize decisions that are based on strategic considerations.

[96] See n 33.

CHAPTER 51

REMOTELY PILOTED WARFARE AS A CHALLENGE TO THE *JUS AD BELLUM*

JORDAN J. PAUST

I. Introduction

THE phrase 'remotely piloted warfare' has several potential meanings depending on what is covered by the phrase 'remotely piloted'[1] and by the

[1] The phrase 'remotely piloted' can pertain with respect to use of land-based, naval, and air and space robotics. Eg remotely controlled robots are used during war and domestic law enforcement to find and dismantle explosives and some can sniff for chemical or bacteriological/biological weaponry. Some fully autonomous vehicles, mines, and other mechanisms are not 'piloted', but are addressed. One publication notes that 'Autonomous systems are also part of the projected ground forces' and that there will be 'a reconfigurable skirmishing vehicle', a 'stealth tank', 'unmanned supply lorries and mine-clearing vehicles', 'a small, tracked robot vehicle that can undertake missions normally done by a single soldier', and 'aerial robots dropping ground robots and using a few special forces to guide them', 'Autonomous Vehicles: Robot Wars' (6 Jun 2011) *Engineer* 20. Concerning various types of military robotics, see Patrick Lin, George Bekey, and Keith Abney, 'Autonomous Military Robotics: Risk, Ethics, and Design' (20 Dec 2008), 1, 5–6, 11–19, available at <http://ethics.calpoly.edu/ONR_report.pdf>. Today, most attention is paid to use of aerial vehicles or drones that are remotely piloted, and these are the vehicles that are primarily addressed in this chapter.

word 'warfare'.[2] These, in turn, can be related to phrases in the UN Charter that are relevant to the overall focus of this volume, such as the use of 'armed force...in the common interest',[3] 'the threat or use of force against' territorial integrity or political independence,[4] Security Council-authorized 'enforcement action',[5] 'regional action' authorized by an appropriate regional organization,[6] and 'self-defense if an armed attack occurs'.[7]

Although use of remotely piloted armed aerial vehicles in combat by the US and the North Atlantic Treaty Organization (NATO) has been relatively new during the last two decades, various present and foreseeable uses of remotely piloted methods and means of armed force and warfare do not appear to necessitate any change in UN Charter precepts regarding the use of force by state and non-state actors. The fact that they will evolve in several ways and become increasingly accessible to states and non-state actors, however, may result in increased permissible use of armed force by states with respect to self-defence, collective self-defence, self-determination assistance,[8] regional action, and enforcement action authorized by the UN Security Council. Their increased use as platforms for armed force during war or relative peace and as methods and means of self-defence has already noticeably resulted in a greater potential for compliance with principles of reasonably necessity, distinction in targeting, and proportionality,[9] which are

[2] There is a difference between use of force and war or 'warfare'. Eg it is widely understood that the use of armed force against certain non-state actors in self-defence can be permissible under the UN Charter but not create an international or non-international armed conflict, however long or short. See also nn 51 and 55. Although war has never been merely state to state, whether a state is at war and it is international in character depends upon the status of opponents (eg whether they are states, nations, peoples, belligerents, or insurgents). This is one reason why the self-defence paradigm is different than the law of war paradigm.

[3] UN Charter, Preamble.

[4] UN Charter, Art 2(4).

[5] UN Charter, Art 42; see also Art 53 ('enforcement action').

[6] UN Charter, Art 52. Concerning permissible 'regional action' taken by NATO and the Organization of American States (OAS), see eg Christine Gray, *International Law and the Use of Force* (Oxford: Oxford University Press, 2000), 113 (the Cuban Missile Crisis was authorized as 'regional peacekeeping under Chapter VIII of the UN Charter'. But see at 40 (NATO authorization regarding Kosovo without Security Council authorization was supposedly of 'doubtful' validity)); Jordan J. Paust, 'Use of Armed Force Against Terrorists in Afghanistan, Iraq, and Beyond' (2002) 35 *Cornell International Law Journal* 533, 545–7; Abram Chayes, 'The Legal Case for U.S. Action in Cuba' (1962) 47 *Department of State Bulletin* 763, 764 (OAS General Assembly resolution authorized forceful interdiction of Soviet vessels heading to Cuba); cf Yoram Dinstein, *War, Aggression and Self-Defence* (4th edn, Cambridge: Cambridge University Press, 2005), 310–14 (missing the point that Art 52 provides for 'regional action' when the Security Council is unable to act and to authorize 'enforcement action' as such).

[7] UN Charter, Art 51.

[8] With respect to permissible self-determination assistance, see eg Paust, 'Use of Armed Force Against Terrorists', 547–8; Jordan J. Paust, 'International Law, Dignity, Democracy, and the Arab Spring' (2012) *Cornell International Law Journal* 46.

[9] See eg Eyal Benvenisti, 'The Legal Battle to Define the Law on Transnational Asymmetric Warfare' (2010) 20 *Duke Journal of Comparative and International Law* 339, 353 fn 40 (computer programs can provide estimates of consequences of drone targeting); Laurie R. Blank, 'After Top Gun: How Drone

general principles that are also relevant to permissibility of the use of armed force under the UN Charter and relevant customary international law or the *jus ad bellum*.[10] However, future application of these principles in connection with use of remotely piloted attacks, self-defence, and warfare might result in challenges regarding interpretation and application around the edges of normative meaning with respect to Article 2(4) of the UN Charter and permissible self-defence under Article 51 of the Charter, especially for those who prefer that there should be

Strikes Impact the Law of War' (2012) 33 *University of Pennsylvania Journal of International Law* 675, 687–9, 691–4, 697–8, 701–2; Aaron M. Drake, 'Current U.S. Air Force Drone Operations and Their Conduct in Compliance with International Humanitarian Law—An Overview' (2011) 39 *Denver Journal of International Law and Policy* 629, 637–40, 642–5; Michael W. Lewis, 'Drones and the Boundaries of the Battlefield' (2012) 47 *Texas International Law Journal* 293, 297–8; Jordan J. Paust, 'Self-Defense Targetings of Non-State Actors and Permissibility of U.S. Use of Drones in Pakistan' (2010) *Journal of Transnational Law and Policy* 237, 274, available at <http://ssrn.com/abstract=1520717>; Jordan J. Paust, 'Permissible Self-Defense Targeting and the Death of bin Laden' (2011) 39 *Denver Journal of International Law and Policy* 569, 572–3 and fn 20; Michael N. Schmitt, 'Drone Attacks Under the *Jus ad Bellum* and *Jus in Bello*: Clearing the "Fog of Law"' (2010) 13 *Yearbook of International Humanitarian Law* 311, 313–14, 320; see also Anna Stolley Persky, 'Lethal Force' (Mar 2012) *Washington Lawyer* 23, 29 (some claim that computers can use face recognition in connection with specific targetings but worry about automated targeting without human direction).

[10] See eg *Case Concerning Oil Platforms (Iran v. US)*, 6 Nov 2003, ICJ Rep 2003, 161, 183, para 43; *Legality of the Threat or Use of Nuclear Weapons*, Advisory Opinion of 8 July 1996, ICJ Rep 1996, 226, 245, para 41 ('submission of the exercise of the right of self-defense to the conditions of necessity and proportionality is a rule of customary international law'), 246, para 46 ('belligerent reprisals... would, like self-defense, be governed *inter alia* by the principle of proportionality'); *Case Concerning Military and Paramilitary Activities in and against Nicaragua (Nicaragua v. US)*, 27 June 1986, ICJ Rep 1986, 14, 94, para 176 (UN Charter, Art 51 does not mention that 'self-defense would warrant only measures which are proportional to the armed attack and necessary to respond to it, a rule well established in customary international law', but this demonstrates the interface that exists between treaty provisions and customary precepts), 103, para 194; Thomas M. Franck, 'On Proportionality of Countermeasures in International Law' (2008) 102 *American Journal of International Law* 715, 719–21 (noting the ICJ's ability to use the general principle of proportionality first, to determine whether there is a right to use force in self-defence (*jus ad bellum*) and, secondly, 'whether the level of countermeasures deployed is permitted by law; whether it is proportionate to the attack itself and to the needs of self-defense (*jus in bello*)'); Paust, 'Self-Defense Targetings of Non-State Actors', 269–76. See also Judith Gardam, *Necessity, Proportionality and the Use of Force by States* (Cambridge: Cambridge University Press, 2004), 30, 141–8.

Since the general principles are the same, it is rational and policy-serving to consider guidance with respect to their meaning and application that is offered in relevant trends in decisions under both the *jus ad bellum* and *jus in bello*, especially regarding measures of self-defence outside the context of war when the laws of war do not apply but offer more detailed interpretive and decisional guidance. See eg Paust, 'Self-Defense Targetings of Non-State Actors', 269–70, 274, 279. For some, this might involve a change from rigid boxed-in thinking as if developments in one box have had no influence and are of no interpretive value within the other box. More generally, 'legal subsystems in isolation from the remaining bulk of international law are inconceivable. There will always be some degree of interaction, at least at the level of interpretation.' Bruno Simma and Dirk Pulkowski, 'Of Planets and the Universe: Self-Contained Regimes in International Law' (2006) 17 *European Journal of International Law* 483, 492.

limitations of the inherent right of self-defence in terms of the character, gravity, area, and scale of state and non-state armed attacks,[11] whether or not the attackers use robotic vehicles.

II. The 'Remotely Piloted' Phenomenon

Drones are the current primary example of remotely piloted aerial vehicles that are used during war and self-defence,[12] what some term unmanned aerial vehicles (UAVs) even though they are not fully automated and are flown by humans situated outside the aerial vehicles. Drones were first used for aerial intelligence, surveillance, and reconnaissance during war.[13] They are also used for intelligence, surveillance, investigation, and related purposes during times of relative peace within a country,[14]

[11] cf *Oil Platforms*, 195, para 72 ('the mining of a single military vessel might be sufficient to bring into play the "inherent right of self-defense" '); see n 48.

[12] Concerning use of the phrase 'remotely piloted aircraft' (RPA) and other acronyms, see eg Drake, 'Current U.S. Air Force Drone Operations and Their Conduct in Compliance with International Humanitarian Law', 630 and fn 2; Chris Jenks, 'Law From Above: Unmanned Aerial Systems, Use of Force, and the Law of Armed Conflict' (2009) 85 *North Dakota Law Review* 649, 653 (using the acronym UAS, for Unmanned Aerial Systems).

[13] See Drake, 'Current U.S. Air Force Drone Operations and Their Conduct in Compliance with International Humanitarian Law', 630 (the US has used drones during the last 50 years for reconnaissance and to safely observe the battlefield), 638–9 (outlining some uses of RPA for intelligence-gathering during war); Jenks, 'Law From Above: Unmanned Aerial Systems, Use of Force, and the Law of Armed Conflict', 654 and fn 22 (Hezbollah used drones along the Israel–Lebanon border during war in 2006).

[14] eg some police departments are keen on acquiring drones for surveillance, investigation, and other law enforcement purposes. Drones will also be used for public and private security and investigation, espionage, news gathering, automobile traffic information, weather monitoring, private witnessing of events, crop dusting, and other purposes. See also 'Video and Human Rights: Visibility Before All', *The Economist*, 14 Jan 2012, 48 ('Organizers of Occupy protests in America have used' drone helicopters 'to spot weaknesses in police lines' and to take aerial pictures); 'Drones Set to Play an Important Role Fighting Terrorism', *China Daily*, 20 May 2011 (online) (China is likely to use more drones for security purposes, including reconnaissance along border areas and in municipalities 'for use in emergencies, for the monitoring of traffic and the pursuit of suspects'); Scanning the Future of Law Enforcement' (2010) 44 *Futurist* 22 ('unmanned robots and drones... could be used by gangs and other criminal elements to attack their prey or one another. Low-cost airships or small submarines could be used to transport narcotics and other contraband... [and] hinder efforts to assign responsibility'); Editorial, 'Big Brother', *National Post*, 7 Oct 2008, A16 ('British police... employ cameras mounted on remote-controlled mini-drones to fly above crowds and look for suspicious activity'); Damian Inwood, 'Massive Security Planned for Games', *Vancouver Province*, 21 May 2008, A3 (use of drones and cameras with face-recognition capabilities during Canadian Olympic Games).

along its borders,[15] and in other countries and over the high seas.[16] For example, it has been reported that the US Central Intelligence Agency (CIA) used an RQ-170 Sentinel drone in Iranian airspace for surveillance of possible nuclear weapons production activities by Iran and that the drone may have been taken down or flown and landed through a cyber-attack, jamming, or hijacked control of the drone.[17] In Afghanistan, soldiers have flown model airplanes over areas that they were about to enter in order to provide needed intelligence. In the future, 'observant machines' that can recognize, observe, and analyse human beings, especially through facial observation and analysis, can be 'Mounted on small robots or drones' and used for law enforcement, national security, and military operations.[18]

III. Possible Challenges to Compliance with Basic Legal Principles that Limit Violence

As noted, drones have been used relatively recently in human history as platforms on which various types of weapons have been utilized during war and measures of self-defence. They can come in various sizes,[19] and in the future some will predictably be the size of a dragonfly. Some drones and other robotics are also likely to use increasingly sophisticated computerized forms of intelligence-gathering and analysis for decision-making with respect to identification and engagement of targets during war and self-defence, perhaps even with a completely autonomous

[15] eg drones have been used along the US border with Mexico for surveillance with respect to smuggling and other unlawful activities.

[16] NGOs can use drones to verify, monitor, and document human rights violations and international crimes. See eg Andrew Stobo Sniderman and Mark Hanis, 'Drones for Human Rights', *New York Times*, 31 Jan 2012, A25 ('Drones are increasingly small, affordable and available to nonmilitary buyers... An environmental group, the Sea Shepherd Conservation Society, has reported that it is using drones to monitor illegal Japanese whaling'). One can predict that state, regional, and UN forces will do the same.

[17] See eg Tim Lister, 'Crashed Drone Was Looking at Iran Nuclear Sites', *CNN*, 15 Dec 2011, available at <http://security.blogs.cnn.com/2011/12/15/crashed-drone-was-looking-at-iran-nuclear-sites>; Rick Gladstone, 'Stop U.S. Drone Flights, Iran Warns Afghanistan', *New York Times*, 16 Dec 2011, A11; 'US, Iran Take War to Cyber Space', *Hindustan Times*, 15 Dec 2011 (online); Saeed Kamali Dehghan, 'Iran Announces Exhibition of US Spy Drone—and Six Others', *The Guardian*, 16 Dec 2011, 33.

[18] Steve Lohr, 'Smarter Than You Think; Computers That See You, Read You and Even Tell You to Wash', *New York Times*, 2 Jan 2011, A1.

[19] See eg Blank, 'After Top Gun', 678; Jenks, "Law From Above', 653; Lin, Bekey, and Abney, 'Autonomous Military Robotics', 11–19; Gary E. Marchant et al, 'International Governance of Autonomous Military Robots' (2011) 12 *Columbia Science and Technology Law Review* 272, 276–8.

decisional, learning, and operational capability.[20] Are there identifiable challenges posed by the foreseeable development and increasing availability and use of drones and other robotics? Will their increased use require changes in the laws of war or the *jus ad bellum*, especially with respect to the need to adhere to basic legal principles that limit violence and its effects?

Presently, it is not generally expected that use of drones for targeting during war will require a change in the laws of war,[21] and it is not generally expected that related use for targeting during permissible measures of self-defence will require a change in the law of self-defence.[22] Nonetheless, their use has raised questions with respect to the ease of going to war,[23] the ease of killing human beings, and application of

[20] See eg Drake, 'Current U.S. Air Force Drone Operations and Their Conduct in Compliance with International Humanitarian Law', 652 (some weapons that are already in use are 'capable of operating, essentially in fully autonomous modes', such as the US Navy's Phalanx Close-In Weapons System (CIWS) that 'automatically performs "search, detect, evaluation, track, engage and kill assessment functions"', and the US Army's Counter Rocket, Artillery, and Mortar system (C-RAM) that is employed on land and that must be used in a manner that does not result in indiscriminate death, injury, or suffering); Michael W. Lewis, 'Response, Law and Ethics for Robot Soldiers', *Opinio Juris Blog*, 2 May 2012 ('CIWS on naval vessels are already examples of automated defensive weapons systems designed to hit incoming missiles, although the decision to turn the CIWS to automatic mode is still made by a human being'), available at <http://opiniojuris.org/2012/05/01/law-and-ethics-for-robot-soldiers>; Lin, Bekey and Abney, 'Autonomous Military Robotics', 7, 11–19; Marchant et al, 'International Governance of Autonomous Military Robots', 276–8, 286–7 (addressing types of lethal autonomous robots (LARS)).

[21] See eg Lewis, 'Drones and the Boundaries of the Battlefield', 295 ('there is nothing legally unique about using unmanned drones as a weapons delivery platform that requires the creation of new or different laws'), 297–8; Michael A. Newton, 'Flying into the Future: Drone Warfare and the Changing Face of Humanitarian Law' (2011) 39 *Denver Journal of International Law and Policy* 601, 605–6; Mary Ellen O'Connell, 'The Resort to Drones Under International Law' (2011) 39 *Denver Journal of International Law and Policy* 585, 599 (current law is adequate); Schmitt, 'Drone Attacks Under the *Jus ad Bellum* and *Jus in Bello*'; Markus Wagner, 'Taking Humans Out of the Loop: Implications for International Humanitarian Law' (2011) 21 *Journal of Law, Science and Technology* (but stating that fully autonomous weapons are unable to make qualitative assessments and are presently 'legally indefensible'); Kenneth Anderson, 'Law and Ethics for Robot Soldiers', *Opinio Juris Blog*, 1 May 2012 (urging 'a gradually evolving pattern of practices of the states developing the systems... through increased reasoned articulation of how and why highly particular technically detailed weapons systems meet fundamental legal standards'); cf Marchant et al, 'International Governance of Autonomous Military Robots', 298 (some call for a new treaty to limit use of lethal autonomous robots).

[22] See generally Blank, 'After Top Gun', 679; Laurie R. Blank and Benjamin R. Farley, 'Characterizing US Operations in Pakistan: Is the United States Engaged in an Armed Conflict?' (2011) 34 *Fordham International Law Journal* 151, 152–3; Paust, 'Permissible Self-Defense Targeting and the Death of bin Laden', 572–3; Schmitt, 'Drone Attacks Under the *Jus ad Bellum* and *Jus in Bello*'.

[23] See eg Afsheen John Radsan and Richard Murphy, 'The Evolution of Law and Policy for CIA Targeted Killing' (2012) 5 *Journal of National Security Law and Policy* 439, 441 ('The lower "costs" of drone strikes... encourage governments to resort to deadly force more quickly—a trend that may accelerate as drone technology rapidly improves and perhaps becomes fully automated through advances in artificial intelligence', and paradoxically, might 'lead to an increase in deadly mistakes'); see also Lin, Bekey, and Abney, 'Autonomous Military Robotics', 46, 75; Marchant et al, 'International Governance of Autonomous Military Robots', 285; O'Connell, 'The Resort to Drones Under International Law', 599 ('We do not have a full study of the psychological impact on operators or on our leaders of this new technology—some indicators suggest it is leading to more killing'); Noel Sharkey, 'Robot Wars as a Reality', *The Guardian*, 18 Aug 2007, 29.

general principles that condition permissible use of force under the laws of war and *jus ad bellum*.

Moreover, there are at least two predictable developments in drone technology that raise concerns whether drones will be sufficiently controlled and permit compliance with general principles of necessity, distinction, and proportionality. First, there is concern that some drones will become completely autonomous and will be used to hunt and quickly eliminate human beings and objects within the matrix of programmed targets. Presently, drones used for targeting during war and self-defence are operated by human beings, and there are often others who can participate in decisions concerning target identification and whether to engage a particular target. Drones often have the capability to fly over an area for hours, allowing nuanced human choice with respect to all features of context,[24] including those concerning identification of the target; the importance of the target; whether equally effective alternative methods of targeting or capture exist; the presence, proximity, and number of civilians who are not targetable; whether some civilians are voluntary or coerced human shields; the precision in targeting that can obtain; and foreseeable consequences with respect to civilian death, injury, or suffering.[25]

Some foresee a growing use of on-board computers to locate targets, provide valuable contextual input, and coordinate with other drones and aircraft, but assume that human beings will still make needed choices concerning proper application of the principles of distinction and proportionality and whether a target should even be engaged under the circumstances.[26] Others foresee a problematic future use of

[24] See n 9.

[25] These are among appropriate considerations for choice and compliance with the principles of reasonable necessity, distinction, and proportionality. See eg Geoffrey S. Corn and Lieutenant Colonel Gary P. Corn, 'The Law of Operational Targeting: Viewing the LOAC Through an Operational Lens' (2012) 47 *Texas International Law Journal* 337, 342–3, 349–53, 362–6, 370–1, 380 (often emphasizing the need for human 'operational art' and adequate awareness of many contextual variables); Amos N. Guiora, 'Determining a Legitimate Target: The Dilemma of the Decision-Maker' (2012) 47 *Texas International Law Journal* 315, 322–3, 331–6; Paust, 'Permissible Self-Defense Targeting and the Death of bin Laden', 576; Paust, 'Self-Defense Targetings of Non-State', 275–7; Afsheen John Radsan and Richard Murphy, 'Measure Twice, Shoot Once: Higher Care for CIA Targeted Killing' (2011) *University of Illinois Law Review* 101 (addressing a six-step US military decisional and review process with respect to drone and related types of targeting and suggesting similar choice-making by CIA personnel); Radsan and Murphy, 'The Evolution of Law and Policy for CIA Targeted Killing', 459, 461–2 (also warning that choice cannot be made 'with mathematical certainty—in part because such judgments implicate contestable facts and competing values'); see also Marchant et al, 'International Governance of Autonomous Military Robots', 285 (doubts exist whether autonomous robots will be capable of making appropriate choices and avoiding indiscriminate killing and wounding).

[26] See eg 'Autonomous Vehicles: Robot Wars' ('Everyone talks about there being a human in the loop', quoting Noel Sharkey, a professor of artificial intelligence and robotics); Marchant et al, 'International Governance of Autonomous Military Robots', 275–6 ('military systems (including weapons) now on the horizon will be too fast, too small, too numerous, and will create an environment too complex for humans to direct', quoting Thomas K. Adams, 'Future Warfare and the Decline of Human Decisionmaking' (2001–2) *Parameters, US Army War College Quarterly* 57–5), 283–5.

drones that are completely autonomous and, if they do not kill and destroy needlessly because of computer glitches,[27] they might kill and destroy without adequate consideration of all relevant features of context despite possible increased sophistication in their programming. Their use would surely be 'smarter' than use of dumb spring-guns,[28] but not without foreseeably deleterious consequences. In fact, some systems can be placed in an autonomous mode by a human decision-maker and then hunt for human or material targets in a defensive or offensive manner.[29] Depending on their capabilities, smart autonomous hunting drones and other hunting robots might be blind with respect to the need to comply with customary principles of distinction and proportionality. When released in an area, they might hunt all humans or all relevant objects indiscriminately, and they might cross borders[30] in ways that violate UN Charter precepts.

One can envision use of fully autonomous aerial, land, and naval mines that do not stay in one place and actually hunt without human supervision. Aerial and naval hunting mines might be used for defensive purposes in an area, but if fully automated they might destroy civilian and neutral governmental aircraft and vessels in violation of international law. If the aircraft or vessels are foreign registered or foreign flagged, their destruction would be the equivalent of destruction of foreign territory[31] and could constitute a use of force in violation of the Charter.[32] Hunting drones might not have the capacity to distinguish between aircraft that have been warned away but keep coming and aircraft that have turned away and are no longer reasonably expected to be engaged in an attack that can trigger the right of self-defence.[33]

With respect to mines, the International Court of Justice (ICJ) has recognized that the laying of mines in the territory of another state can constitute a breach of customary international law prohibiting the use of armed force against another state[34] and that 'the mining of a single military vessel' might trigger the inherent right of self-defence.[35] One remedy with respect to errant drones and mines that are known to be crossing a border or about to unlawfully attack foreign aircraft or

[27] Concerning certain past failures, see eg Lin, Bekey, Abney, 'Autonomous Military Robotics', 7.

[28] As older generations of the legally trained might recall, use of spring-guns to guard property had famously led to criminal prosecutions for reckless and negligent homicide and to private lawsuits.

[29] Recall n 20.

[30] This problem has been recognized. See Lin, Bekey, and Abney, 'Autonomous Military Robotics', 23 (adding that the problem can occur even with aerial robotics that use stored maps and GPS guidance).

[31] That aircraft and vessels are the equivalent of the territory of the flag under international law, see eg *The SS Lotus*, 1927 PCIJ, Ser A, No 10 (a Turkish vessel was assimilated to Turkish territory); *Hirsi Jamaa and Others v. Italy* (App no 27765/09), ECtHR, 23 Feb 2012 (Grand Chamber); Jordan J. Paust et al, *International Criminal Law* (3rd edn, Leiden: Brill, 2007), 175–6; *R v. Anderson* (1868) 11 Cox CC 198 (UK Court of Criminal Appeal).

[32] See Section IV.A.

[33] With respect to such a distinction and self-defence, see eg Jordan J. Paust, 'A Critical Appraisal of the Air and Missile Warfare Manual' (2012) 47 *Texas International Law Journal* 277, 286, and fn 50.

[34] *Nicaragua*, 146, para 292(6).

[35] See n 11.

vessels could involve use of a human override capability to destroy or regain control over an errant drone or mine. An ability to turn off naval and land-based mines would be useful, for example to avoid damage to and destruction of hospital and neutral ships and ambulances.

Secondly, it has been reported that research 'is headed away from single drones and towards a co-ordinated team or swarm of vehicles with a specified mission and location ... a swarm of robots', and that 'inevitably there will be more autonomy; the robots will be required to make more decisions.'[36] It is also foreseeable that with respect to swarms, a human can provide the initial order to a swarm, but 'drones in the armed swarm would work out between them which element would enact an attack order.'[37] Quite possibly, use of a swarm might pose greater danger with respect to computer glitches and the need for nuanced decision-making with respect to identification and engagement of particular targets. Nonetheless, the swarm can prove to be valuable with respect to some forms of lawful uses of offensive and defensive force. Basic legal norms do not need to be changed, but efforts should be made to assure the existence of adequate computerized and human controls and the development of rules of engagement (ROE) to restrain their actual use. Wanton and reckless disregard of consequences can lead to criminal and civil sanctions,[38] but these can occur with respect to misuse of any weapons system.

IV. Drone Targeting and Charter-Based Precepts

A. Challenges to Charter-Based Purposes and Principles

1. *Force in the common interest*

Among general issues identified is concern whether increased availability and use of drones will lead to an increase in the use of armed force by states, either unilaterally or in cooperation with others.[39] If the government of a particular state uses drones to target enemies in war and in self-defence, there can be a lessening of

[36] 'Autonomous Vehicles: Robot Wars'. [37] 'Autonomous Vehicles: Robot Wars'.

[38] See eg Paust et al, *International Criminal Law*, 696–8; Drake, 'Current U.S. Air Force Drone Operations and Their Conduct in Compliance with International Humanitarian Law', 652–3, 657–8.

[39] See n 23.

the loss of lives of its citizens and those of other countries, but will this outcome result in an increased use of armed force by states? Actually, the decision whether to engage in permissible war will likely be far more complex and a state's choice, for example, to merely use drones will not be determinative. Perhaps some states with drone capability will be tempted to use force more readily against weaker enemies, but this remains uncertain.

If drones make it easier for a state to use force or go to war, this will clearly have an impact on a stated purpose of the peoples of the UN 'to save succeeding generations from the scourge of war' and to assure 'that armed force shall not be used, save in the common interest.'[40] It may or may not also impact negatively with respect to decisions of regional organizations to authorize the use of armed force as part of lawful 'regional action' under Article 52 of the Charter or decisions of the Security Council to authorize the use of armed force as part of lawful 'enforcement action' under Article 42 of the Charter. However, at least choice-making by regional organizations and the Security Council will avoid problems connected with unilateralist decision-making and, on balance in specific contexts, might generally serve the common interest despite the fact that forms of violence are being authorized. Moreover, to be lawful measures of violence, regional organizations and the Security Council must make their decisions in accordance with the purposes and principles of the UN Charter.[41]

2. *Force and Article 2(4)*

It may also be the case that some who prefer that minor uses of force across borders should not be of sufficient gravity, expanse, and duration to constitute a use of armed force within the meaning of Article 2(4) of the Charter will be prone to conclude that intentional, short-lived, and precise targeting by a drone across a border will not constitute a violation of Article 2(4). If their viewpoint is generally preferred, this type of conclusion might lead to an increased use of drones for precise cross-border targetings even when targetings are not justifiable as measures of self-defence. With respect to errant hunting, drones that cross into the territory of another state and impermissibly target human beings or objects or that impermissibly destroy civilian and governmental aircraft or vessels, would most likely not come under the first two prohibitions addressed in Article 2(4) because, even if such outcomes were foreseeable or the result of wanton disregard, there

[40] UN Charter, Preamble.

[41] See UN Charter, Art 24(2) ('the Security Council shall act in accordance with the Purposes and Principles of the United Nations'), 25 ('The Members of the United Nations agree to accept and carry out the decisions of the Security Council in accordance with the present Charter'), 52 ('regional action' can be taken by regional organizations, 'provided... [that such] activities are consistent with the Purposes and Principles of the United Nations'). Such purposes and principles include, among others, the need to assure that armed force shall not be used save in the common interest and the need to serve peace, security, self-determination of peoples, and human rights. See Preamble, Arts 1, 55.

would not be an intentional use of armed force 'against' the territorial integrity or political independence of another state or the equivalent of its territory—assuming that the word 'against' requires an intent to do so. Nonetheless, the third (and only other[42]) prohibition addressed in Article 2(4) might not rest on a need for intended outcomes. The third prohibition encompasses the use of force 'in any other manner inconsistent with the Purposes of the United Nations.'[43] The phrase 'inconsistent with' necessarily requires contextual and policy-serving inquiry and may not demand intent to produce such an outcome. Since the purposes of the UN include the need to assure that armed force not be used save in the common interest and the need to serve peace, security, self-determination, and human rights,[44] it may be that the decision to deploy hunter drones in wanton or reckless disregard of foreseeable consequences that are inconsistent with the purposes of the UN will constitute a prohibited use of armed force under the third provision in Article 2(4).

3. *Force in self-defence*

One can assume that use of drones by states in self-defence outside the context of war will not increase the frequency of violent measures of self-defence because permissibility under Article 51 of the Charter is limited by the need for an 'armed attack' to have taken place or for a process of armed attacks to continue,[45] as well as the need for compliance with general principles of reasonable necessity, distinction, and proportionality.[46] Nonetheless, an increased availability of 'weaponized' drones for non-state actors (especially those bent on achieving outcomes of terror) might

[42] Concerning the express prohibition of merely three types of armed force under Art 2(4) of the Charter, see eg Paust, 'Use of Armed Force Against Terrorists', 536–7; see also John Norton Moore et al, *National Security Law* (Durham, NC: Carolina Academic Press, 1990), 131; Anthony D'Amato, 'The Invasion of Panama Was a Lawful Response to Tyranny' (1990) 84 *American Journal of International Law* 516, 520; Michael Reisman and Myres S. McDougal, 'Humanitarian Intervention to Protect the Ibos' in Richard B. Lillich (ed), *Humanitarian Intervention and the United Nations* (Charlottesville, VA: University Press of Virginia, 1973), 166, 177; Carsten Stahn, 'Enforcement of the Collective Will After Iraq' (2003) 97 *American Journal of International Law* 803, 816. But see Dinstein, *War, Aggression and Self-Defence*, 87–8; O'Connell, 'The Resort to Drones Under International Law', 589 (preferring all force above '*de minimis*'); Christian J. Tams, 'The Use of Force Against Terrorists' (2009) 20 *European Journal of International law* 359, 364–5 (also noting early and decades long disagreement), 375.

[43] UN Charter, Art 2(4). To conclude that this phrase precludes all uses of armed force ignores the fact that some armed force may be 'inconsistent with' the purposes of the UN whereas others may, on balance, be consistent. Eg force may thwart peace in the short run but serve peace in the long term as well as regional security, self-determination of peoples, and human rights. Therefore, the phrase 'inconsistent with' necessarily demands awareness of context and whether UN purposes are generally being thwarted or served. See Paust, 'Use of Armed Force Against Terrorists', 536–7 (also noting, however, that mere 'preemptive or retaliatory' uses of force are widely expected to be impermissible).

[44] See n 41.

[45] With respect to the express need for an armed attack, see eg Dinstein, *War, Aggression and Self-Defence*, 183–5; Paust, 'Use of Armed Force Against Terrorists', 534 and fn 2. However, the equally authentic French version of Art 51 speaks about the existence of an *agression armée* (ie an armed aggression). See Paust, 'Self-Defense Targetings of Non-State Actors', 241 fn 4.

[46] See n 10.

lead to an increased use of non-state actor armed attacks on states, their embassies abroad, and their military personnel and other nationals abroad that trigger the inherent right of self-defence,[47] but this is difficult to predict given the fact that over the last few decades several non-state actors have engaged in such armed attacks without the use of drones and it is generally expected that so-called asymmetric warfare and violence will increase in any event. However, some who prefer that an 'armed attack' be of significant gravity[48] before it triggers the inherent right of self-defence may have to change their preference as limited forms of non-state actor armed attacks increase and in reality require immediate and precise responsive uses of force that can be achieved through use of drones, whether or not the non-state actor attacks are terroristic in purpose and effect or amount to measures of asymmetric war across national borders. Restrictivist interpretations can encourage non-state actors to attack across borders and provide functional safe havens.

A hypothetical from another publication demonstrates the point that even a few relatively low-level rocket attacks by non-state actors across borders will likely be considered by states to constitute armed attacks even if others debate whether they are of significant 'gravity' and effect. For real-world decision-makers who see their fellow nationals being killed, injured, and terrorized, a supposed gravity limitation will be simply unavailing.

> Consider the circumstance where a non-state terrorist group acquires rockets capable of striking short-range targets and starts firing them from Mexico (without the consent of the Government of Mexico or prior foreseeability) into Fort Bliss, a U.S. military base near El Paso, Texas. Must the United States actually obtain a special express consent of the Mexican Government or already be engaged in a war with the terrorist group (if that is even possible) before resorting to a selective use of force in self-defense to silence the terrorist attacks on U.S. military personnel and other U.S. nationals? I doubt that any state under such a process of armed attack would wait while the rocket attacks continue or expect that

[47] See Paust, 'Self-Defense Targetings of Non-State Actors', 238–41 and fn 3 (noting that the vast majority of text-writers recognize that armed attacks by non-state actors can trigger the inherent right of self-defence).

[48] See also *Nicaragua*, 101, para 191 (need 'to distinguish the most grave forms of the use of force (those constituting an armed attack) from other less grave forms'); *Oil Platforms*, 187, para 51 (quoting *Nicaragua*, para 72), 195, para 72 (quoted in n 11); Dinstein, *War, Aggression and Self-Defence*, 193, 195 ('it would be fallacious to dismiss automatically from consideration as an armed attack every frontier incident', such as when a soldier fires a single bullet across a border or a small military unit is attacked; 'The gravity of an attack may affect the proper scope of defensive use of force…, but it is not relevant to determining whether there is a right of self-defense in the first instance' (quoting William H. Taft, IV, former Legal Adviser to the US Secretary of State); 'even a small border incident' can constitute an armed attack (quoting J. L. Kunz)), 202 (cumulative 'pin-prick' attacks can be viewed as a process of armed attack), 230–1; Gardam, *Necessity, Proportionality and the Use of Force by States*, 143, 161; Tams, 'The Use of Force Against Terrorists', 370 and fns 69, 71 (noting that a gravity threshold articulated in 1986 'remained controversial', citing Dahm, Dinstein, Feder, Gazzini, and Randelzhofer), 379–81 (noting new practice of states). I agree with Dinstein, Kunz, Taft, and others who recognize the need to abandon an unrealistic gravity limitation.

under international law it must wait to engage in selective self-defense against the attackers. Furthermore, I doubt that any state would expect that it cannot engage in measures of self-defense to stop such rocket attacks if it had not been and cannot be at war with non-state terrorist attackers or that it cannot take such defensive measures if it is not otherwise engaged in a relevant armed conflict.

Certainly the President of the US would try to communicate as soon as possible with the President of Mexico and others concerning what is happening and the fact that the US is not attacking Mexico, but the US President would not have to wait for a formal response while rockets are raining down on US soldiers. Additionally, although it would be polite, the US would not have to warn Mexican authorities before engaging in selective measures of self-defence to stop continuing attacks. Under various circumstances, a warning can be impracticable, futile, and/or create complications threatening the success of a self-defence response, especially in other contexts if a special operations unit is being used for reconnaissance or to carry out the self-defence action.[49]

B. Some Present Applications and Issues Regarding Compliance

Weaponized drones have been used during war and otherwise in self-defence. Has their use necessarily resulted in violations of the UN Charter, as some suggest?[50] Issues have arisen concerning application of various articles of the Charter to actual drone targetings, but it is apparent that whether or not there has been a use of drones should not be critical to informed and policy-serving inquiry—especially since there are and will be various types of drones that might use various types of weapons.

Use of drones for targeting in self-defence (whether or not such occurs also in the context of war) has been controversial for some but has also led to reaffirmation of several important aspects of permissible self-defence. For example, the vast majority of text-writers have affirmed that non-state actor armed attacks can trigger the right of self-defence addressed in Article 51 of the Charter even if selective responsive force directed against a non-state actor occurs within a foreign country,[51] and

[49] Paust, 'Self-Defense Targetings of Non-State Actors', 255–6. See also n 48.

[50] Consider O'Connell, 'The Resort to Drones Under International Law', 589, 592–4, 599.

[51] See n 47. If responsive force is directed merely against the non-state actors who are perpetrating ongoing armed attacks, the use of force against them in a foreign state in compliance with Art 51 of the UN Charter is not a use of force against the foreign state, an attack 'on' or 'against' its territory, or a use of force in violation of its territorial 'integrity' within the meaning of Art 2(4) and, moreover, the two states would not be at war. See eg Paust, 'Self-Defense Targetings of Non-State Actors', 256, 258–9, 279. Importantly, there are no geographic limits with respect to armed attacks that trigger the inherent right of self-defence. Eg an armed attack by a group that initiates a war between a nation or people and a state, a belligerency, or an insurgency within a single state can justify use of responsive

nothing in the language of Article 51 restricts the right to engage in self-defence to circumstances of armed attacks by a state.[52] Moreover, nothing in the language of the Charter requires a conclusion lacking in common sense that a state being attacked can only defend itself within its own borders. General patterns of pre-Charter and post-Charter practice and general patterns of *opinio juris* affirm these points as well as the fact that a state being attacked does not need special express consent of the state from which non-state actor armed attacks emanate and on whose territory a self-defence drone targeting takes place against the non-state actor.[53] Additionally, it would be demonstrably incorrect to claim that a state has no right to defend itself outside its own territory absent (1) attribution or imputation of non-state actor attacks to the foreign state when the foreign state is in control of non-state actor attacks,[54] or (2) the existence of a relevant international or non-international armed conflict.[55] Moreover, the inherent right of self-defence in case of an armed attack is not limited to a circumstance where the state from whose territory a non-state actor armed attack emanates is unwilling or unable to control its territory.[56] Conversely, the mere existence of such a circumstance does not justify the use of armed force in a foreign state without its consent if, for example, the right of self-defence has not been triggered because there has been no armed attack or process of armed attacks.

As noted in another publication, with respect to the need to serve various policies at stake in the context of continual non-state actor armed attacks, including peace,

armed force in self-defence. See also Paust, 'Use of Armed Force Against Terrorists', 534 ('nothing in the language of Article 51 requires that such an armed attack be carried out by another state, nation, or belligerent, as opposed to armed attacks by various other non-state actors'); Jordan J. Paust and Albert P. Blaustein, 'War Crimes Jurisdiction and Due Process: The Bangladesh Experience' (1978) 11 *Vanderbilt Journal of Transnational Law* 1, 11 fn 39 (where an armed attack occurs by a government against a people undergoing a process of self-determination, such people should have the right of self-defense and the right to seek self-determination assistance in accordance with the principles and purposes of the UN Charter).

[52] See eg Dinstein, *War, Aggression and Self-Defence*, 184–5, 204–8; Paust, 'Self-Defense Targetings of Non-State Actors', 241 and fn 5. Importantly also, international law has never been merely state to state. See eg Jordan J. Paust, 'Nonstate Actor Participation in International Law and the Pretense of Exclusion' (2011) 51 *Vanderbilt Journal of International Law* 977; Paust, 'A Critical Appraisal of the Air and Missile Warfare Manual', 279–81.

[53] See Paust, 'Self-Defense Targetings of Non-State Actors', 241–9, 251–2; Paust, 'Permissible Self-Defense Targeting and the Death of bin Laden', 569–70; Michael N. Schmitt, 'Responding to Transnational Terrorism Under the Jus ad Bellum: A Normative Framework' in Michael N. Schmitt and Jelena Pejic (eds), *International Law and Armed Conflict: Exploring the Faultlines: Essays in Honour of Yoram Dinstein* (Leiden: Martinus Nijhoff, 2007), 167–8, 176–7. General consent by all members of the UN exists in advance in Art 51 of the Charter for permissible measures of self-defence and no special ad hoc consent is required.

[54] See Dinstein, *War, Aggression and Self-Defence*, 206; Paust, 'Permissible Self-Defense Targeting and the Death of bin Laden', 570.

[55] Paust, 'Self-Defense Targetings of Non-State Actors', 249–58, 279–80; and see n 51.

[56] Paust, 'Permissible Self-Defense Targeting and the Death of bin Laden', 580–1. Nonetheless, the fact that a non-state actor attack has occurred across a border might be sufficient to demonstrate that the state was unable to control its territory.

security, human rights, and effective opposition to international crime, it is important to note that state sovereignty:

> is not absolute under international law or impervious to its reach, territorial integrity of the state is merely one of the values preferred in the U.N. Charter, and permissible measures of self-defense under Article 51 of the Charter that are reasonably necessary and proportionate against actual armed violence must necessarily override the general impermissibility that attaches to armed intervention.[57]

One should also note that the self-defence paradigm is different from both a mere law of war paradigm applicable during armed conflict and a law enforcement paradigm, and self-defence targetings and captures can occur with respect to those who are direct participants in armed attacks (DPAAs) whether or not an armed conflict exists that would also allow the targeting and capture of persons who are combatants, civilians who are direct participants in hostilities (DPHs), or civilians who are unprivileged fighters engaged in a continuous combat function.[58] Clearly, selective use of armed force as part of permissible self-defence is not simplistically 'law enforcement' or limited by what would only be authorized during law enforcement, whether or not lawful use of force in self-defence is undertaken in time of war or relative peace.

V. Conclusion

Use of remotely piloted and other robotics during war and otherwise outside the context of war during permissible measures of self-defence is likely to increase, and their use by non-state actors is foreseeable. Such uses will pose challenges for some regarding interpretation of Articles 2(4) and 51 of the UN Charter and application of underlying general principles, but it is generally expected that increased use will not require changes in the laws of war or the law of self-defence. Yet, use of autonomous robotics can lead to violations and effort should be made to assure adequate computerized and human controls.

[57] Paust, 'Permissible Self-Defense Targeting and the Death of bin Laden', 570–1; Paust, 'Self-Defense Targetings of Non-State Actors', 256–7 and fns 47–8. Art 51 of the Charter is itself an agreed upon diminution of sovereignty.

[58] See Paust, 'Self-Defense Targetings of Non-State Actors', 260–9, 271–3, 275, 279–80.

CHAPTER 52

THE USE OF CYBER FORCE AND INTERNATIONAL LAW

MICHAEL N. SCHMITT*

I. Introduction

IN the 1990s, a number of advanced states began to focus their military research and development efforts on cyber capabilities. At the same time, the use of cyber force on and off the battlefield captured the attention of war colleges, staff colleges, and other institutions devoted to strategic and operational-level thinking. Unfortunately, the legal community lagged behind. Indeed, the first major conference on cyber operations and international law was not held until 1999.[1] Just as meaningful examination of the normative implications of cyber warfare began, the attacks of 11 September 2001 diverted the legal community's concern to the law of counterterrorism.

* The views expressed in this chapter are those of the author alone and do not necessarily represent those of the US government. The author is grateful for the research and editorial advice offered by First Lieutenant Christopher Markham, USMC.

[1] The Conference was held at the United States Naval War College. See Michel Schmitt and Brian O'Donnell (eds), 'Computer Network Attack and International Law' (2002) 76 *International Law Studies*.

The massive 'hacktivist' cyber operations against Estonia in 2008 refocused the attention of state legal advisers and academia alike.[2] To foster sophisticated analysis of the law governing cyber conflict, in 2009 the North Atlantic Treaty Organization (NATO) Cooperative Cyber Defence Centre of Excellence invited a group of 20 senior international legal practitioners and scholars (the 'International Group of Experts') to explore both the *jus ad bellum* (law governing the use of force) and *jus in bello* (international humanitarian law) aspects of cyberspace. This author served as director of that project, the result of which was the *Tallinn Manual on the International Law Applicable to Cyber Warfare*.[3] As subsequent cyber incidents, from the so-called 'Stuxnet' attacks of 2010 against Iran to the 2013 Mandiant report's allegations of Chinese government complicity in cyber operations against the US, have demonstrated, cyber conflict is an area of legal scholarship that is more relevant today than ever before.[4]

This chapter draws directly on the work of the *Tallinn Manual* to address the *jus ad bellum* issues surrounding cyber operations. There are two central questions in this area. First, when do cyber operations violate the prohibition on the use (or threat) of force set forth in Article 2(4) of the UN Charter and customary international law? Secondly, when may a state against which cyber operations have been used respond with its own use of force? In addressing these issues, it must be noted that the *Tallinn Manual*, and by extension this chapter, is meant to capture the *lex lata* governing cyber operations. Many members of the International Group of Experts that authored the manual, including this author, believe that interpretation and application of the current norms will evolve through state practice, perhaps with some dispatch, as cyber operations play a growing role in interstate relations, are leveraged by non-state actors, and find their way onto the battlefield.

II. The Prohibition of the Use of Cyber Force

Analysis of the *jus ad bellum* in the context of cyber operations necessarily begins with the threshold question of whether that law extends at all to such operations.

[2] For an excellent discussion of the attacks, see Eneken Tikk, Kadri Kaska, and Liis Vihul, *International Cyber Incidents: Legal Considerations* (Tallinn: Cooperative Cyber Defence Centre of Excellence, 2010), 14–33.

[3] Michael Schmitt (ed), *Tallinn Manual on the International Law Applicable to Cyber Warfare* (Cambridge: Cambridge University Press, 2013).

[4] Mandiant Intelligence Center, 'APT1: Exposing one of China's espionage units', 2013, available at <http://intelreport.mandiant.com/Mandiant_APT1_Report.pdf>.

The conventional view, endorsed unanimously by the International Group of Experts, is that the *jus ad bellum* applies to certain cyber operations. This conclusion is based on the International Court of Justice's (ICJ) *Nuclear Weapons* advisory opinion, in which the Court held that the law on the use of force, including in cases of self-defence, governs 'any use of force, regardless of the weapons employed'.[5] By this approach, the *jus ad bellum* reaches qualifying cyber operations launched against a state, whether those operations occur in isolation or as part of an otherwise kinetic operation.[6] It also serves as the legal framework for forceful defensive actions taken by cyber means in the face of a cyber or kinetic armed attack, as well as to kinetic responses to cyber armed attacks. Although this view is almost universally accepted, the question remains as to how these norms apply in cyberspace.[7]

Article 2(4) of the UN Charter sets forth the contemporary international law prohibition of the use of force, and hence cyber uses of force, in interstate relations: 'All Members [of the United Nations] shall refrain in their international relations from the threat or use of force against the territorial integrity or political independence of any State, or in any other manner inconsistent with the Purposes of the United Nations'. In its *Nicaragua* judgment, the ICJ determined that this prohibition constituted a norm of customary international law; in the *Armed Activities* judgment, the Court labelled it 'the cornerstone of the Charter'.[8] The Charter contains two exceptions to the norm—uses of force authorized by the Security Council pursuant to Chapter VII and actions in self-defence in accordance with Article 51, both discussed later in the chapter.

Article 2(4) relates only to cyber operations conducted by states or otherwise attributable to them pursuant to the law of state responsibility.[9] Obviously, any

[5] *Legality of the Threat or Use of Nuclear Weapons*, Advisory Opinion of 8 July 1996, ICJ Rep 1996, 226, para 39.

[6] eg the US has taken the position that 'The development of norms for state conduct in cyberspace does not require a reinvention of customary international law, nor does it render existing international norms obsolete. Long-standing international norms guiding state behavior—in times of peace and conflict—also apply in cyberspace'. US President, *International Strategy for Cyberspace* (May 2011), available at <http://www.whitehouse.gov/sites/default/files/rss_viewer/international_strategy_for_cyberspace.pdf>.

[7] eg the US, has adopted the position that established principles of international law apply in cyberspace. Harold Honju Koh, Legal Adviser, Department of State of the USA, Remarks to the USCYBERCOM Inter-Agency Legal Conference, 18 Sept 2012, reprinted with annotations in (2012) 54 *Harvard International Law Journal Online* 1, 3. For an analysis of Koh's remarks in the light of the *Tallinn Manual* positions, see Michael Schmitt, 'International Law in Cyberspace: The Koh Speech and Tallinn Manual Juxtaposed' (2012) 54 *Harvard International Law Journal Online* 13.

[8] *Military and Paramilitary Activities in and against Nicaragua (Nicaragua v. US)*, Judgment of 27 June 1986, ICJ Rep 1986, 14, paras 188–90. *Armed Activities on the Territory of the Congo (DRC v. Uganda)*, Merits, ICJ Rep 2005, 168, para 148.

[9] *Tallinn Manual*, rule 10, para 4; Albrecht Randelzhofer and Oliver Dörr, 'Article 2(4)' in Bruno Simma et al (eds), *The Charter of the United Nations: A Commentary* (3rd edn, Oxford: Oxford University Press, 2012), 200, 213.

cyber operation carried out by an organ of the state, such as an intelligence agency or the military, is attributable to the state.[10] So too are cyber operations carried out by persons or entities that are empowered by domestic law to exercise 'governmental authority', such as private sector Computer Emergency Response Teams (or CERTS).[11] Beyond these self-evident cases, a cyber operation conducted by a group or by individuals is also attributable to a state when the relevant persons are 'acting on the instructions of, or under the direction or control of, that State in carrying out the conduct'.[12] Such attributability is especially relevant as states turn to the private sector to enhance their cyber capabilities. To the extent the respective state exercises a sufficient level of control over a private actor's activities, it bears legal responsibility for that actor's cyber operations that rise to the level of a use of force.[13]

Unfortunately, no authoritative definition of the use of force exists in international law. Some indication of the parameters of the concept can be derived from the negotiations that occurred during the Charter's drafting conference in 1945. Of particular note is the fact that the delegates rejected an argument that economic coercion should be encompassed in the prohibition.[14] This interpretation was reaffirmed during proceedings leading to the General Assembly's adoption of the Declaration on Friendly Relations, which excluded 'forms of pressure' of 'a political or economic character' from the ambit of a use of force.[15] Further, the ICJ determined in the *Nicaragua* judgment that funding guerrilla operations directed against another state did not rise to the level of a use of force, although it did violate the principle of non-intervention.[16] Drawing on these precedents, the International Group of Experts concluded that neither 'non-destructive cyber psychological operations intended solely to undermine confidence in a government or economy' nor the funding of hacktivist groups (groups conducting cyber operations for political purposes) qualified as uses of force.[17]

Yet, in *Nicaragua* the Court characterized arming and training guerrillas involved in operations against another state as a use of force.[18] This suggests that the concept

[10] International Law Commission (ILC), Responsibility of States for Internationally Wrongful Acts, Art 4, GA Res. 56/83, Annex, A/RES/56/83 (12 Dec 2001).

[11] Articles of State Responsibility, Art 5. [12] Articles of State Responsibility, Art 8.

[13] The requisite level of control is generally understood to be 'effective control'. *Nicaragua*, Judgment, para 115; See also *Application of the Convention on the Prevention and Punishment of the Crime of Genocide (Bosnia and Herzegovina v. Serbia and Montenegro)*, Judgment of 26 Feb 2007, ICJ Rep 2007, 108 paras 399–401.

[14] 6 UNCIO Docs 334, 609 (1945); Doc 2, 617(e)(4), 3 UNCIO Docs 251, 253–4 (1945).

[15] UN GAOR Special Committee on Friendly Relations, A/AC.125/SR.110 to 114 (1970). See also Report of the Special Committee on Friendly Relations and Cooperation Among States, 1969, UN GAOR, 24th Sess, Supp No 19, 12, A/7619 (1969). The draft declaration contained text tracking that of UN Charter, Art 2(4).

[16] *Nicaragua*, Judgment, para 228.

[17] *Tallinn Manual*, rule 11, para 3. For a discussion of the issue of economic and political activities, see Randelzhofer and Dörr, 'Article 2(4)' in Simma et al, *The Charter of the United Nations: A Commentary*, 208–10.

[18] *Nicaragua*, Judgment, para 228. This conclusion draws on the General Assembly's Friendly Relations Declaration, GA Res 2625 (XXV) (24 Oct 1970), A/RES/2625 (XXV).

of a use of force need not necessarily involve direct application of armed force by a state or by groups or individuals under its control. In the cyber context, for instance, providing a rebel group destructive malware and the training necessary to use it effectively could qualify as a use of force.

In the light of the relative paucity of guidance on the precise parameters of a use of force, the International Group of Experts adopted an approach designed to assist states in determining when the international community would likely characterize a cyber operation launched against them, or that they conducted, as a use of force.[19] In doing so, the Experts acknowledged that decisions as to use of force characterizations are often political, as well as normative, in nature. Over time, such decisions and the accompanying state practice inevitably mature into cleaner prescriptive norms. Until that occurs, the best states can do is to intelligently assess the probable depiction of a cyber incident by the international community.

Identification of eight factors likely to influence states in this regard lie at the heart of the approach: severity, immediacy, directness, invasiveness, measurability of effects, military character, state involvement, and presumptive legality.[20] Each assessment is context-dependent, meaning the weight attributed to the various factors depends on the circumstances in which the cyber operation being examined occurs. The factors highlighted are not meant to be exclusive; others may loom large in certain situations.

The most determinative factor is 'severity'. It is the only one that alone suffices to qualify a cyber operation as a use of force. States are highly likely to portray an operation that causes physical harm to individuals and property beyond the *de minimis* level as a use of force. An act not causing physical harm or injury may, as in the case of training and arming cyber activists to target another state, amount to a use of force depending upon its scope, duration, and intensity, when considered in light of, inter alia, the factors set forth later.

Under this approach, the nature of a cyber operation's consequences is highly relevant. The more immediate, direct, invasive, and measurable the attendant effects, the more liable states are to style the operation in question as a use of force. 'Immediacy' refers to the period between execution of the operation and the point at which consequences manifest. 'Directness' refers to the causal relationship between the cyber operation and any harm that ensues. 'Invasiveness' is the extent to which a cyber operation penetrates non-consensually into a state's protected cyber infrastructure. 'Measurability' is the ability to quantify harm caused by an operation.

For example, a cyber operation that immediately interferes with an ongoing operation of critical infrastructure is more likely to be deemed a use of force than one that only achieves the same effect over an extended period. Similarly, a cyber

[19] The approach was originally developed in Michael Schmitt, 'Computer Network and the Use of Force in International Law: Thoughts on a Normative Framework' (1999) 37 *Columbia Journal of Transnational Law* 885.

[20] *Tallinn Manual*, rule 11, para 9(a)–(h).

operation that directly causes massive economic losses by destroying banking data is more likely to be viewed as a use of force than one causing the same losses through undermining confidence in the economy. From a political standpoint, a cyber operation causing effects that can be precisely measured offers decision-makers a more supportable basis for labelling a particular operation a use of force than one with less quantifiable effects.

The 'presumptive legality' of an operation also bears on its characterization. As an example, economic pressure and psychological operations are generally considered lawful. Cyber operations launched with these ends in mind are less likely to be deemed a use of force than, for instance, those that, although not physically destructive, have military objectives. But it must be emphasized that the determination is contextual. Although economic coercion may be presumptively lawful, a cyber operation resulting in massive economic losses may nevertheless be styled by the international community as a use of force. The hypothetical case of a devastating attack on a state's stock market is often offered as the paradigmatic example. Of course, the political environment in which a cyber operation occurs is an important part of the contextual fabric. For instance, a cyber operation conducted by one state against another with which it has recently been involved in an armed conflict is more likely to be judged a use of force by the international community than the same act conducted by a state which has ongoing friendly relations with the target state.

Many other factors can bear on the ultimate depiction of a cyber operation. For instance, states are more likely to see cyber operations of a 'military character', such as those directed against military assets like command-and-control facilities or conducted by cyber units of the armed forces, as a use of force than those that appear civilian. This includes a cyber operation that intrudes into .mil networks as opposed to one that penetrates .edu, .com, or .org networks. Similarly, although a state must be responsible for a cyber operation in order to violate the use of force prohibition, the greater the extent of 'state involvement' in the operation the more likely it is that other states will label it a use of force. As an example, operations conducted by non-state groups controlled by a state are less likely to be so characterized than those conducted by organs of the state, such as military forces or intelligence agencies.

Article 2(4) also bars 'threats' of the use of force. With respect to cyber operations, this element of the prohibition arises both when cyber means are used to threaten an unlawful cyber or kinetic use of force and when a threat to conduct an unlawful cyber use of force is levied by non-cyber means.[21] The threat must be of unlawful actions; there is no violation if the threatened cyber operation would be conducted pursuant to Security Council authorization or by a state engaging in

[21] *Tallinn Manual*, rule 12, para 2.

legitimate self-defence. Furthermore, as contemplated in the prohibition, the threat must be coercive and communicative.[22] In other words, a threat must be designed to cause its target to either engage in, or desist from, particular conduct. There is no requirement that a specific demand be made. The mere acquisition of cyber capabilities without more, however, is not a threat as contemplated by Article 2(4). Rather, the state acquiring the cyber capability must threaten, impliedly or explicitly, to use it.

The fact that a particular cyber operation does not rise to the level of a threat or use of force under Article 2(4) does not mean that the operation is lawful under international law. The action may violate specific bilateral or multilateral treaty obligations or particular aspects of customary international law. Of particular relevance is the prohibition on intervention, which derives from the principle of sovereign equality articulated in Article 2(1) of the UN Charter and numerous other international instruments.[23] The ICJ has similarly recognized non-intervention as a principle of customary international law.[24]

Non-intervention 'forbids States or groups of States to intervene directly or indirectly in the internal or external affairs of other States'.[25] 'Internal or external affairs' refers to those matters about which states, as states, may freely decide. These include such matters as the state's political and economic system and its foreign relations.[26] Cyber means offer many prospects for engaging in intervention. For instance, cyber operations could be used to alter another state's election results or to transfer funds into the accounts of insurgent groups.

Of course, not every cyber operation directed at a state violates the principle of non-intervention. Like threats of the use of force, intervention must in some way be coercive; it must be intended to cause the state to engage in or refrain from particular conduct. As an example, merely intruding into another state's cyber infrastructure to engage in espionage does not qualify as intervention. Moreover, not every coercive cyber operation violates the norm. The International Group of Experts agreed that each cyber operation must be assessed on a case-by-case basis.[27] Taking the election example, it would not constitute intervention merely to express support for a particular candidate on government websites. Such actions are more properly deemed attempts to influence, rather than attempts to coerce. Ultimately, though, the more coercive an action and the more important the interest, the more likely it is that the act will run afoul of the prohibition on intervention.

[22] *Tallinn Manual*, rule 12, para 4.

[23] See eg Declaration on Principles of International Law concerning Friendly Relations and Cooperation among States in accordance with the Charter of the United Nations, GA Res 2625 (XXV), UN GAOR, 25th Sess, Supp No 28, 121, A/8082 (1970).

[24] *Nicaragua*, Judgment, para 202.

[25] *Nicaragua*, Judgment, para 205.

[26] *Nicaragua*, Judgment, para 205.

[27] *Tallinn Manual*, rule 10, para 10.

III. Chapter VII and Cyber Operations

The UN Charter sets forth two exceptions to the prohibition on the use of force. The first, which is relatively uncontroversial, is based in Chapter VII of the Charter. Pursuant to Article 39 of that Chapter, the Security Council may 'determine the existence of any threat to the peace, breach of the peace, or act of aggression'. Once it does so, it may then either 'make recommendations' as to how to resolve the situation or 'decide what measures shall be taken in accordance with Articles 41 and 42, to maintain or restore international peace and security'.[28]

No cyber operation has ever been characterized by the Security Council as meeting the Article 39 criteria. However, the International Group of Experts agreed, 'it is incontrovertible that the Council has the authority to do so'.[29] It is essential to understand that the determination that a cyber action amounts to a threat to the peace, a breach of the peace, or an act of aggression is wholly unrelated to the question of whether it separately qualifies as a use of force under Article 2(4). The former bears on the authority of the Security Council to authorize or mandate remedial actions, whereas the latter deals with whether a state's activities violate international law. Indeed, the Council may label operations falling well below the use of force threshold as the sort of actions encompassed by Article 39. Additionally, whereas Article 2(4) addresses only actions by states, both states and non-state actors may engage in activities falling within the purview of Article 39.

Since there is no procedural mechanism for challenging such a characterization by the Security Council, a cyber operation constitutes a threat to the peace, breach of the peace, or act of aggression whenever the Council so decides.[30] Not only may it decide that Article 39 applies to a particular event (such as a cyber operation by one state against another), it may also determine *ex ante* that a specified type of cyber activity constitutes a threat to the peace, as it has done in the case of transnational terrorism.[31] It could, for instance, decide that any cyber operation directed against critical infrastructure amounts to a threat to the peace and authorize states or international organizations to take immediate remedial measures that might otherwise be unlawful to counteract them.

By making an Article 39 determination, the Security Council accords itself the authority to act pursuant to Articles 41 and 42 of the Charter. Article 41 provides that the Council 'may decide what measures not involving the use of armed force are to be employed to give effect to its decisions, and it may call upon the

[28] UN Charter, Chapter 7, Art 39. [29] *Tallinn Manual*, rule 18, para 1.

[30] Nico Krisch, 'Article 39' in Simma et al, *The Charter of the United Nations: A Commentary*, 1275–6, 1311–12.

[31] See eg SC Res 1373 (28 Sept 2001).

Members of the United Nations to apply such measures'. These may include 'complete or partial interruption of economic relations as well as rail, sea, air, postal, telegraphic, radio, and other means of communication, and the severance of diplomatic relations'.[32]

The phrase 'measures not involving the use of armed force' is generally interpreted as referring to actions that do not rise to the level of a use of force under Article 2(4).[33] There is no reason to exclude cyber measures from its ambit. This conclusion is supported by the article's textual reference to the interruption of 'other means of communication'. The Council could clearly authorize, for example, a total or partial blockage of cyber communications with a state or non-state actor, so long as that action did not rise to the level of a use of force.

Should the Security Council determine that non-forceful measures have proven ineffective, or that their use would be fruitless, it 'may take such action by air, sea, or land forces as may be necessary to maintain or restore international peace and security' under its Article 42 authority.[34] In other words, it may authorize or mandate the use of force such that states employing force in accordance with an Article 42 resolution do not violate the Article 2(4) prohibition.[35] The Council generally does so by providing that 'all necessary means' may be used to effectuate the resolution in question.[36] The International Group of Experts concurred that 'any action undertaken on the basis of this [article] may be implemented by, or against, cyberspace capabilities'.[37] This is only sensible since cyber means or methods of warfare often represent less destructive or injurious options than classic military armed force.

[32] UN Charter, Chapter 7, Art 41.

[33] Krisch, 'Article 39' in Simma et al, *The Charter of the United Nations: A Commentary*, 1311–12.

[34] The Council has wide discretion in this regard. International Criminal Tribunal for the former Yugoslavia, *Prosecutor v. Tadić*, Decision on the Defence Motion for Interlocutory Appeal on Jurisdiction of 2 Oct 1995, IT-94-1-I, para 26. See also Krisch, 'Article 42' in Simma et al, *The Charter of the United Nations: A Commentary*, 1341.

[35] With regard to the terms 'mandate' and 'authorize', the former refers to situations in which the Security Council specifically designates the party (eg NATO) to conduct operations whereas the latter empowers individual states or regional entities to act pursuant to a broader authorization by the Security Council that has not specifically designated it (eg an ad hoc coalition).

[36] An example is SC Res 678 (29 Nov 1991), para 2 (Iraq–Kuwait): 'Authorizes Member States co-operating with the Government of Kuwait, unless Iraq on or before 15 January 1991 fully implements…the above-mentioned resolutions, to use all necessary means to uphold and implement Resolution 660 (1990) and all subsequent relevant resolutions and to restore international peace and security in the area'.

[37] *Tallinn Manual*, rule 18, para 9. Of course, the Security Council may not authorize actions that violate a *jus cogens* norm.

IV. Self-Defence against Cyber Operations

Article 51 of the UN Charter, which reflects customary international law,[38] sets forth the other universally recognized exception to the Article 2(4) prohibition on the use of force. It provides that 'Nothing in the present Charter shall impair the inherent right of individual or collective self-defence if an armed attack occurs against a Member of the United Nations, until the Security Council has taken the measures necessary to maintain international peace and security'.

The textual condition precedent for the exercise of the right of self-defence is an 'armed attack'. This requirement begs the question of when does a cyber operation rise to the level of an armed attack.[39] The prevailing view is that the notion of armed attack and that of the previously discussed use of force are not synonymous.[40] Generally, an armed attack is depicted as of a higher threshold, such that while all armed attacks qualify as uses of force, not every use of force constitutes an armed attack. A gap exists between the two legal concepts, as recognized by the ICJ in its *Nicaragua* judgment.[41] There the Court distinguished uses of force and armed attacks by reference to their 'scale and effects'.[42] In particular, it cited the need to 'distinguish the most grave forms of the use of force (those constituting an armed attack) from other less grave forms'.[43] Unfortunately, the Court provided no guidance for making the distinction.

It must be cautioned that the US does not accept the premise of a distinction between uses of force and an armed attack. In 2012, it confirmed that this position applied equally to cyber uses of force. According to then State Department legal adviser Harold Koh, 'the United States has for a long time taken the position that the inherent right of self-defense potentially applies against any illegal use of force. In our view, there is no threshold for a use of deadly force to qualify as an "armed attack" that may warrant a forcible response'.[44] No member of the International Group of Experts agreed with this position.

[38] *Nicaragua*, Judgment, para 193.

[39] For an interesting discussion of self-defence in the cyber context, see Matthew Waxman, 'Self-Defensive Force against Cyber Attacks: Legal, Strategic and Political Dimensions' (2013) 89 *International Law Studies* 109. For an earlier survey, see Yoram Dinstein, 'Computer Network Attacks and Self-Defence' (2002) 76 *International Law Studies* 99.

[40] Albrecht Randelzhofer and Georg Nolte, 'Article 51' in Simma et al, *The Charter of the United Nations: A Commentary*, 1397, 1401–2.

[41] *Nicaragua*, Judgment, para 191. See also *Oil Platforms (Iran v. US)*, Merits, Judgment of 6 Nov 2003, ICJ Rep 2003, para 51; *Armed Activities*, Merits, para 147.

[42] *Nicaragua*, Judgment, para 195.

[43] *Nicaragua*, Judgment, para 191.

[44] Harold Koh, 'International Law in Cyberspace' (2012) 54 *Harvard International Law Journal Online* 1, 7, citing William Taft IV, 'Self-Defense and the *Oil Platforms* Decision' (2004) 29 *Yale Journal*

The International Group of Experts struggled with this lack of clarity in drafting the *Tallinn Manual*. However, all of the Experts agreed that a cyber operation resulting in significant death of or injury to persons, or damage to or destruction of property, evidenced the requisite scale and effects to qualify as an armed attack.[45] They likewise concurred that the injury or damage in question need not be the first-order effect of the cyber operation in question. To illustrate, a cyber operation that releases water from a dam and subsequently causes widespread downstream damage is an armed attack, as is one that discharges harmful chemicals into a city's water supply thereby poisoning its population.

Whether consequences not clearly crossing the significant death, injury, damage, or destruction threshold are sufficient to render a use of cyber force an armed cyberattack remains unsettled. For example, in *Nicaragua* the ICJ differentiated a 'mere frontier incident' and an armed attack.[46] However, many have criticized this distinction, and numerous members of the International Group of Experts rejected it in the cyber context.[47] For the critics, any physical injury or damage beyond that which is *de minimis* satisfies the scale and effects requirement.

What is unique about cyber operations is the extent to which they can cause immense harm within the target state without producing any physical injuries or damage. This prospect raises the question of whether cyber operations having severe consequences can qualify as armed attacks in the absence of physical effects. In other words, is it the nature of the consequences or their seriousness that determines when an action qualifies as an armed attack as a matter of law? In some cases, focusing solely on the nature of the consequences would seem to produce irrational results. For example, is a cyber operation that opens a dam causing the flooding of several houses really more serious than a cyber operation that crashes a stock market? If we are simply quantifying the damage caused, surely the destruction of several houses, while creating physical damage, is far less 'destructive' than the elimination of billions in wealth.

Although it would appear that the reference to armed attack in Article 51 was originally meant to refer only to actions that are physically harmful or destructive, some members of the International Group of Experts were willing to interpret the norm to include cyber operations that produce particularly severe, albeit not physical, consequences. The paradigmatic cases are cyber operations that, as with the earlier example, seriously disrupt the national economy of the target state or so interfere with its critical infrastructure that daily life is dramatically affected. Other

of International Law 295, 299–302 and Abraham Sofaer, 'The Sixth Annual Waldemar A. Solf Lecture in International Law: Terrorism, the Law, and the National Defense' (1989) 126 *Military Law Review* 89, 93–6.

45 *Tallinn Manual*, rule 13, para 6.

46 *Nicaragua*, Judgment, para 195.

47 *Tallinn Manual*, rule 13, para 7; see also Yoram Dinstein, *War, Aggression and Self-Defence* (5th edn, Cambridge: Cambridge University Press, 2011), 210–11.

experts acknowledged that the norm may evolve towards this standard over time, but argued that it presently represented *lex ferenda, lex lata.*

A related interpretive quandary involves 'pinprick' cyber operations that individually do not cross the armed attack threshold. The legal question is whether their effects may be combined such that they either amount to sufficient physical injury or damage or—for those who take the position that severity alone suffices—have non-physical consequences that are serious enough to merit characterization as an armed attack. The International Group of Experts took the position that such effects may be 'accumulated' for this purpose so long as they are launched by either a single originator (eg a state) or by a group acting in concert (eg cyber terrorists acting cooperatively).[48] For the Experts, the key was whether the cyber operations are sufficiently related to plausibly characterize them as constituent parts of a single broader campaign.

When responding to an armed attack, whether cyber or kinetic, the right to use force in the face of that attack is limited to situations with a transborder element.[49] These include cyber armed attacks conducted by (or attributable to) one state against another or by an external non-state group against a state. The law of self-defence does not apply in situations involving purely intrastate cyberattacks, that is, those launched from within a state against targets in that state. This is so even though the transmission may transit servers located outside the state. Equally, the law of self-defence does not apply to cyber operations launched by one non-state entity against another.

A persistent controversy plaguing the law of self-defence since the terrorist attacks of 9/11 is whether it applies to operations mounted by non-state actors operating transnationally who lack any affiliation with a state. Before 9/11, the prevailing view among international law experts was that the law of self-defence related only to cases of armed attacks launched by states or otherwise attributable to them pursuant to the law of self-defence. With regard to attribution, the ICJ had opined in the *Nicaragua* judgment that 'An armed attack must be understood as including not merely action by regular forces across an international border, but also "the sending by or on behalf of a State of armed bands, groups, irregulars or mercenaries, which carry out acts of armed force against another State of such gravity has amount to" (inter alia) an actual armed attack conducted by regular forces, "or its substantial involvement therein." '[50] Applying this standard in the cyber context, if state A instructs a group of hacktivists to conduct attacks against state B, the right of self-defence allows state B to respond directly against state A, and not simply against the hacktivist group.

State practice in the aftermath of 9/11 appears to support an interpretation of Article 51 that dispenses with any purported requirement for a state to be behind

[48] *Tallinn Manual*, rule 13, para 8. [49] *Tallinn Manual*, rule 13, para 2.
[50] *Nicaragua*, Judgment, para 195.

the attack in question. For instance, the day after the attacks, the Security Council adopted Resolution 1368 (2001), in which it recognized the inherent right of individual or collective self-defence.[51] At the time, there was no suggestion that any state was responsible for the attacks. Two weeks later, the Council affirmed that right of self-defence in Resolution 1373 (2001).[52] No state argued that the counterattacks by UN forces against Al Qaeda violated the law of self-defence. Furthermore, other international organizations and individual states went on to adopt positions consistent with the application of the right of self-defence to attacks mounted by non-state actors,[53] and many states and commentators continue to embrace this interpretation today.[54]

This interpretation applies equally to cyberattacks. Of course, it would relate to cyberattacks by terrorist groups. It would also pertain to cyber operations conducted by private commercial entities, such as information technology companies. For instance, a state victimized by a cyber armed attack conducted by a corporation would be entitled to respond by cyber or kinetic means in self-defence against that corporation itself (at the use of force level). All other requirements of the law of self-defence, especially necessity and proportionality (discussed later), would continue to apply.

On two occasions since the 9/11 attacks, however, the ICJ has adopted a narrower stance. In its *Wall* advisory opinion, the majority took the position that Article 51 was irrelevant where the country acting in self-defence did not claim it was doing so in response to an attack imputable to a foreign state.[55] In that case, Israel sought to create a security fence in order to thwart terrorist attacks, but failed to argue that a foreign state was behind those attacks. The Court appeared unprepared to move beyond the *Nicaragua* threshold of attributability. In the *Armed Activities* judgment, the Court took a roughly analogous position.[56]

[51] SC Res 1368 (12 Sept 2001); SC Res 1373 (28 Sept 2001). [52] SC Res 1373 (28 Sept 2001).

[53] eg both NATO and the Organization of American States (OAS) activated the collective defence provisions of their respective treaties. North Atlantic Treaty, Art 5, 4 Apr 1959, 63 Stat 2241, 2244, 34 UNTS 243, 246; Press Release, NATO, Statement by the North Atlantic Council (12 Sept 2001); Inter-American Treaty of Reciprocal Assistance, Art 3.1, 2 Sept 1947, 62 Stat 1681, 1700, 21 UNTS 77, 93; Terrorist Threat to the Americas, Res 1, Twenty-fourth Meeting of Consultation of Ministers of Foreign Affairs, Terrorist Threat to the Americas, OAS Doc. RC.24/RES.1/01 (21 Sept 2001). As to individual states, see eg Australia's offer of collective defence pursuant to the ANZUS Treaty (ANZUS, Art IV, 1 Sept 1951, 3 UST 3420, 3423, 131 UNTS 83, 86). Brendan Pearson, 'PM commits to mutual defence', *Australian Financial Review*, 15 Sept 2001, 9.

[54] See eg Harold H. Koh, Legal Adviser, Department of State, 'The Obama Administration and International Law', Address Before the American Society of International Law, 25 Mar 2010, available at <http://www.state.gov/s/l/releases/remarks/139119.htm>.

[55] *Legal Consequences of the Construction of a Wall in the Occupied Palestinian Territory*, Advisory Opinion of 9 July 2004, ICJ Rep 2004, 136, para 139. But see Separate Opinion of Judge Higgins, para 33; Separate Opinion of Judge Kooijmans, para 35; Declaration of Judge Buergenthal, para 6.

[56] *Armed Activities*, Merits, paras 146–7. See also Randelzhofer and Nolte, 'Article 51' in Simma et al, *The Charter of the United Nations: A Commentary*, 1414–19.

The International Group of Experts examined this question in depth during its proceedings, with the majority eventually supporting the view that cyber operations conducted by organized non-state groups may sometimes qualify as armed attacks.[57] However, that majority split over whether the law of self-defence also governed cyber operations launched by either an unorganized non-state armed group or individuals, as was often the case during cyber operations against Estonia and Georgia in 2007 and 2008.[58] During those incidents, some individuals acted alone, while others simply responded to a general call to launch attacks. This author is of the view that absent a degree of organization, the law of self-defence does not apply to groups; it never applies to acts of individuals.[59]

Not only does the originator of a cyber operation bear on whether that operation qualifies as an armed attack, but the operation's target and its location also affect its legal character. As a general matter, a cyber operation of the requisite scale and effects against persons or objects within the territory of a state generally constitutes an armed attack against that state. However, the International Group of Experts could not reach consensus regarding cyberattacks motivated by purely private interests.[60] For instance, it is unclear whether a highly destructive operation mounted by a private corporation in state A against a private enterprise located in state B could comprise an armed attack against state B that triggered state B's right of self-defence.

Further complicating this issue is the fact that cyber operations against certain objects located outside a state can in some circumstances qualify as armed attacks against that state. The International Group of Experts concluded that those targeting 'non-commercial government facilities or equipment, and government personnel, certainly qualify as armed attacks' so long as the other criteria have been met.[61] An unassailable example of such an armed attack is a lethal cyberattack directed against another state's head of government or overseas military bases.[62] The legal character of cyber operations against other persons or entities outside a state's territory is uncertain, with determinations made on a case-by-case basis. Relevant factors would include the extent and nature of damage caused, the status of the individuals or objects that have been targeted, and any political motivation to the cyber operations in question.[63]

57 *Tallinn Manual*, rule 13, para 17.

58 Tikk, Kaska, and Vihul, *International Cyber Incidents*.

59 The reference is to the public international law of self-defence, not to the right of individual or unit self-defence.

60 *Tallinn Manual*, rule 13, para 19.

61 *Tallinn Manual*, rule 13, para 20.

62 *Oil Platforms*, para 72. Note that the example of an attack against military forces is contained in the Definition of Aggression, GA Res 3314 (XXIX), Art 3(d). See also Randelzhofer and Nolte, 'Article 51' in Simma et al, *The Charter of the United Nations: A Commentary*, 1411–12.

63 *Tallinn Manual*, rule 13, para 20.

A contentious issue surrounding the right to act in self-defence involves its geographical limitations.[64] In particular, may a state that has been subjected to a cyber armed attack respond against an attacker who is located in another state if the attack cannot be attributed to that state? Obviously, defensive operations are not uses of force against the territorial state or violations of its sovereignty when conducted with that state's consent. Moreover, the majority view among the International Group of Experts was that non-consensual cyber operations may also be permissible as acts of self-defence under certain circumstances. This is so when the state from which the attacks emanate is unable or unwilling to terminate the cyberattacks from its territory despite the legal obligation to do so.[65] For instance, it may lack the technical capability to locate the source of the cyber armed attacks or to take measures to prevent them.

This approach balances the territorial state's sovereignty rights with the self-defence rights of the state under cyberattack. Accordingly, before forceful defensive actions (whether kinetic or cyber) may be conducted, the territorial state must be afforded an opportunity to put an end to the cyberattacks. Of course, it may not be feasible to afford the state an opportunity to do so because cyberattacks can be launched with little warning and have catastrophic effects that manifest instantaneously. In such a situation, the target state may react immediately lest it lose the opportunity to effectively defend itself.[66]

A few of the Experts rejected the notion that a victim state could lawfully conduct kinetic or cyber defensive operations at the use of force level against another state. For them, the principle of sovereignty was impenetrable absent attribution of the attacks in question to the territorial state or Security Council authorization to take action.

Cyber operations in self-defence, like all defensive operations, are subject to the customary international law requirements of necessity and proportionality, acknowledged by the ICJ in the *Nicaragua* judgment, the *Nuclear Weapons* advisory opinion, and the *Oil Platforms* judgment.[67] The principle of necessity in the law of self-defence provides that a use of force in self-defence is only permissible when a response not rising to the level of a use of force is unlikely to prove sufficiently effective to counter a cyber armed attack.[68] For instance, if the victim state's firewalls and anti-malware suffice to defeat an attack, a use of force in response (whether through

[64] Ashley Deeks, 'The Geography of Cyber-Conflict: Through a Glass Darkly' (2013) 89 *International Law Studies* 1.

[65] *Tallinn Manual*, rule 13, para 23. The obligation of a state to ensure cyber infrastructure located on its territory is not used to harm others is set forth in *Tallinn Manual*, rule 5. The seminal case on the subject is *Corfu Channel (UK v. Albania)*, Judgment of 9 Apr 1949, ICJ Rep 1949, 4, 22: A state may not 'allow knowingly its territory to be used for acts contrary to the rights of other States'.

[66] *Tallinn Manual*, rule 13, para 23.

[67] *Nicaragua*, Judgment, paras 174, 196; *Nuclear Weapons*, Advisory Opinion, para 41; *Oil Platforms*, paras 43, 73–4, 76.

[68] *Tallinn Manual*, rule 14, para 2.

defensive cyber or kinetic attacks) is prohibited. However, there is no requirement that forceful measures be the sole option available. Indeed, defensive uses of force are often accompanied by non-forceful measures such as diplomacy, law enforcement, or, in the case of cyberattacks, technical steps such as closing vulnerabilities in the system.

Whereas the necessity criterion determines if forceful defensive measures are permissible, proportionality addresses how the defence may be executed. Proportionality allows only that degree of force necessary to defeat the cyber armed attack in question, and only as long as required by the circumstances.[69] Thus, every use of defensive force is context-specific. As an example, the destructive or injurious effects of a defensive cyber operation must be limited, to the extent feasible in the circumstances, to those systems that will end the cyber armed attack; a general defensive operation against the attacking state's cyber infrastructure would be unlawful if a surgical cyber strike would eliminate the attacking state's ability to continue its cyberattacks. Of course, in certain circumstances, there will be an unavoidable bleed over into systems unconnected with the armed attack. Bleed-over effects would not necessarily prohibit the defensive action if they were unavoidable.

The concept of proportionality in the law of self-defence is often misunderstood. It does not require equivalence between the effects generated by the initial cyber armed attack and the defensive response. For instance, lack of precise knowledge as to the structure of a cyber armed attack may prevent a defending state from fashioning a highly focused response. In such a situation, the only option available to the defending state may be to launch a defensive response (cyber or kinetic) that will have destructive and injurious consequences significantly exceeding those of the original cyber armed attack. So long as the cyber operation is no more extensive than necessary to effectively defend against the cyber armed attack, the operation is a lawful use of force. Yet, if it is possible to effectively defend against the cyber armed attack with a cyber operation that produces destructive or injurious effects well below those of the initial armed attack, it would not be lawful to mount a more destructive or injurious defensive operation.

International law also imposes temporal limitations on the exercise of the right of self-defence. It has long been recognized that the use of force in self-defence is permissible once an armed attack is underway. The concept of being underway includes situations in which the act in question is an integral preliminary step in an overall operation that will qualify as an armed attack. In future warfare, an armed attack by military means conducted by one state against another will likely commence with cyber operations designed to 'prepare the battlefield'. For instance, a state may use cyber operations to shut down enemy command-and-control communications or disable defensive systems such as those affording the enemy early

[69] *Tallinn Manual*, rule 14, para 5.

warning and air defence capability. Such actions initiate an armed attack against which the victim state may respond forcefully.

Whether a state may use force in the face of an attack that is forthcoming, but has not yet been launched, is a question that has evoked great controversy. It is clear that doing so is not permissible if the threat of an attack has not matured, either in terms of the purported attacking state's intent to launch or with respect to its development of a capability to do so. Thus, a defensive use of force against a state that is merely hostile but has not decided to conduct an attack is impermissible, as is one directed against a state that is simply acquiring malware or probing the vulnerabilities of other states' networks.

Beyond these principles, there is a school of thought that goes even further, holding that uses of force in self-defence are only lawful once the armed attack in question has actually begun.[70] Proponents point out that the text of Article 51 ('an armed attack occurs') provides no textual support for the notion of 'anticipatory self-defence'.

The International Group of Experts rejected this position. In their view, a right to use force defensively arises once an armed cyberattack is 'imminent'.[71] This position is based on the well-known 19th-century *Caroline* incident during the Mackenzie Rebellion and the ensuing exchange of diplomatic notes between American and British diplomats. Although the incident did not actually deal with the right of self-defence per se, UN Secretary of State Daniel Webster famously opined, in text that was subsequently cited with approval by the Nuremberg tribunal,[72] that a state may only resort to the use of force when the 'necessity of self-defense [is] instant, overwhelming, leaving no choice of means, and no moment for deliberation'.[73] Reference to the term 'instant' implies a temporal quality that limits exercise of the right of anticipatory self-defence to situations in which an armed attack is imminent.

By one interpretation of imminence, the defensive actions must be temporally proximate to the armed attack. In other words, lawfulness is judged by time. The International Group of Experts, however, adopted an approach that interprets imminence in the contemporary context as a situation in which a victim state's window of opportunity to effectively defend itself is about to close. Restated, imminence refers

[70] Ian Brownlie, *International Law and the Use of Force Between States* (Oxford: Oxford University Press, 1963), 275–8.

[71] *Tallinn Manual*, rule 15. See also Terry Gill and Paul Ducheine, 'Anticipatory Self-Defense in the Cyber Context' (2013) 89 *International Law Studies* 438. For a discussion of anticipatory self-defence generally, see Michael Schmitt, 'Preemptive Strategies and International Law' (2003) 24 *Michigan Journal of International Law* 513.

[72] Judgment of the International Military Tribunal Sitting at Nuremberg, Germany (30 Sept 1946) in (1950) 22 *The Trial of German Major War Criminals: Proceedings of the International Military Tribunal Sitting at Nuremberg, Germany* 435.

[73] Letter from Daniel Webster to Lord Ashburton (6 Aug 1842).

to cases in which a state is faced with the choice of acting defensively or suffering the consequences of the armed attack.

As an example, a state may possess reliable intelligence that its critical infrastructure will be targeted by another state's cyber operations, but lack information as to when the attacks will occur or against which systems. If it can mount cyber or kinetic defensive operations against the cyber capabilities of the latter state, it may do so even though the consequences of the operations would qualify as a use of force. Of course, the defensive action must be both necessary and proportionate.

Limits on post-armed attack defensive responses are imposed by the related principle of immediacy.[74] While a use of force in self-defence need not be contemporaneous with the armed attack to which it responds, there must be sufficient temporal proximity to the attack to distinguish self-defence from mere retaliation. Assessment of the lawfulness of such responses involves a case-by-case analysis. In the cyber context, for instance, reliably identifying the source of an attack may take some time. Moreover, time may be required to identify vulnerabilities in the attacker's cyber systems and develop the malware to exploit them.

The key to the distinction is that an act of self-defence must be motivated by a desire to ensure that the armed attack does not continue. In particular, notice must be taken of the fact that a single cyber operation at the armed attack level may be but one in a series of operations that comprise a campaign against the victim state. That state need not wait to react to determine whether further attacks are forthcoming. So long as it reasonably concludes that the armed attack is not definitively over, it may respond in self-defence.[75] The risk of mistake is borne by the attacker. In situations where it is not reasonable to so conclude, any forceful response would be an unlawful act of retaliation.

Cyber armed attacks are unique in that the victim state may not be aware that it is under attack. In part this was the situation with Stuxnet, which was designed to create the impression that technical flaws in the targeted cyber systems caused the damage. If the victim state subsequently learns that it has been subjected to an armed cyberattack, its right to respond in self-defence will only persist if the attacks are likely to continue. A similar situation is one in which the state knows that it is being subjected to cyber operations at the armed attack level, but is unable to identify the source of the attacks. Once it discovers the identity of the attacker, it may not use force in self-defence if the attacks have clearly ended.

As is clear from the text of Article 51, states may exercise the right of self-defence collectively. In other words, a state may use force to defend another state that is the victim of an armed cyberattack. This treaty law right is universally viewed as reflective of customary international law.[76]

[74] *Tallinn Manual*, rule 15. [75] *Tallinn Manual*, rule 15, para 9.

[76] *Nicaragua*, Judgment, para 193. See also Randelzhofer and Nolte, 'Article 51' in Simma et al, *The Charter of the United Nations: A Commentary*, 1427–8.

A condition precedent to the exercise of collective self-defence is a request from the victim state for assistance.[77] Such a request may either be fashioned in the context of a standing arrangement, such as NATO,[78] or be made on an ad hoc basis in response to a particular cyberattack. The state providing assistance may only act within the scope of the request. For instance, if a state asks for help in the form of cyber operations to bring down systems that are being used to conduct an armed attack, the assisting state would not be able to use kinetic force to achieve that result. A mere request for assistance does not alone justify any action by a state using force in aid of another. The assisting state must itself reasonably conclude that an armed attack has been mounted and that its use of force is necessary, proportionate, and meets the requirements of imminence or immediacy.

The fact that a cyber operation directed against a state does not rise to the level of an armed attack does not leave that state without response options. The victim state could urge the UN Security Council to authorize or mandate remedial action under Chapter VII. It could also engage in classic lawful, albeit 'unfriendly', responses through diplomacy or acts of retorsion. Perhaps most significantly, it could take 'countermeasures' in response to the harmful cyber operations.[79]

Countermeasures are otherwise unlawful actions taken by one state in response to the unlawful actions of another. They are only available in situations in which the offending cyber operations were mounted by a state or are attributable to it pursuant to the law of state responsibility. Countermeasures must be necessary in the sense that lawful actions would not suffice to put an end to the unlawful conduct to which the countermeasures are responding. Further, they must be proportionate to the unlawful conduct that justified them.[80]

There is no requirement that the countermeasure be 'in kind'; cyber countermeasures may be employed to respond to non-cyber unlawful acts and vice versa. Moreover, the countermeasure need only be designed to convince the offending state to desist. Consider a case where one state is conducting cyber operations against the banking system of another. The victim state could direct countermeasures against the cyber infrastructure the other state is using to mount the operation, against the other state's banking system, or against cyber infrastructure that is wholly unrelated to the actions but which impose such costs that the attacking state will likely desist from further actions.

Before countermeasures may be taken, the victim state must first demand that the other state's unlawful cyber operations cease.[81] An exception exists in situations

[77] *Nicaragua*, Judgment, para 199; *Oil Platforms*, para 51.

[78] North Atlantic Treaty (Washington Treaty), Art 5, 34 UNTS 234.

[79] *Tallinn Manual*, rule 9; Articles on State Responsibility, Arts 22 and 49–53.

[80] Articles on State Responsibility, Art 51; *Responsibility of Germany for Damage Caused in the Portuguese Colonies in the South of Africa (Naulilaa Arbitration) (Portugal v. Germany)* (1928) 2 RIAA 1011, 1028; *Gabčíkovo-Nagymoros Project (Hungary/Slovakia)*, Judgment of 25 Sept 1997, ICJ Rep 1997, 7, para 85.

[81] Articles on State Responsibility, Art 52(1)(b).

in which the transmittal of such a demand is not feasible. In particular, cyber operations may unfold so rapidly that it would be unreasonable to require the victim state to demand the cessation before acting.

It may be the case that a state needs to respond to cyber operations conducted by an unknown attacker. Neither countermeasures nor self-defence would be available since the former are only available to react to the acts of states and the latter requires that the armed attack threshold be crossed and that (perhaps) at least an organized armed group be the attacker. In such a case, states may sometimes respond pursuant to the plea of necessity.[82] The plea of necessity justifies protective measures in exceptional situations involving a 'grave and imminent peril' to an 'essential interest'.[83] Measures taken on this basis may affect the interest of other states so long as those interests are not essential and it is apparent that lesser measures would not suffice. For instance, a state sustaining cyberattacks from an unknown source may completely isolate its own cyber infrastructure based on the plea of necessity even though doing so negatively affects cyber activities in other states. The plea could also allow for 'hack-backs' despite uncertainty as to the source of the attacks.

V. Concluding Thoughts

The extent to which the myth of a normative void in cyberspace pervades contemporary discussions about international law is striking. However, measured analysis of the issue inevitably leads to the conclusion that international law governs cyber operations robustly and provides states victimized by them with a range of viable response options.

Of course, unique aspects of cyber operations do affect interpretation of international law norms in the cyber context. The fact that cyber operations can have disastrous results while causing no physical injury or damage heightens the difficulty of determining when the use of force and armed attack thresholds have been crossed. Similarly, the speed with which they unfold and the difficulty of attribution complicate the traditional understandings of anticipatory self-defence and dramatically enhance the importance of response options based on the plea of necessity. The technical complexity of cyber operations and the fact that they take place in a geographically ill-defined environment obscures the duties of states from

[82] *Tallinn Manual*, rule 9, para 10; Articles on State Responsibility, Art 25.

[83] Articles on State Responsibility, Art 25(1)(a).

which the operations are mounted and through which they pass, and shapes application of such legal standards as 'unwilling or unable'.

Finally, it must be admitted that the extant international law may be out of step with shifting community values with respect to cyberspace. In particular, a system of law based in the cognitive shorthand of physical consequences may not pay sufficient due to the values of thoroughly wired societies. To the extent this is so, we can anticipate a fairly rapid evolution of state interpretations of international law's prescriptive norms regarding the use of force when applied to cyberspace.

CHAPTER 53

PRIVATE MILITARY COMPANIES AND THE *JUS AD BELLUM*

IAN M. RALBY

I. Introduction

When Article 2(4) of the UN Charter was adopted in 1945, the world had not yet seen the first 'private military company'. Indeed, it would be another 20 years before the seeds for the industry were planted by the retired Colonel Sir David Stirling when he founded WatchGuard International to advise Middle Eastern states on securing their oil infrastructure;[1] it would be 50 years before the world would witness the combat capabilities of companies like Executive Outcomes and Sandline International;[2] and it would be 60 years before Blackwater Worldwide, a company based in the Great Dismal Swamp of North Carolina, would draw attention to the use of private armed

[1] Kevin A. O'Brien, 'Private Military Companies and African Security 1990–98' in Abdel-Fatau Musah and J. Kayode Fayemi (eds), *Mercenaries: An African Security Dilemma* (London: Pluto Press, 2000), 43, 46.

[2] E. L. Gaston, 'Mercenarism 2.0? The Rise of the Modern Private Security Industry and its Implications for International Humanitarian Law Enforcement' (2008) 49 *Harvard International Law Journal* 221, 225–6.

contractors in the conflicts in Iraq and Afghanistan.[3] The prohibition of the use of force as it intersects with such private companies remains murky. While most of the legal analysis regarding these companies has centred on issues of international humanitarian law and other matters of *jus in bello*, the *jus ad bellum* implications of private military contracting are nevertheless relevant to modern international law and international relations and have the potential to become more so in the coming years.

One of the reasons there has not, as yet, been any literature produced on private military companies and the prohibition on the use of force is that, at first glance, it appears a non-issue. State practice does not indicate any likelihood that a company would be used in lieu of armed forces to attack another state. But international affairs are rarely so simple. The nuances surrounding the use of force by states have caused countless volumes, including the present, to be produced over the last six decades. Private military companies are a relatively new phenomenon. The highest profile issues surrounding their use have concerned violations of international humanitarian law and human rights law. Consequently, accountability and the absence of regulation have dominated the debate and literature surrounding the industry. Many issues pertaining to these companies, however, have yet to be examined. It will only be in niche circumstances that a state could violate the prohibition on the use of force by virtue of its relationship with a private military company. But niche circumstances are precisely what should be given the most attention, as they are the most likely to be exploited by virtue of the inherent uncertainty and twilight which surrounds them.

This chapter begins by differentiating between mercenaries and the various terms applied to private companies that offer services in conflict areas, seeking as well to distinguish myth from reality in terms of what the industry actually does. Once the subject matter has been sufficiently identified and clarified, the attention turns to instances where private military companies have had engagements relevant to questions of prohibited or lawful use of force by states. The real-world examples set the stage for a more in-depth and theoretical examination of the nuances of where private companies may be used by states in a manner contrary to *jus ad bellum*. As this is the first real foray into this topic, this chapter does more to pose questions than offer answers. Significant further analysis will be necessary to comprehensively analyse private military companies and the *jus ad bellum*. The chapter concludes by recognizing that, while most private companies offering armed services are not and will not be used by a state as a means of using force against another state, such companies in certain situations can nevertheless be used by states in a manner that could violate the international legal prohibition on the use of force.

[3] Major Jeffrey S. Thurnher, 'Drowning in Blackwater: How Weak Accountability Over Private Security Contractors Significantly Undermines Counterinsurgency Efforts' (July 2008) *Army Lawyer* 64.

II. The Subject Matter

A. What are Private Military Companies?

Many different terms have been used to describe the activities of private companies that provide military-related services.[4] The expression 'private military and security company' or PMSC is the broadest and most common term, but it has become somewhat controversial and remains an imprecise and colloquial appellation. Many companies today recognize the negative connotations of a privatized military and are thus strongly inclined to abandon the 'military' portion of the expression.[5] The argument is that the services they provide are defensive, rather than combat-oriented, so 'security' is a more accurate description of what they do, and either 'private security company' or 'private security (service) provider' more accurately describes what they are.[6] Critics and commentators, however, maintain the use of the term 'military' (and they often exclude 'security') in part by convention, and in part to indicate that, regardless of the nuances of the services these companies perform, some of what they do falls within the historic ambit of functions performed by the military. Some companies have and still do specifically provide private military services, including training of military personnel and activities that fall in a grey area between defensive and offensive operations.

Some commentators go further and persist in using the term 'mercenary' to describe these companies.[7] While the *Oxford English Dictionary* defines a mercenary as 'a soldier paid to serve in a foreign army or other military organisation',[8] which would include such notable forces as the Nepalese Gurkhas who serve in the British and Indian Armies and the French Foreign Legion,[9] the term 'mercenary' is defined in several different conventions and thus has a specific meaning in international

[4] Todd S. Millard, 'Overcoming Post-Colonial Myopia: A Call to Recognize and Regulate Private Military Companies' (2003) 176 *Military Law Review* 1, 8.

[5] Discussion at the First Meeting of the Security in Complex Environments Group, Aerospace Defence Security Group, Ltd (13 Jan 2011).

[6] Sarah Percy, 'Morality and Regulation' in Simon Chesterman and Chia Lehnardt (eds), *From Mercenaries to Market: The Rise and Regulation of Private Military Companies* (Oxford: Oxford University Press, 2007), 12–14; UK Foreign and Commonwealth Office, Private Military Companies: Options for Regulation, 2002, HC 577, para 9, available at <http://www.globalsecurity.org/military/library/report/2002/mercenaries.pdf>.

[7] See eg Jeremy Scahill, *Blackwater: The Rise of the World's Most Powerful Mercenary Army* (New York: Nation Books, 2007).

[8] *The Oxford English Dictionary Online*, 'Mercenary', Definition 2 (2010), available at <http://www.oed.com/view/Entry/116635?redirectedFrom=mercenary#eid>.

[9] UK Foreign and Commonwealth Office, Private Military Companies: Options for Regulation, para 4. The 2002 Green Paper claims that the *Oxford English Dictionary* defines 'mercenary' as 'a professional soldier serving a foreign power'. This is not accurate.

law.[10] An in-depth analysis of such laws would reveal that these companies are not mercenaries and only in the rarest of cases could the personnel working for them potentially fit the legal criteria for classification as a mercenary.[11] Section III of this chapter will examine the second of the two definitions of 'mercenaries' under the International Convention Against the Recruitment, Use, Financing and Training of Mercenaries, but for a private military company (PMC) contractor to meet the primary definition, they would have to meet a rigid five-prong test.[12] As one commentator boldly claimed: 'any mercenary who cannot exclude himself from this definition deserves to be shot—and his lawyer with him.'[13]

In one of the most in-depth analyses of the terms pertaining to this industry, Sarah Percy distinguishes between 'mercenaries', 'combat PMCs', and 'non-combat PMCs'.[14] Since the present analysis will not address mercenaries, it is useful to look at her nuanced definitions of PMCs. She defines 'combat PMCs' as companies that 'provide military services, including offensive combat, in exchange for payment', and 'non-combat PMCs' as companies 'that exchange military services stopping short of combat for payment'.[15] In evaluating the two variants of PMCs, some, including Percy herself, argue that no 'combat PMCs' still exist.[16] Both Sarah Percy and the UK Foreign and Commonwealth Office in its 2002 Green Paper on options for regulating private military and security companies[17] assert that there have only been two private military companies, Executive Outcomes of South Africa and Sandline of the UK, both of which are now out of business.[18] While this analysis will not specifically seek to refute that statement, anecdotal evidence would suggest that such entities do still exist and are still operating in various parts of the world. While several companies are alleged to have engaged in conduct that is indistinguishable from 'combat', one of the best examples involves a 2004 incident in Najaf that was

[10] International Convention Against the Recruitment, Use, Financing and Training of Mercenaries, GA Res 44/34, A/RES/44/34 (4 Dec 1989), Art 1; Organisation of African Unity, Convention for the Elimination of Mercenarism in Africa (opened for signature), 3 July 1977, OAU Doc CM/817 (XXIX), Annex II, Art 1 (3rd rev 1977) (entered into force 22 Apr 1985); Protocol Additional to the Geneva Conventions of 12 Aug 1949, and Relating to the Protection of Victims of International Armed Conflicts (Protocol I), Art 47, 8 June 1977, 1125 UNTS 17512, available at <http://www.icrc.org/ihl.nsf/FULL/470?OpenDocument>.

[11] See eg Ian Ralby, 'Private Military and Security Companies in the Uncharted Spaces of the Law', unpublished dissertation, Cambridge University Library, 2011, 54–64.

[12] International Convention against the Recruitment, Use, Financing and Training of Mercenaries, GA Res 44/34, A/RES/44/34 (4 Dec 1989), Art 1.

[13] Geoffrey Best, *Humanity in Warfare: The Modern History of the International Law of Armed Conflicts* (London: Routledge, 1980), 328, 374–5 fn 83.

[14] Percy, 'Morality and Regulation' in Chesterman and Lehnardt, *From Mercenaries to Market*, 12–14.

[15] Percy, 'Morality and Regulation' in Chesterman and Lehnardt, *From Mercenaries to Market*, 12–14.

[16] Percy, 'Morality and Regulation' in Chesterman and Lehnardt, *From Mercenaries to Market*, 12–14.

[17] UK Foreign and Commonwealth Office, Private Military Companies: Options for Regulation, para 9.

[18] Percy, 'Morality and Regulation' in Chesterman and Lehnardt, *From Mercenaries to Market*, 12–14; UK Foreign and Commonwealth Office, Private Military Companies: Options for Regulation, para 9.

captured on camera. The video shows contractors, who at the time were working for the American company Blackwater Worldwide, not only participating in a roof-top shoot-out, but actually giving directions to the uniformed US Marines with them.[19]

Other commentators use the terms private military company/PMC versus private security company/PSC to denote a similar distinction as that of Percy's combat versus non-combat PMCs. Consequently, many argue that there are no PMCs, only PSCs left in existence. The line, however, between what is included in military versus security services is virtually impossible to distinguish with any consistently applicable rule. Rather than spending time to set such boundaries, therefore, the present analysis will examine both privatized military and privatized security services in the specific context of the *jus ad bellum* obligations of states. The term 'private military company' or PMC is therefore used, not in an inflammatory way, but to focus on the activities of companies that provide services that might trigger the prohibition on the use of force.

B. What Do PMCs Do?

In 'Politics as a Vocation', Max Weber defines the state as 'a human community that (successfully) claims the monopoly of the legitimate use of physical force within a given territory.'[20] While states may be the only legitimate source of warfare according to Weber, they have long outsourced the performance of violence to private entities.[21] As Peter W. Singer writes in one of the most famous works on private military companies, 'the monopoly of the state over violence is the exception in world history, rather than the rule. The state itself is a rather new unit of governance, appearing only in the last four hundred years. Moreover, it drew from the private violence market to build its public power.'[22] In some ways, states and international organizations have returned to this traditional approach after a relatively short hiatus.

Often called the 'second oldest profession', the earliest evidence of mercenary activity dates to the reign of the Akkadian King Sargon in roughly 2350–2300 BC.[23] Throughout history, private soldiers have been employed to augment, support, and even replace military forces. While the present analysis is about PMCs, not mercenaries, the history of mercenaries colours some of the issues that will be addressed

[19] Video of Blackwater in Najaf, available at <http://www.dailymotion.com/video/x9hi6f_blackwater-sniper-in-najaf_sport>.

[20] Max Weber, 'Politics as a Vocation' in David Owen and Tracey Strong (eds), *The Vocation Lectures* ([1919] Indianapolis, IN: Hackett, 2004), 33.

[21] Anthony Mockler, *Mercenaries* (New York: Macmillan, 1969), 13.

[22] Peter W. Singer, *Corporate Warriors: The Rise of the Privatized Military Industry* (Ithaca, NY: Cornell University Press, 2003), 19.

[23] Serge Yalichev, *Mercenaries of the Ancient World* (London: Constable, 1997), 13.

and is thus worth reviewing. As a fairly central figure in the early days of PMCs has explained: 'Mercenary soldiering has a long and honorable history. . . When something is both widespread and long lasting, there must be some fundamental reason for it.'[24] Despite conflicting views,[25] mercenaries were an integral part of warfare for most of history. Indeed, it has been less than 150 years since, as a result of the Franco-German War, the 'nation-in-arms' concept took hold, dramatically changing the composition of the world's armies.[26] 'The idea, now so widely accepted that a man can be obliged to fight for his country could only be accepted when a man had a country that was more than a geographical expression to fight for.'[27] With this increase in military participation by the citizenry, the role of mercenaries had to be reconsidered, and by the early 20th century, mercenaries constituted perhaps the most minor portion of combat forces at any point in history.[28]

In 1941, Captain David Stirling founded the Special Air Service (SAS) as an elite fighting force within the British military.[29] A quarter-century later, in 1965, Stirling collected a group of ex-SAS personnel and formed the first modern company offering private military services, WatchGuard International.[30] This company sought employment training the armies of Persian Gulf states in Western military tactics. In other words, the ex-SAS personnel were able to draw on their training with the British Army and pass it on to Arab militaries for much higher pay than they had received as uniformed soldiers.[31] Though WatchGuard was never a great success, several SAS alumni spawned other similar companies including Control Risks Group, Keenie Meenie, Saladin Security, and Risk Advisory Group. Many of these British companies founded in the late 1960s and 1970s are still in operation today.

During the same period in which the British PMCs were taking shape, traditional mercenaries, willing to fight in combat for the right price, became involved in African decolonization.[32] In the process, mercenaries garnered a reputation for being cruel and brutal. But the new PMCs managed to stay under the radar as much as possible and sought to offer something different than mercenary outfits.

[24] Lt Col Tim Spicer, *An Unorthodox Soldier: Peace and War in the Sandline Affair* (Edinburgh: Mainstream Publishing, 2000), 29–30.

[25] Compare Thomas More, *Utopia* ([1516] trans Paul Turner, London: Penguin, 2009), 107–9 and Niccolò Machiavelli, *The Prince* ([1532] trans George Bull, London: Penguin, 1999), 51.

[26] Millard, 'Overcoming Post-Colonial Myopia', 6.

[27] Mockler, *Mercenaries*, 13.

[28] G. T. Griffith, *The Mercenaries of the Hellenistic World* (Cambridge: Ares Publishing, 1984), 1.

[29] See eg Virginia Cowles, *The Phantom Major: The Story of David Stirling and the S.A.S. Regiment* (Barnsley: Pen and Sword Military, 2010); Alan Hoe, *David Stirling: The Authorised Biography of the Founder of the SAS* (New York: Time Warner Paperbacks, 1992), 41–225.

[30] Captain Daniel P. Ridlon, 'Contractors or Illegal Combatants? The Status of Armed Contractors in Iraq' (2008) 62 *Air Force Law Review* 199, 215 (citing O'Brien, 'Private Military Companies and African Security 1990–98' in Musah and Fayemi, *Mercenaries*, 43, 46).

[31] Ridlon, 'Contractors or Illegal Combatants?', 199, 215 (citing O'Brien, 'Private Military Companies and African Security 1990–98' in Musah and Fayemi, *Mercenaries*, 43, 46).

[32] Sabelo Gumedze (ed), *Private Security in Africa: Manifestation, Challenges, Regulation* (Pretoria: Institute for Security Studies, 2007), 3.

Consequently, by the beginning of the 1990s, the UN had already drafted a convention outlawing mercenaries but had clearly not considered PMCs in the drafting process.

The end of the Cold War brought about a great sense of hope for peace and stability throughout the world. Suddenly, decades of hardened realist policies appeared obsolete.[33] The collapse of the bipolar balance of powers, which had dominated nearly half a century, left scholars, politicians, and policymakers guessing as to the future of international relations. In 1992, Francis Fukuyama famously wrote 'What we may be witnessing is not just the end of the Cold War, or the passing of a particular period of post-war history, but the end of history as such: that is, the end point of mankind's ideological evolution and the universalisation of Western liberal democracy as the final form of human government.'[34] With the end of the Cold War, and the end of apartheid, the so-called 'peace dividend' led to massive demilitarization policies around the world.[35] National militaries shrank dramatically, leaving highly trained soldiers, sailors, and airmen out of jobs. In this period of transition, private military companies as corporate entities began to enter the fray of international security in a more significant and noticeable way.

Throughout the 1990s, numerous brutal conflicts plagued the African continent. These wars showcased the concept of a private military company equipped to engage in combat. Two companies featured at the forefront of this phenomenon in the 1990s: Sandline International of the UK and Executive Outcomes of South Africa. Both companies were involved primarily in African affairs, though Sandline was infamously involved in Bougainville's self-determination struggle as well.[36] Executive Outcomes (EO) played a major part in ending the war in Angola for the first time (it restarted later), and in fighting against the Revolutionary United Front (RUF) rebels of Sierra Leone (another war which restarted after EO left).[37] In the process, EO caused numerous controversies. According to one scholar, EO found it too difficult to distinguish between combatants and civilians during one

[33] See, generally, Richard Ned Lebow, 'The Long Peace, the End of the Cold War, and the Failure of Realism' (1994) 48 *International Organisation* 249; Jeffrey W. Legro and Andrew Moravcsik, 'Is Anybody Still a Realist?' (1999) 24 *International Security* 5; Bruce Russett, *Grasping the Democratic Peace: Principles for a Post-Cold War Peace* (Princeton, NJ: Princeton University Press, 1993); Paul Schroeder, 'Historical Reality vs. Neo-Realist Theory' (1994) 19 *International Security* 108; John A. Vasquez, 'The Realist Paradigm and Degenerative vs. Progressive Research Programs: An Appraisal of Neotraditional Research on Waltz's Balancing Proposition' (1997) 91 *American Political Science Review* 899.

[34] Francis Fukuyama, 'The End of History?' (Summer 1989) *The National Interest* 4.

[35] David Shearer, 'Private Armies and Military Intervention', International Institute for Strategic Studies, Adelphi Paper 316, 1998, 13–16 and 26–7.

[36] Sean Dorney, *The Sandline Affair: Politics and Mercenaries and the Bougainville Crisis* (Sydney: Australian Broadcasting Commission, 1998).

[37] Jim Hooper, *Bloodsong! An Account of Executive Outcomes in Angola* (London: Harper, 2003); Roelf van Heerden and Andrew Hudson, *Four Ball, One Tracer: Commanding Executive Outcomes in Angola and Sierra Leone* (Solihull: Helion & Co, 2012).

military operation in Sierra Leone, so company officials ordered their employees to initiate air strikes and simply 'kill everybody'.[38] Yet this anecdote is contrasted with the strong and irrefutable evidence that between 250 and 350 employees of EO were able to work with the Republic of Sierra Leone armed forces and, in only a few months, to defeat the RUF rebels more convincingly and successfully than any other intervening force in the course of the decade-long war.[39] The company, which was founded in 1989, dissolved in 1998 when South Africa changed its laws.

Sandline International, headed by former British Army Lieutenant Colonel Tim Spicer and legally based in the Bahamas, was contracted by the government of Papua New Guinea in 1997 for US$36 million to train an elite force and to fight in pursuit of resolving an internal domestic conflict.[40] The contract, however, came to light, causing a major scandal, and was never fully executed.[41] Sandline was also involved in assisting the fighting in Sierra Leone in 1998 and Liberia in 2003. On 16 April 2004, Sandline closed its operations with the following message:

> The general lack of governmental support for Private Military Companies willing to help end armed conflicts in places like Africa, in the absence of effective international intervention, is the reason for this decision. Without such support the ability of Sandline to make a positive difference in countries where there is widespread brutality and genocidal behaviour is materially diminished.[42]

A large number of other companies, however, have found plenty of work in recent years providing armed services in those same areas. Tim Spicer himself went on to found Aegis, one of the largest PMCs currently in operation.[43]

As a result of the wars in Iraq and Afghanistan, the private military industry has boomed since 2001. 'Where, ten years ago, such a category was composed of individuals tasked with personal and installation protection primarily, private security companies have grown to such a degree that many of them now include capabilities in transport, intelligence, combat-firepower, and para-medical skills.'[44] In many ways, developments in this area have occurred so quickly that international policies and existing guidance on the applicability of international law have been outpaced. 'The privatization of [war-fighting and security] activities cannot be controlled in the [traditional] manner, given that enterprises which enter into commercial

[38] Elizabeth Rubin, 'An Army of One's Own: In Africa, Nations Hire a Corporation to Wage War' (Feb 1997) *Harper's* 47; Laura Dickinson, 'Government for Hire: Privatizing Foreign Affairs and the Problem of Accountability under International Law' (2005) 47 *William and Mary Law Review* 137, 153.

[39] Gaston, 'Mercenarism 2.0?', 225–6.

[40] Virginia Newell and Benedict Sheehey, 'Corporate Militaries and States: Actors, Interactions and Reactions' (2006) 41 *Texas International Law Journal* 67, 75.

[41] Newell and Sheehey, 'Corporate Militaries and States', 75.

[42] Sandline International Website, available at <http://www.sandline.com>.

[43] Aegis website, 'Tim Spicer', available at <http://www.aegisworld.com/index.php/tim-spicer>.

[44] Kevin A. O'Brien, 'The New Warrior Class' in Paul B. Rich (ed), *Warlords in International Relations* (Basingstoke: Palgrave Macmillan, 1999), 52, 57.

agreements with other governments have not, traditionally, fallen under the rubric of military oversight or arms control.'[45] While these issues point at the myriad *jus in bello* concerns surrounding PMCs, the present analysis will focus on the force regime of the UN Charter and the *jus ad bellum*.

III. Case Studies

Before delving into a technical legal analysis of PMCs and *jus ad bellum*, it is helpful from a practical standpoint to have a sense of how PMCs have been used and how they could be used by states. To illustrate the ways in which PMCs may trigger the international legal prohibition on the use of force, this analysis will examine three real-world incidents involving companies working at the behest of a state. While the objective is not to claim that these incidents constituted violations of the prohibition on the use of force, Section III will explore how each type of activity represented could be used in a manner contrary to *jus ad bellum*.

A. MPRI in Croatia

In the midst of the Balkan war of 1992–5, the US government licensed an American private military company, Military Professional Resources, Inc (MPRI) to train Croatian forces under a contract with the Croatian government.[46] Shortly after MPRI began performance on the contract, the Croats had tremendous success in repelling Serbian forces from their territory.[47] That success was then augmented in Operation Storm, a major offensive aimed at expelling Serbs from the Krajina region.[48] Operation Storm bore the markings of US strategic preparation and tactical execution, leading many to believe that MPRI provided the planning and support to make the mission possible.[49] Furthermore, Croats involved in the operation

[45] O'Brien, 'The New Warrior Class' in Rich, *Warlords in International Relations*, 58.

[46] Alison Stranger and Mark Williams, 'Private Military Corporations: Benefits and Costs of Outsourcing Sovereignty' (2006) 2 *Yale Journal of International Affairs* 8–9.

[47] Ken Silverstein, 'Privatizing War: How Affairs of State are Outsourced to Corporations Beyond Public Control', *The Nation*, 28 July 1997, available at <https://www.mtholyoke.edu/acad/intrel/silver.htm>.

[48] Deborah D. Avant, *The Market For Force: The Consequences of Privatizing Security* (Cambridge: Cambridge University Press, 2001), 104.

[49] Hannah Tonkin, *State Control Over Private Military and Security Companies in Armed Conflict* (Cambridge: Cambridge University Press, 2011), 48–9; Avant, *The Market For Force*, 104.

attributed their success to the training and assistance received from MPRI.[50] Even MPRI officials themselves bragged of the capacity of the company, calling it 'the greatest corporate assemblage of military expertise in the world'.[51]

The significance of Operation Storm cannot be understated.[52] Not only did it change the course of the war and lead to the reclamation of 30 per cent of Croatian territory, it also proved to observers that a PMC did not have to directly engage in combat (like Executive Outcomes or Sandline) in order to have dramatic effect on a state's use of force. Since Croatia had already been embroiled in conflict prior to hiring MPRI, the prohibition on the use of force was not triggered in this instance. But the potential is unmistakable.

Another dynamic of this particular case study is the role of the US government. Prior to MPRI's contract with the Croatian government, the US had hired the company to provide 45 border monitors to assist with enforcing a UN sanctions regime.[53] On the back of that small contract came the much more extensive relationship between MPRI and the Croats. Commentators and the UK government alike have noted that MPRI's activity in Croatia was tantamount to US 'foreign policy by proxy'.[54] The US was not paying MPRI, but between strong governmental ties and exclusively ex-US military personnel, MPRI seemed to some to be operating as an

[50] Tonkin, *State Control Over Private Military and Security Companies in Armed Conflict*, 48–9, citing Robert Fox, 'Fresh War Clouds Threaten Ceasefire: Secret U.S. Military Advice Helps "Cocky" Croats Push Towards Eastern Slavonia', *Sunday Telegraph*, 15 Oct 1995; Samantha Power et al, 'The Croatian Army's Friends', *US News and World Report*, 21 Aug 1995; Roger Cohen, 'US Cooling Ties to Croatia after Winking at Its Buildup', *New York Times*, 28 Oct 1995, available at <http://www.nytimes.com/1995/10/28/world/us-cooling-ties-to-croatia-after-winking-at-its-buildup.html?pagewanted=all&src=pm>; 'Croatia: Tudjman's New Model Army', *The Economist*, 11 Nov 1995; Ken Silverstein, *Private Warriors* (London: Verso, 2000), 172–3; Singer, *Corporate Warriors*, 5.

[51] Roger Cohen, 'US Cooling Ties to Croatia after Winking at Its Buildup', *New York Times*, 28 Oct 1995.

[52] It is worth noting that, in addition to the points discussed, MPRI's involvement in Croatia also led to an Alien Tort Claims Act claim against MPRI's parent company, L-3 Communications, *Genocide Victims of Krajina v. L-3 Communications*, Complaint Case 1:10-cv-05197 (ND Ill, 2010). The claim alleged:

> Defendant MPRI, a private military contractor subsequently acquired by Defendant L-3 Communications Inc., trained and equipped the Croatian military for Operation Storm and designed the Operation Storm battle plan. Operation Storm became the largest land offensive in Europe since World War II and resulted in the murder and inhumane treatment of thousands of ethnic Serbs, the forced displacement of approximately 200,000 ethnic Serbs from their ancestral homes in Croatian territory, and the pillaging and destruction of hundreds of millions of dollars worth of Serbian-owned property. The victims of Operation Storm and their heirs and next of kin herein claim that Defendants were complicit in genocide.

The case was effectively ended, however, by the US Supreme Court ruling in *Kiobel v. Royal Dutch Petroleum*, 569 US __ (2013) on 17 Apr 2013 which held that the Alien Tort Claims Act does not apply extraterritorially.

[53] Alison Stranger and Mark Williams, 'Private Military Corporations: Benefits and Costs of Outsourcing Sovereignty' (2006) 2 *Yale Journal of International Affairs* 8–9.

[54] Avant, *The Market For Force*, 104.

extension of the US as much as it was a client of Croatia.[55] Indeed, these relationships combined with an express opinion from the US government that MPRI's services were not in violation of an arms embargo has led some to argue that this contract constituted a surreptitious attempt by the US to use force against the Serbs.[56]

B. Blackwater in Colombia

On 1 March 2008, the Colombian military crossed national borders and entered Ecuadorian territory.[57] In what was a planned raid, the military launched an air strike with a coordinated ground attack against the Revolutionary Armed Forces of Colombia (FARC), a paramilitary organization that has been a violent rebel element in Colombia for decades.[58] While the attack was successful with regard to its military objectives, it was a political disaster as it significantly strained relations between the neighbouring countries.[59] Ecuador was exceedingly displeased with the violation of its territorial integrity, especially as the incident was not one of hot pursuit, but of premeditation.[60]

In the Ecuadorian government's report on the incident, however, the most striking and noteworthy revelation was that armed contractors from the PMC Blackwater Worldwide, an American company best known for its activities in Iraq, were accompanying the Colombian forces at the time of the incursion on Ecuadorian soil.[61] Those contractors had been hired not by the Colombian government but by the US government.[62] Section IV will discuss this matter further, but depending on the

[55] Avant, *The Market For Force*, 104.

[56] Samantha Power et al, 'The Croatian Army's Friends', *US News and World Report*, 21 Aug 1995; Roger Cohen, 'US Cooling Ties to Croatia after Winking at Its Buildup', *New York Times*, 28 Oct 1995, available at <http://www.nytimes.com/1995/10/28/world/us-cooling-ties-to-croatia-after-winking-at-its-buildup.html?pagewanted=all&src=pm>; 'Croatia: Tudjman's New Model Army', *The Economist*, 11 Nov 1995; Bradley Graham, 'U.S. Firm Exports Military Expertise; Role in Training Croatian Military Brings Publicity and Suspicions', *Washington Post*, 11 Aug 1995; Charlotte Eager, 'Invisible U.S. Army Defeats Serbs', *The Observer*, 5 Nov 1995.

[57] Christian J. Westra, 'Will the "Bush Doctrine" Survive its Progenitor? An Assessment of Jus ad Bellum Norms for the Post-Westphalian Age' (2009) 32 *Boston College International and Comparative Law Review* 399, 416.

[58] Frank M. Walsh, 'Rethinking the Legality of Colombia's Attack on the FARC in Ecuador: A New Paradigm for Balancing Territorial Integrity, Self-Defense and the Duties of Sovereignty' (2009) 21 *Pace International Law Review* 137, 138.

[59] Walsh, 'Rethinking the Legality', 143–7.

[60] Gabriel Marcella, 'War Without Borders: The Ecuador-Colombia Crisis of 2008 and Inter-American Security', *Air and Space Power Journal*, 1 Apr 2009, available at <http://www.airpower.au.af.mil/apjinternational/apj-s/2009/1tri09/marcellaeng.htm>.

[61] Eva Golinger, 'The Assassinations Next Door: Blackwater in Colombia', *Progresso Weekly*, 15 Dec 2009, available at <http://progreso-weekly.com/2/index.php?option=com_content&view=article&id=1362:the-assassins-next-door-blackwater-in-colombia&catid=40:lastest-news&Itemid=59>.

[62] Eva Golinger, 'Blackwater in Colombia', *Pravda*, 14 Dec 2009, available at <http://english.pravda.ru/hotspots/14-12-2009/111133-columbiaarticle-0/>.

degree of effective control the US government was exercising over the Blackwater personnel, the US may have violated the territorial integrity of Ecuador.[63]

c. CACI and Titan in Iraq

Consolidated Analysis Centers, Inc (CACI),[64] a PMC, and Titan, a translation division of L-3 Communications (which is also now the parent company of MPRI),[65] are companies that have been linked to the Abu Ghraib Prison scandal with allegations that their employees participated in the illegal interrogation tactics for which the Iraqi detention facility has become infamous.[66] According to the US Army's own investigation of the abuses at Abu Ghraib by Major General Antonio Taguba, CACI and Titan employees were directly involved in the violations which took place at the prison.[67] Taguba found that 'U.S. civilian contract personnel (Titan Corporation, CACI, etc. . .), third country nationals, and local contractors do not appear to be properly supervised within the detention facility at Abu Ghraib.'[68] The lack of proper supervision, however, was only a threshold problem, as the report continues to suggest that several employees of CACI and Titan directly participated in the abuse. In fact, he goes on to allege that a CACI civilian interrogator, in addition to making false statements about the activities in which he engaged during the interrogations, actually directed the US Army's Military Police to do things that were not allowed under the applicable regulations or policy. Furthermore, Taguba specifically states: 'he clearly knew his instructions equated to physical abuse.'[69] In addition, an interpreter with Titan lied about having been present for interrogations and was operating without security clearance. A second interpreter with Titan was also suspected of wrongdoing.

According to Colonel Jill Morgenthaler, six soldiers were charged with 'indecent acts, for ordering detainees to publicly masturbate; maltreatment, for non-physical abuse, piling inmates into nude pyramids and taking pictures of them nude; battery, for shoving and stepping on detainees; dereliction of duty; and conspiracy to maltreat detainees.'[70] Colonel Morgenthaler, speaking for US Central Command,

[63] *Case concerning Military and Paramilitary Activities in and against Nicaragua (Nicaragua v. US)*, Merits, Judgment, ICJ Rep 1986, 14, para 115.

[64] CACI website, 'Profile', available at <http://www.caci.com/about/profile.shtml>.

[65] L-3 Communications website, 'Working at L-3 Communications', available at <http://lsgcareers.l-3com.com/careers/>.

[66] Ryan P. Logan, 'The Detainee Treatment Act of 2005: Embodying U.S. Values to Eliminate Detainee Abuse By Civilian Contractors and Bounty Hunters in Afghanistan and Iraq' (2006) 39 *Vanderbilt Journal of Transnational Law* 1605, 1622.

[67] Major General Antonio Taguba, *Article 15-6 Investigation of the 800th Military Police Brigade*, at 'Regarding Part Two of the Investigation, I Make The Following Specific Findings of Fact' (2004), para 30.

[68] Taguba, *Article 15-6 Investigation of the 800th Military Police Brigade*, para 30.

[69] Taguba, *Article 15-6 Investigation of the 800th Military Police Brigade*, paras 11 and 30.

[70] Taguba, *Article 15-6 Investigation of the 800th Military Police Brigade*, paras 11 and 30.

which manages all military operations in the Middle East, said that 'one contractor was originally included with six soldiers, accused for his treatment of the prisoners, but we had no jurisdiction over him. It was left up to the contractor on how to deal with him.'[71] No CACI or Titan employees have been charged with criminal offences in any jurisdiction, though civil claims have been brought against both companies in US domestic courts.[72]

While this incident occurred amid an armed conflict between states, the significance for the present analysis concerns the threat of force. It demonstrates the ability of PMCs to be used extraterritorially in a manner so as to intimidate or display the willingness and ability to use force. Additionally it hints at the 'fly in, fly out' possibilities of using PMCs; namely that a PMC can be hired for a specific purpose, sent in, and brought back out more easily than military personnel in many cases.

IV. Analysis

Having introduced the subject matter and a few instances where PMCs have been used that point further at how they could be used, this section now delves into the question of how PMCs interface with *jus ad bellum*. After a recapitulation of relevant laws, this analysis explores several different issues traditionally discussed in the literature surrounding the prohibition on the use of force. Drawing on the examples presented in the last section, the analysis is enriched by realistic hypotheticals, helping to tease out some of the less obvious ways in which PMCs might end up triggering the prohibition on the use of force.

A. The Prohibition on the Use of Force

Yoram Dinstein describes 1928, the year of the Kellogg–Briand Pact, as 'a watershed date in the history of the legal regulation of the use of inter-State force.'[73] The renunciation of war as an instrument of national policy should have made the remainder

[71] Taguba, *Article 15-6 Investigation of the 800th Military Police Brigade*, paras 11 and 30. It should be noted, however, that in 2007 the Uniform Code of Military Justice was extended by the Military Extraterritorial Jurisdiction Act to cover this sort of conduct under US law.

[72] See eg *Ibrahim v. Titan Corp*, 391 FSupp 2d 10 (DDC, 2005); *Saleh v. Titan Corp*, 436 FSupp 2d 55 (DDC, 2006); *Saleh v. Titan Corp*, 580 F3d 1, 9 (DC Cir, 2009).

[73] Yoram Dinstein, *War, Aggression and Self-Defence* (5th edn, Cambridge: Cambridge University Press, 2011), 85.

of the 20th century one of the most peaceful periods in human history. The Second World War and the numerous conflicts that followed it, however, highlighted the shortcomings of the 1928 Pact. As Dinstein points out, there were four crucial flaws: '(i) the issue of self-defence was not addressed in the text; (ii) no agreed-upon limits were set on the legality of war as an instrument of international policy; (iii) the abnegation of war did not embrace the entire international community; and (iv) forcible measures "short of war" were eliminated from consideration.'[74] The attempt to shift from *jus ad bellum* to *jus contra bellum*, as Dinstein describes, failed to account for the realities of interstate relations.

The UN Charter in 1945 recast the *jus ad bellum* and developed a bifurcated approach to war: prohibition on the one hand and legitimate resort to force on the other. Article 2(4), the centrepiece of the prohibition on the use of force, provides: 'All Members shall refrain in their international relations from the threat or use of force against the territorial integrity or political independence of any state, or in any other manner inconsistent with the Purposes of the United Nations.'[75] As an exception to that prohibition, Article 51 provides:

> Nothing in the present Charter shall impair the inherent right of individual or collective self-defence if an armed attack occurs against a Member of the United Nations, until the Security Council has taken measures necessary to maintain international peace and security. Measures taken by Members in the exercise of this right of self-defence shall be immediately reported to the Security Council and shall not in any way affect the authority and responsibility of the Security Council under the present Charter to take at any time such action as it deems necessary in order to maintain or restore international peace.[76]

These two provisions are further clarified, insofar as interpretation is concerned, by the 1970 Declaration on Principles of International Law concerning Friendly Relations and Co-operation among States in accordance with the UN Charter.

The 1970 Declaration sets forth a series of principles in support of the prohibition on the use of force, clarifying some of the parameters of *jus ad bellum* in the modern legal context. The most obviously relevant to the present analysis is the principle that 'every State has the duty to refrain from organizing or encouraging the organisation of irregular forces or armed bands including mercenaries, for incursion into the territory of another state.'[77] PMCs could potentially fall within the ambit of this principle, suggesting that states are dissuaded from using PMCs for any transnational incursions. Their use, however, is not strictly prohibited. While far more could be said about these cornerstones of *jus ad bellum*, to address the question

[74] Dinstein, *War, Aggression and Self-Defence*, 85. [75] UN Charter, Art 2(4).

[76] UN Charter, Art 51.

[77] Declaration on Principles of International Law Concerning Friendly Relations and Co-operation among States in accordance with the Charter of the United Nations, GA Res 2625, Annex, 25 UN GAOR, Supp No 28, A/5217 (1970), 121.

whether PMCs can be used to violate the prohibition on the use of force, the issues of attribution and state responsibility must first be examined.

B. PMCs and State Responsibility

In the most obvious case of a PMC being used to violate the prohibition on the use of force, a state could hire a company to use armed personnel to enter another country by force in pursuit of a specific mission, possibly even taking control of the foreign state's territory and engaging its armed forces. Not only would this action likely violate the principles of the 1970 Declaration, such activity is highly unlikely as it would almost certainly draw the ire of the international community at large.[78] The first issue in such an instance, however, would be one of attribution. When a state hires a PMC to operate anywhere, it has no doubt 'acted', but the analysis of that action is necessarily different under the law of state responsibility than if the same state had sent its own military to perform the same function. Both Hannah Tonkin and Carsten Hoppe provide excellent analyses of some of the twilight surrounding state responsibility and the use of PMCs.[79] As Hoppe discusses, the International Law Commission's (ILC) Articles on the Responsibility of States for Internationally Wrongful Acts clarify that when a state sends soldiers to a conflict, it does not matter for what specific activity those soldiers are sent; the state is responsible regardless.[80] 'On the other hand, unless incorporation of the personnel into the national army can be proven, attribution of contractor conduct to a state under the conventional reading of the ILC Articles requires a much more complex factual inquiry.'[81] As will be discussed later, de jure incorporation of PMC personnel into the armed forces is extremely unlikely, and the de facto incorporation of PMC personnel into the armed forces can only occur in rare circumstances.[82] Hoppe points out as a preliminary matter, therefore, that since PMCs would not fall under Article 4 responsibility (for organs of a state such as the armed forces),[83] the principles of Articles

[78] Indeed, allegations regarding Russia's use of PMCs in order to be able to deny the involvement of 'troops' in Crimea and Eastern Ukraine in early 2014 underscore the problems that would arise, but furthermore suggest that such activity is not completely outside the realm of possibility. See eg Josh Rogin, 'Russian "Blackwater" Takes Over Ukraine Airport', *Daily Beast*, 28 Feb 2014, available at <http://www.thedailybeast.com/articles/2014/02/28/exclusive-russian-blackwater-takes-over-ukraine-airport.html>.

[79] See generally, Tonkin, *State Control Over Private Military and Security Companies in Armed Conflict*; Carsten Hoppe, 'Passing the Buck: State Responsibility for Private Military Companies' (2008) 19 *European Journal of International Law* 989.

[80] Hoppe, 'Passing the Buck', 990–1.

[81] Hoppe, 'Passing the Buck', 991.

[82] Tonkin, *State Control Over Private Military and Security Companies in Armed Conflict*, 58.

[83] Draft Articles on Responsibility of States for Internationally Wrongful Acts, with commentaries in Report of the International Law Commission on the Work of its Fifty-Third Session, UN GAOR, 56th Sess, Supp No 10, 43, A/56/10 (2001), Art 4, available at <http://www.un.org/law/ilc>; Annex to GA Res 56/83 (12 Dec 2001).

5 (Conduct of persons or entities exercising elements of governmental authority)[84] and 7 (Excess of authority or contravention of instructions)[85] create a situation in which states are responsible for the conduct of soldiers at all times, but would not be responsible for the off-duty actions of PMC personnel.[86] Here there is a legal gap that makes states less responsible for PMCs than for military personnel, but an analysis of state responsibility in triggering the prohibition on the use of force reveals even more problematic ambiguity.

As Hoppe contends, 'there is growing agreement in the literature that the conduct of contractors undertaking combat missions or detention and interrogation for a state in armed conflict or occupation is attributable to the hiring state as exercise of governmental authority.'[87] Article 8 seems to support this notion by pinning responsibility on states for conduct of entities such as PMCs when that conduct is directed or controlled by a state,[88] a position further supported by the International Criminal Tribunal for the former Yugoslavia (ICTY) Appeals Chamber decision in *Prosecutor v. Tadić*.[89] Looking beyond Hoppe and the ILC, in *Nicaragua*, the International Court of Justice (ICJ) held that the crucial matter is whether the state exercises 'effective control' over the party in question.[90] Since it is possible and indeed common for a state to exercise effective control over a PMC, the actions of a PMC could be attributed to the state that has hired it, depending on the particular set of facts. Given that relationship, it would appear that a state could theoretically use force against the territorial integrity or political independence of another state without deploying its military.

Returning to the example of Blackwater in Colombia, several questions arise. Was the US in effective control of the Blackwater contractors when they entered Ecuador? Was the Colombian government exercising effective control over those contractors, even though the US had hired them? Alternatively, were the Colombian forces operating under the control of the PMC? Albrecht Randelzhofer claims 'an incursion into the territory of another State constitutes an infringement of Art 2(4), even if it is not intended to deprive that state of part of its territory and if the invading troops are meant to withdraw immediately after completing a temporary and limited operation. . .'[91] It would appear, therefore, that Blackwater's involvement in this incursion on Ecuadorian soil may have violated the prohibition on the use of force, but it is unclear on whose behalf that violation occurred. In other words, a

[84] Articles on State Responsibility, Art 5. [85] Articles on State Responsibility, Art 7.

[86] Hoppe, 'Passing the Buck', 991. [87] Hoppe, 'Passing the Buck', 991–2.

[88] Articles on State Responsibility, Art 8.

[89] *Prosecutor v. Tadić*, Judgment of 15 July 1999, IT-94-1-A, Appeals Chamber, para 120; Tonkin, *State Control Over Private Military and Security Companies in Armed Conflict*, 87.

[90] *Case concerning Military and Paramilitary Activities in and against Nicaragua (Nicaragua v. US)*, Merits, Judgment, ICJ Rep 1986, 14, para 115.

[91] Albrecht Randelzhofer, 'Article 2(4)' in Bruno Simma et al (eds), *The Charter of the United Nations: A Commentary* (2nd edn, Oxford: Oxford University Press, 2002), vol I, 112, 123.

more in-depth adjudication of the facts would be required to ascertain which, if any, of the governments was responsible for Blackwater's action and thus operating contrary to Article 2(4).

C. PMCs and the Prohibition on the Use of Force

1. *Incorporation into the armed forces*

The analysis of the Blackwater case would be much clearer if the company's personnel had been incorporated into the armed forces of one of the states. Every state has the sovereign right to determine who is and is not a part of its armed forces.[92] Furthermore, 'there is no general obligation on states requiring them to use their public forces rather than private actors to carry out military and security functions.'[93] In Sierra Leone, for example, Executive Outcomes' personnel, mentioned in Section I, were actually brevetted into the Republic of Sierra Leone Armed Forces. While that conflict was a non-international armed conflict, the integration of the PMC personnel meant that, if Sierra Leone had decided to use force against another state and requested the Executive Outcomes personnel to be involved, the PMC would have been directly and unequivocally involved in Sierra Leone's violation of Article 2(4). While such an eventuality remains a theoretical possibility, it is unlikely to arise in reality at this point. Based on customary practices over the last decade, it is doubtful that a state will ever incorporate a PMC into its armed forces, de jure.[94]

Nils Melzer, however, in the International Committee of the Red Cross (ICRC) Interpretive Guidance on Direct Participation in Hostilities, notes that some PMCs are de facto incorporated into the armed forces of a party to non-international armed conflicts by virtue of being given a 'continuous combat function', even when such incorporation does not occur under national law.[95] 'Individuals whose continuous function involves the preparation, execution, or command of acts or operations amounting to direct participation in hostilities are assuming a continuous combat function…even before he or she first carries out a hostile act.'[96] This commentary, however, only applies to non-state parties to a conflict and is, much like Tonkin's analysis of de facto incorporation into the armed forces, a matter primarily of *jus in bello* significance, focused on international humanitarian law. That

92 Richard Morgan, 'Professional Military Firms Under International Law' (2008) 9 *Chicago Journal of International Law* 213, 227 (citing Lassa Oppenheim, 2 *International Law: Disputes, War and Neutrality* 255 (ed H. Lauterpacht, 7th edn, London: Longmans Green, 1952)).

93 Tonkin, *State Control Over Private Military and Security Companies in Armed Conflict*, 173.

94 Hoppe, 'Passing the Buck', 991.

95 ICRC, 'Interpretive Guidance on the Notion of Direct Participation in Hostilities Under International Humanitarian Law', 2009, 39, available at <http://www.icrc.org/eng/resources/documents/feature/direct-participation-ihl-feature-020609.htm>.

96 ICRC, 'Interpretive Guidance', 34.

said, there might arise a strange eventuality whereby a state were to intervene in a conflict without invitation as discussed later, and find itself fighting a belligerent party partially comprised of a PMC. Such a case would require further analysis. In general, however, incorporation, either de jure or de facto into the armed forces could theoretically cause a PMC to be involved in the use of force by a state but, in practice, is unlikely to occur.

2. *Facilitation of the use of force*

Keeping the dynamics of both the Executive Outcomes engagement in Sierra Leone and that of Blackwater in Colombia in mind, the case of MPRI in the Balkans provides another potential point of intersection between PMCs and the *jus ad bellum*: facilitation of the use of force. The Croatian example demonstrates the ability of a PMC to significantly increase a state's military capabilities—strategic, operational, and tactical—in a short amount of time. In that situation, Croatian forces were already involved in an armed conflict before their government hired MPRI to assist them. As the current industry evolves, however, companies are increasingly focused on providing training services, drawing on the elite expertise of ex-military personnel from the world's most advanced national forces. A state with aggressive intention could hire a PMC to assist in building its capacity specifically in order to project force against another state. As will be discussed further later, such an activity could be considered either a form of using force, if the intended target state were known and obvious, or at a minimum, a threat of force. Such arrangements also raise questions of the responsibility of PMCs to vet their clients in order to avoid aiding and abetting illegal activity[97]—a matter beyond the scope of the present analysis, though nevertheless of substantial importance.

3. *Protection of nationals overseas*

The use of force to rescue nationals overseas remains a contentious issue with regard to Article 2(4). The only way force could be legal in such circumstances is if the following criteria are met: (1) the host state must be unable or unwilling to protect the individuals; (2) the individuals must be in immediate danger of life-threatening harm; (3) force is only used as last resort; and (4) the intervening state may only use force that is reasonably necessary and the personnel involved must vacate immediately.[98] Again it would be theoretically possible for a state to use a PMC in such targeted operations. The use of contractors in detention and interrogation operations in Abu Ghraib, as shown by the CACI and Titan case,

[97] The lawsuit against MPRI for complicity to commit genocide, discussed at n 52, further supports this notion.

[98] Martin Dixon, *Textbook on International Law* (6th edn, Oxford: Oxford University Press, 2007), 322.

suggests an appetite to use contractors in contexts where they can be flown in and flown out. While not a completely parallel inference, it could be seen in certain circumstances as politically expedient to use contractors, unaffiliated with the armed forces, to carry out such rescue operations. There would be legal risk, however, as the individuals would almost certainly be operating in violation of other laws, even if the state's own use of force was not strictly prohibited. Unfortunately, it is difficult to discern whether such activity is actually occurring as the contracts to engage in such activity would, if they existed, almost certainly be classified. Nevertheless, it is conceivable that a state might use a PMC in this grey area of the force regime.

As a corollary, it is worth noting that the US Central Intelligence Agency (CIA) has allegedly hired contractors, including from Blackwater, to conduct overseas assassinations on its behalf.[99] This conduct is illegal on several fronts, but it is certainly a violation of the prohibition on the use of force. Consequently, evidence suggests the possibility that PMCs may be used in this manner, as well.

4. *Invitation*

If a state invites another state to assist in an armed conflict or other situation in which force might be necessary, it almost certainly does not expect a PMC to come on behalf of the invited state. The UK government considered such a scenario in 2002, but came to the conclusion that, while the Ministry of Defence effectively outsources support functions like food supply to private companies, security was a different matter. If the UK government has received a formal request from the UN, another state, or another international body to provide support to a humanitarian mission, and has accepted a mandate to do so, the expectation is 'that the front-line tasks will be undertaken by the UK's Armed Forces, with their known skills and experience. The government would therefore not consider it appropriate for the UK to agree to undertake such tasks and then to subcontract them to private companies.'[100] Only if major state militaries became so overstretched as to be unable to provide requested assistance would it be conceivable for a state to send a PMC on its behalf when invited to intervene. This remains, however, a remote possibility.

5. *Self-determination and assistance to rebels*

Another controversial area in the force regime is the use of force in assistance of rebel movements and self-determination efforts. Without exploring the general concerns

[99] Mark Mazzetti, 'C.I.A. Sought Blackwater's Help to Kill Jihadists', *New York Times*, 19 Aug 2009, available at <http://www.nytimes.com/2009/08/20/us/20intel.html?_r=1&hp>.

[100] Response of the Secretary of State for Foreign and Commonwealth Affairs to the Ninth Report of the Foreign Affairs Committee, 'Private Military Companies' (2001–2002, Cm 5642), para (h) (2002).

surrounding such interventions, focusing on the legality of using PMCs in such situations reveals a rather unusual dynamic. As noted in Section I, the personnel of PMCs do not, in most instances, meet the definition of mercenaries, especially the primary definition contained in the UN International Convention Against the Recruitment, Use, Financing and Training of Mercenaries. The Convention, however, has two definitions. The second definition of 'mercenary' is far less restrictive in some ways than the principal definition, though far more restrictive in terms of its scope of application. Article 1.2 provides:

A mercenary is also any person who, in any other situation:

a. is specially recruited locally or abroad for the purpose of participating in a concerted act of violence aimed at:
   i. overthrowing a Government or otherwise undermining the constitutional order of a State; or
   ii. undermining the territorial integrity of a State;
b. is motivated to take part therein essentially by the desire for significant private gain and is prompted by the promise or payment of material compensation;
c. is neither a national nor a resident of the State against which such an act is directed;
d. has not been sent by a State on official duty; and
e. is not a member of the armed forces of the State on whose territory the act is undertaken.[101]

The history behind this provision helps to contextualize it, as fragile African states were calling for a ban on mercenaries who were being hired to fight against self-determination, but were nevertheless also worried about their own ability to stay in power.[102] Oddly, however, this definition, part of a convention whose explicit aim was to protect self-determination efforts, may now actually hinder such movements and other efforts to overthrow oppressive regimes.

If the forces rebelling against the regime of Mu'ammer Gaddafi in Libya—a state party to the UN Mercenary Convention—in March to June 2011, for example, wanted to hire foreign PMCs to assist them, such PMC personnel could potentially be considered mercenaries under Article 1.2 of the UN Convention. They could be deemed to have been recruited to participate in a concerted act of violence aimed at overthrowing a government.[103] They may have been motivated by financial gain,[104] were not sent by a state on official duty,[105] were not residents or nationals of Libya[106] and were not members of the Libyan armed forces.[107] If, on the other hand, an intervening state sent that same company to assist the rebels, the Mercenary Convention would likely not be triggered. The prohibition on the use of force, on the other

[101] International Convention against the Recruitment, Use, Financing and Training of Mercenaries, GA Res 44/34, A/RES/44/34 (4 Dec 1989), Art 1 ('The Mercenary Convention').

[102] Millard, 'Overcoming Post-Colonial Myopia', 61–2.

[103] The Mercenary Convention, Art 1.2(a)(1).

[104] The Mercenary Convention, Art 1.2(b).

[105] The Mercenary Convention, Art 1.2(d).

[106] The Mercenary Convention, Art 1.2(c).

[107] The Mercenary Convention, Art 1.2(e).

hand, might be implicated by such activity, as the legality of the use of force against a legitimate government in support of rebel activities remains an unresolved matter. Interestingly, if the North Atlantic Treaty Organization (NATO) or the UN hired the PMC in these same circumstances, the contract would likely be prohibited, as international organizations are not states, so the personnel of the PMC hired would fall within the definition of mercenaries. This is thus an area of legal twilight that has significant practical implications as the individual members of the PMCs as well as those involved in hiring them could face criminal liability. Ironically, as well, therefore, this definition of 'mercenary' could potentially hinder and inhibit self-determination efforts by denying popular movements the opportunity to seek assistance in their struggle; the exact phenomenon that generated anti-mercenary sentiments in the first place.

6. *Humanitarian intervention*

Another area that requires further exploration is humanitarian intervention—perhaps the most controversial subject within the discourse surrounding the prohibition on the use of force. Adding to the existing controversy as to whether a state can legally intervene to stop a humanitarian crisis is the question of whether a state can do so by way of a PMC. Furthermore, what are the legal implications if a state-funded humanitarian organization hired a PMC to assist in intervening in a humanitarian disaster? What if the PMC hired is fully licensed in the host state and comprised exclusively of local nationals? Is this perhaps a new option for dealing with humanitarian crises? While far more could and indeed should be said on this topic, this is not the venue for a complete explication of the matter. These issues will be at the heart of further investigation into the relationship between PMCs and *jus ad bellum*.

D. PMCs and the Prohibition on the Threat of Force

As Nikolas Stürchler points out, 'even the most comprehensive discussions of the force regime have turned a blind eye to one of its components.'[108] Not only is the use of force prohibited by Article 2(4), but also the *threat* of force. Stürchler examines this matter in considerable depth, engaging in historical, contextual, judicial, and empirical reviews of the law and its implementation in practice. His focus, however, is on military threats. Having established previously that PMCs and their personnel are not likely to be incorporated into the military at this point, especially not in

[108] Nikolas Stürchler, *The Threat of Force in International Law* (Cambridge: Cambridge University Press, 2007), 1–2.

the context of *jus ad bellum*, it is worth examining whether PMCs can be used as a means of threatening force in violation of Article 2(4).

Stürchler makes a distinction between threatening force as a means of upholding the peaceful aims of the UN Charter and threatening force with the intent to use it.[109] Based on his analysis, it seems the first could be legal, as it is a preferable means of avoiding the use of force, whereas the second would always be unlawful. Conceivably, therefore, PMCs could be used in either fashion in certain circumstances. A government could hire PMCs in any number of ways to effectively threaten force without either using its military or even using armed PMCs.

As Stürchler concludes, there is one question that needs to be answered when assessing the threat of force: 'does a state credibly communicate its readiness to use force in a particular instance?'[110] Examples include: an ultimatum;[111] open, explicit, or verbal indications of the use of force;[112] demonstration of force;[113] militarized acts;[114] and the actual use of force.[115] Returning to the three examples from Section III, it is possible to see how PMCs could be used to threaten force. Blackwater accompanying the Colombian forces could be considered a threat by use of force, MPRI's involvement with Croatia could be seen either as militarization or indication of the use of force were the engagement to have begun before the armed conflict, and the CACI and Titan involvement in interrogations could be seen as a demonstration of force or at least an explicit indication of the use of force. This is an area that will need to be explored further, especially as PMCs become more involved in training armed forces and facilitating improved military capacity.

E. PMCs, International Organizations, and the Prohibition on the Use of Force

In addition to the prohibition in Article 2(4) and the exception in Article 51, Chapter VII of the UN Charter in its entirety forms a cornerstone of the force regime. While Chapter VII is less relevant to this discussion in general, it is important to note the relationship between PMCs, the prohibition on the use of force, and the UN itself, as well as other international organizations. Through Chapter VII, the UN Security Council has the power to authorize armed force[116] to 'maintain or restore international peace and security'.[117] While Article 42 of the Charter states that forceful

[109] Stürchler, *The Threat of Force in International Law*, 254.
[110] Stürchler, *The Threat of Force in International Law*, 259.
[111] Stürchler, *The Threat of Force in International Law*, 258.
[112] Stürchler, *The Threat of Force in International Law*, 260.
[113] Stürchler, *The Threat of Force in International Law*, 260.
[114] Stürchler, *The Threat of Force in International Law*, 261.
[115] Stürchler, *The Threat of Force in International Law*, 262.
[116] UN Charter, Art 42.
[117] UN Charter, Art 39.

measures taken by the Security Council may include actions by the 'air, sea or land forces of the Members of the United Nations', nothing in the Charter prohibits using forces that do not belong to the member states. Thus it is theoretically possible that the UN Security Council could, within the force regime, authorize a PMC to use force under Chapter VII. While that may seem far-fetched, it is worth noting that numerous international organizations, including various organs of the UN have contracted and continue to contract with PMCs in a range of areas from de-mining operations to law enforcement to armed security.[118]

The use of PMCs by international organizations raises an important question: could the UN, NATO, or another international organization hire a PMC to do exactly the same thing as a state's military without triggering the prohibition on the use of force? Under basic agency law, it can be assumed that action by a PMC under a contract with an international organization, much like with a private company, would be attributable to the hiring entity.[119] States are prohibited from infringing the territorial integrity or political independence of other states, but international organizations are not subject to Article 2(4).

The military authority of the UN and NATO comes from their member states. A number of commentators and scholars have suggested that these combined state forces use PMCs in place of state forces for certain missions, even amid armed conflicts, and most of these organizations already do hire PMCs to assist their military efforts.[120] If a PMC is working directly for an international organization and not one of its member states, could that organization circumvent the prohibition on the use of force? Long-standing law establishes that multi-state forces like the UN or NATO cannot themselves be party to an armed conflict because they lack legal personality in this context.[121] 'Traditionally, only States and armed groups can be Party to a conflict and have, as such, clear rights and obligations. For armed groups this is only possible under certain conditions. . . . [I]nternational organisations cannot be Party to an armed conflict, despite the fact that they regularly run military operations.'[122] If, therefore, a state hired a PMC to be involved in a multi-state military intervention

[118] Anne-Marie Buzatu and Benjamin Buckland, 'Private Military & Security Companies: Future Challenges in Security Governance', DCAF Horizon 2015 Working Paper No 3, 2010, 15–16.

[119] Cedric Ryngaert, 'Litigating Abuses Committed by Private Military Companies' (2008) 19 *European Journal of International Law* 1035, 1039–40.

[120] See, generally, Malcolm Patterson, 'A Corporate Alternative to United Nations Ad Hoc Military Deployments' (2008) 13 *Journal of Conflict and Security Law* 215; W. Hays Parks, 'Evolution of Policy and Law Concerning the Role of Civilians and Civilian Contractors Accompanying the Armed Forces', 2005, 5–6, available at <http://www.icrc.org/eng/assets/files/other/2005-07-expert-paper-icrc.pdf>; Singer, *Corporate Warriors*, 53–7 and 183.

[121] Proceedings of the Bruges Colloquium, 'Armed Conflicts and Parties to Armed Conflicts Under IHL: Confronting Legal Categories to Contemporary Realities' (22–3 Oct 2009), 10th Bruges Colloquium No 40 Autumn 2010, 109–10, available at <http://www.coleurop.be/file/content/publications/pdf/Collegium40.pdf>.

[122] Proceedings of the Bruges Colloquium, 109–110.

not authorized under Chapter VII, and incorporated the PMC into its armed forces, that PMC could be providing prohibited force. If that same PMC in the exact same operation, however, were hired by NATO rather than one of the member states, it would not be implicating Article 2(4). This inconsistency in international law creates a loophole that could prove significant in the future as multi-state missions are increasingly privatized.

F. The Montreux Document

Just as 1928 was a watershed date insofar as the relationship between states and war was concerned, 2008 was a watershed date for the relationship between states and PMCs. Recognizing the growing need for clarity regarding the place of PMCs in international law, especially given the increased role of such companies in conflict areas around the globe, the Swiss Federal Department of Foreign Affairs and the ICRC jointly initiated in 2006 what has become known as the Montreux Process.[123] Between 2006 and 2008, 17 key countries collaborated via four expert meetings and five intergovernmental meetings in an attempt to clarify what international laws apply to the operation of PMCs in armed conflicts, and what best practices should be in place to ensure that the various entities involved in the private military and security industry maintain compliance with those laws.[124] The participating countries were Afghanistan, Angola, Australia, Austria, Canada, China, France, Germany, Iraq, Poland, Sierra Leone, South Africa, Sweden, Switzerland, Ukraine, the UK, and the US: effectively the countries with the strongest ties to PMSCs.[125] On 17 September 2008, those states ratified the Montreux Document on Pertinent International Legal Obligations and Good Practices for States related to Operations of Private Military and Security Companies during Armed Conflict, the product of their efforts.[126] The Document contains 27 'Pertinent International Legal Obligations' and 73 'Good Practices'.[127]

While the Document expressly 'recalls existing legal obligations of States and PMSCs and their personnel . . . and provides States with good practices

[123] Simon Chesterman, 'Lawyers, Guns and Money: The Governance of Business Activities in Conflict Zones' (2011) 11 *Chicago Journal of International Law* 321, 334.

[124] Press Release, 'The Montreux Document on Private Military and Security Companies', Swiss Federal Department of Foreign Affairs, available at <http://www.eda.admin.ch/psc>.

[125] Report, 'The Montreux Document on Private Military and Security Companies', ICRC, available at <http://www.icrc.org/web/eng/siteengo.nsf/html/montreux-document-170908>.

[126] Press Release, the Montreux Document.

[127] See generally, the Montreux Document on Pertinent International Legal Obligations and Good Practices for States related to Operations of Private Military and Security Companies during Armed Conflict, A/63/467–S/2008/636 (2008).

to promote compliance with international humanitarian law and human rights law during armed conflict',[128] it is a non-binding instrument. The Document explicitly neither creates nor alters any legal obligations.[129] The parties to the Montreux Document specifically state that they do not seek to endorse the use of PMSCs—the term used in the document—but rather to use multilateral collaboration in order to clarify what laws and practices should constrain states and indeed other contracting entities[130] when the decision to use a PMSC has been made.[131]

Unfortunately, however, it appears that only the *jus in bello* aspects of private military contracting were considered when drafting the Montreux Document.[132] While a few provisions obliquely address *jus ad bellum* issues, the prohibition on the use of force is not directly mentioned. As Keiichiro Okimoto explores, there is a relationship between international humanitarian law and the use of force, just as there is a relationship between *jus in bello* and *jus ad bellum*, but the nature of that relationship does not provide for a wholesale application of the Montreux Document to the *jus ad bellum* aspects of private military contracting.[133] A few discrete portions, however, do provide some guidance to states regarding the intersection of PMCs and the force regime. The Document establishes that contracting states retain their international legal obligations even after contracting with a PMSC[134] and thus cannot outsource to PMSCs what they cannot legally do themselves.[135] Beyond this broad platitude, however, most of the more detailed provisions are specific to either international humanitarian law or human rights law.

One of the most significant provisions of the Document, however, regards the responsibility of contracting states for the actions of the PMSCs they hire. Paragraph 7 of the Legal Obligations section reads:

> Although entering into contractual relations does not in itself engage the responsibility of Contracting States, the latter are responsible for violations of international humanitarian law, human rights law, or other rules of international law committed by PMSCs or their personnel where such violations are attributable to the Contracting State, consistent with customary international law, in particular if they are:

[128] The Montreux Document, Preface, para 2.

[129] The Montreux Document, Preface, para 3.

[130] The Montreux Document, Preface, para 8.

[131] The Montreux Document, Preface, para 7.

[132] According to the publicity surrounding the Montreux Process, 'The Montreux Document is the first international document to describe international law as it applies to the activities of private military and security companies (PMSCs) whenever these are present in the context of an armed conflict.' Press Release, the Montreux Document.

[133] Keiichiro Okimoto, *The Distinction and Relationship Between Jus ad Bellum and Jus in Bello* (Oxford: Hart, 2011).

[134] The Montreux Document, Part One, para 1.

[135] The Montreux Document, Part One, para 2.

a. incorporated by the State into its regular armed forces in accordance with its domestic legislation;
b. members of organised armed forces, groups or units under a command responsible to the State;
c. empowered to exercise elements of governmental authority if they are acting in that capacity (i.e. are formally authorised by law or regulation to carry out functions normally conducted by organs of the State); or
d. in fact acting on the instructions of the State (i.e. the State has specifically instructed the private actor's conduct) or under its direction or control (i.e. actual exercise of effective control by the State over a private actor's conduct).[136]

Though this paragraph was undoubtedly focused on *jus in bello* issues, the inclusion of violations of 'other rules of international law' potentially expands this provision to cover the use of PMSCs in situations in which they might be used to violate the prohibition on the use of force. This is a significant statement of obligation, therefore, on the part of the states which endorse the Document.

Finally, out of the 73 paragraphs providing best practices for states, only one is somewhat relevant to the present analysis. 'To determine which services may or may not be contracted out to PMSCs; in determining which services may not be contracted out, Contracting States take into account factors such as whether a particular service could cause PMSC personnel to become involved in direct participation in hostilities.'[137] Before contracting with a PMC to engage in activity that might be attributed to the state as prohibited force being used against another state, the hiring state must first give full consideration to the legal restrictions and implications.

Though the Montreux Document may have been a watershed accomplishment in the regulation of PMCs and in the relationship between states and private companies in armed conflict settings, it provides little guidance on issues of *jus ad bellum*. As the Montreux Document is reviewed and revised, the endorsing states may wish to consider such issues. As yet, however, the issues discussed in this analysis remain, for the most part, open for debate.

V. CONCLUSION

This is a topic that has not been previously explored. While numerous works in recent years have sought to review *jus ad bellum* in light of new developments in international

[136] The Montreux Document, Part One, para 7.

[137] The Montreux Document, Part Two, para 1.

affairs,[138] and numerous more have taken on legal issues surrounding PMCs,[139] there has yet to be an extensive and in-depth study of the intersection of the use of PMCs and the prohibition on the use of force. As the use of PMCs by states continues to evolve, new areas, yet unimagined, may arise, which will further implicate the prohibition on the use of force. One area that needs further examination, for example, is in the context of self-defence. Noam Lubell points out that Article 51 does not restrict the source of the threat against which a state may use force.[140] In other words, non-state actors, potentially including PMCs hired by non-state clients could pose sufficient threat to territorial integrity so as to necessitate the resort to force by a state in self-defence. Could activity in self-defence against a PMC include violating the territorial integrity of another state? This is just one of the many significant questions that will arise when examining the relationship between PMCs and Article 51.

This chapter has perhaps raised more questions than it has answered. It has sought, however, to highlight some of the realistic points of intersection and conflict between states' use of private military companies and their use of force. The various examples and hypotheticals have indicated that, while it may only be in unusual circumstances that the use of a PMC might trigger the prohibition on the threat or use of force, such circumstances are well within the realm of possibility and may already have occurred in several instances. Further research and analysis will be necessary to probe the contours of this issue. As the private military industry continues to develop, evolve, and mature, so too must the legal discourse around it. This chapter, therefore, will hopefully serve as the starting point for an ongoing and rigorous examination of private military companies and the *jus ad bellum* in the coming years and decades.

[138] See eg Lindsay Moir, *Reappraising the Resort to Force: International Law, Jus ad Bellum and the War on Terror* (Oxford: Hart, 2010); Christian Henderson, *The Persistent Advocate and the Use of Force: The Impact of the United States upon the Jus ad Bellum in the Post-Cold War Era* (Farnham: Ashgate, 2010); Noam Lubell, *Extraterritorial Use of Force Against Non-State Actors* (Oxford: Oxford University Press, 2010).

[139] See eg Ian Ralby, 'Private Military and Security Companies in the Uncharted Spaces of the Law', unpublished dissertation, Cambridge University Library, 2011; Tonkin, *State Control Over Private Military and Security Companies in Armed Conflict*, 48–9; Hin-Yan Liu, 'Leashing the Corporate Dogs of War: The Legal Implications of the Modern Private Military Company' (2010) 15 *Journal of Conflict and Security Law* 141; Adam Ebrahim, Note, 'Going to War with the Army You Can Afford: The United States, International Law, and the Private Military Industry' (2010) 28 *Boston University International Law Journal* 181; Amol Mehra, 'Bridging the Accountability Gaps—The Proliferation of Private Military and Security Companies and Ensuring Accountability for Human Rights Violations' (2010) 22 *Pacific McGeorge Global Business and Development Law Journal* 323; Charles Tiefer, 'No More Nisour Squares: Legal Control of Private Security Contractors in Iraq and After' (2009) 88 *Oregon Law Review* 745; Craig S. Jordan, 'Who Will Guard the Guards? The Accountability of Private Military Contractors in Areas of Armed Conflict' (2009) 35 *New England Journal on Criminal and Civil Confinement* 309; Hoppe, 'Passing the Buck', 989; Ridlon, 'Contractors or Illegal Combatants?'; Chia Lehnardt, 'Individual Liability of Private Military Personnel Under International Criminal Law' (2008) 19 *European Journal of International Law* 1015; Gaston, 'Mercenarism 2.0?'; Antenor Hallo de Wolf, 'Modern Condottieri in Iraq: Privatizing War from the Perspective of International and Human Rights Law' (2006) 13 *Indiana Journal of Global Legal Studies* 315.

[140] Lubell, *Extraterritorial Use of Force Against Non-State Actors*, 32.

PART VII

GENERAL PROBLEMS

CHAPTER 54

JUS COGENS AND THE USE OF ARMED FORCE

ANDRÉ DE HOOGH*

I. Introduction

THE concept of *jus cogens*, introduced into positive international law by articles 53 and 64 of the Vienna Convention on the Law of Treaties (VCLT),[1] has captured the imagination of many an international lawyer. Nevertheless, publications focusing on *jus cogens* and the use of armed force tend to be rare.[2] And yet, there are more

* Many thanks to Marcel Brus, Antenor Hallo de Wolf, Jörg Kammerhofer, Abel Knottnerus, and Andrej Zwitter for their detailed comments on an earlier draft, and Patricia Agoncillo for her research assistance. Responsibility is mine alone.

[1] The 1969 Vienna Convention on the Law of Treaties, 1155 UNTS 331–53.

[2] But see Carin Kahgan, '*Jus Cogens* and the Inherent Right to Self-Defense' (1997) 3 *ILSA Journal of International and Comparative Law* 767; Ole Spiermann, 'Humanitarian Intervention as a Necessity and the Threat or Use of *Jus Cogens*' (2002) 71 *Nordic Journal of International Law* 523; Charles Leben, 'Obligations relating to the Use of Force and Arising from Peremptory Norms of International Law' in James Crawford, Alain Pellet, and Simon Olleson (eds), *The Law of International Responsibility* (Oxford: Oxford University Press, 2010), 1197; James Green, 'Questioning the Peremptory Status of the Prohibition of the Use of Force' (2011) 32 *Michigan Journal of International Law* 215; and Alexander Orakhelashvili, 'Changing *Jus Cogens* through State Practice? The Case of the Prohibition of the Use of Force and its Exceptions', Chapter 7 in this volume. Cf also Lauri Hannikainen, *Peremptory Norms (Jus Cogens) in International Law, Historical Development, Criteria, Present Status* (Helsinki: Finnish Lawyers' Publishing Co, 1988), 323–56; and Olivier Corten, *The Law against War: The Prohibition on the Use of Force in Contemporary International Law* (Portland, OR: Hart, 2010), 198–213.

than sufficient reasons to discuss the various legal issues resulting from the claim that the prohibition of the use of armed force in international relations, embodied in Article 2(4) of the UN Charter,[3] constitutes a peremptory norm of general international law.[4]

This chapter will first of all discuss whether or not the prohibition pertaining to the use of armed force can be considered to possess the status of a peremptory norm (Section II). Next, Section III will inquire into the restrictions flowing from the peremptory prohibition of the use of armed force or of aggression and its relationship to accepted or claimed exceptions. It will consider whether the circumstances precluding wrongfulness, namely countermeasures, consent, and necessity allow for use of armed force, and how these relate to the peremptory prohibition. This section will continue to reflect on how specific exceptions to the prohibition, such as the right of self-defence laid down in Article 51 of the Charter, may be accommodated to the peremptory prohibition.

Finally, Section IV will proceed to reflect on demands for forcible action resulting from peremptory norms, such as an armed intervention to stop genocide. First, it will be discussed whether it is admissible to deduce legal effects or consequences directly from the characterization of *jus cogens* norms as hierarchically higher than 'ordinary' norms. Secondly, this section will explore whether the implementation or enforcement of peremptory norms might entail a disregard for the prohibition of the use of armed force in the absence of an accepted conventional or customary justification.

II. The Peremptory Norm(s) Pertaining to the Use of Armed Force

Article 53 VCLT, headed *jus cogens*, stipulates:

A treaty is void if, at the time of its conclusion, it conflicts with a peremptory norm of general international law. For purposes of the present Convention, a peremptory norm of general international law is a norm accepted and recognized by the international community of States as a whole as a norm from which no derogation is permitted and which can be modified only by a subsequent norm of general international law having the same character.

[3] The 1945 Charter of the United Nations, *United Nations Conference on International Organization*, vol XV, 335–54.

[4] eg Corten, *The Law against War*, 201–13; Alexander Orakhelashvili, *Peremptory Norms in International Law* (Oxford: Oxford University Press, 2006), 50–1.

Though the concept of *jus cogens* now appears fully accepted in international law,[5] various issues have engendered debate. One of those concerns the status of the underlying norm of general international law and the way in which such a norm is elevated to peremptory status.

Where Article 53 VCLT stipulates that a norm ought to be accepted and recognized by states as one from which no derogation is permitted, this suggests that a peremptory norm is based on an existing norm. The status of that underlying norm remains unclear, in that Article 53 claims it must be one pertaining to 'general international law'. Some authors have pointed out that it could not singularly refer to multilateral treaties, since those are by nature relative in character, that is, they do not bind states that have refrained from becoming a party to them (Art 34 VCLT).[6] Hence, a sensible construction is that such a norm ought to be based on a universal rule of customary international law.[7]

The determination of the existence of a peremptory norm thus involves a two-stage process: (1) the establishment of a norm of general international law, that is, a universal rule of customary international law; and (2) acceptance and recognition of such a norm as one from which no derogation is permitted.[8] However, this second stage should not be seen to embody simply the criterion of non-derogation,

[5] With even the ICJ now recognizing its existence: *Armed Activities on the Territory of the Congo (New Application: 2002) (DRC v. Rwanda)*, Jurisdiction and Admissibility, Judgment, ICJ Rep 2006, 6, 31–3, paras 64–70; *Application of the Convention on the Prevention and Punishment of the Crime of Genocide (Bosnia and Herzegovina v. Serbia and Montenegro)*, Judgment, ICJ Rep 2007, 43, 104–5 and 110–11, paras 146–8 and 161–2; *Jurisdictional Immunities of the State (Germany v. Italy: Greece Intervening)*, Judgment, ICJ Rep 2012, 99, 140–2, paras 92–7. See also *North Sea Continental Shelf*, Judgment, ICJ Rep 1969, 3, 42; *Barcelona Traction, Light and Power Company, Limited*, Judgment, ICJ Rep 1970, 3, 32, paras 33–4; *Case concerning Military and Paramilitary Activities in and against Nicaragua (Nicaragua v. US)*, Merits, ICJ Rep 1986, 14, 100–1, para 190.

[6] eg Kyoji Kawasaki, 'A Brief Note on the Legal Effects of *Jus Cogens* in International Law' (2006) 34 *Hitotsubashi Journal of Law and Politics* 27, 29. Contrary Malcom Shaw, *International Law* (6th edn, Cambridge: Cambridge University Press, 2008), 127; and Yoram Dinstein, *War, Aggression and Self-Defence* (5th edn, Cambridge: Cambridge University Press, 2012), 105, referring to (quasi-)universal treaties.

[7] cf Władysław Czapliński, '*Jus Cogens* and the Law of Treaties' in Christian Tomuschat and Jean-Marc Thouvenin (eds), *The Fundamental Rules of the International Legal Order,* Jus Cogens *and Obligations* Erga Omnes (Leiden: Martinus Nijhoff, 2006), 83, 89–90; Kawasaki, 'A Brief Note', 29–30; earlier André de Hoogh, *Obligations* Erga Omnes *and International Crimes, A Theoretical Inquiry into the Implementation and the Enforcement of the International Responsibility of States* (The Hague: Kluwer Law International, 1996), 45–6.

[8] See Natalino Ronzitti, 'Use of Force, Jus Cogens and State Consent' in Antonio Cassese (ed), *The Current Legal Regulation of the Use of Force* (Dordrecht: Martinus Nijhoff, 1986), 147, 149; Andreas Paulus, '*Jus Cogens* in a Time of Hegemony and Fragmentation' (2005) 74 *Nordic Journal of International Law* 297, 302; Kawasaki, 'A Brief Note', 30; Shaw, *International Law*, 126–7. For a different view, see Orakhelashvili, *Peremptory Norms in International Law*, 117–20; and Alexander Orakhelashvili, 'Changing *Jus Cogens* through State Practice? The Case of the Prohibition of the Use of Force and its Exceptions', Chapter 7 in this volume, Section III.

but rather that states accept and recognize that a certain norm cannot be derogated from precisely because it is a norm of *jus cogens*. In other words, non-derogability is an attribute, not the defining character, of *jus cogens* in international law.[9]

Certainly, when it comes to the first stage, it can be easily affirmed that the prohibition of the use of armed force in international relations embodied in Article 2(4) of the Charter is also established under customary international law. This was already decided by the International Court of Justice (ICJ) in 1986 in the *Nicaragua* case,[10] and this appears to have been confirmed in the *Armed Activities* case of 2006.[11]

With respect to the second stage, the waters become somewhat muddy. In 1966, the International Law Commission (ILC) in its commentary held that[12] 'the law of the Charter concerning the prohibition of the use of force in itself constitutes a conspicuous example of a rule in international law having the character of *jus cogens*.' Some authors examining a variety of sources and documents have indeed come to the conclusion that the prohibition of the use of armed force is a peremptory norm.[13]

More recently Green has attempted to cast doubt on the prohibition's peremptory status by pointing to various complicating aspects.[14] Moreover, he points to a certain shortage of practice actually showing that states have held the view that the prohibition of the use of armed force is a rule of *jus cogens*.[15] This last feature constitutes a rather problematic aspect in view of the requirement imposed by Article 53 VCLT that a norm must be accepted and recognized as peremptory by the international community of states as a whole.[16] However, Corten recently investigated the matter and came to the conclusion that the prohibition of the threat or use of force, as embodied in Article 2(4), constitutes a peremptory norm.[17]

Be that as it may, for the purposes of this chapter it will be assumed that a peremptory norm exists in relation to the use of armed force. Nevertheless, various questions arise as to the scope of this peremptory norm. Primary among those is how to position existing and possible future exceptions.

[9] See Commentary Art 50 (renumbered 53), *Yearbook of the International Law Commission*, 1966, vol II, 247, 247–248, para 2, noting that a prohibition to derogate from a provision included in a treaty does not endow such a provision with *jus cogens* status.

[10] *Nicaragua*, Merits, 98–102, paras 187–92 (also 92–7, paras 172–82).

[11] *Armed Activities on the Territory of the Congo (DRC v. Uganda)*, Judgment, ICJ Rep 2006, 168, 223–7, paras 148–65.

[12] Commentary Art 50 (renumbered 53) (1966), 247, para 1.

[13] eg Corten, *The Law against War*, 201–13; Orakhelashvili, *Peremptory Norms in International Law*, 50–1.

[14] Green, 'Questioning the Peremptory Status', respectively at 225–9 (use vs threat of force), 229–36 (existing exceptions), and 236–41 (new exceptions or interpretations).

[15] Green, 'Questioning the Peremptory Status', 245–52.

[16] *United Nations Conference on the Law of Treaties*, 1st Sess (New York: United Nations, 1969), 471, para 4. Acceptance and recognition by the 'international community as a whole' has been explained to mean that a very large majority of all states ought to support the peremptory status of a norm (472, para 12). The ILC decided against including any examples, leaving this to state practice and international jurisprudence. Commentary Art 50 (renumbered 53) (1966), 248, para 3.

[17] Corten, *The Law against War*, 201–13.

III. *Jus Cogens* Restrictions on the Use of Armed Force

With respect to the prohibition on the use of armed force a particular problem exists in that it allows for exceptions and this poses some difficulties. Other peremptory norms appear to be based on prohibitions that are absolute in character and these do not raise the same issues.[18] First, the possibility of invoking generally available circumstances precluding wrongfulness will be investigated (Section III.A). Secondly, to accommodate specific exceptions to the prohibition on the use of armed force as a rule of *jus cogens*, three possible avenues of reasoning are feasible: a restrictive interpretation of the word derogation (Section III.B); exceptions as *jus cogens* (Section III.C); and a restrictive scope of the *jus cogens* prohibition (Section III.D).

A. Circumstances Precluding Wrongfulness as General Exceptions

One area where the *jus cogens* status of the prohibition does make a difference relates to the generally accepted circumstances precluding wrongfulness. In this respect Article 26 of the Draft Articles on State Responsibility stipulates that[19] 'Nothing in this chapter precludes the wrongfulness of any act of a State which is not in conformity with an obligation arising under a peremptory norm of general international law.' Among the circumstances precluding wrongfulness adopted by the ILC particularly countermeasures, consent, and necessity, leaving aside self-defence as a specific exception, are particularly relevant to the present inquiry.

In Article 22 of its Draft Articles on State Responsibility, the ILC provided for the enforcement of the responsibility of states through countermeasures: 'The wrongfulness of an act of a State not in conformity with an international obligation towards another State is precluded if and to the extent that the act constitutes a countermeasure taken against the latter State in accordance with chapter II of Part Three.' As such, a state may adopt countermeasures to induce another state to comply with its obligations of continued performance, cessation,

[18] See Leben, 'Obligations relating to the Use of Force', 1202, making a distinction between simple peremptory norms, eg the prohibition on the use of force, and reinforced peremptory norms, eg the prohibition of torture: the first type allows for the same kind of act to be adopted as a sanction, whereas the second type prohibits the act in all circumstances.

[19] Draft articles on responsibility of States for internationally wrongful acts, *Yearbook of the International Law Commission*, 2001, vol II (2), 26–30.

reparation, and assurances or guarantees of non-repetition.[20] However, whether such option is open to states other than injured states is unclear considering the savings clause of Article 54 of the Draft, reserving the matter of 'lawful' measures.[21]

Countermeasures or lawful measures appear to be limited to economic or other 'peaceful' measures.[22] As both countermeasures and lawful measures are set out in the chapter on countermeasures, this could hardly be otherwise since Article 50 requires that countermeasures shall not affect 'the obligation to refrain from the threat or use of force as embodied in the Charter of the United Nations'.[23] The commentary bases this norm directly on Article 2(4) of the Charter and various reaffirmations that armed or forcible reprisals are prohibited.[24] Whether this would follow also from the reference in Article 50(1)(d) to 'other' obligations under peremptory norms is unclear, since the Commission does not specify in its commentary whether the prohibition of the threat or use of force in general constitutes a peremptory norm.[25] If the prohibition in general rather than the prohibition of aggression is a peremptory norm,[26] countermeasures or lawful measures involving the use of armed force would be barred under such norm. This would be different only if the use of armed force were dictated by another peremptory norm, since Article 53 VCLT stipulates that a peremptory norm can only be modified by a norm having the same character (see Section IV.B).

Continuing the discussion of generally available exceptions, the Draft Articles on State Responsibility provide in Article 20:[27] 'Valid consent by a State to the commission of a given act by another State precludes the wrongfulness of that act in relation to the former State to the extent that the act remains within the limits of that consent.' The reference to 'valid' consent may be taken to also express the idea that it is invalid if the act consented to were to conflict with an obligation under a

[20] Commentary Art 49 (2001) in conjunction with Commentaries Arts 29–31 and 34–7, *Yearbook of the International Law Commission*, 2001, vol II (2), respectively 129–31, 88–94, 95–107.

[21] Commentary Art 54, *Yearbook of the International Law Commission*, 2001, vol II (2), 137–9; also Commentary Art 22, *Yearbook of the International Law Commission*, 2001, vol II (2), 75–6, 76, para 6. Cf Jan Wouters and Sten Verhoeven, 'The Prohibition of Genocide as a Norm of *Ius Cogens* and Its Implications for the Enforcement of the Law of Genocide' (2005) 5 *International Criminal Law Review* 401, 413–15.

[22] Commentary Art 22 (2001), 75–6, paras 1, 2, and 5; Commentary Art 54 (2001), 137–9, paras 3–4.

[23] Commentary Art 50, *Yearbook of the International Law Commission*, 2001, vol II (2), 131–4.

[24] Commentary Art 50 (2001), 132, paras 3–4.

[25] Commentary Art 50 (2001), 132–3, para 9. Though the commentary seems to speak against this (ibid), the phrase 'other obligations under peremptory norms' in Art 50(1)(d) has been interpreted to mean that the obligations related to the threat or use of force, the protection of fundamental human rights, and provisions of a humanitarian character prohibiting reprisals also constitute peremptory norms. See Leben, 'Obligations relating to the Use of Force', 1198–9.

[26] In other commentaries the Commission refers to the prohibition of aggression as a peremptory norm: see later in this section and Section III.D.

[27] Commentary Art 20, *Yearbook of the International Law Commission*, 2001, vol II (2), 72–4.

peremptory norm.[28] Otherwise, the conduct of a state undertaken pursuant to consent by another state must remain within the limits of the permission given.[29]

With respect to consent and its relation to the prohibition on the use of armed force, it is generally accepted that a state may invite foreign troops onto its territory.[30] Equally, the prohibitions of the use of armed force and (armed) intervention do not stand in the way of such troops engaging in the use of armed force on a state's territory with a government's consent.[31] Such foreign armed activities are not, however, admissible when based on a request to that effect by the (armed) opposition within a state.[32]

Issues have arisen in relation to the use of armed force for certain purposes, such as the protection of nationals abroad and humanitarian intervention, and in relation to treaties establishing a permanent right of armed intervention. The examination of various situations by Ronzitti and Hannikainen shows that (*ex post facto*) consent will only be invalidated for conflict with obligations under the peremptory prohibition in rather limited circumstances: the purported acquisition of territory, overthrow of a government and consequent installation of another government (in particular when combined with the continued presence of foreign troops on, or outright occupation of, the territory of a state).[33]

Abass has argued that the Economic Community of West African States Protocol and the Constitutive Act of the African Union, establishing legal powers of armed intervention, are not caught by Article 26 of the Draft Articles on State Responsibility.[34] However, his argument in support that these constitute consensual

[28] Commentary Art 20 (2001), 73, para 7; Commentary Art 26, *Yearbook of the International Law Commission*, 2001, vol II (2), 84–5, 85, para 6; Ronzitti, 'Use of Force', 148.

[29] Commentary Art 20 (2001), 72 and 73–4, paras 1 and 9; *Armed Activities*, Judgment, 198–9, para 52, 210–12, paras 98–105, 224, para 149 (more generally, 196–212, paras 42–105).

[30] Commentary Art 20 (2001), 73–4, para 9; Commentary Art 26 (2001), 85, para 6; Paulus, '*Jus Cogens* in a Time', 306–7; Kawasaki, 'A Brief Note', 37 fn 40.

[31] James Crawford, 'Second report on State responsibility', *Yearbook of the International Law Commission*, 1999, vol II (1), 3, 63, para 240(b); Affef Ben Mansour, 'Circumstances Precluding Wrongfulness in the ILC Articles on State Responsibility: Consent' in Crawford, Pellet, and Olleson, *The Law of International Responsibility*, 439, 447, noting that the practice related to consent suggests that the prohibition of the use of armed force is not of peremptory character; and Spiermann, 'Humanitarian Intervention as a Necessity', 535. In *Armed Activities*, Judgment, 196–7, paras 45–7, the Court determined that consent by Congo had been given to certain activities of Uganda, but did not specifically examine the validity of that consent.

[32] *Nicaragua*, Merits, 126, para 246.

[33] Ronzitti, 'Use of Force', 153–63; Hannikainen, *Peremptory Norms (Jus Cogens)*, 349–55. *Ex post facto* consent raises similar issues and relates to acquiescence or a valid waiver of claims and may entail the loss of the right to invoke responsibility. See Commentary Art 46, *Yearbook of the International Law Commission*, 2001, vol II (2), 123–4, para 4, where the ILC indicates that the validity of a waiver arises especially when the situation involves a serious breach of obligation under a peremptory norm.

[34] Ademola Abass, 'Consent Precluding International Responsibility: A Critical Analysis' (2004) 53 *International and Comparative Law Quarterly* 211, 223–4. He does note that a consensual use of force could not be 'directed towards aggressive purposes' (at 224) and that not every obligation under Art 2(4) of the Charter is peremptory (at 225). Art 10 of the 1999 Protocol relating to the Mechanism for Conflict Prevention, Management, Resolution, Peace-Keeping and Security, available at <http://www.

rights of intervention and would not result in coercive use of force may be questioned. The problem with such an argument is that consent is not given in concrete circumstances and intervention can be resorted to against a state rather than at its invitation.[35]

Turning to necessity, this was put forward by the ILC as a circumstance precluding wrongfulness in 1980. The original provision (Art 33) required the existence of a grave and imminent peril to an essential interest of the state, but invoking a state of necessity was barred if this would seriously impair an essential interest of another state.[36] In 2001, the Commission changed the text (Art 25), no longer requiring the essential interest to relate to the state exclusively, stated in the commentary that the essential interest at stake could also relate to the people of a state or to the international community as a whole, and made clear that necessity could not be invoked if it seriously impaired an essential interest of the international community as a whole.[37]

In changing the text of the provision as it did, the Commission therefore appeared to provide more room for the claim that the use of armed force might be resorted to in order to safeguard the essential interests of the international community as a whole.[38] Yet that impression turns out to be false. In its 2001 commentary, the Commission in fact made a volte-face as to whether or not the use of armed force might be claimed under the heading of necessity.

In 1980, the Commission noted in its commentary on necessity that the wrongfulness of conduct could not be precluded if it involved the use of armed force constituting aggression.[39] Referring to attacks on 'the very existence of another State or on the integrity of its territory or the independent exercise of its sovereignty', the Commission claimed that:[40]

> any use by a State of armed force for an assault of the kind mentioned against the sovereignty of another State, indisputably comes within the meaning of the term 'aggression' and, as such, is subject to a prohibition of *jus cogens*—the most typical and incontrovertible prohibition of *jus cogens*.

It proceeded to investigate whether certain armed actions infringing the territorial sovereignty of a state could be considered not to amount to acts of aggression or to

comm.ecowas.int/sec/index.php?id=ap101299&lang=en>; and Art 4(h) of the 2000 Constitutive Act of the Africa Union, 2158 UNTS 33.

[35] In this sense, Corten, *The Law against War*, 254–5.

[36] Commentary Art 33, *Yearbook of the International Law Commission*, 1980, vol II (2), 34–52.

[37] Commentary Art 25, *Yearbook of the International Law Commission*, 2001, vol II (2), 80–4, 83, para 15.

[38] Spiermann, 'Humanitarian Intervention as a Necessity', 527; Gelijn Molier, 'Humanitarian Intervention and the Responsibility to Protect after 9/11' (2006) 53 *Netherlands International Law Review* 37, 53–6.

[39] Commentary Art 33 (1980), 43, para 22 (more broadly 42–5, paras 22–6).

[40] Commentary Art 33 (1980), 43, para 22.

breaches of a *jus cogens* obligation.[41] The situations the Commission had in mind concerned incursions into foreign territory in response to a 'danger to the State, to some of its nationals or simply to human beings', and it continued by pointing out the limited character of such cross-border armed actions in terms of duration and means employed.[42] At that point the Commission expressed doubts whether all obligations to respect the territorial sovereignty of states constituted *jus cogens*.[43] It consequently appeared to envisage the possibility, without committing itself,[44] that necessity might be invoked to allow for preclusion of wrongfulness of conduct otherwise in violation of the prohibition of the use of armed force.

In 2001, the Commission expressed its view on which rules constituted clearly accepted and recognized peremptory norms and included the prohibition of aggression.[45] However, with respect to the possibility of invoking necessity to justify the use of armed force it now claimed:[46]

> the plea of necessity is not intended to cover conduct which is in principle regulated by the primary obligations. This has a particular importance in relation to the rules relating to the use of force in international relations and to the question of 'military necessity'. It is true that in a few cases, the plea of necessity has been invoked to excuse military action abroad, in particular in the context of claims to humanitarian intervention. The question whether measures of forcible humanitarian intervention, not sanctioned pursuant to Chapters VII or VIII of the Charter of the United Nations, may be lawful under modern international law is not covered by article 25.

Thus the Commission backtracked and by its references to 'primary obligations' and 'modern international law' suggested that (forcible) humanitarian intervention is regulated by customary international law and, in any event, not covered by Article 25.

The claim of the Commission that humanitarian intervention is regulated by primary norms rather than secondary norms may be disputed.[47] As a specific armed response to violations of human rights obligations, it falls into the same category as countermeasures and that topic has been included and regulated in the Draft Articles on State Responsibility.[48]

[41] Commentary Art 33 (1980), 43, para 23. See the discussion in Spiermann, 'Humanitarian Intervention as a Necessity', 538–42.

[42] Commentary Art 33 (1980), 44, para 23.

[43] Commentary Art 33 (1980), 44, para 24. [44] Commentary Art 33 (1980), 45, para 24.

[45] Commentary Art 26 (2001), 85, para 5; Commentary Art 40, *Yearbook of the International Law Commission*, 2001, vol II (2), 112–13, 112, para 4.

[46] Commentary Art 25 (2001), 84, para 21 (relevant footnotes omitted).

[47] cf Eric David, 'Primary and Secondary Rules' in Crawford, Pellet, and Olleson, *The Law of International Responsibility*, 27; and Herbert L. A. Hart, *The Concept of Law* (2nd edn, Oxford: Clarendon Press, 1994), 80–1 and 94, for a different perspective on the distinction between primary and secondary rules.

[48] The same issue arises with respect to self-defence. For opposing positions: Spiermann, 'Humanitarian Intervention as a Necessity', 534; David, 'Primary and Secondary Rules', 29–33.

In essence, the Commission's position, correctly in the mind of the present author, appears to be that (customary) international law requires the existence of a specific exception to the peremptory prohibition of the use of armed force.[49] The codification of the secondary rules of state responsibility needs to be based on an analysis of state practice and *opinio juris* and on that basis the conclusion can indeed be drawn that customary international law accepts necessity as a circumstance precluding wrongfulness with its attendant conditions.[50] However, the practice relied upon to support necessity as a circumstance precluding wrongfulness only shows a few examples in which the use of armed force was at stake and only one when the Commission adopted the provision in 1980.[51]

B. Specific Exceptions and Derogation

Regarding specific exceptions to the prohibition on the use of armed force, the ILC indicated in its 1966 commentary on *jus cogens* that states may generally contract out of the majority of general rules of international law and that *jus cogens* rules are precisely those that bar derogation of such a rule 'by agreement *between particular States*'.[52] As the concept of *jus cogens* envisages a limitation to the otherwise existing freedom to contract out of rules of international law, it is intended to disallow states, acting *inter partes*, to derogate from peremptory norms.[53] The basic argument here is that rules that allow all states equally to invoke an exception to the prohibition of the use of armed force simply would not constitute 'derogation'. This could be taken to mean that the right of self-defence, the Security Council's powers under Article 42 of the Charter, and other (potential) justifications recognized under universal rules of customary international law do not transgress the peremptory norm prohibiting the use of armed force.

An advantage of this kind of reasoning is that there is no need to explain a pretend conflict between the peremptory prohibition and the existence of the exception of

[49] Contrary Spiermann, 'Humanitarian Intervention as a Necessity', 543; and Molier, 'Humanitarian Intervention and the Responsibility to Protect', 57.

[50] See *Gabčikovo Nagymaros Project (Hungary/Slovakia)*, Judgment, ICJ Rep 1997, 7, 40–1, paras 51–2.

[51] See Molier, 'Humanitarian Intervention and the Responsibility to Protect', 55; and Sarah Heathcote, 'Circumstances Precluding Wrongfulness in the ILC Articles on State Responsibility: Necessity' in Crawford, Pellet, and Olleson, *The Law of International Responsibility*, 491, 498–9, both mentioning the examples of the Congo (1960) and Kosovo (1999). Corten, *The Law against War*, 225–47, has shown that states have generally not invoked circumstances precluding wrongfulness to justify the use of armed force in situations that might have called for this.

[52] Commentary Art 50 (renumbered 53) (1966), 248, paras 2 and 4 (emphasis added).

[53] Arguing along these lines, Robert Kolb, 'Observation sur l'évolution du concept de *jus cogens*' (2009) 113 *Revue Générale de Droit International Public* 837, 845 and 846–8; Shaw, *International Law*, 125, noting that *jus cogens* will bar the development of local or special custom; and Corten, *The Law against War*, 200–1.

self-defence and Security Council powers under the Charter. If such a conflict were thought to exist, the consequence would be that the Charter ought to be considered void (Art 53 VCLT, first sentence; Art 64 VCLT). It may be noted that the Security Council powers as such do not constitute an exception to the Charter prohibition on the use of armed force, since Article 2(4) addresses the member states and not the UN itself.[54] However, authors do claim that the Security Council is bound by *jus cogens*,[55] and as such the question of conflict with and derogation from the prohibition of the use of armed force cannot be avoided even in relation to its powers under the Charter.[56]

However, this reasoning also makes the limitation as to modification unintelligible. Article 53 VCLT stipulates that a peremptory norm 'can be modified only by a subsequent norm of general international law having the same character.' To argue for a restrictive interpretation of the word derogation also implies that new exceptions may be established through ordinary international lawmaking, that is, through the conclusion of a treaty or development of a (new) rule of customary international law.[57] Leaving aside that a treaty only binds the parties and therefore would constitute an *inter se* arrangement conflicting with the peremptory norm under discussion, admitting this possibility deprives the requirement that a peremptory norm can only be modified by another peremptory norm of its content. Carving out exceptions from the peremptory prohibition would allow for further limitations of that prohibition even when those did not possess peremptory character themselves.

Nevertheless, the Commission had considered that modification of a peremptory norm would likely occur by a general multilateral treaty that would fall outside the scope of the provision, but pointed out that a peremptory norm 'can be modified only by a subsequent norm of general international law having the same character.'[58] This, however, would appear to require that the multilateral treaty would not merely lay down a novel exception, but that it should qualify such an exception as *jus cogens*.

[54] Though Art 24(2) of the Charter does enjoin the Security Council to act in accordance with the purposes and principles of the Charter.

[55] eg Erika de Wet, *The Chapter VII Powers of the United Nations Security Council* (Oxford/Portland, OR: Hart, 2004), 187–91; Orakhelashvili, *Peremptory Norms in International Law*, 413–29. See also *Application of the Convention on the Prevention and Punishment of the Crime of Genocide*, Provisional Measures, Order of 13 Sept 1993, ICJ Rep 1993, 325, Separate Opinion of Judge Lauterpacht, 440–1, paras 100–4, 442, para 106, and 447, para 123.

[56] Note that authorizations of the Security Council to (member) states function as a justification, or circumstance precluding wrongfulness, to use armed force otherwise in violation of the prohibition of the use of force enshrined in Art 2(4) of the Charter and customary international law.

[57] In this sense, Crawford, 'Second Report', 72, para 289, discussing necessity opined: 'it seems enough to say that either modern State practice and *opinio juris* license humanitarian action in certain limited circumstances, or they do not. If they do, then such action would appear to be lawful in those circumstances, and cannot be considered as violating the peremptory norm reflected in article 2(4) of the Charter.'

[58] Commentary Art 50 (renumbered 53) (1966), 248, para 4.

c. Specific Exceptions as *Jus Cogens*

All the same, authors writing on this matter do not generally take the route of interpreting the word derogation restrictively.[59] Rather, some tend to go for a second line of reasoning, namely to argue that not just the prohibition of the use of force is a peremptory norm, but that other rules of the law regulating the use of armed force are also *jus cogens*. Some hold that the entire regime of the *jus ad bellum* as a whole is peremptory,[60] some claim that the right of self-defence is (or exceptions are) necessarily included in the provision of Article 2(4) of the Charter,[61] and some that the right to self-defence is or the exceptions are (a) peremptory norm(s).[62] With respect to these last two perspectives, one may therefore either argue that exceptions are (necessarily) part and parcel of the peremptory prohibition and as such limit its scope, or that such exceptions have independent status as peremptory norms and as such would prevail in the case of conflict.

The first claim, that the entire *jus ad bellum* is part of *jus cogens*, founders because of the objection that many rules contained within that field cannot be shown to have been accepted and recognized by states as norms from which no derogation is permitted.[63]

The second claim, that exceptions form part of the peremptory prohibition and limit its scope, is subject to the same kind of objections as voiced earlier as to the restrictive interpretation of the word derogation. Over and above this, Green has asserted that to incorporate self-defence and Security Council powers to use armed force and all their related conditions and requirements into one peremptory norm, means to produce a lengthy and overcomplicated norm and that such lack of clarity is undesirable for a fundamental peremptory norm.[64]

The third claim, that the right to self-defence, or exceptions more generally, could have a status as independent peremptory norm(s), might of course crumble under the weight of the same objections as those voiced with respect to the first claim.

[59] eg Green, 'Questioning the Peremptory Status', 229, referring to the right of self-defence and authorizations pursuant to the Security Council powers under Art 42 of the Charter, notes that: 'the prohibition of the use of force is a rule from which derogation is explicitly and uncontrovertibly permitted.'

[60] Orakhelashvili, *Peremptory Norms in International Law*, 51.

[61] Kahgan, 'Jus Cogens and the Inherent Right', 783–9. Crawford, 'Second Report', 72, para 288, ranked not only Art 2(4) of the Charter as a peremptory norm but also Art 51. This position is possibly predicated upon the view that the exercise of self-defence cannot be seen as a breach of Art 2(4) (at 74, para 298). See the critique of Jörg Kammerhofer, *Uncertainty in International Law: A Kelsenian Perspective* (London/New York: Routledge, 2011), 49–51.

[62] Commentary Art 34, *Yearbook of the International Law Commission*, 1980, vol II (2), 52–61, 58, para 18. De Wet, *The Chapter VII Powers*, 191; and, critically, Green, 'Questioning the Peremptory Status', 231–2.

[63] Green, 'Questioning the Peremptory Status', 230–1, pointing to the example of the reporting requirement in Art 51 of the Charter and the Court's treatment thereof. Cf *Nicaragua*, Merits, 105, para 200.

[64] Green, 'Questioning the Peremptory Status', 232–4.

Moreover, do states accept and recognize the right to self-defence as a peremptory norm, or to be more exact as a norm from which no derogation is permitted?

And to follow up on this last specification, what would it mean to say that states cannot derogate from the right of self-defence? Derogation in relation to *jus cogens* is taken to mean that a rule of international law cannot be displaced or abrogated by (some) states in their mutual relations. Derogation in relation to the right of self-defence would then suggest that it cannot be renounced or perhaps also that it cannot be alienated. But if such is the case, the limitation imposed in Article 51 of the Charter that nothing in the Charter shall impair the right of self-defence '*until the Security Council has taken measures necessary to maintain international peace and security*' does appear problematic since it provides a restriction to the legitimate exercise of the right of self-defence and, more importantly, subordinates it to the judgement of the Security Council. In the same vein, treaties by which a state outsources the conduct of its international relations and defence could be argued to alienate the right of self-defence and would be in conflict with the peremptory status of the right of self-defence.[65]

D. Specific Exceptions and a Limited Scope of the Peremptory Prohibition

The third and final line of reasoning is linked to the idea that the prohibition on the use of armed force is not in its entirety a peremptory norm, but that the peremptory norm is more restrictive in scope and either limited to the prohibition of aggression or to armed force used against the territorial integrity or political independence of a state. The argument that the peremptory norm is more restrictive in scope and limited to the prohibition of aggression may be supported by pronouncements of the ILC in formulating the circumstances precluding wrongfulness in its work on the responsibility of states.

In 1980, the ILC noted in the commentary on necessity that the wrongfulness of conduct could not be precluded if the use of armed force constituted aggression.[66] The Commission appeared to envisage the possibility that, hence, necessity might be invoked to allow for preclusion of wrongfulness of conduct otherwise in violation of the prohibition of the use of armed force.[67] In 2001, the Commission listed clearly accepted and recognized peremptory norms and included the prohibition of aggression.[68]

[65] Overall of historical interest as regards protectorates, see Mirja Trilsch, 'Protectorates and Protected States' in Rüdiger Wolfrum (ed), *Max Planck Encyclopedia of Public International Law* (Oxford: Oxford University Press, 2008), available at <http://www.mpepil>.

[66] Commentary Art 33 (1980), 43, para 22 (more broadly 42–5, paras 22–6).

[67] See further Section III.A.

[68] Commentary Art 26 (2001), 85, para 5; Commentary Art 40 (2001), 112, para 4.

The choice for the prohibition of aggression as a peremptory norm rather than the prohibition of the use of force seems to be motivated by the perception that aggression is a more limited concept. Whether this is actually the case may be doubted in view of Article 1 of the Definition of Aggression adopted by the General Assembly,[69] which stipulates: 'Aggression is the use of armed force by a State against the sovereignty, territorial integrity or political independence of another State, or in any other manner inconsistent with the Charter of the United Nations, as set out in this Definition.' Article 2 then provides that:

> The first use of armed force by a State in contravention of the Charter shall constitute *prima facie* evidence of an act of aggression although the Security Council may, in conformity with the Charter, conclude that a determination that an act of aggression has been committed would not be justified in the light of other relevant circumstances, including the fact that the acts concerned or their consequences are not of sufficient gravity.

Article 3 then sets out a number of acts that qualify as aggression, such as invasion of or attacks on, or bombardment of or use of weapons against, the territory of another state.

In reading this one is struck by the fact that any use of armed force appears to constitute an act of aggression. This follows from the fact that Article 1 simply recounts the text of Article 2(4) of the Charter (though adding sovereignty), that Article 2 stipulates that a first use of armed force shall be prima facie evidence of an act of aggression, and that the examples of Article 3 are formulated in a manner as to encompass the use of armed force generally. This view may be qualified in some measure by the fact that the Security Council may come to a conclusion, based on all relevant circumstances including the gravity and consequences of the acts concerned, that a determination of aggression is not justified.[70] Similarly, one could also mention that the Preamble observes that 'aggression is the most serious and dangerous form of the illegal use of force', and as such not all (illegal) uses of armed force would fall under the term.[71]

However, all in all, it seems that any use of armed force could be branded as an act of aggression, and as such the prohibition of aggression does not appear to have a less restrictive scope than the prohibition of the use of armed force.[72] A preference

[69] GA Res 3314 (XXIX), Annex, adopted 14 Dec 1974, available at <http://www.un.org/Depts/dhl/resguide/r29.htm>.

[70] In a similar vein, Art 8*bis* (crime of aggression) of the Rome Statute, adopted by the Review Conference in 2010, refers to the character, gravity, and scale of an act of aggression. ICC, Review Conference, Res RC/Res.6, Annex I, available at <http://www.icc-cpi.int/iccdocs/asp_docs/Resolutions/RC-Res.6-ENG.pdf>. See also Annex III, paras 6–7. See also Sean D. Murphy, 'The Crime of Aggression at the International Criminal Court', Chapter 24 in this volume.

[71] Bernard V. A. Röling, 'The 1974 U.N. Definition of Aggression' in Cassese, *The Current Legal Regulation*, 413, 416 and 419.

[72] cf Paulus, '*Jus Cogens* in a Time', 306–7, noting that attempts to distinguish aggression from illegal uses of force have not been successful (fn 29).

for granting peremptory status to the prohibition of aggression rather than the prohibition on the use of armed force cannot be derived from this, and branding the prohibition of aggression as a peremptory norm would then not necessarily accommodate the exceptions to the peremptory prohibition.[73]

Some authors have put forward that the status of the *jus cogens* norm on the use of force is the prohibition of aggressive use of armed force or aggression.[74] Yet what would constitute the distinguishing mark of aggressive force or aggression remains somewhat sketchy.[75] Hannikainen discusses the use of armed force to rescue nationals abroad and armed intervention for humanitarian purposes and comes to the conclusion that these do not constitute *aggressive* use of armed force when limited in duration and the means employed. In his view, such uses of armed force are not of (direct) interest to *jus cogens*.[76] One might be inclined then to see the distinguishing mark between aggression and a 'merely' illegal use of armed force to lie with a 'benevolent' or altruistic motivation.[77] Another option could be to limit the scope of the peremptory prohibition to the use of armed force for certain purposes only, for instance to the use of armed force directed against a state's territorial integrity or political independence.[78]

In conclusion, if the peremptory prohibition were restricted to a suitably and adequately limited notion of aggression, both existing and possible future exceptions to such a prohibition would not normally fall under its scope. However, the absence in law of an *animus aggressionis* or purpose requirement undermines this line of reasoning.

73 Supported by Art 5(1) of the Definition of Aggression, stipulating that political, economic, military, or any other kind of considerations may not serve as a justification for aggression. But note that Art 6 preserves the provisions of the Charter envisaging a lawful use of force.

74 Hannikainen, *Peremptory Norms (Jus Cogens)*, 323–56; Dinstein, *War, Aggression and Self-Defence*, 105–7, discussing the example of a 'pact of aggression'; Molier, 'Humanitarian Intervention and the Responsibility to Protect', 54–5; and, implicitly, Ronzitti, 'Use of Force', 150 and 153–4, 158–60.

75 Note the discussion between Paulus and Kreß on whether the crime of aggression has been properly defined and the difficulties as to the assessment of the character, gravity, and scale of an act of aggression: Andreas Paulus, 'Second Thoughts on the Crime of Aggression' (2010) 20 *Leiden Journal of International Law* 1117, 1119–24, and Claus Kreß, 'Time for Decision: Some Thoughts on the Immediate Future of the Crime of Aggression, A Reply to Andreas Paulus' (2010) 20 *Leiden Journal of International Law* 1129, 1137–42.

76 Hannikainen, *Peremptory Norms (Jus Cogens)*, 336–7 (broader 323–56).

77 In a somewhat different sense, one could say that the state should lack the *animus aggressionis*. See Dinstein, *War, Aggression and Self-Defence*, 146, on individual responsibility for the crime of aggression.

78 Kreß, 'Time for Decision', 1139–40, discussing proposals to limit the crime of aggression to force used for the purpose of annexation or subjugation of a victim state, coercing a state to change government or its political regime, or to attack its military, political, and economic system. See also de Hoogh, Obligations *Erga Omnes*, 181–2, 193–4, 336; Ronzitti, 'Use of Force', 149–52; and Kahgan, 'Jus Cogens and the Inherent Right', 777–81.

IV. *Jus Cogens* Demands for Forcible Action

The introduction of the concept of *jus cogens* into international law and the recognition of specific peremptory norms have led to increased attention to questions of effectiveness and enforcement. The question arises, therefore, whether the *jus cogens* status of a norm may be invoked to justify the use of armed force against a state for the enforcement of a peremptory norm.

Certainly, it seems unlikely that this claim could be made with respect to just any violation of a peremptory norm. In this respect it may be noted that the ILC, discarding the notion of international crimes of state, introduced into Article 40 of its Draft Articles on State Responsibility the conception of *serious breaches of obligation under peremptory norms*.[79] According to paragraph 2 of this provision, a serious breach involves a 'gross or systematic failure' to fulfil the obligation. The commentary specifies that a 'gross' breach refers to the intensity or effects of a violation, whereas a 'systematic' breach entails that the violation is carried out in an organized and deliberate manner.[80] The Commission then lists certain factors that may be relevant to determine the seriousness of the breach:[81] 'intent to violate the norm; the scope and number of individual violations; and the gravity of their consequences for the victims.' The Commission further claims that breaches of the prohibitions of aggression and genocide by their very nature require an intentional and large-scale violation.[82]

The consequences of serious breaches of obligations under peremptory norms are then laid down in Article 41, which in paragraphs 1 and 2 imposes three obligations:[83] (1) to cooperate to bring to an end, through lawful means, the serious breach; (2) not to recognize a situation created by a serious breach; and (3) not to render aid and assistance in maintaining such a situation.[84] For the purposes of this chapter, only the first obligation mentioned is relevant, since the question will be whether the use of armed force may be covered as fulfilment of this obligation.

79 Commentary Art 40 (2001), 112.

80 Commentary Art 40 (2001), 113, para 8.

81 Commentary Art 40 (2001), 113, para 8.

82 Commentary Art 40 (2001), 113, para 8.

83 Commentary Art 41, *Yearbook of the International Law Commission*, 2001, vol II (2), 113–16. It may be noted that these concern obligations for other states rather than the author state of the serious breach and this to a large extent, as the Commission acknowledges, appears to be a matter of progressive development (at 114, para 3). See also Paulus, '*Jus Cogens* in a Time', 315–16.

84 The ICJ recently held, referring to Art 41 of the Draft Articles on State Responsibility, that giving effect to the immunity of a state under customary international law does not imply recognition of, or aid and assistance in maintaining, a situation brought about by a serious breach of obligation under a peremptory norm. *Jurisdictional Immunities*, Judgment, 140, para 93.

In this respect the commentary, invoking the diversity of situations covered, does not provide detail as to the forms that such cooperation might entail, but it continues by specifying that this may entail cooperation with(in) a competent international organization, such as the UN, but also in a non-institutionalized sense.[85] Moreover, the Commission fails to indicate what kinds of measures would be covered by this positive duty, but it observes that they ought to be taken by both individually affected states and other states as part of a joint and coordinated effort.[86] Noticeable in this respect is the reference in the text of the provision to 'lawful means', a phrase that might lead us to the savings clause in Article 54, which states that the chapter on countermeasures is without prejudice to the right of states other than an injured state to take 'lawful measures'.[87]

Two thorny issues will be addressed in this section: first, whether legal consequences may be deduced from the claim that *jus cogens* norms are hierarchically higher than 'ordinary' norms; secondly, what is to be understood by a conflict of norms and whether a duty to prevent breaches of peremptory norms conflicts with the (peremptory) prohibition of the use of armed force or aggression.

A. Legal Consequences Attached to *Jus Cogens* Norms

Legal consequences attached to *jus cogens* norms were laid down initially in Articles 53 and 64 VCLT.[88] The former stipulates that a treaty is void if it conflicts with a peremptory norm. The latter provides that a treaty becomes void and terminates when it conflicts with a new peremptory norm. Over and above the consequences specified in the law of treaties, legal consequences have been included in the Draft Articles on State Responsibility. These are the inability of invoking circumstances precluding wrongfulness with respect to acts that are not in conformity with a peremptory norm (Art 26; see Section III.A); the right of an injured or other state to invoke the responsibility of another state for breaches of obligation owed to the international community as a whole (Arts 42 and 48);[89] and various obligations imposed on states to repress serious breaches of obligations under peremptory norms (Arts 40 and 41). Otherwise, the question whether other states are entitled to adopt countermeasures or lawful measures is reserved (Art 54).

A starting point for discussion of additional legal consequences could be the *Furundžija* case, decided in 1998 by a Trial Chamber of the International Criminal

[85] Commentary Art 41 (2001), 114, para 2. [86] Commentary Art 41 (2001), 114, para 3.

[87] As noted in Section III.A, lawful measures in Art 54 appear to relate exclusively to economic or other measures and not to the use of armed force.

[88] See also Art 71 VCLT for the consequences of the invalidity due to conflict with a peremptory norm.

[89] Commentary Art 42, *Yearbook of the International Law Commission*, 2001, vol II (2), 117–19; Commentary Art 48 (2001), 126–8.

Tribunal for the former Yugoslavia, in which the principle proscribing torture was held to be a peremptory norm.[90] On that basis it continued to argue that this meant:[91]

> a norm that enjoys a higher rank in the international hierarchy than treaty law and even 'ordinary' customary rules. The most conspicuous consequence of this higher rank is that the principle at issue cannot be derogated from by States through international treaties or local or special customs or even general customary rules not endowed with the same normative force.

The Trial Chamber followed up by claiming that it delegitimizes any legislative, judicial, or administrative act authorizing torture, and that individuals remain bound to comply with the prohibition and may be held criminally accountable at the national level.[92] Apparently not satisfied with these already far-reaching consequences, it proceeded to assert that the *jus cogens* nature of the prohibition of torture entitled states to exercise universal jurisdiction, that statutes of limitations may not cover torture, and that political offence exceptions to extradition do not apply.[93]

In 1999, the ILC considered, upon the proposal of Special Rapporteur Crawford,[94] the adoption of a provision in the Draft Articles on State Responsibility that would have introduced compliance with a peremptory norm as a circumstance precluding wrongfulness.[95] The Drafting Committee of the Commission actually adopted a provision to that effect in 2000,[96] though this mysteriously disappeared in the final draft adopted by the Commission in 2001.

Also in 2001, controversy erupted over the question whether a state ought to deny another state's claim of immunity when this obstructs enforcement in relation to breaches under peremptory norms.[97] The debate was sparked, among others, by the *Al-Adsani* case decided by the European Court of Human Rights (ECtHR), in which it held by the narrowest majority possible that by upholding Kuwait's immunity the UK had not violated its obligation to provide access to court under Article 6 of

[90] International Criminal Tribunal for the former Yugoslavia, Trial Chamber, *Prosecutor v. Anton Furundžija*, Judgment of 10 Dec 1998, para 153 (see also para 144), available at <http://www.icty.org/x/cases/furundzija/tjug/en/fur-tj981210e.pdf>.

[91] *Furundžija*, Judgment, para 153.

[92] *Furundžija*, Judgment, paras 154–5.

[93] *Furundžija*, Judgment, paras 156–7.

[94] cf Crawford, 'Second Report', 76–8, paras 308–15, and 87, para 358 (Art 29*bis*).

[95] *Yearbook of the International Law Commission*, 1999, vol II (2), 75–7, paras 306–18.

[96] *Yearbook of the International Law Commission*, 2000, vol II (2), 67 (Art 21 on compliance with a peremptory norm). See Maja Ménard, 'Circumstances Precluding Wrongfulness in the ILC Articles on State Responsibility: Compliance with Peremptory Norms' in Crawford, Pellet, and Olleson, *The Law of International Responsibility*, 449–53.

[97] cf generally Orakhelashvili, *Peremptory Norms in International Law*, 320, and Carlos Espósito, '*Jus Cogens* and Jurisdictional Immunities of States at the International Court of Justice: "A Conflict Does Exist"' (2012) XXI *Italian Yearbook of International Law 2011* 161, favouring the setting aside of state immunity for conflict with *jus cogens*. Otherwise Andrea Gattini, 'The Dispute on Jurisdictional Immunities of the State before the ICJ: Is the Time Ripe for a Change of the Law?' (2011) 24 *Leiden Journal of International Law* 173, and Stefan Talmon, '*Jus Cogens* after *Germany* v. *Italy*: Substantive and Procedural Rules Distinguished' (2012) 25 *Leiden Journal of International Law* 979–1002, rejecting such a position.

the (European) Convention for the Protection of Human Rights and Fundamental Freedoms to a resident Kuwaiti citizen subjected to torture in Kuwait.[98] Though the ECtHR accepted that the prohibition of torture constituted a peremptory norm, it denied that this entailed loss of immunity for civil claims concerning acts taking place abroad.[99] The judges in dissent argued that a state (allegedly) violating the *jus cogens* prohibition of torture 'cannot invoke hierarchically lower rules (in this case, those on state immunity) to avoid the consequences of the illegality of its actions.'[100]

Other legal consequences have been asserted by states drawing logical inferences from the hierarchically higher status of peremptory norms. In 2006, in the *Armed Activities* case, the ICJ rejected an argument by Congo to set aside a Rwandan reservation to the Court's jurisdiction under the Genocide Convention on the basis that such a reservation was incompatible with the peremptory prohibition of genocide.[101] The Court held that even if a dispute relates to compliance with a peremptory norm this does not establish a basis of jurisdiction for the Court to settle such a dispute, and it later noted that no peremptory norm requires a state to consent to the Court's jurisdiction to settle a dispute in relation to the Genocide Convention or the Convention against Racial Discrimination.[102] In addition, the Court found that Article 66(a) VCLT, allowing an application to the Court in respect of the interpretation and application of Articles 53 and 64, could not be invoked to establish its jurisdiction regarding the Conventions mentioned in view of Article 4 establishing the non-retroactivity of the VCLT.[103] The mere fact that peremptory norms are at stake cannot as such constitute an exception to consent as the basis for its jurisdiction.[104] In the *Genocide* case, the Court denied its jurisdiction to settle disputes otherwise unrelated to the Genocide Convention even if the violations alleged concerned obligations arising under peremptory norms.[105]

Focarelli has drawn attention to the tendency of some to use a deductive rather than an inductive approach. The former entails an appeal to the very notion of *jus cogens* justifying 'special' and 'derogatory' effects to effectively safeguard basic human rights or the interstate system without the need to found this in state practice or *opinio juris*.[106] In his view, a fully inductive approach to establish the 'special'

[98] ECtHR, *Al-Adsani v. UK* (App no 35763/97), Judgment of 21 Nov 2001, paras 60–7.

[99] *Al-Adsani*, para 66.

[100] *Al-Adsani*, Joined Dissenting Opinion of Judges Rozakis and Caflisch joined by Judges Wildhaber, Costa, Cabral Barreto, and Vajić, para 3 (broader paras 1–4), and also Dissenting Opinions of Judges Ferrari Bravo and Loucaides.

[101] *Armed Activities (New Application: 2002)*, Jurisdiction and Admissibility, 29–33, paras 56–70.

[102] *Armed Activities (New Application: 2002)*, Jurisdiction and Admissibility, respectively 32, para 64, 33 and 35, paras 69 and 78.

[103] *Armed Activities (New Application: 2002)*, Jurisdiction and Admissibility, 51–2, para 125.

[104] *Armed Activities (New Application: 2002)*, Jurisdiction and Admissibility, 52, para 125.

[105] *Genocide*, Judgment, 104–5, paras 146–8 (see also 110–11, paras 161–2).

[106] Carlo Focarelli, 'Promotional *Jus Cogens*: A Critical Appraisal of *Jus Cogens*' Legal Effects' (2008) 77 *Nordic Journal of International Law* 429, 444–8.

effects of *jus cogens* norms is the only viable methodology, basically requiring such effects to be established on the basis of existing customary international law.[107] Restating the issue, it is therefore not sufficient to establish that *jus cogens* is embodied in positive law, but one must further substantiate that the legal effects flowing from the characterization of a rule as a peremptory norm can be found in applicable treaties or rules of customary international law.[108]

Applying this to the question of demands for forcible action, this entails that the use of armed force to enforce a peremptory norm will require the existence of a justification under the Charter or customary international law. For the latter, it will be necessary to establish state practice and the acceptance of that practice as law (*opinio juris*). Clearly, with respect to armed force in the exercise of the right to self-defence or resorted to pursuant to a Security Council authorization, the Charter provides for an adequate legal basis, and the former is also accepted under customary international law (though the contours and conditions for its exercise are less clearly established).[109] Armed responses to violations of the peremptory prohibition of the use of armed force or aggression are therefore covered, at least when the scale and effects of those violations cross a certain threshold.

The use of armed force to repress (serious) violations of the peremptory prohibitions of genocide, slavery, racial discrimination, torture, and possibly war crimes and crimes against humanity remains problematic from this perspective. Though examples of state practice and *opinio juris* may be found that support a right of humanitarian intervention, on balance genuine humanitarian interventions have been rare, the legal justification(s) offered by intervening state(s) varied and these did not always invoke humanitarian intervention; moreover, overall responses by other states to such interventions have been to condemn such interventions, and hence international law does not provide for a justification of humanitarian intervention.[110]

[107] Focarelli, 'Promotional *Jus Cogens*', 449, emphasizing that this will obviate the need to rely on the *jus cogens* nature of norms as the same effect will then follow based on existing international law (also 450–5). In support of this argument, see Kolb, 'Observation sur l'évolution', 840–1.

[108] Contrary to Focarelli, 'Promotional *Jus Cogens*', 449–59, this aspect does not necessarily entail the uselessness of *jus cogens* or limit it to a promotional role, since some of the legal effects identified may be limited to peremptory norms; however, if international law embodies a certain rule independently from *jus cogens*, this may restrict the utility of the concept.

[109] See *Nicaragua*, Merits, 102–6, paras 193–201.

[110] Anthony C. Arend and Robert J. Beck, *International Law & the Use of Force: Beyond the UN Charter Paradigm* (London/New York: Routledge, 1993), 128–37 (discussion of practice, 114–28); Gelijn Molier, *De (on)rechtmatigheid van humanitaire interventie, Respect voor staatssoevereiniteit versus bescherming van mensenrechten* (Groningen: Boom Juridische Uitgevers, 2003), 217–324, esp 272–3 and 323–4 for conclusions concerning state practice and *opinio juris*; Corten, *The Law against War*, 526–49. Contrary Fernando Téson, *Humanitarian Intervention: An Inquiry into Law and Morality* (3rd edn, Ardsley, NY: Transnational, 2005), 219–78 and 373–413. See also Sir Nigel Rodley, 'Humanitarian Intervention', Chapter 35 in this volume.

The concept and doctrine of Responsibility to Protect, proposed initially by the International Commission on Intervention and State Sovereignty set up by the Canadian government,[111] has not led to any change in this respect. This may be shown especially by reference to the World Summit Outcome document adopted by the General Assembly in 2005.[112] Though accepting a responsibility for states to protect their populations from genocide, crimes against humanity, war crimes, and ethnic cleansing, on the crucial issue of enforcement the General Assembly claimed:

In this context, we are prepared to take collective action, in a timely and decisive manner, through the Security Council, in accordance with the Charter, including Chapter VII, on a case-by-case basis and in cooperation with relevant regional organizations as appropriate, should peaceful means be inadequate and national authorities manifestly fail to protect their populations from genocide, war crimes, ethnic cleansing and crimes against humanity.

On the use of force under the Charter, the General Assembly stressed:[113] 'We reaffirm that the relevant provisions of the Charter are sufficient to address the full range of threats to international peace and security. We further reaffirm the authority of the Security Council to mandate coercive action to maintain and restore international peace and security.' Since then, the Security Council has indeed invoked the concept, most prominently in resolutions concerning the conflict in Libya with respect to which it specifically authorized member states to use force to protect civilians or civilian-populated areas under threat of attack.[114]

However, the interpretation of this last phrase, 'civilians and civilian-populated areas under threat of attack', and the manner of implementation of this authorization, essentially supporting the Libyan armed resistance in overthrowing the Libyan government, now at least partially accounts for the obstruction by Russia and China of more decisive action by the Council in relation to Syria.[115] Moreover, the use of armed force resorted to in the Libyan crisis sits uncomfortably with the peremptory prohibition of aggression, since overthrowing a government appears to endanger the 'political independence' of a state. It may be noted that General Assembly Resolution 2625, the Declaration on Principles of International Law, stipulates that states shall not assist in 'the violent overthrow of the régime of another State'.[116] Surely to overthrow a

[111] International Commission on State Sovereignty and Intervention, Responsibility to Protect, Dec 2001, esp 31–7, available at <http://responsibilitytoprotect.org/ICISS%20Report.pdf>.

[112] GA Res 60/1, 2005 World Summit Outcome, adopted 24 Oct 2005, paras 138–9, available at <http://www.un.org/depts/dhl/resguide/r60.htm>.

[113] GA Res 60/1, para 79.

[114] SC Res 1970, S/RES/1970, adopted 26 Feb 2011, Preamble, para 9; 1973, S/RES/1973, adopted 17 Mar 2011, para 4, both available at <http://www.un.org/en/sc/documents/resolutions/2011.shtml>.

[115] Constantine Antonopoulos, 'The "Legitimacy" to "Legitimise": The Security Council Action under Resolution 1973 (2011)' (2012) 14 *International Community Law Review* 359, 371, 375–7.

[116] GA Res 2625 (XXV), adopted 24 Oct 1970, Annex, Declaration on Principles of International Law concerning Friendly Relations and Co-operation among States in accordance with the Charter of the United Nations, principle of non-intervention, available at <http://www.un.org/Depts/dhl/resguide/r25.htm>.

government must endanger the political independence of a state, even when the use of armed force was authorized by the Council and benevolent motives underlie the choice to support the armed resistance in overthrowing a government.

B. Conflict of (Peremptory) Norms

Without going into detail about the qualification of various rules that have been declared peremptory norms, the proliferation of peremptory norms might suggest a larger potential for conflict. At the same time it may be noted that most of the peremptory norms suggested are grafted upon human rights norms and limited to prohibitions, and as such conflict between such norms is not all that likely. This may appear different when considering the peremptory prohibitions of the use of armed force or aggression on the one hand, and the human rights-oriented peremptory norms on the other hand.

One of the essential attributes of *jus cogens* norms is that they cannot be derogated from and this has led many to argue that they are at the pinnacle of all international law norms, that is, that they are hierarchically higher than 'ordinary' norms.[117] The non-derogability of peremptory norms as the single distinguishing feature of *jus cogens* is widely interpreted as setting substantive limits on the freedom of states to conclude any treaty with whatever content.[118] However, the legal consequence of a treaty being 'void' follows only, according to Articles 53 and 64 VCLT, when a treaty is 'in conflict with' a peremptory norm. This is one of the fault lines of the conflict between proponents and opponents of an enhanced role of *jus cogens*.[119]

The question of conflict has recently been addressed by the ICJ in the case between Germany and Italy on *Jurisdictional Immunities of the State*. Italy claimed that the rules on state immunity conflicted with *jus cogens* rules of international humanitarian law prohibiting murder of civilians in occupied territory and deportation of civilians and prisoners of war for the purposes of slave labour. The Court assumed, for the sake of argument, the *jus cogens* status of the rules concerned, but then bluntly stated that no conflict existed between the rules concerned and maintained:[120]

> The rules of State immunity are procedural in character and are confined to determining whether or not the courts of one State may exercise jurisdiction in respect of another State. They

[117] eg Orakhelashvili, *Peremptory Norms in International Law*, 7–11.

[118] Michael Glennon, 'De l'absurdité du droit impératif (*Jus cogens*)' (2006) 110 *Revue Générale de Droit International Public* 529, 531.

[119] Antonio Cassese, 'For an Enhanced Role of *Jus Cogens*' in Antonio Cassese (ed), *Realizing Utopia: The Future of International Law* (Oxford: Oxford University Press, 2012), 158–71, though he does not address the question of 'conflict'. He does claim, among others, various legal effects of *jus cogens* rules (160–2), the need to submit disputes over, and the determination of, *jus cogens* rules to courts or the ICJ (163–4 and 168–70), and arguing for implementation and integration of *jus cogens* into domestic legal orders at the constitutional level (167–8).

[120] *Jurisdictional Immunities*, Judgment, 140, para 93 (see also 140–1, para 94).

do not bear upon the question whether or not the conduct in respect of which the proceedings are brought was lawful or unlawful.

Following up on this, the Court noted that the same applied with respect to the duty to make reparation for breaches of (*jus cogens*) obligations, and denied, in light of a century of practice of peace treaties and settlements, that the duty to compensate war victims could be said to have been accepted as a rule from which no derogation was permitted.[121]

The Court's judgment has been both criticized and supported, but raises the question how to determine whether a *conflict* exists between norms. In the fragmentation report, a study group of the ILC considered a conflict to be present if:[122] 'two norms that are both valid and applicable point to incompatible decisions so that a choice must be made between them.' The common perspective of norm conflict is perhaps shown by Boudreault, who claims that modern legal theory shows two definitions:[123]

- two norms are 'in a relationship of conflict if one constitutes, has led to, or may lead to, a breach of the other'.
- 'There is a conflict between two norms, one of which may be permissive, if in obeying or applying one norm, the other one is necessarily or possibly violated'.

Be that as it may, the Court is correct in claiming that no conflict exists between the rules of state immunity and *jus cogens* norms. The reason for this is that peremptory norms are, invariably though perhaps not necessarily, based on prohibitive rules.[124] Even the right of peoples to self-determination, already mentioned by the ILC in 1966 (though as a principle)[125] and affirmed by the Court in 1995 as a right *erga omnes*,[126] can be restated to prohibit colonial domination, alien occupation, or

[121] *Jurisdictional Immunities*, Judgment, 140–1, para 94.

[122] ILC, Conclusions of the Study Group on the Fragmentation of International Law: Difficulties arising from the Diversification and Expansion of International Law, in Report of the International Law Commission 2006, A/61/10, 407, 409, point 2, available at <http://untreaty.un.org/ilc/reports/2006/2006report.htm>. See also Report of the Study Group, finalized by Martti Koskenniemi, 'Fragmentation of International Law: Difficulties arising from the Diversification and Expansion of International Law', ILC, A/CN.4/L.682 (13 Apr 2006), 17–20, paras 21–6, available at <http://untreaty.un.org/ilc/sessions/58/58docs.htm>.

[123] François Boudreault, 'Identifying Conflicts of Norms: The ICJ Approach in the Case of the *Jurisdictional Immunities of the State (Germany* v. *Italy: Greece Intervening)*' (2012) 25 *Leiden Journal of International Law* 1003, 1010 (footnotes omitted). See generally Joost Pauwelyn, *Conflict of Norms in Public International Law: How WTO Law Relates to Other Rules of International Law* (Cambridge: Cambridge University Press, 2003), 164–88; Kammerhofer, *Uncertainty in International Law*, 141–6; and Robert Kolb, 'Conflits entre normes de *jus cogens*' in *Droit du pouvoir, pouvoir du droit: mélanges offerts à Jean Salmon* (Brussels: Bruylant, 2007), 481, 483.

[124] Earlier de Hoogh, *Obligations* Erga Omnes, 45, 49, 68.

[125] Commentary Art 50 (renumbered 53) (1966), 248, para 3.

[126] *East Timor (Portugal v. Australia)*, Judgment, ICJ Rep 1995, 90, 102, para 29. Critical André de Hoogh, 'Australia and East Timor, Rights *Erga Omnes*, Complicity and Non-Recognition' (1999) *Australian International Law Journal* 63, 70–5.

racist rule in denial of self-determination,[127] and one might argue that only in case of conflict with those prohibitions would one be able to assert conflict with the peremptory norm of self-determination. The customary rules of state immunity therefore do not violate peremptory prohibitions, since a state giving effect to such rules is not itself committing torture, or violations of international humanitarian law or human rights, etc.

It has been contended by Espósito that, nevertheless, a conflict does exist between the rules concerned. In making this claim, he points to the fact that the distinction between procedural and substantive rules is overly formalistic and that the two categories of rules do not constitute radically differentiated systems of rules.[128] Upon further scrutiny, however, one may note that he makes this criticism because of the obstacle that procedural barriers pose to 'the effective protection of human rights' and that 'peremptory norms impose procedural obligations on international law subjects to prevent their primacy and effectiveness from being undermined by barriers to action aimed at ending violations.'[129]

However, the Court has a different view about rules that pose obstacles to the enforcement of peremptory norms and claimed:[130]

> To the extent that it is argued that no rule which is not of the status of *jus cogens* may be applied if to do so would hinder the enforcement of a *jus cogens* rule, even in the absence of a direct conflict, the Court sees no basis for such a proposition. A *jus cogens* rule is one from which no derogation is permitted but the rules which determine the scope and extent of jurisdiction and when that jurisdiction may be exercised do not derogate from those substantive rules which possess *jus cogens* status, nor is there anything inherent in the concept of *jus cogens* which would require their modification or would displace their application.

Hence, the existence of conflict must be established between a rule or its application and the peremptory norm concerned, but such a conflict does not exist when the conduct in question does not violate the peremptory prohibition. Thus, a conflict of norms will exist only if and when a rule would impose an obligation on a state to violate a peremptory prohibition or the right to do so.[131]

Applying this to the question of *jus cogens* demands for forcible action, it can be said that no such conflict exists. If a state were to consider, or resort to, armed force to enforce a peremptory norm, for instance the prohibition of genocide, the obstacle presented by the prohibition of the use of force does not create a conflict

[127] See Art 1(4) of the Protocol Additional to the Geneva Conventions of 12 Aug 1977, and relating to the victims of international armed conflicts (Protocol I), 1125 UNTS 4.

[128] Espósito, '*Jus Cogens* and Jurisdictional Immunities', 170–1.

[129] Espósito, '*Jus Cogens* and Jurisdictional Immunities', 170, 171 (and also 172–4). He adds, under reference to Art 41 of the Draft on State Responsibility, that such procedural limitations may be understood as assisting in the impunity of violations of peremptory law (at 171–2).

[130] *Jurisdictional Immunities*, Judgment, 141, para 95 (also para 141–2, 96).

[131] Earlier de Hoogh, *Obligations* Erga Omnes, 45–6.

because such a state may refrain from the use of armed force and comply with both prohibitions simultaneously. In other words, complying with the prohibition on the use of armed force does not constitute a violation of the (peremptory) prohibition of genocide.

Not resorting to armed force to stop (an ongoing) genocide might be considered as conflicting with a state's obligation to prevent the commission of genocide,[132] but two qualifications are in order. First, only the prohibition of genocide is considered to constitute a peremptory norm and not also the obligation to prevent genocide.[133] Secondly, although the Court held that a state's obligation to prevent genocide is not limited as such to territories under its jurisdiction or control,[134] and that a state must use all means reasonably available to it,[135] it also noted in respect of a state's capacity to influence another state that[136] 'it is clear that every state may only act within the limits permitted by international law'.

Therefore a state wishing to intervene militarily to stop genocide would have to show, in the absence of a justification for the use of armed force laid down in the Genocide Convention and lacking authorization by the Security Council, that customary international law permits such action. Thus, even if one were to consider that the prohibition of the use of armed force is not a peremptory norm, but rather the prohibition of aggression, this will still not dispense a state from having to invoke a justification for its use of armed force under customary international law. And again the circle is squared: state practice and *opinio juris* are required, but provide insufficient evidence to arrive at such a conclusion.

Theoretically another conflict might exist: one between peremptory norms. Thus, Kolb appears to envisage that a contradiction may exist between the peremptory prohibition on the use of armed force and peremptory norms protecting the most elementary fundamental human rights.[137] However, as with the norm conflict suggested between a peremptory norm and an ordinary norm, it is difficult to see what conflict may be considered to exist. A state resorting to armed force may perhaps be violating the peremptory prohibition of the use of force or of aggression, or neither, but in either (or all) case(s) the choice for that particular state is not which peremptory norm to choose to comply with. In essence, this is a false conflict since the obligations that flow from the peremptory norms address different subjects of law: on the one hand, the state resorting to armed force, and on the other hand, the state that is violating fundamental human rights.

[132] Art 1 of the 1948 Convention on the Prevention and Punishment of the Crime of Genocide, 78 UNTS 277.

[133] *Genocide*, Judgment, 104–5 and 110–11, paras 146–8 and 161–2, and Wouters and Verhoeven, 'The Prohibition of Genocide', 403–6, neither addressing the status of the obligation to prevent genocide as such.

[134] *Genocide*, Judgment, 130, paras 183–4 (see also 107, para 154).

[135] *Genocide*, Judgment, 221, para 430.

[136] *Genocide*, Judgment, 221, para 430.

[137] Kolb, 'Conflits entre normes de *jus cogens*', 495–8.

V. Concluding Observations

This chapter has shown various difficulties related to the proposition that the prohibition of the use of force constitutes a peremptory norm, and other difficulties with the claim that the prohibition of aggression is such a norm. The main problem that arises comes from the necessity to accommodate (existing) exceptions to the prohibition, and none of the lines of argument bar the development of new rules of customary international law that may justify the use of armed force. Nevertheless, it seems likely that any new rule justifying the use of armed force, requiring state practice and *opinio juris*, will be hard to establish. The generally available circumstance precluding wrongfulness of necessity might have filled the gap, but the ILC has plugged this by stating that Article 25 of the Draft Articles on State Responsibility is not intended to cover the use of armed force.

Moreover, even if it is claimed that the prohibition of aggression constitutes *jus cogens*, controversy will persist where the use of armed force intentionally or perchance leads to loss of territory (Serbia and Kosovo) or regime change (Libya). After all, Article 2(4) of the Charter specifically protects a state's territorial integrity and political independence. Therefore, though the peremptory prohibition of the use of force or of aggression does not per se bar the development of international law and hence provides less of a restriction than might be imagined, the onus will lie with states wishing to intervene to state their case and to respect those essential and paramount limitations.

When it comes to demands for forcible action, less again can be gleaned from the status of certain rules as *jus cogens* than one might find desirable. Thus, the hierarchically higher rank of peremptory norms cannot lead one to deductively construe legal effects or consequences to the violation of peremptory norms that are not otherwise established under international law. As such, it will be necessary to find a justification either under the Charter or customary international law for any use of armed force. Such a justification may be extant when acting in the exercise of a right of self-defence against an armed attack or pursuant to Security Council authorization. However, other potential justifications, such as humanitarian intervention, appear to stumble on the insufficiency of state practice and *opinio juris*.

Finally, invoking a conflict of norms to suggest priority for a peremptory norm will in most circumstances not provide any sustenance either. Recent case law of the ICJ has denied the existence of conflict of norms on various grounds. Moreover, any pretended conflict between peremptory norms, for example the prohibitions on the use of armed force and genocide, is false because the prohibitions impose obligations on different states and a state wishing to intervene militarily will not therefore have to choose between complying with either one or the other prohibition.

CHAPTER 55

THE PRINCIPLE OF PROPORTIONALITY FROM A *JUS AD BELLUM* PERSPECTIVE

THEODORA CHRISTODOULIDOU
KALLIOPI CHAINOGLOU

I. Introduction

THE contemporary law of the use of force is codified in the UN Charter which provides that states are prohibited from using force in their international relations,[1] with the exception of military measures which are either mandated by a Chapter VII Security Council resolution[2] or they are taken in self-defence pursuant to Article 51 of the UN Charter. Under the UN Charter the right of self-defence can be exercised when an armed attack occurs and only until the Security Council takes action. The UN Charter nowhere stipulates the conditions which are attached to the exercise of the right of self-defence. It is therefore generally accepted that apart from the UN

[1] UN Charter, Art 2(4). [2] Art 39 and 42.

Charter law, the law of self-defence is also regulated by customary international law.[3] The diplomatic deliberations of the *Caroline* incident of 1837 provide the criteria according to which states may resort to self-defence, namely necessity, imminence, and proportionality.[4]

Today, despite the uncertainty not only with regard to the legal regulation of the use of force but also to the content of the principle of proportionality, all states agree that for any use of force to be lawful it must be both necessary and proportionate. Being in a dialectical relationship with the law of the use of force, proportionality serves as a regulatory and legitimizing factor for any use of force (ie enforcement of a Security Council mandate, self-defence, or use of force to protect human rights). But as states increasingly opt for the use of force in novel situations for which the UN Charter law on the use of force does not provide (ie non-traditional armed conflicts with irregular forces/terrorist groups), proportionality appears to be an evolving concept, the dimensions of which are gradually unveiled. As a consequence, international legal scholars face difficulties in analysing and presenting a satisfactory account of proportionality in the decision-making process of states when they resort to force.[5] Finally, even though proportionality remains a valid principle which still influences the outcome of the diplomatic deliberations within the Security Council, when member states consider whether to grant authorization for the use of force, they appear not to be confident with what proportionality entails.

This chapter addresses the concept of proportionality as it is reflected in the International Court of Justice (ICJ) judicial decisions and the legal opinions of the ICJ judges; the ultimate aim of the present authors is to examine the concept of proportionality in the context of self-defence and use of force to protect human rights by reference to the 'subsidiary means' for the determination of rules of law, namely the findings of the ICJ and selected writings of legal scholars.[6] While these sources are not by themselves international law, when coupled with evidence of international custom as is the case with proportionality, arguably they may provide us with the substance of the principle of proportionality.

[3] See Art 38(1) of the ICJ Statute for the sources of international law.

[4] 'The Caroline Case' (1937) 29 *British and Foreign State Papers* 1137.

[5] See eg Elizabeth Sampson, 'Necessity, Proportionality and Distinction in Nontraditional Conflicts: The Unfortunate Study of the Goldstone Report' in Christopher Ford and Amichai Cohen (eds), *Rethinking the Law of Armed Conflict in an Age of Terrorism* (Lanham, MD: Lexington Books, 2011), 195.

[6] Customary international law is understood to be based on the 'the actual practice and *opinio juris* of States' (see *Continental Shelf (Libyan Arab Jamahiriya v. Malta)*, Judgment of 3 June 1985, ICJ Rep 1985, 29–30, para 27). However, space constraints preclude reference to *opinio juris* and state practice from an analytical point of view and will reflect upon them only briefly.

II. Proportionality in Customary International Law

Proportionality in *jus ad bellum* is traced back to the *Caroline* incident of 1837 and it is premised in customary international law.[7] Although the *Caroline* criteria are universally considered to be a watershed event in the history of *jus ad bellum*, they currently remain vague and do less than little to provide us with the content of the principle of proportionality. Arguably, they provide an unstable 'platform' upon which a state may formulate what should be a necessary and proportional response to a threat that is yet to materialize or to an attack carried out by non-state actors. The fact that the contemporary international environment is permeated by modern security threats, the seriousness of which are amplified by advances in technology and shifts in the nature of warfare (ie cyberwarfare), adds a layer of opaqueness to the conditions of applicability of the *Caroline* criteria outside the traditional interstate setting. Moreover, when states claim to exercise their right to self-defence, they usually avoid clarifying whether their right to self-defence is based on customary and/or UN Charter law. Accordingly, it is observed that for a number of states Article 51 is interpreted to encompass or even impose the customary criteria of necessity, imminence, and proportionality, while not stipulating as such.[8] Similarly, the fact that recent years have seen the active launching of military operations by regional organizations, sometimes mandated by the Security Council and sometimes in the absence of Security Council authorization, raises the question of how proportionality is gauged in these particular uses of force. The ICJ, on the other hand, has approached the applicability of the criterion of proportionality on a case-by-case basis without establishing a general theoretical framework on the content of this criterion and how it applies or should evolve.[9]

The approach of the ICJ to the content of the principle of proportionality could be described as confusing, if not phobic, due to the Court's reluctance to define or even analyse the dimensions of proportionality in *jus ad bellum*. However, where the Court has refrained from providing us with a detailed analysis of the principle of proportionality, the ICJ judges' tendency to append a separate opinion, dissenting opinion, or declaration gives shape to the customary dimensions of proportionality.

In 1989 in the *Nicaragua* case, the ICJ noted that 'there is a specific rule whereby self-defence would warrant only measures which are *proportional to the armed attack* and necessary to respond to it, a rule well established in customary international

[7] *Legality of the Threat or Use of Nuclear Weapons*, Advisory Opinion, ICJ Rep 1996, 226, 256.

[8] Raphaël van Steenberghe, 'Self-Defence in Response to Attacks by Non-State Actors in the Light of Recent Practice: A Step Forward?' (2010) 23 *Leiden Journal of International Law* 183, 186 fn 6.

[9] See the analysis later in the chapter.

law.'[10] According to the Court's finding, a proportionate response in self-defence amounts to *any type* of measures necessary to respond to an armed attack that has taken place or is ongoing. In this case, the defensive measures were found to have failed the test of proportionality due to a combination of factors, for example the selected targets and the scale of the attacks.[11] Given this fact and the fact that the Court did not attempt to specify what type of measures may be acceptable as proportionate (apart from being necessary) in the exercise of the right of self-defence, the Court appears to have interpreted the concept of proportionality against the size and the scope of the armed attack. The *Nicaragua* approach was reaffirmed in the *Nuclear Weapons* case.[12]

In the *Oil Platforms* case what the Court required from the US was to 'show that its actions were necessary and proportional to the armed attack made upon it.'[13] With this statement, the Court clarified that the proportionality of self-defence measures is to be assessed neither in relation to the final objective of the self-defence operation nor in relation to the specific incidents of targeting;[14] instead, proportionality should be assessed by taking into account the scale of the whole operation as well as the necessity of the measures taken in self-defence.[15] The ICJ therefore stated that '*as a response to the mining* by an unidentified agency, of a single United States warship, which was severely damaged but not sunk, and without loss of life, neither "Operation Praying Mantis" as a whole, nor even that part of it that destroyed the Salman and Nasr platforms, can be regarded, in the circumstances of this case, as a proportionate use of force.'[16]

In the *Armed Activities* case, once the Court found that the preconditions for the exercise of self-defence did not exist in the particular case, it refrained from examining whether the alleged actions in self-defence against large-scale attacks by irregular forces were exercised in circumstances of necessity and in a manner that was proportionate. However, the Court was tempted to comment that 'the taking of airports and towns many hundreds of kilometres from Uganda's border would not seem proportionate to the series of trans-border attacks it claimed had given rise to the right of self-defense, nor to be necessary to that end.'[17] In this case, the

[10] *Military and Paramilitary Activities in and against Nicaragua (Nicaragua v. US)*, Merits, Judgment of 27 June 1986, ICJ Rep 1986, 94, para 176.

[11] Judith Gardam, *Necessity, Proportionality and the Use of Force by States* (Cambridge: Cambridge University Press, 2004), 158.

[12] *Nuclear Weapons*, Advisory Opinion, 245 and esp paras 41–3.

[13] *Case Concerning Oil Platforms (Iran v. US)*, Judgment of 6 Nov 2003, ICJ Rep 2003, para 51.

[14] It should be noted that the US and Iran held opposing views as to the meaning of proportionality. See Theodora Christodoulidou and Kalliopi Chainoglou, 'The Principle of Proportionality in Self-Defence and Humanitarian Intervention' (2007) 20 *Journal of International Law of Peace and Armed Conflict* 79, 80–3.

[15] *Oil Platforms*, Judgment, para 72.

[16] *Oil Platforms*, Judgment, para 77.

[17] *Case Concerning Armed Activities on the Territory of the Congo (DRC v. Uganda)*, Judgment of 19 Dec 2005, ICJ Rep 2005, para 147.

Court seemed to imply that the remoteness of the alleged actions in self-defence in relation to the nature of the original attack violated the principles of proportionality and necessity.

The above suggests that proportionality was interpreted by the ICJ as striking a balance between the self-defensive action and the wrong provoking it.

Contrary to the ICJ, Judge Ago had originally provided another interpretation of the principle of proportionality. He had argued that: 'the requirement of the proportionality of the action taken in self-defence ... concerns the relationship between that action and its purpose, namely ... that of halting and repelling that attack. ... It would be mistaken, however, to think that there must be proportionality between the conduct constituting the armed attack and the opposing conduct ... What matters is the result to be achieved by the defensive action, and not the forms, substance and length of the action itself ... Its lawfulness cannot be measured except by its capacity for achieving the desired result.'[18] Judge Ago's position has been upheld by other ICJ judges in their dissenting or separate opinions. For example, Judge Schwebel in the *Nicaragua* case,[19] Judge Higgins in the *Nuclear Weapons* case,[20] and Judge Kooijmans in the *Armed Activities*[21] case connect proportionality with the fulfilment of the general objective of the use of force—that is, the repelling of the attack.

In state practice, states have rarely applied the interpretation of proportionality favoured by the ICJ.[22] Similarly, several scholars argue that the principle of proportionality determines the amount of force that can legitimately be used to achieve the goal pursued.[23]

It seems, therefore, that there are two possible approaches with regard to the interpretation of the principle of proportionality: it could be measures either against

[18] Robert Ago, 'Addendum to the Eighth Report on State Responsibility', *Yearbook of the International Law Commission*, 1980, vol II (1), A/CN.4/318/ADD.5–7, 60, para 121.

[19] *Nicaragua*, Merits, Dissenting Opinion of Judge Schwebel, paras 211–14.

[20] *Nuclear Weapons*, Advisory Opinion, Dissenting Opinion of Judge Higgins, para 5.

[21] *Armed Activities*, Judgment, Separate Opinion of Judge Kooijmans, paras 33–4.

[22] Uganda's oral pleadings in *Armed Activities*, Oral Pleadings, Verbatim Record, 18 Apr 2005, paras 54, 57, 61–7; Iran's memorial in *Oil Platforms*, paras 4.21–4.22; US's Counter Memorial and Counter-Claim in *Oil Platforms*, paras 4.31–4.35 and 5.48; see recently Brazil's statement at the Security Council debate concerning the 2011 NATO military action in Libya, S/PV.6498 (17 Mar 2011). Russia also stated that the said military action was disproportionate because it exceeded the mandate provided under SC Res 1973 (2011), Vladimir Radyuhin, 'Russia condemns NATO's Tripoli bombing', *The Hindu*, 1 May 2011, available at <http:www.thehindu.com/news/international/article1983659.ece>.

[23] Judith Gardam, 'Proportionality and Force in International Law' (1993) 87 *American Journal of International Law* 403; Christopher Greenwood, 'Self-Defense and the Conduct of International Armed Conflict' in Yoram Dinstein and Mala Tabory (eds), *International Law at a Time of Perplexity: Essays in Honour of Shabtai Rosenne* (Dordrecht: Martinus Nijhoff, 1989), 273; Christopher Greenwood, 'The Relationship between *Jus ad Bellum* and *Jus in Bello*' (1985) 9 *Review of International Studies* 224; Olivier Corten, *The Law against War: The Prohibition on the Use of Force in Contemporary International Law* (Oxford: Hart, 2010), 489.

the size and scope of the armed attack (first interpretation of proportionality, favoured by the ICJ) or measures that meet the actual needs of self defence, that is, measures to repel the attack and restore the situation that existed prior to the attack (second interpretation of proportionality, favoured by certain ICJ judges, international scholars, and possibly states).

Nonetheless, the distinction as to the two possible interpretations of proportionality may not be so rigid. Proportionality in *jus ad bellum* should be understood to take the form of a qualified scheme benefiting from two dimensions, better termed as 'double proportionality'.[24] Double proportionality essentially combines the two interpretations of proportionality. One dimension of proportionality is constructively built on the element of necessity to respond to the attack (in terms of its size and scope) while the other dimension of proportionality reflects the fulfilment of the general objective of the use of force—that is, the repelling of the attack.

Double proportionality is likely to be more popular with states due to the political deliberations within national parliaments and the Security Council as well as considerations that fall within the ambit of the defence-budget needs and the contemporary strategic realities. For example, the UK Attorney General on 21 April 2004 in his response to a Parliamentary Question referred to the need for the use of force to be 'proportionate to the threat faced and … limited to what is necessary to deal with the threat.'[25]

III. Measuring Double Proportionality

The question is how can one measure double proportionality and, in particular, how can one measure proportionality of a use of force when its purpose is to meet the

[24] The term 'double proportionality' was first referred to by Vaughan Lowe, 'Clear and Present Danger: Responses to Terrorism' (2005) 54 *International and Comparative Law Quarterly* 192–3.

[25] UK Attorney General Lord Goldsmith, Hansard, HL Deb (21 Apr 2004), vol 660, col 370, available at <http://www.publications.parliament.uk/pa/ld200304/ldhansrd/vo040421/text/40421-07.htm#40421-07_head0>. A couple of years later when the UK Parliament was considering the legality of the military operation in Libya, it was stated that UK forces need to be deployed 'decisively at the right time but only where key UK national interests are at stake; where we have a clear strategic aim; where the likely political, economic and human costs are in proportion to the likely benefits; where we have a viable exit strategy; and where justifiable under international law'. See Defence Committee, Ninth Report: Operations in Libya (25 Jan 2012), para 51 <http://www.publications.parliament.uk/pa/cm201012/cmselect/cmdfence/950/95005.htm>.

general objective of the use of force.[26] The proportionality of the response to the act triggering the right of self-defence depends on the degree of force and consequently on the form of military measures that might lawfully employ. This means that the principle of proportionality imposes an additional level of limitation upon a state's conduct of hostilities, influencing its choice of weapons, targets, and the area of conflict,[27] as well as the geographical[28] and destructive impact of responses on third states, the environment,[29] and people, and even influencing whether the campaign should rely mainly on air strikes and high altitude, rather than on a combination of air and land forces. Judge Greenwood has aptly noted that modern *jus ad bellum* 'is not concerned solely with whether the initial resort to force is lawful; it also has implications for the subsequent conduct of hostilities.'[30]

The measures by which proportionality is calculated have been traditionally analysed from the *jus in bello* perspective. This modern analysis of proportionality in *jus ad bellum* links issues that are traditionally found in *jus in bello* with *jus ad bellum* issues. In fact, it 'picks up' *jus in bello* issues and puts them under the umbrella of the *jus ad bellum*. This has an impact on the legality of the use of force irrespective of whether the state resorting to the use of force complies with the *jus in bello*. Indeed, calculating the principle of proportionality by the means and methods of warfare is an approach that can latently be found in the *Nuclear Weapons* and *Oil Platforms* cases. In the former case, the Court considered whether a nuclear response as a means of warfare is compatible with the principle of proportionality, and stated that 'the very nature of all nuclear weapons and the profound risks associated therewith are further considerations to be born in mind by States believing they can exercise a nuclear response in self-defence in accordance with the requirement of proportionality.'[31] Similarly, in the *Oil Platforms* case, commenting on the criteria of necessity and proportionality, the Court highlighted that one aspect of both of

[26] The measurability of proportionality is of particular concern with respect to the use of non-traditional weapons, ie nuclear weapons, drones, etc. See eg *Nuclear Weapons*, Advisory Opinion, Dissenting Opinion of Judge Schwebel.

[27] Greenwood, 'The Relationship between *Jus ad Bellum* and *Jus in Bello*', 273.

[28] The geographical remoteness of self-defence measures in relation to the original armed attack is a point that has been picked by certain ICJ judges in their dissenting opinions. See Separate Opinion of Judge Simma in *Oil Platforms*, Judgment, and *Armed Activities*, Judgment, paras 13 and 13–14 respectively. See also Christopher Greenwood, 'Self-Defence' in Rüdiger Wolfrum (ed), *Max Planck Encyclopedia of Public International Law* (Oxford: Oxford University Press, 2012), para 29. For this reason Greenwood characterizes proportionality as a 'forward-looking requirement'; the temporal dimension that Judge Greenwood refers to concerns the goal the state seeks to achieve.

[29] In *Nuclear Weapons*, Advisory Opinion, the ICJ noted that 'Respect for the environment is one of the elements that go to assessing whether an action is in conformity with the principles of necessity and proportionality', para 29.

[30] Christopher Greenwood, '*Jus ad Bellum* and *Jus in Bell* in the *Nuclear Weapons Advisory Opinion*' in Laurence Boisson de Chazournes and Philippe Sands (eds), *International Law, the International Court of Justice and Nuclear Weapons* (Cambridge: Cambridge University Press, 1999), 265.

[31] *Nuclear Weapons*, Advisory Opinion, para 43.

these criteria is the 'nature of the *target* of the force used avowedly in self-defence'.[32] The ICJ considered here the lawfulness of the self-defence measures by additionally taking into account whether the selected targets were used for military activities, whether there was sufficient evidence proving it, and whether the alleged victim state took sufficient steps to complain repeatedly to the alleged aggressor state. The approach of the ICJ in *Oil Platforms* has the effect of interweaving issues and considerations of two different and separate bodies of laws—those of *jus ad bellum* and *jus in bello*.

Judge Higgins in her separate opinion in the *Wall* advisory opinion found that even if the construction of the wall were an act of self defence, which seemed to have diminished attacks on Israeli civilians, the question as to why the particular course of action (ie construction of the wall, and route and geographical position of the wall) was chosen as a means of satisfying the criteria of necessity and proportionality over another possible course of action remains unanswered. Both Judge Higgins and Judge Kooijmans drew on the impact of the wall construction on the Palestinians' lives, connecting thus the proportionality issue with the 'attendant hardships' for the Palestinians who were not involved in the attacks.[33]

However, 'picking up' or 'borrowing' *jus in bello* considerations when considering the ambit of *jus ad bellum* proportionality, does not converge the *in bello* with the *ad bellum* proportionality. In the past few years, a small number of scholars seem to disturbingly converge the *jus ad bellum* with the *jus in bello* proportionality.[34] Obviously the use of force is subject to both legal regimes. Their application, however, is neither simultaneous nor parallel. The *jus in bello* rule of proportionality focuses on the regulation of the conduct of the conflict. Proportionality in *jus in bello* determines the balance between the achievement of a military goal and the cost in terms of suffering and loss of civilian life.[35] It weighs the legitimacy of attacking a particular military target, for example collateral damage to civilians, it applies irrespective of whether or not the use of force is deemed lawful, and plays no part whatsoever on the legality of the use of force as a whole. On the other hand, *jus ad bellum* proportionality precedes over *jus in bello* proportionality. Its breach renders

[32] *Oil Platforms*, Judgment, para 74.

[33] *Legal Consequences of the Construction of a Wall in the Occupied Palestinian Territory*, Advisory Opinion, ICJ Rep 2004, Separate Opinion of Judge Higgins and Judge Kooijmans, paras 35 and 34 respectively.

[34] See Sampson, 'Necessity, Proportionality and Distinction in Nontraditional Conflicts'. Cf Solon Solomon, 'The Great Oxymoron: *Jus in Bello* Violations as Legitimate Non-Forcible Measures of Self-Defence: The Post-Disengagement Israeli Measures towards Gaza as a Case Study' (2010) 9 *Chinese Journal of International Law* 501, Raphaël van Steenberghe, 'Proportionality under Jus ad Bellum and Jus in Bello: Clarifying their Relationship' (2012) 45 *Israel Law Review* 107, 112.

[35] See Arts 51(5)(b) and 57(2)(a)(ii), (iii), and (b) of Additional Protocol to the Geneva Conventions of 1949, and relating to the protection of victims of international armed conflicts (Protocol I). Even where the principle of proportionality is not specifically mentioned, it is reflected in many provisions of Additional Protocol I.

illegal an otherwise legal use of force. Even in the scenario where the use of force is considered legal in terms of its proportionality under *jus ad bellum* but illegal in terms of its proportionality under *jus in bello* (or vice versa), the assessment of the proportionality of the actions in question will not be distorted by the applicability of the other legal regime. Hence, the legality of actions in *jus in bello* cannot mitigate their illegality under *jus ad bellum*.

It is noteworthy, for example, that the legality of the Israeli intervention in Lebanon in 2006 primarily failed due to the excessive damage caused to civilians and civilian infrastructure.[36] The Commission of Inquiry on Lebanon, concluded that, albeit the legal justification for self-defence, 'Israel's military actions very quickly escalated from a riposte to a border incident into a general attack against the entire Lebanese territory. Israel's response was considered by the Security Council in its resolution 1701 (2006) as "offensive military operation"'.[37] These actions have the characteristics of an armed aggression, as defined by General Assembly Resolution 3314 (XXIX).

However, it should be admitted that the criterion of proportionality is not perceived as a static legal formality. On the contrary, it is a legal form of conduct which encompasses considerations that may determine or affect to a certain extent the conduct of hostilities, the duration of the military operation, and the choice of means and methods of warfare (eg geographical scope of operations, etc). This means that a state may find itself having limited options in the operational field. In other words, to the extent that the *jus ad bellum* proportionality determines the legality of targeting certain military objectives or using certain weaponry, the measures that a state devises must not exceed those necessary for the state to defend itself against the armed attack. Consequently, the deaths of civilians and destruction of civilian infrastructure which constitute a violation of proportionality under *jus in bello* may indicate (with hindsight or *post facto*) the violation of the *jus ad bellum* proportionality.

[36] See Vaios Koutroulis, 'Of Occupation, *Jus ad Bellum* and *Jus in Bello*: A Reply to Solon Solomon's "The Great Oxymoron: *Jus in Bello* Violations as Legitimate Non-Forcible Measures of Self-Defense: The Post-Disengagement Israeli Measures towards Gaza as a Case Study"' (2011) 10 *Chinese Journal of International Law* 897, 912 ff.

[37] Implementation of GA Res 60/251 of 15 March 2006 entitled 'Human Rights Council', Report of the Commission of Inquiry on Lebanon pursuant to Human Rights Council Resolution S-2/1, A/HRC/3/2, Human Rights Council, 3rd Sess, 23 Nov 2006, 23, para 61.

IV. Proportionality and Self-Defence

According to Article 51 of the UN Charter, states may exercise the inherent right to individual or collective self-defence if an armed attack occurs. This provision has troubled legal scholars and strategists as to whether self-defence can take place before, after, or at the time of the occurrence of the armed attack. As a consequence, the interpretation of Article 51 in different situations has resulted in classifications of self-defence, that is, anticipatory, interceptive, or pre-emptive. These classifications are based on the purpose and time frame of the response to the armed attack or the threat of armed attack. While the purpose of the traditional (restrictive conception of) self-defence is to defend against an armed attack that has already taken place, the purpose of anticipatory self-defence is to pre-empt an imminent or expected attack, and the purpose of pre-emptive self-defence is to deter states or non-state actors from pursuing a specific course of action that, if allowed to evolve/mature, may potentially develop into an armed attack. The various classifications of self-defence are confusing and tend to devalue the customary international law modalities—such as necessity and proportionality—which govern the exercise of the inherent right of self-defence. However, the premise for all these classifications of self-defence is that the defending state, which acts in good faith and on the basis of evidence available at the time, has no choice of other means than to respond with forcible actions. This means that there are no alternative effective and peaceful means to repel or avert the attack in question.

Proportionality in self-defence is concomitant with the size and scope of an armed attack (first interpretation of proportionality) and the overall objective of the defensive responses (second interpretation of proportionality).[38] Proportionality is subject to the balance between the threat and the means and the methods of warfare chosen to deal with the threat. However, the current security milieu faces challenges which may distort the assessment of proportionality. The problem lies mainly in the assessment of what the threat amounts to (within the anticipatory or pre-emptive self-defence context).[39] To a lesser extent, the problem arises when assessing the reasonable means to repel such a threat (ie military measures against non-state actors).

[38] Either interpretation of proportionality is difficult to apply within the context of anticipatory or pre-emptive self-defence. See Christodoulidou and Chainoglou, 'The Principle of Proportionality in Self-Defence and Humanitarian Intervention', 84–8.

[39] In the anticipatory self-defence context, the question is whether proportionality should be measured against the potential impact of the expected threat and the harm caused by the threat and the force necessary to repulse the threat of attack *or* against the purpose of the defensive action only. In the pre-emptive self-defence context, proportionality is even more difficult to measure against the developing threat and/or the impact of the immaterialized and unimaginable harm.

In the contemporary security environment, a number of variables such as the nature of the security threats in terms of their source, the threats' permeability, the international relations of the states concerned, the national security doctrines of the states concerned, as well as the strategy doctrines of international organizations, and the possibilities of resolving peacefully the imminent crisis in question, influence states' perceptions of the imminence of the threat of armed attack or the realization of the armed attack which may, for example, be preceded by a string of cyberattacks.[40] Even though the jurisprudence of the ICJ cannot provide us with a definition of an 'armed attack', states' evolving perceptions of the concept of 'armed attack' as well as of the concepts of necessity and proportionality are reflected in the international fora of international organizations (UN, North Atlantic Treaty Organization (NATO), etc). This explains further why the Security Council has rarely taken action to condemn cases where states used force in self-defence in situations which did not necessarily comply with a restrictive interpretation of Article 51. As has been pointed out, 'usually [the Security Council] affirms the right of self-defence rather than disapplies it'.[41] Despite the fact that the legality of many self-defence cases is not disputed by the Security Council, the proportionality of the use of force in many of those cases was judged by reference to a qualified proportionality scheme (see the previous discussion).

Self-defensive action does not purport to serve as punitive action against the aggressor. Crucially, even in the restrictive interpretation of self-defence under Article 51 the purpose of the use of force is concerned not only with defence against the attack that has taken place but is also future-oriented. Even within the traditional conception of self-defence, the self-defensive response may not only be concerned with the repulsion of an attack but also with the pre-emption of future armed aggression.[42]

Another issue relevant to the assessment of proportionality is the timing of the defensive action and the duration of the action in question. Should the defensive action continue years after the armed attack, or after the first response to an armed attack, or after the end of hostilities or after the period in which any resumed attack could be contemplated? The temporal element of proportionality has been the object of debates among scholars. For example, Gardam argues that proportionality

[40] See Marco Roschini, 'World Wide Warfare *Jus ad Bellum* and the Use of Cyberforce' (2010) 14 *Max Planck Yearbook of United Nations Law* 85, 114 ff. See also Michael N. Schmitt (ed), *Tallinn Manual on the International Law Applicable to Cyber Warfare* (Cambridge: Cambridge University Press, 2012). Eg a number of cyberattacks on Georgia preceded the military invasion that took place in 2008. See Eneken Tikki et al, *Cyber attacks against Georgia: Legal Lessons Identified* (Tallinn: Cooperative Cyber Defence Centre of Excellence, 2008).

[41] Such an exception is Res 1701 (2006) where Hezbollah was requested to cease attacks and Israel was called upon to refrain 'from all offensive military operations'. Christian Tams and James Devaney, 'Applying Necessity and Proportionality to Anti-Terrorist Self-Defence' (2012) 45 *Israel Law Review* 97.

[42] Sean D. Murphy, 'The Doctrine of Preemptive Self-Defense' (2005) 50 *Villanova Law Review* 735.

remains relevant throughout conflict.[43] State practice is inconclusive on the precise conditions required. The essence of the principle of proportionality is a priori based on the relationship between the threat and the defensive response; inherent in this relationship is the temporal element. After all, even Article 51 of the UN Charter verifies the temporal element of the exercise of the right of self-defence as it clearly provides that a state will exercise its inherent right to self-defence until the Security Council steps in. Self-defensive measures in the form of drone attacks against members of Al Qaeda which continue to take place over ten years after Operation Enduring Freedom began in Afghanistan admittedly stretch the temporal element of proportionality. As proportionality is organically time-conditioned, the legality of the defensive measures is dependent on the evidence available at the time of the defensive response.

An important aspect of proportionality is the gathering of qualitative intelligence that will verify the *intent* of the potential aggressor and the *nature* of the threat.[44] From this point of view, intelligence forms an essential part of the criterion of necessity and contributes to a dynamic and pragmatic assessment of proportionality in the sense that throughout the use of force in self-defence the question that ought to be asked is whether there is need for further force to be used. The scope of the response in self-defence will be determined in accordance with the evidence known or reasonably to have been known at the time of response. Such knowledge of evidence, depending on whether the defending state will share it with the rest of the international community, will condition the reaction of third states after the response. The assessment of the principle of proportionality is also dependent on the reaction of third states. However, there are certain issues surrounding the gathering of intelligence that would distort the assessment of proportionality and the identification of the threat in question as well as of the means available in practice to counter it. For example, there is always the possibility that the evidence gathered for intelligence purposes is patchy, due to its nature or source, or even wrong. For this reason in the *Oil Platforms* case the ICJ rejected any margin of appreciation by states and requested clear and objective proof of a threatened attack.[45] However, the ICJ's finding seems not to have taken into consideration certain strategic issues. It is highly questionable what kind of evidence the alleged defending state must produce and at which stages of the defensive action the evidence must be communicated to other states.

43 See eg Judith Gardam, 'Necessity and Proportionality in *Jus ad Bellum* and *Jus in Bello*' in Boisson de Chazournes and Sands, *International Law, the International Court of Justice and Nuclear Weapons*, 275, 280.

44 Robert A. Zayac, Jr, 'United States' Authority to Legally Implement the Self-Defence and Anticipatory Doctrines to Eradicate the Threat Posed by Countries Harbouring Terrorists and Producing Weapons of Mass Destruction' (2005) 29 *Southern Illinois University Law Journal* 452.

45 *Oil Platforms*, Judgment, paras 71–6.

The assessment of proportionality is dependent on the assessment of the timeline of the threatened attack as well as on the gathering of real evidence; the nature of a proportionate defensive response necessitates that the defensive action is planned and carried out with the belief and the intent that any delay in countering the threatened attack will probably result in the defending state's inability to defend itself against the threatened attack and that defending state has considered all the parameters in order to decide whether there is a need for further force to be used. Overall, the impact of the force used must be weighed against and, if possible, be less than the impact of the attack it is intended to preclude or the damage it is likely to prevent. Nevertheless, when the threat targets mainly the survival of a state rather than the less vital interests of the state, the scope of proportionality of the response in self-defence amplifies correspondingly.

V. Proportionality and Anti-Terrorist Operations

Scholarly work until 2001 identified three different approaches to measure proportionality especially against terrorist attacks: first, the 'eye-for-an-eye' approach; secondly, the 'cumulative proportionality' approach; and, thirdly, the 'deterrent' proportionality.[46] The eye-for-an-eye proportionality approach posits that the defensive response be proportionate to the character of the initiating threat[47] (ie first interpretation of proportionality). The second approach posits that in the case of a series of attacks, the cumulative effect of these attacks may justify a single, yet of greater impact, defensive response[48] (ie first interpretation of proportionality). According to this approach, if a state is threatened and harassed by terrorists on a repetitive basis, the state may have only one chance to avert future attacks or to reduce their effectiveness and frequency: that of taking action in self-defence of a greater degree than each terrorist attack in order to eliminate the centre of the terrorist organization.[49] The third approach posits that the defensive response be of sufficient impact to deter terrorists from planning and carrying out future terrorist attacks[50] (ie second interpretation of proportionality). All these approaches have

[46] Arend and Beck, *International Law and the Use of Force*, 165.

[47] Gregory F. Intoccia, 'American Bombing of Libya' (1987) 19 *Case Western Reserve Journal of International Law* 205, 205–6.

[48] Guy Roberts, 'Self-Help in Combating State-Sponsored Terrorism: Self-Defense and Peacetime Reprisals' (1987) 19 *Case Western Reserve Journal of International Law* 282.

[49] Donald W. Greig, *International Law* (London: Butterworths, 1970), 887.

[50] Alberto Coll, 'Military Responses to Terrorism: The Legal and Moral Adequacy of Military Responses to Terrorism' (1987) 81 *American Society International Law Proceedings* 299.

been tested in state practice when terrorism was perceived to be state-supported or state-sponsored.[51]

Proportionality is gauged differently when the defensive measures do not target the host state of the terrorist base but rather the non-state actors operating on the territory of the host state. When the territorial state merely claims to be willing to root terrorists out of its territory but refuses to act alone or join forces with the defending states, the territorial state may even be considered to be an accomplice to the terrorist activities. The sanctuary state will not be targeted, unless the non-state actors' actions are attributable to it.[52]

The selection of targets depends on the degree of state support, sponsorship, or passive toleration of the territorial state towards the non-state actors.[53] In the aftermath of the 11 September 2001 attacks, it is widely accepted that stateless and borderless terrorist organizations threaten not only the survival of certain states but also international peace and security. States have therefore claimed that they have the right to pursue and exercise their inherent right of self-defence against terrorists wherever the latter may be. Anti-terrorist operations have two characteristics. First, their geographical scope may be expanded, for example drone attacks in cross-border operations.[54] Nonetheless, expansion of the geographical scope does not throw the principle of proportionality out of the picture. Secondly, states may be called upon to act during a 'last window of opportunity'—that is, on an early timeline when non-state actors are at the point of acquiring weapons of mass destruction (WMD) pre-capability materials,[55] developing and weaponizing WMD-useable material, or preparing plans for the actual use of WMD.[56]

[51] See generally Richard Erickson, *Legitimate Use of Military Force against State-Sponsored International Terrorism* (Fort Belvoir, VA: Maxwell Air Force Base, Air University Press, 1989).

[52] Michael N. Schmitt, 'Pre-Emptive Strategies in International Law' (2003) 24 *Michigan Journal of International Law* 543.

[53] eg in the case of Afghanistan, the Taliban had fully harmonized the state's operations with Al Qaeda's operations. In those circumstances it was considered lawful not only to destroy the infrastructure and the facilities used by the Taliban, but also to destitute and replace the Taliban government and prevent any other possible future attack emanating from the territory of Afghanistan. Michael C. Bonafede, 'Here, There, and Everywhere: Assessing the Proportionality Doctrine and US Uses of Force in Response to Terrorism After the September 11 Attacks' (2002) 88 *Cornell Law Review* 203; Barry A. Feinstein, 'Operation Enduring Freedom: "Legal Dimensions of an Infinitely Just Operation"' (2002) 11 *Journal of Transnational Law and Policy* 280.

[54] See *Oil Platforms*, Counter-memorial and Counter-claim submitted by the US, 23 June 1997, ICJ Rep 1997, 171, para 4.32; Oscar Schachter, *International Law in Theory and Practice* (Dodrecht: Martinus Nijhoff, 1991), 154.

[55] The benefit of 'last window opportunity' actions provides states with the opportunity to surgically eliminate the threat, ie to target the relevant assets that are the source of the threat and to use limited force for a very short period. It should be noted, though, that the test of proportionality in these cases of action within a specific window of opportunity will be influenced by a balancing-of-costs and a political cost–benefit analysis which would make a state think twice before exercising its right to self-defence at this specific time.

[56] Judith Gardam, 'A Role for Proportionality in the War on Terror' (2005) 74 *Nordic Journal of International Law* 3, 20–1; Elaine Bunn, 'Pre-Emptive Action: When, How, and to What Effect?' (July 2003) 200 *Strategic Forum* 3.

Where a territorial state is willing to take action against terrorists but is unable to do so and its territory continues to be improperly used for a reasonable time (measured by the threat the situation poses to the defending state), the defending state may cross the border of the sanctuary state without its consent and dispatch military units or military drones only for the sole purpose of eliminating the threat; as soon as the threat is eliminated, the military units or military drones must leave the foreign territory. The use of drones is particularly effective when there are inaccessible or remote areas or there is a need for timely and sufficient precision to eliminate the target. Furthermore, the use of drones within the context of cross-border operations limits the scale and the time span of force employed while affording the defending state more consistent compliance with the principle of double proportionality as analysed earlier. Along the same lines, a defending state may employ surgical strikes to neutralize terrorist cells, destroy terrorist training camps actively engaged in hostile activities, and to reduce their capacity for planning, organizing, and conducting future terrorist activities.[57] Assessing the use of drones vis-à-vis other uses of force, Schmitt notes that 'if targeted drone strikes against terrorist camps would suffice to damp down further attacks, [then] it would be unlawful to mount large scale ground operations into the territorial state. The limitation is equally geographical. It would … be unlawful to deploy forces into locations void of terrorists or insurgents.' [58] Therefore, drone attacks against Al Qaeda in Pakistan may be deemed permissible as long as they are treated as self-defensive measures against non-state actors, they are deemed necessary and specific-target, and they do not inflict civilian damage.[59]

In cross-border operations, the proportionality calculation should also take into account the potential effects/consequences of the defensive response, that is, the risk of collateral damage on civilians, on the territory of a state not directly, or not at all, responsible for the threat posed. 'Measures not expected to affect the terrorist network and activities cannot be justified as self-defence as they do not directly contribute to the achievement of the objective.'[60] As Gardam observes, a proportionate action would still have 'to be carefully crafted to achieving the destruction of the group concerned, with the minimum impact on the State concerned, its population and infrastructure.'[61]

[57] Tarcisio Gazzini, *The Changing Rules on the Use of Force in International Law* (Manchester: Manchester University Press, 2005), 198.

[58] Michael N. Schmitt, 'Drone Attacks under the *Jus ad Bellum* and *Jus in Bello*: Clearing the "Fog of Law"' (2011) *Yearbook of International Humanitarian Law* 313, 317.

[59] Andrew Orr, 'Unmanned, Unprecedented and Unsolved. The Status of American Drone Strikes in Pakistan under International Law' (2011) 44 *Cornell International Law Journal* 729, 738: 'The fact that the drone strikes continue to target specific individual fighters (rather than, say, entire villages), however, suggests that their goal is limited to the elimination of ongoing threats to the United States. Such a goal would be *ad bellum* proportionate, but the unavailability of relevant facts precludes a conclusive legal analysis.'

[60] Gazzini, *The Changing Rules on the Use of Force in International Law*, 198.

[61] Gardam, 'A Role for Proportionality in the War on Terror', 17.

Recent practice in anti-terrorist operations has so far indicated that proportionality is measured in the light of the objective of the defensive response, as well as the means and methods employed, by taking into consideration civilian suffering. It has been observed that claims of excessive use of force in anti-terrorist operations have been put forward when the use of force was devoid of a defensive nature (in respect to the purported aim), it lacked a nexus with the temporal limits of self-defence, and when it inflicted unnecessary suffering on the civilian population and damage to the civilian infrastructure.[62] Perhaps we should admit that under *jus ad bellum* proportionality there can never be an absolute or 'a very strict limit on self-defence because it is mainly understood as a prohibition against excesses'. After all, neither the UN nor the ICJ, not even the UN Secretary General or the International Law Commission or any other UN-mandated body, have attempted to formulate guidelines on proportionality. Even though the law of self-defence has been tested significantly in the light of new security threats, the rule of proportionality is not yet dead. Proportionality is evolving and adapting to the new security environment.

VI. Proportionality and the Use of Force to Protect Human Rights

Few topics have raised as much controversy and debate in the use of force area as the issue of the use of force to protect human rights. Taking into consideration that the Security Council can authorize the use of force when widespread human rights violations occur,[63] and the increasing state practice and *opinio juris* favouring the use of force to protect human rights without prior Security Council authorization as part of customary international law[64] (even though the use of force in this regard still remains

[62] This was the case with the Israel–Lebanon war in 2006. See Robert Barnidge, 'The Principle of Proportionality under International Humanitarian Law and Operation Cast Lead' in William C. Banks (ed), *New Battlefields/Old Laws* (New York: Columbia University Press, 2011), 171.

[63] This has been a well-established practice of the Security Council since the 1990s (eg SC Res 794 in Somalia, 929 in Rwanda, 816 and 836 in Bosnia). Any remaining doubts as to whether the Security Council can authorize the use of force to protect human rights were removed by the 2005 World Summit Outcome which introduced the principle of the 'responsibility to protect' (A/60/L.1, para 139) ('we are prepared to take collective action in timely and decisive manner, through the Security Council, in accordance with the Charter, including Chapter VII, on a case-by-case basis … [when] national authorities manifestly fail to protect their populations from genocide, war crimes, ethnic cleansing and crimes against humanity'). The General Assembly adopted the Summit Outcome in GA Res A/RES/60/1.

[64] Theodora Christodoulidou, *The Use of Force and the Promotion and Protection of Human Rights* (Athens: Ant. N. Sakkoulas and Bruylant, 2008).

controversial),[65] the issue of identifying the principle of proportionality when the purpose of the use of force is to protect human rights becomes imminent.

The problems in identifying the principle of proportionality when the purpose of the use of force is to protect human rights are different from those in self-defence and in anti-terrorist operations. First, the ICJ in the jurisprudence referred to previously and in the *Caroline* case proportionality was referred to in self-defence only. This is so because traditionally self-defence has been the only exception to the general prohibition on the use of force enshrined in Article 2(4) of the UN Charter. Secondly, when the Security Council authorizes the use of force the question of whether the states resorting to the use of force have complied with the principle of proportionality is totally ignored by international lawyers, although action mandated by a Chapter VII Security Council resolution constitutes another exception to the general prohibition on the use of force. Thirdly, analysis of the principle of proportionality for the purposes of protecting human rights moves from the just war doctrine to the principle of proportionality in *jus in bello*, totally ignoring the principle of proportionality from a *jus ad bellum* perspective. Although the contribution of the just war doctrine and the *jus in bello* in the principle of proportionality is essential, as the first one refers to the ethical underpinnings of proportionality and the second to the legality of the conduct of a particular means and method of warfare, the principle of proportionality from a *jus ad bellum* perspective determines whether or not the use of force is legal.

The question whether the principle of proportionality imposes additional requirements on the means and methods of warfare is not a new one as it has been tackled several times by international lawyers, but not from a *jus ad bellum* perspective. Rather, they choose to construct their argument either through the *jus in bello*[66] or through the just war doctrine arguing that it falls within the ethical rather than the legal sphere.[67] Even the International Commission on Intervention and State Sovereignty (ICISS) applying the just war tradition states that 'military intervention should only be undertaken when the prospects for success are strong—when the intervention is likely to do more good than harm.'[68] Similarly, the Global Centre for the Responsibility to Protect applying the just war tradition asks 'on balance,

[65] Carlo Focarelli, 'The Responsibility to Protect Doctrine and Humanitarian Intervention: Too Many Ambiguities for a Working Doctrine' (2008) 13 *Journal of Conflict and Security Law* 191.

[66] Michael Bothe, 'The Protection of the Civilian Population and NATO Bombing on Yugoslavia: Comments on a Report to the Prosecutor of the ICTY' (2001) 12 *European Journal of International Law* 535; Independent International Commission on Kosovo, *The Kosovo Report: Conflict, International Response, Lessons Learned* (New York: Oxford University Press, 2000), 179 and 195.

[67] See John F. Murphy, 'Some Legal (And a Few Ethical) Dimensions of the Collateral Damage Resulting from NATO's Kosovo Campaign' (2001) 31 *Israel Yearbook on Human Rights* 76–7; Nicholas J. Wheeler, 'Dying for 'Enduring Freedom': Accepting Responsibility for Civilian Casualties in the War against Terrorism' (2002) 16 *International Relations* 218.

[68] Report of the International Commission on Intervention and State Sovereignty, *The Responsibility to Protect* (Ottawa: International Development Research Centre, 2001), 142.

would the intervention do more good than harm?'[69] This intellectual strand deals with the Sisyphean task of balancing the 'good' versus the harm that is done or is going to be done. Here, the calculation of proportionality is based on the risk taken and the harm inflicted. Accordingly, military measures that carry no risk but result in large-scale destruction, for example through air strikes or psychological operations[70] which subject the population to mental pressure rather than to wholesale killing, will be considered disproportionate.

However, the High-Level Panel on Threats, Challenges and Change in its 2004 report suggested five basic criteria of legitimacy when the Security Council considers whether to authorize the use of military force. Those criteria of legitimacy are reminiscent of the just war doctrine criteria and one of those criteria is proportional means. The High-Level Panel under the title 'proportional means' poses the question: 'Are the scale, duration and intensity of the proposed military action the minimum necessary to meet the threat in question?'[71] Along similar lines is the Secretary-General's report 'In Larger Freedom' where he requested 'the SC to adopt a resolution on the use of force that sets out the principles for the use of force [and] the need to consider—when contemplating whether to authorize the use of force..., whether the military option is proportional to the threat at hand.'[72]

The Security Council has not yet adopted any resolution on the issue, and it remains to be seen whether these criteria will become part of customary international law. Until this is clarified, the question remains as to whether the High-Level Panel introduced just war criteria in its report, which would suggest that the principle of proportionality is an ethical rather than a legal principle, just like the ICISS Report, or whether the High-Level Panel report transformed just war criteria into legal ones, which would suggest that the principle of proportionality is a legal principle. The first alternative, however, seems to be more likely at least for the time being. The 2005 Summit Outcome Document did not include or suggest any criteria of legitimacy when the Security Council considers whether to authorize the use of force. Similarly, the Secretary-General's 2009 report 'Implementing the Responsibility to Protect' merely stated that 'member States may want to consider the principles, rules and doctrine that should guide the application of coercive force in extreme situations relating to the responsibility to protect'.[73]

[69] Global Centre for the Responsibility to Protect, 'The Georgia–Russia Crisis and the Responsibility to Protect: Background Note', 19 Aug 2008, 2.

[70] On this issue, see Kalliopi Chainoglou, 'Psychological Warfare' in Wolfrum, *Max Planck Encyclopedia of Public International Law*, vol VIII, 559–64.

[71] Report of the High-Level Panel on Threats, Challenges and Change, 'A More Secure World: Our Shared Responsibility', A/59/565 (2004), paras 207–8.

[72] Report of the Secretary-General, 'In Larger Freedom: Towards Development, Security and Human Rights for All', A/59/2005 (2005), 58.

[73] Report of the Secretary-General, 'Implementing the Responsibility to Protect', A/63/677 (2009), para 62.

Subsequent reports by the Secretary-General, namely, 'Early Warning, Assessment and the Responsibility to Protect'[74] and 'The Role of Regional and Sub-regional Arrangements in Implementing the Responsibility to Protect'[75] made no reference to these criteria.

Since mainstream analysis on the principle of proportionality ignores the principle of proportionality from a *jus ad bellum* perspective as a condition guiding the application of coercive action, it is imperative to have recourse to customary international law. Judge Greenwood suggested that the limitations imposed by the principles of necessity and proportionality in self-defence would apply *mutatis mutandis* to any other possible justification for the use of force,[76] obviously with the relevant adjustments. This would equally apply to the use of force to protect human rights, whether or not mandated by the Security Council. Building on the principle of proportionality in self-defence (double proportionality) and applying *mutatis mutandis* the principle of proportionality in self-defence, proportionality of the use of force for the purposes of protecting human rights is measured against the size and scope of the human rights violations (ie force that is proportional to the human rights violations—first interpretation of proportionality) and determines the amount of force that can be used to achieve the goal (ie force that is proportional to meet the goal—second interpretation of proportionality).

Therefore, in accordance with the first interpretation of proportionality, the use of force should be proportionate to the human rights violations triggering it, which means that only grave human rights violations warrant a proportionate use of force. This limitation on the use of force is part of a well-established principle in customary international law and not part of the legal literature[77] or the efforts of certain states to initiate more systematic discussion on the use of force to protect human rights.[78] If the use of force is authorized by the Security Council, the 2005 UN Summit specifically stated which human rights violations are considered grave—that is, genocide, war crimes, ethnic cleansing, and crimes against humanity.[79]

With regard to the second interpretation of proportionality, the use of force should also be proportionate to achieve the goal. This means that states should use

[74] Report of the Secretary-General, 'Early Warning, Assessment and the Responsibility to Protect', A/64/864 (2010).

[75] Report of the Secretary-General, 'The Role of Regional and Sub-Regional Arrangements in Implementing the Responsibility to Protect', A/65/877–S/2011/393 (2011).

[76] Greenwood, 'Self-Defense and the Conduct of International Armed Conflict' in Dinstein and Tabory, *International Law at a Time of Perplexity*, 274 fn 9.

[77] In the legal literature, see Antonio Cassese, '*Ex Iniuria Ius Oritur*: Are We Moving Towards International Legitimation of Forcible Humanitarian Countermeasures in the World Community?' (1999) 10 *European Journal of International Law* 23.

[78] See eg the Danish Institute of International Affairs, *Humanitarian Intervention: Legal and Political Aspects* (Copenhagen: Danish Institute of International Affairs, 1999).

[79] World Summit Outcome Document (2005), para 139.

only the amount of force requisite to achieve the goal. Proportionality is weighted not against the military goal but against the 'political goal' of the intervention. The political goal of an intervention the purpose of which is to protect human rights is to stop human rights violations, prevent further human rights violations in the territory in which the states intervene, or even bring to international criminal justice the perpetrators of war crimes and massive human rights violations with links to terrorist organizations. Similarly, the political goal of a Security Council-authorized intervention can be found in the Council resolution authorizing the use of force. Security Council practice shows that the political goal of an intervention can be quite broad, as was the case of Libya in 2011, or more circumscribed, as was the case of Côte d'Ivoire in 2011 and Mali in 2012.[80] Sometimes there are controversies over whether the states or regional arrangements using military force have complied with the Security Council resolution authorizing the use of force or whether they have exceeded the mandate.[81] Yet, it is suggested that the question whether the states using force have complied with the Security Council resolution falls within the analysis of whether the use of force was proportional to the goal of the intervention; thereby whether the use of force meets the requirements of proportionality. It can even be argued that the fact that the Security Council authorized the use of force is indicative of the necessity of the action and the wording of the resolution delimits or circumscribes the principle of proportionality in terms of means and methods of warfare. Therefore, the force used should be proportionate to achieve the goal of stopping human rights violations and preventing further human rights violations in the territory in which the states intervene or achieving the goal specifically referred to in the resolution. Military intervention conducted for the sake of protecting human rights or averting a humanitarian tragedy cannot itself rely on military means which provoke a humanitarian tragedy similar to the original impending tragedy the interventionists sought to avert. Means and methods of warfare that do not aim to prevent further human rights violations and anticipate exacerbation of human suffering (eg the use of air strikes only, flying at high altitude

[80] In the case of Libya, see SC Res 1973 (2011), para 4 where it is stated that the Security Council 'authorizes member states ... to use all necessary measures ... *to protect civilians and civilian populated areas under threat of attack* in the Libyan Arab Jamahiriya including Benghazi'. In the case of Côte d'Ivoire the use of force extended only to 'protect civilians under *imminent threat of physical violence*.' SC Res 1975 (2011), para 6. In the case of Mali, see SC Res 2085 (2012), para 19 where the Security Council 'decides to authorize the deployment of an African-led International Support Mission in Mali (AFISMA) ... *to support the Malian authorities in their primary responsibility to protect the population*' (para 9), and '*calls upon* AFISMA, ... *to bring to justice perpetrators of serious human rights abuses and violations of international humanitarian law in Mali*' (para 19).

[81] Concerning the recent conflicts in Libya and Côte d'Ivoire, see Christian Henderson, 'International Measures for the Protection of Civilians in Libya and Côte d'Ivoire' (2011) 60 *International and Comparative Law Quarterly* 767; Alex J. Bellamy and Paul D. Williams, 'The New Politics of Protection? Côte d'Ivoire, Libya and the Responsibility to Protect' (2011) 87 *International Affairs* 825, 845–6.

during air campaigns, unwillingness to sacrifice one's own soldiers) may violate the principle of proportionality.[82]

This is easier said than done: how does one know which means and methods of warfare would be appropriate to stop human rights violations in a particular conflict? Civil conflicts lead to human rights violations and escalate into international conflicts and certain communities have their most basic human rights suppressed (including the right to life) and are violated by the state itself or other factions within the state, in whose behaviour the state acquiesces or which they cannot control. Finding out which means are appropriate to stop human rights violations in the particular conflict is an extremely difficult and complex task and requires in-depth knowledge of the conflict in question. This suggests that the principle of proportionality when the use of force is to protect human rights, brings under its umbrella issues that have long been considered as non-legal, such as policy considerations and issues of the effectiveness of the intervention. It can even be suggested that the correct application of the principle of proportionality, after examining all the relevant factors, intelligence, and information, will most likely lead to effective interventions.

It is often argued that grave human rights violations are taking place in Chechnya (Russia), in China, and recently in Syria without the option of the use of force being considered seriously by states or the Security Council. However, it seems that the application of the principle of proportionality in such cases leads to the conclusion that use of force to protect human rights in those countries would likely not stop human rights violations and therefore be disproportionate. Indeed, it is difficult to imagine the success of an intervention if military action were taken against a major power or against a state which is suggested as having nuclear weapons. The possible repercussions following a major war, including the use of nuclear weapons and the involvement of more than one state, the increased instability that intervention might cause, the damage to the infrastructure of the target state and to the environment generally, all outweigh such interventions as disproportionate. The application of the principle of proportionality may preclude military action against major powers or states suggested as having nuclear weapons. However, it should be made clear that military action against military powers is precluded based on considerations of proportionality and not on any other political considerations. Hence, the correct application of the principle of proportionality means that uses of force to protect human rights are selective by nature.

Since the principle of proportionality is part of the decision-making process, it is considered in advance of an attack, after analysing all the relevant information and intelligence. One cannot assess the proportionality of an activity by its outcome.

[82] For an analysis of the application of the principle of proportionality in the humanitarian intervention in Kosovo, see Christodoulidou, *The Use of Force and the Promotion and Protection of Human Rights*, 256–62.

Calculations of whether the action is appropriate in terms of proportionality are often easier *ex post facto* than prior to the intervention. If the outcome of the military action did not manage to stop human rights violations, something which had not been anticipated, and the means and methods of warfare were appropriate at that time to achieve the legitimate end, the action will be disproportionate. Such intervention may be a failed or unsuccessful intervention but is not disproportionate. Nonetheless, as explained previously, despite the normative difference between proportionate and successful interventions, the distinction in practice is not, and should not be, so rigid. In fact, these two issues seem interrelated.

VII. Conclusion

Recent state practice and the reaction of the international community to state practice indicates that proportionality is an intuitive yet complex concept susceptible to political manoeuvring. We feel that proportionality is an issue which despite its importance not only in determining the legality of a use of force, but also in circumscribing the scope of the force and limiting the destructive impact of armed conflict, has been sidelined by most legal scholars and international organs such as the ICJ. Proportionality today remains a rather rhetorical tool within a highly politicized sphere of military action that fails to take into consideration complexities surrounding each use of force and each geopolitical environment. For example, civil conflicts in Africa have turned into international conflicts and vice versa for the past few decades without being able to specify their duration, identity the actors and the factions involved or the status of the states involved (ie weak or failed), and the territories in dispute. In these cases, it can be almost impossible to gauge the proportionality of actions taken in self-defence. Also, with regards to the issue of the use of force to protect human rights, the principle of proportionality attempts to put under its umbrella issues that have not traditionally been considered as legal, but rather as moral, or policy, considerations, or issues of the effectiveness of the intervention, and recently issues as to whether states resorting to the use of force have complied with the Security Council resolution authorizing the use of force. To an extent, the principle of proportionality has managed to pull these issues under its umbrella. However, as Michael Ignatieff said: 'moral questions stubbornly resist being reduced to legal ones, and moral exposure is not eliminated when legal exposure is.'[83] We believe that policy considerations and issues of effectiveness also do so.

[83] Michael Ignatieff, *Virtual War: Kosovo and Beyond* (London: Chatto & Windus), 199.

CHAPTER 56

THE RELATIONSHIP BETWEEN *JUS AD BELLUM* AND *JUS IN BELLO*

KEIICHIRO OKIMOTO*

I. INTRODUCTION

THE relationship between *jus ad bellum* (international law regulating the resort to force) and *jus in bello* (law of armed conflict)[1] did not arise as a clearly defined question until the adoption of the General Treaty for Renunciation of War as an Instrument of National Policy[2] (General Treaty) in 1928. The General Treaty, by

* The views expressed herein are those of the author and do not necessarily reflect the views of the United Nations or the International Committee of the Red Cross.

[1] See generally Hersch Lauterpacht, 'The Limits of the Operation of the Laws of War' (1953) 30 *British Yearbook of International Law* 206; Henri Meyrowitz, *Le principe de l'égalité de belligérants devant le droit de la guerre* (Paris: Éditions Pedone, 1970); Christopher Greenwood, 'The Relationship between *Jus ad Bellum* and *Jus in Bello*' (1983) 9 *Review of International Studies* 221; François Bugnion, 'Guerre juste, guerre d'agression et droit international humanitaire' (2002) 847 *Revue internationale de la Croix-Rouge* 523; Marco Sassòli, '*Ius ad Bellum* and *Ius in Bello*–The Separation between the Legality of the Use of Force and Humanitarian Rules to Be Respected in Warfare: Crucial or Outdated?' in Michael Schmitt and Jelena Pejic (eds), *International Law and Armed Conflict: Exploring the Faultlines* (Leiden: Koninklijke Brill, 2007), 241; Adam Roberts, 'The Equal Application of the Laws of War: A Principle under Pressure' (2008) 872 *International Review of the Red Cross* 931; Keiichiro Okimoto, *The Distinction and Relationship between* Jus ad Bellum *and* Jus in Bello (Oxford: Hart, 2011).

[2] General Treaty for Renunciation of War as an Instrument of National Policy, Paris, 27 Aug 1928, 94 LNTS 57. See also Arts 10–16 of the Covenant of the League of Nations, Paris, 28 Apr 1919, 225 CTS 188.

which the parties renounced war as an instrument of national policy in their relations with one another, was the first clear indication of modern *jus ad bellum* which radically changed the legal landscape in many respects.[3] The General Treaty created, inter alia, a distinction between an unlawful party, that is to say, a party that began a war in violation of the General Treaty, and a lawful party to a war. As a consequence, the question arose as to whether *jus in bello*, as it existed at that time, could be applied in its entirety to the unlawful party, including the rules pertaining to the protection of persons *hors de combat* and the limitation on certain means and methods of warfare. This question was raised as it was generally thought that an unlawful party should not be entitled to the 'benefits' of *jus in bello*.

This question persisted even after the adoption of the UN Charter.[4] Article 2(4) of the Charter obliged the UN member states to refrain in their international relations from the threat or use of force. Therefore, the distinction between an unlawful party, that is to say, a party that resorted to force in violation of Article 2(4), and a lawful party was maintained and the question of whether *jus in bello* applied to the unlawful party persisted.

The Charter also specified that use of force is permissible in case of self-defence or when authorized under Chapter VII of the Charter.[5] With the increasing reliance on the right of self-defence to justify the use of force, the regulation of the conduct of self-defence has increasingly become the focus of attention. In this regard, the cumulative requirements imposed on the conduct of self-defence by the customary principles of necessity and proportionality in *jus ad bellum* on the one hand and *jus in bello* on the other have become an important question.

The use of force under Chapter VII poses different types of questions compared to the use of force in self-defence. Practice shows that the use of force is authorized under Chapter VII for a variety of purposes such as to maintain security and stability in a state or to protect civilians in armed conflict. In case such authorizations appeared to modify obligations under *jus in bello*, questions were raised as to whether those authorizations prevailed over the obligations under *jus in bello*.

This chapter sets out the main issues pertaining to the relationship between *jus ad bellum* and *jus in bello* and makes references to state practice, international decisions, and opinions of experts to illustrate how the relationship has been discussed in practice.

[3] For the scope of the prohibition on war in the 1928 General Treaty, see generally Hersch Lauterpacht (ed), *International Law: A Treatise. Vol II: Disputes, War and Neutrality* (7th edn, London: Longmans, Green and Co, 1952), 181 ff.

[4] Charter of the United Nations, San Francisco, 26 June 1945, 59 Stat 1031.

[5] See UN Charter, Arts 51 and 42 in particular. The structure of modern *jus ad bellum* was clearly confirmed by the ICJ in *Legality of the Threat or Use of Nuclear Weapons*, Advisory Opinion of 8 July 1996, ICJ Rep 1996, 226, para 38.

II. Unlawful Party and *Jus in Bello*

So far as *jus in bello* was understood as meaning international humanitarian law (IHL),[6] the question of whether *jus in bello* applied equally to the unlawful and lawful parties to an armed conflict has not been as controversial as it is generally thought.[7] When looking at state practice, international decisions, and opinions of experts, no distinction has been made between the unlawful and lawful parties in terms of the application of IHL. Perhaps the most authoritative statement on the subject could be found in Protocol I[8] Additional to the 1949 Geneva Conventions[9] which provided in its Preamble that 'the provisions of the Geneva Conventions of 12 August 1949 and of this Protocol must be fully applied in all circumstance to all persons who are protected by those instruments, without any adverse distinction based on the nature or origin of the armed conflict or on the causes espoused by or attributed to the Parties to the conflict.'[10]

Experts have unanimously and constantly supported the equal application of IHL to the unlawful and lawful parties.[11] In the pre-UN Charter era, experts of

[6] See generally, Robert Kolb and Richard Hyde, *An Introduction to the International Law of Armed Conflicts* (Oxford: Hart, 2008), 15–19.

[7] For discussions on whether the law of neutrality applies equally to the unlawful and lawful parties, see Lauterpacht, *International Law*, 643 ff; Erik Castrén, *The Present Law of War and Neutrality* (Helsinki: Suomalaisen Tiedeakatemian Toimituksia, 1954); Christopher Greenwood, 'The Concept of War in Modern International Law' (1987) 36 *International and Comparative Law Quarterly* 283. For discussions on 'belligerent rights', see Institut de Droit international (IDI), 'L'égalité d'application des règles du droit de la guerre aux parties à un conflit armé' (1963-I) 50 *Annuaire de l'Institut de Droit International* 14–15, 57–61, 68, 101–2, and 115.

[8] Additional Protocol to the Geneva Conventions of 12 August 1949, and Relating to the Protection of Victims of International Armed Conflicts (Protocol I), Geneva, 8 June 1977, 1125 UNTS 3.

[9] Geneva Conventions, Geneva, 12 Aug 1949, 75 UNTS 31.

[10] See also Geneva Conventions, Common Art 1 and Jean Pictet et al, *Commentary on the Geneva Conventions of 12 August 1949*, vol I (Geneva: ICRC, 1952), 27. See further, Additional Protocol I, Art 96(3)(c).

[11] See Ian Brownlie, *International Law and the Use of Force by States* (Oxford: Clarendon Press, 1963), 406 and fn 3; Meyrowitz, *Le principe*, 78–80; IDI, 'Les conditions d'application des règles humanitaires relatives aux conflits armés aux hostilités dans lesquelles les Forces des Nations Unies peuvent être engagées' (1971-II) 54 *Annuaire de l'Institut de Droit International* 450; Charles Rousseau, *Le droit des conflits armés* (Paris: Pedone, 1983), 24–6; Myres McDougal and Florentino Feliciano, *The International Law of War* (New Haven, CT: New Haven Press, 1994), 530–42; Louise Doswald-Beck (ed), *San Remo Manual on International Law Applicable to Armed Conflicts at Sea* (Cambridge: Cambridge University Press, 1995), 46; Thomas Franck, *Fairness in International Law and Institutions* (Oxford: Clarendon Press, 1995), 275; Christopher Greenwood, 'International Humanitarian Law (Law of War)' in Frits Kalshoven (ed), *The Centennial of the First International Peace Conference: Reports and Conclusions* (Boston, MA: Kluwer Law International, 2000), 173–92; Bugnion, 'Guerre juste', 544–5; Yoram Dinstein, *War, Aggression and Self-Defence* (4th edn, Cambridge: Cambridge University Press, 2005), 156–63; Sassòli, '*Ius ad Bellum* and *Ius in Bello*', 246–9; Roberts, 'The Equal Application of the Laws of War', 961–2.

the International Law Association and the Advisory Committee of the Harvard Research in International Law already explicitly recognized that *jus ad bellum* did not affect the application of IHL in 1934 and 1939 respectively.[12] The question was also discussed extensively at the Institute of International Law in 1963.[13] Although experts who were for[14] or against[15] discriminatory application of *jus in bello* against the unlawful party were deeply divided, they all agreed that the humanitarian rules of *jus in bello* must be applied to the unlawful and lawful parties without distinction, which was also confirmed in the Institute's resolution.[16] To date, writings arguing that IHL does not apply to the unlawful party can hardly be found.

These conclusions on the general principles have constantly been confirmed in state practice and international decisions. In many past armed conflicts, such as the 1950–3 Korean War,[17] 1980–8 Iran–Iraq War,[18] 1990–1 Gulf War,[19] and 2008 Georgia–Russia conflict,[20] and in many international decisions, such as the judgment of

[12] ILA, 'Articles of Interpretation of the Briand–Kellogg Pact' in ILA Report of the Thirty-Eighth Conference (Budapest 1934) (ILA, Budapest 1934), 66, 68; Advisory Committee of the Harvard Research in International Law, 'Draft Convention on Rights and Duties of States in Case of Aggression' (1939) 33 *American Journal of International Law Supp*, 827, 830.

[13] IDI, 'L'égalité d'application'.

[14] See references in n 7 for IDI, 'L' égalité d'application'.

[15] IDI, 'L'égalité d'application' (1963-I) 50 *Annuaire de l'Institut de Droit International* 37, 44, 66, 67, 82, 87, 97, 99, and 108 and (1963-II) 50 *Annuaire de l'Institut de Droit International* 312, 313, 315–16, 320, 330, 332–3, 336–7, 342, 343, 344, 346, and 349.

[16] IDI, 'L'égalité d'application' (1963-II) 50 *Annuaire de l'Institut de Droit International* 368.

[17] For the Security Council's determination of the invasion by the Democratic People's Republic of Korea (DPRK) of the Republic of Korea as a breach of the peace, see SC Res 82 (25 June 1952), SC Res 83 (27 June 1950), and SC Res 84 (7 July 1950). For the recognition of the applicability of the 1949 Geneva Conventions by the US, DPRK, and China, see UN, 'The Question of Korea' (1952) *Yearbook of the United Nations* 155, 185 and 186; UN, 'The Question of Korea' (1953) *Yearbook of the United Nations* 109, 149; GA Res 610 (VII) (3 Dec 1952); and GA Res 804 (VIII) (3 Dec 1953). See also Armistice Agreement (1953) *Yearbook of the United Nations* 136, Annex, paras 3, 8(b), and 15.

[18] For the recognition that Iraq violated the prohibition of the use of force by attacking Iran, see Further Report of the Secretary-General on the Implementation of Security Council Resolution 598 (1987), S/23273 (9 Dec 1991), paras 5 and 6. For violations of the 1925 Gas Protocol by both conflicting parties, see, among others, Report of the Mission Dispatched by the Secretary-General to Investigate Allegations of the Use of Chemical Weapons in the Conflict between the Islamic Republic of Iran and Iraq, S/18852 (8 May 1987), para 66 and SC Res 582 (24 Nov 1986). The Security Council also urged both conflicting parties to release and repatriate prisoners of war without delay in accordance with the Third Geneva Convention. See SC Res 598 (20 July 1987). See also Protocol for the Prohibition of the Use of Asphyxiating, Poisonous or Other Gases, and of Bacteriological Methods of Warfare, Geneva, 17 June 1925, 94 LNTS 65.

[19] For the Security Council's determination that the invasion and occupation of Kuwait by Iraq was a breach of the peace and an armed attack on Kuwait, see SC Res 660 (2 Aug 1990) and SC Res 661 (6 Aug 1990). For the application of the 1949 Fourth Geneva Convention to the actions of Iraq, see, among others, SC Res 666 (13 Sept 1990).

[20] For an implied recognition of a violation of the prohibition on the use of force by Georgia, see Council of the European Union, Independent International Fact-Finding Mission on the Conflict in Georgia, 'Report', vol II (Sept 2009), 265 and 269, Independent International Fact-Finding Mission on the Conflict in Georgia website, at <http://www.ceiig.ch>. For indications of violations of the prohibition on indiscriminate attacks by both conflicting parties, see ibid, 343 and 345.

the International Military Tribunal at Nuremberg,[21] judgment of the US Military Tribunal at Nuremberg in the *Wilhelm List and Others* case,[22] awards of the Eritrea–Ethiopia Claims Commission,[23] and judgment of the International Court of Justice (ICJ) in the *Armed Activities* case,[24] the unlawful parties to the armed conflicts were identified but the application of IHL to all the conflicting parties or specifically to the unlawful party was clearly recognized. During the Vietnam War, the Democratic Republic of Vietnam refused to apply the Third Geneva Convention to US prisoners of war on the basis that the US was waging a war of aggression,[25] but this was an isolated case among other practice to the contrary.

Even when the party that initiated a use of force in violation of *jus ad bellum* could not be clearly determined, the applicability of IHL to the conflicting parties was recognized, such as in the 1967[26] and 1973[27] Middle East conflicts, 1971 India–Pakistan conflict,[28] 1979 China–Vietnam conflict,[29] 1999 Kosovo conflict,[30] 2003 Gulf War,[31]

[21] For violations of the 1928 General Treaty by Germany when it invaded and occupied a number of states, see International Military Tribunal (IMT) in Nuremberg, *Trial of the Major War Criminals before the International Military Tribunal*, vol 1 (1947), 218. For the applicability of the 1907 Hague Regulations to Germany as customary international law, see IMT, *Trial of the Major War Criminals*, vol 1, 253–4 and 334. See also Convention concernant les lois et coutumes de la guerre sur terre, Annexe: Règlement concernant les lois et coutumes de la guerre sur terre, The Hague, 18 Oct 1907, 187 CTS 227. For an English translation, see 9 UKTS 119.

[22] US Military Tribunal in Nuremberg, The Hostages Trial, Trial of Wilhelm List and Others, Judgment (1949) 8 *Law Reports of Trials of War Criminals* 34, 59–60.

[23] For the conclusion that Eritrea began the conflict in violation of Art 2(4) of the UN Charter, see Eritrea–Ethiopia Claims Commission (EECC), Jus ad Bellum: *Ethiopia's Claims 1–8*, Partial Award (2009) XXVI RIAA 457, para 16. For violations of IHL by both Eritrea and Ethiopia, see EECC, *Central Front, Ethiopia's Claim 2*, Partial Award (2009) XXVI RIAA 155, para 113; *Central Front, Eritrea's Claims 2, 4, 6, 7, 8 and 22*, Partial Award (2009) XXVI RIAA, paras 78, 93–105, and 113–14; *Western Front, Aerial Bombardment and Related Claims, Eritrea's Claims 1, 3, 5, 9–13, 14, 21, 25 and 26*, Partial Award (2009) XXVI RIAA 291, para 105; EECC, *Prisoners of War, Eritrea's Claim 17*, Partial Award (2009) XXVI RIAA 23, 71–2; *Prisoners of War, Ethiopia's Claim 4*, Partial Award (2009) XXVI RIAA 73, 113–14.

[24] For the conclusion that Uganda violated Art 2(4) of the UN Charter by invading and occupying some parts of the territory of the Democratic Republic of the Congo (DRC), see *Armed Activities on the Territory of the Congo (DRC v. Uganda)*, Judgment of 19 Dec 2005, ICJ Rep 2000, 168, paras 153 and 165. For violations of IHL by Uganda, see paras 206–8, 211, and 219.

[25] See François Bugnion, '*Jus ad Bellum, Jus in Bello* and Non-International Armed Conflicts' (2003) 6 *Yearbook of International Humanitarian Law* 167, 174–5; ICRC, 'Response to the ICRC's Appeal to Have the Rules of Humanity Respected in Viet Nam' (1965) 54 *International Review of the Red Cross* 477.

[26] Israel, UNSC Verbatim Record, S/PV.1360 (14 June 1967), 12, para 127. See also SC Res 237 (14 June 1967).

[27] Syria, UNSC Verbatim Record, S/PV.1745 (11 Oct 1973), 11, paras 111 and 113; Israel and Egypt, UNSC Verbatim Record, S/PV.1751 (26 Oct 1973), 16, para 156 and 17, para 167 respectively.

[28] India, UNSC Verbatim Record, S/PV.1611 (12 Dec 1971), 13, para 129 and Pakistan, UNSC Verbatim Record, S/PV.1613 (13 Dec 1971), 29, para 291.

[29] ICRC, 'Conflit sino-vietnamien' (1979) 716 *Revue internationale de la Croix-Rouge* 98. See also Bugnion, '*Jus ad Bellum*', 175.

[30] See ICTY, 'Final Report to the Prosecutor by the Committee Established to Review the NATO Bombing Campaign against the Federal Republic of Yugoslavia' (2000) 39 ILM 1257.

[31] SC Res 1472 (28 Mar 2003), particularly para 1; SC Res 1483 (22 May 2003), particularly para 5.

and 2006 Israel–Lebanon conflict.[32] In many of the previously mentioned armed conflicts, the International Committee of the Red Cross (ICRC), as the guardian of IHL and in accordance with its practice, called upon both parties to comply with IHL.[33]

As a result of these discussions and practice, two general principles governing the relationship between *jus ad bellum* and IHL were established: first, that *jus ad bellum* and IHL should be kept separate and, secondly, that IHL applies equally regardless of the status of the conflicting parties under *jus ad bellum*. According to these principles, there is no room for *jus ad bellum* to affect the applicability of IHL to the conflicting parties. The rationale behind the two principles is humanitarian: since the object and purpose of IHL is to alleviate the suffering of individuals during armed conflict, any attempts at curtailing its application, including the discriminatory application of IHL between the unlawful and lawful parties, are seen as contrary to that object and purpose.[34] Moreover, in case both conflicting parties accuse each other as the unlawful party to an armed conflict, and if both parties do not recognize the applicability of IHL to the unlawful party, then none of the parties will be bound by IHL. The repetition of such cases will quickly result in the total irrelevance of IHL and result in armed conflicts which know no limits.[35]

The Preamble to 1977 Additional Protocol I importantly confirmed another principle: IHL does not legitimize or authorize any act of aggression or any other use of force inconsistent with the UN Charter. Indeed, the application of IHL presupposes that force has been resorted to, but such presupposition cannot be construed as tacitly legitimizing or authorizing acts that amount to violations of *jus ad bellum*.[36]

[32] Israel Ministry of Foreign Affairs, 'Responding to Hizbullah Attacks from Lebanon: Issues of Proportionality', 25 July 2006, Israel Ministry of Foreign Affairs website, available at <http://www.mfa.gov.il/MFA/Government/Law/Legal+Issues+and+Rulings>. See also Lebanon, UNSC Verbatim Record, S/PV.5489 (14 July 2006), 5. UN Human Rights Council (HRC), 'Report of the Commission of Inquiry on Lebanon Pursuant to Human Rights Council Resolution S-2/1', A/HRC/3/2 (23 Nov 2006).

[33] See eg ICRC, 'Respect for the Rules of Humanity in Viet Nam' (1965) 53 *International Review of the Red Cross* 417; 'The ICRC and the War in the Near East' (1967) 76 *International Review of the Red Cross* 347, 347; 'The International Committee's Action in the Middle East' (1973) 152 *International Review of the Red Cross* 583, 583–5; 'Iraq–Iran Conflict' (1980) 219 *International Review of the Red Cross* 332; 'Conflict in the Middle East' (1991) 280 *International Review of the Red Cross* 22, 22–8; 'Democratic Republic of the Congo: ICRC Appeals for Compliance with Humanitarian Rules', 19 Aug 1998, News Release 98/32; 'The Balkan Conflict and Respect for International Humanitarian Law' (1999) 834 *International Review of the Red Cross* 408; 'Conflict in Iraq: Memorandum to the Belligerents' (2003) 859 *International Review of the Red Cross* 423; 'Georgia: ICRC Calls on Parties to Respect International Humanitarian Law', 8 Aug 2008, News Release.

[34] See eg Lauterpacht, 'The Limits of the Operation', 212; Bugnion, 'Guerre juste', 542; Dinstein, *War, Aggression and Self-Defence*, 158.

[35] See eg Lauterpacht, 'The Limits of the Operation', 212; Bugnion, 'Guerre juste', 542; Dinstein, *War, Aggression and Self-Defence*, 158.

[36] See also Additional Protocol I, Art 4 and Geneva Conventions, Common Art 3, para 4.

III. Self-Defence and IHL

When a state uses force in violation of Article 2(4) of the UN Charter against a state, this may concurrently be an armed attack within the meaning of Article 51 of the Charter,[37] which would then enable the attacked state to exercise its right of self-defence. In this case, the unlawful party is the state that carried out an armed attack and the lawful party is the state that is taking action in self-defence. An armed attack by a state against a state would often amount to an international armed conflict, to which IHL rules applicable to international armed conflict apply.[38] Whether an attack from a non-state actor, which is not supported by any state, against a state can qualify as an armed attack is still an unsettled question.[39] Supposing that one accepts that it qualifies as an armed attack, the attacked state may lawfully take actions in self-defence against the non-state actor. In terms of IHL, this type of armed conflict is widely considered as a non-international armed conflict where at least Article 3 common to the 1949 Geneva Conventions and customary rules applicable to non-international armed conflict apply.[40] In both of the above scenarios, the equal application of IHL to the conflicting parties is valid as discussed in the previous section.

Over time, the application of *jus ad bellum* and IHL to the lawful party has also become the focus of attention alongside their application to the unlawful party. In this context, the role of the customary principles of proportionality and necessity on the one hand, and the role of IHL on the other in regulating measures taken in self-defence have become more prominent. The two sets of rules were clearly recognized as cumulative requirements imposed on measures taken in self-defence in the ICJ's *Nuclear Weapons* advisory opinion of 1996 in the following terms: 'A use of force that is proportionate under the law of self-defence, must, in order to be lawful, also meet the requirements of the law applicable in armed conflict which comprise in particular the principles and rules of humanitarian law.'[41]

[37] On the relationship between 'use of force' and 'armed attack', see *Case concerning Military and Paramilitary Activities in and against Nicaragua (Nicaragua v. US)*, Merits, Judgment of 27 June 1986, ICJ Rep 1986, 14, para 195.

[38] See Okimoto, *The Distinction and Relationship*, 44–58.

[39] See, on the one hand, *Legal Consequences of the Construction of a Wall in the Occupied Palestinian Territory*, Advisory Opinion of 9 July 2004, ICJ Rep 2004, 136, para 139 and, on the other hand, Thomas Franck, 'Terrorism and the Right of Self-Defense' (2001) 95 *American Journal of International Law* 839, 840.

[40] See ICRC, 'International Humanitarian Law and the Challenges of Contemporary Armed Conflicts', Report prepared by the ICRC for the 31st International Conference of the Red Cross and Red Crescent, Geneva, 2011, 10.

[41] *Nuclear Weapons*, Advisory Opinion, para 42. See also paras 41, 74 ff, and 105(2)(C) and (D). For discussions on the controversial findings in para 105(2)(E), see Yves Sandoz et al, 'Special Issue: The Advisory Opinion on the International Court of Justice on the Legality of Nuclear Weapons and International Humanitarian Law' (1997) 316 *International Review of the Red Cross*.

This principle has been confirmed in other practice[42] and opinions of experts.[43]

The cumulative requirements of *jus ad bellum* and IHL have frequently been discussed in a narrow sense, for example in the context of the overlap between the principle of proportionality in *jus ad bellum* and the principle of proportionality in IHL.[44] However, in order to fully grasp the implications of the ICJ's conclusions in the *Nuclear Weapons* advisory opinion, the whole range of IHL rules, and not just the principle of proportionality within the meaning of IHL, should be taken into account alongside the principle of proportionality in *jus ad bellum*.

The principle of proportionality in *jus ad bellum* requires that the specific measures taken in self-defence must be proportionate to the armed attack[45] or the aim to halt and repel the armed attack.[46] Factors such as the nature of the target,[47] effects of attacks on civilians and civilian objects,[48] and geographical[49] and temporal[50] extent of self-defence measures are taken into account to measure the proportionality.

The principle of proportionality in *jus ad bellum* has a direct bearing on the conduct of hostilities while acting in self-defence, which is concurrently regulated by IHL, particularly by the rules concerning methods and means of warfare and occupation. Part of the legal consequences of the concurrent application of the principle of proportionality and IHL is that a particular measure in self-defence must be discontinued immediately if it violates either the principle of proportionality or IHL.[51]

The separation between *jus ad bellum* and *jus in bello* requires that an assessment of whether a measure taken in self-defence is proportionate or is in conformity with

[42] *Nuclear Weapons*, Oral Statement of Iran, 6 Nov 1995, para 28 and Dissenting Opinion of Judge Koroma; *Case concerning Oil Platforms (Iran v. US)*, Merits, Judgment of 6 Nov 2003, ICJ Rep 2003, 161, Counter-Memorial of the US, para 4.01; *Wall*, Written Statements of Malaysia, para 150; Saudi Arabia, para 31; League of Arab States, para 9.6; Switzerland, para 27. The oral and written statements can be found at the ICJ website, <http://www.icj-cij.org>.

[43] Greenwood, 'International Humanitarian Law', 184. See also Yves Sandoz et al (eds), *Commentary on the Additional Protocols of 8 June 1977 to the Geneva Conventions of 12 August 1949* (Geneva: ICRC, 1987), para 3598; Judith Gardam, *Necessity, Proportionality and the Use of Force* (Cambridge: Cambridge University Press, 2004), 168–9.

[44] Jasmine Moussa, 'Can *Jus ad Bellum* Override *Jus in Bello*? Reaffirming the Separation of the Two Bodies of Law' (2008) 872 *International Review of the Red Cross* 963, 975–9. The principle of proportionality in IHL usually refers to the rule reflected in Additional Protocol I, Art 51(1)(b). See also Rule 14 in Jean-Marie Henckaerts and Louise Doswald-Beck, *Customary International Humanitarian Law. Vol I: Rules* (Geneva: ICRC and Cambridge, Cambridge University Press, 2005), 46.

[45] *Nicaragua*, Merits, para 176; *Oil Platforms*, Merits, para 77; *Armed Activities*, Judgment, para 147.

[46] See eg ILC, *Yearbook of the International Law Commission*, 1980, vol II (1), 69–70; *Armed Activities*, Judgment, para 304.

[47] See eg *Oil Platforms*, Merits, paras 51, 74, and 76.

[48] See eg the statements in the Security Council of China, the Republic of the Congo, France, Greece, Japan, the Russian Federation, and Tanzania, during the 2006 Lebanon conflict, UNSC Verbatim Record, S/PV.5489 (14 July 2006), 7, 11, 12, 13, and 17.

[49] See eg *Armed Activities*, Judgment, para 147.

[50] See Okimoto, *The Distinction and Relationship*, 71–5.

[51] See generally Keiichiro Okimoto, 'The Cumulative Requirements of *Jus ad Bellum* and *Jus in Bello* in the Context of Self-Defence' (2012) 11 *Chinese Journal of International Law* 45.

IHL must be conducted separately. Such assessment could result in three situations. First, a particular measure taken in self-defence violates IHL but not the principle of proportionality; secondly, it violates the principle of proportionality but not IHL; and, thirdly, it violates both the principle of proportionality and IHL. In the third situation, there is no doubt that the measure taken in self-defence must cease immediately. In case of the first scenario, some have stated that even if a measure taken in self-defence violates IHL, it could still be continued by justifying it as a proportionate measure in self-defence under *jus ad bellum*.[52] However, this position is not consistent with the obligation to cease an act which amounts to a breach of an international obligation, as provided in Article 30 of the Draft Articles on the Responsibility of States for Internationally Wrongful Acts.[53] The violations of IHL oblige the state concerned to cease the particular self-defence measure immediately. Even if the measure is proportionate within the meaning of *jus ad bellum*, the violations of IHL cannot be nullified and the obligation to cease that particular measure in self-defence remains intact. The same can be said for the second scenario mentioned above. Therefore, a violation of the principle of proportionality obliges the state to cease its measure in self-defence immediately, even if such measure is in conformity with IHL.

For example, in the *Wall* advisory opinion, the ICJ rejected the applicability of Article 51 of the UN Charter[54] but found that the construction of the wall violated international humanitarian and human rights law,[55] including Article 53 of the 1949 Fourth Geneva Convention which prohibits the destruction of private and public property in occupied territories,[56] and ruled that Israel must cease the construction of the wall and dismantle it.[57] Even if Israel had claimed that the construction of the wall was a proportionate measure in self-defence,[58] the Court made it clear that the construction must cease and the wall must be dismantled, since it already violated the Fourth Geneva Convention. Such legal consequences pursuant to violations of IHL could not have been nullified by claiming that the construction of the wall was a proportionate measure in self-defence.

In the *Armed Activities* case, Uganda argued that its invasion and military actions in the DRC from 1998 onwards were carried out in self-defence and proportionate to the alleged armed attack by the armed groups supported by the DRC.[59] The Court rejected this argument,[60] whilst concluding that Uganda's use of force could not have been proportionate, even if it had been qualified as lawful self-defence.[61]

[52] See eg Solon Solomon, 'The Great Oxymoron: *Jus in Bello* Violations as Legitimate Non-Forcible Measures of Self-Defense: The Post-Disengagement Israeli Measures towards Gaza as a Case Study' (2010) 9 *Chinese Journal of International Law* 501.

[53] Art 30(a) in ILC, Articles on Responsibility of States for Internationally Wrongful Acts, A/56/10 Supp 10 (2001), 40, 51.

[54] *Wall*, Advisory Opinion, para 139. [55] *Wall*, Advisory Opinion, paras 114–37.

[56] *Wall*, Advisory Opinion, paras 132–3 and 135. [57] *Wall*, Advisory Opinion, para 163(3)(B).

[58] Israel stated that the construction of the wall was justified by the right of self-defence, by which it implicitly accepted that its use of force had to be proportionate to the perceived armed attack. Israel, 'Summary Legal Position of the Government of Israel', A/ES-10/248 (24 Nov 2003), Annex I.

[59] *Armed Activities*, Rejoinder of Uganda, 119–26. [60] *Armed Activities*, Judgment, para 147.

[61] *Armed Activities*, Judgment, para 147.

Even if the Court concluded otherwise, namely that Uganda's use of force was proportionate self-defence, the Court's later findings that Uganda violated the rules of IHL pertaining to methods and means of warfare and occupation at various times during its use of force[62] meant that those military operations that violated IHL had to cease immediately. The proportionality of the use of force could not have nullified the legal consequences of violations of IHL and allowed Uganda to continue the military operations concerned. However, the fact that some of the military operations violated IHL at specific moments during a long-term use of force in self-defence does not necessarily mean that the entire use of force in self-defence must be ceased altogether. Whether the entire self-defence measures must be ceased or not must be assessed against *jus ad bellum*, namely the customary principles of proportionality and necessity. However, the role of IHL during self-defence should not be understated since, as in the *Wall* advisory opinion, violations of IHL could lead to a legal consequence where the state must cease its entire measures in self-defence.[63]

On the other hand, self-defence measures that violate the principle of proportionality oblige the state to cease those measures, even if they were conducted in conformity with IHL. In the *Armed Activities* case, the ICJ concluded that the use of force by Uganda would have been disproportionate to the initial armed attack, even if it was qualified as a lawful measure in self-defence, particularly because Uganda took over airports and towns, many hundreds of kilometres from Uganda's border in response to a series of transborder attacks.[64] However, the military operations in these towns could have been conducted in conformity with the rules of IHL. Even if that were the case, the obligation to cease its use of force due to its disproportionate nature within the meaning of *jus ad bellum* could not have been nullified. In other words, Uganda would have been obliged to cease the military operations and withdraw from the towns, which were distant and irrelevant to the initial armed attack, even if those military operations could have been in conformity with IHL.

IV. Military Enforcement Measures under Chapter VII of the UN Charter and IHL

The relationship between *jus ad bellum* and *jus in bello* has been mostly discussed in the context of use of force in violation of Article 2(4) of the UN Charter or use of force in self-defence, as well as whether IHL applies to those types of use of

[62] See n 24. [63] See n 57. [64] See n 24.

force. However, the other exception to the prohibition on the use of force, military enforcement measures under Chapter VII of the Charter, also forms an indispensable part of *jus ad bellum*. Therefore, its relation to IHL must be considered in order to grasp the overall picture of the relationship between *jus ad bellum* and *jus in bello*.

As noted earlier, a use of force that violates Article 2(4) of the Charter could simultaneously be an armed attack, but it can also constitute a threat to the peace, breach of the peace, or an act of aggression within the meaning of Article 39 of the Charter. For example, the Security Council determined that the armed attack by DPRK on the Republic of Korea and the armed attack by Iraq against Kuwait constituted a breach of the peace[65] and a breach of international peace and security[66] respectively.[67] A determination of a breach of the peace or an act of aggression by the Security Council would effectively distinguish the unlawful party from the lawful party to an armed conflict. The applicability of IHL between the unlawful and lawful parties will not be discussed here since it was already clarified earlier. With respect to a situation which is determined as a 'threat to the peace', the unlawful and lawful parties to an armed conflict are not necessarily determined since the overall situation is often qualified as a threat to the peace without identifying which party is unlawful or lawful.[68] However, even if the unlawful and lawful parties are not identified, the Security Council has recognized the applicability of IHL to all the parties to the armed conflict without distinction.[69] Therefore, the mere determination of an action or a situation under Article 39 of the Charter does not affect the application of IHL to the conflicting parties.

However, when the Security Council decides to take measures necessary to maintain or restore international peace and security, particularly those measures involving use of force under Chapter VII, the question of whether the application of IHL will be affected by such Chapter VII decisions could arise. Military enforcement measures under Chapter VII have, in practice, been carried out by two types of UN forces: first, directly by UN member states, individually or collectively (state-led UN forces) or, secondly, by forces established as a subsidiary organ of the Security Council which are under the command and control of the UN (UN-commanded forces). Both types of UN forces are cumulatively bound by IHL[70] and the Security

[65] See n 17. [66] See n 19.

[67] See further, UNGA, 'Definition of Aggression', GA Res 3314 (XXIX) (14 Dec 1974); *Nicaragua*, Merits, para 195; *Armed Activities*, Judgment, para 146.

[68] See eg SC Res 1234 (9 Apr 1999) on the armed conflicts in the DRC.

[69] See eg SC Res 1234, para 6. See generally, Okimoto, *The Distinction and Relationship*, 133–7.

[70] See generally Luigi Condorelli et al (eds), *Nations Unies et le droit international humanitaire* (Paris: Éditions Pedone, 1996); Christopher Greenwood, 'International Humanitarian Law and United Nations Military Operations' (1998) 1 *Yearbook of International Humanitarian Law* 3; Alexandre Faite and Jérémie Labbé (eds), *Expert Meeting on Multinational Peace Operations: Applicability*

Council resolutions authorizing military enforcement measures[71] when they become parties to an armed conflict.

Security Council resolutions adopted under Chapter VII are generally considered as decisions that should be accepted and carried out by the UN member states by virtue of Article 25 of the Charter[72] and, at the same time, constitute obligations under the Charter that prevail over obligations under other international agreements, in case of a conflict between the former and the latter, by virtue of Article 103 of the Charter.[73] Therefore, a question arises as to whether Chapter VII decisions authorizing military enforcement measures could prevail over IHL-related treaties in case of a conflict between the two. However, since the Security Council is obliged to act in accordance with the Purposes and Principles of the UN under Article 24(2) of the Charter, which includes the promotion and respect for human rights,[74] this provision, in general terms, obliges the Security Council not to authorize military enforcement measures that would be in conflict with IHL, taking into account that the term 'human rights' in the UN is now understood as including IHL through its subsequent practice.[75]

In practice, only a few cases have given rise to a potential conflict between Chapter VII decisions and IHL-related treaties. For example, questions were raised as to whether Resolutions 1483 (2003)[76] and 1511 (2003),[77] which set out how the occupying powers and the multinational force which they formed part of should administer and maintain security and stability in Iraq, permitted actions that go beyond the status quo,[78] which is the cornerstone of the law of

of International Humanitarian Law and International Human Rights Law to UN Mandated Forces (Geneva: ICRC, 2004); Keiichiro Okimoto, 'Violations of International Humanitarian Law by United Nations Forces and Their Legal Consequences' (2003) 6 *Yearbook of International Humanitarian Law* 199; Marten Zwanenburg, *Accountability of Peace Support Operations* (Leiden: Martinus Nijhoff, 2005).

[71] See generally Niels Blokker, 'Is the Authorization Authorized? Powers and Practice of the Security Council to Authorize the Use of Force by "Coalitions of the Able and Willing"' (2000) 11 *European Journal of International Law* 541. See also Okimoto, *The Distinction and Relationship*, 173–7.

[72] On the effects of Security Council resolutions authorizing the use of force, see eg Linos-Alexandre Sicilianos, 'Entre multilatéralisme et unilatéralisme: L'autorisation par le Conseil de Sécurité de recourir à la force' (2008) 339 *Recueil des cours de l'Académie de droit international* 9, 125–30.

[73] *Questions of Interpretation and Application of the 1971 Montreal Convention Arising from the Aerial Incident at Lockerbie (Libyan Arab Jamahiriya v. UK)*, Order of 14 Apr 1992, ICJ Rep 1992, 3, para 39.

[74] See UN Charter, Art 1(3). See also *Application of the Convention on the Prevention and Punishment of the Crime of Genocide (Bosnia and Herzegovina v. Serbia and Montenegro)*, Order of 13 Sept 1993, ICJ Rep 1993, Separate Opinion of Judge Lauterpacht, para 101.

[75] See eg GA Res 2444 (XXIII) (19 Dec 1968), A/RES/2444 (XXIII).

[76] SC Res 1483 (22 May 2003), S/RES/1483.

[77] SC Res 1511 (16 Oct 2003), S/RES/1511.

[78] See generally David Scheffer, 'Beyond Occupation Law' (2003) 97 *American Journal of International Law* 842; Marten Zwanenburg, 'Existentialism in Iraq: Security Council Resolution 1483 and the Law of Occupation' (2004) 856 *International Review of the Red Cross* 745; Adam Roberts, 'Transformative Military Occupation: Applying the Law of War and Human Rights' (2006) 100 *American Journal of International Law* 580; Robert Kolb, 'Occupation in Iraq since 2003 and the Powers of the UN Security Council' (2006) 869 *International Review of the Red Cross* 29.

occupation.[79] However, since Resolution 1483 (2003) already explicitly required the occupying powers to comply fully with the law of occupation[80] and the mandate in Resolution 1511 (2003) was generally in line with the primary duty of occupying powers,[81] neither of the resolutions prevailed over the law of occupation.[82]

So far as UN-commanded forces are concerned, similar questions do not arise in most cases since the UN obtains consent of the host state when deploying such forces.[83] The United Nations Operation in Somalia II (UNOSOM II) could have been an exception where consent of the host state could not be obtained due to the absence of a government[84] and when it was carrying out extensive operations to restore security and law and order in Mogadishu,[85] which would have brought the law of occupation into operation. Although the mandates of UNOSOM II[86] were narrower than the obligations under the law of occupation, if a situation of occupation existed on the ground, the law of occupation applied in its entirety.

The relationship between Chapter VII authorization to take military enforcement measures and IHL could also be problematic in cases where UN forces are given mandates that appear to enforce IHL.[87] IHL itself does not envisage use of force as a means to enforce IHL but Article 89 of 1977 Additional Protocol I is an exception which envisages UN actions, including the use of force, in case of serious violations of IHL.[88] However, Article 89 itself does not automatically permit the use of force to enforce IHL.[89] The procedures in Chapter VII must be followed.

In the case of the former Yugoslavia, 'safe areas' were established for six towns in Bosnia and Herzegovina by Chapter VII resolutions in response to violations of

[79] See Hague Regulations, Art 43. For the exception to the status quo, see Fourth Geneva Convention, Art 64. 'Law of occupation' here refers particularly to Hague Regulations, Arts 42–56, the Fourth Geneva Convention, and customary international law.

[80] SC Res 1483 (22 May 2003), S/RES/1483, para 5.

[81] See Hague Regulations, Art 43.

[82] Zwanenburg, 'Existentialism in Iraq', 768; Roberts, 'Transformative Military Occupation', 613; Kolb, 'Occupation in Iraq', 49. In this sense, some 'Orders' issued by the Coalition Provisional Authority (CPA) went beyond the law of occupation. See eg Order Number 1 (De-Ba'athification of Iraqi Society), Number 2 (Dissolution of Entities), Number 37 (Tax Strategy for 2003), Number 39 (Foreign Investment), and Number 64 (Amendment to the Company Law No. 21 of 1997). See the website of the CPA at <http://www.iraqcoalition.org/regulations>.

[83] UN Secretariat, *United Nations Peacekeeping Operations: Principles and Guidelines* (New York: United Nations, 2008), 31–2. See Hague Regulations, Art 42.

[84] UNSC, Further Report of the Secretary-General Submitted in Pursuance of Paragraphs 18 and 19 of Resolution 794 (1992), S/25354 (3 Mar 1993), para 41.

[85] See UNGA, 'Somalia' (1993) *Yearbook of the United Nations* 288. See also UNSC, Report of the Commission of Inquiry Established Pursuant to Security Council Resolution 885 (1993) to Investigate Armed Attacks on UNOSOM II Personnel Which Led to Casualties among Them, S/1994/653 (1 June 1994).

[86] See SC Res 814 (26 Ma 1993), S/RES/814, para 5 and S/25354, para 57(b)–(f).

[87] eg MONUSCO (DRC), SC Res 1925 (28 May 2010), S/RES/1925 and the French forces in Côte d'Ivoire, SC Res 1528 (27 Feb 2004), S/RES/1528.

[88] Additional Protocol I, Art 89 provides: 'In situations of serious violations of the [Geneva] Conventions or of this Protocol, the High Contracting Parties undertake to act, jointly or individually, in co-operation with the United Nations and in conformity with the United Nations Charter.'

[89] Sandoz et al, *Commentary*, paras 35–98.

IHL.[90] The conflicting parties were obliged to refrain from attacking them and the UN Protection Force (UNPROFOR) was authorized to use force to protect the safe areas.[91] At the same time, UNPROFOR brokered two agreements between the conflicting parties which established demilitarization zones in Srebrenica[92] and Zepa,[93] one of which made specific reference to Article 60 of 1977 Additional Protocol I. The 'safe areas' and demilitarization zones were incompatible concepts since the former imposed obligations on the conflicting parties under Chapter VII not to attack the 'safe areas' whereas the latter required the consent of the parties.[94] The events that ensued in Srebrenica, which were later qualified by the ICJ[95] and the International Criminal Tribunal for the Former Yugoslavia (ICTY)[96] as genocide, partly reflected the danger of adopting conflicting measures in parallel.

In the former Yugoslavia, offensive force was also used by the North Atlantic Treaty Organization (NATO) to protect the 'safe areas'. Such offensive use of force authorized by the Security Council to protect civilians has been highlighted by the UN in recent years,[97] although its mode of implementation is largely undefined[98] and its employment is subject to very strict conditions.[99] The term 'civilians' is defined in IHL as persons not taking a direct part in hostilities.[100] Therefore, IHL generally defines which persons are to be protected in case the Security Council authorizes use of force to protect civilians. At the same time, the concept of civilians in IHL defines not only whom UN forces should protect, but also whom they must not target when they are using force to protect civilians. However, the distinction between civilians and persons taking a direct part in hostilities can be extremely difficult, particularly in non-international armed conflict,[101] which could cause serious

[90] SC Res 819 (16 Apr 1993), S/RES/819, paras 1 and 2; SC Res 824 (6 May 1993), S/RES/824, paras 3 and 5.

[91] SC Res 836 (4 June 1993), S/RES/836, paras 5 and 9.

[92] Agreement for the Demilitarization of Srebrenica, S/25700 (30 April 1993), Annex II.

[93] Report of the Secretary-General Pursuant to General Assembly Resolution 53/35: The Fall of Srebrenica, A/54/549 (15 Nov 1999), para 65.

[94] A/54/549, para 499. [95] *Genocide*, Order, para 297.

[96] ICTY, *Prosecutor v. Krstić*, Judgment of the Trial Chamber of 2 Aug 2001, IT-98-33-T, para 599 and Judgment of the Appeals Chamber of 19 Apr 2004, IT-98-33-A, para 38.

[97] GA Res 60/1 (16 Sept 2005), A/RES/60/1, para 139; Report of the Secretary-General to the Security Council on the Protection of Civilians in Armed Conflict, S/1999/957 (8 Sept 1999), 22; High-Level Panel on Threats, Challenges and Change, 'A More Secure World: Our Shared Responsibility', A/59/565 (2 Dec 2004), 203; Report of the Secretary-General, 'In Larger Freedom: Towards Development, Security and Human Rights for All', A/59/2005 (21 Mar 2005), paras 125–6.

[98] Report of the Secretary-General on the Protection of Civilians in Armed Conflict, S/2009/277 (29 May 2009), para 52.

[99] See n 97.

[100] See Additional Protocol I, Arts 50(1) and 51(3); Art 13(3) of Additional Protocol to the Geneva Conventions of 12 August 1949, and Relating to the Protection of Victims of Non-International Armed Conflicts (Protocol II), Geneva, 8 June 1977, 1125 UNTS 609; and Geneva Conventions, Common Art 3. For customary law status, see rules 5 and 6 in Henckaerts and Doswald-Beck, *Customary International Humanitarian Law*, 17 and 19.

[101] See the proceedings of the Expert Meetings on the Notion of Direct Participation in Hostilities organized by the ICRC and the TMC Asser Instituut held between 2003 and 2008,

difficulties for the UN forces. It is also worth noting that all other applicable rules of IHL, including the rules on means and methods of warfare, apply when the UN forces are using force to protect civilians.

In addition to IHL, the relevant Security Council resolutions determine which persons and objects can be attacked in order to carry out the mandate to protect civilians. A UN report seems to indicate some kind of proportionality between the use of force by UN forces and the threats posed by the conflicting parties on civilians.[102] This implies that the use of force against specific persons and objects would have to contribute directly to the prevention of attacks against civilians rather than to weaken the general military capacity of the conflicting parties. For example, the air strikes undertaken by NATO in 1995 against the Bosnian Serb Army were initially aimed specifically at protecting the 'safe areas'[103] but when they extended to areas beyond the vicinity of the 'safe areas', concerns were raised.[104]

In this sense, IHL and the relevant Security Council resolutions constitute cumulative requirements on the use of force under Chapter VII to protect civilians. Therefore, if, for example, a particular target does not qualify as a military objective within the meaning of IHL, even if the target falls under the scope of the relevant Security Council resolutions, it must not be attacked. Conversely, if a target does not meet the terms of the relevant Security Council resolutions, even if the target fully qualifies as a military objective within the meaning of IHL, it must not be attacked.

V. Conclusion

The discussions on the relationship between *jus ad bellum* and *jus in bello* have come a long way, and the separation between *jus ad bellum* and *jus in bello* and the equal application of *jus in bello* to the conflicting parties are now well-established rules of customary international law. However, the range of consequences arising from the concurrent application of *jus ad bellum* and *jus in bello* and the relationship between the use of force authorized under Chapter VII of the UN Charter and IHL are areas that merit further analyses in the light of further practice and international decisions.

available on the ICRC website at <http://www.icrc.org/eng/resources/documents/article/other/direct-participation-article-020709.htm>. See also Nils Melzer, *Interpretive Guidance on the Notion of Direct Participation in Hostilities under International Humanitarian Law* (Geneva: ICRC, 2009).

[102] A/59/2005, para 126. [103] A/54/549, paras 189, 190, 412, and 444.

[104] A/54/549, 455 and 457.

CHAPTER 57

CONSEQUENCES FOR THIRD STATES AS A RESULT OF AN UNLAWFUL USE OF FORCE

PAOLO PALCHETTI

I. Introduction

In case of an unlawful use of force by a state against another state, the use of the term 'third states' may be regarded as questionable, if not incorrect. It might convey the idea that a breach of the obligation not to use force gives rise exclusively to a bilateral relation between the two states involved in armed conflict. As is all too well known, this is not the case. The obligation not to use force in international relations being an obligation *erga omnes*, 'all States can be held to have an interest in [its] protection'[1] and are entitled to take certain steps to react against its breach. While,

[1] *Barcelona Traction, Light and Power Company, Limited (Belgium v. Spain)*, ICJ Rep 1970, 32, para 33. In this judgment the Court expressly recognized that obligations *erga omnes* 'derive, for example, in contemporary international law, from the outlawing of acts of aggression' (para 34). On the *erga omnes* character of the obligation not to use force, see also the International Law Commission's Commentary to the Articles on the Responsibility of States for Internationally Wrongful Acts, *Yearbook of the International Law Commission*, 2001, vol II (2), 127.

admittedly, the *erga omnes* character of this obligation may render inappropriate the terminology of 'third states', it is essential for this chapter to draw a distinction between those states which are directly involved in conflict either as the author or as the victim of the unlawful armed intervention, on the one hand, and all other states, on the other hand. The term 'third states' will be used loosely to refer to this latter category of states.

Different sets of legal rules concur to define the legal position of third states in situations arising out of an unlawful use of force. Traditionally, the law of neutrality provided the main legal framework governing the question of the rights and duties of third states vis-à-vis the belligerent states. Under the law of neutrality, a state has the right not to be adversely affected by the conflict if it complies with the duty of non-participation and impartiality. Thus, the neutral state must refrain from assisting one party to the conflict and must ensure equal treatment of the belligerents.[2] While the law of neutrality aims at the containment of the conflict and appears to be incompatible with the possibility of third party responses against an aggressor, with the crystallization of the rule prohibiting the use of force and the establishment by the UN Charter of a system of collective security, third states have been given the power, and under certain circumstances the duty, to react against an unlawful use of force. Thus, under Article 51 of the UN Charter, which reflects customary international law, third states are entitled to assist the victim of an armed attack by using force in collective self-defence against the attacking state. Under Chapter VII of the UN Charter, the Security Council has the power to oblige member states to take enforcement measures in order to put to an end a situation of threat to peace, breach of the peace, or aggression. Moreover, under Article 2(5) of the Charter, member states have a general duty to 'give the United Nations every assistance in any action it takes in accordance with the present Charter' and to 'refrain from giving assistance to any state against which the United Nations is taking preventive or enforcement action'. Lastly, a further development is the emergence of the category of obligations *erga omnes* and of a comprehensive set of rules establishing the consequences arising out of a breach of this category of obligations. As the Articles on State Responsibility adopted in 2001 by the International Law Commission (ILC) make clear, these legal consequences concern to a great extent the position of third states. They have the right to invoke the responsibility of the wrongdoing state, and in particular the right to ask for the cessation of the wrongful conduct and the performance of the obligation of reparation in the interest of the injured state.[3] At the same time, when peremptory rules—such as the one which prohibits

[2] See Yoram Dinstein, *War, Aggression and Self-Defence* (5th edn, Cambridge: Cambridge University Press, 2011), 25 ff; Michael Bothe, 'The Law of Neutrality' in Dieter Fleck (ed), *Handbook of International Humanitarian Law* (2nd edn, Oxford: Oxford University Press, 2008), 571 ff.

[3] Articles on the Responsibility of States for Internationally Wrongful Acts, Art 48. See also the ILC's Commentary, 126 ff.

aggression[4]—are breached, states are required to abide by a number of duties. These include the duty to cooperate to bring to an end the breach, the duty not to recognize as lawful a situation created by such a breach, and the duty not to render aid and assistance in maintaining that situation.[5]

This brief survey testifies to the variety of possible responses that third states are entitled, and under certain circumstances obliged, to take when confronted with situations of unlawful use of force. The picture which emerges is by no means a tidy one and reveals a certain tension between different approaches to the position of third states. Responses by third states may have the form of a centralized reaction against the wrongdoing state under the aegis of the UN Security Council, or may consist of unilateral actions aimed at enforcing community interests in accordance with the rules on state responsibility. Third states, at least in principle, appear to be entitled to invoke the legal protection ensured by the general rules of neutrality or, on the contrary, may decide to use force against the aggressor by acting in collective self-defence. All this raises evidently a problem of coexistence, if not of consistency, between the various rules dealing with the position of third states in situations of an unlawful use of force.

This chapter does not aim to examine in any detail the rights and duties of third states under each of the previously mentioned sets of rules but, rather, to provide an analysis of the possible interplay between these different rules, as well as to identify potential areas of friction. In particular, the main focus will be on the rules on state responsibility and on the impact of these rules on, and their mutual interaction with, other rules dealing with the position of third states. The focus on the law on state responsibility appears to be justified by the increasing importance of this body of rules in the determination of the legal consequences stemming from the notion of *erga omnes* obligations.

While this chapter will only deal with the rights and duties of third states, it seems appropriate to make a cursory reference to the position of entities other than states. In particular, it may be observed that, like states, international organizations are also to be regarded as affected by a breach of the obligation not to use force. The ILC Articles on the Responsibility of International Organizations recognize that, in cases of breaches of obligations owed to the international community as a whole, international organizations are entitled to invoke the responsibility of the wrongdoing states. However, this entitlement is subject to the requirement that 'safeguarding the interest of the international community as a whole underlying the obligation

[4] As the ILC observed, 'it is generally agreed that the prohibition of aggression is to be regarded as peremptory': *Yearbook of the International Law Commission*, 2001, vol II (2), 112. See also the ICJ's position in *Military and Paramilitary Activities in and against Nicaragua (Nicaragua v. US)*, ICJ Rep 1986, 100–1, para 190.

[5] Articles on State Responsibility, Art 41. See also the ILC's Commentary, *Yearbook of the International Law Commission*, 2001, vol II (2), 114 ff.

breached is within the functions of the international organization invoking responsibility'.[6] According to these Articles, when a serious breach of peremptory rules has taken place international organizations have the same duties as states.[7] Moreover, in the case of an armed attack, international organizations appear to be entitled to act in collective self-defence to support the victims of such an attack.[8] Since in this regard the position of 'third international organizations' does not substantially differ from that of third states, it will be assumed that the situation stated in regard to the latter category of subjects equally applies, *mutatis mutandis*, to international organizations.

II. The Narrowing of the Scope of Applicability of the Law of Neutrality

In its 1997 advisory opinion on the *Legality of the Threat or Use of Nuclear Weapons*, the International Court of Justice (ICJ), while recognizing that the principle of neutrality is 'of fundamental character', was careful to stress that its applicability to situations of international armed conflict was 'subject to the relevant provisions of the United Nations Charter'.[9] The question of the compatibility of the law of neutrality with the system of collective security established under the UN Charter has long been discussed in legal literature.[10] The prevailing view, which finds confirmation in state practice as well as in the position of the ICJ, is that the UN Charter does not prevent a state from invoking the principle of neutrality other than in specific circumstances in which the respect of the duty of impartiality or of non-participation

[6] See Articles on the Responsibility of International Organizations, Art 49, para 3, A/66/10, paras 88 ff.

[7] Articles on State Responsibility, Art 42.

[8] Art 21 provides that 'The wrongfulness of an act of an international organization is precluded if and to the extent that the act constitutes a lawful measure of self-defence under international law'. On the possibility of international organizations using force in self-defence, see Pierre Klein, *La responsabilité des organisations internationales* (Brussels: Bruylant, 1998), 419 ff; Christian Dominicé, 'La responsabilité internationale des Nations Unies' in Jean-Pierre Cot et al (eds), *La Charte des Nations Unies, Commentaire article par article* (3rd edn, Paris: Economica, 2005), 158; Emmanuel Roucounas, 'Present Problems of the Use of Force in International Law: Sub-Group on Self-Defence: Provisional Draft' (2006) 72-I *Annuaire de l'Institut de droit international* 127.

[9] *Legality of the Threat or Use of Nuclear Weapons*, ICJ Rep 1997, 261, para 89.

[10] See Dietrich Schindler, 'Aspects contemporains de la neutralité' (1961) 121 *Recueil des cours de l'Académie de droit international* 221; Charles G. Fenwick, 'Is Neutrality still a Term of Present Law?' (1969) 63 *American Journal of International Law* 100; Christine Chinkin, *Third Parties in International*

appears to be incompatible with the duty to comply with enforcement measures adopted by the Security Council.[11] This is the case, for instance, when member states are bound to comply with a Security Council decision imposing economic or other kinds of measures against the aggressor state. Equally, when the Security Council authorizes the use of force against an aggressor, while member states are not bound to take part in the military action against that state, they have at least an obligation, under Article 2(5) of the Charter, to assist those states which act in pursuance of the objectives indicated by the Council.

It is more uncertain to what extent the law of neutrality is applicable in situations in which the Security Council remains inactive. Without entering into the much debated question whether third states are entitled in this type of situation to adopt a position of 'non-belligerency',[12] it may be observed that those who admit the possibility of third states being able to invoke the status of neutrality even in cases of a flagrant breach of the prohibition to use force, mainly rely on the rather formalistic argument that neutrality is not per se incompatible with the current rules of international law outlawing the use of force. In particular, reference is made to the fact that while third states, by acting in collective self-defence, have the right to assist the victim of the armed attack, under general international law they do not have a duty to do so. Thus, in the absence of a legal duty to discriminate between the belligerents, a state would be free to choose non-involvement and to seek the legal protection assured by the law of neutrality.[13]

Even if this view is well founded in regard to compatibility between the principle of neutrality and the rule on collective self-defence, it is doubtful whether the same argument is equally applicable when it comes to assessing the compatibility of this principle with the rules on state responsibility dealing with the consequences arising out of a grave breach of peremptory rules. As already mentioned, these rules do not simply confer rights on third states towards the wrongdoing state; they also impose on them a number of duties. Under certain circumstances, compliance with these duties might require states to adopt conduct which is incompatible with the duties arising from the law of neutrality. Thus, Article 41(1) of the ILC Articles on State Responsibility provides that 'States shall cooperate to bring an end through

Law (Oxford: Oxford University Press, 1993), 313; Maria Gavouneli, 'Neutrality—A Survivor?' (2012) 23 *European Journal of International Law* 267.

[11] For this view, see Bothe, 'The Law of Neutrality', 575; Wolff Heintschel von Heinegg, '"Benevolent" Third States in International Armed Conflicts: The Myth of the Irrelevance of the Law of Neutrality' in Michael N. Schmitt and Jelena Pejic (eds), *International Law and Armed Conflict: Exploring the Faultlines. Essays in Honour of Yoram Dinstein* (Leiden: Martinus Nijhoff, 2007), 543.

[12] Non-belligerency would imply the possibility of third states supporting one of the belligerent states without becoming a party to the conflict. See Schindler, 'Aspects contemporains de la neutralité', 266 ff; Heintschel von Heinegg, '"Benevolent" Third States in International Armed Conflicts', 548 ff.

[13] Ian Brownlie, *International Law and the Use of Force by States* (Oxford: Oxford University Press, 1963), 403; Gavouneli, 'Neutrality—A Survivor?', 272.

lawful means any serious breach' of obligations arising under a peremptory norm of general international law. While, admittedly, this obligation to cooperate is rather vague, and while, as the ILC itself recognized, it might not reflect an already established rule of general international law,[14] it is difficult not to see the tension existing between a duty to cooperate to bring an aggression to an end and the duty of impartiality required under the law of neutrality. It could be held that strict compliance with the duty of impartiality may lead to a breach of the obligation of cooperation, particularly when this may have the effect of undermining the attempt by the state which was the object of the armed attack, or of the states acting in collective self-defence, to put to an end to the unlawful use of force by the wrongdoing state.[15] Reference may also be made to the obligation not to recognize as lawful a situation created by a serious breach of peremptory rules and to the obligation not to render aid or assistance in maintaining that situation, both set forth in Article 41(2) of the ILC Articles. Unlike the obligation provided under paragraph 1 of Article 42, the obligations of non-recognition and of non-assistance are certainly prescribed by rules having a customary nature.[16] Again, compliance with these obligations may conflict with the duties incumbent on a neutral state. Thus, for instance, the duty of impartiality implies that the neutral state cannot change its commercial relations with the belligerent parties so as to favour one party over the other;[17] however, continuing existing commercial relations with the aggressor state might entail a breach of the obligation not to aid or assist a state in maintaining a situation of occupation of a territory brought about by an unlawful use of force.

In all likelihood, it cannot yet be said that the development of rules establishing the legal consequences arising for third states in a case where grave breaches of peremptory rules have been committed has led to a complete obsolescence of the law of neutrality. However, this development marks a significant move away from the importance traditionally accorded to the non-involvement of third states as a means of restraining conflicts. The main emphasis appears nowadays to be on the effective enforcement of rules aiming to protect the common interests of the international community and on the role which third states may play in that regard. To the extent that this trend will find further confirmation in state practice and will lead to the development of stricter rules imposing duties on third states, the law of neutrality—the scope of applicability of which has already been reduced by the

[14] *Yearbook of the International Law Commission*, 2001, vol II (2), 114, para 3.

[15] See Nina Jorgensen, 'The Obligation of Cooperation' in James Crawford, Alain Pellet, and Simon Olleson (eds), *The Law of State Responsibility* (Oxford: Oxford University Press, 2010), 700; Karl Doehring, 'Neutralität und Gewaltverbot' (1993) 31 *Archiv des Völkerrechts* 199.

[16] See, in this respect, the position held by the ICJ in its advisory opinions on *Legal Consequences for States of the Continued Presence of South Africa in Namibia (South West Africa) notwithstanding Security Council Resolution 276 (1970)*, ICJ Rep 1970, 54, and *Legal Consequences of the Construction of a Wall in the Occupied Palestinian Territory*, ICJ Rep 2004, 200, para 159.

[17] Bothe, 'The Law of Neutrality', 572.

system of collective security established by the UN Charter—appears destined to find still less room for application, if not to vanish entirely through obsolescence.

III. Collective Self-Defence and Enforcement of *Erga Omnes* Obligations: Common Purpose but Different Conditions?

When the unlawful use of force reaches the level of an act of aggression, third states may rely on two sets of rules to justify their unilateral reaction against the aggressor state. As we have seen, they may base their response on the primary rules on the use of force, which confer on them the right to act in collective self-defence.[18] Alternatively, third states may rely on the secondary rules dealing with the legal consequences arising from a serious breach of a peremptory rule. Among these consequences, reference must be made, in particular, to the possibility of third states taking countermeasures against the wrongdoing state. As is well known, the existence of a right of third states to adopt countermeasures in response to a breach of an *erga omnes* obligation has proved to be a controversial issue; and one on which the ILC has refrained from taking a stand.[19] However, state practice appears to support this possibility, at least in those cases—such as in case of aggression—where the wrongful conduct amounts to a serious breach of peremptory rules.[20]

[18] A response in collective self-defence certainly comprises a use of force against the aggressor. However, as observed in the Commentary on Art 21 of the Articles on State Responsibility, 'Self-defence may justify non-performance of certain obligations other than that under Article 2, paragraph 4, of the Charter of the United Nations, provided that such non-performance is related to the breach of that provision'. *Yearbook of the International Law Commission*, 2001, vol II (2), 74, para 2. Admittedly, when third party responses take the form of non-military reactions, the distinction between action in self-defence and countermeasures becomes blurred. On this point, see also Brownlie, *International Law and the Use of Force*, 404, and Christian Hillgruber, 'The Right of Third States to Take Countermeasures' in Christian Tomuschat and Jean-Marc Thouvenin (eds), *The Fundamental Rules of the International Legal Order* (Leiden: Brill, 2006), 281.

[19] Art 54 simply provides that 'This chapter does not prejudice the right of any State, entitled under article 48, paragraph 1, to invoke the responsibility of another State, to take lawful measures against that State to ensure cessation of the breach and reparation in the interest of the injured State or of the beneficiaries of the obligation breached'. It is not clear whether, by using the expression 'lawful measures', Art 54 refers to countermeasures or to measures of retortion which are per se lawful. On this issue, see Denis Alland, 'Countermeasures of General Interest' (2002) 13 *European Journal of International Law* 1121.

[20] See Art 5 of the resolution on 'Obligations *erga omnes* in international law', adopted in 2005 by the Institute of International Law (2005) 71-I *Annuaire de l'Institut de droit international* 135. For an

An enforcement action in response to a serious breach of peremptory rules differs in some respects from an action in collective self-defence. A first difference concerns the means available to third states: while in a self-defence scenario the response includes the possibility of military actions against the aggressor, under the law of state responsibility there is a prohibition on resort to forcible countermeasures. Another difference relates to their respective purposes. Collective self-defence is primarily aimed at assisting the victim state in order to put to an end to the aggression; whereas an enforcement action has a broader purpose in that it aims at procuring not only cessation but also reparation for the internationally wrongful act. Notwithstanding these distinctive features, it is clear that these two forms of reaction are strictly related as they both aim at countering acts of aggression by the unilateral actions of third states. Taking into account their strict relation, it may be asked whether, for the sake of consistency, these two sets of reactions should not be subjected to the same or similar conditions or, to put it differently, whether certain requirements which limit the possibility of acting in collective self-defence should also apply to countermeasures taken by third states on the basis of the *erga omnes* character of the obligation breached.

One of the main issues in this regard concerns the importance given to the consent of the state which is the victim of aggression.[21] In its judgment in the *Nicaragua* case, the ICJ stated that 'there is no rule permitting the exercise of collective self-defence in the absence of a request by the state which regards itself as the victim of an armed attack'.[22] While this requirement is not set forth under Article 51 of the Charter, it appears to find its basis in customary rules on the use of force.[23] Accordingly, under these rules the attitude of the victim state is decisive for all other states: without its request, third states are not entitled to act in collective self-defence. To what extent, in the case of aggression, can the attitude of the victim state affect the rights and

extensive survey of state practice, see Christian Tams, *Enforcing Obligations Erga Omnes in International Law* (Cambridge: Cambridge University Press, 2010), 207 ff.

[21] As regards the question of whether third states are entitled to take countermeasures once the Security Council has taken 'measures necessary to maintain international peace and security', see Section IV. Another interesting issue is whether the distinction between an armed attack and minor breaches of the prohibition not to use force, which is relevant for the purpose of determining whether a state is entitled to use force in self-defence, is also relevant for the purpose of determining whether third states are entitled to take countermeasures. On this issue, see Jochen A. Frowein, 'Reactions by Not Directly Affected States to Breaches of Public International Law' (1994) 248 *Recueil des cours de l'Académie de droit international* 373; Santiago Villalpando, *L'émergence de la communauté internationale dans la responsabilité des Etats* (Paris: PUF, 2005), 254 ff.

[22] *Military and Paramilitary Activities in and against Nicaragua (Nicaragua v. US)*, ICJ Rep (1986, 105, para 199. According to the Court, 'the requirement of a request by the State which is the victim of the alleged attack is additional to the requirement that such State should have declared itself to have been attacked'.

[23] For a different view, however, see Christine Gray, *International Law and the Use of Force* (3rd edn, Oxford: Oxford University Press, 2008), 185 ff; Dinstein, *War, Aggression and Self-Defence*, 294 ff.

duties arising for third states under the law of state responsibility? State practice does not provide a clear answer to this question; which is not surprising since in most cases victim states are willing to accept the response of third states against the aggressor. While this issue will only rarely arise in practice, the problem remains whether the absence of an express request by the victim state, or a passive attitude of such state towards the unlawful conduct of the aggressor state, may preclude third states from taking countermeasures or even from invoking the responsibility of the aggressor state.

A first problem concerns the possibility that the victim state waives its claims towards the aggressor. It may be asked whether this waiver, which obviously must be validly given and cannot be imposed by coercion, has the effect of extinguishing any claim by third states relating to the cessation of the act of aggression or the reparation due to the victim state. Article 45 of the ILC Articles on State Responsibility does not take a clear stand on this issue. Addressing this point, the ILC commentary simply observes, in rather obscure terms, that since a serious breach of obligations arising from peremptory norms of general international law 'engages the interest of the international community as a whole, even the consent or the acquiescence of the injured state does not preclude that interest from being expressed in order to ensure a settlement in conformity with international law'.[24] According to one view, where a serious breach of a peremptory rule specially affects one state—as occurs in the case of aggression—priority must be given to the position held by that state for the purposes of determining the legal consequences arising from such a breach. This would imply that a waiver by the victim state would have the effect of precluding third states from invoking the responsibility of the aggressor state.[25] However, this view appears to narrow down excessively the legal entitlements of third states. Since the obligation not to use force is held by all states, it seems that all states are at least entitled to determine whether that obligation has been breached and to request cessation if the breach continues. In other words, the very notion of obligations *erga omnes* appears to entail that every state is entitled to claim compliance with this type of obligation, independent of the attitude taken by the state which has been specially affected by the breach of that obligation.[26] Significantly, Article

[24] *Yearbook of the International Law Commission*, 2001, vol II (2), 122, para 4.

[25] Christian Tams, 'Waiver, Acquiescence, and Extinctive Prescription' in Crawford, Pellet, and Olleson, *The Law of State Responsibility*, 1041. See also the more nuanced view of Iain Scobbie, 'The Invocation of Responsibility for the Breach of "Obligations under Peremptory Norms of General International Law"' (2002) 13 *European Journal of International Law* 214.

[26] For this view, see Giorgio Gaja, 'Obligations and Rights *Erga Omnes* in International Law: First Report' (2005) 71-I *Annuaire de l'Institut de Droit International* 119; Enzo Cannizzaro, *Corso di diritto internazionale* (Turin: Giappichelli, 2012), 437; Villalpando, *L'émergence de la communauté internationale*, 327 ff. According to Paolo Picone, 'Il ruolo dello Stato leso nelle reazioni collettive alle violazioni di obblighi *erga omnes*' (2012) 96 *Rivista di diritto internazionale* 957, states, including the injured state, are not entitled to waive their recognized powers to protect the interests of the international community.

48 of the ILC Articles does not subject the right of third states to claim the cessation of the wrongful conduct to the position eventually adopted by the victim state. The attitude of the victim state appears instead to be relevant only as far as claims for reparation are concerned. Since, as provided for under Article 48, reparation may be claimed only 'in the interest of the injured State', a waiver by that state of its right to invoke responsibility appears to entail a correspondent loss by third states of their right to claim reparation.[27]

It remains to be seen whether third states are entitled to take countermeasures against the aggressor state only following a prior request by the victim state or whether instead countermeasures may be taken even in the absence of a prior request. While the ILC Articles on State Responsibility do not address this issue, a brief remark in the commentary to Article 54 appears to suggest that the ILC was rather inclined to support the former solution. Referring to the practice concerning countermeasures taken by third states in response to breaches of *erga omnes* obligations, it observed that 'in those cases where there was, identifiably, a State primarily injured by the breach in question, other States have acted at the request and on behalf of that State'.[28] Interestingly, to support this statement the ILC made reference to the fact that, in its *Nicaragua* judgment, the ICJ indicated in the prior request of the victim state an indispensable requirement for action in collective self-defence, thereby suggesting that this condition also applies by analogy to countermeasures based on the *erga omnes* character of the obligation breached.[29] The possibility of applying by analogy the condition indicated in *Nicaragua* with regard to the exercise of the right of collective self-defence was also advocated in more precise terms by the Commission's Special Rapporteur, James Crawford, according to whom 'If State A cannot act in collective self-defence of State B without State B's consent, it does not seem appropriate to hold that it could take (collective) countermeasures in cases where State B is the victim, irrespective of State B's wishes'.[30] Leaving aside the question whether this view finds confirmation in state practice, it can be observed, however, that this extension by analogy of the requirement of the prior request of the victim state does not seem to rely on solid arguments. The fact that an action in collective self-defence is subject to such a requirement may be explained by the need to limit the recourse to force by third states, which could abuse this right for

[27] For the view that 'if the injured State, however, decides not to claim reparation, other States cannot do more than claim cessation of the internationally wrongful act and, if circumstances so require, appropriate assurances and guarantees of non-repetition', see Stefan Talmon, 'Jus Cogens after *Germany v. Italy*: Substantive and Procedural Rules Distinguished', Bonn Research Papers on International Law, Paper 2/4, 2012, 24.

[28] *Yearbook of the International Law Commission*, 2001, vol II (2), 139, para 5.

[29] *Yearbook of the International Law Commission*, 2001, vol II (2), 139, para 5 fn 861.

[30] James Crawford, Third Report on State Responsibility, A/CN.4/507/Add.4, 19, para 400. For the view that countermeasures are only permitted if the injured state has called upon third states to adopt them, see also Hillgruber, 'The Right of Third States to Take Countermeasures', 291.

purposes other than the protection of the victim state. While resort to countermeasures by third states may also be a source of abuse, it seems apparent that the possibility of a military response poses greater risks than countermeasures. This may justify a difference in the conditions required for these two sets of reactions by third states. Moreover, if it is admitted that third states have an autonomous right to claim the cessation of the wrongful conduct by the aggressor state, it seems reasonable to say that, in principle, they should also be entitled to take countermeasures in order to enforce the obligation breached, irrespective of the attitude of the victim state.[31] The recognition of this entitlement would ensure that, even in cases where the victim state remains passive, breaches of *erga omnes* obligations are effectively countered.

IV. Centralized vs Decentralized Response by Third States: To What Extent May Security Council's Measures Limit Unilateral Responses by Third States?

Under Article 51 of the Charter, third states are entitled to act in collective self-defence 'until the Security Council has taken measures necessary to maintain international peace and security'. Does the same limit apply when third states, acting under the law of state responsibility, adopt unilateral countermeasures to react against an aggression? Or does this limit only apply to military actions based on the right to collective self-defence, third states' right to take peaceful countermeasures being not affected, at least in principle, by Security Council measures? Here again, the question revolves around the differences and analogies between the conditions required for these two sets of reactions by third states. From a broader perspective, it raises the problem of the relationship between the state responsibility regime and the UN collective security system.

The Articles on State Responsibility do not provide clear indications on this issue;[32] the only provision dealing with this problem is Article 59, which simply

[31] Villalpando, *L'émergence de la communauté internationale*, 338 ff.

[32] For an overview of the different positions which emerged during the debate in the ILC, see Maurizio Arcari, 'Responsabilità dello Stato per violazioni gravi di norme fondamentali e sistema di sicurezza collettiva delle Nazioni Unite' in Marina Spinedi, Alessandra Gianelli, and Maria Luisa Alaimo (eds),

states that 'These articles are without prejudice to the Charter of the United Nations'. The main point which can be drawn from this provision is that, in the case of conflict between the obligations flowing from the Charter or from binding acts taken by a UN organ and the rules on state responsibility, the former obligations prevail.

When acting under Chapter VII, the Security Council may certainly exclude the adoption of countermeasures against a state. Such exclusion may be expressly stated or, alternatively, it may be inferred from the text of the resolution that the measures adopted by the Security Council were intended to be exclusive. In such situations, the obligations resulting from the decision of the Security Council prevail and states are under a duty not to take countermeasures or to suspend the countermeasures which they have already taken. This does not mean that whenever the Security Council takes measures which are binding on states, unilateral countermeasures by third states are ruled out irrespective of the content of the measures adopted.[33] The view that third states cannot resort to unilateral countermeasures once the Security Council has made use of its powers under Chapter VII, is premised on the idea that a centralization in the hands of the Security Council of the response against grave breaches of peremptory rules would allow for defusing the risk of abuse inherent in a system which allocates to each and every state the power to react to those breaches. However, this view does not take into due account the fact that the Security Council is a political body whose main task is to maintain peace and not to enforce law, and that effective enforcement of obligations *erga omnes* may necessitate giving third states the possibility of going beyond the measures adopted by the Security Council. Whether third states are entitled to adopt countermeasures after an intervention by the Security Council appears to depend in each case on the specific content of the decisions taken by the Council.[34] However, in principle, the fact that the Security Council is actively seized of a certain situation does not prevent third states from resorting to countermeasures. State practice appears to support this conclusion as in several instances third states have taken countermeasures to react to breaches of *erga omnes* obligations even in cases where the Security Council has already intervened.[35]

La codificazione della responsabilità internazionale degli Stati alla prova dei fatti (Milan: Giuffrè, 2006), 291 ff; Vera Gowlland-Debbas, 'Responsibility and the United Nations Charter' in Crawford, Pellet, and Olleson, *The Law of State Responsibility*, 115.

[33] For a different view, see Frowein, 'Reactions by Not Directly Affected States', 371. According to Linos-Alexandre Sicilianos, 'Countermeasures in Response to Grave Violations of Obligations Owed to the International Community' in Crawford, Pellet, and Olleson, *The Law of State Responsibility*, 142, 'the triggering of Chapter VII ends the power of States not individually injured to react as they please at the individual level'.

[34] See Villalpando, *L'émergence de la communauté internationale*, 448 ff; Pierre Klein, 'Responsibility for Serious Breaches Deriving from Peremptory Norms of International Law and United Nations Law' (2002) 13 *European Journal of International Law* 1254; Hillgruber, 'The Right of Third States to Take Countermeasures', 288.

[35] Martin Davidowicz, 'Public Law Enforcement without Public Law Safeguards? An Analysis of State Practice on Third-Party Countermeasures and their Relationship to the UN Security Council' (2006) 77 *British Yearbook of International Law* 417; Tams, *Enforcing Obligations Erga Omnes*, 267 ff.

Apart from the limitation flowing from the Charter, the intervention of the Security Council may have other consequences. In particular, it may have an indirect impact on the power of third states to adopt countermeasures as it may call into question the issue of proportionality.[36] When considering whether to take countermeasures in addition to the measures adopted by the Security Council, third states must take into account the need to comply with the requirement of the proportionality of the overall response against the wrongdoing state. In this respect, an intervention by the Security Council will normally have the effect of reducing the room for manoeuvre for third states.

In the case of aggression, third states are entitled to take countermeasures against the aggressor state even if the Security Council remains inactive. As we have seen, if the Security Council intervenes by adopting 'measures necessary to maintain international peace and security', as a matter of principle this intervention does not imply that third states are precluded from acting unilaterally. Also in this respect, therefore, the rules on collective self-defence differ from the rules governing the legal entitlements of third states in the case of grave breaches of peremptory rules. As with the requirement of the prior consent of the victim state, such difference may be explained by the fact that collective self-defence involves the possibility of third states using military force in order to repel aggression. This justifies tighter control by the Security Council over the action of third states.[37] When peaceful countermeasures are at stake, considerations based on the need for effective enforcement of community values appear to prevail over the risks inherent in a decentralized response. While the Security Council may limit or rule out third party countermeasures, such limitations may not be presumed and only operate if they are clearly imposed by a binding decision.

V. Concluding Remarks

As has emerged from this brief analysis of some of the problems which concern the role of third states in situations of unlawful use of force, this is an area of law where a number of important issues still remain controversial and where the diversity of approaches underlying the various rules applicable in this type of situation add to the complexity of the legal regime governing the conduct of third states. Nowadays, through the development of rules which specify the legal consequences

[36] On the requirement of proportionality of countermeasures, see the Articles on State Responsibility, Art 51.

[37] Cannizzaro, *Corso di diritto internazionale*, 441.

flowing from the concept of *erga omnes* obligations, the primary emphasis is generally placed on the role of third states as guardians of community interests, including the fundamental interest of preserving peace and security. However, while international law has gone a long way towards accommodating the protection of community interests, the development of these rules has not yet led to the displacement of the older rules on neutrality, which give priority to the containment of conflict and the protection of bilateral interests. Nor is it clear to what extent, if any, in the case of aggression, the law on the use of force governing collective self-defence has an impact on the rules governing third parties' responses based on the *erga omnes* concept. From a different perspective, it can be said that the uncertainties surrounding the question of the role of third states in situations of unlawful use of force simply reflect the still uncertain status of the law governing many aspects of third states' enforcement of community interests.

Among the problems which still remain to be fully resolved, three can be singled out as most relevant for the definition of the role of third states in situations of unlawful use of force. They relate to the relationship of third states, respectively, with the wrongdoing state, with the direct victim of the unlawful use of force, and with the Security Council.

The first issue concerns the existence of third states' duties aimed at ensuring compliance with *erga omnes* obligations. As we have seen, while the ILC has recognized the existence of duties to this effect, their precise content is rather vague and states are left with a significant measure of discretion in relation to the type of conduct they must take in order to comply with these duties. Whether international law will develop stricter legal standards is uncertain; but at present this appears unlikely. Practice supporting the existence of these duties is rather limited and states do not show any signs pointing towards their readiness to accept stricter standards.[38] However, if a development in this direction does take place, the emergence of stricter duties will have a significant impact on third states, as they, in most cases, would be prevented from taking a position of neutrality in their relationship with the aggressor state.

The second point concerns the possibility for third states to invoke the responsibility of the aggressor state, and to take countermeasures against it, irrespective of the attitude of the state which is the direct victim of the aggression. As we have seen, there is in this respect an opposition between a more traditional view which, by upholding a bilateralist paradigm, identifies the consent of the injured state as a necessary requirement for a response by third parties, and a view which, by relying on the communitarian character of the interests involved, denies the existence of

[38] See Christian Tams, 'Individual States as Guardians of Community Interests' in Ulrich Fastenrath et al (eds), *From Bilateralism to Community Interest: Essays in Honour of Bruno Simma* (Oxford: Oxford University Press, 2011), 400.

such a requirement. If the development of international law goes in the direction of placing greater importance on the enforcement of community interests, and therefore accepting a third party response in the absence of a request by the victim state, the role of third states would be further enhanced.

This leads to a last point, which concerns the relationship between the unilateral responses of third states against serious breaches of peremptory rules and the centralized mechanism of reaction established by the UN Charter. As has already been stated, in principle the fact that the Security Council has adopted measures to address a certain matter does not preclude the possibility of third states taking countermeasures. So far, the coexistence between the collective security system and the possibility of a decentralized reaction by third states has not given rise to major problems. However, this state of affairs may change if resort to collective countermeasures becomes more widespread in the future. While the Security Council certainly has the power to decide on the suspension of unilateral countermeasures, it remains to be seen whether it will make use of this power, thereby accepting that it plays an effective role as an institutional safeguard against the risk of improper resort to countermeasures. The solution to this dilemma, however, lies in the realm of politics, not in that of law.

Index

Introductory Note

References such as '178–9' indicate (not necessarily continuous) discussion of a topic across a range of pages. Wherever possible in the case of topics with many references, these have either been divided into sub-topics or only the most significant discussions of the topic are listed. Because the entire work is about 'use of force', the use of this term (and certain others which occur constantly throughout the book) as an entry point has been restricted. Information will be found under the corresponding detailed topics.

B

C

F

G

H

O

Q

R

S

U

Y

Z